Introduction
to Psychology

Introduction to Psychology

9e

JAMES W. KALAT

North Carolina State University

WADSWORTH
CENGAGE Learning

Australia • Brazil • Japan • Korea • Mexico • Singapore • Spain • United Kingdom • United States

WADSWORTH
CENGAGE Learning™

Introduction to Psychology, **Ninth Edition**
James W. Kalat

Senior Publisher: Linda Schreiber

Executive Editor: Jon-David Hague

Senior Sponsoring Psychology Editor: Jane Potter

Associate Developmental Editor: Tali Beesley

Assistant Editor: Rebecca Rosenberg

Editorial Assistant: Alicia Mclaughlin

Media Editor: Rachel Guzman and Lauren Keyes

Executive Marketing Manager: Kim Russell

Marketing Associate: Molly Felz

Marketing Assistant: Anna Anderson

Executive Marketing Communications Manager: Talia Wise

Senior Content Project Manager: Pat Waldo

Creative Director: Rob Hugel

Art Director: Vernon Boes

Print Buyer: Karen Hunt

Rights Acquisitions Account Manager, Text: Tim Sisler

Rights Acquisitions Account Manager, Image: Don Schlotman

Production Service: Nancy Shammas, New Leaf Publishing Services

Text Designer: Jeanne Calabrese

Photo Researcher: Martha Hall, Image Services Director, Pre-PressPMG

Copy Editor: Frank Hubert

Illustrator: Precision Graphics

Cover Designer: Jeanne Calabrese Design, Inc.

Cover Image: © Moodboard/Corbis

Compositor: Graphic World, Inc.

For product information and technology assistance, contact us at
Cengage Learning Customer & Sales Support, 1-800-354-9706.

For permission to use material from this text or product,
submit all requests online at **www.cengage.com/permissions.**

Further permissions questions can be e-mailed to
permissionrequest@cengage.com.

Library of Congress Control Number: 2009938502

Student Edition:
ISBN-10: 0-495-81091-6
ISBN-13: 978-0-495-81091-9

Paper Edition:
ISBN-10: 0-495-81076-2
ISBN-13: 978-0-495-81076-6

Loose-leaf Edition:
ISBN-10: 0-495-81092-4
ISBN-13: 978-0-495-81092-6

Wadsworth
10 Davis Drive
Belmont, CA 94002-3098
USA

Cengage Learning is a leading provider of customized learning solutions with office locations around the globe, including Singapore, the United Kingdom, Australia, Mexico, Brazil, and Japan. Locate your local office at **www.cengage.com/global.**

Cengage Learning products are represented in Canada by Nelson Education, Ltd.

To learn more about Wadsworth, visit **www.cengage.com/Wadsworth**

Purchase any of our products at your local college store or at our preferred online store **www.ichapters.com**.

Printed in the United States of America

1 2 3 4 5 6 7 13 12 11 10 09

To my grandchildren: Ann, Liam, and Max.

JAMES W. KALAT (rhymes with ballot) is Professor of Psychology at North Carolina State University, where he teaches Introduction to Psychology and Biological Psychology. Born in 1946, he received an AB degree summa cum laude from Duke University in 1968 and a PhD in psychology from the University of Pennsylvania, under the supervision of Paul Rozin. He is also the author of *Biological Psychology*, 10th Edition (Belmont, CA: Wadsworth, 2009), and co-author with Michelle N. Shiota of *Emotion* (Belmont, CA: Wadsworth, 2007). In addition to textbooks, he has written journal articles on taste-aversion learning, the teaching of psychology, and other topics. A remarried widower, he has three children, two stepsons, and three grandchildren. When not working on something related to psychology, his hobby is bird-watching.

brief contents

contents

3 Biological Psychology 61

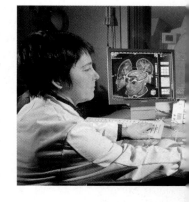

4 Sensation and Perception 96

5 Nature, Nurture, and Human Development 143

8 Cognition and Language 272

11 Motivated Behaviors 373

12 Emotions, Stress, and Health 410

13 Social Psychology 451

A few years ago, I was on a plane that had to turn around shortly after takeoff because one of its two engines had failed. When we were told to get into crash position, the first thing I thought was, "I don't want to die yet! I was looking forward to writing the next edition of my textbook!" True story.

I remember taking my first course in psychology as a freshman at Duke University in 1965. Frequently, I would describe the fascinating facts I had just learned to my roommate, friends, relatives, or anyone else who would listen. I haven't changed much since then. When I read about new research or think of a new example to illustrate some point, I want to tell my wife, children, colleagues, and students. Through this textbook, I can tell even more people. I hope my readers will share this excitement and want to tell still others.

Ideally, a course or textbook in psychology should accomplish two goals. The first is to instill a love of learning so that our graduates will continue to update their education. Even if students remembered everything they learned in this text—and I know they won't—their understanding would gradually go out of date unless they continue to learn about new developments. I fantasize that some of my former students occasionally read *Scientific American Mind* or similar publications. The second goal is to teach people skills of evaluating evidence and questioning assertions, so that when they do read or hear about some newly reported discovery, they will ask the right questions and draw the appropriate conclusions (or draw no conclusion if the evidence is weak). That skill can carry over to fields other than psychology.

Throughout this text, I have tried to model the habit of critical thinking or evaluating the evidence, particularly in the **What's the Evidence** features, which describe research studies in some detail. I have pointed out the limitations of the evidence and the possibilities for alternative interpretations. The goal is to help students ask their own questions, distinguish between good and weak evidence, and ultimately, appreciate the excitement of psychological inquiry.

APPROACHES, FEATURES, AND STUDENT AIDS

Many years ago, I read an educational psychology textbook that said children with learning disabilities and attention problems learn best from specific, concrete examples. I remember thinking, "Wait a minute. I do, too! Don't we *all* learn best from specific, concrete examples?" For this reason, science classes use laboratories, to let students try demonstrations and experiments. Few introductory psychology classes offer laboratories, but we can nevertheless encourage students to try procedures that require little or no equipment. At various points, the text describes simple **Try It Yourself** exercises, such as negative afterimages, binocular rivalry, encoding specificity, and the Stroop effect. Some of these activities are available as **Online Try It Yourself** activities on the companion website at **www.cengage.com/psychology/kalat**. Students who try these activities will understand and remember the concepts far better than if they read about them only in abstract terms. A few of the online activities enable students to collect and report their own data.

Reading the material is good, but using it is better. Researchers find that we learn more if we alternate between reading and testing than if we spend the same amount of time reading. The **Concept Checks** pose questions that attentive readers should be able to answer with a little thought. Students who answer correctly can feel encouraged; those who miss a question should use the feedback to reread the relevant passages.

Education was long a very traditional field in which the procedures hardly changed since the invention of chalk and desks. Recently, however, educators have been learning to use the power of new technologies, and this text offers several important technological enhancements. The website already mentioned includes the Online Try It Yourself exercises as well as flash cards, quizzes, an online glossary, and links to other interesting sites related to each chapter. An eBook (electronic version of the text) is available at **www.ichapters.com**. In addition to the usual text material, it includes links to videos, animations, and Online Try

It Yourself activities. It also includes multiple-choice questions with feedback. If a student chooses an incorrect answer, the eBook explains why it was wrong and then explains the correct answer.

Each chapter of this text is divided into two to five modules, each with its own summary. Modules provide flexibility for the instructor who wishes to take sections in a different order—for example, operant conditioning before classical conditioning—or who wishes to omit a section. Modular format also breaks up the reading assignments so that a student reads one or two modules for each class. Key terms are listed at the end of each module, and a list with definitions can be downloaded from the website. At the end of the text, a combined Subject Index and Glossary provides definitions of key terms as well as page references for those terms and others.

WHAT'S NEW
IN THE NINTH EDITION

Does psychology really change fast enough to justify a new edition of an introductory text every 3 years? Some areas of psychology admittedly do not, but others do. This edition has more than 600 new references, including more than 500 from 2006 or later. The chapter on memory was substantially reorganized. A few new topics have been added, such as the Myers-Briggs and NEO-PI-R personality tests. Many of the figures are new or revised. Two of the "What's the Evidence?" sections are new, dealing with criminal profiling (chapter 13) and the problems of a before-and-after study without a control group (chapter 2). Even in topics where the content has not changed much, an author always finds many small ways to improve the presentation. Here are a few of my favorite new studies:

- People show a slight preference for a job that sounds similar to their own name (e.g. Larry and lawyer), as well as a place to live, employer, or spouse who shares their initials. (chapter 1)
- If students take a test with the instructions in red letters, or any other red mark on the test, their scores suffer. Evidently, the red discourages students by reminding them of teachers' corrections on past tests and papers. (chapter 1)
- If you measure how strongly various people's brains respond to somewhat frightening pictures, you can predict their political leanings with moderate accuracy. (chapter 3)
- Although males and females differ on the average in their interests, even in early childhood, supposed differences in abilities are either absent or elusive. In cultures where women have low status, males do better than females in mathematics, but where status is about equal, so is math performance. (chapter 5)
- After you have learned something, such as a vocabulary list, additional study at the same time is nearly a complete waste of time. Study is much more effective if you go away from it for a day or so and then return to review. (chapter 7)
- People often do not know why they made a decision. If you ask, "Why did you choose this picture instead of the other one?" and then show the picture that the person *didn't* choose, the person often doesn't recognize that you made a switch and confidently describes plausible reasons for the choice. (chapter 8)
- The Flynn effect is the observation that mean IQ performance has increased from one generation to the next for several generations. New data show a similar generational increase in developmental milestones of the first 2 or 3 years. Because health and nutrition seem the preeminent explanations for this change in early development, they become likely candidates to explain the Flynn effect, too. (chapter 9)
- If you monitor people's brain activity while they are about to make a "spontaneous" decision to press the left or right key, you can predict their choice 5 to 10 seconds before they are conscious of their decision. (chapter 10)
- When an area shifts to daylight savings time, people's alertness and performance suffer for a week or two. The effects are greatest for people who were already sleep deprived, such as most college students. (chapter 10)
- Men with higher testosterone levels are less likely than other men to marry, and if they do marry, they are less likely to be faithful. (chapter 11)
- After you make a decision about anything, even something trivial, you become more likely than before to take action on other matters instead of procrastinating. (chapter 11)
- Spending a little money on a gift for someone else raises your happiness more than spending that money on yourself would. (chapter 12)
- Happiness is contagious. If your friends become happier, you probably will, too, and then you may spread it to still other people. (chapter 12)
- Becoming familiar with someone does not necessarily increase liking. You find out what you have in common but also what you don't have in common, and you discover the other person's flaws. (chapter 13)
- Psychologists have long assumed that no one would ever again replicate Milgram's obedi-

ence experiment, but J. M. Burger did, in part. He asked people to deliver shocks only up to 150 volts, relieving the serious ethical problem of the original study. He found that people obeyed authority almost as much today as they did in the 1960s. (chapter 13)

- If you ask people in different countries to rate how conscientious they are, the reports don't differ much from one country to another. However, direct observations of conscientious behaviors show clear differences among countries. (chapter 14)
- People with early-onset depression usually have other relatives with the same or other psychiatric conditions. People with late-onset depression usually have relatives with blood circulation disorders. (chapter 16)
- Apparently, schizophrenia can be caused by mutations (including new mutations) in so many different genes that no one gene will emerge as consistently linked to schizophrenia. (chapter 16)

TEACHING AND LEARNING SUPPLEMENTS

You're familiar with those television advertisements that offer something, usually for $19.95, and then say, "But wait, there's more!" Same here. In addition to the text, the publisher offers many supplements:

Study Guide, revised by Mark Ludorf, provides learning objectives, chapter outlines, other study aids, and practice test items, with an explanation of why each wrong answer is wrong. It also includes a language-building component especially helpful for nonnative speakers of English.

Test Bank, revised by Ralf Greenwald, includes questions from the previous edition, hundreds of new items contributed by James Kalat and tested in his classes, and many new ones by Ralf Greenwald. That bank is also available in ExamView® electronic format. Many of the items have already been tested with classes at North Carolina State University, and the Test Bank indicates the percentage correct and point biserial. Note also that the Test Bank includes a special file of items that cut across chapters, intended for a comprehensive final exam.

Instructor's Resource Manual, revised by Nancy Jo Melucci, is both thorough and creative. It includes suggestions for class demonstrations and lecture material. It also contains the author's suggested answers to the Step Further questions available online.

PowerLecture with JoinIn and ExamView is designed to facilitate an instructor's assembly of PowerPoint® or similar demonstrations and contains lecture slides, figures and tables from the text, the Instructor's Resource Manual and Test Bank, and Resource Integration Guide. With PowerLecture, all of your media resources are in one place, including an image library with graphics from the book itself, video clips, and more. ExamView® includes all of the test items from the printed Test Bank in electronic format and enables you to create customized tests in print or online, and JoinIn™ Student Response System offers instant assessment and better student results.

CengageNOW with Critical Thinking Videos is an online self-study and assessment system that helps students study efficiently and effectively while allowing instructors to easily manage their courses. CengageNOW analyzes student performance and discovers which areas students need the most help with. Students take a pretest, and based on their answers, the system creates a personalized learning plan unique to each student. This learning plan is full of engaging pedagogy that aids student understanding of core concepts in psychology. After completing the personalized learning plan, the student follows up with a posttest to ensure mastery of the material. The self-study and assessment questions were revised for this edition by Alisha Janowsky.

Available on the website, WebTutor, and CengageNow for *Introduction to Psychology,* 9th Edition, **Online Try It Yourself** exercises illustrate concepts and promote critical thinking about various topics in the text.

ACKNOWLEDGMENTS

To begin the job of writing a textbook, a potential author needs self-confidence bordering on arrogance and, to complete it, the humility to accept criticism of favorite ideas and carefully written prose. A great many people provided helpful suggestions that made this a far better text than it would have been without them.

During preparation of this edition, I have worked with three acquisition editors, Erik Evans, Michelle Sordi, and Jane Potter. The transition proceeded as smoothly as I could hope, and I particularly thank Jane Potter for guiding the text through most of the process. Tali Beesley served as developmental editor, offering detailed suggestions ranging from organization of a chapter to choice of words to new and improved figures. I thank each of these people for their tireless help.

Rebecca Rosenberg supervised the supplements, a task that grows bigger with each edition. I have now had the pleasure to work with Frank Hubert as my copy editor for several editions, and I greatly appreciate his careful reading and attention to detail. Nic Albert secured numerous quality peer reviews throughout the entire project. Nancy Shammas and Pat Waldo did a marvelous job of supervising the production, a complicated task with a book such as this. Vernon Boes, who managed the design development, Lisa Torri, who managed the art development, and Jeanne Calabrese, who designed the interior and the cover, had the patience and artistic judgment to counterbalance their very nonartistic author. Tierra Morgan planned and executed the marketing strategies. Martha Hall, the photo researcher, found an amazing variety of wonderful photographs and managed the permissions requests. To each of these, my thanks and congratulations.

My wife, Jo Ellen Kalat, not only provided support and encouragement, but also listened to my attempts to explain concepts and offered many helpful suggestions and questions. My son Samuel Kalat provided many insightful ideas and suggestions. I thank my department head, Douglas Gillan, and my N.C. State colleagues—especially David Martin, Bob Pond, Bart Craig, and Rupert Nacoste—for their helpful suggestions.

Many reviewers provided helpful and insightful comments. I thank the following people, as well as those who wish to remain anonymous: Jennifer Ackil, Gustavus Adolphus College; Melanie M. Arpaio, Sussex County Community College; Thomas Carskadon, Mississippi State University; Alicia M. Doerflinger, Marietta College; Andrew Johnson, Park University; Jonathan Lytle, Temple University; Michelle Merwin, University of Tennessee at Martin; Todd Nelson, California State University; William Price, North Country Community College; and Robert A. Rosellini, University at Albany.

Each edition builds on contributions from reviewers of previous editions. I would also like to thank the following reviewers who contributed their insight to previous editions: Jeffrey Adams, Trent University; Judi Addelston, Valencia Community College; Mark Affeltranger, University of Pittsburgh; Catherine Anderson, Amherst College; Susan Anderson, University of South Alabama; Bob Arkin, Ohio State University; Susan Baillet, University of Portland; Cynthia Bane, Denison University; Joe Bean, Shorter College; Mark Bodamer, John Carroll University; Richard W. Bowen, Loyola University Chicago; Michael Brislawn, Bellevue Community College; Delbert Brodie, St. Thomas University; John Broida, University of Southern Maine; Gordon Brow, Pasadena City College; Gregory Bushman, Beloit College; James Calhoun, University of Georgia; Bernardo Carducci, Indiana University Southeast; Mar Casteel, Pennsylvania State University, York Campus; Liz Coccia, Austin Community College; Karen Couture, Keene State College; Deana Davalos, Colorado State University; Patricia Deldin, Harvard University; Katherine Demitrakis, Albuquerque Technical Vocational Institute; Janet Dizinno, St. Mary University; Kimberly Duff, Cerritos College; Darlene Earley-Hereford, Southern Union State Community College; David J. Echevarria, University of Southern Mississippi; Vanessa Edkins, University of Kansas; Susan Field, Georgian Court College; Deborah Frisch, University of Oregon; Gabriel Frommer, Indiana University; Rick Fry, Youngstown State University; Robe Gehring, University of Southern Indiana; Judy Gentry, Columbus State Community College; Anna L. Ghee, Xavier University; Bill P. Godsil, Santa Monica College; Kerri Goodwin, Loyola College in Maryland; Joel Grace, Mansfield University; Troianne Grayson, Florida Community College at Jacksonville; Joe Grisham, Indiana River Community College; Julie A. Gurner, Quinnipiac University; Community College of Philadelphia; Alexandria E. Guzmán, University of New Haven; Richard Hanson, Fresno City College; Richard Harris, Kansas State University; Wendy Hart-Stravers, Arizona State University; W. Bruce Haslam, Weber State University; Christopher Hayashi, Southwestern College; Bert Hayslip, University of North Texas; Manda Helzer, Southern Oregon University; W. Elaine Hogan, University of North Carolina Wilmington; Debra Hollister, Valencia Community College; Susan Horton, Mesa Community College; Charles Huffman, James Madison University; Linda Jackson, Michigan State University; Alisha Janowsky, University of Central Florida; Robert Jensen, California State University, Sacramento; James Johnson, Illinois State University; Craig Jones, Arkansas State University; Lisa Jordan, University of Maryland; Dale Jorgenson, California State University, Long Beach; Jon Kahane, Springfield College; Peter Kaplan, University of Colorado, Denver; Arthur Kemp, Central Missouri State University; Mark J. Kirschner, Quinnipiac University; Kristina T. Klassen, North Idaho College; Martha Kuehn, Central Lakes College; Cindy J. Lahar, University of Calgary; Chris Layne, University of Toledo; Cynthia Ann Lease, Virginia Polytechnic Institute and State University; Chantal Levesque, University of Rochester; John Lindsay, Georgia College and State University; Mary Livingston, Louisiana Technical University; Linda Lockwood, Metropolitan State College of Denver; Sanford

Lopater, Christopher Newport University; Mark Ludorf, Stephen F. Austin State University; Pamelyn M. MacDonald, Washburn University; Steve Madigan, University of Southern California; Don Marzoff, Louisiana State University; Christopher Mayhorn, North Carolina State University; Michael McCall, Ithaca College; David G. McDonald, University of Missouri; Tracy A. McDonough, College of Mount St. Joseph; J. Mark McKellop, Juniata College; Mary Meiners, San Diego Miramar College; Dianne Mello-Goldner, Pine Manor College; Nancy J. Melucci, Long Beach City College; Rowland Miller, Sam Houston State University; Gloria Mitchell, De Anza College; Paul Moore, Quinnipiac University; Anne Moyer, Stony Brook University; Jeffrey Nagelbush, Ferris State University; Bethany Neal-Beliveau, Indiana University-Purdue University at Indianapolis; Jan Ochman, Inver Hills Community College; Wendy Palmquist, Plymouth State College; Elizabeth Parks, Kennesaw State University; Gerald Peterson, Saginaw Valley State University; Brady Phelps, South Dakota State University; Shane Pitts, Birmingham Southern College; Thomas Reig, Winona State University; David Reitman, Louisiana State University; Bridget Rivera, Loyola College in Maryland; Jeffrey Rudski, Muhlenberg College; Linda Ruehlman, Arizona State University; Richard Russell, Santa Monica College; Mark Samuels, New Mexico Institute of Mining and Technology; Kim Sawrey, University of North Carolina at Wilmington; Troy Schiedenhelm, Rowan-Cabarrus Community College; Michele N. Shiota, University of California, Berkeley; Noam Shpancer, Purdue University; Eileen Smith, Fairleigh Dickinson University; James Spencer, West Virginia State College; Jim Stringham, University of Georgia; Robert Stawski, Syracuse University; Whitney Sweeney, Beloit College; Alan Swinkels, St. Edward's University; Natasha Tokowicz, University of Pittsburgh; Patricia Toney, Sandhills Community College; Warren W. Tryon, Fordham University; Katherine Urquhart, Lake Sumter Community College; Stavros Valenti, Hofstra University; Suzanne Valentine-French, College of Lake County; Douglas Wallen, Mankato State University; Michael Walraven, Jackson Community College; Donald Walter, University of Wisconsin–Parkside; Jeffrey Weatherly, University of North Dakota; Ellen Weissblum, State University of New York Albany; Fred Whitford, Montana State University; Don Wilson, Lane Community College; David Woehr, Texas A&M University; Jay Wright, Washington State University; John W. Wright, Washington State University.

James Kalat

Welcome to introductory psychology! I hope you will enjoy reading this text as much as I enjoyed writing it. When you finish, I hope you will send me your comments via email at **psych.feedback@ cengage.com** or by mail using the student reply page at the end of this book. The publisher will pass your comments along to me.

The first time I taught introductory psychology, several students complained that the book we were using was interesting to read but impossible to study. What they meant was that they had trouble finding and remembering the main points. I have tried to make this book interesting and as easy to study as possible.

FEATURES OF THIS TEXT

Modular Format

Each chapter is divided into two or more modules so that you can study a limited section at a time. Each chapter begins with a table of contents to orient you to the topics considered. At the end of each module is a list of key terms and a summary of some important points, each with page references. If a point is unfamiliar, you should reread the appropriate section. At the end of a chapter, you will find suggestions for further reading, a few Internet sites to visit, and other suggestions.

Key Terms

When an important term first appears in the text, it is highlighted in boldface and defined in *italics*. All the boldface terms are listed in alphabetical order at the end of each module. They appear again with definitions in the combined Subject Index and Glossary at the end of the book. You might want to find the Subject Index and Glossary right now and familiarize yourself with it. You can also consult or download a list of key terms with their definitions from this Internet site: **www.cengage.com/psychology/kalat.**

I sometimes meet students who think they have mastered the course because they have memorized the definitions. You do need to understand the defined words, but don't memorize the definitions word for word. It would be better to try to use each word in a sentence or think of examples of each term. Better yet, when appropriate, think of evidence for or against the concept that the term represents.

Questions to Check Your Understanding

People remember material better if they alternate between reading and testing than if they spend the whole time reading. (We'll consider that point again in the chapter on memory.) At various points in this text are Concept Checks, questions that ask you to use or apply the information you just read. Try to answer each of them before reading the answer. If your answer is correct, you can feel encouraged. If it is incorrect, you should reread the section.

Try It Yourself Activities

The text includes many items marked Try It Yourself. Most of these can be done with little or no equipment in a short time. You will understand and remember the text far better if you try these exercises. Online Try It Yourself activities are also available at **www.cengage.com/psychology/kalat.** The purpose of these is the same as the Try It Yourself activities in the text; the difference is that online activities can include sounds and motion. The description of a research study will be easier to understand and remember after you have experienced it yourself.

What's the Evidence Sections

Every chapter except the first includes a section titled What's the Evidence? These sections highlight research studies in more than the usual amount of detail, specifying the hypothesis (idea being tested), research methods, results, and interpretation. In some cases, the discussion also mentions the limitations of the study. The purpose of these sections is to provide examples of how to evaluate evidence.

Internet Site

The text website is **www.cengage.com/psychology/ kalat.** This site offers flash cards, quizzes, interactive art, an online glossary, and links to other interesting websites related to each chapter. The site also includes the Online Try It Yourself activities. All of these opportunities are highly recommended; please explore them.

Indexes and Reference List

A list of all the references cited in the text is at the back of the book in case you want to check something for more details. The combined Subject Index and Glossary defines key terms and indicates where in the book to find more information. The name index provides the same information for all names mentioned in the text.

Optional Study Guide

Also available is a Study Guide to accompany this text, written by Mark Ludorf. It provides detailed chapter outlines, learning objectives, study hints, and other helpful information. The most valuable part for most students is the sample test questions, with an answer key that explains not only which answer is right but also why each of the others is wrong. The website offers some sample questions but not as many. The Study Guide also includes a language-building component. The Study Guide is recommended for students who have struggled with multiple-choice tests in the past and who are willing to spend some time in addition to reading the book and studying lecture notes. If your bookstore does not stock the Study Guide, you can ask them to order a copy. The ISBN is **0495909475.**

ANSWERS TO SOME FREQUENTLY ASKED QUESTIONS

Do you have any useful suggestions for improving study habits? Whenever students ask me why they did badly on the last test, I ask, "When did you read the assignment?" Many answer, "Well, I didn't exactly read *all* of the assignment," or "I read it the night before the test." If you want to learn the subject matter well, read the assigned material before the lecture, review it again after the lecture, and quickly go over it again a few days later. Then reread the textbook assignments and your lecture notes before a test. Memory researchers have established that you will understand and remember something better by studying it several times spread out over days than by studying the same amount of time all at once. Also, of course, the more total time you spend studying, the better.

When you study, don't just read the text but stop and think about it. The more actively you use the material, the better you will remember it. One way to improve your studying is to read by the SPAR method: **S**urvey, **P**rocess meaningfully, **A**sk questions, **R**eview.

Survey: Know what to expect so that you can focus on the main points. When you start a chapter, first look over the outline to get a preview of the contents. When you start a new module, turn to the end and read the summary.

Process meaningfully: Read the chapter carefully, stopping to think from time to time. Tell your roommate something you learned. Think about how you might apply a concept to a real-life situation. Pause when you come to the Concept Checks and try to answer them. Do the Try It Yourself exercises. Try to monitor how well you understand the text and adjust your reading accordingly. Good readers read quickly through easy, familiar content but slowly through difficult material.

Ask questions: When you finish the chapter, try to anticipate what you might be asked later. You can use questions in the Study Guide, on the website, or compose your own. Write out the questions and think about them, but do not answer them yet.

Review: Pause for at least an hour, preferably a day. Now return to your questions and try to answer them. Check your answers against the text or the answers in the Study Guide. Reinforcing your memory a day or two after you first read the chapter will help you retain the material longer and deepen your understanding. If you study the same material several times at lengthy intervals, you increase your chance of remembering it long after the course is over.

What do those parentheses mean, as in "(Baumeister, 2008)"? Am I supposed to remember the names and dates? Psychologists generally cite references in the text in parentheses rather than in footnotes. "**(Baumeister, 2008)**" refers to an article written by Baumeister, published in 2008. All the references cited in the text are listed in alphabetical order (by the author's last name) in the References section at the back of the book.

You will also notice a few citations that include two dates separated by a slash, such as "(Wundt, 1862/1961)." This means that Wundt's document was originally published in 1862 and was republished in 1961.

No, you should not memorize the parenthetical source citations. They are provided so an interested reader can look up the source of a statement and check for further information. The names that *are* worth remembering, such as B. F. Skinner, Jean Piaget, and Sigmund Freud, are emphasized in the discussion itself.

Can you help me read and understand graphs? The graphs in this book are easy to follow. Just take a minute or so to study them carefully. You will encounter four kinds: pie graphs, bar graphs, line graphs, and scatter plots. Let's look at each kind.

Pie graphs show how a whole is divided into parts. Figure 1 shows the proportion of psychologists who work in various settings. It shows that many are self-employed, almost as many work in colleges and other educational institutions, and a slightly smaller number work in hospitals and other health-care institutions.

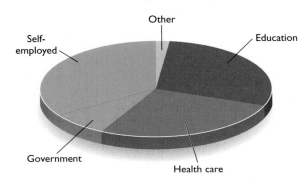

FIGURE 1

Bar graphs show measurements for two or more groups. Figure 2 shows how much unpleasantness three groups of women reported while they were waiting for a painful shock. The unpleasantness was least if a woman could hold her husband's hand while waiting, intermediate if she held a stranger's hand, and most if she was by herself.

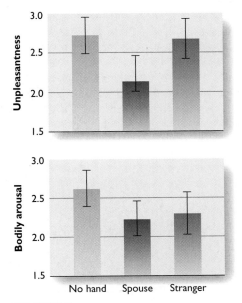

FIGURE 2

Line graphs show how one variable relates to another variable. Figure 3 shows measurements of narcissism (self-centeredness) for young adults tested in various years. The upward trend of the line indicates that over the years, young adults have become more self-centered than in previous generations.

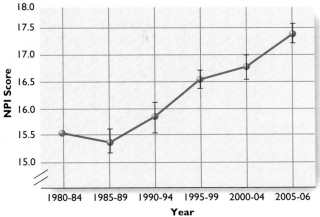

FIGURE 3

Scatter plots are similar to line graphs, with this difference: A line graph shows averages, whereas a scatter plot shows individual data points. By looking at a scatter plot, we can see how much variation occurs among individuals.

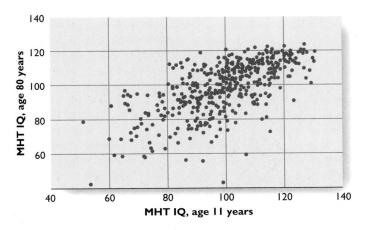

FIGURE 4

To prepare a scatter plot, we make two observations about each individual. In Figure 4, each person is represented by one point. If you take that point and scan down to the *x*-axis, you find that person's score on an IQ test at age 11. If you then scan across to the *y*-axis, you find that person's score on a similar test at age 80. You can see about how consistent most people's scores are over a lifetime.

We may have to take multiple-choice tests on this material. How can I do better on those tests?

1. Read each choice carefully. Do not choose the first answer that looks correct; first make sure that the other answers are wrong. If two answers seem reasonable, decide which of the two is better.

2. If you don't know the correct answer, make an educated guess. Eliminate answers that are clearly wrong. An answer that includes absolute words such as *always* or *never* is probably wrong; don't choose it unless you have a good reason to support it. Also eliminate any answer that includes unfamiliar terms. If you have never heard of something, it is probably not the right answer.

3. After you finish, don't be afraid to go back and reconsider your answers. Students have been telling each other for decades that "you should stick with your first answer," but research says that most people who change their answers improve their scores. When you examine a question a second time, you sometimes discover that you misunderstood it the first time.

LAST WORDS BEFORE WE START . . .

Most of all, I hope you enjoy the text. I have tried to include the liveliest examples I can find. The goal is not just to teach you some facts but also to teach you a love of learning so that you will continue to read more and educate yourself about psychology long after your course is over.

James Kalat

© Matthieu Spohn/Getty Images

What Is Psychology?

Consider This:

If you are like most students, you start off assuming that nearly everything you read in your textbooks and everything your professors tell you must be true. What if it isn't? Suppose impostors have replaced the faculty of your college. They pretend to know what they are talking about and they all vouch for one another's competence, but in fact, they are all unqualified. They have managed to find textbooks that support their prejudices, but those textbooks are full of false information, too. If so, how would you know?

While we are entertaining such skeptical thoughts, why limit ourselves to colleges? When you read books and magazines or listen to political commentators, how do you know who has the right answers?

The answer is that *no one* has the right answers all of the time. Professors, textbook authors, advice columnists, politicians, and others have strong reasons for some beliefs and weak reasons for others. Sometimes, they think they have strong reasons but discover to their embarrassment that they were wrong. I don't mean to imply that you should disregard everything you read or hear. But you should expect people to tell you the reasons for their conclusions so that you can draw your own conclusions. At least if you make a mistake, it will be your own and not someone else's.

You have just encountered the theme of this book: Evaluate the evidence. You will hear all sorts of claims concerning psychology. Some are valid, others are wrong, many are valid under certain conditions, and some are too vague to be either right or wrong. When you finish this book, you will be in a better position to examine evidence and decide which claims to take seriously.

Who has the correct answers? None of us do, at least not always. Even when people we trust seem very confident of their opinions, we should ask for their evidence or reasoning.

Psychologists' Goals

- What is psychology?
- What philosophical questions motivate psychologists?
- What do various kinds of psychologists do?
- Should you consider majoring in psychology?

Your history text probably doesn't spend much time discussing what the term *history* means, and I doubt that a course on English literature spends the first day defining *literature*. Psychology is different because so many people have misconceptions. I remember a student who asked when we were going to get to the kind of psychology he could "use on" people. Another young man bluntly asked me (in my office, not publicly) whether I could teach him tricks to seduce his girlfriend. I told him (a) psychologists don't try to trick people into doing something against their better judgment, (b) if I did know tricks like that, ethically I couldn't tell him about them, and (c) if I knew powerful tricks to control behavior, *and* I had no ethics, I would probably use my powers to manipulate governments and industry instead of teaching introduction to psychology!

The term *psychology* derives from the Greek roots *psyche,* meaning "soul" or "mind," and *logos,* meaning "word." Psychology is literally the study of the mind or soul, and people defined it that way until the early 1900s. Around 1920, psychologists became disenchanted with the idea of studying the mind. First, research deals with what we observe, and the mind is unobservable. Second, talking about "the mind" implies it is a thing or object. Mental activity is a process. It is not like the river but like the flow of the river; not like the automobile but like the movement of the automobile. Beginning in the early 1900s, psychologists defined their field as the study of behavior.

However, we care about what we see, hear, and think, not just about what we do. When you look at this optical illusion and say that the horizontal part of the top line looks longer than that of the bottom line (although really they are the same length), the question is why it *looks* longer, not just why you *said* it looks longer. So for a compromise, let's define **psychology** as *the systematic study of behavior and experience.* The word *experience* lets us discuss your perceptions without implying that a mind exists independently of your body.

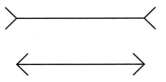

When most people think of psychologists, they think of clinical psychologists—those who try to help worried, depressed, or otherwise troubled people. Clinical psychology is only one part of psychology. Psychology also includes research on sensation and perception, learning and memory, hunger and thirst, sleep, attention, child development, and more. You might expect that a course in psychology will teach you to "analyze" people or decipher hidden aspects of their personality. It will not. You will learn to understand many aspects of behavior, but you will gain no dazzling powers. Ideally, you will become more skeptical of those who claim to analyze people's personality from small samples of their behavior.

GENERAL POINTS ABOUT PSYCHOLOGY

Psychology is a huge, diverse field that is difficult to summarize. Nevertheless, let's start with three of the most general statements about psychology. Each of these will arise repeatedly throughout this text.

"It Depends."

Hardly anything is true about the behavior of all people at all times. Almost every aspect of behavior depends on age. Behavior also varies with people's genetics, health, past experiences, and whether they are currently awake or asleep. In some ways, behavior differs between males and females or from one culture to another. Some aspects depend on the time of day, the temperature of the room, or how recently someone ate. The way people answer a question depends on exactly how the question is worded, what other questions they have already answered, and who is asking the question.

When I describe "it depends" as a general truth of psychology, you may think I am suggesting that psychology has no real answers. On the contrary, "it depends" is a serious point. The key is to know *what* it depends on. The further you pursue your studies of psychology, the more you will become attuned to the wealth of subtle influences that most people overlook. For example, suppose you are about to take a test. At the top of the test, the instructor has put the instructions in bright red letters to make sure you read them. What will be the result? The bright red letters might get you to read the instructions, but you will do less well than usual on this test! Ever since you started school, your teachers have been marking your errors with red ink. Just seeing red ink at the top of a test reminds you of failure. Psychologists have found that even a small red letter or number at the top of a test slightly impairs students' performance (Elliot, Maier, Moller, Friedman, & Meinhardt, 2007).

Another example of "it depends": Decades ago, two psychology laboratories were conducting similar studies on human learning but reporting contradictory results. Both researchers were experienced and highly respected, they thought they were following the same procedures, and they did not understand why their results differed. Eventually, one of them traveled to the other's university to watch the other in action. Almost immediately, he noticed a key difference in procedure: the chairs in which the participants sat! His colleague at the other university had obtained chairs from a retired dentist. So the research participants were sitting in *dentist's* chairs, which reminded them of visits to the dentist. They were sitting there in a state of heightened anxiety, which altered their behavior (Kimble, 1967).

Still another example of "it depends": When you choose a career or a place to live, you can cite all sorts of logical reasons, but you might overlook a subtle, unconscious influence: your name! People named Dennis or Denise are slightly more likely than others to become a dentist, apparently just because they like the sound of the word "dentist," which is similar to their own name. People named Laura or Larry are more likely than others to become a lawyer. People named Louis or Louise are more likely than others to move to Louisiana, and people named George or Georgia are more likely to move to Georgia. People who were born on March 3 (3/3) are more likely than others to move to a town like Three Forks, Montana, or Three Oaks, Michigan (Pelham, Mirenberg, & Jones, 2002). People have a slight tendency to marry someone with the same first initial or last initial as their own (J. T. Jones, Pelham, Carvallo, & Mirenberg, 2004) and a slight tendency to take a job with a company that starts with the same letter as their last name (Anseel & Duyck, 2008). For example, if your name is Jim Davis, you might want to marry Josephine Dillon and work for John Deere company, without realizing that your initials had anything to do with your choices. Much of psychology is about discovering the little, easily ignored factors that influence your actions.

Research Progress Depends on Good Measurement

Nobel Prize–winning biologist Sidney Brenner was quoted as saying, "Progress in science depends on new techniques, new discoveries, and new ideas, probably in that order" (McElheny, 2004, p. 71). Psychologists' understanding has advanced fastest on topics such as sensory processes, learning, and memory, which researchers can measure fairly easily. On topics such as emotion and personality, research progress has been slower because of the difficulty of measurement. As you proceed through this text, especially in the second half, you will note occasional interruptions asking, "Wait . . . how well do IQ scores really measure intelligence?" or "Are people as happy as they say they are?" Areas of psychology with less certain measurement have less definite conclusions and slower progress.

Some Conclusions Reflect Stronger Evidence Than Others

Authors revise psychology textbooks because of new research, and psychologists conduct new research because of everything that we don't know. Unfortunately, people sometimes express strong opinions even about the things we don't know. Admittedly, we sometimes have to make decisions without complete evidence. Still, it is important to distinguish between opinions based on strong evidence and those based on less. For example, solid evidence indicates that a woman who drinks much alcohol during pregnancy risks damage to her infant's brain. Therefore, we try to discourage pregnant women from drinking. On the other hand, is it always a bad idea to spank a child? Is it okay to let children watch television hour after hour? Are men and women biologically predisposed to behave differently? On these issues and others, many people have strong opinions despite the weakness or uncertainty of the evidence. People who express an opinion should describe their evidence (or lack of it) so that others can evaluate it and perhaps overrule it in the light of newer, better evidence.

MAJOR PHILOSOPHICAL ISSUES IN PSYCHOLOGY

Many psychological questions date back to Aristotle and other ancient philosophers. Although psychology has moved away from the methods of philosophy, it addresses many of the same issues. Three of the most profound are free will versus determinism, the mind–brain problem, and the nature–nurture issue.

Free Will versus Determinism

The scientific approach seeks the immediate causes of an event (what led to what). That is, scientists assume determinism, *the idea that everything that happens has a cause, or determinant, that one could observe or measure.* This view is an assumption, not an established fact, but the success of scientific research attests to its value.

Does it apply to human behavior? We are, after all, part of the physical world, and our brains are made of chemicals. According to the determinist assumption, everything we do has causes. This view seems to conflict with the impression all of us have that "*I* make the decisions about my actions. Sometimes, when I am making a decision, like what to eat for lunch or which sweater to buy, I am in doubt right up to the last second. The decision could have gone either way. I wasn't controlled by anything, and no one could have predicted what I would do." *The belief that behavior is caused by a person's independent decisions* is known as free will.

Some psychologists maintain that free will is an illusion (Wegner, 2002): What you call a conscious intention is more a prediction than a cause of your behavior. When you have the conscious experience of "deciding" to move a finger, the behavior is already starting to happen. We shall explore the evidence for this idea later, in the module on consciousness.

Other psychologists and philosophers reply that you do make decisions, in the sense that something within you initiates the action (Baumeister, 2008). Your brain actually burns more calories than usual while making difficult decisions (Masicampo & Baumeister, 2008). (Although it's a measurable effect, it's a small one. You won't lose weight by sitting around thinking deep thoughts.) Even though your brain is made of chemicals, no one could predict your decisions by mapping out all the atoms in your brain. The system as a whole has emergent properties that go beyond the sum of all of its components (Kauffman, 2008).

Nevertheless, the "you" that makes your decisions is itself a product of your heredity and the events of your life. (You did not create yourself.) In a sense, yes, you have a will, an ability to make choices (Dennett, 2003). But your will is not independent of all causes. A computer or robot can also be programmed to make choices. Your heredity and experiences programmed you, and your makeup determines your decisions.

The test of determinism is ultimately empirical: If everything you do has a cause, your behavior should be predictable. In some cases, it definitely is. For example, after a sudden, unexpected, loud noise, the prediction is that you will immediately tense your muscles (unless you are deaf, in a coma, or paralyzed). However, in most cases, psychologists' predictions are more like those of a meteorologist who predicts that tomorrow's weather will be, "High temperature around 30, low temperature around 20, with a 10% chance of precipitation." The imprecision and occasional errors do not mean that the weather is "free" but only that it is subject to so many influences that no one can predict it exactly.

Behavior is guided by external forces, such as waves, and by forces within the individual. According to the determinist view, even those internal forces follow physical laws.

A psychologist trying to predict your behavior will want to know as much as possible about your past behavior, your environment, your current health, your genetics, where you live, and a great deal more. Even with all that information, no one can predict perfectly, any more than physicists can predict exactly where a leaf will fall.

Researchers admit one point: Although determinism makes sense theoretically and leads to good research, it doesn't work well as a philosophy of life. Psychologists asked people to read a passage arguing for determinism or one on an irrelevant topic and then put them in a situation in which it would be easy to "cheat" to gain a personal advantage. A higher percentage of those who read the determinism essay cheated (Vohs & Schooler, 2008). Apparently, they felt less sense of personal responsibility.

The Mind–Brain Problem

Everything you experience or do depends on the physics and chemistry of your nervous system. Then what, if anything, is the mind? The *philosophical question of how experience relates to the brain* is the mind–brain problem (or mind–body problem). In a universe composed of matter and energy, why is there such a thing as a conscious mind? One view, called dualism, holds that *the mind is separate from the brain but somehow controls the brain and therefore the rest of the body.* However, dualism contradicts the law of conservation of matter and energy, one of the cornerstones of physics. According to that principle, the only way to influence any matter or energy, including

Figure 1.1 These PET scans show the brain activity of normal people during different activities. Red indicates the highest activity, followed by yellow, green, and blue. Arrows indicate the most active areas. (Courtesy of Michael E. Phelps and John C. Mazziotta, University of California, Los Angeles, School of Medicine)

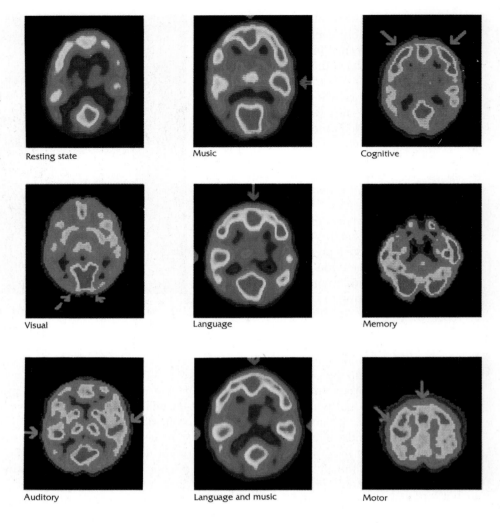

Resting state Music Cognitive

Visual Language Memory

Auditory Language and music Motor

the matter and energy that compose your body, is to act on it with other matter or energy. If the mind isn't composed of matter or energy, it can't *do* anything. For that reason, nearly all brain researchers and philosophers favor monism, *the view that conscious experience is inseparable from the physical brain.* Either the mind is something the brain produces, or mind and brain activity are just two terms for the same thing. The mind–brain problem is a thorny philosophical issue, but it does lend itself to research, some of which we shall consider in chapter 3 on the brain and chapter 10 on consciousness.

The photos in Figure 1.1 show brain activity while a person engages in nine tasks, as measured by a technique called positron-emission tomography (PET). Red indicates the highest degree of brain activity, followed by yellow, green, and blue. As you can see, the various tasks increase activity in different brain areas, although all areas show some activity at all times (Phelps & Mazziotta, 1985). Data such as these show a close relationship between brain activity and psychological events. You might ask: Did the brain activity cause the thoughts, or did the thoughts cause the

brain activity? Most brain researchers reply, "Neither," because brain activity and mental activity are the same thing.

Even if we accept this position, we are still far from understanding the mind–brain relationship. What type of brain activity is associated with consciousness? Why does conscious experience exist at all? Could a brain get along without it? Research studies are not about to resolve these questions and put philosophers out of business, but research results do constrain the philosophical answers that we can seriously consider.

The Nature–Nurture Issue

Why do most little boys spend more time than little girls with toy guns and trucks and less time with dolls? Is it because of biological differences or because of the way parents rear their sons and daughters?

Alcohol abuse is common in some cultures and rare in others. Are these differences entirely a matter of social custom, or do genes influence alcohol use also?

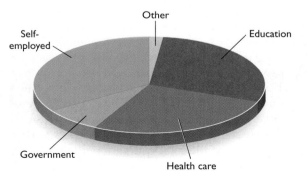

Why do different children develop different interests? They may have had different hereditary tendencies, but they have also experienced different environmental influences. Separating the roles of nature and nurture is difficult.

Certain psychological disorders are more common in large cities than in small towns and in the countryside. Does life in crowded cities cause psychological disorders? Or do people develop such disorders because of a genetic predisposition and then move to big cities in search of jobs, housing, and welfare services?

Each of these questions relates to the **nature–nurture issue** (or heredity–environment issue): *How do differences in behavior relate to differences in heredity and environment?* The nature–nurture issue shows up in various ways throughout psychology, and it seldom has a simple answer. It is the central issue of chapter 5 (development) and also important in several other chapters.

1. In what way does all scientific research presuppose determinism?
2. What is one major objection to dualism?

Concept Check

Answers

1. Any attempt to make discoveries about nature presupposes that we live in a universe of cause and effect.
2. Dualism conflicts with the principle of the conservation of matter and energy. A nonmaterial mind could not influence anything in the universe.

WHAT PSYCHOLOGISTS DO

We have considered some major philosophical issues related to psychology in general. However, most psychologists deal with smaller questions and specialize in narrower fields. They work in many occupational settings, as shown in Figure 1.2. The most common settings are colleges and universities, private practice, hospitals and mental health clinics, and government agencies.

Service Providers to Individuals

It is important to distinguish among several types of mental health professionals. Some of the main kinds of service providers for people with psychological troubles are clinical psychologists, psychiatrists, social workers, and counseling psychologists.

Clinical Psychology

Clinical psychologists *have an advanced degree in psychology, with a specialty in understanding and helping people with psychological problems.* Those problem range from depression, anxiety, and substance abuse to marriage conflicts, difficulties making decisions, or even the feeling that "I should be getting more out of life." Clinical psychologists try, in one way or another, to understand why a person is having problems and then help that person overcome the difficulties. Some clinical psychologists are college professors and researchers, but most are full-time practitioners.

Figure 1.2

Psychologists work in a variety of settings. (Based on data from U.S. Department of Labor, 2008)

Other · Self-employed · Education · Government · Health care

Psychiatry

Psychiatry is a *branch of medicine that deals with emotional disturbances.* To become a psychiatrist, someone first earns an MD degree and then takes an additional 4 years of residency training in psychiatry. Because psychiatrists are medical doctors, they can prescribe drugs, such as tranquilizers and antidepressants, whereas in most places psychologists cannot. Some states now permit psychologists with additional specialized training to prescribe drugs. More psychiatrists than clinical psychologists work in mental hospitals, and psychiatrists more often treat clients with severe disorders.

Does psychiatrists' ability to prescribe drugs give them an advantage over psychologists in places where psychologists cannot prescribe them? Not always. Drugs can be useful, but relying entirely on them can be a mistake. Whereas a typical visit to a clinical psychologist includes an extensive discussion of the issues troubling the client, many visits to a psychiatrist are briefer sessions that focus on checking the effectiveness of a drug and evaluating its side effects. A survey found that over the years, fewer and fewer psychiatrists have been providing talk therapy to their clients (Mojtabai & Olfson, 2008).

Other Mental Health Professionals

Several other kinds of professionals also provide help and counsel. **Psychoanalysts** are *therapy providers who rely heavily on the theories and methods pioneered by the early 20th-century Viennese physician Sigmund Freud and later modified by others.* Freud and his followers attempted to infer the hidden, unconscious, symbolic meaning behind people's words and actions, and psychoanalysts today continue that effort.

There is some question about who may rightly call themselves psychoanalysts. Some people apply the term to anyone who attempts to uncover unconscious thoughts and feelings. Others apply the term only to graduates of a 6- to 8-year program at an institute of psychoanalysis. These institutes admit only people who are already either psychiatrists or clinical psychologists. Thus, people completing psychoanalytic training will be at least in their late 30s.

A **clinical social worker** *is similar to a clinical psychologist but with different training.* In most cases, a clinical social worker has a master's degree in social work with a specialization in psychological problems. Many health maintenance organizations (HMOs) steer most of their clients with psychological problems toward clinical social workers instead of psychologists or psychiatrists because the social workers, with less formal education, charge less per hour. Some psychiatric nurses (nurses with additional training in psychiatry) provide similar services.

Counseling psychologists *help people with educational, vocational, marriage, health-related, and other decisions.* A counseling psychologist has a doctorate degree (PhD, PsyD, or EdD) with supervised experience in counseling. The activities of a counseling psychologist overlap those of a clinical psychologist, but the emphasis is different. Whereas a clinical psychologist deals mainly with anxiety, depression, and other emotional distress, a counseling psychologist deals mostly with life decisions and family or career readjustments, which, admittedly, can cause anxiety or depression. Counseling psychologists work in educational institutions, mental health centers, rehabilitation agencies, businesses, and private practice.

You may also have heard of **forensic psychologists,** *who provide advice and consultation to police, lawyers, and courts.* Forensic psychologists are, in nearly all cases, trained as clinical or counseling psychologists with additional training in legal issues. They help with such decisions as whether a defendant is mentally competent to stand trial or whether someone eligible for parole is dangerous (Otto & Heilbrun, 2002). Several popular films and television series have depicted forensic psychologists helping police investigators develop a "psychological profile" of a serial killer. That may sound like an exciting, glamorous profession, but few psychologists engage in such activities (and the accuracy of their profiles is uncertain, as discussed in chapter 14). Most criminal profilers today have training and experience in law enforcement, not psychology.

Table 1.1 compares various types of mental health professionals.

3. Can psychoanalysts prescribe drugs?

Answer

3. Psychoanalysts begin by receiving a degree in either psychiatry or clinical psychology. Those trained in psychiatry can prescribe drugs because psychiatrists are medical doctors. However, in most states, psychoanalysts trained in clinical psychology cannot prescribe drugs.

Service Providers to Organizations

Psychologists also work in business, industry, and school systems, doing work you might not recognize as psychology. The job prospects in these fields have been good, and you might find these fields interesting.

Table 1.1 Several Types of Mental Health Professionals

Type of Therapist	Education
Clinical psychologist	PhD with clinical emphasis or PsyD plus internship. Ordinarily, 5+ years after undergraduate degree.
Psychiatrist	MD plus psychiatric residency. Total of 8 years after undergraduate degree.
Psychoanalyst	Psychiatry or clinical psychology plus 6–8 years in a psychoanalytic institute. Many others who rely on Freud's methods also call themselves psychoanalysts.
Psychiatric nurse	From 2-year (AA) degree to master's degree plus supervised experience.
Clinical social worker	Master's degree plus 2 years of supervised experience. Total of at least 4 years after undergraduate degree.
Counseling psychologist	PhD, PsyD, or EdD plus supervised experience in counseling.
Forensic psychologist	Doctorate, ordinarily in clinical psychology or counseling psychology, plus additional training in legal issues.

Industrial/Organizational Psychology

The psychological study of people at work is known as **industrial/organizational (I/O) psychology**. It deals with such issues as hiring the right person for a job, training people for jobs, developing work teams, determining salaries and bonuses, providing feedback to workers about their performance, planning an organizational structure, and organizing the workplace so that workers will be productive and satisfied. I/O psychologists study the behavior of both the individual and the organization, including the impact of economic conditions and government regulations. We shall consider work motivation in chapter 11.

Here's an example of a concern for industrial/organizational psychologists (Campion & Thayer, 1989): A company that manufactures complex electronic equipment needed to publish reference and repair manuals for its products. The engineers who designed the devices did not want to spend their time writing the manuals, and none of them were skilled writers anyway. So the company hired a technical writer to prepare the manuals. After a year, she received an unsatisfactory performance rating because the manuals she wrote contained too many technical errors. She countered that, when she asked various engineers in the company to check her manuals or to explain technical details to her, they were always too busy. She found her job complicated and frustrating. Her office was badly lit, noisy, and overheated, and her chair was uncomfortable. Whenever she mentioned these problems, she was told that she "complained too much."

In a situation such as this, an industrial/organizational psychologist helps the company evaluate the problem and consider solutions. Maybe the company hired the wrong person for this job. If so, they should fire her and hire some expert on electrical engineering who is also an outstanding writer and *likes* a badly lit, noisy, overheated, uncomfortable office. However, if the company cannot find or afford such a person, then it needs to improve the working conditions and provide the current employee with more training and help.

Human Factors

Many years ago, my son Sam, then 16 years old, turned to me as he rushed out the door and asked me to turn off his stereo. I went to his room and tried to find a power switch on the stereo. No such luck. I looked in vain for the manual. Finally, in desperation, I had to unplug the stereo.

Learning to operate our increasingly complex machinery is one of the struggles of modern life. Sometimes, the consequences are serious. Imagine an airplane pilot who intends to lower the landing gear and instead raises the wing flaps. Or a worker in a nuclear power plant who fails to notice a warning signal. A type of psychologist known as a **human factors specialist** (or **ergonomist**), *attempts to facilitate the operation of machinery so that ordinary people can use it efficiently and safely.* The term *ergonomics* is derived from Greek roots meaning "laws of work." Ergonomics was first used in military settings, where complex technologies sometimes required soldiers to spot nearly invisible targets, understand speech through deafening noise, track objects in three dimensions, and make life-or-death decisions in a split second. The military turned to psychologists to determine what skills their personnel could master and to redesign the tasks to fit those skills.

Human factors specialists help redesign machines to make them easier and safer to use. This field uses principles of both engineering and psychology.

Human factors specialists soon applied their experience not only to business and industry but also to everyday devices, such as cameras, computers, microwave ovens, and cell phones. At various universities, the human factors program is part of the psychology department, engineering, or both. Regardless of who administers the program, it combines features of psychology, engineering, and computer science. It is a growing field with many jobs available.

School Psychology

Many if not most children have academic problems at one time or another. Some children have trouble sitting still or paying attention. Others get into trouble for misbehavior. Some have specialized problems with reading, spelling, arithmetic, or other academic skills. Others master their schoolwork quickly and become bored. They too need special attention.

School psychologists are *specialists in the psychological condition of students,* usually in kindergarten through the 12th grade. Broadly speaking, school psychologists identify the educational needs of children, devise a plan to meet those needs, and then either implement the plan themselves or advise teachers how to implement it.

School psychology can be taught in a psychology department, a branch of an education department, or a department of educational psychology. In some countries, it is possible to practice school psychology with only a bachelor's degree. In the United States, the minimum is usually a master's degree, but a doctorate may become necessary in the future. Job opportunities in school psychology have been strong and continue to grow. Most school psychologists work for a school system; others work for mental health clinics, guidance centers, and other institutions.

Psychologists in Teaching and Research

Many psychologists, especially those who are not clinical psychologists, have positions in colleges and universities where they teach and conduct research. Most of this text deals with that research. To some extent, different kinds of psychologists study different topics. For example, a develop-

mental psychologist might observe children's attempts to control their emotions, and biological psychologists might examine the consequences of brain damage. However, different kinds of psychologists also sometimes study the same questions, approaching them in different ways. To illustrate, let's consider one example: how we select what to eat. Different kinds of psychologists seek different kinds of explanations.

Developmental Psychology

Developmental psychologists *study how behavior changes with age,* "from womb to tomb." For example, they might examine language development from age 2 to 4 or memory from age 60 to 80. They try to explain the changes over age, frequently dealing with the nature–nurture issue. They also examine to what extent behavior is stable over time and to what extent it changes.

With regard to food selection, some taste preferences are present from birth. Newborns prefer sweet tastes and avoid bitter and sour substances. However, they appear indifferent to salty tastes, as if they could not yet taste salts (Beauchamp, Cowart, Mennella, & Marsh, 1994). Toddlers around the age of $1^1/_2$ will try to eat almost anything they can fit into their mouths, unless it tastes sour or bitter. For that reason, parents need to keep dangerous substances like furniture polish out of toddlers' reach. Older chil-

Infants and young children will try to eat almost anything. As they grow older, they learn to avoid foods for reasons other than just taste.

If you ate corn dogs and cotton candy and then got sick on a wild ride, something in your brain would blame the food, regardless of what you think consciously. Ordinarily, however, this kind of learning teaches us to avoid harmful substances.

dren become increasingly selective, even "picky" about what foods they will accept. However, even up to age 7 or 8, about the only reason children give for refusing to eat something is that they think it would taste bad (Rozin, Fallon, & Augustoni-Ziskind, 1986). As they grow older, they cite more complex reasons for rejecting foods, such as health concerns.

Learning and Motivation

The research field of **learning and motivation** studies *how behavior depends on the outcomes of past behaviors and current motivations.* How often we engage in any particular behavior depends on the results of that behavior in the past.

We learn our food choices largely by learning what *not* to eat. For example, if you eat something and then feel sick, you form an aversion to the taste of that food, especially if it was unfamiliar. It doesn't matter whether you consciously think the food made you ill. If you eat something at an amusement park and then go on a wild ride and get sick, you may dislike that food, even though you know the ride was at fault.

Cognitive Psychology

Cognition refers to *thought and knowledge.* A **cognitive psychologist** *studies those processes.* (The root *cogn-* also shows up in the word *recognize,* which literally means "to know again.") Cognitive psychologists emphasize how our thinking influences our behaviors. Typical research for cognitive psychologists focuses on memory, language, problem solving, and decision making. Possible research questions include, "What does it take to become an expert in a certain field? What does an expert do that other people don't, and how do experts solve problems in their field?"

Applying cognitive psychology to food selection is a bit of a stretch, but our cognitions about food do enter into our food decisions. For example, people often refuse an edible food just because of the very idea of it (Rozin & Fallon, 1987; Rozin, Millman, & Nemeroff, 1986). Most people in the United States refuse to eat meat from dogs, cats, or horses. Vegetarians reject all meat, not because they think it would taste bad, but because they dislike the idea of eating animal parts. The longer people have been vegetarians, the more firmly they tend to regard meat eating as not only undesirable but also immoral (Rozin, Markwith, & Stoess, 1997).

How would you like to try the tasty morsels in Figure 1.3? Most people are repulsed by the idea of eating insects or reptiles, even if they are germ-free (Rozin & Fallon, 1987). Would you be willing to drink a glass of apple juice after a cockroach had been dipped into it? What if the cockroach had been carefully sterilized? Some people not only refuse to drink that glass of apple juice but say they have lost their taste for apple juice in general (Rozin et al., 1986). Would you drink pure water from a brand-new, never-used toilet bowl? Would you eat a piece of chocolate fudge shaped like dog feces? If not, you are guided by the idea of the food, not its taste or safety.

Biological Psychology

A **biopsychologist** (or **behavioral neuroscientist**) *explains behavior in terms of biological factors, such as electrical and chemical activities in the nervous system, the effects of drugs and hormones, genetics, and evolutionary pressures.* How would a biological psychologist approach the question of how people (or animals) select foods?

A major contributor to food selection is taste, and we have some built-in taste preferences. From birth on, people (and nearly all other mammals) avidly consume sweets but spit out anything sour or bitter.

A small part of the difference among people in their taste preferences relates to the fact that some people have up to three times as many taste buds as others do, mostly for genetic reasons. The genes vary within each population, although the relative frequencies of strong tasters and weak tasters are fairly similar for Asia, Europe, and Africa (Wooding et al., 2004). People with the most taste buds usually have the least tolerance for strong tastes, including black coffee, black breads, hot peppers, grapefruit, radishes, and Brussels sprouts (Bartoshuk, Duffy, Lucchina, Prutkin, & Fast, 1998; Drewnowski, Henderson, Shore, & Barratt-Fornell, 1998). They are generally

Figure 1.3 Different cultures have different food taboos. Here is an assortment of insect and reptile dishes. (Yum, yum?)

satisfied with small portions of desserts, as they don't need much sugar to satisfy their craving.

Hormones also affect taste preferences. Many years ago, one child showed a strong craving for salt. As an infant, he licked the salt off crackers and bacon without eating the food itself. He put a thick layer of salt on everything he ate, and sometimes, he swallowed salt directly from the shaker. When deprived of salt, he stopped eating and began to waste away. At the age of $3^1/_2$, he was taken to the hospital and fed the usual hospital fare. He soon died of salt deficiency (Wilkins & Richter, 1940).

The reason was that he had defective adrenal glands, which secrete the hormones that enable the body to retain salt (Verrey & Beron, 1996). He craved salt because he had to consume it fast enough to replace what he lost in his urine. (Too much salt is bad for your health, but too little salt is also dangerous.) Later research confirmed that salt-deficient animals immediately show an increased preference for salty tastes (Rozin & Kalat, 1971). Apparently, becoming salt deficient causes salty foods to taste especially good (Jacobs, Mark, & Scott, 1988). People often report salt cravings after losing salt by bleeding or sweating.

Cassava, a root vegetable native to South America, is now a staple food in much of Africa as well. It grows in climates not suitable for most other crops. However, people must pound and wash it for days to remove the cyanide.

Evolutionary Psychology

An **evolutionary psychologist** *tries to explain behavior in terms of the evolutionary history of the species, including reasons evolution might have favored a tendency to act in particular ways.* For example, *why* do people and other animals crave sweets and avoid bitter tastes? Here, the answer is easy: Most sweets are nutritious and almost all bitter substances are poisonous (T. R. Scott & Verhagen, 2000). Ancient animals that ate fruits and other sweets survived to become our ancestors. Animals that ate bitter substances were likely to die before they could reproduce.

However, although some evolutionary explanations of behavior are persuasive, others are debatable (de Waal, 2002). Yes, the brain is the product of evolution, just as any other organ is, but the question is whether evolution has micromanaged our behavior. The research challenge is to separate the evolutionary influences on our behavior from what we have learned during a lifetime. Chapter 13 on social psychology will explore this question in more detail.

Social Psychology and Cross-Cultural Psychology

Social psychologists *study how an individual influences other people and how the group influences an individual.* For example, people usually eat together, and on the average we eat about twice as much when we are in a large group than we do when eating alone (de Castro, 2000). If you invite guests to your house, you offer them something to eat or drink as an important way of strengthening a social relationship.

Cross-cultural psychology *compares the behavior of people from different cultures.* It overlaps social psychology, except that it compares one culture to another. Comparing people from different cultures is central to determining what is truly characteristic of humans and what varies depending on our background.

Cuisine is one of the most stable and defining features of any culture. In one study, researchers interviewed Japanese high school and college students who had spent a year in another country as part of an exchange program. The satisfaction reported by students with their year abroad had little relationship to the educational system, religion, family life, recreation, or dating customs of the host country. The main determinant of their satisfaction was the food: Students who could sometimes eat Japanese food had a good time. Those who could not became homesick (Furukawa, 1997).

The similarity between the words *culture* and *agriculture* is no coincidence, as cultivating crops was a major step toward civilization. We learn

from our culture what to eat and how to prepare it (Rozin, 1996). Consider, for example, cassava, a root vegetable that is poisonous unless someone washes and pounds it for 3 days. Can you imagine discovering that fact? Someone had to say, "So far, everyone who ate this plant died, but I bet that if I wash and pound it for 3 days, then it will be okay." Our culture also teaches us good ways of combining foods. American corn (maize) is deficient in certain nutrients and beans are deficient in others, but corn and beans together make a good combination—as the Native Americans discovered long ago.

Table 1.2 summarizes some of the major fields of psychology, including several that have not been discussed.

Concept Check

4. **a.** Of the kinds of psychological research just described—developmental psychology, learning and motivation, cognitive psychology, biological psychology, evolutionary psychology, social psychology, and cross-cultural psychology—which field concentrates most on children?
   b. Which two are most concerned with how people behave in groups?
   c. Which concentrates most on thought and knowledge?
   d. Which is most interested in the effects of brain damage?
   e. Which is most concerned with studying the effect of a reward on future behavior?
5. Why do many menstruating women crave potato chips?

TABLE 1.2 Some Major Specializations in Psychology

Specialization	General Interest	Example of Interest or Research Topic
Biopsychologist	Relationship between brain and behavior	What body signals indicate hunger and satiety?
Clinical psychologist	Emotional difficulties	How can people be helped to overcome severe anxiety?
Cognitive psychologist	Memory, thinking	Do people have several kinds of memory?
Community psychologist	Organizations and social structures	Would improved job opportunities decrease psychological distress?
Counseling psychologist	Helping people make important decisions	Should this person consider changing careers?
Developmental psychologist	Changes in behavior over age	At what age can a child first distinguish between appearance and reality?
Educational psychologist	Improvement of learning in school	What is the best way to test a student's knowledge?
Environmental psychologist	How noise, heat, crowding, etc. affect behavior	What building design can maximize the productivity of the people who use it?
Evolutionary psychologist	Evolutionary history of behavior	How did people evolve their facial expressions of emotion?
Human factors specialist	Communication between person and machine	How can an airplane cockpit be redesigned to increase safety?
Industrial/organizational psychologist	People at work	Should jobs be made simple and foolproof or interesting and challenging?
Learning and motivation specialist	Learning in humans and other species	What are the effects of reinforcement and punishment?
Personality psychologist	Personality differences	Why are certain people shy and others gregarious?
Psychometrician	Measuring intelligence, personality, interests	How fair are current IQ tests? Can we devise better tests?
School psychologist	Problems that affect schoolchildren	How should the school handle a child who regularly disrupts the classroom?
Social psychologist	Group behavior, social influences	What methods of persuasion are most effective for changing attitudes?

Answers

4. **a.** Developmental psychology. **b.** Social psychology and cross-cultural psychology. **c.** Cognitive psychology. **d.** Biological psychology. **e.** Learning and motivation.
5. By losing blood, they also lose salt, and a deficiency of salt triggers a craving for salty tastes.

SHOULD YOU MAJOR IN PSYCHOLOGY?

Can you get a job if you major in psychology? Psychology is one of the most popular majors in the United States, Canada, and Europe. So if psychology majors cannot get jobs, a huge number of people are going to be in trouble!

The bad news is that few jobs specifically advertise for college graduates with a bachelor's degree in psychology. The good news is that an enormous variety of jobs are available for graduates with a bachelor's degree, not specifying any major. If you earn a degree in psychology, you will compete with history majors, English majors, astronomy majors, and everyone else for jobs in government, business, and industry. According to one survey, only 20 to 25% of psychology majors took a job closely related to psychology, such as personnel work or social services (Borden & Rajecki, 2000). Still, many other jobs were good ones, even if they were not in psychology.

Even if you get a job that seems remote from psychology, your psychology courses will have taught you much about how to evaluate evidence, organize and write papers, handle statistics, listen carefully to what people say, understand and respect cultural differences, and so forth. You will, of course, also gain useful background in your other courses. Regardless of your major, you should develop your skills in communication, mathematics, and computers. (If you don't have those skills, you will work for someone who does.)

Psychology also provides a good background for people entering professional schools. Many students major in psychology and then apply to medical school, law school, divinity school, or other programs. Find out what coursework is expected for the professional program of your choice and then compare the coursework required for a psychology major. You will probably find that the psychology major is compatible with your professional preparation.

Suppose you want a career as a psychologist. The educational requirements vary among countries, but in the United States and Canada, nearly all jobs in psychology require education beyond the bachelor's degree. People with a master's degree can get jobs in mental health or educational counseling, but in most states, they must work under the supervision of someone with a doctorate. People with a PhD (doctor of philosophy) in clinical psychology or a PsyD (doctor of psychology) degree can provide mental health services. The main difference between the PhD and PsyD degrees is that the PhD includes an extensive research project, leading to a dissertation, whereas the PsyD degree does not. PsyD programs vary strikingly, including some that are academically strong and others with low standards (Norcross, Kohout, & Wicherski, 2005). A college teaching or research position almost always requires a PhD.

An increasing percentage of doctorate-level psychologists now work in business, industry, and the military doing research related to practical problems. If you are a first- or second-year college student now, it is hard to predict what the job market will be by the time you finish an advanced degree. If you are just looking for a safe, secure way to make a living, psychology offers no guarantees. A career in psychology is for those whose excitement about the field draws them irresistibly to it.

For more information about majoring in psychology, prospects for graduate school, and a great variety of jobs for psychology graduates, visit the American Psychological Association's website. To find the most current link to the APA site, visit **www.cengage.com/psychology/kalat**.

1.1   module

In Closing

Types of Psychologists

An experimental psychology researcher, a clinical psychologist, a human factors specialist, and an industrial/organizational psychologist are all psychologists, even though their daily activities have little in common. What unites psychologists is a dedication to progress through research.

I have oversimplified this discussion of the various psychological approaches in several ways. In particular, biological psychology, cognitive psychology, social psychology, and the other fields overlap significantly. Nearly all psychologists combine insights and information gained from several approaches. Many like to hyphenate their self-description to emphasize the overlap. For example, "I'm a social-developmental-cognitive neuroscientist."

As we proceed through this book, we shall consider one type of behavior at a time and, generally, one approach at a time. That is simply a necessity; we cannot talk intelligently about many topics at once. But bear in mind that all these processes do ultimately fit together. What you do at any given moment depends on a great many influences.

SUMMARY

The page number after an item indicates where the topic is first discussed.

- *What is psychology?* Psychology is the systematic study of behavior and experience. Psychologists deal with both theoretical and practical questions. (page 3)
- *Three general themes.* Almost any statement in psychology depends on many factors, and few statements apply to everyone all the time. Research progress depends on good measurement. Some conclusions in psychology are based on stronger evidence than others. (page 3)
- *Determinism–free will.* Determinism is the view that everything that occurs, including human behavior, has a physical cause. This view is difficult to reconcile with the conviction that humans have free will—that we deliberately, consciously decide what to do. (page 4)
- *Mind–brain.* The mind–brain problem is the question of how conscious experience relates to the activity of the brain. (page 5)
- *Nature–nurture.* Behavior depends on both nature (heredity) and nurture (environment). The relative contributions of nature and nurture vary from one behavior to another. (page 6)

- *Psychology and psychiatry.* Clinical psychologists have a PhD, PsyD, or master's degree. Psychiatrists are medical doctors. Both clinical psychologists and psychiatrists treat people with emotional problems, but psychiatrists can prescribe drugs and other medical treatments, whereas in most states, psychologists cannot. Counseling psychologists help people deal with difficult decisions, and they less often deal with serious disorders. (page 7)
- *Service providers to organizations.* Nonclinical fields of application include industrial/organizational psychology, human factors, and school psychology. (page 8)
- *Research fields in psychology.* Psychology as an academic field has many subfields, including biological psychology, learning and motivation, cognitive psychology, developmental psychology, and social psychology. (page 10)
- *Job prospects.* People with a bachelor's degree in psychology enter a wide variety of careers or continue their education in professional schools. Those with a doctorate in psychology have additional possibilities depending on their area of specialization. In psychology, as in any other field, job prospects can change between the start and finish of one's education. (page 13)

KEY TERMS

You can check the page listed for a complete description of a term. You can also check the glossary/index at the end of the text for a definition of a given term, or you can download a list of all the terms and their definitions for any chapter at this website: **www.cengage.com/ psychology/kalat**

biopsychologist (or behavioral neuroscientist) (page 11)

clinical psychologist (page 7)

clinical social worker (page 8)

cognition (page 11)

cognitive psychologist (page 11)

counseling psychologist (page 8)

cross-cultural psychology (page 12)

determinism (page 4)

developmental psychologist (page 10)

dualism (page 5)

evolutionary psychologist (page 12)

forensic psychologist (page 8)

free will (page 5)

human factors specialist (or ergonomist) (page 9)

industrial/organizational (I/O) psychology (page 9)

learning and motivation (page 11)

mind–brain problem (page 5)

monism (page 6)

nature–nurture issue (page 7)

psychiatry (page 8)

psychoanalyst (page 8)

psychology (page 3)

school psychologist (page 10)

social psychologist (page 12)

Psychology Then and Now

- How did psychology get started?
- What were the interests of early psychologists?
- How has psychology changed over the years?

Imagine yourself as a young scholar in 1880. Enthusiastic about the new scientific approach in psychology, you have decided to become a psychologist. Like other early psychologists, you have a background in either biology or philosophy. You are determined to apply the scientific methods of biology to the problems of philosophy.

So far, so good. But what questions will you address? A good research question is interesting and answerable. (If it can't be both, it should at least be one or the other!) In 1880 how would you choose a research topic? You cannot get research ideas from a psychological journal because the first issue won't be published until next year. (Incidentally, it will be in German.) You cannot follow in the tradition of previous researchers because there haven't *been* any previous researchers. You are on your own.

In the next several pages, we shall explore some of the changes in what psychologists considered good research topics, including projects that dominated psychology for a while and then faded. We shall discuss additional historical developments in later chapters. Figure 1.4 outlines some major historical events inside and outside psychology. For additional information about the history of psychology, visit **www.cengage.com/psychology/kalat** for current links to helpful websites.

THE EARLY ERA

At least since Aristotle (384–322 B.C.), philosophers and writers have debated why people act the way they do, why they have the experiences they do, and why one person is different from another. Without discounting the importance of these great thinkers, several 19th-century scholars advocated a scientific approach. Impressed by the great strides made in physics, chemistry, and biology, they hoped for similar progress in psychology.

Wilhelm Wundt and the First Psychological Laboratory

The origin of psychology as we now know it is generally dated to 1879, when medical doctor and sensory researcher Wilhelm Wundt (pronounced *voont*) set up the first psychology laboratory in Leipzig, Germany. People had been interested in psychological questions throughout history, and occasionally, biologists and others had done research related to these questions, but Wundt was the first person to establish a laboratory intended exclusively for psychological research.

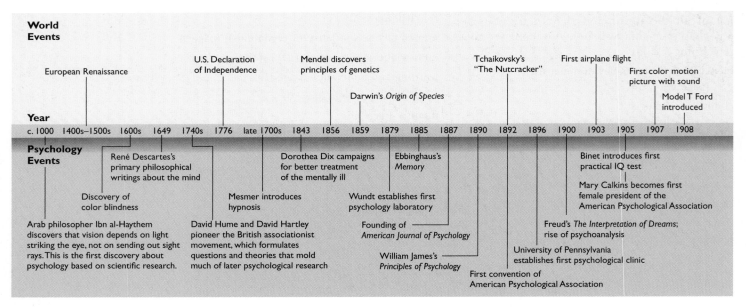

Figure 1.4 Dates of some important events in psychology and elsewhere. (Based partly on Dewsbury, 2000a)

Figure 1.5 (Left) In one of Wilhelm Wundt's earliest studies, the pendulum struck the metal balls (b and d), making a sound each time. To an observer, however, the ball appeared to be somewhere else at the time of the sound, approximately the distance that it would travel in $1/8$ of a second. Wundt inferred that a person needs that much time to shift attention from one stimulus to another. (Right) Animated cartoonists rediscovered Wundt's observation decades later: The character's mouth movements seem to be in synchrony with the sounds if the movements precede the sounds by $1/8$ to $1/6$ of a second.

Wundt's interests ranged from sensory physiology and the timing of conscious experience (Figure 1.5) to cultural differences in behavior, with emphases on motivation, voluntary control, and cognitive processes (Zehr, 2000). One of Wundt's fundamental questions was: What are the components of experience, or mind? He proposed that experience is composed of elements and compounds, like those of chemistry. Psychology's elements were, he maintained, sensations and feelings (Wundt, 1896/1902).[1] At any moment, you might experience the taste of a fine meal, the sound of good music, and a certain degree of pleasure. These would merge into a single experience (a compound) based on the separate elements. Furthermore, Wundt maintained, your experience is partly under your voluntary control; you can shift your attention from one element to another and get a different experience.

[1] A reference citation containing a slash between the years, such as this one, refers to a book originally published in the first year (1896) and reprinted in the second year (1902). All references are listed at the end of the book.

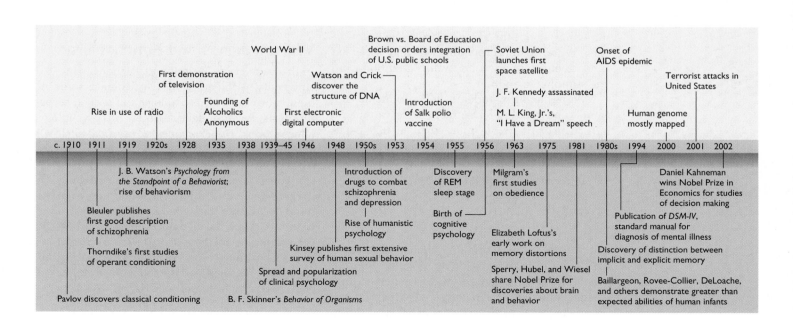

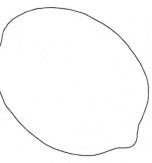

Edward Titchener asked subjects to describe their sensations. For example, they might describe their sensation of shape, their sensation of color, and their sensation of texture while looking at a lemon. Titchener had no way to check the accuracy of these reports, however, so later psychologists abandoned his methods.

Wundt tried to test his idea about the components of experience by collecting data. He presented various kinds of lights, textures, and sounds and asked subjects to report the intensity and quality of their sensations. That is, he asked them to introspect—*to look within themselves.* He recorded the changes in people's reports as he changed the stimuli.

Wundt demonstrated the possibility of meaningful psychological research. For example, in one of his earliest studies, he set up a pendulum that struck metal balls and made a sound at two points on its swing (points b and d in Figure 1.5). People would watch the pendulum and indicate where it appeared to be when they heard the sound. Often, the pendulum appeared to be slightly in front of or behind the ball when people heard the strike. The apparent position of the pendulum at the time of the sound differed from its actual position by an average of $^1/_8$ of a second (Wundt, 1862/1961). Apparently, the time we think we see or hear something is not the same as when the event occurs. Wundt's interpretation was that a person needs about $^1/_8$ of a second to shift attention from one stimulus to another.

Wundt and his students were prolific investigators, and the brief treatment here cannot do him justice. He wrote more than 50,000 pages about his research, but his main impact came from setting the precedent of collecting scientific data to answer psychological questions.

Edward Titchener and Structuralism

At first, most of the world's psychologists received their education from Wilhelm Wundt himself. One of Wundt's students, Edward Titchener, came to the United States in 1892 as a psychology professor at Cornell University. Like Wundt, Titchener believed that the main question of psychology was the nature of mental experiences.

Titchener (1910) typically presented a stimulus and asked his subject to analyze it into its separate features—for example, to look at a lemon and describe its yellowness, brightness, shape, and other characteristics. He called his approach structuralism, *an attempt to describe the structures that compose the mind,* particularly sensations, feelings, and images. For example, imagine you are the psychologist: I look at a lemon and try to describe my experience of its brightness to you separately from my experience of its yellowness.

You see the problem. How do you know whether my reports are accurate? After Titchener died in 1927, psychologists virtually abandoned both his questions and his methods. Why? Remember that a good scientific question is both interesting and answerable. Regardless of whether Titchener's questions about the elements of the mind were interesting, they seemed unanswerable.

William James and Functionalism

In the same era as Wundt and Titchener, Harvard University's William James articulated some of the major issues of psychology and earned recognition as the founder of American psychology. James's book *The Principles of Psychology* (1890) defined many of the questions that still dominate psychology today.

James had little patience with searching for the elements of the mind. He focused on what the mind *does* rather than what it *is.* That is, instead of trying to isolate the elements of consciousness, he preferred *to learn how people produce useful behaviors.* For this reason, we call his approach functionalism. He suggested the following examples of good psychological questions (James, 1890):

● How can people strengthen good habits?
● Can someone attend to more than one item at a time?

- How do people recognize that they have seen something before?
- How does an intention lead to action?

James proposed possible answers but did little research of his own. His main contribution was to inspire later researchers to address the questions that he posed.

Studying Sensation

One of early psychologists' main research topics was the relationship between physical stimuli and psychological sensations. To a large extent, the study of sensation *was* psychology. The first English-language textbook of the "new" scientifically based psychology devoted almost half of its pages to the senses and related topics (Scripture, 1907). By the 1930s, psychology textbooks devoted less than 20% of their pages to these topics (Woodworth, 1934), and today, the proportion is 5–10%. Why were early psychologists so interested in sensation?

One reason was philosophical: They wanted to understand mental experience, and experience consists of sensations. Another reason was strategic: A scientific psychology had to begin with answerable questions, and questions about sensation are more easily answerable than those about, say, personality.

Early psychologists discovered that what we see, hear, and otherwise experience is not the same as the physical stimulus. For example, a light that is twice as intense as another one does not look twice as bright. Figure 1.6 shows the relationship between the intensity of light and its perceived brightness. *The mathematical description of the relationship between the physical properties of a stimulus and its perceived properties* is called the psychophysical function because it relates psychology to physics. Such research demonstrated that, at least in the study of sensation, scientific methods provide nonobvious answers to psychological questions.

----

6. What topic was the main focus of research for the earliest psychologists and why?
7. What was the difference between structuralists and functionalists?

Concept Check

Answers

6. Early psychological research focused mainly on sensation because sensation is central to experience and because the early researchers believed that sensation questions were answerable.
7. Structuralists wanted to understand the components of the mind. They based their research mainly on introspection. Functionalists wanted to explore what the mind could *do*, and they focused mainly on behavior.

Darwin and the Study of Animal Intelligence

Charles Darwin's theory of evolution by natural selection (Darwin, 1859, 1871) had an enormous impact on psychology as well as biology. Darwin argued that humans and other species share a remote common ancestor. This idea implied that each species has specializations adapted to its own way of life but also that all vertebrate species have many features in common. It further implied that nonhuman animals should exhibit varying degrees of human characteristics, including intelligence.

Based on this last implication, early comparative psychologists, *specialists who compare different animal species,* did something that seemed more reasonable then than it does now: They set out to measure animal intelligence. They apparently imagined that they could rank-order animals from the smartest to the dullest. Toward that goal, they set various species to such tasks as the delayed-response problem and the detour problem. In the *delayed-response problem,* an animal sees or hears a signal indicating where it can find food. Then the signal ends, and the animal is restrained for a delay to see how long it remembers the signal (Figure 1.7). In the *detour problem,* an animal is separated from food by a barrier to see whether it takes a detour away from the food to reach it (Figure 1.8).

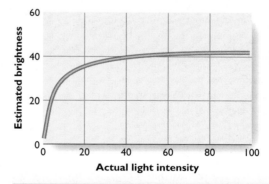

Figure 1.6 This graph of a psychophysical event shows the perceived intensity of light versus its physical intensity. When a light becomes twice as intense physically, it does not seem twice as bright. (Adapted from Stevens, 1961)

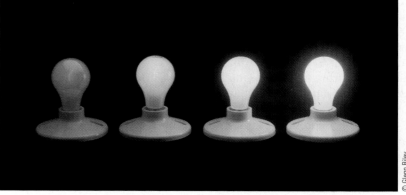

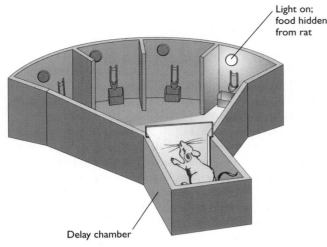

Light on; food hidden from rat

Delay chamber

Figure 1.7 Early comparative psychologists assessed animal intelligence with the delayed-response problem. Variations on this delayed-response task are still used today.

Food

Figure 1.8 Another task popular among early comparative psychologists was the detour problem. An animal must go away from the food to move toward it.

Psychologists today continue to study animal learning and intelligence, but the emphasis has changed. The questions are now, "What can we learn from animal studies about the mechanisms of intelligent behavior?" and "How did each species evolve the behavioral tendencies it shows?"

Measuring Human Intelligence

While some psychologists studied animal intelligence, others pursued human intelligence. Francis Galton, a cousin of Charles Darwin, was among the first to try to measure intelligence and to ask whether intellectual variations were based on heredity. Galton was fascinated with measurement (Hergenhahn, 1992). For example, he invented the weather map, measured degrees of boredom during lectures, suggested the use of fingerprints to identify individuals, and—in the name of science—attempted to measure the beauty of women in different countries.

In an effort to determine the role of heredity in human achievement, Galton (1869/1978) examined whether the sons of famous and accomplished men tended to become eminent themselves. (Women in 19th-century England had little opportunity for fame.) Galton found that the sons of judges, writers, politicians, and other noted men had a high probability of similar accomplishment themselves. He attributed this edge to heredity. (I'll leave this one for you to judge: Did he have adequate evidence for his conclusion? If the sons of famous men become famous themselves, is heredity the only explanation?)

Galton also tried to measure intelligence using simple sensory and motor tasks, but his measurements were unsatisfactory. In 1905 a French

However, measuring animal intelligence turned out to be more difficult than it sounded. Often, a species seemed dull-witted on one task but brilliant on another. For example, zebras are generally slow to learn to approach one pattern instead of another for food unless the patterns happen to be narrow stripes versus wide stripes, in which case they suddenly excel (Giebel, 1958) (Figure 1.9). Rats seem unable to find food hidden under the object that looks different from the others, but they easily learn to choose the object that *smells* different from the others (Langworthy & Jennings, 1972).

Eventually, psychologists realized that the relative intelligence of nonhuman animals was probably a meaningless question. The study of animal learning illuminates general principles of learning and sheds light on evolutionary questions (Papini, 2002), but a dolphin is neither more nor less intelligent than a chimpanzee. It is intelligent in different ways.

Figure 1.9 Zebras learn rapidly when they have to compare stripe patterns. (Giebel, 1958)

researcher named Alfred Binet devised the first useful intelligence test, which we shall discuss further in chapter 9. At this point, just note that the idea of testing intelligence became popular in the United States and other Western countries. Psychologists, inspired by the popularity of intelligence tests, later developed tests of personality, interests, and other psychological characteristics. Note that measuring human intelligence faces some of the same problems as animal intelligence: People have a great many intelligent abilities, and it is possible to be more adept at one than another. Much research goes into trying to make tests of intelligence fair and accurate.

THE RISE OF BEHAVIORISM

Earlier in this chapter, I casually defined psychology as "the systematic study of behavior and experience." For a substantial period of psychology's history, most experimental psychologists would have objected to the words "and experience." Some psychologists still object today, though less strenuously. During the mid-1900s, most researchers described psychology as the study of behavior, period. They had little to say about minds, experiences, or anything of the sort. (According to one quip, psychologists had "lost their minds.") Why?

Recall the failure of Titchener's effort to analyze experience into its components. Most psychologists concluded that questions about mind were unanswerable. Instead, they addressed questions about what they observed: What do people and other animals do and under what circumstances? How do changes in the environment alter what they do? What is learning and how does it occur?

John B. Watson

Many regard John B. Watson as the founder of behaviorism, *a field of psychology that concentrates on observable, measurable behaviors and not on mental processes.* Watson was not the first behaviorist, but he systematized the approach and popularized it (Watson, 1919, 1925). Here are two quotes from Watson:

> Psychology as the behaviorist views it is a purely objective experimental branch of natural science. Its theoretical goal is the prediction and control of behavior. (1913, p. 158)

> The goal of psychological study is the ascertaining of such data and laws that, given the stimulus, psychology can predict what the response will be; or, on the other hand, given the response, it can specify the nature of the effective stimulus. (1919, p. 10)

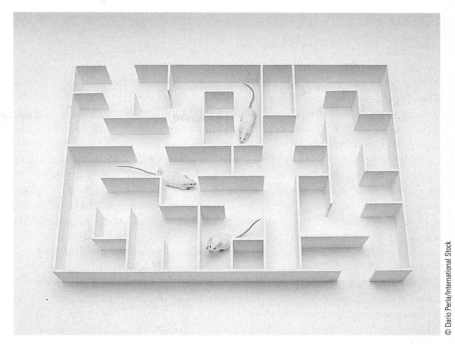

© Dario Perla/International Stock

Early behaviorists studied rats in mazes. As they discovered that this behavior was more complicated than they supposed, their interest turned to other topics.

Studies of Learning

Inspired by Watson, many researchers set out to study animal behavior, especially animal learning. One advantage of studying nonhuman animals is that the researcher can control the animals' diet, waking/sleeping schedule, and so forth far more completely than with humans. The other supposed advantage was that nonhuman learning might be simpler to understand. Many psychologists optimistically expected to discover simple, basic laws of behavior. Just as physicists could study gravity by dropping any object in any location, many psychologists in the mid-1900s thought they could learn all about behavior by studying rats in mazes. One highly influential psychologist, Clark Hull, wrote, "One of the most persistently baffling problems which confronts modern psychologists is the finding of an adequate explanation of the phenomena of maze learning" (1932, p. 25). Another wrote, "I believe that everything important in psychology (except perhaps . . . such matters as involve society and words) can be investigated in essence through the continued experimental and theoretical analysis of the determiners of rat behavior at a choice-point in a maze" (Tolman, 1938, p. 34).

As research progressed, psychologists found that the behavior of a rat in a maze was more complicated than they had expected, and such research declined in popularity. Just as psychologists of the 1920s abandoned the structuralist approach to the mind, later psychologists abandoned the hope that studying rats in mazes would quickly uncover universal principles of behavior. Psychologists continue to study animal learning, but the goals and methods have changed.

The behaviorist approach is still alive and well today, as we shall see in chapter 6, but it no longer dominates experimental psychology as it once did. The rise of computer science showed that it was possible to talk about memory, knowledge, and information processing in machines, and if machines can have such processes, presumably humans can, too. Psychologists demonstrated the possibilities of meaningful research on topics that behaviorists had avoided.

FROM FREUD TO MODERN CLINICAL PSYCHOLOGY

In the early 1900s, clinical psychology was a small field devoted largely to visual, auditory, movement, and memory disorders (Routh, 2000). The treatment of psychological disorders (or mental illness) was the province of psychiatry, a branch of medicine. The Austrian psychiatrist Sigmund Freud revolutionized and popularized psychotherapy with his methods of analyzing patients' dreams and memories. He tried to trace current behavior to early childhood experiences, including children's sexual fantasies. We shall examine Freud's theories in much more detail in chapter 13. Although his evidence was weak, he was a persuasive speaker and writer, and his influence was enormous. By the mid-1900s, most psychiatrists in the United States and Europe were following his methods.

During World War II, more people wanted help, especially soldiers traumatized by war experiences. Because psychiatrists could not keep up with the need, psychologists began providing therapy. Clinical psychology became a more popular field and more similar to psychiatry. Research began to compare the effectiveness of different methods, with newer methods becoming more prominent, as we shall see in chapters 15 and 16.

RECENT TRENDS

Psychology today ranges from the study of simple sensory processes to interventions intended to change communities. Today's research encompasses both basic and applied science. **Basic research** seeks theoretical knowledge for its own sake, such as understanding the processes of learning and memory. **Applied research** deals with practical problems, such as how to help children with learning disabilities. The two kinds of research are mutually supportive. Understanding the basic processes helps applied researchers develop effective interventions. Work toward practical solutions sometimes discovers principles that are theoretically important.

Recall that some of the earliest psychological researchers wanted to study the conscious mind but became discouraged with Titchener's introspective methods. Since the 1960s, cognitive psychology (the study of thought and knowledge) has gradually gained in prominence (over behaviorist approaches) and now dominates experimental psychology. Instead of asking people about their thoughts, today's cognitive psychologists carefully measure the accuracy and speed of responses under various circumstances to draw inferences about the underlying processes.

Another rapidly growing field is neuroscience. Research on the nervous system has advanced rapidly in recent decades. For instance, new techniques of brain scanning now enable researchers to compare brain activity while people engage in different tasks. Today, neuroscience influences nearly every aspect of psychology, and psychologists in almost any field of specialization need to be aware of the field's developments and their theoretical implications (Norcross et al., 2005).

Evolutionary psychology is another new emphasis. Animals that were capable of behaving in certain ways survived, reproduced, and became our ancestors. Those whose behaviors did not lead to reproductive success failed to pass on their genes. In some cases, we can cautiously infer the selective pressures that led to our current behaviors.

For many decades, researchers interested in personality concentrated on fear, anger, sadness, and other disorders or problems. Since the 1990s, a growing field has been **positive psychology**, which *studies the predispositions and experiences that make people happy, productive, and successful.* We turn to this topic in chapter 12.

Figure 1.10 Mary Calkins, one of the first prominent women in U.S. psychology.

New fields of application have also arisen. Health psychologists study how people's health is influenced by their behaviors, such as smoking, drinking, sexual activities, exercise, diet, and reactions to stress. They also try to help people change their behaviors to promote better health. Sports psychologists apply psychological principles to help athletes set goals, train, and concentrate their efforts.

Psychologists today have also broadened their scope to include more of human diversity. In its early days, around 1900, psychology was more open to women than most other academic disciplines, but even so, the opportunities for women were limited (Milar, 2000). Mary Calkins (Figure 1.10), an early memory researcher, was regarded as the Harvard psychology department's best graduate student, but she was denied a PhD because Harvard enforced its tradition of granting degrees only to men (Scarborough & Furomoto, 1987). She did, however, serve as president of the American Psychological Association, as did Margaret Washburn, another important woman in the early days of psychology.

As of 2005, women are receiving more than 70% of new PhDs in psychology (Cynkar, 2007). Women heavily dominate some fields, such as developmental psychology, and hold many leadership roles in psychological organizations. Minority students receive bachelor's and master's degrees almost in proportion to their numbers in the total population. However, the number of African American and Hispanic students receiving PhD degrees lags behind the population norms, as

U.S. population

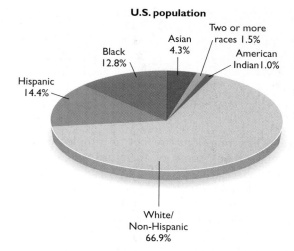

Black 12.8%
Asian 4.3%
Two or more races 1.5%
American Indian 1.0%
Hispanic 14.4%
White/Non-Hispanic 66.9%

Recent psychology doctorates

Hispanic 6.2%
Asian 6.0%
Black 4.4%
Two or more races 4.4%
American Indian 0.4%
White/Non-Hispanic 66.9%

Figure 1.11 Ethnic groups as a percentage of the U.S. population and as a percentage of people receiving doctorate degrees in psychology during 2005. (Source: U.S. Census Bureau population estimates for 2005; Center for Psychology Workforce Analysis and Research. 2005 Doctorate Employment Survey, APA, 2007)

shown in Figure 1.11 (Center for Psychology Workforce Analysis and Research, 2007).

What will psychology be like in the future? We don't know, of course, but we assume it will reflect the changing needs of humanity. A few likely trends are foreseeable. Because advances in medicine have enabled people to live longer, the psychology of aging is increasingly important. Because of depletion of natural resources and climate change, people will need to change their way of life in many ways that we cannot fully anticipate. Persuading people to change their behavior is a task for both politicians and psychologists. See the end-of-chapter section called *Why Does This Matter to Me? Social Responsibility and Psychology* for tips on how psychology can help the world become greener.

8. Why did behaviorists avoid the topics of thought and knowledge?
9. What event led to the rise of clinical psychology as we know it today?

Concept Check

Answers

9. During and after World War II, the need for services was greater than psychiatrists could provide. Clinical psychologists began providing treatment for psychological distress.

8. Behaviorists concentrate on observable behaviors, whereas thought and knowledge are unobservable processes within the individual.

We learn about what is or is not a stable feature of human nature by comparing people of different cultures.

In Closing

Psychology through the Years

Throughout the early years of psychology, many psychologists devoted enormous efforts to projects that produced disappointing results. Not all the efforts of early psychologists were fruitless, and in later chapters, you will encounter many classic studies that have withstood the test of time. Still, if psychologists of the past spent much of their time on projects we now consider misguided, can we be sure that many of today's psychologists aren't on the wrong track?

We can't, of course. In later chapters, you will read about research that has amassed what seems in many cases to be strong evidence, but you are welcome to entertain doubts. Maybe some psy-

chologists' questions are not as simple as they seem; perhaps some of their answers are not solid; perhaps you can think of a better way to approach certain topics. Psychologists have better data and firmer conclusions than they used to, but still, they do not have all the answers.

That is not a reason for despair. Much like a rat in a maze, researchers make progress by trial and error. They pose a question, try a particular research method, and discover what happens. Some results support fascinating and important conclusions; others disconfirm old conclusions and lead to replacements. In either case, the research leads to better questions and better answers.

SUMMARY

- *Choice of research questions.* During the history of psychology, researchers have several times changed their opinions about what constitutes an interesting, important, answerable question. (page 16)
- *First research.* In 1879 Wilhelm Wundt established the first laboratory devoted to psychological research. He demonstrated the possibility of psychological experimentation. (page 16)
- *Limits of self-observation.* One of Wundt's students, Edward Titchener, attempted to analyze the elements of mental experience, relying on people's own observations. Other psychologists became discouraged with this approach. (page 18)
- *The founding of American psychology.* William James, the founder of American psychology, focused attention on how the mind guides useful behavior rather than on the contents of the mind. By doing so, he paved the way for the rise of behaviorism. (page 18)
- *Early sensory research.* In the late 1800s and early 1900s, many researchers concentrated on studies of the senses, partly because sensation is central to mental experience. (page 19)

- *Darwin's influence.* Charles Darwin's theory of evolution by natural selection influenced psychology in many ways. It prompted some prominent early psychologists to compare the intelligence of different species. That question turned out to be more complicated than expected. (page 19)
- *Intelligence testing.* The measurement of human intelligence was one concern of early psychologists that has persisted through the years. (page 20)
- *The era of behaviorist dominance.* As psychologists became discouraged with their attempts to analyze the mind, they turned to behaviorism. For many years, psychological researchers studied behavior, especially animal learning, to the virtual exclusion of mental experience. (page 21)
- *Maze learning.* Clark Hull exerted a great influence on psychology for a number of years. Eventually, his approach became less popular because rats in mazes did not seem to generate simple or general answers to major questions. (page 21)
- *Freud.* Sigmund Freud's theories heavily influenced the early development of psychotherapy, although other methods are more widespread today. (page 22)

- *Clinical psychology.* At one time, psychiatrists provided nearly all the care for people with psychological disorders. After World War II, clinical psychology began to assume much of this role. (page 22)

- *Psychological research today.* Today, psychologists study a wide variety of topics. Cognitive psychology has replaced behaviorist approaches to learning as the dominant field of experimental psychology. Neuroscience now influences researchers in almost all fields. Other new approaches are also becoming widespread. (page 22)

KEY TERMS

You can check the page listed for a complete description of a term. You can also check the glossary/index at the end of the text for a definition of a given term, or you can download a list of all the terms and their definitions for any chapter at this website: **http://psychology.wadsworth.com/ kalat_intro9e/.**

applied research (page 22)

basic research (page 22)

behaviorism (page 21)

comparative psychologist (page 19)

functionalism (page 18)

introspection (page 17)

positive psychology (page 22)

psychophysical function (page 19)

structuralism (page 17)

exploration and study

Why Does This Matter to Me?

SOCIAL RESPONSIBILITY AND PSYCHOLOGY

Many environmental problems are caused by human behavior. Psychologists can help steer the course of our future toward more socially responsible and sustainable outcomes. Students of today need to be ever mindful of the link between human behavior and its impact on the environment and our communities.

"What Is Psychology?" and Social Responsibility: A Step Further

Many prominent psychologists have been interested in the impact humans have on their environment. What environmental issues can you think of that a psychologist might address?

Want Some Tips on How to Live Green?

Find current weblinks on www.cengage.com/psychology/kalat for the following informational websites:
- New American Dream
- The Green Guide
- Ecomall
- EarthEasy: Ideas for Environmentally Sustainable Living
- Green Matters: The Busy Person's Guide to Greener Living

Join the iChapters Plant a Tree Drive!

To show its support of the environmental movement, iChapters is planting a tree on behalf of each fan of the iChapters Facebook Page and for every 10 questions answered correctly in our quiz.
http://www.ichapters.com/plantatree/

Exploration and Study

SUGGESTIONS FOR FURTHER EXPLORATION

In addition to the study materials provided at the end of each module, you may supplement your review of this chapter with the following book and website suggestions or by using one or more of the book's electronic resources, which include its companion website, interactive Cengage Learning eBook, and CengageNOW. Brief descriptions of these resources follow. For more information, visit **www.cengage.com/psychology/kalat.**

ADDITIONAL RESOURCES

The book's companion website, accessible from **www.cengage.com/psychology/kalat,** provides a wide range of study resources such as an interactive glossary, flashcards, tutorial quizzes, updated web links, and Try It Yourself activities.

CengageNOW with Critical Thinking Videos is an easy-to-use resource that helps you study in less time to get the grade you want. An online study system, CengageNOW gives you the option of taking a diagnostic pretest for each chapter. The system uses the results of each pretest to create personalized chapter study plans for you. The Personalized Study Plans

- Help you save study time by identifying areas on which you should concentrate and give you one-click access to corresponding pages of the interactive Cengage Learning eBook;
- Provide interactive exercises and study tools to help you fully understand chapter concepts; and
- Include a posttest for you to take to confirm that you are ready to move on to the next chapter.

Find critical thinking videos in your CengageNOW product, which offer an opportunity for you to learn more about psychological research on different topics.

Books

Sechenov, I. (1965). *Reflexes of the brain.* Cambridge, MA: MIT Press. (Original work published 1863). One of the first attempts to deal with behavior scientifically and still one of the clearest arguments for determinism in human behavior.

Websites

Links to the websites described below are kept current and can be found at **www.cengage.com/psychology/kalat.**

Careers in Psychology

Clinical psychologist Lynn Friedman offers advice on majoring in psychology, going to graduate school, and starting a career.

Nontraditional Careers in Psychology

Advice and information for students from the American Psychological Association.

Today in the History of Psychology

Warren Street, at Central Washington University, offers a sample of events in the history of psychology for every day of the year. Pick a date from the History of Psychology Calendar and see what happened on that date. The APA sponsors this site, which is based on Street's book, *A Chronology of Noteworthy Events in American Psychology.*

More about the History of Psychology

The University of Akron has assembled a museum of old psychology laboratory equipment and other mementos from psychology's past.

What Else Would You Like to Know?

This online library offers many of the most famous books and articles ever written in psychology.

Annotated Links

Both of these sites provide annotated links to a vast array of information about psychology.

© Biosphoto / Ruoso Cyril / Peter Arnold Inc.

Scientific Methods in Psychology

© Panoramic Images/Getty Images

Consider This: Years ago, I was watching a Discovery Channel nature documentary about elephants. After the narrator discussed the enormous amount of food elephants eat, he started on their digestive system. He commented that the average elephant passes enough gas in a day to propel a car for 20 miles (32 km). I thought, "Wow, isn't that amazing!" and I told a couple of other people about it.

Later I started to think, "Wait a minute. *How did someone measure that?* Did someone really attach a balloon to an elephant's rear end and collect gas for 24 hours? And then put it into a car to see how far the car would go? Was it a full-sized car or an economy car? City traffic or highway? How do they know they measured a typical elephant? Did they determine the mean for a broad sample of elephants?" The more I thought about it, the more skeptical I became.

"Oh, well," you might say. "Who cares?" You're right; how far you could propel a car on elephant gas doesn't matter. However, my point is not to ridicule the makers of this documentary but to ridicule *me*. Remember, I said I told two people about this claim before I started to doubt it. For decades, I have been teaching students to question assertions and evaluate the evidence, and here I was, uncritically accepting a silly statement and telling other people, who for all I know, may have gone on to tell other people. The point is that all of us yield to the temptation to accept unsupported claims, and we all need to discipline ourselves to question the evidence, especially for the interesting or exciting claims that we would like to believe. This chapter concerns the evaluation of evidence in psychology.

Thinking Critically and Evaluating Evidence

- How do scientists evaluate theories?

- Why are most scientists so skeptical of theories and claims that contradict our current understanding?

The American comedian and politician Will Rogers once said that what worried him was not the things that people don't know but the things they *think* they know that really aren't so. You have heard people make countless claims about psychology, medicine, politics, religion, and so forth, but frequently, one confident claim contradicts another. How can you know what is true?

It is difficult to be sure, except in mathematics. For that reason, most scientists avoid the word *prove*. The lack of absolute certainty, however, does not mean that "you may as well believe anything you want" or that "anything has as much chance of being true as anything else." Some conclusions are backed by much stronger evidence than others.

EVIDENCE AND THEORY IN SCIENCE

People sometimes say "I have a theory . . ." when they mean they have a guess. A scientific **theory** is more than a guess. It is *an explanation or model that fits many observations and makes valid predictions.* Agreeing with old observations is important, but predicting new ones is more important (Lipton, 2005). It is easy to offer an explanation for what happened yesterday but more impressive if you can predict what will happen tomorrow.

Can we ever be sure a theory is "true"? The philosopher Karl Popper argued that because no observation proves a theory to be correct, the purpose of research is to find which theories are *incorrect*. That is, the point of research is to *falsify* the incorrect theories, and a good theory is one that withstands all attempts to falsify it. In other words, it wins by a process of elimination.

A well-formed theory, therefore, is **falsifiable**—that is, *stated in such clear, precise terms that we can see what evidence would count against it*—if, of course, such evidence existed. For example, the theory of gravity makes precise predictions about falling objects. Because people have tested these predictions many times, and none of the observations have disconfirmed the predictions, we have high confidence in the theory.

This point is worth restating because "falsifiable" sounds like it should be a bad thing. Falsifiable does not mean we actually have evidence against a theory. (If we did, it would be falsi*fied*.) Falsifiable means we can imagine something that would count as evidence against the theory. A theory that makes no predictions or only vague ones is *not* falsifiable because no conceivable evidence would count against it. For example, Sigmund Freud claimed that all dreams are motivated by wish fulfillment, although a "censor" in the head disguises the wish. If you have a happy dream, it appears to be a wish fulfillment. If you have an unhappy dream, then evidently a censor in your brain disguised the wish. As Domhoff (2003) noted, Freud stated his theory in such a way that any possible observation was evidence for it or at least not against it.

However, when Popper wrote that research is *always* an attempt to falsify a theory, he went too far. "All objects fall" (the law of gravity) is falsifiable. "Some objects fall" is not falsifiable. If it *were* false, you could not *demonstrate* it to be false! You also could not falsify the idea that "there is a monster in Loch Ness, Scotland." No matter how many observers fail to find a monster, we can't be sure. (Maybe it hides deep in the mud and comes out every few hundred years.) Similarly, consider the statement, "Some people have psychic powers that enable them to get information without using their senses." No matter how many people fail to show psychic powers, the possibility remains that someone else might be different. We cannot expect anyone to falsify this claim.

Instead of insisting that all research is an effort to falsify a theory, another approach is to discuss **burden of proof,** *the obligation to present evidence to support one's claim.* In a criminal trial, the burden of proof is on the prosecution. If the prosecution does not make a convincing case, the defendant goes free. The reason is that the prosecution should be able to find convincing evidence if someone is guilty, but many innocent defendants could not possibly demonstrate their innocence.

Similarly in science, the burden of proof is on anyone who makes a claim that should be demonstrable if it is true. A claim that "some objects fall" or "some people have psychic powers" should be demonstrable if true. A claim that "*every* object falls" cannot be demonstrated, so the burden of proof is on someone who doubts it.

STEPS FOR GATHERING AND EVALUATING EVIDENCE

The word *science* derives from a Latin word meaning "knowledge." Scientific reasoning is like other kinds of problem solving, but it is based on carefully observed and recorded information. Science is distinguished by the fact that scientists generally agree on how to evaluate theories. Whereas most people can hardly imagine evidence that would change their religious or political views, scientists can generally imagine evidence that would disconfirm their favorite theories. (Oh, not always, I admit. Some can be stubborn.)

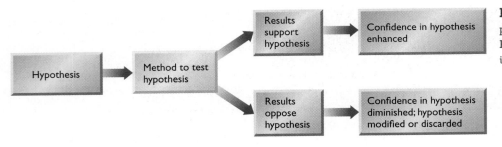

Figure 2.1 An experiment tests the predictions that follow from a hypothesis. Results either support the hypothesis or indicate a need to revise or abandon it.

In that sense, psychologists—most of them, anyway!—follow the scientific method. Obviously, our knowledge of psychology lacks the precision of physics or chemistry. But psychologists do generally agree on what constitutes good evidence.

The simplest kind of evidence is careful observation. The sciences of astronomy and anatomy are based almost entirely on observation and description. In psychology, too, researchers observe what people do and under what circumstances and how one person differs from another. For example, Robert Provine (2000) studied laughter by visiting shopping malls and recording who laughed and when.

Eventually, we want to go beyond observations to find explanations. To evaluate competing explanations, researchers collect new data, guided by a **hypothesis**, which is *a clear predictive statement*. A test of a hypothesis goes through the series of steps described in the following four sections (see also Figure 2.1). Articles in most scientific publications follow this sequence, too. In each of the remaining chapters of this book, you will find at least one example of a psychological study described in a section entitled "What's the Evidence?" Each of those will go through the sequence from hypothesis to interpretation.

Hypothesis

A hypothesis can be based on your own casual observations, such as noticing that some children who watch much televised violence are themselves aggressive. You might then form a hypothesis that watching violence leads to violence. A hypothesis can also be based on a larger theory, such as "children tend to imitate the behavior they see," which might include televised violence. A hypothesis can also emerge from trends in society. It has been estimated that the average child, before graduating from elementary school, will have watched 8,000 murders and 100,000 other violent acts on television (Bushman & Anderson, 2001) in addition to countless violent acts in video games (Anderson & Bushman, 2001). Presumably, all those experiences produce *some* effect.

A good hypothesis leads to predictions. For example, "if we let children watch violent television, they will behave more aggressively," or "if we decrease the amount of violence on television, the crime rate will decrease."

Method

Any hypothesis could be tested in many ways. One way to test the effects of televised violence would be to examine whether children who watch more violent programs engage in more violent behavior. However, a study of this type could not tell us about cause and effect: Watching violence may lead to violence, but people who are already violent probably like to watch violence. Another method is to see whether violent behavior increases after an increase in the availability of televised violence. However, other social, economic, and political events may occur at the same time, and we cannot separate the effects of televised violence from the other factors. A better method is to take a set of children, such as those attending a summer camp, randomly assign them to two groups and let one group watch violent programs while the other group watches nonviolent programs, and see whether the two groups differ in their violent behaviors. If the groups differ, that kind of study can justify a cause-and-effect conclusion (Parke, Berkowitz, Leyens, West, & Sebastian, 1977). The limitation is that researchers control what people watch for only a few days.

Because any method has strengths and weaknesses, researchers vary their methods. If studies using different methods all point to the same conclusion, we increase our confidence in that conclusion.

Results

Fundamental to any research is measuring the outcome. A phenomenon such as "violent behavior" is tricky to measure. (Do threats count? Does verbal abuse? When does a push or shove cross the line between playfulness and violence?) It is important for an investigator to set clear rules about measurements. After making the measurements, the investigator determines whether the results are impressive enough to call for an explanation or whether the apparent trends might have been due to chance.

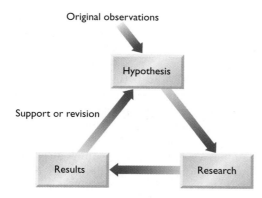

Figure 2.2 A hypothesis leads to research. The results either support the hypothesis or imply a need to revise or abandon it.

Interpretation

The final task is to consider what the results mean. If they contradict the hypothesis, researchers should abandon or modify the original hypothesis (see Figure 2.2). Maybe it applies only to certain kinds of people or only under certain circumstances. If the results match the prediction, investigators gain confidence in the hypothesis, but they also should consider other hypotheses that fit the results.

REPLICABILITY

Most scientific researchers are scrupulously honest in reporting their results. Distortions of data are rare and scandalous. A major reason for the honesty is that other researchers can check their results. A person who reports a scientific study must include the methods in enough detail for other people to repeat the study. If other researchers get similar results, they presumably will be persuaded. If not, they distrust the original finding.

Replicable results are *those that anyone can obtain, at least approximately, by following the same procedures,* and scientists insist on replicable results. Consider an example of a nonreplicable result. In the 1960s and early 1970s, several researchers reported that they trained rats to do something, chopped up the rats' brains, extracted certain chemicals, and injected those chemicals into untrained animals. The recipients then apparently remembered what the first group of rats had learned to do. From what we know of brain functioning, theoretically this procedure shouldn't work, but if it did, imagine the possibilities. Some people proposed, semiseriously, that someday we might be able to offer people an injection of desirable memories. Instead of going to class for a semester, you could get an injection of European

history or introduction to calculus. Alas, the results were not replicable. When other researchers repeated the procedures, they found no consistent effect (L. T. Smith, 1975).

So, what conclusion should we draw? Until or unless someone finds conditions under which the phenomenon is replicable (consistently repeatable), we do not take it seriously. This rule may seem harsh, but it is our best defense against error.

Often, however, an effect is small but real. For example, one method of teaching might work better than another, but only slightly, so we do not see the advantage in every study. The same is true for research on how to run an organization, how to deliver psychotherapy, and many other complex human behaviors. When we are looking at small trends in the data, researchers use a **meta-analysis,** *which combines the results of many studies and analyzes them as though they were all one very large study.* A meta-analysis also determines which variations in procedure increase or decrease the effects.

CRITERIA FOR EVALUATING SCIENTIFIC THEORIES

After investigators identify replicable findings, what do they do with the results? One goal is to establish theories. A good theory starts with as few assumptions as possible and leads to many correct predictions. In that way, it reduces the amount of information we must remember. The periodic table in chemistry is an excellent example: From the information about the elements, we can predict the properties of an enormous number of compounds.

What do we do if several theories fit the known facts? For example, suppose you notice that a picture on your wall is hanging on an angle. You consider three possible explanations:

- A mild earth tremor shook the picture.
- One of your friends bumped it without telling you.
- A ghost moved it.

All three explanations fit the observation, but we don't consider them on an equal basis. *When given a choice among explanations that seem to fit the facts, we prefer the one whose assumptions are fewer, simpler, or more consistent with other well-established theories.* This is known as the principle of **parsimony** (literally "stinginess") or *Occam's razor* (after the philosopher William of Occam). The principle of parsimony is a conservative idea: We stick with ideas that work and try as hard as we can to avoid new assumptions (e.g., ghosts).

Parsimony and Degrees of Open-Mindedness

The principle of parsimony tells us to adhere to what we already believe, to resist radically new hypotheses. You might protest: "Shouldn't we remain open-minded to new possibilities?" Yes, if open-mindedness means a willingness to consider proper evidence, but not if it means the assumption that "anything has as much chance of being true as anything else." The stronger the reasons behind our current opinion, the more evidence we should need before replacing it. Consider two examples:

Visitors from outer space. There are good reasons to doubt the idea of visitors from other planets. To get from one solar system to another in less than thousands of years, you need to travel at nearly the speed of light. At that speed, a collision with a dust particle would be catastrophic. However, we could imagine alien life forms whose biology enables them to survive a journey of thousands of years or whose technology permits greater speed than seems possible to us today. If weird-looking beings stepped out of an odd-looking spacecraft, we should consider the possibility of a hoax by other people, but solid evidence could persuade us of visitors from outer space. So, we remain—cautiously—open-minded.

Perpetual motion machines. A "perpetual motion machine" is one that generates more energy than it uses. For centuries, people have attempted and failed to develop such a machine. (Figure 2.3 shows one example.) The U.S. Patent Office is officially closed-minded on this issue, refusing even to consider patent applications for such machines, because a perpetual motion machine violates what physicists call *the second law of thermodynamics.*

According to that law, within a closed system, entropy (disorder) can never decrease. A more casual statement is that any work wastes energy, and therefore, we need to keep adding energy to keep any machine going. Could the second law of thermodynamics be wrong? I recommend only the slightest amount of open-mindedness. An enormous amount of data supports the second law of thermodynamics, as do logical arguments about why it must be true. If someone shows you what appears to be a perpetual motion machine, look carefully for a hidden battery or other power source—that is, a simple, parsimonious explanation. Even if you don't find a hidden power source, it is vastly more likely that you over-looked one than that the second law of thermodynamics is wrong. A claim as extraordinary as a perpetual motion machine requires extraordinary evidence.

What does all this discussion have to do with psychology? Sometimes, people claim spectacular results that seem impossible based on what we know of biology or physics. Although it is fair to examine the evidence, it is also important to maintain a skeptical attitude and look as closely as possible for a simple, parsimonious explanation. We shall consider two examples.

Applying Parsimony: Clever Hans, the Amazing Horse

Early in the 20th century, Mr. von Osten, a German mathematics teacher, set out to demonstrate the intellectual ability of his horse, Hans. To teach Hans arithmetic, he first showed him an object, said "one," and lifted Hans's foot once. He raised Hans's foot twice for two objects and so on. Eventually, when von Osten presented a set of objects, Hans learned to tap his foot by himself, and with practice he managed to tap the correct number of times. Soon it was no longer necessary for Hans to see the objects. Von Osten would just call out a number, and Hans would tap the appropriate number.

Mr. von Osten moved on to addition and then to subtraction, multiplication, and division. Hans caught on quickly, soon responding with 90 to 95% accuracy. Then von Osten and Hans began touring Germany. Hans's abilities grew until he could add fractions, convert fractions to decimals or vice versa, do simple algebra, tell time to the minute, and give the values of all German coins. Using a letter-to-number code, he could spell out the names of objects and identify musical notes such as B-flat. (Evidently, Hans had perfect pitch.) He was usually correct even when questions were put to him by people other than von Osten, in unfamiliar places, with von Osten out of sight.

Given this evidence, many people were ready to believe that Hans had great intellectual powers. But others sought a more parsimonious explanation. Oskar Pfungst (1911) observed that Hans could not answer a question correctly unless the questioner knew the answer. Apparently, the questioner was doing something to give away the answer. Then Pfungst found that Hans was accurate only when the questioner stood in plain sight.

Eventually, Pfungst observed that anyone who asked Hans a question would lean forward to watch Hans's foot. Hans had simply learned to start tapping whenever someone stood next to his forefoot and leaned forward. As soon as Hans had given the correct number of taps, the questioner

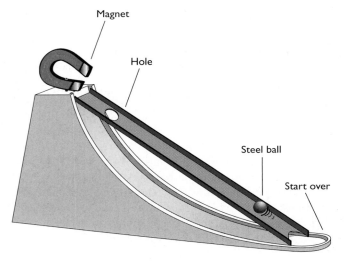

Figure 2.3 A proposed perpetual motion machine: The magnet pulls the metal ball up the inclined plane. When the ball reaches the top, it falls through the hole and returns to its starting point, from which the magnet will again pull it up. Can you see why this device is sure to fail? (See answer A on page 36.)

Magnet

Hole

Steel ball

Start over

Clever Hans and his owner, Mr. von Osten, demonstrated that the horse could answer complex mathematical questions with great accuracy. The question was, "How?" (After Pfungst, 1911, in Fernald, 1984)

would give a slight upward jerk of the head and a change in facial expression, anticipating that this might be the last tap. (Even skeptical scientists who tested Hans did this involuntarily. After all, they thought, wouldn't it be exciting if Hans got it right?) Hans simply continued tapping until he saw that cue.

In short, Hans was indeed a clever horse, but we do not believe that he understood mathematics. Note that Pfungst did not demonstrate that Hans *didn't* understand mathematics. Pfungst merely demonstrated that he could explain Hans's behavior in the parsimonious terms of responses to facial expressions, and therefore, no one needed to assume anything more complex. The same principle applies in general: Whenever possible, we seek a simple explanation that requires no new assumptions. We adopt new assumptions only if the simple, familiar ones fail.

Applying Parsimony: Extrasensory Perception

The possibility of **extrasensory perception (ESP)** has long been controversial in psychology. Supporters of extrasensory perception claim that *at least some people, some of the time, can acquire information without using any sense organ and without receiving any form of physical energy.* For example, supporters claim that people with ESP can identify someone else's thoughts (telepathy) just as accurately from a great distance as from an adjacent room, in apparent violation of the inverse-square law of physics, and that their accuracy is not diminished by a lead shield that would interrupt any known form of energy. Some ESP supporters also claim that certain people can perceive inanimate objects that are hidden from sight (clairvoyance), predict the future (precognition), and influence such physical events as a roll of dice by mental concentration (psychokinesis).

Acceptance of any of these claims would require us not only to overhaul major concepts in psychology but also to discard the most fundamental tenets of physics, even the idea that we live in a universe of matter and energy. What evidence is there for ESP?

Anecdotes

One kind of evidence consists of anecdotes—people's reports of isolated events, such as an amazing coincidence or a dream or hunch that comes true. Such experiences often seem impressive, but they are not scientific evidence. Sooner or later, occasional bizarre coincidences are almost sure to occur, and people

tend to remember them. For example, as you have probably heard, people have found many parallels between the lives of Presidents Abraham Lincoln and John Kennedy, including the following:

- Lincoln was elected to Congress in 1846 and elected president in 1860; Kennedy was elected to Congress in 1946 and elected president in 1960.
- The names Lincoln and Kennedy each contain seven letters.
- Both Lincoln and Kennedy were shot in the head on a Friday while seated next to their wives.
- Lincoln was shot in the Ford's Theatre, and Kennedy was shot while in a Ford Lincoln.
- Both were succeeded in office by a southerner named Johnson.

The problem is, if you try hard enough, you can find parallels for many pairs of people. Consider Attila the Hun and former U.S. President Harry S Truman:

- Attila the Hun was king of the Huns from 445 until 453; Harry S Truman was president of the United States from 1945 until 1953.
- Both Attila and Truman took office upon the death of the previous leader; both were succeeded in office by a military general.
- The initials for "The Hun" are T. H. The initials for "Harry Truman" are H. T.
- Both the name Attila the Hun and Harry S Truman consist of 12 letters and 2 spaces.
- Both had a middle name that is meaningless out of context ("The" and "S").

Pick two people in history, or two people you know, and see how many "uncanny" similarities you can find.

Furthermore, we tend to remember and talk about the hunches and dreams that *do* come true and forget the others. People hardly ever say, "Strangest thing! I had a dream, but then nothing like it actually happened!" People also exaggerate the coincidences that occur and sometimes misremember them. We could evaluate anecdotal evidence only if people recorded their hunches and dreams *before* the predicted events and then determined how many unlikely predictions actually came to pass.

You may have heard of the "prophet Nostradamus," a 16th-century French writer who allegedly predicted many events of later centuries. Figure 2.4 presents four samples of his writings. All of his "predictions" are at this level of vagueness. After something happens, people imaginatively reinterpret his writings to fit the event. (If we don't know what a prediction means until *after* it occurs, is it really a prediction?)

Figure 2.4 According to the followers of Nostradamus, each of these statements is a specific prophecy of a 20th-century event (Cheetham, 1973). What do you think the prophecies mean? Compare your answers to answer B on page 36.

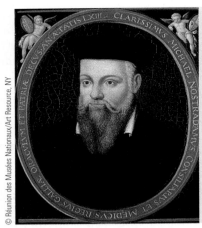

1. The great man will be struck down in the day by a thunderbolt. An evil deed, foretold by the bearer of a petition. According to the prediction another falls at night time. Conflict at Reims, London, and pestilence in Tuscany.

2. When the fish that travels over both land and sea is cast up on to the shore by a great wave, its shape foreign, smooth, and frightful. From the sea the enemies soon reach the walls.

3. The bird of prey flying to the left, before battle is joined with the French, he makes preparations. Some will regard him as good, others bad or uncertain. The weaker party will regard him as a good omen.

4. Shortly afterwards, not a very long interval, a great tumult will be raised by land and sea. The naval battles will be greater than ever. Fires, creatures which will make more tumult.

Magician Lance Burton can make people and animals seem to suddenly appear, disappear, float in the air, or do other things that we know are impossible. Even if we don't know how he accomplishes these feats, we take it for granted that they are based on methods of misleading the audience.

someone says that Nostradamus predicted violence in the Middle East next year, we need not be impressed if that prediction comes true.)

Professional Psychics

Various stage performers claim to read other people's minds and perform other amazing feats. The Amazing Kreskin has consistently denied doing anything supernatural. He prefers to talk of his "extremely sensitive" rather than "extrasensory" perception (Kreskin, 1991). Still, part of his success as a performer comes from allowing people to believe he has uncanny mental powers.

After carefully observing Kreskin and others, David Marks and Richard Kammann (1980) concluded that they used the same kinds of deception commonly employed in magic acts. For example, Kreskin sometimes begins his act by asking the audience to read his mind. Let's try to duplicate this trick right now: Try to read my mind. I am thinking of a number between 1 and 50. Both digits are odd numbers, but they are not the same. For example, it could be 15 but it could not be 11. (These are the instructions Kreskin gives.) Have you chosen a number? Please do.

All right, my number was 37. Did you think of 37? If not, how about 35? You see, I started to think 35 and then changed my mind, so you might have got 35.

If you successfully "read my mind," are you impressed? Don't be. At first, it seemed that you had many numbers to choose from (1 to 50), but by the end of the instructions, you had only a few. The first digit had to be 1 or 3, and the second had to be 1, 3, 5, 7, or 9. You eliminated 11 and 33 because both digits are the same, and you probably eliminated 15 because I cited it as a possible example. That leaves only seven possibilities. Most people stay far away from the example given and tend to avoid the highest and lowest possible

1. How could someone scientifically evaluate the accuracy of Nostradamus's predictions?

Answer

1. To evaluate Nostradamus's predictions, we would need to ask someone to tell us precisely what his predictions mean before the events they supposedly predict. Then we would ask someone else to estimate the likelihood of those events. Eventually, we would compare the accuracy of the predictions to the advance estimates of their probability. (For example, if

choices. That leaves 37 as the most likely choice and 35 as the second most likely.

Second act: Kreskin asks the audience to write down something they are thinking about while he walks along the aisles talking. Then, back on stage, he "reads people's minds." He might say something like, "Someone is thinking about his mother . . ." In any large crowd, someone is bound to shout, "Yes, that's me. You read my mind!" On occasion he describes something that someone has written out in great detail. That person generally turns out to be someone sitting along the aisle where Kreskin was walking.

After a variety of other tricks (see Marks & Kammann, 1980), Kreskin goes backstage while the mayor or some other dignitary hides Kreskin's paycheck somewhere in the audience. Then Kreskin comes back, walks up and down the aisles, across the rows, and eventually shouts, "The check is here!" The rule is that if he guesses wrong, then he does not get paid. (He hardly ever misses.)

How does he do it? It is a Clever Hans trick. Kreskin studies people's faces. Most people want him to find the check, so they get more excited as he gets close to it and more disappointed or distressed if he moves away. In effect they are saying, "Now you're getting closer" and "Now you're moving away." At last he closes in on the check.

Of course, someone always objects, "Well, maybe you've explained what some professional psychics do. But there's this other guy you haven't investigated yet. Maybe he really does possess psychic powers." Well, maybe, but it is simpler (more parsimonious) to assume that other performers are also using illusion and deception.

Experiments

Because stage performances and anecdotal events occur under uncontrolled conditions, we cannot determine the probability of coincidence or the possibility of deception. Laboratory experiments provide the only evidence about ESP worth serious consideration.

For example, consider the *ganzfeld* procedure (from German words meaning "entire field"). A "sender" is given a photo or film, selected at random from four possibilities, and a "receiver" in another room is asked to describe the sender's thoughts and images. Typically, the receiver wears half Ping-Pong balls over the eyes and listens to static noise through earphones to minimize normal stimuli that might overpower the presumably weak extrasensory stimuli (Figure 2.5). Later, a judge examines a transcript of what the receiver said and compares it to the four photos or films, determining which one it matches most closely. On the average, it should match the target about one in four times. If a receiver "hits" more often than one in four, we can calculate the probability of accidentally doing that well. (ESP re-

Figure 2.5 In the ganzfeld procedure, a "receiver," who is deprived of most normal sensory information, tries to describe the photo or film that a "sender" is examining.

searchers, or parapsychologists, use many other procedures, but in each case, the goal is to determine whether someone answers more correctly than could be explained by chance.)

Over the decades, ESP researchers reported many apparent examples of telepathy or clairvoyance, none of which were replicable under well-controlled conditions. In the case of the ganzfeld studies, one review reported that 6 of the 10 laboratories using this method found positive results (Bem & Honorton, 1994). However, 14 later studies from 7 laboratories failed to find evidence that the receiver chose the target stimulus any more often than one would expect by chance (Milton & Wiseman, 1999). In short, the ganzfeld phenomenon, like other previous claims of ESP, is nonreplicable.

The lack of replicability is one major reason to be skeptical of ESP, but it is not the only one. The other is parsimony. If someone claims that a horse does mathematics or a person reads the minds of other people far away, we should search thoroughly for a simple explanation. Even if some new result seemed difficult to explain, the "ESP" explanation is hard to consider until someone specifies it clearly. Saying that a result demonstrates "an amazing ability that science cannot explain" is not a testable theory.

Would you like to test your own ability to find a parsimonious explanation for apparent mind-reading? Go to **www.cengage.com/psychology/ kalat.** Navigate to the student website, then to the Online Try It Yourself section, and click Psychic Phenomenon.

In Closing

Scientific Thinking in Psychology

What have we learned about science in general? Science does not deal with proof or certainty. All scientific conclusions are tentative and are subject to revision. Nevertheless, this tentativeness does not imply a willingness to abandon well-established theories without excellent reasons.

Scientists always prefer the most parsimonious theory. Before they accept any claim that requires a major new assumption, they insist that it be supported by replicable experiments that rule out simpler explanations and by a new theory that is clearly superior to the theory it replaces.

SUMMARY

- *Burden of proof.* In any dispute, the side that should be capable of presenting clear evidence has the obligation to do so. (page 29)
- *Steps in a scientific study.* A scientific study goes through the following sequence of steps: hypothesis, method, results, and interpretation. Because almost any study is subject to more than one possible interpretation, we base our conclusions on a pattern of results from many studies. (page 29)
- *Replicability.* The results of a given study are taken seriously only if other investigators following the same method obtain similar results. (page 31)

- *Criteria for evaluating theories.* A good theory agrees with observations and leads to correct predictions of new information. All else being equal, scientists prefer the theory that relies on simpler assumptions. (page 31)
- *Skepticism about extrasensory perception.* Psychologists carefully scrutinize claims of extrasensory perception because the evidence reported so far has been unreplicable and because the scientific approach includes a search for parsimonious explanations. (page 33)

KEY TERMS

burden of proof (page 29)

extrasensory perception (ESP) (page 33)

falsifiable (page 29)

hypothesis (page 30)

meta-analysis (page 31)

parsimony (page 31)

replicable result (page 31)

theory (page 29)

ANSWERS TO OTHER QUESTIONS IN THE MODULE

A. Any magnet strong enough to pull the metal ball up the inclined plane would not release the ball when it reached the hole at the top. It would be strong enough to pull the ball across the hole. (page 32)

B. The prophecies of Nostradamus (see page 34), as interpreted by Cheetham (1973), refer to the following: (1) the assassinations of John F. Kennedy and Robert F. Kennedy, (2) Polaris ballistic missiles shot from submarines, (3) Hitler's invasion of France, and (4) World War II.

Conducting Psychological Research

- How do psychological researchers study processes that are difficult to define?
- How do they design their research, and what special problems can arise?
- How do psychologists confront the ethical problems of conducting research?

A radio talk show featured two psychologists as guests. The first argued that day care was bad for children because she had seen in her clinical practice many sadly disturbed adults who had been left in day care as children. The second psychologist, researcher Sandra Scarr (1997), pointed out that the clinician had no way of knowing about the well-adjusted adults who had also been left in day care as children. Scarr described eight well-designed research studies, examining thousands of people in four countries, which found no evidence of harmful consequences from day care.

Which type of evidence strikes you as stronger, the anecdotes or the eight research studies? To Scarr's dismay, the people who called in to the program seemed to find both kinds of evidence about equally convincing.

Psychology, like any other field, makes progress only by distinguishing between strong evidence and weak evidence. In this module, we consider some of the special problems encountered when applying scientific methods to psychological phenomena.

GENERAL PRINCIPLES OF PSYCHOLOGICAL RESEARCH

The primary goal of this module is not to prepare you to conduct psychological research but to help you be an intelligent interpreter of research. When you hear about some new study, you should be able to ask pertinent questions to decide how good the evidence is and what conclusion (if any) it justifies.

Operational Definitions

Suppose a physicist asks you to measure the effect of temperature on the length of an iron bar. You ask, "What do we *really mean* by temperature?" The physicist replies, "Don't worry about it. Temperature really is the rate of motion of molecules, but for practical purposes what I mean by temperature is the reading on the thermometer."

We need the same strategy in psychology. If we want to measure the effect of hunger on students' ability to concentrate, we could spend forever attempting to define what hunger and concentration really are, or we could say, "Let's measure hunger by the hours since the last meal and concentration by the length of time that the student continues reading without stopping to do something else." By doing so, we are using an **operational definition,** *a definition that specifies the operations (or procedures) used to produce or measure something, ordinarily a way to give it a numerical value.* An operational definition is not like a dictionary definition. You might object that "time since the last meal" is not what hunger really *is.* Of course not, but the reading on a thermometer is also not what temperature really is. An opera-

tional definition just says how to measure something. It lets us get on with research.

Suppose we want to investigate friendliness. We would need an operational definition of friendliness—that is, a way to measure it. We might define it as the number of people someone smiles at during an hour or the number of people someone lists as close friends. Or we might operationally define *love* as "how many hours you spend with someone who asks you to stay nearby."

2. Which of the following is an operational definition of intelligence?
   a. the ability to comprehend relationships,
   b. a score on an IQ test,
   c. the ability to survive in the real world, or
   d. the product of the cerebral cortex of the brain.
3. What would you propose as an operational definition of sense of humor?

Answers

2. A score on an IQ test is an operational definition of intelligence. (Whether it is the *best* operational definition is a different question.) None of the other definitions tells us how to measure or produce intelligence.
3. We might define it as the number of times someone laughs during a movie or the number of times someone says something that makes other people laugh. Other definitions are possible if they include a method of measurement.

Population Samples

A **population** *is the entire group of individuals to be considered.* Researchers generally wish to draw conclusions that apply to a large population, such as all 3-year-olds or all people with depression or all adult human beings. Because it is not practical to examine everyone in the population, researchers study a *sample* of people and assume that the results for the sample apply to the whole population.

For example, pollsters ask 1,000 or so voters which candidate they support and then project

College students are often used as convenience samples. However, college students are atypical in many ways, making this kind of sample less desirable than a representative or random sample for many research purposes.

the probable result for the entire city, state, or country. Of course, the prediction can go wrong if some last-minute event changes many people's voting decision or if the ballot is confusing.

For some purposes, almost any sample is satisfactory. For example, investigators interested in basic sensory processes do not worry much about sampling problems. The eyes, ears, and other sense organs operate similarly in all people, with obvious exceptions of those with visual or hearing impairments. Similarly, many of the principles of hunger, thirst, and so forth are similar enough among all people that an investigator can study almost any group—students in an introductory psychology class, for example. Indeed, for many purposes, researchers use laboratory animals. We refer to *a group chosen because of its ease of study* as a convenience sample.

To study behaviors that vary from one group to another, we need a broader sample of people. A representative sample closely resembles the population in its percentage of males and females, Blacks and Whites, young and old, city dwellers and farmers, or whatever other characteristics are likely to affect the results. To get a representative sample of the people in a given region, an investigator first determines what percentage of the residents belong to each category and then selects people to match those percentages. Of course, a sample that is representative in some ways might not be representative in others.

In a random sample, *every individual in the population has an equal chance of being selected.* To produce a random sample of Toronto residents, an investigator might start with a map of Toronto and select a certain number of city blocks at random, randomly select one house from each of those blocks, and then randomly choose one person from each of those households. *Random* here has a special meaning. If you simply say, "Okay, I'll pick this block, this block, and this block," you may have chosen without any conscious plan, but the results are not random. When people try to choose randomly, they almost always follow certain biases, such as spacing their choices out almost evenly. It is best to let a machine select choices at random. A random sample has this advantage: The larger a random sample, the smaller the probability that its results differ substantially from the whole population. However, although a random sample is theoretically the best, it is difficult to achieve.

If a researcher wants to compare two groups, it is important to use the same kind of sample from both groups. Every fall, the newspapers report the average SAT scores for different American states. The problem is that the samples are different. In some states, most high school students take the SAT. In other states, where most colleges require the ACT instead, students take the SAT only if they plan to apply to out-of-state schools such as MIT, the Ivy League universities, and so forth. We cannot meaningfully compare the results for different states if we have a wide sample from some states and an elite sample from others.

What if we want to draw generalizations about all humans, everywhere? Could we do a study of a couple of hundred Americans and then generalize to the rest of the world? If you are an American, you might easily overlook that issue, but you would probably raise questions if someone studied only people in China or India—even though far more of humanity lives in China and India than in the United States. It is tempting to see one's own culture as "normal." If we want to learn what is true of humans in general, as opposed to a single culture, what should we do? Just imagine trying to get a random sample of all the people on the planet. Although that goal is impractical, it is useful to study cross-cultural samples, *groups of people from at least two cultures.* Consider questions about human nature: Do people learn facial expressions of emotions, or are the expressions built-in? Are boys naturally more aggressive than girls? Are people biologically predisposed to marriage? Cross-cultural data

© Paul Chesley/Getty Images

© Tannen Maury/The Image Works

A psychological researcher can test generalizations about human behavior by comparing people from different cultures.

Table 2.1 Types of Samples

Sample	Individuals Included	Advantages and Disadvantages
Convenience sample	Anyone who is available	Easiest to get, but results may not generalize to the whole population
Representative sample	Same percentage of male/female, White/Black, etc. as the whole population	Results probably similar to whole population, although sample may be representative in some ways but not others
Random sample	Everyone in population has same chance of being chosen	Difficult to get this kind of sample, but it is the best suited for generalizing to the whole population
Cross-cultural	People from different cultures	Difficulties include language barriers, cooperation problems, etc., but essential for studying many issues

bers of another culture to cooperate. Table 2.1 reviews the major types of samples.

4. Suppose I compare the interests and abilities of male and female students at my university. If I find a consistent difference, can I assume that it represents a difference between men and women in general? (Obviously, the answer is no, or else I would not have asked the question.) Why not?

Concept Check

Answer

4. Clearly not. It is unlikely that the men at a given college are typical of men in general or that the women are typical of women in general. Moreover, at some colleges, the men are atypical in some respects and the women atypical in different ways.

Eliminating the Influence of Expectations

Because researchers cannot ethically do research with people without first obtaining their consent, all the people in a research study know they are being studied. If they think they know what the experimenter hopes to find, that expectation influences their behavior. Experimenters are human beings, too, and their expectations may influence how they record the data. Good research requires finding ways to reduce the influence of all these expectations.

Experimenter Bias and Blind Studies

Experimenter bias is *the tendency of an experimenter (unintentionally, in most cases) to distort or misperceive the results of an experiment based on the expected outcome.* Imagine that you, as a psychological investigator, are testing the hypothesis that left-handed children are more creative than right-handed children. (I don't know why you would be testing this silly hypothesis, but suppose you are.) If the results support your hypothesis, you expect to be on your way to fame and success as a psychology re-

are essential for dealing with issues such as these. However, cross-cultural sampling is difficult (Matsumoto, 1994). Obvious problems include the expense, language barriers, and convincing mem-

Table 2.2 Single-Blind and Double-Blind Studies

Who is aware of which participants are in which group?

	Experimenter Who Organized the Study	Observer	Participants
Single-blind	aware	unaware	aware
Single-blind	aware	aware	unaware
Double-blind	aware	unaware	unaware

Figure 2.6 In experiments on sensory deprivation, people who are deprived of most sensory stimulation often report disorientation and sometimes hallucinations. But might these results depend partly on people's expectations of distorted experience?

searcher. Now you see a left-handed child do something, and you are trying to decide whether it counts as "creative." You want to be fair. You don't want your hypothesis to influence your decision about whether to consider the act creative. Just try to ignore your hypothesis.

To minimize the influence of expectations, it is best to use a **blind observer**—*an observer who records data without knowing the researcher's predictions.* For example, we might ask someone to record creative acts by a group of children without any hint that we are interested in the effects of handedness. Because blind observers do not know the hypothesis, they record their observations fairly.

Ideally, the experimenter conceals the procedure from the participants as well. Suppose experimenters give one group of children a pill that is supposed to increase their creativity. If those children know the prediction, maybe they act differently just because of their expectation. Or maybe the children not receiving the pill are disappointed and therefore don't try hard.

The solution is to give the drug to one group and a **placebo** (*a pill with no known pharmacological effects*) to another group without telling the children which pill they are taking or what results the experimenter expects. Then any difference between the two groups cannot be due to their expectations.

In a **single-blind study**, *either the observer or the participants are unaware of which participants received which treatment* (Table 2.2). In a **double-blind study**, *both the observer and the participants are unaware.* Of course, the experimenter who organized the study would need to keep records of which participants received which procedure. (A study in which *everyone* loses track of the procedure is known jokingly as "triple blind.")

Demand Characteristics

Many people who know they are part of an experiment figure out, or think they have figured out, the point of the experiment. Sometimes, those expectations produce big effects.

To illustrate, in some well-known studies of sensory deprivation in the 1950s, people were placed in an apparatus that minimized vision, hearing, touch, and other sensory stimulation (Figure 2.6). Many participants reported that they experienced hallucinations, anxiety, and difficulty concentrating. Suppose after hearing about these studies, you agree to participate in an experiment described as a study of "meaning deprivation." The experimenter asks you about your medical history and then asks you to sign a form agreeing not to sue if you have a bad experience. You see an "emergency tray" containing medicines and instruments, which the experimenter assures you is there "just as a precaution." The experimenter tells you about medical personnel who are available in an emergency "just in case." Now you enter an "isolation chamber," which is actually an ordinary room with two chairs, a desk, a window, a mirror, a sandwich, and a glass of water. You are shown a microphone you can use to report any hallucinations or other distorted experiences and a "panic button" you can press for escape if the discomfort becomes unbearable.

Staying in a room for a few hours should hardly be a traumatic experience. But all the preparations suggested that terrible things were about to happen, and when this study was conducted, several people reported that they were hallucinating "multicolored spots on the wall," that "the walls of the room are starting to waver," or that "the objects on the desk are becoming animated and moving about." Some complained of anxiety, restlessness, difficulty concentrating, and spatial disorientation. One pressed the panic button to demand release (Orne & Scheibe, 1964).

Students in a control group were led to the same room, but they were not shown the "emergency tray," were not asked to sign a release form, and were given no other indication that anything unusual was likely to happen. None of them reported any unusual experiences.

Sensory deprivation probably does influence behavior. But as this experiment illustrates, sometimes what appears to be the result of a procedure is really due to people's expectations. Martin Orne (1969) defined demand characteristics as *cues that tell participants what is expected of them and what the experimenter hopes to find.* To minimize demand characteristics, many experimenters take steps to conceal the purpose of the experiment. A double-blind study also serves the purpose: If two groups share the same expectations but behave differently because of a treatment, then the differences are not due to their expectations.

OBSERVATIONAL RESEARCH DESIGNS

The general principles that we just discussed apply to many kinds of research. Psychologists use various methods of investigation, each with its advantages and disadvantages. Most research starts with description: What happens and under what circumstances? Let's first examine several kinds of observational studies. Later we consider experiments, which are designed to illuminate cause-and-effect relationships.

Naturalistic Observations

A naturalistic observation is *a careful examination of what happens under more or less natural conditions.* For example, biologist Jane Goodall (1971) spent years observing chimpanzees in the wild, recording their food habits, their social interactions, their gestures, and their whole way of life (Figure 2.7).

Figure 2.7 In a naturalistic study, observers record the behavior of people or other species in a natural setting. Here, noted biologist Jane Goodall records her observations on chimpanzees. By patiently staying with the chimps, Goodall gradually won their trust and learned to recognize individual animals. In this manner, she was able to add enormously to our understanding of chimpanzees' natural way of life.

Similarly, psychologists sometimes try to observe human behavior "as an outsider." A psychologist might observe what happens when two unacquainted people get on an elevator together: Do they stand close or far apart? Do they speak? Do they look toward each other or away? Does it matter whether they are both men, both women, or a man and a woman? Does their ethnic background make a difference?

Case Histories

Some fascinating conditions are rare. For example, some people are almost completely insensitive to pain. People with Capgras syndrome believe that some of their relatives have been replaced with impostors, who look, sound, and act like the real people. People with Cotard's syndrome insist that they are dead or do not exist. A psychologist who encounters someone with a rare condition may report a case history, *a thorough description of the person, including abilities and disabilities, medical condition, life history, unusual experiences, and whatever else seems relevant.* It is, of course, possible to report a case history of any person, not just the unusual, but the unusual cases attract more attention. A case history is a kind of naturalistic observation, but we distinguish it because it focuses on a single individual.

A case history can be valuable, but it runs the risk of being just an anecdote. Unless other observers examine this person or someone similar, we are at the mercy of the original investigator, who may have overlooked important points, exaggerated, or misunderstood. A good case history guides further research, but we should interpret a single report cautiously.

Surveys

A survey is *a study of the prevalence of certain beliefs, attitudes, or behaviors based on people's responses to questions.* Surveys are common in Western society. In fact, no matter what your occupation, at some time you will probably conduct a survey of your employees, your customers, your students, your neighbors, or fellow members of an organization. You will also frequently read survey results in the newspaper or hear them reported on television. You should be aware of the ways in which survey results can be misleading.

Sampling

Getting a random or representative sample is important in research, particularly with surveys. In 1936 the *Literary Digest* mailed 10 million postcards, asking people their choice for president of the United States. Of the 2 million responses, 57% preferred the Republican candidate, Alfred Landon.

Later that year, the Democratic candidate, Franklin Roosevelt, defeated Landon by a wide margin. The problem was that the *Literary Digest* had selected names from the telephone book and automobile registration lists. In 1936, at the end of the Great Depression, few poor people (who were mostly Democrats) owned telephones or cars.

With any survey, researchers should acknowledge the limitations of their sample. Even if one had a random sample of all adults in an entire country, the results apply only to that country at the time of the survey. It would be unwarranted to draw conclusions about other countries or other times.

The Seriousness of Those Being Interviewed

When you answer a survey, do you carefully consider your answers, or do you answer impulsively? In one survey, only 45% of the respondents said they believed in the existence of intelligent life on other planets. However, a few questions later on the survey, 82% said they believed the U.S. government was "hiding evidence of intelligent life in space" (Emery, 1997). Did 37% of the people *really* think that the U.S. government is hiding evidence of something that doesn't exist? More likely, they were answering without much thought.

Here's another example: Which of the following programs would you most like to see on television reruns? Rate your choices from highest (1) to lowest (10). (Please fill in your answers, either in the text or on a separate sheet of paper, before continuing to the next paragraph.)

___ South Park   ___ *Xena, Warrior Princess*

___ *Lost*   ___ *The X-Files*

___ *Cheers*   ___ *Teletubbies*

___ *Seinfeld*   ___ *Space Doctor*

___ *I Love Lucy*   ___ *Homicide*

When I conducted this survey with my own students at North Carolina State University, nearly all did exactly what I asked—they gave every program a rating, including *Space Doctor,* a program that never existed. Most rated it toward the bottom, but more than 10% rated it in the top five, and a few ranked it as their top choice. (This survey was inspired by an old *Candid Camera* episode in which interviewers asked people their opinions of the nonexistent program *Space Doctor* and received many confident replies.)

Students who rated *Space Doctor* did nothing wrong, of course. I asked them to rank programs, and they did. The fault lies with anyone who interprets such survey results as if they represented informed opinions. People frequently express opinions based on little or no knowledge.

The Wording of the Questions

Let's start with a little demonstration. Please answer these two questions:

1. I oppose raising taxes. (Circle one.)
   1   2   3   4   5   6   7
   Strongly agree   Strongly disagree
2. I make it a practice to never lie. (Circle one.)
   1   2   3   4   5   6   7
   Strongly agree   Strongly disagree

Now cover up those answers and reply to these similar questions:

3. I would be willing to pay a few extra dollars in taxes to provide high-quality education to all children. (Circle one.)
   1   2   3   4   5   6   7
   Strongly agree   Strongly disagree
4. Like all human beings, I occasionally tell a white lie. (Circle one.)
   1   2   3   4   5   6   7
   Strongly agree   Strongly disagree

Some odd survey results merely reflect the fact that people did not take the questions seriously or did not understand the questions.

Most students at one college indicated agreement to all four items (Madson, 2005). Note that item 1 contradicts 3, and 2 contradicts 4. You can't be opposed to raising taxes and in favor of raising taxes. You can't be honest all the time and occasionally lie. However, the wording of a question changes its connotation. Question 3 talks about raising taxes "a few extra dollars" for a worthy cause. That differs from raising taxes in general by some unknown amount for unknown reasons. Similarly, depending on what you mean by a "white lie," you might tell one occasionally while still insisting that you "make it a practice to never lie"—at least not much. Still, the point is that someone can bias your answers one way or the other by rewording a question.

Here is another example. Some students are offered the first pair of questions, and others are offered the second pair:

1. Suppose your professor tells you your rank in the class so far, on a scale from 1st percentile (worst) to 99th percentile (best). How would you feel if you were told you were in the 10th percentile? (Circle one.)
   1 (worst)   2   3   4   5   6   7 (best)

   How would you feel if you were told you were in the 90th percentile?
   1 (worst)   2   3   4   5   6   7 (best)

2. Suppose your professor tells you your rank in the class so far, on a scale from 1st percentile (worst) to 99th percentile (best). How would you feel if you were told you were in the 91st percentile? (Circle one.)
   1 (worst)   2   3   4   5   6   7 (best)

   How would you feel if you were told you were in the 99th percentile?
   1 (worst)   2   3   4   5   6   7 (best)

On the average, students offered the first pair of questions rated their happiness 6.46 if they were told they were in the 90th percentile. Students offered the second pair of questions rated their happiness 5.89 if they were told they were in the 91st percentile (Hsee & Tang, 2007). Obviously, it doesn't make sense to be happier about being in the 90th percentile than the 91st. The wording of the question sets up an implicit comparison: The 90th percentile is much better than the 10th, but the 91st is worse than the 99th.

In short, the next time you hear the results of some survey, be skeptical. Ask how the question was worded and what choices were offered. Even a slightly different wording could yield a different percentage.

Surveyor Biases

Sometimes, an organization words the questions of a survey to encourage the answers they hope to receive. Here is an example: According to a 1993 survey, 92% of high school boys and 98% of high school girls said they were victims of sexual harassment (Shogren, 1993). Shocking, isn't it? However, perhaps the designers of the survey *wanted* to show that sexual harassment is rampant. The survey defined sexual harassment by a long list of acts ranging from serious offenses (e.g., having someone rip your clothes off in public) to minor annoyances. For example, if you didn't like the sexual graffiti on the restroom wall, you could consider yourself sexually harassed. If you tried to make yourself look sexually attractive (as most teenagers do, right?) and then attracted a suggestive look from someone you *didn't* want to attract, that stare would count as sexual harassment. (I worry about those who said they *weren't* sexually harassed! They liked *all* the graffiti on the restroom walls? No one *ever* looked at them in a sexual way?) Sexual harassment is, of course, a serious problem, but a survey that combines major and minor offenses is likely to mislead.

Figure 2.8 shows the results for two surveys conducted on similar populations at about the same time. The issue is whether stem cells derived from aborted fetuses can be used in medical research. The question on the left was written by an organization opposed to abortion and stem cell research. The question on the right was worded by an organization that is either neutral or favorable to stem cell research (Public Agenda, 2001). As you can see, the wording of the question influenced the answers.

Correlational Studies

Another type of research is a correlational study. A **correlation** is *a measure of the relationship between two variables.* (A variable is anything measurable that differs among individuals, such as age, years of education, or reading speed.) A **correlational study** is *a procedure in which investigators measure the correlation between two variables without controlling either of them.* For example, investigators have observed correlations between people's height and weight. Similarly, one can find a correlation between scores on personality tests and how many friends someone has.

The Correlation Coefficient

We would probably find a strong positive correlation between hours per week reading and scores on a vocabulary test. We would expect a lower correlation between reading hours and scores on a chemistry test. To measure the strength of a correlation, researchers use a **correlation coefficient,**

Figure 2.8 The question on the left, written by opponents of stem cell research, led most people to express opposition. The question on the right, worded differently, led most people to express support. (From ICR/National Conference of Catholic Bishops, 2001 and ABC News/Bellnet, June 2001, © 2004 by Public Agenda Foundation. Reprinted by permission.)

Stem cells are the basic cells from which all of a person's tissues and organs develop. Congress is considering whether to provide federal funding for experiments using stem cells from human embryos. The live embryos would be destroyed in their first week of development to obtain these cells. Do you support or oppose using your federal tax dollars for such experiments?

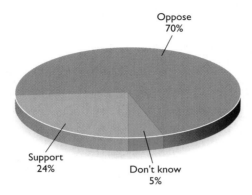

Sometimes fertility clinics produce extra fertilized eggs, also known as embryos, that are not implanted in a woman's womb. These extra embryos either are discarded, or couples can donate them for use in medical research called stem cell research. Some people support stem cell research, saying it's an important way to find treatments for many diseases. Other people oppose stem cell research, saying it's wrong to use any human embryos for research purposes. What about you — do you support or oppose stem cell research?

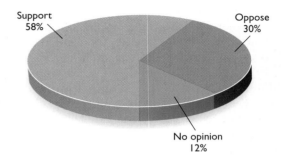

a mathematical estimate of the relationship between two variables. The coefficient can range from +1 to −1. A correlation coefficient indicates how accurately we can use a measurement of one variable to predict another. A correlation coefficient of +1, for example, means that as one variable increases, the other increases also. A correlation coefficient of −1 means that as one variable increases, the other decreases. A correlation of either +1 or −1 enables us to make perfect predictions of one variable from measurements of the other one. (In psychology you probably will never see a perfect +1 or −1 correlation coefficient.) A negative correlation is just as useful as a positive correlation and can indicate just as strong a relationship. For example, the more often people practice golf, the lower their golf scores, so golf practice is negatively correlated with scores.

In nations where people eat more seafood, depression is less common, so seafood consumption is negatively correlated with depression, as shown in Figure 2.9 (Gómez-Pinilla, 2008).

A 0 correlation indicates that measurements of one variable have no linear relationship to measurements of the other variable. As one variable goes up, the other does not consistently go up or down. A correlation near 0 can mean that two variables really are unrelated or that one or both of them were poorly measured. (If something is inaccurately measured, we can hardly expect it to predict anything else.)

Figure 2.10 shows scatter plots for three correlations (real data). In a scatter plot, *each dot represents a given individual, with one measurement for that individual on the x-axis (horizontal) and another measurement on the y-axis (vertical).* In Figure 2.10, each dot represents one student in an introductory psychology class. The value for that student along the y-axis represents percentage correct on the final exam. In the first graph, values along the x-axis represent scores on the first test in the course. Here the correlation is +.72, indicating a fairly strong relationship. Most of the students who did well on the first test also did well on the final, and most who did poorly on the first test also did poorly on the final. In the second graph, the x-axis represents times absent out of 38 class meetings. Here you see a correlation of −.44. This negative correlation indicates that, in general, those with more absences had lower exam scores. The third graph shows how the final exam scores related to the last three digits of each student's social security number. We would not expect a meaningful relationship, and we do not see one. The correlation is −.08, close to

Figure 2.9 Each dot represents one country. The value along the x-axis indicates the amount of seafood that an average person eats in a year. The value along the y-axis indicates the probability of developing major depression. As seafood consumption increases, the probability of depression decreases. (Gómez-Pinilla, 2008)

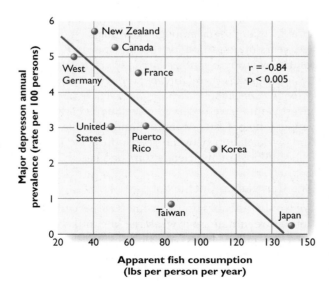

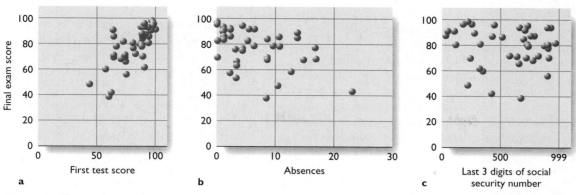

Figure 2.10 Scatter plots for three correlations. (a) Scores on first test and scores on final exam (correlation = + .72). (b) Times absent and scores on final exam (correlation = −.44). (c) Last three digits of social security number and scores on final exam (correlation = −.08). (In a scatter plot, each dot represents the measurements of two variables for one person.)

0. The small negative correlation in the actual data represents a random fluctuation. If we examined the data for larger and larger populations of students, the correlation would no doubt come closer and closer to 0.

Concept Check

5. Identify each of these as a positive, zero, or negative correlation:
   a. The more crowded a neighborhood, the lower the income.
   b. People with high IQ scores are neither more nor less likely than other people to have high telephone numbers.
   c. People who awaken frequently during the night are more likely than other people to feel depressed.
6. Which indicates a stronger relationship between two variables, a +.50 correlation or a −.75 correlation?
7. The correlation between students' grades and their scores on a self-esteem questionnaire is very low, not much above 0. Why might that be?

Answers

5. **a.** Negative correlation between crowdedness and income. **b.** Zero correlation between telephone numbers and IQ scores. **c.** Positive correlation between awakenings and depression. **6.** The −.75 correlation indicates a stronger relationship—that is, a greater accuracy of predicting one variable based on measurements of the other. A negative correlation is just as useful as a positive one. **7.** One possibility is that grades are unrelated to self-esteem. Another possibility is that we used an inaccurate measurement of either self-esteem or grades or both. If anything is measured poorly, it cannot correlate strongly with anything else.

Illusory Correlations

Sometimes with unsystematic observations, we "see" a correlation that doesn't really exist. For example, many people believe that consuming sugar makes children hyperactive. However, extensive research found little effect of sugar on activity levels, and some studies found that sugar *calms* behavior (Milich, Wolraich, & Lindgren, 1986; Wolraich et al., 1994). How, then, do we handle reports that sugar makes children hyperactive? Researchers watched two sets of mothers with their 5- to 7-year-old sons after telling one group that they had given the sons sugar and the other that they had given the sons a placebo. In fact, they had given both a placebo. The mothers who *thought* their sons had been given sugar rated their sons hyperactive during the observation period, whereas the other mothers did not (Hoover & Milich, 1994). That is, people see what they expect to see.

When people expect to see a connection between two events (e.g., sugar and activity levels), they remember the cases that support the connection and disregard the exceptions, thus perceiving an illusory correlation, *an apparent relationship based on casual observations of unrelated or weakly related events.* Many stereotypes about groups of people can be regarded as illusory correlations.

People's expectations and faulty memories produce illusory correlations, such as that between the full moon and abnormal behavior.

As another example, consider the widely held belief that a full moon affects human behavior. For hundreds of years, many people have believed that crime and various kinds of mental disturbance are more common under a full moon than at other times. In fact, the term *lunacy* (from the Latin word *luna*, meaning "moon") originally meant mental illness caused by the full moon. Some police officers claim that they receive more calls on nights with a full moon, and some hospital workers say they have more emergency cases on such nights.

However, careful reviews of the data have found no relationship between the moon's phases and either crime or mental illness (Raison, Klein, & Steckler, 1999; Rotton & Kelly, 1985). Why, then, does the belief persist? People remember events that fit the belief and disregard those that do not.

Correlation and Causation

As mentioned, a correlation tells us how strongly two variables are related to each other. It does not tell us *why*. If two variables—let's call them A and B—are positively correlated, it could be that A causes B, B causes A, or some third variable, C, causes both of them. Therefore, a correlational study does not justify a cause-and-effect conclusion.

For example, there is a strong positive correlation between the number of books people own about chess and how good they are at playing chess. Does owning chess books make someone a better chess player? Does being a good chess player cause someone to buy chess books? Both hypotheses are partly true. People who start to like chess usually buy chess books, which improve their game. As they get better, they become even more interested and buy more books. But neither the chess books nor the skill exactly causes the other.

"Then what good is a correlation?" you might ask. The simplest answer is that correlations help us make useful predictions. If your friend has just challenged you to a game of chess, you could scan your friend's bookshelves and estimate your chances of winning.

Here are three more examples to illustrate why we cannot draw conclusions regarding cause and effect from correlational data (see also Figure 2.11):

- *Unmarried men are more likely than married men to spend time in a mental hospital or prison.* That is, marriage is negatively correlated with men's mental illness and criminal activity. Does the correlation mean that marriage leads to mental health and good social adjustment? Or does it mean that the men in mental hospitals and prisons are unlikely to marry? (The second conclusion is certainly true. The first may be also.)

- *According to one study, people who sleep about 7 hours a night are less likely to die within the next few years than those who sleep either more or less* (Kripke, Garfinkel, Wingard, Klauber, & Marler, 2002). It's easy to believe that sleep deprivation impairs your health, but should we conclude (as some people did) that sleeping too much also impairs your health? Here is an alternative explanation: People who already have life-threatening illnesses tend to sleep more than healthy people. So perhaps illness causes extra sleep rather than extra sleep causing illness. Or perhaps advancing age increases the probability of both illness and extra sleep. (The study included people ranging from young adulthood through age 101!)

- *On the average, the more often parents spank their children, the worse their children misbehave.* Does this correlation indicate that spankings lead to misbehavior? Possibly, but an alternative explanation is that the parents resorted to spanking because their children were already misbehaving (Larzelere, Kuhn, & Johnson, 2004). Yet another possibility is that the parents had genes for "hostile" behavior that led them to spank, and the children inherited those genes, which led to misbehaviors.

Now, let me tell you a dirty little secret: In rare circumstances, correlational results *do* imply cause and effect. It is a "dirty little secret" because professors want students to avoid cause-and-effect conclusions from correlations, and mentioning the exceptions is risky. Still, consider the fact that

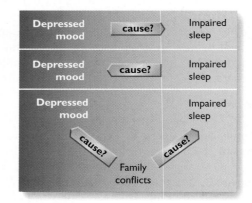

Figure 2.11 A strong correlation between depression and impaired sleep does not tell us whether depression interferes with sleep, poor sleep leads to depression, or whether another problem leads to both depression and sleep problems.

people are generally in a better mood when the weather improves (Keller et al., 2005). A likely explanation is that the weather changes your mood. What other possibility is there? Your mood changes the weather? Hardly. Might something else control the weather and your mood independently? If so, what? In the absence of any other hypothesis, we conclude that the weather changes your mood. Also consider that how often a U.S. congressional representative votes a profeminist position (as defined by the National Organization for Women) correlates with how many daughters the representative has (Washington, 2006). It is implausible that someone's voting record would influence the sex of children born many years previously; it is highly likely that having daughters could influence political views. Again, the results suggest cause and effect. Nevertheless, the point remains: We should almost always be skeptical of causal conclusions that anyone draws from a correlational study.

To determine causation, an investigator needs to manipulate one of the variables directly through a research design known as an *experiment*. When an investigator manipulates one variable and then observes corresponding changes in another variable, a conclusion about causation can be justified, presuming, of course, that the experiment is well designed.

8. Suppose we find a .8 correlation between students' reported interest in psychology and their grades on a psychology test. What conclusion can we draw?

9. On the average, the more medicines people take, the more likely they are to die young. Propose alternative explanations for this correlation.

10. On the average, drug addicts who regularly attend counseling sessions are more likely to stay drug-free than those who drop out. Propose alternative explanations for this correlation.

Answers

8. We can conclude only that if we know either someone's interest level or test score, we can predict the other with reasonably high accuracy. We *cannot* conclude that an interest in psychology will help someone learn the material or that doing well on psychology tests increases someone's interest in the material. Either conclusion might be true, of course, but neither conclusion follows from these results. A correlational study cannot demonstrate a cause-and-effect relationship.

9. Perhaps people get sick from complications caused by taking too many pills. Or maybe the people who take many medicines are those who already had serious illnesses.

10. Perhaps the counseling sessions are helpful to people who want to quit drugs. Or perhaps the people with the most serious addictions are the ones who quit.

EXPERIMENTS

An **experiment** is *a study in which the investigator manipulates at least one variable while measuring at least one other variable.* Experimental research in psychology and biology faces problems that are not common in the physical sciences. Suppose physicists measure the length of a metal bar at one temperature, increase the temperature, and then find that the bar has lengthened. They conclude that a higher temperature caused the bar to expand. Now imagine a comparable procedure in psychology: Researchers measure the language skills of some 5-year-old children, provide them with a 6-month special training program, and then find that the children have increased their language skills. Can we conclude that the training program was effective? No, because the children probably would have improved their language during 6 months even without the training. (Physicists don't worry that a metal bar might grow on its own.)

Instead of a before-and-after study, a better design is to compare two groups: An investigator might assemble a group of 5-year-old children, randomly divide them into two groups, and provide the training for one group (the *experimental group*) and not the other (the *control group*). Someone, preferably a blind observer, evaluates the language skills of the two groups. If the two groups become different in some consistent way, then the difference is probably the result of the experimental procedure. Table 2.3 contrasts experiments with observational studies.

With an experiment, as with any research, we should beware of generalizing the results too far. If the researchers studied 5-year-old children in the United States, the results might not apply, or might not apply equally well, to children in another country or even to children in the same country many years later. We gain confidence in the generalizability of the results if researchers obtain similar results from a variety of samples, especially if they come from different cultures.

Some Important Terms

An experiment is an attempt to measure how changes in one variable affect one or more other variables. The **independent variable** is *the item*

Table 2.3 Comparison of Five Methods of Research

Observational Studies	
Case study	Detailed description of single individual; suitable for studying rare conditions.
Naturalistic observation	Description of behavior under natural conditions.
Survey	Study of attitudes, beliefs, or behaviors based on answers to questions.
Correlation	Description of the relationship between two variables that the investigator measures but does not control; determines whether two variables are closely related but does not address questions of cause and effect.
Experiment	
Determination of the effect of a variable controlled by the investigator on some other variable that is measured; the only method that can inform us about cause and effect.	

that an experimenter changes or controls—for example, the type of training that people receive or the wording of the instructions before they start some task. The *dependent variable is the item that an experimenter measures to determine how it was affected*—for example, how many questions people answer correctly or how rapidly they respond to signals. If the procedure causes different groups to behave differently, you can think of the independent variable as the cause and the dependent variable as the effect

An **experimental group** *receives the treatment that an experiment is designed to test.* For example, the experimental group might receive some special experience that we think will influence later behavior. The **control group** is *a set of individuals treated in the same way as the experimental group except for the procedure that the experiment is designed to test.* If the people in the experimental group received a special experience, those in the control group would do something else during the same time.

Suppose we conduct a study comparing the mental health of people who use illegal drugs and those who don't. We find that nonusers have better mental health on the average. What conclusion should we draw? None. It is tempting to assume that drug use impaired mental health, but it is equally plausible that impaired mental health leads people to try illegal drugs. A research study does not qualify as an experiment unless it has **random assignment** of participants to groups: *The experimenter uses a chance procedure, such as drawing names out of a hat, to make sure that every participant has the same probability as any*

other participant of being assigned to a given group. (Of course, for ethical reasons, it would be impossible to assign people randomly to use or not use illegal drugs!)

11. Which of the following would an experimenter try to minimize or avoid? falsifiability, independent variables, dependent variables, blind observers, demand characteristics.

12. An instructor wants to find out whether the frequency of testing in an introductory psychology class influences students' final exam performance. The instructor gives weekly tests in one class, just three tests in a second class, and only a single midterm exam in the third class. All three classes take the same final exam, and the instructor then compares their performances. Identify the independent variable and the dependent variable.

Answers

11. Of these, only demand characteristics are to be avoided. If you did not remember that falsifiability is a good feature of a theory, check page 29. Every experiment must have at least one independent variable (what the experimenter controls) and at least one dependent variable (what the experimenter measures). Blind observers provide an advantage.

12. The independent variable is the frequency of tests during the semester. The dependent variable is the students' performance on the final exam.

What's the Evidence?
Inheritance of *Acquired Characteristics?*

We have discussed research procedures in general. Now let's examine a specific example in more detail. The example relates to a couple of very old studies that deserve to be better known. The research topic pertains to evolution, but the point here is not so much evolution itself as some pitfalls of research. I hope you will see how these studies illustrate some of the points we have been studying about research.

Charles Darwin's theory of evolution by natural selection makes a simple point: If individuals with one kind of genes reproduce more than those with other genes, then the first set of genes will become more common from one generation to the next. Eventually, the whole population will resemble those who were most successful at reproducing. Prior to Darwin, Jean-Baptiste Lamarck had offered a different theory, evolution by inheritance of acquired characteristics. According to that theory, if you exercise your muscles, your children will be born with larger muscles. If you fail to use your little toe, your children will be born with a smaller little toe than you had. The evidence never supported that theory, and nearly all biologists of the late 1800s and early 1900s abandoned it in favor of Darwin's theory. However, a few holdouts continued defending Lamarckian evolution.

First Study (McDougall, 1938)

Hypothesis If rats learn to swim through a maze, their offspring will learn the maze more quickly.

Method The researcher set up a simple maze in a water tank, such that rats had to learn to swim a particular route to get out of the water. He trained them day after day until each rat was consistently swimming quickly the correct route. Then he let them breed the next generation. He did not select the best learners for breeding. He simply chose rats at random. When rats of the next generation were old enough, he trained them and let them reproduce. This procedure continued for one generation of rats after another.

Results Consistent with Lamarck's theory, the average performance of the rats improved from one generation to the next for the first few generations. That is, the second generation learned faster than the first, the third faster than the second, and so on for a few generations. Later, the results fluctuated.

Interpretation These results are consistent with the hypothesis, but we should consider other hypotheses, too. If these results really indicate inheritance of acquired characteristics, we would have to imagine that the experience of learning the maze somehow directed the genes to mutate in the right way to help the next generation learn the same maze. It is difficult to imagine how this could happen.

When results conflict so strongly with what we think we know, scientists ask these questions: Are the results replicable? Is there a more parsimonious explanation? And is there any flaw in the design of the study?

Do you, in fact, see anything wrong with the procedure? It does have a serious but subtle problem. If you don't see it, don't feel bad. At the time of this study, hardly anyone saw what was wrong. However, one group of researchers noticed that this is a before-and-after study with no control group. What would happen, they wondered, if they repeated the study using a control group that never received training in the maze? Would their offspring improve as much as the offspring of the trained rats?

Second Study (Agar, Drummond, Tiegs, & Gunson, 1954)

Hypothesis If it is possible to replicate McDougall's results, the improvement will also occur in a control group that receives no training in the maze.

Method Rats in the trained group were treated the same as those in McDougall's study: Rats learned the maze and then mated. Rats of the next generation also learned the maze and then mated and so forth.

In the control group, the rats used for training were not used for breeding. Young, healthy rats typically have a litter of about 12 babies. In each generation, a few rats were trained in the maze but not used for breeding. Other rats from the same litter were not trained and were permitted to breed. So in each generation, the researchers obtained a measure of maze learning, but because only untrained rats mated, all the rats in the control group were descended from untrained rats. Any improvement over generations could not be due to the training. The experiment continued for 18 years, with a few generations of rats per year. (Rats reach sexual maturity at about age 60 days.)

Results Figure 2.12 shows the results. For the first few years, on the average, both the trained group and the control group showed improvement from one generation to the next in their maze learning. In later years, the results fluctuated. The two groups performed similarly throughout the study.

Interpretation To most people's surprise, McDougall's results were replicable. However, because the trained group did not differ from the control group, training had nothing to do with the improvement over generations. That is, the results showed no evidence for inheritance of acquired characteristics.

How, then, can we explain the improvement over generations? One possibility is that rats of the first generation were stressed. They had just been shipped in by train, in crowded boxes, from rat-breeding facilities to McDougall's laboratory. (Yes, there are companies that specialize in breeding and selling rats.) The second generation grew up in the laboratory, but they were the offspring of highly stressed parents. Conceivably, those effects could persist for several generations.

Another possibility is that the experimenters gradually got better at taking care of rats and running the experiment. We might be seeing a change in the experimenters, not a change in the rats.

A third possibility is that because the experimenters always mated brother with sister, later generations may have become less vigorous. Ordinarily, we expect inbreeding to be a disadvantage, but perhaps less vigorous rats

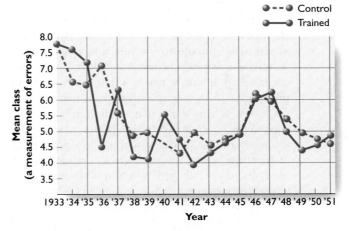

Figure 2.12 Rats in the experimental group and the control group improved at equal rates from one generation to the next. (From Agar, W. E., Drummond, F. H., Tiegs, O. W., & Gunson, M. M. (1954). Fourth (final) report on a test of McDougall's Lamarckian experiment on the training of rats. *Journal of Experimental Biology, 31,* 307–321)

swam more slowly and therefore had more time to consider which direction to turn in the maze. This idea sounds a little far-fetched but not impossible.

We don't know which explanation is correct. The question isn't important enough for anyone to do the additional research necessary to find out. The main conclusion is that we can account for the results without assuming inheritance of acquired characteristics.

This episode emphasizes several points about research: (a) If the results seem unlikely, look for a more parsimonious explanation. (b) Beware of before-and-after studies. Without a control group, we don't know what they mean. In other chapters of this book, we encounter other examples that make the same point. Chapter 9 includes a study in which slow-learning 2-year-old children received a prolonged enrichment experience and appeared to improve in intelligence. Do you see what might be wrong with that study? (c) If behavior changes from one generation to the next, the explanation doesn't have to be genetic. It might reflect a change in the environment. We shall see several examples of this idea, especially in the chapter on development (chapter 5).

ETHICAL CONSIDERATIONS IN RESEARCH

In any experiment, psychologists manipulate a variable to determine how it affects behavior. Perhaps you object to the idea of someone trying to alter your behavior. If so, consider that every time you talk to people, you are trying to alter their behavior at least slightly. Most experiments in psychology are no more manipulative than a conversation. Still, some experiments do raise difficult issues, and researchers are bound by both law and conscience to treat their participants ethically.

Ethical Concerns with Humans

Consider the question of televised violence. If psychologists believed that watching violent programs might really transform viewers into murderers, it would be unethical to conduct experiments to find out for sure. It would also be unethical to perform procedures likely to cause significant pain, embarrassment, or any other harm. In chapter 16, we consider a famous, very old experiment designed to cause phobias (extreme fears) in children. Even at the time, many psychologists condemned the study as unethical, and by today's standards, we would certainly prohibit it.

The central ethical principle is that research should include only procedures to which people would agree. Psychologists ask prospective participants to give their informed consent before proceeding, *a statement that they have been told what to expect and that they agree to continue.* When researchers ask for volunteers, they de-

scribe what will happen. Most procedures are innocuous, such as tests of perception, memory, or attention. Occasionally, however, the procedure includes something that people might not wish to do, such as examining disgusting photographs, drinking concentrated sugar water, or receiving electrical shocks. Participants are told they have the right to quit if they find the procedure too disagreeable.

Special problems arise in research with children, people who are mentally retarded, or others who might not understand the instructions well enough to provide informed consent (Bonnie, 1997). Individuals with severe depression pose a special problem (Elliott, 1997) because some seem to have lost interest in protecting their own welfare. In such cases, researchers either consult the person's guardian or nearest relative or simply decide not to proceed.

Research at a college must first be approved by an Institutional Review Board (IRB). An IRB judges whether the proposed studies include procedures for informed consent and whether they safeguard each participant's confidentiality. An IRB also tries to prevent risky procedures. It probably would reject a proposal to offer cocaine, even if people were eager to give their informed consent. A committee would also ban procedures that they consider seriously embarrassing or degrading. Many "reality television" shows would be banned if they needed approval from an IRB (Spellman, 2005).

The committee also judges procedures in which investigators want to deceive participants temporarily. Suppose a researcher wants to test whether it is harder to persuade people if they know someone is trying to persuade them. The researcher wants to use one group that is informed of the upcoming persuasion and one that is not. The researcher cannot fully inform all participants without losing the whole point of the study. The institutional committee would have to decide whether this temporary deception is acceptable.

The American Psychological Association (APA) published a book discussing the proper ethical treatment of volunteers in experiments (Sales & Folkman, 2000). The APA censures or expels any member who disregards these principles.

Ethical Concerns with Nonhumans

Some psychological research deals with nonhuman animals, especially research on basic processes such as sensation, hunger, and learning (Figure 2.13). Researchers use nonhumans if they want to control aspects of life that people will not let them control (e.g., who mates with whom), if they want to study behavior continuously over months or years (longer than people are willing to participate), or if the research poses health risks. Animal research has long been essential for preliminary testing of most new drugs, surgical procedures, and methods of relieving pain. People with untreatable illnesses argue that they have the right to hope for cures that might result from animal research (Feeney, 1987). Much of our knowledge in psychology, biology, and medicine made use of animal studies at some point.

Nevertheless, some people oppose much or all animal research. Animals, after all, cannot give informed consent. Some animal rights supporters insist that animals should have the same rights as humans, that keeping animals (even pets) in cages is slavery, and that killing any animal is murder. Others oppose some kinds of research but are willing to compromise about others.

Psychologists vary in their attitudes. Most support some kinds of animal research but draw a line somewhere separating acceptable from unacceptable research (Plous, 1996). Naturally, different psychologists draw that line at different places.

In this debate, as in so many other political controversies, one common tactic is for each side to criticize the most extreme actions of its opponents. For example, animal rights advocates point to studies that exposed monkeys or puppies to painful procedures that seem difficult to justify. Researchers point to protesters who have vandalized laboratories, planted bombs, banged on a researcher's children's windows at night, and inserted a garden hose through a window to flood a house (G. Miller, 2007a). Some protesters have stated that they oppose using any drug, even a medication for AIDS, if its discovery came from research with animals. Unfortunately, when both sides concentrate on criticizing their most extreme opponents, they make points of agreement harder to find.

One careful study by a relatively unbiased outsider concluded that the truth is messy: Some

Figure 2.13 One example of animal research: A mirror mounted on a young owl's head enables investigators to track the owl's head movements and thereby discover how it localizes sounds with one ear plugged. The findings may help researchers understand how people with visual loss use their hearing to compensate.

research is painful to the animals *and* nevertheless valuable for scientific and medical progress (Blum, 1994). We must, most people conclude, seek a compromise.

Professional organizations such as the Neuroscience Society and the American Psychological Association publish guidelines for the proper use of animals in research. Colleges and other research institutions maintain laboratory animal care committees to ensure that laboratory animals are treated humanely, that their pain and discomfort are kept to a minimum, and that experimenters consider alternatives before imposing potentially painful procedures.

How can we determine in advance whether the value of the expected experimental results (which is hard to predict) will outweigh the pain the animals will endure (which is hard to measure)? As is common with ethical decisions, reasonable arguments can be raised on both sides of the question, and no compromise is fully satisfactory.

module 2.2

In Closing

Psychological Research

As you read at the beginning of this chapter, most scientists avoid the word *prove*. Psychologists certainly do. (The joke is that psychology courses don't have true–false tests, just maybe–perhaps tests.) The most complex and most interesting aspects of human behavior are products of genetics, a lifetime of experiences, and countless current influences. Given the practical and ethical limitations, it might seem that psychological researchers would become discouraged. However, because of these difficulties, researchers have been highly inventive in designing complex methods. A single study rarely answers a question decisively, but many studies converge to increase our total understanding.

SUMMARY

- *Operational definitions.* For many purposes, psychologists prefer operational definitions, which state how to measure a phenomenon or how to produce it. (page 37)

- *Sampling.* Because psychologists hope to draw conclusions that apply to a large population, they try to select a sample that resembles the total population—either a representative sample or a random sample. To apply the results to people worldwide, they need a cross-cultural sample. (page 37)

- *Experimenter bias and blind observers.* An experimenter's expectations influence the interpretations of behavior and the recording of data. To ensure objectivity, investigators use blind observers who do not know what results are expected. In a double-blind study, neither the observer nor the participants know the researcher's predictions. Researchers try to minimize the effects of demand characteristics, which are cues that tell participants what the experimenter expects them to do. (page 39)

- *Naturalistic observations.* Naturalistic observations provide descriptions of humans or other species under natural conditions. (page 41)

- *Case histories.* A case history is a detailed research study of a single individual, generally someone with unusual characteristics. (page 41)

- *Surveys.* A survey is a report of people's answers on a questionnaire. It is easy to conduct a survey and, unfortunately, easy to get misleading results. (page 41)

- *Correlations.* A correlational study is a study of the relationship between variables that are outside the investigator's control. The strength of this relationship is measured by a correlation coefficient, which ranges from 0 (no relationship) to plus or minus 1 (a perfect relationship). (page 43)

- *Illusory correlations.* Beware of illusory correlations—relationships that people think they observe between variables after casual observation. (page 45)

- *Inferring causation.* A correlational study cannot uncover cause-and-effect relationships, but an experiment can. (page 46)

- *Experiments.* In an experiment, the investigator manipulates an independent variable to determine its effect on the dependent variable. A before-and-after study often leads to results that are hard to interpret. It is better to compare the results for different groups. (page 47)

- *Random assignment.* An experimenter should randomly assign individuals to form experimental and control groups. All participants should have an equal probability of being chosen for the experimental group. (page 48)

- *Ethics of experimentation.* Research on human participants should not proceed until the participants have given their informed consent. Psychologists try to minimize risk to their participants, but they sometimes face difficult ethical decisions. (page 50)

KEY TERMS

blind observer (page 40)

case history (page 41)

control group (page 48)

convenience sample (page 38)

correlation (page 43)

correlation coefficient (page 43)

correlational study (page 43)

cross-cultural samples (page 38)

demand characteristics (page 41)

dependent variable (page 48)

double-blind study (page 40)

experiment (page 47)

experimental group (page 48)

experimenter bias (page 39)

illusory correlation (page 45)

independent variable (page 47)

informed consent (page 50)

naturalistic observation (page 41)

operational definition (page 37)

placebo (page 40)

population (page 37)

random assignment (page 48)

random sample (page 38)

representative sample (page 38)

scatter plot (page 44)

single-blind study (page 40)

survey (page 41)

Measuring and Analyzing Results

- How can researchers state the "average" results in a study?

- How can researchers describe the variations among individuals?

- How can researchers determine whether the results represent something more than chance fluctuations?

Some years ago, a television program reported that 28 young people known to have played the game Dungeons and Dragons had committed suicide. Alarming, right?

Not necessarily. At that time, at least 3 million young people played the game regularly. The reported suicide rate among D&D players—28 per 3 million—was considerably *less* than the suicide rate among teenagers in general.

So do these results mean that playing D&D *prevents* suicide? Hardly. The 28 reported cases are probably an incomplete count. Besides, no matter what the correlation between playing D&D and committing suicide, it could not tell us about cause and effect. Maybe the kinds of young people who play D&D are simply different from those who do not.

Then what conclusion should we draw? *None.* When the data are incomplete or the method is flawed, no conclusion follows. (Even when the data are acceptable, people sometimes present them in a confusing or misleading manner, as shown in Figure 2.14.) In this module, we consider proper ways to analyze and interpret results.

DESCRIPTIVE STATISTICS

To explain the meaning of a study, an investigator must summarize the results. If a researcher observes 100 people, we do not want the details about every person. We want to know the general trends or averages. An investiga-

tor provides descriptive statistics, which are *mathematical summaries of results*. The correlation coefficient, discussed earlier in this chapter, is an example of a descriptive statistic.

Measures of the Central Score

We care about the central score—that is, the middle or average score. Three ways of representing it are the mean, median, and mode. The **mean** is *the sum of all the scores divided by the total number of scores.* When people say "average," they generally refer to the mean. For example, the mean of 2, 10, and 3 is 5 ($15 \div 3$). The mean is especially useful if the scores approximate the normal distribution (or normal curve), *a symmetrical frequency of scores clustered around the mean.* A normal distribution is often described as a bell-shaped curve. For example, if we measure how long it takes various students to complete some task, their times usually follow a pattern similar to the normal distribution.

The mean can be misleading, however, in certain cases. For example, *every* student in my class this semester has a greater than average number of arms and legs! It's true. Think about it. What is the average (mean) number of arms or legs for a human being? It is not 2, but 1.99 . . . because a few people have had an arm or leg amputated. So if the "average" refers to the mean, it is possible for the vast majority to be above or below average. Here is another example: A survey

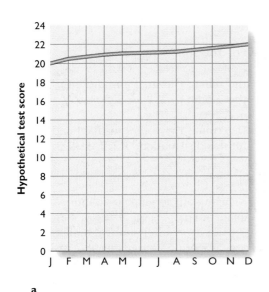

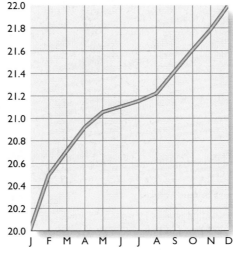

Figure 2.14 Statistics can be misleading: Both graphs present the same data, an increase from 20 to 22 over 1 year's time. But graph (b) makes that increase look dramatic by ranging from 20 to 22 (rather than 0 to 22). (After Huff, 1954)

a

b

asked people how many sex partners they hoped to have, ideally, over the next 30 years. The mean for women was 2.8 and the mean for men was 64.3 (L. C. Miller & Fishkin, 1997). But those means are extremely misleading. Almost two thirds of women and about half of men replied "1." They wanted a loving relationship with one partner. Most of the others said they hoped for a few partners during their lifetime, but a small number of men said they hoped for hundreds, thousands, or tens of thousands. If most men reply "1" or "2," but a few reply with huge numbers, a mean such as "64.3" can be misleading.

When the population distribution is far from symmetrical, we can better represent the typical scores by the median instead of the mean. To determine the median, *we arrange the scores in order from the highest to the lowest. The middle score is the median.* For example, for the set of scores 2, 10, and 3, the median is 3. For the set of scores 1, 1, 1, and 3.5×10^5, the median is 1. In short, extreme scores greatly affect the mean but not the median.

The third way to represent the central score is the mode, *the score that occurs most frequently.* For example, in the distribution of scores 2, 2, 3, 4, and 10, the mode is 2. The mode is seldom useful except under special circumstances. Suppose we asked college students how much they study and gathered the results shown in Figure 2.15. Half of the students at this college study a great deal, and half study very little. The mean for this distribution is 4.28 hours per day, a very misleading number because all the students study either much more or much less than that. The median is no better as a representation of these results: Because we have an even number of students, there is no

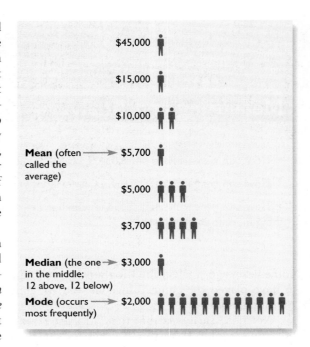

Figure 2.16 The monthly salaries of the 25 employees of company X, showing the mean, median, and mode. (After Huff, 1954)

middle score. We could take a figure midway between the two scores nearest the middle, but in this case those scores are 2 and 7, so we would compute a median of 4.5, again misleading. A distribution like this is called a *bimodal distribution* (one with two common scores); the researcher might describe the two modes and not even mention the mean or the median.

To summarize: The mean is what most people intend when they say "average." It is the sum of the scores divided by the number of scores. The median is the middle score after the scores are ranked from highest to lowest. The mode is the most common score (Figure 2.16).

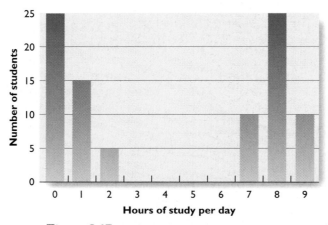

Figure 2.15 Results of an imaginary survey of study habits at one college. In this case, both the mean and the median are misleading. This distribution has two modes, which are 0 and 8.

13. **a.** For the following distribution of scores, determine the mean, the median, and the mode: 5, 2, 2, 2, 8, 3, 1, 6, 7.
    b. Determine the mean, median, and mode for this distribution: 5, 2, 2, 2, 35, 3, 1, 6, 7.

Concept Check

Answer

13. **a.** mean = 4; median = 3; mode = 2. **b.** mean = 7; median = 3; mode = 2. Note that changing just one number in the distribution from 8 to 35 greatly altered the mean without affecting the median or the mode.

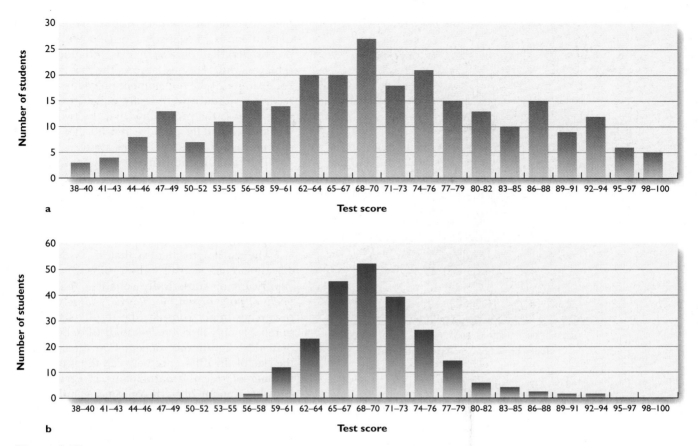

Figure 2.17 These two distributions of test scores have the same mean but different variances and different standard deviations.

Measures of Variation

Figure 2.17 shows two distributions of scores, which might be the results for two introductory psychology tests. Both tests have the same mean, 70, but different distributions. If you had a score of 80, you would beat only 75% of the other students on the first test, but with the same score, you would beat 95% on the second test.

To describe the difference between Figure 2.17a and b, we need a measurement of the variation (or spread) around the mean. The simplest such measurement is the range of a distribution, *a statement of the highest and lowest scores.* The range in Figure 2.17a is 38 to 100, and in Figure 2.18b, it is 56 to 94.

The range is a simple but not very useful calculation because it reflects only the extremes. The most useful measure is the standard deviation (SD), *a measurement of the amount of variation among scores in a normal distribution.* In the appendix to this chapter, you will find a formula for calculating the standard deviation. For present purposes, you can simply remember that when the scores are closely clustered near the mean, the standard deviation is small. When the scores are more widely scattered, the stan-

dard deviation is large. So, Figure 2.17a has a larger standard deviation; Figure 2.17b has a smaller standard deviation.

As Figure 2.18 shows, the Scholastic Assessment Test (SAT) was designed to produce a mean of 500 and a standard deviation of 100. Of all people taking the test, 68% score within 1 standard deviation above or below the mean (400–600), and 95% score within 2 standard deviations (300–700). Only 2.5% score above 700. Another 2.5% score below 300.

Standard deviations enable us to compare scores on different tests. For example, if you scored 1 standard deviation above the mean on the SAT, you tested about as well as someone who scored 1 standard deviation above the mean on a different test, such as the American College Test.

---

14. Suppose that you score 80 on your first psychology test. The mean for the class is 70, and the standard deviation is 5. On the second test, you receive a score of 90. This time the mean for the class is also 70, but the standard deviation is 20. Compared to the other students in your class, did your performance improve, deteriorate, or stay the same?

Answer

14. Even though your score rose from 80 on the first test to 90 on the second, your performance actually deteriorated in comparison to other students' scores. A score of 80 on the first test was 2 standard deviations above the mean, better than 98% of all other students. A 90 on the second test was only 1 standard deviation above the mean, a score that beats only 84% of the other students.

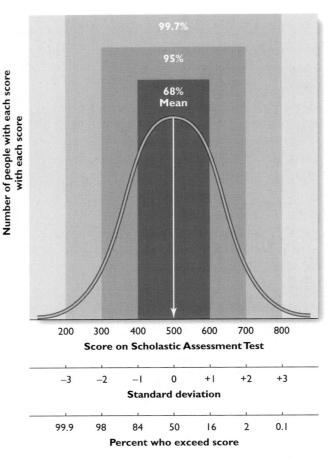

Figure 2.18 In a normal distribution of scores, the amount of variation from the mean can be measured in standard deviations. In this example, scores between 400 and 600 are said to be within 1 standard deviation from the mean; scores between 300 and 700 are within 2 standard deviations.

EVALUATING RESULTS: INFERENTIAL STATISTICS

Suppose researchers randomly assign people to two groups to help them quit smoking cigarettes. One group receives punishments for smoking, and the other group gets rewards for not smoking. Before treatment, both groups average about 10 cigarettes per day. At the end of 6 weeks of therapy, those in the punishment group average 7.5 cigarettes per day, whereas those in the reward group average 6.5 cigarettes per day. How seriously should we take this difference?

To answer this question, we obviously need to know more than just the numbers 7.5 and 6.5. How many smokers were in the study? (Just a few? Hundreds? Thousands?) Also, how much variation occurred within each group? Are most people's behaviors close to the group means, or did a few extreme scores distort the averages?

We evaluate the results with inferential statistics, which are *statements about a large popula-tion based on an inference from a small sample.* Certain kinds of statistical tests determine the probability that purely chance variation would achieve a difference as large as the one observed. For example, if the punishment procedure and the reward procedure were really equal in effective-ness, what is the probability that the two groups would accidentally produce results that differed as much as what we saw in this study?

The result is summarized by a p (as in *prob-ability*) value. For example, $p < .05$ indicates that *the probability that randomly generated results would resemble the observed results is less than 5%.* The smaller the p value, the more impressive the results.

The usual agreement is that, if p is less than .05, researchers consider the results statistically significant or statistically reliable—that is, *un-likely to have arisen by chance.* A more cautious researcher might consider the results significant or reliable only if p were less than .01 or even .001. Statistical significance depends on three factors: the size of the difference between the groups, the number of research participants in each group, and the amount of variation among individuals within each group.

If the results are not statistically significant, what then? We should draw no conclusion. We should *not* conclude that the hypothesis was wrong or that the procedure had no effect. Sometimes, a hypothesis is correct but difficult to demonstrate, and sometimes, a procedure appears to be ineffec-tive just because our measurements are inaccurate (Kluger & Tikochinsky, 2001). Of course, the more often researchers have failed to find a significant effect, the more skeptical we should become.

For a variety of reasons, many scientists rec-ommend that instead of (or in addition to) stating the p value, researchers should show the means and 95% confidence intervals for each group, as shown in Figure 2.19 (Cumming, 2008). The 95% confidence interval is *the range within which the true population mean lies, with 95% certainty.*

"Wait a minute," you protest. "We already know the means: 7.5 and 6.5. Aren't *those* the 'true' population means?" No, those are the means for particular samples of the population. Someone who studies another group of smokers may not get the same results. What we care about is the mean for all smokers. It is impractical to measure that mean, but if we know the sample mean, the size of the sample, and the standard deviation, we can es-timate how close the sample mean is to the popula-tion mean. Figure 2.19 presents two possibilities.

In part **a,** the 95% confidence intervals are small. In other words, the standard deviations were small, the samples were large, and the sam-ple means are almost certainly close to the true population means. In part **b,** the confidence intervals are larger, so the sample means are just rough approximations of the true population means. Presenting data with confidence intervals enables readers to see how large and impressive the difference is between two groups (Hunter, 1997; Loftus, 1996).

15. Should we be more impressed with results when the 95% confidence intervals are large or small? Should we be more impressed if the *p* value is large or small?

Answer

merely by chance.
probability of getting such a large difference
low *p* value indicates a low
the results. A small *p* value indicates a low
dence interval indicates high confidence in
15. In both cases, smaller. A small 95% confi-

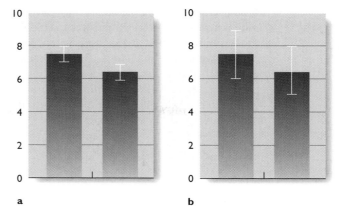

Figure 2.19 The vertical lines indicate 95% confidence intervals. The pair of graphs in part a indicate that the true mean has a 95% chance of falling within a very narrow range. The graphs in part b indicate a wider range.

module 2.3

In Closing

Statistics and Conclusions

Sometimes, psychological researchers get such consistent effects that they need no statistics: If you turn out the lights in a sealed room, people will no longer be able to see. If you add sugar to your iced tea, it tastes sweet. Statistical tests are critical for evaluating smaller effects: Does a change in wording alter people's responses to a survey? Does the use of an electronic study guide improve students' test scores? Does family therapy provide better results than individual therapy

to treat drug abuse? Most psychological researchers deal with small effects and therefore need a solid understanding of statistics.

Examining the statistics is only the first step toward drawing a conclusion. To say that an experiment has statistically significant or reliable results means only that we would be unlikely to get such results merely by chance. At that point, psychologists use their knowledge to seek the most likely interpretation of the results.

SUMMARY

* *Mean, median, and mode.* One way of presenting the central score of a distribution is via the mean, determined by adding all the scores and dividing by the number of individuals. Another way is the median, which is the middle score after all the scores have been arranged from highest to lowest. The mode is the score that occurs most frequently. (page 53)
* *Standard deviation (SD).* To indicate whether most scores are clustered close to the mean or

whether they are spread out, psychologists report the range of scores called the standard deviation. If we know that a given score is a certain number of standard deviations above or below the mean, then we can determine what percentage of other scores it exceeds. (page 55)
* *Inferential statistics.* Inferential statistics are attempts to deduce the properties of a large population based on the results from a small sample of that population. (page 56)

- *Probability of chance results.* The most common use of inferential statistics is to calculate the probability that a given research result could have arisen by chance. That probability is low if the difference between the two groups is large, if the variability within each group is small, and if the number of individuals in each group is large. (page 56)

- *Statistical significance.* When psychologists say $p < .05$, they mean that the probability that accidental fluctuations could produce the kind of results they obtained is less than 5%. They generally set a standard of 5% or less. If the results meet that standard, they are then said to be statistically significant or reliable. (page 56)

KEY TERMS

95% confidence interval (page 56)

descriptive statistics (page 53)

inferential statistics (page 56)

mean (page 53)

median (page 54)

mode (page 54)

normal distribution (or normal curve) (page 53)

$p < .05$ (page 56)

range (page 55)

standard deviation (SD) (page 55)

statistically significant (or statistically reliable) results (page 56)

exploration and study

Why Does This Matter to Me?

SOCIAL RESPONSIBILITY AND PSYCHOLOGY

Many environmental problems are caused by human behavior. Psychologists can help steer the course of our future toward more socially responsible and sustainable outcomes. Students of today need to be ever mindful of the link between human behavior and its impact on the environment.

"Scientific Methods in Psychology" and Social Responsibility: A Step Further

If one person claims that the Greenhouse Effect exists and someone else doubts it, which side has the burden of proof? If you have an opinion on this topic, how did you form it?

Find Your Carbon Footprint

Your carbon footprint is a measure of how much your everyday activities can affect the environment. There are many available websites that can help you calculate your impact and offer suggestions on ways you can contribute to a more sustainable future. As you use the tools provided on these websites, think about what evidence would be needed to demonstrate that measurements are accurate and useful. Go to www.cengage.com/psychology/kalat to find a current link to a carbon footprint calculator.

Join the iChapters Plant a Tree Drive!

To show its support of the environmental movement, iChapters is planting a tree on behalf of each fan of the iChapters Facebook Page and for every 10 questions answered correctly in our quiz.
http://www.ichapters.com/plantatree/

Exploration and Study

SUGGESTIONS FOR FURTHER EXPLORATION

In addition to the study materials provided at the end of each module, you may supplement your review of this chapter with the following book and website suggestions or by using one or more of the book's electronic resources, which include its companion website, interactive Cengage Learning eBook, and CengageNOW. Brief descriptions of these resources follow. For more information, visit **www.cengage.com/psychology/kalat**

ADDITIONAL RESOURCES

The book's companion website, accessible from **www.cengage.com/psychology/kalat,** provides a wide range of study resources such as an interactive glossary, flashcards, tutorial quizzes, updated web links, and Try It Yourself activities. For example, the exercise on Psychic Phenomenon ties to what you've learned in this chapter.

CengageNOW with Critical Thinking Videos is an easy-to-use resource that helps you study in less time to get the grade you want. An online study system, CengageNOW gives you the option of taking a diagnostic pretest for each chapter. The system uses the results of each pretest to create personalized chapter study plans for you. The Personalized Study Plans

- Help you save study time by identifying areas on which you should concentrate and give you one-click access to corresponding pages of the interactive Cengage Learning eBook;
- Provide interactive exercises and study tools to help you fully understand chapter concepts; and
- Include a posttest for you to take to confirm that you are ready to move on to the next chapter.

Find this Try-It-Yourself activity, as well as critical thinking videos and more, in your CengageNOW product, which offers an opportunity for you to learn more about psychological research on different topics.

Books

Martin, D. (2007). *Doing psychology experiments* (7th ed.). Pacific Grove, CA: Brooks/Cole. A discussion of all aspects of research, including methods of conducting research and statistical analyses of results.

Stanovich, K. E. (2004). *How to think straight about psychology* (7th ed.). Boston: Pearson, Allyn & Bacon. An excellent discussion of how to evaluate evidence and avoid pitfalls.

Websites

Links to the websites described below are kept current and can be found at **www.cengage.com/psychology/kalat.**

HyperText Psychology_BASICS

This site walks you through the basics of research: social science methods; field studies, surveys, and experiments; and the use of statistics in interpreting results.

Statistical Assessment Service (STATS)

Here you'll learn how statistical and quantitative information and research are represented (and misrepresented) by the media and how journalists can learn to convey such material more accurately and effectively.

Psychological Research Opportunities

The Psychology Department at the University of Mississippi invites you to participate in some of their research projects online.

Psychic Phenomenon

Flash Mind Reader

Do you believe that it is possible for someone to read your mind? You will choose a number, find the symbol that corresponds to that number (between 1 and 100), then concentrate on that symbol. No matter how many times you go through the procedure, this program will unerringly tell you what symbol you selected! Unconvinced? Click the "crystal ball" to try it yourself.

BEGIN

Psychic Phenomenon

Statistical Calculations

This appendix shows you how to calculate a few of the statistics mentioned in chapter 2. It is intended primarily to satisfy your curiosity. Ask your instructor whether you should use this appendix for any other purpose.

STANDARD DEVIATION

To determine the standard deviation (SD):

1. Determine the mean of the scores.
2. Subtract the mean from each of the individual scores.
3. Square each of those results, add the squares together, and divide by the total number of scores.

The result is called the *variance.* The standard deviation is the square root of the variance. Here is an example:

Individual scores	Each score minus the mean	Difference squared
12.5	−2.5	6.25
17.0	+2.0	4.00
11.0	−4.0	16.00
14.5	−0.5	0.25
16.0	+1.0	1.00
16.5	+1.5	2.25
17.5	+2.5	6.25
105		36.00

The mean is 15.0 (the sum of the first column, divided by 7). The variance is 5.143 (the sum of the third column, divided by 7). The standard deviation is 2.268 (the square root of 5.143).

CORRELATION COEFFICIENTS

To determine the correlation coefficient, we designate one of the variables x and the other one y. We obtain pairs of measures, x_i and y_i. Then we use the following formula:

$$r = \frac{[\Sigma x_i y_i) - n \cdot \bar{x} \cdot \bar{y}]}{n \cdot sx \cdot sy}$$

In this formula, $(\Sigma x_i y_i)$ is the sum of the products of x and y. For each pair of observations (x, y), we multiply x times y and then add together all the products. The term $n \cdot \bar{x} \cdot \bar{y}$ means n (the number of pairs) times the mean of x times the mean of y. The denominator, $n \cdot sx \cdot sy$, means n times the standard deviation of x times the standard deviation of y.

WEB/TECHNOLOGY RESOURCES

Introductory Statistics: Concepts, Models, and Applications

You can read an entire statistics textbook by David W. Stockburger, Southwest Missouri State University, on the web or download it, free! The link to this website is kept current and can be found at **www.cengage.com/psychology/kalat.**

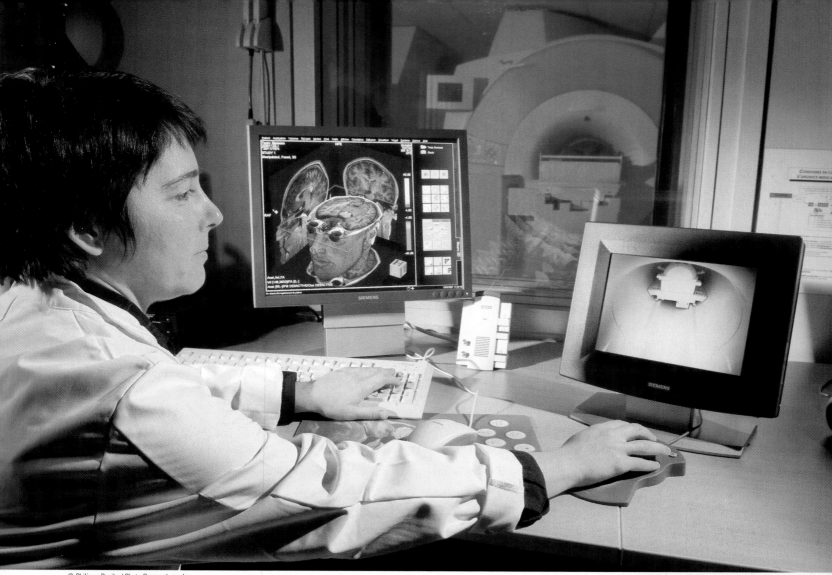

© Philippe Psaila / Photo Researchers, Inc.

Biological Psychology

A bee has amazingly complex behavior, but we have no way to get inside the bee's experience to know what (if anything) it feels like to be a bee.

© T. Dickinson/The Image Works

Consider This:

Every year, computers get smaller and smarter. Brains have always been small and smart. A human brain weighs only 1.2 to 1.4 kg (2.5 to 3 lb), and a bee's brain weighs only a milligram. With that tiny brain, a bee locates food, evades predators, finds its way back to the hive, and then does a dance that directs other bees to the food. It also takes care of the queen bee and protects the hive against intruders.

Everything you perceive or do is a product of your brain activity. How does the brain do all that? We would like to know for both practical and theoretical reasons. Some of the practical issues relate to abnormal behavior. Are psychological disorders biological in origin? Can we treat them effectively with drugs or other biological interventions? Can we prevent brain deterioration in old age? Theoretical issues relate to what makes us tick. How does brain activity relate to consciousness? Do people differ in personality because of differences in their brains? The fascination of such questions impels researchers to tireless efforts.

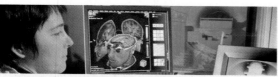
Neurons and Behavior

> • To what extent can we explain our experiences and behavior in terms of the actions of individual cells in the nervous system?

What constitutes an explanation? Consider the following quote ("The Medals and the Damage Done," 2004):

> In 2002, [Michael] Brennan was a British national rowing champion . . . As the UK Olympic trials loomed, Brennan was feeling confident. But . . . for much of the past 12 months, Brennan's performance has been eroded by constant colds, aching joints and fatigue . . . When the trials rolled round this April, Brennan . . . finished at the bottom of the heap. "I couldn't believe it," he says. To an experienced sports doctor, the explanation is obvious: Brennan has "unexplained underperformance syndrome" (UPS).

What do you think? Is "unexplained underperformance syndrome" an *explanation?*

Consider another example: Young birds, born in the far north and now just months old, migrate south for the winter. In some species, the parents migrate before the youngsters are ready, so the young birds cannot follow experienced leaders. How do the young birds know when to migrate, which direction, and how far? How do they know they should migrate at all? "It's an instinct," someone replies. Is that an explanation? Or is it no better than unexplained underperformance syndrome?

Explanations take many forms. We could explain behavior in terms of the biological mechanisms that make it happen, how and why the organism evolved as it did, or how it developed over time (Tinbergen, 1951).

A **physiological explanation** *describes the mechanisms that produce a behavior.* In the case of a migrating bird, researchers identify which signals tell the bird to migrate, such as changes in the amount of sunlight per day. They also identify whether the bird finds south by watching the sun, watching the stars, detecting the earth's magnetic field, or something else. The next step is to discover how these signals alter the bird's hormones and stimulate various brain areas to produce the behaviors.

An **evolutionary explanation** *relates behavior to the evolutionary history of the species.* At any point in time, various members of a species behave differently, partly because of their genetics. Some behaviors help individuals survive, find mates, take care of their young, and therefore pass on their genes to the next generation. Individuals with less successful behaviors are less likely to pass on their genes. Consequently, later generations come to resemble those who behaved most successfully. This process is what Charles Darwin called "descent with modification" and later biologists called *evolution.*

In the case of bird migration, we cannot actually observe how the behavior evolved because behavior—unlike bones—leaves no fossils (with rare exceptions such as footprints, which identify the animal's gait). However, researchers can try to understand why some species evolved the ability to migrate whereas others did not. They also explore the adaptations that make migration possible, such as a light, streamlined body to facilitate long-distance flight and the ability to tolerate sleep deprivation during the long journey (Rattenborg et al., 2004).

A **developmental** (or *ontogenetic*) **explanation** deals with changes over age. No animal or person is literally born with a behavior. We are born with

the capacity to develop a behavior. A baby bird cannot learn to migrate, at least not in any usual sense of the word *learn.* Still, various experiences are undoubtedly important. Researchers investigate the role of the bird's early visual experience, flight experience, and so forth.

In this chapter and parts of the next, we concentrate on physiological explanations. In this module, we consider the individual cells that compose the nervous system. To what extent can we explain behavior in terms of those cells and the connections among them?

NERVOUS SYSTEM CELLS

You experience your "self" as a single entity that senses, thinks, and remembers. However, your brain consists of an enormous number of separate cells called **neurons** (NOO-rons). Figure 3.1 shows estimates of the numbers of neurons in various parts of the human nervous system (R. W. Williams & Herrup, 1988). The nervous system also contains other kinds of cells called **glia** (GLEE-uh), *which support the neurons in many ways such as by insulating them, synchro-*

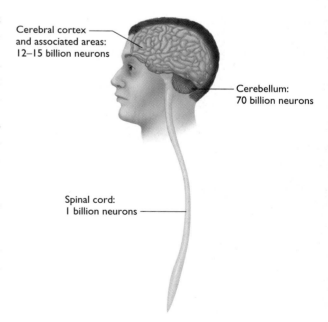

Cerebral cortex and associated areas: 12–15 billion neurons

Cerebellum: 70 billion neurons

Spinal cord: 1 billion neurons

Figure 3.1 Estimated distribution of the neurons in the adult human central nervous system. An exact count is not feasible, and the number varies from one person to another. (Based on data of R. W. Williams & Herrup, 1988)

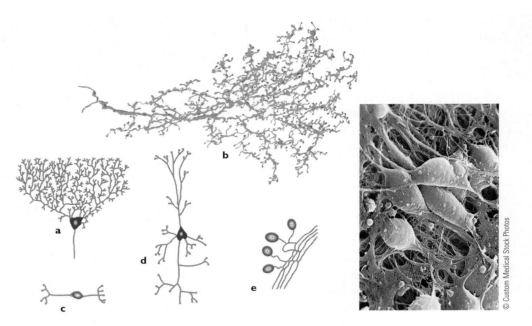

Figure 3.2 Neurons vary enormously in shape. The neurons in (a) and (b) receive input from many sources, the neuron in (c) from only a few sources, and the neuron in (d) from an intermediate number of sources. The sensory neurons (e) carry messages from sensory receptors to the brain or spinal cord. Inset: Electron micrograph showing cell bodies in brown and axons and dendrites in green. The color was added artificially; electron micrographs are made with electron beams, not light, and therefore, they show no color.

© Custom Medical Stock Photos

nizing activity among neighboring neurons, and removing waste products. The glia are smaller but more numerous than neurons.

How do so many separate neurons and glia combine forces to produce the single stream of experiences that is you? The answer is communication. Sensory neurons carry information from the sense organs to the central nervous system, where neurons compare it to past information and exchange information with other neurons.

To understand our nervous system, we must understand the properties of the individual neurons and the connections among them. Neurons vary in shape depending on whether they receive information from a few sources or many and whether they send impulses over a short or a long distance (Figure 3.2).

A neuron consists of three parts: a cell body, dendrites, and an axon (Figure 3.3). The **cell body** *contains the nucleus of the cell.* The **dendrites** (from a Greek word meaning "tree") are *widely branching structures that receive input from other neurons.* The **axon** is a *single, long, thin, straight fiber with branches near its tip.* Some vertebrate axons are covered with **myelin,** *an insulating sheath that speeds up the transmission of impulses along an axon.* As a rule, an axon transmits information to other cells, and the dendrites or cell body receives that information. The information can be either

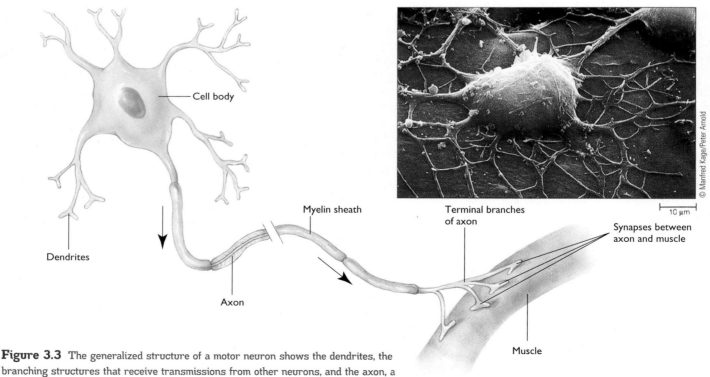

© Manfred Kage/Peter Arnold

Figure 3.3 The generalized structure of a motor neuron shows the dendrites, the branching structures that receive transmissions from other neurons, and the axon, a long fiber with branches near its tip. Inset: A photomicrograph of a neuron.

excitatory or inhibitory. That is, it can increase or decrease the probability that the next cell will send a message of its own. Inhibitory messages are important for many purposes. For example, during a period of painful stimulation, your brain has mechanisms to inhibit further sensation of pain. If you step on a tack and reflexively raise your foot, inhibitory synapses prevent you from trying to raise your other foot at the same time.

....

1. Which part of a neuron receives input from other neurons? Which part sends messages to other cells?

Concept Check

Answer

1. Dendrites receive input from other neurons. An axon sends messages.

....

THE ACTION POTENTIAL

Axons are specialized to convey information over long distances, such as from the skin to the spinal cord. Imagine what would happen if axons relied on electrical conduction: Electricity is extremely fast, but because animal bodies are poor conductors, electrical impulses would weaken rapidly during travel. Short people would feel a pinch on their toes more intensely than tall people would—if either felt their toes at all.

Instead, axons convey information by a combination of electrical and chemical processes called an **action potential**, *an excitation that travels along an axon at a constant strength, no matter how far it must travel.* An action potential is a yes–no or on–off message, like a standard light switch (without a dimmer). This principle is known as the *all-or-none law.*

The advantage of an action potential over simple electrical conduction is that action potentials from distant places like your toes reach your brain at full strength. The disadvantage is that action potentials are slower than electrical conduction. Your knowledge of what is happening to your toes is at least a 20th of a second out of date. Pain and itch sensations are even slower. A 20th of a second is seldom worth worrying about, but your information about different body parts is out of date by different delays. Consequently, if you are touched on two or more body parts at almost the same time, your brain cannot accurately gauge which touch came first.

Here is a quick description of how the action potential works:

1. When the axon is not stimulated, its membrane has a **resting potential**, *an electrical polarization across the membrane (or covering) of an axon.* Typically, the inside has a charge of about –70 millivolts relative to the outside. It gets this value from the negatively charged proteins inside the axon. In addition, a mechanism called the sodium-potassium pump pushes sodium ions out of the axon while pulling potassium ions in. Consequently, sodium ions are more concentrated outside the axon and potassium ions are more concentrated inside.

2. An action potential starts in either of two ways: First, many axons produce spontaneous activity. Second, input from other neurons can excite a neuron's membrane. In either case, if the excitation reaches the *threshold* of the axon (variable but typically about –55 millivolts), the result is to open (briefly) some *gates* (or *channels*) at the start of the axon. Through those gates sodium and potassium ions can flow. Sodium ions, which are highly concentrated outside the membrane, rush into the cell, attracted by the negative charge inside. The influx of positively charged sodium ions is the action potential. As the positive charge enters the axon at one point, it stimulates the next point along the axon, which then starts opening sodium channels and repeating the process, as shown in Figure 3.4.

3. After the sodium gates have been open for a few milliseconds, they snap shut. However, the potassium gates remain open. Potassium does not flow out as rapidly as sodium flowed in, but it continues longer. The potassium ions carry a positive charge, so their exit drives the inside of the axon back to its resting potential (Figure 3.5b).

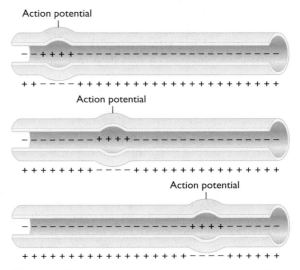

Figure 3.4 Ion movements conduct an action potential along an axon. At each point along the membrane, sodium ions enter the axon. As each point along the membrane returns to its original state, the action potential flows to the next point.

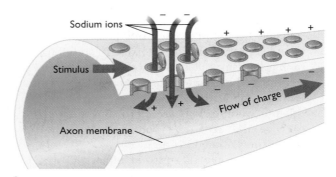

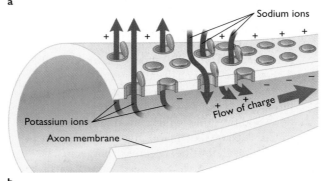

Figure 3.5 (a) During an action potential, sodium gates open, and sodium ions enter the axon, bearing a positive charge. (b) After an action potential occurs, the sodium gates close at that point and open at the next point along the axon. As the sodium gates close, potassium gates open, and potassium ions flow out of the axon. (Modified from Starr & Taggart, 1992)

4. Eventually, the sodium-potassium pump removes the extra sodium ions and recaptures the escaped potassium ions.

A review of the highlights: Sodium enters the cell (excitation). Then potassium leaves (return to the resting potential).

Conduction along an axon is analogous to a fire burning along a string: The fire at each point ignites the next point, which in turn ignites the next point. In an axon, after sodium ions enter the membrane, some of them diffuse to the neighboring portion of the axon, exciting it enough to open its own sodium gates. The action potential spreads to this next area and so on down the axon, as shown in Figure 3.5. In this manner, the action potential remains equally strong all the way to the end of the axon.

Here is how this information relates to psychology: First, it explains why sensations from your fingers and toes do not fade away by the time they reach your brain. Second, an understanding of action potentials is one step toward understanding the communication between neurons. Third, anesthetic drugs (e.g., Novocain) operate by clogging sodium gates and therefore silencing neurons. When your dentist drills a tooth, the receptors in your tooth send out the message "Pain!

Pain! Pain!" But that message does not reach your brain because the sodium gates are blocked.

....

2. If a mouse and a giraffe both get pinched on the toes at the same time, which will respond faster? Why?

3. Fill in these blanks: When the axon membrane is at rest, the inside has a _____ charge relative to the outside. When the membrane reaches its threshold, _____ ions enter from outside to inside, bringing with them a _____ charge. That flow of ions constitutes the _____ _____ of the axon.

Answers

....

SYNAPSES

Communication between one neuron and the next is not like transmission along an axon. At a synapse (SIN-aps), *the specialized junction between one neuron and another* (Figure 3.6), *a neuron releases a chemical that either excites or inhibits the next neuron.* That is, the chemical makes the next neuron either more or less likely to produce an action potential. Synapses regulate everything your nervous system accomplishes.

A typical axon has several branches, each ending with a little bulge called a *presynaptic ending,* or terminal bouton, as shown in Figure 3.7. When an action potential reaches the terminal bouton, it releases a neurotransmitter, *a chemical that acti-*

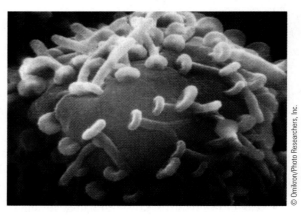

Figure 3.6 This synapse is magnified thousands of times in an electron micrograph. The tips of axons swell to form terminal boutons.

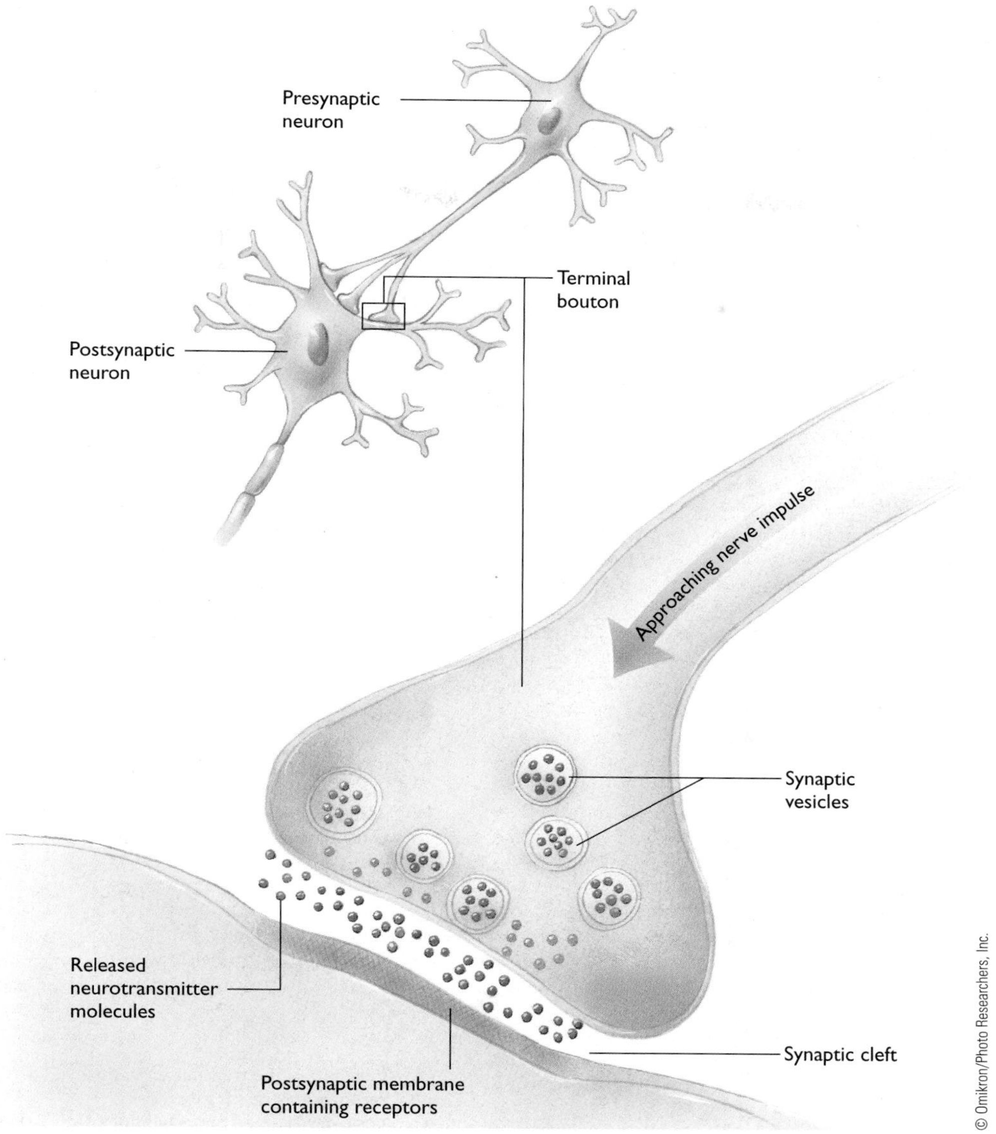

Figure 3.7 The synapse is the junction of the presynaptic (message-sending) cell and the postsynaptic (message-receiving) cell. At the end of the presynaptic axon is the terminal bouton, which contains molecules of the neurotransmitter.

Presynaptic neuron

Terminal bouton

Postsynaptic neuron

Approaching nerve impulse

Synaptic vesicles

Released neurotransmitter molecules

Synaptic cleft

Postsynaptic membrane containing receptors

© Omikron/Photo Researchers, Inc.

vates receptors on other neurons (Figure 3.7). Several dozen chemicals are used as neurotransmitters in various brain areas, although any given neuron releases only one or a few of them. The neurotransmitter molecules diffuse across a narrow gap to receptors on the **postsynaptic neuron**, *the neuron on the receiving end of the synapse*. A neurotransmitter fits into its receptor like a key fits into a lock. Its presence there either excites or inhibits the postsynaptic neuron. Depending on the receptor, the effect might last just milliseconds, many seconds, or minutes. (For vision or hearing, you want moment-by-moment information. You don't need such rapid updating of information about hunger or thirst.) Figure 3.8 summarizes the process.

Depending on the neurotransmitter and the type of receptor, the attachment enables either positively charged or negatively charged ions to enter the postsynaptic cell. If the positive charges

sufficiently outweigh the negative charges, the cell produces an action potential. The process is like a decision: You weigh the pluses and minuses and act if the pluses are stronger.

Inhibition is not the absence of excitation; it is like stepping on the brakes. For example, when a pinch on your foot stimulates a reflex that contracts one set of muscles, inhibitory synapses in your spinal cord block activity in the muscles that would move your leg in the opposite direction.

After a neurotransmitter excites or inhibits a receptor, it separates from the receptor, ending the message. From that point on, the fate of the receptor molecule varies. It could return to reexcite the postsynaptic receptor, it could diffuse away from the synapse, or it could be reabsorbed by the axon that released it (through a process called *reuptake)*. Most antidepressant drugs act by blocking reuptake, thus prolonging a transmitter's effects.

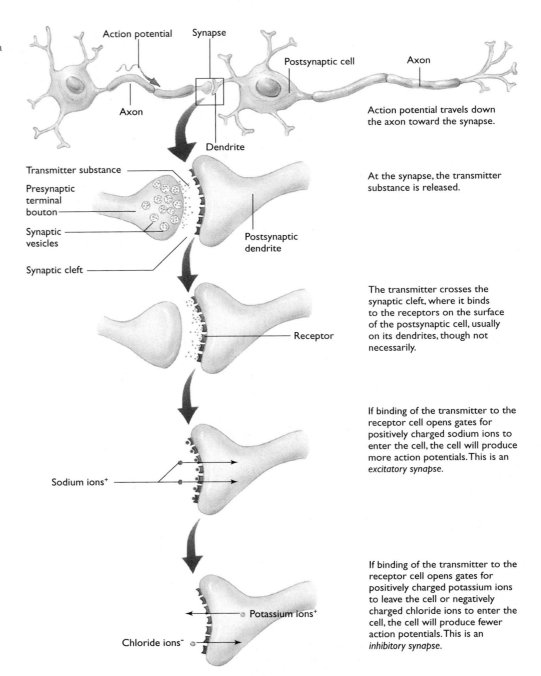

Figure 3.8 The complex process of neural communication takes only 1–2 milliseconds.

Action potential

Synapse

Axon

Postsynaptic cell

Axon

Action potential travels down the axon toward the synapse.

Dendrite

Transmitter substance

Presynaptic terminal bouton

Synaptic vesicles

Synaptic cleft

Postsynaptic dendrite

At the synapse, the transmitter substance is released.

Receptor

The transmitter crosses the synaptic cleft, where it binds to the receptors on the surface of the postsynaptic cell, usually on its dendrites, though not necessarily.

Sodium ions⁺

If binding of the transmitter to the receptor cell opens gates for positively charged sodium ions to enter the cell, the cell will produce more action potentials. This is an *excitatory synapse.*

Potassium ions⁺

Chloride ions⁻

If binding of the transmitter to the receptor cell opens gates for positively charged potassium ions to leave the cell or negatively charged chloride ions to enter the cell, the cell will produce fewer action potentials. This is an *inhibitory synapse.*

---

4. What is the difference between the presynaptic neuron and the postsynaptic neuron?
5. GABA is a neurotransmitter that inhibits postsynaptic neurons. If a drug prevents GABA from attaching to its receptors, what will happen to the postsynaptic neuron?

Answers

4. The presynaptic neuron releases a neurotransmitter that travels to the postsynaptic neuron, where it activates an excitatory or inhibitory receptor.
5. If a drug prevents GABA from attaching to its receptors, the postsynaptic neuron will receive less inhibition. It will therefore produce more action potentials than usual.

What's the Evidence?
Neurons Communicate Chemically

You have just learned that neurons communicate by releasing chemicals at synapses. What evidence led to this important conclusion?

Today, neuroscientists have a wealth of evidence that neurons release chemicals at synapses. They radioactively trace where chemicals go and what happens when they get there. They also inject purified chemicals and use extremely fine electrodes to measure the responses of neurons. In 1920 Otto Loewi conducted a clever experiment with only the simplest technology and demonstrated that neurons communicate with chemicals, as he later described in his autobiography (Loewi, 1960).

Hypothesis If a neuron releases chemicals, an investigator should be able to collect some of those chemicals, transfer them to another animal, and thereby get the second animal to do what the first animal had been doing. Loewi could not collect chemicals within the brain, so he worked with axons communicating with the heart muscle. (A neuron stimulates a muscle at a junction that is like the synapse between two neurons.)

Method Loewi electrically stimulated certain axons that slowed a frog's heart. As he continued the stimulation, he collected fluid around that heart and transferred it to the heart of a second frog.

Results When Loewi transferred the fluid from the first frog's heart, the second frog's heart rate also slowed (Figure 3.9).

Interpretation Evidently, the stimulated axons had released a chemical that slows heart rate. At least in this case, neurons send messages by releasing chemicals.

Loewi eventually won a Nobel Prize in physiology for this and related research. Even outstanding experiments have limitations, however. Loewi's results did not indicate whether axons release chemicals at all synapses, most, or only a few. Answering that question required technologies not available until several decades later. The answer is that *most* neuronal communication uses chemicals, although a few synapses communicate electrically.

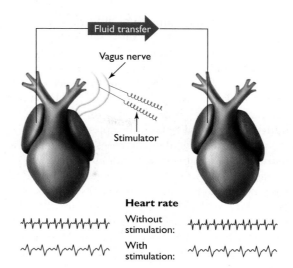

Figure 3.9 Otto Loewi electrically stimulated axons known to decrease a frog's heart rate. He collected fluid from around the heart and transferred it to another frog's heart. When that heart slowed its beat, Loewi concluded that the axons in the first heart released a chemical that slows heart rate.

NEUROTRANSMITTERS AND BEHAVIOR

The brain has dozens of neurotransmitters, each of which activates many kinds of receptors. Table 3.1 lists some of the most abundant transmitters. For example, serotonin activates at least 15 kinds, probably more (Roth, Lopez, & Kroeze, 2000). Each re-

Table 3.1 Some of the Most Important Neurotransmitters

Neurotransmitter	Functions	Comment
Glutamate	The brain's main excitatory transmitter, present at most synapses. Essential for almost all brain activities, including learning.	Strokes kill neurons mostly by overstimulation, due to excess release of glutamate.
GABA (gamma-amino-butyric acid)	The brain's main inhibitory transmitter.	Antianxiety drugs and antiepileptic drugs increase activity at GABA synapses.
Acetylcholine	Increases brain arousal.	Acetylcholine is also released by motor neurons to stimulate skeletal muscles.
Dopamine	One path is important for movement (damaged in Parkinson's disease). Another path is important for memory and cognition.	Most antipsychotic drugs decrease activity at dopamine synapses. L-dopa, used for Parkinson's disease, increases availability of dopamine.
Serotonin	Modifies many types of motivated and emotional behavior.	Most antidepressant drugs prolong activity at serotonin synapses.
Norepinephrine	Enhances storage of memory of emotional or otherwise meaningful events.	All or nearly all axons releasing norepinephrine originate from one small brain area, called the locus coeruleus.
Histamine	Increases arousal and alertness.	Antihistamines (for allergies) block histamine and therefore lead to drowsiness.
Endorphins	Decrease pain and increase pleasure.	Morphine and heroin stimulate the same receptors as endorphins.
Nitric oxide	Dilates blood vessels in the most active brain areas.	The only known transmitter that is a gas.
Anandamide, 2AG, and others	Sent by the postsynaptic neuron back to the presynaptic neuron to decrease further release of transmitters.	THC, the active chemical in marijuana, stimulates these same presynaptic receptors.

ceptor type controls somewhat different aspects of behavior. For example, because serotonin type 3 receptors are responsible for nausea, researchers have developed drugs to block nausea without much effect on other aspects of behavior (Perez, 1995). However, with a few exceptions such as nausea, most complex behaviors rely on several transmitters and several types of receptors.

Still, a disorder that increases or decreases a particular transmitter or receptor alters behavior in predictable ways. One example is **Parkinson's disease,** *a condition that affects about 1% of people over the age of 50. The main symptoms are difficulty in initiating voluntary movement, slow movement, tremors, rigidity, and depressed mood.* All of these symptoms can be traced to a gradual decay of a pathway of axons that release *the neurotransmitter* **dopamine** (DOPE-uh-meen). Whereas most medications that affect the brain were discovered by accident, the treatment for Parkinson's disease was the first case in which knowledge of the underlying mechanism led to finding a successful drug. Researchers knew they needed to increase dopamine levels in the brain. Dopamine pills or injections would not work because dopamine (like many other chemicals) is unable to cross from the blood into the brain. However, a drug called L-dopa does cross into the brain. Neurons absorb L-dopa, convert it to dopamine, and thereby increase their supply of dopamine.

As we shall see in chapter 16, drugs that alleviate depression and schizophrenia also act on dopamine and serotonin synapses, although the relationship between the neurotransmitters and the behavior is complex. We still have much to learn about the relationship between synapses and their behavioral outcomes.

----

6. People suffering from certain disorders are given haloperidol, a drug that blocks activity at dopamine synapses. How would haloperidol affect someone with Parkinson's disease?

Answer

6. Haloperidol would increase the severity of Parkinson's disease. In fact, large doses of haloperidol induce symptoms of Parkinson's disease in anyone.

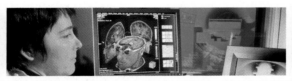

3.1 module

In Closing

Neurons, Synapses, and Behavior

Behavior is complicated. You might describe some action in just a few words ("I ate a meal" or "I argued with my roommate"), but that short description corresponds to an immensely complicated sequence of coordinated and well-timed movements. Each complex behavior emerges from synapses, which in their basic outline are simple processes: A cell releases a chemical, which excites or inhibits a second cell for various periods of time. Then the chemical washes away or reenters the first cell to be used again.

Complex behavior emerges from those simple synapses because of the connections among huge numbers of neurons. No one neuron or synapse does much by itself. Your experience results from dozens of types of neurotransmitters, billions of neurons, and trillions of synapses, each contributing in a small way.

SUMMARY

- *Neuron structure.* A neuron, or nerve cell, consists of a cell body, dendrites, and an axon. The axon conveys information to other neurons. (page 63)
- *The action potential.* Information is conveyed along an axon by an action potential, which is regenerated without loss of strength at each point along the axon. (page 65)
- *Mechanism of the action potential.* An action potential depends on the entry of sodium into the axon. Anything that blocks this flow blocks the action potential. (page 65)

- *How neurons communicate.* A neuron communicates with another neuron by releasing a chemical called a neurotransmitter at a specialized junction called a synapse. A neurotransmitter can either excite or inhibit the next neuron. (page 66)
- *Neurotransmitters and behavioral disorders.* An excess or deficit of a particular neurotransmitter can lead to abnormal behavior, such as that exhibited by people with Parkinson's disease. (page 69)

KEY TERMS

action potential (page 65)

axon (page 64)

cell body (page 64)

dendrite (page 64)

developmental explanation (page 63)

dopamine (page 70)

evolutionary explanation (page 63)

glia (page 63)

myelin (page 64)

neuron (page 63)

neurotransmitter (page 66)

Parkinson's disease (page 70)

physiological explanation (page 63)

postsynaptic neuron (page 67)

resting potential (page 65)

synapse (page 66)

terminal bouton (page 66)

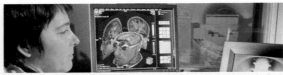

3.2 module

Drugs and Their Effects

- How do drugs affect synapses?
- How do they affect behavior?

Imagine you are typing a paper at your computer, except that you have extra fingers that sometimes do things you hadn't planned. Sometimes, they press the Caps Lock key AND EVERYTHING COMES OUT IN CAPITAL LETTERS. They press other keys and your words come out **boldface,** *italicized,* underlined, enlarged, or distorted in other ways. Your extra fingers delete lettrs, add exxtras, and add spaces in the mid dle of words. **Psychoactive drugs** have analogous effects on behavior. They *enhance certain experiences, weaken others, and garble thinking and speech by their effects on synapses.* In chapter 16, we shall consider drug abuse and addiction, including alcoholism. Here the emphasis is on how drugs operate.

Psychoactive drugs affect synapses in many ways. Some attach to receptors and activate them. Some attach imperfectly, like an almost-fitting key that gets stuck in a lock. Drugs increase or decrease the release of transmitters or decrease reuptake (the return of released transmitters to the neuron that released them). A drug that increases activity at a synapse is called an *agonist,* based on the Greek word for a contestant or fighter. A drug that decreases activity at a synapse is an *antagonist,* from the Greek word for an enemy.

STIMULANTS

Stimulants are *drugs that increase energy, alertness, and activity.* Amphetamine, methamphetamine, and cocaine prevent neurons from reabsorbing dopamine or serotonin after releasing them. As a result, they prolong the effects of those transmitters at their receptors (Volkow, Wang, & Fowler, 1997; Volkow et al., 1998). Amphetamine and methamphetamine not only block reuptake but also increase the release of the transmitters (Giros et al., 1996; Paladini, Fiorillo, Morikawa, & Williams, 2001). Dopamine synapses are critical for almost anything that strongly motivates people, ranging from sex and food to gambling and video games (Koepp et al., 1998; Maldonado et al., 1997). By increasing the activity at dopamine synapses, stimulant drugs hijack the brain's motivational system.

Cocaine has long been available in the powdery form of cocaine hydrochloride, which can be sniffed. Before 1985, the only way to get a more intense effect from cocaine hydrochloride was to transform it into *freebase cocaine*—cocaine with the hydrochloride removed. Freebase cocaine enters the brain rapidly, and fast entry intensifies the experience. *Crack cocaine,* which first became available in 1985, is cocaine that has already been converted into freebase rocks, ready to be smoked (Brower & Anglin, 1987; Kozel & Adams, 1986). It is called "crack" because it makes popping noises when smoked. Crack produces a rush of potent effects within a few seconds.

The behavioral effects of stimulant drugs depend on the dose. Low levels enhance attention. In fact, amphetamine is often prescribed for attention deficit disorder, under the trade name Adderall. At higher doses, amphetamine and cocaine lead to confusion, impaired attention, and impulsiveness (Simon, Mendez, & Setlow, 2007; Stalnaker et al., 2007). A study of twins, in

which one abused cocaine or amphetamine and the other did not, found that the one who used the drugs had impaired motor skills and attention lasting a year or more after quitting the drugs (Toomey et al., 2003). Physical effects include higher heart rate, blood pressure, and body temperature, and sometimes tremors, convulsions, lung damage, and heart attack.

Stimulant effects from amphetamine or cocaine increase gradually after one takes the drug. However, because they act by inhibiting the reuptake of dopamine and other transmitters, the transmitters wash away from the synapse faster than the presynaptic neuron can resynthesize them. Consequently, the availability of the transmitters declines over the next few hours, and the user experiences lethargy and mild depression, more or less the opposite of the high feeling shortly after taking the drug.

Methylphenidate (Ritalin), a drug often prescribed for people with attention deficit disorder, works the same way as cocaine, at the same synapses (Volkow et al., 1997, 1998). The difference is that methylphenidate, taken as pills, reaches the brain gradually over an hour or

Crack cocaine reaches the brain much faster than other forms of cocaine. All else being equal, the faster a drug reaches the brain, the more intense the experience will be and the greater the probability of addiction.

more and declines slowly over hours. Therefore, it does not produce the sudden "rush" that makes crack cocaine so addictive.

Tobacco delivers nicotine, which increases wakefulness and arousal by stimulating *acetylcholine* synapses. (Acetylcholine is one of the common neurotransmitters in the nervous system.) Although nicotine is classed as a stimulant, most smokers say it relaxes them. The research suggests an explanation for this paradox. Although smoking increases tension levels, abstaining from cigarettes increases tension even more. Smoking another cigarette relieves the withdrawal symptoms and restores the usual mood (Parrott, 1999). Nicotine also produces mixed effects on motivation: It decreases energy and motivation in low-reward situations but increases activity in high-reward situations (Rice & Cragg, 2004). It also increases activity and responsiveness in novel situations (Fagen, Mitchum, Vezina, & McGehee, 2007). We consider nicotine addiction again in chapter 16.

7. The drug AMPT (alpha-methyl-para-tyrosine) prevents the body from making dopamine. How would a large dose of AMPT affect someone's later responsiveness to cocaine, amphetamine, or methylphenidate?

8. Some people with attention deficit disorder report that they experience benefits for the first few hours after taking methylphenidate pills but begin to deteriorate in the late afternoon and evening. Why?

Concept Check

Answers

8. Remember what happens after taking cocaine: Neurons release dopamine and other transmitters faster than they resynthesize them. Because cocaine blocks reuptake, the supply of transmitters dwindles, and the result is lethargy and mild depression. The same process occurs with methylphenidate but more slowly and to a smaller degree.

7. Someone who took AMPT would become much less responsive than usual to amphetamine, cocaine, or methylphenidate. These drugs increase the release of dopamine or prolong its effects, but if the neurons cannot make dopamine, they cannot release it.

DEPRESSANTS

Depressants are *drugs that decrease arousal,* such as alcohol and *anxiolytics* (anxiety-reducing drugs). People have been using alcohol since prehistoric times. When archeologists unearthed a

Neolithic village in Iran's Zagros Mountains, they found a jar that had been constructed about 5500–5400 B.C., one of the oldest human-made crafts ever found (Figure 3.10). Inside the jar, especially at the bottom, the archeologists found a yellowish residue. They were curious to know what the jar had held, so they sent some of the residue for chemical analysis. The unambiguous answer came back: The jar had been a wine vessel (McGovern, Glusker, Exner, & Voigt, 1996).

Alcohol is a *class of molecules that includes methanol, ethanol, propyl alcohol (rubbing alcohol), and others. Ethanol is the type that people drink.* Alcohol is a depressant that acts as a relaxant at moderate doses. In greater amounts, it increases risk-taking behaviors, including aggression, by suppressing the fears and inhibitions that ordinarily limit such activities. In still greater amounts, as in binge drinking, alcohol leads to unconsciousness and death. Excessive use damages the liver and other organs, aggravates medical conditions, and impairs memory and motor control. A woman who drinks alcohol during pregnancy risks damage to her baby's brain, health, and appearance.

Anxiolytic drugs or **tranquilizers** *help people relax.* The most common examples are *benzodiazepines,* including diazepam (Valium) and alprazolam (Xanax). Benzodiazepines calm people by facilitating transmission at synapses that use GABA, the brain's main inhibitory transmitter. Alcohol facilitates transmission at the same synapses by a different mechanism (Sudzak et al., 1986). Taking alcohol and tranquilizers together is dangerous because the combination suppresses the brain areas that control breathing and heartbeat.

One benzodiazepine drug, flunitrazepam (Rohypnol), has attracted attention as a "date rape drug." Flunitrazepam, which dissolves quickly in water, has no color, odor, or taste to warn the person who is consuming it. The effects of this drug, like those of other anxiolytics, include drowsiness, poor muscle coordination, and memory impairment (Anglin, Spears, & Hutson, 1997; Woods & Winger, 1997). Someone under the influence of the drug does not have the strength to fight off an attacker and may not remember the event clearly. A hospital that suspects someone has been given

Figure 3.10 This wine jar, dated about 5500–5400 B.C. is one of the oldest human crafts ever found.

© University of Pennsylvania Museum

this drug can detect its presence with a urine test. Another "date rape drug," GHB (gamma hydroxybutyrate), has become widespread because it can be made easily (though impurely) with household ingredients. Like flunitrazepam, it relaxes the body and impairs muscle coordination. Large doses induce vomiting, tremors, coma, and death.

9. Which kind of synapses do alcohol and anxiolytic drugs (tranquilizers) facilitate?

Answer

9. They facilitate synapses using GABA, the brain's main inhibitory transmitter.

NARCOTICS

Narcotics are *drugs that produce drowsiness, insensitivity to pain, and decreased responsiveness.* The classic examples, **opiates**, are *either natural drugs derived from the opium poppy or synthetic drugs with a chemical structure resembling natural opiates.* Opiates make people feel happy, warm, and content, with little anxiety or pain. Morphine (named after Morpheus, the Greek god of dreams) has important medical use as a painkiller. Undesirable consequences include nausea and withdrawal from the world. After the drug leaves the brain, the affected synapses become less responsive, and elation gives way to anxiety, pain, and exaggerated responsiveness to sounds and other stimuli.

Opiate drugs such as morphine, heroin, methadone, and codeine bind to specific receptors in the brain (Pert & Snyder, 1973). The discovery of neurotransmitter receptors demonstrated that opiates block pain in the brain, not in the skin. Neuroscientists then found that the brain produces several chemicals, called **endorphins**, that *bind to the opiate receptors* (Hughes et al., 1975). Endorphins inhibit chronic pain. The brain also releases endorphins during pleasant experiences, such as the "runner's high" or the chill you feel down your back when you hear especially thrilling music (A. Goldstein, 1980).

MARIJUANA

Marijuana (*cannabis*) is difficult to classify. It is certainly not a stimulant. It has a calming effect but not like that of alcohol or tranquilizers. It softens pain but not as powerfully as opiates. It produces sensory distortions, especially an illusion that time is passing more slowly than usual, but not distortions like those from LSD. Because marijuana does not closely resemble any other drug, we discuss it separately.

The disadvantageous effects of marijuana include memory impairments and decreased drive. Many studies reporting memory problems in marijuana users are hard to interpret. Does marijuana impair memory or do people with memory problems like to use marijuana? As always, correlation does not indicate causation. However, one study found that a few months after people quit using marijuana, their memory improved (Pope, Gruber, Hudson, Huestis, & Yurgelun-Todd, 2001). This result strongly suggests that poor memory was a result of marijuana use, not a lifelong characteristic of those who chose to use marijuana.

Marijuana has several potential medical uses. It reduces nausea, suppresses tremors, reduces pressure in the eyes, and decreases cell loss in the brain after a stroke (Glass, 2001; Panikashvili et al., 2001). Because of legal restrictions in the United States, research on these medical uses has been limited. On the negative side, marijuana increases the risk of Parkinson's disease (Glass, 2001), and long-term use probably increases the risk of lung cancer, as tobacco cigarettes do.

You may have heard that marijuana is dangerous as a "gateway drug." That is, many heroin and cocaine users had used marijuana first. True,

After California legalized marijuana for medical uses, many clubs and stores opened for the sale and distribution of the drug.

but they also tried cigarettes and alcohol first, as well as other risky experiences. It is unclear whether the use of marijuana encourages the use of other drugs.

The active ingredient in marijuana is THC, or tetrahydrocannabinol. THC attaches to receptors that are abundant throughout the brain (Herkenham, Lynn, deCosta, & Richfield, 1991). The brain produces large amounts of its own chemicals that attach to those receptors. Two of those chemicals are *anandamide* (from *ananda*, the Sanskrit word for "bliss") and 2-AG (short for *sn*-2 arachidonylglycerol) (Devane et al., 1992; Stella, Schweitzer, & Piomelli, 1997). These receptors are abundant in brain areas that control memory and movement, but they are nearly absent from the medulla, which controls heart rate and breathing (Herkenham et al., 1990). In contrast, the medulla has many opiate receptors.

Unlike most other neurotransmitter receptors, those for anandamide and 2-AG (and therefore marijuana) are located on the *pre*synaptic neuron. When the presynaptic neuron releases a transmitter, such as glutamate or GABA, the postsynaptic (receiving) cell releases anandamide or 2-AG, which returns to the presynaptic cell to inhibit further release (Kreitzer & Regehr, 2001; Oliet, Baimoukhametova, Piet, & Bains, 2007; R. I. Wilson & Nicoll, 2002). In effect it says, "I received your signal. You can slow down on sending any more of it." Marijuana, by resembling these natural reverse transmitters, has the same effect, except that it slows the signal even before it has been sent. It is as if the presynaptic cell "thinks" it has sent a signal when in fact it has not.

Marijuana has many behavioral effects, which researchers are beginning to explain. It decreases nausea by blocking the type of serotonin receptor responsible for nausea (Fan, 1995). It increases activity in brain areas responsible for feeding and appetite (DiMarzo et al., 2001). How it produces the illusion that time is passing slowly is hard to explain, but the same phenomenon occurs in laboratory animals. Under the influence of marijuana smoke, rats show impairments when they have to respond at certain time intervals. They respond too quickly, as if 10 seconds felt like 20 seconds (Han & Robinson, 2001).

Answer

HALLUCINOGENS

Drugs that induce sensory distortions are called **hallucinogens** (Jacobs, 1987). Many of these drugs are derived from mushrooms or plants, and others are manufactured. Hallucinogenic drugs such as LSD (lysergic acid diethylamide) distort sensations and sometimes produce a dreamlike state or an intense mystical experience. Peyote, a hallucinogen derived from a cactus plant, has a long history of use in Native American religious ceremonies (see Figure 3.11).

LSD attaches mainly to one kind of serotonin receptor (Jacobs, 1987). It stimulates those receptors at irregular times and prevents neurotransmitters from stimulating them at the normal times. We have an interesting gap in our knowledge at this point: We know *where* LSD exerts its effects, but we do not understand *how* altering those receptors leads to the experiences.

© Manu Sassoonian/Art Resource, NY

Figure 3.11 Tablas, or yarn paintings, created by members of the Huichol tribe (Mexico) evoke the beautiful lights, vivid colors, and "peculiar creatures" experienced after the people eat the hallucinogenic peyote cactus in ritualized ceremonies.

10. An overdose of opiates produces a life-threatening decrease in breathing and heart rate. Large doses of marijuana do not produce those effects. Why not?

Concept Check

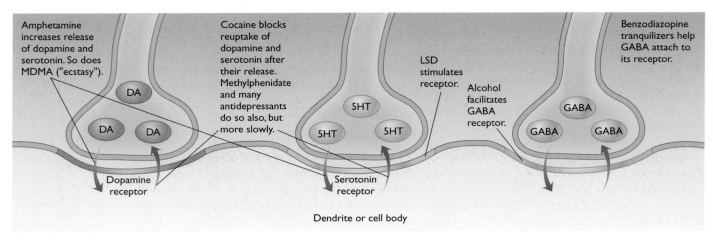

Amphetamine increases release of dopamine and serotonin. So does MDMA ("ecstasy").

DA

DA DA

Dopamine receptor

Cocaine blocks reuptake of dopamine and serotonin after their release. Methylphenidate and many antidepressants do so also, but more slowly.

5HT

5HT 5HT

Serotonin receptor

LSD stimulates receptor.

Alcohol facilitates GABA receptor.

Benzodiazopine tranquilizers help GABA attach to its receptor.

GABA

GABA GABA

Dendrite or cell body

Figure 3.12 Both legal and illegal drugs operate at the synapses. Drugs can increase the release of neurotransmitters, block their reuptake, or directly stimulate or block their receptors.

The drug MDMA (methylenedioxymethamphetamine), better known as "ecstasy," produces stimulant effects similar to amphetamine at low doses and hallucinogenic effects similar to LSD at higher doses. Many young adults use MDMA at parties to increase their energy. However, as the drug wears off, people feel depressed and lethargic. Repeated users show increased anxiety and depression and impairments of attention, memory, and sleep, which persist a year or more after they quit using the drug (Montoya, Sorrentino, Lukas, & Price, 2002; Reneman et al., 2001).

Several studies with laboratory animals have found that MDMA damages neurons' mitochondria, impairing neurons' function and sometimes killing them (Alves et al., 2007). A study of 27 people at one dance party found that 6 of them had MDMA levels within the range found to produce damage in the laboratory (Irvine et al., 2006).

Other studies have shown that repeated heavy users of MDMA lose brain serotonin, regaining it slowly over months after quitting the drug (Cowan, 2006; Reneman, de Win, van den Brink, Booij, & den Heeten, 2006). However, most of these people used other drugs, too, which may have contributed to the loss. The possible dangers of MDMA remain controversial, but the research implies a need for great caution.

Another hallucinogen, phencyclidine (PCP, or "angel dust") acts by inhibiting receptors for the neurotransmitter glutamate. At low doses, PCP's effects resemble those of alcohol. At higher doses, it produces hallucinations, thought disorder, memory loss, and loss of emotions.

Figure 3.12 diagrams the effects of several drugs. Table 3.2 summarizes the drugs we have been considering. The list of risks is incomplete because of space. Large or repeated doses of any drug can be life-threatening.

Table 3.2 Commonly Abused Drugs and Their Effects

Drug Category	Effects on the Nervous System	Short-term Effects	Risks (partial list)
Stimulants Amphetamine	Increases release of dopamine and decreases reuptake, prolonging effects	Increases energy and alertness	Psychotic reaction, agitation, heart problems, sleeplessness, stroke
Cocaine	Decreases reuptake of dopamine, prolonging effects	Increases energy and alertness	Psychotic reaction, heart problems, crime to pay for drugs, death
Methylphenidate (Ritalin)	Decreases reuptake of dopamine but with slower onset and offset than cocaine	Increases alertness; much milder withdrawal effects than cocaine	Increased blood pressure
Caffeine	Blocks a chemical that inhibits arousal	Increases energy and alertness	Sleeplessness
Nicotine	Stimulates some acetylcholine synapses; stimulates some neurons that release dopamine	Increases arousal; abstention by a habitual smoker produces tension and depression	Lung cancer from the tars in cigarettes
Depressants Alcohol	Facilitates effects of GABA, an inhibitory neurotransmitter	Relaxation, reduced inhibitions, impaired memory and judgment	Automobile accidents, loss of job
Benzodiazepines	Facilitate effects of GABA, an inhibitory neurotransmitter	Relaxation, decreased anxiety, sleepiness	Dependence. Life-threatening if combined with alcohol or opiates
Narcotics Morphine, heroin, other opiates	Stimulate endorphin synapses	Decrease pain; withdrawal from interest in real world; unpleasant withdrawal effects during abstention	Heart stoppage; crime to pay for drugs
Marijuana Marijuana	Excites negative feedback receptors of both excitatory and inhibitory transmitters	Decreases pain and nausea; distorted sense of time	Impaired memory; lung diseases; impaired immune response
Hallucinogens LSD	Stimulates serotonin type 2 receptors at inappropriate times	Hallucinations, sensory distortions	Psychotic reaction, accidents, panic attacks, flashbacks
MDMA ("ecstasy")	Stimulates neurons that release dopamine; at higher doses also stimulates neurons that release serotonin	At low doses increases arousal; at higher doses hallucinations	Dehydration, fever, lasting damage to serotonin synapses
Rohypnol and GHB	Facilitate action at GABA synapses (which are inhibitory)	Relaxation, decreased inhibitions	Impaired muscle coordination and memory
Phencyclidine (PCP or "angel dust")	Inhibits one type of glutamate receptor	Intoxication, slurred speech; at higher doses hallucinations, thought disorder, impaired memory and emotions	Psychotic reaction

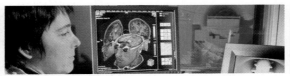

In Closing

Drugs and Synapses

If you were to change a few of a computer's connections at random, you could produce an "altered state," which would almost certainly not be an improvement. Giving drugs to a human brain is a little like changing the connections of a computer, and almost any drug at least temporarily impairs brain functioning in some way. By examining the effects of drugs on the brain, we gain greater insight into the brain's normal processes and functions.

SUMMARY

- *Stimulants.* Stimulant drugs such as amphetamines and cocaine increase activity levels and pleasure by increasing the release, and decreasing reuptake, of dopamine and certain other neurotransmitters. Compared to other forms of cocaine, crack enters the brain faster and therefore produces more intense effects. (page 72)
- *Alcohol.* Alcohol, the most widely abused drug in our society, relaxes people and relieves their inhibitions. It can also impair judgment and reasoning. (page 73)
- *Anxiolytics.* Benzodiazepines, widely used to relieve anxiety, can also relax muscles and promote sleep. (page 73)
- *Opiates.* Opiate drugs bind to endorphin receptors in the nervous system. The immediate effect of opiates is pleasure and relief from pain. (page 74)
- *Marijuana.* Marijuana's active compound, THC, acts on abundant receptors, found mostly in the hippocampus and certain brain areas important for the control of movement. Marijuana acts on receptors on the presynaptic neuron, putting the brakes on release of both excitatory and inhibitory transmitters. (page 74)
- *Hallucinogens.* Hallucinogens induce sensory distortions. LSD acts at one type of serotonin synapse. MDMA produces stimulant effects at low doses and hallucinogenic effects at higher doses. (page 75)

KEY TERMS

alcohol (page 73)

anxiolytic drugs (tranquilizers) (page 73)

depressant (page 73)

endorphins (page 74)

hallucinogens (page 75)

narcotics (page 74)

opiates (page 74)

psychoactive drugs (page 72)

stimulants (page 72)

module 3.3

Brain and Behavior

• If you lose part of your brain, do you also lose part of your mind?

Why do psychologists need to know about brain functioning? Let's consider an example: political persuasion. Some people favor vigorous efforts to protect themselves and society against possible threats. They advocate capital punishment, own guns to protect themselves against intruders, urge readiness for military action, and desire strong barriers against immigration. At the other end of the political spectrum are those who oppose capital punishment, advocate gun control, wish to avoid military conflict whenever possible, and are more willing to permit immigration. If we try to explain the range of views, we might point to differences in people's education, socioeconomic status, or early experiences. An additional factor is brain physiology! Some people's brains react strongly to any signal of danger. An easy way to test this difference is to make a sudden loud sound. The people who react with the strongest eye blinks, and who continue reacting strongly after repeated sounds, tend to be political conservatives, who favor capital punishment, military action, and so forth. Those with the least reactions tend to take the opposite positions (Oxley et al., 2008). Figure 3.13 shows the results of one study. So, if you and I argue about what is the "logical" solution to some political problem, we may really be disagreeing because of differences in our brain chemistry.

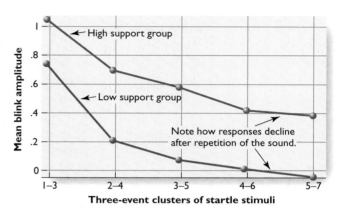

Figure 3.13 People with high support for military action, capital punishment, and immigration control show enhanced eye-blink responses to a sudden loud noise relative to those with low support for these positions. Those with low support show a more rapid decline in response as the noise is repeated.

THE MAJOR DIVISIONS OF THE NERVOUS SYSTEM

Of all the insights that researchers have gained about the nervous system, one of the most profound is that different parts perform different functions. Your perception and thinking seem like a single, integrated process, but it is possible for you to lose one part or another of that process after brain damage.

Biologists distinguish between the central nervous system and the peripheral nervous system. The **central nervous system** consists of *the brain and the spinal cord*. The central nervous system communicates with the rest of the body by the **peripheral nervous system**, which consists of *bundles of nerves between the spinal cord and the rest of the body*. We distinguish two parts of the peripheral nervous system, the *somatic nervous system*, which connects to the skin and muscles, and the *autonomic nervous system*, which connects to the heart, stomach, and other organs. Sensory nerves bring information from other body areas to the spinal cord; motor nerves take information from the spinal cord to the muscles, where they cause muscle contractions. Figure 3.14 summarizes these major divisions of the nervous system.

The central nervous system begins its embryological development as a tube with three lumps, as shown in Figure 3.15. These lumps develop into the *forebrain, midbrain,* and *hindbrain*. The rest of the tube develops into the spinal cord (Figure 3.16). The forebrain, which contains the cerebral cortex and other structures, is the dominant portion of the human brain.

The Forebrain: Cerebral Cortex

The forebrain consists of two **hemispheres**, *left and right* (Figure 3.17). Each hemisphere controls sensation and movement on the opposite side of the body. (Why does it control the opposite side instead of its own side? No one knows.) We shall consider the differences between the left and right hemispheres later in this module. The *outer covering of the forebrain*, known as the **cerebral cortex**, is especially prominent in humans. To compare the brain anatomy of humans and many other species, visit the Brain Museum website. Go to **www.cengage.com/psychology/kalat** for a current link to this website.

For the sake of convenience, we describe the cerebral cortex in terms of four *lobes*: occipital, parietal, temporal, and frontal, as shown in Figure 3.18. The **occipital lobe**, *at the rear of the head, is specialized for vision*. People with damage in this area have *cortical blindness*: They have no conscious vision, no object recognition, and no visual imagery (not even in dreams), although they still have eye blinks and other visual reflexes that do not require the cerebral cortex. Also, they wake up in the day and get sleepy at night because an area outside the cerebral cortex controls wake–sleep cycles.

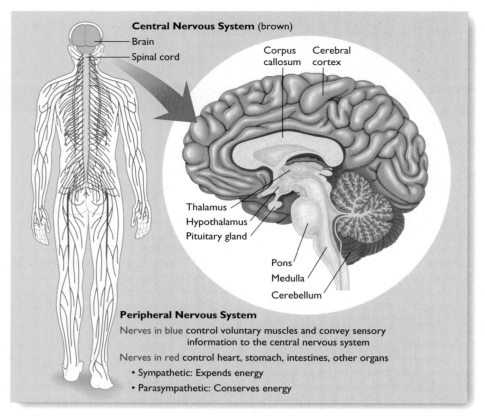

Figure 3.14 The major components of the nervous system are the central nervous system and the peripheral nervous system, which includes the somatic nervous system and the autonomic nervous system.

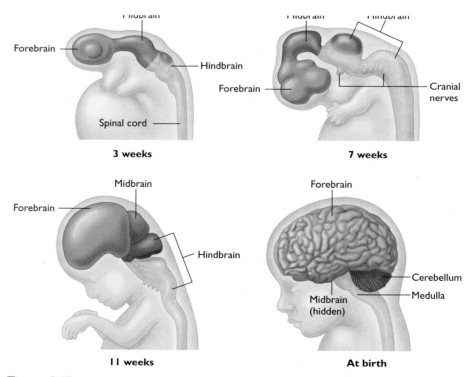

Figure 3.15 The human brain begins development as three lumps. By birth, the forebrain has grown much larger than the midbrain or the hindbrain.

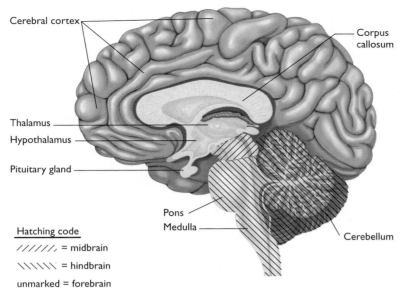

Cerebral cortex

Corpus callosum

Thalamus

Hypothalamus

Pituitary gland

Pons

Medulla

Cerebellum

Hatching code

////// = midbrain

\\\\\\ = hindbrain

unmarked = forebrain

Figure 3.16 The major divisions of the human central nervous system as seen from the midline.

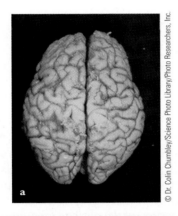

a

© Dr. Colin Chumbley/Science Photo Library/Photo Researchers, Inc.

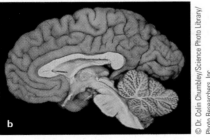

b

© Dr. Colin Chumbley/Science Photo Library/ Photo Researchers, Inc.

Figure 3.17 The human cerebral cortex: (a) left and right hemispheres; (b) a view from inside. The folds greatly extend the brain's surface area.

The **temporal lobe** of each hemisphere, *located toward the left and right sides of the head, is the main area for hearing and some of the complex aspects of vision.* Damage to parts of the temporal lobe sometimes produces striking and specialized deficits. One area in the temporal lobe, found in monkeys as well as humans, responds only to the sight of faces (Tsao, Freiwald, Tootell, & Livingstone, 2006). People with damage in that area no longer recognize faces, although they see well in other regards and recognize people by their voices (Tarr & Gauthier, 2000). People with damage to another part of the temporal lobe become motion blind: Although they can see the size, shape, and color of an object, they do not track its speed or direction of movement (Zihl, von Cramon, & Mai, 1983).

People with damage in the auditory parts of the temporal lobe do not become deaf, but they are impaired at recognizing sequences of sounds, as in music or speech. Just as damage in one area makes people motion blind, damage in another area makes them motion deaf. The source of a sound seems never to be moving (Ducommun et al., 2004).

Language comprehension depends on part of the temporal lobe, in the left hemisphere for most people. People with damage in that area have trouble understanding speech and remembering the names of objects. Their own speech, largely lacking nouns and verbs, is hard to understand, resembling that of normal people who are pressured to talk faster than usual (Dick et al., 2001).

Other parts of the temporal lobe are critical for certain aspects of emotion. The **amygdala** (Figure 3.19), *a subcortical structure deep within the temporal lobe, responds strongly to emotional situations.* People with damage to the amygdala are slow to process emotional information, such as facial expressions and descriptions of emotional situations (Baxter & Murray, 2002). In contrast, people with an easily aroused amygdala tend to be shy and fearful throughout their lives (Hariri et al., 2002; Rhodes et al., 2007).

The **parietal lobe,** *just anterior (forward) from the occipital lobe, is specialized for the body*

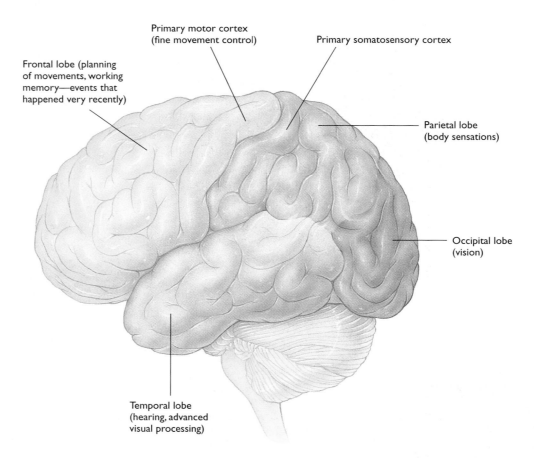

Frontal lobe (planning of movements, working memory—events that happened very recently)

Primary motor cortex (fine movement control)

Primary somatosensory cortex

Parietal lobe (body sensations)

Occipital lobe (vision)

Temporal lobe (hearing, advanced visual processing)

Figure 3.18 The four lobes of the human forebrain, with some of their functions.

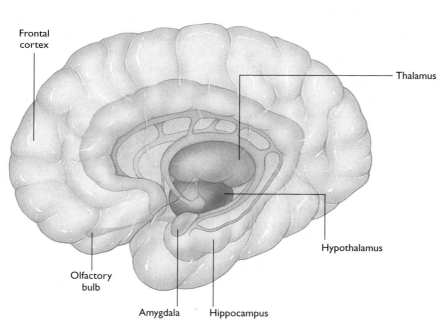

Frontal cortex

Thalamus

Hypothalamus

Olfactory bulb

Amygdala

Hippocampus

Figure 3.19 A view of the forebrain, showing internal structures as though the outer structures were transparent.

senses, including touch, pain, temperature, and awareness of the location of body parts in space. The primary somatosensory (so-ma-toh-SEN-so-ree, meaning body-sensory) cortex, *a strip in the anterior portion of the parietal lobe, has cells sensitive to touch in different body areas,* as shown in Figure 3.20. In that figure, note that the largest areas are devoted to touch in the most sensitive areas, such as the lips and hands. Damage to any part of the somatosensory cortex impairs sensation from the corresponding body part. Extensive damage also interferes with spatial attention. After parietal damage, people see an object but cannot determine where it is. They have trouble reaching toward it, walking around it, or shifting attention from one object to another.

Although the somatosensory cortex is the primary site for touch sensations, touch also activates areas that are important for emotional responses. Consider someone who has lost input to the somatosensory cortex. You gently stroke her arm, and she smiles without knowing why. She has the pleasant emotional experience without any touch sensation (Olausson et al., 2002). You see again that brain damage produces surprisingly specialized changes in behavior and experience.

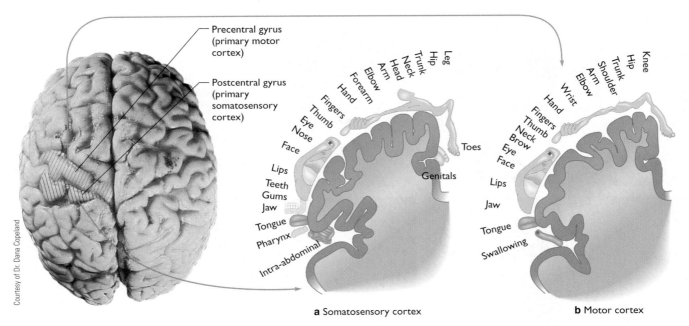

Courtesy of Dr. Dana Copeland

a Somatosensory cortex   **b** Motor cortex

Figure 3.20 (a) The primary somatosensory cortex and (b) the primary motor cortex, illustrating which part of the body each brain area controls. Larger areas of the cortex are devoted to body parts that need to be controlled with great precision, such as the face and hands. (parts a and b after Penfield & Rasmussen, 1950)

The frontal lobe, *at the anterior (forward) pole of the brain,* includes the **primary motor cortex,** *important for the planned control of fine movements,* such as moving one finger at a time. As with the primary somatosensory cortex, each area of the primary motor cortex controls a different part of the body, and larger areas are devoted to precise movements of the tongue and fingers as opposed to, say, the shoulder and elbow muscles, which have smaller representations. The *anterior sections of the frontal lobe,* called the **prefrontal cortex,** contribute to certain aspects of memory and to the planning of movements—that is, decision making. Suppose you have a choice between going to a movie tonight and finishing a paper that is due tomorrow, which will have a big effect on your grade at the end of the semester. Passing up the immediate pleasure in favor of the delayed reward depends on your prefrontal cortex (Frank & Claus, 2006). People with impairments of the prefrontal cortex often make impulsive decisions because they have trouble imagining how good they might feel after one outcome and how sad or guilty they might feel after another (S. W. Anderson, Bechara, Damasio, Tranel, & Damasio, 1999; Damasio, 1999). In short, the prefrontal cortex is important for many key aspects of human behavior.

Since the late 1990s, psychologists have become excited about **mirror neurons,** which are found in several brain areas but especially the frontal cortex. Mirror neurons *are active when you make a movement and also when you watch some-* one else make a similar movement (Dinstein, Hasson, Rubin, & Heeger, 2007). Do mirror neurons enable you to copy other people's actions? Do they enable you to identify with other people and understand them better? Autistic children, who show little activity in their "mirror neurons" of the frontal cortex while they watch other people, seldom imitate others or even show much interest in them (Dapretto et al., 2006). You can see how psychologists would speculate that mirror neurons are the basis for human civilization.

However, before we speculate too far, researchers need to address some important questions. In particular, were you born with mirror neurons? If so, they were probably an important basis for your social learning. The other possibility is that you learned to copy other people. After that learning, whenever you saw someone do something, it reminded you of your own ability to do the same thing and therefore activated neurons responsible for those actions. That is, you gradually *developed* mirror neurons as a *result* of imitation and identification. By this hypothesis, the distinctive feature of autistic children is that they fail to learn to identify with others and therefore fail to *develop* mirror neurons.

We probably have several kinds of mirror neurons. Infants just a few days old do (in some cases) imitate a few facial movements, as shown in Figure 3.21. That result implies built-in mirror neurons that connect the sight of a movement to the movement itself (Meltzoff & Moore, 1977). Also, children laugh when others laugh and cry when others cry,

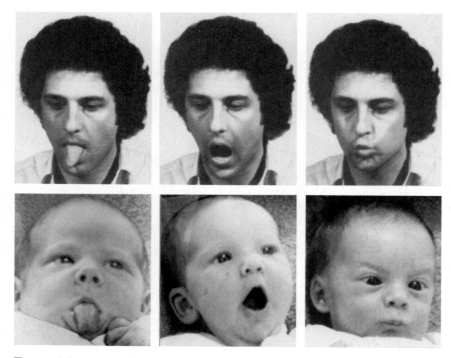

Figure 3.21 Newborn infants sometimes imitate facial expressions. Because they have not had an opportunity to learn to imitate, their behavior implies built-in mirror neurons. (From: A. N. Meltzoff & M. K. Moore, "Imitation of facial and manual gestures by human neonates." *Science*, 1977, 198, 75–78. Used by permission of Andrew N. Meltzoff, Ph.D.)

even at an early age. However, other mirror neurons develop their properties by learning. If you consistently watch someone else move the little finger every time you move your index finger, some of the cells in your frontal cortex will come to respond whenever you move your *index* finger or see someone else move the *little* finger (Catmur, Walsh, & Heyes, 2007). In other words, at least some—probably many—neurons develop their mirror quality (or in this case an antimirror quality) by learning.

11. The following five people have suffered damage to the forebrain. From their behavioral symptoms, state the probable location of each one's damage:
   Concept Check
   a. impaired touch sensations and spatial localization
   b. impaired hearing and some changes in emotional experience
   c. inability to make fine movements with the right hand
   d. loss of vision in the left visual field
   e. difficulty planning movements and remembering what has just happened.
12. What evidence suggests that imitation produces mirror neurons as opposed to the idea that mirror neurons produce imitation?

Answers

11. a. parietal lobe; b. temporal lobe; c. primary motor cortex of the left frontal lobe; d. right occipital lobe; e. prefrontal cortex.
12. It is possible to train neurons to respond to one kind of movement the person produces and a different movement the person watches. If people can learn to develop these "antimirror" neurons, then presumably, they could also learn to develop mirror neurons.

The Forebrain: Subcortical Areas

The interior of the forebrain includes several other structures, some of which are shown in Figure 3.19. At the center is the *thalamus*, which is the last stop for almost all sensory information on the way to the cerebral cortex. Surrounding the thalamus are other areas called the *limbic system*. (A limbus is a margin or border.) One of these areas, the hippocampus, is important for memory and will appear again in chapter 7. The **hypothalamus**, *located just below the thalamus, is important for hunger, thirst, temperature regulation, sex, and other motivated behaviors*. The hypothalamus will appear again in chapter 11. The amygdala is a key area for emotion (chapter 12).

Motor Control

The cerebral cortex does not directly control the muscles. It sends some of its output to the **pons** and **medulla** (parts of the hindbrain), *which control the muscles of the head* (e.g., for chewing, swallowing, breathing, and talking). The rest of its output passes through the pons and medulla to the **spinal cord**, *which controls the muscles from the neck down* (Figures 3.16 and 3.22). The spinal cord also controls many reflexes, such as the knee-jerk reflex, without relying on input from the brain. A **reflex** is a *rapid, automatic response to a stimulus*, such as unconscious adjustments of your legs while you are walking or quickly jerking your hand away from something hot.

The **cerebellum** (Latin for "little brain"), *part of the hindbrain*, is important for any behavior that requires aim or timing, such as tapping out a rhythm, judging which of two visual stimuli is mov-

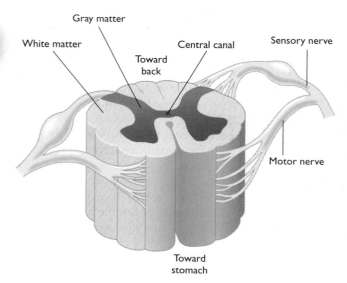

Figure 3.22 The spinal cord receives sensory information from all body parts except the head. Motor nerves in the spinal cord control the muscles and glands.

ing faster, and judging whether one musical tempo is faster or slower than another (Ivry & Diener, 1991; Keele & Ivry, 1990). It is also essential to learned responses that require precise timing (Krupa, Thompson, & Thompson, 1993). People with damage to the cerebellum show motor problems like those of alcoholic intoxication, including slurred speech, staggering, and inaccurate eye movements. The reason for the similarity is that alcohol suppresses activity in the cerebellum.

13. Someone with a cut through the upper spinal cord still shows many reflexive movements but no voluntary movements of the arms or legs. Why not?

Concept Check

Answer

13. The spinal cord controls many reflexes by itself. However, voluntary control of muscles depends on messages from the brain to the spinal cord, and a cut through the upper spinal cord interrupts those messages.

MEASURING BRAIN ACTIVITY

We have been considering the functions of different brain areas, but how did researchers discover those functions? For decades, nearly all of the conclusions came from studies of patients with brain damage, and much of it still does. However, researchers now also have modern techniques that examine brain anatomy and activity in healthy people.

An **electroencephalograph (EEG)** *uses electrodes on the scalp to record rapid changes in brain electrical activity* (Figure 3.23). A similar method is a **magnetoencephalograph (MEG)**, *which records magnetic changes.* Both methods provide data on a millisecond-by-millisecond basis, so they measure the brain's reactions to lights, sounds, and other events. However, because they record from the surface of the scalp, they provide little precision about the location of the activity.

Another method offers much better anatomical localization but less information about timing: **Positron-emission tomography (PET)** *records radioactivity of various brain areas emitted from injected chemicals* (Phelps & Mazziotta, 1985). First, someone receives an injection of a radioactively labeled compound such as glucose. The brain's most active areas rapidly absorb glucose, a sugar that is the brain's main fuel (almost its only fuel). Therefore, the labeled glucose emits radioactivity primarily from those areas. Detectors around the head record the radioactivity and send the results to a computer that generates an image such as the

one in Figure 3.24. Red indicates areas of greatest activity, followed by yellow, green, and blue. Unfortunately, PET scans require exposing the brain to radioactivity.

Another technique, **functional magnetic resonance imaging (fMRI),** *uses magnetic detectors outside the head to compare the amounts of hemoglobin with and without oxygen in different brain areas* (J. D. Cohen, Noll, & Schneider, 1993). (Adding or removing oxygen changes the response of hemoglobin to a magnetic field.) The most active brain areas use the most oxygen and therefore decrease the oxygen bound to the blood's hemoglobin. The fMRI technique indicates which brain areas are currently the most active on a second-by-second basis, as in Figure 3.25.

For more detail about brain scan techniques, visit "The Secret Life of the Brain: Scanning the Brain" on PBS's website. Go to **www.cengage.com/psychology/kalat** for a current link to this website.

If we want to use a PET or fMRI scan to measure the brain activity provoked by a certain task, the data tell us nothing except by comparison to how much activity would occur otherwise. For example, suppose we want to determine which brain areas are important for recent

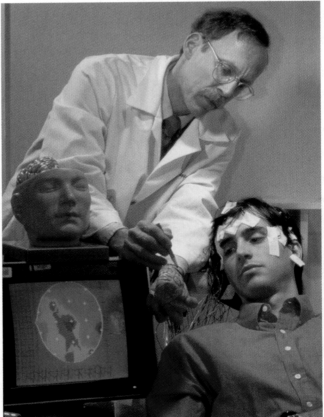

© Richard T. Nowitz/Photo Researchers, Inc.

Figure 3.23 An EEG records momentary changes in electrical potential from the scalp, revealing an average of the activity of brain cells beneath each electrode.

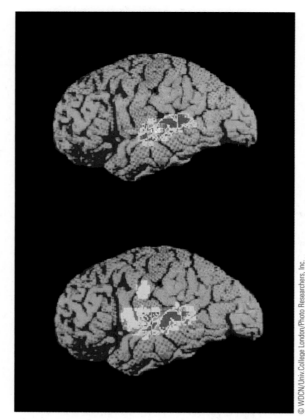

Figure 3.24 A PET scan of the human brain. Red shows areas of most-increased activity during some task; yellow shows areas of next most-increased activity.

memory. We record activity while someone is engaged in a memory task and compare that activity to times when the person is doing . . . what? Doing nothing? That comparison wouldn't work; the memory task presumably includes sensory stimuli, motor responses, attention, and other processes. Besides that, "doing nothing" (mind wandering) activates certain brain areas,

too (Mason et al., 2007). Researchers must design a comparison task that requires attention to the same sensory stimuli, the same hand movements, and so forth as the memory task. Then they set a computer to subtract the activity in the comparison task from the activity in the memory task. The areas with the largest difference between the tasks are presumably important for some aspect of memory.

Brain scans are a potentially powerful research tool, and they provide impressive and beautiful illustrations, but interpreting the results is tricky (Logothetis, 2008). Sometimes, researchers find greater activity in some brain area among people who perform some task best. That makes sense: Those who showed more brain activity performed the task better. But sometimes, researchers find greater brain activity among people who perform the task *worse* (Gigi, Babai, Katzav, Atkins, & Hendler, 2007; Pexman, Hargreaves, Edwards, Henry, & Goodyear, 2007). Now the interpretation is that those who performed worse had to work their brains harder because the task was more difficult for them. In short, brain scans tell us which areas increased their activity, but they don't tell us *why*.

THE AUTONOMIC NERVOUS SYSTEM AND ENDOCRINE SYSTEM

The **autonomic nervous system**, closely associated with the spinal cord, *controls the internal organs such as the heart.* The term *autonomic* means involuntary, or automatic, in the sense that we have little voluntary control of it. A sudden loud noise increases your heart rate, but you can't decide to increase your heart rate in the same way that you could decide to wave your hand. Your brain does, nevertheless, receive information from, and send information to, the autonomic nervous system. For example, if you are nervous about something, your autonomic nervous system reacts more strongly than usual; if you are relaxed, it responds less.

The autonomic nervous system has two parts: (a) The *sympathetic nervous system,* controlled by a chain of cells lying just outside the spinal cord, increases heart rate, breathing rate, sweating, and other processes that are important for vigorous fight-or-flight activities. It inhibits digestion, sexual arousal, and other activities not important to an emergency situation. (b) The *parasympathetic nervous system,* controlled by cells at the top and bottom levels of the spinal cord, decreases heart rate, increases digestive activities, and in general, promotes activities of the body that take place during rest

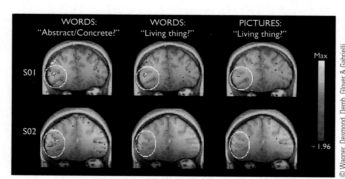

Figure 3.25 This brain scan was made with functional magnetic resonance imaging (fMRI). Participants looked at words or pictures and judged whether each item was abstract or concrete, living or nonliving. Yellow shows the areas most activated by this judgment; red shows areas less strongly activated. (From Wagner, Desmond, Demb, Glover, & Gabrieli, 1997. Photo courtesy of Anthony D. Wagner)

and relaxation (Figure 3.26). If you are driving and you see a police car with its siren on behind you, your sympathetic nervous system arouses. Your heart starts racing, you breathe heavily, and you start sweating. Then the police car passes, and you see that it is chasing someone else. Ah. Your parasympathetic nervous system kicks in, and you suddenly relax. We shall return to this topic in more detail in the discussion of emotions (chapter 12).

The autonomic nervous system influences the endocrine system, *a set of glands that produce hormones and release them into the blood.* Hormones controlled by the hypothalamus and *pituitary gland* also regulate the other endocrine organs. Figure 3.27 shows some of the endocrine glands. Hormones are *chemicals released by glands*

and conveyed via the blood to alter activity in various organs. Some hormonal effects are brief, such as a change in heart rate or blood pressure. In other cases, hormones prepare a body for pregnancy, migration, hibernation, or long-lasting activities. A woman's menstrual cycle depends on hormones and so does the onset of puberty. Within the brain, hormones can produce temporary changes in the excitability of cells, and they also influence the survival, growth, and connections of cells. The sex hormones (*androgens* and *estrogens*) have particularly strong effects during early development, when they are responsible for many differences, on the average, between male and female brains as well as external anatomy (Cahill, 2006). Module 11.3, sexual motivation, considers the role of sex hormones in more detail.

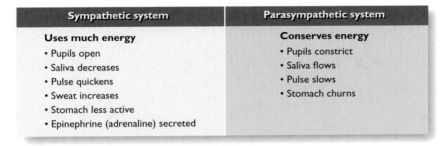

Sympathetic system	Parasympathetic system
Uses much energy	**Conserves energy**
• Pupils open	• Pupils constrict
• Saliva decreases	• Saliva flows
• Pulse quickens	• Pulse slows
• Sweat increases	• Stomach churns
• Stomach less active	
• Epinephrine (adrenaline) secreted	

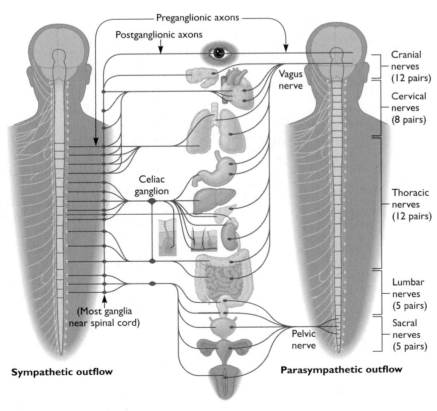

Figure 3.26 The sympathetic nervous system prepares the body for brief bouts of vigorous activity. The parasympathetic nervous system promotes digestion and other nonemergency functions. Although both systems are active at all times, one or the other can predominate at a given time.

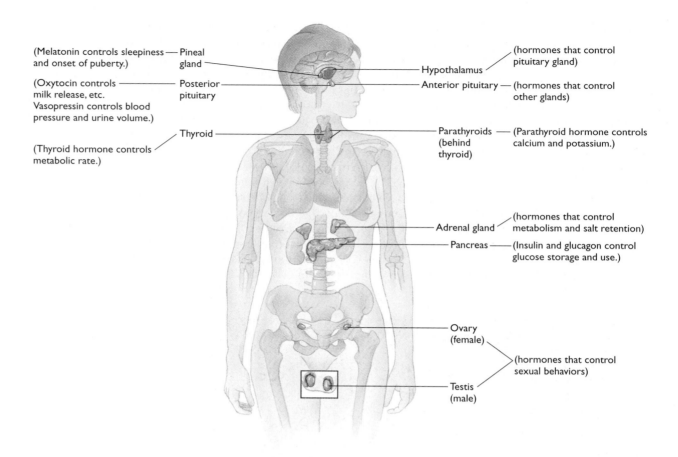

(Melatonin controls sleepiness and onset of puberty.) — Pineal gland

(Oxytocin controls milk release, etc. Vasopressin controls blood pressure and urine volume.) — Posterior pituitary

(Thyroid hormone controls metabolic rate.) — Thyroid

Hypothalamus — (hormones that control pituitary gland)

Anterior pituitary — (hormones that control other glands)

Parathyroids (behind thyroid) — (Parathyroid hormone controls calcium and potassium.)

Adrenal gland — (hormones that control metabolism and salt retention)

Pancreas — (Insulin and glucagon control glucose storage and use.)

Ovary (female)

Testis (male)

(hormones that control sexual behaviors)

Figure 3.27 Glands in the endocrine system produce hormones and release them into the bloodstream. This figure shows some of the glands and hormones.

---

14. While someone is trying to escape danger, the heart rate and breathing rate increase. After the danger passes, heart rate and breathing rate fall below normal. Which part of the autonomic nervous system is more active during the danger, and which is more active after it?

Concept Check

Answer

14. The sympathetic nervous system predominates during the danger, and the parasympathetic system predominates afterward.

EXPERIENCE AND BRAIN PLASTICITY

When we talk about brain anatomy, it is easy to get the impression that the structures are fixed. In fact, brain structure shows considerable plasticity—that is, *change as a result of experience.*

For many decades, researchers believed that the nervous system produced no new neurons after early infancy. Later researchers found that *undifferentiated cells called* stem cells can develop into additional neurons in certain brain areas (Gage, 2000; Graziadei & deHan, 1973; Song, Stevens, & Gage, 2002). New neurons in the hippocampus are important for memory formation (Kee, Teixeira, Wang, & Frankland, 2007; Meshi et al.,

2006; Ramirez-Amaya, Marrone, Gage, Worley, & Barnes, 2006). New neurons evidently do *not* form in the cerebral cortex (Spalding, Bhardwaj, Buchholz, Druid, & Frisén, 2005).

New experiences produce huge effects on synapses, as axons and dendrites expand and withdraw their branches. These changes, which occur more rapidly in young people but continue throughout life, enable the brain to adapt to changing circumstances (Boyke, Driemeyer, Gaser, Büchel, & May, 2008). For example, one man lost his hand in an accident at age 19. Thirty-five years later, surgeons grafted a new hand onto his arm. A few months later, axons had grown into the new hand, with proper connections to the brain, and he regained partial sensation from the hand (Frey, Bogdanov, Smith, Watrous, & Breidenbach, 2008).

Consider also the changes that accompany blindness. Ordinarily, the occipital cortex at the rear of the head is devoted to vision alone. For people who are born blind, axons from other systems gradually invade the occipital cortex and displace the inactive axons representing visual input. Within years, the occipital cortex becomes responsive to touch and language. The behavioral effects include an enhanced ability to make fine distinctions by touch, as in reading Braille, as well as enhanced language skills (Amedi, Floel, Knecht, Zohary, & Cohen, 2004; Burton et al., 2002; Sadato et al., 1996, 1998). For someone who becomes blind later in life, the occipital cortex reorganizes less extensively (Gothe et al., 2002).

Some changes in the nervous system are large enough for the unaided eye to see. For example, one part of the temporal cortex (devoted to hearing) is 30% larger in professional musicians than in other people (Schneider et al., 2002). We can't be sure whether that difference was a result of training, but other studies have reported that the brains of children who are starting musical training appear indistinguishable from those of children not in musical training (Norton et al., 2005). Also, piano training in adulthood lasting only 2 weeks induces changes in the way the brain responds to music (Lappe, Herholz, Trainor, & Pantev, 2008). These results imply that musical training alters the brain rather than the alternative idea that musicians' brains differed from the start.

---

15. On the average, blind people do better than sighted people at using their hands to recognize shapes, even though the touch receptors themselves do not change. What accounts for this advantage?

Concept Check

Answer

15. If someone is blind from birth, touch sensation invades the occipital cortex as well as its normal site in the parietal cortex. The greater brain representation of touch enables the person to attend to fine details of touch that a sighted person would not notice.

THE TWO HEMISPHERES AND THEIR CONNECTIONS

Let's focus on one type of brain damage that produces results of widespread interest. As mentioned, each hemisphere of the brain gets sensory input mostly from the opposite side of the body and controls muscles on the opposite side. The hemispheres differ in other ways, too. For almost all right-handed people and more than 60% of

left-handed people, parts of the left hemisphere control speech. For most other left-handers, both hemispheres control speech. Few people have complete right-hemisphere control of speech. The right hemisphere is more important for certain other functions, including the ability to imagine what an object would look like after it rotated and the ability to understand the emotional connotations of facial expressions or tone of voice (Stone, Nisenson, Eliassen, & Gazzaniga, 1996). People with right-hemisphere damage often can't tell when a speaker is being sarcastic, and they frequently don't understand jokes (Beeman & Chiarello, 1998).

In one study, people watched videotapes of 10 people speaking twice. In one speech, they described themselves honestly, and in the other case, they told nothing but lies. Do you think you could tell the difference between truth and lies? You probably couldn't. The average for MIT undergraduates was 47% correct, slightly less than they should have done by random guessing. The only group that did better than chance was a set of people with left-hemisphere brain damage! They understood almost nothing of what people were saying, so they relied on gestures and facial expressions—which the right hemisphere interprets quite well (Etcoff, Ekman, Magee, & Frank, 2000).

The two hemispheres constantly exchange information. If you feel something with the left hand and something else with the right hand, you can tell whether they are made of the same material because the hemispheres pass information back and forth through the **corpus callosum,** *a set of axons that connect the left and right hemispheres of the cerebral cortex* (Figure 3.28). What would happen if the corpus callosum were cut?

Occasionally, brain surgeons cut it to relieve **epilepsy,** *a condition in which cells somewhere in the brain emit abnormal rhythmic, spontaneous impulses.* Most people with epilepsy respond well to antiepileptic drugs and live normal lives. A few, however, continue having frequent major seizures. When all else fails, surgeons sometimes recommend cutting the corpus callosum. The original idea was that epileptic seizures would be limited to one hemisphere and therefore be less incapacitating.

The operation was more successful than expected. Not only are the seizures limited to one side of the body, but they also become less frequent. Apparently, the operation interrupts a feedback loop that allows an epileptic seizure to echo back and forth between the two hemispheres. However, although these split-brain patients resume a normal life, they show some fascinating behavioral effects.

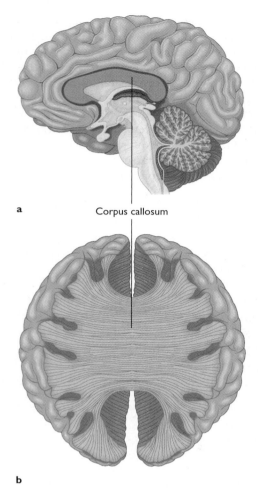

a

Corpus callosum

b

Figure 3.28 The corpus callosum is a large set of fibers that convey information between the two hemispheres of the cerebral cortex. (a) A midline view showing the location of the corpus callosum. (b) A horizontal section showing how each axon of the corpus callosum links one spot in the left hemisphere to a corresponding spot in the right hemisphere.

If you have left-hemisphere control of speech, like most people, your talking hemisphere easily describes what you feel on either side of the body or see in either half of the visual field. The information that enters your right hemisphere passes quickly across the corpus callosum to your left (speaking) hemisphere. However, a split-brain patient (someone whose corpus callosum has been cut) who feels something with the left hand cannot describe it. The information went to the right (nonspeaking) hemisphere, which cannot communicate with the left hemisphere (Nebes, 1974; Sperry, 1967). If asked to point to it, the person might point correctly with the left hand while saying, "I have no idea what it was. I didn't feel anything." The right hemisphere understood the instructions and answered with the hand it controls but could not talk.

Now consider what happens when a split-brain patient sees something (Figure 3.29). The person in Figure 3.29 focuses on a point in the middle of the screen. The investigator flashes a word such as *hatband* on the screen for a split second, too briefly for an eye movement, and asks for the word. The person replies, "band," which is what the left hemisphere saw. (The left hemisphere sees the right side of the world.) To the question of what *kind* of band, the reply is, "I don't know. Jazz band? Rubber band?" However, the left hand (controlled by the right hemisphere) points to a hat (which the right hemisphere saw).

Shortly after the surgery, some individuals report conflicts between the two sides, as if people with different plans were occupying the same body. One person reported that his left hand sometimes changed the channel or turned off the television set while he (the talking side, the left

Figure 3.29 (a) When the word *hatband* is flashed on a screen, a split-brain patient reports only what the left hemisphere saw, *band*, and (b) writes *band* with the right hand. However, (c) the left hand (controlled by the right hemisphere) points to a hat, which is what the right hemisphere saw.

hemisphere) was enjoying the program. Once he was going for a walk and the left leg refused to go any farther and would move only if he turned around to walk home (Joseph, 1988). In some ways, it is as if the person has two "minds" occupying one skull.

16. After damage to the corpus callosum, a person can describe some, but not all, of what he or she feels. With which hand must the person feel an object before speaking about it?

Answer

16. The person must feel something with the right hand, the hand that the left hemisphere feels.

Split-brain surgery is rare. We study such patients not because you are likely to meet one but because they teach us something about brain organization: We see that our experience of a unified consciousness depends on communication across brain areas. If communication between the two hemispheres is lost, then each hemisphere becomes partly independent of the other.

THE BINDING PROBLEM

Even if someone has a unified brain, with the corpus callosum intact, how do the different brain areas combine to produce the experience of a single self? One part of your brain is responsible for hearing, another for touch, others for various aspects of vision, and so forth, and those areas have few connections with one another. When you play a piano, how do you know that the piano you see is also what you hear and feel? *The question of how separate brain areas combine forces to produce a unified perception of a single object* is the **binding problem** (Treisman, 1999). The binding problem relates to the mind–brain problem mentioned in chapter 1.

A naive explanation would be that all the various parts of the brain funnel their information to a "little person in the head" who puts it all together. However, research on the cerebral cortex has found no central processor that could serve that purpose. Few cells receive information from more than one sense. In fact, the mystery deepens: When you see a brown rabbit hopping, one brain area detects the shape, another the movement, and another the brownness. How do you put them together?

Part of the answer lies with the parietal cortex, important for spatial perception. Consider the piano: If you identify the location of the hand that you feel, the piano you see, and the sound you hear, and all those locations are the same, you link the sensations together. The parietal cortex is important for localizing sensations. If, like someone with parietal cortex damage, you cannot locate anything in space, you probably won't bind sensations into a single experience. You might look at a yellow lemon and a red tomato and report seeing a yellow tomato and no lemon at all (L. C. Robertson, 2003).

We also know that binding occurs only for precisely simultaneous events. Have you ever watched a film or television show in which the soundtrack is noticeably ahead of or behind the picture? If so, you knew that the sound wasn't coming from the performers on screen. You get

We hear the sound as coming from the dummy's mouth only if sound and movements are synchronized. In general, binding depends on simultaneity of two kinds of stimuli.

the same experience watching a poorly dubbed foreign-language film. However, when you watch a ventriloquist, the motion of the dummy's mouth simultaneous with the sound lets you perceive the sound as coming from the dummy. Even young infants figure out who is talking based on whose lip movements synchronize with the sounds (Lickliter & Bahrick, 2000).

You can experience a demonstration of binding with an Online Try It Yourself activity. Go to **www.cengage. com/psychology/kalat.** Navigate to the student website, then to the Online Try It Yourself section, and click Illustration of Binding.

You can also try the following (I. H. Robertson, 2005): Stand or sit by a large mirror as in Figure 3.30, watching both your right hand and its reflection in the mirror. Hold your

left hand out of sight. Then repeatedly clench and unclench both hands, and touch each thumb to your fingers and palm, in unison. You will feel your left hand doing the same thing that you see the hand in the mirror doing. After a couple of minutes, you may start to experience the hand in the mirror as your own left hand. You might even feel that you have three hands—the right hand, the real left hand, and the apparent left hand in the mirror. You are binding your touch and visual experiences because they occur at the same time, apparently in the same location. For most people, this procedure is just an amusing demonstration, but it is valuable in certain cases. For someone who has had an arm amputated, this procedure helps the person feel an artificial arm as being part of the body.

People with parietal lobe damage have trouble binding aspects of a stimulus, such as color and shape, because they do not perceive visual locations accurately (Treisman, 1999; Wheeler & Treisman, 2002). People with intact brains experience the same problem if they see something very briefly while distracted (Holcombe & Cavanagh, 2001). What would it be like to see objects without binding them? You can get some feel for this experience with an Online Try It Yourself activity. Go to **www.cengage.com/psychology/kalat.** Navigate to

Figure 3.30 Move your left and right hands in synchrony while watching the image of one hand in a mirror. Within minutes, you may experience the one in the mirror as being your own hand. This demonstration illustrates how binding occurs.

the student website, then to the Online Try It Yourself section, and click Possible Failure of Binding.

---

17. What is the binding problem?
18. What two elements must take place for binding to occur?

Answer

17. The binding problem is the theoretical question of how the brain creates a unified experience, given that different brain areas analyze different aspects of a stimulus.
18. For binding to occur, the brain must be able to identify that different aspects of the stimulus come from the same location. Also, the different aspects must occur simultaneously.

In Closing

Brain and Experience

This module has stressed that mind and brain activity are tightly linked—indeed, synonymous. If you lose part of your brain, you lose part of your mind. If you activate some aspect of your mental experience, you simultaneously increase activity in some part of your brain. The study of brain activity helps us understand the components that combine to form our behavior.

Another major point is that although different brain areas handle different functions without feeding into a central processor, they still manage to function as an organized whole. When we perceive two events simultaneously in the same location, we bind them together as a single object. Brain areas act separately and nevertheless produce a single experience.

Research on brain functioning is challenging because the brain itself is so complex. Just think about all that goes on within this 1.3 kg mass of tissue composed mostly of water. It is an amazing structure.

SUMMARY

- *Central and peripheral nervous systems.* The central nervous system consists of the brain and the spinal cord. The peripheral nervous system consists of nerves that communicate between the central nervous system and the rest of the body. (page 79)
- *The cerebral cortex.* The four lobes of the cerebral cortex and their primary functions are: occipital lobe, vision; temporal lobe, hearing and some aspects of vision; parietal lobe, body sensations; frontal lobe, preparation for movement. Damage in the cerebral cortex can produce specialized deficits depending on the location of damage. (page 79)
- *Communication between the cerebral cortex and the rest of the body.* Information from the cerebral cortex passes to the medulla and then into the spinal cord. The medulla and spinal cord receive sensory input from the periphery and send output to the muscles and glands. (page 84)
- *Learning about brain functions.* Modern technology enables researchers to develop images showing the structure and activity of various brain areas in living, waking people. (page 85)
- *Autonomic nervous system and endocrine system.* The autonomic nervous system controls the body's organs, preparing them for emergency activities or for vegetative activities. The endocrine system consists of organs that release hormones into the blood. (page 86)

- *Brain plasticity.* Experiences alter brain connections. Prolonged unusual experiences—such as in people born blind or musicians who practice many hours per day—change the brain in profound ways. (page 88)
- *Hemispheres of the brain.* Each hemisphere of the brain controls the opposite side of the body. In addition, the left hemisphere of the human brain is specialized for most aspects of language in most people. The right hemisphere is important for understanding spatial relationships and for understanding the emotional aspects of communication. (page 89)
- *Corpus callosum.* The corpus callosum enables the left and right hemispheres of the cortex to communicate with each other. If the corpus callosum is damaged, information that reaches one hemisphere cannot be shared with the other. (page 89)
- *Split-brain patients.* The left hemisphere is specialized for language in most people, so split-brain people can describe information only if it enters the left hemisphere. Such people show signs of having separate fields of awareness. (page 89)
- *The binding problem.* We develop a unified experience of an object even though our registers of hearing, touch, vision, and so forth occur in different brain areas that do not connect directly to one another. Binding requires perception of the location of various aspects of a sensation. It also requires simultaneity of various sensory events. (page 91)

KEY TERMS

amygdala (page 81)

autonomic nervous system (page 86)

binding problem (page 91)

central nervous system (page 79)

cerebellum (page 84)

cerebral cortex (page 79)

corpus callosum (page 89)

electroencephalograph (EEG) (page 85)

endocrine system (page 87)

epilepsy (page 89)

frontal lobe (page 83)

functional magnetic resonance imaging (fMRI) (page 85)

hemisphere (page 79)

hormone (page 87)

hypothalamus (page 84)

magnetoencephalograph (MEG) (page 85)

medulla (page 84)

mirror neurons (page 83)

occipital lobe (page 79)

parietal lobe (page 81)

peripheral nervous system (page 79)

plasticity (page 88)

pons (page 84)

positron-emission tomography (PET) (page 85)

prefrontal cortex (page 83)

primary motor cortex (page 83)

primary somatosensory cortex (page 82)

reflex (page 84)

spinal cord (page 84)

stem cells (page 88)

temporal lobe (page 81)

exploration and study

Why Does This Matter to Me?

SOCIAL RESPONSIBILITY AND PSYCHOLOGY

Many environmental problems are caused by human behavior. Psychologists can help steer the course of our future toward more socially responsible and sustainable outcomes. Students of today need to be ever mindful of the link between human behavior and its impact on the environment and our communities.

"Biological Psychology" and Social Responsibility: A Step Further

Many household products are pollutants that could negatively affect one's synapses, not to mention that they can be very unhealthy for the environment. However, many people feel that they must use these harmful products to keep their houses clean or their lawns green. How can people be encouraged to stop using these harmful products when they see a demand from society to maintain a certain level of upkeep in and outside their homes?

Learn More about Pollutants Found in Households

Up Close and Toxic is a film about the many toxic pollutants found in our homes and ways that we can reduce their presence. To find out more about the film visit Bullfrog Film's website. Go to www.cengage.com/psychology/kalat for a current link to this website.

Join the iChapters Plant a Tree Drive!

To show its support of the environmental movement, iChapters is planting a tree on behalf of each fan of the iChapters Facebook Page and for every 10 questions answered correctly in our quiz.
http://www.ichapters.com/plantatree/

Exploration and Study

SUGGESTIONS FOR FURTHER EXPLORATION

In addition to the study materials provided at the end of each module, you may supplement your review of this chapter with the following book and website suggestions or by using one or more of the book's electronic resources, which include its companion website, interactive Cengage Learning eBook, and CengageNOW. Brief descriptions of these resources follow. For more information, visit **www.cengage.com/psychology/kalat.**

ADDITIONAL RESOURCES

The book's companion website, accessible from **www.cengage.com/psychology/kalat,** provides a wide range of study resources such as an interactive glossary, flashcards, tutorial quizzes, updated web links, and Try It Yourself activities. For example, the exercises on Illustration of Binding and Possible Failure of Binding tie to what you've learned in this chapter.

CengageNOW with Critical Thinking Videos is an easy-to-use resource that helps you study in less time to get the grade you want. An online study system, CengageNOW gives you the option of taking a diagnostic pretest for each chapter. The system uses the results of each pretest to create personalized chapter study plans for you. The Personalized Study Plans

- Help you save study time by identifying areas on which you should concentrate and give you one-click access to corresponding pages of the interactive Cengage Learning eBook;
- Provide interactive exercises and study tools to help you fully understand chapter concepts; and
- Include a posttest for you to take to confirm that you are ready to move on to the next chapter.

Find critical thinking videos like this one in your CengageNOW product, which offer an opportunity for you to learn more about psychological research on different topics.

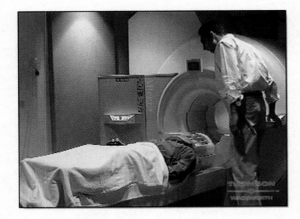

Neural Networks

Books

Kalat, J. W. (2009). *Biological psychology* (10th ed.). Belmont, CA: Wadsworth. Chapters 2 through 4 deal with the material discussed in this chapter in more detail.

Klawans, H. L. (1996). *Why Michael couldn't hit.* New York: W. H. Freeman. Informative and entertaining account of how the rise and fall of various sports heroes relates to what we know about the brain.

Websites

Links to the websites described below are kept current and can be found at **www.cengage.com/psychology/kalat.**

The Whole Brain Atlas

Stunning photographs of both normal and abnormal brains.

Brain Anatomy of Various Species

Compare the brains of humans, chimpanzees, dolphins, weasels, hyenas, polar bears, and a great many other mammals.

Web of Addictions

Andrew L. Homer and Dick Dillon provide factual information about alcohol and other abused drugs. Fact sheets and other material are arranged by drug, with links to net resources related to addictions, in-depth information on special topics, and a list of places to get help with addictions.

National Clearinghouse for Alcohol and Drug Information

News reports about drug and alcohol abuse, with links to many other sites.

© Lynn Rogers

4 chapter

Sensation and Perception

No matter how exotic some other planet might be, it could not have colors we do not have here. The reason is that our eyes can see only certain wavelengths of light, and color is the experience our brains create from those wavelengths.

Consider This:

When my son Sam was 8 years old, he asked me, "If we went to some other planet, would we see different colors?" He meant colors that were as different from familiar colors as yellow is from red or blue. I told him that would be impossible, and I tried to explain why. No matter where we go in outer space, we could never experience a color, sound, or other sensation that would be fundamentally different from what we experience on Earth. Different combinations, yes, but not fundamentally different sensory experiences.

Three years later, Sam told me he wondered whether people who look at the same thing are all having the same experience: When different people look at something and call it "green," how can we know whether they are having the same experience? I agreed that there is no way to be sure.

Why am I certain that colors on a different planet would look the same as on Earth but uncertain whether colors look the same to different people here? If the answer isn't clear to you, perhaps it will be after you read this chapter.

Sensation is the *conversion of energy from the environment into a pattern of response by the nervous system.* It is the registration of information. Perception is *the interpretation of that information.* For example, light rays striking your eyes produce sensation. Your experience of recognizing your roommate is a perception. In practice, the distinction between sensation and perception is often difficult to make.

Vision

- How do our eyes convert light into something we can experience?
- How do we perceive colors?

The comic book superhero Superman is said to have x-ray vision. Would that be possible? Never mind whether a biological organism could generate x-rays. If you *could* send out x-rays, would your vision improve?

What is vision, anyway? It is the detection of light. Sensation in general is the detection of **stimuli**—*energies from the world around us that affect us in some way.* Our eyes, ears, and other sensory organs are packed with **receptors**—*specialized cells that convert environmental energies into signals for the nervous system.* You probably already learned this account in an elementary or high school science class. But did you believe it? Evidently, not everyone does. One survey posed the questions, "When we look at someone or something, does anything such as rays, waves, or energy go out of our eyes? Into our eyes?" Among first graders (about age 6), 49% answered (incorrectly) that energy went out of the eyes, and 54% answered (correctly) that energy came into the eyes. (It was possible to say *yes* to both.) Among college students, 33% said that energy went out of the eyes; 88% said that energy came in (Winer & Cottrell, 1996).

Follow-up studies revealed that the college students had not misunderstood the question. They really believed that their eyes sent out something that was essential to vision. Even after reading a textbook chapter that explained vision, they did no better. After a psychologist patiently explained that the eyes do *not* send out sight rays (or anything else), most answered correctly, but when asked again a few months later, almost half of those who had changed their answers went back to their original, wrong answers, saying their eyes sent out sight rays (Winer, Cottrell, Gregg, Fournier, & Bica, 2002).

Back to Superman: X-rays do not bounce off objects and come back. Even if he sent out x-rays, his brain would receive no sensation from the rays. The x-rays would accomplish nothing, except perhaps to cause cancer!

Many people have other misconceptions about vision. We are often led astray because we imagine that what we see is a copy of the outside world. It is not. Just as a computer translates a sight or sound into a series of 1s and 0s, your brain *translates* stimuli into very different representations.

THE DETECTION OF LIGHT

What we call *light* is part of the **electromagnetic spectrum,** *the continuum of all the frequencies of radiated energy*—from gamma rays and x-rays with very short wavelengths, through ultraviolet, visible light, and infrared, to radio and TV transmissions with very long wavelengths (Figure 4.1). What makes light visible? The answer is our receptors, which are equipped to respond to wavelengths from 400 to 700 nanometers (nm). With different receptors, we would see a different range of wavelengths. Many insects and birds, for example, see ultraviolet wavelengths, which are invisible to humans.

The Structures of the Eye

When we see an object, light reflected from that object passes through the **pupil,** an *adjustable opening in the eye.* The pupil widens and narrows to control the amount of light entering the eye. The **iris** is the *colored structure on the surface of the eye surrounding the pupil.* It is the structure we describe when we say someone has brown, green, or blue eyes.

Light that passes through the pupil travels through the *vitreous humor* (a clear jellylike substance) to strike the retina at the back of the eyeball. The **retina** is a *layer of visual receptors covering the back surface of the eyeball.* The cornea and the lens focus the light on the retina, as shown in Figure 4.2. The **cornea,** *a rigid transparent structure on the outer surface of the eyeball,* always focuses light in the same way. The **lens** is a *flexible structure that can vary in thickness,* enabling the eye to **accommodate,** that is, *to adjust its focus for objects at different distances.* When we look at a distant object, for example, our eye muscles relax

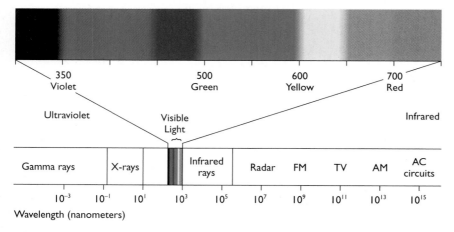

Figure 4.1 Visible light is a small part of the electromagnetic spectrum. We see these wavelengths because we have receptors that respond to them.

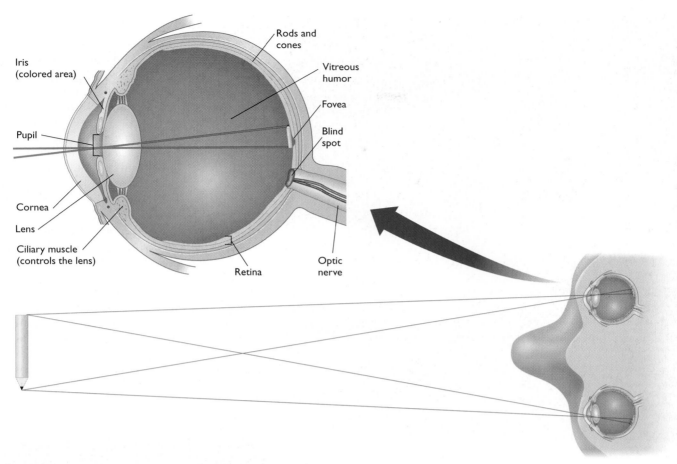

Figure 4.2 The lens gets its name from the Latin word *lens*, meaning "lentil." This reference to its shape is an appropriate choice, as this cross-section of the eye shows. The names of other parts of the eye also refer to their appearance.

and let the lens become thinner and flatter, as shown in Figure 4.3a. When we look at a close object, our eye muscles tighten and make the lens thicker and rounder (Figure 4.3b). In old age, the lens becomes rigid, and people find it harder to focus on nearby objects.

The **fovea** (FOE-vee-uh), *the central area of the human retina,* is adapted for highly detailed vision (see Figure 4.2). Of all retinal areas, the fovea has the greatest density of receptors. Also, more of the cerebral cortex is devoted to analyzing input from the fovea than input from other areas. When you want to see something in detail, you look at it so the light focuses on the fovea.

Hawks, owls, and other predatory birds have a greater density of receptors on the top of the retina (for looking down) than on the bottom of the retina (for looking up). When these birds fly, this arrangement lets them see the ground beneath them in detail. When on the ground, however, they have trouble seeing above themselves (Figure 4.4).

Some common disorders of vision are located in Table 4.1.

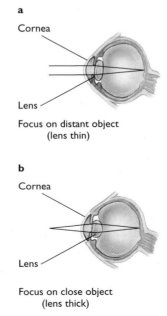

Figure 4.3 The flexible, transparent lens changes shape so that objects (a) far and (b) near can come into focus. The lens bends entering light rays so that they fall on the retina.

Figure 4.4 Birds of prey, such as these owlets, can see down much more clearly than up. In flight that arrangement is helpful. On the ground, they have to turn their heads almost upside down to see above them.

Table 4.1 Common Disorders of Vision

Disorder	
Presbyopia	Impaired ability to focus on nearby objects because of decreased flexibility of the lens.
Myopia	Nearsightedness—impaired ability to focus on distant objects.
Hyperopia	Farsightedness—impaired ability to focus on close objects.
Glaucoma	Condition characterized by increased pressure within the eyeball, which can sometimes impair vision.
Cataract	A disorder in which the lens becomes cloudy.

1. As people grow older, the lens becomes more rigid. How would that rigidity affect vision?

Concept Check

Answer

1. Because the lens is more rigid, older people have less ability to change their focus for objects at different distances. In particular, they find it more difficult to focus on nearby objects—they develop hyperopia.

The Visual Receptors

The visual receptors of the eye, specialized neurons in the retina at the back of the eyeball, are so sensitive that they can respond to a single photon, the smallest possible quantity of light. The two types of visual receptors, cones and rods, differ in function and appearance, as Figure 4.5 shows. The **cones** are *adapted for color vision, daytime vision, and detailed vision.* The **rods** are *adapted for vision in dim light.*

Of the visual receptors in the human retina, about 5% are cones. Although 5% may not sound like much, the parts of the retina containing cones send far more axons to the brain than do the rod-rich areas. Consequently, cone responses dominate the visual parts of the human brain. Most birds have the same or a higher proportion of cones and good color vision. Species that are active mostly at night—rats and mice, for example—have mostly rods, which facilitate detection of faint light.

The proportion of cones is highest toward the center of the retina. The fovea consists solely of cones (see Figure 4.2). Away from the fovea, the proportion of rods increases sharply. For that reason, your color vision becomes weaker toward the periphery of your eye.

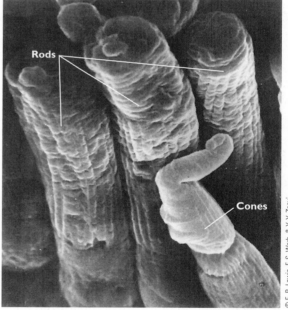

Figure 4.5 Rods and cones seen through a scanning electron micrograph. The rods, which number over 120 million in humans, provide vision in dim light. The 6 million cones in the retina distinguish gradations of color in bright light, enabling us to see that roses are red, magenta, ruby, carmine, cherry, vermilion, scarlet, and crimson—not to mention pink, yellow, orange, and white. (Reprinted from *Brain Research*, Vol. 15, 1969, E. R. Lewis, F. S. Werb, & Y. Y. Zeevi, Scanning electron microscopy of vertebrate visual receptors, pp. 559–562. Copyright 1969, with permission from Elsevier.)

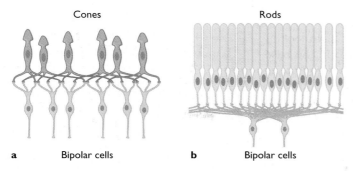

Cones   Rods

a   Bipolar cells   **b**   Bipolar cells

Figure 4.6 Because so many rods converge their input into the next layer of the visual system, known as bipolar cells, even a small amount of light falling on the rods stimulates the bipolar cells. Thus, the periphery of the retina, with many rods, readily detects faint light. However, because bipolars in the periphery get input from so many receptors, they have only imprecise information about the location and shape of objects.

Try this experiment: Hold several pens or pencils of different colors behind your back. (Any objects will work if they are similar in size, shape, and brightness.) Pick one at random without looking at it. Hold it behind your head and bring it slowly into your field of vision. When you just barely begin to see it, you will probably not see its color. You can also try an Online Try It Yourself activity. Go to **www.cengage.com/kalat.** Navigate to the student website, then to the Online Try It Yourself section, and click Color Blindness in Visual Periphery.

Rods are more effective than cones for detecting dim light for two reasons: First, a rod is more responsive to faint stimulation than a cone is. Second, the rods pool their resources. Only a few cones converge their messages onto the next cell, called a *bipolar cell,* whereas many rods converge their messages. In the far periphery of the retina, more than 100 rods send messages to a bipolar cell (Figure 4.6). Thus, faint stimulation of a few rods can combine forces to stimulate the bipolar cell. Table 4.2 summarizes some of the key differences between rods and cones.

2. Why is it easier to see a faint star in the sky if you look slightly to the side of the star instead of straight at it?

Answer

2. The center of the retina consists entirely of cones. If you look slightly to the side, the light falls on an area of the retina that consists partly of rods, which are more sensitive to faint light.

Table 4.2 Differences between Rods and Cones

	Rods	Cones
Shape	Nearly cylindrical	Tapered at one end
Prevalence in human retina	90–95%	5–10%
Abundant in	All vertebrate species	Species active during the day (birds, monkeys, apes, humans)
Area of the retina	Toward the periphery	Toward the fovea
Important for color vision?	No	Yes
Important for detail?	No	Yes
Important in dim light?	Yes	No
Number of types	Just one	Three

Dark Adaptation

Suppose you go into a basement at night looking for a flashlight. The only light bulb in the basement is burned out. A little moonlight comes through the basement windows, but not much. At first, you hardly see anything, but as time passes, your vision gradually improves. *Gradual improvement in the ability to see in dim light* is called **dark adaptation.**

Here is the mechanism: Exposure to light chemically alters molecules called *retinaldehydes,* thereby stimulating the visual receptors. (Retinaldehydes are derived from vitamin A.) Under moderate light the receptors *regenerate* (rebuild) the molecules as fast as the light alters them, and the person maintains a constant level of visual sensitivity. In darkness or dim light, however, the receptors regenerate their molecules without interruption, and the ability to detect faint light improves.

Cones and rods adapt at different rates. When we enter a dark place, our cones regenerate their retinaldehydes faster than the rods do, but by the time the rods finish their regeneration, they are far more sensitive to faint light than the cones are. At that point, we see mostly with rods.

Here is how a psychologist demonstrates dark adaptation (E. B. Goldstein, 2007): You enter a room that is completely dark except for a tiny flashing light. You use a knob to continually adjust the light so that you can barely see it. Over 3 or 4 minutes, you gradually decrease the intensity of the light, as shown in Figure 4.7a. Note that a decrease in the intensity of the light indicates increased sensitivity of your eyes. If you stare straight at the point of light, your results demonstrate the adaptation of your cones to the dim light. (You are focusing the light on your fovea, which has no rods.)

Now the psychologist repeats the study with a change in procedure: You stare at a faint light while another light flashes to the side, where it stimulates both rods and cones. You adjust a knob until the flashing light in the periphery is barely visible. (Figure 4.7b shows the results.) During the first 7 to 10 minutes, the results are the same as before. But then your rods become more sensitive than your cones, and you begin to see even fainter lights. Your rods continue to adapt over the next 20 minutes or so.

To demonstrate dark adaptation without any apparatus, try this: At night, turn on one light in your room. Close one eye and cover it tightly with your hand for a minute or more. Your covered eye will adapt to the dark while your open eye remains adapted to the light. Then turn

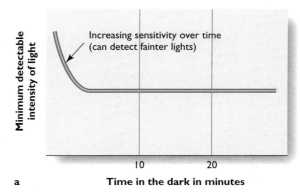

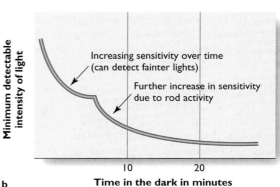

Figure 4.7 These graphs show dark adaptation to (a) a light you stare at directly, using only cones, and (b) a light in your peripheral vision, which you see with both cones and rods. (Based on E. B. Goldstein, 1989)

off the light and open both eyes. You will see better with your dark-adapted eye than with the light-adapted eye. (This instruction assumes you still have some faint light coming through a window. In a *completely* dark room, of course, you see nothing.)

3. You may have heard people say that cats can see in total darkness. Is that possible?

4. After you have thoroughly adapted to extremely dim light, will you see more objects in your fovea or in the periphery of your eye?

Answers

3. Like people, cats adapt to dim light. No animal, however, can see in complete darkness. Vision is the detection of light that strikes the eyes.

4. You will see more objects in the periphery. The fovea contains only cones, which cannot become as sensitive as the rods in the periphery.

The Visual Pathway

If you or I were designing an eye, we would probably run connections from the receptors directly back to the brain. Your eyes are built differently. The visual receptors send their impulses *away from* the brain, toward the center of the eye, where they make synaptic contacts with neurons called bipolar cells. The bipolar cells make contact with still other neurons, the ganglion cells, which are *neurons that receive their input from the bipolar cells.* The *axons from the ganglion cells join to form* the optic nerve, *which turns around and exits the eye,* as Figures 4.2 and 4.8 show. Half of each optic nerve crosses to the opposite side of the brain at the optic chiasm (KI-az-m). Most axons of the optic nerve go to the thalamus, which then sends information to the primary visual cortex in the occipital lobe. People vary in the number of axons in the optic nerve. Some have up to three times as many as others. Those with the thickest optic nerves detect fainter or briefer lights and smaller amounts of movement (Andrews, Halpern, & Purves, 1997; Halpern, Andrews, & Purves, 1999).

The *retinal area where the optic nerve exits* is called the blind spot. That part of the retina has no room for receptors because the exiting axons take up all the space. Also, blood vessels enter the eye at this point. Ordinarily, you are unaware of your blind spot.

To illustrate, close your left eye and stare at the center of Figure 4.9; then slowly move the page forward and backward. When your eye is about 25 to 30 cm (10 to 12 inches) away from the page, the lion disappears because it falls into your blind spot. In its place you perceive a continuation of the circle. Also, go to **www.cengage. com/psychology/kalat.** Navigate to the student website, then to the Online Try It Yourself section, and click Filling in the Blind Spot.

In fact, you have tiny "blind spots" throughout your retina because many receptors lie in the shadow of the retina's blood vessels. Your brain fills in the gaps with what "must" be there (Adams & Horton, 2002).

We become aware of visual information when it reaches the cerebral cortex. Someone with a damaged visual cortex has no conscious visual perception, even in dreams, despite normal eyes. However, someone with damaged eyes and an intact brain can still imagine visual scenes. One

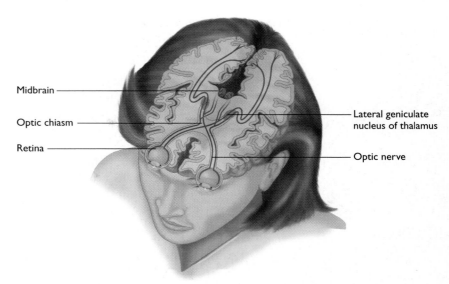

Figure 4.8 Axons from ganglion cells in the retina depart the eye at the blind spot and form the optic nerve. In humans, about half the axons in the optic nerve cross to the opposite side of the brain at the optic chiasm.

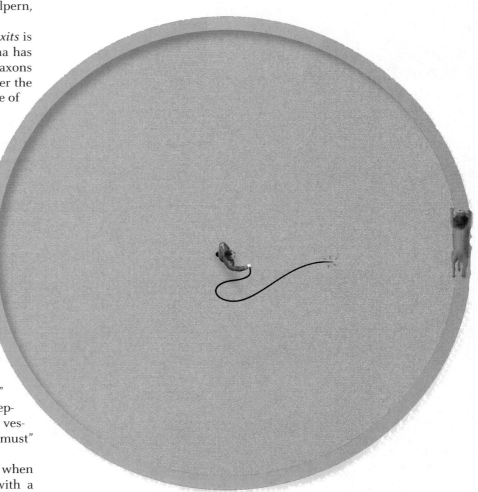

Figure 4.9 Close your left eye and focus your right eye on the animal trainer. Move the page toward your eyes and away from them until the lion on the right disappears. At that point, the lion is focused on the blind spot of your retina, where you have no receptors.

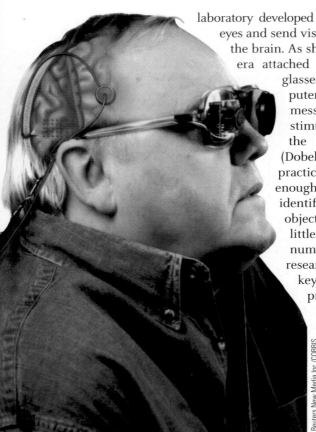

laboratory developed a way to bypass damaged eyes and send visual information directly to the brain. As shown in Figure 4.10, a camera attached to a blind person's sunglasses sends messages to a computer, which then sends messages to electrodes that stimulate appropriate spots in the person's visual cortex (Dobelle, 2000). After hours of practice, such people see well enough to find their way around, identify simple shapes, and count objects. However, the vision has little detail because of the small number of electrodes. Further research is underway with monkeys in hopes of developing a practical aid for people who are blind (Bradley et al., 2005).

Figure 4.10 William Dobelle developed an apparatus that takes an image from a camera attached to sunglasses, transforms it, and sends a message to electrodes in the visual cortex. By this means, someone with damaged eyes regains partial vision.

COLOR VISION

How does the visual system convert different wavelengths into a perception of color, as in Figure 4.1? The process begins with three kinds of cones. Later, cells in the visual path code this wavelength information in terms of pairs of opposites—red versus green, yellow versus blue, and white versus black. Finally, cells in the cerebral cortex compare the input from various parts of the visual field to synthesize a color experience. Let's examine these stages in turn.

The Trichromatic Theory

Thomas Young was an English physician of the 1700s who, among other accomplishments, helped to decode the Rosetta stone (making it possible to understand Egyptian hieroglyphics), introduced the modern concept of energy, revived and popularized the wave theory of light, showed how to calculate annuities for insurance, and offered the first theory about how people perceive color (Martindale, 2001). His theory, elaborated and modified by Hermann von Helmholtz in the 1800s, came to be known as the **trichromatic theory,** or the **Young-Helmholtz theory.** It is called *trichromatic* because it states that our receptors respond to three primary colors. In modern terms, we say that *color vision depends on the response rates of three types of cones* (Figure 4.11). One type is most sensitive to short wavelengths (which we generally see as blue), another to medium wavelengths (green), and another to long wavelengths (red). Each wavelength prompts varying levels of activity in the three types of cones. For example, green light excites mostly the medium-wavelength cones, red light excites mostly the long-wavelength cones, and yellow light excites the medium-wavelength and long-wavelength cones about equally. Every wavelength of light produces its own distinct ratio of responses by the three kinds of cones. White light excites all three kinds equally.

Young and Helmholtz proposed their theory long before anatomists confirmed the existence of three types of cones (Wald, 1968). Helmholtz found that observers could mix various amounts of three wavelengths of light to match all other colors. (Mixing lights is different from mixing paints. Mixing yellow and blue *paints* produces green; mixing yellow and blue *lights* produces white.)

The short-wavelength cones, which respond most strongly to blue, are less numerous than the other types of cones. Consequently, a tiny blue point may look black. For the retina to detect blueness, the blue must extend over a moderately large area. *Try It Yourself* Figure 4.12 illustrates this effect.

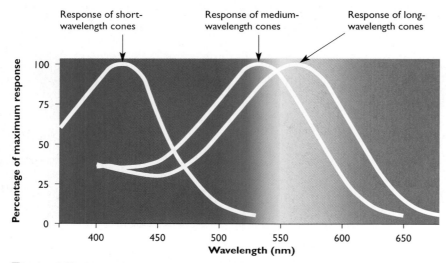

Figure 4.11 Sensitivity of three types of cones to different wavelengths of light. (Based on data of Bowmaker & Dartnall, 1980)

Figure 4.12 Blue dots look black unless they cover a sizable area. Count the red dots; then count the blue dots. Try again while standing farther from the page. You will probably see as many red dots as before but fewer blue dots.

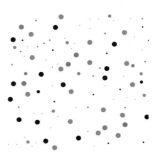

5. According to the trichromatic theory, how does our nervous system tell the difference between bright yellow-green and dim yellow-green light?

Answer

5. Although bright yellow-green and dim yellow-green light evoke the same ratio of activity by the three cone types, the total activity is greater for bright yellow-green light.

The Opponent-Process Theory

Young and Helmholtz were right about how many cones we have, but our perception of color has features that the trichromatic theory does not easily handle. For example, four colors, not three, *seem* primary or basic to most people: red, green, yellow, and blue. Yellow does not seem like a mixture of reddish and greenish experiences, nor is green a yellowish blue. More important, if you stare for a minute or so at something red and look away, you see a green afterimage. If you stare at something green, yellow, or blue, you see a red, blue, or yellow afterimage. The trichromatic theory does not easily explain these afterimages.

Therefore, a 19th-century scientist, Ewald Hering, proposed the **opponent-process theory** of color vision: *We perceive color in terms of paired*

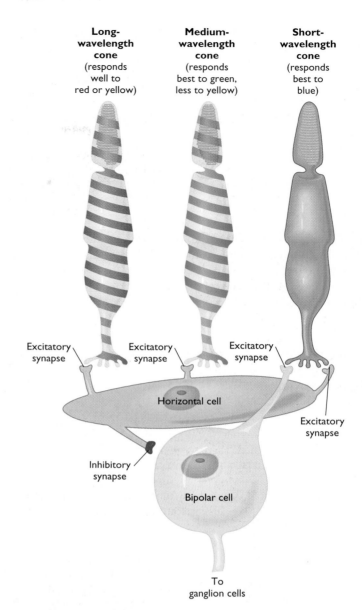

Figure 4.14 A hypothetical way to explain negative afterimages in terms of cells in the retina. Input from short-wavelength cones excites this bipolar cell, and input from other wavelengths inhibits it. If prolonged stimulation with short wavelengths (blue) fatigues the bipolar cell, it will rebound to decreased activity, perceived as yellow.

Figure 4.13 Stare at one of Daffy's pupils for a minute or more under a bright light without moving your eyes. Then look at a plain white or gray background. You will see a negative afterimage.

opposites—red versus green, yellow versus blue, and white versus black. This idea is best explained with the example in Figure 4.13. *Please do this now.*

When you looked away, you saw the cartoon in its normal coloration. After staring at something blue, you get a yellow afterimage. After staring at yellow, you see blue; after red, you see green; after green, you see red; after white, black; and after black, white. *Experiences of one color after the removal of another* are called **negative afterimages.**

Presumably, the explanation depends on cells somewhere in the nervous system that increase their activity in the presence of, say, blue, and decrease it in the presence of yellow. Figure 4.14 shows a possible wiring diagram. However, this simple explanation faces a problem: Stare at the center of Figure 4.15 for a minute or more, and then look at a white surface. The afterimage you see is red on the outside, as expected. But you see *green,* not gray

Figure 4.15 Stare at the center for a minute or more and then look at a white surface. What color do you see in the center?

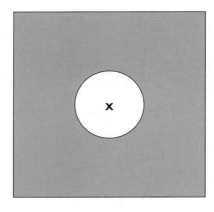

or black, for the inside circle. Your perception of the inside depended on the surrounding context. That result strongly implies that the negative afterimage, and indeed color perception in general, depends on the cerebral cortex, not just interactions within the retina.

try it yourself

6. Which theory explains negative color afterimages?
7. The negative afterimage that you created by staring at Figure 4.13 may seem to move against the background. Why doesn't it stay in one place?

Concept Check

Answers

6. The opponent-process theory most easily explains negative color afterimages because it assumes that we perceive colors in terms of paired opposites, such as red vs. green.
7. The afterimage is on your eye, not on the background. When you try to focus on a different part of the afterimage, you move your eyes and the afterimage moves with them.

Figure 4.16 (a) When the block is under yellow light (left) or blue light (right), you still recognize the colors of individual squares. Parts b and c show what happens if we remove the context: The "blue" squares in the left half of part a and the "yellow" squares in the right half are actually grayish. (*Why We See What We Do*, by D. Purves and R. B. Lotto, figure 6.10, p. 134. Copyright 2003 Sinauer Associates, Inc. Reprinted by permission.)

The Retinex Theory

Suppose you look at a large white screen illuminated with green light in an otherwise dark room. How would you know whether this is a white screen illuminated with green light or a green screen illuminated with white light? Or a blue screen illuminated with yellow light? You wouldn't know. Now someone wearing a brown shirt and blue jeans stands in front of the screen. Suddenly, you see the shirt as brown, the jeans as blue, and the screen as white, even though all the objects are reflecting mostly green light. The point is we perceive color by comparing the light one object reflects to the light that other objects reflect. As a result, we perceive blue jeans as blue and bananas as yellow regardless of the type of light. This *tendency of an object to appear nearly the same color under a variety of lighting conditions* is called **color constancy** (Figure 4.16).

In response to such observations, Edwin Land (the inventor of the Polaroid Land camera) proposed the **retinex theory.** According to this theory, *we perceive color when the cerebral cortex compares various retinal patterns.* (*Retinex* is a combination of the words *retina* and *cortex*.) The cerebral cortex compares the patterns of light coming from different areas and synthesizes a color perception for each area (Land, Hubel, Livingstone, Perry, & Burns, 1983; Land & McCann, 1971).

As Figure 4.16 emphasizes, we should not call short-wavelength light "blue" or long-wavelength light "red." A gray square can look blue in one context and yellow in another (Lotto & Purves, 2002; Purves & Lotto, 2003). The color is something our brain constructs, not a property of the light itself.

Vision researchers consider the trichromatic, opponent-process, and retinex theories correct with regard to different aspects of vision. The trichromatic correctly states that human color vision starts with three kinds of cones. The opponent-process theory explains how later cells organize color information. The retinex theory adds the final touch, noting that the cerebral cortex compares color information from various parts of the visual field.

Color Vision Deficiency

Centuries ago, people assumed that anyone who was not blind could see and recognize colors (Fletcher & Voke, 1985). Then during the 1600s, the phenomenon of color vision deficiency (or colorblindness) was unambiguously recognized. Here was the first clue that color vision is a function of our eyes and brains and not just of the light itself.

The older term color*blindness* is misleading because very few people are totally unable to dis-

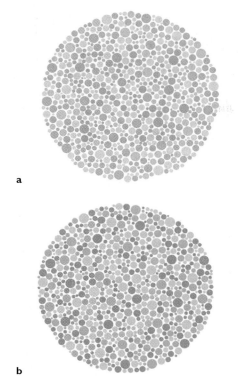

a

b

Figure 4.17 These items provide an informal test for red-green color vision deficiency, an inherited condition that mostly affects men. What do you see? Compare your answers to answer A on page 108. (Reproduced from *Ishihara's Test for Colour Deficiency*, Isshinkai Foundation, Tokyo, Japan. A test for color deficiency cannot be conducted with this material. For accurate testing, the original plate should be used. The reproduced figures are not good for examining the individual's color sensation.)

need two such genes to develop the condition because they have two X chromosomes. Red-green color-deficient people have only two kinds of cones, the short-wavelength cone and either the long-wavelength or the medium-wavelength cone (Fletcher & Voke, 1985).

Figure 4.17 gives a crude but usually satisfactory test for red-green color vision deficiency. What do you see in each part of the figure?

How does the world look to people with color vision deficiency? They describe the world with all the usual color words: Roses are red, bananas are yellow, and grass is green. But their answers do not mean that they perceive colors the same as other people do. Most cannot tell us what a "red" rose actually looks like. Certain rare individuals, however, are red-green color deficient in one eye but have normal vision in the other eye. Because they know what the color words really mean (from experience with their normal eye), they can describe what their deficient eye sees. They say that objects that look red or green to the normal eye look yellow or yellow-gray to the other eye (Marriott, 1976).

If you have normal color vision, Figure 4.18 will show you what it is like to be color deficient. First, cover part b, a typical item from a color deficiency test, and stare at part a, a red field, under a bright light for about a minute. (The brighter the light and the longer you stare, the greater the effect will be.) Then look at part b. Staring at the red field fatigued your long-wavelength cones, weakening your red sensation.

Now stare at part c, a green field, for about a minute and look at part b again. Because you have fatigued your green cones, the figure in b will stand out even more strongly than usual. In fact certain people with red-green color deficiency may be able to see the number in b only after staring at c.

tinguish colors. About 8% of men and less than 1% of women have difficulty distinguishing red from green (Bowmaker, 1998). The cause is a recessive gene on the X chromosome. Because men have only one X chromosome, they need just one gene to become red-green color deficient. Women

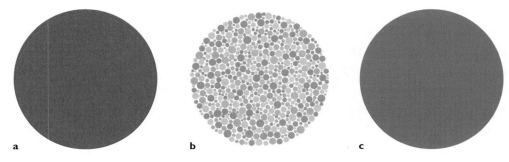

a   **b**   **c**

Figure 4.18 First, stare at pattern (a) under bright light for about a minute and then look at (b). What do you see? Next stare at (c) for a minute and look at (b) again. Now what do you see? See answer B on page 108. (Reproduced from *Ishihara's Test for Colour Deficiency*, Isshinkai Foundation, Tokyo, Japan. A test for color deficiency cannot be conducted with this material. For accurate testing, the original plate should be used. The reproduced figures are not good for examining the individual's color sensation.)

In Closing

Vision as an Active Process

Before the existence of people or other color-sighted animals on Earth, was there any color? *No.* Light was present, to be sure, and different objects reflected different wavelengths of light, but color exists only in brains.

If you take additional courses on sensation and perception, you will discover that the visual system is immensely complex and different from common sense. Your brain has to do an enormous amount of processing to determine what you are seeing. Imagine building a robot with vision. Light strikes the robot's visual sensors, and then . . . what? How will the robot know what objects it sees or what to do about them? All those processes—which we currently can mimic only slightly in a robot—happen in your brain within a fraction of a second.

SUMMARY

- *Common misconceptions.* The eyes do not send out "sight rays," nor does the brain build little copies of the stimuli it senses. It converts or translates sensory stimuli into a code that represents the information. (page 98)
- *Focus.* The cornea and lens focus the light that enters through the pupil of the eye. (page 98)
- *Cones and rods.* The retina contains two kinds of receptors: cones and rods. Cones are specialized for detailed vision and color perception. Rods detect dim light. (page 100)
- *Blind spot.* The blind spot is the area of the retina through which the optic nerve exits. This area has no visual receptors and is therefore blind. (page 103)

- *Color vision.* Color vision depends on three types of cones, each sensitive to a particular range of light wavelengths. The cones transmit messages so that later cells in the visual system indicate one color (e.g., blue) by an increase in activity and another color (e.g., yellow) by a decrease. The cerebral cortex compares responses from different parts of the retina to determine color experiences. (page 104)
- *Color vision deficiency.* Complete colorblindness is rare. Certain people have difficulty distinguishing reds from greens for genetic reasons. (page 106)

KEY TERMS

accommodation of the lens (page 98)

blind spot (page 103)

color constancy (page 106)

cone (page 100)

cornea (page 98)

dark adaptation (page 102)

electromagnetic spectrum (page 98)

fovea (page 99)

ganglion cells (page 103)

iris (page 98)

lens (page 98)

negative afterimage (page 105)

opponent-process theory (page 105)

optic nerve (page 103)

perception (page 97)

pupil (page 98)

receptor (page 98)

retina (page 98)

retinex theory (page 106)

rod (page 100)

sensation (page 97)

stimulus (page 98)

trichromatic theory
(or Young-Helmholtz theory)
(page 104)

ANSWERS TO OTHER QUESTIONS IN THE MODULE

A. In Figure 4.17a, a person with normal color vision sees the numeral 74; in Figure 4.17b, the numeral 8.

B. In Figure 4.18b, you should see the numeral 29. After you have stared at the red circle in part a, the 29 in part b may look less distinct than usual, as though you were red-green color defi-

cient. After staring at the green circle, the 29 may be even *more* distinct than usual. If you do not see either of these effects at once, try again, but this time stare at part a or c longer *and* continue staring at part b a little longer. The effect does not appear immediately.

The Nonvisual Senses

• How do hearing, the vestibular sense, skin senses, pain, taste, and smell work?

Consider these common expressions:

- I *see* what you mean.
- I *feel* your pain.
- I am deeply *touched* by everyone's support and concern.
- The Senate will *hold* hearings on the budget proposal.
- She is a person of fine *taste.*
- He was *dizzy* with success.
- The policies of this company *stink.*
- That *sounds* like a good job offer.

Each sentence expresses an idea in terms of sensation. The metaphorical use of sensation terms is no accident. Our thinking and brain activity deal mostly or entirely with sensory stimuli. Perhaps you doubt that assertion: "What about abstract concepts?" you might object. "Sometimes, I think about numbers, time, love, justice, and all sorts of other nonsensory concepts." Yes, but how did you learn those concepts? Didn't you learn numbers by counting objects you could see or touch? Didn't you learn about time by observing changes in sensory stimuli? Didn't you learn about love and justice from specific events that you saw, heard, and felt? Could you explain any abstract concept without referring to something you detected with your senses?

We have already considered how we detect light. Now let's discuss how we detect sounds, head tilt, skin stimulation, and chemicals.

HEARING

What we familiarly call the "ear" is a fleshy structure technically known as the *pinna.* It funnels sounds to the inner ear, where the receptors lie. The mammalian ear converts sound waves into mechanical displacements along a row of receptor cells. Sound waves are *vibrations of the air or of another medium.* They vary in frequency and amplitude (Figure 4.19). The frequency of a sound wave is the number of *cycles (vibrations) that it goes through per second,* designated hertz (Hz). Pitch is a *perception closely related to frequency.* We perceive a high-frequency sound wave as high pitched and a low-frequency sound as low pitched.

Loudness is a *perception that depends on the amplitude of sound waves*—that is, their intensity. Other things being equal, the greater the amplitude of a sound, the louder it sounds. Because loudness is a psychological experience, however, other factors influence it also. For example, someone who speaks rapidly seems louder than someone speaking slowly at the same amplitude.

The ear converts relatively weak sound waves into more intense waves of pressure in the *fluid-filled canals of the snail-shaped organ* called the cochlea (KOCK-lee-uh), *which contains the receptors for hearing* (Figure 4.20). When sound waves strike the eardrum, they cause it to vibrate. The eardrum connects to three tiny bones: the hammer, the anvil, and the stirrup (also known by their Latin names: malleus, incus, and stapes). As the weak vibrations of the large eardrum travel through these bones, they are transformed into stronger vibrations of the much smaller stirrup. The stirrup in turn transmits the vibrations to the fluid-filled cochlea, where the vibrations displace hair cells along the basilar (BASS-uh-ler) membrane in the cochlea. These hair cells, which act like touch receptors on the skin, connect to neurons whose axons form the auditory nerve. The auditory nerve transmits impulses to the brain areas responsible for hearing.

Understanding the mechanisms of hearing helps us explain hearing loss. One kind of hearing loss is conduction deafness, which *results when the bones connected to the eardrum fail to transmit sound waves properly to the cochlea.*

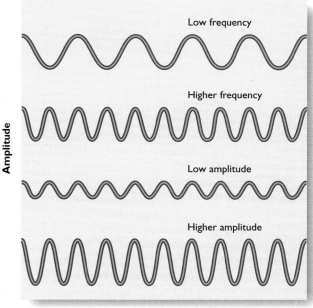

Low frequency

Higher frequency

Low amplitude

Higher amplitude

Amplitude

0.1 second

Figure 4.19 The period (time) between the peaks of a sound wave determines the frequency of the sound. We experience frequencies as different pitches. The vertical range, or amplitude, of a wave determines the sound's intensity and loudness.

Figure 4.20 Sound waves vibrate the eardrum (a). Three tiny bones—the hammer, anvil, and stirrup—convert the eardrum's vibrations into vibrations in the fluid-filled cochlea (b). These vibrations displace hair cells along the basilar membrane in the cochlea, which is aptly named after the Greek word for *snail*. Here, the dimensions of the cochlea have been changed to make the general principles clear.

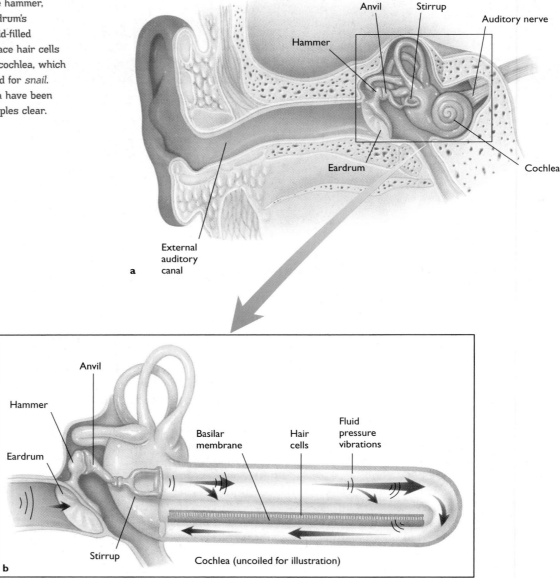

Surgery can sometimes correct conduction deafness by removing whatever is obstructing the bones' movement. People with conduction deafness still hear their own voice because it is conducted through the skull bones to the cochlea, bypassing the eardrum altogether. The other type of hearing loss is nerve deafness, which *results from damage to the cochlea, the hair cells, or the auditory nerve.* Nerve deafness can result from disease, heredity, or exposure to loud noises. Surgery cannot correct nerve deafness. Hearing aids can compensate for hearing loss in most people with either type of deafness (Moore, 1989). Hearing aids merely increase the intensity of the sound, however, so they do not help in cases of severe nerve deafness.

People with damage to certain parts of the cochlea have trouble hearing only the high or medium-range frequencies. Modern hearing aids can be adjusted to intensify one set of frequencies and not another.

Pitch Perception

Adult humans hear sound waves from about 15–20 hertz to about 15,000–20,000 Hz (cycles per second). The upper limit of hearing declines with age and also after exposure to loud noises. Thus, children hear higher frequencies than adults do. Low frequencies are perceived as low pitch, and high frequencies are perceived as high pitch, but frequency is not the same as pitch. For example, doubling the frequency doesn't make the pitch seem twice as high; it makes it one octave higher.

We hear pitch by different mechanisms at different frequencies. At low frequencies (up to about 100 Hz), *a sound wave through the fluid of the cochlea vibrates all the hair cells, which produce action potentials in synchrony*

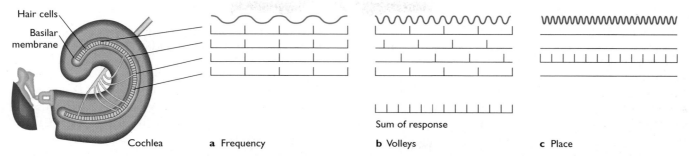

Figure 4.21 (a) At low frequencies, hair cells along the basilar membrane produce impulses in synchrony with the sound waves. (b) At medium frequencies, different cells produce impulses in synchrony with different sound waves, but a volley (group) produces one or more impulses for each wave. (c) At high frequencies, only one point along the basilar membrane vibrates.

with the sound waves. This is the frequency principle. For example, a sound at a frequency of 50 Hz makes each hair cell send the brain 50 impulses per second.

Beyond about 100 Hz, hair cells cannot keep pace. Even so, each sound wave excites at least a few hair cells, and *"volleys" of them (groups) respond to each vibration by producing an action potential* (Rose, Brugge, Anderson, & Hind, 1967). This is known as the volley principle. Thus, a tone at 1000 Hz might send 1,000 impulses to the brain per second, even though no single neuron fires that rapidly. Volleys keep up with sounds up to about 4000 Hz, good enough for almost all speech and music. (The highest note on a piano is 4224 Hz.)

At still higher frequencies, we rely on a different mechanism. At each point along the cochlea, the hair cells are tuned resonators that vibrate only for sound waves of a particular frequency. That is, *the highest frequency sounds vibrate hair cells near the stirrup end, and lower frequency sounds (down to about 100–200 Hz) vibrate hair cells at points farther along the membrane* (Warren, 1999). This is the place principle. Tones less than about 100 Hz excite all hair cells equally, and we hear them by the frequency principle. We identify tones from 100 to 4000 Hz by a combination of the volley principle and the place principle. Beyond 4000 Hz, we identify tones only by the place principle. Figure 4.21 summarizes the three principles of pitch perception.

8. Suppose a mouse emits a soft high-frequency squeak in a room full of people. Which kinds of people are least likely to hear the squeak?

9. When hair cells at one point along the basilar membrane become active, we hear a tone at 5000 Hz. What do we hear when the same hair cells double their rate of activity?

Answers

8. Obviously, the people farthest from the mouse are least likely to hear it. In addition, older people would be less likely to hear the squeak because of declining ability to hear high frequencies. Another group unlikely to hear the squeak are those who had damaged their hearing by repeated exposure to loud noises, including loud music.

9. We still hear a tone at 5000 Hz, but it is louder than before. For high-frequency tones, the pitch we hear depends on which hair cells are most active, not on how many impulses per second they fire.

You have heard of people who can listen to a note and identify its pitch by name: "Oh, that's a C-sharp." People either name pitches well or not at all. Hardly anyone is intermediate. The main influence is early, extensive training in music. Not everyone with musical training develops absolute pitch,

Hearing is the sensing of vibrations. Evelyn Glennie, profoundly deaf since childhood, has become a famous percussionist. She detects the vibrations through her stocking feet.

but almost everyone with absolute pitch had extensive musical training (Athos et al., 2007). The ability is more widespread among people who speak tonal languages, such as Vietnamese and Mandarin Chinese, in which children learn from the start to pay close attention to the pitch of a word (Deutsch, Henthorn, Marvin, & Xu, 2006). For example, in Mandarin Chinese, dá (with a rising tone) means dozen, and dà (with a falling tone) means big. You can test yourself for absolute pitch at UCSF Pitch Perfect's website. Go to **www.cengage.com/psychology/kalat** for a current link to this site.

If you are amazed at absolute pitch, your own ability to recognize (though not name) a specific pitch might surprise you. In one study, 48 college students with no special talent or training listened to 5-second segments from television theme songs, played in their normal key or one-half or one note higher or lower. The students usually chose the correct version, but only of programs they had watched (Schellenberg & Trehub, 2003). That is, they remembered the familiar pitches.

You probably also have heard of people who are "tone-deaf." Anyone who is *completely* tone-deaf could not understand speech, as slight pitch changes differentiate one speech sound from another. However, for unknown reasons, some people are impaired at detecting pitch changes and poor at detecting notes that are out of tune (Hyde & Peretz, 2004). Many tone-deaf people have relatives with the same condition, so it probably has a genetic basis (Peretz, Cummings, & Dube, 2007). You can test yourself for tone-deafness at Amusia's website. Go to **www.cengage.com/psychology/kalat** for a current link to this site.

Localization of Sounds

When you hear, the activity is actually in your ear, but you experience the sound as "out there," and you can generally estimate its place of origin. What cues do you use?

The auditory system determines the direction of a sound source by comparing the messages from the two ears. If a sound is coming from a source in front, the messages reach the two ears simultaneously at equal intensity. If it comes from the left, it reaches the left ear first and is more intense there (Figure 4.22). The timing is important for localizing low-frequency sounds. Intensity helps us localize high-frequency sounds.

You also detect the approximate distance of sound sources. If a sound grows louder, you interpret it as coming closer. If two sounds differ in pitch, you assume the higher frequency tone is closer. (Low-frequency tones carry better over distance, so if you hear a high-frequency tone, its source is probably close.) However, loudness and frequency tell you only the *relative* distances, not *absolute* distances. The only cue for absolute distance is the amount of reverberation (Mershon & King, 1975). In a closed room, you first hear the sound waves coming directly from the source and then the waves that reflected off the walls, floor, ceiling, or other objects. If you hear many echoes, you judge the source of the sound to be far away. It is hard to localize sound sources in a noisy room where echoes are hard to hear (McMurtry & Mershon, 1985).

10. Why is it difficult to tell whether a sound is coming from directly in front of or directly behind you?
11. If someone who needs hearing aids in both ears wears one in only the left ear, what will be the effect on sound localization?
12. Suppose you are listening to a monaural (nonstereo) radio. Can the station play sounds that you will localize as coming from different directions, such as left and right? Can it play sounds that you will localize as coming from different distances? Why or why not?

Answers

10. We localize sounds by comparing the input into the left ear with the input into the right ear. If a sound comes from straight ahead or from directly behind us (or from straight above or below), the input into the left and right ears will be identical.
11. Sounds will be louder in the left ear than in the right, and therefore, they may seem to be coming from the left side even when they aren't. (However, a sound from the right will still strike the right ear before the left, so time of arrival at the two ears will compete against the relative loudness.)
12. Various sounds from the radio cannot seem to come from different directions because your localization of a sound depends on comparing the responses of the two ears. However, the radio can play sounds that seem to come from different distances because distance localization depends on the amount of reverberation, loudness, and high-frequency tones, all of which can vary with a single speaker. Consequently, the radio can easily give an impression of people walking toward you or away from you, but not of people walking from side to side.

Figure 4.22 The ear located closest to the sound receives the sound waves first. That cue is important for localizing low-frequency sounds.

THE VESTIBULAR SENSE

Imagine yourself riding a roller coaster with your eyes closed. The up and down, back and forth sensations you feel come from structures called *vestibules* in the inner ear on each side of your head. The **vestibular sense** detects *the tilt of the head, acceleration of the head, and orientation of the head with respect to gravity.* It plays a key role in posture and balance. Intense vestibular sensations are responsible for motion sickness.

The vestibular sense also enables you to keep your eyes fixated on a target as your head moves. When you walk down the street, you can keep your eyes fixated on a street sign, even though your head is bobbing up and down. The vestibular

The vestibular sense plays a key role in posture and balance as it reports the position of the head.

sense detects head movements and compensates with eye movements.

To illustrate, try to read this page while you jiggle the book up and down or side to side, keeping your head steady. Then hold the book steady and move your head up and down and from side to side. You probably find it much easier to read when you are moving your head than when you are jiggling the book. The reason is that your vestibular sense keeps your eyes fixated on the print during head movements. After damage to the vestibular sense, people report blurry vision while they are walking. To read street signs, they must come to a stop.

The vestibular system is composed of three semicircular canals, oriented in three separate directions, and two otolith organs (Figure 4.23b). The *semicircular canals* are lined with hair cells and filled with a jellylike substance. When the body accelerates in any direction, the jellylike substance in the corresponding semicircular canal pushes against the hair cells, which send messages to the brain. The *otolith organs* shown in Figure 4.23b also contain hair cells (Figure 4.23c), which lie next to the *otoliths* (calcium carbonate particles). Depending on which way the head tilts, the particles excite different sets of hair cells. The otolith organs report the direction of gravity and therefore which way is up.

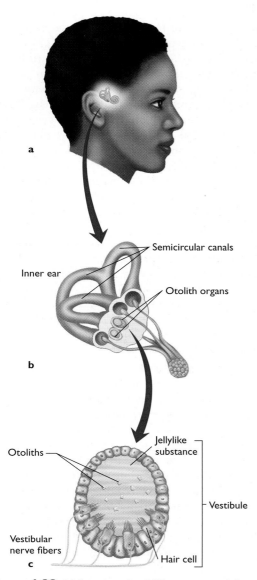

Figure 4.23 (a) Location of and (b) structures of the vestibule. (c) Moving your head or body displaces hair cells that report the tilt of your head and the direction and acceleration of movement.

If the otoliths provide unreliable information, we rely on vision. For astronauts in the zero-gravity environment of outer space, the up–down dimension becomes meaningless. Instead, they learn to rely on visual signals, such as the walls of the ship (Lackner, 1993).

THE CUTANEOUS SENSES

What we commonly think of as touch consists of several partly independent senses: pressure on the skin, warmth, cold, pain, itch, vibration, movement across the skin, and stretch of the skin. These sensations depend on several kinds of receptors, as Figure 4.24 shows (Iggo & Andres, 1982). A pinprick on the skin feels different from a light touch, and both feel different from a burn because each excites different receptors. Collectively, these sensations are known as the **cutaneous senses,** meaning the *skin senses.* Although they are most prominent in the skin, we also have them in our internal organs. Therefore, the cutaneous senses are also known as the *somatosensory system,* meaning *body-sensory system.*

Have you ever wondered about the sensation of itch? Is it a kind of touch, pain, or what? The receptors have not been identified, but we know they are of two kinds. One is stimulated by histamine, a chemical released by tissues recovering from an injury or reacting to a mosquito bite. The other kind responds to chemicals in certain plants (Johanek et al., 2007). Itch is unlike pain; in fact, it is inhibited by pain (Andrew & Craig, 2001). When you scratch an itchy spot, you have to produce some pain to relieve the itch. For example, if

a dentist anesthetizes your mouth for dental surgery, as the anesthesia wears off, the itch receptors recover before the pain and touch receptors. If you scratch the itchy spot, you don't feel the scratch and it does not relieve the itch.

Tickle is another kind of cutaneous sensation. Have you ever wondered why you can't tickle yourself? Some people can, a little, especially when they are just starting to wake up, but it's not the same as when someone else tickles them. The reason is that tickle requires surprise. When you are about to touch yourself, certain parts of your brain build up an anticipation response that is similar to the actual stimulation (Carlsson, Petrovic, Skare, Petersson, & Ingvar, 2000). When you try to tickle yourself, the sensation is no surprise.

Pain

Pain is important for its own sake and because of its relation to depression and anxiety. The experience of pain is a mixture of sensation (information about tissue damage) and emotion (an unpleasant reaction). The sensory and emotional qualities depend on different brain areas (Craig, Bushnell, Zhang, & Blomqvist, 1994; Fernandez & Turk, 1992). The brain area responsive to the emotional aspect—the *anterior cingulate cortex*—also responds to the emotional pain of feeling rejected by other people (Eisenberger, Lieberman, & Williams, 2003) or of watching someone else get hurt (Singer et al., 2004). Physical pain can be very intense at the moment, but emotional pain is more enduring. Try to remember how you felt during a painful injury. Then try to remember how you felt when someone insulted you in public or when a boyfriend or girlfriend broke up with you. Most people relive the emotional pain more intensely (Chen, Williams, Fitness, & Newton, 2008).

The Gate Theory of Pain

You visit a physician because of severe pain, but as soon as the physician tells you the problem is nothing to worry about, the pain starts to subside. Have you ever had such an experience?

Recall the term *placebo* from chapter 2: A placebo is a drug or other procedure that has no important effects other than those that result from people's expectations. Placebos have little effect on most medical conditions, but they often significantly relieve pain, at least its emotional aspect (Hróbjartsson & Gøtzsche, 2001). Even the effects of medicines depend partly on expectations. When people have a catheter in their arm and receive painkilling medicine without knowing it, the drug is less effective than when people know they are receiving it (Amanzio, Pollo, Maggi, & Benedetti, 2001).

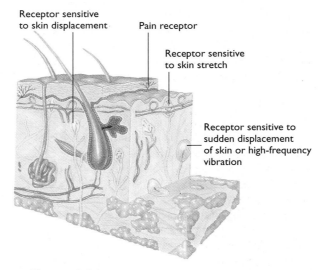

Receptor sensitive to skin displacement

Pain receptor

Receptor sensitive to skin stretch

Receptor sensitive to sudden displacement of skin or high-frequency vibration

Figure 4.24 Cutaneous sensation is the product of many kinds of receptors, each sensitive to a particular kind of information.

In one experiment, college students had a smelly brownish liquid rubbed onto one finger. It was in fact a placebo, but they were told it was a painkiller. Then they were painfully pinched on that finger and a finger of the other hand. They consistently reported less pain on the finger with the placebo (Montgomery & Kirsch, 1996). How placebos work is unclear, but these results eliminate mere relaxation, which should affect both hands equally.

Because of observations such as these, Ronald Melzack and P. D. Wall (1965) proposed the gate theory of pain, the idea that *pain messages must pass through a gate, presumably in the spinal cord, that can block the messages.* That is, other kinds of input close the gate, preventing pain messages from advancing to the brain. For example, if you injure yourself, rubbing the surrounding skin sends inhibitory messages to the spinal cord, closing the pain gates. Pleasant or distracting events also send inhibitory messages. The gate can also enhance the pain messages. For example, inflamed skin (e.g., after sunburn) increases sensitivity of the spinal cord neurons so that almost any stimulation becomes painful (Malmberg, Chen, Tonegawa, & Basbaum, 1997). In short, the activities of the rest of the nervous system facilitate and inhibit pain messages (Figure 4.25).

Ways to Decrease Pain

Some people are completely insensitive to pain. Before you start to envy them, consider: They often burn themselves by picking up hot objects, scald their tongues on hot coffee, cut themselves without realizing it, and sometimes bite off the tip of the tongue. They fail to learn to avoid danger, and many of them die young (Cox et al., 2006).

Although it would be a mistake to rid ourselves of pain altogether, we would like to limit it. One way is to provide distraction. For example, postsurgery patients in a room with a pleasant view complain less about pain, take less painkilling medicine, and recover faster than do patients in a windowless room (Ulrich, 1984). Some hospitals have started simulating natural environments, as postsurgery patients in a room with a view complain less about pain.

Several medications also reduce pain. All pains release the neurotransmitter glutamate, and *intense pain also releases a neurotransmitter called substance P.* Mice that lack substance P receptors react to all painful stimuli as if they were mild (DeFelipe et al., 1998). Other neurons release endorphins, *neurotransmitters that inhibit the release of substance P and thereby weaken pain sensations* (Pert & Snyder, 1973) (see Figure 4.26). The term *endorphin* is a combination of the terms *endogenous*

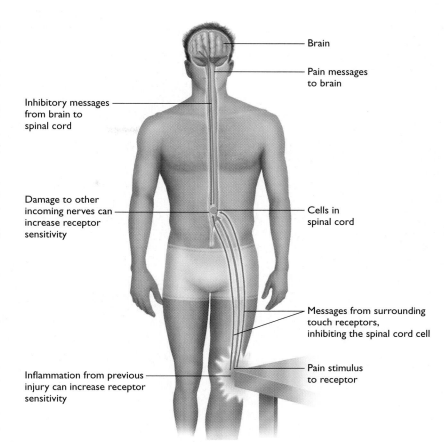

Figure 4.25 Pain messages from the skin are relayed from spinal cord cells to the brain. According to the gate theory of pain, those spinal cord cells serve as a gate that can block or enhance the signal. Green lines indicate axons with excitatory inputs; red lines indicate axons with inhibitory inputs.

(self-produced) and *morphine.* The drug morphine, which stimulates endorphin synapses, has long been known for its ability to inhibit dull, lingering pains. Pleasant experiences, such as sexual activity or thrilling music, also release endorphins (A. Goldstein, 1980). (That effect helps explain why a pleasant view eases postsurgical pain.) In short, endorphins are a powerful way to close pain gates.

Paradoxically, another method of decreasing pain begins by inducing it. The *chemical capsaicin stimulates receptors that respond to painful heat* (Caterina, Rosen, Tominaga, Brake, & Julius, 1999). Capsaicin is the chemical that makes jalapeños and similar peppers taste hot. Injecting capsaicin or rubbing it on the skin produces a temporary burning sensation (Yarsh, Farb, Leeman, & Jessell, 1979). However, as that sensation subsides, the skin loses some of its pain sensitivity. Several skin creams with capsaicin are used to relieve aching muscles. Capsaicin decreases pain because it releases substance P faster than the neurons can resynthesize it. Also, high doses of capsaicin damage pain receptors.

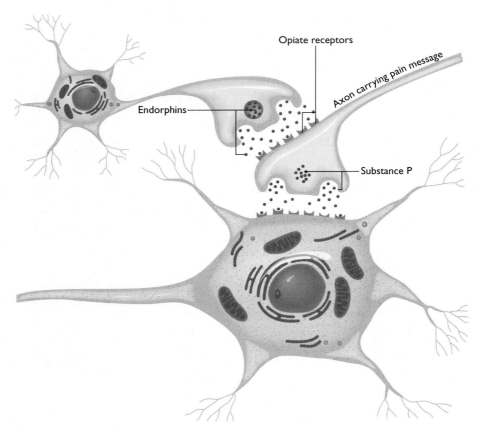

Figure 4.26 Substance P is the neurotransmitter responsible for intense pain sensations. Endorphins block the release of substance P, thereby decreasing pain sensations. Opiates imitate the effects of endorphins.

13. Naloxone, a drug used as an antidote for an overdose of morphine, is known to block the endorphin synapses. How could we use naloxone to determine whether a pleasant stimulus releases endorphins?

14. Psychologist Linda Bartoshuk recommends candies containing moderate amounts of jalapeño peppers as a treatment for pain in the mouth. Why?

Answers

13. Determine how much the pleasant stimulus decreases pain for several people. Then give half of them naloxone and half of them a placebo. Again measure how much the pleasant stimulus decreases the pain. If the pleasant stimulus decreases pain by releasing endorphins, then naloxone should impair its pain-killing effects.

14. The capsaicin in the jalapeño peppers will release substance P faster than it can be resynthesized, thus decreasing the later sensitivity to pain in the mouth.

Phantom Limbs

Some people report *continuing sensations, including pain, in a limb long after it has been amputated.* This phenomenon, known as a **phantom limb**, might last days, weeks, or years after the amputation (Ramachandran & Hirstein, 1998). Physicians and psychologists have long wondered about the cause. Research in the 1990s established that the problem lies within the brain.

Figure 3.20 showed how each part of the somatosensory cortex gets input from a different body area. Figure 4.27a repeats part of that illustration. Part b shows what happens immediately after a hand amputation: The hand area of the cortex becomes inactive because the axons from the hand are inactive. (You might think of the neurons in the hand area of the cortex as "widows" that have lost their partners.) As time passes, axons from the face, which ordinarily excite only the face area of the cortex, grow connections to the nearby hand area of the cortex. From then on, any stimulation of the face continues to excite the face area but now also excites the hand area. When the axons from the face area stimulate the hand area, they produce a hand experience—that is, a phantom limb (Flor et al., 1995; Ramachandran & Blakeslee, 1998).

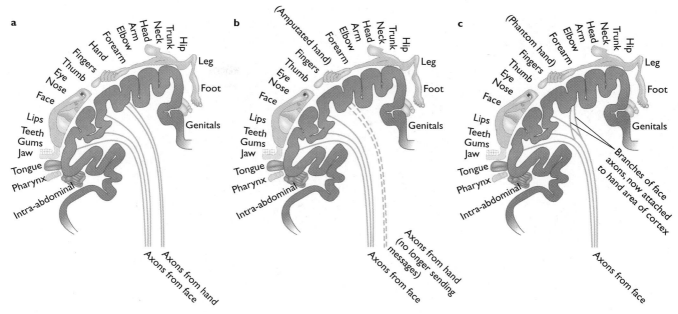

Figure 4.27 (a) Each area in the somatosensory cortex gets input from a different part of the body. (b) If one body part, such as the hand, is amputated, its area of the cortex no longer gets its normal input. (c) However, the axons from a neighboring area branch out to excite the vacated area. Now, any stimulation of the face excites both the face area and the hand area. When the stimulation spreads to the hand area, the sensation feels as if it came from the hand and the face.

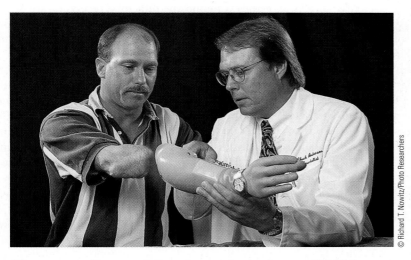

After someone with an amputation gains experience using an artificial limb, phantom limb sensations fade or disappear.

It is possible to relieve phantom sensations: People who learn to use an artificial limb lose their phantoms (Lotze et al., 1999). Evidently, the relevant areas of the cortex start reacting to the artificial limb, and this sensation displaces the abnormal sensations.

15. When would a phantom hand sensation be strongest?

Answer

15. The phantom hand sensation would be strongest when something touches the face.

Concept Check

THE CHEMICAL SENSES

Humans' heavy reliance on vision and hearing is unusual compared to most animals. Most life on Earth consists of small invertebrates that depend on taste and smell to find food and mates. Even most mammals rely heavily on smell. We humans often overlook the importance of these sensations.

Taste

The sense of **taste,** which *detects chemicals on the tongue,* serves just one function: It governs our eating and drinking. The *taste receptors are* in the **taste buds,** *located in the folds on the surface of the tongue,* almost exclusively along the outside edge of the tongue in adults (Figure 4.28). (Children's taste buds are more widely distributed.)

Try this demonstration (based on Bartoshuk, 1991): Soak something small (a cotton swab will do) in sugar water, salt water, or vinegar. Then touch it to the center of your tongue, not too far back. You will feel it but taste nothing. Then slowly move the soaked substance toward the side or front of your tongue. Suddenly, you taste it. If you go in the other direction (first touching the side of the tongue and then moving toward the center), you will continue to taste the substance even at the center of your tongue. The explanation is that your taste buds do not tell you

try it yourself

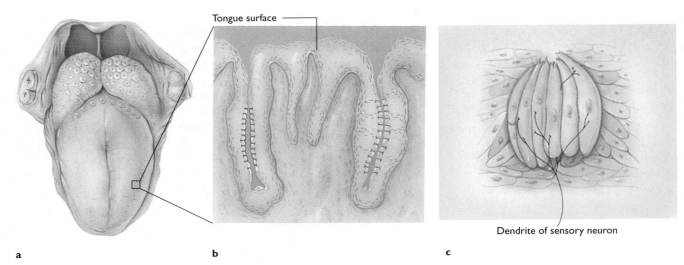

Tongue surface

Dendrite of sensory neuron

a   b   c

Figure 4.28 (a) Taste buds, which react to chemicals dissolved in saliva, are located along the edge of the tongue in adult humans. (b) A cross section through part of the surface of the tongue showing taste buds. (c) A cross section of one taste bud. Each taste bud has about 50 receptor cells within it.

where you taste something. When you stimulate touch receptors on your tongue, your brain interprets the taste perception as coming from the spot where it feels touch.

Types of Taste Receptors

Traditionally, Western cultures have talked about four primary tastes: sweet, sour, salty, and bitter. However, the taste of monosodium glutamate (MSG), common in Asian cuisines, cannot be described in these terms (Kurihara & Kashiwayanagi, 1998; Schiffman & Erickson, 1971), and researchers found a taste receptor specific to MSG (Chaudhari, Landin, & Roper, 2000). English had no word for the taste of MSG (similar to the taste of unsalted chicken soup), so researchers adopted the Japanese word *umami*. Further research found that rodents also have a receptor for the taste of fats (Laugerette, Gaillard, Passilly-Degrace, Niot, & Besnard, 2007). Perhaps humans do, too.

Bitter taste is puzzling because such diverse chemicals taste bitter. The only thing they have in common is being poisonous or at least harmful in large amounts. How could such diverse chemicals all excite the same receptor? The answer is, they don't. We have 25 or more kinds of bitter receptors, each sensitive to different types of chemicals (Adler et al., 2000; Behrens, Foerster, Staehler, Raguse, & Meyerhof, 2007; Matsunami, Montmayeur, & Buck, 2000). Any chemical that excites any of these receptors produces the same bitter sensation. One consequence is that a wide variety of harmful chemicals taste bitter. Another consequence is that we do not have many of any one kind of bitter receptor, and we do not detect low concentrations of bitter chemicals.

Smell

The *sense of smell* is known as olfaction. The olfactory receptors, located on the mucous membrane in the rear air passages of the nose (Figure 4.29), detect the presence of certain airborne molecules. Chemically, olfactory receptors are much like synaptic receptors. The axons of the olfactory receptors form the olfactory tract, which extends to the olfactory bulbs at the base of the brain.

The human sense of smell is not as good as that of dogs or many other species, but it is better than we might guess. We watch a dog track someone through the woods and think, "Wow, I could never do that." Well, of course not, if you stand up with your nose far above the ground. Experimenters asked young adults to get down on all fours, touch their nose to the ground, and try to follow a scent trail, blindfolded. Most succeeded, as shown in Figure 4.30 (J. Porter et al., 2007).

How many kinds of olfactory receptors do we have? Until 1991, researchers did not know. In contrast, researchers in the 1800s established that people have three kinds of color receptors. They used behavioral methods, showing that people can mix three colors of light in various amounts to match any other color. Regarding olfaction, however, no one reported comparable studies. Can people match all possible odors by mixing appropriate amounts of three, four, seven, ten, or some other number of odors?

It is good that no one spent a lifetime trying to find out. Linda Buck and Richard Axel (1991), using modern biochemical technology, demonstrated that the human nose has hundreds of types of olfactory receptors. Rats and mice have about a thousand (Zhang & Firestein, 2002). Each

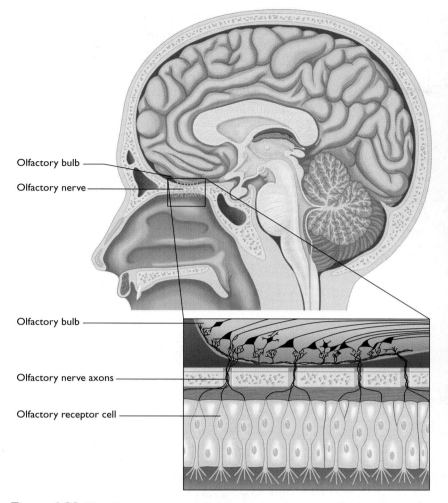

Olfactory bulb
Olfactory nerve

Olfactory bulb

Olfactory nerve axons

Olfactory receptor cell

Figure 4.29 The olfactory receptor cells lining the nasal cavity send information to the olfactory bulb in the brain.

Figure 4.30 The yellow line shows a path of chocolate odor. The red line is the path traced by a person trying to follow the odor. (Reprinted by permission from Macmillan Publishers Ltd. From *Nature Neuroscience, 10,* 27–29, Mechanisms of scent-tracking in humans, J. Porter, et. al, 2007.)

olfactory receptor detects only a few closely related chemicals (Araneda, Kini, & Firestein, 2000). Much remains to be learned about how the brain processes olfactory information (Figure 4.31).

Many odors produce strong emotional responses. People who lose the sense of smell lose much of their joy in life and in many cases become more and more depressed (Herz, 2007). Food without its smell loses much of its flavor. Intimate contact with a loved one becomes less enjoyable.

Our emotional reactions to odors are not built-in, however. Americans experience wintergreen odor only in association with candy. In Britain, wintergreen is often included in rub-on pain medications. Guess what: Most Americans like the odor, and British people do not. That is, culture does not modify the sensation itself but modifies the emotional reaction to it. One woman reported hating the smell of roses because she first smelled them at her mother's funeral. Another woman reported liking the smell of skunk

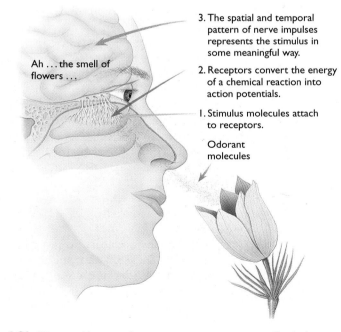

Ah ... the smell of flowers ...

3. The spatial and temporal pattern of nerve impulses represents the stimulus in some meaningful way.

2. Receptors convert the energy of a chemical reaction into action potentials.

1. Stimulus molecules attach to receptors.

Odorant molecules

Figure 4.31 Olfaction, like any other sensory system, converts physical energy into a complex pattern of brain activity.

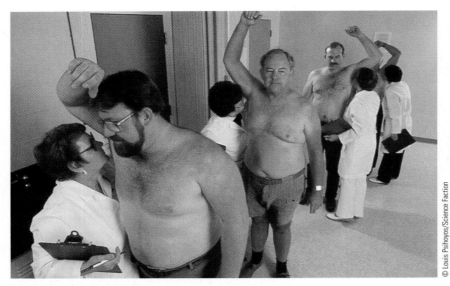

Professional deodorant tester: That's a career option you probably never considered. U.S. industries spend millions of dollars to eliminate the kinds of personal odors that are essential to other mammalian species.

ably as a result of pheromones they secrete (McClintock, 1971).

One study examined women in Bedouin Arab families. In that culture, an unmarried woman has extensive contact with her mother and sisters, almost none with men, and does not use oral contraceptives. Thus, pheromones have a maximum opportunity to show their effects. The results showed that the women within a family usually menstruate within a day or two of one another (Weller & Weller, 1997).

16. How many kinds of taste receptors do we have? How many kinds of olfactory receptors?

Answer

16. We have five kinds of taste receptors (sweet, sour, salty, bitter, and umami). We have hundreds of kinds of olfactory receptors.

SYNESTHESIA

We end our tour of the senses with synesthesia, a *condition in which a stimulus of one type, such as sound, also elicits another experience, such as color.* Researchers estimate that one person in 500 has synesthesia, but the actual number may be higher because some people try to hide an experience that others regard as a sign of mental illness (Day, 2005). (It is not.)

No two people with synesthesia have quite the same experience. In fact, people with this condition sometimes argue about the color of Tuesday or the taste of a melody. It is, however, a real phenomenon, and it is quick and automatic. In one study, people listened to sentences such as, "The clear lake was the most beautiful hue of 7." For people with synesthesia who experienced 7 as "blue," this sentence evoked a strong brain response within a tenth of a second after hearing the 7. For those who experienced 7 as yellow, orange, or some other color, the response was weaker, as it is for people without synesthesia (Brang, Edwards, Ramachandran, & Coulson, 2008). One person with a word-taste synesthesia reported tasting a word before he could think of it. He said he couldn't quite remember what the word was, but it tasted like tuna (Simner & Ward, 2006). One man reported seeing synesthetic colors that he never saw in real life because he was red-green color deficient. He called them "Martian colors" (Ramachandran, 2003). Evidently, although his retina could not send messages for those colors, the brain was organized to perceive them.

For another example, find the 2s and As in the following displays as quickly as possible.

try it yourself

(from a distance) because it reminded her of a joyful trip through the country when she was a child (Herz, 2007).

Suppose I ask you to smell something labeled "odor of Parmesan cheese." You say you like it. Then I say, "Oops, I'm sorry, that was mislabeled. It's actually the smell of vomit." Oh, no! Now you hate the smell—the same smell! "Wait, my mistake. I was right the first time. It really is Parmesan." Now do you like it or not? Your emotional reaction to an odor depends on what you think it is (Herz & von Clef, 2001).

Olfaction serves important social functions, especially in nonhuman mammals that identify one another by means of pheromones, which are *chemicals they release into the environment* (Brennan & Zufall, 2006). For example, a female dog in her fertile and sexually responsive time of year emits pheromones that attract every male dog in the neighborhood. Pheromones act on the vomeronasal organ, a set of receptors near, but separate from, the standard olfactory receptors (Monti-Bloch, Jennings-White, Dolberg, & Berliner, 1994). Each of those receptors responds to one and only one chemical, identifying it at extremely low concentrations (Leinders-Zufall et al., 2000).

Most humans prefer *not* to recognize one another by smell. The deodorant and perfume industries exist for the sole purpose of removing and covering up human odors. But perhaps we respond to pheromones anyway, unconsciously. For example, young women who are in frequent contact, such as roommates in a college dormitory, tend to synchronize their menstrual cycles, prob-

```
55555555555  55555555555  55555555555  5555555525555
55555555555  555555555525  55555555555  55555555555555
55555555555  55555555555  55525555555  55555555555555
552555555555  55555555555  55555555555  55555555555555
55555555555  55555555555  55555555555  5555555555555

44444444444  44444444444  44444444444  4444444444444
44444444444  44A444444444  44444444444  4444444444444
44444A444444  44444444444  44444444444  4444444A44444
44444444444  44444444444  44444444444  4444444444444
44444444444  44444444444  444444444A44  4444444444444
```

One person with synesthesia found it just as hard as anyone else to find the As among 4s because both looked red to her. However, because 2s look violet and 5s look yellow to her, she was quicker than average to find the 2s, almost as if—but not quite as if—the displays had been printed like this (Laeng, Svartdal, & Oelmann, 2004):

```
555555555555  555555555555  555555555555  5555555525555
555555555555  5555555555525  555555555555  5555555525555
555555555555  555555555555  5552555555555  5555555555555
552555555555  555555555555  555555555555  5555555555555
555555555555  555555555555  555555555555  5555555555555
```

These results are surprising. The colors helped her find the 2s, but somehow her brain had to know the 2s from the 5s *before* it could produce the color experiences. At this point, synesthesia remains a fascinating mystery. Researchers have a few hypotheses about possible causes and brain mechanisms, but so far none are supported strongly.

module 4.2

In Closing

Sensory Systems

The world as experienced by a bat (which hears frequencies up to 100,000 Hz) or a mouse (which depends on its whiskers to explore the world) is in many ways a different world from the one that you and I experience. The function of our senses is not to tell us about everything in the world but to alert us to the information we are most likely to use, given our way of life.

SUMMARY

- *Pitch.* At low frequencies of sound, we identify pitch by the frequency of vibrations of hair cells in our ears. At intermediate frequencies, we identify pitch by volleys of responses from many neurons. At high frequencies, we identify pitch by the location where the hair cells vibrate. (page 110)
- *Localizing sounds.* We localize the source of a sound by detecting differences in the time and loudness of the sounds our two ears receive. We localize the distance of a sound source primarily by the amount of reverberation, or echoes, following the main sound. (page 112)

- *Vestibular system.* The vestibular system tells us about the movement of the head and its position with respect to gravity. It enables us to keep our eyes fixated on an object while the rest of the body is in motion. (page 113)
- *Cutaneous receptors.* We experience many types of sensation on the skin, each dependent on different receptors. Itch is a sensation based on tissue irritation, inhibited by pain. Tickle depends on the unpredictability of the stimulus. (page 114)
- *Pain.* The experience of pain can be greatly inhibited or enhanced by other simultaneous experiences, including touch to surrounding skin or a person's expectations. (page 114)

- *Phantom limbs.* After an amputation, the corresponding portion of the somatosensory cortex stops receiving its normal input. Soon axons from neighboring cortical areas form branches that start exciting the silenced areas of cortex. When they receive the new input, they react in the old way, which produces a phantom sensation. (page 116)
- *Taste receptors.* People have receptors sensitive to sweet, sour, salty, bitter, and umami (MSG) tastes, and possibly fat. We have many kinds of bitter receptors, but not many of any one kind. (page 117)
- *Olfactory receptors.* The olfactory system—the sense of smell—depends on hundreds of types of receptors. Olfaction is important for many behaviors, including food selection and (especially in nonhuman mammals) identification of potential mates. We have strong emotional reactions to many odors based on previous experiences. (page 118)
- *Synesthesia.* Some people have consistent experiences of one sensation evoked by another. For example, they might experience particular letters or numbers as having a color. (page 120)

KEY TERMS

capsaicin (page 115)

cochlea (page 109)

conduction deafness (page 109)

cutaneous senses (page 114)

endorphin (page 115)

frequency principle (page 111)

gate theory (page 115)

hertz (Hz) (page 109)

loudness (page 109)

nerve deafness (page 110)

olfaction (page 118)

phantom limb (page 116)

pheromone (page 120)

pitch (page 109)

place principle (page 111)

sound waves (page 109)

substance P (page 115)

synesthesia (page 120)

taste (page 117)

taste bud (page 117)

vestibular sense (page 113)

volley principle (page 111)

The Interpretation of Sensory Information

- What is the relationship between the world and our perceptions of it?
- Why are we sometimes wrong about what we think we see?

According to a popular expression, "a picture is worth a thousand words." If so, what is a thousandth of a picture worth? One word? Perhaps not even that.

Printed photographs, such as the one on page 120, are composed of a great many dots, which you can see if you magnify the photo, as in Figure 4.32. Although one dot by itself tells us nothing, the pattern of many dots becomes a meaningful picture.

Actually, our vision is like this all the time. Your retina includes about 126 million rods and cones, each of which sees one dot of the visual field. What you perceive is not dots but lines, curves, and objects. Your nervous system starts with a vast amount of information and extracts what is important.

PERCEPTION OF MINIMAL STIMULI

Some of the earliest psychological researchers tried to determine the weakest sounds, lights, and touches that people could detect. They also measured the smallest difference that people could detect between one stimulus and another—the *just noticeable difference* (JND). We considered a little of this research in chapter 1. As is often the case, however, the questions were more complicated than they seemed.

Sensory Thresholds and Signal Detection

Imagine a typical experiment to determine the threshold of hearing—that is, the minimum intensity that one can hear: Participants are presented with tones of varying intensity in random order and sometimes no tone at all. Each time, the participants say whether they heard anything. Figure 4.33 presents typical results. Notice that no sharp line separates sounds that people hear from sounds they do not. Researchers therefore define an absolute sensory threshold as the *intensity at which a given individual detects a stimulus 50% of the time.* However, people sometimes report hearing a tone when none was present. We should not be surprised. Throughout the study, they have been listening to faint tones and saying "yes" when they heard almost nothing. The difference between nothing and almost nothing is slim. Still, if they sometimes report a tone when none was present, we have to be cautious in interpreting all their responses.

When people try to detect weak stimuli, they can be correct in two ways: reporting the presence of a stimulus (a "hit") and reporting its absence (a "correct rejection"). They can also be wrong in two ways: failing to detect a stimulus when present (a "miss") and reporting a stimulus when none was present (a "false alarm"). Figure 4.34 outlines these possibilities.

Signal-detection theory is the *study of people's tendencies to make hits, correct rejections, misses, and false alarms* (D. M. Green & Swets, 1966). The theory originated in engineering, where it applies to such matters as detecting radio signals in the presence of noise. Suppose someone reports a stimulus present on 80% of the trials when it is actually present. That statistic is meaningless unless

Figure 4.32 From a photograph composed of dots, we see objects and patterns.

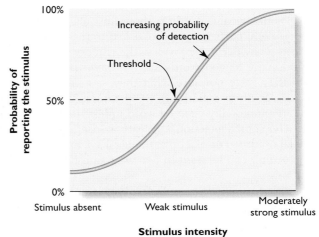

Figure 4.33 Typical results of an experiment to measure an absolute sensory threshold. No sharp boundary separates stimuli that you perceive from those you do not.

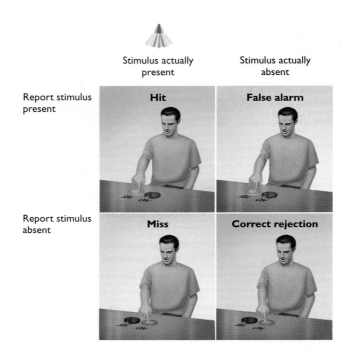

	Stimulus actually present	Stimulus actually absent
Report stimulus present	**Hit**	**False alarm**
Report stimulus absent	**Miss**	**Correct rejection**

Figure 4.34 People make two kinds of correct judgments (green backgrounds) and two kinds of errors (yellow backgrounds). If you tend to say the stimulus is present when you are in doubt, you will get many hits but also many false alarms.

we also know how often the person said it was present when it was not. If the person also reported it present on 80% of trials when it was absent, then the person is just guessing and not really detecting anything at all.

In a signal-detection experiment, people's responses depend on their willingness to risk misses or false alarms. (When in doubt, you have to risk one or the other.) Suppose you are the participant and I tell you that you will receive a 10-cent reward whenever you correctly report that a light is present, but you will be fined 1 cent if you say "yes" when it is absent. When you are in doubt, you guess "yes," with results like those in Figure 4.35a. Then I change the rules: You will receive a 1-cent reward for correctly reporting the presence of a light, but you will suffer a 10-cent penalty and an electrical shock if you report a light when none was present. Now you say "yes" only when you are certain, and the results look like those in Figure 4.35b. In short, people's answers depend on the instructions and their strategies, not just their senses.

People become cautious about false alarms for other reasons, too. In one experiment, participants were asked to read words that flashed briefly on a screen. They performed well with ordinary words such as *river* or *peach*. For emotionally loaded words such as *penis* or *bitch,* however, they generally said they were not sure what they saw. Several explanations are possible (e.g., G. S. Blum & Barbour, 1979). One is that participants hesitate to blurt out an emotionally charged word unless they are certain they are right.

The signal-detection approach is useful in many settings remote from the laboratory. For example, the legal system is also a signal-detection situation. A jury can be right in two ways and wrong in two ways:

	Defendant is guilty	Defendant is innocent
Jury votes "guilty"	Hit	False alarm
Jury votes "not guilty"	Miss	Correct rejection

If you were on a jury and you were unsure, which mistake would you be willing to risk? Most people agree that you should vote "not guilty" because a "miss" (setting a guilty person free) is less bad than a false alarm (convicting an innocent person).

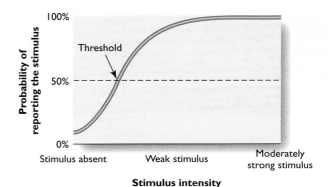

Instructions: You will receive a 10-cent reward for correctly reporting that a light is present. You will be penalized 1 cent for reporting that a light is present when it is not.

a

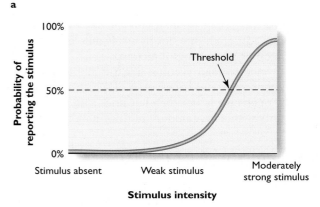

Instructions: You will receive a 1-cent reward for correctly reporting that a light is present. You will be penalized 10 cents *and* subjected to an electric shock for reporting that a light is present when it is not.

b

Figure 4.35 Results of measuring a sensory threshold with different instructions.

Another example is screening baggage at an airport. Because the x-ray images are often ambiguous, the screeners are sure to make mistakes of both kinds—missing dangerous items and issuing false alarms (Wolfe, Horowitz, & Kenner, 2005).

17. Suppose we find that nearly all drug abusers have a particular pattern of brain waves. Can we now use that pattern as a way to identify people with a drug problem? Think about this problem in terms of signal detection.

Concept Check

Answer

17. We have been told the hit rate, but we cannot evaluate it unless we also know the false alarm rate. That is, how many people without a drug problem have this same pattern of brain waves? If that percentage is large, the test is useless.

Subliminal Perception

Subliminal perception is the idea that *stimuli sometimes influence our behavior even when they are presented so faintly or briefly that we do not perceive them consciously.* (*Limen* is Latin for "threshold." Thus, *subliminal* means "below the threshold.") Is subliminal perception powerful, impossible, or something in between?

What Subliminal Perception Cannot Do

Many years ago, claims were made that subliminal messages could control people's buying habits. For example, a theater owner might insert a single frame, "EAT POPCORN," in the middle of a film. Customers who were not aware of the message could not resist it, so they would flock to the concession stand to buy popcorn. Many tests of this hypothesis found little or no effect (Cooper & Cooper, 2002), and the advertiser eventually admitted he had no evidence (Pratkanis, 1992).

Another claim is that certain rock-'n'-roll recordings contain "satanic" messages that were recorded backward and superimposed on the songs. Some people allege that listeners unconsciously perceive these messages and then follow the evil advice. Researchers cannot say whether any rock band ever inserted such a message. (There are a lot of rock bands, after all.) The issue is whether a backward message has any influence. If people hear a backward message, does it influence their behavior? Researchers have recorded various messages (nothing satanic) and asked people to listen to them backward. They have found that people listening to a backward message cannot determine what it would sound like forward, and the messages do not influence behavior in even the subtlest ways (Kreiner, Altis, & Voss, 2003; Vokey & Read, 1985).

A third unsupported claim: "Subliminal audiotapes" with faint, inaudible messages can help you improve your memory, quit smoking, lose weight, raise your self-esteem, and so forth. In one study, psychologists asked more than 200 volunteers to listen to a popular brand of audiotape. However, they intentionally mislabeled some of the self-esteem tapes as "memory tapes" and some of the memory tapes as "self-esteem tapes." After 1 month of listening, most people who *thought* they were listening to self-esteem tapes said they had improved their self-esteem, and those who *thought* they were listening to memory tapes said they had improved their memory. The actual content made no difference. The improvement depended on people's expectations, not the tapes (Greenwald, Spangenberg, Pratkanis, & Eskanazi, 1991).

What Subliminal Perception Can Do

Subliminal messages do produce effects, although most are brief and subtle. For example, people in one study viewed a happy, neutral, or angry face flashed on a screen for less than one thirtieth of a second, followed immediately by a neutral face. Under these conditions, no one reports seeing a happy or angry face, and even if asked to guess, people do no better than chance. However, when they see a happy face, they slightly and briefly move their facial muscles in the direction of a smile. After seeing an angry face, they tense their muscles slightly and briefly in the direction of a frown (Dimberg, Thunberg, & Elmehed, 2000). In a similar study, people viewed subliminal stimuli related to fear (e.g., a growling dog) or disgust (an unflushed toilet). Shortly afterward, they were asked to choose between watching a scary movie and eating a "strange food." Those primed with the subliminal fear stimuli avoided the scary movie, and those primed with the disgust stimuli avoided the strange food (Ruys & Stapel, 2008). In another study, a screen flashed a signal for a participant to make a handgrip response. Shortly prior to this stimulus was a much briefer stimulus indicating whether the reward on that trial could be 1 British pound or 1 British penny. Although people had no conscious perception of the brief stimulus, they made stronger handgrip responses after the signal for the larger reward (Pessiglione et al., 2007).

These effects emerge only as small changes in average performance over many individuals or many trials. However, the fact that subliminal perception affects behavior at all demonstrates the possibility of unconscious influences (Greenwald & Draine, 1997).

....

18. Suppose someone claims that the subliminal words "Don't shoplift," intermixed with music at a store, decrease shoplifting. What would be the best way to test that claim?

Answer

18. Play that message on half of all days, randomly chosen, for a period of weeks. On other days, play no subliminal message or an irrelevant one. See whether the frequency of shoplifting decreases on days with the message.

....

PERCEPTION AND THE RECOGNITION OF PATTERNS

How do you know what you're seeing? Let's start with an apparently simple example: When you look at a light, how does your brain decide how bright it is? We might guess that the more intense the light, the brighter the appearance.

However, perceived brightness depends on comparison to the surrounding objects. Brightness contrast *is the increase or decrease in an object's apparent brightness by comparison to objects around it.* Consider Figure 4.36. Compare the pink bars in the middle left section to those in the middle right. The ones on the right probably look darker, but in fact, they are the same. Also go to **www.cengage.com/psychology/kalat**. Navigate to the student website, then to the Online Try It Yourself section, and click Brightness Contrast.

If two spots on the page reflect light equally, why don't they look the same? When the brain sees something, it uses its past experience to calculate how that pattern of light probably was generated, taking into account all the contextual information (Purves, Williams, Nundy, & Lotto, 2004). In Figure 4.36, you see what appears to be a partly clear white bar covering the center of the left half of the grid, and the pink bars look light. The corresponding section to the right also has pink bars, but these appear to be under the red bars and on top of a white background. Here the pink looks darker because you contrast the pink against the white background above and below it.

If perceiving brightness is that complicated, you can imagine how hard it is to explain face recognition. People are amazingly good at recognizing familiar faces, even after not seeing someone in years (Bruck, Cavanagh, & Ceci, 1991). For a demonstration, go to **www.cengage.com/psychology/kalat**. Navigate to the student website, then to the Online Try It Yourself section, and click Matching High School Photos.

We recognize faces by whole patterns, based on specialized brain areas that are fine-tuned by early experience (Farah, 1992; Kanwisher, 2000;

Figure 4.37 Who is this? We recognize people by hair as well as facial features. If you're not sure who it is, check answer C, page 140.

La Grand, Mondloch, Maurer, & Brent, 2004). Although we attend mostly to facial features, we attend to the hair also. Can you identify the person in Figure 4.37?

The Feature-Detector Approach

How do we recognize patterns? According to one explanation, we begin by breaking a stimulus into its parts. For example, when we look at a letter of the alphabet, *specialized neurons in the visual cortex,* called feature detectors, *respond to the presence of simple features, such as lines and angles.* One neuron might detect the feature "horizontal line," while another detects a vertical line, and so forth.

What's the Evidence?
Feature Detectors

What evidence do we have for feature detectors in the brain? The evidence includes studies of laboratory animals and humans.

First Study

Hypothesis Neurons in the visual cortex of cats and monkeys respond only when light strikes the retina in a particular pattern.

Method Two pioneers in the study of the visual cortex, David Hubel and Torsten Wiesel (1981 Nobel Prize winners in physiology and medicine), inserted thin electrodes into cells of the occipital cortex of cats and monkeys and then recorded the activity of those cells when various light patterns struck the animals' retinas. At first, they used mere

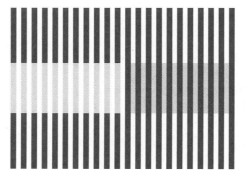

Figure 4.36 The pink bars in the left center area are in fact the same as the pink bars in the right center area, but those on the left seem lighter.

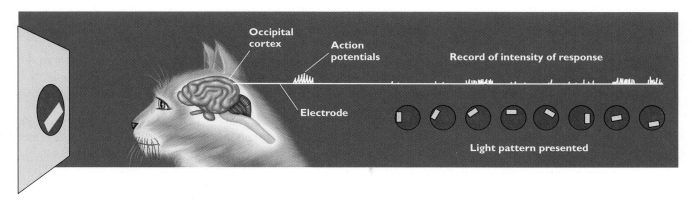

Figure 4.38 Hubel and Wiesel implanted electrodes to record the activity of neurons in the visual cortex. In most cases, a neuron responded vigorously when a portion of the retina saw a bar of light oriented at a particular angle. When the angle changed, that cell became silent but another cell responded.

points of light, which produced little response. Later they tried lines (Figure 4.38).

Results They found that each cell responds best in the presence of a particular stimulus (Hubel & Wiesel, 1968). Some cells become active only when a vertical bar of light strikes a given portion of the retina. Others become active only for a horizontal bar. In other words, such cells appear to be feature detectors. In later experiments, investigators found cells that respond to other features, such as movement in a particular direction.

Interpretation Hubel and Wiesel reported feature-detector neurons in cats and monkeys. If the organization of the visual cortex is similar in species as distantly related as cats and monkeys, it is likely (though not certain) to be similar in humans as well.

A second line of evidence follows this reasoning: If the human cortex contains feature-detector cells, we should be able to fatigue certain cells by overstimulating them. When we look away, we should see an aftereffect created by the inactivity of that type of cell. (Recall the negative afterimage in color vision, as shown by Figure 4.13.) An example is the waterfall illusion: *If you stare at a waterfall for a minute or more and then turn your eyes to nearby cliffs, the cliffs appear to flow upward.* Staring at the waterfall fatigues neurons that respond to downward motion. When you look away, those neurons become inactive, while neurons that respond to upward motion remain active. The difference in relative responses produces an illusion of upward motion. To observe a similar illusion, try the Online Try It Yourself activity. Go to **www.cengage.com/ psychology/kalat**. Navigate to the student website, then to the Online Try It Yourself section, and click Motion Aftereffect.

Here is another demonstration:

Second Study

Hypothesis After you stare at a set of vertical lines, you fatigue the feature detectors that respond to lines of that width. If you then look at wider or narrower lines, they will appear to be even wider or narrower than they really are.

Method Cover the right half of Figure 4.39 and stare at the little rectangle in the middle of the left half for a minute or more. Do not stare at one point, but move your focus around within the rectangle. Then look at the square in the center of the right part of the figure and compare the spacing between the lines of the top and bottom gratings (Blakemore & Sutton, 1969).

Results What did you perceive in the right half? People generally report that the top lines look narrower and the bottom lines look wider.

Interpretation Staring at the left part of the figure fatigues neurons sensitive to wide lines in the top part of the figure and neurons sensitive to narrow lines in the bottom part. Then, when you look at lines of medium width, the fatigued cells become inactive. Therefore, cells sensitive to

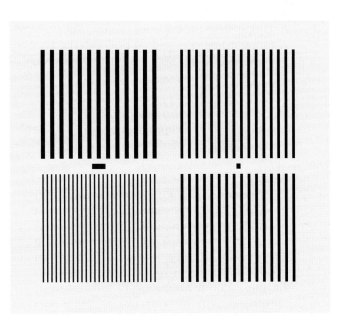

Figure 4.39 To fatigue your feature detectors and create an afterimage, follow the directions in the second study. (From Blakemore & Sutton, 1969)

narrower lines dominate your perception in the top part, and those sensitive to wider lines dominate in the bottom part.

To summarize, two types of evidence support the existence of visual feature detectors: (a) The brains of other species contain cells with the properties of feature detectors, and (b) after staring at certain patterns, we see aftereffects that imply fatigue of feature-detector cells in the brain.

The research just described started an enormous amount of activity by laboratories throughout the world. Later results revised our views of what the earlier results mean. For example, even though certain neurons respond well to a single vertical line,

most respond even more strongly to a sine-wave grating of lines:

Thus, the feature that cells detect is probably more complex than just a line. Furthermore, because each cell responds to a range of stimuli, no cell provides an unambiguous message about what you see at any moment.

An important point about scientific advances: A single line of evidence—even Nobel Prize–winning evidence—seldom provides the final answer to a question. We look for multiple ways to test a hypothesis.

19. What is a feature detector, and what evidence supports the idea of feature detectors?

Concept Check

Answer

19. A feature detector is a neuron that responds mostly in the presence of a particular visual feature, such as a straight horizontal line. One kind of evidence is that recordings from neurons in laboratory animals indicate that each cell responds mainly to a particular kind of stimulus. Another line of evidence is that people who have stared at a stimulus become temporarily less sensitive to that kind of stimulus, implying fatigue of the feature detectors for that stimulus.

Do Feature Detectors Explain Perception?

The neurons just described are active in the early stages of visual processing. Do we simply add up the responses from various feature detectors to perceive a face?

No, feature detectors cannot completely explain how we perceive letters, much less faces. For example, we perceive the words in Figure 4.40a as CAT and HAT, even though the H and A symbols are identical and therefore stimulate the same feature detectors. Likewise, the character in the center of Figure 4.40b can be read as either B or 13. Perception of a pattern requires more than just simple feature detectors.

Gestalt Psychology

Your ability to perceive something in more than one way, as in Figure 4.40, is the basis of Gestalt psychology, *a field that focuses on our ability to perceive overall patterns. Gestalt* (geh-SHTALT) is a German word meaning pattern or configuration. The founders of Gestalt psychology rejected the idea that a perception can be broken down into its component parts. A melody broken up into individual notes is no longer a melody. Their slogan was, "The whole is different from the sum of its parts."

Gestalt psychology does not deny the importance of feature detectors. It merely insists that feature detectors are not enough. Feature detectors represent a bottom-up process, *in which tiny elements combine to produce larger items.* However, perception also includes a top-down process, *in which you apply your experience and expectations to interpret what each item must be in context.* Here are some examples.

In Figure 4.41, you may see animals or you may see meaningless black and white patches. You might see only patches for a while and then

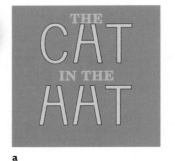

a   b

Figure 4.40 Context determines our perception. In (a) we see the same item as A or H depending on context. In (b) the central character can appear as B or the number 13 depending on whether we read horizontally or vertically. (Part b from *Inversions*, by S. Kim. Copyright © 1989 by Scott Kim. NY: W. H. Freeman.)

a

b

Figure 4.41 Do you see an animal in each picture? If not, check answer D on page 140. (From *American Journal of Psychology*. Copyright 1930 by the Board of Trustees of the University of Illinois. Used with permission of the author and the University of Illinois Press.)

one or both animals suddenly emerge. To perceive the animals, you separate figure and ground— that is, you distinguish the *object from the background.* Ordinarily, you make that distinction almost instantly. You become aware of the process only when it is difficult (as it is here).

Figure 4.42 shows five reversible figures, *stimuli that can be perceived in more than one way.* In effect, we test hypotheses: "Is this the front of the object or is that the front? Is this section the foreground or the background?" The longer you look at a reversible figure, the more frequently you alternate between one perception and another (Long & Toppine, 2004). Part a of Figure 4.42 is called the *Necker cube,* after the psychologist who first called attention to it. Which is the front face of the cube? You can see it either way. Part b is either a vase or two profiles. In part c, you might see a woman's face or a man blowing a horn. Does part d show an old woman or a young woman? Almost everyone sees one or the other immediately, but many people lock into one perception so tightly that they do not see the other one. The 8-year-old girl who drew part e intended it as a face. Can you find another possibility? If you have trouble with parts c, d, or e, check answers E, F, and G on page 140. The point of the reversible figures is that we perceive by imposing order (top-down), not just by adding up lines and points (bottom-up).

20. In what way does the phenomenon of reversible figures conflict with the idea that feature detectors fully explain vision?

Concept
Check

Answer

20. If vision were simply a matter of stimulating feature detectors and adding up their responses, then a given display would always produce the same perception.

The Gestalt psychologists described several principles of how we organize perceptions into meaningful wholes, as illustrated in Figure 4.43. Proximity is the *tendency to perceive objects that are close together as belonging to a group.* The objects in part a form two groups because of their proximity. The *tendency to perceive objects that resemble each other as a group* is called similarity. In part b, we group the Xs together and the ●s together because of similarity.

When lines are interrupted, as in part c, we perceive continuation, *a filling in of the gaps.* You probably perceive this illustration as a rectangle covering the center of a very long hot dog.

When a familiar figure is interrupted, as in part d, we perceive a closure of the figure; that is, *we imagine the rest of the figure* to see something that is simple, symmetrical, or consistent with our past experience (Shimaya, 1997). For example, you probably see the following as an

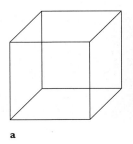    

a   b   c   d   e

Figure 4.42 Reversible figures: (a) The Necker cube. Which is the front face? (b) Faces or a vase. (c) A sax player or a woman's face ("Sara Nader"). (d) An old woman or a young woman. (e) A face or what? (Part b: "Faces or Vase" from *Mind Sights*, by Roger Shepard. Copyright 1990 by Roger N. Shepard. Reprinted by arrangement with Henry Holt & Company, LLC; part c: A sax player or a woman's face ("Sara Nader") from *Mind Sights*, by Roger Shepard. Copyright 1990 by Robert N. Shepard. Reprinted by arrangement with Henry Holt and Company, LLC; part d: From *American Journal of Psychology*. Copyright 1930 by the Board of Trustees of the University of Illinois. Used with permission of the author and the University of Illinois Press."

a

b

c

Figure 4.43 Gestalt principles of (a) proximity, (b) similarity, (c) continuation, (d) closure, and (e) good figure.

Imagine yourself in a crowded place, such as a park or a shopping mall. From a distance you see someone with features that look familiar. By the principle of closure, you fill in the gaps and recognize the person . . . or perhaps you incorrectly think you recognize the person.

Another Gestalt principle is **common fate**: *We perceive objects as part of the same group if they change or move in similar ways at the same time.* Suppose you see two or more objects. If they move in the same direction and speed, you see them as parts of the same object or group. Figure 4.44 illustrates. Also, if they grow brighter or darker at the same time, you see them as related (Sekuler & Bennett, 2001).

a

b

c

Figure 4.44 If two items move together, we see them as parts of the same object or group. If one item moves and the other does not, we perceive them as separate.

orange rectangle overlapping a blue diamond, although you don't really know what, if anything, is behind the rectangle:

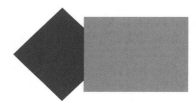

The principle of closure resembles continuation. With a complicated pattern, however, closure deals with more information. For example, in Figure 4.43c, you fill in the gaps to perceive one long hot dog. With additional context, you might perceive the same pattern as two shorter hot dogs:

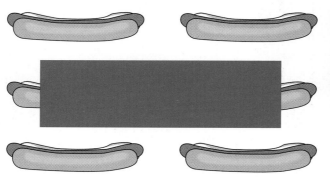

Finally, when possible, we tend to perceive a **good figure**—*a simple, familiar, symmetrical figure.* Many important, familiar objects in the world are geometrically simple or close to it: The sun and moon are round, tree trunks meet the ground at almost a right angle, faces and animals are nearly symmetrical, and so forth. If we can interpret something as a circle, square, or straight line, we do. In Figure 4.43e, the part on the left could represent a red square overlapping a green one or a green backward L overlapping a red object of almost any shape. We are powerfully drawn to the first interpretation because it includes "good," regular, symmetrical objects.

In Figure 4.45a, we perceive a white triangle overlapping three ovals (Singh, Hoffman, & Albert, 1999). That perception is so convincing that you may have to look carefully to persuade yourself that no line establishes a border for the triangle. However, if we tilt the blue objects slightly, as in Figure 4.45b, the illusion of something on top of them disappears. We "see" the overlapping object only if it is a symmetrical, good figure.

Similarities between Vision and Hearing

The perceptual organization principles of Gestalt psychology apply to hearing also. Analogous to reversible figures, some sounds can be heard in more than one way. You can hear a clock going "tick, tock, tick, tock" or "tock, tick, tock, tick." You can hear your windshield wipers going "dunga, dunga" or "gadung, gadung."

The Gestalt principles of continuation and closure work best when we see something that has interrupted something else. For example, consider Figure 4.46. In parts c and d, the context suggests objects partly blocking our view of a three-dimensional cube. In parts a and b, we are much less likely to see a cube, as nothing suggests an object occluding the view. Similarly, in Figure 4.47a, we see a series of meaningless patches. In Figure 4.47b, the addition of some black glop helps us see these patches as the word *psychology* (Bregman, 1981). We get continuation or closure mainly when we see that something has blocked the presumed object in the background.

The same is true in hearing. If a speech or song is broken up by periods of silence, we do not fill in the gaps and find the utterance hard to understand. However, if the same gaps are filled by noise, we "hear" what probably occurred during those gaps. That is, we apply continuation and closure (C. T. Miller, Dibble, & Hauser, 2001; Warren, 1970).

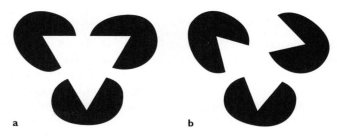

Figure 4.45 In (a) we see a triangle overlapping three irregular ovals. We see it because triangles are "good figures" and symmetrical. If we tilt the ovals, as in (b), they appear as irregular objects. (From "Contour Completion and Relative Depth: Petter's Rule and Support Ratio," by M. Singh, D. D. Hoffman, & M. K. Albert, *Psychological Science*, 1999, 10, 423–428. Copyright © 1999 Blackwell Publishers Ltd. Reprinted by permission.)

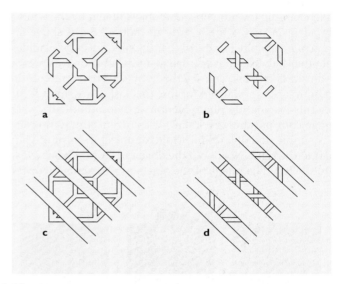

Figure 4.46 (a) and (b) appear to be arrays of flat objects. Introducing a context of overlapping lines causes a cube to emerge in (c) and (d). (From *Organization in Vision: Essays on Gestalt Perception*, by Gaetano Kanizsa, pp. 7–9. Copyright © 1979 by Gaetano Kanizsa. Reproduced with permission of Greenwood Publishing Group, Westport, CT.)

Figure 4.47 Why is the word *psychology* easier to read in (b) than in (a)? (After Bregman, 1981)

PERCEIVING MOVEMENT AND DEPTH

As an automobile moves away from us, its image on the retina grows smaller, yet we perceive it as moving, not as shrinking. That perception illustrates **visual constancy**—our *tendency to perceive objects as keeping their shape, size, and color, despite certain distortions in the light pattern reaching our retinas.* Figure 4.48 shows examples of two visual constancies: shape constancy and size constancy. Constancies depend on our familiarity with objects and on our ability to estimate distances and angles of view. For example, we know that a door is still rectangular even when we view it from an odd angle. But to recognize that an object keeps its shape and size, we have to perceive movement or changes in distance. How do we do so?

Perception of Movement

Moving objects capture our attention for a good reason. Throughout our evolutionary history, moving objects have been more likely than stationary objects to require immediate action. A moving object could be a person (either friend or foe), a lion charging toward you, or an object blown by the wind. People are particularly adept at perceiving a body in motion. Suppose we attach small lights to someone's shoulders, elbows, hands, hips, knees, and ankles. Then we turn out all other lights so that you see just the lights on this person. As soon as the person starts to walk, you see the lights as a person in motion. In fact, you have a brain area specialized for just this task (Grossman & Blake, 2001). You can see this fascinating phenomenon at Biomotion Lab's website. Go to **www.cengage.com/psychology/kalat** for a current link to this site.

Try this simple demonstration: Hold an object in front of your eyes and then move it to the right. Now hold the object in front of your eyes and move your eyes to the left. The image of the object moves across your retina in the

same way when you move the object or move your eyes. Yet you perceive the object as moving in one case but not in the other. Why?

The object looks stationary when you move your eyes for two reasons. One is that the vestibular system informs the visual areas of the brain about your head and eye movements. When your brain knows that your eyes have moved to the left, it interprets what you see as being a result of the movement. One man with a rare kind of brain damage could not connect his eye movements with his perceptions. Whenever he moved his head or eyes, the world appeared to be moving. Frequently, he became dizzy and nauseated (Haarmeier, Thier, Repnow, & Petersen, 1997).

Furthermore, we perceive motion when an object moves *relative to the background* (Gibson, 1968). For example, when you walk forward, stationary objects in your environment move across your retina but do not move relative to the background.

What do we perceive when an object is stationary and the background moves? In that unusual case, we *incorrectly perceive the object as moving against a stationary background,* a phenomenon called **induced movement.** For example, when you watch clouds moving slowly across the moon, you might perceive the clouds as stationary and the moon as moving. Induced movement is a form of *apparent movement,* as opposed to *real movement.*

You have already read about the waterfall illusion (page 127), another example of apparent movement. Yet another is **stroboscopic movement,** an *illusion of movement created by a rapid succession of stationary images.* When a scene is flashed on a screen and is followed a split second later by a second scene slightly different from the first, you perceive the objects as having moved smoothly from their location in the first scene to their location in the second scene (Figure 4.49). Motion pictures are actually a series of still photos flashed on the screen.

Our ability to detect visual movement played an interesting role in the history of astronomy. In 1930 Clyde Tombaugh was searching the skies for a possible undiscovered planet beyond Neptune. He photographed each region of the sky twice, several days apart. A planet, unlike a star, moves from one photo to the next. However, how would he find a small dot that moved among all the countless unmoving dots in the sky? He put each pair of photos on a machine that would flip back and forth between one photo and the other. When he came to one pair of photos, he immediately noticed one dot moving as the machine flipped back and forth

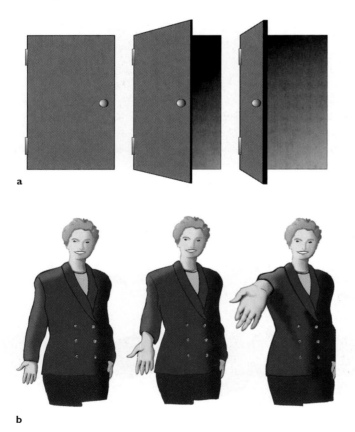

a

b

Figure 4.48 (a) Shape constancy: We perceive all three doors as rectangles. (b) Size constancy: We perceive all three hands as equal in size.

Figure 4.49 A movie consists of a series of still photographs flickering at 86,400 per hour. Here you see a series of stills spread out in space instead of time.

(Tombaugh, 1980). He identified that dot as Pluto, which astronomers now list as a dwarf planet (Figure 4.50).

Perception of Depth

Although we live in a world of three dimensions, our retinas are in effect two-dimensional surfaces. **Depth perception**, our *perception of distance,* enables us to experience the world in three dimensions. This perception depends on several factors.

One factor is **retinal disparity**— *the difference in the apparent position of an object as seen by the left and right retinas.* Try this: Hold a finger at arm's length. Focus on it with one eye and then the other. Note that the apparent position of your finger shifts with respect to the background. Now hold your finger closer to your face and repeat. The apparent position of your finger shifts even more. The amount of discrepancy between the two eyes is one way to gauge distance.

A second cue for depth perception is the **convergence** of the eyes—that is, the *degree to which they turn in to focus on a close object* (Figure 4.51). When you focus on a distant object, your eyes look in almost parallel directions. When you focus on something close, your eyes turn in, and you sense the tension of your eye muscles. The more the muscles pull, the closer the object must be.

Retinal disparity and convergence are called **binocular cues** because they *depend on both eyes.* **Monocular cues** enable someone to *judge depth and distance with just one eye* or when both eyes see the same image, as when you look at a picture, such as Figure 4.52. The ability to interpret depth in a picture depends on experience. For example, in Figure 4.53 does it appear to you that the hunter is aiming his spear at the antelope? When this drawing was shown to African people who had seldom or never seen drawings, many said the hunter was aiming at a baby elephant (Hudson, 1960).

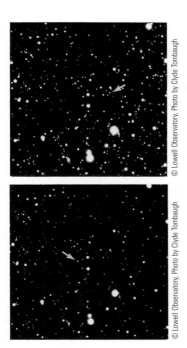

Figure 4.50 Clyde Tombaugh photographed each area of the sky twice, several days apart. Then he used a machine to flip back and forth between the two photos of each pair. When he came to one part of the sky, he immediately noticed one dot that moved between the two photos. That dot was Pluto.

Figure 4.51 The more the viewer converges her eyes toward each other to focus on an object, the closer the object must be.

Figure 4.52 We judge depth and distance in a photograph using monocular cues (those that would work even with just one eye). Closer objects occupy more space on the retina (or in the photograph) than do distant objects of the same type. Nearer objects show more detail. Closer objects overlap distant objects. Objects in the foreground look sharper than objects do on the horizon.

If you were a passenger on this train looking toward the horizon, the ground beside the tracks would appear to pass by more quickly than the more distant elements in the landscape. In this photo's version of motion parallax, the ground is blurred and more distant objects are crisp.

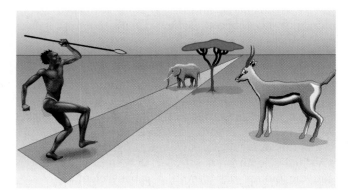

Figure 4.53 Which animal is the hunter attacking? Many people unfamiliar with drawings and photographs said he was attacking a baby elephant. (From Hudson, 1960)

Let's consider some of the monocular cues we use to perceive depth:

Object size: Other things being equal, a nearby object produces a larger image than a distant one. This cue helps only for objects of known size. For example, the jogger in Figure 4.52 produces a larger image than do any of the houses, which we know are actually larger. So we see the jogger as closer. However, the mountains in the background differ in actual as well as apparent size, so we cannot assume the ones that look bigger are closer.

Linear perspective: As parallel lines stretch out toward the horizon, they come closer together. Examine the road in Figure 4.52. At the bottom of the photo (close to the viewer), the edges of the road are far apart. At greater distances they come together.

Detail: We see nearby objects, such as the jogger, in more detail than distant objects.

Interposition: A nearby object interrupts our view of a more distant object. For example, the closest telephone pole (on the right) interrupts our view of the closest tree, so we see that the telephone pole is closer than the tree.

Texture gradient: Notice the distance between one telephone pole and the next. At greater distances, the poles come closer and closer together. The "packed together" appearance of objects gives us another cue to their approximate distance.

Shadows: Shadows help us gauge sizes as well as locations of objects.

Accommodation: The lens of the eye *accommodates*—that is, it changes shape—to focus on nearby objects, and your brain detects that change and thereby infers the distance to an object. Accommodation could help tell you how far away the photograph itself is, although it provides no information about the relative distances of objects in the photograph.

Motion parallax. Another monocular cue helps us perceive depth while we are moving, although it does not help with a photograph. If you are walking or riding in a car and fixating at the horizon, nearby objects move rapidly across the retina, while those farther away move less. The *difference in speed of movement of images across the retina as you travel* is the principle of **motion parallax.** Television and film crews use this principle. If the camera moves slowly, you see closer objects move more than distant ones and get a sense of depth.

---

21. Which monocular cues to depth are available in Figure 4.53?
22. With three-dimensional photography, cameras take two views of the same scene from different locations through lenses with different color filters or with different polarized-light filters. The two views are then superimposed. The viewer looks at the composite view through special glasses so that one eye sees the view

Concept Check

taken with one camera and the other eye sees the view taken with the other camera. Which depth cue is at work here?

Answers

OPTICAL ILLUSIONS

Our vision is well adapted to understanding what we see, but it is not always perfect. An **optical illusion** is a *misinterpretation of a visual stimulus.* Figure 4.54 shows a few examples. For many more optical illusions, visit the websites of the Exploratorium or Michael Bach. Go to **www.cengage .com/psychology/kalat** for current links to these websites. Psychologists would like to explain the optical illusions as simply as possible. (Remember the principle of parsimony from chapter 2.) One approach, which applies to some of the illusions but not all, pertains to mistakes of depth perception.

Depth Perception and Size Perception

As you see in Figure 4.55, a given image on the retina may represent either a small, close object or a large, distant object. If you know either the size

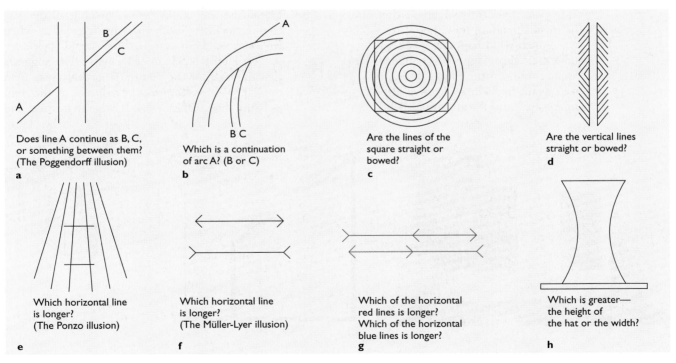

Does line A continue as B, C, or something between them? (The Poggendorff illusion)
a

Which is a continuation of arc A? (B or C)
b

Are the lines of the square straight or bowed?
c

Are the vertical lines straight or bowed?
d

Which horizontal line is longer? (The Ponzo illusion)
e

Which horizontal line is longer? (The Müller-Lyer illusion)
f

Which of the horizontal red lines is longer? Which of the horizontal blue lines is longer?
g

Which is greater— the height of the hat or the width?
h

Figure 4.54 These geometric figures illustrate optical illusions. Answers (which you are invited to check with ruler and compass): (a) B, (b) B, (c) straight, (d) straight, (e) equal, (f) equal, (g) equal, (h) equal.

Figure 4.55 Because fish come in many sizes, we can estimate the size of a fish only if we know how far away it is or if we compare its size to other nearby objects. See what happens when you cover the man and then cover the hand.

or the distance, you can estimate the other one. However, if you misperceive either one, you will be mistaken about the other also.

Watch what happens when you take a single image and change its apparent distance: Stare at Figure 4.13 again to form a negative afterimage. Examine the afterimage while

you are looking at a sheet of paper. As you move the paper backward and forward, you can make the apparent size change.

The real world provides many cues about the size and distance of objects. However, the cues are occasionally inadequate. I once was unsure whether I was watching a nearby toy airplane or a distant, full-size airplane. A similar issue arises in reported sightings of UFOs. When people see an unfamiliar object in the sky, they often misjudge its distance. If they overestimate its distance, they also overestimate its size and speed.

Certain optical illusions occur when we misjudge distance and therefore size. For example, Figure 4.56a shows people in the Ames room (named for its designer, Adelbert Ames). The room is designed to look like a normal rectangular room, although, as Figure 4.56b shows, one corner is much closer than the other. The two young women are actually the same height. If we eliminated all the background cues, we would correctly perceive the women as being the same size but at different distances. However, the apparently rectangular room provides such powerful (though misleading) cues to distance that the women appear to differ greatly in height.

Even a two-dimensional drawing on a flat surface offers cues that lead to erroneous depth perception. Because of your long experience with photos and drawings, you interpret most drawings as representations of three-dimensional scenes. Figure 4.57 shows a bewildering two-prong/three-prong device and a round staircase that seems to run uphill all the way clockwise or downhill all the way counterclockwise. Both drawings puzzle us when we try to see them as three-dimensional objects.

In Figure 4.58, linear perspective suggests that the right of the picture is farther away than the left. We therefore see the cylinder on the right as being the farthest away. If it is the farthest and

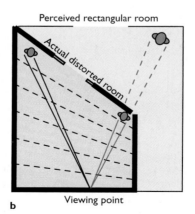

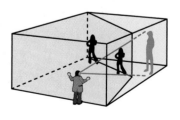

Figure 4.56 The Ames room is designed to be viewed through a peephole with one eye. (a) Both people are the same height, although they appear very different. (b) This diagram shows how the shape of the room distorts the viewer's perception of distance. (Part b from J. R. Wilson et al., 1964)

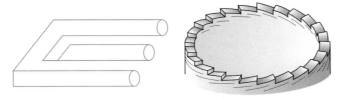

Figure 4.57 These two-dimensional drawings puzzle us because we try to interpret them as three-dimensional objects.

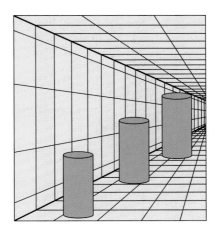

Figure 4.58 The cylinder on the right seems larger because the context makes it appear farther away.

still produces the same size image on the retina as the other two, then it would have to be the largest. When we are misled by the cues that ordinarily ensure constancy in size and shape, we experience an optical illusion (Day, 1972).

Figure 4.59 shows the tabletop illusion (Shepard, 1990). Here, almost unbelievably, the vertical dimension of the blue table equals the horizontal dimension of the yellow table, and the horizontal dimension of the blue table equals the vertical dimension of the yellow table. (Take measurements at the center of each table. The shapes of the tables are not exactly the same.) The yellow table appears long and thin compared to the blue one because we interpret it in depth. In effect, your brain constructs what each table would have to really *be* to look this way (Purves & Lotto, 2003).

Purves's Empirical Approach to Optical Illusions

The tabletop illusion suggests another approach to optical illusions. You see the tables in depth, to be sure, but in more general terms, you call on all your experience to see what the object probably *is*.

For example, this object △ might be a flat triangle, a long rectangle trailing off toward the horizon, or other possibilities. When the context does not dictate a particular option, you unconsciously calculate, "When I have seen

something like this in the past, what has it usually been?" According to Dale Purves and his colleagues, your perception is wholly empirical—that is, based on the statistics of your experience (Howe & Purves, 2005; Purves & Lotto, 2003).

For example, consider the Poggendorff illusion, as in Figure 4.60. The diagonal lines are actually straight, but they do not appear to be. Researchers photographed about a hundred scenes of many types and then had a computer analyze all the lines. They found that when a line slanting downward went behind a barrier, more often than not, when it emerged on the other side, it was slightly higher than would happen with a truly

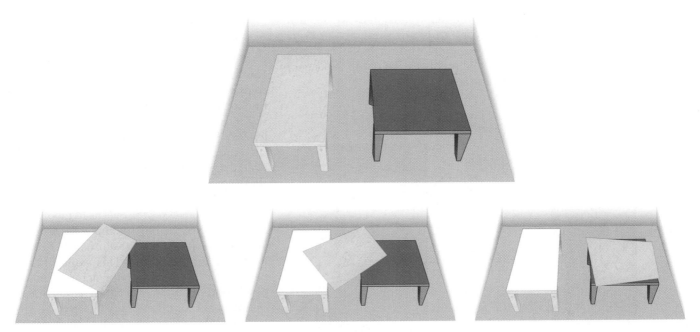

Figure 4.59 The tabletop illusion. The blue table is as wide as the yellow table is long, and as long as the yellow table is wide, if you measure in the middle of each table. The parts below show rotation of the yellow table to overlap the blue one.

straight line (Howe, Yang, & Purves, 2005). That is, in nature,

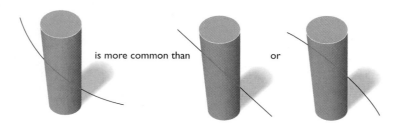

is more common than

or

Therefore, when you see something like the diagrams in Figure 4.60, your visual system sees the slanted line on the right as "lower than expected." Application of the same approach accounts for many other optical illusions.

The Moon Illusion

To most people, the *moon at the horizon appears about 30% larger than it appears when it is higher in the sky.* This moon illusion is so convincing that many people have tried to explain it by referring to the bending of light rays by the atmosphere or other physical phenomena. However, if you photograph the moon and measure its image, you will find that it is the same size at the horizon as it is higher in the sky. Figure 4.61 shows the moon at two positions in the sky. You can measure the two images to demonstrate that they are really the same size. (The atmosphere's bending of light rays makes the moon look orange near the horizon, but it does not increase the size of the image.) However, photographs do not capture the full strength of the moon illusion as we see it in real life. In Figure 4.61 or any similar pair of photos, the moon looks almost the same at each position. In the actual night sky, the moon looks enormous at the horizon.

Figure 4.61 Ordinarily, the moon looks much larger at the horizon than it does overhead. In photographs this illusion disappears almost completely, but the photographs demonstrate that the physical image of the moon is the same in both cases. The moon illusion requires a psychological explanation, not a physical one.

One explanation is size comparison. When you see the moon low in the sky, it seems large compared to the tiny buildings or trees you see at the horizon. When you see the moon high in the sky, it appears small compared to the vast, featureless sky (Baird, 1982; Restle, 1970).

A second explanation is that the terrain between the viewer and the horizon gives an impression of great distance. When the moon is high in the sky, we have no basis to judge distance, and we unconsciously see the overhead moon as closer. Because we see the horizon moon as more distant, we perceive it as larger (Kaufman & Rock, 1989; Rock & Kaufman, 1962). This explanation is appealing because it relates the moon illusion to our perception of distance, a factor already accepted as important for other illusions.

Many psychologists are not satisfied with this explanation, however, because they are not convinced that the horizon moon looks farther away than the overhead moon. If we ask which looks

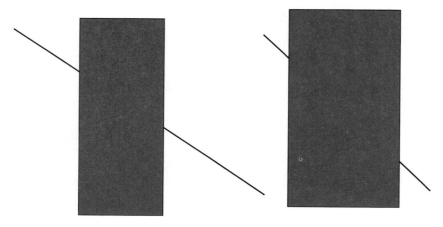

Figure 4.60 Two versions of the Poggendorff illusion.

farther away, many people say they are not sure. If we insist on an answer, most say the horizon moon looks *closer,* contradicting the theory. Some psychologists reply that the situation is complicated: We unconsciously perceive the horizon as farther away. Consequently, we perceive the horizon moon as very large. Then, because of the perceived large size of the horizon moon, we consciously say it looks closer, while continuing unconsciously to perceive it as farther (Rock & Kaufman, 1962).

Studies of optical illusions confirm what other phenomena already indicated: What we perceive is not the same as what is "out there." Our visual system does an amazing job of providing us with useful information about the world around us, but under unusual circumstances, we have distorted perceptions.

module 4.3

In Closing

Making Sense of Sensory Information

You have probably heard the expression, "Seeing is believing." The saying is true in many ways, including that what you believe influences what you see. Perception is not just a matter of adding up all the events striking the retina. We look for what we expect to see, we impose order on haphazard patterns, we see three dimensions in two-dimensional drawings, and we see optical illusions. The brain does not compute what light is striking the retina but tries to learn what objects are present and what they are doing.

SUMMARY

- *Perception of minimal stimuli.* No sharp dividing line distinguishes sensory stimuli that can be perceived and sensory stimuli that cannot be perceived. (page 123)

- *Signal detection.* To determine how accurately someone detects a signal, we need to consider not only the ratio of hits to misses when the stimulus is present but also the ratio of false alarms to correct rejections when the stimulus is absent. (page 123)

- *Subliminal perception.* Under some circumstances, a weak stimulus that we do not consciously identify can influence our behavior, at least weakly or briefly. (page 125)

- *Face recognition.* People are amazingly good at recognizing faces. (page 126)

- *Detection of simple visual features.* In the first stages of the process of perception, feature-detector cells identify lines, points, and simple movement. Visual aftereffects can be interpreted in terms of fatiguing certain feature detectors. (page 126)

- *Perception of organized wholes.* According to Gestalt psychologists, we perceive an organized whole by identifying similarities and continuous patterns across a large area of the visual field. (page 128)

- *Visual constancies.* We ordinarily perceive the shape, size, and color of objects as constant, even when the pattern of light striking the retina varies. (page 132)

- *Motion perception.* We perceive an object as moving if it moves relative to its background. We can distinguish between an object that is actually moving and a similar pattern of retinal stimulation that results from our own movement. (page 132)

- *Depth perception.* To perceive depth, we use the accommodation of the eye muscles and retinal disparity between the views that our two eyes see. We also learn to use other cues that are just as effective with one eye as with two. (page 133)

- *Optical illusions.* Some optical illusions occur because we misperceive the relative distances of objects. We perceive displays by comparing them to our previous experiences with similar objects. (page 135)

KEY TERMS

absolute sensory threshold (page 123)

binocular cues (page 133)

bottom-up process (page 128)

brightness contrast (page 126)

closure (page 129)

common fate (page 130)

continuation (page 129)

convergence (page 133)

depth perception (page 133)

feature detector (page 126)

figure and ground (page 129)

Gestalt psychology (page 128)

good figure (page 131)

induced movement (page 132)

monocular cues (page 133)

moon illusion (page 138)

motion parallax (page 135)

optical illusion (page 135)

proximity (page 129)

retinal disparity (page 133)

reversible figure (page 129)

signal-detection theory (page 123)

similarity (page 129)

stroboscopic movement (page 132)

subliminal perception (page 125)

top-down process (page 128)

visual constancy (page 132)

waterfall illusion (page 127)

ANSWERS TO OTHER QUESTIONS IN THE MODULE

C.

© Exploratorium, www.exploratorium.edu

D.

E.

F.

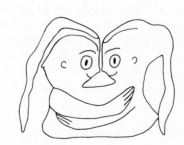

Eye
Ear
Cheek
Jaw
Necklace

Eye
Nose
Mouth
Chin

Young woman   Old woman

G.

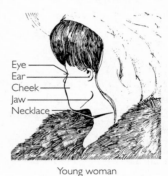

exploration and study

Why Does This Matter to Me?

SOCIAL RESPONSIBILITY AND PSYCHOLOGY

Many environmental and societal problems are caused by human behavior. Psychologists can help steer the course of our future toward more socially responsible and sustainable outcomes. Students of today need to be ever mindful of the link between human behavior and its impact on the environment and our communities.

"Sensation and Perception" and Social Responsibility: A Step Further

Imagine how your life would change if you lost one of your senses or had an impaired sense. Which parts of your life would change the most? Many of you may already wear eyeglasses. People the world over can benefit from your old prescription lenses. Consider donating your old eyeglasses. Many charity shops and prescription eyeglass stores include collection facilities. Items also can be sent in padded envelopes or boxes to:

New Eyes for the Needy:
549 Millburn Avenue
P.O. Box 332
Short Hills, NJ 07078
(A current link to New Eyes for the Needy's website can be found at www.cengage .com/psychology/kalat.)

Want to See the World through an Animal's Point of View?

National Geographic's Crittercam allows us to see the world from the backs of different kinds of animals. Just as psychologists study how humans sense and perceive the world, biologists study how animals sense and perceive it. As we learn about the ecosystems that surround us, we learn how our actions affect them. (For a current link to National Geographic's Crittercam, go to www.cengage.com/psychology/kalat.)

Join the iChapters Plant a Tree Drive!

To show its support of the environmental movement, iChapters is planting a tree on behalf of each fan of the iChapters Facebook Page and for every 10 questions answered correctly in our quiz. http://www.ichapters.com/plantatree/

Exploration and Study

SUGGESTIONS FOR FURTHER EXPLORATION

In addition to the study materials provided at the end of each module, you may supplement your review of this chapter with the following book and website suggestions or by using one or more of the book's electronic resources, which include its companion website, interactive Cengage Learning eBook, and CengageNOW. Brief descriptions of these resources follow. For more information, visit **www.cengage.com/psychology/kalat**.

ADDITIONAL RESOURCES

The book's companion website, accessible from **www.cengage.com/psychology/kalat,** provides a wide range of study resources such as an interactive glossary, flashcards, tutorial quizzes, updated web links, and Try It Yourself activities. For example, these exercises tie to what you've learned in this chapter: color blindness, filling in the blind spot, brightness contrast, matching high school photos, and motion aftereffect

CengageNOW with Critical Thinking Videos is an easy-to-use resource that helps you study in less time to get the grade you want. An online study system, CengageNOW  gives you the option of taking a diagnostic pretest for each chapter. The system uses the results of each pretest to create personalized chapter study plans for you. The Personalized Study Plans

- Help you save study time by identifying areas on which you should concentrate and give you one-click access to corresponding pages of the interactive Cengage Learning eBook;
- Provide interactive exercises and study tools to help you fully understand chapter concepts; and
- Include a posttest for you to take to confirm that you are ready to move on to the next chapter.

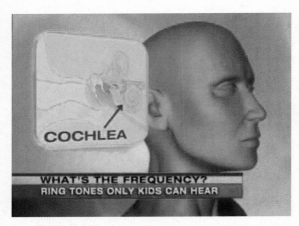

WHAT'S THE FREQUENCY?
RING TONES ONLY KIDS CAN HEAR

COCHLEA

ABC Video: Ringtones and the Cochlea

Find critical thinking videos like this one in your CengageNOW product, which offer an opportunity for you to learn more about psychological research on different topics.

Books

Herz, R. (2007). *The scent of desire.* New York: HarperCollins. A delightful exploration of the role of smell in human behavior, including romantic relationships.

Purves, D., & Lotto, R. B. (2003). *Why we see what we do.* Sunderland, MA: Sinauer Associates. Insightful and creative account of human perception.

Ramachandran, V. S., & Blakeslee, S. (1998). *Phantoms in the brain.* New York: Morrow. Fascinating explanation of phantom limbs and related phenomena.

Websites

Links to the websites described below are kept current and can be found at www.cengage.com/psychology/kalat.

Vision Science Demonstrations

Links to many fascinating demonstrations, mostly visual but a few auditory. It's one amazing experience after another.

More Illusions

Here are wonderful illusions, both visual and auditory. Enjoy.

Seeing, Hearing, and Smelling

Elaborate psychological and medical information, courtesy of the Howard Hughes Medical Institute.

Smells and Flavors

Rich source of information about olfaction, ranging from the chemistry of perfumes to the olfactory receptors and how our brains handle olfaction.

© Ariel Skelley/CORBIS

Nature, Nurture, and Human Development

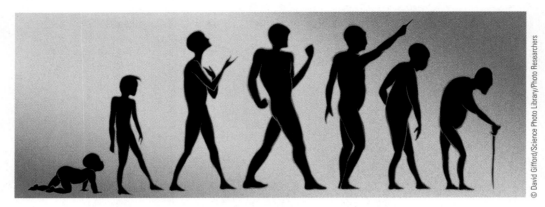

As we grow older, our behavior changes in many ways. Developmental psychologists seek to describe and understand these changes.

Consider This: Suppose you buy a robot. When you get home, you discover that it does nothing useful. It cannot even maintain its balance. It makes irritating, high-pitched noises, moves its limbs haphazardly, and leaks. The store you bought it from refuses to take it back. And you're not allowed to turn it off. So you are stuck with this useless machine.

A few years later, your robot walks and talks, reads and writes, draws pictures, and does arithmetic. It follows your directions (usually) and sometimes does useful things without being told. It beats you at memory games.

How did all this happen? After all, you knew nothing about how to program a robot. Did your robot have some sort of built-in programming that simply took a long time to phase in? Or was it programmed to learn all these skills?

Children are like that robot. Parents wonder, "How did my children get to be the way they are?" The goal of developmental psychology is to understand how nature and nurture combine to produce human behavior "from womb to tomb."

Genetics and Evolution of Behavior

• How do genes influence behavior?

Everyone has tens of thousands of genes that control development. If we could go back in time and change just one of the genes you were born with, how would your experience and personality be different?

Obviously, it depends! *Which* gene? Hundreds of your genes control olfactory receptors. A mutation in one of them would decrease your sensitivity to a few smells, and you might not even notice your deficiency. Mutations in certain other genes would change your life drastically or end it early.

The effect of changing a gene also depends on your environment. Suppose you had a gene that magnifies your reactions to stressful experiences. How would that have changed your life? If you had a low-stress life, the gene would do no harm. If you encountered severe stress, you could be seriously impaired.

Psychologists widely agree that both heredity and environment are essential for everything you do. Nevertheless, in some cases, the *differences* among people relate mainly to *differences* in their heredity or environment. For analogy, we cannot meaningfully ask whether a computer's activity depends on its hardware or software because both are essential. However, two computers might differ because of differences in their hardware, their software, or both. Similarly, the difference between having color vision and lacking it depends almost entirely on genetics, whereas the difference between speaking English and speaking some other language depends on where you were reared. Most behavioral differences depend on differences in both heredity and environment.

The study of genetics has become increasingly important for citizens of the 21st century. Because biologists have mapped the human genome (the set of all genes on our chromosomes), physicians who examine your chromosomes can predict your likelihood of getting various diseases. Laboratories use samples of blood or sperm to determine which suspect might have committed some crime. The possibilities for further applications are huge. Let's first review some basic points about genetics and then explore their application to human behavior.

GENETIC PRINCIPLES

Except for your red blood cells, all of your cells contain a nucleus, which includes *strands of hereditary material* called **chromosomes** (Figure 5.1). Each human nucleus has 23 pairs of chromosomes, except those in egg and sperm cells, which have 23 unpaired chromosomes. At fertilization, the 23 chromosomes from an egg cell combine with the 23 of a sperm cell to form 23 pairs for the new person (Figure 5.2).

Sections along each chromosome, known as **genes**, *control the chemical reactions that direct development*—for example, controlling height or hair color. Genes are composed of the chemical DNA, which controls the production of another chemical called RNA, which among other functions controls the production of proteins. The proteins either become part of the body's structure or control the rates of chemical reactions in the body. To explain

the concept of genes, educators often use an example such as eye color. If you have either one or two genes for brown eyes, you will have brown eyes because the brown-eye gene is **dominant**— *that is, a single copy of the gene is sufficient to produce its effect.* The gene for blue eyes is

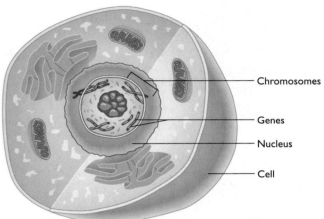

Figure 5.1 Genes are sections of chromosomes in the nuclei of cells. (Scale is exaggerated for illustration purposes.)

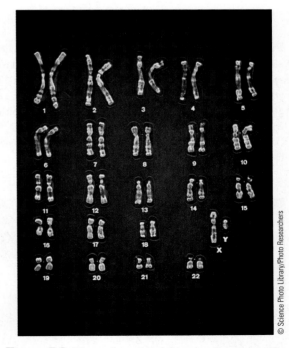

Figure 5.2 The nucleus of each human cell contains 46 chromosomes, 23 from the sperm and 23 from the ovum, united in pairs.

recessive—its effects appear only if the dominant gene is absent. You have blue eyes only if you have two genes for blue eyes.

However, examples like this are misleading because they imply that each gene has only one effect, which it controls completely. Most behaviors depend on contributions from many genes as well as the environment. Furthermore, the actual nature of genes is more complicated than we once thought. In some cases, part of one gene overlaps part of another one, or parts of a single gene are located on different parts of a chromosome or even on different chromosomes. Also, the product of a gene can be modified by neighboring parts of the chromosome. For example, different species of voles (similar to mice) vary genetically with regard to a brain chemical called *vasopressin*. They have the same genes for vasopressin itself and for vaso-

pressin receptors, but they vary in some nearby chromosomal material that modifies the quantity of vasopressin receptors. In voles that make high quantities, males help their mates build nests and take care of their babies. In voles with low quantities, males mate and then desert, showing no further interest in the female or her babies (Lim et al., 2004) (see Figure 5.3). Thus, talking about "the gene" for vasopressin receptors is ambiguous: Do we mean the part of the chromosome that builds the receptor or all parts of all chromosomes that modify the production of that receptor? Curiously, something similar has been found in humans: Men who make greater amounts of vasopressin receptors have closer relationships with their wives and express less likelihood of divorce (Walum et al., 2008). For $99 (as of 2008), you can send your DNA or that of your prospective partner to a lab to test the vasopressin receptors. (I recommend you save your money. The gene makes a difference on the average for humans but not consistently enough to make good predictions for each person.)

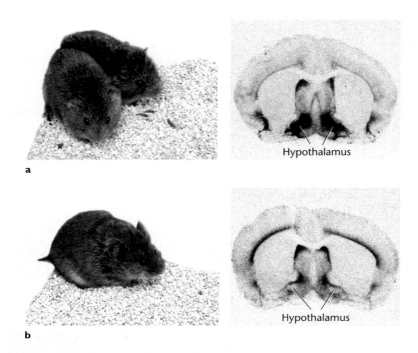

a

Hypothalamus

b

Hypothalamus

Figure 5.3 (a) Prairie voles form long-term pair bonds. Staining of their brain shows much expression of the hormone vasopressin in the hypothalamus. (b) A closely related species, meadow voles, mate but then the male deserts his mate and has less brain vasopressin. Researchers found that if they increased the vasopressin levels, they could get meadow voles to become devoted fathers, like their prairie vole relatives. (Reprinted with permission from Lim, M. M., Wang, Z., Olazábal, D. E., Ren, X., Terwilliger, E. F., & Young, L. J., 2004. Enhanced partner preference in a promiscuous species by manipulating the expression of a single gene. *Nature, 429,* 754–757.)

1. Why is it generally misleading to talk about "the gene" for some behavior or ability?

Concept Check

Answer

1. Almost every aspect of behavior depends on the combined influence of many genes and environmental influences. Also, the exact borders of a gene are ambiguous. Portions of the chromosome that do not code for any proteins of their own can modify the effectiveness of a portion that does.

Sex-Linked and Sex-Limited Genes

Because chromosomes come in pairs (one from the mother and one from the father), you have two of almost all genes. The exceptions are those on the **sex chromosomes**, which *determine*

a   b   c

Albinos occur in many species, always because of a recessive gene. (a) Striped skunk. (b) American alligator. (c) Mockingbird.

whether an individual develops as a male or as a female. Mammals' sex chromosomes are known as X and Y (Figure 5.4). *A female has two X chromosomes* in each cell; *a male has one X chromosome and one Y chromosome.* The mother contributes an X chromosome to each child, and the father contributes either an X or a Y. Because men have one X chromosome and one Y chromosome, they have unpaired genes on these chromosomes. Women have two X chromosomes, but in each cell, one of the X chromosomes is activated and the other is silenced, apparently at random.

Genes located on the X chromosome are known as sex-linked *or* X-linked genes. Genes on the Y chromosome are also sex-linked, but the Y chromosome has fewer genes. An X-linked recessive gene shows its effects more in men than in women. For example, red-green color deficiency depends on an X-linked recessive gene. A man with that gene on his X chromosome will be red-green deficient because he has no other X chromosome. A woman with that gene probably has a gene for normal color vision on her other X chromosome. Consequently, far more men than women have red-green deficiency (Figure 5.5).

A sex-limited gene *occurs equally in both sexes but exerts its effects mainly or entirely in one or the other.* For example, both men and women have the genes for facial hair, but men's hormones activate those genes. Both men and women have the genes for breast development, but women's hormones activate those genes.

estimate how much of the variation in some behavior depends on differences in genes. The answer is summarized by the term heritability, *an estimate of the variance within a population that is due to heredity.* Heritability ranges from 1, indicating that heredity controls all the variance, to 0, indicating that it controls none of it. For example, red-green deficiency has a heritability of almost 1. Note that the definition of heritability includes the phrase "within a population." For example, in a population with little genetic diversity, heritability is low because whatever differences occur can't be due to differences in genes. In some other population with great genetic diversity, the genetic variations produce major differences among individuals, so heritability is likely to be higher. To estimate the heritability of a behavior, researchers rely on evidence from twins and adopted children.

However, estimates of heritability are often misleading because we cannot fully separate the effects of heredity and environment. For example, imagine you have a gene that makes you tall. If you live where people play basketball, you probably spend much time playing basketball. You will be on basketball teams, you will receive coaching, and your skills will improve. As your skills improve, you experience more success and receive further encouragement. What started as a small genetic increase in height develops into a huge advantage in basketball skill that reflects environmental influences as well as genetics. Researchers call this tendency a multiplier effect: *A small ini-*

Figure 5.4 An electron micrograph shows that the X chromosome is longer than the Y chromosome. (From Ruch, 1984)

---

2. Suppose a father is red-green deficient and a mother has two genes for normal color vision. What sort of color vision will their children have?

Concept Check

Answer

2. The sons receive a gene for normal color vision from the mother, and a Y chromosome (irrelevant to color vision) from the father. They will have normal color vision. The daughters receive a gene for normal color vision from the mother and a gene for red-green color deficiency from the father. They will also have normal color vision, but they will be carriers who can pass the red-green deficiency gene to some of their children.

Estimating Heritability in Humans

As discussed in the section on nature and nurture in chapter 1, all behavior depends on both heredity and environment, but variation in a given behavior might depend more on the variation in genes or variations in the environment. Suppose we want to

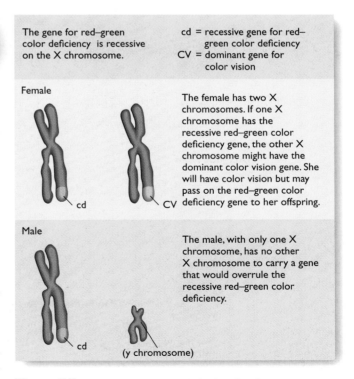

The gene for red–green color deficiency is recessive on the X chromosome.

cd = recessive gene for red–green color deficiency
CV = dominant gene for color vision

Female

The female has two X chromosomes. If one X chromosome has the recessive red–green color deficiency gene, the other X chromosome might have the dominant color vision gene. She will have color vision but may pass on the red–green color deficiency gene to her offspring.

cd   CV

Male

The male, with only one X chromosome, has no other X chromosome to carry a gene that would overrule the recessive red–green color deficiency.

cd   (y chromosome)

Figure 5.5 Why males are more likely than females to be red-green color deficient.

tial advantage in some behavior, possibly genetic in origin, alters the environment and magnifies that advantage (Dickens & Flynn, 2001).

Genes $\longrightarrow$ Initial tendencies $\longrightarrow$ Learning and encouragement

Improvements in the behavior

3. If our society changed so that it provided an equally good environment for all children, would the heritability of behaviors increase or decrease?

Answer

3. If all children had equally supportive environments, the heritability of behaviors would *increase*. Remember, heritability refers to how much of the difference among people is due to hereditary variation. If the environment is practically the same for all, then environmental variation cannot account for much of the variation in behavior. Whatever behavioral variation still occurs would be due mostly to hereditary variation.

Twin Studies

One kind of evidence for heritability comes from studies of twins. **Monozygotic** (mon-oh-zie-GOT-ik) **twins** *develop from a single fertilized egg (zygote) and therefore have identical genes.* Most people call them "identical" twins, but that term is misleading. Some monozygotic twins are mirror images—one right-handed and the other left-handed. It is also possible for a gene to be activated in one twin and suppressed in the other. You should therefore learn the somewhat awkward term *monozygotic.* **Dizygotic** (DIE-zie-GOT-ik) **twins** *develop from two eggs and share only half their genes, like any brother and sister* (Figure 5.6). They are often called "fraternal" twins because they are only as closely related as brother and sister. If dizygotic twins resemble each other almost as much as monozygotic twins do in some trait, then we conclude that the heritability of that trait is low because the amount of genetic similarity did not have much influence on the outcome. If monozygotic twins resemble each other much more strongly, then the heritability is high. This procedure is based on the assumption that both kinds of twins share their environment to the same extent. That assumption is approximately correct but not entirely, as other people tend to treat monozygotic twins more similarly than they do dizygotic twins.

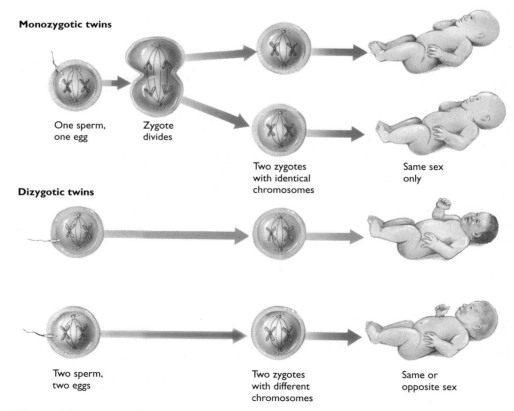

Figure 5.6 Monozygotic twins develop from the same fertilized egg. Dizygotic twins grow from two eggs fertilized by different sperm.

Researchers also examine pairs of monozygotic twins who grew up in separate environments. In the United States and Europe today, adoption agencies place both twins in one family, but in previous times, many twins were adopted separately. One pair of monozygotic twins were reunited in adulthood after being reared in different western Ohio cities (Figure 5.7). They quickly discovered that they had much in common: Both had been named Jim by their adoptive parents. Each liked carpentry and drafting, had built a bench around a tree in his yard, and worked as a deputy sheriff. Both chewed their fingernails, gained weight at the same age, smoked the same brand of cigarettes, drove Chevrolets, and took their vacations in western Florida. Each married a woman named Linda, divorced her, and married a woman named Betty. One had a son named James Alan and the other had a son named James Allen, and both had a pet dog named Toy.

How many of these similarities are mere coincidences? Chevrolets are popular cars, for example, and many people from western Ohio vacation in western Florida. It's hard to believe these twins had genes forcing them to marry a Linda and divorce her to marry a Betty. (If they had been adopted in Afghanistan, they would have had trouble finding a Linda or a Betty.)

All right, but consider other monozygotic twins separated at birth. One pair of women each wore rings on seven fingers. A pair of men discovered that they used the same brands of toothpaste, shaving lotion, hair tonic, and cigarettes. When they sent each other a birthday present, their presents crossed in the mail, and each received the same present he had sent. Another pair reported that when they went to the beach, they waded into the water backward and only up to their knees (Lykken, McGue, Tellegen, & Bouchard, 1992).

Researchers examined about 100 pairs of twins, some monozygotic and others dizygotic, who were reared separately and reunited as adults. On the average, the monozygotic twins resembled each other more strongly with regard to hobbies, vocational interests, answers on personality tests, tendency to trust other people, political beliefs, probability of voting, job satisfaction, life satisfaction, probability of mental illness, consumption of coffee and fruit juices, and preference for awakening early in the morning or staying up late at night (Bouchard & McGue, 2003; Cesarini et al., 2008; DiLalla, Carey, Gottesman, & Bouchard, 1996; Fowler, Baker, & Dawes, 2008; Hur, Bouchard, & Eckert, 1998; Hur, Bouchard, & Lykken, 1998; Lykken, Bouchard, McGue, & Tellegen, 1993; McCourt, Bouchard, Lykken, Tellegen, & Keyes, 1999). This pattern is more convincing than the anecdotes from any single pair. The implication is that genes influence a wide variety of behaviors.

Studies of Adopted Children

Another kind of evidence for heritability comes from studies of adopted children. Resemblance to their adopting parents implies an environmental influence. Resemblance to their biological parents implies a genetic influence.

However, the results are sometimes hard to interpret. For example, consider the evidence that many adopted children with an arrest record had biological mothers with a criminal history (Mason & Frick, 1994). The resemblance could indicate a genetic influence, but the mothers also provided the prenatal environment. Chances are, many of the mothers with a criminal record smoked, drank alcohol, perhaps used other drugs, and in other ways endangered the fetus's brain development. The importance of prenatal environment is easily overlooked. For example, malnourished female rats give birth to babies that show learning impairments. In some cases, even the grandchildren are impaired (Harper, 2005).

Another point to remember is that adoption agencies consistently place children in the best possible homes. That policy is certainly good for the children, but from a scientific standpoint, it means that we have little variance in the quality of adopting families. Does growing up with an alcoholic parent increase the probability of alco-

Figure 5.7 Monozygotic twins Jim Lewis and Jim Springer were separated at birth, reared in separate cities of western Ohio, and reunited in adulthood.

© Enrico Ferorelli

hol abuse? Probably, but we can't easily test this hypothesis with adopted children because few of their adopting parents are alcohol abusers (Stoolmiller, 1999).

4. Suppose someone studies a group of adopted children who developed severe depression and finds that many of their biological parents had depression, whereas few of their adopting parents did. One possible interpretation is that genetic factors influence depression more than family environment does. What is another interpretation?

Concept Check

Answer

4. Perhaps biological mothers who are becoming depressed eat less healthy foods, drink more alcohol, or in some other way impair the prenatal environment of their babies.

HOW GENES INFLUENCE BEHAVIOR

Based on studies of twins and adopted children, researchers have found at least moderate heritability for almost every behavior they have examined, including loneliness (McGuire & Clifford, 2000), neuroticism (Lake, Eaves, Maes, Heath, & Martin, 2000), time spent watching television (Plomin, Corley, DeFries, & Fulker, 1990), and religious devoutness (Waller, Kojetin, Bouchard, Lykken, & Tellegen, 1990). About the only behavior for which researchers have reported zero heritability is choice of religious denomination (Eaves, Martin, & Heath, 1990). That is, genes apparently influence how often you attend religious services but not which services you attend. How could genes influence this range of behaviors?

Direct and Indirect Influences

Genes control maturation of brain structures, production of neurotransmitters, and production of neurotransmitter receptors. They also influence behavior by altering organs outside the nervous system. Consider dietary choices: Almost all infants can digest *lactose,* the sugar in milk. As they grow older, nearly all Asians and many others lose the ability to digest it. (The loss depends on genes, not on how often people drink milk.) The ability to digest milk in adulthood varies sharply from place to place within Africa. Different African populations that started tending cattle independently evolved different genetic adaptations for digesting milk (Tishkoff et al., 2006). People who cannot digest lactose enjoy a little milk and more readily enjoy cheese and yogurt, which are easier to digest, but they get gas and cramps from consuming too much milk or ice cream (Flatz, 1987; Rozin & Pelchat, 1988). Figure 5.8 shows how the ability to digest dairy products varies among ethnic groups. The point is that a gene can affect

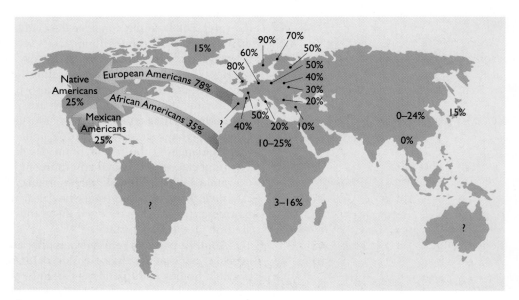

Figure 5.8 Adult humans vary in their ability to digest lactose, the main sugar in milk. The numbers refer to the percentage of each population's adults that can easily digest lactose. (Based on Flatz, 1987; Rozin & Pelchat, 1988)

behavior—in this case, consumption of dairy products—by altering chemical reactions outside the brain.

Genes also influence behaviors by altering body anatomy. Consider genes that make you unusually good-looking. Because many people smile at you, invite you to parties, and try to become your friend, you develop increased self-confidence and social skills. The genes changed your behavior by changing how other people treated you.

Interactions between Heredity and Environment

A software program might run faster on one computer than another depending on their hardware. Similarly, the way you react to some experience depends on your heredity. This kind of effect is an interaction—*an instance in which the effect of one variable depends on some other variable.* For example, people with different genes react differently to marijuana and tobacco (Moffitt, Caspi, & Rutter, 2006).

One study found that how children react to social support depends on a gene that controls reuptake of the neurotransmitter serotonin. Recall from chapter 3 that a neurotransmitter, after its release from an axon, returns to that axon for reuse. A gene that controls serotonin reuptake comes in two forms, *long* and *short.* In children with the long form, social support increases shyness, but in those with the short form, social support decreases shyness (Fox et al., 2005). We shall need more research to understand why this interaction occurs, but for present purposes, the point is that sometimes neither heredity nor environment by itself has a predictable effect. The outcome depends on the combination.

Shyness relates to temperament—*the tendency to be active or inactive, outgoing or reserved, and to respond vigorously or quietly to new stimuli.* Temperament depends partly on genetics. Studies of monozygotic and dizygotic twins show a strong influence of genetics on temperament (Bouchard, Lykken, McGue, Segal, & Tellegen, 1990; Matheny, 1989). Environmental influences magnify the genetic tendencies. For example, someone who is inclined to be active and vigorous tends to choose outgoing friends and stimulating social situations. Someone with a more reserved temperament gravitates toward quiet activities and smaller social groups.

Temperament is fairly consistent over the years for most people (Durbin, Hayden, Klein, & Olino, 2007). Infants who frequently kick and cry are termed "difficult" or "inhibited," whereas those who seldom kick or cry are called "easy" or "uninhibited" (Thomas & Chess, 1980). Those with a difficult or inhibited temperament are more likely than others to be frightened by unfamiliar events at ages 9 and 14 months (Kagan & Snidman, 1991). They tend to be shy and nervous in a playground at age 7½ years (Kagan, Reznick, & Snidman, 1988). As adults, they react to photographs of unfamiliar people with strong responses in the amygdala, a brain area that processes anxiety-related information (Schwartz, Wright, Shin, Kagan, & Rauch, 2003) (see Figure 5.9). For another example, children who are rated "impulsive" at 30 months are likely to have more teenage sex partners than average (Zimmer-Gembeck, Siebenbruner, & Collins, 2004).

Here is another example: Phenylketonuria (PKU) is *an inherited condition that, if untreated, leads to mental retardation.* About 2% of people with European or Asian ancestry, and almost no Africans, have the recessive gene that leads to PKU, but because the gene is recessive, one copy is nearly harmless. People with copies from both parents cannot metabolize *phenylalanine,* a common constituent of proteins. On an ordinary diet, an affected child accumulates phenylalanine in the brain and becomes mentally retarded. However, a diet low in phenylalanine protects the brain. Thus, a special diet prevents a disorder that would otherwise show high heritability.

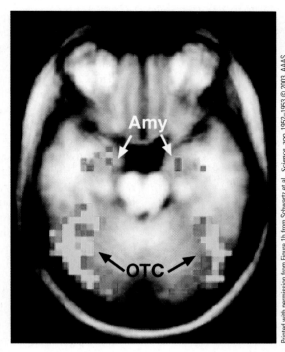

Figure 5.9 This horizontal section shows the result of functional magnetic resonance imaging (fMRI). Two brain areas were more active than average in adults with an inhibited temperament, marked in red for a large difference and in yellow for an even larger difference. "Amy" indicates the amygdala (on each side of the brain). OTC indicates the occipital and temporal areas of the cortex.

5. Some people assume that if something is under genetic control, we can't do anything about it. Cite an example that contradicts this idea.

Answer

5. Phenylketonuria is a genetic condition that would cause mental retardation, but a special diet minimizes the problem.

EVOLUTION AND BEHAVIOR

Why do you have the genes that you do? Simply, your parents had those genes and survived long enough to reproduce. So did your parents' parents and so on. Ancient people whose genes did not enable them to survive and reproduce failed to become your ancestors.

Let's say it in a different way: At any time, individuals within any population of any species vary in their genes. Gene mutations supply the population with new variations. Individuals with certain genes reproduce more than those with other genes, and the successful genes become more prevalent in the next generation. The consequence is *a gradual change in the frequency of various genes from one generation to the next*, otherwise known as evolution.

In a small population, a gene might spread accidentally, even if it is neutral or harmful. For example, imagine a population of insects on a small island. Some reproduce more than others just because they happened to settle in a place with better food or fewer predators. The ones that reproduce most successfully may or may not have the best genes. You can see this in an Online Try It Yourself activity.

Go to **www.cengage.com/psychology/kalat**. Navigate to the student website, then to the Online Try It Yourself section, and click Genetic Generations.

Still, a gene that is common in a large population almost certainly had benefits in the past, though not necessarily today. Evolutionary psychologists try to infer the benefits that favored certain genes. For example, many people have genes that cause them to overeat and become obese, a clear disadvantage. Such genes might have been advantageous in previous times when food shortages were common. If food is scarce, you should eat all you can. We shall encounter other speculations like this later in the text. However, we need to be cautious, as some of the speculations are uncertain and difficult to test (de Waal, 2002).

Nevertheless, evolutionary thinking helps us understand certain aspects of development (Bjorklund & Pellegrini, 2000). For example, consider a human infant's grasp reflex: An infant grasps tightly onto anything placed into the palm of the hand. As the infant grows older, that reflex is suppressed. For humans today, the function is far from obvious, but for our ancient ancestors,

the grasp reflex helped the infant hold onto the mother as she traveled (Figure 5.10).

6. Suppose we find that some gene that is widespread in the population appears to be useless or disadvantageous. How can we explain the spread of a harmful gene?

Concept Check

Answer

6. The disadvantageous gene could have spread randomly within a small population, perhaps because individuals with this gene happened to be in a good location. Another possibility is that the gene was beneficial at a previous time. (Another possibility, not already mentioned, is that the gene is useless or harmful in one way but produces another, valuable effect that we haven't yet discovered.)

THE FETUS AND THE NEWBORN

Genes control development of the body, which in turn provides for behavior. Let's focus briefly on very early development. During prenatal development, everyone starts as a *fertilized egg cell,* or zygote, which develops through its first few stages until the stage of fetus *about 8 weeks after conception.* As soon as 6 weeks after conception, the brain is mature enough to produce a few movements. Later, but still before birth, the head and eyes turn toward sounds, and the brain alternates between waking and sleeping (Joseph, 2000).

© Charles Gupton/Stock, Boston, Inc.

© Courtesy of Jo Ellen Kalat

Figure 5.10 Human infants tightly grasp anything in the palm of their hands. Today, this reflex has no obvious value, but in our remote ancestors, it helped infants hold onto their mothers.

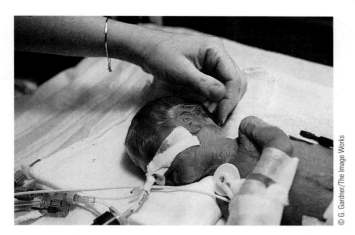

Figure 5.11 Babies with low birth weight are susceptible to physical and behavioral difficulties, but we cannot be sure that low birth weight causes the problems.

The growing body receives nutrition from the mother. Undernourished mothers generally give birth to small babies (Figure 5.11). The lower the birth weight, the greater the risk of impaired cognitive ability later in life (Shenkin, Starr, & Deary, 2004). Those who are born very premature are also at risk for long-lasting deficits in learning and emotional self-control (Clark, Woodward, Horwood, & Moor, 2008). These facts are clear, but their meaning is not.

The apparently obvious interpretation is that being born very small or very premature impairs brain development. However, we have to ask *why* the baby was born so small or so premature. In some cases, the mother was ill nourished, unhealthy, or disadvantaged in other ways (Garcia Coll, 1990; McCormick, 1985). One way to study the effect of birth weight separately from other influences is to examine pairs of twins where one twin was born heavier than the other. In most cases, the one with lower birth weight develops about as well as the heavier one (R. S. Wilson, 1987).

A more severe risk arises if the fetus is exposed to alcohol or other substances. Any drugs that the mother takes reach the fetus's brain while it is highly vulnerable (Hubbs-Tait, Nation, Krebs, & Bellinger, 2005). *If the mother drinks alcohol during pregnancy,* the infant may develop fetal alcohol syndrome, *a condition marked by stunted growth of the head and body; malformations of the face, heart, and ears; and nervous system damage, including seizures, hyperactivity, learning disabilities, and mental retardation* (Streissguth, Sampson, & Barr, 1989). The more alcohol the mother drinks during pregnancy, the greater the damage (Figure 5.12).

The reason for the nervous system damage is now understood: Developing neurons require persistent excitation to survive. Without it, they activate a self-destruct program. Alcohol interferes with the brain's main excitatory neurotransmitter (glutamate) and facilitates the main inhibitory neurotransmitter (GABA). It therefore decreases neurons' arousal and makes them self-destruct (Ikonomidou et al., 2000).

Still, it is remarkable that an occasional "high-risk" child—small at birth, exposed to alcohol or other drugs before birth, from an impoverished or turbulent family, a victim of prejudice, and so forth—overcomes all odds to become healthy and successful. Resilience (the ability to overcome obstacles) is poorly understood (Luthar, Cicchetti, & Becker, 2000), but it relates partly to temperament and genetic influences, education, and supportive relatives and friends (Bonanno & Mancini, 2008).

7. Anti-anxiety drugs increase activity at GABA synapses. Why should a pregnant woman avoid taking them?

Answer

7. These drugs decrease brain stimulation, and neurons that fail to receive enough stimulation self-destruct.

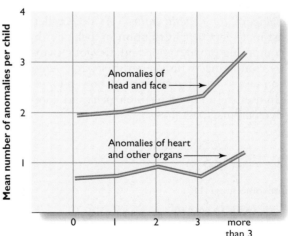

a

b

Figure 5.12 (a) The more alcohol a woman drinks during pregnancy, the more likely her baby is to have anomalies of the head, face, and organs. (Based on data of Ernhart et al., 1987) (b) A child with fetal alcohol syndrome: Note the wide separation between the eyes, a common feature of this syndrome.

In Closing

Getting Started in Life

Physicists say that the development of the universe depended on its "initial conditions"—the array of matter and energy a fraction of a second after the "big bang." The outcome of any experiment in physics or chemistry depends on the initial conditions—the type of matter, its temperature and pressure, and so forth. You had initial conditions, too—your genetics and prenatal environment. Understanding those initial conditions is critical to understanding you, but it would not be enough. At any point in your life, your behavior depends on a complex combination of your predispositions, past experiences, and current environment.

SUMMARY

- *Genes.* Genes control heredity. However, the process is complicated, as each strand of chromosome is modified by other sections. (page 145)
- *Sex-linked and sex-limited genes.* Genes on the X or Y chromosome are sex linked. An X-linked recessive gene will show its effects more frequently in males than in females. A sex-limited gene is present in both sexes, but it affects one more than the other. (page 146)
- *Heritability.* Researchers study twins and adopted children to estimate the heritability of various traits. However, the result of a gene can influence the environment in ways that magnify the effects of the gene. Therefore, heritability estimates are sometimes misleading. (page 147)
- *Evidence for genetic influences.* Researchers estimate genetic contributions to behavior by comparing monozygotic and dizygotic twins, by comparing twins reared in separate environments, and by examining how adopted children resemble their biological and adoptive parents. (page 148)

- *How genes affect behavior.* Genes affect behaviors by altering the chemistry of the brain. They also exert indirect effects by influencing some aspect of the body that in turn influences behavior. (page 150)
- *Interactions between heredity and environment.* In many cases, the effect of a gene depends on some aspect of the environment. For example, social support increases shyness in people with one form of a particular gene and decreases shyness in people with a different form of the gene. The phenylketonuria gene would lead to mental retardation, but a special diet minimizes its effects. (page 151)
- *Evolution.* Genes that increase the probability of survival and reproduction become more common in the next generation. Psychologists explain some aspects of behavior in terms of evolutionary trends that favored certain genes in our ancestors. (page 151)
- *Prenatal development.* The brain begins to mature long before birth. Exposure to drugs such as alcohol decreases brain activity and releases neurons' self-destruct programs. Some people manage to do well in life despite unpromising circumstances. (page 152)

KEY TERMS

chromosome (page 145)

dizygotic twins (page 148)

dominant (page 145)

evolution (page 152)

fetal alcohol syndrome (page 153)

fetus (page 152)

gene (page 145)

heritability (page 147)

interaction (page 151)

monozygotic twins (page 148)

multiplier effect (page 147)

phenylketonuria (PKU) (page 151)

recessive (page 146)

sex chromosomes (page 146)

sex-limited gene (page 147)

sex-linked (or X-linked) gene (page 147)

temperament (page 151)

X chromosome (page 147)

Y chromosome (page 147)

zygote (page 152)

Cognitive Development

- How can we know about an infant's abilities and experiences?
- How do children's thought processes differ from adults'?

The artwork of young children is amazingly inventive and revealing. One toddler, 1½ years old, proudly showed off a drawing that consisted only of dots. Adults were puzzled. It is a rabbit, the child explained, while making more dots: "Look: hop, hop, hop . . ." (Winner, 1986). When my daughter, Robin, was 6 years old, she drew a picture of a boy and a girl wearing Halloween costumes and drawing pictures (Figure 5.13). For the little girl's drawing, Robin pasted on some wildlife photos that, she insisted, were the little girl's drawings. The little boy's drawing was just a scribble. When I asked why the little girl's drawing was so much better than the little boy's, Robin replied, "Don't make fun of him, Daddy. He's doing the best he can."

Often, as in this case, a drawing expresses the child's worldview. As children grow older, their art becomes more

Figure 5.13 A drawing of two children drawing pictures, courtesy of 6-year-old Robin Kalat.

skillful, but it often becomes less expressive. The point is this: As we grow older, we gain many new abilities and skills, but we lose something, too.

Studying the abilities of young children is challenging. They misunderstand our questions and we misunderstand their answers. Developmental psychologists have made progress by devising increasingly careful methods of measurement.

INFANCY

As stressed in chapter 1, research progress depends on good measurement. How can we measure psychological processes in infants? A newborn is like a computer that is not attached to a monitor or printer: It processes information, but it cannot tell us about it. The challenge is to figure out how to attach some sort of monitor to find out what is happening inside. Researchers rely on the few responses that infants do control, such as eye and mouth movements.

Infants' Vision

William James, the founder of American psychology, said that as far as an infant can tell, the world is a "buzzing confusion," full of meaningless sights and sounds. Since James's time, psychologists have substantially increased their estimates of infants' vision.

As we grow older, we mature, but we revert to childlike behaviors when such behavior is acceptable.

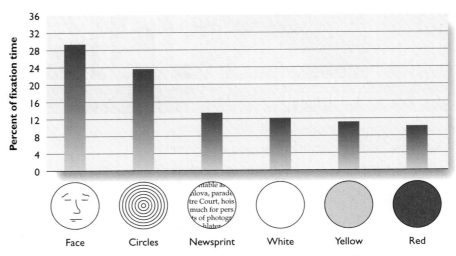

Figure 5.14 Infants pay more attention to faces than to other patterns. These results suggest that infants are born with certain visual preferences. (Based on Fantz, 1963)

We can start by recording an infant's eye movements. Even 2-day-old infants spend more time looking at drawings of human faces than at other patterns with similar areas of light and dark (Fantz, 1963) (see Figure 5.14). However, infants do not have the same concept of "face" that adults do. Figure 5.15 shows the results of distorting a face. Newborns gaze equally at distorted and normal faces. However, they gaze longer at right-side-up faces than upside-down faces regardless of distortion. Evidently, the newborn's concept of face is simply an oval with most of its content toward the top (Cassia, Turati, & Simion, 2004). Even at age 3 to 4 months old, an infant's concept of face differs from an adult's: Infants look longer at female than male faces and recognize female faces more easily than male faces (Ramsey-Rennels & Langlois, 2006). Presumably, the explanation is that most infants have more experience with female faces.

The ability to recognize faces continues developing for years. Parents in one study repeatedly read a storybook with photographs of two children's faces from many angles and with many expressions. After 2 weeks, 4-year-old children easily recognized pictures of the two children. However, when they had to choose between a normal picture and one with altered spacing among the features, they guessed randomly (Mondloch, Leis, & Maurer, 2006). Most people 6 years old or older easily see the difference between the photos in Figure 5.16, but 4-year-olds evidently do not.

By age 5 months, infants have had extensive visual experience but almost no experience at crawling or reaching for objects. Over the next several months, they increase their control of arm and leg movements. They learn to pick up toys, crawl around objects, avoid crawling off ledges, and in other ways coordinate what they see with

what they do. Apparently, they need that experience to learn a fear of heights (Adolph, 2000). Those who crawl early develop a fear of heights early; those who are late to crawl are also late to develop a fear of heights (Campos, Bertenthal, & Kermoian, 1992).

Infants' Hearing

It might seem difficult to measure newborns' responses to sounds because we cannot observe anything like eye movements. However, infants suck more vigorously when they are aroused, and certain sounds arouse them more than others do.

In one study, the experimenters played a brief sound and noted how it affected infants' sucking rate (Figure 5.17). On the first few occasions, the sound increased the sucking rate. A repeated sound produced less and less effect. We say that the infant became *habituated* to the sound. **Habituation** is *decreased response to a repeated stimulus.* When the experimenters substituted a new sound, the sucking rate increased. Evidently, the infant was aroused by the unfamiliar sound. *When a change in a stimulus increases a previously habituated response,* we say that the stimulus produced **dishabituation.**

Psychologists monitor habituation and dishabituation to determine whether infants hear a difference between two sounds. For example, infants who have become habituated to the sound *ba* will increase their sucking rate when they hear the sound *pa* (Eimas, Siqueland, Jusczyk, & Vigorito, 1971). Apparently, even month-old infants notice the difference between *ba* and *pa,* an important distinction for later language comprehension.

Similar studies have shown that infants who have habituated to hearing one language, such as

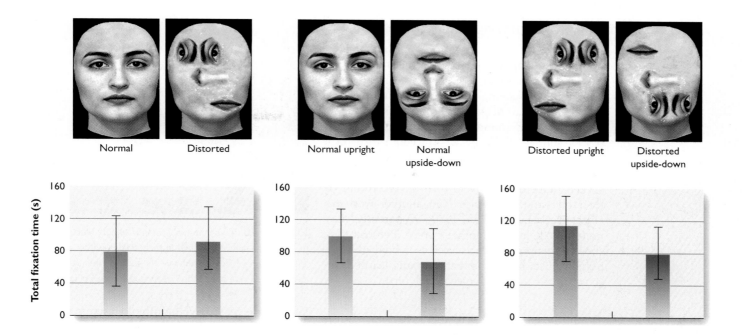

| Normal | Distorted | Normal upright | Normal upside-down | Distorted upright | Distorted upside-down |

Figure 5.15 Infants gaze about equally at normal and distorted faces, but they stare longer at upright than upside-down faces. (Cassia, V. M., Turati, C., & Simion, F., 2004. Can a nonspecific bias toward top-heavy patterns explain newborns' face preferences? *Psychological Science, 15,* 379–383)

Dutch, dishabituate when they hear a different language, such as Japanese. At first, they show no response to a shift between Dutch and English, presumably because the sounds and rhythms are similar. By age 5 months, however, they dishabituate when they hear a change from a British accent to an American accent (Jusczyk, 2002). Studies of this sort show that children discriminate relevant language sounds long before they know what the words mean.

8. Suppose an infant habituates to the sound *ba,* but when we substitute the sound *bla,* the infant fails to increase its sucking rate. What interpretation would be likely?

Concept Check

Answer

8. Evidently, the infant does not hear a difference between *ba* and *bla.* (This is a hypothetical result; the study has not been done.)

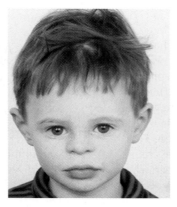

Figure 5.16 These faces are the same except for the positions of the eyes, nose, and mouth. Four-year-olds do not recognize which of these faces is familiar. ("Recognizing the face of Johnny, Suzy, and me: Insensitivity to the spacing among features at 4 years of age," by C. J. Mondloch, A. Leis, & D. Maurer. (2006). *Child Development, 77,* 234–243. Blackwell Publishers)

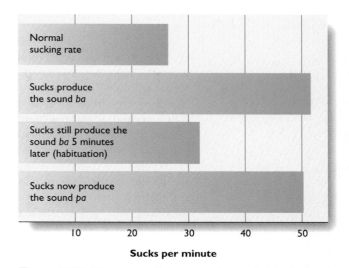

Normal sucking rate

Sucks produce the sound *ba*

Sucks still produce the sound *ba* 5 minutes later (habituation)

Sucks now produce the sound *pa*

Sucks per minute

Figure 5.17 After repeatedly hearing a *ba* sound, the infant's sucking habituates. When a new sound, *pa,* follows, the sucking rate increases. (Based on results of Eimas, Siqueland, Jusczyk, & Vigorito, 1971)

Infants' Learning and Memory

How could we measure learning and memory in infants who cannot speak? Several studies have used the fact that infants learn to suck harder on a nipple if their sucking turns on a sound. Investigators then tried to determine whether infants suck harder for some sounds than others. In one study, babies younger than 3 days old could turn on a tape recording of a woman's voice by sucking on a nipple at certain times or rates. The results: They sucked more frequently to turn on recordings of their own mother's voice than another woman's voice (DeCasper & Fifer, 1980). Apparently, they preferred their own mother's voice. Because they showed this preference as early as the day of birth, psychologists believe that the infants learned the sound of the mother's voice before birth.

Figure 5.18 Two-month-old infants rapidly learn to kick to activate a mobile attached to their ankles with a ribbon. They remember how to activate the mobile when tested days later. (From Hildreth, Sweeney, & Rovee-Collier, 2003)

9. Suppose a newborn sucks to turn on a tape recording of its father's voice. Eventually, the baby habituates and the sucking frequency decreases. Now the experimenters substitute the recording of a different man's voice. What would you conclude if the sucking frequency increased? What if it remained the same? What if it decreased?

Concept Check

Answer

9. If the frequency increased, we would conclude that the infant recognizes the difference between the father's voice and the other voice. If the frequency remained the same, we would conclude that the infant did not notice a difference. If it decreased, we would assume that the infant preferred the sound of the father's voice.

Using slightly older infants, researchers examined responses to changing and unchanging visual stimuli. Suppose an infant can see two monitors. One of them shows a simple display for half a second, then goes blank for a quarter of a second, then shows the same display again, and so forth. The other monitor shows a display, goes blank, shows a different display, and so on. Four-month-old infants look mostly toward the changing display, indicating that they remember what they had seen, at least for a quarter of a second (Oakes, Ross-Sheehy, & Luck, 2007). Also, when they are viewing changing displays, their brain waves show increased activity (Bauer, 2007).

Carolyn Rovee-Collier (1997, 1999) demonstrated an ability to remember a new response for days. She attached a ribbon to an ankle so that an infant could activate a mobile by kicking with one leg (Figure 5.18). Two-month-old infants quickly learned this response and generally kept the mobile going nonstop for a full 45-minute session. (Infants have little control over their leg muscles, but they don't need much control to keep the mobile going.) Once they have learned, they quickly remember what to do when the ribbon is reattached several days later—to the infants' evident delight. Six-month-old infants remembered the response for 2 weeks. Even after forgetting it, they could relearn it in 2 minutes and then retain it for an additional month or more (Hildreth, Sweeney, & Rovee-Collier, 2003).

RESEARCH DESIGNS FOR STUDYING DEVELOPMENT

As we move beyond the study of infancy, we begin to compare one age with another, and we encounter special research problems that go beyond the general issues raised in chapter 2. Do we study older and younger people at the same time, or do we study one group of people when they are younger, and then the same group again after they have grown older? Each method has its strengths and limitations.

Cross-Sectional and Longitudinal Designs

A **cross-sectional study** *compares groups of individuals of different ages at the same time.* For example, we could compare the drawing abilities of 6-year-olds, 8-year-olds, and 10-year-olds. A weakness of cross-sectional studies is the difficulty of obtaining equivalent samples at different ages. For example, suppose you want to compare 20-year-olds and 60-year-olds. If you study 20-year-olds from the local college, where do you find an equivalent group of 60-year-olds?

A longitudinal study *follows a single group of individuals as they develop.* For example, we could study one group of children from, say, 6 to 12. Table 5.1 contrasts the two kinds of studies. Longitudinal studies face practical difficulties. A longitudinal study necessarily takes years, and not everyone who participates the first time is willing and available later.

Furthermore, those who remain in a study may differ in important ways from those who leave. Suppose a visitor from outer space observes that about 50% of young adult humans are males, but among 70-, 80-, and 90-year-olds, the percentage of men steadily declines. The visitor concludes that, as humans grow older, males transform into females. You know why that conclusion is wrong. On the average, men die earlier, leaving a greater percentage of older females. Selective attrition is *the tendency for certain kinds of people to drop out of a study.* People drop out for many reasons, including health, moving far away, or loss of interest. Psychologists can compensate for selective attrition by discarding the data for people who left the study.

A longitudinal study also faces the difficulty of separating the effects of age from the effects of changes in society. For example, suppose we find that most 20-year-olds in the United States in 1970 were politically liberal, but 30 years later, most of those individuals became more conservative. Did they become more conservative because of age or because the country as a whole became more conservative?

Nevertheless, certain questions logically require a longitudinal study. For example, to study the effects of divorce on children, researchers compare how each child reacts at first with how that same child reacts later. To study whether happy children become happy adults, we would follow a single group of people over time.

10. Suppose you study the effect of age on artistic abilities, and you want to be sure that any apparent differences depend on age and not differences among generations. Should you use a longitudinal study or a cross-sectional study?

11. At Santa Enigma College, the average first-year student has a C-minus average, and the average senior has a B-plus average. An observer concludes that, as students progress through college, they improve their study habits. Based on the idea of selective attrition, propose another possible explanation.

Concept Check

Table 5.1 Cross-Sectional and Longitudinal Studies

	Description	Advantages	Disadvantages	Example
Cross-sectional	Several groups of subjects of various ages studied at one time	1. Quick 2. No risk of confusing age effects with effects of changes in society	1. Risk of sampling error by getting different kinds of people at different ages 2. Risk of cohort effects	Compare memory abilities of 3-, 5-, and 7-year-olds
Longitudinal	One group of subjects studied repeatedly as the members grow older	1. No risk of sampling differences 2. Can study effects of one experience on later development 3. Can study consistency within individuals over time	1. Takes a long time 2. Some participants quit 3. Sometimes hard to separate effects of age from changes in society	Study memory abilities of 3-year-olds, and of the same children again 2 and 4 years later

Answers

10. ¹¹ gnol sroines emoceb ot hguone

11. for first-year students) do not stay in school (and therefore pull down the grade average year students who have the lowest grades Another possible explanation is that the first-born at different times.

10. Use a longitudinal study, which studies the same people repeatedly instead of people

Sequential Designs

A sequential (or "cross-sequential") design combines cross-sectional and longitudinal designs. In a sequential design, *researchers start with groups of people of different ages, studied at the same time, and then study them again at one or more later times.* For example, imagine we study the drawings of 6-year-olds and 8-year-olds and then examine the drawings by those same children 2 years later:

First study	2 years later
Group A, age 6 years	Group A, now 8 years old
Group B, age 8 years	Group B, now 10 years old

If Group A at age 8 resembles Group B at age 8, we can feel confident that the groups are comparable. We can then compare Group A at 6, both groups at 8, and Group B at 10.

12. In the sectional design just described, what would we conclude if Group A at age 8 years differed from Group B at 8 years?

Answer

12. One hypothesis is different sampling. Perhaps one group was healthier, came from a better school, or had some other advantage. Another possibility is that society as a whole had changed during the 2 years in some way that affected children's drawings.

Cohort Effects

Suppose you had been born in 1940. Your childhood and adolescence would have been very different from today: no Internet, computers, iPods, cell phones, air conditioners, automatic dishwashers, or appliances for washing and drying clothes. You would have listened to radio instead of watching television. Long-distance telephone calls were a luxury. Few women or minorities went to college, and those few had limited job opportunities afterward. If you had lived then, how would you have been different?

People of different generations differ in many ways, which psychologists call *cohort effects* (Figure 5.19). A **cohort** is *a group of people born at a particular time or a group of people who enter an organization at a particular time.*

The era in which you grew up is a powerful influence on your personality, social behavior, and attitudes. For example, people whose youth spanned the Great Depression and World War II learned to save money and to sacrifice their own

Figure 5.19 People born at different times grow up with different customs, education, nutrition, and health care. Such influences are called *cohort effects.*

pleasures for the needs of the country. Even after the war was over and prosperity reigned, most remained thrifty and cautious (Rogler, 2002). In contrast, young people of today have had much more leisure time (Larson, 2001). Jean Twenge (2006) has compared cohort effects to the differences among cultures. Indeed, the technology you have grown up with may seem unfamiliar and alien to your grandparents, who in some ways are like "immigrants" to modern culture. Many aspects of intellect and personality differ between generations, as we shall examine in later chapters.

. . . .

13. Suppose you want to study the effect of age on choice of clothing. Would cohort effects have greater influence on a longitudinal study or a cross-sectional study?

Answer

13. A cross-sectional study would show cohort effects. If older people dress differently from younger people, it may be that the older generation has always had different standards or tastes.

. . . .

JEAN PIAGET'S VIEW OF COGNITIVE DEVELOPMENT

Now armed with an understanding of research methods for studying development, let's proceed with cognitive development. Attending a political rally has a profound effect on a young adult, less effect on a preteen, and none on an infant. Playing with a pile of blocks is a more stimulating experience for a young child than for anyone older. The effect of any experience depends

Jean Piaget (on the left) demonstrated that children with different levels of maturity react differently to the same experience.

on someone's maturity. The theorist who made this point most influentially was Jean Piaget (pee-ah-ZHAY) (1896–1980).

Early in his career, while administering IQ tests to French-speaking children in Switzerland, Piaget was fascinated that so many children of a given age gave the *same* incorrect answer to a given question. He concluded that children have qualitatively different thought processes from adults. Piaget made extensive longitudinal studies of children, especially his own. According to Piaget, intellectual development is not merely an accumulation of experience. Rather, the child constructs new mental processes as he or she interacts with the environment.

In Piaget's terminology, behavior is based on schemata (the plural of *schema*). A **schema** is *an organized way of interacting with objects.* For instance, infants have a grasping schema and a sucking schema. Older infants gradually add new schemata to their repertoire and adapt their old ones. The adaptation takes place through the processes of assimilation and accommodation.

Assimilation means *applying an old schema to new objects or problems.* For example, a child who observes that animals move on their own may believe that the sun and moon, which seem to move, must be alive also. (Many ancient adults believed the same thing.) **Accommodation** means *modifying an old schema to fit a new object or problem.* For example, a child may learn that "only living things move on their own" is a rule with exceptions and that the sun and moon are not alive.

Infants shift back and forth between assimilation and accommodation. **Equilibration** is *the establishment of harmony or balance between the two,* and according to Piaget, equilibration is the key to intellectual growth. A discrepancy occurs between the child's current understanding and some evidence to the contrary. The child accommodates to that discrepancy and achieves an equilibration at a higher level.

The same processes occur in adults. When you see a new mathematical problem, you try several methods until you hit upon one that works. In other words, you assimilate the new problem to your old schema. However, if the new problem is different from previous problems, you modify (accommodate) your schema to find a solution. Through processes like these, said Piaget, intellectual growth occurs.

Piaget contended that children progress through four major stages of intellectual development:

1. *The sensorimotor stage* (from birth to almost 2 years)
2. *The preoperational stage* (from just before 2 to 7 years)

3. *The concrete operations stage* (from about 7 to 11 years)
4. *The formal operations stage* (from about 11 years onward)

The ages are variable, and not everyone reaches the formal operations stage. However, apparently, everyone progresses through the stages in the same order. Let us consider children's capacities at each of Piaget's stages.

INFANCY: PIAGET'S SENSORIMOTOR STAGE

Piaget called the first stage of intellectual development the sensorimotor stage because *at this early age (the first 1½ to 2 years) behavior is mostly simple motor responses to sensory stimuli*—for example, the grasp reflex and the sucking reflex. According to Piaget, infants respond only to what they see and hear at the moment. In particular, he believed that children during this period fail to respond to objects they remember seeing even a few seconds ago. What evidence could he have for this view?

What's the Evidence?
The Infant's Concept of Object Permanence

Piaget argued that infants in the first few months of life lack the concept of object permanence, *the idea that objects continue to exist even when we do not see or hear them.* That is, for an infant, "Out of sight, out of existence."

Piaget drew his inferences from observations like this: Place a toy in front of a 6-month-old infant, who reaches out for it. Later, place a toy in the same place, but before the infant has a chance to grab it, cover it with a clear glass. No problem; the infant removes the glass and takes the toy. Now repeat that procedure but use an opaque (nonclear) glass. The infant, who watched you place the glass over the toy, makes no effort to remove the glass and obtain the toy. Next, place a thin barrier between the infant and the toy. An infant who cannot see the toy does not reach for it (Piaget, 1937/1954) (see Figure 5.20).

According to Piaget, the infant does not know that the hidden toy continues to exist. However, the results vary depending on circumstances. For example, if you show a toy and then turn out the lights, a 7-month-old infant reaches out toward the unseen toy if it was a familiar toy but not if it was unfamiliar (Shinskey & Munakata, 2005). A study by Renee Baillargeon (1986) also suggests that infants show signs of understanding object permanence when they are tested differently.

Hypothesis An infant who sees an event that would be impossible (if objects are permanent) will be surprised and therefore will stare longer than will an infant who sees a similar but possible event.

Method Infants aged 6 or 8 months watched a series of events. The infant watched the experimenter raise a screen to show the track and then watched a toy car go down a slope and emerge on the other side of the screen, as shown here. This was called a "possible" event.

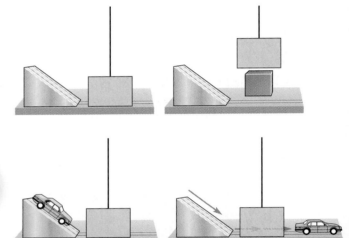

Possible event. The box is behind the track, and the car passes by the box.

The researchers measured how long the child stared after the car passed by. They repeated the procedure until the child's staring time decreased for three trials in a row (showing habituation). Then the experimenters presented a series of "possible" events, as just described, and "impossible" events like this:

 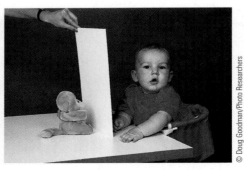

Figure 5.20 (a) A 6- to 9-month-old child reaches for a visible toy but not one that is hidden behind a barrier (b) even if the child sees someone hide the toy. According to Piaget, this observation indicates that the child hasn't yet grasped the concept of object permanence.

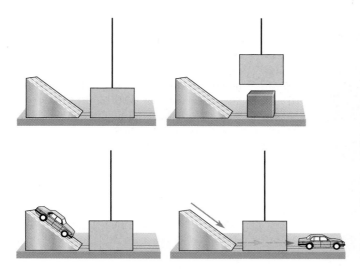

Impossible event. The raised screen shows a box on the track where the car would pass. After the screen lowers, the car goes down the slope and emerges on the other side.

In an impossible event, the raised screen showed a box on the track where the car would pass. After the screen lowered, the car went down the slope and emerged on the other side. (The experimenters pulled the box off the track after lowering the screen.) The experimenters measured each child's staring times after both kinds of events. They repeated both events two more times, randomizing the order of events.

Results Figure 5.21 shows the mean looking times. Infants stared longer after seeing an impossible event than after seeing a possible event. They also stared longer after the first pair of events than after the second and third pairs (Baillargeon, 1986).

Interpretation Why did the infants stare longer at the impossible event? The inference—admittedly only an inference—is that the infants found the impossible event surprising. To be surprised, the infants had to expect that the box would continue to exist and that a car could not go through it. If this inference is correct, even 6-month-old infants have some understanding of object permanence, as well as elementary physics. A later study with a slightly different method demonstrated object permanence in infants as young as 3 1/2 months (Baillargeon, 1987).

Still, remember that 9-month-olds failed Piaget's object permanence task of reaching out to pick up a hidden object. Do infants understand object permanence or not? Evidently, the question is not well phrased. Infants use a concept in some situations and not others. The same is true for all of us. Have you ever stated a grammatical rule correctly in English class and then violated the rule in your own speech? Have you ever learned a formula in a math or physics class and then failed to apply it to a new situation?

Other psychologists have modified Baillargeon's procedure to test many other aspects of infants' cognition. For example, researchers put five objects behind a screen, added five more, and removed the screen. Nine-month-olds stared longer when they saw just five objects than when they saw ten, suggesting some understanding of addition (McCrink &

Wynn, 2004). Researchers buried a ball in the sand and then retrieved apparently the same ball from the same or a different location. Infants stared longer when the ball emerged from the different location (Newcombe, Sluzenski, & Huttenlocher, 2005). In another study, infants stared (suggesting surprise) when a toy hung mostly over a table without falling. They reached for a toy in the middle of a table rather than one hanging way over the edge, suggesting that they knew the one hanging over the edge must be glued or attached in some way (Hespos & Baillargeon, 2007). If we assume that staring means surprise and surprise implies an understanding of mathematics and physics, then infants understand far more than we previously imagined. However, infants as old as 12 months show no surprise if you place a toy into a container, where it just barely fits, and then pull out a toy of different shape or color (Baillargeon, Li, Ng, & Yuan, 2009). Evidently, infants imagine that objects can magically change shape or color.

Here are two conclusions: First, we should be cautious about inferring what infants or anyone else can or cannot do; the results depend on the procedures. Second, concepts develop gradually; it is possible to show a concept in one situation and not another.

Sense of Self

Another aspect of children's progress through the sensorimotor stage is that they appear to gain some concept of "self." Here is the evidence: A mother puts a spot of unscented rouge on an infant's nose and then places the infant in front of a mirror. Infants younger than 1½ years old either ignore the red spot on the baby in the mirror or reach out to touch the mirror. At some point after age 1½ years, infants instead touch themselves on the nose, indicating that they recognize themselves in the mirror (Figure 5.22). Infants show this sign of self-recognition at varying ages; the age when they first show self-recognition is about the same as when they begin to act embarrassed (M. Lewis, Sullivan, Stanger, & Weiss, 1991). They show a sense of self in both situations or neither.

Before this time, do they fail to distinguish between self and other? Perhaps, but we cannot be sure. Before age 1½, we see no evidence for a sense of self, but absence of evidence is not evidence of absence. Perhaps younger infants would show a sense of self in some other test that we have not yet devised.

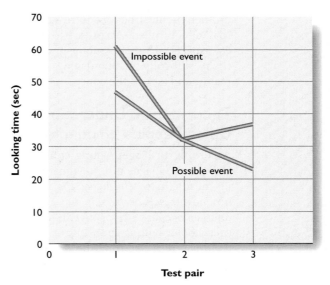

Figure 5.21 Mean looking times of 6- and 8-month-old infants after they had watched either possible or impossible events. (From Baillargeon, 1986)

Figure 5.22 If someone places a bit of unscented rouge on a child's nose, a 2-year-old looking at a mirror shows self-recognition by touching his or her own nose.

EARLY CHILDHOOD: PIAGET'S PREOPERATIONAL STAGE

By age 1½ to 2, children begin speaking. A child who asks for a toy obviously understands object permanence. Nevertheless, young children still misunderstand much. They do not understand how a mother can be someone else's daughter. A boy with one brother will assert that his brother has no brother. Piaget refers to this period as the **preoperational stage** because *the child lacks operations, which are reversible mental processes.* For a boy to understand that his brother has a brother, he must be able to reverse the concept of "having a brother." According to Piaget, three typical aspects of preoperational thought are egocentrism, difficulty distinguishing appearance from reality, and lack of the concept of conservation.

Egocentrism: Understanding Other People's Thoughts

According to Piaget, young children's thought is **egocentric**. Piaget did *not* mean selfish. Instead, he meant that *a child sees the world as centered around himself or herself and cannot easily take another person's perspective.* If you sit opposite a preschooler with a set of blocks between you, the child can describe how the blocks look from the child's side but not how they would look from your side.

Another example: Young children hear a story about a little girl, Lucy, who wants her old pair of red shoes. Part way through the story, Lucy's brother Linus enters the room, and she asks him to bring her red shoes. He goes and brings back her new red shoes, and she is angry because she wanted the old red shoes. Young children hearing the story are surprised that he brought the wrong shoes because *they* knew which shoes she wanted (Keysar, Barr, & Horton, 1998).

However, young children do understand another person's perspective on simple tasks. In one study, 5- and 6-year-old children had to tell an adult to pick up a particular glass. If a child saw that the adult could see two glasses, the child usually said to pick up the "big" or "little" glass to identify the right one. If the child saw that the adult could see only one glass, the child often said just "the glass" (Nadig & Sedivy, 2002) (see Figure 5.23).

14. Which of the following is the clearest example of egocentric thinking?

   a. A writer who uses someone else's words without giving credit.

   b. A politician who blames others for everything that goes wrong.

   c. A professor who gives the same complicated lecture to a freshman class as to a convention of professionals.

Answer

14. c is a case of egocentric thought, a failure to recognize another person's point of view.

To say that a child is egocentric means that he or she does not understand what other people know and don't know. Psychologists say that a young child lacks, but gradually develops, **theory of mind**, which is *an understanding that other people have a mind, too, and that each person knows some things that other people don't know.* How can we know whether a child has this understanding? Here is one example of a research effort.

What's the Evidence?
Children's Understanding of Other People's Knowledge

How and when do children first understand that other people have minds and knowledge? Researchers have devised some clever experiments to address this question.

Hypothesis A child who understands that other people have minds will distinguish between someone who knows something and someone who could not.

Method A 3- or 4-year-old child sat in front of four cups (Figure 5.24) and watched as one adult hid a candy or toy

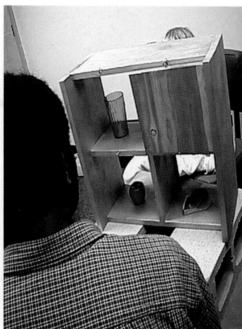

Figure 5.23 Sometimes, a child saw that the adult could see two glasses. At other times, it was clear that the adult could see only one. If two glasses were visible, the child usually told the adult which glass to pick up, instead of saying, "pick up the glass." (Based on research by Nadig, A. & Sedivy, J. (2002). Evidence of perspective-taking constraints in children's on-line reference resolution. *Psychological Science, 13 (4)*, pp. 329–336. Used by permission of the author.)

under one of the cups, although a screen prevented the child from seeing which cup. Then another adult entered the room. The "informed" adult pointed to one cup to show where he or she had just hidden the surprise; the "uninformed" adult pointed to a different cup. The child then had an opportunity to look under one cup for the treat.

This procedure was repeated 10 times for each child. The two adults alternated roles, but on each trial, one or the other hid the treat while the other was absent. That is, one was informed and the other was not.

Results Of the 4-year-olds, 10 of 20 consistently chose the cup indicated by the informed adult. (The other 10 showed no consistent preference.) That is, they understood who had the relevant knowledge and who did not. However, the 3-year-olds were as likely to follow the lead of one adult as the other (Povinelli & deBlois, 1992).

Interpretation Evidently, 4-year-olds are more likely than 3-year-olds to understand other people's knowledge (or lack of it). Psychologists have found similar results for children in five cultures (Callaghan et al., 2005).

Distinguishing Appearance from Reality

Piaget and many other psychologists have contended that young children do not distinguish clearly between appearance and reality. For example, a child who sees you put a white ball behind a blue filter will say that the ball is blue. When you ask, "Yes, I know the ball *looks* blue, but what color is it *really*?" the child replies that it really *is* blue (Flavell, 1986). Similarly, a 3-year-old who encounters a sponge that looks like a rock will say that it really is a rock, but a child who says it is a sponge will also insist that it *looks like* a sponge.

Other psychologists have argued that the 3-year-old's difficulty is more with language than with the appearance–reality distinction. (After all, 3-year-olds do play games of make-believe, so they sometimes distinguish appearance from reality.) In one study, psychologists showed 3-year-olds a sponge that looked like a rock and let them touch it. When the investigators asked what it looked like and what it was *really*, most of the children said "rock" both times or "sponge" both times. However, if the investigators asked, "Bring me something so I can wipe up some spilled water," the children brought the sponge. And when the investigators asked, "Bring me something so I can take a picture of a teddy bear with something that looks like a rock," they brought the same object. So evidently, they did understand that something could be a sponge and look like a rock, even if they didn't say so (Sapp, Lee, & Muir, 2000).

Also consider this experiment: A psychologist shows a child a playhouse room that is a scale model of a full-size room. The psychologist hides a tiny toy in the small room while the child watches and explains that a bigger toy just like it is "in the same place" in the bigger room. (For example, if the little toy is behind the sofa in the little room, the big toy is behind the sofa in the big room.) Then the psychologist asks the child to find the big toy in the big room. Most 3-year-olds go to the correct place at once (DeLoache, 1989). Most 2½-year-old children, however, search haphazardly (Figure 5.25a). If the experimenter shows the child the big toy in the big room and asks the child to find the little toy "in the same place" in

Figure 5.24 A child sits in front of a screen covering four cups and watches as one adult hides a surprise under one cup. Then that adult and another (who had not been present initially) point to one of the cups to signal where the surprise is hidden. Many 4-year-olds, unlike 3-year-olds, consistently follow the advice of the informed adult.

the little room, the results are the same: Most 3-year-olds find it, and most 2½-year-olds do not (DeLoache, 1989).

Before we conclude what a 2½-year-old cannot do, consider this clever follow-up study: The psychologist hides a toy in the small room while the child watches. Then both step out of the room, and the psychologist shows the child a "machine that can make things bigger." The psychologist aims a beam from the machine at the room and takes the child out of the way. They hear some chunkata-chunkata sounds, and then the psychologist shows the full-size "blown-up" room and asks the child to find the hidden toy. Even 2½-year-olds go immediately to the correct location (DeLoache, Miller, & Rosengren, 1997) (Figure 5.25b). (Incidentally, hardly any of the children doubted that the machine had expanded the room. Many continued to believe it even after the psychologist explained what really happened!) The overall conclusion is that a child shows or fails to show an ability depending on how we ask the question.

Developing the Concept of Conservation

According to Piaget, preoperational children lack the concept of conservation. They fail to *understand that objects conserve such properties as number, length, volume, area, and mass after changes in the shape or arrangement of the objects.* They cannot perform the mental operations necessary to understand the transformations. Table 5.2 shows typical conservation tasks. For example, if we show two equal glasses with the same amount of water and then pour the contents of one glass into a taller, thinner glass, preoperational children say that the second glass contains more water (Figure 5.26).

I once thought perhaps the phrasing of the questions tricks children into saying something they do not believe. If you have the same doubts, borrow a 6-year-old child and try it yourself with your own wording. Here's my experience: Once when I was discussing Piaget in my introductory psychology class, I invited my son Sam, then 5½ years old, to take part in a class demonstration. I started with two glasses of water, which he agreed contained equal amounts of water. Then I poured the water from one glass into a wider glass, lowering the water level. When I asked Sam which glass contained more water, he confidently pointed to the tall, thin one. After class he complained, "Daddy, why did you ask me such an easy question? Everyone could see that there was more water in that glass! You should have asked me something harder to show how smart I am!" The following year, I brought Sam, now 6½ years old,

a A 2¹/₂-year-old is shown a small room where a stuffed animal is hidden.

Child is unable to find the stuffed animal in the larger room.

b Child is shown a small room where a stuffed animal is hidden.

Child is told that the machine expands the room. Child stands out of the way during some noises and then returns.

Child is able to find the stuffed animal in the "blown-up" room.

Figure 5.25 If an experimenter hides a small toy in a small room and asks a child to find a larger toy "in the same place" in the larger room, most 2½-year-olds search haphazardly (a). However, the same children know where to look if the experimenter says this is the same room as before, but a machine has expanded it (b).

Table 5.2 Typical Tasks Used to Measure Conservation

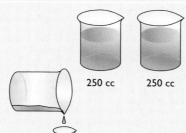

Conservation of number
Preoperational children say that these two rows contain the same number of pennies.
Preoperational children say that the second row has more pennies.

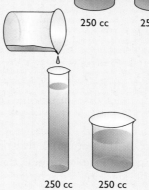

Conservation of volume
Preoperational children say that the two same-size containers have the same amount of water.

250 cc   250 cc

Preoperational children say that the taller, thinner container has more water.

250 cc   250 cc

Conservation of mass
Preoperational children say that the two same-size balls of clay have the same amount of clay.
Preoperational children say that a squashed ball of clay contains a different amount of clay than the same-size round ball of clay.

Figure 5.26 Preoperational children don't understand that the volume of water remains constant despite changes in its appearance. During the transition to concrete operations, a child finds conservation tasks difficult and confusing.

to class for the same demonstration. I poured the water from one of the tall glasses into a wider one and asked him which glass contained more water. He looked and paused. His face turned red. Finally, he whispered, "Daddy, I don't know!" After class he complained, "Why did you ask me such a hard question? I'm never coming back to any of your classes again!" The question that used to be embarrassingly easy had become embarrassingly difficult.

The next year, when he was 7½, I tried again (at home). This time he answered confidently, "Both glasses have the same amount of water, of course. Why? Is this some sort of trick question?"

LATER CHILDHOOD AND ADOLESCENCE: PIAGET'S STAGES OF CONCRETE OPERATIONS AND FORMAL OPERATIONS

At about age 7, children enter the stage of concrete operations and begin to understand the conservation of physical properties. The transition is gradual, however. For instance, a 6-year-old child may understand that squashing a ball of clay does not change its weight but may not realize until years later that squashing the ball does not change the volume of water it displaces when it is dropped into a glass.

According to Piaget, during the stage of concrete operations, *children perform mental operations on concrete objects but still have trouble with abstract or hypothetical ideas.* For example, ask this question: "How could you move a 4-mile-high mountain of whipped cream

from one side of the city to the other?" Older children enjoy devising imaginative answers, but children in the concrete operations stage complain that the question is silly.

Or ask, "If you could have a third eye anywhere on your body, where would you put it?" Children in this stage generally respond immediately that they would put it right between the other two, on their foreheads. Older children suggest more imaginative ideas such as on the back of their head, in the stomach (so they could watch food digesting), or on the tip of a finger (so they could peek around corners).

Finally, in Piaget's stage of formal operations, adolescents develop *the mental processes that deal with abstract, hypothetical situations. Those processes demand logical, deductive reasoning and systematic planning.* According to Piaget, children reach the stage of formal operations at about age 11. Later researchers found that many people reach this stage later or not at all.

Thinking with formal operations demonstrates planning. For example, we set up five bottles of clear liquid and explain that it is possible to mix some combination to produce a yellow liquid. The task is to find that combination. Children in the concrete operations stage plunge right in with no plan. They try combining bottles A and B, then C and D, then perhaps A, C, and E. Soon they have forgotten which combinations they've already tried. Adolescents in the formal operations stage approach the problem more systematically. They may first try all the two-bottle combinations: AB, AC, AD, AE, BC, and so forth. If those fail, they try three-bottle combinations: ABC, ABD, ABE, ACD, and so on. By trying every possible combination only once, they are sure to succeed. Table 5.3 summarizes Piaget's four stages.

Table 5.3 Summary of Piaget's Stages of Cognitive Development

Stage and Approximate Age	Achievements and Activities	Limitations
Sensorimotor (birth to 1½ years)	Reacts to sensory stimuli through reflexes and other responses	Little use of language; seems not to understand object permanence in the early part of this stage
Preoperational (1½ to 7 years)	Develops language; can represent objects mentally by words and other symbols; can respond to objects that are remembered but not present	Lacks operations (reversible mental processes); lacks concept of conservation; focuses on one property at a time (such as length or width), not on both at once; still has trouble distinguishing appearance from reality
Concrete operations (7 to 11 years)	Understands conservation of mass, number, and volume; can reason logically with regard to concrete objects that can be seen or touched	Has trouble reasoning about abstract concepts and hypothetical situations
Formal operations (11 years onward)	Can reason logically about abstract and hypothetical concepts; develops strategies; plans actions in advance	None beyond the occasional irrationalities of all human thought

15. You are given the following information about four children. Assign each of them to one of Piaget's stages of intellectual development.

Concept Check

a. Child has mastered the concept of conservation but has trouble with abstract and hypothetical questions.

b. Child performs well on tests of object permanence but has trouble with conservation.

c. Child has schemata but does not speak in complete sentences and fails tests of object permanence.

d. Child performs well on tests of object permanence, conservation, and hypothetical questions.

Answers

15. **a.** concrete operations stage; **b.** preoperational stage; **c.** sensorimotor stage; **d.** formal operations stage.

Are Piaget's Stages Distinct?

Piaget regarded the four stages of intellectual development as distinct. He believed a transition from one stage to the next required a major reorganization of thinking, almost as a caterpillar metamorphoses into a chrysalis and a chrysalis metamorphoses into a butterfly. That is, intellectual growth has periods of revolutionary reorganization.

Later research has cast much doubt on this conclusion. If it were true, then a child in a given stage of development—say, the preoperational stage—should perform consistently at that level. In fact, children fluctuate as a task is made more or less difficult. For example, consider the conservation-of-number task, in which an investigator presents two rows of seven or more objects, spreads out one row, and asks which row has more. Preoperational children reply that the spread-out row has more. However, when Rochel Gelman (1982) presented two rows of only three objects each (Figure 5.27) and then spread out one of the rows, even 3- and 4-year-old children usually answered that the rows had the same number of items. After much

a

b

Figure 5.27 (a) With the standard conservation-of-number task, preoperational children answer that the spread-out row has more items. (b) With a simplified task, the same children say that both rows have the same number of items.

practice with short rows, most of the 3- and 4-year-olds also answered correctly that a spread-out row of eight items had the same number of items as a tightly packed row of eight.

Whereas Piaget believed children made distinct jumps from one stage to another, most psychologists today see development as gradual and continuous (Courage & Howe, 2002). That is, the difference between older children and younger children is not so much a matter of *having* or *lacking* some ability. Rather, older children extend their abilities to more and more situations.

Differing Views: Piaget and Vygotsky

One implication of Piaget's view is that children must discover certain concepts, such as the concept of conservation, mainly on their own. Teaching a concept means directing children's attention to the key aspects and letting them discover the concept. In contrast, Russian psychologist Lev Vygotsky (1978) argued that educators should not wait for children to rediscover the principles of physics and mathematics. Indeed, he argued, the distinguishing characteristic of human thought is that language and symbols let us profit from the experience of previous generations.

When Vygotsky said that adults should teach children, he did not mean that adults should ignore the child's developmental level. Rather, every child has a **zone of proximal development**, which

is *the distance between what a child can do alone and what the child can do with help.* Instruction should remain within that zone. For example, one should not try to teach a 4-year-old the concept of conservation of volume. However, a 6-year-old who does not yet understand the concept might learn it with help and guidance. Similarly, children improve their recall of lists or stories if adults help them understand and organize the information (Larkina, Güler, Kleinknecht, & Bauer, 2008). Vygotsky compared this help to *scaffolding,* the temporary supports that builders use during construction: After the building is complete, the scaffolding is removed. Good advice for educators, therefore, is to be sensitive to a child's zone of proximal development and pursue how much further they can push a child.

16. What would Piaget and Vygotsky think about the feasibility of teaching the concept of conservation?

Answer

16. Piaget would recommend waiting for the child to discover the concept by himself or herself. According to Vygotsky, the answer depends on the child's zone of proximal development. An adult can help a child who is at the right age.

HOW GROWN UP ARE WE?

Both Piaget and Vygotsky implied that we start with infant cognition and eventually attain adult thinking, which we practice from then on. Are they right, or do we sometimes slip into childish ways of thought?

Consider egocentric thinking. Young children seem to assume that whatever they know or understand, other people will know or understand also. Sometimes, adults make the same mistake. Suppose you say, "The daughter of the man and the woman arrived." Did one person arrive (who is the daughter of the man and the woman) or two people (the man's daughter and some other woman)? Presumably, you know what you meant, but you probably overestimate how well other people understand you (Keysar & Henly, 2002).

Another example: According to Piaget, after about age 7, we all understand conservation of number, volume, and so forth. If we show two equally tall, thin containers of water and pour the water from one of them into a wider container, older children and adults confidently say that the two containers have equal amounts of water.

The zone of proximal development is the gap between what a child does alone and what the child can do with help.

© Laura Dwight/PhotoEdit

However, let's test in a different way: We give people a tall, thin glass or a short, wide glass and invite them to add as much juice as they want. Adults as well as children usually put more juice into the short, wide glass, while thinking that they are getting less juice than usual. Even professional bartenders generally pour more liquor into a short, wide glass than into a tall, thin one (Wansink & van Ittersum, 2003). Evidently, even adults don't fully understand conservation of volume if they are tested in this way.

Here is a different kind of childlike thinking in adults: Suppose you are given a stack of cards with designs varying in shape and color, including these:

First, you are told to sort them into stacks according to either shape or color. (The experimenter randomly assigns half the participants to each rule.) Then the experimenter shuffles the stack and asks you to sort them the other way. (If shape the first time, then color now.) Children find it very difficult to switch rules until age 4 or 5. Do we ever completely succeed? No. Even college students slow down when they change to the second rule. When they switch back and forth repeatedly, they are a bit faster, on the average, whenever they use the same rule they used the first time (Diamond & Kirkham, 2005). In short, as we grow older, we learn to suppress our childlike ways of thinking, but we don't lose them completely. A bit below the surface, there is a child's mind inside each of us.

17. How could you get someone to pour you a larger than average drink?

Concept Check

Answer

17. Ask to have the drink in a short, wide glass.

module 5.2

In Closing

Developing Cognitive Abilities

Jean Piaget had an important influence on developmental psychology by calling attention to the ways in which infants and young children differ from adults. They are not just slower or less well informed; they process information differently. Everything that we do develops over age, and we shall return to developmental issues repeatedly in later chapters. In particular, chapter 6 (learning) discusses the role of imitation in the development of social behaviors and personality; chapter 8 (cognition) discusses the development of language; and chapter 13 (social psychology) includes the development of moral reasoning and prosocial behaviors.

However, Piaget overstated the distinctness between one stage and the next. Whether an infant displays egocentric thinking, object permanence, theory of mind, the appearance–reality distinction, or conservation of number and volume depends on how we run the test. Even adults, who have supposedly mastered all these concepts, revert to childlike thinking at times. Development is not a matter of suddenly gaining cognitive skills and then using them consistently. It is a matter of applying skills more consistently and under a wider variety of conditions.

SUMMARY

- *Inferring infant capacities.* We easily underestimate newborns' capacities because they have so little control over their muscles. Careful testing demonstrates greater abilities than we might have supposed. (page 155)
- *Infant vision and hearing.* Newborns stare at some visual patterns longer than others. They habituate to a repeated sound but dishabituate to a slightly different sound, indicating that they hear a difference. (page 155)

- *Infant memory.* Newborns suck more vigorously to turn on a recording of their own mother's voice than some other woman's voice, indicating that they recognize the sound of the mother's voice. Infants store visual memories, at least briefly. Infants just 2 months old learn to kick and move a mobile, and they remember how to do it several days later. (page 158)

- *Cross-sectional and longitudinal studies.* Psychologists study development by cross-sectional studies, which examine people of different ages at the same time, and by longitudinal studies, which look at a single group of people at various ages. A sequential design combines both methods. (page 158)
- *Cohort effects.* Some of the differences between young people and old people are not due to age but to era of birth. (page 160)
- *Piaget's view of children's thinking.* According to Jean Piaget, children's thought differs from adults' thought qualitatively as well as quantitatively. He believed children grew intellectually through accommodation and assimilation. (page 161)
- *Piaget's stages of development.* Children in the sensorimotor stage respond to what they see, hear, or feel at the moment. In the preoperational stage, they lack reversible operations. In the concrete operations stage, children reason about concrete problems but not

abstractions. Adults and older children are in the formal operations stage, in which they can plan strategies and deal with hypothetical or abstract questions. (page 162)
- *Egocentric thinking.* Young children sometimes have trouble understanding other people's point of view. The results depend on the testing procedure. (page 164)
- *Appearance and reality.* Young children sometimes seem not to distinguish between appearance and reality. However, with a simpler task, they do distinguish. In many cases, children show a concept under some conditions and not others. (page 165)
- *Vygotsky.* According to Lev Vygotsky, children must learn new abilities from adults or older children, but we should be aware of their zone of proximal development. (page 170)
- *Adults.* Adults revert to childlike reasoning in certain situations. (page 170)

KEY TERMS

accommodation (page 161)

assimilation (page 161)

cohort (page 160)

conservation (page 166)

cross-sectional study (page 158)

dishabituation (page 156)

egocentric (page 164)

equilibration (page 161)

habituation (page 156)

longitudinal study (page 159)

object permanence (page 162)

operation (page 164)

preoperational stage (page 164)

schema (pl. schemata) (page 161)

selective attrition (page 159)

sensorimotor stage (page 162)

sequential design (page 160)

stage of concrete operations (page 168)

stage of formal operations (page 168)

theory of mind (page 164)

zone of proximal development (page 170)

Social and Emotional Development

> • How does our social and emotional behavior change as we grow older?

You are a contestant on a new TV game show, *What's My Worry?* Behind the curtain is someone you can't see, who has an overriding concern. You are to identify that concern by questioning a psychologist who knows this person well. You must ask questions that can be answered with a single word or phrase. Here's the catch: The more questions you ask, the smaller the prize. If you guess correctly after the first question, you win $64,000. After two questions, you win $32,000 and so on. Your best strategy is to ask as few questions as possible and then make an educated guess.

What would your first question be? Mine would be: "How old is this person?" The principal worries of teenagers are different from those of 20-year-olds, which in turn differ from those of still older people. Each age has its own concerns, opportunities, and pleasures.

ERIKSON'S DESCRIPTION OF HUMAN DEVELOPMENT

Erik Erikson divided the human life span into eight periods that he called ages or stages. At each stage, he said, people have specific tasks to master, and each stage generates its own social and emotional conflicts. Table 5.4 summarizes Erikson's stages.

Erikson suggested that failure to master the task of a particular stage meant unfortunate consequences that would carry over to later stages. For example, the newborn infant deals with basic trust versus mistrust. An infant whose early environment is supportive forms a strong parental attachment that positively influences future relationships with other people (Erikson, 1963). An infant who is mistreated fails to form a trusting rela-

Erik Erikson argued that each age has its own social and emotional conflicts.

tionship and has trouble developing close ties with people later. We shall consider some of the relevant research later in this module.

In adolescence, the key issue is identity. Most adolescents in Western societies consider many options of how they will spend the rest of their lives. It is possible to delay a decision but not forever. You can't achieve your goals until you set them.

Table 5.4 Erikson's Stages of Human Development

Stages	Main Conflict	Typical Question
Infant	Basic trust versus mistrust	Is my social world predictable and supportive?
Toddler (ages 1–3)	Autonomy versus shame and doubt	Can I do things by myself or must I always rely on others?
Preschool child (ages 3–6)	Initiative versus guilt	Am I good or bad?
Preadolescent (ages 6–12)	Industry versus inferiority	Am I successful or worthless?
Adolescent (early teens)	Identity versus role confusion	Who am I?
Young adult (late teens and early 20s)	Intimacy versus isolation	Shall I share my life with another person or live alone?
Middle adult (late 20s to retirement)	Generativity versus stagnation	Will I succeed in my life, both as a parent and as a worker?
Older adult (after retirement)	Ego integrity versus despair	Have I lived a full life or have I failed?

According to Erikson, the key decision of young adulthood is intimacy or isolation—that is, sharing your life with someone else or living alone. Obviously, forming a good relationship benefits the rest of your life and a bad decision hurts.

If you live a full life span, you will spend about half your life in "middle adulthood," where the issue is generativity (producing something important, e.g., children or work) versus stagnation (not producing). If all goes well, you take pride in your success. If not, then the difficulties and disappointments continue into old age.

It is possible to disagree with various points in Erikson's description. For example, you might describe the main concerns of certain ages differently from what he said. Nevertheless, two of his general points do seem valid: Each stage has its own special difficulties, and an unsatisfactory resolution to the problems of one age produces extra difficulty in later life.

Let's examine in more detail some of the major social and emotional issues of particular ages. Beyond the primary conflicts that Erikson highlighted, development is marked by a succession of other significant issues.

INFANCY AND CHILDHOOD

An important aspect of human life at any age is attachment—*a long-term feeling of closeness toward another person*. The first attachments begin in infancy. John Bowlby (1973) proposed that infants who develop one or more good attachments have a sense of security and safety. They explore the world and return to their attachment figure when frightened or distressed. Those who do not develop strong early attachments have trouble developing close relations later as well (Mikulincer, Shaver, & Pereg, 2003).

How can we measure strength of attachment to test and extend this theory? Most work has used the Strange Situation (usually capitalized), pioneered by Mary Ainsworth (1979). In this procedure, *a mother and her infant* (typically 12 to 18 months old) *come into a room with many toys. Then a stranger enters the room. The mother leaves and then returns. A few minutes later, both the stranger and the mother leave; then the stranger returns, and finally, the mother returns.* Through a one-way mirror, a psychologist observes the infant's reactions to each coming and going. Observers classify infants' responses in the following categories.

- *Securely attached.* The infant uses the mother as a base of exploration, cooing at her, showing her toys, and making eye contact with her. The infant shows some distress when the mother leaves but cries only briefly if at all. When she returns, the infant goes to her with apparent delight, cuddles for a while, and then returns to the toys.

- *Anxious (or resistant).* Responses toward the mother fluctuate between happy and angry. The infant clings to the mother and cries profusely when she leaves, as if worried that she might not return. When she does return, the infant clings to her again but does not use her as a base to explore the toys. A child with an anxious attachment typically shows many fears, including a strong fear of strangers.

- *Avoidant.* While the mother is present, the infant does not stay near her and does not interact much with her. The infant may or may not cry when she leaves and does not go to her when she returns.

- *Disorganized.* The infant seems not even to notice the mother or looks away while approaching her or covers his or her face or lies on the floor. The infant alternates between approach and avoidance and shows more fear than affection.

The prevalence of the various attachment styles differs from one population to another, but the secure pattern is the most common in the United States and most other countries (Ainsworth, Blehar, Waters, & Wall, 1978). Of course, many children do not fit neatly into one category or another, and some who are classified as "secure" or "avoidant" are more secure or avoidant than others. Still, most children remain stable in their classification from one time to another (Moss, Cyr, Bureau, Tarabulsy, & Dubois-Comtois, 2005).

The Strange Situation also can be used to evaluate the relationship between child and father (Belsky, 1996), child and grandparent, or other relationships. As a rule, the quality of one relationship correlates with the quality of others. For example, most children who have a secure relationship with the mother also have a secure relationship with the father, and chances are the parents are happy with each other as well (Elicker, Englund, & Sroufe, 1992; Erel & Burman, 1995). Beyond about age 18 months, the Strange Situation is no longer a useful tool, as children show little distress at being left alone or with a stranger. The attachment patterns continue, though, and can be measured in other ways. For example, most infants who have a secure relationship with their parents at age 12 months continue to have a close relationship with them decades later (Waters, Merrick, Treboux, Crowell, & Albersheim, 2000). Those who show a secure attachment in infancy are more likely than others to form high-quality romantic attachments in adulthood (Roisman,

Collins, Sroufe, & Egeland, 2005). They are also likely to form close and mutually supportive relationships with friends and romantic partners, whereas those with anxious or avoidant attachments worry excessively about rejection or fail to seek others' support in times of distress (Mikulincer et al., 2003).

Why do some children develop more secure attachments than others? One possibility is that children differ genetically in their tendency to fear the unfamiliar. Several studies with older children and adults support this idea (Gillath, Shaver, Baek, & Chun, 2008; McGuire, Clifford, Fink, Basho, & McDonnell, 2003; Schwartz et al., 2003). However, the variance in attachment style relates more strongly to how responsive the parents are to the infants' needs, including holding and touching. Gentle touch can be very reassuring (Hertenstein, 2002). Programs that teach parents to be more responsive produce significant increases in secure attachments by the infants (Bakermans-Kranenburg, van IJzendoorn, & Juffer, 2003).

Patterns of attachment are largely the same across cultures, with a few apparent exceptions. However, what appears to be a difference in attachment sometimes reflects difficulties in measurement. In one study, Western psychologists observing Black children in South Africa found low consistency between measurements of attachment in one situation and another. When they enlisted local people as coinvestigators, the local observers, who understood the local customs, reported data with much greater consistency (Minde, Minde, & Vogel, 2006). One study reported an unusually high prevalence of "anxious attachment" among Japanese infants. However, Japanese mothers customarily stay with their babies almost constantly, including bathing with them and sleeping in the same bed. When the Japanese mothers were persuaded to leave their infants alone with a stranger, it was in many cases the first time the infant had ever had such an experience, and the infant reacted with horror. The same reaction by a U.S. child would have a different meaning (Rothbaum, Weisz, Pott, Miyake, & Morelli, 2000). By age 6, most Japanese children have secure relationships with their parents, like those in other countries (Behrens, Hesse, & Main, 2007).

....

18. If a child in the Strange Situation clings tightly to the mother and cries furiously when she leaves, which kind of attachment does the child have?

19. What attachment style is most likely in a child who tends to have strong anxieties?

Answers

18. In the United States, this pattern would indicate an anxious or insecure attachment. In Japan, however, this behavior is an understandable reaction to a surprising experience.

19. A child with strong anxieties would probably show an anxious (or resistant) attachment style, clinging to the mother and being distressed when she leaves.

SOCIAL DEVELOPMENT IN CHILDHOOD AND ADOLESCENCE

The social and emotional development of children and adolescents depends largely on their friendships. As they grow older, they come to identify more and more with their own age group instead of their parents.

Adolescence begins when the body reaches *puberty,* the onset of sexual maturation. The role of adolescents varies among cultures. In most nontechnological societies, most teenagers are married and working. They move quickly from childhood into adulthood. The same was true in Europe and America in the 1800s. In Western culture today, our improved health and nutrition have lowered the average age of puberty (Okasha, McCarron, McEwen, & Smith, 2001), but our economic situation encourages young people to stay in school and postpone marriage, family, and career (Arnett, 2000). The result is a long period of physical maturity without adult status. Imagine if our society decided that people should stay in college even longer. Would this policy bring out the best behavior in 25- to 30-year-olds?

Adolescence is sometimes portrayed as a time of "storm and stress." Most adolescents report increased moodiness and occasional conflict with their parents in early adolescence, though the conflicts decrease in later adolescence (Laursen, Coy, & Collins, 1998). Comparisons of monozygotic and dizygotic twins suggest a genetic contribution to the conflicts (McGue, Elkins, Walden, & Iacono, 2005). However, storm and stress also depend on family and cultural influences. Adolescents who receive sympathetic support and understanding experience less conflict with their parents (R. A. Lee, Su, & Yoshida, 2005).

Adolescence is also a time of risk-taking behaviors, not only in humans but in other species, too (Spear, 2000). Adolescents are certainly aware of the dangers. If asked about the advisability of drunk driving, unprotected sex, and so forth, they describe the dangers as well as adults do. Why, then, don't they behave like adults? Part of the explanation lies in the powerful effect of peer pressure. In one study, researchers asked people to play the video game Chicken, in which they guide a car on the screen. When a traffic light turns

Children learn social skills by interacting with brothers, sisters, and friends close to their own age.

(a) American teenagers are financially dependent on their parents but have the opportunity to spend much time in whatever way they choose. (b) In many nontechnological societies, teenagers are expected to do adult work and accept adult responsibilities.

yellow, a participant can earn extra points by getting through the light but at the risk of a game-ending crash if the light turns red before the car gets through the light. Adolescents are more likely than adults to race through yellow lights, and if several of their friends were watching, that tendency increases (Gardner & Steinberg, 2005).

Most adults dismiss risky options almost at once. Suppose you are asked questions like these:

Swimming with alligators: Good idea or bad idea?

Eating salads: Good idea or bad idea?

Setting your hair on fire: Good idea or bad idea?

Nearly all adolescents and adults make the same decisions, but adults decide more quickly. Adults' emotions scream, "No, of course I don't want to swim with alligators!" Adolescents think about it first (Reyna & Farley, 2006). In short, it is pointless to teach adolescents to think through their decisions and evaluate the risks. They do that already. The task is to get adolescents to transfer their rational decisions into action and to make risk-related decisions quickly and automatically.

Identity Development

As Erikson pointed out, adolescence is a time of "finding yourself," determining "who am I?" or "who will I be?" It is when most people first construct a coherent "life story" of how they got to be the way they are (Habermas & Bluck, 2000).

In some societies, most people enter the same occupation as their parents and live in the same town. The parents may even choose their children's marriage partners. Western society offers young people far more choices about education, career, marriage, political and religious affiliation, where to live, sexual activity, and so forth. All that freedom is invigorating but also somewhat frightening.

An adolescent's *concern with decisions about the future and the quest for self-understanding* has been called an **identity crisis**. The term *crisis* implies more emotional turbulence than is typical. Identity development has two major elements: whether one is actively exploring the issue and

whether one has made any decisions (Marcia, 1980). We can diagram the possibilities using the following grid:

	Has explored or is exploring the issues	Has not explored the issues
Decisions already made	Identity achievement	Identity foreclosure
Decisions not yet made	Identity moratorium	Identity diffusion

Those who have not yet given any serious thought to making any decisions and who have no clear sense of identity are said to have **identity diffusion**. They are not actively concerned with their identity at the moment. Identity diffusion is more common among people with low self-esteem and a hopeless, pessimistic attitude toward life (Phillips & Pittman, 2007). People in **identity moratorium** are *considering the issues but not yet making decisions*. They experiment with various possibilities and imagine themselves in different roles before making a choice. Researchers distinguish between two kinds of moratorium—simply delaying a decision and actively searching for a decision (Crocetti, Rubini, Luyckx, & Meeus, 2008).

Identity foreclosure is a state of *reaching firm decisions without much thought*. For example, a young man might be told that he is expected to go into the family business with his father, or a young woman might be told that she is expected to marry and raise children. Decrees of that sort were once common in North America and Europe, and they are still common in other societies today. Someone who accepts such decisions has little reason to explore alternative possibilities.

Finally, **identity achievement** is *the outcome of having explored various possible identities and then making one's own decisions.* Identity achievement does not come all at once. For example, you might decide about your career but not about marriage. You might also reach identity achievement and then rethink a decision years later.

The "Personal Fable" of Teenagers

Answer the following items true or false:

- Other people may fail to realize their life ambitions, but I will realize mine.
- I understand love and sex in a way that my parents never did.
- Tragedy may strike other people but probably not me.
- Almost everyone notices how I look and how I dress.

According to David Elkind (1984), teenagers are particularly likely to harbor such beliefs. Taken together, he calls them the "personal fable," the conviction that "I am special—what is true for everyone else is not true for me." Up to a point, this fable supports an optimistic outlook on life, but it becomes dangerous if it leads people to take foolish risks.

According to David Elkind, one reason for risky behavior is the "personal fable," the secret belief that "nothing bad can happen to me."

© Patrick Ward/Stock Boston

This attitude is hardly unique to teenagers, however. Most middle-aged adults regard themselves as more likely than other people to succeed on the job and as less likely than average to have a serious illness (Quadrel, Fischhoff, & Davis, 1993). They also overestimate their own chances of winning a lottery, especially if they get to choose their own lottery ticket (Langer, 1975). That is, few people fully outgrow the personal fable.

ADULTHOOD

From early adulthood until retirement, the main concern of most adults is, as Erikson noted, "What will I achieve and contribute to society and my family? Will I be successful?"

Adulthood extends from one's first full-time job until retirement—for most people, most of the lifespan. We lump so many years together because it seems that little is changing. During your childhood and adolescence, you grew taller each year. During adulthood, the changes in your appearance are slow and subtle. From infancy until early adulthood, each new age brought new privileges, such as permission to stay out late, your first driver's license, the right to vote, and the opportunity to go to college. After early adulthood, one year blends into the next. Children and teenagers know exactly how old they are, but adults sometimes have to think about it. Important changes do occur during adulthood, but most of them are self-initiated. When adults describe the "turning points" in their lives, they generally mention the choices they made, such as getting married, having children, changing jobs, or moving to a new location (Rönkä, Oravala, & Pulkkinen, 2003).

The behavioral changes during childhood depend mostly on developing new abilities. During adulthood, behavior changes because of new situations or roles. Daniel Levinson (1986) describes adult development in terms of a series of overlapping eras. After the transition into adulthood at about age 20, give or take a couple of years, comes early adulthood, which lasts until about age 40–45. During early adulthood, people make big decisions about career, marriage, and having children. Once people have chosen a career, they usually stay with it or something closely related, as vocational interests are highly stable (Low, Yoon, Roberts, & Rounds, 2005). During early adulthood, people devote maximum energy to pursuing their goals. However, buying a house and raising a family on a young person's salary are difficult and stressful.

During middle adulthood, extending from about age 40 to 65, physical strength and health begin to decline but probably not enough to interfere with an active personal and professional life. At this point, people have already achieved success at work or have come to accept whatever status they have. Many people become more accepting of themselves and others at this time and feel less tyrannized by the stress of the job. In most cases, they also face less day-to-day stress of caring for small children.

In middle adulthood, according to Levinson (1986), people go through a **midlife transition,** *a time when they reassess their personal goals, set new ones, and prepare for the rest of life.* This transition often occurs in response to a divorce, illness, death in the family, a career change, or some other event that causes the person to question past decisions and current goals (Wethington, Kessler, & Pixley, 2004). Just as the adolescent identity crisis is a bigger issue in cultures that offer many choices, the same is true for the midlife transition. If you lived in a society that offered no choices, you would not worry about the paths not taken! In Western society, however, you enter adulthood with high hopes. You hope to earn an advanced degree, excel at an outstanding job, marry a wonderful person, have marvelous children, become a leader in your community, run for political office, write a great novel, compose great music, travel the world. . . . You know you are not working on all of your goals right now, but you tell yourself, "I'll do it later." As you grow older, you realize that you are running out of "later." Some of your early ambitions have become unrealistic, and others will be, too, if you don't start on them soon.

People deal with their midlife transitions in many ways. Most of them abandon unrealistic goals and set new goals consistent with the direction their lives have taken. Others decide that they have been ignoring dreams that they are not willing to abandon. They go back to school, set up a business of their own, or try something else they have always wanted to do. The least satisfactory outcome is to decide, "I can't abandon my dreams, but I can't do anything about them either. I can't take the risk of changing my life, even though I am dissatisfied with it." People with that attitude become discouraged and depressed.

The advice is clear: To increase your chances of feeling good in middle age and beyond, make good decisions when you are young. If you care about something, don't wait for a midlife crisis. Get started now.

20. How does a midlife transition resemble an adolescent identity crisis?

Answer

20. In both cases, people examine their lives, goals, and possible directions for the future.

OLD AGE

Finally, people reach late adulthood, which begins around age 65. According to Erikson, those who feel satisfied with their lives experience "ego integrity," and those who are not satisfied feel "despair." How you feel in old age depends on what happened long before.

People age in different ways. Some deteriorate in intellect, coordination, and ability to care for themselves, while others remain alert and active. Memory usually remains reasonably intact among older people who are healthy and active. Programs that increase older people's physical exercise improve their memory and cognition (Colcombe & Kramer, 2003; Mattson & Magnus, 2006).

Memory in old age differs across situations. Everyone remembers interesting material better than something that seems unimportant, but the difference is larger for older people, who tend to focus their attention and resources more narrowly on topics likely to bring them pleasure or topics of practical importance to them. Thus, they overlook details that a younger person would remember. When older people can't remember a detail, they fill in the gap with an educated guess of what "must have happened" (Hess, 2005). As you will see in the memory chapter, all people fill in their memory gaps with inferences. The difference is that older people tend to face memory gaps more frequently.

As we shall see in chapter 12 (emotion), several kinds of evidence indicate that healthy older people are, on the average, happier and more satisfied with life than younger people are. That result may seem surprising. However, young people face many pressures from work and raising children, whereas older people have more leisure. Furthermore, older people deliberately focus their attention on family, friends, and other events that bring them pleasure (Carstensen, Mikels, & Mather, 2006).

Your satisfaction in old age will depend largely on how you live while younger. Some older people say, "I hope to live many more years, but even if I don't, I have lived my life well. I did everything that I really cared about." Others say, "I wanted to do so much that I never did." Feeling dignity in old age also depends on how people's families, communities, and societies treat them. Some cultures, such as Korea, observe a special ceremony to celebrate a person's retirement or 70th birthday (Damron-Rodriguez, 1991). African American and Native American families traditionally honor their elders, giving them a position of status in the family and calling on them for advice. Japanese families follow a similar tradition, at least publicly (Koyano, 1991).

In Tibet and many other cultures, children are taught to treat old people with respect and honor.

Although an increasing percentage of people over 65 remain in the work force, most people eventually retire. Retirement is another transition, analogous to an adolescent identity crisis or a midlife transition. Retirement decreases stress, but it also brings a sense of loss to those whose lives had focused on their work (Kim & Moen, 2001). Loss of control becomes a serious issue when health begins to fail. Consider someone who spent half a century running a business and now lives in a nursing home where staff members make all the decisions. Leaving even a few of the choices and responsibilities to the residents improves their self-respect, health, alertness, and memory (Rodin, 1986; Rowe & Kahn, 1987).

THE PSYCHOLOGY OF FACING DEATH

A man who has not found something he is willing to die for is not fit to live.

—Martin Luther King Jr. (1964)

This is perhaps the greatest lesson we learned from our patients: LIVE, so you do not have to look back and say, "God, how I have wasted my life!"

—Elisabeth Kübler-Ross (1975, p. xix)

The worst thing about death is the fact that when a man is dead it's impossible any longer to undo the harm you have done him, or to do the good you haven't done him. They say: live in such a way as to be always ready to die. I would say: live in such a way that anyone can die without you having anything to regret.

—Leo Tolstoy (1865/1978, p. 192)

Have you ever heard the advice, "Live each day as if it were going to be your last"? The point is to appreciate every moment, but the advice would be terrible if you took it seriously. If you really believed you would die today, you certainly wouldn't plan for the future. You wouldn't save money or worry about the long-term health consequences of what you ate or drank. You probably wouldn't be studying this textbook.

Just thinking about the fact of eventual death evokes distress, and to go on with life effectively, we try to shield ourselves from thinking too much about dying. According to **terror-management theory**, *we cope with our fear of death by avoiding thoughts about death and by affirming a worldview that provides self-esteem, hope, and value in life* (Pyszczynski, Greenberg, & Solomon, 2000). When something reminds you of your mortality, you do whatever you can to reduce your anxiety. You reassure yourself that you still have many years to live. "My health is good, I don't smoke, I don't drink too much, and I'm not overweight." If that isn't true, you tell yourself that you plan to quit smoking, you are going to cut down on your drinking, and any day now you are going to start losing weight. You also think about the good job you have (or hope to have), the high salary you earn (or expect to earn), and the exciting things you will do during the rest of your life (Kasser & Sheldon, 2000).

Still, even excellent health merely postpones death, so a reminder of death redoubles your efforts to defend a belief that life is important. You reaffirm your religious beliefs, your patriotism, or other views that help you make sense of life and find meaning in it (Greenberg et al., 2003). You become more dutiful than usual in upholding the customs of your society (Gailliot, Stillman, Schmeichel, Maner, & Plant, 2008). You also take pride in how you have contributed to your family, your profession, or something else that will continue after you are gone (Pyszczynski et al., 2000). Up to a point, these affirmations are good, although it is also true that people who are reminded of their own mortality sometimes become hostile to those who disagree with or challenge their beliefs (Hayes, Schimel, & Williams, 2008).

The advances in modern medicine have raised new ethical issues with regard to dying. We can now keep people alive long after they have lost most of their physical and mental capacities. Should we? If someone is bedridden and in pain, with little hope of recovery, is it acceptable to help the person hasten death? A growing number of people have to face these difficult decisions for themselves and family members.

5.3 module

In Closing

Social and Emotional Issues through the Life Span

Let's close by reemphasizing a key point of Erik Erikson's theory: Each age or stage builds on the previous ones. The quality of your early attachments to parents and others correlates with your ability to form close, trusting relationships later. How well you handle the identity issues of adoles-cence affects your adult life. Your productivity as an adult determines how satisfied you will feel in old age. Life is a continuum, and the choices you make at any age are linked with those you make before and after.

SUMMARY

- *Erikson's view of development.* Erik Erikson described the human life span as a series of eight ages or stages, each with its own social and emotional conflicts. (page 173)
- *Infant attachment.* Infants can develop several kinds of attachment to significant people in their lives, as measured in the Strange Situation. (page 174)
- *Adolescent identity crisis.* Adolescents have to deal with the question "Who am I?" Many experiment with several identities before deciding. (page 176)

- *Adults' concerns.* A major concern of adults is productivity in family and career. Many adults undergo a midlife transition when they re-evaluate their goals. (page 177)
- *Old age.* Dignity and independence are key concerns of old age. (page 178)
- *Facing death.* People at all ages face the anxieties associated with the inevitability of death. A reminder of death influences people to defend their worldviews. (page 179)

KEY TERMS

attachment (page 174)

identity achievement (page 177)

identity crisis (page 176)

identity diffusion (page 176)

identity foreclosure (page 176)

identity moratorium (page 176)

midlife transition (page 178)

Strange Situation (page 174)

terror-management theory (page 179)

Diversity: Gender, Culture, and Family

> • What factors influence development of personality and social behavior?

The start of the first module in this chapter began by asking how you would be different if we could go back and change one of your genes. Suppose we changed you from male to female or female to male. Or suppose we changed your ethnicity or culture. Perhaps we trade you to a different family. Then how would you be different?

With such drastic changes, it is not clear that it would still be *you*! Gender, culture, and family are integral parts of anyone's development and identity.

GENDER INFLUENCES

Males and females differ biologically in many ways that influence behavior. The male and female brains differ more strongly than you might guess, with some brain areas being proportionately larger in men and other areas proportionately larger in women (Cahill, 2006). Certain genes are more active in male brains, and other genes are more active in female brains on the average (Reinius et al., 20008).

How do men and women differ behaviorally? Men, being generally larger and stronger, throw harder and get into fights more often (Hyde, 2005). On the average, boys are more active, whereas girls have better self-control (Else-Quest, Hyde, Goldsmith, & Van Hulle, 2006). Men are more likely to help a stranger change a flat tire, but women are more likely to provide long-term nurturing support (Eagly & Crowley, 1986). The more pairs of shoes you own, the higher is the probability that you are female. Men and women tend to carry books in different ways, as shown in Figure 5.28. A list of miscellaneous and not necessarily important differences could go on and on.

On the average, girls and women are better than boys and men at detecting emotions from nonverbal signals (Chen & Haviland-Jones, 2000; Hall & Matsumoto, 2004). People have long noted how often men misinterpret a woman's smile, thinking she is showing sexual interest when in fact she is only being friendly. Psychologists used to interpret this trend as wishful thinking until they discovered that the opposite is also true: When a woman really is trying to signal sexual interest, many men misinterpret the expression as mere friendliness (Farris, Treat, Viken, & McFall, 2008). Evidently, men are just less accurate at recognizing all emotional expressions, one way or the other.

When giving directions, men are more likely to use directions and distances—such as "go four blocks east . . ."—whereas women are more likely to use landmarks—such as "go until you see the library . . ." (Saucier et al., 2002).

Figure 5.29 shows the relative frequency with which men and women used different ways of giving directions (Rahman, Andersson, & Govier, 2005). This tendency is not unique to humans. In monkeys, mice, and several other species, males perform better than females in mazes without landmarks, whereas females remember the landmarks better (C. M. Jones, Braithwaite, & Healy, 2003; C. L. Williams, Barnett, & Meck, 1990). However, men are capable of following landmarks, and women are capable of following directions and distances. When only one or the other is available, both men and women find their way (Spelke, 2005).

Figure 5.28 Men usually carry books and similar objects at their sides. Women beyond the age of puberty usually carry them at their chest. Of course, this generalization does not apply to people wearing backpacks.

Men often fail to read other people's emotions.
(© *ZITS PARTNERSHIP*, King Features Syndicate. Reprinted by permission.)

Okay, so men and women differ in miscellaneous behavioral ways. However, to what extent do males and females differ in intellectual abilities? The answer is not much, if at all (Halpern et al., 2007; Hyde, 2005; Levine, Vasilyeva, Lourenco, Newcombe, & Huttenlocher, 2005; Spelke, 2005). For example, most people believe that men outperform women in mathematics. Males significantly outperform females in math in countries where men have greater economic and political status than women. In countries where men and women have nearly equal status, the difference in average math performance disappears (Guiso, Monte, Sapienza, & Zingales, 2008). In the United States, on the average, females' standardized math test scores and grades in nearly all math courses are equal to or better than those of males from elementary school through college (Hyde, Lindberg, Linn, Ellis, & Williams, 2008; Spelke, 2005).

An exception to this rule is that males do better at certain aspects of geometry, such as the tasks in Figure 5.30. With much simpler tasks, we see a hint of a male advantage even among infants a few months old (Moore & Johnson, 2008; Quinn & Liben, 2008). Do these results reflect a

difference in inborn ability? Not necessarily. Boys usually spend more time on activities that require attention to angles and directions, and they have much opportunity to learn relevant skills. Young women who spent 10 hours playing action video games significantly narrowed the male–female gap on visuospatial tasks (Feng, Spence, & Pratt, 2007). Thus, it appears that men and women differ more in interests than abilities.

Vastly more men than women become grand masters in chess. However, a study found that boys and girls started at an equal level in chess and progressed at equal rates. The main reason more men than women reached the highest level was that vastly more boys than girls *started* playing chess (Chabris & Glickman, 2006).

Most people believe that women talk much more than men. Perhaps they do in certain situations or in certain populations but not universally. In one study, male and female college students wore devices that recorded what they said at unpredictable times, without their knowing when the device was operating. Extrapolating from the samples, the investigators estimated that the average woman spoke 16,215 words per day compared to 15,669 for men—a statistically

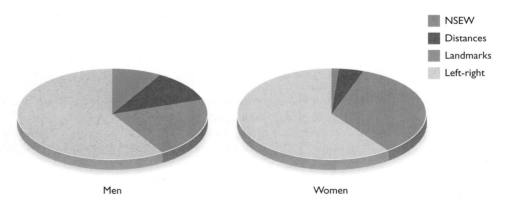

Figure 5.29 When giving directions, men refer to distances and north-south-east-west more often than women do. Women describe more landmarks. Men and women refer to left and right about equally. (Based on data of Rahman, Andersson, & Govier, 2005)

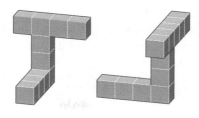

Can the set of blocks on the left be rotated to match the set at the right?

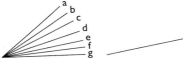

Which of the lines at the left has the same angle as the one at the right?

Figure 5.30 On the average, men perform slightly better than women on tasks like these. (The answers are given below.)

Answers: No, the set on the left cannot be rotated to match the one on the right. For the second question, line e matches the model to its right.

insignificant difference. Both groups showed much variation (Mehl, Vazire, Ramirez-Esparza, Slatcher, & Pennebaker, 2007).

Males and females do show differences in interests, however, from childhood through adulthood. The way people rear children certainly contributes to those differences. For example, children who watch a television commercial showing just boys playing with a particular toy say that this is a toy "just for boys" (Pike & Jennings, 2005). However, biological tendencies may contribute also. One study found that male monkeys preferred to play with what people consider "boys' toys," such as a ball and a toy car, and female monkeys preferred to play with "girls' toys," such as a soft doll (Alexander & Hines, 2002). Researchers have also found that girls who were exposed to higher than average levels of the male hormone testosterone during prenatal development tend to play with boys' toys more than the average for other girls (Berenbaum, Duck, & Bryk, 2000; Nordenström, Servin, Bohlin, Larsson, & Wedell, 2002; Pasterski et al., 2005).

Sex Roles and Androgyny

Much research interest has focused on sex roles, *the different activities expected of males and females.* Sex roles attract research interest because of their potential to constrain people's behaviors. For example, women who feel bound by traditional sex roles may fail to pursue interests or career opportunities that are considered too masculine. Sex roles can be a problem for men, too. In many cultures, men are required to kill a large animal or withstand great pain to prove their manhood before they are eligible to marry or

become a father. In the United States, the customs are not so demanding, but some men feel a need to get into fights or engage in other risky behaviors to prove their manhood (Vandello, Bosson, Cohen, Burnaford, & Weaver, 2008).

A few aspects of sex roles are biologically determined: For example, only women can nurse babies, and men are more likely than women to do jobs requiring physical strength. However, many of our sex roles are customs set by our society. Do you regard building a fire as mostly men's work or women's? What about basket weaving? Planting crops? Milking cows? People's answers vary from one society to another (Wood & Eagly, 2002). Cultures also determine the relative status of men and women. Generally, if a culture lives in conditions that require hunting, vigorous defense, or other use of physical strength, men have greater status than women. When food is abundant and enemies are few, men and women have more equal status.

Cultural traditions last long after the end of the conditions that established them (D. Cohen, 2001), but they do gradually change. Within most technologically advanced countries since the 1960s, a much higher percentage of women have taken jobs in fields previously dominated by men—such as law, medicine, government, and business administration (Eagly, Johannesen-Schmidt, & van Engen, 2003). Simultaneously, most men have increased the amount of time they spend on child care (Barnett & Hyde, 2001).

Given that sex roles can be flexible, Sandra Bem (1974) proposed that the ideal would be a personality capable of alternating between stereotypically male and stereotypically female traits depending on the situation. For example, you might be ambitious and assertive (male traits) but also sympathetic to the feelings of others (female). Androgyny is *the ability to display both male and female characteristics.* The word comes from the Greek roots *andr-*, meaning "man" (as in the words *androgen* and *android*), and *gyn-*, meaning "woman" (as in the word *gynecology*).

The idea sounds good, but the evidence has not strongly indicated that androgynous people are mentally healthier, more successful, or better adjusted than other people. Part of the problem has to do with measuring androgyny. Originally, the idea was to give people a questionnaire about masculine traits (ambitious, competitive, independent, willing to take risks, etc.) and a questionnaire about female traits (affectionate, cheerful, loyal, sympathetic, etc.). An androgynous person was someone who checked about an equal number of masculine and feminine traits. The problem with this approach is that someone could be equal on both by being equally *low* on both! Imagine someone who is not ambitious, not independent, not cheerful, and not sympathetic.

Later researchers therefore defined androgyny as being above average on both masculine and feminine traits. However, another problem arose: Lists of masculine and feminine traits include both favorable and unfavorable items. Independence and ambition (masculine traits) are generally good, as are compassion and tolerance (feminine traits). However, selfishness is an undesirable masculine trait, and submissiveness is an undesirable feminine trait. Thus, an improved definition is that androgyny consists of being above average on both desirable masculine traits and desirable feminine traits. Using that definition, psychologists find that most androgynous people are mentally healthy with high self-esteem (Woodhill & Samuels, 2003).

However, that demonstration still does not document the usefulness of the androgyny concept. Positive masculine traits (independence, ambition, etc.) are beneficial, and so are positive feminine traits (compassion, tolerance, etc.). So it is no surprise that having both positive masculine and positive feminine traits is beneficial. To be a useful concept, androgyny should provide a benefit above what the masculine and feminine characteristics provide. Researchers have occasionally demonstrated that androgynous people show much flexibility (Cheng, 2005), but most research suggests that the benefits of androgyny are simply the sum of the benefits from masculine and feminine traits (Marsh & Byrne, 1991; Spence, 1984).

....

21. Research finds that androgynous people tend to be successful and mentally healthy. Why does this finding, by itself, fail to demonstrate the usefulness of the concept of androgyny?

Answer

21. Androgyny is defined as being above average on both favorable masculine traits and favorable feminine traits. It's obvious that the sum of two sets of favorable traits should be favorable. The important question is whether androgyny provides any benefit that goes beyond the sum of masculine and feminine.

....

Reasons Behind Gender Differences

It is easy to list differences between males and females but more difficult to explain them. Let's start with biological factors. If nothing else, males

are on the average taller and more muscular. Physical differences predispose each gender to certain behavioral differences that alter the ways other people react, and other people's reactions alter further behavior.

Social influences are powerful, too. Even with 6- and 9-month-old infants, mothers talk to their daughters in a more conversational way and give more instructions to their sons, such as "come here" (Clearfield & Nelson, 2006). At this age, the infants themselves are neither walking nor talking, so the difference demonstrates the mother's own behavior, not her reaction to the infants' behavior.

In one fascinating study, researchers set up cameras and microphones to eavesdrop on families in a science museum. Boys and girls spent about equal time looking at each exhibit, and the parents spent about equal time telling boys and girls how to use each exhibit, but on the average, the parents provided about three times as much scientific explanation to the boys as to the girls, regardless of how many questions the children themselves asked (Crowley, Callanen, Tenenbaum, & Allen, 2001).

CULTURAL AND ETHNIC INFLUENCES

If you had grown up in a different culture, your attitudes, beliefs, and behaviors would be vastly different from what they are today. However, categorizing and describing the effects of culture are not easy. One of the most popular generalizations is that Western culture, such as the United States, Canada, and most of Europe, is "individualistic." People value independence, strive for individual achievements, and take pride in personal accomplishments. In "collectivist" cultures such as China and much of the rest of Asia, people emphasize dependence on one another, strive for group advancement, and take pride in their family's or group's accomplishments more than their own. This generalization is useful in some ways, but it is vague and overstated (Brewer & Chen, 2007). In many ways, Americans care about group success as much as Chinese people do, and Chinese people can compete individually as much as Americans do. We don't need to abandon the individualistic versus collectivist distinction, but we need to refine and clarify it.

Consider this example of the difficulty of interpreting a cultural difference: Suppose you fill out a survey questionnaire. As a reward, the interviewer offers you a choice of five pens. Four of them are the same color and one is different. As a rule, would you prefer the unusual one or the more common type? Americans are more likely to pick the unusual color, whereas Japanese choose the common color. But why? The initial interpretation was that Japanese tend to be conformist and want to be the same as everyone else. Can you imagine another explanation?

Researchers suggested that the Japanese were being polite: "If I take the last available pen of this color, then the next person, who might really like this color, can't have it!" If researchers told a Japanese person, "all the others have already chosen and you are the last one to choose," then the Japanese were as likely as Americans to choose the unusual color (Yamagishi, Hashimoto, & Schug, 2008).

Growing up as a member of an ethnic minority poses special issues. Achieving ethnic identity is comparable to the process adolescents go through in finding an individual identity. In most cases, minority-group members who achieve a strong, favorable ethnic identity have high self-esteem (Phinney, 1990). Many people enhance their group evaluation during adolescence and thereby solidify their self-esteem (French, Seidman, Allen, & Aber, 2006). However, the outcome depends on the status of one's group. In Miami, Florida, researchers found that Cuban Americans with a strong ethnic identification had high self-esteem, but Nicaraguan Americans with a strong ethnic identification had low self-esteem (Cislo, 2008). Cuban Americans dominate Miami politics and culture, so it is easy to see how ethnic identification would work differently for the Cuban and Nicaraguan Americans.

It is possible to identify with both one's own group and the nation as a whole, and some maintain double identifications more strongly than others do (Gong, 2007). Muslim Americans faced a serious problem in this regard after the terrorist attacks in September 2001: Suddenly, they became targets of hostility and prejudice, and most found it more difficult to feel both Muslim and American (Sirin & Fine, 2007).

Ethnic identity is especially salient for immigrants to a country. In addition to language problems, many face prejudices and questions about whether they have entered the country legally. They also have to deal with an unfamiliar culture. Immigrants, their children, and sometimes further generations experience biculturalism, *partial identification with two cultures.* For example, Mexican immigrants to the United States speak Spanish and follow Mexican customs at home but switch to the English language and U.S. customs in other places. People maintain some parts of their original culture longer than others. For example, most immigrants to the United States maintain their ethnic food preferences long after they have switched to American customs of dress and entertainment (Ying, Han, & Wong, 2008).

Many immigrants are bicultural, being familiar with two sets of customs. These immigrant children attend middle school in Michigan.

Mexican American youth report difficulty understanding U.S. culture, problems of not fitting in with others at school, and either difficulties in school because of poor English or difficulties at home because of poor Spanish (Romero & Roberts, 2003). Some Chinese Americans who consider being Chinese part of their "essence" as a person find it particularly difficult to deal with a different culture (Chao, Chen, Roisman, & Hong, 2007). However, the situation is not entirely bleak. In many places, bicultural youth tend to have low rates of substance use, delinquency, and depression (Coatsworth, Moldonado-Molina, Pantin, & Szapocznik, 2005). One reason is that their parents maintain close supervision (Fuligni, 1998). Another reason is that by not feeling fully part of U.S. youth culture, bicultural adolescents are less subject to its peer pressures.

At least to a small extent, nearly all of us learn to function in multiple subcultures. Unless you live in a small town where everyone has the same background, religion, and customs, you learn to adjust what you say and do in different settings and with different groups of people. The transitions are more noticeable and more intense for ethnic minorities.

Analogous to biculturalism is biracialism. A growing percentage of people in the United States have parents from different racial or ethnic origins, such as African and European, European and Hispanic, or Asian and Native American. People of biracial or multiracial backgrounds are especially common in Hawaii, California, and Puerto Rico. Decades ago, psychologists believed that biracial children and adolescents were at a serious disadvantage because they would not feel accepted by either group. The research, however, finds that most biracial people today are pleased with their

Many biracial people have achieved great success. President Barack Obama and professional golfer Tiger Woods are prominent examples.

mixed background, which enables them to see the best in both cultures, to accept all cultures, and to overcome prejudice and discrimination. Most biracial youth say they feel reasonably well accepted by both groups. They show no special problems in academic performance or mental health. The one problem they often mention is how to label themselves. If a form asks for a racial/ethnic identity, they don't want to check just one identity because that would deny the other part of themselves (Shih & Sanchez, 2005). Many give one answer at one time and a different answer at a different time (Doyle & Kao, 2007). The U.S. Census form now permits people to check more than one category.

22. In what way is biracialism similar to biculturalism?

Answer

22. A bicultural person identifies to some extent with two cultures. A biracial person has two kinds of ethnic background and identifies to some extent with each.

THE FAMILY

In early childhood, our parents and other relatives are the most important people in our lives. How do those early family experiences mold our personality and social behavior?

Birth Order and Family Size

You have no doubt heard people say that firstborn children are more successful and ambitious than later-borns. Firstborns also rate themselves as more honest and conscientious (e.g., Paulhus, Trapnell, & Chen, 1999). On the other hand, later-born children are said to be more popular, more independent, less conforming, less neurotic, and possibly more creative.

Most of the studies supporting these generalizations used flawed research methods (Ernst & Angst, 1983; Schooler, 1972). A common way to do the research is this: Ask people to tell you their birth order and something else about themselves, such as their grade point average in school. Then measure the correlation between the measurements. Do you see a possible problem here?

The problem is that many firstborns come from families with only one child, whereas later-born children necessarily come from larger families. Many highly educated and ambitious parents have only one child and provide that child with many advantages. Therefore, what appears to be a difference between first- and later-born children could be a difference between small and large families (Rodgers, 2001).

A better method is to compare first- and second-born children in families with at least two children, first- and third-born children in families with at least three children, and so forth. Figure 5.31 shows the results of one study. As you can see, the average IQ was higher in small families than in large families. However, within a family of a given size, birth order made little difference (Rodgers, Cleveland, van den Oord, & Rowe, 2000).

Most other studies have also found that apparent differences between firstborn and later-born children are really differences between small and large families (Wichman, Rodgers, & MacCallum, 2006). However, a large Norwegian study found that firstborn children did score slightly higher on IQ tests than later-born children, even within the

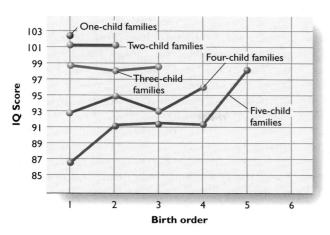

Figure 5.31 Children from small families tend to score higher on IQ tests than children from large families. However, within a family of a given size, birth order is not related to IQ. (From "Resolving the Debate Over Birth Order, Family Size, and Intelligence" by J. L. Rodgers, *American Psychologist*, 55(6), 2000, 599–612. Copyright © 2000 by the American Psychological Association. Adapted by permission of the author.)

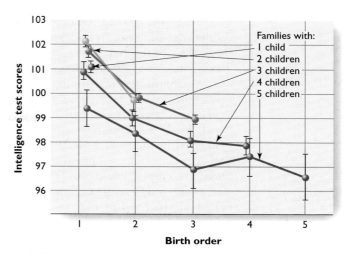

Figure 5.32 In a Norwegian study, children from small families scored higher than those from larger families. In addition, earlier-born children scored higher than later-born children, even when considering family size. (Modified from Figure 1 from Bjerkedal, T., Kristensen, P., Skjeret, G. A., & Brevik, J. I. (2007). Intelligence test scores and birth order among young Norwegian men (conscripts) analyzed within and between families. *Intelligence*, 35, 503–514. Reprinted with permission from Elsevier.)

same family (Bjerkedal, Kristensen, Skjeret, & Brevik, 2007). Contrast the results in Figure 5.32 to those in Figure 5.31. Given this contradiction in results, the true relationship between birth order and IQ is still uncertain, as is the relationship between birth order and personality. However, two points are clear: The effect of birth order, if any, is small. And research on this topic must be done carefully to separate the effects of birth order from those of family size.

- -

23. Suppose someone found that last-born children (those with no younger brothers or sisters) do better in school than second-to-last-borns. What would be one likely explanation?

Concept Check

Answer

23. An only child is a last-born as well as a first-born. A large sample of last-borns will include many children from single-child families, which are often characterized by high IQ and ambitions. Second-to-last-borns necessarily come from larger families.

- -

Effects of Parenting Styles

If you have children of your own, will you be loving and kind or strict and distant? Will you give the children everything they want or make them work for rewards? Will you encourage their independence or enforce restrictions? Moreover, how much does your behavior matter?

Psychologists have done a great deal of research comparing parenting styles to the behavior and personality of the children. Much of this research is based on four parenting styles described by Diana Baumrind (1971):

Authoritative parents: These parents *set high standards and impose controls, but they are also warm and responsive to the child's communications.* They set limits but adjust them when appropriate. They encourage their children to strive toward their own goals.

Authoritarian parents: Like the authoritative parents, authoritarian parents set firm controls, but they tend to be *emotionally more distant from the child. They set rules without explaining the reasons behind them.*

Permissive parents: Permissive parents are *warm and loving but undemanding.*

Indifferent or uninvolved parents: These parents *spend little time with their children and do little more than provide them with food and shelter.*

Parenting styles are reasonably consistent within a family. For example, most parents who are permissive with one child are permissive with the others, too (Holden & Miller, 1999). The research has found small but reasonably consistent links between parenting style and children's behavior. For example, most children of authoritative parents are self-reliant, cooperate with others, and do well in school. Children of authoritarian parents tend to be law-abiding but distrustful and not very independent. Children of permissive parents are often socially irresponsible. Children of indifferent parents tend to be impulsive and undisciplined.

However, the "best" style of parenting depends on the child. Children with a somewhat fearful temperament respond well to mild discipline, developing a strong conscience. Children with a fearless temperament respond poorly to any kind of discipline and respond better to rewards (Kochanska,

Aksan, & Joy, 2007). If you become a parent, use some trial and error to find what works best with your children rather than relying on what some authority says is the "right" way to rear children.

Furthermore, interpreting the results about parenting is not as easy as it may appear. For years, psychologists assumed that parental indifference *leads to* impulsive, out-of-control children. However, as Judith Rich Harris (1998) pointed out, other explanations are possible. Maybe impulsive, hard-to-control children cause their parents to withdraw into indifference. Or maybe the parents and children share genes that lead to uncooperative behaviors. Similarly, the kindly behaviors of authoritative parents could encourage well-mannered behaviors in their children, but it is also possible that these children were well behaved from the start, thereby encouraging kindly, understanding behaviors in their parents.

A better approach is to study adopted children, who are genetically unrelated to the parents rearing them. One study of adult twins who had been adopted by separate families found that the parenting style described by one twin correlated significantly with the parenting style described by the other twin, especially for pairs of monozygotic twins (Krueger, Markon, & Bouchard, 2003). That is, if one twin reported being reared by kindly, understanding adoptive parents, the other usually did also, even though they were reared in separate families. The twins had similar personalities, which affected their adopting parents, as well as affecting how the twins perceived their environments.

If we examine long-term personality traits of adopted children and their adopting parents, the results surprise most people: The children's personalities correlate almost zero with the parents' personalities (Heath, Neale, Kessler, Eaves, & Kendler, 1992; Loehlin, 1992; Viken, Rose, Kaprio, & Koskenvuo, 1994). For this reason, Harris (1995, 1998) argued that parenting style has little influence on most aspects of personality. Much personality variation depends on genetic differences, and the rest of the variation, she argued, depends mostly on the influence of other children. For more information, visit this website: **home.att. net/~xchar/tna/.**

As you can imagine, not everyone happily accepted Harris's conclusion. Psychologists who had spent a career studying parenting styles were not pleased to be told that their results were inconclusive. Parents were not pleased to be told that they had little influence on their children's personalities. Harris (2000), however, chose her words carefully. She did not say that it makes no difference how you treat your children. For one thing, obviously, if you treat your children badly, they won't like you!

Also, parents control where the children live and therefore influence their choice of peers, and parents influence some choices that most peers don't care about, such as religion and music lessons. Psychologists using improved research methods have shown real, though not huge, effects of parenting style (Collins, Maccoby, Steinberg, Hetherington, & Bornstein, 2000). The quality of parenting is especially important for high-risk children, such as adopted children who spent the first few months of life in low-quality orphanages (Stams, Juffer, & van IJzendoorn, 2002). Still, parents do not have as much control over their children's psychological development as psychologists once assumed.

24. Why is a correlation between parents' behavior and children's behavior inconclusive concerning how parents influence their children? Why would a correlation between adoptive parents' behavior and that of their adopted children provide more useful information?

Answer

24. Children can resemble their parents' behavior because of either genetics or social influences. Adoptive children do not necessarily resemble their adopted parents genetically, so any similarity in behavior would reflect environmental influences. Of course, the question would remain as to whether the parents influenced the children or the children influenced the parents.

Parental Employment and Child Care

What is the normal way to rear infants and young children? The customs vary so widely that "normal" has no clear meaning. In subsistence cultures, a mother returns to her tasks of gathering food and so forth shortly after giving birth, leaving her infant most of the day with other women and older children (McGurk, Caplan, Hennessy, & Moss, 1993). Within the first few months, the infant establishes strong attachments to several adults and children (Tronick, Morelli, & Ivey, 1992).

Still, many psychologists in Europe and North America maintained that healthy emotional development required an infant to establish a strong attachment to a single caregiver—ordinarily, the mother. When more and more families began placing infants in day care so that both parents could return to work shortly after their infant's

In many cultures, it has long been the custom for a mother to leave her infant for much of the day with friends, relatives, and other children.

birth, a question arose about the psychological effects on those children.

Many studies compared children who stayed with their mothers and those who entered day care within their first year or two of life. The studies examined attachment (as measured by the Strange Situation or in other ways), adjustment and well-being, play with other children, social relations with adults, and intellectual development. The results were that most children develop satisfactorily if they receive adequate day care (Scarr, 1998). Later studies have confirmed that children in dual-income families do just as well academically as those with a parent at home (Goldberg, Prause, Lucas-Thompson, & Himsel, 2008). One exception to this rule is that if both parents return to work full time within the first year of an infant's life, the child later shows a slightly increased probability of problem behaviors toward both children and adults (Hill, Waldfogel, Brooks-Gunn, & Han, 2005; NICHD Early Child Care Research Network, 2006). As always, we cannot be sure about cause and effect from data such as these. Perhaps the families that use full-time day care in the first year differ from other families in ways that influence the results.

Older children are less affected, and perhaps positively affected, by having both parents employed. One longitudinal study of 2,402 low-income families examined preschoolers and older children before and after their mothers took jobs. The preschoolers showed no behavioral changes, and the older children showed slight benefits in some aspects of adjustment (Chase-Lansdale et al., 2003).

Nontraditional Families

Western society has considered a traditional family to be a mother, a father, and their children. A nontraditional family is, therefore, anything else. Psychologists have compared children reared by single mothers to those reared by a father and mother. On the average, single mothers are more likely to have financial difficulties, and many are undergoing the emotional trauma of divorce. However, if we limit our attention to single mothers with good incomes and no recent divorce, their children show about the same social and emotional development as those in two-parent homes (MacCallum & Golombek, 2004; Weissman, Leaf, & Bruce, 1987). Children reared by gay and lesbian parents also develop about the same as those reared by heterosexuals in terms of social and emotional development, psychological adjustment, and romantic relationships (Golombok et al., 2003; MacCallum & Golombok, 2004; Patterson, 1994; Silverstein & Auerbach, 1999; Wainwright, Russell, & Patterson, 2004).

Many children today are reared by a single parent or grandparent. Some are reared by gay parents. The research indicates that who rears the child has little influence on long-term personality development if the caregivers are loving and dependable.

However, we should be cautious about our conclusions. The studies failing to find significant differences between children reared in traditional and nontraditional families have examined small numbers of children and have measured only limited aspects of behavior (Redding, 2001). Some of the studies had methodological weaknesses that could hide small but noteworthy effects (Schumm, 2008). At most, we can say that being reared by a single parent or by gays or lesbians does not produce a big enough effect to be clear in small samples of people. We need more research before dismissing the possibility of any effect at all.

Parental Conflict and Divorce

In an earlier era, people in the United States considered divorce shameful. Political commentators attributed Adlai Stevenson's defeat in the presidential campaign of 1952 to the fact that he was divorced. Americans would never vote for a divorced candidate, the commentators said. "Never" didn't last very long. By 1980, when Ronald Reagan was elected president, voters hardly noticed his divorce and remarriage.

Mavis Hetherington and her associates conducted longitudinal studies of middle-class children and their families following a divorce (Hetherington, 1989). Compared to children in intact families, those in divorced families showed

Many sons of divorced parents go through a period when they act out their frustrations by starting fights.

more conflicts with their parents and other children. They pouted and sought attention, especially in the first year after a divorce. Later studies found that divorce has the strongest emotional effect on elementary schoolchildren but impairs academic performance more strongly for teenagers (Lansford et al., 2006).

Hetherington's studies concentrated on White middle-class children, and the results differ for other cultures. Divorce is more common in Black families, but in most regards, divorced Black women adjust better than White women do (McKelvey & McKenry, 2000). Many Black families ease the burden of single parenthood by having a grandmother or other relative help with child care.

Exceptions occur to almost any generalization about the effects of divorce on children (Hetherington, Stanley-Hagan, & Anderson, 1989). Some children remain distressed for years, whereas others recover quickly. A few seem to do well at first but become more distressed later. Other children are resilient throughout their parents' divorce and afterward. They keep their friends, do all right in school, and maintain good relationships with both parents. In fact, even some children who are seriously maltreated or abused develop far better than one might expect (Caspi et al., 2002).

None of this research implies that parents should always stay together for their children's benefit. Children do not fare well if their parents are constantly fighting. Children who observe much conflict between their parents tend to be nervous, unable to sleep through the night (El-Sheikh, Buckhalt, Mize, & Acebo, 2006), and prone to violent and disruptive behaviors (Sternberg, Baradaran, Abbott, Lamb, & Guterman, 2006).

25. You may hear someone say that the right way to rear children is with both a mother and a father. Based on the evidence, what would be a good reply?

Concept Check

Answer

25. According to the evidence so far, children reared by a single parent, divorced parents, or a gay couple develop about normally.

In Closing

Many Ways of Life

This module began with the question of how you would have been different if you had been born into a different gender, ethnic group, or family. In some ways, it is obvious that the differences would have been drastic. You would have had different friends, different activities, and different experiences with sexism and racism. However, most of the research described in this module indicates that your intellect and many aspects of your personality would have been about the same. Our group identities affect us enormously in some regards and much less in others.

SUMMARY

- *Gender influences.* Men and women differ on the average in brain anatomy and miscellaneous aspects of behavior, including interests. However, researchers have found no clear evidence of differences in intellectual abilities. (page 181)
- *Androgyny.* Psychologists have proposed that people should benefit from androgyny, the ability to alternate between masculine and feminine traits. However, so far the demonstrated benefits of androgyny seem to be the sum of the benefits of masculinity and femininity. (page 183)
- *Ethnic and cultural differences.* Being a member of an ethnic minority raises special issues for identity development. Immigrant children have special difficulties as they try to participate in two cultures. Most bicultural and biracial children develop well. (page 184)
- *Birth order.* Most studies comparing firstborn versus later-born children do not separate the effects of birth order from the effects of family size. If we disregard families with only one child, most differences are small between firstborns and later-borns. (page 186)
- *Parenting styles.* Parenting style correlates with the behavior of the children. For example, caring, understanding parents tend to have well-behaved children. However, children affect the parents as much as parents affect the children. Also, within biological families, children's behavior can correlate with parenting style because of genetic influences. (page 187)
- *Nontraditional child care.* A child's normal personality and social development require at least one caring adult, but the number of caregivers and their gender and sexual orientation apparently matter little. (page 188)
- *Effects of divorce.* Children of divorced parents often show signs of distress, but the results vary across families and over time. (page 190)

KEY TERMS

androgyny (page 183)

authoritarian parents (page 187)

authoritative parents (page 187)

biculturalism (page 185)

indifferent or uninvolved parents (page 187)

permissive parents (page 187)

sex roles (page 183)

Why Does This Matter to Me?

SOCIAL RESPONSIBILITY AND PSYCHOLOGY

Many environmental problems are caused by human behavior. Psychologists can help steer the course of our future toward more socially responsible and sustainable outcomes. Students of today need to be ever mindful of the link between human behavior and its impact on the environment and our communities.

"Nature, Nurture, and Human Development" and Social Responsibility: A Step Further

Toward the end of Module 5.2, the text noted, "A bit below the surface, there is a child's mind inside each of us." What are some ways in which we easily become childish? What brings out the child within us, and what brings out the adult? If wasting natural resources is childlike, how could we elicit more adult approaches? Conversely, how can we encourage childlike enthusiasm for nature and its wonder?

Start Young

There are many organizations that focus on promoting green habits in children. For a list of current interactive websites for kids, visit **www.cengage.com/psychology/kalat**, and share the activities and tips you find with the young people in your life.

Join the iChapters Plant a Tree Drive!

To show its support of the environmental movement, iChapters is planting a tree on behalf of each fan of the iChapters Facebook Page and for every 10 questions answered correctly in our quiz.
http://www.ichapters.com/plantatree/

Exploration and Study

SUGGESTIONS FOR FURTHER EXPLORATION

In addition to the study materials provided at the end of each module, you may supplement your review of this chapter with the following book and website suggestions or by using one or more of the book's electronic resources, which include its companion website, interactive Cengage Learning eBook, and CengageNOW. Brief descriptions of these resources follow. For more information, visit www.cengage.com/psychology/kalat.

ADDITIONAL RESOURCES

The book's companion website, accessible from **www.cengage.com/psychology/kalat**, provides a wide range of study resources such as an interactive glossary, flashcards, tutorial quizzes, updated web links, and Try It Yourself activities. For example, the exercise on Genetic Generations ties to what you've learned in this chapter.

CengageNOW with Critical Thinking Videos is an easy-to-use resource that helps you study in less time to get the grade you want. An online study system, CengageNOW gives you the option of taking a diagnostic pretest for each chapter. The system uses the results of each pretest to create personalized chapter study plans for you. The Personalized Study Plans

- Help you save study time by identifying areas on which you should concentrate and give you one-click access to corresponding pages of the interactive Cengage Learning eBook;
- Provide interactive exercises and study tools to help you fully understand chapter concepts; and
- Include a posttest for you to take to confirm that you are ready to move on to the next chapter.

Find critical thinking videos like this one in your CengageNOW product, which offer an opportunity for you to learn more about psychological research on different topics.

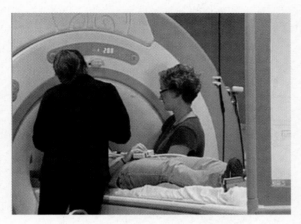

Visual-Spatial Processing

Books

Twenge, J. M. (2006). *Generation Me.* New York: Free Press. Provocative description of generational differences, especially the effects on today's young adults.

Websites

Links to the websites described below are kept current and can be found at **www.cengage.com/ psychology/kalat.**

Human Genome Project

This is the definitive site for understanding the Human Genome Project, from the basic science to ethical, legal, and social considerations to the latest discoveries.

The Child Psychologist

Rene Thomas Folse's site focuses on children with disorders or other causes for concern.

American Academy of Child & Adolescent Psychiatry

Check this site for information about common psychological disorders of children and teenagers.

The Nurture Assumption

Judith Rich Harris maintains this web page about her controversial book on the importance of peers and the relative unimportance of parenting styles.

The Child Artist Grown Up

Did you like Robin Kalat's drawing at the start of Module 5.2? Check out her adult art at this site.

© China Daily/Reuters/CORBIS

Learning

Consider This:

Newborn humans have almost no control of their muscles, except for their eyes and mouth. Imagine a baby born with complete control of all muscles, including arms, hands, legs, and feet. Would that be a good thing?

After the parents stopped bragging about their precocious youngster, they would discover what a nightmare they had. An infant with extreme mobility but no experience would get into every imaginable danger. From the start, people need to learn what is safe to touch and what isn't, where we can go and where we shouldn't. Just about everything we do requires constant learning and relearning.

Psychologists have devoted an enormous amount of research to learning, and in the process, they developed and refined research methods that they now routinely apply in other areas of psychological investigation. This chapter is about the procedures that change behavior—why you lick your lips at the sight of tasty food, why you turn away from a food that once made you sick, why you handle sharp knives cautiously, and why you shudder if you see someone charging toward you with a knife. In chapter 7, we proceed to the topic of memory, including the ability to recall specific events.

© Andrea Chu/Getty Images

6.1 module

Behaviorism

- How and why did the behaviorist viewpoint arise?
- What is its enduring message?

When you drop an object, why does it fall? In ancient times, people said it falls because it wants to be on the ground, its natural resting place. Why is the water level about equal throughout a lake? According to the ancients, it is because nature abhors a vacuum. If a gap started to occur anywhere on the lake, water would rush in to prevent a vacuum.

Today's physicists do not talk about objects wanting to be on the ground or about nature abhorring a vacuum. Their explanations rely on natural processes such as gravity and the motion of molecules. The same is true in botany. When a flower bends toward the sun, botanists do not say the flower is trying to face the sun. They say the light triggered a mechanism that caused cells on the darker side of the stem to expand, thereby tilting the flower toward the sun.

Beginning in the 1800s, researchers began applying the same approach to animal behavior, seeking the mechanisms behind the behavior instead of guessing what an animal thinks or wants. Consider this example: When a monitor lizard sees a smaller lizard (a possible prey), the monitor does not start chasing at once. Instead, it heads for the nearest pile of rocks, which would have been a good hiding place for the smaller lizard. From that position, the monitor attacks, and its prey has no escape (Sweet & Pianka, 2003). Did the monitor devise this plan as an intelligent strategy? Or did it simply learn by trial and error that it catches more prey if it starts from a pile of rocks?

Psychologists who study animal learning and behavior seek simple explanations, such as trial-and-error learning. The **behaviorists**, who have dominated the study of animal learning, *insist that psychologists should study only observable, measurable behaviors, not mental processes.* Behaviorists seek the simplest possible explanation for behavior and resist interpretations in terms of understanding or insight. At least, they insist, we should exhaust attempts at simple explanations before we adopt more complex ones. You will recognize this idea as the principle of parsimony from chapter 2.

The term *behaviorist* applies to theorists and researchers with quite a range of views. Two major categories are *methodological behaviorists* and *radical behaviorists.* Methodological behaviorists *study only the events that they can measure and observe*—in other words, the environment and the individual's actions—*but they sometimes use those observations to infer internal events* (Day & Moore, 1995). For example, depriving an animal of food, presenting it with appealing food, or making it exercise increases the probability that the animal will eat or will engage in acts that have in the past led to food. From such observations, a psychologist infers hunger, which is an **intervening variable**, *something that we cannot directly observe but that links a variety of procedures to a variety of possible responses:*

Similarly, one could use other observations to infer intervening variables such as thirst, sex drive, anger, and fear. We infer intervening variables from behavior and do not observe them directly. A methodological behaviorist uses such terms only after anchoring them to observable procedures and responses—that is, after giving them a clear operational definition (as discussed in chapter 2). Many psychological researchers are methodological behaviorists, even if they do not use that term.

Radical behaviorists do not deny that private events such as hunger or fear exist, but they consider the terms unhelpful. Radical behaviorists *deny that hunger, fear, or other internal, private events cause behavior* (Moore, 1995). For example, they maintain, if food deprivation leads to hunger and hunger leads to eating, why not just say that food deprivation leads to eating? What do we gain from the word *hunger?* According to radical behaviorists, any internal state is caused by events in the environment (in combination with the individual's genetics). Therefore, the cause of a behavior lies in the events, not the internal states that resulted from them.

According to this point of view, discussions of mental events are just sloppy language. For example, as B. F. Skinner (1990) argued, when you say, "I *intend* to . . . ," what you really mean is "I am about to . . . " or "In situations like this, I usually . . . " or "This behavior is in the preliminary stages of happening . . . ." Any statement about mental experiences can be converted into a description of behavior.

Operation	Intervening Variable	Observable Response
Food deprivation		Increased protein intake
Prolonged exercise	Any of these can increase → Hunger (an intervening variable) → Increases any of these	Increased carbohydrate intake
Presence of other animals that are eating		Increased fat intake
Presence of highly appealing food		Increased work on tasks that have previously produced food
Certain medical conditions		

A methodological behaviorist might observe facial expressions to make inferences about sadness. A radical behaviorist, however, would study the facial expressions themselves, not as a means of inferring something else.

1. How does a radical behaviorist differ from a methodological behaviorist?

Concept Check

Answer

1. All behaviorists insist that conclusions must be based on measurements or observations of behavior. However, a methodological behaviorist sometimes uses behavioral observations to make inferences about motivations or other internal states. A radical behaviorist avoids discussion of internal events and insists that internal events are never the cause of behavior.

THE RISE OF BEHAVIORISM

We should understand behaviorism within the historical context in which it arose. In the early 1900s, one highly influential group within psychology, the *structuralists* (see chapter 1), studied thoughts, ideas, and sensations by asking people to describe them. Behaviorists protested that it is useless to ask people to report their private experiences. If someone says, "My idea of roundness is stronger than my idea of color," we cannot check the accuracy of the report. We are not even certain what it means. If psychology is to be a scientific enterprise, behaviorists insisted, it must deal with observable events—that is, behavior and its rela-

tion to the environment. This point remains valid, and even a century later, many psychologists are still scolded for relying too much on self-reports instead of observing behavior (Baumeister, Vohs, & Funder, 2007).

Some behaviorists went to extremes to avoid any mention of mental processes. Jacques Loeb (1918/1973) argued that much of animal behavior, perhaps including human behavior, could be described as simple responses to simple stimuli—for example, approaching light, turning away from strong smells, clinging to surfaces, walking toward or away from moisture, and so forth (see Figure 6.1). Complex behavior, he surmised, is the result of adding together the changes of speed and direction elicited by various stimuli. Loeb's view of behavior was an example of stimulus–response psychology, *the attempt to explain behavior in terms of how each stimulus triggers a response.*

Although the term *stimulus–response psychology* was appropriate for Loeb, it is a misleading description of today's behaviorists. Behaviorists believe that behavior is a product of

FIGURE 6.1 Jacques Loeb, an early student of animal behavior, argued that much or all of invertebrate behavior could be described as responses to simple stimuli, such as approaching light or moving opposite to the direction of gravity.

not only the current stimuli but also the individual's history of experiences, plus such factors as wakefulness or sleepiness (Staddon, 1999).

If behaviorists are to deal successfully with complex behaviors, the greatest challenge is to explain learning. The behaviorist movement became the heir to a tradition of animal learning research that began for other reasons. Charles Darwin's theory of evolution by natural selection inspired many early psychologists to study animal learning and intelligence (Dewsbury, 2000b). At first, they were interested in comparing the intelligence of various species. By about 1930, however, interest faded because the question seemed unanswerable. (A species that seems more intelligent on one task can be less intelligent on another.) The behaviorists continued studying animal learning, with some of the same methods, but they asked different questions.

If nonhumans learn in more or less the same way as humans do, behaviorists reasoned, then it should be possible to discover the basic laws of learning by studying the behavior of a convenient laboratory animal, such as a pigeon or a rat. This enterprise was ambitious and optimistic. Its goal was to find basic laws of behavior, analogous to the laws of physics. Most of the rest of this chapter will deal with behaviorists' research about learning.

THE ASSUMPTIONS OF BEHAVIORISM

Behaviorists make several assumptions, including determinism, the ineffectiveness of mental explanations, and the power of the environment to select and mold behaviors (Moore, 1995). Let's consider each of these points.

Behaviorists emphasize the role of experience in determining our actions—both our current experience and our past experiences in similar situations.

Determinism

Behaviorists accept the idea of *determinism* as described in chapter 1, the idea that we live in a universe of cause and effect. Given that our behavior is part of the universe, it too must have causes, such as "animals deprived of food will increase the rates of behaviors that lead to food." The goal of behaviorism is to determine more and more detailed laws of behavior.

The Ineffectiveness of Mental Explanations

In everyday life, we commonly refer to our motivations, emotions, and mental state. Behaviorists insist that such statements explain nothing:

Q: Why did she yell at him?

A: She yelled because she was angry.

Q: How do you know she was angry?

A: We know she was angry because she was yelling.

Here, the reference to mental states lured us into circular reasoning. Behaviorists prefer simply to describe what the individuals *do* instead of inferring what they are *trying* to do or what they are *feeling* while they do it.

The same insistence on description is central to the British and American legal systems: A witness is asked, "What did you see and hear?" An acceptable answer might be, "The defendant was sweating and trembling, and his voice was wavering." A witness should not say, "The defendant was nervous and worried," because that statement requires an inference that the witness is not entitled to make. (Of course, the jury might draw an inference.)

The Power of the Environment to Mold Behavior

Behaviors produce outcomes. Eating your carrots has one kind of outcome, and insulting your roommate has another. The outcome determines how often the behavior will occur in the future. In effect, our environment selects successful behaviors, much as evolution selects successful animals. The most extreme statement of environmental determinism came from John B. Watson, one of the founders of behaviorism, who said,

> Give me a dozen healthy infants, well-formed, and my own specified world to bring them up in and I'll guarantee to take any one at random and train him to become any type of specialist I might select—doctor, lawyer, artist, merchant-chief, and yes, even beggar-man thief—regardless of his tal-

ents, penchants, tendencies, abilities, vocations, and race of his ancestors. I am going beyond my facts and I admit it, but so have the advocates of the contrary. (1925, p. 82)

Today, few psychologists would claim that variations in behavior depend entirely on the environment (or that they depend entirely on heredity, for that matter). Although behaviorists do not deny the importance of heredity, they generally emphasize how the environment selects one behavior over another, and their explanations of individual differences concentrate on people's different learning histories.

2. Why do behaviorists reject explanations in terms of thoughts?

Concept Check

Answer

2. We cannot observe or measure thoughts or other internal events. We infer them from observed behaviors, and therefore, it is circular to use them as an explanation of behavior.

module 6.1

In Closing

Behaviorism as a Theoretical Orientation

Many students dismiss behaviorism because, at least at first glance, it seems so ridiculous: "What do you *mean,* my thoughts and beliefs and emotions don't cause my behavior?!" The behaviorists' reply is, "Exactly right. Your thoughts and other internal states do not cause your behavior because events in your environment caused your thoughts. The events that caused the thoughts are therefore the real causes of your behavior, and psychologists should spend their time trying to understand the influence of the events, not trying to analyze your thoughts." Don't be too quick to agree or disagree. Just contemplate this: If you believe that your thoughts or other internal states cause behaviors *independently* of your previous experiences, what evidence could you provide to support your claim?

SUMMARY

- *Methodological and radical behaviorists.* Behaviorists insist that psychologists should study behaviors and their relation to observable features of the environment. Methodological behaviorists use these observations to draw inferences about internal states. Radical behaviorists insist that internal states are of little scientific use and that they do not control behavior. The causes of the internal states themselves, as well as of the behaviors, lie in the environment. (page 196)
- *The origins of behaviorism.* Behaviorism began as a protest against structuralists, who asked people to describe their own mental processes. Behaviorists insisted that the structuralist approach was futile and that psychologists should study observable behaviors. (page 197)
- *Behaviorists' interest in learning.* Before the rise of the behaviorist movement, other psychologists had studied animal intelligence. Behaviorists adapted some of the methods used in previous studies but changed the questions, concentrating on the basic mechanisms of learning. (page 198)
- *Behaviorists' assumptions.* Behaviorists assume that all behaviors have causes (determinism), that mental explanations are unhelpful, and that the environment acts to select effective behaviors and suppress ineffective ones. (page 198)

KEY TERMS

behaviorist (page 196)

intervening variable (page 196)

methodological behaviorist (page 196)

radical behaviorist (page 196)

stimulus–response psychology (page 197)

Classical Conditioning

• When we learn a relationship between two stimuli, what happens?

You are sitting in your room when your roommate flicks a switch on the stereo. You know that the stereo is set to a deafening level. You flinch not because of the soft flicking sound of the switch itself but because of the loud noise it predicts.

You are driving on the highway when you see a car behind you with flashing lights. You get a sinking feeling in your stomach because you recognize the lights as the sign of a police car.

You enter a room and look around. A very attractive person from one of your classes, who you thought had never noticed you, smiles and says hello. Ooh, what a nice feeling!

Many aspects of our behavior consist of responses to signals. We respond to what each signal means, what it predicts. Psychologists' efforts to understand this kind of learning have led them to conduct thousands of experiments on both humans and nonhumans. For many kinds of learning, the similarities among species are more impressive than the differences. Often, it is easier to study nonhumans because a researcher can better control the variables likely to influence performance.

PAVLOV AND CLASSICAL CONDITIONING

In the late 1800s and early 1900s, behaviorism was starting to dominate experimental psychology. Researchers sought simple, mechanical explanations to displace what they considered unscientific accounts of thoughts, ideas, and other mental processes. The mood of the time was ripe for the theories of Ivan P. Pavlov, a Russian physiologist who had won a Nobel Prize in

physiology in 1904 for his research on digestion. As Pavlov continued his digestion research, he noticed that a dog would salivate or secrete stomach juices as soon as it saw the lab worker who customarily fed the dogs. Because this secretion undoubtedly depended on the dog's previous experiences, Pavlov called it a "psychological" secretion. He enlisted the help of other specialists, who discovered that "teasing" a dog with the sight of food produced salivation that was as predictable and automatic as any reflex. Pavlov adopted the term *conditional reflex,* implying that he only *conditionally* (or tentatively) accepted it as a reflex (Todes, 1997). However, the term has usually been translated as *conditioned reflex,* and that term is now well established in the literature.

Pavlov's Procedures

Pavlov presumed that animals are born with certain *automatic connections*—called **unconditioned reflexes**—*between a stimulus such as food and a response such as secreting digestive juices.* He conjectured that animals acquire new reflexes by transferring a response from one stimulus to another. For example, if a neutral stimulus (e.g., a sound) always precedes food, an animal would respond to the sound as it responds to food. The sound would elicit digestive secretions.

The *process by which an organism learns a new association between two stimuli—a neutral stimulus and one that already evokes a reflexive response*—is known as **classical conditioning**, or **Pavlovian conditioning**. (It is called classical because it has been known and studied for a long time.)

Pavlov selected dogs with a moderate degree of arousal. (Highly excitable dogs would not hold still long enough, and highly inhibited dogs would fall asleep.) Then he attached a tube to one of the salivary ducts in a dog's mouth to measure salivation, as shown in Figure 6.2. He could have measured stomach secretions, but measuring salivation was easier.

Whenever Pavlov gave a dog food, the dog salivated. The food → salivation connection was automatic, requiring no training. Pavlov called food the unconditioned stimulus, and he called

Ivan P. Pavlov (with the white beard) with students and a dog. Pavlov devised simple principles to describe learned changes in a dog's behavior.

At first,

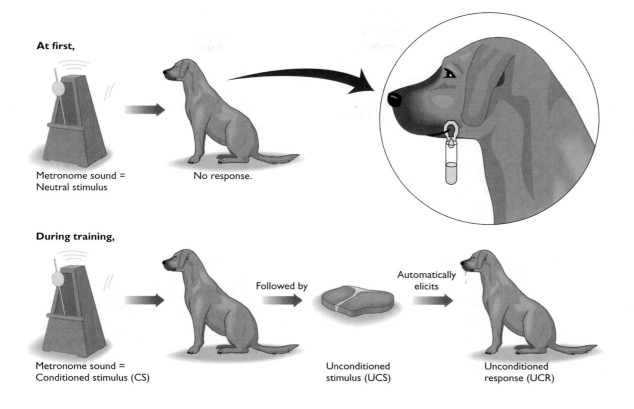

Metronome sound = Neutral stimulus

No response.

During training,

Metronome sound = Conditioned stimulus (CS)

Followed by

Unconditioned stimulus (UCS)

Automatically elicits

Unconditioned response (UCR)

After some number of repetitions,

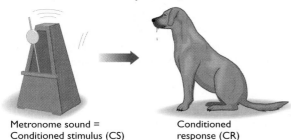

Metronome sound = Conditioned stimulus (CS)

Conditioned response (CR)

Figure 6.2 A conditioned stimulus precedes an unconditioned stimulus. At first, the conditioned stimulus elicits no response, and the unconditioned stimulus elicits the unconditioned response. After sufficient pairings, the conditioned stimulus begins to elicit the conditioned response, which can resemble the unconditioned response. In Pavlov's studies, the response was salivation, which Pavlov measured with a pouch attached to a dog's cheek.

salivation the unconditioned response. The **unconditioned stimulus (UCS)** is *an event that automatically elicits an unconditioned response,* and the **unconditioned response (UCR)** is *an action that the unconditioned stimulus elicits.*

Next Pavlov introduced a new stimulus, such as a metronome. Upon hearing the metronome, the dog lifted its ears and looked around but did not salivate, so the metronome was a neutral stimulus with regard to salivation. Pavlov sounded the metronome a couple of seconds before giving food to the dog. After a few pairings of the metronome with food, the dog began to salivate as soon as it heard the metronome (Pavlov, 1927/1960).

We call the metronome the **conditioned stimulus (CS)** because a dog's *response to it depends on the preceding conditions*—that is, the pairing of the CS with the UCS. The salivation that follows the metronome is the **conditioned response (CR).** The conditioned response is *whatever response the conditioned stimulus begins to elicit as a result of the conditioning (training) procedure.* At the start of the conditioning procedure, the conditioned stimulus does *not* elicit a conditioned response. After conditioning, it does.

In Pavlov's experiment, the conditioned response was salivation and so was the unconditioned response. However, in some cases, the conditioned response differs from the unconditioned response. For example, the unconditioned response to an electric shock includes shrieking and jumping. The conditioned response to a stimulus paired with shock (i.e., a warning signal for shock) is a tensing of the muscles and lack of activity (e.g., Pezze, Bast, & Feldon, 2003).

To summarize, the *unconditioned stimulus* (UCS), such as food, automatically elicits the *unconditioned response* (UCR), such as salivating. A neutral stimulus, such as a sound, that is paired with the UCS becomes a *conditioned stimulus* (CS). At first, this neutral stimulus elicits either no response or an irrelevant response, such as looking around. After some number of pairings of the CS with the UCS, the conditioned stimulus elicits the *conditioned response* (CR), which usually resembles the UCR. The key difference between the CR and UCR is that the CS (conditioned stimulus) elicits the CR (conditioned response) and the UCS (unconditioned stimulus) elicits the UCR (unconditioned response). Figure 6.2 diagrams these relationships.

As a rule, conditioning occurs more rapidly if the conditioned stimulus is unfamiliar. If you have heard a tone many times (followed by nothing) and now start hearing the tone followed by a puff of air to your left eye, you will be slow to show signs of conditioning. Similarly, imagine two people who are bitten by a snake. One has never been near a snake before, and the other has spent years tending snakes at the zoo. You can guess which one will learn a greater fear.

More Examples of Classical Conditioning

Here are more examples of classical conditioning:

- Your alarm clock makes a faint clicking sound a couple of seconds before the alarm goes off. At first, the click by itself does not awaken you, but the alarm does. After a week or so, you awaken when you hear the click.

| Unconditioned stimulus | = | alarm | → | Unconditioned response | = | awakening |
| Conditioned stimulus | = | click | → | Conditioned response | = | awakening |

- You hear the sound of a dentist's drill shortly before the unpleasant experience of the drill on your teeth. From then on, the sound of a dentist's drill arouses anxiety. Many fears and anxieties develop by classical conditioning.

| Unconditioned stimulus | = | drilling | → | Unconditioned response | = | tension |
| Conditioned stimulus | = | sound of the drill | → | Conditioned response | = | tension |

- A nursing mother responds to her baby's cries by putting the baby to her breast, stimulating the flow of milk. After a few days of repetitions, the sound of the baby's cry is enough to start the milk flowing.

| Unconditioned stimulus | = | baby sucking | → | Unconditioned response | = | milk flow |
| Conditioned stimulus | = | baby's cry | → | Conditioned response | = | milk flow |

- An African bird, the white-breasted go-away bird (yes, that's its real name), perches on treetops and utters an alarm call to alert its relatives when it sees an eagle, leopard, or other dangerous predator. Dik-diks are tiny antelopes that live in the same forests. They learn a conditioned fear response to the sound of the go-away bird's alarm call. When they hear it, they stop eating, look around, and run for cover (Lea, Barrera, Tom, & Blumstein, 2008).

| Unconditioned stimulus | = | sight of dangerous predator | → | Unconditioned response | = | running for cover |
| Conditioned stimulus | = | go-away bird's call | → | Conditioned response | = | running for cover |

Note the usefulness of classical conditioning: It prepares individuals for likely events. In some cases, however, the effects can be unwelcome. For example, many cancer patients who have had repeated chemotherapy or radiation become nauseated when they approach or even imagine the building where they received treatment (Dadds, Bovbjerg, Redd, & Cutmore, 1997).

| Unconditioned stimulus | = | chemotherapy or radiation | → | Unconditioned response | = | nausea |
| Conditioned stimulus | = | approaching the building | → | Conditioned response | = | nausea |

Form an image of a lemon, a nice fresh juicy one. You cut it into slices and then suck on a slice. Imagine that sour taste. As you imagine the lemon, do you notice yourself salivating? If so, your imagination produced enough resemblance to the actual sight and taste of a lemon to serve as a conditioned stimulus.

3. At the start of training, the CS elicits _____ and the UCS elicits _____ . After many repetitions of the CS followed by the UCS, the CS elicits _____ and the UCS elicits _____ .

4. In this example, identify the CS, UCS, CR, and UCR: Every time an army drill sergeant calls out "Ready, aim, fire," the artillery shoots, making a painfully loud sound that causes you to flinch. After a few repetitions, you tense your muscles after the word "fire," before the shot itself.

Answers

3. No response (or at least nothing of interest) . . . the UCR . . . the CR . . . still the UCR. 4. The conditioned stimulus is the sound "Ready, aim, fire." The unconditioned stimulus is the artillery shot. The unconditioned response is flinching; the conditioned response is tensing.

The Phenomena of Classical Conditioning

Let's start with laboratory studies and later discuss how they apply to human experiences. The *process that establishes or strengthens a conditioned response* is known as **acquisition**. Figure 6.3 shows how the strength of a conditioned response increases after pairings of the conditioned and unconditioned stimuli.

Once Pavlov had demonstrated classical conditioning, curious psychologists explored what would happen after various changes in procedure. Here are a few of the main phenomena.

Extinction

Suppose I sound a buzzer and then blow a puff of air into your eyes. After a few repetitions, you start to close your eyes as soon as you hear the buzzer (Figure 6.4). Now I sound the buzzer repeatedly without the puff of air. What do you do?

You blink your eyes the first time and perhaps the second and third times, but before long,

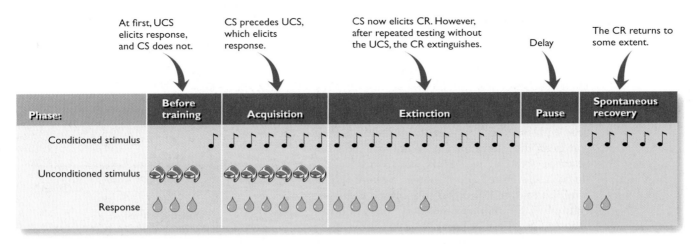

Phase:	Before training	Acquisition	Extinction	Pause	Spontaneous recovery
	At first, UCS elicits response, and CS does not.	CS precedes UCS, which elicits response.	CS now elicits CR. However, after repeated testing without the UCS, the CR extinguishes.	Delay	The CR returns to some extent.
Conditioned stimulus	♪	♪ ♪ ♪ ♪ ♪ ♪	♪ ♪ ♪ ♪ ♪ ♪ ♪ ♪ ♪ ♪		♪ ♪ ♪ ♪ ♪
Unconditioned stimulus	🫘🫘🫘	🫘🫘🫘🫘🫘			
Response	💧💧💧	💧💧💧💧💧💧	💧💧💧💧 💧		💧💧

Figure 6.3 If the conditioned stimulus regularly precedes the unconditioned stimulus, acquisition occurs. If the conditioned stimulus is presented by itself, extinction occurs. A pause after extinction yields a brief spontaneous recovery.

you stop. This decrease of the conditioned response is called **extinction** (see Figure 6.3). *To extinguish a classically conditioned response, repeatedly present the conditioned stimulus (CS) without the unconditioned stimulus (UCS).* That is, acquisition of a response (CR) occurs when the CS predicts the UCS; extinction occurs when the CS no longer predicts the UCS.

Extinction is not the same as forgetting. Both weaken a learned response, but they arise in different ways. You forget during a long period without reminders or practice. Extinction occurs as the result of a specific experience—perceiving the conditioned stimulus without the unconditioned stimulus.

When we talk about the extinction of an animal or plant species, we mean it is gone for-

ever. In classical conditioning, extinction does *not* mean complete obliteration. Extinction suppresses a response. You can think of acquisition as learning to make a response and extinction as learning to inhibit it. For example, suppose you go through original learning in which a tone regularly predicts a puff of air to your eyes. You learn to blink your eyes at the tone. Then you go through an extinction process in which you hear the tone many times but receive no air puffs. You extinguish, so the tone no longer elicits a blink. Now, without warning, you get another puff of air to your eyes. As a result, the next time you hear the tone, you blink your eyes. Extinction inhibited your conditioned response, but a sudden puff of air weakens that inhibition (Bouton, 1994).

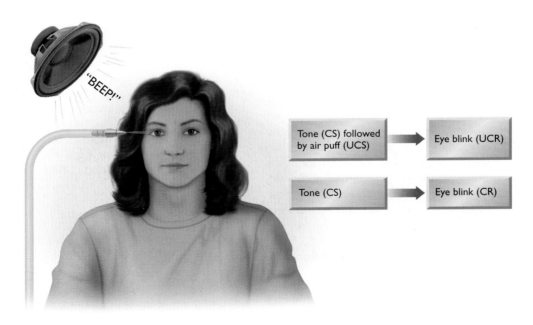

Tone (CS) followed by air puff (UCS) → Eye blink (UCR)

Tone (CS) → Eye blink (CR)

Figure 6.4 Classical conditioning of the eye-blink response.

Spontaneous Recovery

Suppose you are in a classical-conditioning experiment. At first, you repeatedly hear a buzzer (CS) that precedes a puff of air to your eyes (UCS). Then the buzzer stops predicting an air puff. After a few trials, your response to the buzzer extinguishes. Now, suppose you sit there for a long time with nothing happening and then suddenly you hear the buzzer again. What will you do? Chances are, you will blink your eyes at least slightly. **Spontaneous recovery** is *a temporary return of an extinguished response after a delay* (see Figure 6.3). Spontaneous recovery requires no additional CS–UCS pairings.

Why does spontaneous recovery take place? Think of it this way: At first, the buzzer predicted a puff of air to your eyes, and then it didn't. You behaved in accordance with the more recent experiences. Hours later, neither experience is much more recent than the other, and the effects of acquisition and extinction are about equally strong.

5. In Pavlov's experiment on conditioned salivation in response to a buzzer, what procedure produces extinction? What procedure produces spontaneous recovery?

Answer

5. To bring about extinction, present the buzzer repeatedly without presenting food. To bring about spontaneous recovery, first bring about extinction; then wait hours or days and present the buzzer again.

Stimulus Generalization

Suppose a bee stings you, and you learn to fear bees. Now you see a wasp or hornet. Will you fear that, too?

You probably will. However, you probably will not show any fear of ants, fleas, or other insects that don't resemble bees. The more similar a new stimulus is to the conditioned stimulus, the more likely you are to show a similar response (Figure 6.5). **Stimulus generalization** is the *extension of a conditioned response from the training stimulus to similar stimuli.*

This definition may sound straightforward, but psychologists find it difficult to specify exactly what "similar" means (Pearce, 1994). For example, after a bee stings you, you might fear

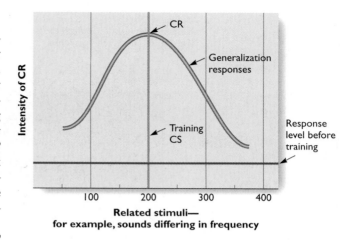

Figure 6.5 Stimulus generalization is the process of extending a learned response to new stimuli that resemble the one used in training. A less similar stimulus elicits a weaker response.

the sound of buzzing bees when you are walking through a forest but not when you hear the same sounds as part of a nature documentary on television. Your response depends on the total configuration of stimuli.

Discrimination

Suppose your alarm clock makes one kind of click when the alarm is about to ring and a different kind of click at other times. You will learn to **discriminate** between the two clicks: You *respond differently because the two stimuli predict different outcomes.* You awaken when you hear one click but you stay asleep when you hear the other. Similarly, you discriminate between a bell that signals time for class to start and a different bell that signals a fire alarm.

Discrimination training enhances our sensitivity to sensory cues. In one study, people sniffed two almost identical chemicals. At first, they could not smell any difference. However, one chemical always preceded an electrical shock, and the other always preceded a safe interval without shock. As training proceeded, people began to detect the difference, and they reacted to the smell that predicted shock (Li, Howard, Parrish, & Gottfried, 2008).

What's the Evidence?

Emotional Conditioning Without Awareness

In many situations, conditioning occurs fastest when people are aware of the connection between the CS and UCS (Knuttinen,

Power, Preston, & Disterhoft, 2001). (With laboratory animals, it is hard to ask!) However, emotional responses sometimes become conditioned without awareness. The implications are far-reaching. We shall examine one study in detail. In some ways, this discussion will seem out of place: The whole idea of discussing attitudes, emotions, and so forth is contrary to the customs of radical behaviorism. Nevertheless, we see here how other psychologists have taken the idea of classical conditioning and applied it more broadly.

Hypothesis People will form favorable attitudes toward items paired with something they like and unfavorable attitudes toward items paired with something they dislike, even if they are not aware of the connection (Olson & Fazio, 2001).

Method Forty-five female college students viewed a series of slides. Most included a Pokemon image, as shown in Figure 6.6, although a few were blank. Most of those with a Pokemon also included another picture or a word. Each student's task was to look for a particular "target" image and press a computer key whenever she saw it, ignoring all the other pictures and words. Most of the other images were paired with neutral words and pictures, but one of them was always paired with something likable (e.g., a picture of tasty food or the word "excellent"), and one was always paired with something negative (e.g., a picture of a cockroach or the word "terrible"). After viewing all the slides repeatedly, each student was asked to look at all the Pokemon images (by themselves) and rate how pleasant or unpleasant they were. They were also asked whether they remembered what other items had paired with each Pokemon.

Results On the average, the participants gave a higher pleasantness rating to the Pokemon that had been associated with favorable words and pictures and lower ratings to the one associated with unfavorable words and pictures.

However, they did not remember what words or pictures had been associated with each Pokemon. (They hadn't been told to remember those pairings, and they didn't.)

Interpretation These results show classical conditioning alters people's emotional responses to pictures, even though people did not notice them enough to report explicit memories.

Additional research has shown conditioning of other kinds of emotional responses. In one study, people saw words paired with pictures of faces, some of which were smiling or frowning. For some participants, personally relevant words (their name, their birth date, etc.) were consistently paired with smiling faces. As a result of this pairing, they showed increases in several measures of self-esteem! Evidently, the pairings enhanced emotional responses to reminders of the participants themselves (Baccus, Baldwin, & Packer, 2004).

DRUG TOLERANCE AS AN EXAMPLE OF CLASSICAL CONDITIONING

Classical conditioning shows up in places you might not expect. One example is **drug tolerance**: *Users of certain drugs experience progressively weaker effects after taking the drugs repeatedly.* Some longtime users inject themselves with more heroin than it would take to kill an average person, while experiencing relatively mild effects.

Drug tolerance results partly from automatic chemical changes that occur in cells throughout the body (Baker & Tiffany, 1985). It also depends partly on classical conditioning. Consider: When drug users inject themselves with morphine or heroin, the drug injection procedure is a complex

Figure 6.6 Each participant was asked to press a key whenever she saw a particular Pokemon image; she was to ignore the other Pokemon images. Some of these other Pokemon images were paired with pleasant or unpleasant words or images, as shown above.

stimulus that includes the time and place as well as the needle injection. This total stimulus predicts a second stimulus, the drug's entry into the brain, which triggers a variety of body defenses, including changes in hormone secretions, heart rate, and breathing rate.

First stimulus	→	Second stimulus	→	Automatic response
(Injection procedure)		(Drug enters brain)		(Body's defenses)

Whenever one stimulus predicts a second stimulus that produces an automatic response, classical conditioning can occur. The first stimulus becomes the CS, the second becomes the UCS, and the response is the UCR. Let's relabel as follows:

Conditioned stimulus	→	Unconditioned stimulus	→	Unconditioned response
(Injection procedure)		(Drug enters brain)		(Body's defenses)

If conditioning occurs here, what would be the consequence? Suppose the CS (drug injection) produces a CR that resembles the UCR (the body's defenses against the drug). As a result, when the person starts the injection, before the drug enters the body, the body starts mobilizing its defenses against the drug. Therefore, the drug has less effect—the body develops tolerance. Shepard Siegel (1977, 1983) conducted several experiments to confirm that classical conditioning occurs during drug injections. That is, after many drug injections, the injection procedure by itself evokes the body's antidrug defenses:

Conditioned stimulus	→	Conditioned response
(Injection procedure)		(Body's defenses)

One prediction was this: If the injection procedure serves as a conditioned stimulus, then the body's defense reactions should be strongest if the drug is administered in the usual way, in the usual location, with as many familiar stimuli as possible. (The entire experience constitutes the conditioned stimulus.)

The evidence supports this prediction for a variety of drugs (Marin, Pérez, Duero, & Ramirez, 1999; Siegel, 1983). Furthermore, the brain mechanisms responsible for learning are also necessary for the development of drug tolerance (Pérez, Maglio, Marchesini, Molina, & Ramirez, 2002).

Understanding drug tolerance is theoretically interesting, and this research eventually led to applications to helping people quit their addictions. People with a history of addiction to alcohol or other drugs experience cravings in the presence of sights, sounds, and smells that remind them of their drug experiences. When psychologists present those stimuli under conditions where the person is able to resist the temptation, the result is a partial extinction of the cravings (Loeber, Croissant, Heinz, Mann, & Flor, 2006).

6. When someone develops tolerance to the effects of a drug injection, what are the conditioned stimulus, the unconditioned stimulus, the conditioned response, and the unconditioned response?

7. Within the classical-conditioning interpretation of drug tolerance, what procedure should extinguish tolerance?

6. The conditioned stimulus is the injection procedure. The unconditioned stimulus is the entry of the drug into the brain. Both the conditioned response and the unconditioned response are the body's defenses against the drug.

7. To extinguish tolerance, present the injection procedure (conditioned stimulus) without injecting the drug (unconditioned stimulus). Instead, inject water or salt water. Siegel (1977) demonstrated that repeated injections of salt water do reduce tolerance to morphine in rats.

EXPLANATIONS OF CLASSICAL CONDITIONING

What is classical conditioning, really? As is often the case, the process appeared simple at first, but later investigation found it to be a more complex and more interesting phenomenon.

Pavlov noted that conditioning depended on the timing between CS and UCS, as shown here:

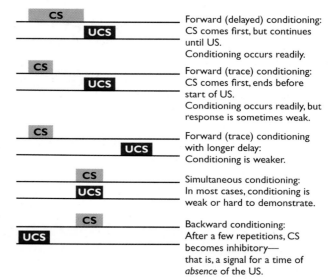

In these displays, read time left to right. Pavlov surmised that presenting the CS and UCS at nearly the same time caused a connection to grow in the brain so that the animal treated the CS as if it were the UCS. Figure 6.7a illustrates the connections before the start of training: The UCS excites a UCS center in the brain, which immediately stimulates the UCR center. Figure 6.7b illustrates connections that develop during conditioning: Pairing the CS and UCS develops a connection between their brain representations. After this connection develops, the CS excites the CS center, which excites the

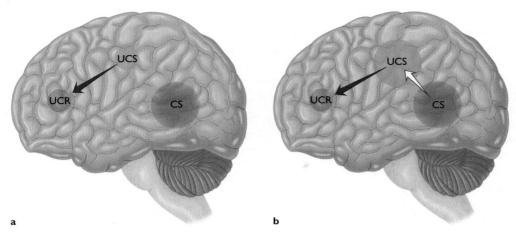

Figure 6.7 According to Pavlov, (a) at the start of conditioning, activity in the UCS center automatically activates the UCR center. (b) After sufficient pairings of the CS and UCS, a connection develops between the CS and UCS centers. Afterward, activity in the CS center flows to the UCS center and therefore excites the UCR center.

UCS center, which excites the UCR center and produces a response.

Later studies contradicted that idea. For example, a shock (UCS) causes rats to jump and shriek, but a conditioned stimulus paired with shock makes them freeze in position. They react to the conditioned stimulus as a danger signal, not as if they felt a shock. Also, in delay conditioning (Figure 6.7), where a delay separates the end of the CS from the start of the UCS, the animal does not make a conditioned response immediately after the conditioned stimulus but instead waits until almost the end of the usual delay between CS and UCS. Again, it is not treating the CS as if it were the UCS; it is using it as a predictor, a way to prepare for the UCS (Gallistel & Gibbon, 2000).

It is true, as Pavlov suggested, that the longer the delay between the CS and the UCS, the weaker the conditioning, other things being equal. However, just having the CS and UCS close together in time is not enough. It is essential that they occur more often together than they occur apart. That is, the CS must be a good predictor of the UCS. Consider this experiment: For rats in both Group 1 and Group 2, every pre-

sentation of a CS is followed by a UCS, as shown in Figure 6.8. For Group 2, the UCS also appears at many other times without the CS. In other words, for this group, the UCS happens every few seconds anyway, and it isn't much more likely with the CS than without it. Group 1 learns a strong response to the CS, and Group 2 does not (Rescorla, 1968, 1988).

8. If classical conditioning depended *entirely* on presenting the CS and UCS at nearly the same time, what result should the experimenters have obtained in Rescorla's experiment?

 Concept Check

Answer

8. If classical conditioning depended entirely on presenting the CS and UCS at nearly the same time, the rats in both groups would have responded equally to the conditioned stimulus, regardless of how often they received the unconditioned stimulus at other times.

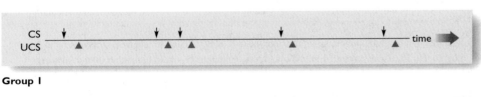

Group 1

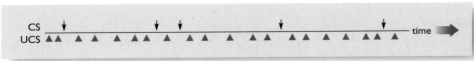

Group 2

Figure 6.8 In Rescorla's experiment, the CS always preceded the UCS in both groups, but Group 2 received the UCS frequently at other times also. Group 1 developed a strong conditioned response to the CS, and Group 2 did not.

Now consider this experiment: Rats receive a light (CS) followed by shock (UCS) until they respond consistently to the light. (Their response is to freeze in place.) Then they get a series of trials with both a light and a tone, again followed by shock. Do they learn a response to the tone? No. The same pattern occurs with the reverse order: First, rats learn a response to the tone, and then they get light–tone combinations before the shock. They continue responding to the tone but not to the light (Kamin, 1969) (see Figure 6.9). These results demonstrate the **blocking effect**: *The previously established association to one stimulus blocks the formation of an association to the added stimulus.* Research supports two explanations: First, if the first stimulus predicts the outcome, the second stimulus adds no new information. Second, the rat attends strongly to the stimulus that already predicts the outcome and therefore pays less attention to the new stimulus.

The same principle holds in human reasoning. Suppose you have several experiences when you eat something with peppers and have an allergic reaction. Then you have several experiences when you eat peppers and nuts and have the same reaction. You have already decided to try to avoid peppers. Do you now avoid nuts as strongly as the peppers? Probably not (Melchers, Ungor, & Lachnit, 2005).

9. Suppose you have already learned to flinch when you hear the sound of a dentist's drill. Now your dentist turns on some soothing background music during the drilling. The background music is paired with the pain just as much as the drill sound is. Will you learn to flinch at the sound of that background music?

Answer

9. You will not learn to flinch at the sound of the background music. Because the drill sound already predicted the pain, the new stimulus is uninformative and will not be strongly associated with the pain.

Group 1

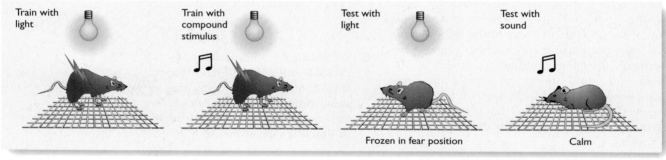

Group 2

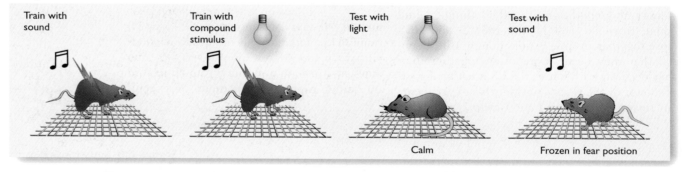

Figure 6.9 Each rat first learned to associate either light or sound with shock. Then it received a compound of both light and sound followed by shock. Each rat continued to show a strong response to the old stimulus (which already predicted shock) but little to the new one.

In Closing

Classical Conditioning Is More Than Drooling Dogs

If someone had asked you, when you first decided to study psychology, to list the main things you hoped to learn, you probably would not have replied, "I want to learn how to make dogs salivate!" I hope you have seen that the research on dog salivation is just a way to explore fundamental mechanisms, much as genetics researchers have studied the fruit fly *Drosophila* or neurophysiologists have studied the nerves of squid. Classical conditioning plays an important role in a wide variety of important behaviors, ranging from emotional responses to drug tolerance.

People sometimes use the term "Pavlovian" to mean simple, mechanical, robotlike behavior. Pavlovian or classical conditioning is not a mark of stupidity. It is a way of responding to relationships among events, a way of preparing us for what is likely to happen.

SUMMARY

- *Classical conditioning.* Ivan Pavlov discovered classical conditioning, the process by which an association forms between a neutral stimulus (the conditioned stimulus) and one that initially evokes a reflexive response (the unconditioned stimulus). The result is a new response (the conditioned response) to the conditioned stimulus. (page 200)
- *Extinction.* A conditioned response can be extinguished by repeatedly presenting the conditioned stimulus by itself. (page 203)
- *Spontaneous recovery.* If the conditioned stimulus is not presented at all for some time after extinction and is then presented again, the conditioned response may return. The return is called spontaneous recovery. (page 204)
- *Stimulus generalization.* A conditioned response to a stimulus will extend to other stimuli to the extent that they resemble the trained stimulus. (page 204)
- *Discrimination.* Animals (including people) learn to respond differently to stimuli that predict different outcomes. (page 204)
- *Emotional conditioning without awareness.* Emotional responses can be conditioned even if the learner is not aware of the connection. (page 205)
- *Drug tolerance.* Drug tolerance results in part from classical conditioning. The drug administration procedure comes to evoke defensive responses. (page 205)
- *Basis for classical conditioning.* Pavlov believed that conditioning occurred because presenting two stimuli close to each other in time developed a connection between their brain representations. Later research showed that animals do not treat the conditioned stimulus as if it were the unconditioned stimulus. Also, being close in time is not enough; learning requires that the first stimulus predict the second stimulus. (page 206)

KEY TERMS

acquisition (page 203)

blocking effect (page 208)

classical conditioning (or Pavlovian conditioning) (page 200)

conditioned response (CR) (page 201)

conditioned stimulus (CS) (page 201)

discrimination (page 204)

drug tolerance (page 205)

extinction (page 203)

spontaneous recovery (page 204)

stimulus generalization (page 204)

unconditioned reflex (page 200)

unconditioned response (UCR) (page 201)

unconditioned stimulus (UCS) (page 201)

Operant Conditioning

• How do the consequences of our behaviors affect future behaviors?

Sometimes, a simple idea can be amazingly powerful. In this module, we consider the simple but powerful idea that behaviors become more likely or less likely because of their consequences. We repeat or cease a behavior depending on the outcome.

THORNDIKE AND OPERANT CONDITIONING

Shortly before Pavlov's research, Edward L. Thorndike (1911/1970), a Harvard graduate student, began training cats in a basement. Saying that earlier experiments had dealt only with animal intelligence, not animal stupidity, he sought a simple behaviorist explanation of learning. He put cats into puzzle boxes (Figure 6.10) from which they could escape by pressing a lever, pulling a string, or tilting a pole. Sometimes, he placed food outside the box, but usually, cats worked just to escape from the box. The cats learned to make whatever response opened the box, especially if the box opened quickly.

They learned by trial and error. When a cat had to tilt a pole to escape from the box, it might at first paw or gnaw at the door, scratch the walls, or pace back and forth. Eventually, it bumped against the pole and the door opened. The next time, the cat went through a similar repertoire of behaviors but might bump against the pole a little sooner. Over many trials, the cat gradually yet inconsistently improved its speed of escape. Figure 6.11 shows a learning curve to represent this behavior. A learning curve is *a graph of the changes in behavior that occur over the course of learning.*

Did the cat understand the connection between bumping against the pole and opening the door? No, said Thorndike. If the cat had gained a new insight at some point, its escape should have been quick and consistent from that point on. The cat's gradual, inconsistent improvement suggested no point of insight or understanding.

Thorndike concluded that learning occurs when certain behaviors are strengthened at the expense of others. An animal enters a situation with a repertoire of responses such as pawing the door, scratching the walls, pacing, and so forth (labeled R_1, R_2, R_3, etc. in Figure 6.12). It starts with its most probable response (R_1). If nothing special happens, it proceeds to other responses, eventually reaching one that opens the door—for example, bumping against the pole (R_7 in this example). Opening the door is a reinforcement.

A reinforcement is *the process of increasing the future probability of the most recent response.* Thorndike said that it "stamps in," or strengthens, the response. The next time the cat is in the puzzle box, it has a slightly higher probability of the effective response. If it receives reinforcement again, the probability goes up another notch (Figure 6.12c).

Thorndike summarized his views in the law of effect (Thorndike, 1911/1970, p. 244):

Of several responses made to the same situation, those which are accompanied or closely followed by satisfaction to the animal will, other things being equal, be more firmly connected with the situation, so that, when it recurs, they will be more likely to recur.

Figure 6.10 Each of Thorndike's puzzle boxes had a device that could open it. Here, tilting the pole will open the door. (Based on Thorndike, 1911/1970)

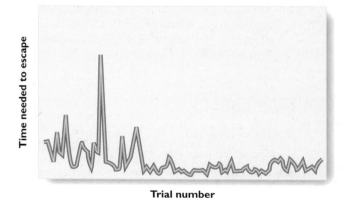

Figure 6.11 As the data from one of Thorndike's experiments show, a cat gradually and inconsistently decreases the time for escape from a box. Thorndike concluded that the cat did not at any point "get the idea." Instead, reinforcement gradually increased the probability of the successful behavior.

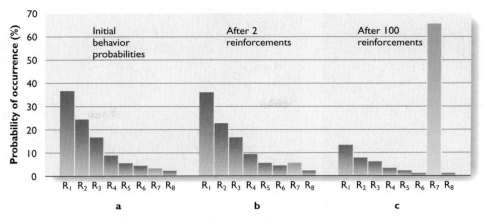

Figure 6.12 According to Thorndike, a cat starts with many potential behaviors in a given situation. When one of these leads to reinforcement, the future probability of that behavior increases. We need not assume that the cat understands what it is doing or why.

Hence, the animal becomes more likely to repeat the responses that led to favorable consequences even if it does not understand why. In fact, it doesn't need to "understand" anything at all. A machine could be programmed to produce random responses and then repeat the ones that led to reinforcement.

Was Thorndike's interpretation correct? Another way of putting this question: When an animal learns to make a response that produces some outcome, does it "expect" that outcome, or does it simply register, "This is the response to make in this situation"? There is no simple way to answer this question (Burke, Franz, Miller, & Schoenbaum, 2008).

Thorndike revolutionized the study of animal learning, substituting experimentation for collections of anecdotes. He also demonstrated the possibility of simple explanations for apparently complex behaviors (Dewsbury, 1998). On the negative side, his example of studying animals in contrived laboratory situations led researchers to ignore many interesting phenomena about animals' natural way of life (Galef, 1998).

The kind of learning that Thorndike studied is called **operant conditioning** (because the subject *operates* on the environment to produce an outcome) or **instrumental conditioning** (because the subject's behavior is *instrumental* in producing the outcome). Operant or instrumental conditioning is *the process of changing behavior by providing a reinforcement after a response*. The defining difference between operant conditioning and classical conditioning is the procedure: *In operant conditioning, the subject's behavior produces an outcome that affects future behavior. In classical conditioning, the subject's behavior has no effect on the outcome (the presentation of either the CS or the UCS)*. For example, in classical conditioning, the experimenter (or the world) presents two stimuli at particular times, regardless of what the individual does or doesn't do. Those stimuli change future behaviors, but the behaviors do not change the stimuli. In operant conditioning, the individual has to make some response before it receives reinforcement.

In general, the two kinds of conditioning also affect different behaviors. Classical conditioning applies mainly to **visceral responses** (i.e., *responses of the internal organs*), such as salivation and digestion, whereas operant conditioning applies mainly to **skeletal responses** (i.e., *movements of leg muscles, arm muscles, etc.*). However, this distinction sometimes breaks down. For example, if a tone predicts an electric shock (a classical-conditioning procedure), the tone makes the animal freeze in position (a skeletal response) as well as increase its heart rate (a visceral response).

10. When I ring a bell, an animal sits up on its hind legs and drools; then I give it some food. Is the animal's behavior an example of classical conditioning or operant conditioning? So far, you do not have enough information to answer the question. What else do you need to know before you can answer?

Answer

10. You need to know whether the bell always predicts food (classical conditioning) or whether the animal receives food only when it sits up (operant conditioning).

What serves as a reinforcer for one person might not for another. Lucy Pearson (left) has collected more than 110,000 hubcaps. Jim Hambrick (right) collects Superman items.

REINFORCEMENT AND PUNISHMENT

What constitutes reinforcement? From a practical standpoint, a reinforcer is *an event that follows a response and increases the later probability or frequency of that response.* From a theoretical standpoint, we would like to predict what would be a reinforcer and what would not. We might guess that reinforcers are biologically useful to the individual, but many are not. For example, saccharin, a sweet but biologically useless chemical, can be a reinforcer. For many people, alcohol and tobacco are stronger reinforcers than vitamin-rich vegetables. So biological usefulness doesn't define reinforcement.

Thorndike described reinforcers as events that brought "satisfaction." That definition won't work either. How could you know what brings a rat or a cat satisfaction? Also, people work hard for a paycheck, a decent grade in a course, and other outcomes that don't produce clear evidence of pleasure (Berridge & Robinson, 1995).

According to the disequilibrium principle of reinforcement, *each of us has a normal "equilibrium" state in which we divide our time among various activities. If you have had a limited opportunity to engage in one of your behaviors, you are in disequilibrium, and an opportunity to increase that behavior, getting back to equilibrium, will be reinforcing* (Farmer-Dougan, 1998; Timberlake & Farmer-Dougan, 1991). For example, suppose that when you can do whatever you choose, you spend 30% of your day sleeping, 10% eating, 12% exercising, 11% reading, 9% talking with friends, 3% grooming, 3% playing the piano, and so forth. If you have been unable to spend this much time on one of those activities, then the opportunity to engage in that activity will be reinforcing. Even a rare behavior, such as clipping your toenails, can be reinforcing if you have not had an opportunity to do it recently. Of course, the demand for certain behaviors is more insistent than others. If you have been deprived of oxygen, the opportunity to breathe will be extremely reinforcing. If you have been deprived of reading time or telephone time, the reinforcement value will be less.

....

11. Suppose you want to reinforce a child for doing chores around the house, and you don't know what would be a good reinforcer. According to the disequilibrium principle, how should you proceed?

Concept Check

Answer

11. Begin by determining how the child ordinarily spends his or her time when given unlimited opportunities. Then find which of these activities the child has been deprived of recently. The opportunity to do one of those activities should be reinforcing.

....

Primary and Secondary Reinforcers

Psychologists distinguish between primary reinforcers (or *unconditioned reinforcers), which are reinforcing because of their own properties,* and secondary reinforcers (or *conditioned reinforcers), which became reinforcing because of previous experiences.* Food and water are primary reinforcers. Money (a secondary reinforcer) becomes reinforcing because we can exchange it for food or other primary reinforcers.

Many secondary reinforcers are surprisingly powerful. Consider how hard children work for a little gold star that the teacher pastes on an assignment.

A student learns that a good grade wins approval, and an employee learns that increased productivity wins the employer's praise. In these cases, *secondary* means "learned." It does not mean weak or unimportant. We spend most of our time working for secondary reinforcers.

Punishment

In contrast to a *reinforcer*, a punishment *decreases the probability of a response*. A reinforcer can be either the presentation of something (e.g., food) or the removal of something (e.g., stopping pain). A punishment can be either the presentation of something (e.g., pain) or the removal of something (e.g., withholding food). Punishment is most effective when it is quick and predictable. If you might or might not get punished a long time from now, the effects are weak and variable.

Punishments are not always effective. If the threat of punishment were always effective, the crime rate would be zero. B. F. Skinner (1938) tested punishment in a famous laboratory study. He first trained food-deprived rats to press a bar to get food and then stopped reinforcing their presses. For the first 10 minutes, some rats not only failed to get food, but every time they pressed the bar, the bar slapped their paws. The

punished rats temporarily suppressed their pressing, but in the long run, they pressed as many times as did the unpunished rats. Skinner concluded that punishment temporarily suppresses behavior but produces no long-term effects.

That conclusion, however, is an overstatement (Staddon, 1993). A better conclusion would have been that punishment does not greatly weaken a response when no other response is available. Skinner's food-deprived rats had no other way to seek food. (If someone punished you for breathing, you would continue breathing but not because you were a slow learner.)

Is physical punishment of children, such as spanking, a good or bad idea? Most American parents spank their children at times, whereas spanking is rare or illegal in many other countries. Many psychologists strongly discourage spanking, recommending that parents simply reason with the child or use nonphysical methods of discipline, such as time out. Those approaches work fine with some children, but what about children who do not respond well and continue to misbehave? Would spanking be appropriate for them or not?

Nearly all the research is correlational. (Try to imagine randomly assigning some parents to spank their children and other parents not to.) The results say that children who are frequently spanked tend to be ill behaved. You probably see the problem in interpreting this result: It might mean that spanking causes misbehavior, or it might mean that ill-behaved children provoke their parents to spank them (Baumrind, Larzelere, & Cowan, 2002). Researchers find that parents who frequently use time out or other nonphysical means of discipline *also* have children with much misbehavior (Larzelere & Kuhn, 2005). So the clearest conclusion is that if a child seldom misbehaves, the parents seldom use any discipline at all. Big surprise.

A more fruitful approach is to compare children who are spanked to children who are equally often subjected to time out or some other form of discipline. The results vary. As you might guess, what works with one child may not work with another. However, the summary is this: If parents rely on spanking as their main or exclusive response to a child's misbehavior, or if they use severe punishment, the child is likely to react badly. Possible outcomes include antisocial behavior and low self-esteem. However, if parents use mild spanking, and only after other attempts at discipline have failed, the spanking usually halts the immediate misbehavior without producing any demonstrable long-term harm (Larzelere & Kuhn, 2005).

12. The government imposes strict punishments for selling illegal drugs. Based on what you have read, why are those punishments ineffective for many people?

Answer

12. To be effective, punishments must be quick and predictable. Punishments for drug dealing are neither. Furthermore, punishment most effectively suppresses a response when the individual has alternative responses that can gain reinforcements. Many people who sell drugs have no alternative way to gain similar profits.

Categories of Reinforcement and Punishment

As mentioned, a reinforcer can be either the onset of something like food or the removal of something like pain. A punishment also can be either the onset or offset of something. Psychologists use different terms to distinguish these possibilities, as shown in Table 6.1.

Table 6.1 Four Categories of Operant conditioning

	Event Such as Food	Event Such as Pain
Behavior leads to the event	**Positive Reinforcement** *Result:* Increase in the behavior, reinforced by presentation of food. *Example:* "If you clean your room, I'll get you a pizza tonight."	**Punishment = Passive Avoidance Learning** *Result:* Decrease in the behavior, and therefore a decrease in pain. *Example:* "If you insult me, I'll slap you."
Behavior avoids the event	**Negative Punishment = Omission Training** *Result:* Decrease in the behavior, and therefore food continues to be available. *Example:* "If you hit your little brother again, you'll get no dessert."	**Negative Reinforcement = Escape or Avoidance Learning** *Result:* Increase in the behavior, and therefore a decrease in pain. *Example:* "If you go into the office over there, the doctor will remove the thorn from your leg."

Note that the upper left and lower right of the table both show reinforcement. Either gaining food or preventing pain *increases* the behavior. The items in the upper right and lower left are both punishment. Gaining pain or preventing food *decreases* the behavior. Food and pain are, of course, just examples. Many other events serve as reinforcers or punishers. Let's go through these terms and procedures, beginning in the upper left of the table and proceeding clockwise.

Positive reinforcement is the *presentation of an event* (e.g., food or money) *that strengthens or increases the likelihood of a behavior.* Punishment occurs when a response is followed by an event such as pain. You put your hand on a hot stove, burn yourself, and learn to stop doing that. Punishment is also called passive avoidance learning because *the individual learns to avoid an outcome by being passive* (e.g., by *not* putting your hand on the stove).

Try not to be confused by the term negative reinforcement. Negative reinforcement is *a kind of reinforcement (not a punishment), and therefore, it increases the frequency of a behavior. It is "negative" because the reinforcement is the absence of something.* For example, you learn to apply sunscreen to avoid skin cancer, and you learn to brush your teeth to avoid tooth decay. Negative reinforcement increases the behavior and decreases the undesirable outcome. Negative rein-

forcement is also known as escape learning *if the response stops an outcome* or avoidance learning *if it prevents the outcome altogether.* Far more researchers use the terms escape learning and avoidance learning than the potentially confusing term negative reinforcement.

If reinforcement by avoiding something bad is negative reinforcement, then *punishment by avoiding something good* is negative punishment. The term negative punishment is seldom used. The practice is more often known simply as punishment or as omission training *because the omission of the response leads to restoration of the usual privileges.* If your parents punished you by taking away your allowance or privileges ("grounding you"), they were using omission training. Another example is a teacher punishing a child by a time-out session away from classmates.

Classifying a procedure in one of these four categories is often tricky. If you adjust the thermostat in a cold room to increase the heat, are you working for increased heat (positive reinforcement) or decreased cold (negative reinforcement)? Because of this ambiguity, several authorities recommend abandoning the term negative reinforcement (Baron & Galizio, 2005; Kimble, 1993). The ambiguity gets even worse: If you are told you can be suspended from school for academic dishonesty, you can think of it as being honest to stay in school (positive reinforcement), being honest to avoid suspension (negative reinforcement/avoidance learning), decreasing dishonesty to avoid suspension (punishment/ passive avoidance), or decreasing dishonesty to stay in school (negative punishment/omission training). Sorry about that! We simplify matters by using just the terms *reinforcement* (to increase a behavior) and *punishment* (to decrease it). Nevertheless, you should understand all of the terms, as they appear in many psychological publications. Attend to how something is worded: Are we talking about increasing or decreasing a behavior? Are we increasing or decreasing the outcome? Practice with the concept check that follows.

13. Identify each of the following examples using the terms in Table 6.1:
    a. Your employer gives you bonus pay for working overtime.
    b. You learn to stop playing your accordion at 5 A.M. because your roommate threatens to kill you if you do it again.
    c. You turn off a dripping faucet, ending the "drip drip drip" sound.
    d. You learn to drink less beer than you once did because you have felt sick after drinking too much.
    e. Your swimming coach says you cannot go to the next swim meet (which you are looking forward to) if you break a training rule.
    f. If you get a speeding ticket, you will temporarily lose the privilege of driving the family car.
    g. You learn to come inside when a storm is brewing to avoid getting wet.

Answers

13. **a.** positive reinforcement; **b.** punishment or passive avoidance; **c.** escape learning or negative avoidance; **d.** punishment or passive avoidance; **e.** omission training or negative punishment; **f.** omission training or negative punishment; **g.** avoidance learning or negative reinforcement.

ADDITIONAL PHENOMENA OF OPERANT CONDITIONING

Recall the concepts of extinction, generalization, and discrimination in classical conditioning. The same concepts apply to operant conditioning, although the procedures are different.

Extinction

No doubt you have heard the saying, "If at first you don't succeed, try, try again." The comedian W. C. Fields said, "If at first you don't succeed, try, try again. Then quit. There's no point in being a damn fool about it."

In operant conditioning, **extinction** *occurs if responses stop producing reinforcements.* For example, you were once in the habit of asking your roommate to join you for supper. The last few times you asked, your roommate said no, so you stop asking. In classical conditioning, extinction is achieved by presenting the CS without the UCS. In operant conditioning, the procedure is response without reinforcement. Table 6.2 compares classical and operant conditioning.

Table 6.2 Classical Conditioning and Operant Conditioning

	Classical Conditioning	Operant Conditioning
Terminology	CS, UCS, CR, UCR	Response, reinforcement
Behavior	Does not control UCS	Controls reinforcement
Paired during acquisition	Two stimuli (CS and UCS)	Response and reinforcement (in the presence of certain stimuli)
Responses	Mostly visceral (internal organs)	Mostly skeletal muscles
Extinction procedure	CS without UCS	Response without reinforcement

Generalization

Someone who receives reinforcement for a response in the presence of one stimulus will probably make the same response in the presence of a similar stimulus. *The more similar a new stimulus is to the original reinforced stimulus, the more likely is the same response.* This phenomenon is known as **stimulus generalization.** For example, you might reach for the turn signal of a rented car in the same place you would find it in your own car.

Many animals have evolved an appearance that takes advantage of their predators' stimulus generalization (Darst & Cummings, 2006). A predatory bird that learns to avoid a poisonous snake probably also avoids a harmless look-alike snake. A bird that learns to avoid a bad-tasting butterfly will also avoid other butterflies of similar appearance. Figure 6.13 shows one example.

Poisonous   Harmless

© David Cannatella/University of Texas, Austin

Figure 6.13 The harmless frog evolved an appearance that resembles a poisonous species, taking advantage of the way birds generalize their learned avoidance responses. (Source: Darst & Cummings, 2006)

Discrimination and Discriminative Stimuli

If reinforcement occurs for responding to one stimulus and not another, the result is **discrimination** between them, yielding *a response to one stimulus and not the other.* For example, you smile and greet someone you think you know, but then you realize it is someone else. After several such experiences, you learn to recognize the difference between the two people.

A stimulus that indicates which response is appropriate or inappropriate is called a **discriminative stimulus.** A great deal of our behavior is governed by discriminative stimuli. For example, you learn ordinarily to be quiet during a lecture but to talk when the professor encourages discussion. You learn to drive fast on some streets and slowly on others. Throughout your day, one stimulus after another signals which behaviors will yield reinforcement, punishment, or neither. *The ability of a stimulus to encourage some responses and discourage others* is known as **stimulus control.**

B. F. SKINNER AND THE SHAPING OF RESPONSES

The most influential radical behaviorist, B. F. Skinner (1904–1990), demonstrated many uses of operant conditioning. Skinner was an ardent practitioner of parsimony (chapter 2), always seeking simple explanations in terms of reinforcement histories rather than complex mental processes.

One problem confronting any behavior researcher is how to define a response. Imagine watching children and trying to count "aggressive behaviors." What is an aggressive act and what isn't? Skinner simplified the measurement by simplifying the situation (Zuriff, 1995): He set up a box, called an *operant-conditioning chamber* (or *Skinner box,* a term that Skinner himself never used), in which a rat presses a lever or a pigeon pecks an illuminated "key" to receive food (Figure 6.14). He operationally defined the response as anything that the animal did to depress the lever or key. So if the rat pressed the lever with its snout instead of its paw, the response still counted. If the pigeon batted the key with its wing instead of pecking it with its beak, it still counted. The behavior was defined by its outcome, not by muscle movements.

Does that definition make sense? Skinner's reply was that it did because it led to consistent results in his research. Skinner's procedures became standard in many laboratories. When deciding how to define a term (e.g., *response*), the best definition is the one that produces the clearest results.

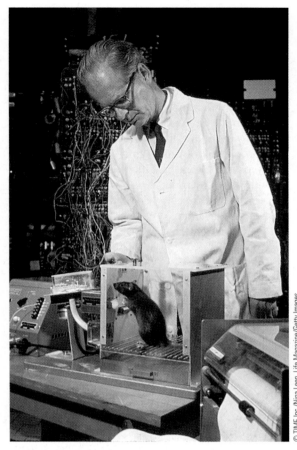

FIGURE 6.14 B. F. Skinner examines a rat in an operant-conditioning chamber. When the light above the bar is on, pressing the bar is reinforced. A food pellet rolls out of the storage device (left) and down the tube into the cage.

© TIME Inc./Nina Leen, Life Magazine/Getty Images

Shaping Behavior

When Thorndike wanted to train a cat to push a pole or pull a string, he simply put the cat in a puzzle box and waited. Skinner wanted to train rats to push levers and pigeons to peck at keys. These behaviors are not part of the animals' normal routine. If he simply put an animal into a box and waited, he might be in for a very long wait. To speed the process, Skinner introduced a powerful technique, called **shaping,** for *establishing a new response by reinforcing successive approximations to it.*

To *shape* a rat to press a lever, you might begin by reinforcing the rat for standing up, a common behavior in rats. After a few reinforcements, the rat stands up more frequently. Now you change the rules, giving food only when the rat stands up while facing the lever. Soon it spends more time standing up and facing the lever. (It extinguishes its behavior of standing and facing in other directions because those responses are not reinforced.)

Next you provide reinforcement only when the rat stands facing the correct direction while in the half of the cage nearer the lever. You gradually move the boundary, and the rat moves closer to the lever. Then the rat must touch the lever and, finally, apply weight to it. Through a series of short, easy steps, you shape the rat to press a lever.

Shaping works with humans, too, of course. All of education is based on the idea of shaping: First, your parents or teachers praise you for counting your fingers. Later, you must add and subtract to earn their congratulations. Step by step, your tasks become more complex until you are doing calculus.

Chaining Behavior

Ordinarily, you don't do just one action and then stop. You do a long sequence of actions. To produce a sequence, psychologists use a procedure called chaining. Assume you want to train a show horse to go through a sequence of actions. You could *chain* the behaviors, *reinforcing each one with the opportunity to engage in the next one.* The animal starts by learning the final behavior. Then it learns the next to last behavior, which is reinforced by the opportunity to perform the final behavior. And so on.

For example, a rat might be placed on the top platform, as in Figure 6.15f, where it eats. Then it is put on the intermediate platform with a ladder leading to the top platform. The rat learns to climb the ladder. Then it is placed again on the intermediate platform but without the ladder. It must learn to pull a string to raise the ladder so that it can climb to the top platform. Then the rat is placed on the bottom platform (Figure 6.15a). It now has to learn to climb the ladder to the intermediate platform, pull a string to raise the ladder, and then climb the ladder again. A chain like this can go on and on. Each behavior is reinforced with the opportunity for the next behavior, except for the final behavior, which is reinforced with food.

People learn chains of responses, too. You learn to eat with a fork and spoon. Then you learn to put your own food on the plate before eating. Eventually, you learn to plan a menu, go to the store, buy the ingredients, cook the meal, put it on the plate, and then eat it. Each behavior is reinforced by the opportunity to engage in the next behavior.

To show the effectiveness of shaping and chaining, Skinner performed a demonstration:

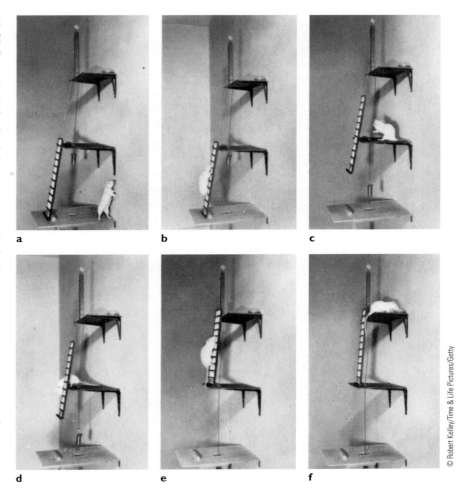

FIGURE 6.15 In chaining, each behavior is reinforced by the opportunity to engage in the next behavior. To reach food on the top platform, this rat must climb a ladder and pull a string to raise the ladder so that it can climb up again

First, he trained a rat to go to the center of a cage. Then he trained it to do so only when he played a certain piece of music. Next he trained it to wait for the music, go to the center of the cage, and sit up on its hind legs. Step by step, he eventually trained the rat to wait for the music (the "Star-Spangled Banner"), move to the center of the cage, sit up on its hind legs, put its claws on a string next to a pole, pull the string to hoist the U.S. flag, and then stand back and salute. Only then did the rat get its reinforcement. Needless to say, patriotism is not part of a rat's usual repertoire.

Schedules of Reinforcement

The simplest procedure in operant conditioning is to *provide reinforcement for every correct response*, a procedure known as continuous reinforcement. However, in the real world, continuous reinforcement is not common.

Reinforcement for some responses and not for others is known as intermittent reinforcement or partial reinforcement. We behave differently when we learn that only some of our responses will be reinforced. Psychologists have investigated the effects of many schedules of reinforcement, which are *rules for the delivery of reinforcement*. Four schedules for the delivery of intermittent reinforcement are fixed ratio, fixed interval, variable ratio, and variable interval (see Table 6.3). A ratio schedule provides reinforcements depending on the number of responses. An interval schedule

Table 6.3 Some Schedules of Reinforcement

Type	Description
Continuous	Reinforcement for every response of the correct type
Fixed ratio	Reinforcement following completion of a specific number of responses
Variable ratio	Reinforcement for an unpredictable number of responses that varies around a mean value
Fixed interval	Reinforcement for the first response that follows a given delay since the previous reinforcement
Variable interval	Reinforcement for the first response that follows an unpredictable delay (varying around a mean value) since the previous reinforcement

provides reinforcements depending on the timing of responses.

Fixed-Ratio Schedule

A **fixed-ratio schedule** *provides reinforcement only after a certain (fixed) number of correct responses*—after every sixth response, for example. We see similar behavior among pieceworkers in a factory whose pay depends on how many pieces they turn out or among fruit pickers who get paid by the bushel.

A fixed-ratio schedule usually produces rapid, steady responding. Researchers sometimes graph the results with a *cumulative record,* in which the line is flat when the animal does not respond, and it moves up with each response. For a fixed-ratio schedule, a typical result would look like this:

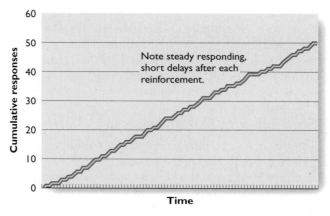

However, if the schedule requires a large number of responses for reinforcement, the individual pauses after each reinforced response. For example, if you have just completed 10 calculus problems, you pause briefly before starting your next assignment. After completing 100 problems, you pause even longer.

Variable-Ratio Schedule

A **variable-ratio schedule** is similar to a fixed-ratio schedule, except that *reinforcement occurs after a variable number of correct responses.* For example, reinforcement sometimes occurs after one or two responses and sometimes after a great many. Variable-ratio schedules generate steady response rates.

Variable-ratio schedules, or approximations of them, occur whenever each response has about an equal probability of success. For example, when you apply for a job, you might or might not be hired. The more times you apply, the better your chances, but you cannot predict how many applications you need to submit before receiving a job offer.

Fixed-Interval Schedule

A **fixed-interval schedule** *provides reinforcement for the first response after a specific time interval.* For instance, an animal might get food for the first response it makes after a 15-second interval. Then it would have to wait another 15 seconds before another response is effective. Animals (including humans) on such a schedule learn to pause after each reinforcement and begin to respond again toward the end of the time interval. The cumulative record would look like this:

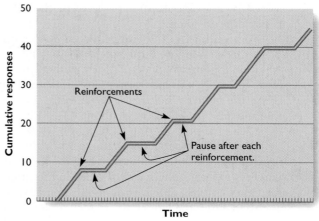

Checking your mailbox is an example of behavior on a fixed-interval schedule. If your mail is delivered at about 3 P.M. and you are eagerly awaiting an important package, you might begin to check around 2:30 and continue checking every few minutes until it arrives.

Variable-Interval Schedule

With a **variable-interval schedule,** *reinforcement is available after a variable amount of time.* For example, reinforcement may come for the first response after 2 minutes, then for the first response after the next 7 seconds, then after 3 minutes 20 seconds, and so forth. You cannot know how long before your next response is reinforced. Consequently, responses on a variable-interval schedule occur slowly but steadily. Checking your e-mail is an example: A new message could appear at any time, so you check occasionally.

Stargazing is also reinforced on a variable-interval schedule. The reinforcement for stargazing —finding a comet, for example—appears at unpredictable intervals. Consequently, both professional and amateur astronomers scan the skies regularly.

Extinction of Responses Reinforced on Different Schedules

Suppose you have two friends, Beth and Becky. Beth has been highly reliable. Whenever she says she will do something, she does it. Becky, on the other hand, sometimes keeps her word and sometimes doesn't. Now both of them go through a period of untrustworthy behavior. With whom will you lose patience sooner? It's Beth. One explanation is that you notice the change more quickly. Because Becky has been unreliable in the past, a new stretch of similar behavior is not really new.

Another example: You and a friend go to a gambling casino and bet on the roulette wheel. Amazingly, your first 10 bets are all winners. Your friend wins some and loses some. Then both of you go into a prolonged losing streak. Presuming both of you have the same amount of money, which of you will probably continue betting longer?

Your friend will, even though you had a more favorable early experience. Responses extinguish more slowly after intermittent reinforcement (either a ratio schedule or an interval schedule) than after continuous reinforcement. Someone who has received intermittent reinforcement is accustomed to playing without winning and persists longer.

14. Identify which schedule of reinforcement applies to each of the following examples:

Concept Check

   a. You attend every new movie that appears at your local theater, although you enjoy about one fourth of them.
   b. You phone your best friend and hear a busy signal. You don't know how soon your friend will hang up, so you try again every few minutes.
   c. You tune your television set to an all-news cable channel, and you look up from your studies to check the sports scores every 30 minutes.

15. Stargazing in the hope of finding a comet was cited as an example of a variable-interval schedule. Why is it *not* an example of a variable ratio?
16. A novice gambler and a longtime gambler both lose 20 bets in a row. Which one is more likely to continue betting? Why?

Answers

14. **a.** variable ratio. (You will be reinforced for about one fourth of your entries to the theater but on an irregular basis.) **b.** variable interval. (Calling will become effective after some interval of time, but the length of that time is unpredictable.) **c.** fixed interval.

15. In a variable-ratio schedule, the number of responses matters, but the timing does not. If you have already checked the stars tonight and found no comets, checking three more times tonight will probably be fruitless. Checking at a later date gives you a better chance.

16. The longtime gambler will continue longer because he or she has a history of being reinforced for gambling on a variable-ratio schedule, which retards extinction. For the same reason, an alcoholic who has had both good experiences and bad experiences while drunk is likely to keep on drinking after several bad experiences.

APPLICATIONS OF OPERANT CONDITIONING

Although operant conditioning arose from purely theoretical concerns, it has a long history of applications. Here are three examples.

Animal Training

Most animal acts are based on training methods like Skinner's. To induce an animal to perform a trick, the trainer first trains it to perform something simple. Gradually, the trainer shapes the animal to perform more complex behaviors. Most animal trainers rely on positive reinforcement and seldom if ever use punishment.

Sometimes, what an animal learns is not exactly what the trainer intended (Rumbaugh & Washburn, 2003). Psychologists tried to teach a chimpanzee to urinate in a pan instead of on the floor. They gave her some chocolate candy every time she used the pan. Quickly, she learned to urinate just a few drops at a time, holding out her hand for candy each time. When at last she could urinate no more, she *spat* into the pan and again held out her hand for candy!

Persuasion

How could you persuade someone to do something objectionable? To use an extreme example, could you convince a prisoner of war to cooperate with the enemy?

The best way is to start by reinforcing a slight degree of cooperation and then working up to the goal little by little. This principle was applied by people who probably never heard of B. F. Skinner, positive reinforcement, or shaping. During the Korean War, the Chinese Communists forwarded some of the letters written home by prisoners of war but intercepted others. (The prisoners could tell from the replies which letters had been forwarded.) The prisoners suspected that they could get their letters through if they wrote something mildly favorable about their captors. So they began including occasional remarks that the Communists were not really so bad, that certain aspects of the Chinese system seemed to work pretty well, or that they hoped the war would end soon.

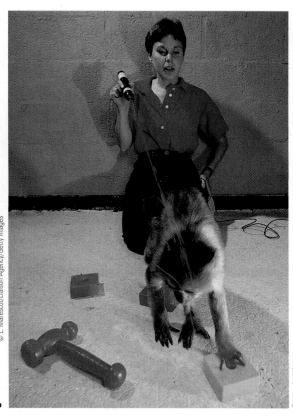

Monkeys can be trained to help people with disabilities. (a) Monkeys assist people with limited mobility. (b) This monkey is being trained to retrieve objects identified with a laser beam.

After a while, the Chinese started essay contests, offering extra food or other privileges to the soldier who wrote the best essay in the captors' opinion. Most of the winning essays contained a statement or two that offered a minor compliment to the Communists or a minor criticism of the United States. Gradually, more and more soldiers started including such statements. Then the Chinese might ask, "You said the United States is not perfect. Could you tell us some of the ways in which it is not perfect, so that we can better understand your system?" As time passed, without torture and with only modest reinforcements, the Chinese induced prisoners to denounce the United States, make false confessions, inform on fellow prisoners, and reveal military secrets (Cialdini, 1993).

The point is clear: Whether we want to get rats to salute the flag or soldiers to denounce it, the most effective training technique is to start with easy behaviors, reinforce those behaviors, and then gradually shape more complex behaviors.

Applied Behavior Analysis/ Behavior Modification

In one way or another, people almost constantly try to influence other people's behavior. Psychologists have applied operant conditioning to enhance that influence.

In applied behavior analysis, also known as behavior modification, a *psychologist tries to remove the reinforcers for unwanted behaviors and provides reinforcers for more acceptable behaviors.* For example, school psychologists instituted a program to encourage children with attention-deficit disorder to complete more school assignments. In addition to verbal praise, children received points for each assignment completed and additional points for completing it accurately. They lost points for any rule violation, such as being out of the seat. At the end of each week, those who had accumulated enough points could go to a party or take a field trip. The result of this program was a significant increase in completion of assignments and better in-class behavior (Fabiano et al., 2007).

Another example: Many children hurt themselves on playgrounds, often by using equipment improperly, such as going down the slide head first. The reinforcer for this risky behavior is simply the thrill of it. To stop such behavior, a safety officer talked to elementary school classes about playground safety and offered rewards to the whole class if everyone shifted to safer playground behaviors. College students observed the children in the playground and reported instances of risky behavior. The reinforcers here were almost trivial, such as a blue ribbon for every student or a colorful poster for the door. Nevertheless, the result was decreased risky behaviors, and the improved safety continued for weeks afterward (Heck, Collins, & Peterson, 2001).

....

17. Of the procedures characterized in Table 6.1, which one applies to giving more attention to someone's appropriate speech? Which one applies to decreasing attention to inappropriate speech?

Concept Check

Answer

17. Increasing attention for appropriate speech is positive reinforcement. Decreasing attention for inappropriate speech is omission training or negative punishment. (If you called it "lack of positive reinforcement," you would not be wrong, and calling it simply "punishment" is acceptable.)

....

module 6.3

In Closing

Operant Conditioning and Human Behavior

Suppose one of your instructors announced that everyone in the class would receive the same grade at the end of the course, regardless of performance on tests and papers. Would you study hard in that course? Probably not. Or suppose your employer said that all raises and promotions would be made at random, with no regard to how well you do your job. Would you work as hard as possible? Not likely. Our behavior depends on its consequences, just like that of a rat or pigeon. That is the main point of operant conditioning.

SUMMARY

- *Reinforcement.* Edward Thorndike defined reinforcement as the process of increasing the future probability of the preceding response. (page 210)
- *Operant conditioning.* Operant conditioning is the process of controlling the rate of a behavior through its consequences. (page 211)
- *The nature of reinforcement.* The opportunity to engage in a behavior that has recently been deprived is reinforcing. Also, something that an individual can exchange for a reinforcer becomes a reinforcer itself. (page 212)
- *Reinforcement and punishment.* Behaviors are reinforced by presenting favorable events or omitting unfavorable events. Behaviors are punished by presenting unfavorable events or omitting favorable events. (page 213)
- *Extinction.* In operant conditioning, a response is extinguished if it is no longer followed by reinforcement. (page 215)

- *Shaping.* Shaping is a technique for training subjects to perform acts by reinforcing them for successive approximations to the desired behavior. (page 216)
- *Schedules of reinforcement.* The frequency and timing of a response depend on the schedule of reinforcement. In a ratio schedule of reinforcement, an individual is given reinforcement after a fixed or variable number of responses. In an interval schedule of reinforcement, an individual is given reinforcement after a fixed or variable period of time. (page 217)
- *Applications.* People have applied operant conditioning to animal training, persuasion, and applied behavior analysis. (page 219)

KEY TERMS

applied behavior analysis (or behavior modification) (page 220)

avoidance learning (page 214)

chaining (page 217)

continuous reinforcement (page 217)

discrimination (page 216)

discriminative stimulus (page 216)

disequilibrium principle (page 212)

escape learning (page 214)

extinction (page 215)

fixed-interval schedule (page 218)

fixed-ratio schedule (page 218)

intermittent reinforcement (page 217)

law of effect (page 210)

learning curve (page 210)

negative punishment (page 214)

negative reinforcement (page 214)

omission training (page 214)

operant conditioning (or instrumental conditioning) (page 211)

passive avoidance learning (page 214)

positive reinforcement (page 214)

primary reinforcer (page 212)

punishment (page 213)

reinforcement (page 210)

reinforcer (page 212)

schedule of reinforcement (page 217)

secondary reinforcer (page 212)

shaping (page 216)

skeletal responses (page 211)

stimulus control (page 216)

stimulus generalization (page 215)

variable-interval schedule (page 218)

variable-ratio schedule (page 218)

visceral responses (page 211)

Variations of Learning

- In what way is learning specialized for particular needs?

- How do we learn from the successes and failures of others without trying every response ourselves?

Thorndike, Pavlov, and the other pioneers of learning assumed that learning was the same in all situations. If so, researchers could study any convenient example, such as salivary conditioning or the responses of pigeons in a Skinner box, and discover all the principles of learning.

However, from the start, researchers encountered reasons to doubt this assumption that learning is always the same. At a minimum, some things are easier to learn than others. For example, Thorndike's cats learned to push and pull various devices in their efforts to escape from his puzzle boxes. But when Thorndike tried to teach them to scratch or lick themselves for the same reinforcement, they learned slowly and performed inconsistently (Thorndike, 1911/1970). Why?

One explanation is preparedness, the *concept that evolution has prepared us to learn some associations more easily than others* (Seligman, 1970). Presumably, cats and their ancestors since ancient times have encountered many situations in which pushing or pulling something produced a useful outcome. It makes sense for them to have evolved predispositions to facilitate this kind of learning. However, when in nature would licking or scratching yourself move an obstacle and get you out of confinement? For good reasons, cats are not prepared for this kind of learning.

Similarly, if you hear a sound coming from your left, depending on the sound, it might be a good idea to approach the sound (to your left) or go away from it (to your right). But when in nature would one kind of sound (such as a high pitch) mean "turn to the left" (regardless of where the sound came from) and a different sound (maybe a low pitch) mean "turn to the right"? Dogs readily learn that a sound coming from one location means "raise your left leg" and a sound coming from another location means "raise your right leg." They are slow to learn that a ticking metronome means raise the left leg and a buzzer means raise the right leg (Dobrzecka, Szwejkowska, & Konorski, 1966) (see Figure 6.16). Again, these results make sense if we assume that animals are evolutionarily prepared to learn the associations that are likely to be useful in their natural habitat. In chapter 16, we shall consider the hypothesis that people are evolutionarily prepared to learn phobias of objects that have been dangerous throughout human existence, such as snakes and spiders.

The idea of preparedness has many practical applications. People learn more easily to turn a wheel clockwise to move something to the right and counterclockwise to move it to the left (as when turning the steering wheel of a car). When engineers design machines, they often consult with human-factors psychologists about how to set up the controls so that people can easily learn to use them.

CONDITIONED TASTE AVERSIONS

If a sound (CS) predicts food (UCS), learning proceeds most quickly if the CS precedes the UCS by about half a second. If a rat receives food after pressing a bar, learning is fastest if the reinforcement occurs within a second or two after the response. Based on research of this type, psychologists were at one time convinced that learning could occur only be-

Dog easily learns to raise the leg closer to the sound source.

Dog does not easily learn to raise one leg when it hears a metronome and a different leg when it hears a buzzer.

Figure 6.16 According to the principle of preparedness, evolution has prepared us to learn some associations more easily than others. Dogs easily learn to use the direction of a sound as a signal for which leg to lift. They have trouble using the type of sound as a signal for the same response.

FIGURE 6.17 This coyote previously fell ill after eating sheep meat containing lithium salts. Now it reacts with revulsion toward both live and dead sheep.

tween events that occurred within seconds of each other (Kimble, 1961).

However, that generalization fails if we look at some other situations. Consider eating in particular. You eat something—let's say it's something you have never tried before—and you get sick to your stomach later. Food poisoning is a slow process, so you might not begin to feel symptoms until hours after your meal. You nevertheless form an aversion to that food. If you try eating it again, you find it repulsive. *Associating a food with illness* is **conditioned taste aversion**, first documented by John Garcia and his colleagues (Garcia, Ervin, & Koelling, 1966). One of its special features is that it occurs reliably after a single pairing of food with illness, even with a long delay between them. It occurs if the food itself made you sick or if you got sick from something else. Even if you know you got sick from something else, such as riding a roller coaster, you learn a food aversion anyway. Some part of your brain reacts, "I don't care about that roller coaster. I feel sick, and I'm not taking any chances. From now on, that food is taboo." You can learn taste aversions to a familiar food, but you acquire much stronger aversions if you had no previous safe experience with the food. If you eat several foods before becoming ill, you learn aversions mainly to the unfamiliar ones, even if you ate familiar foods closer in time to the illness.

For example, a rat drinks a saccharin solution, which it has never tasted before. Saccharin tastes sweet, and in moderate amounts, it is neither healthful nor harmful. After the rat has drunk it for a few minutes, the experimenter removes the bottle, waits minutes or hours, and then injects a small amount of lithium or other substance that makes the rat moderately ill. The experimenter waits days for the rat to recover and then offers it a choice between the saccharin solution and unflavored water. The rat strongly prefers the unflavored water (Garcia et al., 1966).

In contrast, rats that did not become ill, or that became ill after drinking something else, strongly prefer the saccharin solution. We can interpret this result as an evolutionary specialization of learning: Although animals (including people) usually associate events that occurred at about the same time, they associate food with illness despite long delays.

An animal that learns a conditioned taste aversion to a food treats it as if it tasted bad (Garcia, 1990). Some ranchers in the western United States have used this type of learning to deter coyotes from eating sheep (Figure 6.17). They offer the coyotes sheep meat containing enough lithium salts to produce nausea but not enough to be dangerous. Afterward, the coyotes become less likely to attack sheep, although they continue to hunt rabbits and other prey. One study reported that this method reduced coyotes' sheep kills to about half of what had occurred the previous year (Gustavson, Kelly, Sweeney, & Garcia, 1976). This technique has the potential of protecting sheep without killing the coyotes, which are a threatened species.

Conditioned taste aversions account for some of our choices of food and beverage. One way of treating alcoholism is to ask people to drink some alcohol and then administer a drug that causes nausea. This treatment is not widely used today, but when it has been used, it has been more effective, and quicker, than other treatments for alcoholism (Revusky, 2009). Most pregnant women experience food cravings, mainly for fruits and sweets, and food aversions, mainly to meats and eggs. Most women also experience nausea ("morning sickness") during the first few weeks of pregnancy. A likely explanation for the food aversions is that women associate something they ate with subsequent nausea, and several lines of evidence support this interpretation. For example, women with the most pregnancy nausea tend to be those with the strongest food aversions (Bayley, Dye, &

Hill, 2009). Similarly, many cancer patients learn aversions to foods they ate just prior to chemotherapy or radiation therapy (Bernstein, 1991; Scalera & Bavieri, 2009).

Besides the fact that conditioned taste aversions link events separated by hours, they are special in another regard as well: When an animal becomes ill, it has had many experiences over the last several hours, but it associates the illness almost exclusively with something it ate. In a classic experiment (Garcia & Koelling, 1966), rats were allowed to drink saccharin-flavored water from tubes that were set up to turn on a bright light and a loud noise whenever the rats licked the water. Some of the rats were exposed to x-rays (which induce nausea) while they drank. Others were given electric shocks to their feet when they drank. After the training was complete, each rat was tested separately with a tube of saccharin-flavored water and a tube of unflavored water that produced lights and noises. (Figure 6.18 illustrates the experiment.)

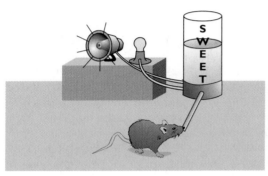
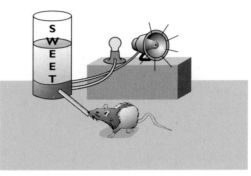

Rats drink saccharin-flavored water. Whenever they make contact with the tube, they turn on a bright light and a noisy buzzer.

Then

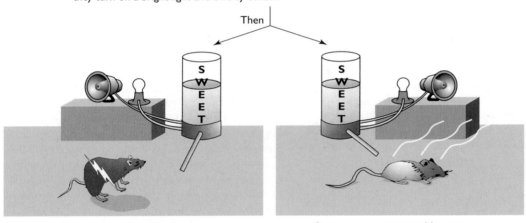

Some rats get electric shock.

Some rats are nauseated by x-rays.

Next day: Rats are given a choice between a tube of saccharin-flavored water and a tube of unflavored water hooked up to the light and the buzzer.

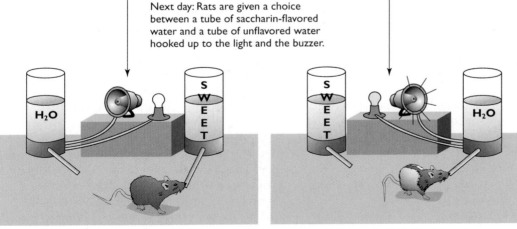

Rats that had been shocked avoid the tube with the lights and noises.

Rats that had been nauseated by x-rays avoid the saccharin-flavored water.

FIGURE 6.18 An experiment by Garcia and Koelling (1966): Rats "blame" an illness on what they ate. They blame pain on what they saw or heard or where they were.

The rats that received x-rays avoided the flavored water. The rats that received shocks avoided the tube that produced lights and noises. Evidently, animals are predisposed to associate illness with what they eat or drink. They associate skin pain mostly with what they see or hear. This tendency is an excellent example of preparedness. This predisposition is beneficial because foods are more likely to cause internal events, and lights and sounds are more likely to signal external events.

One further oddity: Rats voluntarily exercise, especially in a running wheel, and learn a preference for a cage with a running wheel. Nevertheless, running or swimming evidently produces mild stomach distress (analogous to riding a roller coaster), and rats learn to avoid the taste of anything they drank just before running or swimming (Boakes & Nakajima, 2009; Lett, Grant, Koh, & Smith, 2001). The fact that exercise simultaneously increases preference for the cage and decreases preference for a food indicates that conditioned taste aversion is a special kind of learning. It also indicates that a single event can be reinforcing for one response and punishing for another!

18. Which kind of learning takes place despite a long delay between the events to be associated?
19. What evidence indicates that conditioned taste aversion is different from other kinds of learning?
20. People used to advise children not to swim within an hour after eating. Although the risk of cramps is doubtful, what is one valid reason to avoid swimming after a meal?

Concept Check

Answers

18. Conditioned taste aversions develop despite a long delay between food and illness.

19. In addition to the fact that conditioned taste aversion occurs over long delays, animals are predisposed to associate foods and not other events with illnesses. Also, an event such as running in a wheel can be reinforcing for other responses but simultaneously decrease preference for a taste associated with it.

20. It is possible to learn an avoidance of the food one ate before swimming.

BIRDSONG LEARNING

Birdsongs brighten the day for people who hear them, but they are earnest business for the birds themselves. For most species, song is limited to males during the mating season. As a rule, a song indicates, "Here I am. I am a male of species _____. If you're a female of my species, please come closer. If you're a male of my species, go away."

© Joe McDonald/CORBIS

A male white-crowned sparrow learns his song in the first months of life but does not begin to sing it until the next year.

(Among the delights of birdsongs are the exceptions to the rule. Mockingbirds copy all the songs they hear and defend their territory against intruders of all species—sometimes even squirrels, cats, people, and automobiles. Carolina wrens sing male-and-female duets throughout the year. Woodpeckers don't sing but rely on the rhythm and loudness of their pecks to signal others. That woodpecker banging on the metal siding of your house in spring is *trying* to make a racket to impress the females. But on to more relevant matters.)

If you reared an infant songbird in isolation from others of its species, would it develop a normal song on its own? It depends. Some species have a built-in song, but others have to learn it. In several sparrow species, a male develops a normal song only if he hears the song of his own species. He *learns most readily during a sensitive period early in his first year of life.* The young bird learns better from a live tutor, such as his father, than from a tape-recorded song in a laboratory (Baptista & Petrinovich, 1984; Marler & Peters, 1987, 1988). He will not learn at all from the song of another species. Evidently, a fledgling sparrow produces approximately the right song and identifies which songs to imitate to improve his song (Marler, 1997).

Birdsong learning resembles human language learning in that both take place in a social context, both occur most easily in early life, both start with babbling and gradually improve, and both deteriorate gradually if the individual becomes deaf later (Brainard & Doupe, 2000). We shall consider language learning in more detail in chapter 8. Song learning is unlike standard examples of classical and operant conditioning. During the sensitive period, the infant bird only listens. We cannot call the song he hears an unconditioned stimulus because it elicits no apparent response. At no time in this sensitive period does the bird receive any reinforcement.

Nevertheless, he learns a representation of how his song should sound. The following spring, when the bird starts to sing, we see a trial-and-error process. At first, his song is a mixture of sounds, like a babbling human infant. As time passes, he eliminates some sounds and rearranges others until he matches the songs he heard the previous summer (Marler & Peters, 1981, 1982). But his only reinforcer is recognizing that he has sung correctly.

The point is that the principles of learning vary from one situation to another. If a situation poses special problems (e.g., food selection, song learning in birds, or language learning in humans), we can expect to find evolutionary specializations to facilitate learning (Rozin & Kalat, 1971).

Answer

21. The most distinctive feature is that birdsong learning occurs when the learner makes no apparent response and receives no apparent reinforcement. In certain sparrow species, birdsong learning occurs most readily during an early sensitive period, and the bird is capable of learning its own species' song but not the song of another species.

SOCIAL LEARNING

Just as many birds learn their song from other birds, humans obviously learn much from each other also. Just think of all the things you did *not* learn by trial and error. You don't throw on clothes at random and wait to see which clothes bring the best reinforcements. You mostly copy what other people are wearing. If you are cooking, you don't make up recipes at random. You start with what other people have recommended. If you are dancing, you don't randomly try every possible muscle movement. You primarily copy what other people do.

According to the social-learning approach (Bandura, 1977, 1986), *we learn about many behaviors by observing the behaviors of others.* For example, if you want to learn to drive a car, you start by watching people who are already skilled. When you try to drive yourself, you receive reinforcement for driving well and punishments (possibly injuries!) if you drive badly, but you will be facilitated by your observations of others.

Social learning is a type of operant conditioning, and the underlying mechanisms are similar. If your task is to determine whether the green cards or the blue cards are more valuable, you can try choosing cards and see which one usually produces more reinforcement. Or you can take advice from another person who claims to know. Your own experience and the other person's advice produce similar outcomes, and they activate some of the same brain areas (Behrens, Hunt, Woolrich, & Rushworth, 2008). However, in many circumstances, social information is much quicker and more efficient than trying to learn something from scratch on your own.

Modeling and Imitation

If you visit another country with customs unlike your own, you find much that seems bewildering. Even the way to order food in a restaurant may be unfamiliar. A hand gesture such as

is considered friendly in some countries but rude and vulgar in others. Many visitors to Japan find the toilets confusing. With effort, you learn foreign customs either because someone explains them to you or because you watch and copy. You *model* your behavior after others or *imitate* others.

In high school, what made certain students popular? I'm sure you could cite many reasons, but once they became popular, simply being the center of attention increased their popularity. In fact, whenever a friend showed interest in some boy or girl, you started to notice that person, too.

A Japanese toilet is a hole in the ground with no seat. Western visitors usually have to ask how to use it. (You squat.)

According to the social-learning approach, we learn many behaviors by observing what others do, imitating behaviors that are reinforced and avoiding behaviors that are punished. This girl is being blessed by the temple elephant. Others who are watching may later imitate her example.

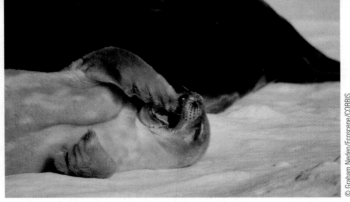

FIGURE 6.19 Does looking at this photo make you want to yawn?

You modeled or imitated your friend's interest. The same is true in nonhumans. If one female shows an interest in mating with a particular male, other females increase their interest in him also (Dubois, 2007).

Why do we imitate? Other people's behavior often provides information. Did you ever have this experience? You tell your parents you want to do something because "everyone else" is doing it. They scream, "If everyone else were jumping off a cliff, would you do it, too?" Well, let's think about it. If literally *everyone* were jumping off a cliff, maybe they have a reason! Maybe you're in great danger where you are, and it would be safer to jump. Maybe if you jump, you won't fall very far, and you'll land on something soft. If everyone is doing it, you should at least consider the possibility that they know something you don't.

Another reason for imitation is that other people's behavior establishes a norm or rule. For example, you wear casual clothing where others dress casually and formalwear where others dress formally. You drive on the right side of the road in America or on the left side in Britain. Copying other people helps in many situations.

You also imitate automatically in some cases. If someone yawns, you become more likely to yawn yourself. Even seeing a photo of an animal yawning may have the same result (Figure 6.19). You are not intentionally copying, and you haven't received any new information. You imitate because seeing a yawn suggested the idea of yawning.

You automatically imitate many other actions that you see, often with no apparent motivation (Dijksterhuis & Bargh, 2001). If you see someone smile or frown, you briefly start to smile or frown. Your expression may be a quick, involuntary twitch that is hard to notice, but it does occur. Spectators at an athletic event sometimes move their arms or legs slightly in synchrony with what some athlete is doing. When expert pianists listen to a composition they have practiced, they start involuntarily tapping their fingers as if they were playing the music (Haueisen & Knösche, 2001). People also copy the hand gestures they see (Bertenthal, Longo, & Kosobud, 2006). You can demonstrate by telling someone, "Please wave your hands" while you clap your hands. Many people copy your actions instead of following your instructions.

Albert Bandura, Dorothea Ross, and Sheila Ross (1963) studied the role of imitation for learning aggressive behavior. They asked two groups of children to watch films in which an adult or a cartoon character violently attacked an inflated "Bobo" doll. Another group watched a different film. They then left the children in a room with a Bobo doll. Only the children who had watched films with attacks on the doll attacked the doll themselves, using many of the same movements they had just seen (Figure 6.20). The clear implication is that children copy the aggressive behavior they have seen in others.

- - - - - - - - - - - - - - - - - - - -

22. Many people complain that they cannot find much difference between the two major political parties in the United States because so many American politicians campaign using similar styles and take similar stands on the issues. Explain this observation in terms of social learning.

Concept Check

Answer

22. One reason that most American politicians run similar campaigns and take similar stands is that they all tend to copy the same models—candidates who have won recent elections. Another reason is that they all pay attention to the same public opinion polls.

- - - - - - - - - - - - - - - - - - - -

FIGURE 6.20 This girl attacks a doll after seeing a film of a woman hitting it. Witnessing violence increases the probability of violent behavior.

We tend to imitate the actions of successful people but only if we feel self-efficacy, a belief that we could perform the task well.

States that sponsor lotteries provide publicity and an exciting atmosphere for each big payoff. They hope this publicity will provide vicarious reinforcement that encourages other people to buy lottery tickets.

Vicarious Reinforcement and Punishment

Six months ago, your best friend quit a job with Consolidated Generic Products to open a restaurant. Now you are considering quitting your job and opening your own restaurant. How do you decide what to do?

You probably start by asking how successful your friend has been. You imitate behavior that has been reinforcing to someone else. That is, you learn by vicarious reinforcement or vicarious punishment—by *substituting someone else's experience for your own.*

Whenever a new business venture succeeds, other companies copy it. For example, the first few successful Internet companies were followed by a horde of imitators. When a sports team wins consistently, other teams copy its style of play. When a television program wins high ratings, other producers are sure to present look-alikes the following year. Politicians imitate the campaign tactics of candidates who were previously elected.

Advertisers depend heavily on vicarious reinforcement. They show happy, successful people using their product, with the implication that if you use their product, you too will be happy and

successful. The people promoting state lotteries show the ecstatic winners—never the losers!—suggesting that if you play the lottery, you too can win.

Vicarious punishment is generally less effective for nonhumans as well as humans (Kuroshima, Kuwahata, & Fujita, 2008). If you see someone succeed, you copy the technique as well as you can. If you see people fail, you don't know why they failed or what would work better. Furthermore, most of us are optimistic about our own future, and we do not identify with people who have failed. We know others suffer because of heavy drinking, cigarette smoking, obesity, risky sex, lack of exercise, or failure to wear seat belts, but we tell ourselves, "It won't happen to me."

Self-Efficacy in Social Learning

We primarily imitate successful people. So, when you watch an Olympic diver win a gold medal, why do you (I assume) *not* try to imitate those dives? We imitate someone else's behavior only if we have a sense of self-efficacy—*the belief of being able to perform the task successfully.* You consider your strengths and weaknesses, compare yourself to the successful person, and estimate your chance of success.

We see this effect in children's life aspirations. Nearly anyone would like a high-paying, high-prestige profession, but many think they could never rise to that level, so they don't try

Self-Reinforcement and Self-Punishment in Social Learning

We learn by observing people who are doing what we would like to do. If our sense of self-efficacy is strong enough, we try to imitate their behavior. But actually succeeding often requires prolonged efforts. People typically set a goal for themselves and monitor their progress toward that goal. They provide reinforcement or punishment for themselves, just as if they were training someone else. They say to themselves, "If I finish this math assignment on time, I'll treat myself to a movie and a new magazine. If I don't finish on time, I'll make myself clean the stove and the sink." (Nice threat, but people usually forgive themselves without imposing the punishment.)

Some therapists teach clients to use self-reinforcement. One 10-year-old boy had a habit of biting his fingernails, sometimes down to the skin and even drawing blood. He learned to keep records of how much nail-biting he did at various times of day, and then he set goals for himself. If he met the goals of reducing his nail-biting, he wrote compliments such as "I'm great! I did wonderful!" The penalty for doing worse was that he would return his weekly allowance to his parents. An additional reinforcement was that his father promised that if the son made enough progress, he would let the son be the "therapist" to help the father quit smoking. Over several weeks, the boy quit nail-biting altogether (Ronen & Rosenbaum, 2001).

One amusing anecdote shows how self-reinforcement and self-punishment can fail: To try to quit smoking cigarettes, psychologist Ron Ash (1986) vowed to smoke only while he was reading *Psychological Bulletin* and other highly respected but tedious journals. He hoped to associate smoking with boredom. Two months later, he was smoking as much as ever, but he was starting to *enjoy* reading *Psychological Bulletin*!

We acquire a sense of self-efficacy mainly through our own successes but also partly by watching and identifying with role models.

(Bandura, Barbaranelli, Caprara, & Pastorelli, 2001). One value of getting women and minorities into high-visibility leadership jobs is that they provide role models, showing others that the opportunity is available. Athletic teams and other groups also differ in their feeling of efficacy. A group confident of its abilities accomplishes much more than a group with doubts. Especially in the early stages of his presidential campaign, Barack Obama energized his supporters with chants of "Yes, we can!"

6.4   module

In Closing

All Learning Is Not the Same

When investigators examine how synapses change during learning, they find similar mechanisms in all species and a wide variety of situations. Nevertheless, we find multiple variations on the theme. The ways we learn are adapted to different situations, such as food choice and birdsong. We use social mechanisms to facilitate and hasten learning. The outcome of these specializations is learning that is highly efficient for many purposes.

SUMMARY

- *Preparedness.* Evolution has prepared us (and other animals) to learn some associations more readily than others. (page 223)
- *Conditioned taste aversions.* Animals, including people, learn to avoid foods, especially unfamiliar ones, if they become ill afterward. This type of learning occurs reliably after a single pairing, even with a long delay between the food and the illness. Illness is as-

sociated much more strongly with foods than with other stimuli. (page 223)
- *Birdsong learning.* Infant birds of some species must hear their songs during a sensitive period early in life if they are to develop a fully normal song the following spring. During the early learning, the bird makes no response and receives no reinforcement. (page 226)

- *Imitation.* We learn much by observing other people's actions and their consequences. (page 227)
- *Vicarious reinforcement and punishment.* We tend to imitate behaviors that lead to reinforcement for other people. We are less consistent in avoiding behaviors that are unsuccessful for others. (page 229)
- *Self-efficacy.* Whether we imitate a behavior depends on whether we believe we are capable of duplicating it. (page 229)
- *Self-reinforcement and self-punishment.* Once people have decided to try to imitate a certain behavior, they set goals for themselves and may even provide their own reinforcements. (page 230)

KEY TERMS

conditioned taste aversion (page 224)

preparedness (page 223)

self-efficacy (page 229)

sensitive period (page 226)

social-learning approach (page 227)

vicarious reinforcement or vicarious punishment (page 229)

exploration and study

Why Does This Matter to Me?

SOCIAL RESPONSIBILITY AND PSYCHOLOGY

Many environmental problems are caused by human behavior. Psychologists can help steer the course of our future toward more socially responsible and sustainable outcomes. Students of today need to be ever mindful of the link between human behavior and its impact on the environment and our communities.

"Learning" and Social Responsibility: A Step Further

What are some potential reinforcers for living a greener life? For instance, if you were to start a Ride Your Bike/Don't Drive campaign, what would be some of the perks that you would highlight?

Green Tip

Some companies offer incentives, a form of positive reinforcement, for recycling old goods. Before you throw away your old TV or PC or even your old MP3 player, check with the manufacturer to see if they offer store credit toward a new purchase if you bring them your old product.

Join the iChapters Plant a Tree Drive!

To show its support of the environmental movement, iChapters is planting a tree on behalf of each fan of the iChapters Facebook Page and for every 10 questions answered correctly in our quiz. http://www.ichapters.com/plantatree/

Exploration and Study

SUGGESTIONS FOR FURTHER EXPLORATION

In addition to the study materials provided at the end of each module, you may supplement your review of this chapter with the following book and website suggestions or by using one or more of the book's electronic resources, which include its companion website, interactive Cengage Learning eBook, and CengageNOW. Brief descriptions of these resources follow. For more information, visit **www.cengage.com/psychology/kalat.**

ADDITIONAL RESOURCES

The book's companion website, accessible from **www.cengage.com/psychology/kalat**, provides a wide range of study resources such as an interactive glossary, flashcards, tutorial quizzes, updated web links, and Try It Yourself activities.

CengageNOW with Critical Thinking Videos is an easy-to-use resource that helps you study in less time to get the grade you want. An online study system, CengageNOW gives you the option of taking a diagnostic pretest for each chapter. The system uses the results of each pretest to create personalized chapter study plans for you. The Personalized Study Plans

Critical Thinking

- Help you save study time by identifying areas on which you should concentrate and give you one-click access to corresponding pages of the interactive Cengage Learning eBook;
- Provide interactive exercises and study tools to help you fully understand chapter concepts; and
- Include a posttest for you to take to confirm that you are ready to move on to the next chapter.

Find critical thinking videos like this one in your CengageNOW product, which offer an opportunity for you to learn more about psychological research on different topics.

Books

Bandura, A. (1986). *Social foundations of thought and action.* Upper Saddle River, NJ: Prentice Hall. A review of social learning by its most influential investigator.

Kroodsma, D. (2005). *The singing life of birds.* New York: Houghton Mifflin. Thorough account of research on a fascinating kind of animal learning.

Websites

Links to the websites described below are kept current and can be found at **www.cengage.com/psychology/kalat**.

Positive Reinforcement

Lyle K. Grant of Athabasca University helps students understand what does and what does not constitute positive reinforcement. Be sure you understand the examples before you begin the practice exercise.

B. F. Skinner

Skinner's daughter provides a biography of a highly influential psychologist.

Albert Bandura

C. George Boeree of Shippensburg University provides a short biography of Albert Bandura, a pioneer in the field of social learning.

Timing

©David Woolley/Getty Images

Memory

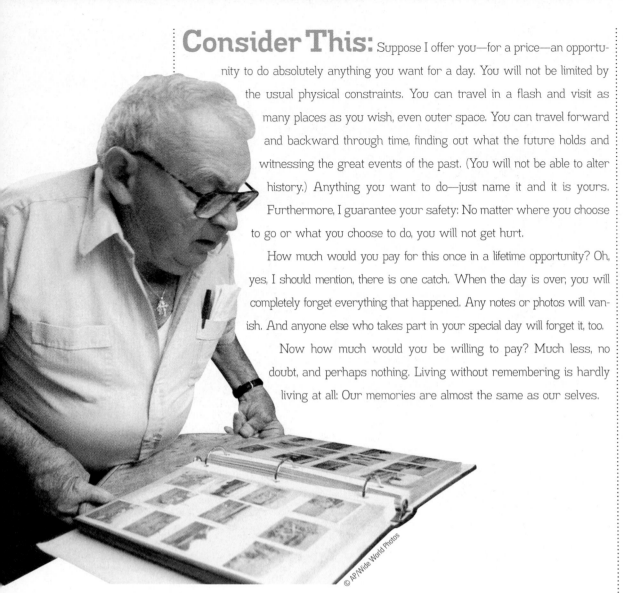

Consider This:

Suppose I offer you—for a price—an opportunity to do absolutely anything you want for a day. You will not be limited by the usual physical constraints. You can travel in a flash and visit as many places as you wish, even outer space. You can travel forward and backward through time, finding out what the future holds and witnessing the great events of the past. (You will not be able to alter history.) Anything you want to do—just name it and it is yours. Furthermore, I guarantee your safety: No matter where you choose to go or what you choose to do, you will not get hurt.

How much would you pay for this once in a lifetime opportunity? Oh, yes, I should mention, there is one catch. When the day is over, you will completely forget everything that happened. Any notes or photos will vanish. And anyone else who takes part in your special day will forget it, too.

Now how much would you be willing to pay? Much less, no doubt, and perhaps nothing. Living without remembering is hardly living at all: Our memories are almost the same as our selves.

With a suitable reminder, you remember some events distinctly, even after a long delay. Other memories are lost or distorted.

Types of Memory

- Do we have different kinds of memory?
- If so, what is the best way to describe those differences?

Every year, people compete in the World Memory Championship in Britain. (You can read about it at their website; this link can be found at **www.cengage.com/psychology/kalat**.) One event is speed of memorizing a shuffled deck of 52 cards. The all-time record is 26.28 seconds. Another is memorizing a long number within 1 hour. The record is a 1,949-digit number. (The winner took almost 2 hours to recite it.) People also compete at memorizing dates of fictional events, names of unfamiliar faces in photos, and so forth. Dominic O'Brien, eight-time world champion, gives speeches and writes books about how to train your memory. However, he admits that one time while he was practicing card memorization, an irate friend called from an airport to complain that O'Brien had forgotten to pick him up. O'Brien apologized and drove to London's Gatwick Airport, practicing card memorization along the way. When he arrived, he remembered that his friend was at Heathrow, London's other major airport (Johnstone, 1994).

Anyone—you, me, or Dominic O'Brien—remembers some information and forgets the rest. Like O'Brien, we mostly remember what we paid attention to, the material we considered interesting or important.

Memory is *the retention of information.* It includes skills such as riding a bicycle or eating with chopsticks. It also includes facts that never change (your birthday), facts that seldom change (your mailing address), and facts that frequently change (where you last parked your car). You remember the most important events of your life and some of the less important events. You remember many interesting and important facts you learned in school and a few of the less useful ones. (I learned that "Polynesians eat poi and breadfruit." That fact will come in handy the next time I plan a meal for some Polynesians . . . if I can find some poi or breadfruit, whatever that is.)

Some advice: This chapter, like chapters 4 and 8, includes many Try It Yourself activities. You will gain much more from this chapter if you take the time to try them.

Dominic O'Brien, eight-time winner of the World Memory Championship and author of several books on training your memory, admits he sometimes forgets practical information, such as promising to meet a friend at Heathrow Airport.

© Rupert Watts

EBBINGHAUS'S PIONEERING STUDIES OF MEMORY

Suppose you wanted to study memory, but no one had ever done memory research before. Where would you start? Some of the earliest psychological researchers asked people to describe their memories. The problem was that the researchers did not know when the memories had formed, how often people had rehearsed them, or whether the memories were correct. German psychologist Hermann Ebbinghaus (1850–1909) avoided these problems by an approach that we now take for granted: He taught new material so that he knew exactly what someone had learned and when. Then he measured memory after various delays. To be sure the material was new, he used lists of nonsense syllables, such as GAK or JEK. He wrote out 2,300 syllables, assembled them randomly into lists (Figure 7.1), and then set out to study memory. He had no cooperative introductory psychology students or friends eager to memorize nonsense syllables, so he ran all the tests on himself. For 6 years, he memorized thousands of lists of nonsense syllables. (He was either very dedicated to his science or uncommonly tolerant of boredom.)

Many of his findings were hardly surprising. For example, as shown in Figure 7.2, he took longer

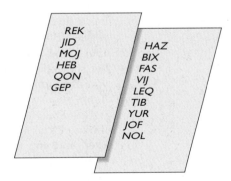

REK
JID
MOJ
HEB
QON
GEP

HAZ
BIX
FAS
VIJ
LEQ
TIB
YUR
JOF
NOL

Figure 7.1 Hermann Ebbinghaus pioneered the scientific study of memory by observing his own capacity for memorizing lists of nonsense syllables.

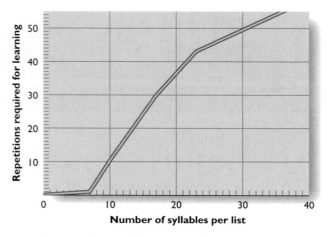

Figure 7.2 Ebbinghaus counted how many times he had to read a list of nonsense syllables before he could recite it once correctly. For a list of seven or fewer, one reading was usually enough. Beyond seven, the longer the list, the more repetitions he needed. (From Ebbinghaus, 1885/1913)

to memorize longer lists than shorter lists. "Of course!" you might scoff. But Ebbinghaus was not just demonstrating the obvious. He measured *how much* longer it took to memorize a longer list. You might similarly object to the law of gravity: "Of course the farther something falls, the longer it takes to hit the ground!" Nevertheless, measuring the acceleration of gravity was essential to progress in physics. In the same way, measuring how long it takes to learn a list enables researchers to compare learning under different conditions: Do adults learn faster than children? Do we learn some kinds of lists faster than other lists? Ebbinghaus's approach led to all the later research on memory, including findings that were not so obvious.

METHODS OF TESTING MEMORY

Nearly everyone occasionally has a tip-of-the-tongue experience (Brown & McNeill, 1966). You want to remember someone's name, and all you can think of is a similar name that you know isn't right. You will probably think of the correct name later, and you are sure you would recognize it if you heard it.

In other words, memory is not an all-or-none thing. You might or might not remember something depend-

ing on how someone tests you. Let's survey the main methods of testing memory. Along the way, we begin to distinguish among different types of memory.

Free Recall

The simplest method for the tester (though not for the person tested) is to ask for **free recall**. To recall something is *to produce a response, as you do on essay tests or short-answer tests.* For instance, "Please name all the children in your second-grade class." You probably will not name many, partly because you confuse the names of the children in your second-grade class with those you knew in other grades.

Cued Recall

You will do better with **cued recall**, in which you *receive significant hints about the material.* For example, a photograph of the children in your second-grade class (Figure 7.3) or a list of their initials will help you remember. Try this: Cover the right side of Table 7.1 with a piece of paper and try to identify the authors of each book on the left. (This method is free recall.) Then uncover the right side, revealing each author's initials, and try again. (This method is cued recall.)

Recognition

With **recognition**, a third method of testing memory, someone *chooses the correct item among several options.* People usually recognize more items than they recall. For example, I might give you a list of 60 names and ask you to check off

Figure 7.3 Can you recall the names of the students in your second-grade class? Trying to remember without any hints is *free recall.* Using a photo or a list of initials is *cued recall.*

Table 7.1 The Difference Between Free Recall and Cued Recall

Instructions: First try to identify the author of each book listed in the left column while covering the right column (free recall method). Then expose the right column, which gives each author's initials, and try again (cued recall).

Book	Author
Moby Dick	H. M.
Emma and *Pride and Prejudice*	J. A.
Hercule Poirot stories	A. C.
Sherlock Holmes stories	A. C. D.
I Know Why the Caged Bird Sings	M. A.
War and Peace	L. T.
This textbook	J. K.
The Canterbury Tales	G. C.
The Origin of Species	C. D.
Gone with the Wind	M. M.
Les Miserables	V. H.

(For answers, see page 246, answer A.)

the correct names of children in your second-grade class. Multiple-choice tests use the recognition method.

Savings

A fourth method, the **savings method** (also known as the **relearning method**), detects weak memories *by comparing the speed of original learning to the speed of relearning.* Suppose you cannot name the children in your second-grade class and cannot even pick out their names from a list of choices. You would nevertheless learn a correct list of names faster than a list of people you had never met. That is, you save time when you relearn something. The amount of time saved (time needed for original learning minus the time for relearning) is a measure of memory.

Implicit Memory

Free recall, cued recall, recognition, and savings are tests of **explicit** (or **direct**) **memory**. That is, *someone who states an answer regards it as a product of memory.* In **implicit memory** (or **indirect memory**), *an experience influences what you say or do even though you might not be aware of*

the influence. If you find that definition unsatisfactory, you are not alone (Frensch & Rünger, 2003). Defining something in terms of a vague concept like "awareness" is not a good habit. This definition is tentative until we develop a better one.

The best way to explain implicit memory is by example: Suppose you are in a conversation while other people nearby are discussing something else. You ignore the other discussion, but a few words from that background conversation probably creep into your own. You do not even notice the influence, although an observer might.

Here is a demonstration of implicit memories. For each of the following three-letter combinations, fill in additional letters to make any English word:

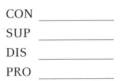

CON _____
SUP _____
DIS _____
PRO _____

You could have thought of any number of words—the dictionary lists well over 100 familiar CON_____ words alone. Did you happen to write any of the following: *conversation, suppose, discussion,* or *probably?* Each of these words appeared in the paragraph before this demonstration. *Reading or hearing a word temporarily **primes** that word and increases the chance that you will use it yourself,* even if you are not aware of the influence (Graf & Mandler, 1984; Schacter, 1987). This demonstration works better if you listen to spoken words than if you read them. To get a better sense of priming, try an Online Try It Yourself activity. Go to **www.cengage.com/ psychology/kalat.** Navigate to the student website, then to the Online Try It Yourself section, and click Implicit Memories. Table 7.2 contrasts some memory tests.

Procedural memories, *memories of motor skills* such as walking or eating with chopsticks, are another kind of implicit memories. Psychologists distinguish procedural memories from **declarative memories,** *memories we can readily state in words.* To illustrate the difference, take some motor skill you have mastered—such as riding a bicycle, using in-line skates, or tying a necktie—and try explaining it in words (no gestures!) to someone who has never done it before. You will quickly discover how much you do without thinking about it verbally. Also, if you type, you know the locations of the letters well enough to press the right key at the right time, but can

Table 7.2 Several Ways to Test Memory

Title	Description	Example
Recall	You are asked to say what you remember.	Name the Seven Dwarfs.
Cued recall	You are given significant hints to help you remember.	Name the Seven Dwarfs. Hint: One was always smiling, one was smart, one never talked, one always seemed to have a cold . . .
Recognition	You are asked to choose the correct item from among several items.	Which of the following were among the Seven Dwarfs: Sneezy, Sleazy, Dopey, Dippy, Hippy, Happy?
Savings (relearning)	You are asked to relearn something: If it takes you less time than when you first learned that material, some memory has persisted.	Try memorizing this list: Sleepy, Sneezy, Doc, Dopey, Grumpy, Happy, Bashful. Can you memorize it faster than this list: Sleazy, Snoopy, Duke, Dippy, Gripey, Hippy, Blushy?
Implicit memory	You are asked to generate words, without necessarily regarding them as memories.	You hear the story "Snow White and the Seven Dwarfs." Later you are asked to fill in these blanks to make any words that come to mind: _ L _ P _ _ N _ Z _ _ _ C _ _ O _ EY _ R _ P _ _ _ P P _ _ A _ H _ U _

you state that knowledge explicitly? For example, which letter is directly to the right of C? Which is directly to the left of P?

1. For each of these examples, identify the type of memory test—free recall, cued recall, recognition, savings, or implicit.
   a. Although you thought you had forgotten your high school French, you do better in your college French course than your roommate, who never studied French before.
   b. You are trying to remember the phone number of the local pizza parlor without looking it up in the phone directory.
   c. You hear a song on the radio without paying much attention to it. Later, you find yourself humming a melody, but you don't know what it is or where you heard it.
   d. You forget where you parked your car, so you scan the parking lot hoping to pick yours out among all the others.
   e. Your friend asks, "What's the name of our chemistry lab instructor? I think her name starts with an S."
2. Is remembering how to tie your shoes a procedural memory or a declarative memory? Is remembering the color of your shoes a procedural or a declarative memory?

Concept Check

Answers

1. **a.** savings; **b.** free recall; **c.** implicit; **d.** recognition; **e.** cued recall.
2. Remembering how to tie your shoes is a procedural memory. Remembering their appearance is a declarative memory (one you could express in words).

APPLICATION: SUSPECT LINEUPS AS RECOGNITION MEMORY

Suppose you witness a crime, and now the police want you to identify the guilty person. They ask you to look at suspects in a lineup or examine a book of photos. Your task is a clear example of recognition memory, as you try to identify the correct item among distracters.

The task raises a problem, familiar from your own experience. When you take a multiple-choice test—also recognition memory—you pick the best available choice. Sometimes, none of the choices is exactly right, but you select the best one available. Now, imagine doing the same with a book of photos. You look through the choices and pick the one who looks most like the perpetrator of the crime. You tell the police you think suspect 42 is the guilty person. "Think?" the police ask. "Your testimony won't be worth much in court unless you're sure." You look again, eager to cooperate. Finally, you say yes, you're sure. The police say, "Good, that's the person we thought did it." The feedback reinforces your belief in the validity of your choice, and your memory of the original event may change to accommodate your choice. You testify in court, and the suspect is convicted. But is justice done? Many people have been convicted of crimes because of eyewitness testimony and later exonerated by DNA evidence.

Psychologists have proposed ways to improve suspect lineups. One is for the officer supervising the lineup to be a blind observer (see chapter 2). An officer who knows which person is the suspect might unintentionally bias the witness into identifying someone the witness didn't really remember. A second recommendation is to postpone as long as possible any feedback about whether the witness chose the person the police suspected (Wells, Olson, & Charman, 2003; Zaragoza, Payment, Ackil, Drivdahl, & Beck, 2001). Any sign of agreement adds to a witness's confidence, even if the witness was wrong (Semmler, Brewer, & Wells, 2004; Wright & Skagerberg, 2007).

Another more controversial recommendation is to present the lineup sequentially—that is, one suspect at a time, instead of viewing several suspects simultaneously (Wells et al., 2000; Wells, Memon, & Penrod, 2006). In a sequential lineup, the witness says "yes" or "no" to each suspect. As soon as the witness says yes, the procedure is finished. After all, there is no point in looking at additional suspects if the witness has already decided. Also, the witness has no opportunity to go back and reexamine photos after rejecting them. The witness should make a definite identification or none at all, and not just choose the best suspect available. A sequential lineup greatly decreases the number of false identifications. When witnesses view a simultaneous lineup that does not include the guilty person, most witnesses identify someone anyway (the one who looks closest to the culprit). With a sequential lineup, witnesses less often choose an innocent person. However, the cost is that witnesses also frequently fail to identify guilty people. That is, with a sequential lineup, witnesses become cautious and frequently fail to choose anyone (Malpass, 2006). The advantages and disadvantages of the two types of lineup depend on how we weigh the risk of setting a guilty person free versus the risk of imprisoning an innocent person.

....

3. How does a sequential lineup avoid one of the problems inherent in a multiple-choice test?

Answer

3. With a multiple-choice test, a person chooses the best available answer, even if it is not exactly correct. The same is often true in a simultaneous lineup. With a sequential lineup, a person chooses only when confident.

....

CHILDREN AS EYEWITNESSES

While we are discussing eyewitness memory, let's consider the special case of young children. Should we trust their reports when they are witnesses or victims of a crime? One research approach is to ask a child to recall a medical or dental examination. How well can the child report those events? In such studies, researchers find that children as young as 3 years old report with reasonable accuracy even 6 weeks later (Baker-Ward, Gordon, Ornstein, Larus, & Clubb, 1993).

Several factors influence the accuracy of young children's reports:

- **Delay of questioning.** Imagine a doctor who usually takes a child's temperature during a physical exam but did not do so in the most recent exam. A child who is asked immediately after an exam reports the events correctly. If asked 3 months later, the child confuses one exam with another and reports that the doctor did take the child's temperature (Ornstein et al., 2006).

- **Type of question.** To an open-ended question such as, "Tell me what happened," a young child's answer is usually short but accurate. After a suggestive question such as, "Did he touch you under your clothing?" children's accuracy is less dependable (Lamb, Orbach, Hershkowitz, Horowitz, & Abbott, 2007). A suggestive question is especially dangerous months after an event, when the child's memory has weakened (Quas et al., 2007).

- **Hearing other children.** A child who hears other children reporting something is likely to make the same report, even if it is wrong (Principe, Kanaya, Ceci, & Singh, 2006).

- **Repeating the question.** If someone asks a child the same question two or three times within a session, the child often changes answers, apparently assuming that the first answer must have been wrong (Krähenbühl & Blades, 2006; Poole & White, 1993). However, repeated open-ended questioning by different interviewers, or by the same interviewer on different days, helps remind the child and sometimes elicits new information (Hershkowitz & Terner, 2007).

- **Using doll props.** To investigate suspicions of sexual abuse, some psychologists try to prod a child's memory by providing anatomically detailed dolls and asking the child to act out some event. The idea sounds reasonable, but when researchers ask children to act out a doctor's exam (where they know what happened), children often act out events that did not happen (Greenhoot, Ornstein, Gordon, & Baker-Ward, 1999).

- **Understanding a question.** If I ask you whether you ever saw anyone imbosk a lecythus, I assume you would say you don't know, or you would ask me to explain the question. A 3-year-old child who doesn't understand a question usually answers "yes" (Imhoff & Baker-Ward, 1999).

Adults easily overestimate a child's understanding. Once my son and his wife took my granddaughter, then age 3, on a trip. They told her they would stop at a barbecue restaurant for dinner. She was so excited that she could hardly wait. She spent most of the trip asking, "Now how long till barbecue?" As they finally approached the restaurant, she asked, "Will other children be there too, with their Barbies?"

Can we trust a child's testimony? In short, it depends. With proper questioning, even a 3-year-old provides accurate information. With delayed or biased questioning, the accuracy declines.

THE INFORMATION-PROCESSING VIEW OF MEMORY

Over the years, psychologists have repeatedly tried to explain the mechanisms of behavior by analogy to the technologies of their time. In the 1600s, René Descartes compared animal behavior to the actions of a hydraulic pump. Psychologists of the early 1900s suggested that learning worked like a telephone switchboard. In the early days of radio, some researchers compared the nervous system to a radio. The information-processing model compares human memory to that of a computer: *Information that enters the system is processed, coded, and stored,* as in Figure 7.4. When you type something on the keyboard, the computer stores it in a temporary memory. When you store something on the hard drive, you set up a stable, long-lasting representation. According to the information-processing model, information first enters short-term memory (a temporary store), and some short-term memory transfers into long-term memory (like a hard disk). Eventually, a cue from the environment prompts the system to retrieve stored information (Atkinson & Shiffrin, 1968). Let's examine this model.

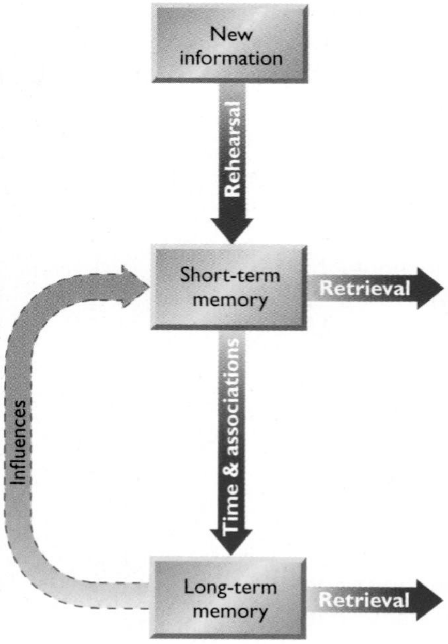

Figure 7.4 The information-processing model of memory resembles a computer's memory system, including temporary and permanent memory.

[Figure 7.4 diagram: New information → (Rehearsal) → Short-term memory ↔ Retrieval; Short-term memory → (Time & associations) → Long-term memory → Retrieval; Influences]

4. In what ways is the analogy between computer memory and human memory imperfect? (You can't look this one up. Think about it.)

Answer

4. A computer reports its memory exactly, even after not opening a file in years. Human memory becomes less detailed and less accurate over time. It is possible to delete memories from the hard drive of a computer but not easy to delete human memories. You can probably think of other differences.

Short-Term and Long-Term Memory

Information-processing theory distinguishes between short-term memory, *temporary storage of recent events,* and long-term memory, *a relatively permanent store.* For example, while you are playing tennis, the current score is in your short-term memory, and the rules of the game are in your long-term memory.

Psychologists distinguish two major types of long-term memory: semantic and episodic. Semantic memory is *memory of principles and facts,* like nearly everything you learn in school. Episodic memory is *memory for specific events in your life* (Tulving, 1989). For example, your memory of the law of gravity is a semantic memory, whereas remembering the time you dropped your grandmother's vase is an episodic memory. Remembering the rules of tennis is a semantic memory, and your memory of a particular time you played tennis is an episodic memory.

Episodic memories are more fragile than semantic memories. If you don't play tennis for a few years, you will still remember the rules, but your memory of particular tennis games will fade. Older people are especially likely to forget specific episodes, despite retaining semantic memories (Piolino, Desgranges, Benali, & Eustache, 2002). People with certain kinds of brain damage lose most of their episodic memories but keep their semantic memories.

5. Classify each of these as semantic memory or episodic memory: (a) Naming the first president of the United States. (b) Defining "classical conditioning." (c) Describing your trip to Disney World. (d) Remembering where you had dinner last night, who ate with you, and what you ate.

Answer

5. (a) semantic. (b) semantic (c) episodic. (d) episodic.

You might remember something you have heard (a semantic memory) but forget where you heard it (an episodic memory). *Forgetting where or how you learned something* is source amnesia. Suppose you hear a rumor or read an e-mail from someone you don't know. At first, you dismiss the statement because you know it came from an unreliable source. Later, you forget the source and start to take the statement seriously (M. K. Johnson, Hashtroudi, & Lindsay, 1993; Riccio, 1994). In chapter 13 on social psychology, we return to this phenomenon, known as the *sleeper effect.*

In one study, students read fictional stories that included such facts as "a sextant is a tool used at sea to navigate by the stars." Later, they were asked such questions as, "what tool is used at sea to navigate by the stars?" People who had just read that fact were more likely than other people to answer correctly. Most remembered seeing it in the story, but many said they had already known the fact before reading the story. Another group of students read stories with misinformation such as "a compass is a tool used at sea to navigate by the stars." Many of these students later answered the question incorrectly, saying that a compass is a tool to navigate by the stars. Although most said they remembered seeing this fact in the story, many insisted that they too had "already" known this fact before reading the story! This example illustrates another type of source amnesia (Marsh, Meade, & Roediger, 2003).

Psychologists have traditionally drawn several distinctions between short- and long-term memory. Two of the differences are capacity and decay over time.

Differences in Capacity

Long-term memory has a vast, hard-to-measure capacity. Asking how much information you could store in long-term memory is like asking how many books you could fit into a library. The answer depends on the size of the books and how you arrange them. Short-term memory, in contrast, has a limited capacity. Read each of the following sequences of letters and then look away and try to repeat them from memory. Or read each aloud and ask a friend to repeat it.

> try it
> yourself

E H G P H

J R O Z N Q

S R B W R C N

M P D I W F B S

Z Y B P I A F M O

Most normal adults can repeat a list of about seven letters, numbers, or words. Some remember eight or nine; others only five or six. George Miller (1956) referred to the short-term memory capacity as "the magical number seven, plus or minus two." When people try to repeat a longer list, they may fail to remember even the first seven items. It is like trying to hold objects in one hand: If you try to hold too many, you drop them all.

You can store more information in short-term memory by a process called chunking—*grouping items into meaningful sequences or clusters*. For example, the sequence "ventysi" has seven letters, at the limit of most people's capacity. However,

"seventysix" with three additional letters can be easily remembered as "76," a two-digit number. "Seventeenseventysix" is even longer, but if you think of it as 1776, an important date in U.S. history, it is a single item to store. Because people are so good at chunking, sometimes without realizing that they are doing it, psychologists are not certain that short-term memory really does hold seven items. When you remembered S R B W R C N, did you really remember it as seven items? Or did you group them, such as SR . . . B . . . WR . . . CN? Many researchers now believe the true limit of human short-term memory is closer to four than to seven (Saults & Cowan, 2007).

One college student in a lengthy experiment initially could repeat about seven digits at a time (Ericsson, Chase, & Faloon, 1980). Over a year and a half, working 3 to 5 hours per week, he gradually improved until he could repeat 80 digits, as shown in Figure 7.5, by using elaborate strategies for chunking. He was a competitive runner, so he might store the sequence "3492 . . ." as "3 minutes, 49.2 seconds, a near world-record time for running a mile." He might store the next set of numbers as a good time for running a kilometer, a mediocre marathon time, or a date in history. With practice, he started recognizing larger and larger chunks of numbers. However, when he was tested on his ability to remember a list of letters, his performance was only average because he had not developed any chunking strategies for letters.

One cautionary point: We talk about storing a memory as if you were holding objects in your hand or placing books on a library shelf. This is only a loose analogy. Memory depends on changes in synapses spread out over a huge population of cells. It is not like something you put in one place.

Short-term memory is like a handful of objects. It can hold only a limited number.

Kutbidin Atamkulov travels from one Central Asian village to another singing from memory the tale of the Kirghiz hero, Manas. The song, which lasts 3 hours, has been passed from master to student for centuries.

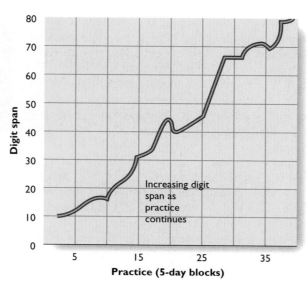

Figure 7.5 A college student gradually increased his ability to repeat a list of numbers. However, his short-term memory for letters or words did not increase. (From Ericsson, Chase, & Faloon, 1980)

Decay of Memories over Time

A short-term memory, by definition, doesn't last very long. To say it more accurately, short-term memory doesn't last long without repetition. Here is the classic demonstration: Lloyd Peterson and Margaret Peterson (1959) presented meaningless sequences of letters, like HOXDF, and then tested people's memory after various delays. If you were in this study, knowing that the experimenter was going to ask you to repeat the letters, you would spend the delay rehearsing, "HOXDF, HOXDF, . . ." To prevent rehearsal, the experimenters included a second task. When they presented the letters, they also presented a number, such as 231. The instruction was to start with that number and count backward by 3s, such as "231, 228, 225, 222, 219, . . ." until the experimenter signaled the end of the delay. At that point, the participant was to say the letters.

Figure 7.6 shows the results. Only about 10% of the participants could recall the letters after 18 seconds. In other words, a short-term memory fades rapidly. You can demonstrate this phenomenon yourself with an Online Try It Yourself activity Decay of Short-Term Memory.

Do not take that figure of 18 seconds too seriously. Peterson and Peterson were dealing with nonsense information, such as HOXDF. The results are different with more meaningful material.

Exactly why do short-term memories fade? The simplest hypothesis is that the brain representation decays over time. Neuroscientists have identified a protein that the brain makes after an experience that weakens the memory trace, presumably to avoid permanently storing unimportant information (Genoux et al., 2002). Another hypothesis is that short-term memories only appear to fade because we confuse one with another. If you read a series of letters and then count backward by 3s, your memory of those letters fades rapidly on the average. However, it does not fade rapidly on the first trial. On the first trial, you remember the letters much longer than you will on later trials, when you confuse that set of letters (HOXDF) with all the other sets from previous trials (Keppel & Underwood, 1962).

Here is further evidence: Suppose you go through a series of trials. First it's HOXDF, a delay of counting backward by 3s, and then trying to recite the letters. Then it's BKLRE, a different delay, and answering. And so forth. After many trials, your average results begin to look like those in Figure 7.6. You seldom remember the letters when the delay is more than 6 to 9 seconds. Now we give you a 1-minute rest period and start again. On your first trial after that rest period, your chance of remembering improves dramatically (Unsworth, Heitz, & Parks, 2008). The implication is that short-term memories fade partly, if not entirely, because we confuse the most recent one with all the preceding ones.

If short-term memory is what has just happened, long-term memory is everything else. How long does a long-term memory last? It depends. You have many memories that you keep as long as they are current, updating them with new information as often as necessary (Altmann & Gray, 2002). If you are playing basketball, you remember

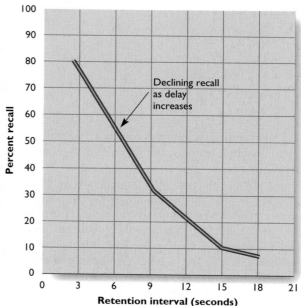

Figure 7.6 In a study by Peterson and Peterson (1959), people remembered a set of letters well after a short delay, but their memory faded quickly if they were prevented from rehearsing.

the score, approximately how much time is left in the game, what defense your team is using, what offense, how many fouls you have committed, and so forth. You won't (and wouldn't want to) remember that information for the rest of your life, but you also don't need to rehearse it constantly to prevent it from fading. Similarly, right now you probably remember approximately how much money is in your wallet, where and when you plan to meet someone for dinner, what you plan to do next weekend, how long until your next psychology test, and much other information you need to store until you update it with new information.

Many long-term memories last a lifetime. Old people can describe events that happened in their childhood. Harry Bahrick (1984) found that people who had studied Spanish 1 or 2 years ago remembered more than those who had studied it 3 to 6 years ago, but beyond 6 years, the retention appeared to be stable (Figure 7.7).

6. How does the capacity of short-term memory compare with that of long-term memory?

7. Studies in the 1950s indicated that short-term memories, unless rehearsed, decay within seconds. Why is that conclusion no longer certain?

Concept Check

Answers

7. If interference from previous trials is minimized, short-term memory lasts longer.

6. Short-term memory has a capacity limited to only about seven items, possibly less, in the average adult, whereas long-term memory has a huge, difficult-to-measure capacity.

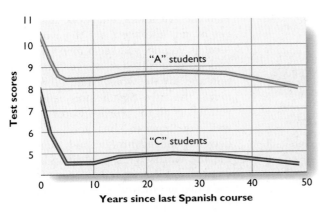

Figure 7.7 Spanish vocabulary as measured by a recognition test declines in the first few years but then becomes stable. The students who received an "A" performed better, but each group showed similar rates of forgetting. (From "Semantic memory content in permastore: Fifty years of memory for Spanish learned in school" by H. P. Bahrick, *Journal of Experimental Psychology,* 1984, pp. 1–29.)

WORKING MEMORY

"Clarence Birdseye patented a method for selling frozen fish." I bet you didn't know that. It is now a short-term memory, which may or may not become a long-term memory.

"Go straight until the first intersection, then turn right and go two blocks." We might also describe this statement as a short-term memory, but it's not the same as the one about Birdseye, because you have probably heard the same instruction, or a similar one, many times before. Here's another example: "Read the first three paragraphs on page 42, and then close your book and summarize what you read." You want to store this information temporarily, but it's hardly in the same category as something you had never heard before.

Originally, psychologists thought of short-term memory as the way to store something while moving it into long-term storage. That is, you gradually **consolidate** your memory by *converting a short-term memory into a long-term memory.* One problem for this idea is that *how long* information remains in short-term memory is a poor predictor of whether it becomes a long-term memory. You might watch a hockey game in which the score remains 1-0 for 2 hours, but you don't store that score permanently. In contrast, if someone tells you, "Your sister just had a baby," you form a lasting memory quickly.

Today, most researchers emphasize temporary memory storage as the information you are using at the moment. To emphasize this different perspective, they speak of *working* memory instead of short-term memory. Working memory doesn't have to be new to you, and it doesn't have to be on the way to permanent memory. It includes something like "go to the first intersection and turn right," which you have heard many times before, need to use now, and will disregard after you no longer need it.

Working memory is *a system for working with current information.* It is almost synonymous with one's current sphere of attention. Theorists have proposed that working memory contains several components (Baddeley, 2001; Baddeley & Hitch, 1994; Repovš & Baddeley, 2006):

• A *phonological loop,* which stores and rehearses speech information. Your phonological loop enables you to repeat seven or so unrelated items immediately after hearing them. It is essential for understanding a long sentence. You have to remember the words at the start of the sentence long enough to connect them to the words at the end.

- *A visuospatial sketchpad,* which temporarily stores and manipulates visual and spatial information (Luck & Vogel, 1997). You use this process for recognizing pictures or imagining what an object looks like from another angle.

Researchers distinguish between the phonological and visuospatial stores because of evidence that different brain areas mediate the two kinds of memory (Zimmer, 2008) and that people can do an auditory word task and a visuospatial task at the same time without much interference between them (Baddeley & Hitch, 1974). Similarly, within the visuospatial realm, tasks that interfere with visual memory don't interfere with spatial processing, and vice versa (Repovš & Baddeley, 2006). People presumably have additional stores for touch, smell, and taste memory, although few researchers have examined those types.

- *A central executive,* which governs shifts of attention. The hallmark of good working memory is the ability to shift attention as needed among different tasks. A hospital nurse has to keep track of the needs of several patients, sometimes interrupting the treatment of one patient to take care of an emergency and then returning to complete the first patient. Also imagine yourself driving a car, monitoring the oncoming traffic, the cars in your lane, the gauges on your dashboard, traffic signs, and a conversation with a passenger.
- *An episodic buffer,* which binds together the various parts of a meaningful experience. For example, recall your dinner last night. You

probably remember where you were, what you ate, who else was present, what they said, and perhaps what music was in the background. The episodic buffer is the hypothetical device that puts these items together. Figure 7.8 summarizes this model.

Here is one simple way to measure shifting attention, which is a major component of the central executive: Recite aloud some poem, song, or other passage that you know well. (If you can't think of a more interesting example, you can recite the alphabet.) Time how long it takes. Then measure how long it takes you to say the same thing silently. Finally, time how long it takes you to alternate—the first word aloud, the second silent, the third aloud, and so forth. Alternating takes longer because you keep shifting attention.

Here is another way to measure executive processes: You hear a list of words such as *maple, elm, oak, hemlock, chestnut, birch, sycamore, pine, redwood, walnut, dogwood, hickory.* After each word, you are supposed to say the *previous* word. So after "maple, elm," you should say "maple." After "oak" you reply "elm." If you do well on that task, proceed to a more difficult version: You should repeat what you heard *two* words ago. So you wait for "maple, elm, oak" and reply "maple." Then you hear "hemlock" and reply "elm." You need to shift back and forth between listening to the new word and repeating something from memory.

Another example: An investigator flashes on the screen a simple arithmetic question and a word, such as

$$(2 \times 3) + 1 = 8? \quad \text{SPRING}$$

As quickly as possible, you should read the arithmetic question, answer it yes or no, and then say the word. As soon as you do, you see a new question and word; again, you answer the question and say the word. After a few such items, the investigator stops and asks you to say all the words in order. To do well, you have to shift your attention between the arithmetic and memorizing the words. This is a difficult task. Some people have trouble remembering even two words under these conditions. Remembering five or six is an excellent score.

People vary in their performance on tasks like this partly for genetic reasons (Parasuraman, Greenwood, Kumar, & Fossella, 2005). Those who do well on this task are considered to have a "high

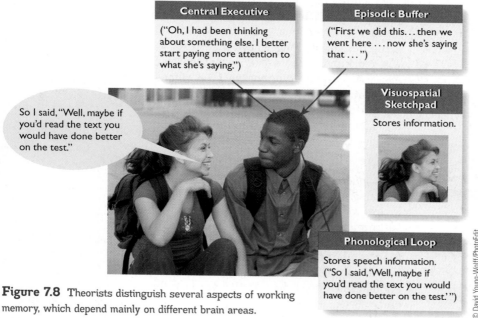

Figure 7.8 Theorists distinguish several aspects of working memory, which depend mainly on different brain areas.

capacity" of working memory. They generally do well on many other tasks, including intelligence tests (Engle, Tuholski, Laughlin, & Conway, 1999; Oberauer, Süss, Wilhelm, & Wittman, 2003), understanding other people's point of view (Barrett, Tugade, & Engle, 2004), and ignoring distraction when they need to focus attention (Heitz & Engle, 2007). They have less than average "mind wandering" while they need to concentrate on a difficult task but more than average mind wandering when performing easy tasks (Kane et al., 2007). However, it is not certain how much of these benefits result from executive function (the ability to shift attention) and how much result simply from good memory in general (Mogle, Lovett, Stawski, & Sliwinski, 2008).

What enables some people to have a greater than average capacity of working memory? According to one study, the key is attention. Participants were instructed to watch two displays on a screen and say whether the red rectangles were the same for the two displays, ignoring the blue rectangles. Brain recordings indicated that the people with less working memory responded to both the red and blue rectangles, while those with more working memory screened out the blue

ones, as if they weren't there at all (Vogel, McCollough, & Machizawa, 2005). That is, good working memory requires attending to the relevant and screening out the irrelevant.

Interestingly, if people have to perform an additional constantly distracting task, such as tapping a rhythm with their fingers, everyone's performance suffers, but those with the best working memory suffer the most (Kane & Engle, 2000; Rosen & Engle, 1997). They still perform better than people with less working memory but not by as much as usual. Of course, one reason is that those with poor working memory weren't doing well anyway, so they had less room to get worse. Another reason is that people with good working memory usually do well by attending to the most important information. When they are distracted, they lose that advantage.

8. Some students listen to music while studying. Is the music likely to help or impair their study? (What might the answer depend on?)

Answer

8. If the music attracts attention or evokes any response, such as singing along or tapping a foot, it will impair attention. The best students will notice the biggest difference. Background music with no words and no tendency to evoke responses might provide a slight benefit if it prevents the student from noticing other more distracting sounds.

module 7.1

In Closing

Varieties of Memory

Although researchers cannot clearly say what memory is, they agree about what it is *not*: Memory is not a single store into which we simply dump things and later take them out. When Ebbinghaus conducted his studies of memory in the late 1800s, he thought he was measuring the properties of memory, period. We now know that the properties of memory depend on the type of material memorized, the individual's experience with similar materials, the method of testing, and the recency of the event. Memory is not one process, but many.

SUMMARY

- *Ebbinghaus's approach.* Hermann Ebbinghaus pioneered the experimental study of memory by testing his own ability to memorize and retain lists of nonsense syllables. (page 235)
- *Methods of testing memory.* The free recall method reveals only relatively strong memories. Progressively weaker memories can be demonstrated by the cued recall, recognition, and savings methods. Implicit memories are changes in behavior under conditions in which the person cannot verbalize the memory or is unaware of the influence. (page 236)

- *Suspect lineups.* Suspect lineups are an example of the recognition method of testing memory. Unfortunately, witnesses sometimes choose the best available choice and then decide they are sure. Psychologists have recommended ways to decrease inaccurate identifications. (page 238)
- *Children as eyewitnesses.* Even young children can provide accurate eyewitness reports if they are asked unbiased questions soon after the event. (page 239)

- *The information-processing model.* According to the information-processing model, information progresses from short-term memory to long-term memory. (page 240)
- *Short-term and long-term memory.* Short-term memory has a capacity of only a few items in normal adults, although chunking can enable us to store much information in each item. Long-term memory has a huge capacity. Short-term memories fade over time if not rehearsed, partly because of interference from similar memories. Long-term memories last varying periods, up to a lifetime. (page 240)
- *Working memory.* Current researchers identify working memory as a system for dealing with current information, including the ability to shift attention back and forth among tasks as necessary. (page 243)

KEY TERMS

chunking (page 241)

consolidation (page 243)

cued recall (page 236)

declarative memory (page 237)

episodic memory (page 240)

explicit memory (or direct memory) (page 237)

free recall (page 236)

implicit memory (or indirect memory) (page 237)

information-processing model (page 240)

long-term memory (page 240)

memory (page 235)

priming (page 237)

procedural memory (page 237)

recognition (page 236)

savings method (or relearning method) (page 237)

semantic memory (page 240)

short-term memory (page 240)

source amnesia (page 240)

working memory (page 243)

ANSWERS TO OTHER QUESTION IN THE MODULE

A. Herman Melville, Jane Austen, Agatha Christie, Arthur Conan Doyle, Maya Angelou, Leo Tolstoy, James Kalat, Geoffrey Chaucer, Charles Darwin, Margaret Mitchell, Victor Hugo. (page 237)

Encoding, Storage, and Retrieval

• How can we improve our memories?

Have you ever felt distressed because you can't remember some experience? One woman reports feeling distressed because she can't stop remembering! When she sees or hears a date—such as April 27, 1994—a flood of episodic memories descends on her. "That was Wednesday. . . . I was down in Florida. I was summoned to come down and to say goodbye to my grandmother who they all thought was dying but she ended up living. My Dad and my Mom went to New York for a wedding. Then my Mom went to Baltimore to see her family. I went to Florida on the 25th, which was a Monday. This was also the weekend that Nixon died. And then I flew to Florida and my Dad flew to Florida the next day. Then I flew home and my Dad flew to Baltimore to be with my Mom" (Parker, Cahill, & McGaugh, 2006, p. 40). Tell her another date, and she might describe where she went to dinner, and with whom, as well as the major news event of that day. The researchers studying her checked her reports against her extensive diaries and a book of news events. She was almost always correct for any date since she was 11 years old. For one test, they asked her to give the date (e.g., April 7) for every Easter between 1980 and 2003. She was right on all but one and later corrected herself on that one. What makes this feat even more impressive is that she is Jewish and therefore doesn't celebrate Easter (Parker et al., 2006).

You might not want to have the detailed episodic memory of this woman, who says her memories so occupy her that she can hardly focus on the present. Still, it would be good to improve your memory for what you want to remember. Memory consists of three aspects—encoding the memory, storing and maintaining it, and retrieving it. The main point of this module is simple: When you want to retrieve a memory, it's too late if you didn't encode it well in the first place. To improve your memory, improve the way you study.

ENCODING

If you want to memorize a definition, would you repeat it over and over? Other things being equal, repetition helps, but repetition by itself is a poor study method.

To illustrate, examine Figure 7.9, which shows a real U.S. penny and 14 fakes. If you live in the United States, you have seen pennies countless times, but can you now identify the real one? Most U.S. citizens guess wrong (Nickerson & Adams, 1979). (If you do not have a penny in your pocket, check answer B on page 258. If you are not from the United States, try drawing the front or back of a common coin in your own country.) In short, mere repetition, such as looking at a coin many times, does not guarantee a strong memory.

Meaningfulness and Other Influences on Encoding

One of the most powerful influences on how well you encode a memory is obvious: attention. Your working memory can deal with a limited amount of information, and even a mild distraction interferes with learning. Older adults are particularly vulnerable to the effects of distraction (Stevens,

Most actors preparing for a play spend much time thinking about the meaning of what they will say (a deep level of processing) instead of just repeating the words.

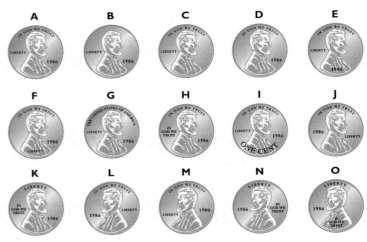

Figure 7.9 Can you spot the genuine penny among 14 fakes? (From "Long-term memory for a common object" by R. S. Nickerson and M. J. Adams in *Cognitive Psychology*, 1979, pp. 287–307. Reprinted by permission of Elsevier.)

People recall emotionally arousing events in great detail, although not always accurately.

slapping schoolchildren's hands with a stick to make them pay attention.

Many people report intense, detailed "flashbulb" memories of hearing highly emotional news, in which they remember where they were, what they were doing, and even the weather and other irrelevant details. However, although flashbulb memories are intense, they are not always accurate. In one study, U.S. students reported their memories of where they were, what they were doing, and so forth at the time of hearing about the terrorist attacks on September 11, 2001. They reported their memories on the day after the attacks and then again weeks or months later. Over time, the students continued to report highly vivid memories, but their accuracy gradually declined (Talarico & Rubin, 2003).

Emotional arousal affects memory in at least two ways. First, emotional arousal increases the release of the hormones cortisol and epinephrine (adrenaline) from the adrenal gland. Moderate increases in cortisol and epinephrine stimulate the amygdala and other brain areas that enhance memory storage (Andreano & Cahill, 2006).

Second, if you feel emotion when you recall something, the emotion increases your confidence that the memory must be right. In one study, people viewed a series of neutral and unpleasant photos. Then they examined another series of photos and tried to identify which ones had been in the first set and which ones were new. They were equally accurate at identifying neutral and unpleasant photos, but they reported greater confidence in their memory for the unpleasant ones (Sharot, Delgado, & Phelps, 2004).

Hasher, Chiew, & Grady, 2008). We consider attention in more detail in chapter 8.

Emotional arousal also enhances memory encoding. Chances are you vividly remember your first day of college, your first kiss, the time your team won the big game, and times you were frightened. Extreme panic interferes with memory, but emotion within normal limits benefits memory.

The effects of arousal on memory have been known for centuries. In England in the early 1600s, when people sold land, they did not yet have the custom of recording the sale on paper. Paper was expensive and few people could read anyway. Instead, local residents would gather while someone announced the sale and instructed everyone to remember it. Of all those present, whose memory of the sale was most important? The children, because they would live the longest. And of all those present, who were least interested? Right, again, it's the children. To increase the chances that the children would remember, the adults would kick them while telling them about the business deal. The same idea persisted in the custom, still common in the early 1900s, of

9. Most people with posttraumatic stress disorder have lower than normal levels of cortisol. What would you predict about their memory?

Answer

9. Because of the lower cortisol levels, they should have trouble storing memories and therefore report frequent memory lapses.

In addition to attention and emotion, many other factors influence how well you store your memories. To illustrate, read the following list, close the book, and write as many of the words as you can. The demonstration would work better if you saw the words one at a time on a screen. You can approximate that procedure by covering the list with a sheet of paper and pulling it down to reveal one word at a time.

LEMON
GRAPE
POTATO
COCONUT
CUCUMBER
TOMATO
BROCCOLI
APPLE
SPINACH
TOMATO
ORANGE
LETTUCE
CARROT
STRAWBERRY
BANANA
TOMATO
PEACH
NAKED
LIME
PINEAPPLE
TURNIP
MANGO
TOMATO
BLUEBERRY
TOMATO
APRICOT
WATERMELON

© UPI/Bettmann/CORBIS

© Remi Benali/Gamma Presse

Bob Williams was one of 40 aging former paratroopers who reenacted his parachute jump on the 50th anniversary of D-Day. We forget most events from long ago but remember the most distinctive ones.

I hope you tried the demonstration. If so, TO-MATO was probably one of the words you remembered because it occurred five times instead of just once. Other things being equal, repetition helps. But all other things are not equal. You probably also remembered LEMON and WATER-MELON because they were the first and last items on the list. The **primacy effect** *is the tendency to remember well the first items.* The **recency effect** *is the tendency to remember the final items.* The primacy and recency effects are robust for almost any type of memory. If you try to list all the people you have ever dated, all the vacations you have ever taken, or all the sporting events you have ever watched, you will probably include the earliest ones and the most recent.

You probably also remembered CARROT and NAKED. The word CARROT was distinctive because of its size, color, and font. NAKED stood out as the only item on the list that was neither a fruit nor a vegetable. In a list of mostly similar items, the distinctive ones are easier to remember. We also tend to remember unusual people. If you meet several men of ordinary appearance with similar names, like John Stevens, Steve

Johnson, and Joe Stevenson, you will have trouble remembering their names. You will more quickly remember a 7-foot-tall, redheaded man named Stinky Rockefeller.

You might not have remembered MANGO if you didn't grow up eating mangoes in childhood. People find it easier to remember words they learned in early childhood (e.g., APPLE, ORANGE, and BANANA) than words they learned later (Juhasz, 2005). Similarly, if you grew up watching *Sesame Street,* you can probably name Bert, Ernie, and Oscar the Grouch more quickly than most of the characters you have watched on television more recently.

Did you remember the word LIME? Probably not, because it came right after the word NAKED. When people see an unexpected sex-related word, it grabs attention so strongly that they pay less attention to the next word and sometimes up to the next four or five words (Arnell, Killman, & Fijavz, 2007). The effect would be even stronger if you were watching a series of slides, and one of them had a photo of naked people. Some people also forget the word that came *before* a highly emotional word or image (Strange, Kroes, Roiser, Yan, & Dolan, 2008).

....

10. What are some factors that increase or decrease your probability of remembering a word on a list?

Answer

10. Moderate emotion enhances memory and distraction impairs it. Memory is enhanced by repetition, distinctiveness, and being either first or last on a list. We also tend to remember words we learned early in life more easily than those we learned later.

....

Let's try another demonstration. Below are two lists. As you read through one of the lists—I don't care which one—repeat each word for a couple of seconds. So, if the word were "insect," you would say, "Insect, insect, insect . . ." and then proceed to the next word. For the other list, imagine yourself stranded in the middle of a vast grassland in some foreign country, where you need to find food and water and protect yourself from snakes, lions, and whatever other dangers might appear. As you go through the list, again spend a couple of seconds on each word, thinking about how useful it would be for survival under these conditions. Give it a rating from 1 (useless) to 5 (extremely valuable). You choose whether to do the repetition list first or the rating for survival list first.

List A	List B
toothbrush	firecracker
thermometer	rollerblades
marionette	umbrella
jewelry	hammock
tuxedo	binoculars
washcloth	encyclopedia
bandage	saxophone
trampoline	camera
metronome	mirror
flashlight	scissors
chain	string
knife	bottle
balloon	radio
carpet	envelope
overcoat	candy
matches	pencil

In experiments like this, people usually remember far more words from the survival list than from the repetition list (Nairne, Pandeirada, & Thompson, 2008; Nairne, Thompson, & Pandeirada, 2007). If, instead of rating the words for survival relevance, you rated them for pleasantness or for how much they pertain to your own experience, that procedure would help, too, but not as much as rating words for survival. Evidently, thinking about survival engages attention and memory better than anything else does. Certainly, it makes sense for our brains to have evolved this way.

Moreover, simply repeating the words is one of the least effective ways to study. According to the **levels-of-processing principle** (Craik & Lockhart, 1972), *how easily you retrieve a memory depends on the number and types of associations you form.* When you read a list or read a chapter, simply reading the words without much thought is "shallow processing," which produces only weak, fleeting memories. Alternatively, you might stop and consider various points that you read, relate them to your own experiences, and think of your own examples to illustrate each principle. The more ways you think about the material, the deeper is your processing and the more easily you will remember later. Because you form many associations, many possible *reminders*—called **retrieval cues**—will stimulate your memory later. Table 7.3 summarizes this model.

....

11. Many students who get the best grades in a course read the assigned text chapters more slowly than average. Why?

Table 7.3 Levels-of-Processing Model of Memory

Superficial processing	Simply repeat the material to be remembered: "Hawk, Oriole, Tiger, Timberwolf, Blue Jay, Bull."
Deeper processing	Think about each item. Note that two start with T and two with B.
Still deeper processing	Note that three are birds and three are mammals. Also, three are major league baseball teams and three are NBA basketball teams. Use whichever associations mean the most to you.

Students who pause to think about the meaning are engaging in deep processing. They will remember the material better than those who read a chapter quickly.

Encoding Specificity

When you encode something, you form associations. According to the **encoding specificity principle** (Tulving & Thomson, 1973), *the associations you form at the time of learning will be the most effective retrieval cues later* (Figure 7.10). Here is an example (modified from Thieman, 1984). First, read the pairs of words (which psychologists call *paired associates*) in Table 7.4A. Then turn to Table 7.4B on page 252. For each of the words on that list, try to recall a related word on the list you just read. *Please do this now.* (The answers are on page 258, answer C.)

Most people find this task difficult. Because they initially coded the word *cardinal* as a type of clergyman, for example, they do not think of it when they see the retrieval cue *bird*. If they had thought of it as a bird, then *clergyman* would not have been a good reminder.

The principle of encoding specificity extends to other aspects of experience at the time of storage. In one study, college students who were fluent in both English and Russian were given a list of words such as *summer, birthday,* and *doctor,* some in English and some in Russian. For each word, they were asked to describe any related event they remembered. In response to Russian words, they recalled mostly events that happened

Table 7.4A

Clergyman—Cardinal	Geometry—Plane
Trinket—Charm	Tennis—Racket
Type of wine—Port	Music—Rock
U.S. politician—Bush	Magic—Spell
Inch—Foot	Envelope—Seal
Computer—Apple	Graduation—Degree

when they were speaking Russian. In response to English words, they recalled mostly events when they were speaking English (Marian & Neisser, 2000).

More examples: If you experience something while you are sad, you will recall it better when you are sad again (Eich & Macaulay, 2000). If you learn something while frightened, you will recall it better when you are frightened again, and if you learn while calm, you will remember better when calm (Lang, Craske, Brown, & Ghaneian, 2001). Strong drugs can induce this effect also. **State-dependent memory** is *the tendency to remember something better if your body is in the same condition during recall as it was during the original learning.* State-dependent memory, however, is a fragile and inconsistent effect (Eich, 1995; Mitte, 2008).

The encoding specificity principle has this implication: If you want to remember something at a particular time and place, make your study conditions similar to the conditions when you will try to remember. However, if you want to remember something always, then you should vary your study habits.

12. Suppose someone cannot remember what happened at a party last night. What steps might help improve the memory? Concept Check

Answer

12. Often, someone who claims not to remember simply does not want to talk about it. Presuming the person really wants to remember, it would help to return to the place of the party with the same people present, perhaps even at the same time of day. If he or she used alcohol or other drugs, take them again. The more similar the conditions of original learning and later recall, the better the probability of remembering.

Figure 7.10 According to the principle of encoding specificity, how you code a word during learning determines which cues will remind you of that word later. If you think of the word *queen* as *queen bee,* then the cue *playing card* will not remind you of it later. If you think of the *queen of England,* then *chess piece* will not be a good reminder.

Table 7.4B

Instructions: For each of these words, write one of the second of the paired terms from the list in Table 7.4a.

Animal—	Stone—
Part of body—	Personality—
Transportation—	Write—
Temperature—	Bird—
Crime—	Harbor—
Shrubbery—	Fruit—

THE TIMING OF STUDY SESSIONS

If you have an upcoming test, should you study a little at a time or wait until shortly before the test? You know that waiting until just before the test is risky. An unexpected interruption might prevent you from studying at all. Let's change the question to make the answer less obvious: Suppose you don't wait until the day before the test, but you nevertheless study all at once. Will your result be better, worse, or about the same as if you had studied a little at a time over several days?

The answer is that studying all at once is worse for every kind of material that researchers have tested (Cepeda, Pashler, Vul, Wixted, & Rohrer, 2006; Kornell & Bjork, 2008). Suppose you are trying to learn a foreign language. You study a list of words until you know their meanings. Now, you spend another 10 minutes going over the same list again and again. How much do you gain? The research says that the extra 10 minutes is almost completely wasted (Rohrer & Pashler, 2007). You would do much better to stop now and study another 10 minutes tomorrow.

If you are going to wait to study again, how long should you wait? As you might guess, it depends. If you want to remember something as well as possible a week after your initial study, you will get the best results if you review 1 day later. To remember something a month later, you should wait about 11 days before you review. To remember after a year, separate your study sessions by about 3 weeks. In each case, it is better to wait longer than the recommended time than to wait less (Cepeda, Vul, Rohrer, Wixted, & Pashler, 2008). Best of all, of course, is to review several times.

When you study something all at once, it *seems* that you are learning well because the material is so fresh in your memory at the time. However, people almost always underestimate how much they are going to forget (Koriat, Bjork, Sheffer, & Bar, 2004). To remember something well, you need to practice retrieving the memory—that is, finding it. While you are reading something over and over, it is so fresh in your memory that you gain no practice at retrieving it. If you go away and come back later, you need some effort to refresh the ideas, and that effort strengthens the memory.

You can gain some of that same advantage by alternating between reading and testing yourself. A test forces you to generate the material instead of passively reading it. Students in one experiment read a page about sea otters. Half of them spent the whole time rereading that page. The other half spent part of their time reading it and part taking a test (on which they received no feedback). Two days later, the group that took the test remembered more of the material (Roediger & Karpicke, 2006). The questions called their attention to details in the essay that they overlooked, and the act of generating answers helped solidify their memories.

....

13. So, why is it a good idea to answer Concept Checks like this one?

Answer

13. Practicing the retrieval of a memory strengthens it. Students who spent part of their study time answering test questions did better than those who spent the whole time reading.

....

Another reason for spreading out your study is that if you study under a variety of conditions, you remember under more conditions (Schmidt & Bjork, 1992). Varying the conditions of learning slows the original learning and makes the task seem more difficult, but in the long run, it helps. In one experiment, a group of 8-year-old children practiced throwing a small beanbag at a target on the floor 3 feet away. Another group practiced with a target sometimes 2 feet away and sometimes 4 feet away but never 3 feet away. Then both groups were tested with the target 3 feet away. The children who had been practicing with the 3-foot target missed it by a mean of 8.3 inches. The children who had been practicing with 2-foot and 4-foot targets actually did better, missing by a mean of only 5.4 inches, even though they were aiming at the 3-foot target for the first time (Kerr & Booth, 1978). In another experiment, young adults practiced a technique for mentally squaring two-digit numbers—for example, $23 \times 23 = 529$. Those who practiced with a small range of numbers

People need to monitor their understanding to decide whether to continue studying or whether they already understand it well enough. Most readers have trouble making that judgment correctly.

learned the technique quickly but forgot it quickly. Those who practiced with a wider range of numbers learned more slowly but remembered better later (Sanders, Gonzalez, Murphy, Pesta, & Bucur, 2002).

The conclusions: (a) It is hard to judge how well you have learned something if you haven't waited long enough to see how much you will forget. (b) Studying something once is seldom effective, no matter how hard you study that one time. (c) You will remember better if you test yourself. (d) Varying the conditions of studying improves long-term memory.

THE SPAR METHOD

One systematic way to organize your study is the SPAR method:

Survey. Get an overview of what the passage is about. Scan through it; look at the boldface headings; try to understand the organization and goals of the passage.

Process meaningfully. Think about how you could use the ideas or how they relate to other things you know. Evaluate the strengths and weaknesses of the argument. The more you think about what you read, the better you will remember it.

Ask questions. If the text provides questions, like the Concept Checks in this text, answer them. Then pretend you are the instructor, write questions you would ask on a test, and answer them yourself. In the process, you discover which sections of the passage you need to reread.

Review. Wait a day or more and retest your knowledge. Spreading out your study over time increases your ability to remember the material.

14. If you want to do well on the final exam in this course, what should you do now—review this chapter or review the first three chapters in the book?

15. How does the advice to spread out your study over a long time instead of doing it all at one sitting fit or contrast with the encoding specificity principle?

Answers

14. To prepare well for the final exam, you should review all the material at irregular intervals. You might profit by skimming chapters 1, 2, and 3 right now. Of course, if you have a test on chapter 7 in a day or two, your goal and your strategy are different.

15. The ideas are compatible. If you study all at one sitting, you encode the memory to what you are thinking about at that time. If you study at several times, the memory attaches to a greater variety of retrieval cues.

MNEMONIC DEVICES

If you need to memorize something lengthy and not especially exciting—for example, a list of all the bones in the body—how would you do it? One effective strategy is to attach systematic retrieval cues to each term so that you can remind yourself of the terms when you need them.

A **mnemonic device** is *any memory aid that relies on encoding each item in a special way.* The word *mnemonic* (nee-MAHN-ik) comes from a Greek root meaning "memory." (The same root appears in the word *amnesia,* "lack of memory.") Some mnemonic devices are simple, such as "Every Good Boy Does Fine" to remember the notes EGBDF on the treble clef in music. If you have to remember the functions of various brain areas, you might try links like those shown in Figure 7.11 (Carney & Levin, 1998).

Suppose you had to memorize a list of Nobel Peace Prize winners (Figure 7.12). You might try making up a little story: "Dun (Dunant) passed (Passy) the Duke (Ducommun) of Gob (Gobat) some cream (Cremer). That made him internally ILL (Institute of International Law). He suited (von Suttner) up with some roses (Roosevelt) and spent some money (Moneta) on a Renault (Renault) . . ." You still have to study the names, but your story helps.

Another mnemonic device is the **method of loci** (method of places). *First, you memorize a series of places, and then you use a vivid image to associate*

Figure 7.11 One mnemonic device is to think of an image that will remind you of what you need to remember, such as the functions of different parts of the nervous system.

A parachute lets you coast down slowly, like the parasympathetic nervous system.

If the symphony excites you, it arouses your sympathetic nervous system.

each location with something you want to remember. For example, you might start by memorizing every location along the route from your dormitory room to your psychology classroom. Then you link the locations, in order, to the names.

Suppose the first three locations you pass are the desk in your room, the door to your room, and the corridor. To link the first Nobel Peace Prize winners, Dunant and Passy, to your desk, you might imagine a Monopoly game board on your desk with a big sign "DO NOT (Dunant) PASS (Passy) GO." Then you link the second pair of names to the second location, your door: A DUKE student (as in Ducommun) is standing at the door, giving confusing signals. He says "DO COME IN (Ducommun)" and "GO BACK (Gobat)." Then you link the corridor to Cremer, perhaps by imagining someone has spilled CREAM (Cremer) all over the floor (Figure 7.13). You continue in this manner until you have linked every name to a location. Now, if you can remember all those locations in order and if you have good visual images for each one, you can recite the list of Nobel Peace Prize winners.

Simpler mnemonic devices can help in many cases, such as remembering people's names. You might remember someone named Harry Moore by picturing him as "more hairy" than everyone else. If you want to recite a traditional wedding vow by memory, you might remember "BRISTLE" to remind you of "**B**etter or worse, **R**icher or poorer, **I**n **S**ickness and health, **T**o **L**ove and to cherish."

STORAGE

Most of the work of forming a memory pertains to encoding. Storing or maintaining a memory sounds like a passive process, but important things happen here, too. As time passes after initial learning, some memories change in ways that make them available much later, perhaps forever. This process is called consolidation, as mentioned earlier. As a memory consolidates, different brain

Nobel Peace Prize Winners

1901	H. Dunant and F. Passy
1902	E. Ducommun and A. Gobat
1903	Sir W. R. Cremer
1904	Institute of International Law
1905	Baroness von Suttner
1906	T. Roosevelt
1907	E. T. Moneta and L. Renault
1908	K. P. Arnoldson and F. Bajer
1909	A. M. F. Beernaert and Baron d'Estournelles de Constant

1998	John Hume and David Trimble
1999	Doctors Without Borders
2000	Kim Dae Jung
2001	Kofi Annan
2002	Jimmy Carter, Jr.
2003	Shirin Ebadi
2004	Wangari Maathai
2005	International Atomic Energy Agency and Mohamed ElBaradei
2006	Mohammad Yunus
2007	Al Gore and the Intergovernmental Panel on Climate Change
2008	Martti Ahtisaari

Figure 7.12 A list of Nobel Peace Prize winners: Mnemonic devices can be useful when people try to memorize long lists like this one.

Figure 7.13 With the method of loci, you first learn a list of places, such as "my desk, the door of my room, the corridor, . . ." Then you link each place to an item on a list.

areas become essential for its storage, as we shall consider in the next module.

Decades ago, psychologists imagined consolidation as a simple process that took a fixed amount of time. Gradually, researchers discovered it to be a diverse and complicated process (Meeter & Murre, 2004). Some memories consolidate much more easily than others. When you hear, "Jakarta is the capital of Indonesia," you might have to repeat this fact several times, spread out over days or weeks, to form a lasting memory. If someone tells you, "Yes, I will go with you to the dance on Friday," you store the memory almost immediately. If you have a strong interest and background in some topic, you learn new information on that topic quickly compared to a topic that is new to you. Something similar is true of rats: If they have had previous training on a particular kind of problem, they quickly learn to solve similar problems, and they remember it well later (Tse et al., 2007).

How long does consolidation continue? Certain kinds of evidence suggest that it continues for decades, but the interpretation of that evidence is ambiguous. Several studies have found that people in their 60s and 70s remember events from their adolescence and early adulthood better than more recent events (Haist, Gore, & Mao, 2001; Maguire & Frith, 2003; Niki & Luo, 2002). For example, older adults generally remember the music, movies, and politicians from their youth better than they remember comparable items from recent years. Possibly, memories continue to consolidate over a lifetime, or perhaps they form more strongly when people are younger (Berntsen & Rubin, 2002).

. . . .

16. Which kinds of memory consolidate fastest?

Answer

16. If you already know a topic well, you learn and consolidate new information about it quickly. If something is highly interesting and important to you, you consolidate that material rapidly also.

. . . .

RETRIEVAL

If you store a book on a library shelf, you can retrieve the book intact and the same as when you put it there. Human memory isn't the same. When you try to retrieve a memory of some experience, you will start with the details that you remember clearly and reconstruct the rest to fill in the gaps: *During an original experience, we con-* *struct a memory. When we try to retrieve that memory, we reconstruct an account based partly on surviving memories and partly on our expectations of what must have happened.* For example, you might recall studying in the library three nights ago. With a little effort, you might remember where you sat, what you were reading, who sat next to you, and where you went for a snack afterward. If you aren't quite sure, you fill in the gaps with what usually happens during an evening at the library. Within weeks, you gradually forget that evening, and if you try to remember it, you will rely more and more on "what must have happened," omitting more and more details (Schmolck, Buffalo, & Squire, 2000). If you happen to fall in love with the person who sat next to you that evening, the evening is important enough to become a lifetime memory. Still, when you try to recall it, you reconstruct the details. You remember where you went for a snack and some of what the two of you said, but if you want to recall the book you were reading, you have to reason it out: "Let's see, that semester I was taking a chemistry course that took a lot of study, so maybe I was reading a chemistry book. No, wait, I remember. When we went out to eat, we talked about politics. So maybe I was reading my political science text."

Reconstruction and Inference in List Memory

Try this demonstration: Read the words in list A once; then turn away from the list, pause for a few seconds, and write as many of the words as you can remember. Repeat the same procedure for list B. *Please do this now, before reading the following paragraph.*

List A	List B
bed	candy
rest	sour
weep	sugar
tired	dessert
dream	salty
wake	taste
snooze	flavor
keep	bitter
doze	cookies
steep	fruits
snore	chocolate
nap	yummy

After you have written your lists, check how many of the words you got right. If you omitted many, you are normal. The point of this demonstration is not how many you got right but whether you included *sleep* on the first list or *sweet* on the second. Many people include one of these words (which are not on the lists), and some do so with confidence (Deese, 1959; Roediger & McDermott, 1995; Watson, Balota, & Roediger, 2003). Apparently, while learning the individual words, people also learn the gist of what they are all about, and when they are trying to retrieve the list later, they reconstruct a memory of a word that the list implied (Seamon et al., 2002). We reconstruct what "must have" been on the list.

In list B, *sweet* is related to the other words in meaning. In list A, *sleep* is related to most of the words in meaning, and the list also includes three words that rhyme with sleep (*weep, keep,* and *steep*). This combined influence is even more effective, producing false recall in a higher percentage of people. Young children are particularly prone to the effects of rhyming words and less sensitive to words with related meanings (Dewhurst & Robinson, 2004).

If you did not include *sleep* or *sweet,* try an Online Try It Yourself activity False Memories. Hearing a list (as you can with the online demonstration) produces a bigger effect than reading a list. Of course, the effect will also be weaker because now you have been warned about what to expect (Roediger & McDermott, 2000; Westerberg & Marsolek, 2006).

This effect occurs mainly when people have a memory of intermediate strength. If a list is short or if you learn it well, you do not add an extra word not on the list. However, if you had such a defective memory that you could not remember any of the words on the list, you could not use them to infer another word on the list, and again you would not show a false memory (Schacter, Verfaellie, Anes, & Racine, 1998).

17. If you studied a list such as "candy, sour, sugar, dessert, salty, taste, . . . " thoroughly instead of hearing it just once, would you be more likely or less likely to include "sweet," which isn't on the list? Why?

Answer

17. You would be less likely to add a word not on the list. We rely on inferences mostly when the actual memory is weak.

Reconstructing Stories

Suppose you listen to a story about a teenager's day, including both normal events (watching television) and oddities (parking a bicycle in the kitchen). Which would you remember better—the normal events or the oddities? It depends. If you are tested immediately, while your memory is still strong, you remember the unusual and distinctive events best. However, as you start forgetting the story, you begin to omit the unlikely events, reconstructing a more typical day for the teenager, including likely events that the story omitted, such as "the teenager went to school in the morning." In short, the less certain your memory is, the more you rely on your expectations (Heit, 1993; Maki, 1990). If you retell something repeatedly—either a story you heard or an event from your own experience—the retellings gradually become more coherent (Ackil, Van Abbema, & Bauer, 2003; Bartlett, 1932). They make more sense because you rely more on the gist, keeping the details that fit the overall theme and omitting or modifying the others.

In a study that highlights the role of expectations, U.S. and Mexican adults tried to recall three stories. Some were given U.S. versions of the stories, and others were given Mexican versions. (For example, in the "going on a date" story, the Mexican version had the man's sister go along as a chaperone.) On the average, U.S. participants remembered the U.S. versions better, whereas Mexicans remembered the Mexican versions better (R. J. Harris, Schoen, & Hensley, 1992). This is one way culture influences memory.

18. In books about history, it seems that one event led to another in a logical order, but in everyday life, events seem illogical, unconnected, and unpredictable. Why?

Answer

18. Long after the fact, a historian puts together a coherent story based on the gist of events, emphasizing details that fit the pattern and omitting others. In your everyday life, you are aware of all the facts, including those that do not fit any pattern.

Hindsight Bias

Three weeks before the impeachment trial of U.S. President Clinton in 1999, college students were asked to predict the outcome. On the average, they estimated the probability of a conviction at 50.5%. A week and a half after Clinton was not convicted, they were asked, "What would you have said 4 $\frac{1}{2}$ weeks ago was the chance [of a conviction]?" On the average, they reported a 42.8% estimate (Bryant & Guilbault, 2002). Their behavior illustrates **hindsight bias,** *the tendency to mold our recollection of the past to fit how*

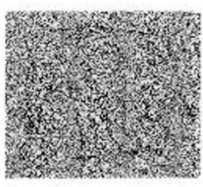

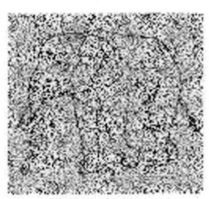

events later turned out. Something happens and we then say, "I *knew* that was going to happen!"

Another example: As you can see in Figure 7.14, an image gradually morphs from a blur to an elephant. At what point do you think the average person would identify it as an elephant? It is hard to imagine not knowing it will be an elephant. On this and similar sequences, most people overestimate how soon people will recognize the image (Bernstein, Atance, Loftus, & Meltzoff, 2004). That is, they show hindsight bias.

Hindsight bias affects judgments in legal cases. In one study, people were told about the possible hazards of a train going around a mountain track. Some participants were asked whether the company should cease operations for safety reasons. One third said "yes." The other participants were told, in addition, that a train had derailed, spilling toxic chemicals into a river. They were asked whether the company should pay punitive damages for irresponsibly continuing operations in spite of foreseeable dangers. Two thirds said "yes" (Hastie, Schkade, & Payne, 1999). That is, after people knew about the accident, they thought it was foreseeable.

Hindsight bias is not altogether irrational. When you make a prediction, you receive a huge array of information, some of it unimportant or wrong. When you get the outcome, you reasonably conclude that the information that had pointed in the correct direction was the best. You want to focus on that information so you can pay more attention to it in the future (Hoffrage, Hertwig, & Gigerenzer, 2000). In the process, you convince yourself that you were already strongly influenced by that information.

Figure 7.14 At what point in this sequence do you think the average person would recognize it as an elephant? (Source: From Bernstein, Atance, Loftus, & Meltzoff, 2004)

7.2  module

In Closing

Improving Your Memory

If you would like to improve your memory for something that happened years ago, what could you do? Not much. You might try returning to the place where the event happened or finding some other reminder, but your prospects for finding a lost memory are limited. To improve your memory, by far the best strategy is to improve your storage. Think carefully about anything you want to remember, study it under a variety of conditions, and review frequently.

SUMMARY

- *Influences on memory encoding.* Moderate emotion enhances memory encoding, and distraction impairs it. Memory is best for the first and last items of a list, anything that is unusual, and items familiar since childhood. (page 247)
- *Levels of processing.* A memory becomes stronger and easier to recall if you think about the meaning of the material and relate it to other material. A memory is particularly enhanced if you think about how it could pertain to your survival. (page 250)
- *Encoding specificity.* When you form a memory, you store it with links to the way you thought about it at the time. When you try to recall the memory, a cue is most effective if it resembles the links you formed at the time of storage. (page 251)
- *Timing of study.* Spreading out your study is more effective than a single session for several reasons. During a single session, you underestimate how much you will forget later, and you ordinarily do not get to practice retrieving a memory because it is still fresh. Also, studying at several times provides a variety of cues that will be helpful in retrieval. (page 252)
- *Advantages of testing.* Someone who alternates between reading and testing remembers the material better than someone who spent the same amount of time just reading. (page 252)
- *The SPAR method.* One method to improve study is to Survey, Process meaningfully, Ask questions, and Review. (page 253)
- *Mnemonics.* Specialized techniques for using systematic retrieval cues help people remember lists of items. (page 253)
- *Storage and consolidation.* Whereas some memories are lost, others gradually strengthen and change. (page 254)
- *Retrieval.* Few memories are recalled intact. Ordinarily, we recall parts of an event and fill in the rest with logical reconstructions. (page 255)
- *Reconstructions from a word list.* If people read or hear a list of related words and try to recall them, they are likely to include closely related words that were not on the list. They have remembered the gist and reconstructed what else must have been on the list. (page 255)
- *Story memory.* Someone who tries to retell a story after memory of the details has faded relies on the gist, omits details that seemed irrelevant, and adds or changes other facts to fit the logic of the story. (page 256)
- *Hindsight bias.* People often revise their memories, saying that how an event turned out was what they expected all along. (page 257)

KEY TERMS

encoding specificity principle (page 251)

hindsight bias (page 257)

levels-of-processing principle (page 250)

method of loci (page 253)

mnemonic device (page 253)

primacy effect (page 249)

recency effect (page 249)

reconstruction (page 255)

retrieval cue (page 250)

SPAR method (page 253)

state-dependent memory (page 251)

ANSWERS TO OTHER QUESTIONS IN THE MODULE

B. The correct coin is A. (page 247)

C. Animal—Seal; Part of body—Foot; Transportation—Plane; Temperature—Degree; Crime—Racket; Shrubbery—Bush; Stone—Rock; Personality—Charm; Write—Spell; Bird—Cardinal; Harbor—Port; Fruit—Apple. (page 251)

Forgetting

> • Why is memory retrieval sometimes difficult?
>
> • Why do we sometimes report confident but inaccurate memories?
>
> • Why do some people have severe memory problems?

He: We met at nine.

She: We met at eight.

He: I was on time.

She: No, you were late.

He: Ah, yes! I remember it well. We dined with friends.

She: We dined alone.

He: A tenor sang.

She: A baritone.

He: Ah, yes! I remember it well. That dazzling April moon!

She: There was none that night. And the month was June.

He: That's right! That's right!

She: It warms my heart to know that you remember still the way you do.

He: Ah, yes! I remember it well.

—"I Remember It Well" from the musical *Gigi*. ("I Remember It Well" lyrics by Alan Jay Lerner. Music by Frederick Loewe. Copyright © 1957, 1958 (renewed) Chappell & Co. All rights reserved. Used by permission of Alfred Publishing Co., Inc.)

We all forget, and forgetting doesn't surprise us. A little more surprising is the fact that sometimes we think we remember something clearly, though we are wrong. Here we explore some of the ways that memory fails.

RETRIEVAL AND INTERFERENCE

Human memory sometimes confuses the sought material with similar information. The first experimental demonstration of this principle was accidental. Remember Hermann Ebbinghaus, who pioneered memory research. Ebbinghaus measured how long he could remember various lists of 13 nonsense syllables. The results appear as the green line on Figure 7.15. On the average, he forgot more than half of each list within the first hour (Ebbinghaus, 1885/1913). What a discouraging graph! If people typically forget that fast, then education would be pointless. However, most college students remember nearly 90% of a list of nonsense syllables 24 hours later, as shown in the purple line of Figure 7.15 (Koppenaal, 1963).

Why do you suppose most college students remember a list so much better than Ebbinghaus did? You may be tempted to say that college students are very intelligent. Well, yes, but Ebbinghaus was no dummy either. Or you might suggest that college students "have had so much practice at memorizing nonsense." (Sorry if you think so.) The explanation is the opposite: Ebbinghaus had memorized *too much* nonsense—thousands of lists of syllables. If you memorize large amounts of similar material, your memory becomes

Ebbinghaus quickly forgot new lists of nonsense syllables because of interference from all the previous lists he had learned.

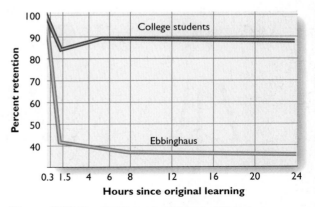

Figure 7.15 Recall of lists of syllables by Ebbinghaus (1885/1913) and by college students after delays of various lengths (based on Koppenaal, 1963). Ebbinghaus learned as fast as other people but forgot faster.

like a cluttered room: The clutter doesn't prevent you from bringing in still more clutter, but it interferes with finding the item you want. Ebbinghaus forgot new lists quickly because of interference from older lists.

If you learn several sets of related materials, the old interferes with the new and the new interferes with the old. The *old materials increase forgetting of the new materials* through **proactive interference** (acting forward in time). The *new materials increase forgetting of the old materials* through **retroactive interference** (acting backward in time). Figure 7.16 contrasts the two kinds of interference.

Interference is a major cause of forgetting. You forget where you parked your car because of proactive interference from all the previous times you parked your car. You forget last week's French vocabulary list because of retroactive interference from this week's list.

- - - - - - - - - -

19. Professor Tryhard learns the names of his students every semester. After several years, he learns them as quickly as ever but forgets them faster. Does he forget because of retroactive or proactive interference?

20. Remember the concept of spontaneous recovery from chapter 6? Can you explain it in terms of proactive interference? (Hint: Original learning comes first and extinction comes second. What would happen if the first interfered with the second?)

21. How does interference explain the primacy effect and recency effect in list learning?

Concept Check

Answers

19. It is due to proactive interference—interference from memories learned earlier.

20. First, someone learns the response; the second learning is the extinction of the response. If the first learning proactively interferes with the later extinction, spontaneous recovery will result.

21. The first item on a list is spared from proactive interference. The last is spared from retroactive interference. However, low interference is not the only explanation for these effects.

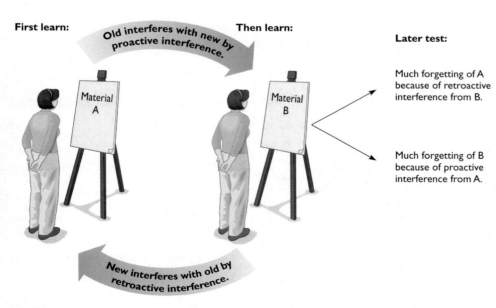

First learn: *Old interferes with new by proactive interference.* **Then learn:**

Material A

Material B

Later test:

Much forgetting of A because of retroactive interference from B.

Much forgetting of B because of proactive interference from A.

New interferes with old by retroactive interference.

Figure 7.16 If you learn similar sets of materials, each interferes with retrieval of the other.

A CONTROVERSY: "RECOVERED MEMORIES" OR "FALSE MEMORIES"?

Frequently when you forget something, the memory is not totally lost. If you had less interference or if you had the right reminder, the memory could come back. Would it be possible for therapists to help people recover lost memories of important, possibly traumatic, experiences?

Suppose someone tells a therapist about vague unpleasant feelings, and the therapist replies, "Symptoms like yours are usually found among people who were abused, especially sexually abused, in childhood. Do you think you were?" In some cases, although the client says "no," the therapist persists: "The fact that you can't remember doesn't mean that it didn't happen. It may have been so painful that you repressed the memory." The therapist recommends hypnosis, repeated attempts to remember, or other techniques. A few sessions later, the client says, "It's starting to come back to me. . . . I think I do remember. . . . " Most therapists would not use such aggressive techniques to try to recover old memories, but some do. *Reports of long-lost memories, prompted by clinical techniques,* are known as **recovered memories.**

Sexual abuse in childhood does occur, and no one knows how often. Some abused children develop long-lasting psychological scars. But when people claim to recover long-forgotten memories, has the therapist uncovered the truth, distorted the truth, or convinced the client to believe something that never happened? Since the early 1990s, this issue has been one of the most heated debates in psychology.

Some reports are bizarre. In one case, two sisters accused their father of repeatedly raping them both vaginally and anally, bringing his friends over on Friday nights to rape them, and forcing them to participate in satanic rituals that included cannibalism and the slaughter of babies (Wright, 1994). The sisters had not remembered any of these events until repeated sessions with a therapist. In another case, a group of 3- and 4-year-old children, after repeated urgings from a therapist, accused their Sunday school teacher of sexually abusing them with a curling iron, forcing them to drink blood and urine, hanging them upside down from a chandelier, dunking them in toilets, and killing an elephant and a giraffe during Sunday school class (M. Gardner, 1994). No one found any physical evidence to support the claims, such as scarred tissues or giraffe bones.

Even when recovered-memory claims are much less bizarre, their accuracy is uncertain. Researchers studied two groups of adults—some who spontaneously remembered an episode of childhood sexual abuse that they hadn't thought about in years, and some who recovered a memory during therapy. In most cases, when someone spontaneously reported a long-lost memory, investigators found supporting evidence, such as other people who reported being abused by the same perpetrator. For the people who reported recovering a memory only as a result of therapy, investigators could not find supporting evidence in a single case (Geraerts et al., 2007).

When people have abusive experiences, are they likely to forget them for years? And is it possible to persuade someone to "remember" an event that never actually happened just by suggesting it?

Memory for Traumatic Events

Sigmund Freud, whom we consider more fully in chapter 14, introduced the term **repression** as *the process of moving an unbearably unacceptable memory or impulse from the conscious mind to the unconscious mind.* Although many therapists continue to use the concept of repression, researchers have found no clear evidence for the idea (Holmes, 1990). Experiments designed to demonstrate repression have produced small, ambiguous effects that do not necessarily require the concept of repression. Many clinicians now prefer the term **dissociation**, referring to *memory that one has stored but cannot retrieve* (Alpert, Brown, & Courtois, 1998). However, most of the doubts about the term *repression* also apply to the similar concept of *dissociation*.

Do people ever forget highly emotional events? It depends on what we mean by "forget." Students in one experiment viewed 24 lists of words. Each list had a distinct category. For example, one was a list of 10 tools. Most of the lists were normal sorts of categories, but one was a list of "dirty" words. I won't give you examples, but you can probably guess. If you went through this procedure, and then the researcher asked you to name the categories, wouldn't you be sure to remember that one list was a bunch of dirty words? Ordinarily, yes, but after reading through all 24 lists once, the students had a distractor task and then examined 21 of the lists again—not including the dirty words. Then when they were asked to name the categories of all the 24 lists they had read, most of them forgot to mention "dirty words." So, does this result mean that the students managed to forget this presumably emotional experience? Not exactly. When they were reminded that they had read a list of dirty words, most said,

"Oh, yeah," and then recited most of the words on that list (S. M. Smith & Moynan, 2008). This study illustrates the difficulty psychologists sometimes encounter in determining whether something was really forgotten or not.

What about traumatic events? One study examined 16 children who had witnessed the murder of one of their parents. All had recurring nightmares and haunting thoughts of the experience, and none had forgotten (Malmquist, 1986). Other studies have examined prisoners of war who had been severely mistreated (Merckelbach, Dekkers, Wessel, & Roefs, 2003), children who had been kidnapped or forced to participate in pornographic movies (Terr, 1988), and people with other horrible experiences. People almost always remembered the events, or they forgot only about as much as one might expect for childhood events. Evidently, if repression of traumatic experiences occurs at all, it does so only under rare and undefined circumstances.

Memory for a traumatic experience depends on someone's age at the time of the event, its severity, and the reaction of other family members. Several studies examined young adult women who had been victims of childhood sexual abuse, documented by either hospital records or criminal proceedings. In each study, those who were older at the time of the offense remembered it better than those who were younger. Memory was better among those who had more severe or repeated abuse and those who received more family support and encouragement (Alexander et al., 2005; Goodman et al., 2003; L. M. Williams, 1994). These results suggest that early traumatic memories are similar to other memories. They also suggest that repression of such memories is rare, if it occurs at all.

Areas of Agreement and Disagreement

Psychologists agree that some people do not remember abusive childhood experiences. However, in most of these cases, the abusive events happened in early childhood, a period that most people remember poorly or not at all. Even when someone does forget a horrible experience, the question is why. Many clinicians believe that repression or dissociation is a possible explanation. If so, then attempts to recover the memory are at least a theoretical possibility (Alpert et al., 1998). (Whether recovering them would be *beneficial* is uncertain.) The alternative view, favored by most memory researchers, is that traumatic memories are like other memories: If we don't think about something for a long time, we find it harder to retrieve, and if we try to reconstruct the event later, the result is a mixture of truth and distortion.

22. Based on material earlier in this chapter, why should we expect traumatic events to be remembered better than most other events?

Concept Check

Answer

22. Emotionally arousing memories are usually more memorable than other events. Any emotionally arousing event stimulates cortisol release and in other ways activates the amygdala, a brain area that helps store memories.

What's the Evidence?

Suggestions and False Memories

Critics of attempts to recover lost memories have suggested that a therapist who repeatedly encourages a client to recall lost memories can unintentionally implant a **false memory** (or false report), *a report that someone believes to be a memory but that does not correspond to real events* (Lindsay & Read, 1994; Loftus, 1993). Early research found that asking misleading questions about a videotape, such as "Did you see the children getting on the school bus?" caused many people falsely to report that they remembered seeing a school bus (Loftus, 1975). Could an experimenter mislead people into reporting false memories for their own lives? Let's examine two experiments.

First Study

Hypothesis People who are told about a childhood event will come to remember it as something they experienced, even if in fact they did not.

Method The participants, aged 18 to 53, were told that the study concerned their childhood memories. Each participant was given paragraphs describing four events. Three of the events had actually happened. (The experimenters had contacted parents to get descriptions of childhood events.) A fourth event was a plausible but false story about getting lost. An example for one Vietnamese woman: "You, your Mom, Tien, and Tuan, all went to the Bremerton Kmart. You must have been 5 years old at the time. Your Mom gave each of you some money to get a blueberry ICEE. You ran ahead to get into the line first, and somehow lost your way in the store. Tien found you crying to an elderly Chinese woman. You three then went together to get an ICEE." After reading the four paragraphs, each participant was asked to write whatever additional details he or she could remember of the event. Participants were asked to try again 1 week later and then again after another week (Loftus, Feldman, & Dashiell, 1995).

Results Of 24 participants, 6 reported remembering the suggested false event. Participants generally described these events in fewer words than their correct memories, but some did provide additional details. The woman in the foregoing example said, "I vaguely remember walking around Kmart crying and looking for Tien and Tuan. I thought I was lost forever. I went to the shoe department, because we always spent a lot of time there. I went to the handkerchief place because we were there last. I circled all over the store it seemed 10 times. I just remember walking around crying. I do not remember the Chinese woman, or the ICEE (but it would be raspberry ICEE if I was getting an ICEE) part. I don't even remember being found."

Interpretation A suggestion can provoke some people to report a personal experience in moderate detail, even though the event never happened. Granted, the suggestion influenced only a quarter of the people tested, and most of them reported only vague memories. Still, the researchers achieved this effect after only a single brief suggestion. In a similar study, 13 of 47 participants reported detailed false memories of getting lost or getting attacked by an animal or another child, and 18 more participants reported partial recollection (Porter, Birt, Yuille, & Lehman, 2000). After a suggestion that "you got sick as a child after eating egg salad," many participants avoided eating egg salad for months afterward (Geraerts et al., 2008).

One objection is that perhaps these "false" memories were not entirely false. Maybe the young woman *was* lost at some point—if not in a Kmart at age 5, then somewhere else at some other age. Maybe some of these people did get sick after eating something in childhood, even if it wasn't egg salad. In other studies, researchers suggested virtually impossible events. For example, college students read fake advertisements for Disneyland that depicted people meeting and shaking hands with Bugs Bunny, a Warner Brothers character who would never appear at Disneyland. About 30% of those who read this ad later reported that they too had met Bugs Bunny at Disneyland. Some reported touching his ears or tail (Loftus, 2003). In another study, British students who were asked to imagine certain experiences later reported that they actually remembered those experiences, including "having a nurse remove a skin sample from my little finger"—a procedure that British physicians never use (Mazzoni & Memon, 2003). In short, suggestions can lead people to report memories of events that never happened.

Second Study

Some therapists recommend that their clients examine photographs from their childhood to help evoke old memories. They are certainly right that photographs bring back memories. The question, however, is whether old photographs might also facilitate reports of false memories.

Hypothesis A false suggestion about a childhood event will evoke more memory reports if people have examined photographs from that time period.

Method The researchers contacted the parents of 45 college students and asked each to provide a report of some event that happened while these students were in third or fourth grade and another that happened in fifth or sixth grade. Both were supposed to be events that the student might or might not remember rather than events the family had repeatedly discussed. The researchers also asked the parents to confirm that the following "false memory" event—the one they planned to suggest—had *not* happened: In the first grade, the child took a "Slime" toy to school, and then she and another child slid it into the teacher's desk and received a mild punishment later. Finally, the researchers asked the parents for copies of class photographs from first grade, third or fourth, and fifth or sixth.

After all these preparations, they brought in the students and briefly described for each student the two correct events (provided by the parents) and the one false event. For each, they asked the students to provide whatever additional information they remembered. Half of them (randomly selected) were shown their class photographs and half were not. At the end of the session, they were asked to think about the first-grade event for the next week and try to remember more about it. Those in the photograph group took the photo with them. A week later, the students returned and again reported whatever they thought they remembered (Lindsay, Hagen, Read, Wade, & Garry, 2004).

Results Most students reported clear memories of the two real events. For the false event of first grade, Figure 7.17 shows the percentage of students who reported the event in the first and second sessions. Memories increased from the

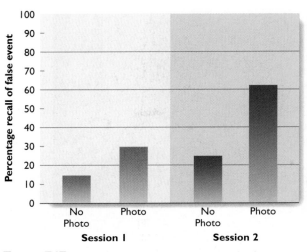

Figure 7.17 More students who saw a first-grade class photograph reported remembering the suggested (false) event. (From "True photographs and false memories" by D. S. Lindsay, L. Hagen, J. D. Read, K. A. Wade, and M. Garry from *Psychological Science*, Vol. 9, No. 6. Copyright © 2004 Blackwell Publishing. Reprinted with permission.)

first to the second session, and students who saw the photographs reported more memories than those who did not see photographs. By the second session, almost two thirds of the students who saw a class photograph reported some memory of the false event.

At the end of the study, the researchers explained that the first-grade event did not really happen. Many of the students expressed surprise, such as, "No way! I remember it! That is so weird!" (Lindsay et al., 2004, p. 153).

Interpretation Examining an old photograph evokes old memories but also increases suggestibility for false memories. Looking at the photo helps the person remember, "Oh, yes, that's what my first-grade teacher looked like. And that was my closest friend back then . . ." If the person tries to remember acting with a friend to pull a prank on the teacher, the visual image becomes more vivid and more convincing.

In related studies, researchers manipulated photos by computers, showing childhood pictures of people having tea with Prince Charles of England or riding with their families in a hot-air balloon—false events for each of the participants. Many of the participants claimed to remember the events and provided additional details (Strange, Sutherland, & Garry, 2004; Wade, Garry, Read, & Lindsay, 2002).

The question still remains, however, about clinicians' reports of recovering lost memories of early trauma. Many clinicians object that the kinds of false memories implanted in research settings (being lost in a mall, first-grade mischief, etc.) are different from emotionally intense memories of sexual abuse. To this criticism researchers reply that ethical concerns prevent them from suggesting memories of traumatic abuse.

If someone reports remembering an event after many years of not remembering it, we may

never know whether the event actually happened. No one recommends rejecting all such reports (Pope, 1996). The recommendation is to withhold judgment about the accuracy of a recovered memory unless independent evidence supports it. A further recommendation is to avoid using repeated suggestions, photographs, or other techniques that increase the probability of a false memory report.

23. In what way is hindsight bias similar to an implanted "false memory"?

Answer

23. In a case of hindsight bias, something that you learn later operates like a suggestion, so that when you try to remember what you previously thought, you are influenced by that suggestion and change your reported memory to fit it.

AMNESIA

Imagine you defied the advice given to computer owners and passed your computer through a powerful magnetic field. Chances are you would erase the memory, but suppose you found that you had erased only the text files and not the graphics files. Or suppose the old memories were intact but you could no longer store new ones. From the damage, you would gain hints about how your computer's memory works.

The same is true of human memory. Various kinds of brain damage impair one kind of memory but not another, enabling us to draw inferences about how memory is organized.

Amnesia After Damage to the Hippocampus

Amnesia is a *loss of memory*. Even in the most severe cases, people don't forget everything they ever learned. They don't forget how to walk, talk, or eat. (If they did, we would call it *dementia,* not amnesia.) And they usually don't forget all their factual knowledge. What they most often forget is their personal experiences. Amnesia results from many kinds of brain damage, including damage to the hippocampus.

In 1953 Henry Molaison, known in the research literature by his initials H. M., was suffering from many small daily epileptic seizures and about one major seizure per week. He did not respond to any antiepileptic drugs, and in desperation, surgeons removed most of his **hippocampus,** *a large forebrain structure in the interior of the*

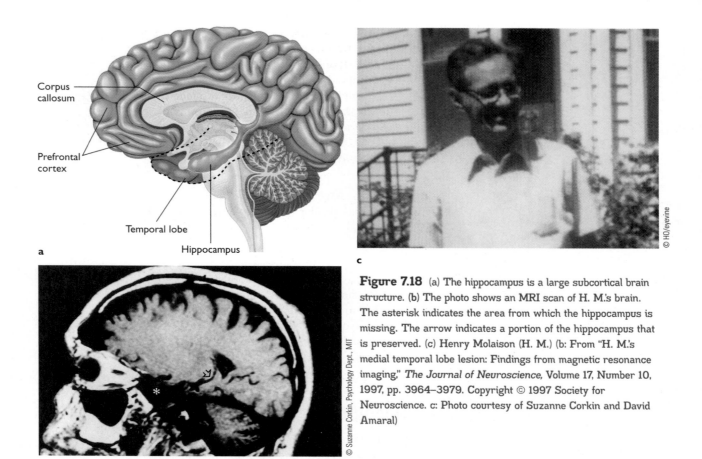

Corpus callosum

Prefrontal cortex

Temporal lobe

Hippocampus

a

b

c

Figure 7.18 (a) The hippocampus is a large subcortical brain structure. (b) The photo shows an MRI scan of H. M.'s brain. The asterisk indicates the area from which the hippocampus is missing. The arrow indicates a portion of the hippocampus that is preserved. (c) Henry Molaison (H. M.) (b: From "H. M.'s medial temporal lobe lesion: Findings from magnetic resonance imaging," *The Journal of Neuroscience*, Volume 17, Number 10, 1997, pp. 3964–3979. Copyright © 1997 Society for Neuroscience. c: Photo courtesy of Suzanne Corkin and David Amaral)

temporal lobe (Figure 7.18), where they believed his epileptic seizures were originating. They also removed some surrounding brain areas. At the time, researchers knew little about the hippocampus and did not know what to expect. Since then, animal research has established that the hippocampus is active during both encoding and retrieving memories (Eldridge, Engel, Zeineh, Bookheimer, & Knowlton, 2005). It is one of the very few brain areas that make new neurons, which aid memory storage, and it is the brain area where researchers most easily demonstrate changes in synapses during learning (Kee, Teixeira, Wang, & Frankland, 2007; Kerchner & Nicoll, 2008; Tashiro, Makino, & Gage, 2007). Had the surgeons known the importance of the hippocampus, they would not have recommended this operation, and H. M. almost certainly would not have agreed to it.

The surgery greatly decreased the frequency and severity of H. M.'s seizures. His personality remained the same, but he became more passive (Eichenbaum, 2002). His IQ score increased slightly, presumably because he had fewer epileptic seizures. However, he suffered severe memory problems (Corkin, 1984; Milner, 1959). H. M. suffered a massive anterograde (ANT-eh-ro-grade) amnesia, *inability to store new long-term memories.* For years after the operation, he cited the year as 1953 and his own age as 27. Later, he took wild guesses (Corkin, 1984). He would read the same issue of a magazine repeatedly without recognizing it. He could not even remember where he had lived. He also suffered a moderate retrograde amnesia, *loss of memory for events that occurred shortly before the brain damage* (Figure 7.19). That is, he had trouble recalling events that happened before the operation. (Any loss of consciousness, such as after a concussion or excessive alcohol intake, produces at least brief retrograde amnesia; Riccio, Millin, & Gisquet-Verrier,

2003.) Initial reports said that H. M.'s retrograde amnesia was limited to the last couple of years before the surgery. Later reports said it extended much further, especially for episodic (autobiographical) memories. Another person with amnesia following injury to his hippocampus and other brain areas suffered a complete loss of his episodic memory. When he looks at old family photos, he names the people, but he cannot describe the event in the photo or any other event including those people (Rosenbaum et al., 2005).

H. M. had normal short-term memory and working memory, as do most other patients with amnesia (Shrager, Levy, Hopkins, & Squire, 2008). However, any distraction erased his memory. He often told the same person the same story several times within a few minutes, forgetting that he had told it before (Eichenbaum, 2002).

Like Rip van Winkle, the story character who slept for 20 years and awakened to a vastly changed world, H. M. became more and more out of date with each passing year (Gabrieli, Cohen, & Corkin, 1988; M. L. Smith, 1988). He did not recognize people who became famous after the mid-1950s, although when given a famous person's name—such as John Glenn or Mikhail

Figure 7.19 Brain damage induces retrograde amnesia (loss of old memories) and anterograde amnesia (difficulty storing new memories).

Gorbachev—he could provide a bit of more-or-less correct information (O'Kane, Kensinger, & Corkin, 2004). He did not understand the meaning of words and phrases that entered the English language after his surgery. For example, he treated *Jacuzzi* and *granola* as nonwords (Corkin, 2002). He guessed that *soul food* means "forgiveness" and that a *closet queen* might be "a moth" (Gabrieli et al., 1988).

In spite of H. M.'s massive memory difficulties, he could still acquire and retain new skills. Recall the distinction between procedural memory (skills) and declarative memory (facts). H. M. learned to read material written in mirror fashion (N. J. Cohen & Squire, 1980), such as shown below. However, he did not remember having learned this or any other new skill and always expressed surprise at his success.

He could read sentences written backwards, like this.

The results for H. M. led researchers to study both people and laboratory animals with similar damage. The following points have emerged:

- Storing declarative memory requires the hippocampus. Procedural memories do not.
- The hippocampus is more important for explicit memory than for implicit memory and more important for difficult tasks than for easy tasks (Reed & Squire, 1999; J. D. Ryan, Althoff, Whitlow, & Cohen, 2000).
- The hippocampus is especially important for spatial memories—remembering where something is (Kumaran & Maguire, 2005).
- Patients with hippocampal damage have trouble imagining the future, just as they have trouble recalling the past. When you imagine a future event, such as a trip to the beach or a visit to a museum, you rearrange and modify your recollections of similar events in the past. If you can't remember your past, you can't put much detail into your imagined future (Hassabis, Kumaran, Vann, & Maguire, 2007). A patient with amnesia truly lives in the present moment, without a past or a future.

Exactly what is the role of the hippocampus in memory? According to one influential theory, the hippocampus is critical for remembering the details and context of a memory. When you recall something you did yesterday, your memory is rich in details, including who, what, where, and when. Those details depend on the hippocampus. As time passes, your memory consolidates, but as it consolidates, it changes. You remember the "gist" of what happened but fewer details. Your memory becomes more dependent on other brain areas, especially the prefrontal cortex (Takehara-Nishiuchi & McNaughton, 2008). Episodic memories necessarily include details and context. Without a healthy hippocampus, you would not store the details and context of an event in the first place, and you would have trouble recalling them later (Winocur, Moscovitch, & Sekeres, 2007).

24. Which kinds of memory are most impaired in H. M.? Which kinds are least impaired?

Answers

24. H. M. is greatly impaired at forming new declarative memories. His short-term memory is intact, as is his memory for events long before the operation and his ability to form new procedural memories.

Amnesia After Damage to the Prefrontal Cortex

Damage to the prefrontal cortex also produces amnesia (see Figure 7.18). Because the prefrontal cortex receives extensive input from the hippocampus, the symptoms of prefrontal cortex damage overlap those of hippocampal damage. However, some special deficits also arise.

Prefrontal cortex damage can be the result of a stroke, head trauma, or **Korsakoff's syndrome,** *a condition caused by a prolonged deficiency of vitamin B₁ (thiamine), usually as a result of chronic alcoholism.* This deficiency leads to widespread loss or shrinkage of neurons, especially in the prefrontal cortex. Patients suffer apathy, confusion, and amnesia (Squire, Haist, & Shimamura, 1989). If given a list of words to remember, they forget those at the beginning of the list before they reach the end and soon forget those at the end also (Stuss et al., 1994).

Patients with prefrontal cortex damage answer many questions with **confabulations,** *which* *are attempts to fill in the gaps in their memory.* Most confabulations include out-of-date information (Schnider, 2003). They usually replace the current reality with something more pleasant from the past (Fotopoulou, Solms, & Turnbull, 2004). For example, an aged hospitalized woman might insist that she had to go home to feed her baby. Confabulations are not exactly attempts to hide an inability to answer a question, as Korsakoff's patients almost never confabulate on a question such as "Where is Premola?" or "Who is Princess Lolita?" (Schnider, 2003). That is, someone who never knew the answer freely admits not knowing. The following interview is a typical example (Moscovitch, 1989, pp. 135–136). Note the mixture of correct information, confabulations that were correct at some time in the past, and imaginative attempts to explain the discrepancies between one answer and another:

Psychologist: How old are you?

Patient: I'm 40, 42, pardon me, 62.

Psychologist: Are you married or single?

Patient: Married.

Psychologist: How long have you been married?

Patient: About 4 months.

Psychologist: What's your wife's name?

Patient: Martha.

Psychologist: How many children do you have?

Patient: Four. (He laughs.) Not bad for 4 months.

Psychologist: How old are your children?

Patient: The eldest is 32; his name is Bob. And the youngest is 22; his name is Joe.

Psychologist: How did you get these children in 4 months?

Patient: They're adopted.

Psychologist: Who adopted them?

Patient: Martha and I.

Psychologist: Immediately after you got married you wanted to adopt these older children?

Patient: Before we were married we adopted one of them, two of them. The eldest girl Brenda and Bob, and Joe and Dina since we were married.

Psychologist: Does it all sound a little strange to you, what you are saying?

Patient: I think it is a little strange.

Psychologist: I think when I looked at your record it said that you've been married for over 30 years. Does that sound more reasonable to you if I told you that?

Patient: No.

Psychologist: Do you really believe that you have been married for 4 months?

Patient: Yes.

Patients with prefrontal cortex damage confidently defend their confabulations and often maintain the same confabulation from one time to the next. Actually, the same is true of normal people who learn something poorly. In one study, college students listened to complicated 2-minute descriptions of topics they knew little about and then answered detailed questions. Once a week for the next 4 weeks, they heard the same description and answered the same questions. Most people repeated the same incorrect guesses from one week to the next (Fritz, Morris, Bjork, Gelman, & Wickens, 2000).

Why do people with prefrontal damage confabulate so much more than the rest of us? According to Morris Moscovitch (1992), the prefrontal cortex is necessary for *working with memory,* the strategies we use to reconstruct memories that we cannot immediately recall. If you are asked what is the farthest north that you have ever traveled or how many salads you ate last week, you reason out your answer. People with prefrontal cortex damage have difficulty making reasonable inferences.

Despite their impoverished memory in other regards, people with brain damage perform well on most tests of implicit memory. For example, after hearing a list of words, a patient may not be able to say any of the words on the list and may not even remember that there was a list. However, when given a set of three-letter stems such as CON—, the patient completes them to make words that were on the list (Hamann & Squire, 1997).

Another example: After patients repeatedly practiced playing the video game Tetris, they said they did not remember playing the game before, although they did improve from one session to the next. When they closed their eyes to go to sleep at night, they said they saw little images of

People who spend many hours playing the game Tetris report seeing images of Tetris blocks, especially as they are falling asleep. The same is true of people with severe amnesia, even though they don't remember playing the game.

blocks and wondered what they were (Stickgold, Malia, Maguire, Roddenberry, & O'Connor, 2000).

One important conclusion emerges from all the studies of brain damage and amnesia: We have several different types of memory. It is possible to impair one type without equally damaging another.

25. Although confabulation is a kind of false memory, how does it differ from the suggested false memories discussed earlier in this module?

Answer

25. Most confabulated statements were true at one time, though not now. Also, people with brain damage seldom confabulate answers to questions they never could have answered in the past. That is, they seldom make up totally new information.

Memory Impairments in Alzheimer's Disease

A more common cause of memory loss is Alzheimer's (AHLTZ-hime-ers) disease, *a condition occurring mostly in old age, characterized by increasingly severe memory loss, confusion, depression, disordered thinking, and impaired attention.* Although several genes have been linked to an onset of Alzheimer's disease before age 60, more than 99% of the people with Alzheimer's disease have a later onset, and most cases of the late-onset form are not linked with any identified gene. Moreover, the genes' effects are not inevitable. The Yoruba people of Nigeria almost never get Alzheimer's disease, even if they have the genes that predispose Americans to this disease (Hendrie, 2001). Which aspect of their culture shields them from Alzheimer's is uncertain, although diet is a likely candidate.

Alzheimer's disease is marked by a gradual accumulation of harmful proteins in the brain and deterioration of brain cells, leading to a loss of arousal and attention. The memory problem includes both anterograde and retrograde amnesia. Because the areas of damage include the hippocampus and the prefrontal cortex, their memory deficits overlap those of H. M. and patients with Korsakoff's syndrome. For example, like Korsakoff's patients, they often confabulate (Nedjam, Dalla Barba, & Pillon, 2000). Like H. M., as a rule they learn new skills, such as how to use a cell phone (Lekeu, Wojtasik, Van der Linden, & Salmon, 2002). Their mixture of memory problems should not be surprising, given the overall decrease of arousal and attention. Weak arousal and impaired attention cause problems for almost any aspect of memory.

26. What kinds of memory are impaired in patients with Alzheimer's disease?

Answer

26. Patients with Alzheimer's disease have weaknesses in almost all types of memory, although they can learn new skills (procedural memory).

Infant Amnesia

How much do you remember from when you were 6 years old? How about age 4? Age 2? Although 2- and 3-year-olds remember events that happened months ago, these memories fade over time, and most adults report at most a few fragmentary memories of early childhood (Bauer, Wenner, & Kroupina, 2002; K. Nelson & Fivush, 2004). The *scarcity of early episodic memories* is known as infant amnesia, or childhood amnesia. Although psychologists have proposed many theories of infant amnesia, none are fully persuasive (Howe & Courage, 1997).

In what may have been the earliest proposal on this issue, Sigmund Freud suggested that children go through emotionally difficult experiences at ages 4 to 5 that are so disturbing that a child represses everything experienced at that time or before. However, neither Freud nor anyone else has provided persuasive evidence for this idea.

A more modern proposal is that the hippocampus, known to be important for memory, is slow to mature, so memories from the first few years are not stored well (Moscovitch, 1985). Furthermore, most of the memories that we can readily demonstrate in infants are either procedural memories (how to do something) or semantic memories (such as where to find certain things or what acts are safe and unsafe). It is not clear that infants form many episodic memories, which depend heavily on the hippocampus (Newcombe, Lloyd, & Ratliff, 2007). However, even the memories that infants do form do not last long. Patricia Bauer (2005) provided novel experiences to preschool children of various ages and tested their recollections later. Although all the children learned well enough, the youngest children forgot fastest. That is, the problem is not just that young children fail to form memories. They forget rapidly.

Another proposal is that a permanent memory of an experience requires a "sense of self" that develops between ages 3 and 4 (Howe & Courage,

1993). However, rats, pigeons, and other nonhuman species develop long-lasting memories. If we want to avoid saying that rats have more sense of self than 3-year-old children, we could argue that rats' memories aren't the same as the kind of memory we are discussing for adult humans. However, at best, this idea is not convincing.

Another possibility is that after we come to rely on language, we lose access to memories encoded earlier. That idea will not explain why a 4-year-old can describe what happened at age 3, whereas a 7-year-old cannot. Still, some interesting research supports the onset of language as one factor in infant amnesia: Psychologists let some 3-year-olds play with a "magic shrinking machine." A child could place a large toy into a slot, crank a handle, and then see a smaller version of the same toy come out, as if the machine had shrunk the toy. When the children returned 6 months or a year later, they clearly remembered the machine and how to work it. However, when they were asked to describe how the machine worked or to name the toys that it shrank, the children described their experience using only the words they had known at the time they originally played with the machine (Simcock & Hayne, 2002). For example, a child who knew the word "teddy bear" at age 3 would use it later, but a child who did not know the term at age 3 would not, even after learning it in the meantime. In a similar study, 2-year-old children learned that only one color of fluid would operate a "magic bubble machine." Of those who did not know the name of that color at the time but who learned it within the next 2 months, 30% could then name the color that operated the machine (Morris & Baker-Ward, 2007). So it appears that children sometimes apply newly learned words to old memories.

One more possibility is that infant amnesia relates to encoding specificity. If we learn something in one time, place, physiological condition, or state of mind, we remember it more easily under the same or similar conditions. Maybe we forget our early years just because we don't have enough of the right retrieval cues to find those infant memories.

At this point, none of these hypotheses is well established. Infant amnesia probably has several explanations, not just one.

....

27. What evidence indicates that infant amnesia is not due to a failure to establish long-term memories?

Answer

27. Young children remember events that happened months or even years ago. However, a few years later, they lose those memories.

....

7.3 module

In Closing

Memory Loss and Distortion

The first part of this module presented evidence that when we try to recall something from long ago, we often find that the details have faded and we need to infer or reconstruct much of the information. The material on amnesia shows a mechanism: Recent memories depend on the hippocampus, which binds all the details and context of an event. Later, as the representation in the hippocampus fades, memory depends more on the cerebral cortex and other areas that store the gist of the event, without much detail. The fact that we are built this way is not really a failing. Computers store every detail that we give them indefinitely, but our brains don't need to. The older some experience is, the less likely we are to need its details. If we do need the details, we can usually reason them out well enough for most purposes.

SUMMARY

- *Interference.* When someone learns several similar sets of material, the earlier ones interfere with retrieval of later ones by proactive interference. The later ones interfere with earlier ones by retroactive interference. Interference is a major cause of forgetting. (page 259)

- *The "recovered memory" versus "false memory" debate.* Some therapists have used hypnosis or suggestions to try to help people remember painful experiences. Many researchers doubt the accuracy of those recovered memories. Suggestions can induce people to distort memories or report events that did not happen. It is difficult to distinguish accurate memories from distorted or false ones. (page 260)

- *Amnesia after damage to the hippocampus.* H. M. and other patients with damage to the hippocampus have great difficulty storing new long-term declarative memories, especially episodic memories, although they form normal short-term, procedural, and implicit memories. (page 263)

- *Role of the hippocampus.* The hippocampus serves many functions in memory. One is to bind together all the details and context of an event. In the absence of a healthy hippocampus or after the information in the hippocampus weakens, one is left with only the "gist" of the event, stored in the cerebral cortex or elsewhere. (page 265)

- *Damage to the prefrontal cortex.* Patients with damage to the prefrontal cortex give confident wrong answers, known as confabulations. Most confabulations were correct information earlier in the person's life. (page 265)

- *Alzheimer's disease.* Patients with Alzheimer's disease, a condition that occurs mostly after age 60 to 65, have a variety of memory problems, although implicit and procedural memory are more intact than explicit, declarative memory. Their problems stem largely from impairments of arousal and attention. (page 267)

- *Infant amnesia.* Most people remember little from early childhood, even though preschoolers have clear recollections of experiences that happened months or even years ago. No explanation is fully convincing. (page267)

KEY TERMS

Alzheimer's disease (page 267)

amnesia (page 263)

anterograde amnesia (page 264)

confabulations (page 265)

dissociation (page 261)

false memory (page 262)

hippocampus (page 263)

infant amnesia (or childhood amnesia) (page 267)

Korsakoff's syndrome (page 265)

proactive interference (page 260)

recovered memory (page 260)

repression (page 261)

retroactive interference (page 260)

retrograde amnesia (page 264)

Why Does This Matter to Me?

SOCIAL RESPONSIBILITY AND PSYCHOLOGY

Many environmental problems are caused by human behavior. Psychologists can help steer the course of our future toward more socially responsible and sustainable outcomes. Students of today need to be ever mindful of the link between human behavior and its impact on the environment.

"Memory" and Social Responsibility: A Step Further

What do you do to help yourself remember to follow through on green practices every day? For instance, if you wanted to remember to take canvas bags with you every time you went to the grocery store, what could you do?

Join the iChapters Plant a Tree Drive!

To show its support of the environmental movement, iChapters is planting a tree on behalf of each fan of the iChapters Facebook Page and for every 10 questions answered correctly in our quiz.
http://www.ichapters.com/plantatree/

Exploration and Study

SUGGESTION FOR FURTHER EXPLORATION

In addition to the study materials provided at the end of each module, you may supplement your review of this chapter with the following book and website suggestions or by using one or more of the book's electronic resources, which include its companion website, interactive Cengage Learning eBook, and CengageNOW. Brief descriptions of these resources follow. For more information, visit **www.cengage.com/psychology/kalat**.

ADDITIONAL RESOURCES

The book's companion website, accessible from **www.cengage.com/psychology/kalat**, provides a wide range of study resources such as an interactive glossary, flashcards, tutorial quizzes, updated web links, and Try It Yourself activities. For example, the exercises on decay of short-term memory, false memory, and implicit memories tie to what you've learned in this chapter.

CengageNOW with Critical Thinking Videos is an easy-to-use resource that helps you study in less time to get the grade you want. An online study system, CengageNOW gives you the option of taking a diagnostic pretest for each chapter. The system uses the results of each pretest to create personalized chapter study plans for you. The Personalized Study Plans

Critical Thinking

- Help you save study time by identifying areas on which you should concentrate and give you one-click access to corresponding pages of the interactive Cengage Learning eBook;
- Provide interactive exercises and study tools to help you fully understand chapter concepts; and
- Include a posttest for you to take to confirm that you are ready to move on to the next chapter.

Find critical thinking videos like this one in your CengageNOW product, which offer an opportunity for you to learn more about psychological research on different topics.

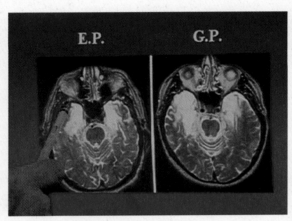

Amnesia and Different Types of Changes

Books

Eichenbaum, H. (2002). *The cognitive neuroscience of memory.* New York: Oxford University Press. An engaging account of memory and its impairments.

Schacter, D. L. (2001). *The seven sins of memory.* Boston: Houghton Mifflin. Discusses common mistakes that interfere with memory.

Websites

Links to the websites described below are kept current and can be found at **www.cengage.com/psychology/kalat**.

Amnesia and Patient H. M.

This site gives a good history of the patient and what his condition told us about memory.

Mnemonics

A thorough review of many techniques for memorizing.

The World Memory Championship

Check out the latest results on this memory contest.

So her story is known
around the world.

the newspapers.

© Aflo/Getty Images

8 chapter

Cognition and Language

Consider This: Consider the statement, "This sentence is false." Is the statement itself true or false? Declaring the statement true agrees with its own assessment that it is false. But declaring it false would make its assessment correct. A sentence about itself, called a *self-referential* sentence, can be confusing. It can be true (like this one!). It can be false ("Anyone who reads this sentence will be transported suddenly to the planet Neptune"), untestable ("Whenever no one is reading this sentence, it changes its font"), or amusing ("This sentence no verb").

In this chapter, you will be asked to think about thinking. Doing so is self-referential, and if you try to "think about what you are thinking now," you can go into a confusing loop like the one in "This sentence is false." Thus, psychological researchers focus as much as possible on results obtained from carefully controlled experiments, not just on what people say that they think about their thought processes.

Cognitive psychology studies how people think and what they know.

- What is attention?
- How can we study concepts?

Cognition means *thinking and using knowledge.* This is the field of cognitive psychologists, who also deal with how people organize their thoughts into language. Cognition begins with attending to something and categorizing what it is. How can researchers learn about cognitive processes? During the era when behaviorists dominated experimental psychology, researchers devoted little effort to cognition. Since about 1970, research has increased substantially, as psychologists developed ways to infer the unobservable.

RESEARCH IN COGNITIVE PSYCHOLOGY

Perhaps it seems that cognitive psychology should be simple. "If you want to find out what people think or what they know, why not ask them?" Sometimes, psychologists do ask, but people don't always know their own thought processes. Consider this experiment: The experimenter presents two cards at a time, each showing a female face, and asks which one looks more attractive. After the participant chooses, the experimenter sometimes asks for an explanation. Occasionally, the experimenter surreptitiously switches cards, so he

asks why the participant chose the face that he or she had, in fact, *not* chosen, as shown in Figure 8.1. People seldom (13% of the time) notice the switch, and on the average, their "explanations" are just as long, just as specific, and just as confident for the switched cards as for the originally chosen cards. Sometimes, they give reasons such as "I like her earrings" or "I like her blonde hair," which applied to the switched face and not to the one originally chosen (Johansson, Hall, Sikström, & Olsson, 2005). In those cases, clearly, people are stating reasons that they made up afterward, not at the time of the original choice. Therefore, we suspect that even on the trials when no switch occurred, the stated reasons are frequently made up after the fact. People choose without knowing the reason and then make up a reasonable-sounding explanation afterward.

So, if we can't always find out people's thought processes just by asking them, how can we discover them? Much research relies on careful measurements of timing. Let's consider one of the first experiments that showed how to measure a mental process.

Fig. 1, from Johansson, Hall, Sikström, & Olsson, 2005, *Science, 310,* 116–119. Used by permission of the author.

a **b** **c** **d**

Figure 8.1 The participant identified the face considered more attractive. Then the experimenter switched cards and asked why this face seemed more attractive.

What's the Evidence?
Mental Imagery

If you look at something and try to describe what it would look like from a different angle, you probably say you answered the question by imagining a mental rotation of the object. Roger Shepard and Jacqueline Metzler (1971) reasoned that if people visualize mental images, then the time it takes them to rotate a mental image should be similar to the time needed to rotate a real object.

Hypothesis When people have to rotate a mental image to answer a question, the farther they have to rotate it, the longer it will take them to answer the question.

Method Participants examined pairs of drawings of three-dimensional objects, as in Figure 8.2, and indicated whether it would be possible to rotate one object to match the other. (Try to answer this question yourself before reading further.)

People pulled one lever to indicate *same* and another lever to indicate *different.* When the correct answer was *same,* someone might determine that answer by rotating a mental image of the first picture until it matched the second.

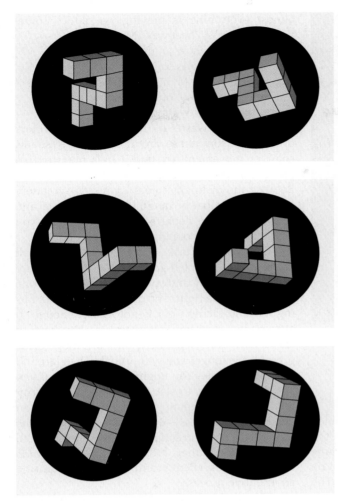

Figure 8.2 Examples of pairs of drawings used in an experiment by Shepard and Metzler (1971). Do the drawings for each pair represent the same object being rotated, or are they different objects? (See answer A on page 285.) (From "Mental rotation of three-dimensional objects" by R. N. Shepard and J. N. Metzler from *Science*, 1971, pp. 701–703. Copyright © 1971. Reprinted with permission from AAAS.)

If so, the delay should depend on how far the image had to be rotated.

Results Participants answered nearly all items correctly. As predicted, their reaction time when they responded *same* depended on the angular difference in orientation between the two views. If the first object had to be rotated 30 degrees to match the second one, people needed a certain amount of time to pull the *same* lever. If an image had to be rotated 60 degrees to match the other, people took twice as long to pull the lever. That is, they reacted as if they were watching a model of the object rotate at a constant speed.

Interpretation Viewing a mental image is partly like real vision. In this case, common sense appears to be correct. However, the main point is that researchers can infer thought processes from people's delay in answering a question. Most research in cognitive psychology measures the accuracy and timing of responses.

ATTENTION

You are constantly bombarded with more sights, sounds, smells, and other stimuli than you can process. **Attention** is *your tendency to respond to and to remember some stimuli more than others at a given time.*

Sometimes, something (e.g., a loud noise) suddenly grabs your attention. Psychologists call this a "bottom-up" process because the peripheral stimuli control it. Magicians use this tendency. A magician pulls a rabbit or a dove out of a hat, and the surprised viewers automatically watch the rabbit hop away or the dove fly away. During the brief time that their attention is occupied, the magician sets up the next trick, unnoticed (Macknik et al., 2008).

In contrast to a bottom-up process, you can deliberately decide to shift your attention in a "top-down" process. To illustrate, fixate your eyes on the x in the center and then, without moving your eyes, read the letters in the circle around it clockwise:

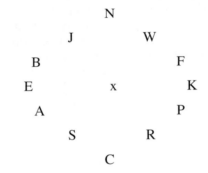

As you see, it is possible to control your attention without moving your eyes. When you increase your attention to something in your visual field, the part of your visual cortex sensitive to that area becomes more active and receives more blood flow (Müller, Malinowski, Gruber, & Hillyard, 2003). If you focus on a word, such as THIS, and attend to the letters, you increase activity in the language areas of the brain, but if you attend to the color, you shift activity to the color-detecting areas (Polk, Drake, Jonides, Smith, & Smith, 2008).

Let's go back to bottom-up processes, in which a stimulus automatically grabs your attention. Hearing your name or seeing your photograph is almost sure to attract your attention (Brédart, Delchambre, & Laureys, 2006; K. L. Shapiro, Caldwell, & Sorensen, 1997). Your attention also flows to anything unusual. I once watched a costume contest in which people were

almost everything is moving, we notice something that isn't (Theeuwes, 2004).

To illustrate how an unusual object draws attention, examine Figure 8.3, which shows a huge flock of sandhill cranes and one whooping crane. Find the whooping crane. That was easy, wasn't it? When an object differs drastically from those around it in size, shape, color, or movement, we find it by a **preattentive process**, meaning that it *stands out immediately*. Because the distinctive item jumps out preattentively, the number of sandhill cranes is irrelevant. If some of them departed or more arrived, you would find the whooping crane just as fast.

Contrast that task with Figure 8.4. Here, all the birds are marbled godwits. Most of them are facing to your left, and your task is to find the one that faces to the right. The difference between facing left and facing right is not salient enough to attract your attention automatically. You have to check each bird separately, and the more birds present, the longer you will probably need to find the unusual one. (You might find it quickly if you are lucky enough to start your search in the correct corner of the photograph.) You had to rely on an **attentive process**—*one that requires searching through the items in series* (Enns & Rensink, 1990; Treisman & Souther, 1985). The *Where's Waldo* books are an excellent example of a task requiring an attentive process.

The distinction between attentive and preattentive processes has practical applications. Imagine yourself as a human factors psychologist designing machinery with several gauges. When the apparatus is running safely, the first gauge should read about 70, the second 40, the third 30, and the fourth 10. If you arrange the gauges as in the top row of Figure 8.5, then people using this machine must check each gauge separately to find any-

Figure 8.3 Demonstration of preattentive processes: You would find the one whooping crane just as fast in a larger flock of sandhill cranes.

told to dress so distinctively that their friends could find them in a crowd as quickly as possible. The winner was a young man who came onto the stage naked. Although I concede that he earned the prize, this contest had a problem: The most distinctive clothing (or lack of it) depends on what everyone else is wearing. A naked person is easy to spot in most places, but at a nudist beach, you would be more likely to notice a man in a coat and tie. What is unusual depends on the context. Ordinarily, we notice something that is flashing on and off, but if almost everything is flashing on and off, something that remains steady draws our attention (Pashler & Harris, 2001). If

Figure 8.4 Demonstration of attentive processes: Find the marbled godwit that is facing to the right. In this case, you need to check the birds one at a time.

Figure 8.5 Each gauge represents a measurement of a different variable in a machine. For the top row, the operator must check gauges one at a time. In the bottom row, all the safe ranges are in the same direction. The operator detects an unsafe reading preattentively.

thing dangerous. In the bottom row of Figure 8.5, the gauges are arranged so that all the safe ranges are on the right. Now someone glances at the display and quickly (preattentively) notices anything out of position.

1. Suppose you are in a field of brownish bushes and one motionless brown rabbit. Will you find the rabbit by attentive or preattentive processes? If the rabbit starts hopping, will you find it by attentive or preattentive processes?

Answer

1. Finding a motionless brown rabbit in a field of brown objects requires attentive processes, but you could use preattentive processes to find a hopping rabbit. (For this reason, animals in danger of predation stay motionless when they can.)

The Attention Bottleneck

Much evidence indicates that attention is limited, and various items compete for attention. If two or three objects flash briefly on a screen, you can identify their colors. If six objects flash on a screen, you know the colors of two or three of them, but you could only guess at the others (Zhang & Luck, 2008).

Imagine yourself in the control room of the Three Mile Island nuclear power plant, the site of a nearly disastrous accident in 1979. Figure 8.6 shows a small portion of the room as it appeared then, with an enormous number of knobs and gauges. (Since then, the controls have been redesigned to simplify the task.) A poorly designed control system overwhelms someone's ability to pay attention. Let's consider examples of the limits of human attention.

Conflict in Attention

Can you do two things at once? Sure, you can *do* two things at once, such as walk and chew gum. However, if you closely watch someone who is walking and chewing at the same time, you may notice that the activities are synchronized. The person might chew once per footstep, once per two footsteps, two times per three footsteps, or whatever, but the activities are linked. More important, you cannot *plan* two actions at once. To illustrate, put a pen or pencil in each of your two hands. Now draw ∪ with one hand and ⊃ with the other hand. Either you will draw them slowly, or you will draw at least one of them sloppily. You

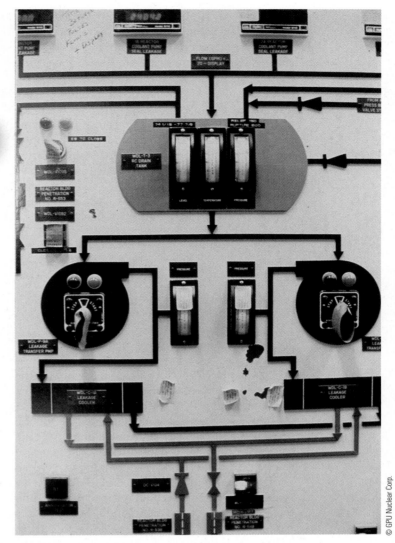

Figure 8.6 The Three Mile Island TMI-2 nuclear power plant had a confusing control system, a small portion of which is shown here. Some of the important gauges were not easily visible, some were poorly labeled, and many alarm signals had ambiguous meanings. After the accident in 1979, the system was redesigned.

© GPU Nuclear Corp.

can't plan separate movements for your two hands at once (Lien, Ruthruff, & Johnston, 2006). However, after you have carefully drawn ∪ and ⊃, you can easily trace one with the left hand and the other with the right. When you trace, you follow the guide of what you see.

Even simple activities interfere with each other. Suppose you have these two simple tasks: You will hear a tone, and you are to judge whether it is a lower pitch (440 Hz, the A above middle C on the scale) or 880 Hz (one octave higher). Less than a second after the onset of the tone, you see a two-digit number, and you are to indicate whether it is higher or lower than 45. Your response to the second task will be slower than it would have been without the first task. You needed time to shift attention from one task to the other. Most people are not aware of this delay (Corallo, Sackur, Dehaene, & Sigman, 2008). To experience another example of attentional bottleneck, visit Dual Task's website, which can be found at **www.cengage.com/psychology/kalat**.

Many years ago, when automobile radios were introduced, people worried that listening to the radio would distract drivers and cause accidents. We no longer worry about radio, but we do worry about drivers using cell phones. Conversations require more attention than a radio, and a cell-phone conversation is more distracting than one with a passenger in the car because most passengers pause a conversation when driving conditions are difficult (Drews, Pasupathi, & Strayer, 2008). Research on simulated driving finds that a cell-phone conversation decreases a driver's visual attention and increases the risk of accidents (Kunar, Carter, Cohen, & Horowitz, 2008). Even such a simple task as saying whether you heard one tone or two significantly slows drivers' responses when they need to hit the brakes (Levy, Pashler, & Boer, 2006).

The Stroop Effect

Read the following instructions and then examine Figure 8.7: Notice the blocks of color at the top of the figure. Scanning from left to right, name each color as fast as you can. Then notice the nonsense syllables in the center of the figure. Again, say the color of each one as fast as possible. Then turn to the real words at the bottom. Instead of reading them, quickly state each one's color.

Most people read the colors quickly for the first two parts, but they slow down greatly for the colored words (which happen to be the names of colors). After all of your years of reading, you can hardly bring yourself to look at RED and say "green." The words attract your attention and therefore distract from attention to the colors. *The tendency to read the words instead of saying the color of ink* is known as the Stroop effect, after the

psychologist who discovered it. People do better on this task if they blur their vision, say the colors in a different language, or manage to regard the color words as meaningless (Raz, Kirsch, Pollard, & Nitkin-Kaner, 2006).

Do words always take priority over colors? It depends. Try the following: Go back to Figure 8.7 and notice the red, green, blue, and yellow patches at the four corners. This time, instead of saying anything, point to the correct color patch. When you come to RED, point to the blue patch in the lower left. Then try this demonstration again but point to the color corresponding to the *meaning* of the word. That is, when you come to RED, point to the red patch in the upper left. Try it now.

You probably found it easy to point to the patch that matches the color of the ink and harder to point to the color matching the word meaning (Durgin, 2000). When you are speaking, you are primed to read the words you see, but when you are pointing, you are more primed to attend to nonverbal cues, such as ink color.

Change Blindness

Movie directors discovered long ago that if they shot different parts of a scene on different days, few viewers noticed the changes in the cloud pattern, the background props, or the actors' clothes (Simons & Levin, 2003). Why is that? Most people believe they see a whole scene at once, but in fact, your vision detects only a few details at a time. When you look at a complex scene, your eyes usually dart around from one fixation point

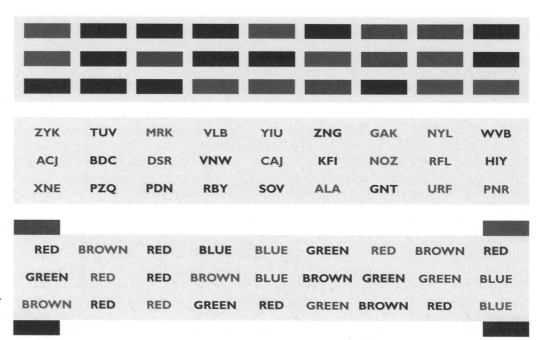

Figure 8.7 Read (left to right) the color of the ink in each part. Try to ignore the words themselves.

to another, fixating about three times per second (Henderson, 2007). You would notice anything that changed at the point where you fixate at a given moment, and a big, sudden change somewhere else might grab your attention, but you cannot attend to every detail at once.

Psychologists call this phenomenon change blindness—*the failure to detect changes in parts of a scene*. If anything moves or changes its appearance suddenly, it automatically draws your attention, but you seldom notice similar changes that occur slowly or while you are moving your eyes (Henderson & Hollingworth, 2003). You are especially unlikely to notice changes if your working memory is occupied with other matters, such as the plot of a movie (Todd, Fougnie, & Marois, 2005). Have you ever seen one of those puzzles that ask you to "find ten differences between these two pictures"? The difficulty of finding them indicates that you don't simultaneously pay attention to everything you see. Figure 8.8 shows two pairs of photos. In each pair, one differs from the other in a single regard. How quickly can you find those differences? Most people need 10 seconds or longer (Rensink, O'Regan, & Clark, 1997). For an Online Try It Yourself activity, go to **www. cengage.com/psychology/kalat**. Navigate to the student website, then to the Online Try It Yourself section, and click Change Blindness.

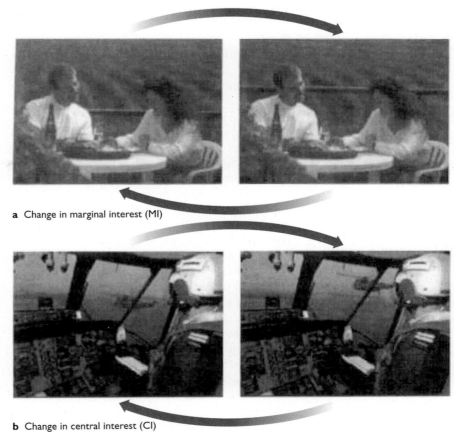

a Change in marginal interest (MI)

b Change in central interest (CI)

Figure 8.8 How quickly can you find the difference in each pair of pictures? If you need help, check answer B, page 285 (From Rensink, O'Regan & Clark, *Science*, vol. 8 number 5, 368–373. Photo reprinted with permission from the publisher and the author.)

2. Did you find the changes in Figure 8.8 by a preattentive or an attentive mechanism?

Answer

2. The changes did not jump out by a preattentive mechanism. You had to use an attentive process to check each part of the scene one at a time.

The conclusion is that you do not maintain a detailed representation of what you see or hear. You hold a few details, which vary from one time to another. Change blindness is another phenomenon that magicians exploit (Macknik et al., 2008). A magician throws a ball into the air and catches it a few times and then pretends to throw it again, "watching" it go up. Many viewers do not immediately notice the change. They "see" the ball going up . . . and then disappearing!

The Attentional Blink

It takes time to shift attention from one item to another, as we see in the **attentional blink**: *During a brief time after perceiving one stimulus, it is*

difficult to attend to something else. You probably don't blink your eyes, but you "blink" your attention. Suppose you watch a screen that displays a series of letters, one at a time for 90 milliseconds (ms) each. Every series includes one letter in blue ink, and it may or may not include the letter T. Your task is to name the blue letter and say whether or not a T appeared. Here are three series and their correct answers:

D S R B J A O E C V   "B, no."

X F D P N S J V N T   "F, yes."

Y L H F X G W K T Q   "G, yes."

In the third example, most people miss the T (and say "no") because it appeared during a period between 100 to 700 ms after the blue letter. Your attention gets so absorbed in the letter G that it does not shift easily to another letter (Nieuwenstein & Potter, 2006). The G so strongly activates the visual cortex that it blots out the response to the next few letters (M. A. Williams, Visser, Cunnington, & Mattingley, 2008).

3. Suppose you are playing a video game and you see two brief signals, about a quarter-second apart, telling you to do two things. You respond to the first one but not to the second. Why?

Answer

3. The second fell within the attentional blink.

ATTENTION-DEFICIT DISORDER

People vary in their ability to maintain attention, as in anything else. **Attention-deficit disorder (ADD)** is characterized by *easy distraction, impulsiveness, moodiness, and failure to follow through on plans* (Wender, Wolf, & Wasserstein, 2001). **Attention-deficit hyperactivity disorder (ADHD)** is *the same except with excessive activity and "fidgetiness."* The symptoms vary considerably in type and intensity. Some people have problems mostly with attention, some mainly with impulsivity, and some with both. The underlying causes almost certainly vary also. Although a genetic tendency is evident (Blasi et al., 2005), no one gene is common to all people diagnosed with ADD or ADHD. Brain scans show minor abnormalities in several brain areas for most people diagnosed with ADD or ADHD (Seidman, Valera, & Makris, 2005), but none of these abnormalities are consistent from one person to another. In many cases, the problem can be described as a delay in brain maturation (Shaw et al., 2007). For these reasons, many psychologists doubt that we are dealing with a single disorder (Furman, 2008). Rather, the labels ADD or ADHD are given to people with various problems that impair attention and impulse control. In some cases, those problems result from fetal alcohol exposure, lead poisoning, epilepsy, sleep deprivation, emotional stress, and other environmental causes (Pearl, Weiss, & Stein, 2001). In most cases, the cause is unknown.

What exactly do we mean by "attention deficit"? It is certainly not a complete lack of attention. When people are asked to respond whenever they see or hear a particular signal, most ADHD children perform well enough, but what psychologists note is high variability. A child might respond as fast as anyone else on some trials but occasionally show long delays (Cao et al., 2008).

The problem is not an inability to pay attention. People with ADD or ADHD easily pay attention to something they care about. The problem relates to shifting attention. For example, recall the attentional blink. After detecting a target on a screen, anyone has trouble detecting another target a half-second later, but many people with ADD or ADHD have trouble for a full second or more (Hollingsworth, McAuliffe, & Knowlton, 2001). That is, they do not quickly shift their attention from one item to another. Here are two more tasks sensitive to attention-deficit disorder:

- **The Choice-Delay Task** Would you prefer a small reward now or a bigger reward later? Obviously, it depends on *how much* bigger and *how much* later. On the average, people with ADD or ADHD are more likely than other people to opt for the immediate reward

(Solanto et al., 2001). Researchers found that 4-year-olds who choose the immediate reward have difficulties with attention and self-control both at age 4 and during adolescence (Eigsti et al., 2006).

- **The Stop Signal Task** Suppose your task is to press the X key whenever you see an X on the screen and the O key whenever you see an O, but if you hear a "beep" shortly after you see either letter, then you should not press. If the letter and beep occur simultaneously, you easily inhibit your urge to press the button. If the beep occurs after you have already started to press, it's too late. The interesting results are with short delays: After how long a delay could you still manage to stop your finger from pressing the button? Most people with ADD or ADHD have trouble inhibiting their response, even after short delays (Rubia, Oosterlaan, Sergeant, Brandeis, & v. Leeuwen, 1998; Solanto et al., 2001). Try the Online Try It Yourself exercise Stop Signal Task to get an idea of this task. However, remember that you should try to press the X or O as quickly as possible after you see a letter. Some people wait a second or two to find out whether a beep is coming. If you *always* inhibit your responses, even with long delays between a letter and a beep, then you are "cheating." Try to press as fast as you can.

The Choice-Delay task and Stop Signal task measure different types of attentional problems. Some children show impairments on one task but not the other (Solanto et al., 2001; Sonuga-Barke, 2004).

4. Describe one of the behavioral tests used to measure deficits of attention or impulse control.

Answer

4. In the Choice-Delay task, the question is under what conditions someone will sacrifice a reward now for a larger one later. In the Stop Signal task, one signal calls for a response and a second signal cancels the first signal; the question is under what circumstances a person can inhibit the response.

The most common treatment for ADD or ADHD is stimulant drugs such as methylphenidate (Ritalin) (Elia, Ambrosini, & Rapoport, 1999). Stimulant drugs improve school performance and everyday behaviors (de Wit, Crean, & Richards,

2000; Jerome & Segal, 2001). However, the fact that stimulant drugs appear to help a given child does not confirm a diagnosis of ADD or ADHD. Stimulant drugs also increase the attention span of normal children (R. Elliott et al., 1997; Zahn, Rapoport, & Thompson, 1980).

Behavioral methods are also helpful in dealing with ADD/ADHD (Pelham & Fabiano, 2008). Those methods include classroom use of rewards for good behavior and time outs for inappropriate behavior. People who play action video games for many hours also improve their ability to focus attention (Boot, Kramer, Simons, Fabiani, & Gratton, 2008). Another way to enhance attention is by interacting with nature (Berman, Jonides, & Kaplan, 2008). If you walk along a city street, you are surrounded by traffic and other items that demand your attention and leave you mentally exhausted. If you walk through a forest, you replenish your resources, enhancing your later ability to control your attention.

CATEGORIZATION

After you have attended to something, you want to know what it is. You put it into a category of some type, such as *building, tree,* or *river.* The ancient Greek philosopher Heraclitus said that you cannot step into the same river twice. The river constantly changes, so that today's Mississippi River is not the same as yesterday's. Furthermore, the "you" that steps into a river now is different from the "you" of an earlier time. Nevertheless, to think and communicate about anything, we have to group items into categories, and the formation of categories or concepts is a major step in cognition.

Ways to Describe a Category

Do we look up our concepts in a mental dictionary to determine their meaning? A few words have simple, unambiguous definitions. For example, a *line* is the shortest distance between two points.

Many concepts are hard to define, however. You can probably recognize country music, but can you define it? What's the border between being bald and not bald? Is a man who loses one hair bald? Of course not. Then he loses one more hair, then another, and another. Eventually, he *is* bald. At what point did losing one more hair make him bald? Similar problems arise if we try to classify everyone as depressed or not, schizophrenic or not, or alcoholic or not.

Eleanor Rosch (1978; Rosch & Mervis, 1975) argued that many categories are best described by *familiar or typical examples* called **prototypes.** We decide whether an object belongs to a category by determining how well it resembles the prototypes

of that category. For example, we define the category "vehicle" by examples: *car, bus, train, airplane, boat,* and *truck.* Is an *escalator* also a vehicle? What about *water skis*? These items are not exactly vehicles and not exactly nonvehicles.

However, some categories cannot be described by prototypes (Fodor, 1998). For example, we can think about "bug-eyed monsters from outer space" without ever encountering a prototype of that category.

Conceptual Networks and Priming

Try to think about one word and nothing else. It's impossible. You can't think without relating something to something else. For example, when you think about *bird,* you link it to more specific terms, such as *sparrow,* more general terms, such as *animals,* and related terms, such as *flight* and *eggs.*

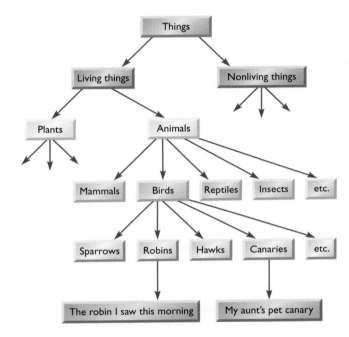

We naturally organize items into hierarchies, such as animal as a higher level category, bird as intermediate, and sparrow as a lower level category. Researchers demonstrate the reality of this kind of hierarchy by measuring the delay for people to answer various questions (A. M. Collins & Quillian, 1969, 1970). Answer the following true–false questions as quickly as possible:

- Canaries are yellow.
- Canaries sing.
- Canaries lay eggs.
- Canaries have feathers.
- Canaries have skin.

All five items are true, but people usually answer some faster than others. Most people answer fastest on the *yellow* and *sing* items, slightly slower on the *eggs* and *feathers* items, and still slower on the *skin* item. Why? Yellowness and singing are distinctive of canaries. Because you do not think of eggs or feathers specifically as canary features, you reason, "Canaries are birds, and birds lay eggs. So canaries must lay eggs." For skin, you have to reason, "Canaries are birds and birds are animals. Animals have skin, so canaries must have skin." This way of categorizing things saves you enormous effort overall. When you learn some new fact about birds or animals in general, you don't have to learn it again separately for every species.

5. Which would people answer faster: whether politicians give speeches or whether they sometimes eat spaghetti? Why?

Answer

5. It would take longer to answer whether politicians eat spaghetti. Giving speeches is a distinctive feature of politicians. Eating spaghetti is not. To answer the second question, you have to reason that politicians are people, and most people eat spaghetti.

We also link a word or concept to related concepts. Figure 8.9 shows a possible network of conceptual links that someone might have at a particular moment (A. M. Collins & Loftus, 1975). Suppose this network describes your own concepts. *Thinking about one of the concepts shown in*

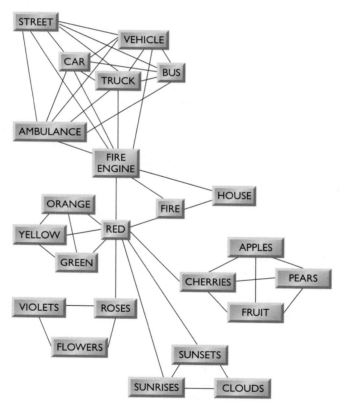

Figure 8.9 We link each concept to a variety of other related concepts. Any *stimulus* that activates one of these concepts will also partly activate (or prime) the ones that are linked to it. (From "A spreading-activation theory of semantic processing" by A. M. Collins and E. F. Loftus in *Psychological Review*, 1975, pp. 407–428. Reprinted by permission of Elizabeth Loftus.)

this figure will activate, or prime, the concepts linked to it through a process called **spreading activation** (A. M. Collins & Loftus, 1975). For example, if you hear *flower,* you are primed to think of *rose, violet,* and other flowers. If you also hear *red,* the combination of *flower* and *red* primes you to think of *rose.* You would recognize that word more easily than usual if it were flashed briefly on a screen or spoken very softly.

The idea of priming a concept is analogous to priming a pump: If you put some water in the pump to get it started, you can continue using the pump to draw water from a well. Similarly, priming *a concept gets it started. Reading or hearing one word makes it easier to think or recognize a related word. Seeing something makes it easier to recognize a related object.* Priming is important during reading. When you come to a word that you barely know, you find it easier to understand if the preceding sentences were about closely related concepts (Plaut & Booth, 2000). They provide hints about the meaning of the new word.

Priming occurs in many situations. If you were asked what you plan to do tomorrow, the odor of cleaning fluid in the room would prime you to think of cleaning your room, even if you were not conscious of the odor (Holland, Hendriks, & Aarts, 2005). If you view photos of famous people, you will more easily remember the name Brad Pitt if you had recently thought about cherry pits, just because of the similarity between pit and Pitt (Burke, Locantore, Austin, & Chae, 2004). If you look at pictures and try to identify the people or objects in the foreground, you will find the task easier if the background primes the same answer as the object in the foreground (Davenport & Potter, 2004) (see Figure 8.10). Most kinds of priming have brief effects, but some effects last surprisingly long (Mitchell, 2006).

Here is an illustration that can be explained in terms of spreading activation. Quickly answer each of the following questions (or ask someone else):

1. How many animals of each kind did Moses take on the ark?
2. What was the famous saying uttered by Louis Armstrong when he first set foot on the moon?
3. Some people pronounce St. Louis "saint loo-iss" and some pronounce it "saint loo-ee." How would you pronounce the capital city of Kentucky?

You can check answer C at the end of this module, page 285. Many people who miss these

Figure 8.10 A football stadium background primes identification of "football player," and a church primes identification of "priest/clergyman." When the people are placed in the opposite settings, they are harder to identify. (Davenport, J. L. & Potter, M. C. (2004). Scene consistency in object and background perception. *Psychological Science*, 15, 559–564. Used by permission.)

questions are embarrassed or angry. Figure 8.11 offers an explanation in terms of spreading activation (Shafto & MacKay, 2000): The question about Louis Armstrong activates a series of sounds and concepts that are linked to one another and to other items. The sound *Armstrong* and the ideas *first astronaut on the moon* and *famous sayings* are all linked to "One small step for a man . . ." Even the name *Louis Armstrong* is loosely linked to *Neil Armstrong* because both are famous people. The combined effect of all these influences automatically triggers the answer, "One small step for a man . . ." The name *Louis* in the second question helps prime the answer *Louisville* in the third.

6. Suppose someone says "cardinal" and then briefly flashes the word *bird* on a screen. Some viewers identify the word correctly, suggesting priming, and some do not. Considering both priming and the encoding specificity idea from chapter 7, how might you explain why some people and not others identified the word *bird*?

Answer

6. People who heard "cardinal" and thought of it as a bird would have spreading activation to prime the word *bird*. However, other people who thought of "cardinal" as an officer in the Catholic church would have spreading activation to prime a very different set of words and not *bird*.

Figure 8.11 According to one explanation, the word *Armstrong* and the ideas *astronaut, first person on the moon*, and *famous sayings* all activate the linked saying "One small step for a man . . ."

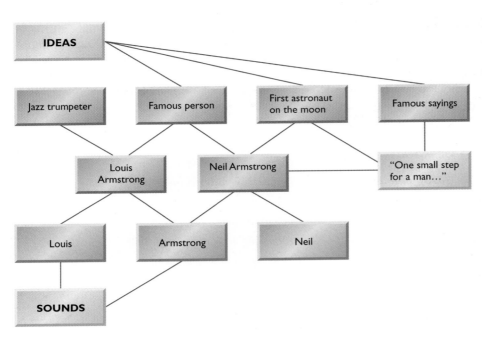

In Closing

Thinking About Attention and Concepts

Behaviorists have traditionally avoided the topic of cognition because thinking and knowledge are unobservable. Although I hope this module has demonstrated that scientific research on cognition is possible and leads to new understanding, I also hope you see that the behaviorists' objections were not frivolous. Research on cognition is difficult, and each advance requires many experiments to check and recheck each conclusion and compare alternative explanations. The results can have practical as well as theoretical benefits. For example, the better we can specify what we mean by "attention," the better we can deal with those who have attention deficits.

SUMMARY

- *Research methods in cognitive psychology.* Researchers infer mental processes from measurements of speed and accuracy. (page 274)
- *Mental imagery.* Mental images resemble vision in certain respects. The time required to answer questions about a rotating object depends on how far the object would actually rotate between one position and another. (page 274)
- *Top-down and bottom-up processes.* Some stimuli grab our attention automatically. We also control our attention, deliberately shifting it from one item to another. (page 275)
- *Attentive and preattentive processes.* We quickly notice items that are unusual in certain salient ways, regardless of potential distracters. Noticing less distinct items requires attention to one target after another. (page 276)
- *Attention bottleneck.* Attention is limited, and items compete for it. (page 277)
- *Conflict.* Adding attention to one item means subtracting it from another. For example, talking on a cell phone distracts from attention to driving. (page 277)

- *The Stroop effect.* When we are speaking, written words grab attention, making it difficult to attend to the color of the letters. (page 278)
- *Change blindness.* We often fail to detect changes in a scene if they occur slowly or during an eye movement. (page 278)
- *Attentional blink.* We frequently fail to detect a stimulus that appears 100 to 700 ms after a first stimulus that required attention. (page 279)
- *Attention-deficit disorder.* People with attention-deficit disorder have trouble shifting attention. Two tests of attention problems are the Choice-Delay task and the Stop Signal task. (page 280)
- *Categorization.* People use many categories that are hard to define. Many items are marginal examples of a category, so we cannot insist on a yes–no decision. (page 281)
- *Conceptual networks and priming.* We represent words or concepts with links to related concepts. Thinking about a concept primes one to think of related concepts. (page 281)

KEY TERMS

attention (page 275)

attention-deficit disorder (ADD) (page 280)

attention-deficit hyperactivity disorder (ADHD) (page 280)

attentional blink (page 279)

attentive process (page 276)

change blindness (page 279)

Choice-Delay task (page 280)

cognition (page 274)

preattentive process (page 276)

priming (page 282)

prototype (page 281)

spreading activation (page 282)

Stop Signal task (page 280)

Stroop effect (page 278)

ANSWERS TO OTHER QUESTIONS IN THE MODULE

A. The objects in pair a are the same; in b they are the same; and in c they are different. (page 275)

B. In the top scene, a horizontal bar along the wall has changed position. In the lower scene, the location of the helicopter has changed. (page 279)

C. 1. None. Moses didn't have an ark; Noah did. 2. Louis Armstrong never set foot on the moon; it was Neil Armstrong. 3. The correct pronunciation of Kentucky's capital is "frank-furt." (Not "loo-ee-ville"!) (page 282)

Solving Problems, Making Decisions, and Thinking

- How do we solve problems?
- What are some common errors of thinking?
- To what extent do we make decisions consciously or unconsciously?

Here is an example of creative problem solving: A college physics exam asked how to use a barometer to determine the height of a building. One student answered that he would tie a long string to the barometer, go to the top of the building, and carefully lower the barometer until it reached the ground. Then he would cut the string and measure its length.

When the professor marked this answer incorrect, the student asked why. "Well," said the professor, "your method would work, but it's not the method I wanted you to use." When the student objected, the professor offered as a compromise to let him try again.

"All right," the student said. "Take the barometer to the top of the building, drop it, and measure the time it takes to hit the ground. Then, from the formula for the speed of a falling object, using the gravitational constant, calculate the height of the building."

"Hmmm," replied the professor. "That too would work. And it does make use of physical principles. But it still isn't what I had in mind. Can you think of another way?"

"Another way? Sure," he replied. "Place the barometer next to the building on a sunny day. Measure the height of the barometer and the length of its shadow. Also measure the length of the building's shadow. Then use this formula":

height of barometer ÷ height of building = length of barometer's shadow ÷ length of building's shadow

The professor was impressed but still reluctant to give credit, so the student persisted with another method: "Measure the barometer's height. Then walk up the stairs of the building, marking it off in units of the barometer's height. At the top, take the number of barometer units and multiply by the height of the barometer to get the height of the building."

The professor sighed: "Give me one more way—any other way—and I'll give you credit, even if it's not the answer I wanted."

"Really?" asked the student with a smile. "*Any* other way?"

© David Burnett/Contact Press Images

How would you carry 98 water bottles—all at once, with no vehicle? When faced with a new problem, sometimes people find a novel and effective solution.

"Yes, any other way."

"All right," said the student. "Go to the man who owns the building and say, 'Hey, buddy, if you tell me how tall the building is, I'll give you this cool barometer!'"

Sometimes, people develop creative, imaginative solutions like the ones that the physics student proposed. Sometimes, they think they have a wonderful, creative idea, although the idea couldn't possibly work. Figure 8.12 shows an example. People sometimes make good decisions and sometimes make decisions they regret. Psychologists study problem-solving behavior and decision making partly to understand the thought processes and partly to look for ways to help people reason more effectively.

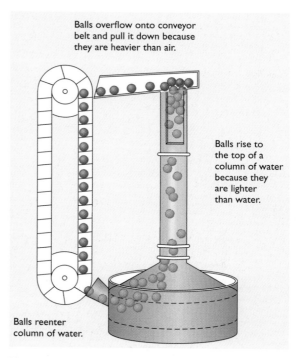

Figure 8.12 An inventor applied for a patent on this "perpetual motion machine." Rubber balls, being lighter than water, rise in a column of water and flow over the top. The balls are heavier than air, so they fall, thus moving a belt and generating energy. At the bottom, they reenter the water column. Do you see why this system could never work? (Check answer D on page 297.)

Balls overflow onto conveyor belt and pull it down because they are heavier than air.

Balls rise to the top of a column of water because they are lighter than water.

Balls reenter column of water.

ALGORITHMS AND HEURISTICS

We solve problems by means of algorithms and heuristics. Suppose you are a traveling salesperson living in Ames, Iowa (Figure 8.13). You want to visit 10 other cities and then return home by the shortest route. To find that route, you might list all possible routes, measure them, and determine which one is shortest. *A mechanical, repetitive procedure for solving a problem or testing every hypothesis* is called an **algorithm.**

However, you would probably want to simplify the problem. You would not bother checking routes that zigzag back and forth from one end of Iowa to the other. If instead of visiting 10 cities you had to visit hundreds of cities, simplifying the problem would be even more important. **Heuristics** are *strategies for simplifying a problem and generating a satisfactory guess.* These strategies provide quick guidance when you are willing or forced to accept some possibility of error, and they work more often than not (Gigerenzer, 2008). One heuristic: If you want to guess which child is oldest, choose the tallest. Another: If you want to guess which of two cities has a larger population, choose the one you have heard of or the one you have heard of more often (D. G. Goldstein & Gigerenzer, 2002). Still another: If the instructions for some task are difficult to understand, the task itself is probably difficult to do. Each heuristic works most of the time but not always. For example, *if the instructions are written in an unfamiliar or unclear font,* people find them difficult to read and therefore overestimate the difficulty of the task (Song & Schwarz, 2008). If a medicine or food additive has a name that is difficult to pronounce, you probably assume it is unsafe (Song & Schwarz, 2009).

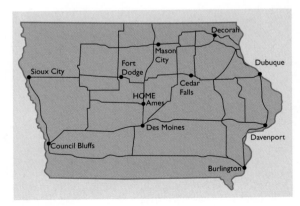

Figure 8.13 In the traveling salesperson task, you want to find the shortest route connecting all the points you need to visit.

Maximizing and Satisficing

You also use heuristics for questions that have no single correct answer, such as, "Which job shall I take?" or "Whom if anyone shall I marry?" or "How shall I spend my money?" On these questions, some people are willing to settle for "good enough," whereas others want to research every possibility to make the best choice. Do you channel-surf through hundreds of cable channels to find the program you like best, or do you stop as soon as you find one that looks interesting? Do you go from store to store in search of the best bargain, or do you buy as soon as you find something you like? One strategy, **maximizing,** means *thoroughly considering every possibility to find the best one.* **Satisficing** is *searching only until you find something satisfactory.* The maximizing strategy approximates the use of an algorithm. Satisficing is more of a heuristic approach.

Some people rely mostly on maximizing, and others prefer satisficing, although of course you might switch strategies depending on the situation. Researchers classify people as mainly maximizers or satisficers based on questions of the following type (Schwartz et al., 2002). For each item, rate yourself from 1 (not at all true) to 7 (definitely true):

- When I listen to the car radio, I frequently check other stations.
- I shop at many stores before deciding which clothes to buy.
- I expect to interview for many jobs before I accept one.

Researchers find that high maximizers usually make better choices, at least according to certain criteria. For example, they get jobs with higher starting pay than do satisficers, in spite of being about equal in their college grade-point average. However, they have more difficulty making a choice (Paivandy, Bullock, Reardon, & Kelly, 2008), and they are *less* satisfied with their choices! Satisficers look for something "good enough" and find it. Maximizers look for "the best" and continue to wonder whether they were right (Iyengar, Wells, & Schwartz, 2006). Whatever they choose, maximizers regret the opportunities they missed. In short, seeking the best possible choice sets you up for disappointment.

In many situations today, the maximizing strategy is difficult, just because of the huge number of choices available. In one study, researchers set up a booth at a supermarket offering free samples of jams. At various times, they offered either 6 kinds of jam or 24. As shown in

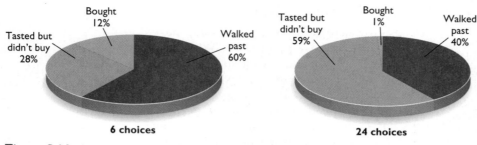

Figure 8.14 When people were offered 24 choices of jams, many stopped to taste, but few bought. (Based on data from Iyengar & Lepper, 2000)

Figure 8.14, offering 24 jams attracted more people to stop and taste, but almost none of them bought any. With fewer choices, more people selected one to buy. Too many choices inhibit people from making any decision at all, especially people who are looking for the best possible choice (Schwartz, 2004).

Having too few choices is disadvantageous also. Most Americans like making choices, and anything they choose becomes immediately more valuable in their eyes (Szrek & Baron, 2007). Many Asians are just as pleased to receive an item without having any choice (Savani, Markus, & Conner, 2008). If you have a decision to make, how many choices would you like to have? If we have too few choices, we wish there was more variety, but with too many choices, we feel overwhelmed. On an Internet dating service, the average person prefers to see profiles of 20 or more potential partners before making a choice, although people who are offered fewer choices are usually just as happy with their decisions (Lenton, Fasolo, & Todd, 2008). For a less important decision such as which kind of jam to buy, young adults prefer about 10 choices, and older adults prefer even fewer choices, about 5 (Reed, Mikels, & Simon, 2008; Shah & Wolford, 2007).

7. Based on this research, would you expect someone who dates a great many people before marriage to be happier or less happy with the eventual marriage partner?

Concept Check

Answer

7. Someone who dates a great many people is probably a maximizer, looking for the perfect match. If so, we would predict that this person will make a good choice but probably feel less satisfied, wondering whether this was really the perfect choice.

The Representativeness Heuristic and Base-Rate Information

Although heuristic thinking is often helpful, it leads us astray when we rely on it inappropriately. In 2002 Daniel Kahneman won the Nobel Prize in economics for research showing examples of inappropriate use of heuristics. For example, consider the saying: "If something looks like a duck, waddles like a duck, and quacks like a duck, chances are it's a duck." This saying is an example of the representativeness heuristic, *the assumption that an item that resembles members of some category is probably also in that category.* This heuristic is usually correct, except when we deal with uncommon categories. If you see something that looks like a rare bird, you should check carefully to make sure it isn't a similar, more common species. In general, to decide whether something belongs in one category or another, you should consider

the base-rate information—that is, *how common the two categories are.*

When people apply the representativeness heuristic, they frequently overlook base-rate information. For example, consider the following question (modified from Kahneman & Tversky, 1973):

Psychologists have interviewed 30 engineers and 70 lawyers. One of them, Jack, is a 45-year-old married man with four children. He is generally conservative, cautious, and ambitious. He shows no interest in political and social issues and spends most of his free time on home carpentry, sailing, and solving mathematical puzzles. What is the probability that Jack is one of the 30 engineers in the sample of 100?

Most people estimate a rather high probability—perhaps 80 or 90%—because the description sounds more like engineers than lawyers. That estimate isn't wrong, as we do not know the true probability. The key point is that if some people are told the sample included 30 engineers and 70 lawyers and others are told it included 70 engineers and 30 lawyers, both groups make about the same estimate for Jack (Kahneman & Tversky, 1973). Certainly, the base-rate information should have some influence.

In 2002 Princeton psychologist Daniel Kahneman (left) won the Nobel Prize in economics. (There is no Nobel Prize in psychology.) Although others have won Nobel Prizes for research related to psychology, Kahneman was the first winner who had a PhD in psychology.

Here is another example of misusing the representativeness heuristic:

> Linda was a philosophy major. She is 31, bright, outspoken, and concerned about issues of discrimination and social justice.

What would you estimate is the probability that Linda is a bank teller? What is the probability that she is a feminist bank teller? (Answer before you read on.)

The true probabilities, hard to estimate, are not the point. The interesting result is that many people estimate a higher probability that Linda is a *feminist* bank teller than the probability that she is a bank teller (Tversky & Kahneman, 1983). However, every feminist bank teller is a bank teller. Apparently, people regard this description as fairly typical for a feminist and thus for a feminist bank teller (or feminist anything else) but not typical for bank tellers in general (Shafir, Smith, & Osherson, 1990).

---

8. A device was built to protect airplanes by detecting explosives in people's luggage. It detects 95% of bombs. When luggage has no explosives, it has a false alarm (falsely detecting a bomb) 5% of the time. Is this device good enough to use? (Hint: Think about the base-rate probability of the presence of a bomb.)

Concept Check

Answer

8. A false-alarm rate of 5% is far too high. Imagine a plane with 100 innocent passengers, each checking two bags. Of the 200 innocent bags, this device will identify 5%—that is, 10 bags—as containing a bomb! Speer (1989) estimated that this device (which the Federal Aviation Administration considered using) would have 5 million false alarms for every bomb it found.

The Availability Heuristic

When you estimate how common something is, you usually start by thinking of examples. If you remember enjoying your astronomy class more times than you remember enjoying any other class, probably that astronomy class really was interesting. If you remember many summer days when mosquitoes bit you and no winter days when they bit you, you conclude that mosquitoes are more common in summer. The availability heuristic is *the tendency to assume that if we easily think of examples of a category, then that category must be common.* However, this heuristic leads us astray when uncommon events are highly memorable (Table 8.1). During the months after the terrorist attacks of September 11, 2001, people thought frequently about airplane disasters, and most Americans avoided air travel. They traveled by car instead, although the risk of a fatal crash is far greater in cars than in airplanes (Gigerenzer, 2004).

Other examples: How would you feel if your favorite team wins its next game? How would you feel if you missed your bus? How would you feel if your professor complimented you on good work? Most people overestimate how good they would feel after good events and how bad they would feel after bad events because the most extreme memories are easily available. You remember the most intense joy you ever felt when your team won a big game, the worst you ever felt when you missed the bus, and so forth (Morewedge, Gilbert, & Wilson, 2005). In addition, anticipated future events are more arousing than almost any memory of the past, just because the future is uncertain (Van Boven & Ashworth, 2007).

Also, consider the widespread belief that "you should always stick with your first impulse on a multiple-choice test." Researchers have consistently found this claim to be wrong (J. J. Johnston, 1975; Kruger, Wirtz, & Miller, 2005). Changing an answer helps for several reasons. You sometimes discover that you misread a question the first time

Table 8.1 The Representativeness Heuristic and the Availability Heuristic

	A Tendency to Assume That	Leads Us Astray When	Example of Error
Representativeness Heuristic	An item that resembles members of a category probably belongs to that category.	Something resembles members of a rare category.	Something looks like it might be a UFO, so you decide it is.
Availability Heuristic	The more easily we can think of members of a category, the more common the category is.	One category gets more publicity than another or is more memorable.	You remember more reports of airplane crashes, than car crashes so you think air travel is more dangerous.

or that you wrote down the wrong answer accidentally. Sometimes, a question later in the test reminds you of the correct answer to an earlier item. Why, then, do most students believe that their first impulse is correct? Think of what happens when you get your test back. You check the questions you got wrong, and you notice anything you changed from right to wrong. You don't notice the ones you changed from wrong to right. Your availability heuristic leads you to believe that changing an answer hurts you.

OTHER COMMON ERRORS IN HUMAN COGNITION

In addition to relying inappropriately on the representativeness heuristic and availability heuristic, people consistently make several other kinds of errors. For decades, college professors have emphasized critical thinking, *the careful evaluation of evidence for and against any conclusion.* However, even those who teach critical thinking sometimes find themselves accepting nonsense that they should have questioned. Why do intelligent people sometimes make major mistakes? Here are a few of the reasons.

Overconfidence

How long is the Nile River? "I don't know!" you reply. I didn't expect you to know, but guess an approximate range, such as "between X and Y" in either miles or kilometers. Then note how confident you are that the actual answer is

within the range you guessed. If you say "0%," you mean that you *know* your range is wrong, in which case you should widen the range until you are fairly confident you must be right.

On difficult questions like this, most people are overconfident of their answers. For example, when they say they are 90% confident, they are actually correct far less than 90% of the time (Plous, 1993). On easy questions, the trend is reversed and people tend to be underconfident (Erev, Wallsten, & Budescu, 1994; Juslin, Winman, & Olsson, 2000). You can try additional items with the Online Try It Yourself exercise Overconfidence. (Incidentally, the Nile River is 4,187 miles long, or 6,738 kilometers.)

Philip Tetlock (1994) studied government officials and consultants, foreign policy professors, newspaper columnists, and others who make their living by analyzing and predicting world events. He asked them to predict world events over the next several years—such as what would happen in Korea, the Middle East, and so forth—and to state their confidence in their predictions (e.g., 70%). Five years later, he compared predictions to actual results and found very low accuracy, especially among those who were the most confident.

Confirmation Bias

We often err by *accepting a hypothesis and then looking for evidence to support it instead of considering other possibilities.* This tendency is the confirmation bias. For example, examine the poorly focused photo in Figure 8.15a and guess what it depicts. Then see Figures 8.15b and 8.15c on the following pages. Seeing the extremely out-of-focus photo makes it harder to identify the second photo. When people see the first photo, they form a hypothesis, probably a wrong one, which interferes with correctly perceiving a later photo (Bruner & Potter, 1964).

Peter Wason (1960) asked students to discover a certain rule he had in mind for generating sequences of numbers. One example of the numbers the rule might generate, he explained, was "2, 4, 6." He told the students that they could ask about other sequences, and he would tell them whether or not those sequences fit his rule. They should tell him as soon as they thought they knew the rule.

Most students started by asking, "8, 10, 12?" When told "yes," they proceeded with "14, 16, 18?" Each time, they were told, "Yes, that sequence fits the rule." Soon most of them guessed, "The rule is three consecutive even numbers." "No," came the reply. "That is not the rule." Many

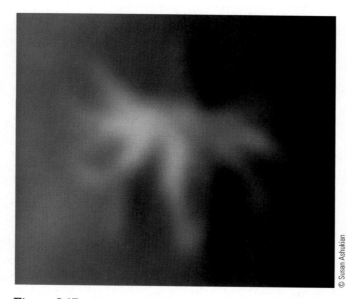

Figure 8.15a Guess what this shows. Then examine parts b and c on pages 292 and 294.

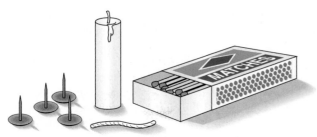

Figure 8.16 Given only these materials, what is the best way to attach the candle to a wall so that it can be lit?

3. There are some students in a room. All but two of them are psychology majors, all but two are chemistry majors, and all but two are history majors. How many students are present? (If your first impulse is to say "two of each," try it out: It doesn't work.) Now here's the interesting part: There are two possible solutions. After you have found one solution, discard it and find another. After you have either found solutions or given up, check answer E on page 297. (Solve these problems before reading further.)

Question 1 was difficult because most people think of the matchbox as a container for matches, not as a tool on its own. The box is "functionally fixed" for one way of using it. A similar question was put to people in a subsistence society with few tools. They were given a set of objects and asked how they could use them to build a tower to reach a person in distress. If the objects included an empty box, they used it, but if the box contained other objects, they didn't quickly think of emptying the box and using it (German & Barrett, 2005).

Question 2 was difficult because most people assume that the lines must remain within the area defined by the nine dots. On question 3, it is difficult to think of even one solution, and after thinking of it, it is hard to abandon it to think of a different approach.

students persisted, trying "20, 22, 24?" "26, 28, 30?" "250, 252, 254?" They continued testing sequences that fit their rule, ignoring other possibilities. The rule Wason had in mind was, "Any three positive numbers of increasing magnitude." For instance, 1, 2, 3 would be acceptable, and so would 21, 25, 601.

A special case of confirmation bias is functional fixedness, *the tendency to adhere to a single approach or a single way of using an item.* Here are three examples:

1. You are provided with a candle, a box of matches, some thumbtacks, and a tiny piece of string, as shown in Figure 8.16. Using no other equipment, find a way to mount the candle to the wall so that it can be lit.

2. Consider an array of nine dots:

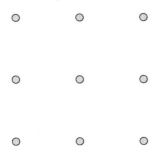

Connect all nine dots with a series of connected straight lines, such that the end of one line is the start of the next. For example, one way would be:

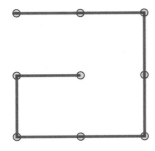

But use the fewest lines possible.

Framing Questions

A logical person should give the same answer no matter how a question is worded, right? However, most people change their answers depending on the wording of the questions, as you may recall from the discussion of surveys in chapter 2.

For example, which would you rather receive, $5 now or $6.20 four weeks from now? Many people choose $5 now. Let's rephrase: Which would you prefer, $5 today and $0 a month from now or $0 today and $6.20 a month from now? The second phrasing increases the percentage of people who choose the delayed reward (Magen, Dweck, & Gross, 2008).

Another example: Suppose you have been appointed head of the Public Health Service, and you need to choose a plan to deal with a disease that has endangered the lives of 600 people. If you adopt plan A, you will save the lives of 200 people. If you adopt plan B, you have a 33% chance to save all 600 and a 67% chance to save no one. *Choose plan A or B before reading further.*

Now another disease breaks out, and again, you must choose between two plans. If you adopt plan C, 400 people will die. If you adopt plan D, there is a 33% chance that no one will die and a 67% chance that 600 will die. *Choose plan C or D now.*

Figure 8.17 shows the results for a large group of people. Most chose A over B and D over C. However, plan A is exactly the same as C (200 live, 400 die), and plan B is exactly the same as D. Why then did so many people choose both A and D? According to Tversky and Kahneman (1981), most people avoid taking a risk to gain something (e.g., saving lives) but willingly take a risk to avoid loss (e.g., not letting people die). *The tendency to answer a question differently when it is framed (phrased) differently* is called the framing effect. See also the Online Try It Yourself activity Framing Effect.

Do losses always seem more salient than gains? It depends! A loss of $10,000 seems bigger than a gain of $10,000, and it will alter your mood for longer. But the effect reverses at small amounts. If you find a coin or small bill, you are pleased at your good fortune. If you lose the same amount, you shrug it off as not worth worrying about (Harinck, Van Dijk, Van Beest, & Mersmann, 2007).

Plan	How question was framed	Plan preferred by	Outcome
A	Save 200 people	72%	
C	400 people will die	22%	200 live, 400 die
B	33% chance of saving all 600; 67% chance of saving no one	28%	
D	33% chance no one will die; 67% chance all 600 will die	78%	33% chance 600 live or 67% chance 600 die

Figure 8.17 Most people chose plan A over B and D over C, although A produces the same result as C and B produces the same result as D. Amos Tversky and Daniel Kahneman (1981) proposed that most people play it safe to gain something but accept a risk to avoid a loss.

The Sunk Cost Effect

The sunk cost effect is a special case of the framing effect. Suppose that months ago you bought an expensive ticket to a football game, but the game is today and the weather is miserably cold. You wish you hadn't bought the ticket. Do you go to the game?

Figure 8.15b

© Susan Ashukian

Many people say they will go to the football game in the bad weather because they don't want to waste the money. This example illustrates the sunk cost effect, *the willingness to do something because of money or effort already spent* (Arkes & Ayton, 1999). This tendency arises in many situations. A company continues investing vast amounts of money in an unsuccessful project because it doesn't want to admit it has wasted so much money. A professional sports team gives someone a huge signing bonus, and later finds the player's performance disappointing, but keeps using that player to avoid wasting the money.

9. When students estimate their grades for the coming semester or athletic coaches estimate their teams' success for the coming year, what mistake is likely?

10. Someone says, "More than 90% of all college students like to watch late-night television, but only 20% of adults over 50 do. Therefore, most watchers of late-night television are college students." What error in thinking has this person made?

11. Someone tells me that if I say "abracadabra" every morning, I will stay healthy. I say it daily, and sure enough, I stay healthy. I conclude that this magic word ensures health. What error in thinking have I made?

12. Which of the following offers by your professor would probably be more persuasive? **(a)** "If you do this extra project, there's a small chance I will add some points to your grade." **(b)** "I'm going to penalize this whole class for being inattentive today, but if you do this extra project, there's a chance I won't subtract anything from your grade."

Answers

9. Both are likely to be overconfident. Generally, the weakest students and teams are most likely to overestimate their success.

10. Failure to consider the base rate: 20% of all older adults is a larger number than 90% of all college students.

11. Premature commitment to one hypothesis without testing the hypothesis that one could stay healthy without the magic word.

12. Probably **(b)**. People are generally more willing to take a risk to avoid losing something than to gain something.

EXPERTISE

How can we overcome the errors of human reasoning? Although all of us make mistakes in our reasoning, some develop expertise within a given field that enables them to solve problems quickly with a minimum of error. They apply the appropriate algorithms quickly, and they recognize which heuristics work in a particular situation. Reaching that point requires enormous effort.

Practice Makes (Nearly) Perfect

Expert performance is extremely impressive. Researchers asked people to watch video clips showing basketball free throws. The clips were interrupted at various points before the ball reached the net, and the observers were to guess whether the ball would go through the hoop. Professional basketball players, unlike other people, were remarkably accurate even with very short clips that stopped before the ball left the shooter's hand (Aglioti, Cesari, Romani, & Urgesi, 2008).

It is tempting to assume that experts were born with special talent. Not so, say psychologists who have studied expertise. In fields ranging from chess to sports to violin playing, the rule is that expertise requires about 10 years of intense practice (Ericsson & Charness, 1994; Ericsson, Krampe, & Tesch-Römer, 1993). The top violin players say they have practiced 3 to 4 hours every day since early childhood. A world-class tennis player spends hours at a time working on backhand shots, and a golfer spends similar efforts on chip shots. Hungarian author Laszlo Polgar set out to demonstrate his conviction that almost anyone can achieve expertise with sufficient effort. He devoted enormous efforts to nurturing his three daughters' chess skills. All three became outstanding chess players, and one, Judit, was the first woman and the youngest person ever to reach grand master status.

When we look at brain anatomy, we find that developing expertise expands the axons and dendrites of neurons relevant to a skill. Professional musicians show expansions in the brain areas important for hearing (Schneider et al., 2002) and timing (Gaser & Schlaug, 2003). The areas representing finger sensations expand in people who read Braille (Pascual-Leone, Wasserman, Sadato, & Hallett, 1995). The longer someone has been a London taxi driver, the larger the posterior hippocampus, which is important for spatial memory (Maguire et al., 2000).

Brain autopsies have shown that people with more education and mental activity tend to have greater branching in their dendrites (Jacobs, Schall, & Scheibel, 1993). However, although it is possible that education and mental activity pro-

Judit Polgar confirmed her father's confidence that prolonged effort could make her a grand master chess player.

mote brain growth, it is also possible that people who started with more dendritic branching succeeded well in their education and were drawn to more intellectual activities. Older adults who spend much time on crossword puzzles and similar activities improve their performance on those tasks but not on other tasks (Salthouse, 2006). In short, practice of any skill improves performance of that skill, but we have no clear evidence that mental exercise improves performance of skills one has not practiced.

Expert Pattern Recognition

What exactly do experts do that sets them apart from others? Primarily, they can look at a pattern and recognize its important features quickly.

In a typical experiment (de Groot, 1966), chess experts and novices briefly examined pieces on a chessboard, as in Figure 8.18, and then tried to recall the positions. When the pieces were arranged as they might be in an actual game, expert players recalled 91% of the positions correctly, whereas novices recalled only 41%. When the pieces were arranged randomly, however, the expert players did no better than average. That is, they do not have a superior memory overall, but through long practice, they have learned to recognize common chessboard patterns. (Recall the concept of chunking from chapter 7—the process of recognizing a large cluster of items and then remembering them as a unit.) The top players do almost as well in blitz chess—where they have only a few seconds to choose each move—as in normal chess. That is, they make most of their moves by memory, not reasoning (Burns, 2004). In a wide variety of other areas, from bird identifica-

Figure 8.18 Master chess players quickly recognize and memorize chess pieces arranged as they might occur in a normal game (a). However, they are no better than average at memorizing a random pattern (b).

tion to reading x-rays to judging gymnastic competitions, experts learn to recognize important details almost immediately (Murphy & Medin, 1985; Ste-Marie, 1999; Tanaka, Curran, & Sheinberg, 2005).

Figure 8.15c

13. The introduction to module 7.1 mentioned the World Memory Championship, in which contestants compete at memorizing long lists of words, numbers, or cards. How would practice enable them to develop this kind of expertise? That is, what must they do differently from other people?

Answer

13. As with other kinds of expertise, experts at memorizing learn to recognize patterns. Whereas most people would see "King of hearts, two of spades, three of clubs, seven of clubs, ace of diamonds" as five items, someone who has practiced memorizing cards might see this as a single familiar pattern or as a part of an even larger pattern.

UNCONSCIOUS THINKING AND PROBLEM SOLVING

Consider this problem (M. Gardner, 1978): Figure 8.19 shows an object that was made by cutting and bending an ordinary piece of cardboard. How was it made? Take a piece of paper and try to make it yourself. (The solution is on page 297, answer F.)

This is an "insight" or "aha!" problem. You can't go through a set formula to solve it, and if you do solve it, you probably don't know how

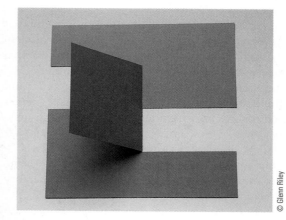

Figure 8.19 This object was made by cutting and folding an ordinary piece of cardboard with nothing left over. How was it done?

you found the answer. You say, "It just came to me." The processes in your head were apparently unconscious.

Unconscious thoughts enter into our decisions—unconscious in the sense that we can't verbalize them. Here is one demonstration: You see a series of words on the screen. When you see a "good" word (e.g., *love* or *happy*), tap a key with your left finger. When you see a "bad" word (e.g., *hate* or *angry*), tap a key with your right finger. After you learn this task well, the rule changes: Tap with your left finger when you see either a good word *or* a photo of the U.S. military. Tap with your right finger when you see a bad word. Then we try the reverse: Tap with your left finger when you see a good word. Tap with your right finger when you see a bad word or a photo of the U.S. military. On the average, people with high respect for the U.S. military answer faster when the instructions pair military pictures with good words. People who dislike the U.S. military answer faster when the instructions pair military pictures with bad words. *This task, based on relative speed of response to different pairs of stimuli,* is one version of the Implicit Association Test (IAT). We shall encounter more examples in chapters 13 and 14. Now, what about people who say they are neutral toward the U.S. military? At one time, the U.S. military wanted to expand its bases in Vicenza, Italy, and the proposal was intensely controversial among people there. Some of the people said they were neutral on this issue. However, on the IAT, nearly all of them responded faster to either the good word/military combination or the bad word/military combination. (The differences are small, and people don't monitor their reaction times well enough to detect the difference.) Their responses on this task, revealing preferences that they did not express consciously, accurately predicted changes they would express in their conscious opinions a few weeks later (Galdi, Arcuri, & Gawronski, 2008). Evidently, many people who claim to be undecided on a political issue are merely unconscious of their decision.

Here is another example of unconscious processing: Suppose you are registering for next semester's courses, and you are debating between a course in anthropology and one in economics. You receive a flood of information: The anthropology course sounds more interesting, it meets at a more convenient time, and your boyfriend or girlfriend is planning to take it, but the textbook is more expensive. The economics course is more useful for your career plans, and your adviser recommends it, but the professor teaching the course next semester has a reputation for being boring, and the class meets in a room that is a long walk from your dormitory. How do you decide? Researchers gave participants a series of scenarios like this. Sometimes, they asked for a quick decision. Sometimes, they let a person think about it deliberately for 3 minutes. Sometimes, they distracted the person for 3 minutes, allowing time for unconscious processing. On the average, people made the best decisions when they processed the information unconsciously during a 3-minute distraction. The decisions were best according to two criteria: People were more likely to choose the item with more positive features and fewer negatives, as counted by the researchers. Also, when asked about their choice later, the participants were more likely to be happy with their choices. When making a conscious decision, participants usually focused on a single attribute that was easy to defend, such as "the economics course is better for my career plans," whereas unconscious heuristic thinking weighed a combination of factors (Dijksterhuis & Nordgren, 2006).

However, it is not always better to think about decisions unconsciously. Another study contrasted three procedures: Ponder a decision unconsciously (as in the example just given), think about it consciously for a few minutes, or think about it consciously for as long as you want (usually *less* time than the group required to think about it for a few minutes). Those who considered their decision consciously for only as long as they wanted did at least as well as the unconscious thinking group and maybe a bit better. Those required to think about their decision consciously for a longer time did the worst. They often talked themselves out of the decision they wanted to make based on one or two attributes of a particular choice (Payne, Samper, Bettman, & Luce, 2008). Still, the point is that unconscious processes are helpful for much decision making.

· ·

14. Sometimes, people say they are going to "sleep on it" before making a decision. For what kind of decision might that be a good strategy?

Answer

14. It might be a good strategy for someone who needs to weigh large quantities of information about several choices.

· ·

In Closing

Successful and Unsuccessful Problem Solving

In this module, we have considered thinking at its best and worst—expertise and error. Experts polish their skills through extensive practice. Of course, we all have to make decisions about topics in which we are not experts. Without insisting on perfection, we can at least hold ourselves to the standard of not doing anything foolish. Perhaps if we become more aware of common errors, we can be more alert to avoid them.

SUMMARY

- *Algorithm and heuristics.* People solve problems by algorithms (repetitive means of checking every possibility) and heuristics (ways of simplifying a problem). (page 287)
- *Maximizing and satisficing.* The maximizing strategy is to consider thoroughly every possible choice to find the best one. The satisficing strategy is to accept the first choice one finds that is good enough. People using the maximizing strategy usually make good choices but are often not fully pleased with them. That strategy is especially problematic when too many choices are available. (page 287)
- *Representativeness heuristic and base-rate information.* If something resembles members of some category, we usually assume it too belongs to that category. However, that assumption is risky if the category is a rare one. (page 288)
- *Availability heuristic.* We generally assume that the more easily we can think of examples of some category, the more common that category is. However, this heuristic misleads us when items in rare categories get much publicity. (page 289)

- *Critical thinking.* Even people who try conscientiously to evaluate the evidence for every claim sometimes find themselves repeating a nonsensical statement that they know they should have doubted. (page 290)
- *Some reasons for errors.* People tend to be overconfident about their own judgments on difficult questions. They tend to look for evidence that confirms their hypothesis instead of evidence that might reject it. They answer the same question differently when it is framed differently. They sometimes take unpleasant actions to avoid admitting that previous actions were a waste of time or money. (page 290)
- *Expertise.* Becoming an expert requires years of practice and effort. Experts recognize and memorize familiar and meaningful patterns more rapidly than less experienced people do. (page 293)
- *Unconscious decision making.* When confronted with conflicting information, we sometimes make better decisions by thinking about the problem unconsciously while doing other things than by debating the possibilities directly. (page 294)

KEY TERMS

algorithm (page 287)

availability heuristic (page 289)

base-rate information (page 288)

confirmation bias (page 290)

critical thinking (page 290)

framing effect (page 291)

functional fixedness (page 291)

heuristics (page 287)

Implicit Association Test (IAT) (page 295)

maximizing (page 287)

representativeness heuristic (page 288)

satisficing (page 287)

sunk cost effect (page 292)

D. Any membrane heavy enough to keep the water in would also keep the rubber balls out. (page 286)

E. (1) The best way to attach the candle to the wall is to dump the matches from the box and thumbtack the side of the box to the wall, as shown in this picture. The tiny piece of string is irrelevant.

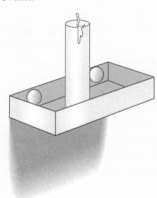

(2) The dots can be connected with four lines:

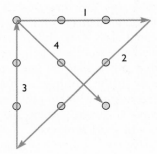

(3) One answer is three students: one psychology major, one chemistry major, and one history major. The other possibility is two students who are majoring in something else—music, for example. (If there are two music majors, all but two of them are indeed majoring in psychology, etc.). (page 291)

F. This illustration shows how to cut and fold an ordinary piece of paper or cardboard to match the figure with nothing left over. (page 294)

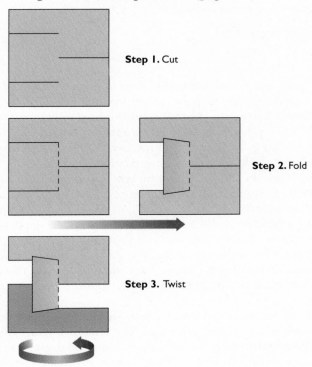

Step 1. Cut

Step 2. Fold

Step 3. Twist

- To what extent can other species learn language?
- What specializations enable humans to learn language?
- How do we understand words and sentences?
- What do we do when we read?

Language enables us to learn from the experiences of people who lived far away or long ago. Languages have the property of productivity, *the ability to combine our words into new sentences that express an unlimited variety of ideas* (Deacon, 1997). Every day, you say and hear a few stock sentences like, "Nice weather we're having" or "I can't find my keys," but you also invent new sentences that no one has ever said or heard before.

You might ask, "How do you know that no one has ever said that sentence before?!" Well, of course, no one can be certain that a particular sentence is new, but we can be confident that many sentences are new (without specifying which ones) because of the vast number of possible ways to rearrange words. Imagine this exercise (but don't really try it unless you have nothing else to do with your life): Pick a sentence of more than 10 words from any book you choose. How long would you need to keep reading, in that book or any other, until you found the exact same sentence again?

In short, we do not memorize all the sentences we use. Instead, we learn rules for making and understanding sentences. The famous linguist Noam Chomsky (1980) described those rules as a transformational grammar, *a system for converting a deep structure into a surface structure.* The deep structure is the underlying logic or meaning of a sentence. The surface structure is the sequence of words as they are actually spoken or written (Figure 8.20). According to this theory, when-

ever we speak, we transform the deep structure of the language into a surface structure.

Two surface structures can resemble each other without representing the same deep structure, or they can represent the same deep structure without resembling each other. For example, "John is easy to please" has the same deep structure as "pleasing John is easy" and "it is easy to please John." These sentences represent the same idea. In contrast, consider the sentence, "Never threaten someone with a chain saw." The surface structure of that sentence maps into two deep structures, as shown in Figure 8.21.

NONHUMAN PRECURSORS TO LANGUAGE

Language researcher Terrence Deacon once presented a talk about language to his 8-year-old's elementary school class. One child asked whether other animals have their own languages. Deacon explained that other species communicate but without the productivity of human language. The child persisted, asking whether other animals had at least a *simple* language, perhaps one with only a few words and short sentences. No, he replied, they do not have even a simple language.

Deep Structure No. 1:
You are holding a chain saw. Don't threaten to use it to attack someone!

Deep Structure No. 2:
Some deranged person is holding a chain saw. Don't threaten him!

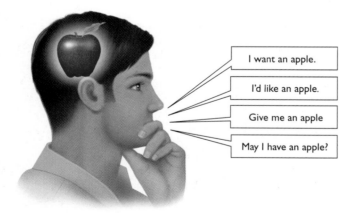

Figure 8.20 According to transformational grammar, we can transform a sentence with a given deep structure into any of several other sentences with different surface structures.

Figure 8.21 The sentence "Never threaten someone with a chain saw" has one surface structure but two deep structures, corresponding to different meanings.

Then another child asked, "Why not?" (Deacon, 1997, p. 12). Deacon paused. Why not, indeed? If language is so extremely useful to humans, why haven't other species evolved at least a little of it? And what makes humans so good at learning language?

One way to examine humans' language specialization is to ask how far another species could progress toward language. Beginning in the 1920s, several psychologists reared chimpanzees in their homes and tried to teach them to talk. The chimpanzees learned many human habits but understood only a few words.

Part of the problem is that chimpanzees cannot make human sounds. They make their sounds while inhaling, whereas humans speak while exhaling. (Try to speak while inhaling!) However, chimpanzees do make hand gestures in nature. R. Allen Gardner and Beatrice Gardner (1969) taught a chimpanzee named Washoe to use the sign language of the American deaf (Ameslan). Washoe eventually learned the symbols for about 100 words, and other chimps learned to communicate with other visual symbols (Figure 8.22).

How much do these gestures resemble language? Washoe and other chimpanzees trained in this way used their symbols almost exclusively to make requests, not to describe, and rarely in original combinations (Pate & Rumbaugh, 1983; Terrace, Petitto, Sanders, & Bever, 1979; C. R. Thompson & Church, 1980). By contrast, a human child with a vocabulary of 100 words or so links them into short sentences and frequently uses words to describe. However, Washoe did show at least limited understanding of language. She usually answered "Who" questions with names, "What" questions with objects, and "Where" questions with places, even when she did not specify the correct name, object, or place (Van Cantfort, Gardner, & Gardner, 1989).

a

b

c

d

Images courtesy of Ann Premack

Figure 8.22 Psychologists have tried to teach chimpanzees to communicate with gestures or symbols. (a) A chimp arranges plastic chips to request food. (b) Viki in her human home, helping with the housework. She learned to make a few sounds similar to English words. (c) Kanzi, a bonobo, presses symbols to indicate words. (d) A chimp signing *toothbrush*.

More impressive results have been reported for another species, the bonobo chimpanzee, *Pan paniscus*. Bonobos' social behavior resembles that of humans in several regards: Males and females form strong attachments; females are sexually responsive outside their fertile period; males contribute to infant care; and adults often share food with one another. Like humans, they stand comfortably on their hind legs, and they often copulate face-to-face. Several bonobos have learned to press keys on a board to make short sentences, as in Figure 8.22c and Figure 8.23. Unlike Washoe and other common chimpanzees, bonobos sometimes use symbols to describe events, without requesting anything. One with a cut on his hand explained that his mother had bitten him. They also make original, creative requests, such as asking one person to chase another.

The most proficient bonobos seem to comprehend symbols about as well as a 2- to 2 $\frac{1}{2}$-year-old child understands language (Savage-Rumbaugh et al., 1993). They also show considerable understanding of spoken English, following such odd commands as "bite your ball" and "take the vacuum cleaner outside" (Savage-Rumbaugh, 1990; Savage-Rumbaugh, Sevcik, Brakke, & Rumbaugh, 1992). They passed a test of responding to commands issued over earphones, eliminating the possibility of unintentional "Clever Hans"–type signals, as discussed in chapter 2 (Figure 8.23).

Why have bonobos been more successful with language than common chimpanzees? Apparently, bonobos have a greater predisposition for this type of learning. Also, they learned by observation and imitation, which promote better understanding than the formal training methods that previous studies used (Savage-Rumbaugh et al., 1992). Finally, the bonobos began their language experience early in life. Humans learn language more easily when they are young, and bonobos probably do, too.

....

15. Based on the studies with bonobos, can you offer advice about how to teach language to children with impaired language learning?

Answer

15. Start language learning when a child is young. Rely on imitation as much as possible instead of providing direct reinforcements for correct responses.

....

HUMAN SPECIALIZATIONS FOR LEARNING LANGUAGE

Humans are clearly more adapted for language than any other species, including bonobos. Why do we learn language so easily?

Language and General Intelligence

Did we evolve language as an accidental by-product of evolving big brains? Several observations argue strongly against this idea. Dolphins and whales have even larger brains but do not develop language. They communicate but not in a flexible system resembling human language. Some people with massive brain damage have less total brain mass than a chimpanzee but continue to speak and understand language.

Also, some children, up to 7% by some estimates, have normal intelligence in other ways but noticeable limitations in language. For example, they don't understand the difference between "Who was the girl pushing?" and "Who was pushing the girl?" (Leonard, 2007). People in one family having a particular gene have even greater language impairments despite otherwise normal intelligence (Fisher, Vargha-Khadem, Watkins, Monaco, & Pembrey, 1998; Lai, Fisher, Hurst, Vargha-Khadem, & Monaco, 2001). They do not fully master even simple rules, such as how to form plurals of nouns. So normal human brain size and normal intelligence do not automatically produce language.

At the opposite extreme, consider Williams syndrome, *a genetic condition characterized by mental retardation in most regards but skillful use of language.* Before the discovery of Williams syn-

Figure 8.23 Kanzi, a bonobo, points to answers on a board in response to questions he hears through earphones. Experimenter Rose Sevcik does not hear the questions, so she cannot signal the correct answer.

drome, psychologists assumed that language was impossible without normal intelligence. Although people with Williams syndrome typically do not master language perfectly (Meyer-Lindenberg, Mervis, & Berman, 2006), their speech is remarkably good compared to their other abilities. One 14-year-old with Williams syndrome wrote creative stories and songs but in other ways performed like a 5- to 7-year-old and could not be left alone without a babysitter. Another child, when asked to name as many animals as he could, started with "ibex, whale, bull, yak, zebra, puppy, kitten, tiger, koala, dragon . . ." Another child could sing more than 1,000 songs in 22 languages (Bellugi & St. George, 2000). However, these children prefer 50 pennies to 5 dollars and, when asked to estimate the length of a bus, give answers such as "3 inches or 100 inches, maybe" (Bellugi, Lichtenberger, Jones, Lai, & St. George, 2000). Evidently, language ability is not the same as overall intelligence.

Language Learning as a Specialized Capacity

Susan Carey (1978) calculated that children between the ages of 1 ½ and 6 learn an average of nine new words per day. But how do they infer the meanings of all those words? A parent points at a frog and says "frog." How does the child guess that the word means *frog* rather than *small thing, green thing,* or *this particular frog*? More important, how does the child know the sound means anything at all?

Noam Chomsky has argued that people learn language so easily that children must begin with preconceptions. Chomsky and his followers suggest that people are born with a language acquisition device or "language instinct," *a built-in mechanism for acquiring language* (Pinker, 1994). One line of evidence for this idea is that deaf children who are not taught a sign language invent one of their own and try to teach it to their parents or to other deaf children (Goldin-Meadow, McNeill, & Singleton, 1996; Goldin-Meadow & Mylander, 1998). Further evidence is that children learn to use complex grammatical structures, such as "Is the boy who is unhappy watching Mickey Mouse?" even though they don't hear that kind of expression very often. To pick up that kind of grammar so quickly, they must have some predispositions to guide them.

Other psychologists counter that we are underestimating children's opportunity to learn. Parents throughout the world simplify the language-learning task by speaking to their infants in *parentese*—a pattern of speech that prolongs the vowels, making clearer than usual the difference between words such as *cat* and *cot* (Kuhl et al.,

1997). Several studies found that even infants younger than 1 year old detect the regularities of the language they hear (Marcus, Vijayan, Rao, & Vishton, 1999; Saffran, 2003). For example, when adults speak, they usually run all their words together without pausing between them: "Lookattheprettybaby." The infant detects which sounds go together as words by statistical relations. For example, the infant frequently hears the two-syllable combination "pret-ty" and frequently hears "ba-by" but less often hears the combination "ty-ba" and concludes that the word break comes between *pretty* and *baby*. We can infer that infants draw this conclusion because infants react to "ty-ba" as a new, attention-getting sound and don't react the same way to "pretty" or "baby" (Saffran, Aslin, & Newport, 1996). In short, infants learn the basics of language from regularities in what they hear.

- -

16. Suppose biotechnologists manipulate some genes to create a new breed of raccoons with brains as large as humans'. Should we expect these raccoons to develop language?

Answer

16. Probably not. Several species already have brains larger than those of humans without showing language. Some humans have nearly normal intelligence, and others have limited language despite low overall intelligence. Brain size, intelligence, and language are not the same thing.

- -

Language and the Human Brain

What aspect of the human brain enables us to learn language so easily? Studies of people with brain damage have long pointed to two brain areas as particularly important for language. People with damage in the frontal cortex, including *Broca's area* (Figure 8.24), develop Broca's aphasia, *a con-*

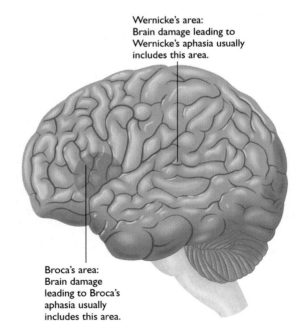

Wernicke's area: Brain damage leading to Wernicke's aphasia usually includes this area.

Broca's area: Brain damage leading to Broca's aphasia usually includes this area.

Figure 8.24 Brain damage that produces major deficits in language usually includes the left-hemisphere areas shown here. However, the deficits are severe only if the damage is more extensive, including these areas but extending to others as well.

dition characterized by difficulties in language production. Serious language impairment occurs only if the damage extends well outside Broca's area, but that area seems to be central. The person speaks slowly and inarticulately and is no better with writing or typing. Someone with Broca's aphasia is especially impaired with using and understanding grammatical devices, such as prepositions, conjunctions, word endings, and complex sentences. For example, one person who was asked about a dental appointment slowly mumbled, "Yes . . . Monday . . . Dad and Dick . . . Wednesday nine o'clock . . . 10 o'clock . . . doctors . . . and . . . teeth" (Geschwind, 1979, p. 186). People with an intact brain sometimes have similar difficulties putting together a clear grammatical sentence if they try to talk while concentrating on some other very trying task (Blackwell & Bates, 1995).

People with damage in the temporal cortex, including *Wernicke's area* (see Figure 8.24), develop **Wernicke's aphasia,** *a condition marked by impaired recall of nouns and impaired comprehension of language, despite the ability to speak fluently and grammatically.* Difficulty with nouns and impaired comprehension fit together: If you have trouble remembering what something is called, you will have trouble processing a sentence based on that word. Because these people omit most nouns, their speech is hard to understand. For example, one patient responded to a question about his health, "I felt worse because I can no longer keep in mind from the mind of the minds to keep me from mind and up to the ear which can be to find among ourselves" (J. Brown, 1977, p. 29). Temporary impairment of the temporal cortex also leads to speech problems like this, but as the cortex returns to normal, so does speech (Hillis et al., 2006).

Our language areas of the brain evolved from precursors in other species. Areas approximately corresponding to Wernicke's area and Broca's area in monkeys respond to monkey vocalizations (Gilda-Costa et al., 2006; Petkov et al., 2008). However, the structure of those areas evolved considerably from monkeys to apes to humans (Rilling et al., 2008). Furthermore, language depends on far more than just these two areas. Reading the word *kick* activates not only Wernicke's area but also the part of the motor cortex controlling foot movements. Reading *lick* activates the part of the motor cortex responsible for tongue movements (Hauk, Johnsrude, & Pulvermüller, 2004). Reading other words activates brain areas responsible for color perception, facial recognition, emotion, and so forth. It is hardly an exaggeration to say that the whole human brain is specialized to make language possible.

LANGUAGE DEVELOPMENT

Brain specializations facilitate language learning, but we still have to learn. Children's language learning is amazing. Virtually every child learns language, even if the parents know nothing about how to teach it.

Language in Early Childhood

Table 8.2 lists the average ages at which children reach various stages of language ability (Lenneberg, 1969; Moskowitz, 1978). Progression through these stages depends largely on maturation (Lenneberg, 1967, 1969). Parents who expose their children to as much language as possible increase the children's vocabulary, but they hardly affect the rate of progression through language stages (Figure 8.25). Hearing children of deaf parents are exposed to much less spoken language, but they too progress almost on schedule.

Deaf infants babble as much as hearing infants do for the first 6 months and then start to decline. At first, hearing infants babble only haphazard sounds, but soon they start repeating the sounds that are common in the language they have been hearing. If a parent responds to an infant's sounds by replying, the infant approximately copies the type of reply, such as consonant-vowel (Goldstein & Schwade, 2008). By age 1 year, an infant babbles mostly sounds that resemble whatever language the family speaks (Locke, 1994).

One of an infant's first sounds is *muh,* and that sound or something similar has been adopted by many of the world's languages to mean "mother." Infants also make the sounds *duh, puh,* and *buh.* In many languages, the word for father is similar to *dada* or *papa. Baba* is the word for father in Chinese and for grandmother in several

Table 8.2 Stages of Language Development

Age	Typical Language Abilities (Much Individual Variation)
3 months	Random vocalizations.
6 months	More distinct babbling.
1 year	Babbling that resembles the typical sounds of the family's language; probably one or more words including "mama"; language comprehension much better than production.
1½ years	Can say some words (mean about 50), mostly nouns; few or no phrases.
2 years	Speaks in two-word phrases.
2½ years	Longer phrases and short sentences with some errors and unusual constructions. Can understand much more.
3 years	Vocabulary near 1,000 words; longer sentences with fewer errors.
4 years	Close to adult speech competence.

other languages. In effect, infants tell their parents what words to use for important concepts.

By age 1 ½, most toddlers have a vocabulary of about 50 words, but they seldom link words together. A toddler says "Daddy" and "bye-bye" but not "Bye-bye, Daddy." In context, parents can usually discern considerable meaning in these single-word utterances. *Mama* might mean, "That's a picture of Mama," "Take me to Mama," "Mama went away and left me here," or "Mama, I'm hungry." Toddlers do, however, combine a word with a gesture, such as pointing at something while saying "mine" (Iverson & Goldin-Meadow, 2005). The word and gesture constitute a primitive kind of sentence.

Figure 8.25 This child may enjoy the attention, but extremely early practice has little effect on language development.

By age 2, children start producing telegraphic phrases of two or more words, such as "more page" (read some more), "allgone sticky" (my hands are now clean), and "allgone outside" (someone has closed the door). Note the originality of such phrases. It is unlikely that the parents ever said "allgone sticky"!

By age 2 ½ to 3 years, most children generate full sentences but with some idiosyncrasies. Many young children have their own rules for forming negative sentences. A common one is to add *no* or *not* to the beginning or end of a sentence, such as, "No I want to go to bed!" One little girl formed her negatives just by saying something louder and at a higher pitch. If she shrieked, "I want to share my toys!" she meant, "I do *not* want to share my toys." She had learned this rule by noting that people screamed when they told her not to do something. My son Sam made negatives for a while by adding the word *either* to the end of a sentence: "I want to eat lima beans either." Apparently, he had heard people say, "I don't want to do that either."

When young children speak, they apply grammatical rules, although of course they cannot state those rules. For example, they learn the way English usually forms plurals of nouns and past tenses of verbs. Then they apply those rules to produce such sentences as "the womans goed and doed something," or "the mans getted their foots wet." We say that children *overregularize* or *overgeneralize* the rules. My son David invented the word *shis* to mean "belonging to a female." (He had apparently generalized the rule "He–his, she–shis.") These inventions show that children are not just repeating what they have heard.

Apparently, we have an "optimal period" for learning language in early childhood. The start and end of this period are gradual, but language learning is easiest in early childhood (Werker & Tees, 2005). Much of the evidence for this conclusion comes from people who learn a second language. Adults learn the vocabulary of a second language faster than children do, but children learn the pronunciation better, as well as difficult aspects of the grammar. Even those who overheard another language in childhood without paying much attention to it learn it more easily later in life (Au, Knightly, Jun, & Oh, 2002). However, researchers find no sharp age cutoff when language becomes more difficult. That is, learning a second language is easier for 2-year-olds than 4-year-olds but also easier for 13-year-olds than 16-year-olds (Hakuta, Bialystok, & Wiley, 2003; Harley & Wang, 1997).

18. At what age do children begin to string words into combinations they have never heard before? Why do psychologists believe that even very young children learn rules of grammar?

Answer

18. Children begin to string words into novel combinations as soon as they begin to speak two words at a time. Children show that they learn rules of grammar when they overgeneralize those rules, creating such words as *womans* and *goed*.

Children Exposed to No Language or Two Languages

Would children who were exposed to no language at all make up a new one? In rare cases, an infant who was accidentally separated from other people grew up in a forest without human contact until discovered years later. Such children not only fail to show a language of their own but also fail to learn much language after they are given the chance (Pinker, 1994). However, their development is so abnormal and their early life so unknown that we should hesitate to draw conclusions.

The best evidence comes from studies of children who are deaf. Children who cannot hear well enough to learn speech and who are not taught sign language invent their own sign language (Senghas, Kita, & Özyürek, 2004). Observations in Nicaragua found that sign language evolved over the decades. Deaf people learned sign language and taught it to the next generation, who, having learned it from early childhood, elaborated on it, made it more expressive, and then taught the enhanced sign language to the next generation, and so on (Senghas & Coppola, 2001).

Most sign languages share some interesting similarities. For example, most include a marker to distinguish between a subject that is acting on an object ("the mouse eats the cheese") and a subject that is acting without an object ("the mouse is moving"). The sign languages invented by children in Taiwan resemble those of children in the United States, even though the spoken languages of those countries—Chinese and English—have very different grammars (Goldin-Meadow & Mylander, 1998).

If a deaf child starts to invent a sign language and no one responds to it, because the child meets no other deaf children and the adults fail to learn, the child gradually abandons it. If such a child is exposed to sign language much later, such as age 12, he or she struggles to develop signing skills and never catches up with those who started earlier (Harley & Wang, 1997; Mayberry, Lock, & Kazmi, 2002). This observation is our best evidence for the importance of early development in language learning: A child who doesn't learn a language while young is permanently impaired at learning one.

Some children grow up in a bilingual environment, *learning two languages.* Bilingualism is especially common among immigrant children, who are generally bicultural as well, learning both their parents' customs and those of their new country. The brain areas responding to words in one language are the same as those for words of the other language (Perani & Abutalebi, 2005). As a result, parts of the left hemisphere grow thicker than average among people who develop high flu-

ency in two or more languages from childhood onward (Mechelli et al., 2004). However, if the brain representations of the two languages overlap heavily, how do bilingual people keep their two languages separate? They don't, at least not completely (Thierry & Wu, 2007). For example, people who are fluent in both English and American Sign Language often make the facial gestures appropriate to sign language while they are speaking English (Pyers & Emmorey, 2008). However, one brain area, the caudate nucleus, is strongly activated while the person shifts from one language to the other (Crinion et al., 2006). Evidently, it primes one set of word representations and inhibits the other.

Bilingualism has two disadvantages: Children take longer to master two languages than to master one (of course), and they usually don't master either one as well as a person who spoke only one language. Even adult bilinguals get confused when they switch between languages (Levy, McVeigh, Marful, & Anderson, 2007). In each language, most bilinguals have a smaller than average vocabulary and take longer than average to think of a word (Bialystok, Craik, & Luk, 2008).

The primary advantage of bilingualism is obvious: If you learn a second language, you can communicate with more people. A second advantage is that bilingual people gain practice in controlling their attention, shifting from one language frame to another. In the process, they improve the skills needed for controlling attention in other areas, such as the Stroop task, tasks that require someone to ignore distractions, and tasks in which the instructions change suddenly (Bialystok et al., 2008; Bialystok, Craik, & Ryan, 2006; Carlson & Meltzoff, 2008).

....

19. What is the most convincing evidence that early exposure to language is necessary for language development?

20. What are the advantages and disadvantages of bilingualism?

Answers

20. Advantages: It becomes possible to speak with more people, and the ability to control attention improves. Disadvantages: It takes longer to learn two languages than one, and it is difficult to master either language as well as a person who is learning only one.

19. Deaf children who cannot learn spoken language and who have no opportunity to communicate with signs early in life are permanently disadvantaged in learning sign language.

....

UNDERSTANDING LANGUAGE

When we speak, we usually don't clarify every detail, and we often use words with ambiguous meanings. For instance, the word *peck* can mean one fourth of a bushel or to strike with a beak. *Rose* can mean a flower or the past tense of the verb *to rise*. *Desert* can mean an area of land that gets very little rain or to abandon someone or something. In context, however, listeners usually understand what we mean.

We become even more aware of the importance of context when we compare languages. Consider: Mandarin Chinese draws no distinctions for noun number or verb tense, and it lacks words for *a* and *the*. Thus, the sentence for "A man is buying an apple" is also the sentence for "The men bought apples," "A man will buy apples," and so forth. Despite this ambiguity, listeners ordinarily guess what someone means based on context. (If the context is insufficient, a speaker adds a word such as *tomorrow* or *yesterday*.) The Malay language has one word for "you and I" and a different word for "someone else and I." English translates both words as "we." The Malaysians wonder how listeners know what someone means by this ambiguous word, just as English speakers wonder how the Chinese get by without indications of number or tense.

Understanding a Word

The context not only determines how we interpret a word, but it also primes us to hear an ambiguous sound one way or another. For example, a computer generated a sound halfway between a normal *s* sound and a normal *sh* sound. When this intermediate sound replaced the *s* sound at the end of the word *embarrass,* people heard it as an *s* sound. When the same sound replaced *sh* at the end of *abolish,* people heard the same sound as *sh* (Samuel, 2001).

We also use lip-reading more than we realize to understand what we hear. If lip movements do not match the sound, we sometimes strike a compromise between what we see and what we hear (McGurk & MacDonald, 1976). To experience this phenomenon, go to the Online Try It Yourself activity McGurk Effect.

In one study, students listened to a tape recording of a sentence with a sound missing (Warren, 1970). The sentence was, "The state governors met with their respective legislatures convening in the capital city." However, the sound of the first *s* in the word *legislatures,* along with part of the adjacent *i* and *l,* had been replaced by a cough or a tone. The students were asked to listen to the recording and try to identify the location of the cough or tone.

None of the 20 students identified the location correctly, and half thought the cough or tone interrupted one of the other words on the tape. Even those who were told that the *s* sound was missing insisted that they clearly heard the sound *s*. The brain uses the context to fill in the missing sound.

Just as we hear the word *legislatures* as a whole, not as a string of separate letters, we interpret a sequence of words as a whole, not one at a time. Suppose you hear a tape-recorded word that is carefully engineered to sound halfway between *dent* and *tent*. The way you perceive it depends on the context:

1. When the *ent in the fender was well camouflaged, we sold the car.
2. When the *ent in the forest was well camouflaged, we began our hike.

Most people who hear sentence 1 report the word *dent.* Most who hear sentence 2 report *tent.* Now consider two more sentences:

3. When the *ent was noticed in the fender, we sold the car.
4. When the *ent was noticed in the forest, we stopped to rest.

For sentences 3 and 4, the context comes too late to help. People are as likely to report hearing *dent* in one sentence as in the other (Connine, Blasko, & Hall, 1991). Consider what this means: In the first two sentences, the fender or forest showed up three syllables after *ent. In the second pair, the fender or forest appeared six syllables later. Evidently, when you hear an ambiguous sound, you hold it in a temporary "undecided" state for about three syllables for the context to clarify it. Beyond that point, it is too late. You hear it one way or the other and stick with your decision.

Although a long-delayed context cannot help you hear an ambiguous word correctly, it does help you understand its meaning. Consider the following sentence from Karl Lashley (1951):

> Rapid righting with his uninjured hand saved from loss the contents of the capsized canoe.

If you hear this sentence spoken aloud so that spelling is not a clue, you are likely at first to interpret the second word as *writing,* until you reach the final two words of the sentence. Suddenly, the phrase *capsized canoe* tells you that *righting* meant "pushing with a paddle." Only the immediate context can influence what you hear, but even a delayed context can change the word's meaning.

Understanding Sentences

Making sense of language requires knowledge about the world. For example, consider the following sentences (from Just & Carpenter, 1987):

- That store sells horse shoes.
- That store sells alligator shoes.

You interpret *horse shoes* to mean "shoes for horses to wear," but you don't interpret *alligator shoes* as "shoes for alligators to wear." Your understanding of the sentences depended on your knowledge of the world, not just the syntax of the sentences.

Here is another example:

- I'm going to buy a pet hamster at the store, if it's open.
- I'm going to buy a pet hamster at the store, if it's healthy.

Nothing about the sentence structure told you that *it* refers to the store in the first sentence and a hamster in the second sentence. You understood because you know that stores but not hamsters can be open, whereas hamsters but not stores can be healthy.

In short, understanding a sentence depends on your knowledge of the world and all the assumptions that you share with the speaker or writer of the

Figure 8.26 In England, a *football coach* is a bus full of soccer fans. In the United States, it's the person who directs a team of American football players.

sentence. Sometimes, you even have to remember where you are because the meaning of a word differs from one place to another (Figure 8.26).

Now consider this sentence: *While Anna dressed the baby played in the crib.* Quickly: Whom did Anna dress? And who played in the crib? The addition of a comma would simplify the sentence, but even without it, English grammar prohibits "baby" from being both the object of *dressed* and the subject of *played.* If the baby played in the crib (as you no doubt answered), Anna must have dressed herself. Nevertheless, many people misunderstand and think Anna dressed the baby (Ferreira, Bailey, & Ferraro, 2002). Remember the example from earlier in the chapter about how many animals Moses took on the ark? That was another example in which many people overlook the details of the sentence and construct a "good enough" interpretation of the sentence's meaning based on their knowledge and reasonable expectations.

Limits to Our Language Understanding

Some sentences are grammatical but almost incomprehensible. One example is a doubly embedded sentence—a sentence within a sentence within a sentence. A singly embedded sentence is understandable, though not simple:

> The dog the cat saw chased a squirrel.

> The squirrel the dog chased climbed the tree.

In the first sentence, "the cat saw the dog" is embedded within "the

dog chased a squirrel." In the second, "the dog chased the squirrel" is embedded within "the squirrel climbed the tree." So far, so good, but now consider a doubly embedded sentence:

> The squirrel the dog the cat saw chased climbed the tree.

Doubly embedded sentences overburden our memory. In fact, if your memory is already burdened with other matters, you may have trouble understanding a singly embedded sentence (Gordon, Hendrick, & Levine, 2002).

Double negatives are also difficult to understand. "I would not deny that . . ." means that I agree. "It is not false that . . ." means that something is true. People understand such sentences with difficulty. Have you ever seen a multiple-choice test item that asks "Which of the following is not true . . ." and then one of the choices has a *not* in it? With such items, confusion is almost certain.

Triple negatives are still worse. Consider the following sentence, which includes *four* negatives (emphasis added): "If you do *not* unanimously find from your consideration of all the evidence that there are *no* mitigating factors sufficient to *preclude* the imposition of a death sentence, then you should sign the verdict requiring the court to impose a sentence *other than* death." In Illinois, a judge reads those instructions to a jury in a capital punishment case to explain how to decide between a death penalty and life in prison. Do you think many jurors understand?

With a single negative, people often don't fully accept the meaning of the word *not.* Suppose you are trying to decide whether to buy a product at the supermarket. The package says, "Contains no rat pieces!" Does that notice encourage you to buy the product? Hardly! After all, why would the manufacturer mention the absence of something unless it might be present? I was once on an airplane that turned around shortly after departure because one of its two engines failed. The attendant told the passengers what was happening, but until she said, "Please don't panic," we didn't realize there might be a reason to panic.

In one clever experiment, students watched an experimenter pour sugar into two jars. The students were then told to label one jar "sucrose, table sugar" and the other "not sodium cyanide, not poison." Then the experimenter made two cups of Kool-Aid, one from each jar of sugar, and asked the students to choose one cup to drink (Figure 8.27). Almost half expressed no preference, but of the 44 who did have a preference, 35 wanted Kool-Aid made from the jar marked "sucrose," not from the one that denied cyanide and poison (Rozin, Markwith, & Ross, 1990).

Figure 8.27 Most students preferred Kool-Aid made with sugar labeled "sugar" instead of sugar labeled "not cyanide," even though they had placed the labels themselves. People don't always trust the word *not.* (Based on results of Rozin, Markwith, & Ross, 1990)

READING

Students of language distinguish between phonemes and morphemes. A **phoneme** is *a unit of sound*, such as *f* or *sh*. A **morpheme** is *a unit of meaning*. For example, the noun *thrills* has two morphemes (*thrill* and *s*). The final *s* is a unit of meaning because it indicates that the noun is plural (Figure 8.28). *Harp* has one morpheme, *harping* has two, *harper* has two, but *harpoon* has just one, as it is not derived from *harp*. Readers of English and other European languages are accustomed to the idea that a letter or combination of letters represents a phoneme. However, other languages are written in different ways. In the Japanese *hiragana* style of writing, each character represents a syllable. In Chinese, each character represents a morpheme and ordinarily a whole word.

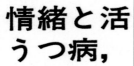
Japanese hiragana

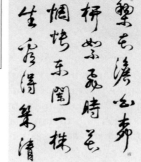
Chinese characters

21. How many phonemes are in the word *thoughtfully?* How many morphemes?

Concept Check

Answer

21. It has seven phonemes: th-ough-t-f-u-ll-y. It has three morphemes: thought-ful-ly.

As you will recall, expertise develops from many years of practice, enabling someone to recognize complex patterns at a glance. Because you have been reading for hours a day, almost every day since childhood, you have developed expertise at reading. You may not think of yourself as an expert because we usually reserve the term *expert* for someone who is far more skilled than others. Nevertheless, you recognize words instantaneously, like an expert who recognizes chess patterns at a glance.

Phonemes (units of sound):

SHAMELESSNESS

Morphemes (units of meaning):

Figure 8.28 The word *shamelessness* has nine phonemes (units of sound) and three morphemes (units of meaning).

Word Recognition

Consider the following experiment: The investigator flashes a letter on a screen for less than a quarter-second, shows an interfering pattern, and asks, "Was it C or J?" Then the experimenter flashes an entire word on the screen under the same conditions and asks, "Was the first letter of the word C or J?" (Figure 8.29). Which question is easier? Most people *identify the letter more accurately when it is part of a word than when it is presented by itself* (Reicher, 1969; Wheeler, 1970). This is known as the **word-superiority effect**. You can experience it yourself with the Online Try It Yourself activity Word-Superiority Effect.

In further research, James Johnston and James McClelland (1974) briefly flashed words on the screen and asked students to identify one letter (whose position was marked) in each word (Figure 8.30). On some trials, the experimenters told the students to try to see the whole word. On other trials, they showed the students exactly where the critical letter would appear on the screen and told them to focus on that spot and ignore the rest of the screen. Most students identified the critical letter more successfully when they looked at the whole word than when they focused on just the letter itself. This benefit oc-

RIVER*

a

SVLEJ*

b

Figure 8.30 Students identified an indicated letter better when they focused on an entire word (a) than on a single letter in a designated spot among random letters (b).

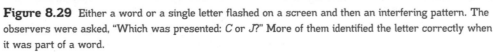

Figure 8.29 Either a word or a single letter flashed on a screen and then an interfering pattern. The observers were asked, "Which was presented: *C* or *J*?" More of them identified the letter correctly when it was part of a word.

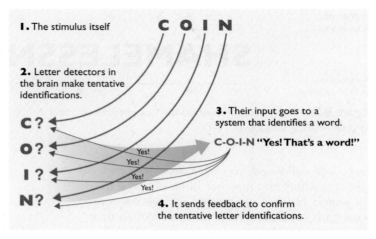

Figure 8.31 According to one model, a visual stimulus activates certain letter units, some more strongly than others. Those letter units then activate a word unit, which in turn strengthens the letter units that compose it. For this reason, we recognize a whole word more easily than a single letter.

the feedback strengthens the activity of the *R*, *E*, and *D* units. Word recognition can become more complex. Consider the following sentence:

> The boy cuold not slove the porblem so he aksed for help.

Most readers "recognize" the words *could, solve, problem, and asked,* although of course they read faster when all words are spelled correctly (Rayner, White, Johnson, & Liversedge, 2006; White, Johnson, Liversedge, & Rayner, 2008). When we read, we process the whole context so that even out-of-place letters activate identification of the correct words. (This tendency can pose a probelm for proofreaders, who sometimes fail to notice a misspelling!)

....

22. What evidence indicates that we do *not* read a word one letter at a time?

Answer

out of order.

spelled word even when certain letters are

Also, a reader sometimes "recognizes" a mis-

and another letter in a different context.

8.32, appear to be one letter in one context

22. Ambiguous letters, such as those in Figure

....

curs only with a real word, like COIN, not with a nonsense combination, like CXQF (Rumelhart & McClelland, 1982).

You may have experienced the word-superiority effect yourself. To pass time on long car trips, people sometimes try to find every letter of the alphabet on the billboards. It is usually easier to spot a letter by reading complete words than by checking letter by letter.

What accounts for the word-superiority effect? According to one model (McClelland, 1988; Rumelhart, McClelland, & the PDP Research Group, 1986), our perceptions and memories are represented by connections among "units" corresponding to sets of neurons. Each unit connects to other units (Figure 8.31). Any activated unit excites some of its neighbors and inhibits others. Suppose units corresponding to the letters C, O, I, and N are moderately active. They excite a higher order unit corresponding to the word COIN. Although none of the four letter units sends a strong message by itself, the collective impact is strong (McClelland & Rumelhart, 1981). The perception COIN then feeds excitation back to the individual letter-identifying units and confirms their tentative identifications.

This model helps explain our perception of Figure 8.32. Why do you see the top word in that figure as *RED* instead of *PFB*? After all, in the other words, those letters do look like *P*, *F*, and *B*. In the top word, one ambiguous figure activates some *P* units and some *R* units; the next figure activates *E* and *F* units, and the third figure activates *D* and *B* units. All of those units in turn activate other units corresponding to *RFB, PFB, PFD,* and *RED*. As you tentatively perceive the word as *RED* (the only English word among those choices),

Figure 8.32 The combination of possible letters enables us to identify a word. Word recognition in turn helps to confirm the letter identifications. (From "Parallel Distributed Processing: Explorations in the Microstructure of Cognition," Vol. 1: Foundations, by David E. Rumelhart et al., p. 8, figure 2. [Series in Computational Models of Cognition and Perception.] Copyright 1986 by MIT Press. Used by permission of the publisher.)

Reading and Eye Movements

Reading requires eye movements, of course. When psychologists monitored eye movements, they discovered that a reader's eyes move in a jerky fashion. You move your eyes steadily to follow a moving object, but when scanning a stationary object, such as a page of print, you alternate between fixations, *when your eyes are stationary,* and saccades (sa-KAHDS), *quick eye movements from one fixation point to another.*

You read during your fixations only. You are virtually blind during the saccades. To illustrate this point, try the following demonstration: Look at yourself in the mirror and focus on your left eye. Then move your focus to the right eye. Do you see your eyes moving in the mirror? (Go ahead; try it.) People almost always agree that they do not see their eyes move.

"Oh, but wait," you say. "That movement in the mirror was simply too quick and too small to see." Wrong. Get someone else to look at your left eye and then shift gaze to your right eye. You *do* see the other person's eye movement. Go back and try your own eyes in the mirror again and observe the difference. You see someone else's eyes move, but you do not see your own eyes move in the mirror.

Why not? Certain neurons in the parietal cortex monitor impending eye movements and send a message to the visual cortex, in effect saying, "The eyes are about to move, so decrease activity for a moment." Even in total darkness, the visual cortex decreases its activity 75 milliseconds (ms) before the eye movement and remains depressed throughout the movement (Burr, Morrone, & Ross, 1994; Paus, Marrett, Worsley, & Evans, 1995; Vallines & Greenlee, 2006). Blood flow to the visual cortex decreases, and responsiveness to light decreases (Irwin & Brockmole, 2004). Activity is especially suppressed in the brain areas responsible for detecting visual movement (Kleiser, Seitz, & Krekelberg, 2004).

In short, your visual cortex takes a brief vacation during a saccadic eye movement, and so you read only during fixations. For an average adult reader, most fixations last about 200 to 250 ms. We have briefer fixations on familiar words like *legal* than on harder words like *luau* or words with more than one meaning like *lead* (Rodd, Gaskell, & Marslen-Wilson, 2002). Because saccades are brief (25 to 50 ms), a normal pace is about four fixations per second (Rayner, 1998).

How much can a person read during one fixation? Research indicates that we read only about 11 characters—one or two words—at a time. To demonstrate this limitation, focus on the letter *i* marked by an arrow (↓) in these two sentences:

↓
1. This is a sentence with no misspelled words.

↓
2. Xboc tx zjg rxunce with no mijvgab zucn.

If you permit your eyes to wander back and forth, you notice the gibberish in sentence 2. But as long as you dutifully keep your eyes on the fixation point, the sentence looks all right. You read the letter on which you fixated plus about three or four characters (including spaces) to the left and about seven to the right. The rest is too blurry to make it out. Therefore, you see —*ce with no m*— or possibly —*nce with no mi*—.

This limit of about 11 letters depends partly on the lighting. In faint light, your span decreases to as little as 1 or 2 letters, and your reading ability suffers accordingly (Legge, Ahn, Klitz, & Luebker, 1997). The limit does not depend on how much fits into the fovea of your eyes. In the following display, again focus on the letter *i* in each sentence and check how many letters you can read to its left and right:

↓
This is a sentence with no misspelled words.

↓
This is a sentence with no misspelled words.

↓
is a sentence with no misspelled

If your reading span were limited by how many letters can fit into the fovea of your retina, you would read fewer letters as the print gets larger. In fact, you do at least as well, maybe even better, with larger print (up to a point).

What we can see at a glance also depends on our habits of reading. In Japanese and Chinese, where each character conveys more information than English letters do, readers see fewer letters per fixation (Rayner, 1998). In Hebrew and Farsi, which are written right to left, readers read more letters to the left of fixation and fewer to the right (Brysbaert, Vitu, & Schroyens, 1996; Faust, Kravetz, & Babkoff, 1993; Malamed & Zaidel, 1993).

You might wonder how speed-readers differ from normal readers. An average adult reader has about four or five fixations per second with occasional backtracks, for an overall rate of about 200 words per minute. Speed-readers have briefer fixations with fewer backtracks. With practice, they double or triple their reading speed with normal comprehension of most material. However, understanding difficult material requires a reader to slow down and think about it. When speed-readers read college textbooks, they either slow their reading (Just & Carpenter, 1987) or fail the tests (Homa, 1983).

23. If a word is longer than 11 letters, will a reader need more than one fixation to read it?

Answer

23. Sometimes, but not always. Suppose your eyes fixate on the fourth letter of *memorization*. You should be able to see the three letters to its left and the seven to its right—that is, all except the final letter. Because there is only one English word that starts *memorizatio-*, you already know the word.

8.3 module

In Closing

Language and Humanity

At the start of this module, we considered the question, "If language is so useful to humans, why haven't other species evolved at least a little of it?" None of the research answers this question, but we can speculate.

Many adaptations are much more useful on a large scale than on a small scale. For example, stinkiness is extremely useful to skunks. Being slightly stinky wouldn't help much. Porcupines survive because of their long quills. Having a few short quills could be slightly helpful, but not very. Similarly, a little bit of language development is probably an unstable condition, evolutionarily speaking. Once a species such as humans had evolved a little language, those individuals with still better language abilities would have a huge selective advantage over the others.

SUMMARY

- *Language productivity.* Human languages enable us to create new words and phrases to express new ideas. (page 298)
- *Language training in nonhumans.* Bonobos, and to a smaller extent other species, have learned certain aspects of language. Human evolution evidently elaborated on potentials found in our apelike ancestors but developed that potential further. (page 298)
- *Language and intelligence.* It is possible to have intelligence without language or language without other aspects of intelligence. Therefore, many psychologists regard language as a specialized capacity, not just a by-product of overall intelligence. (page 300)
- *Predisposition to learn language.* Noam Chomsky and others have argued that the ease with which children acquire language indicates that they are born with a predisposition that facilitates language. (page 301)
- *Brain organization and aphasia.* Brain damage, especially in the left hemisphere, impairs people's ability to understand or use language. Many brain areas contribute to language in varied ways. (page 301)
- *Stages of language development.* Children advance through several stages of language development, reflecting maturation of brain structures. From the start, children's language is creative, using the rules of language to make new word combinations and sentences. (page 302)
- *Children exposed to no language or two.* If deaf children are not exposed to language, they invent a sign language of their own. However, a deaf child who learns neither spoken language nor sign language in childhood is impaired on learning any language later. Children in a bilingual environment sometimes have trouble keeping the two languages separate but gain increased ability to control and shift attention. (page 304)
- *Understanding language.* Much of speech is ambiguous. We understand words and sentences in context by applying the knowledge we have about the world in general. (page 305)
- *Limits to our language understanding.* Many sentences are difficult to understand, especially those with embedded clauses or more than one negative. Difficult grammar places a burden on our working memory. (page 306)
- *Reading.* When we read, we alternate between fixation periods and saccadic eye movements. We read during the fixations, not during the saccades. An average adult reads about 11 letters per fixation. People increase their speed of reading by increasing the number of fixations per second. (page 307)

KEY TERMS

exploration and study

Why Does This Matter to Me?

SOCIAL RESPONSIBILITY AND PSYCHOLOGY

Many environmental and societal problems are caused by human behavior. Psychologists can help steer the course of our future toward more socially responsible and sustainable outcomes. Students of today need to be ever mindful of the link between human behavior and its impact on the environment and our communities.

"Cognition and Language" and Social Responsibility: A Step Further

People for the Ethical Treatment of Animals (PETA) has a new campaign to rename fish "sea kittens." They say that fish can perceive as much about their environment as kittens can. A current link to their campaign can be found at www.cengage.com/psychology/kalat. It seems that PETA is interested in changing the conceptual category for fish. Do you think it is possible for an organization to change the way people form categories and concepts? Whether you agree or disagree with PETA's campaign, do you think their belief in the power of naming is well founded?

Put Your English Language Skills to Use

Whether you stay close to home or travel abroad for the summer or after you graduate, chances are your English language skills will be considered a valuable commodity —one that you could share. Visit www.cengage.com/psychology/kalat for links to an extensive list of programs and organizations that can help you find opportunities to teach others.

Join the iChapters Plant a Tree Drive!

To show its support of the environmental movement, iChapters is planting a tree on behalf of each fan of the iChapters Facebook Page and for every 10 questions answered correctly in our quiz.
http://www.ichapters.com/plantatree/

Exploration and Study

SUGGESTIONS FOR FURTHER EXPLORATION

In addition to the study materials provided at the end of each module, you may supplement your review of this chapter with the following book and website suggestions or by using one or more of the book's electronic resources, which include its companion website, interactive Cengage Learning eBook, and CengageNOW. Brief descriptions of these resources follow. For more information, visit **www.cengage.com/psychology/kalat**.

ADDITIONAL RESOURCES

The book's companion website, accessible from **www.cengage.com/psychology/kalat**, provides a wide range of study resources such as an interactive glossary, flashcards, tutorial quizzes, updated web links, and Try It Yourself activities. Each of the following activities tie to what you've learned in this chapter: change blindness, framing questions, McGurk effect, overconfidence, Stop Signal task, and word superiority effect.

CengageNOW with Critical Thinking Videos is an easy-to-use resource that helps you study in less time to get the grade you want. An online study system, CengageNOW gives you the option of taking a diagnostic pretest for each chapter. The system uses the results of each pretest to create personalized chapter study plans for you. The Personalized Study Plans

- Help you save study time by identifying areas on which you should concentrate and give you one-click access to corresponding pages of the interactive Cengage Learning eBook;
- Provide interactive exercises and study tools to help you fully understand chapter concepts; and
- Include a posttest for you to take to confirm that you are ready to move on to the next chapter.

Find critical thinking videos like this one in your CengageNOW product, which offer an opportunity for you to learn more about psychological research on different topics.

Books

Pinker, S. (1999). *Words and rules: The ingredients of language.* New York: Basic Books. A discussion of language by a writer with a keen eye for excellent examples.

Schwartz, B. (2004). *The paradox of choice: Why more is less.* New York: HarperCollins. Fascinating, entertaining discussion of why too many choices or too much effort to find the best choice can work to our disadvantage.

Websites

Links to the websites described below are kept current and can be found at **www.cengage.com/psychology/kalat**.

Attention

You can try some demonstrations that show how hard it is to plan two actions at once.

Human Language

This site has links to many sources of information about languages.

Situated Cognition

Intelligence

Consider This: Alan Turing, a famous mathematician and pioneer in computer science, bicycled to and from work each day. Occasionally, the chain fell off his bicycle, and he had to replace it. Turing kept records and noticed that the chain fell off at regular intervals, after exactly a certain number of turns of the front wheel. He calculated that this number was the product of the number of spokes in the front wheel times the number of links in the chain times the number of cogs in the pedal. He deduced that the chain came loose whenever a particular link in the chain came in contact with a particular bent spoke on the wheel. He identified that spoke, repaired it, and had no more trouble with his bicycle (I. Stewart, 1987).

© Bernd Opitz/Getty Images

To repair a bicycle, you could use general problem-solving skills or specific expertise about bicycles. Either approach shows a kind of intelligence.

Turing's solution to his problem is impressive, but hold your applause. Your local bicycle mechanic could have solved the problem without using mathematics at all. So, you might ask, what's my point? Was Turing unintelligent? Of course not. The point is that intelligence includes both the ability to solve unfamiliar problems, as Turing showed, and practiced skills, such as those of a bicycle mechanic.

Intelligence and Intelligence Tests

- What do we mean by "intelligence"?
- Is there more than one kind of intelligence?

Is there intelligent life in outer space? For decades, people have pointed huge arrays of dishes toward the stars, hoping to detect signals from alien civilizations. If we did intercept signals, would we make any sense of them? The enterprise assumes that intelligent life in outer space would be similar to us. It is a remarkable assumption, considering how different human intelligence is from that of, say, dolphins here on Earth.

WHAT IS INTELLIGENCE?

Intelligence clearly has something to do with learning, memory, and cognition—the topics of the last three chapters. Defining it more precisely is not easy. Here are some attempts to define intelligence (Kanazawa, 2004; Sternberg, 1997; Wolman, 1989):

- The mental abilities that enable one to adapt to, shape, or select one's environment.
- The ability to deal with novel situations.
- The ability to judge, comprehend, and reason.
- The ability to understand and deal with people, objects, and symbols.
- The ability to act purposefully, think rationally, and deal effectively with the environment.

Note that these definitions use such terms as *judge, comprehend, understand,* and *think rationally*—terms that are just as poorly defined as intelligence. To advance our understanding, we need research on intelligent behaviors. Psychological researchers have followed a circuitous route: They began with tests of intellectual abilities, defined as the ability to do well in school. Then they conducted research to find out what the tests measure. Do they measure a single skill or a variety of separate skills? It may strike you as odd to measure something before figuring out what it is. However, physicists used the same approach with electricity, magnetism, gravity, and other phenomena.

Spearman's Psychometric Approach and the *g* Factor

One of the earliest research studies in psychology was Charles Spearman's (1904) **psychometric approach** to intelligence, based on *the measurement of individual differences in performance.* Spearman began by measuring how well a group of people performed various tasks, such as following directions, judging musical pitch, matching colors, and doing arithmetic. He found that performance on any of his tasks correlated positively with performance on any of the others. Spearman therefore inferred that all the tasks have something in common. To perform well on any test of mental ability, Spearman argued, people need a *"general" ability,* which he called

g. The symbol *g* is italicized and always lowercase, like the mathematical terms *e* (the base of natural logarithms) and *i* (the square root of -1).

To account for the fact that performances on various tasks do not correlate perfectly, Spearman suggested that each task also requires a *"specific" ability, s* (Figure 9.1). Thus, intelligence consists of a general ability plus an unknown number of specific abilities, such as mechanical, musical, arithmetical, logical, and spatial abilities. Spearman called his theory a "monarchic" theory of intelligence because it included a dominant ability, or monarch (*g*), that ruled over the lesser abilities.

Later researchers confirmed that scores on virtually all kinds of cognitive tests correlate positively with one another within any representative sample of the population (W. Johnson, Bouchard, Krueger, McGue, & Gottesman, 2004; W. Johnson, te Nijenhuis, & Bouchard, 2008). You have probably noticed this trend yourself: A student who does well in one course generally does well in other courses. Only under special conditions do the individuals who perform well on one test tend to score below average on another. For example,

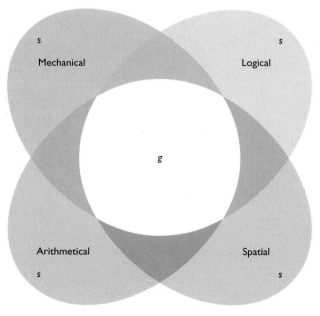

Figure 9.1 According to Spearman (1904), all intelligent abilities have an area of overlap, which he called *g* (for "general"). Each ability also depends on an *s* (for "specific") factor.

in one study, rural Kenyan children who did well on an academic test did poorly on a test of knowledge about traditional herbal medicines, and those who did well on the test of herbal medicines did poorly on the academic test (Sternberg et al., 2001). Presumably, the two groups of children had been exposed to different types of experiences.

Possible Explanations for *g*

The observations underlying *g* indicate that whatever causes people to do well on one test also increases their probability of doing well on other tests. But what contributes to good performance on so many kinds of tests? The simplest interpretation is that all the tasks measure a single underlying ability. Consider an analogy with the tasks shown in Figure 9.2: Most people who excel at running a 100-meter race also do well at the high jump and the long jump. We can hardly imagine an outstanding high jumper who could not manage a better than average long jump. The reason

Figure 9.2 Measurements of sprinting, high jumping, and long jumping correlate with one another because they all depend on the same leg muscles. Similarly, the *g* factor that emerges in IQ testing could reflect a single ability.

for this high correlation is that all three events depend on the same leg muscles.

Similarly, people might perform well on a variety of intellectual tests because all the tests depend on one underlying skill. If so, what might that skill be? One possibility is that *g* depends mainly on working memory or some aspect of it (e.g., Martínez & Colom, 2009). For almost any intellectual task, holding information in memory is important, as is the ability to shift attention from one part of the task to another.

An alternative explanation for *g* is that we have several types of intelligence that correlate because they grow in the same ways (Petrill, Luo, Thompson, & Detterman, 1996). By analogy, consider the lengths of three body parts—the left leg, the right arm, and the left index finger: As a rule, most people with a long left leg also have a long right arm and a long left index finger. Although the three lengths correlate strongly, they do not measure the same thing. Amputating one of them would not affect the others. Lengths of leg, arm, and finger correlate because the factors that increase the growth of one also help the others grow—factors such as genes, health, and nutrition. Similarly, all forms of intelligence depend on genes, health, nutrition, and education. Most people who have good support for developing one intellectual skill also have good support for developing others.

Which of these examples applies to intelligence? Do the various intellectual skills correlate with one another because they all measure a single underlying ability (as do running and jumping, which require good leg muscles) or because they all grow together (as do your arms, legs, and fingers)?

To some extent, both hypotheses are probably correct. Most intellectual tasks require attention and working memory. Also, independent brain functions do correlate with one another because most factors that promote good development of one area promote good development of all.

1. What evidence did Spearman have in favor of the concept of *g*?
2. What are two possible explanations for *g*?

Concept Check

Answers

1. Scores on many different kinds of tests correlate positively with one another.
2. Different kinds of intellectual tests may all tap the same underlying ability, such as working memory. Or they may depend on different abilities that tend to develop together because they all depend on the same influences, including health, nutrition, education, and genetics.

Hierarchical Models of Intelligence

Although Spearman and most of the later researchers have regarded *g* as the key to intelligence, it does not account for everything. Spearman suggested the existence of specific (*s*) factors, but the task fell on other psychologists to try to describe them.

One important distinction those psychologists have made is between fluid intelligence and crystallized intelligence (Cattell, 1987). The analogy is to water: Fluid water fits into any shape of container, whereas an ice crystal has a fixed shape. **Fluid intelligence** is *the power of reasoning and using information*. It includes the ability to perceive relationships, solve unfamiliar problems, and gain new knowledge. **Crystallized intelligence** consists of *acquired skills and knowledge and the ability to apply that knowledge in specific situations*. Fluid intelligence enables you to learn new skills in a new job, whereas crystallized intelligence includes the job skills you have already acquired. The ability to learn new words is an example of fluid intelligence, and the words already learned are part of your crystallized intelligence. Expertise, as discussed in chapter 8, is an example of crystallized intelligence. One type of evidence supporting the fluid versus crystallized distinction is that fluid intelligence correlates mainly with the ability of certain brain areas to increase their activity, whereas crystallized intelligence correlates more strongly with the actual size of certain brain areas (Choi et al., 2008).

Fluid intelligence reaches its peak before age 20, remains nearly steady for decades, and declines on the average in old age, although more in some people than others (Horn, 1968). Crystallized intelligence, on the other hand, continues to increase as long as people are active and alert (Cattell, 1987; Horn & Donaldson, 1976). A 20-year-old may be more successful than a 65-year-old at solving a new, unfamiliar problem, but the 65-year-old excels on problems in his or her area of specialization. However, the distinction between fluid and crystallized intelligence is sharper in theory than in practice. Any task taps both crystallized and fluid intelligence to some extent.

Other researchers have described intelligence in terms of a hierarchy, or a series of levels. According to one view, *g* consists of eight or more subabilities, including fluid intelligence (reasoning), crystallized intelligence, memory, visual perception, auditory perception, retrieval fluency, cognitive speed, and processing speed (Carroll, 1993, 2003). Other researchers, noting that many of these subabilities correlate strongly with one another, proposed a simpler hierarchy, in which *g*

consists of three major aspects: verbal processing (language), perceptual processing (dealing with vision and hearing), and image rotation (spatial relationships). Each of these major abilities could be subdivided further (W. Johnson & Bouchard, 2005).

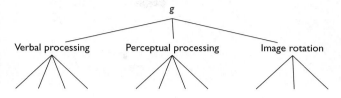

3. Was Alan Turing's solution to the slipping bicycle chain, from the introduction to this chapter, an example of fluid or crystallized intelligence? Was the solution provided by a bicycle mechanic an example of fluid or crystallized intelligence?

4. What kind of evidence indicates how many subabilities compose *g*?

Answers

3. Turing's solution reflected fluid intelligence, a generalized ability that could apply to any topic. The solution provided by a bicycle mechanic reflected crystallized intelligence, an ability developed in a particular area of experience.

4. The number of subabilities is the number of clusters of skills, where items within a cluster correlate with each other, but each cluster does not correlate strongly with the others.

Gardner's Theory of Multiple Intelligences

Certain critics propose to dispense with, or at least deemphasize, the concept of *g*. According to this view, scores on all kinds of intellectual tests correlate with one another for extraneous reasons, such as the fact that all of the tests require the use of language or all of them require logical reasoning. According to Howard Gardner (1985, 1999), if we could test intellectual abilities in pure form, we might find **multiple intelligences**— *unrelated forms of intelligence,* consisting of language, musical abilities, logical and mathematical reasoning, spatial reasoning, ability to recognize and classify objects, body movement skills, self-control and self-understanding, and sensitivity to other people's social signals. Gardner argues that people can be outstanding in one type of intelli-

According to Howard Gardner, we have many intelligences, including mathematical ability, artistic skill, muscle skills, and musical abilities.

gence but not others. For example, an athlete can excel at body movement skills but lack musical abilities. Someone who seems intelligent in one way may be mediocre or worse in another because different skills require not only different kinds of practice but also, perhaps, different brain specializations.

Gardner certainly makes the important point that each person has different skills. However, the question is whether those skills represent different types of intelligence. To defend them as being different, someone needs to demonstrate that they are not strongly correlated with one another. However, each of Gardner's proposed types of intelligence does correlate positively with the others, with the exception of body movement skills and possibly music (Visser, Ashton, & Vernon, 2006). Therefore, it would seem that language, logic, spatial reasoning, and all the others are simply different manifestations of *g*. Gardner's idea is that these abilities would stop correlating so strongly if we could measure them in pure form, without the contribution of language and so forth. Perhaps it's true, but no one knows how to measure these abilities in pure form. At this point, Gardner's theory is an appealing idea without solid evidence to support it.

In Garrison Keillor's fictional *Lake Wobegon*, "all the children are above average." In one sense, this statement is true: Almost everyone is above average at something.

Sternberg's Triarchic Theory of Intelligence

Regardless of exactly why *g* emerges or what it means, we often need to know about more than overall ability. For example, many children labeled "learning disabled" have serious difficulties on one or two kinds of skills while performing at an average or above-average level on others. To help these children, psychologists and teachers want to determine exactly *why* a child is struggling (Conners & Schulte, 2002; Das, 2002).

Spearman's concept of intelligence has been called "monarchic" because it proposes *g* as a "monarch" that rules over the more specialized abilities. Robert Sternberg (1985) attempted to go beyond this view by proposing a triarchic theory that deals with *three aspects of intelligence: (a) cognitive processes, (b) identifying situations that require intelligence, and (c) using intelligence in practical ways.* He tried to analyze the cognitive processes into smaller components. For example, he suggested that when solving certain kinds of problems we go through several stages that include encoding the information, drawing inferences, mapping relationships, and applying the knowledge. If so, it might make sense for intelligence tests to measure each of these processes separately. The goal was an intelligence test with a theoretical relationship to cognitive psychology. Unfortunately, when Sternberg tried to develop tests of encoding, inferring, mapping, and so forth, he found that all the measures correlated fairly highly with each other (Deary, 2002). In other words, he rediscovered *g*.

Sternberg has explored other possible distinctions among types of intelligence. He argued that we have at least three types of intelligence: *analytical* (or academic), *creative* (planning approaches to new problems), and *practical* (actually doing something). While criticizing standard IQ tests for concentrating only on analytical intelligence, Sternberg tried to develop new tests that tap creative and practical aspects as well. Controversy persists regarding the status of creative and practical intelligence. On the one hand, we have all known people who seem high in academic intelligence but not in creativity or practical intelligence. On the other hand, thinking of examples is not enough; the question is whether analytical intelligence is strongly or weakly correlated with creativity and practical intelligence *in general*. Furthermore, measuring creativity and practical intelligence is easier said than done.

Sternberg and his colleagues have argued that their tests of creative and practical intelligence are better predictors of intelligence in everyday life than are standard IQ tests (Sternberg, 2002). However, many other researchers remain unconvinced, arguing as follows (Brody, 2003; Gottfredson, 2003; Koke & Vernon, 2003):

- Sternberg has overstated the success of his tests at predicting performance.
- The tests that claim to measure analytical, creative, and practical intelligence produce scores that correlate highly with one another, and with the scores on more standard IQ tests, so it is not clear that they are measuring different processes. Sternberg apparently rediscovered *g* one more time.
- The analytical scores (similar to standard IQ tests) predict people's creative and practical behaviors about as well as scores on the creative and practical tests do. Evidently, what are claimed to be three different kinds of tests seem to be measuring the same processes.

5. What evidence would we need to determine whether music, mathematics, social sensitivity, and so forth are really different kinds of intelligence or just different aspects of a single type? Concept Check

Answer

5. We would need to determine whether ability at each kind of intelligence correlates highly with the others. If they all correlate highly with one another, they are simply different aspects of *g*. If they do not, and if the differences reflect more than just different amounts of practice at different skills, then they are separate kinds of intelligence.

Table 9.1 Four Theories of Intelligence

Theory	Theorist	Key Ideas and Terms
Psychometric approach	Charles Spearman	*g* factor: general reasoning ability
		s factor: specific ability required for a given task
Fluid and crystallized intelligence	Raymond Cattell	Fluid intelligence: solving unfamiliar problems
		Crystallized intelligence: highly practiced skills
Multiple intelligences	Howard Gardner	Music, social attentiveness, dancing, mathematics, and all other skills that society values
Triarchic theory	Robert Sternberg	Analytical, creative, and practical intelligence

IQ TESTS

We have been discussing intelligence and IQ tests in general, and the idea of IQ tests is no doubt familiar to you, as such tests are commonplace in education. However, the time has come to examine several examples in more detail.

Let's start with this analogy: You have just been put in charge of choosing the members of your country's next Olympic team. However, the Olympic rules have been changed: Each country will send only 30 men and 30 women, and each athlete must compete in every event. The Olympic committee will not describe those events until all the athletes have been chosen. Clearly, you cannot hold the usual kind of tryouts, but neither will you choose people at random. How will you proceed?

Your best bet would be to devise a test of "general athletic ability." You might measure the abilities of applicants to run, jump, change direction, maintain balance, throw and catch, kick, lift weights, respond rapidly to signals, and perform other athletic feats. You would choose the applicants with the best scores.

No doubt, your test would be imperfect. But if you want your team to do well, you need some way to measure athletic ability. Later, other people begin to use your test also. Does its wide acceptance mean that athletic ability is a single quantity? Of course not. You found it useful to treat athletic ability as a single quantity, but you know that most great basketball players are not great swimmers or gymnasts. Does your test imply that athletic ability reflects innate talent? No, it merely measures athletic skills. It says nothing about how they developed.

Intelligence tests resemble this imaginary test of athletic ability. If you were in charge of choosing which applicants a college should admit, you would want to select those who will be the best students. Because students will study subjects that they have not studied before, it makes sense to measure a range of academic skills, not knowledge of a single topic. That is, you want a test of **aptitude** (*ability to learn, or fluid intelligence*) rather than **achievement** (*what someone has already learned, or crystallized intelligence*). Aptitude and achievement are hard to separate. Aptitude leads to achievement, and past achievement increases future ability to learn. One way to measure the ability to learn is to measure how much someone has already learned. Still, we make an effort to separate the two.

The original goal of intelligence tests was to identify the *least* capable children, who could not learn from ordinary schooling. Later, the tests were also used to identify the best students, who would profit from accelerated classes. Similar tests are used for selecting among applicants to colleges and professional schools. Grades are useful, too, but the grades at one school may not be entirely comparable to those at another. Teachers' recommendations are useful up to a point, but teachers have their own biases. Objective tests help compare students from different schools.

Intelligence quotient (IQ) tests attempt to *measure an individual's probable performance in school and similar settings*. The term *quotient* dates from when IQ was determined by dividing mental age by chronological age and then multiplying by 100. **Mental age** is *the average age of children who perform as well as this child*. Chronological age is actual age, or time since birth. For example, an 8-year-old who performs like an average 10-year-old has a mental age of 10, a chronological age of 8, and an IQ of $10 \div 8 \times 100 = 125$. That method is now obsolete, but the term remains.

Two French psychologists, Alfred Binet and Theophile Simon (1905), devised the first IQ tests. The French Ministry of Public Instruction wanted a fair way to identify children who had such serious intellectual deficiencies that they should not be placed in the same classes with other students. The task of identifying such children had formerly been left to medical doctors, but the school system wanted an impartial test. Binet and Simon's test measured the skills that children need for success in school, such as understanding and using language, computational skills, memory, and the ability to follow instructions.

Their test and others like it make reasonably accurate predictions. But suppose a test correctly predicts that one student will perform better than another in school. Can we then say that the first student did better in school *because of* a higher IQ score? No, an IQ score does not explain school performance any more than a basketball player's shooting average explains how many shots he makes. An IQ score, like a shooting average, is a measurement, not an explanation.

The Stanford-Binet Test

The test that Binet and Simon designed was later modified for English speakers by Stanford psychologists and published as the **Stanford-Binet IQ test**. The test's items are designated by age (Table 9.2). An item designated as "age 8," for example, will be answered correctly by 60 to 90% of 8-year-olds. (A higher percentage of older children answer it correctly and a lower percentage of younger children.) A child who answers correctly most of the age 8 items, but not the age 9 items, has a mental age of 8.

School psychologists are carefully trained on how to administer the test items and score the answers. A psychologist testing an 8-year-old might start with the items designated for 7-year-olds. Unless the child misses many of the 7-year-old items, the psychologist gives credit for all the 6-year-old items without testing them. If the child answers most of the 7-year-old items correctly, the psychologist proceeds to the items for 8-year-olds, 9-year-

TABLE 9.2 Examples of the Types of Items on the Stanford-Binet Test

Age	Sample Test Item	
2	Test administrator points at pictures of everyday objects and asks, "What is this?" "Here are some pegs of different sizes and shapes. See whether you can put each one into the correct hole."	
4	"Why do people live in houses?" "Birds fly in the air; fish swim in the _____."	
6	"Here is a picture of a horse. Do you see what part of the horse is missing?" "Here are some candies. Can you count how many there are?"	
8	"What should you do if you find a lost puppy?" "Stephanie can't write today because she twisted her ankle. What is wrong with that?"	
10	"Why should people be quiet in a library?" "Repeat after me: 4 8 3 7 1 4."	
12	"What does regret mean?" "Here is a picture. Can you tell me what is wrong with it?"	
14	"What is the similarity between high and low?" "Watch me fold this paper and cut it. Now, when I unfold it, how many holes will there be?"	
Adult	"Make up a sentence using the words *celebrate, reverse,* and *appointment.*" "What do people mean when they say, 'People who live in glass houses should not throw stones'"?	

Source: Modified from Nietzel and Bernstein, 1987.

olds, and so forth, until the child begins to miss most items. At that point, the psychologist ends the test. This method is known as *adaptive testing*. Individuals proceed at their own pace, usually finishing in somewhat over an hour (V. W. McCall, Yates, Hendricks, Turner, & McNabb, 1989).

Stanford-Binet IQ scores are computed from tables set up to ensure that a given IQ score means the same at different ages. The mean IQ at each age is 100. A 6-year-old with an IQ score of, say, 116 has performed better on the test than 84% of other 6-year-olds. Similarly, an adult with an IQ score of 116 has performed better than 84% of other adults. The Stanford-Binet provides subscores reflecting visual reasoning, short-term memory, and other specialized skills (Daniel, 1997; V. W. McCall et al., 1989).

Figure 9.3 Most IQ tests are administered individually. Here, a psychologist (left) records the responses by a participant (right).

The Wechsler Tests

Two IQ tests originally devised by David Wechsler, and later modified by others, known as the Wechsler Adult Intelligence Scale–Fourth Edition (WAIS–IV) and the Wechsler Intelligence Scale for Children–Fourth Edition (WISC–IV), produce the same average, 100, and almost the same distribution of scores as the Stanford-Binet. The WISC is given to children up to age 16, and the WAIS is for everyone older. As with the Stanford-Binet, the Wechsler tests are administered to one person at a time. The Stanford-Binet and Wechsler tests are the most widely used IQ tests in the English language.

A Wechsler test provides an overall score and four major subscores. One is the Verbal Comprehension Index, based on such items as "Define the word *letter*" and "How are a peach and a plum similar?" A second part is the Perceptual Reasoning Index, which calls for nonverbal answers. For example, the examiner might arrange four blocks in a particular pattern and then ask the child to arrange four other blocks to match the pattern (Figure 9.3).

A third part, the Working Memory Index, includes such items as "Listen to these numbers and then repeat them: 3 6 2 5" and "Listen to these numbers and repeat them in reverse order: 4 7 6." The fourth part is Processing Speed. An example of an item is "Here is a page full of shapes. Put a slash (/) through all the circles and an X through all the squares." This task is simple, but the question is how quickly someone can proceed accurately.

△ ○ □ ▱ ○ △ ▱ □ ○

Each part of the WISC–IV or the WAIS–III begins with simple questions and progresses to more difficult ones. The inclusion of several subscores calls attention to someone's strengths and weaknesses. For example, a child who learned

English as a second language might do poorly on the Verbal Comprehension Index but much better on Perceptual Reasoning and Processing Speed, which do not require verbal answers. People with certain disabilities perform slowly on the Processing Speed tasks but do well on other parts of the test. A low score on one part of the WISC helps identify a problem for which teachers can provide help or special consideration.

Culture-Reduced Testing

The Stanford-Binet and Wechsler tests, though useful for many purposes, have a major limitation: Because they require use of the English language, they are unfair to immigrants, people with hearing impairments, and anyone else who does not speak English well. "Why not simply translate the tests into other languages, including sign language?" you might ask. Psychologists sometimes do, but a translated item may be easier or harder than the original. For example, one part of the Stanford-Binet presents words and asks for words that rhyme with them. Generating rhymes is moderately easy in English, easier in Italian, but almost impossible in Zulu (M. W. Smith, 1974).

To overcome such problems, psychologists have tried to devise a culture-fair or culture-reduced test. Although no task is free of cultural influences (Rosselli & Ardila, 2003), some tests are fairer than others. A test without language is reasonably fair to more people, especially immigrants and people who are deaf. *The most widely used culture-reduced test* is the Progressive Matrices test devised by John C. Raven. These matrices, which *progress* gradually from easy to difficult items, attempt to measure abstract reasoning. That is, they measure mostly fluid intelligence, whereas the Stanford-Binet and Wechsler tests measure a combination of fluid and crystallized intelligence. To answer questions on the Progressive Matrices, a person must generate hypotheses, test them, and infer rules. Figure 9.4 presents three matrices similar to those on this test. The first is relatively easy, the second is harder, and the third is harder still.

The Progressive Matrices require no verbal responses or factual information, and the instructions are simple. It therefore provides a fair opportunity to people from different cultures, who speak different languages. The main disadvantage is that this test provides only a single score instead of identifying someone's strengths and weaknesses.

How culture-fair is the Progressive Matrices test? It requires less information than the Wechsler or Stanford-Binet tests, but it does assume familiarity with pencil-and-paper, multiple-choice tests. The Progressive Matrices

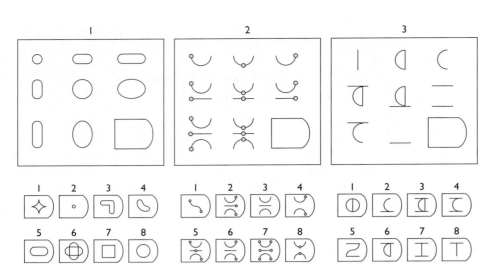

Figure 9.4 Items similar to those on Raven's Progressive Matrices test. Each pattern has a piece missing. From the choices provided, select the one that completes the pattern both going across and going down. (You can check your answers against answer A on page 323.)

Many immigrants to the United States settle in ethnic neighborhoods where they can use their original language. Most first-generation immigrants do not score highly on English-language intelligence tests. As a rule, their children and grandchildren get higher scores.

test has less cultural content than the other tests, but no test can be totally free of cultural influences.

6. What is one advantage of the Wechsler IQ tests over Raven's Progressive Matrices? What is an advantage of the Progressive Matrices?

Answer

6. The Wechsler tests provide separate scores for different tasks and therefore identify someone's strengths and weaknesses. Raven's Progressive Matrices are fairer for someone who is not a native speaker of English.

9.1 | module

In Closing

Measuring Something We Don't Fully Understand

The standard IQ tests were devised by trial and error long before most of the discoveries about memory and cognition that we discussed in the last two chapters. We still do not understand intelligence very well. Can we measure intelligence without understanding it? Possibly so; physicists measured gravity and magnetism long before they understood them theoretically. Maybe psychologists can do the same with intelligence.

Or maybe not. Measuring a poorly understood phenomenon is risky. Many psychologists who are dissatisfied with the current tests are striving toward better ones. Producing a significantly improved IQ test is not as easy as it may sound.

In the meantime, the current tests have both strengths and weaknesses. An IQ test, like any other tool, can be used in constructive or destructive ways. The next module explores ways of evaluating IQ tests.

SUMMARY

- *Defining intelligence.* Intelligence is difficult to define, given our current understanding. Psychological researchers have begun by trying to measure it, hoping to learn something from the measurements. (page 315)
- *g factor.* People's scores on almost any test of "intelligent" abilities correlate positively with scores on other tests. The overlap among tests is referred to as *g,* meaning the general factor in intelligence. (page 315)
- *Possible explanations for* g. Many psychologists believe the *g* factor corresponds to an ability that underlies all kinds of intelligence, such as mental speed or working memory. Another possibility is that all kinds of intellectual abilities correlate with one another because the same growth factors that promote any one of them also support the others. (page 316)
- *Fluid and crystallized intelligence.* Psychologists distinguish between fluid intelligence (reasoning ability) and crystallized intelligence (acquired and practiced skills). (page 317)
- *Intelligence as a hierarchy.* The *g* factor can be subdivided into more specific categories, such as verbal, perceptual, and image rotation. (page 317)
- *One or many types of intelligence?* Howard Gardner argued that people have many independent types of intelligence, including social attentiveness, musical abilities, and motor skills. However, so far, no one has demonstrated that different types of intelligence are independent of one another. (page 317)
- *Triarchic theory.* According to Sternberg's triarchic theory, intelligence consists of analytical, creative, and practical abilities. Again, the issue is whether these constitute independent abilities or whether they are different manifestations of a single process, *g.* (page 318)
- *IQ tests.* The Stanford-Binet, Wechsler, and other IQ tests were devised to predict the level of performance in school. Culture-reduced tests such as Raven's Progressive Matrices can be used to test people who are unfamiliar with English. (page 319)

KEY TERMS

aptitude (page 319)

achievement (page 319)

crystallized intelligence (page 317)

fluid intelligence (page 317)

g (page 315)

intelligence quotient (IQ) tests (page 320)

mental age (page 320)

multiple intelligences (page 317)

Progressive Matrices (page 321)

psychometric approach (page 315)

s (page 315)

Stanford-Binet IQ test (page 320)

triarchic theory (page 318)

Wechsler Adult Intelligence Scale–Fourth Edition (WAIS–IV) (page 321)

Wechsler Intelligence Scale for Children–Fourth Edition (WISC–IV) (page 321)

ANSWERS TO OTHER QUESTION IN THE MODULE (PAGE 322)

A. 1. (8); 2. (2); 3. (4)

Evaluation of Intelligence Tests

- How accurate, useful, and fair are IQ tests?
- Why do some people score higher than others?

> Whatever exists at all exists in some amount.
>
> —E. L. Thorndike (1918, p. 16)

> Anything that exists in amount can be measured.
>
> —W. A. McCall (1939, p. 15)

> Anything which exists can be measured incorrectly.
>
> —D. Detterman (1979, p. 167)

All three of these quotes apply to intelligence: If intelligence exists, it must exist in some amount, and therefore, it must be measurable, but it can also be measured incorrectly. The challenge is to evaluate the accuracy, usefulness, and fairness of IQ tests. Because much is at stake here, the conclusions are often controversial.

THE STANDARDIZATION OF IQ TESTS

In the first module, we considered examples of IQ tests. To evaluate them or any other test, we need to go beyond impressions of whether they look reasonable. The evaluation begins with standardization, *the process of evaluating the questions, establishing rules for administering a test, and interpreting the scores.* One main step is to find the norms, which are *descriptions of how frequently various scores occur.* Psychologists try to standardize a test on a large sample of people who are as representative as possible of the entire population.

You may sometimes hear someone use the term *standardized test* in a way that makes it sound threatening. The opposite of a standardized test is an unstandardized test—one for which no one has verified that the questions are clear, and no one is sure what constitutes an excellent score or an average score. Standardizing a test improves it.

The Distribution of IQ Scores

Binet, Wechsler, and the others who devised IQ tests chose items and arranged the scoring method to establish a mean score of 100. The standard deviation is 15 for the Wechsler test, and 16 for the Stanford-Binet. (As discussed in chapter 2, the standard deviation measures the variability of performance. It is small if most scores are close to the mean and large if scores vary widely.) The scores for a large population approximate a *normal distribution,* or bell-shaped curve, as shown in Figure 9.5. The distribution is symmetrical, and most scores are close to the mean.

In a normal distribution, 68% of all people fall within 1 standard deviation above or below the mean, and about 95% are within 2 standard deviations. Someone with a score of 115 on the Wechsler test exceeds the scores of people within 1 standard deviation from the mean plus all of those more than 1 standard deviation below the mean—a total of 84%, as shown in Figure 9.5. We say that such a person is "in the 84th percentile." Someone with an IQ score of 130 is in the 98th percentile, with a score higher than those of 98% of others.

In fact, however, although the distribution of IQ scores approximates a normal distribution, it doesn't quite match it. As shown in Figure 9.6, the actual distribution appears to be a combination of two distributions. One has a mode (most common score) of about 108 or 109, and another has a mode around 79 (W. Johnson, Carothers, & Deary, 2008). If we add the two distributions together, we get something close to a normal distribution, but with a bulge on the lower end and a mode (109) that is higher than the mean (100).

The bulge at the lower end represents people with various kinds of disabilities, described as mentally challenged. For example, people with Down syndrome *have a variety of physical and medical impairments as a result of having an extra*

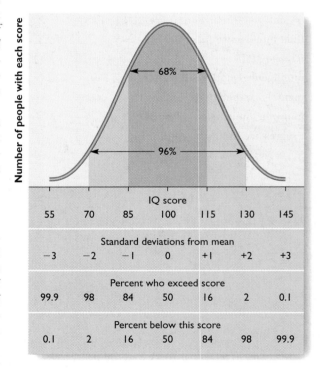

IQ score						
55	70	85	100	115	130	145

Standard deviations from mean						
−3	−2	−1	0	+1	+2	+3

Percent who exceed score						
99.9	98	84	50	16	2	0.1

Percent below this score						
0.1	2	16	50	84	98	99.9

Figure 9.5 The curve shown here represents scores on the Wechsler IQ test, with a standard deviation of 15 (15 points above and below the mean, which is 100).

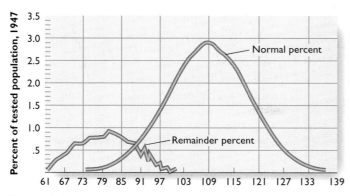

Figure 9.6 Although the actual distribution of IQ scores has a mean of 100, there is a bulge of lower scores, implying that we are observing a superimposition of one distribution centered around 79 and another centered around 109. (Source: Johnson, W., Carothers, A., & Deary, I. J., 2008. Sex differences in variability in general intelligence. *Perspectives on Psychological Science, 3,* 518–531.)

copy of chromosome #21. They have delays in speech development, poor motor skills, and limitations in memory and cognition. Some do much better than others, and some do get jobs, but most remain at a level where people would not want to leave them unsupervised for more than an hour (Carr, 2008).

The term *mentally challenged* or *mentally disabled* refers to people more than two standard deviations below average, corresponding to an IQ score of 68 or 70, depending on the test. This cutoff is arbitrary, and a psychologist considers other observations of the person's level of functioning before making a diagnosis. In the United States, the Individuals with Disabilities Education Act requires public schools to provide "free and appropriate" education for all children regardless of their limitations. Children with mild physical or intellectual disabilities are mainstreamed as much as possible—that is, placed in the same classes as other children but given special consideration. The results of mainstreaming have been mixed. On the plus side, children in mainstream classes develop better language abilities than those in classes limited to children with disabilities (Laws, Byrne, & Buckley, 2000). However, most children with disabilities have few friends, especially as they advance to the later grades (Hall & McGregor, 2000).

Psychologists refer to people more than 2 standard deviations above the mean—with an IQ of 130 or more—as "gifted." However, being gifted requires more than a high IQ score. Gifted children learn rapidly and without much help, seek to master knowledge, ask deep philosophical questions, and develop new ideas (Winner, 2000a). Many become extremely adept in an area of interest, such as mathematics (Sweetland, Reina, &

Taffi, 2006). Often, they have trouble finding friends their own age with similar interests, and they spend most of their time alone.

Since the first IQ tests, psychologists have found that girls tend to do better than boys on certain kinds of language tasks, especially relating to verbal fluency, as well as certain memory tests. Boys tend to do better than girls on visuospatial rotations. On attention tasks, the genders tend to differ in strategy, with males more often focusing on one item at a time and females spreading their attention more broadly (W. Johnson & Bouchard, 2007). None of these differences are huge. However, by loading IQ tests with one type of item or another, test authors could have produced results showing that girls are smarter than boys or that boys are smarter than girls. Instead, they balanced various types of items to ensure that the mean scores of both females and males would be 100, and they continue to be equal today (Colom, Juan-Espinosa, Abad, & García, 2000).

Males show greater individual variability. On several intellectual measures, more males than females appear at the extreme top and bottom of the range (Arden & Plomin, 2006; Hedges & Nowell, 1995). A study of 41 countries found that males showed more variability than females in 35

A person with Down syndrome.

Many children with low IQ scores can be mainstreamed in regular classes. Those with more severe disabilities are taught in special classes.

countries on verbal scores and in 37 countries on math scores (Machin & Pekkarinen, 2008). *Why males are more variable we do not know.* However, this tendency is not huge. In some types of science and math jobs, men outnumber women by more than ten to one. The difference in variability of scores is not nearly large enough to account for this discrepancy (W. Johnson et al., 2008).

Restandardizations and the Flynn Effect

In 1920 a question that asked people to identify Mars was considered difficult because most people knew little about the planets. Today, the same question is easy. Researchers periodically restandardize tests to keep the overall difficulty about the same.

Those who restandardized the IQ tests eventually realized that they were consistently making the tests more difficult to keep the mean score from rising. That is, *decade by decade, generation by generation, people's raw scores on IQ tests have gradually increased, and test makers have had to make the tests harder to keep the mean score at 100.* This tendency is known as the **Flynn effect,** after James Flynn, who called attention to it (Flynn, 1984, 1999). The results vary across countries, tests, and periods of time, but a typical figure is just above 3 IQ points per 10 years. So if you took the same IQ test as your parents, and your parents are 25 years older than you, then your score would be about 8 points higher than theirs. If you took an IQ test from your grandparents' era, your score would be still higher.

One consequence is that if you take an IQ test and later take a restandardized form, your score will probably drop! You did not deteriorate, but you are being compared to a higher standard. For most people, a few points' change makes little difference, but for people at the lower end of the distribution, the loss of a few points might qualify them for special services (Kanaya, Scullin, & Ceci, 2003).

The Flynn effect—increase in IQ scores over generations—has occurred across ethnic groups (Raven, 2000), over many decades, and in every country for which we have data, including the United States, Canada, Europe, Australia, New Zealand, Israel, Japan, urban areas of Brazil and China, and even rural Kenya (Daley, Whaley, Sigman, Espinosa, & Neumann, 2003; Flynn, 1998; Must, te Nijenhuis, Must, & van Vianen, 2009). However, several studies suggest that the Flynn effect was strongest in the early and middle 1900s and that it has slowed or stopped since about 1990, at least in parts of Europe (Sundet, Barlaug, & Torjussen, 2004; Teasdale & Owen, 2005, 2008).

The effect has occurred for a wide variety of IQ tests, including the Wechsler tests (Kaufman, 2001), Raven's Progressive Matrices (Pind, Gunnarsdóttir, & Jóhannesson, 2003), and others (Colom & García-López, 2003). The increase is greatest on reasoning tasks, such as Raven's Progressive Matrices, and weak or absent on tests of knowledge (Flynn, 1999; Rodgers & Wänström, 2006) and speed of responding (Nettelbeck & Wilson, 2004). On conservation of volume and weight tasks, like those that Jean Piaget studied (chapter 5), researchers reported *decreased* performance between 1976 and 2003 (Shayer, Ginsburg, & Coe, 2007). So, many mental abilities have improved, but not all.

What accounts for the Flynn effect? Psychologists have no consensus. One hypothesis points to improved education and test-taking skills (W. M. Williams, 1998). When later generations show an increase in semantic (factual) memory, education is a major contributor (Rönnlund & Nilsson, 2008). However, most studies show the greatest gains on reasoning tests (such as Raven's Progressive Matrices) and the fewest gains on factual knowledge. Besides, the IQ improvement is evident in 6-year-old children, who have just started school, and in rural Kenyan children, who have little schooling (Daley et al., 2003).

Another possibility is exposure to increasing technology, beginning with movies and radio in the early 1900s and progressing through television, video games, and the Internet. These kinds of experiences stimulate visuospatial thinking, probably related to performance on Raven's Progressive Matrices and similar tests (Neisser, 1997). Even in rural Kenya, the least technological place in which the Flynn effect has been demonstrated, some homes now have television (Daley et al., 2003).

Much evidence points to a contribution from improved health and nutrition (Sigman & Whaley, 1998). People have been getting taller over the years also, and a likely explanation for that trend is advances in health and nutrition. Also, many infants in the United States, Britain, and Australia have been evaluated for their developmental quotient from ages 6 to 22 months. *This score is based on the ages at which an infant holds the head up, sits up, stands, walks, jumps, shows curiosity, says a first word, responds to requests, and so forth.* Developmental quotient scores have also increased at a rate of just over 3 points per decade (Lynn, 2009). Developmental quotient is not the same as IQ, but the two scores are positively correlated. The most parsimonious explanation is that whatever is responsible for increases in the developmental quotient is also responsible for increases in IQ scores. Age of holding the head up or sitting up clearly has nothing to do with education or test-taking strategy, but it could have much to do with prenatal and early postnatal health and nutrition. Vitamin and mineral deficiencies were common in the early 1900s, but no more. Decades ago, it was common for women to smoke and drink during pregnancy, but today, such practices are strongly discouraged. Improved nutrition is a particularly appealing explanation for the decrease in mental retardation over the years.

For years, psychologists dismissed genetics as a contributing factor. Evolution simply does not operate fast enough to explain changes from one decade to another. Besides, less educated, lower IQ parents tend to have more than the average number of children. Therefore, from a genetic standpoint, we would have to predict if anything a decrease in IQ scores over generations, not an increase (Lynn & Harvey, 2008). However, a different kind of genetic explanation is possible (Mingroni, 2004): Heterosis is *improvement due to outbreeding.* We don't know much about the genes that influence intelligence, but apparently, hundreds of genes have small effects (Plomin & Kovas, 2005). Imagine a series of genes, and suppose in each case the dominant form of the gene promotes higher IQ development. Genetic diversity is limited in any small community, so if people mate with others nearby, many couples will have the dominant form of the same genes and the recessive form of other genes. If people start choosing partners from other villages, maybe even other countries or other ethnic groups, then someone with the dominant form of one gene mates with someone who has the dominant form of another gene. Their children therefore have a dominant form of more genes than either parent. The result could be increased IQ scores, height, developmental quotients, and so forth.

Here is one observation that heterosis explains and other hypotheses do not: If a couple has children born many years apart, the oldest might be, say, 10 years older than the youngest, but on the average, the youngest child does *not* have a higher IQ than the oldest. If the Flynn effect were entirely due to improved health, nutrition, or technology over the years, we should expect the latest-born to have an advantage. But if the effect depends on heterosis, birth order within a family should have no effect.

Although IQ test performance has been increasing, actual intelligence may not have been. It is possible to argue that young adults today are somewhat smarter than those of previous generations (Cocodia et al., 2003; R. W. Howard, 1999; Schooler, 1998), but it is difficult to believe that today's young people deserve IQ scores 15 to 20 points higher than their grandparents. Flynn (1998) therefore argued that we have seen an increase in IQ scores, but not intelligence, over time. If so, what exactly do IQ scores mean? At a minimum, we should beware of comparing two people's scores if they took different forms of the test in different eras.

EVALUATION OF TESTS

Have you ever complained about a test in school that seemed unfair? *Seeming* unfair doesn't necessarily make a test unfair—and seeming fair doesn't necessarily make it fair. When psychologists want to evaluate the accuracy or fairness of a test, they examine specific kinds of evidence. The main ways of evaluating any test are to check its reliability and validity.

Reliability

The reliability of a test is defined as *the repeatability of its scores* (T. B. Rogers, 1995). A reliable test produces consistent, repeatable results. To determine the reliability of a test, psychologists calculate a correlation coefficient. (Recall from chapter 2 that a correlation coefficient measures how accurately we can use one measurement to predict another.) Psychologists may test the same people twice, either with the same test or with equivalent versions of it, and compare the two sets of scores. Or they may compare the scores on the first and second halves of the test or the scores on the test's odd-numbered and even-numbered items. If all items measure approximately the same thing, one set of scores should correlate highly with the other set. Correlation coefficients theoretically range from +1 to −1. In the real world, however, a reliability coefficient is always either zero or positive. A negative reliability would mean that most people who score high the first time they take some test do worse than average the second time. That pattern simply never happens. Figure 9.7 illustrates test–retest reliability, *the correlation between scores on a first test and a retest.*

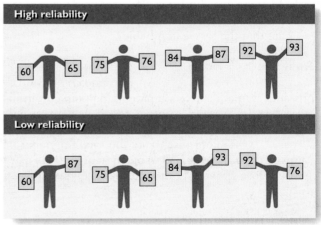

Figure 9.7 On a test with high reliability, people who score high the first time will score high when they take the test again. On a test with low reliability, scores fluctuate randomly.

If a test's reliability is perfect (+1), the person who scores the highest on the first test also scores highest on the retest, the person who scores second highest on the first test also scores second highest on the retest, and so forth. If the reliability is 0, scores vary randomly from one test to another. The WISC, Stanford-Binet, Progressive Matrices, and other commonly used intelligence tests all have reliabilities above .9.

IQ scores are reasonably stable over time for most individuals. Many studies have found correlations near .9 for people taking the same test at times 10 to 20 years apart (Larsen, Hartmann, & Nyborg, 2008), and one study found that IQ scores at age 11 correlated .66 with scores at age 80 (Deary, Whiteman, Starr, Whalley, & Fox, 2004). Figure 9.8 shows the results.

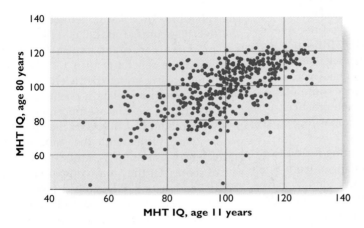

Figure 9.8 In this scatter plot, each point represents one person. The distance along the x-axis shows the IQ score at age 11, and the y-axis shows the IQ score at age 80. The correlation is relatively high (.66). (MHT = the Moray House Test, a type of IQ test.) (Source: Deary, I. J., Whiteman, M. C., Starr, J. M., Whalley, L. J., & Fox, H. C., 2004. The impact of childhood intelligence on later life: Following up the Scottish mental surveys of 1932 and 1947. *Journal of Personality and Social Psychology*, 86, 130–147. Reproduced by permission of the American Psychological Association.)

7. I have just devised a new "intelligence test." I measure your intelligence by dividing the length of your head by its width and then multiplying by 100. Will the scores on this test be reliable?

8. Most students find that their scores on any standardized test increase the second time they take it. Does the improvement indicate that the test is unreliable?

Answers

7. Yes! To say that a test is "reliable" is simply to say that its scores are repeatable. My test will give highly reliable (repeatable) scores. True, they will be useless, but reliability does not measure usefulness.
8. Not necessarily. If the rank order of scores remains about the same, the test is reliable. That is, if most people's scores improve by about the same amount, then those who had the highest scores the first time still have the highest scores the second time.

Validity

A test's **validity** is defined as *the degree to which evidence and theory support the interpretations of test scores for its intended purposes* (Joint Committee on Standards, 1999). In simpler terms, validity is a determination of how

well the test measures what it claims to measure. To determine the validity of a test, researchers examine five types of evidence:

Content. The content of a test should match its stated purposes. For example, a test given to job applicants should include only tasks that are important for the job. A test to determine which children have successfully completed fifth grade should correspond to the main aspects of the fifth-grade curriculum.

Response processes. If a test claims to measure a certain skill, then the test-takers should need to use that skill to answer the questions. This criterion seems obvious, but cases arise in which people find shortcuts to answering questions. For example, some tests of reading comprehension include a paragraph or two to read, followed by multiple-choice questions. Often, people with previous knowledge can guess the answer without reading the passage (Katz, Lautenschlager, Blackburn, & Harris, 1990). Unfortunately, few research studies have examined the processes that people use to answer test questions (Braden & Niebling, 2005).

Internal structure. If a test claims to measure a single skill, such as working memory, then all the items should correlate with one another. That is, people who answer one item correctly should be more likely than average to answer the other items correctly. If a test claims to test two or more abilities, then we should expect to find two or more clusters of items that correlate strongly with one another.

Relation to other variables. If a test is valid, the scores predict important kinds of performance. Scores on an interest inventory should predict which jobs or activities someone would enjoy. Results of a personality test should predict which people might develop anxiety problems or depression. Scores on an IQ test should predict grades in school. In fact, they do. The scores correlate positively with grades and achievement tests in all academic subjects (Deary, Strand, Smith, & Fernandes, 2007).

IQ tests were designed to predict school performance. Later results showed that they predicted other outcomes as well to the surprise of almost everyone, including the authors of the tests. On the average, people with higher IQ scores get better jobs than most other people and earn higher salaries (Strenze, 2007). They also have fewer automobile accidents than others do (O'Toole, 1990) and are less likely to suffer post-traumatic stress disorder (Vasterling et al., 2002). They do better than others at reading maps, understanding order forms, reading bus schedules, and taking their medicines correctly (Gottfredson, 2002a). They are more likely than average to forego a smaller pleasure now in favor of a larger one later (Shamosh et al., 2008). Health and life span are greater than average among people with high IQ, especially those who are also high in conscientiousness (Deary, Batty, Pattie, & Gale, 2008; Gottfredson, 2004). Although some of these correlations are small, they indicate that IQ scores relate to real-world outcomes outside the classroom.

As you might expect, very high IQ test scores predict success in scientific fields. Even among those with a master's or PhD degree, those with higher IQ scores usually have more patents and scientific publications (Park, Lubinski, & Benbow, 2008). IQ scores also predict success on a wide variety of other jobs, especially if combined with other information (Schmidt & Hunter, 1998). According to Linda Gottfredson (2002b, pp. 25, 27), "The general mental ability factor—*g*—is the best single predictor of job performance . . . [It] enhances performance in all domains of work." According to Frank Schmidt and John Hunter (1981, p. 1128), "Professionally developed cognitive ability tests are valid predictors of performance on the job . . . for all jobs . . . in all settings." That is probably an overstatement. (It could hardly be an understatement!) For example, IQ scores are probably not useful predictors of success as a singer or professional athlete. Still, for many jobs, using some type of cognitive test score to select employees increases the chances that those who are hired will learn their jobs quickly and succeed at them.

Do IQ tests measure everything that we care about intellectually? Of course not. One study found that eighth graders' performance in school correlated highly with questionnaire measurements of their self-discipline (Duckworth & Seligman, 2005). College grades correlate highly with measures of study skills and study habits (Credé & Kuncel, 2008). People also vary in initiative, creativity, motivation, and other variables, many of which are hard to measure but certainly important.

Consequences of testing. Finally, we need to consider IQ tests' costs and benefits. Test publishers claim that their tests enable schools to choose the right students for advanced placement courses, help colleges admit the best applicants, and help employers fill jobs. Do the tests actually accomplish those goals well enough to be worth the cost and effort? Some colleges require all applicants to take both the general part of the SAT and several SAT subject tests. Because the subject tests correlate highly with the general test, it is not clear why any college needs both general and subject test scores (Baron & Norman, 1992).

Critics raise other issues about the consequences of testing. For example, in the U.S. public school system, students' scores on end-of-grade tests determine whether they advance to the next grade. The scores also influence the teachers' salaries for the next year and the amount of government support that a school receives. As a result, the best qualified teachers don't want to work at schools with low-performing students (Tuerk, 2005). Many students and teachers concentrate heavily on preparing for the tests at the expense of other educational goals. Do the tests accomplish enough good to outweigh these costs? Although opinions are strong, good research on these issues is rare (Braden & Niebling, 2005).

Special Problems in Measuring Validity

Measuring the validity of a test can be tricky. For example, consider data for the Graduate Record Examination (GRE), a test taken by applicants to most graduate schools in the United States. According to one large study, grades for first-year graduate students in physics correlated .13 with their GRE quantitative scores and .19 with their verbal scores. That is, verbal scores were better predictors than quantitative scores for students in physics. For first-year students in English, the pattern was reversed. Their grades correlated .29 with their quantitative scores and .23 with their verbal scores (Educational Testing Service, 1994). These scores surprise most people because physics is such a quantitative field and English is such a verbal field.

The explanation is simple. Almost all graduate students in physics have nearly the same (very high) score on the quantitative test, and almost all English graduate students have nearly the same

In some countries, test scores determine a student's future almost irrevocably. Students who perform well are almost assured future success, and those who perform poorly have limited opportunities.

(very high) score on the verbal test. If almost all the students in a department have nearly the same score, their scores cannot predict who will succeed. A test predicts performance only for a population whose scores vary over a substantial range.

9. Can a test have high reliability and low validity? Can a test have low reliability and high validity?

10. If physics graduate departments tried admitting some students with low quantitative scores on the GRE and English departments tried admitting some students with low verbal scores, what would happen to the predictive validity of the tests?

11. Would you expect the SAT scores to show higher predictive validity at a college with extremely competitive admissions standards or at a college that admits almost every applicant?

Answers

9. Yes, a test can have high reliability and low validity. A measure of intelligence determined by dividing head length by head width has high reliability (repeatability) but presumably no validity. A test with low reliability cannot have high validity, however. Low reliability means that the scores fluctuate randomly. If the test scores cannot even predict a later score on the same test, then they can hardly predict anything else.

10. The predictive validity of the tests would increase. The predictive validity tends to be low when almost all students have practically the same score. It is higher when students' scores are highly variable.

11. The predictive validity of SAT scores will be higher at the college that admits almost anyone. At the college with extremely competitive admissions standards, almost all students have nearly the same SAT scores, and the slight variation in scores cannot predict who will get the best grades.

Interpreting Fluctuations in Scores

Suppose on the first test in your psychology course you get 94% correct. On the second test (which was equally difficult), your score is only 88%. Does that score indicate that you studied harder for the first test than for the second test? Not necessarily. When you take tests that are not perfectly reliable, your scores fluctuate. The lower the reliability, the greater the fluctuation.

When people lose sight of this fact, they sometimes draw unwarranted conclusions. In one study, Harold Skeels (1966) tested infants in an orphanage and identified those with the lowest IQ scores. He then transferred those infants to an institution that provided more attention. Several years later, most of them showed major increases in their IQ scores. Should we conclude, as many psychologists did, that the extra attention improved the children's IQ performances? Not necessarily (Longstreth, 1981). IQ tests for infants have low reliability. The scores fluctuate widely from one time to another, even from one day to the next. If someone selects infants with low scores and retests them later, their mean IQ score is almost certain to improve simply because the scores had nowhere to go but up.

ARE IQ TESTS BIASED?

In addition to being reliable and valid, a test should also be unbiased—that is, equally fair and accurate for all groups. A **biased** test *overstates or understates the true performance of one or more groups.* We cannot insist that all groups score equally well on a test. If groups really do differ in some kind of performance, the test should report that fact, and we should not blame the test for what it tells us. However, it should not exaggerate a difference or give unfair advantages to one group or another.

Because this concept is easily misunderstood, let's illustrate with an example. Imagine a store that sells DVDs. The management determines that the best salespeople are those who know the most about contemporary popular culture. The company develops a test of knowledge about recent movies, television, and music and offers sales jobs only to people who do well on this test. Suppose we find that, on the average, young adults do better on this test than older adults. Is this test, therefore, biased against older adults?

This is an empirical question—that is, one to be decided by the evidence—but the answer is probably no. Most older adults have below-average scores on the test because they really do not know as much about popular culture. Using the test to select employees at this store is not biased if the test results correctly predict who will be good salespeople. Note that it does not prevent all older people from getting the job. Those older adults who do know much about popular culture will succeed on both the test and the job.

Now suppose an employer down the street takes this "unbiased" test and uses it to select employees for a shoe store. A reasonable prediction is that this test, which is unbiased for choosing employees at a DVD store, will be highly bi-

Women who return to school after age 25 usually get better grades than their SAT scores predict. The tests are "biased" against them in the sense of underpredicting their performance.

ogists conduct several kinds of research. They try to identify bias both in individual test items and in the test as a whole.

Evaluating Possible Bias in Single Test Items

Suppose on a test with 100 items, one item is the 10th easiest for one group but only the 42nd easiest for some other group. This pattern suggests that the item taps information or skills that are more available to one group than the other. If so, the item is biased (Schmitt & Dorans, 1990). For example, Figure 9.9, an item that once appeared on the SAT, diagrams an American football field and asks for the ratio of the distance between the goal lines to the distance between the sidelines. For men, this was one of the easiest items on the test. Many women missed it, including some of the brightest women who missed almost no other questions.

The reason was that some women had so little interest in football that they did not know which were the goal lines and which were the sidelines. The publishers of the SAT determined that this item was biased and removed it from the test.

ased for choosing salespeople at a shoe store. How much you know about popular culture is important for selling DVDs but not for selling shoes. Therefore, the test would unfairly penalize older job applicants at the shoe store. Furthermore, the older adults who did well on the test, and therefore got hired, would in fact be no better qualified for this job than the ones the test rejected. The point is that bias means unfairness for a particular purpose. Researchers need to determine the bias, or lack of it, for any potential use of any test.

For what purposes, if any, are IQ tests or other tests biased? Women who enter college or graduate school after age 25 generally receive better grades than their SAT scores predict (Swinton, 1987). Therefore, the tests are biased against them, even though in fact most of them have good scores. The tests are biased in the sense that a given SAT score means something different for a 25-year-old woman than for a 20-year-old. Why do older women get better grades than their test scores predict? Here are three hypotheses: (a) Because they have been away from school for a while, their test-taking skills are rusty. (b) Anyone who returns to school at that point must have strong motivation, whereas some younger students do not. (c) A few extra years of experiences give them some advantages.

To determine whether a test is biased against groups, psychol-

Evaluating Possible Bias in a Test as a Whole

By definition, a biased test systematically misestimates the performance by members of some group. For example, if an IQ test is biased against Black students, then Black students who score, say, 100 will do *better* in school than White students with the same score.

However, the evidence indicates that Black students with a given IQ score generally do about the same in school as do White students with the same score and sometimes worse (Pesta & Poznanski, 2008; Sackett, Borneman, & Connelly, 2008). The same is true for SAT scores (McCornack, 1983). The unpleasant fact is that over many years White students have usually had better grades in school than Black students. The difference in IQ scores approximately matches the difference in performance. The tests report a difference; they don't create one.

"Students will rise to your level of expectation," says Jaime Escalante (left), the high school teacher portrayed by Edward James Olmos (right) in *Stand and Deliver.* The movie chronicles Escalante's talent for inspiring average students to excel in calculus.

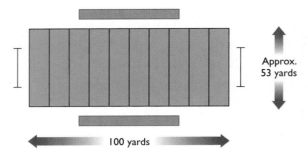

Approx.
53 yards

100 yards

The diagram above represents a football field. What is the ratio of the distance between the goal lines to the distance between the sidelines?

a. 1.89
b. 1.53
c. 0.53
d. 5.3
e. 53

Figure 9.9 This item was eliminated from the SAT when researchers determined that it was biased against women. Some women who did very well on the rest of the test did not know which were the goal lines and which were the sidelines.

Since about 1970, Black students have increased their scores on IQ tests. In comparison to the mean of 100 for White children, the mean for Black students increased from about 83 in 1970 to about 88 in 2000, according to the Stanford-Binet and Wechsler tests, as shown in Figure 9.10 (Dickens & Flynn, 2006). Other studies suggest an increase in scores from 1970 to 1990 and a leveling off since then (Magnuson & Duncan, 2006). On the average, Black students also increased their grades in school since 1970 (Grissmer, Williamson, Kirby, & Berends, 1998). The fact that grades and test scores improved simultaneously supports the idea that the tests predict performance validly. The improvement of Black students' IQ scores

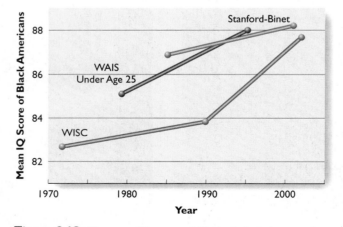

Figure 9.10 The mean IQ scores of Black students increased relative to White students from 1970 to 2000, according to the results of the two most widely used IQ tests. (Modified from Dickens & Flynn, 2006)

and grades presumably relates to improved educational and occupational opportunities for most Black families.

If IQ and SAT scores predict school performance as accurately for Blacks as for Whites, then by the usual definition of bias, the tests are not biased. However, another possibility remains: If many Black students have not been exposed to all the same opportunities as the average White student, then Black students' performance might be impaired on the tests and in school as well. Several studies indicate that, relative to the average for White students, Black students do better on tests of learning new information than on tests of what they have learned in the past (Fagan & Holland, 2007). For example, a Black student with a mediocre score on a vocabulary test might do better on items like these (Fagan & Holland, 2009):

> It costs 1500 BEZANTS to buy the rug in Byzantium. What is a BEZANT?
>
> a. hotel   b. coin   c. mill   d. harbor
>
> Big drills went into the earth hoping to find shiny KODT or energy-rich, flowing VALD. KODT is to silver as VALD is to
>
> a. gold   b. Mecca   c. oil   d. eggs
>
> (Check answer B on page 337.)

What we can conclude is that whatever causes Black students to do less well in school also leads them to do less well on IQ tests. Researchers still need to uncover the underlying reasons. Poverty (which leads to poor prenatal health and nutrition, as well as high levels of stress) is an obvious hypothesis (Evans & Schamberg, 2009). However, it is probably not the whole explanation. If we compare Blacks and Whites of the same socioeconomic status, a difference in scores remains, although it is smaller than usual (Magnuson & Duncan, 2006). A related hypothesis is that growing up in a White family gives a child more familiarity with the skills and content that the tests (and schools) measure. One study found that Black children adopted by White families performed higher on IQ tests than did Black children adopted by Black families (Moore, 1986). Another possibility is impairment by low expectations and aspirations. If you think you don't have a chance anyway, maybe you don't try. On the average, Black men score lower than Black women, and Black women are significantly more likely to attend college, strongly suggesting that many Black men are not giving a full effort academically (McKinnon & Bennett, 2005). It will be interesting to see whether the election of Barack Obama as U.S. president leads to greater aspirations among young Blacks and perhaps higher performances.

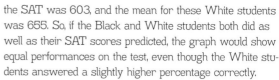

12. A test of driving skills includes items requiring good vision. People with visual impairments score lower than people with good vision. Is the test therefore biased against people with visual impairments?

13. Suppose on some new IQ test tall people generally get higher scores than short people. How could we determine whether this test is biased against short people?

Answers

12. No, this test is not biased against people with visual impairments. It correctly determines that they are likely to be poor drivers. A *difference* between groups does not constitute bias; only an *inaccurate difference* in scores constitutes bias.

13. We would need to determine whether the test accurately predicts the school performances of both short and tall people. If short people with, say, an IQ score of 100 perform better in school than tall people with the same score, then the test underpredicts the short people's performances, and inaccurate prediction means bias. (The fact that tall people do better on this test does not *by itself* demonstrate bias.)

What's the Evidence?
Stereotype Threat

The possible bias of a test depends not only on the test's questions but also on how the test is administered. If members of one group feel especially nervous or uncomfortable, their performance will suffer. In some (but not all) studies, children who were tested by an interviewer of their own ethnic group scored higher than those tested by someone of another group (Kim, Baydar, & Greek, 2003).

A related but subtler influence is what Claude Steele termed **stereotype threat**—*people's perceived risk of performing poorly and thereby supporting an unfavorable stereotype about their group.* For example, Black students who take an IQ test may fear that a poor score would support prejudices against Blacks in general. They may become distracted and upset, or they may decide not to try. Let's examine Steele's study and its results.

Hypothesis Suppose a group of Black students are about to take a test. If they believe that this is the kind of test on which Black students in general do not perform well, then they will worry that their own performance may reflect poorly on their group. As a result, they will fail to perform up to their abilities. If they are freed from this kind of worry, their performance may improve.

Method Participants were 20 Black and 20 White undergraduate students at Stanford University, a prestigious and highly selective institution. They were given a set of 27 difficult verbal questions from the Graduate Record Exam, a test similar to the SAT but intended for college seniors applying to graduate schools. Prior to starting the test, different groups (randomly assigned) received different instructions. Those in the "nondiagnostic" group were told that the research was an attempt to study the psychological factors related to solving difficult verbal problems, not an attempt to evaluate anyone's abilities. In contrast, participants in the "diagnostic" group were told that the research was an attempt to find each participant's "strengths and weaknesses" in solving verbal problems. This latter instruction was an attempt to increase students' nervousness about being evaluated.

Results Instead of simply presenting the number of correct answers for each group, the researchers adjusted the scores based on participants' SAT scores. The results in Figure 9.11 show the number of correct answers for each group *relative to the scores predicted by their SAT scores.* The mean for these Black students on the SAT was 603, and the mean for these White students was 655. So, if the Black and White students both did as well as their SAT scores predicted, the graph would show equal performances on the test, even though the White students answered a slightly higher percentage correctly.

The results for the "nondiagnostic" group do in fact show this pattern. However, for students who were given the "diagnostic" instructions, Black students had lower scores than their SAT scores predicted. They answered fewer questions overall, and answered fewer correctly, than Black students given the "nondiagnostic" instructions. The type of instructions did not significantly affect the White students.

When interviewed afterward, the Black students who received the "diagnostic" instructions said that they felt strongly aware of the stereotype about Black students taking ability tests. They also said they felt self-doubts and worries about possibly conforming to this stereotype (Steele & Aronson, 1995). An additional study by the same researchers found that simply asking participants to indicate their race prior to the test produced a significant decrease in Black students' performances (Steele & Aronson, 1995).

Interpretation The results confirmed that many Black students are sensitive to a suggestion that they are taking a test on which Black students in general do not excel. Presumably, the worry distracts from their ability to concentrate on the problems.

Many further studies have been conducted on stereotype threat, and most (though not all) replicate the general finding (Nguyen & Ryan, 2008). Stereotype threat also ap-

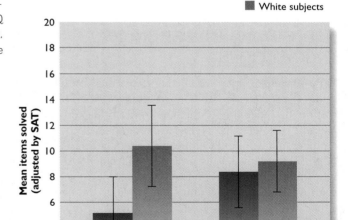

Figure 9.11 Black students who believed the test would identify their strengths and weaknesses failed to live up to their abilities. (From Claude M. Steele & Joshua Aronson, 1995. "Stereotype threat and the intellectual test performance of African Americans." *Journal of Personality and Social Psychology, 69,* 797–811. Reproduced by permission of the American Psychological Association.)

plies to other groups. For example, on the average, women's performance on a math test deteriorates if someone highlights the stereotype that women don't do well at math. Their anxiety increases, and their concentration decreases (Krendl, Richeson, Kelley, & Heatherton, 2008). However, women do better if they don't believe the stereotype about women doing poorly at math or if they don't believe that stereotype applies to them personally (Dar-Nimrod & Heine, 2006; Kiefer & Sekaquaptewa, 2007; Lesko & Corpus, 2006).

Three fascinating studies presented math problems to Asian women. For some of the women, the researchers primed their attention to being female by first giving them a questionnaire about being female. Those women did less well than usual on the test. For other women, the researchers primed their attention to being Asian. (The stereotype—probably false—is that women are not so good at math, but Asians are especially good.) Focusing their attention on being Asian improved their math performance in two of the three studies (Ambady, Shih, Kim, & Pittinsky, 2001; Cheryan & Bodenhausen, 2000; Shih, Pittinsky, & Ambady, 1999).

Given the goal of helping all people live up to their abilities, how can we combat stereotype threat? One approach is simply to tell people about stereotype threat! In one study, researchers described math problems as diagnostic of abilities that differ between men and women. But then they told some of the women (randomly assigned) about stereotype threat and urged them not to let the stereotype bother them. Those women performed as well as men did on the average (Johns, Schmader, & Martens, 2005). In another study, researchers presented math problems as diagnostic of people's abilities but then instructed some of the women to engage in "self-affirmation" by briefly writing about their most valuable characteristic, such as creativity, social skills, or sense of humor. These women approached the test with confidence and performed well (Martens, Johns, Greenberg, & Schimel, 2006).

....

14. How does stereotype threat affect the validity of a test?

Answer

14. Stereotype threat leads some people to perform at a lower level than they would otherwise. It therefore decreases the validity of the test.

....

Because no IQ test has perfect reliability, someone taking a test on two occasions gets slightly different scores. The scores of monozygotic ("identical") twins correlate with each other about .85, not much below the reliability of the test (McGue & Bouchard, 1998). Monozygotic twins resemble each other in overall IQ, as well as in brain volume (Posthuma et al., 2002) and in specific skills such as working memory and processing speed (Luciano et al., 2001). They continue to resemble each other throughout life, even beyond age 80 (Petrill et al., 1998). Dizygotic twins and nontwin siblings resemble each other in cognitive abilities but less closely than monozygotic twins (Bishop et al., 2003). The greater similarity between monozygotic twins implies a probable genetic basis.

Monozygotic Twins Reared Apart

In Figure 9.12, note the high correlation between monozygotic twins reared apart. That is, monozygotic twins who have been adopted by different parents and reared in separate environments strongly resemble each other in IQ scores (Bouchard & McGue, 1981; Farber, 1981).

These results imply a genetic contribution, but they may overstate it. Recall the multiplier effect from chapter 5: Slightly better than average performance early in life, perhaps genetically based, leads to encouragement and support, which leads to still better performance. So if twins begin life with a small intellectual advantage, their envi-

INDIVIDUAL DIFFERENCES IN IQ SCORES

Why do some people score higher than others on IQ tests? The British scholar Francis Galton (1869/1978)[1] was the first to argue for the importance of heredity. His evidence was that politicians, judges, and other eminent and distinguished people generally had distinguished relatives. I assume you will quickly see why this evidence does not justify a conclusion about the importance of genetics. Let's consider the evidence we have today, which is certainly stronger than it was in Galton's time.

Family Resemblances

Figure 9.12, based on an extensive literature review (Plomin, DeFries, McClearn, & McGuffin, 2001), shows the correlations of IQ scores for people with various degrees of genetic relationship. These data are based mostly on European or American families.

[1] Remember, a slash like this indicates original publication date and the date of a revised printing. It does not represent Galton's birth and death dates.

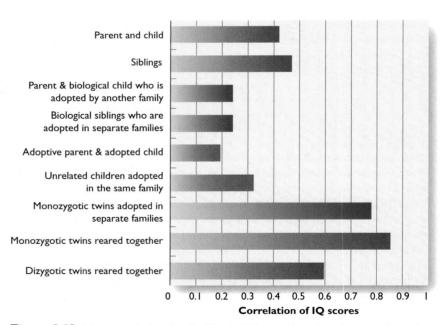

Figure 9.12 Mean correlations for the IQs of children with various degrees of genetic and environmental similarity. (Siblings are nontwin brothers or sisters.) (Modified from Figure 9.7, page 168, in Plomin, R., DeFries, J. C., McClearn, G. E., & McGuffin, P. (Eds.) 2001. *Behavioral Genetics* (4th ed.). New York: Worth.)

ronment may encourage and magnify that effect, turning an initially small advantage into a larger one (Dickens & Flynn, 2001).

A further problem is that most twin studies rely primarily on data from middle-class families. Studies of impoverished families find much less evidence for a genetic influence. That is, monozygotic twins in those families resemble each other about the same as dizygotic twins do (Turkheimer, Haley, Waldron, D'Onofrio, & Gottesman, 2003). The probable meaning is this: For people living in a terrible environment, the genes don't make as much difference. Their chance for intellectual development is limited. For people in a satisfactory environment, genetic differences have more impact.

Twins and Single Births

In Figure 9.12, notice that dizygotic twins resemble each other more closely than single-birth siblings do. This finding suggests an influence from being born at the same time and therefore sharing more of their environment. Supporting this conclusion, researchers have found a higher correlation between the IQs of brothers born within a couple of years of each other than those born further apart (Sundet, Eriksen, & Tambs, 2008).

Adopted Children

In Figure 9.12, note the positive correlation between unrelated children adopted into the same family. This correlation indicates an influence from shared environment. However, this correlation is lower than the correlation between biological brothers or sisters. The IQs of young adopted children correlate moderately with those of their adoptive parents. As the children grow older, their IQ scores gradually correlate more with those of their biological parents and less with those of their adoptive parents (Loehlin, Horn, & Willerman, 1989; Plomin, Fulker, Corley, & DeFries, 1997) (see Figure 9.13). Other studies confirm that parental environment has a strong influence on the cognitive performance of young children, but the contribution of heredity increases in middle childhood and beyond (Davis, Arden, & Plomin, 2008).

These results imply a genetic influence from the biological parents. However, another interpretation is possible. Some of the low-IQ parents who put their children up for adoption are impoverished and probably do not provide good prenatal care. The mother may have poor nutrition, may smoke and drink, or may in other ways put her infant at risk for reasons other than genetics. Poor prenatal care correlates with decreased IQ for the offspring throughout life (Breslau, Dickens, Flynn, Peterson, & Lucia, 2006). In short, adopted children can resemble their biological parents for nongenetic reasons.

Gene Identification

The Human Genome Project and related research now make it possible to identify particular genes that promote intelligence. The outline of the research is to determine whether any gene is more common among those with higher IQ scores than those with lower scores. Similar research has been done with laboratory animals, comparing fast learners to slow learners. Dozens of genes have been found to correlate with human performance, and dozens with mice, some of them the same genes that were identified in humans. However, so far, researchers have not found a gene that is strongly associated with intelligence (Butcher, Davis, Craig, & Plomin, 2007; Plomin & Spinath, 2004). Evidently, intelligence depends on the combined influence of hundreds of genes as well as environmental influences. The task now is to learn more about *how* various genes contribute and *which* environmental influences are most important. A few genes have been identified that influence IQ through effects on specific neurotransmitter receptors in the brain (Bertolino et al., 2006; de Quervain & Papassotiropoulos, 2006). For the most part, we don't know how the genes contribute to intellect or how they interact with the environment.

The heritability of variations in IQ scores does not mean that genes dictate people's intellectual accomplishments. Obviously, if we gave every child either an extremely good or extremely bad environment, we could raise or lower everyone's IQ scores. Positive heritability of IQ scores merely means that when children grow up in the

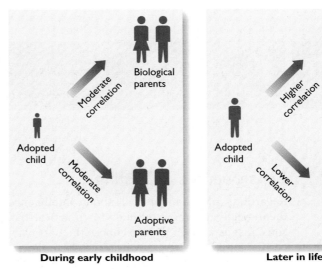

During early childhood **Later in life**

Figure 9.13 As adopted children grow older, their IQs begin to correlate more strongly with those of their biological parents.

same environment, some do better than others, and part of that difference relates to genetics.

Environmental Interventions

Although psychologists agree that both heredity and environment are important for intellectual development, we do not yet know much in detail about the critical aspects of the environment. If simply growing up in a family of people with high IQ scores were a major influence, we should expect to find a higher correlation between the IQs of adopting parents and their adopted children. Other aspects of the environment need more careful research attention, including the role of prenatal health and nutrition.

A variety of programs have attempted to take children from extremely deprived homes and give them special intervention to improve their intellectual development. People who hoped that brief intervention might lead to huge long-term gains have been disappointed. Just as no one gene produces a huge effect, no single environmental intervention does either. However, intensive programs occupying many hours per week for several years do produce significant, lasting benefits (Ramey & Ramey, 1998). One interesting intervention is music lessons. In one study, 6-year-olds who were randomly assigned to receive music lessons showed a gain of 1 to 2 IQ points, on the average, compared to other children (Schellenberg, 2004). Additional research indicates that children with music training show IQ advantages beyond what we can explain in terms of parental income and education (Schellenberg, 2006).

Interventions work best if they start early. Some orphanages provide a particularly deprived environment, including poor nutrition and minimal intellectual stimulation. Most children who remain in the orphanages perform poorly on tests and in school. Those who leave the orphanages and enter adoptive families show clear improvement, with the greatest improvement evident among children adopted before age 6 months (Beckett et al., 2006; van IJzendoorn, Juffer, & Poelhuis, 2005).

....

15. What types of evidence support a genetic contribution to individual differences in IQ scores? What are some reasons to suspect that the evidence overstates the role of genetics?

16. Under what circumstances do environmental interventions most strongly influence intellectual development?

Answers

15. One type of evidence is that monozygotic twins resemble each other in IQ more than dizygotic twins do. However, this observation may overstate the role of genetics because twins that show early talent in some area such as academics, possibly for genetic reasons, receive encouragement to develop that ability, so environmental factors strengthen the early tendency. Also, monozygotic twins correlate with each other more strongly in middle-class environments than in poor environments. A second type of evidence is that IQs of adopted children correlate significantly with those of their biological parents. The limitation here is that the biological mother provides the prenatal environment as well as genetics.

16. Environmental interventions are most effective if they start early, preferably before age 6 months.

In Closing

Consequences of Testing

Regardless of what we say about intelligence theoretically, testing continues for practical reasons. Just as a coach tries to choose the best players for an athletic team, colleges and employers try to choose the applicants who will learn the fastest. If people are going to make those judgments—as they no doubt will—we want them to use the best available tests and evaluate the results accurately.

Testing has consequences for the individuals who take them and the institutions that evaluate the scores, but it can also have another kind of consequence: If we begin to better understand the factors that influence intelligence, we may be able to do something about them. As a society, we would like to intervene early to help children develop as well as possible, but to make those interventions work, we need research. How important are prenatal health and early childhood nutrition? Which kinds of environmental stimulation are most effective? Are different kinds of stimulation better for different kinds of children? To answer these questions, we need good measurements—measurements that can come only from testing of some kind.

SUMMARY

- *Standardization.* To determine the meaning of a test's scores, the authors of a test determine the mean and the distribution of scores for a random or representative sample of the population. IQ tests are revised periodically. (page 324)
- *Distribution of IQ scores.* IQ tests have a mean of 100 and a standard deviation of about 15 or 16, depending on the test. However, the mode (most frequent score) is higher than 100, and a bulge of lower scores exists. (page 324)
- *The Flynn effect.* To keep the mean score at 100, authors of IQ tests have had to revise the tests periodically, always making them more difficult. That is, raw performance has been increasing steadily. The reasons for this trend are unknown. (page 326)
- *Reliability and validity.* Tests are evaluated in terms of reliability and validity. Reliability is a measure of the repeatability of a test's scores. Validity is a determination of how well a test measures what it claims to measure. (page 327)
- *Measuring validity.* To evaluate a test's validity for a given purpose, researchers examine its content, the response processes people use while taking the test, the internal structure of the test, the scores' relationship to other variables, and the consequences of using the test. (page 328)
- *Test bias.* Bias means inaccuracy of measurement. Psychologists try to remove from a test any item that tends to be easy for one group of people to answer but difficult for another. They also try to evaluate whether the test as a whole makes equally accurate predictions for all groups. (page 330)
- *Test anxiety and stereotype threat.* Many Black students perform worse on tests after any reminder of the stereotype of Black students scoring poorly on such tests. However, some simple procedures can weaken this threat. (page 333)
- *Hereditary and environmental influences.* Several kinds of evidence point to both hereditary and environmental influences on individual differences in IQ performance. (page 334)

KEY TERMS

bias (page 330)

developmental quotient (DQ) (page 327)

Down syndrome (page 324)

Flynn effect (page 326)

heterosis (page 327)

norms (page 324)

reliability (page 327)

standardization (page 324)

stereotype threat (page 333)

test–retest reliability (page 327)

validity (page 328)

ANSWERS TO OTHER QUESTION IN THE MODULE (PAGE 332)

B. The correct answers are (b) coin and (c) oil.

Why Does This Matter to Me?

SOCIAL RESPONSIBILITY AND PSYCHOLOGY

Many environmental and societal problems are caused by human behavior. Psychologists can help steer the course of our future toward more socially responsible and sustainable outcomes. Students of today need to be ever mindful of the link between human behavior and its impact on the environment and our communities.

"Intelligence" and Social Responsibility: A Step Further

Though it may be limited, Gardner's theory of multiple intelligences at least makes the point that we all have varying skill sets. What are your strengths, and how can you use your strengths to benefit those around you? Are you strong mathematically? If so, could you tutor young children in your neighborhood? Are you artistic? If so, could you set up an art program at a local nursing home?

Your Skills Applied

U.S. President Barack Obama has called for a new spirit of service. For many ideas on how you can help, visit the USA Service website. A current link can be found at www.cengage.com/psychology/kalat.

Join the iChapters Plant a Tree Drive!

To show its support of the environmental movement, iChapters is planting a tree on behalf of each fan of the iChapters Facebook Page and for every 10 questions answered correctly in our quiz.
http://www.ichapters.com/plantatree/

Exploration and Study

SUGGESTIONS FOR FURTHER EXPLORATION

In addition to the study materials provided at the end of each module, you may supplement your review of this chapter with the following book and website suggestions or by using one or more of the book's electronic resources, which include its companion website, interactive Cengage Learning eBook, and CengageNOW. Brief descriptions of these resources follow. For more information, visit **www.cengage.com/psychology/kalat**.

ADDITIONAL RESOURCES

The book's companion website, accessible from **www.cengage.com/psychology/kalat**, provides a wide range of study resources such as an interactive glossary, flashcards, tutorial quizzes, updated web links, and Try It Yourself activities.

CengageNOW with Critical Thinking Videos is an easy-to-use resource that helps you study in less time to get the grade you want. An online study system, CengageNOW gives you the option of taking a diagnostic pretest for each chapter. The system uses the results of each pretest to create personalized chapter study plans for you. The Personalized Study Plans

Critical Thinking

- Help you save study time by identifying areas on which you should concentrate and give you one-click access to corresponding pages of the interactive Cengage Learning eBook;
- Provide interactive exercises and study tools to help you fully understand chapter concepts; and

- Include a posttest for you to take to confirm that you are ready to move on to the next chapter.

Find critical thinking videos like this one in your CengageNOW product, which offer an opportunity for you to learn more about psychological research on different topics.

Stereotype Threat

Book

Nisbett, R. E. (2009). *Intelligence and how to get it.* New York: W. W. Norton. The author discusses research on hereditary and environmental contributors to intelligence, focusing on the value of schools and culture.

Websites

Links to the websites described below are kept current and can be found at **www.cengage.com/ psychology/kalat**.

Sample IQ Tests

Take a variety of IQ and personality tests. Some are serious and some are obviously fake. None of these are the best established tests, but you might find them interesting.[2]

The Flynn Effect

Read about research concerning the Flynn effect, including data from various countries.

---

[2] Any psychological test that is readily available to the public, while entertaining and possibly informative, should not be used to make important decisions. The most powerful, valid, and reliable psychological assessment devices are usually kept under the tight control of their creators or copyright holders.

© Ghislain & Marie David de Lossy/Cultura/Jupiter Images

10 chapter

Consciousness

Consider This: Today's computers play chess, predict the weather, and perform many other tasks as well as or better than people can. Still, we can list areas in which we greatly outperform the machines—such as recognizing faces and understanding humor. Suppose some future computer masters all these tasks. Would it then be conscious? How would we know? Indeed, how do you know that I am conscious, or how do I know that you are? We don't! I infer that other people are conscious because they look and act much like me, but I cannot be certain. Are newborns conscious? Nonhuman animals? We make inferences, but we can't observe consciousness.

Many psychologists have despaired of any scientific approach to consciousness. As Karl Lashley (1923) observed, some psychologists have gone so far as to imply that consciousness does not exist at all. Some philosophers have suggested wishfully that a future psychology may dispense altogether with any concept of mind or consciousness so that we shall not need to explain it (Churchland, 1986).

Nevertheless, researchers have begun to answer a few questions about consciousness. Although we cannot say much about what it is, we can answer a few questions about the conditions necessary for its occurrence. We also know some of the ways in which it varies during sleep, dreams, and hypnosis. This chapter attempts to answer a variety of scientific questions but leaves unanswered this fundamental philosophical question: In a universe composed of matter and energy, why is there such a thing as consciousness?

Sleep and dreams are alterations of consciousness.

Conscious and Unconscious Processes

- What brain activity is necessary for consciousness?
- How does consciousness relate to action?

What is consciousness, anyway? As William James (1892/1961) said about consciousness, "Its meaning we know so long as no one asks us to define it" (p. 19).

We might define **consciousness** as *the subjective experience of perceiving oneself and one's surroundings.* This definition is only marginally useful, however, as it relies on the undefined phrase "subjective experience." For practical purposes, researchers use the operational definition that *you are conscious of something if you can report it in words.* This definition works only for people who speak. One-year-olds do not talk, but we don't assume they are unconscious. Similarly, nonhuman animals do not talk, nor do adults with brain damage, people when they are dreaming, or monks of certain religious orders. Silence does not always mean unconsciousness.

BRAIN MECHANISMS NECESSARY FOR CONSCIOUSNESS

Not all nervous system activity is conscious. Your spinal cord controls reflexes, your hypothalamus regulates body temperature, and many other processes occur without your awareness. Among the sensory stimuli striking your receptors at any moment, you are conscious of only a few. Right now, what do you hear? Do you smell or taste anything? What sensation do you feel in your left leg? Your right elbow? The back of your neck? As you turn your attention to one sensation after another, you become aware of much that had been present but unconscious until then (Lambie & Marcel, 2002). Chapter 8 discussed several examples of unconscious processing.

In terms of brain activity, how does a stimulus that becomes conscious differ from one that remains unconscious? A good research design is to present a stimulus under conditions where people report it (conscious) and the same stimulus under conditions where they cannot report it (unconscious). Brain scans then measure how brain activity differs under the two conditions. Participants in one study watched words flash on a screen for just 29 milliseconds (ms) each. On some trials, a blank screen preceded and followed the word:

Under those conditions, people usually identified the word, even though it flashed so briefly. On other trials, a masking pattern preceded and followed the word:

Under those conditions, people almost never saw the word. Under both conditions, the light struck the retina for 29 ms, so we can ask what happened to that information. Brain recordings indicated that the stimuli activated the same areas of the visual cortex in both conditions but produced greater activation on trials when people became conscious of the word. Also, on those trials, the activation spread from the visual cortex to more of the rest of the brain (Dehaene et al., 2001). These data imply that consciousness of a stimulus depends on the amount of brain activity. At any moment, many stimuli compete for your attention. You become conscious of something when its information takes over much of your brain's activity.

Let's consider another example. Each cell in the visual cortex receives input from one part of the left retina and a corresponding part of the right retina. Ordinarily, two retinas see almost the same thing. Examine Figure 10.1 to see what happens when the images conflict.

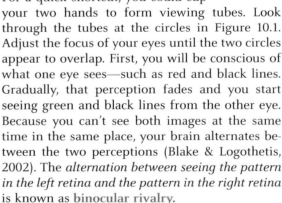

Find or make tubes like those in a roll of paper towels, so your left eye can look through one and your right eye can look through the other. For a quick shortcut, you could cup your two hands to form viewing tubes. Look through the tubes at the circles in Figure 10.1. Adjust the focus of your eyes until the two circles appear to overlap. First, you will be conscious of what one eye sees—such as red and black lines. Gradually, that perception fades and you start seeing green and black lines from the other eye. Because you can't see both images at the same time in the same place, your brain alternates between the two perceptions (Blake & Logothetis, 2002). The *alternation between seeing the pattern in the left retina and the pattern in the right retina* is known as **binocular rivalry.**

During binocular rivalry, input from one eye is unconscious, although it continues to reach the brain and your brain continues processing it. Suppose your two eyes view different scenes on a computer screen, so an experimenter can alter one scene while you are conscious of the other one. When you report being conscious of the right eye, the experimenter gradually changes the scene in the left eye to show a face. Your attention will shift to the left eye faster if the face is right-side-up rather than upside-down. A face with an emotional expression will capture your attention faster

Figure 10.1 To produce binocular rivalry, look through tubes and alter the focus of your eyes until the two circles seem to merge. You will alternate between seeing red lines and green lines.

CAN WE USE BRAIN MEASUREMENTS TO INFER CONSCIOUSNESS?

A stimulus becomes conscious when it excites activity over much of the cortex. Being conscious at all differs from unconsciousness with regard to total brain activity. Might we be able to use brain measurements to infer the presence of consciousness?

Physicians distinguish various gradations of brain activity. In **brain death,** *the brain shows no activity and no response to any stimulus.* Most people consider it ethical to remove life support for someone in this condition, although physicians usually wait for 24 hours to be certain. In a **coma** (KOH-muh), *caused by trauma or damage to the brain, the brain shows a steady but low level of activity and no response to any stimulus,* including potentially painful stimuli. People starting to emerge from a coma enter a **vegetative state,** *in which they respond to some stimuli (at least with changes in heart rate and breathing) but show no purposeful actions.* For a person in this state, brain activity is higher than in a coma but still lower than normal, especially in the parietal and frontal lobes of the cortex (Alkire, Hudetz, & Tononi, 2008). Someone in a **minimally conscious state** has brief periods of purposeful actions and speech comprehension. A vegetative or minimally conscious state can last for months or years.

Physicians and others have traditionally assumed that people in a vegetative state are unconscious, but new research methods have challenged that assumption. One young woman was in a vegetative state for months after a traffic accident. Researchers used fMRI to record her brain activity. In a critical test, they instructed her to imagine certain activities. An instruction to imagine tennis activated the same motor areas of the cortex that it did for a group of uninjured people. An instruction to imagine walking through her house activated brain areas responsible for spatial navigation, again as it would for uninjured people (Owen et al., 2006). Figure 10.2 shows the results. Tests of other people in a vegetative state found that some showed these kinds of brain responses to instructions, but most didn't (K. Smith, 2007). The results suggest the possibility of using brain scans to measure consciousness in an unresponsive person or of identifying patients who have the best potential to recover from a vegetative state.

than a neutral face will (Alpers & Gerdes, 2007). Also, if the experimenter changes the scene to show a Chinese or Hebrew word, your attention will shift to the left faster if you read that language than if you don't (Jiang, Costello, & He, 2007). That is, something meaningful to you captures your attention even before you are conscious of what it is!

Researchers use fMRI and similar devices, as described in chapter 3, to measure the resulting brain activity. To identify the patterns of brain activity, researchers might make one stimulus flash a few times per second while the other stimulus remains constant. Then they look for patterns of brain activity that pulsate at the same frequency as the one stimulus. When research participants say they see the flashing stimulus, researchers see that rhythm of activity over a large portion of the brain (Cosmelli et al., 2004; S. H. Lee, Blake, & Heeger, 2005). As that perception fades and the other replaces it, the rhythmic activity subsides, and a steadier pattern spreads over the brain. In short, a conscious perception controls the activity over a large portion of the brain. We begin to understand why it is hard to be conscious of several things at the same time: At any moment, much of your brain is occupied with whatever is at that time conscious.

....

1. How did researchers arrange for a stimulus to be conscious on some trials and not others?

Answer

were not conscious of it.

fore and after the word. In those cases, people

cases, researchers put interfering patterns be-

the word, most people identified it. In other

tion of a second. When they simply presented

1. Researchers presented a word for a small frac-

....

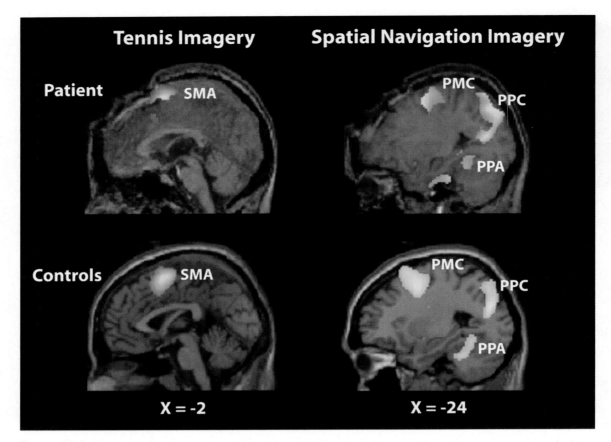

Figure 10.2 The brain areas marked in red and yellow showed increased activity after instructions to imagine playing tennis or imagine walking through the house. Note the similarities between a patient in a persistent vegetative state and uninjured people. SMA = supplementary motor cortex, an area important for planning complex movements. PMC, PPC, and PPA = three areas responsible for spatial imagery and memory. (Figure 1 from Owen, A. M., Coleman, M. R, Boly, M., Davis, M. H., Laureys, S., & Pickard, J. D. (2006). Detecting Awareness in the vegetative state. *Science, 313,* 1402. Used by permission, AAAS.)

2. What evidence suggested that some people in a vegetative state are conscious?

Answer

2. One woman in a vegetative state responded to instructions with brain activity that resembled that of uninjured people who heard the same instructions.

CONSCIOUSNESS AS A THRESHOLD PHENOMENON

Does consciousness develop gradually? Suppose some stimulus produces a very low level of brain activity. If the activity increases, might you first report being a "little bit" conscious of it and then more and more? A fascinating study suggests on the contrary that consciousness is an all-or-none process. Words appeared for various brief times (less than a twentieth of a second) with various degrees of masking, such as ▮mere▮ and ▨▨▨▨. A related study used the attentional blink procedure described in chapter 8 to make a word hard to identify. Both studies adjusted the procedures such that peo-

ple identified the words sometimes but not always. Researchers asked what each word was and also, "On a scale from 0 to 100, how visible was the word?" Most people rated nearly every word either 0 or 100 (Sergent & Dehaene, 2004). People seldom said they were partly aware of a word. These results suggest that brain activity below a certain threshold is unconscious. Above that threshold, it spreads, reverberates, occupies much of the brain, and becomes conscious.

Another study suggests the same conclusion. Occasionally, it is possible to insert electrodes into single cells in human brains while people are undergoing certain kinds of brain surgery. (Brain surgery can be done with local anesthesia to the scalp because the brain itself has no pain receptors.) Researchers identified cells in the temporal cortex that responded when the person saw a particular stimulus, such as a picture. Then they showed that stimulus repeatedly at very brief durations under conditions where people sometimes reported being conscious of it and sometimes not. The cells responsive to a particular picture showed a strong, lasting response on every trial when the person reported awareness of the stimulus. They responded only briefly and weakly when the person reported no awareness. Intermediate responses did not occur (Quiroga, Mukamel, Isham, & Fried, 2008). Again, the conclusion is that a stimulus either reaches a certain threshold, producing a sustained response associated with consciousness, or it fails to do so.

....

3. What evidence suggests that consciousness is an all-or-none matter?

Answer

3. Participants viewed words under difficult conditions and reported how visible they were. People usually reported a word as either 0% or 100% visible; they rarely reported partial consciousness of a stimulus. Also, individual cells in the temporal cortex either responded strongly to a stimulus (on trials when someone reported being conscious of the stimulus), or they responded only weakly.

CONSCIOUSNESS AS A CONSTRUCTION

When you see or hear something, you believe that you see or hear it *as it happens.* However, if you consider the experiments with very brief presentations of stimuli, you see a reason to doubt that assumption: Suppose a word flashes on a screen for 29 ms with interfering stimuli before, after, or superimposed on the word, such that you are not aware of seeing any word. Now the experimenter presents words with similar interference but extends the duration to 50 ms. With this longer presentation, you do see the word. More important, you see it for the whole 50 ms. It is not as if you had 29 ms of unconscious perception and 21 ms of conscious perception. Rather, the final part of that 50-ms presentation enabled you to become conscious of the first part retroactively! In some way, your brain constructed an experience of a 50-ms stimulus, even though it had to wait until the second half of the stimulus to perceive the first part at all.

Here is a related phenomenon. Suppose you see a light alternating between two locations, like this:

With proper timing between the lights, you experience an *illusion of the light moving back and forth between the two locations,* known as the **phi effect.** Some signs in front of restaurants or motels use this effect. The light appears to move smoothly and gradually through intermediate positions where it never occurred.

The illusion can become more elaborate: Suppose you see a small bright line alternating with a longer bright line:

You perceive the line not only as moving back and forth but also growing gradually longer and shorter (Jancke, Chavane, Naaman, & Grinvald, 2004). So when the longer line appears, you construct a conscious perception of an intermediate length line *earlier* than the long line. Evidently, consciousness does not occur at exactly the same time as the events. We construct a conscious perception of events that already happened.

....

4. What is the phi effect and what does it tell us about consciousness?

Answer

4. The phi effect is an illusion of movement when a stimulus alternately blinks on and off in two locations. The fact that we perceive gradual movement between the two locations implies that the later perception induced a conscious perception prior to itself. That is, we sometimes experience consciousness retroactively, not simultaneously with the events.

UNCONSCIOUS OR ALTERED PERCEPTION

Given that only some of the information reaching the brain becomes conscious, what happens to the rest of it? The brain does use it to a limited degree. Recall subliminal perception from chapter 4: A brief, faint stimulus that you do not detect primes you to detect something similar. Also recall the discussion of implicit memory from chapter 7: You might not remember seeing or hearing some word, but you become more likely than usual to think of that word and use it.

Spatial Neglect

Striking examples of unconscious perception arise in patients with damage to parts of the right hemisphere who show spatial neglect—*a tendency to ignore the left side of the body, the left side of the world, or the left side of objects* (Buxbaum, 2006). (Damage in the left hemisphere seldom yields neglect of the right side. Apparently, an intact right hemisphere attends to both sides of the world.) Symptoms are severest shortly after a right-hemisphere stroke, with partial recovery over the next few weeks (Farnè et al., 2006).

Many people with spatial neglect eat food from only the right side of the plate, read only the right side of the page, or read only the right side of words. When copying a picture, they draw only the right side of the object (Driver & Mattingley, 1998). If asked to point "straight ahead," they usually point to the right of center (Richard, Honoré, Bernati, & Rousseaux, 2004). Although some patients have a partial loss of sensation from the left side, the problem for most patients relates to attention. Even when describing something from memory, they describe only the right side.

One person was shown a letter E composed of small Hs, as in Figure 10.3c. She identified it as a big E composed of small Hs, indicating that she saw the whole figure. However, when she was then asked to cross off all the Hs, she crossed off only the ones on the right (J. C. Marshall & Halligan, 1995).

You can demonstrate something similar to this experience for yourself. Stare straight ahead and describe what you see *without moving your eyes*. Then hold a white napkin or similar object a little more than a finger's length in front of your eyes so that it covers the center of your vision. Again describe what you see without moving your eyes. You will find yourself including more of the objects in the periphery of your view. You saw them before, but you were attending so much to the objects in the center that you ignored those around the sides.

Patients with neglect show similar tendencies. They report the objects on the left when they see nothing on the right. They usually notice a face on the left, even if they do not detect words or shapes (Vuilleumier, 2000). They briefly attend to the left side when someone asks them to, just as you can look straight ahead but make a special effort to attend to objects in the periphery.

5. What evidence indicates that people with spatial neglect have a deficit in attention and not just sensation? **Concept Check**

Answer

5. They neglect the left side of objects when describing them from memory. Also, it is possible to increase their attention to the left side in various ways.

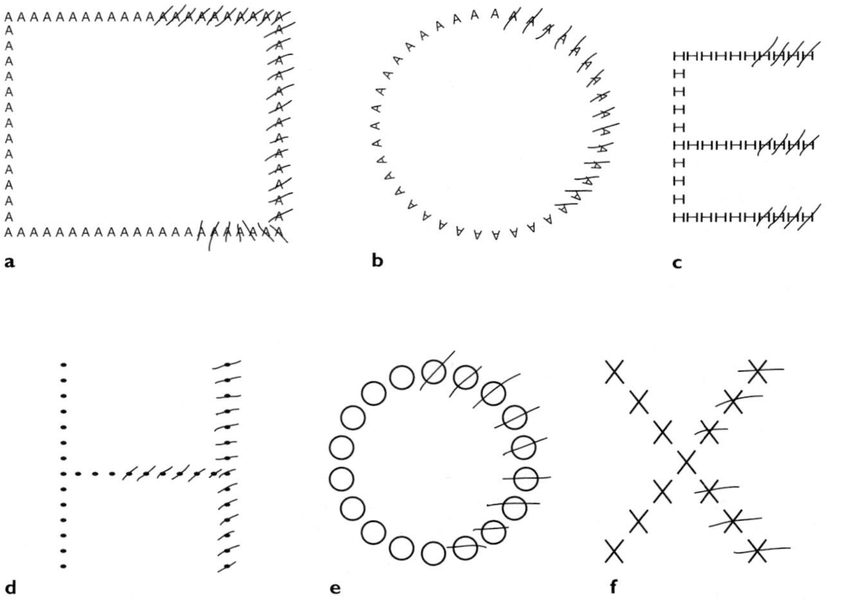

a   b   c

d   e   f

Figure 10.3 A patient with spatial neglect identified the overall figures, implying that she saw both sides. However, when she tried to cross off the elements within each letter, she crossed off only the parts on the right. (Source: Reprinted by permission from Macmillan Publishers Ltd: *Nature 373*, 521–523. Marshall, J. C., & Halligan, P. W. 1995. Seeing the forest but only half the trees?)

The Déjà vu Experience

The déjà vu experience is the *sense that an event is uncannily familiar*. The experience is fairly common in young adults and becomes less so as people grow older (A. S. Brown, 2003). Because it takes several forms, a single explanation may not suffice. Occasionally, someone is in a place for the first time and sees everything as familiar, as if he or she had been there before. Perhaps the person really had seen something similar, possibly in a movie or photo, but forgot when and where.

However, much more commonly, people report déjà vu in a familiar setting. You might be sitting in your room, walking down a familiar road, or having an everyday conversation, when you suddenly feel, "This has happened before!" In a sense, of course it has happened before, but your sense is not of doing something similar to what you have done in the past. Instead, it seems *this particular event has happened before*. As people talk, you feel, "I knew they were going to say that!" You could not really have predicted the words, but after you hear

dé·jà vu

WENDELL HAS A STRANGE FEELING THAT HE HAS SEEN THIS WORD BEFORE.

DaveCarpenter

© Dave Carpenter/www.cartoonstock.com

them, you feel that you had been *about to* predict them. Apparently, something is triggering the brain to signal "familiar."

One man with epilepsy originating in his temporal cortex had a special feeling, an *aura*, before each of his seizures. Each aura included a strong sense of déjà vu that lasted long enough for him to move around and shift his attention from one item to another. During the aura, *whatever* he looked at seemed strangely familiar (O'Connor & Moulin, 2008). In a case like this, we can discard the hypothesis that everything he saw was actually familiar. Many other people with abnormalities in the temporal lobe also experience intense feelings of déjà vu (Moulin, Conway, Thompson, James, & Jones, 2005).

....

6. What evidence shows that déjà vu does not always indicate that an experience was actually familiar?

Concept Check

Answer

6. A person with temporal lobe epilepsy reported an intense déjà vu experience immediately before his seizures, regardless of where he was or what he was seeing at the time.

....

CONSCIOUSNESS AND ACTION

Given that some sensations become conscious and others don't, but the unconscious information still influences behavior, the question arises: Exactly what does consciousness do, if anything? Does it control our decisions and actions?

What's the Evidence?
Consciousness and Action

Each of us has the impression that "I make a conscious decision, and then I act." But does your consciousness *cause* your actions? In a scientifically and philosophically important study, researchers measured the time when someone made a conscious decision to act, the time when brain activity preparing for the movement started, and the time when the act itself started. What would you guess was the order of the three events in time?

Critical Thinking

Hypothesis The researchers were interested in three hypotheses, any one of which would be interesting: (a) A person becomes aware of a decision to act before relevant brain activity begins, (b) awareness occurs at the same time as the brain activity, and (c) the brain activity responsible for a movement starts before any awareness of a decision.

Method People were instructed to make a simple movement—flexion of the wrist. Although they had no choice over the type of movement, they had complete freedom over the timing. The instruction was to flex the wrist whenever they decided to, but as spontaneously as possible, with no planning. While waiting for that spontaneous urge to occur, they were to watch a special clock like the one in Figure 10.4, on which a spot of light moved around the edge every 2.56 seconds. At whatever time they suddenly decided to flex the wrist, they were to note the exact position of the light at that moment, so they could report it later. In this way, the study measured, as well as anyone knows how, the time of the conscious decision. Meanwhile, researchers used electrodes on the scalp to detect increased activity in the motor cortex (see Figures 3.18 and 3.20), which is the brain area responsible for initiating muscle movements. *The increased motor cortex activity prior to the start of the movement* is known as the **readiness potential.** Researchers also measured the time the wrist muscles began to flex. On certain trials, the participants were told to report when they felt the wrist actually start to flex instead of the time they felt the intention to move it.

Results It is not easy to report the exact moment when you form an intention, and the results varied from person to person and from trial to trial. Figure 10.5 shows the means for a large sample. On the average, people reported forming an intention of movement 200–300 ms before the movement (Libet, Gleason, Wright, & Pearl, 1983). (They noted the time on the clock then. They did not report it until later.) For example, someone might report that he or she formed an intention when the light was at location 25 on the clock, 200 ms before the movement began at location

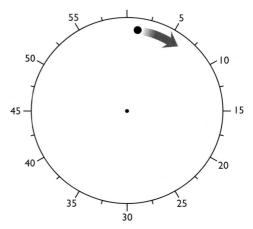

Figure 10.4 A spot of light rotated around the clock once every 2.56 seconds. Participants made a spontaneous decision to flex the wrist and noted the location of the light at the time of the decision. They remembered that time and reported it later. (From Libet, Gleason, Wright, & Pearl, 1983)

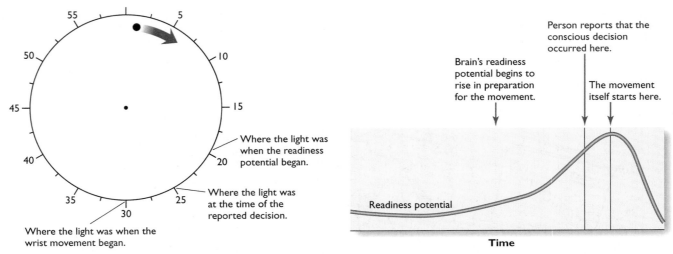

Figure 10.5 On the average, the brain's readiness potential began 300 ms or more prior to the reported decision, which occurred 200–300 ms before the movement.

30. (Remember, the light zooms around the circle in 2.56 seconds.) In contrast, the readiness potential in the brain began 300–800 ms before the reported intention. Several other laboratories replicated this finding with varying procedures, confirming that the readiness potential comes before any awareness of conscious intention (Haggard & Eimer, 1999; Lau, Rogers, Haggard, & Passingham, 2004; Pockett & Miller, 2007; Trevena & Miller, 2002).

How accurate are people's reports of the time of their actions? Recall that on certain trials the participants reported the time of the wrist motion. On these trials, people usually reported feeling the movement within 100 ms of the actual time (Lau et al., 2004; Libet et al., 1983). From this finding, the researchers concluded that people can report the time of an experience with moderate accuracy.

Interpretation These results indicate that your brain starts producing a voluntary movement before you are conscious of it. If so, your consciousness does not cause your action.

7. In this experiment, what did participants report, and when did they report it?
8. What was the order of these events: Conscious decision to move, brain activity relevant to movement, and the movement itself?

Concept Check

Answers

7. Participants watched a special fast clock and noted the time when they made a spontaneous decision to flex the wrist. They reported it a few seconds later.
8. Measurable brain activity came first, then the perception of the conscious decision, and then the movement.

Imagine yourself in this follow-up study: You watch a screen that displays a different letter of the alphabet every half-second. You choose not only when to act but which of two acts to do. At whatever time you wish, you decide whether to press a button on the left or one on the right. As soon as you decide, you press it, and you remember what letter is on the screen at the time you decided which button to press. The researchers record activity from several areas of your cortex. The result: You usually report a letter you saw within 1 second of making the response. The letters changed only twice per second, so the researchers could not determine the time of decision with greater accuracy. However, it wasn't necessary because areas in the frontal and parietal cortex showed activity related to the left or right hand 7 to 10 seconds before your response (Soon, Brass, Heinze, & Haynes, 2008). That is, someone monitoring your cortex could predict which choice you were going to make a few seconds before you were aware of your decision.

So, the next time you are thinking about what to do next, relax! Just tell yourself, "My brain probably already decided a few seconds ago. I'm just waiting for it to tell me!"

Seriously, what happens to the concept of free will? It depends on what you mean by free will. This study does not conflict with the idea that you make a voluntary decision. The choice of when to flex your wrist definitely originates within you. However, the results imply that the voluntary decision is at first unconscious. Earlier in this module, we considered evidence that a sensory stimulus must produce a certain strength of brain activity to become conscious. Presumably, the same is true for an intention to make a movement. In support of this idea, one study found that mild electrical stimulation of certain brain areas caused people to report "feeling an urge" to make some movement, and slightly stronger stimulation caused actual movements (Fried et al., 1991).

Most people are surprised to hear that their brains start a voluntary movement before they make a conscious decision. One legitimate criticism is that the task requires people to make a decision and then shift their attention to noting the position of a spot on the clock. Shifting attention takes time, and for that reason and others, people cannot precisely report when they made their decision (Haggard & Libet, 2001; Lau, Rogers, & Passingham, 2006; Wundt, 1862/1961). However, when people try to report the time of their wrist movement, they also have to shift attention, and yet their reports are within 100 ms of the actual time. The onset of the brain's readiness potential precedes the reported conscious decision by at least 300 ms and often by more.

A different kind of challenge asks whether people really know the time of their conscious decision at all or whether they are just guessing. If two events, such as a light and a noise, occur at almost the same time, we tend to perceive them as being closer in time than they really were. Similarly, if you press a button that makes a noise 250 ms later, you perceive your button press slightly later than it really was and the tone slightly earlier than it was, making them closer together (Haggard, Clark, & Kalogeras, 2002). That tendency also modifies perceived time of an intention. Researchers repeated Libet's experiment, except that a computer generated a beep a few milliseconds after the response. Under these circumstances, people reported the times of their conscious decisions later than usual and close to the time of both the response and the beep (Banks & Isham, 2009). Even when researchers don't present a beep, do people report their decision as coming closer to the movement than it actually was? Do they really perceive the time of their decision at all, or do they just guess?

module | 10.1

In Closing

The Role of Consciousness

Since the dawn of psychology, most researchers have considered consciousness an impossible topic to research. As you have read in this module, it is a very difficult topic, but it no longer seems impossible. We begin to answer some of the questions about consciousness, and if we can't answer all the questions, at least we clarify them.

What outcomes can result from research? If we better understand what brain activity is associated with consciousness, we will be in a better position to infer consciousness, or lack of it, in brain-damaged people, coma patients, infants, fetuses, and nonhuman animals. We may also be in a position to improve our speculations on the age-old question of the relationship between mind and brain.

SUMMARY

- A stimulus presented under different conditions may become conscious in some cases and not others. When it becomes conscious, it activates neurons more strongly, and their activity reverberates through other brain areas. (page 342)
- In binocular rivalry, we see how two stimuli compete for conscious awareness and for dominance of brain activity. (page 342)
- Brain scans provide suggestions of consciousness in some patients who seem unresponsive to their environment. (page 343)

- On any given trial, people rate a weak stimulus either completely visible (100%) or not visible at all (0%). Recordings from single brain cells also indicate that a faint stimulus produces a strong response on trials when it becomes conscious and a weak response on all other trials. These results suggest that consciousness requires a stimulus to pass an all-or-nothing threshold. (page 344)
- Unconscious stimuli also influence behavior in several ways. (page 345)

- Some people with damage in parts of the right hemisphere seem to be unconscious of the left side of their world, but it is possible to direct their attention to information on the left and make it conscious. (page 346)
- In déjà vu, people experience a sense of extreme familiarity for a new event. (page 346)
- People's reports of the time of onset of a conscious decision place it later than when brain activity in preparation for the movement begins. These results suggest that the first part of a decision process is unconscious. (page 342)
- Some research promotes skepticism that people can report their decision times at all. When they report the time of a decision, they may be to some extent guessing. (page 349)

KEY TERMS

binocular rivalry (page 342)

brain death (page 343)

coma (page 343)

consciousness (page 342)

déjà vu experience (page 346)

minimally conscious state (page 343)

phi effect (page 345)

readiness potential (page 347)

spatial neglect (page 346)

vegetative state (page 343)

Sleep and Dreams

- Why do we sleep?
- What accounts for the content of our dreams?

Consciousness and alertness cycle daily between wakefulness and sleep. During sleep, we become less aware of our surroundings. Dreams take us to a fantasy world where impossible events seem possible. Why do we have these periods of altered consciousness?

OUR CIRCADIAN RHYTHMS

Animal life follows biological cycles. Consider hibernation. Ground squirrels hibernate in winter, when they would have trouble finding food. The females awaken in spring as soon as food is available. The males also need to eat, but they have a reason to awaken earlier: The females are ready to mate as soon as they come out of their winter burrows, and each female mates only once a year. A male who awakens after the females pays for his extra rest by missing his only mating opportunity of the *entire year.* To avoid that risk, males awaken a week before the females do. They spend that week waiting—with no females, nothing to eat, and little to do except fight with one another (French, 1988).

The point is that animals have evolved internal timing mechanisms to prepare them for predictable needs. Male ground squirrels awaken not in response to their current situation but in preparation for what will happen a few days later. Similarly, birds start migrating south in the fall long before their northern homes become inhospitable.

Humans have mechanisms that prepare us for activity during the day and sleep at night. Like other animals, we generate a circadian rhythm, a *rhythm of activity and inactivity lasting about a day.* (The term *circadian* comes from the Latin roots *circa* and *dies,* meaning "about a day.") The rising and setting of the sun provide cues to reset our rhythm, but we generate the rhythm ourselves. In an environment with no cues for time, such as near-polar regions in summer or winter, most people generate a waking– sleeping rhythm a little longer than 24 hours, which gradually drifts out of phase with the clock (Palinkas, 2003). That is, we generate circadian rhythms within ourselves, and we don't require the rising and setting of the sun to do so.

The genes that control circadian rhythms vary, like any other gene. Certain mice have genes that cause their circadian rhythms to run faster or slower than 24 hours (Siepka et al., 2007), and so do some people. People with a faster than average rhythm go to sleep earlier than other people and wake up earlier (Toh et al., 2001). Whereas most people enjoy weekends and vacations as an opportunity to stay up late, people with fast-running rhythms enjoy the opportunity to go to bed even earlier than usual!

Sleepiness and alertness depend on one's position within the circadian rhythm. If you have ever gone all night without sleep—as most college students do at one time or another—you probably grew very sleepy between 2 and 6 A.M. But in the morning, you began feeling less sleepy, not more. You became more alert because of your circadian rhythm, even though your sleep deprivation continued.

In one study, volunteers went without sleep for three nights. Their body temperature and performance on reasoning tasks declined during the first night and then increased the next morning. During the second and third nights, their temperature and reasoning decreased more than on the first night, but they rebounded in the day (Figure 10.6). Thus, sleep deprivation produces a pattern of progressive deterioration superimposed on the normal circadian cycle of rising and falling body temperature and alertness (Babkoff, Caspy, Mikulincer, & Sing, 1991). In short, sleepiness apparently depends partly on how long one has gone without sleep and partly on the time of day (i.e., circadian rhythm).

The rising and setting of the sun do not produce our daily rhythm of wakefulness and sleepiness, but they synchronize the rhythm. We adjust our internally generated cycles so that we feel alert during the day and sleepy at night.

© Jeff Greenberg/The Image Works

Figure 10.6 Cumulative effects of three nights without sleep: Body temperature and reasoning decrease each night and increase the next morning. They also deteriorate from one day to the next. (From Babkoff, Caspy, Mikulincer, & Sing, 1991)

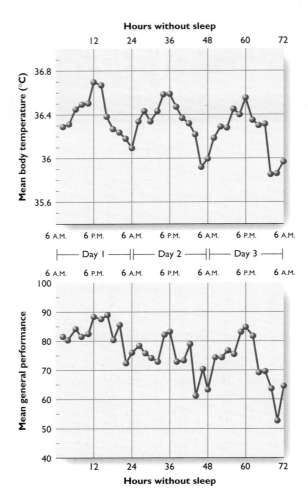

Hours without sleep

Mean body temperature (°C)

Day 1 — Day 2 — Day 3

Mean general performance

Hours without sleep

Concept Check

9. If you were on a submarine deep in the ocean with only artificial light that was the same at all times, what would happen to your rhythm of wakefulness and sleepiness?

Answer

9. You would continue to produce a 24-hour circadian rhythm. The sun resets the rhythm, but you generate it within your own body.

Morning People and Evening People

People vary in their circadian rhythms. "Morning people" awaken easily, become alert quickly, and do their best work early. "Evening people" take longer to warm up in the morning (literally as well as figuratively) and do their best work in the afternoon or evening (Horne, Brass, & Pettitt, 1980). Most people are consistent, and you probably know whether you are a morning person, evening person, or neutral (in between).

Most young adults are either evening people or neutral, whereas nearly all people over age 65 are morning people. If you ask people at what time they like to go to bed on days when they have no obligations, their mean answer shifts later and later during the teenage years, reaches 1–2 A.M. at age 20, and then starts reversing, slowly and steadily over decades (Roenneberg et al., 2004). If the shift toward earlier bedtimes after age 20 were entirely a reaction to job requirements, we might expect it to be a sudden change, and we should predict the trend to reverse at retirement. The fact that the trend continues gradually over a lifetime suggests a biological basis. Furthermore, the same pattern occurs in other species. Older rats wake up promptly and reach their peak performance quickly, whereas younger rats awaken more slowly and improve their performance later (Winocur & Hasher, 1999, 2004).

Age differences in circadian rhythms are important for research. For example, researchers have often reported memory losses in older people. But young graduate students do much of the research, usually in the late afternoon—a fine time for young adults but not for the elderly. Researchers in one study compared the memories of young adults (18–22 years old) and older adults (66–78 years old) at different times of day. Early in the morning, the older adults did about as well as the younger ones. Later in the day, the younger adults remained steady or improved, whereas the older adults deteriorated (May, Hasher, & Stoltzfus, 1993). Figure 10.7 shows the results.

Shifting Sleep Schedules

Ordinarily, the light of early morning resets the body's clock each day to keep it in synchrony with the outside world. If you travel across time zones, your internal rhythm is temporarily out of phase

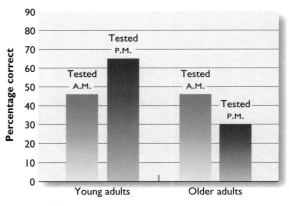

Figure 10.7 Early in the morning, older people perform as well as younger people on memory tasks. Later in the day, young people improve and older people deteriorate.

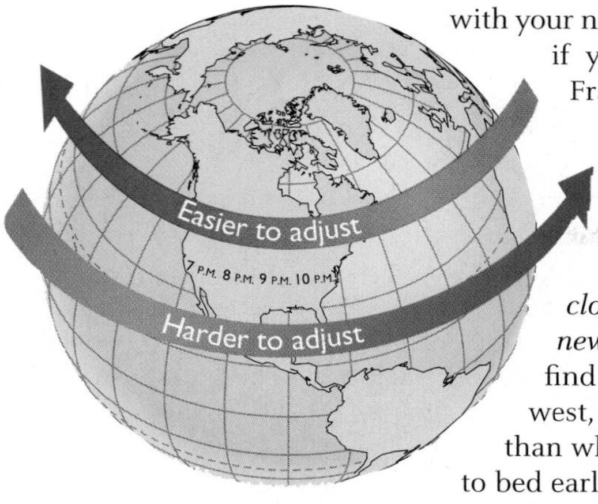

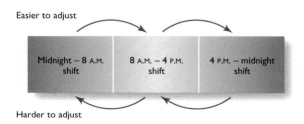

Figure 10.8 People traveling east suffer more serious jet lag than people traveling west.

with your new environment. For example, if you travel from California to France, it is 7 A.M. (time to wake up) when your body says it is 10 P.M. (close to bedtime). You experience jet lag, *a period of discomfort and inefficiency while your internal clock is out of phase with your new surroundings.* Most people find it easier to adjust when flying west, where they go to bed later, than when flying east, where they go to bed earlier (Figure 10.8).

People voluntarily control their sleeping and waking times based on when they have to go to school or work, but the sun continues to rule the internal clock. Researchers asked people in Germany the times they prefer to go to bed and wake up. On business days, people throughout Germany have to awaken at the same time because they are all in the same time zone. However, on weekends and holidays, people in eastern Germany prefer to go to bed and wake up about half an hour earlier than those in western Germany, corresponding to the fact that the sun rises half an hour earlier in eastern Germany (Roenneberg, Kumar, & Merrow, 2007).

People in most parts of the United States have to shift their clock ahead an hour on one Sunday in March because of daylight savings time. On Monday, they awaken when the room clock tells them to, even though their internal clock thinks it is an hour earlier. The act of waking up early, while the sky is still dark, doesn't effectively reset the internal clock. During the week or two after the shift to daylight savings time, people feel ill rested and perform less efficiently than usual (Lahti et al., 2006; Monk & Aplin, 1980). That tendency is strongest for people who were already somewhat sleep deprived, including most college students.

Some businesses run three work shifts, such as midnight–8 A.M., 8 A.M.–4 P.M., and 4 P.M.–midnight. Because few people want to work regularly on the midnight–8 A.M. shift, many companies rotate their workers among the three shifts. Employers can ease the burden on their workers in two ways: First, when they transfer workers from one shift to another, they should transfer them to a *later* shift (Czeisler, Moore-Ede, & Coleman, 1982) (see Figure 10.9). That is, someone working the 8 A.M.–4 P.M. shift switches to the 4 P.M.–midnight shift (equivalent to traveling west) instead of the midnight–8 A.M. shift (equivalent to traveling east). Second, employers can help workers adjust to the night shift by providing bright lights that resemble sunlight. In one study, young people exposed to very bright lights at night adjusted well to working at night and sleeping during the day. Within 6 days, their circadian rhythms shifted to the new schedule. Another group who worked the same schedule under dimmer lights showed no indications

Easier to adjust

| Midnight – 8 A.M. shift | 8 A.M. – 4 P.M. shift | 4 P.M. – midnight shift |

Harder to adjust

Figure 10.9 The graveyard shift is aptly named: Serious industrial accidents usually occur at night, when workers are least alert. As in jet lag, the direction of change is critical. Moving forward—clockwise—is easier than going backward.

of altering their circadian rhythms (Czeisler et al., 1990).

10. Suppose you are the president of a U.S. company, negotiating a business deal with someone from the opposite side of the world. Should you prefer a meeting place in Europe or on an island in the Pacific Ocean?

Answer

10. You should prefer to meet on a Pacific island so that you will travel west.

Brain Mechanisms of Circadian Rhythms

The circadian rhythm of sleep and wakefulness is generated by a tiny structure at the base of the brain known as the *suprachiasmatic nucleus.* If that brain area is damaged, the body's activity cycles become erratic (Rusak, 1977). If cells from that area are kept alive outside the body, they generate a 24-hour rhythm on their own (Earnest, Liang, Ratcliff, & Cassone, 1999; Inouye & Kawamura, 1979). Cells in other areas also produce daily rhythms, but the suprachiasmatic nucleus is the body's main clock (Figure 10.10).

The suprachiasmatic nucleus exerts its control partly by regulating the pineal gland's secretions of the hormone *melatonin,* which is important for both the daily rhythm of sleep and certain animals' annual rhythm of hibernation (Lincoln, Clarke, Hut, & Hazlerigg, 2006). Ordinarily, the human pineal gland starts releasing melatonin 2 or 3 hours before bedtime. Taking a melatonin pill in the evening has little effect because you are already producing melatonin. However, if you have just flown a few time zones east and want to get to bed soon, but you're not sleepy yet, then a melatonin pill can help (Deacon & Arendt, 1996).

11. Suppose you are required to work the midnight–8 A.M. shift, and you would like to go to sleep at 4 P.M. Would a melatonin pill help? If so, when should you take it?

Answer

11. Try a melatonin pill between 1 P.M. and 2 P.M.

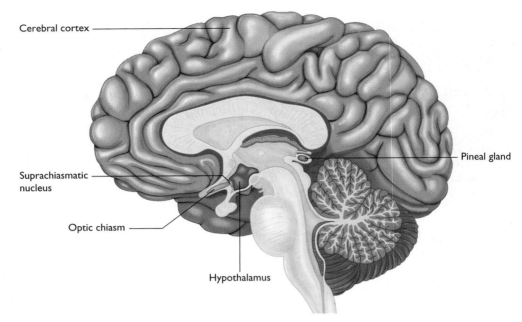

Figure 10.10 The suprachiasmatic nucleus, a small area at the base of the brain, produces the circadian rhythm. Information from the optic nerves resets the circadian rhythm but doesn't produce it.

Cerebral cortex

Pineal gland

Suprachiasmatic nucleus

Optic chiasm

Hypothalamus

WHY WE SLEEP

We would not have evolved a mechanism that forces us to spend one third of our lives sleeping unless sleep did us some good. But what good does it do? Scientists have identified several benefits.

The simplest is that sleep saves energy. When NASA sent a robot to explore Mars, they programmed it to shut down at nights, when exploration would only waste energy. Presumably, our ancient ancestors evolved sleep for the same reason. Sleeping mammals and birds lower their body temperatures, and all animals decrease muscle activity, saving energy. When food is scarce, people sleep longer and at a lower body temperature (Berger & Phillips, 1995).

Various animal species differ in their amount of sleep per day in ways that make sense based on their way of life (Campbell & Tobler, 1984; Siegel, 2005). Predatory animals, including cats and bats, sleep most of the day. They get the nutrition they need from brief, energy-rich meals, and they face little danger of attack during their sleep. In contrast, prey species like horses need to spend many hours grazing, and their survival depends on running away from attackers, even at night (Figure 10.11). They sleep fewer hours and rouse easily. Woody Allen once wrote, "The lion and the calf shall lie down together, but the calf won't get much sleep."

Animals show many other sleep specializations. Migratory birds forage for food during the day and do their migratory flying at night. That schedule leaves little time for sleep, and furthermore, they would have trouble finding a safe place to sleep at unfamiliar sites along their migratory path. Their solution is simple: They hardly sleep at all during migration. A caged bird during the migration season paces back and forth all day and all night, except for occasional periods of drowsiness when it closes one eyelid for a few seconds (Fuchs, Haney, Jechura, Moore, & Bingman, 2006). The bird shows no sign of sleep deprivation, although forcing it to stay awake at other times of year would produce the predictable impairments of learning and performance. In some way—which we haven't figured out how to bottle and sell—birds actually decrease their need for sleep during the migratory season (Rattenborg et al., 2004).

Whales and dolphins face a different problem: Throughout the night, they have to swim to the surface to breathe. Their solution is to sleep in half of the brain at a time so that one half or the other is always alert enough to enable breathing (Lyamin et al., 2002; Rattenborg, Amlaner, & Lima, 2000). Seals sleep like this also when they are at sea, but they shift to sleeping on both sides when they are on land (Lyamin, Kosenko, Lapierre, Mukhametov, & Siegel, 2008). During the first month after a baby whale or dolphin is born, it doesn't sleep at all, and neither does its mother (Lyamin, Pryaslova, Lance, & Siegel, 2005). Evidently, like migratory birds, they have found the secret to decreasing the need for sleep.

In addition to saving energy, we accomplish other functions during sleep. Sleep provides an occasion for restorative functions in the brain. When people are deprived of sleep, inhibitory transmitters accumulate in the brain, interfering with attention and learning (Åkerstedt, 2007; Gvilia, Xu, McGinty, & Szymusiak, 2006). Well-rested people notice when their attention lapses, and they nudge themselves back onto a task, but sleep-deprived

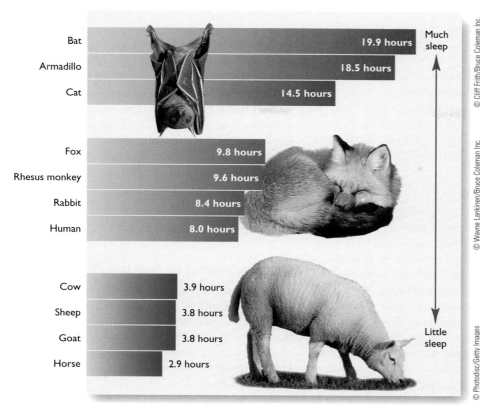

Bat — 19.9 hours — Much sleep
Armadillo — 18.5 hours
Cat — 14.5 hours

Fox — 9.8 hours
Rhesus monkey — 9.6 hours
Rabbit — 8.4 hours
Human — 8.0 hours

Cow — 3.9 hours
Sheep — 3.8 hours
Goat — 3.8 hours
Horse — 2.9 hours — Little sleep

Figure 10.11 Predatory mammals sleep more than prey animals. Predators are seldom attacked during their sleep, but prey species need to arouse quickly from sleep to avoid being attacked. (Based on data from Zepelin & Rechtschaffen, 1974)

When people learn a difficult new motor task, such as a video game skill, the brain areas active during the learning become reactivated during sleep that night, replaying the same patterns they had during the day, only faster. The amount of activity in those areas during sleep predicts the amount of improvement the next day (Euston, Tatsuno, & McNaughton, 2007; Huber, Ghilardi, Massimini, & Tononi, 2004; Maquet et al., 2000; Peigneux et al., 2004). Wakefulness and sleep play complementary roles in learning. Animal researchers have demonstrated that learning strengthens the appropriate synapses during wakefulness and weakens other synapses during sleep (Vyazovskiy, Cirelli, Pfister-Genskow, Faraguna, & Tononi, 2008).

12. Name two important functions of sleep.

Concept Check

Answer

12. Sleep conserves energy, and memories strengthen during sleep.

people do not (Chee et al., 2008). A sleep-deprived driver is as dangerous as a drunk driver (Falleti, Maruff, Collie, Darby, & McStephen, 2003).

However, some people need less sleep than others. Some get by fine with 3 or 4 hours of sleep, and one healthy 70-year-old woman slept only about 1 hour per night (Meddis, Pearson, & Langford, 1973). Some people tolerate sleep deprivation better than others (Figure 10.12). In 1965 a San Diego high school student, Randy Gardner, stayed awake for 11 days as a high school science project and suffered no apparent harm (Dement, 1972). On the last night, he played about 100 arcade games against sleep researcher William Dement and won every game. Just before the end of the ordeal, he held a press conference and handled himself well. He then slept for 14 hours and 40 minutes and awoke refreshed.

If a torturer prevented you from sleeping for the next 11 days, would you do as well as Randy Gardner? Probably not, for two reasons: First, Gardner knew he could quit. A sense of control makes any experience less stressful. Second, people vary in their ability to tolerate sleep deprivation. We heard about Gardner only because he tolerated it so well. We have no idea how many other people tried to deprive themselves of sleep but gave up. As a rule, "evening people," who tend to waken late and stay up late, tolerate sleep deprivation better than morning people (Caldwell et al., 2005).

Sleep also strengthens learning and memory, including both motor skills and language-related tasks (L. Marshall, Helgadóttir, Mölle, & Born, 2006; Stickgold, 2005). When you learn something, your memory improves if you go to sleep within the next 3 hours (even a nap), and it deteriorates after a sleepless night (Hu, Stylos-Allan, & Walker, 2006; Korman et al., 2007; Rasch & Born, 2008; Yoo, Hu, Gujar, Jolesz, & Walker, 2007). A good night's sleep also improves learning the next day (Van der Werf et al., 2009). So beware of those all-night study sessions.

Figure 10.12 Even near the end of Randy Gardner's 264 consecutive sleepless hours, he performed tasks of strength and skill. Observers dutifully recorded his every move.

STAGES OF SLEEP

In the mid-1950s, American and French researchers independently discovered a stage of sleep called *paradoxical sleep,* or **rapid eye movement (REM) sleep** (Dement & Kleitman, 1957a, 1957b; Jouvet, Michel, & Courjon, 1959). *During this stage of sleep, the sleeper's eyes move rapidly back and forth under the closed lids.* (The other stages of sleep are known as non-REM, or NREM, sleep.) A paradox is an apparent contradiction. REM sleep is paradoxical because it is light in some ways and deep in others. It is light because the brain is active and the body's heart rate, breathing rate, and temperature fluctuate substantially (Parmeggiani, 1982). It is deep because the large muscles of the body that control posture and locomotion are deeply relaxed. Indeed, the nerves to those muscles are virtually paralyzed at this time. REM also has features that are hard to classify as deep or light, such as penis erections and vaginal lubrication.

William Dement's early research indicated that people who were awakened during REM sleep usually reported dreaming, but people who were awakened during other periods seldom reported dreaming. Later research weakened that link, however. Adults who are awakened during REM sleep report dreams about 85 to 90% of the time, whereas those awakened during NREM (non-REM) sleep report dreams on 50 to 60% of occasions (Foulkes, 1999). REM dreams are on the average longer, more complicated, and more visual, with more action by the dreamer, but not always (McNamara, McLaren, Smith, Brown, & Stickgold, 2005). Furthermore, some people with brain damage have REM sleep but no dreams, and others have dreams but no REM sleep (Solms, 1997). Thus, REM is not synonymous with dreaming (Domhoff, 1999).

Nevertheless, because vivid dreams are most common during REM sleep and because the postural muscles are paralyzed during REM sleep, people typically do not act out their dreams. A small number of people, with a condition called *REM behavior disorder,* fail to inhibit their muscular activity during REM, and as a result, they sometimes walk around flailing their arms. The opposite can also occur, in which the muscles remain paralyzed after arousal from REM sleep. Have you ever had the experience of waking up and finding yourself unable to move? If so, don't be alarmed. The explanation is that the brain does not wake up all at once (Silva & Duffy, 2008). If your cerebral cortex is more or less awake, but certain areas in your pons and medulla remain in the REM stage, you will find yourself alert, with your eyes open, but temporarily unable to move your arms or legs.

Sleep Cycles During the Night

The brain is more active than you might guess during sleep. Neurons' metabolic rate, spontaneous activity, and responsiveness to stimuli decrease less than 20% (Hobson, 2005). The main characteristic of sleep is an increase of inhibitory messages, preventing brain messages from reverberating widely (Massimini et al., 2005). Anesthetic drugs given to surgical patients also increase inhibition and prevent messages from spreading around the brain

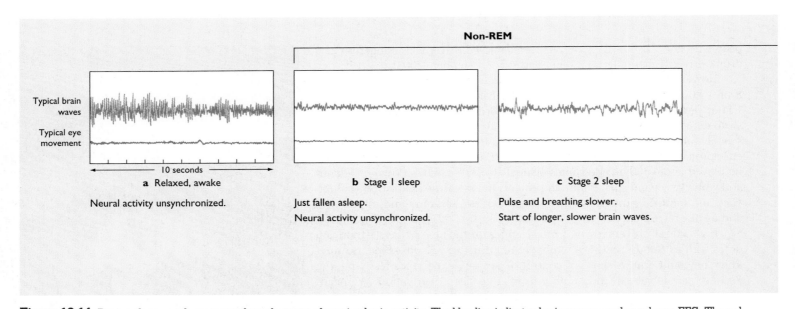

Figure 10.14 During sleep, people progress through stages of varying brain activity. The blue line indicates brain waves, as shown by an EEG. The red line shows eye movements. REM sleep resembles stage 1 sleep, except for the addition of rapid eye movements. (Courtesy of T. E. Le Vere)

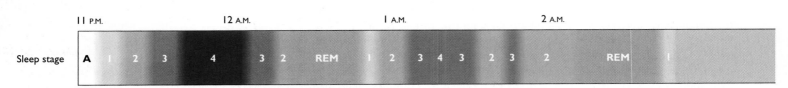

Figure 10.15 This sleeper had five cycles of REM and non-REM sleep and awakened (A) briefly three times during the night. Stage 4 occupies more time earlier in the night than later. REM becomes more prevalent as the night progresses. (From Dement, 1972)

(Alkire et al., 2008). As noted in the first module of this chapter, a spread of messages through the brain is central to conscious experience.

Sleep researchers distinguish among sleep stages by recording brain waves with electrodes attached to the scalp (Figure 10.13). *A device* called an electroencephalograph (EEG) *measures and amplifies tiny electrical changes on the scalp that reflect patterns of brain activity.* Sleep researchers *combine an EEG measure with a simultaneous measure of eye movements to produce a* polysomnograph (literally, "many-sleep measure"), as shown in Figure 10.14. Upon falling asleep, one enters stage 1, when the eyes are nearly motionless and the EEG shows many short, choppy waves (Figure 10.14a). These small waves indicate a fair amount of brain activity. Because brain cells fire out of synchrony, their activities nearly cancel each other out, like the sound of many people talking at the same time.

As sleep continues, a person progresses into stages 2, 3, and 4, as shown in Figure 10.14b–e. These stages differ in the number of long, slow waves. Stage 2 has the fewest and stage 4 has the most. These waves indicate synchrony among neurons, which occurs during *decreased* brain activity. The waves grow larger because the little brain activity that does occur drives many neurons in syn-

chrony. Stage 2 is also marked by sleep spindles, *waves of activity at about 12–14 per second.* Sleep spindles result from an exchange of information between the cerebral cortex and the underlying thalamus. Sleep spindles are important for storing memory (Eschenko, Mölle, Born, & Sara, 2006), and counts of people's spindles per night correlate surprisingly highly (.7) with their IQ scores (Fogel, Nader, Cote, & Smith, 2007).

Someone who progresses through stages 2, 3, and 4 then gradually moves back through stages 3 and 2, and then to REM sleep, not stage 1. In Figure 10.14f, the EEG in REM sleep resembles that of stage 1, but the eyes move steadily. At the end of REM sleep, the sleeper cycles again through stages 2, 3, 4 and then back to 3, 2, and REM. In a healthy young adult, each cycle lasts 90 to 100 minutes on average. As shown in Figure 10.14, over the course of the night, stages 3 and 4 become shorter while REM and stage 2 increase in duration. Figure 10.15 represents sleep under quiet, undisturbed conditions.

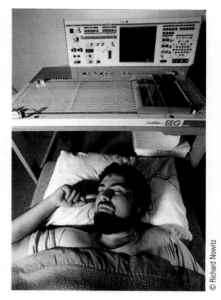

Figure 10.13 Electrodes monitor the activity in a sleeper's brain, and an EEG then records and displays brain-wave patterns.

© Richard Nowitz

Non-REM

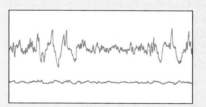

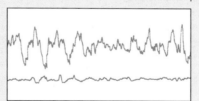

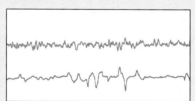

Typical brain waves

Typical eye movement

d Stage 3 sleep

Pulse, breathing, and brain activity slower yet.

Neural activity more synchronized.

Stages 3 and 4 dominate first half of night.

e Stage 4 sleep

Pulse, breathing, and brain activity slowest.

Brain waves highly synchronized, indicating low overall neuron activity.

f REM (paradoxical) sleep

Eyes move back and forth.

Dreams more frequent, vivid, complex.

Brain waves desynchronized.

Postural muscles most relaxed.

Duration gets longer toward morning.

---

3 A.M.   4 A.M.   5 A.M.   6 A.M.   7 A.M.

2   3   2   REM   1   2   3 2 A 1   REM   A A   2   REM

13. During which sleep stage is the brain least active? During which stage are the muscles least active?

Answer

13. The brain is least active during stage 4 sleep. The muscles are least active during REM sleep.

The Functions of REM Sleep

Given that people spend 20 to 25% of an average night in REM sleep, REM presumably serves an important function, but what? One approach is to determine which people get more REM sleep than others. Infants get more REM sleep than children, and children get more than adults. That observation might suggest that REM sleep serves a function that is more acute in younger people. However, infants not only get more REM sleep but also more total sleep (Figure 10.16). If we compare species, we find that the species that get the most sleep (e.g., cats) also generally have the greatest percentage of REM sleep.

Adult humans who sleep 9 or more hours per night spend a large percentage of that time in REM sleep. Those who sleep 6 hours or less get less REM sleep. In short, those who sleep the most spend the greatest percentage of that time in REM. It is as though a certain amount of *non*-REM sleep is necessary each night, and additional amounts of REM sleep are added if sleep continues long enough (Horne, 1988).

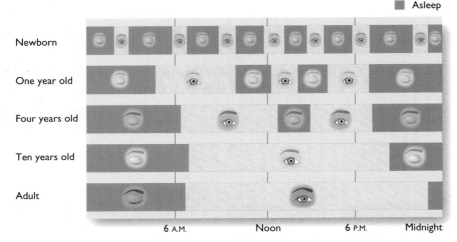

Figure 10.16 Newborns' sleep alternates between wakefulness and naps throughout the day. Within a few months, infants consolidate most of their sleep into one longer period at night, although they continue having one or two naps during the day. As people grow older, the amount of sleep decreases. (Based on Kleitman, 1963)

ABNORMALITIES OF SLEEP

Comedian Steven Wright says that someone asked him, "Did you sleep well last night?" He replied, "No, I made a few mistakes."

We laugh because sleep isn't the kind of activity on which people make mistakes. Sometimes, however, we fail to sleep, feel poorly rested, or have bad dreams. These experiences are not "mistakes," but our sleep is not what we wanted it to be.

For more information in general about sleep disorders, visit The Sleep Site. The link to this website can be found at **www.cengage.com/ psychology/kalat**.

Insomnia

Insomnia means "lack of sleep." A better definition of insomnia is *not enough sleep for the person to feel rested the next day*. Insomnia can result from many causes, including noise, worries, indigestion, uncomfortable temperatures, use of alcohol or caffeine, and medical or psychological disorders (Ohayon, 1997). If you have persistent insomnia, consult a physician, but for occasional or minor insomnia, you can try a few things yourself (Hauri, 1982; Lilie & Rosenberg, 1990):

- Keep a regular time schedule for going to bed and waking up each day.
- Avoid caffeine, nicotine, and other stimulants, especially in the evening.
- Don't rely on alcohol or tranquilizers to fall asleep. After repeated use, you may be unable to sleep without them.
- Keep your bedroom cool and quiet.
- Exercise daily but not shortly before bedtime.

Sleep Apnea

One type of insomnia is sleep apnea (AP-nee-uh). *Apnea* means "no breathing." Many people have occasional brief periods without breathing during their sleep. People with **sleep apnea**, however, *fail to breathe for a minute or more and then wake up gasping for breath*. They may lie in bed for 8 to 10 hours but sleep less than half that time. During the following day, they feel sleepy and may have headaches.

Although many people with sleep apnea have mild brain abnormalities (Macey et al., 2002), some of the brain abnormalities are probably the result of persistent poor sleep rather than the cause of it (Zhu et al., 2007). The most common cause of apnea is obstructions in the breathing passages. When someone with a large abdomen— usually, a middle-aged man—lies on his back, the abdomen's weight interferes with the diaphragm muscles that control breathing. Also the airways

Insomnia is identified by how sleepy the person is the following day.

and blocks the attacks of muscle weakness. Future research may develop medications based on orexin, but none are available currently.

Sleep Talking, Sleepwalking, Nightmares, and Night Terrors

Many people have unsettling experiences during their sleep. Sleep talking is the most common and least troublesome. It ranges from a grunted word to a clear paragraph. Most people talk in their sleep more often than they realize because they do not remember sleep talking and usually no one else hears them. Sleep talking is most common during stage 2 sleep, but it occurs in all stages (Moorcroft, 2003). Sleep talkers sometimes pause between utterances, as if they were carrying on a conversation. In fact, it is possible to engage some sleep talkers in a dialogue. Sleep talking is not related to mental or emotional disorders, and sleep talkers rarely say anything embarrassing.

become narrow, especially while lying in a sleeping position (Mezzanotte, Tangel, & White, 1992).

Treatment includes recommendations to lose weight and to avoid alcohol and tranquilizers, which slow breathing. Surgeons can remove tissue to widen the airways. Some people with sleep apnea use a device that pumps air into a mask covering the nose and mouth during sleep, forcing the person to breathe.

Narcolepsy

People with narcolepsy experience *sudden attacks of extreme sleepiness in the middle of the day.* They also experience sudden attacks of muscle weakness or paralysis and occasional dreamlike experiences while awake. These symptoms can be interpreted as a sudden intrusion of REM sleep into the waking period of the day (Guilleminault, Heinzer, Mignot, & Black, 1998).

Dogs with a particular gene also develop narcolepsy. This gene impairs the brain receptors for a transmitter called *orexin*, also known as *hypocretin* (Lin et al., 1999). Other researchers found that preventing the production of orexin causes narcolepsy in mice (Chemelli et al., 1999). People with narcolepsy have fewer than the normal number of neurons that produce orexin (Thanickal et al., 2000). Orexin does not wake people up, but it helps keep them awake (M. G. Lee, Hassani, & Jones, 2005). People lacking orexin alternate between wakefulness and sleepiness repeatedly over a day instead of remaining awake during the day and remaining asleep at night (Mochizuki et al., 2004).

A combination of stimulant and antidepressant drugs maintains wakefulness during the day

Sleepwalking tends to run (walk?) in families, mostly in children and mainly during stage 4 sleep (Dement, 1972). Some adults sleepwalk also, mostly during the first half of the night's sleep. The person engages in clumsy, apparently purposeless movements with only limited responsiveness to surroundings. Contrary to what you may have heard, wakening a sleepwalker is not dangerous, although it is not particularly helpful either (Moorcroft, 2003). A better idea is to guide the person gently back to bed. In addition to walking during sleep, some people have been known to eat, rearrange furniture, drive cars, and engage in sex (either by masturbation or with a partner) during sleep (Mangan, 2004). You might wonder how all this is possible. Is the person really asleep? The answer is "sort of." The entire brain does not wake up or go to sleep all at once. Sometimes, one part awakens and another part remains asleep (Krueger et al., 2008). For most people most of the time, the lag is short. You might get out of bed without being fully awake, but the other brain areas catch up quickly. Sleepwalking occurs when certain brain areas remain awake for minutes while others remain asleep.

Other concerns include nightmares and night terrors. Nightmares are merely unpleasant dreams, common for anyone. A night terror, however, *causes someone to awaken screaming and sweating with a racing heart rate, sometimes flailing with the arms and pounding the walls.* Night terrors occur during stage 3 or stage 4 sleep, not REM, and their dream content, if any, is usually simple, such as a single image. Comforting or reassuring people during a night terror is futile, and the terror simply has to run its course. Many children have night terrors, as do nearly 3% of adults (Mahowald & Schenck, 2005). Treatments include psychotherapy, antidepressant and antianxiety drugs, and advice to minimize stress.

14. Why would sleepwalking be unlikely during REM sleep?

Answer

14. The major muscles are relaxed and inactive during REM sleep.

Concept Check

Leg Movements While Trying to Sleep

Do you ever lie in bed, trying to fall asleep, when suddenly one leg kicks? An occasional leg jerk while trying to fall asleep is common and no cause for concern. In contrast, some people have *prolonged "creepy-crawly" sensations in their legs, accompanied by repetitive leg movements strong enough to awaken the person, especially during the first half of the night* (Moorcroft, 1993). This condition, known as periodic limb movement disorder (or more informally as restless leg syndrome), interrupts sleep in many people, mostly over age 50. The causes are unknown, and the best advice is to avoid factors that make the condition worse, such as caffeine, stress, or fatigue. Tranquilizers sometimes suppress these leg movements (Schenck & Mahowald, 1996).

THE CONTENT OF OUR DREAMS

Even a saint is not responsible for what happens in his dreams.

—St. Thomas Aquinas

In ancient times, people believed that dreams foretold the future. Occasionally, of course, they do, either by coincidence or because the dreamer had a reason to expect some outcome. Today, scientists do not believe dreams tell us about the future, although many other people in both Eastern and Western societies do. If you dream about a plane crash tonight, will you hesitate to take a plane trip tomorrow? If you dream your friend treats you badly or your lover is unfaithful, will you become suspicious in real life? If so, you have plenty of company (Morewedge & Norton, 2009).

If, as scientists believe, dreams do not tell us the future, what do they tell us? Can we explain or interpret dreams? Let's start with a description of dream content and then consider three theories.

Descriptive Studies of Dreaming

To determine dream content, some studies ask people to keep dream diaries. Another approach is to awaken people in the laboratory and ask for immediate dream reports (Domhoff, 2003). Table 10.1 lists common dream themes

Table 10.1 Percentages of College Students Who Reported Certain Dream Topics

Dream Topic	U.S. 1958	Japan 1958	Canada 2003
Falling	83%	74%	74%
Being attacked or pursued	77%	91%	82%
Trying to do something again and again	71%	87%	54%
Schoolwork	71%	86%	67%
Sex	66%	68%	76%
Arriving too late	64%	49%	60%
Eating delicious food	62%	68%	31%
Frozen with fright	58%	87%	41%
Loved one dying	57%	42%	54%

Based on Griffith, Miyagi, & Tago (1958); Nielsen et al. (2003)

of college students in the United States and Japan in 1958 and Canada in 2003. Note the similarity across the three samples.

Researchers have demonstrated a few differences in dreams between one culture and another, none of which are very surprising (Domhoff & Schneider, 2008). For example, people in hunter-gatherer societies dream about animals more often than city dwellers do. People in dangerous societies dream more frequently than others do about being victims of violent aggression. Still, the cross-cultural similarities in dream content are striking.

Are dreams mostly happy? In the Disney movie, Cinderella sings, "A dream is a wish your heart makes." Martin Luther King Jr.'s famous "I Have a Dream" speech described a wonderful future. Calling your boyfriend or girlfriend "dreamy" would be a compliment. In these ways and others, common usage implies that dreams are happy. However, Table 10.1 shows that much or most of dream content is unpleasant, such as falling, being chased, or being unable to do something. When a group of college students recorded their dreams and their daytime experiences, 73% of their dreams included something threatening, as opposed to only 15% of their daytime activity reports. Furthermore, many of the unpleasant experiences in their dreams were life-threatening events or potential catastrophes, whereas most of their daytime threats were milder, such as the possibility of a failing grade or a broken friendship (Valli, Strandholm, Sillanmäki, & Revonsuo, 2008). Curiously, 11- to 13-year-olds have the happiest dreams on the average (Foulkes, 1999). From then on, dreams get worse and worse. Sorry about that.

Although some dreams are bizarre, most are commonplace and similar to what we think about in everyday life (Domhoff, 1996; Hall & Van de Castle, 1966). For example, preteens seldom dream about the opposite sex, but teenagers do (Strauch & Lederbogen, 1999). Blind people frequently dream about difficulties in locomotion or transportation (Hurovitz, Dunn, Domhoff, & Fiss, 1999). In one study, young adults checked off from a list of topics (e.g., marriage, family, friends, and hobbies) those that were concerns to them and others that were matters of indifference. Then they reported their dreams over three nights. They frequently dreamed of the concerns and rarely of the indifferent topics (Nikles, Brecht, Klinger, & Bursell, 1998). However, we do not dream about everything we do in daily life. People seldom dream about reading, writing, using a computer, or watching television (Schredl, 2000). They do dream about sexual and other fantasies that they have never acted on in real life. For the best research on dream content, visit the UCSC psychology department's website on dream research. A current link to this website can be found at **www.cengage.com/psychology/kalat**.

SLOW WAVE

SLOW WAVE

These comic strips represent actual dreams as described to the artist. Dreams often mix possible with impossible events and frequently explore the theme of "things that could go wrong." (Reprinted with permission of Jesse Reklaw)

Many questions about dreaming are difficult to answer. For example, "How accurately do we remember our dreams?" Well, how would we find out? With real events, we compare people's memories to what actually happened, but we have no way to compare reported dreams to the originals. Or consider this apparently simple question: "Do we dream in color?" People ask because they do not remember whether their dreams were in color. But how could an investigator determine whether people dream in color except by asking them to remember? The best evidence we have is that, when people are awakened during REM sleep, when their recall is at its best, they report color at least half of the time (Herman, Roffwarg, & Tauber, 1968; Padgham, 1975). This result does not mean that other dreams are in black and white. Perhaps the colors in those dreams are not memorable.

You might wonder whether people who are blind have visual dreams. It depends. People who experienced eye damage after about age 5 to 7 continue to have visual dreams. However, people who were born blind or who became blind in early childhood have no visual imagery in their dreams. Instead, they dream of sounds, touch, smells, and tastes (Hurovitz et al., 1999). Sighted people rarely dream of smells or tastes (Zadra, Nielsen, & Donderi, 1998). People who become blind because of damage to the visual cortex lose visual dreaming as well as visual imagery.

15. How is the content of dreams similar to waking thoughts, and how is it different?

Concept Check

Answer

15. We mostly dream about the same topics we think about, but dreams usually feature less happy emotions.

Freud's Approach

The Austrian physician and founder of psychoanalysis, Sigmund Freud, maintained that dreams reveal the dreamer's unconscious thoughts and motivations. To understand a dream, he said, one must probe for hidden meanings. Each dream has a **manifest content**—*the content that appears on the surface*—and a **latent content**—*the hidden ideas that the dream experience represents symbolically.*

For example, Freud (1900/1955) once dreamed that one of his friends was his uncle. He worked out these associations: Both this friend and another one had been recommended for an appointment as professor at the university. Both had been turned down, probably because they were Jews. Freud himself had been recently recommended for the same appointment, and he feared that he too would be rejected because he was Jewish. Freud's only uncle had once been convicted of illegal business dealings. Freud's father had said, however, that the uncle was not bad but just a simpleton.

How did the two friends relate to the uncle? One of the friends was in Freud's judgment a bit simpleminded. The other had once been accused of sexual misconduct, although he was not convicted. By linking these two friends to his uncle, Freud interpreted the dream as meaning, "Maybe they didn't get the university appointment because one was a simpleton (like my uncle) and the other was regarded as a criminal (like my uncle). If so, my being Jewish might not stop me from getting the appointment."

In some cases, Freud relied on individual associations, as in the dream just described, but he also assumed that certain elements have predictable meanings for most people. For example, he claimed that the number three in a dream represents a man's penis and testes. Anything long, such as a stick, represents a penis. So does anything that could penetrate the body, anything from which water flows, anything that can be lengthened, almost any tool, and anything that can fly or float—because rising is like an erection (Freud, 1935). He admitted that if you dream about a knife or an airplane, you really might be dreaming about a knife or airplane instead of a penis, but he was confident that a skilled psychoanalyst could tell the difference (even if the dreamer could not).

One of Freud's most famous dream analyses concerned a man who reported remembering a dream from when he was 4 years old (!) in which he saw six or seven white dogs with large tails sitting motionlessly in a tree outside his window. (The actual dream was of spitz dogs, although Freud wrote about them as wolves.) After a laborious line of reasoning, Freud concluded that the child had dreamed about his parents in their bedclothes—presumably white, like the dogs in the dream. The dogs' lack of motion represented its opposite—frantic sexual activity. The big tails also represented their opposite—the boy's fear of having his penis cut off. In short, said Freud, the boy had dreamed about watching his parents have sex, doggy style. Decades later, researchers located the man who had told this dream to Freud. He reported that (a) he regarded Freud's interpretation of his dream as far-fetched and (b) Freud's treatment did him no apparent good, as he spent many later years in continued treatment (Esterson, 1993).

Can anyone listen to dreams and determine hidden aspects of the dreamer's personality? Many therapists offer dream interpretations that their clients find meaningful. However, psychoanalysts offer no evidence to back their conclusions, and Freud's approach to dream analysis has been on the decline (Domhoff, 2003).

....

16. Are Freud's ideas on dreaming falsifiable in the sense described in chapter 2?

Concept Check

Answer

16. No. A falsifiable theory makes specific predictions so that we could imagine evidence that would contradict it. Freud's dream theories make no clear predictions.

....

The Activation-Synthesis Theory

A modern theory relates dream content to spontaneous activity that arises in the brain during REM sleep. According to the **activation-synthesis theory of dreams**, *input arising from the pons (Figure 3.16) activates the brain during REM sleep. The cortex takes that haphazard activity plus whatever stimuli strike the sense organs and does its best to synthesize a story to make sense of this activity* (Hobson & McCarley, 1977). The activation-synthesis theory

does not regard our dreams as meaningless. Even if dreams begin with random brain activity, the dreamer's interpretations of this activity reflect his or her personality, motivations, and previous experiences. Still, the activation-synthesis theory sees meaning as an accidental by-product, not the cause, of the dream.

Some aspects of dreams do appear to relate to spontaneous brain activity. For example, input from the pons activates the visual areas of the brain, especially during the first minutes of a REM period, and nearly all dreams include visual content (Amzica & Steriade, 1996). Also, when people dream of using a toilet or trying to find a toilet, they often awake and discover that they really do need to use a toilet. Many people occasionally dream of flying or falling, possibly because the vestibular system detects the body's horizontal position and the brain interprets this sensation as floating or falling (Hobson & McCarley, 1977; Velluti, 1997).

Do you ever dream that you are trying to walk or run, but you cannot move? One explanation is that the major postural muscles are really paralyzed during REM sleep. Your brain sends messages telling your muscles to move but receives sensory feedback indicating they have not moved.

The main problem is that the activation-synthesis theory makes no clear, testable predictions. For example, people almost always sleep horizontally but only occasionally dream of flying or falling. Why not always? Our muscles are always paralyzed during REM sleep. Why don't we always dream that we can't move? *After* a dream, the activation-synthesis theory sometimes provides an explanation, but it offers few predictions.

The Neurocognitive Theory

Sometimes, you may have a dream that strikes you as so odd that you never would have thought of such a thing in waking life. Nevertheless, you did think of it while dreaming. The **neurocognitive theory** *treats dreams as a kind of thinking that occurs under special conditions* (Domhoff, 2001; Foulkes, 1999; Solms, 2000). These conditions include:

• persisting activity of much of the cortex
• reduced sensory stimulation, especially in the brain's primary sensory areas
• loss of voluntary control of thinking

The brain is active enough to engage in imagination that sensory information does not override. According to this theory, REM sleep is not necessary for dreaming, although the arousal associated with REM intensifies dreams. As with Freud's theory and the activation-synthesis theory, the problem with the neurocognitive theory is that it makes few testable predictions.

17. According to the neurocognitive theory of dreaming, how does dreaming differ from other thinking?

 Concept Check

Answer

17. According to the neurocognitive theory, dreaming is like other thinking, except that it occurs during a time of decreased sensory input and loss of voluntary control of thinking.

module 10.2

In Closing

The Mysteries of Sleep and Dreams

Sleep and dreams are not a state of unconsciousness but a state of reduced or altered consciousness. For example, a parent will awaken at the sound of a child softly crying. A healthy brain is never completely off duty, never completely relaxed.

Although our understanding of sleep and dreams continues to grow, major questions remain. Even such basic issues as the function of REM sleep remain in doubt. People have long found their dreams a source of wonder, and researchers continue to find much of interest and mystery.

SUMMARY

- *Circadian rhythms.* Sleepiness depends on the time of day. Even in an unchanging environment, people become sleepy in cycles of approximately 24 hours. (page 351)
- *The need for sleep.* Sleep serves several functions, including conservation of energy, restorative functions in the brain, and an opportunity to strengthen memories. (page 354)
- *Sleep stages.* During sleep, people cycle through sleep stages 1 through 4 and back through stages 3 and 2 to 1 again. The cycle beginning and ending with stage 1 lasts about 90 to 100 minutes. (page 356)
- *REM sleep.* A special stage known as REM sleep replaces many of the stage 1 periods. REM sleep is characterized by rapid eye movements, a high level of brain activity, and re-

laxed muscles. People usually dream during this stage but dream in other stages also. (page 356)
- *Insomnia.* Insomnia—subjectively unsatisfactory sleep—can result from many influences, including sleep apnea and narcolepsy. (page 358)
- *Dream content.* More dreams are more threatening than pleasant. Freud proposed that dreams are the product of unconscious motivations. The activation-synthesis theory claims that dreams are an accidental by-product of arousal during REM sleep. The neurocognitive theory states that dreaming is just thinking, except that it occurs under conditions of low sensory input and no voluntary control of thinking. (page 360)

KEY TERMS

activation-synthesis theory of dreams (page 362)

circadian rhythm (page 351)

electroencephalograph (EEG) (page 357)

insomnia (page 358)

jet lag (page 353)

latent content (page 361)

manifest content (page 361)

narcolepsy (page 359)

neurocognitive theory (page 362)

night terror (page 359)

periodic limb movement disorder (page 360)

polysomnograph (page 357)

rapid eye movement (REM) sleep (page 356)

sleep apnea (page 358)

sleep spindles (page 357)

- What can hypnosis do?
- What are its limitations?

Truth is nothing but a path traced between errors.[1]

—Franz Anton Mesmer

If a hypnotist told you that you were 4 years old and you suddenly starting acting like a 4-year-old, we would say that you are a good hypnotic subject. If the hypnotist told you that your cousin was sitting in the empty chair in front of you and you said that you see her, then again, we would remark on the depth of your hypnotism.

But what if you had *not* been hypnotized and you suddenly started acting like a 4-year-old or insisted that you saw someone in an empty chair? Then psychologists would suspect that you were suffering from a serious psychological disorder. Hypnosis induces a temporary state that is sometimes bizarre. No wonder we find it so fascinating.

Hypnosis is *a condition of increased suggestibility that occurs in the context of a special hypnotist–subject relationship.* The term *hypnosis* comes from Hypnos, the Greek god of sleep, although the similarity between hypnosis and sleep is superficial. People in both states lose initiative, and hypnotized people, like dreamers, accept contradictory information without protest. Hypnotized people, however, walk around and respond to objects in the real world. Also, their EEG is not like that of sleepers. It is more like that of a relaxed wakeful person (Rainville, Hofbauer, Bushnell, Duncan, & Price, 2002).

Hypnosis was introduced by Franz Anton Mesmer (1734–1815), an Austrian physician. When treating medical problems, Mesmer would pass a magnet back and forth across the patient's body to redirect the flow of blood, nerve activity, and undefined "fluids." Some patients reported dramatic benefits. Later, Mesmer discovered that he could dispense with the magnet and use only his hand. From this observation, you or I would conclude that the phenomenon related to the power of suggestion instead of magnetism. Mesmer, however, drew the quirky conclusion that he did not need a magnet because *he himself* was a magnet. With that claim, he gave us the term *animal magnetism*.

After his death, others studied "animal magnetism" or "Mesmerism," eventually calling it "hypnotism." By that time, many physicians and scientists had already associated hypnosis with charlatans and hocus-pocus. Still today, some stage performers use hypnosis for entertainment. We should carefully distinguish the exaggerated claims from the legitimate use of hypnosis by licensed therapists.

WAYS OF INDUCING HYPNOSIS

Mesmer thought hypnosis was a power emanating from his body. If so, only special people could hypnotize others. Today, we believe that becoming a successful hypnotist requires practice but no unusual powers.

The first step toward being hypnotized is agreeing to give it a try. Contrary to what you may have heard, no one can hypnotize an uncooperative person. The hypnotist tells you to sit down and relax, and you do so because you would like to experience hypnosis. The whole point of hypnosis is following the hypnotist's suggestions, and when you sit down and relax, you are already starting to follow suggestions.

A hypnotist might then monotonously repeat something like, "You are starting to fall asleep. Your eyelids are getting heavy. Your eyelids are getting very heavy. They are starting to close. You are falling into a deep, deep sleep." In another technique (Udolf, 1981), the hypnotist suggests, "After you go under hypnosis, your arm will begin

Although Mesmer is often depicted as irresistibly controlling people, hypnosis depends on the person's willingness.

© Mary Evans Picture Library

---

[1] Does this seem profound? Or is it nonsense? Many statements sound profound until we try to figure out exactly what they mean.

A hypnotist induces hypnosis by repeating suggestions, relying on the hypnotized person's cooperation and willingness to accept suggestions.

to rise automatically." (Some people, eager for the hypnosis to succeed, shoot their arm up immediately and have to be told, "No, not yet. Just relax. That will happen later.") Then the hypnotist encourages you to relax and suggests that your arm is starting to feel lighter, as if it were tied to a helium balloon.

The hypnotist might suggest that your arm is beginning to feel strange and is beginning to twitch. The timing of this suggestion is important because when you stand or sit in one position long enough, your limbs really do feel strange and twitch. If the hypnotist's suggestion comes at just the right moment, you think, "Wow, that's right. My arm does feel strange. This is starting to work!" Believing that you are being hypnotized is a big step toward actually being hypnotized.

THE USES AND LIMITATIONS OF HYPNOSIS

Hypnosis can produce relaxation, concentration, and changes in behavior, some of which persist after the end of the hypnotic state. Hynotizability resembles ordinary suggestibility. If I asked you to imagine a bright, sunny day, you almost certainly would, even without being hypnotized. If I asked you to please stand and put your hands on your head, you probably would (if I asked nicely), again without being hypnotized. If I asked you to stand, flap your arms, and cluck like a chicken, you might or might not. People vary in how far they will follow suggestions without hypnosis, and suggestibility without hypnosis correlates with hypnosis. People follow suggestions a little more with hypnosis than without, but only a little (J. Kirsch & Braffman, 2001). If you are easily hypnotizable, you probably also respond strongly to books and movies, reacting almost as if the events were really happening. That is, hypnotizability is a variation on people's normal suggestibility.

What Hypnosis Can Do

One well-established effect of hypnosis is to inhibit pain. Some people can undergo medical or dental surgery with only hypnosis and no anesthesia. The benefits of hypnosis are most easily demonstrated for acute (sudden) pains, but hypnosis can help with chronic pains, too (Patterson, 2004). Hypnosis is particularly helpful for people who react unfavorably to anesthetic drugs and those who have developed a tolerance for painkilling opiates.

Recall from chapter 4 that pain has both sensory and emotional components. Hypnosis alters mostly the emotional components. Even when a hypnotized person says that he or she feels no pain, the heart rate and blood pressure still increase (Hilgard, 1973). Under hypnotic suggestion to feel no unpleasantness, a person subjected to painful stimuli shows high arousal in the parietal cortex areas responsive to body sensations but not in the frontal cortex areas responsive to unpleasant emotions (Rainville, Duncan, Price, Carrier, & Bushnell, 1997) (see Figure 10.17).

Another use of hypnosis is the **posthypnotic suggestion**, *a suggestion to do or experience something after coming out of hypnosis.* Suppose you receive a suggestion under hypnosis that whenever you see the number 1, it will look red, and when you see the number 2, it will look yellow. After you emerge from hypnosis, the researcher shows you black numbers on various backgrounds

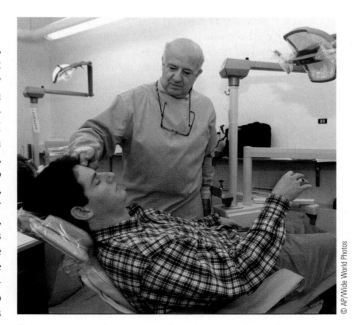

Some dentists use hypnosis to relieve pain, even for tooth extractions and root canal surgery.

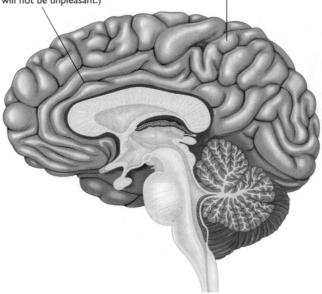

Area of frontal cortex responsive to emotional distress. (Activity decreased by hypnotic suggestion that stimulus will not be unpleasant.)

Area of parietal cortex responsive to painful stimulation.

Figure 10.17 A hypnotic suggestion to experience less pain decreases activity in the frontal cortex areas associated with emotional distress but has little effect on the sensory areas in the parietal cortex.

and asks you to press a key as soon as you see a number. You will have no trouble seeing 1 or **2**, but you will usually fail to see **1** or 2. (Cohen Kadosh, Henik, Catena, Walsh, & Fuentes, 2009). Until the hypnotist cancels the suggestion or it wears off, you will be like the people with synesthesia, as discussed in chapter 4.

In one study, adults known to be easily hypnotized were randomly assigned to different groups. One group was handed a stack of 120 addressed stamped postcards and asked (without being hypnotized) to mail one back each day until they exhausted the stack. Another group was given a posthypnotic suggestion to mail one card per day. The nonhypnotized group actually mailed back more cards, but they reported that they had to remind themselves each day to mail a card. Those given the posthypnotic suggestion said they never made a deliberate effort. The idea of mailing a card just "popped into mind," providing a sudden compulsion to mail one (Barnier & McConkey, 1998).

Many therapists have given cigarette smokers a posthypnotic suggestion that they will not want to smoke. The results are mixed. Some studies report significant benefits, but placebo treatments also produce benefits (Elkins, Marcus, Bates, Rajab, & Cook, 2006; J. P. Green, Lynn, & Montgomery, 2008). That is, much of the improvement depends on expectations.

Perceptual Distortions Under Hypnosis

A few people report visual or auditory **hallucinations** *(sensory experiences not corresponding to reality)* under hypnosis, and many report touch hallucinations after being told, "your nose itches" or "your left hand feels numb" (Udolf, 1981). When hypnotized people report hallucinations, are they telling the truth or are they just saying what the hypnotist wants them to say?

People are often telling the truth. In one study, researchers performed brain scans while people listened to sounds, imagined them, or hallucinated them under hypnotic suggestion. The hypnotic experiences activated some of the same brain areas as actual sounds did, but imagining sounds did not (Szechtman, Woody, Bowers, & Nahmias, 1998). Evidently, hypnotic hallucinations are more like real experiences than like imagination.

However, when hypnotized people claim that they don't see or hear something, careful testing demonstrates that the information does register partly. In one study, people who were highly susceptible to hypnosis looked at the optical illusion shown in Figure 10.18a. They were hypnotized and told not to see the radiating lines but to see only the two horizontal ones. Those who said that they no longer saw the radiating lines still perceived the top line as longer than the bottom one, as in the usual optical illusion

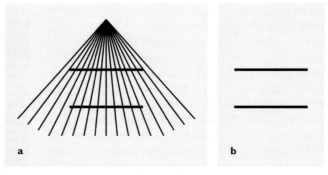

a   b

Figure 10.18 Horizontal lines of equal length in (a) the Ponzo illusion and (b) without the optical illusion. Researchers employ such stimuli to determine how hypnosis alters sensory perception.

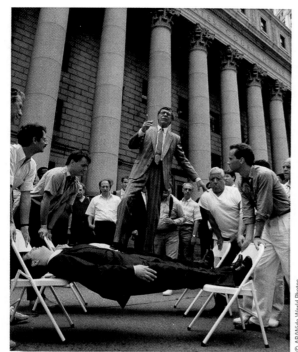

Figure 10.19 The U.S. Supreme Court ruled in 1987 that criminal defendants may testify about details they recalled under hypnosis. Its decision sparked this protest by the magician known as The Amazing Kreskin, who borrowed a stunt commonly used to demonstrate the power of hypnosis—standing on a person suspended between two chairs.

(R. J. Miller, Hennessy, & Leibowitz, 1973). If the radiating lines had truly disappeared, they would have seen something like Figure 10.18b, where the horizontal lines look equal. So these people did see the radiating lines to some extent.

What Hypnosis Does Not Do

Many of the spectacular claims made for the power of hypnosis turn out to be less impressive on closer scrutiny. For instance, as in Figure 10.19, people under hypnosis can balance their head and neck on one chair and their feet on another chair and even allow someone to stand on their body! Amazing? Not really. It's easier than it looks, even without hypnosis. Give it a try. (But don't invite someone to stand on you. Someone who does not balance correctly could injure you.)

Many people have attempted to use hypnosis to enhance memory. For example, a distressed person tells a psychotherapist, "I don't know why I have such troubles. Maybe I had some bad experience when I was younger. I just can't remember." Or a witness to a crime says, "I saw the culprit for a second or two, but now I can't give you a good description." Therapists and police officers have sometimes turned to hypnotism in the hope of

uncovering lost memories. However, hypnotized people are highly suggestible. When given a suggestion such as "you will remember more than you told us before," hypnotized people report more information, some of it correct and most of it incorrect, with increased confidence in both the correct and the incorrect (Fligstein, Barabasz, Barabasz, Trevisan, & Warner, 1998; J. P. Green & Lynn, 2005; Wagstaff et al., 2004). Let's consider a typical study.

What's the Evidence?
Hypnosis and Memory

The design of this study and many like it is simple: The experimenter presents material, tests people's memory of it, and then hypnotizes them and tests their memory again (Dywan & Bowers, 1983).

Hypothesis People will remember some of the material without hypnosis and more of it after hypnosis.

Method Fifty-four people looked at a series of 60 slides with drawings of simple objects (e.g., pencil, hammer, or bicycle), one every 3.5 seconds. Then they were given a sheet with 60 blank spaces and asked to recall as many of the items as possible. The slides were presented a second and third time, and after each session, the participants had another chance to recall items. Each day for the next week, they again wrote a list of all the items they could remember (but without seeing the slides again). Finally, a week after the original slide sessions, they returned to the laboratory. Half of them, selected at random, were hypnotized and the others were just told to relax. All were asked to recall as many of the drawings as possible.

Results Figure 10.20 shows the means for the two groups. The hypnotized people reported some items that they had not recalled before and more than the nonhypnotized group did. However, the hypnotized group reported more incorrect items than the nonhypnotized group did.

Interpretation These results show no evidence that hypnosis improves memory. Rather, it decreases people's usual hesitance about reporting uncertain or doubtful memories. It may also cause people to confuse imagination with reality.

You might note that this study is an example of the signal-detection issue discussed in chapter 4: A reported new memory is a "hit," but the number of hits, by itself, is useless information unless we also know the number of "false alarms"—reported memories that are incorrect.

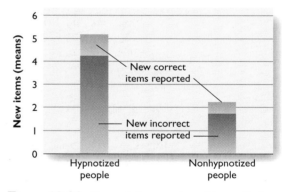

Figure 10.20 Hypnosis increased people's recall of items they had not recalled before. However, most of the new "memories" they confidently reported were incorrect. (From "The Use of Hypnosis to Aid Recall" by J. Dywan and K. Bowers in *Science*, 1981, pp. 184–185. Copyright © 1981. Reprinted by permission of AAAS.)

Many other studies have produced similar conclusions: Hypnosis sometimes increases the number of correct items recalled, but it also increases the number of incorrect items recalled. People who have been hypnotized continue to report both the correct and incorrect items with high confidence, long after the hypnotic session (Steblay & Bothwell, 1994). Curiously, although hypnosis is unreliable for enhancing memory, a posthypnotic suggestion can cause people to forget something (Mendelsohn, Chalamish, Solomonovich, & Dudai, 2008).

In response to such findings, a panel appointed by the American Medical Association (1986) recommended that courts of law should refuse to admit any testimony that was elicited under hypnosis, although hypnosis might be used as an investigative tool if all else fails. For example, if a hypnotized witness reports a license plate number and the police track down the car and find blood on it, the blood is certainly admissible evidence, even if the hypnotized report is not. Success stories of that type are rare.

Another doubtful claim is that hypnosis can help people recall their early childhood. A hypnotist might say, "You are getting younger. It is now the year . . . ; now it is . . . ; now you are only 6 years old." A hypnotized person may act like a young child, playing with teddy bears and blankets (Nash, Johnson, & Tipton, 1979). But is he or she reliving early experiences? Evidently not.

- The reported memories, such as the names of friends and the details of birthday parties, are generally inaccurate, according to records that parents or others have kept (Nash, 1987).
- Someone who has presumably regressed under hypnosis to early childhood retains spelling and other skills learned later in life. When asked to draw a picture, he or she does not draw as children draw but as adults imagine that children draw (Orne, 1951) (see Figure 10.21).

- Hypnotized subjects who are given a suggestion that they are growing older give a convincing performance of being an older person and report memories of what has happened to them in old age (Rubenstein & Newman, 1954). Because their reports of the future can only be imagination, we should assume the same for their past.

You may even encounter the astounding claim that hypnosis can help someone recall memories from a previous life. Hypnotized young people who claim to be recollecting a previous life most often describe the life of someone similar to themselves and married to someone remarkably similar to their current boyfriend or girlfriend. If they are asked whether their country (in their past life) is at war or what kind of money is in use, their guesses are seldom correct (Spanos, 1987–1988).

19. Does hypnosis improve memory?

Answer

19. No. People under hypnosis confidently report more details, but most of them are wrong.

What's the Evidence?
Hypnosis and Risky Acts

Most hypnotists agree, "You don't have to worry. People will not do anything under hypnosis that they would ordinarily refuse to do." That reassurance is an important strategy in persuading you to agree to hypnosis. But is it true? How would anyone know? Do you suppose hypnotists ask clients to perform immoral acts, meet with refusals, and then report the results of these unethical experiments? Not likely. Furthermore, on the rare occasions when investigators have asked hypnotized people to perform dangerous acts, the results have been hard to interpret. Here is an example.

Hypothesis Hypnotized people will sometimes perform acts that people would refuse to do otherwise.

Method Eighteen college students were randomly assigned to three groups. The investigator hypnotized those in one group, instructed the second group to pretend they were hypnotized, and simply asked the third group to participate in the study (without mentioning hypnosis). Each student was then asked to perform three acts: First, pick up a poisonous snake from a box. The snake really was poisonous, and anyone who got too close was restrained at the last moment. Second, reach into a vat of fuming nitric acid to retrieve a coin (which was already starting to dissolve). Here, there was no last-second restraint. Anyone who followed the instructions was told to wash his or her hands in warm

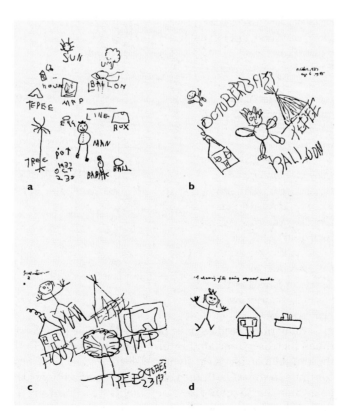

Figure 10.21 One person made drawing (a) at age 6 and the other three drawings (b, c, d) as a college student while hypnotized and told to regress to age 6. Orne (1951) concluded that hypnotized students drew as they thought a child would.

Will hypnotized people do anything that they would otherwise refuse to do? The problem is that nonhypnotized people will sometimes perform some strange and dangerous acts either because an experimenter asked them to or on their own.

soapy water immediately afterward. (Today's ethical procedures would prevent this study.) Third, throw the nitric acid into the face of the hypnotist's assistant. While the participant was washing hands, the researcher had replaced the nitric acid with water, but the participant had no way of knowing that.

Results Five of the six hypnotized students followed all three directions (Orne & Evans, 1965). Moreover, so did all six of those who were pretending to be hypnotized! So did two of the six who were just told to take these actions as part of an experiment with no mention of hypnosis. (Nonhypnotized subjects did, however, hesitate longer than the hypnotized subjects.)

Why would people do such extraordinary things? They explained that they trusted the experimenter: "If he tells me to do something, it can't really be dangerous."

Interpretation We do not have adequate evidence to decide whether people under hypnosis will do anything that they would refuse to do otherwise because it is difficult to find anything that people will refuse to do!

Notice the importance of control groups: We cannot simply assume what people would do without hypnosis. We need to test them.

IS HYPNOSIS AN ALTERED STATE OF CONSCIOUSNESS?

If a hypnotist tells you, "Your hand is rising; you can do nothing to stop it," your hand might indeed rise. If you were later asked why, you might reply that you lost control of your own behavior. Still, you were not a puppet. Was the act voluntary, involuntary, or something in between? To put the question differently, is hypnosis really different from normal wakefulness?

At one extreme, some psychologists regard hypnosis as a special state of consciousness characterized by increased suggestibility. At the other extreme, some psychologists emphasize the similarities between hypnosis and normal wakeful consciousness, including the fact that people who respond well to hypnosis also respond strongly to suggestions without hypnosis. Most psychologists take intermediate positions, noting that hypnotized people are neither "pretending to be hypnotized" nor under a hypnotist's control. That is, hypnosis is a special state in some ways but not others (I. Kirsch & Lynn, 1998).

One way to determine whether hypnosis is a special state of consciousness is to find out whether nonhypnotized people can do everything that hypnotized people do. How convincingly could you act like a hypnotized person?

How Well Can Someone Pretend to Be Hypnotized?

In several experiments, some college students were hypnotized and others pretended they were hypnotized. An experienced hypnotist then examined them and tried to determine which ones were really hypnotized.

Fooling the hypnotist turned out to be easier than expected. The pretenders tolerated sharp pain without flinching and pretended to recall old memories. They made their bodies as stiff as a board and lay rigid between two chairs. When standing people were told to sit down, they did so immediately (as hypnotized people do) without first checking to make sure they had a chair behind them (Orne, 1959, 1979). When told to experience anger or another emotion, they exhibited physiological changes such as increased heart rate and sweating, just as hypnotized people do (Damaser, Shor, & Orne, 1963). Even experienced hypnotists could not identify the pretenders.

Only a few differences between the hypnotized people and pretenders emerged (Orne, 1979). The pretenders failed to match some of the behaviors of hypnotized people, simply because they did not know how a hypnotized subject would act. For instance, when the hypnotist suggested, "You see Professor Schmaltz sitting in that chair," people in both groups reported seeing the professor. Some of the hypnotized subjects, however, asked with puzzlement, "How is it that I see the professor there, but I also see the chair?" Pretenders never reported seeing this double reality. At that point in the experiment, Professor Schmaltz walked into the room. "Who is that entering the room?" asked the hypnotist. The pretenders would either say they saw no one, or they would identify Schmaltz as someone else. The hypnotized subjects would say, "That's Professor Schmaltz." Some then said that they were confused about seeing the same person in two places. For some of them, the hallucinated professor faded at that moment. Others continued to accept the double image.

One study reported a way to distinguish hypnotized people from pretenders more than 90% of the time. But it might not be the way you would expect. Simply ask people how deeply hypnotized they thought they were, how relaxed they were, and whether they were aware of their surroundings while hypnotized. People who rate themselves as "extremely" hypnotized, "extremely" relaxed, and "totally unaware" of their surroundings are almost always pretenders. Those who were really hypnotized rate themselves as only mildly influenced (Martin & Lynn, 1996).

So, what is our conclusion? Apparently, people pretending to be hypnotized can mimic almost any effect of hypnosis that they know about. However, hypnosis is ordinarily not just role-playing. The effects that role-players learn to imitate happen spontaneously for the hypnotized people.

10. Does hypnosis give people the power to do anything they could not do otherwise? Does it cause them to do anything they would be unwilling to do otherwise?

Answer

10. No evidence indicates that hypnosis empowers people to do anything they could not do otherwise if sufficiently motivated. People pretending to be hypnotized can imitate what hypnotized people do, and the only exceptions are things that the imitators did not know about. As to whether hypnosis can make people do something they would ordinarily refuse to do, we do not know. In certain experiments, hypnotized people have done some strange things, but so have nonhypnotized people.

Meditation excludes the worries and concerns of the day and thereby induces a calm, relaxed state.

MEDITATION AS AN ALTERED STATE OF CONSCIOUSNESS

Hypnosis is not the only method of inducing a relaxed and possibly altered state of consciousness. Meditation, *a systematic procedure for inducing a calm, relaxed state through the use of special techniques,* follows traditions that have been practiced in much of the world for thousands of years, especially in India. Meditation takes many forms. One variety seeks "thoughtless awareness," in which the person is aware of the sensations of the moment but otherwise completely passive. While seeking this state, the per-

son might concentrate on a single image, repeat a simple sound (e.g., "om"), or repeat a short religious statement (e.g., "God is good"). Meditators may observe their own thoughts, attempt to modify them, or distance themselves from certain thoughts. Goals of meditation vary from the development of wisdom to general well-being (Walsh & Shapiro, 2006).

Many studies document that meditation increases relaxation, decreases pain, decreases anxiety, and alleviates problems related to anxiety, including migraine headaches (Wachholtz & Pargament, 2008; Yunesian, Aslani, Vash, & Yazdi, 2008). It also improves attention and concern for others (Walsh & Shapiro, 2006). However, most studies fail to control for participants' expectations of benefits. Few studies have used double-blind procedures. The medical and psychological benefits appear attributable to relaxation (Holmes, 1987).

10.3 | module

In Closing

What Hypnosis Is and Isn't

Researchers agree on a few general points: Hypnosis is not faking or pretending to be hypnotized, and it does not give people mental or physical powers that they otherwise lack. Hypnosis enables people to relax, concentrate, and follow suggestions better than they usually do. Be skeptical of anyone who claims much more than that for hypnosis.

SUMMARY

- *Nature of hypnosis.* Hypnosis is a condition of increased suggestibility that occurs in the context of a special hypnotist–subject relationship. Psychologists try to distinguish the genuine phenomenon, which deserves serious study, from exaggerated claims. (page 364)
- *Hypnosis induction.* To induce hypnosis, a hypnotist asks a person to concentrate and then makes repetitive suggestions. The first steps toward being hypnotized are the willingness to be hypnotized and the belief that one is becoming hypnotized. (page 364)
- *Uses.* Hypnosis can alleviate pain, and through posthypnotic suggestion, it sometimes helps people combat bad habits. (page 365)
- *Sensory distortions.* Hypnosis can induce hallucinations and other sensory distortions. However, when hypnotized people are told not to see something, even when they claim not to see it, enough aspects of the information get through to the brain to influence other perceptions. (page 366)
- *Nonuses.* Hypnosis does not give people special strength or unusual powers. When asked to report their memories under hypnosis, people report a mixture of correct and incorrect information with much confidence. (page 367)
- *Uncertain limits.* Although many hypnotists insist that hypnotized people will not do anything that they would refuse to do when not hypnotized, little evidence is available to support this claim. (page 368)
- *Hypnosis as an altered state.* Controversy continues about whether hypnosis is a special state of consciousness. (page 369)
- *Meditation.* Meditation increases relaxation and decreases anxiety. (page 370)

KEY TERMS

hallucination (page 366)

hypnosis (page 364)

meditation (page 370)

posthypnotic suggestion (page 365)

exploration and study

Why Does This Matter to Me?

SOCIAL RESPONSIBILITY AND PSYCHOLOGY

Many environmental and societal problems are caused by human behavior. Psychologists can help steer the course of our future toward more socially responsible and sustainable outcomes. Students of today need to be ever mindful of the link between human behavior and its impact on the environment and our communities.

"Consciousness" and Environmental Responsibility: A Step Further

Now that we see what kind of brain activity is necessary for consciousness, could we examine brain activity to determine the presence of consciousness in nonhuman animals? What are the implications of humans believing that nonhuman animals are or are not conscious? How do beliefs about animal consciousness affect attitudes toward habitat loss, species depletion, and animal research? *Activity adapted from http://www.teachgreenpsych.com/tg_cognition.html#belief.*

As Dangerous As Drunk Driving

Check out the Drowsy Driving website to see if you are at risk for becoming a drowsy driver and find ways that you can help raise awareness. A current link to this site can be found at www.cengage.com/psychology/kalat.

Join the iChapters Plant a Tree Drive!

To show its support of the environmental movement, iChapters is planting a tree on behalf of each fan of the iChapters Facebook Page and for every 10 questions answered correctly in our quiz.
http://www.ichapters.com/plantatree/

SUGGESTIONS FOR FURTHER EXPLORATION

In addition to the study materials provided at the end of each module, you may supplement your review of this chapter with the following book and website suggestions or by using one or more of the book's electronic resources, which include its companion website, interactive Cengage Learning eBook, and CengageNOW. Brief descriptions of these resources follow. For more information, visit **www.cengage.com/psychology/kalat**.

ADDITIONAL RESOURCES

The book's companion website, accessible from **www.cengage.com/psychology/kalat**, provides a wide range of study resources such as an interactive glossary, flashcards, tutorial quizzes, updated web links, and Try It Yourself activities.

CengageNOW with Critical Thinking Videos is an easy-to-use resource that helps you study in less time to get the grade you want. An online study system, CengageNOW gives you the option of taking a diagnostic pretest for each chapter. The system uses the results of each pretest to create personalized chapter study plans for you. The Personalized Study Plans

- Help you save study time by identifying areas on which you should concentrate and give you one-click access to corresponding pages of the interactive Cengage Learning eBook;
- Provide interactive exercises and study tools to help you fully understand chapter concepts; and
- Include a posttest for you to take to confirm that you are ready to move on to the next chapter.

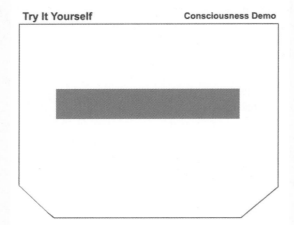

Try It Yourself: Consciousness Demonstration

Find this Try-It-Yourself activity, as well as critical thinking videos and more, in your CengageNOW product, which offers an opportunity for you to learn more about psychological research on different topics.

Books

Domhoff, G. W. (2003). *The scientific study of dreams.* Washington, DC: American Psychological Association. A review of the best research on dreams.

Koch, C. (2004). *The quest for consciousness.* Englewood, CO: Roberts. A scientific approach to the mind–brain issue.

Moorcroft, W. (2003). *Understanding sleep and dreaming.* New York: Kluwer. An excellent review of research on many aspects of sleep and dreams.

Websites

Links to the websites described below are kept current and can be found at **www.cengage.com/psychology/kalat**.

Binocular Rivalry

Demonstrations and discussion of binocular rivalry and its implications for consciousness.

Sleep Disorders

Learn more about sleep disorders and treatment.

Dream Research

The best scientific work on the content of dreams.

Sleep Research

Links to all kinds of information about sleep.

© Frank & Helena/Getty Images

Motivated Behaviors

Consider This: During the summer of 1996, the proprietors of London's Kew Gardens announced that an unusual plant, native to Sumatra and rarely cultivated elsewhere, was about to bloom for the first time since 1963. If you had been in London then, would you have made a point of visiting Kew Gardens to witness this rare event? No? What if I told you that it was a truly beautiful flower? With a lovely, sweet smell? Still no?

Then what if I told you the truth—that the flower is called the *stinking lily* or *corpse plant* because it smells like a huge, week-old carcass of rotting meat or fish. One whiff of it can make a person retch. Now would you

This flower is seldom cultivated, for good reasons. Would you stand in line to visit it?

want to visit it? If so, you would have to wait in line. When Kew Gardens announced that the stinking lily was about to bloom, an enormous crowd gathered, forming a line that stretched to the length of a soccer field (MacQuitty, 1996). When another stinking lily bloomed in Davis, California, more than 3,000 visitors came in the 5 days it was in bloom (Cimino, 2007).

The visitors' behavior is not unusual. People seek new and interesting experiences just out of curiosity. Even motivations with obvious biological value, such as hunger and sex, sometimes produce puzzling behaviors. Researchers have nevertheless made progress in understanding many aspects of motivation. We begin this chapter with an overview of general principles of motivation. Then we explore three representative and important motivations: hunger, sex, and work.

General Principles of Motivation

> • What is motivation?
> • What is the difference between motivated and unmotivated behaviors?

You are sitting quietly, reading a book, when suddenly you hear a loud noise. You jump a little and gasp. Was your action motivated? "No," you say. "I jumped involuntarily." Now I tell you that I want to do a little experiment. As soon as you hear me tap my pencil, you should try to jump and gasp just as you did the first time. I tap my pencil, and sure enough, you jump and gasp. Was that action motivated? "Yes," you reply.

So, what appears to be approximately the same behavior can be motivated at one time and unmotivated at another time. Can we trust people to tell us their motivations? No, we can't. Someone accused of murder says, "I didn't mean to kill. It was an accident." Your friend, who promised to drive you somewhere and then left without you, says, "I didn't do it on purpose. I just forgot." We need to study how motivated behaviors differ from unmotivated behaviors, but even then, we will frequently be uncertain whether someone's behavior was motivated or accidental.

VIEWS OF MOTIVATION

Like many other important terms in psychology, motivation is difficult to define. Let's consider several possibilities: "Motivation is what activates and directs behavior." This description fits many examples, but it also fits some other phenomena. For instance, light activates and directs plant growth, but we wouldn't say that light motivates plants.

"Motivation is what makes our behavior more vigorous and energetic." The problem with this definition is that some motivated behavior is not vigorous at all. For example, you might be motivated to spend the next few hours sleeping.

How about this: Based on the concept of reinforcement from chapter 6, we could define motivation as *the process that determines the reinforcement value of an outcome.* In more everyday language, motivation is what makes you want something more at one time and less at another. For example, food is more reinforcing at some times than others. Motivated behavior is goal-directed behavior. If you are motivated by hunger, you try one approach after another until you find food. If you are too cold, you put on heavier clothing, find a nice fireplace, or do whatever else is available to get warmer.

This definition works as a description, but it offers no theory. Let's briefly consider some influential theories with their strengths and weaknesses.

Drive Theories

One view regards motivation as a drive, *a state of unrest or irritation that energizes one behavior after another until one of them removes the irritation* (Hull, 1943). For example, if you get a splinter in your finger, the discomfort motivates you to try various actions until you remove the splinter.

According to the *drive-reduction theory* that was popular among psychologists of the 1940s and 1950s, humans and other animals eat to reduce their hunger, drink to reduce their thirst, and have sexual activity to reduce their sex drive. By this view, if you satisfy all your needs, you will then become inactive. People's search for new experiences—riding roller coasters or smelling odd flowers, for example—is a problem for this view.

Homeostasis

An important advance upon the idea of drive reduction is the concept of homeostasis, *the maintenance of an optimum level of biological conditions within an organism* (Cannon, 1929). The idea of homeostasis recognizes that we are motivated to seek a state of equilibrium, which is not zero stimulation. For example, people make an effort to maintain a fairly constant body temperature, a steady body weight, a certain amount of water in the body, a moderate amount of sensory experience, and so on.

Motivated behaviors do not maintain exact constancy because our behavior often anticipates future needs. For example, you might eat a large breakfast even though you are not hungry, just because you know you will be too busy to stop for lunch. If you are angry or frightened, you start sweating before you begin the vigorous actions that might heat your body. (We call it a "cold sweat.") Many animals put on extra fat and fur to protect against winter's cold weather and then lose weight and shed the extra fur in spring. A revised concept of homeostasis is allostasis, *defined as maintaining levels of biological conditions that vary according to an individual's needs and circumstances.*

Incentive Theories

The drive-reduction and homeostasis concepts overlook the power of new stimuli to arouse behaviors. For example, why do you sometimes eat tasty-looking foods even when you are not hungry? Motivation includes more than the internal forces that push us toward certain behaviors. It also includes incentives—*external stimuli that pull us toward certain actions.* Most motivated behaviors are controlled by a combination of drives and incentives. You eat because you are hungry (a drive) and because you see appealing food in front of you (an incentive). You jump into a swimming pool on a hot day to cool your body (a drive) and because you will enjoy splashing around in the water with friends (an incentive).

The artist who created this wooden cow probably hoped for recognition and money (an extrinsic motivation) but also must have enjoyed the creative process itself (an intrinsic motivation). The back of the cow folds out to reveal a desk.

Intrinsic and Extrinsic Motivations

Similar to the distinction between drives and incentives, psychologists also distinguish between intrinsic and extrinsic motivations. An **intrinsic motivation** is *a motivation to do an act for its own sake.* An **extrinsic motivation** is *based on the reinforcements and punishments that the act may bring.* For example, reading a book for enjoyment displays an intrinsic motivation, whereas reading a book to pass a test depends on an extrinsic motivation. The two kinds of motivation frequently combine. For instance, an artist paints for the joy of creation (intrinsic) and for the hope of profit (extrinsic).

Does a combination of intrinsic and extrinsic motivations lead to more persistent and effective performance than, say, intrinsic motivation alone? Not always. In a classic study, researchers let monkeys play with a device like the one in Figure 11.1. To open it, a monkey had to remove the pin, lift the hook, and then lift the hasp. The monkeys played with the device for 10 days just for fun (an intrinsic motivation). Then the device was placed over a food well containing a raisin. When monkeys opened the device to get raisins (an extrinsic motivation), their performance deteriorated. Instead of patiently removing the pin, the hook, and the hasp as before, monkeys attacked the hasp forcefully. They took longer to open the device for food than they did for play. Later, when they were offered the device by itself with no food available, they played with it less than before (Harlow, Harlow, & Meyer, 1950). It had become work, not play.

The same principle applies to human behavior. In a typical experiment, college students were asked to try to arrange plastic pieces with complex shapes to match figures in a drawing. For a while, students in the experimental group were paid $1 for each correct match. (Students in the control group did not know that the others were paid.) Later, the experiment continued without pay for anyone. When pay was suspended, the experimental group decreased their efforts (Deci, 1971). As with the monkeys, once you have been paid, the task is work rather than play. Results such as these illustrate the **overjustification effect:** *When people receive more extrinsic motivation than necessary to perform a task, their intrinsic motivation declines* (Ryan & Deci, 2000).

One explanation for the overjustification effect is that after working hard on a task, you become tired of it. However, even after a rest period, people still show a decreased interest in the task. According to another explanation, people ask themselves, "Why am I doing this?" They answer, "It's because I'm being paid." Therefore, they no longer do it for the sheer joy it brings.

The overjustification effect applies under some conditions but not others, and it is often a weak effect (Eisenberger & Cameron, 1996). For example, would you guess that praising a child for work well done would strengthen or weaken intrinsic motivation? The results vary from one study to another (Henderlong & Lepper, 2002). As a rule, praise helps if the recipient thinks the praise was deserved. Someone who is praised after a mediocre effort concludes, "They expected very little of me."

Table 11.1 summarizes three views of motivation.

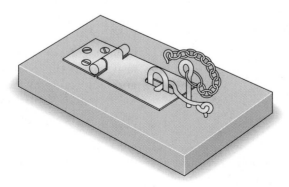

FIGURE 11.1 Monkeys learned to remove the pin, hook, and hasp to open this device. When they received a raisin instead of opening it just for fun, their performance deteriorated.

....

1. Suppose you want to encourage your younger cousin to continue taking piano lessons. Based on the overjustification effect, is it wise to pay him for practicing?

TABLE 11.1 Three Views of Motivation

View	Basic Position	Major Weaknesses
Drive Theories According to drive theories, motivation is an irritation that continues until we find a way to reduce it.	Motivations are based on needs or irritations that we try to reduce; they do not specify particular actions.	Implies that we always try to reduce stimulation, never to increase it. Also overlooks importance of external stimuli.
Homeostasis (plus anticipation) Homeostasis is the process of maintaining a variable such as body temperature within a set range.	Motivations tend to maintain body states near some optimum intermediate level. They may react to current needs and anticipate future needs.	Overlooks importance of external stimuli.
Incentive Theories Incentives are external stimuli that attract us even if we have no biological need for them.	Motivations are responses to attractive stimuli.	Incomplete theory unless combined with drive or homeostasis.

Answer

1. According to the overjustification effect, you should not pay enough that your cousin practices only for the reward. However, sincere verbal praise would be good.

CONFLICTING MOTIVATIONS

You almost always feel more than one motivation. Sometimes, those motivations are in harmony. Imagine yourself outside on a hot day. You would like to cool off, you are thirsty and a bit hungry, and you would like to be with your friends. One of your friends suggests going somewhere for a snack and a cool glass of lemonade. You agree, satisfying all four motives—temperature regulation, thirst, hunger, and socialization. At another time, you might have motivations in conflict. For example, suppose you are hungry but your friends want to play tennis. You have to choose between eating and socializing. How do we resolve such conflicts?

Maslow's Hierarchy of Needs

Abraham Maslow (1970) proposed that we resolve conflicts by a **hierarchy of needs,** *an organization from the most insistent needs to the ones that receive attention only when all others are under control,* as shown in Figure 11.2. If you need to breathe, fighting for oxygen takes priority over all else. If you are hungry, thirsty, or too hot or too cold, you pursue those needs until you satisfy them. After you satisfy your basic physiological needs, you move on to your safety needs, such as security from attack and avoidance of pain. Next come your social needs, followed by your need for self-esteem. At the apex of the hierarchy is the need for **self-actualization,** *the need for creative activities to fulfill your potential.* Maslow further proposed

that people who satisfy more of their higher needs tend to be mentally healthier than others.

As a generalization, Maslow's hierarchy makes the valid point that all needs are not equal. Ordinarily, certain motivations take priority over others. However, the theory fails if we take it literally. Sometimes, escaping pain or avoiding danger is more urgent than seeking food. Might you walk through bitter cold, passing up opportunities to eat or drink, to be with someone you love? It depends: How cold is it, how hungry and thirsty are you, and how much do you love that person? Might you risk your life to advance a cause you believe in? Some people do. Although the lower-level needs *usually* take priority over the higher needs, exceptions are common. Under certain circumstances, almost any need takes priority over another.

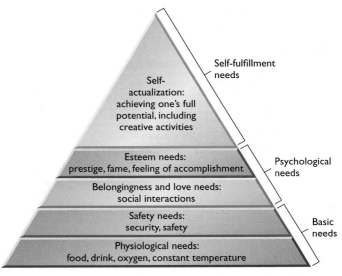

FIGURE 11.2 According to Maslow's hierarchy of needs, you satisfy your lower needs before moving on to your higher needs. (Based on Maslow, 1970)

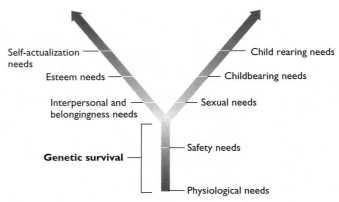

FIGURE 11.3 According to a revised model, people who satisfy their physiological and safety needs can branch off in two directions, expressing themselves as individuals or concentrating on care for their children. Although most people follow both sets of motivations, the emphasis can shift more in one direction or the other.

A further criticism is that Maslow's theory is culture specific. For people in much of North America and Europe, self-esteem and self-actualization are important goals. For people in China, the individual's accomplishments are less important than the sense of belonging to one's group and one's family. Figure 11.3 presents an alternative hierarchy of needs (Yang, 2003). According to this model, everyone has to satisfy the survival needs at the bottom. Having satisfied them, a person can branch off in either of two directions or a combination of both. The arm at the right pertains to reproduction, an essential goal for all human cultures, although not for every person within a given culture. The arm at the left pertains to expressing one's own needs. Relating to other people and belonging to a family or group are important to everyone, especially people in collectivist cultures. Self-esteem and self-actualization needs are important for people in some cultures but not others.

2. What are two criticisms of Maslow's hierarchy?

Answer

2. First, a lower level of need does not always take precedence over one at a higher level. Second, self-esteem and self-actualization are more important in some cultures than others.

Motivation Conflict as a Way to Measure Motivation

Psychological researchers sometimes measure the strength of someone's motivation by self-reports. A researcher might ask, "On a scale from 1 to 7, how motivated are you to achieve excellence on your job?" Would you trust people to give completely accurate answers? Probably not. Furthermore, self-reports are impossible for nonhuman animals and very young children. Another way to measure motivation is to offer a reinforcement for certain levels of work. For example, a researcher might measure your motivation for money by seeing how much work you are willing to do for $10 or might measure a rat's hunger by seeing how many times it will press a lever for a small piece of food.

Researchers also make use of conflicts. Suppose a rat can get food only by running across a floor that delivers mild electrical shocks. We can measure the rat's hunger by how long a runway it will cross. We compare that distance to how far it will run to reach a sexual partner, how far a mother rat will run to reach her babies, or any other possible reward.

3. Is the use of this conflict method consistent or inconsistent with Maslow's hierarchy of needs?

Answer

3. If Maslow's hierarchy were literally true, this method would fail because a rat would always prefer food to the avoidance of shock and would never prefer a sexual partner to the avoidance of shock.

Delay of Gratification

Here is another kind of motivation conflict: You could enjoy a big cheeseburger and hot fudge sundae for dinner or eat light and hope to lose a little weight. You could relax with friends tonight or study and get a better grade on the test next week. People differ in how well they *defer gratification*—that is, choose the action that produces the bigger payoff later instead of the smaller pleasure now (Simpson & Vuchinich, 2000). Recall the Choice-Delay task from chapter 8: You might be offered a choice between a small, immediate reward and a larger, delayed one. You would like to wait for the delayed reward, but that immediate reward is tempting.

Sometimes, people choose an immediate pleasure while promising themselves to be virtuous later. For example, suppose you can choose a movie to borrow for this weekend, and your choices include some lowbrow comedies and some movies that would be thought provoking and intellectually stimulating. You might go either way on this choice. Suppose you get to choose one this week and one next week. That instruction greatly increases the probability you will go for the lowbrow comedy this week (Khan & Dhar, 2007). You justify your choice by thinking (perhaps incorrectly) that next week you'll choose the more intellectual film. Another factor: If you already made the "virtuous" choice in some other setting—for example, you ate a light meal for dinner and passed up the chance for a rich dessert—you decide you owe yourself a favor, and you opt for the lowbrow comedy (Milkman, Rogers, & Bazerman, 2008).

One way to overcome the temptation to choose the immediate reward is to commit to an action well in advance. You know you would choose an immediate $500 over $750 a year later. You can make the wiser decision if you choose far in advance. For example, which would you prefer, $500 a year from now or $750 two years from now? You know that when you get to one year from now, you will wish you could have the $500 right away, but if you choose now, you can commit to the better but delayed reward.

We don't always prefer a reward now to a bigger one later. Most people would prefer a passionate kiss from their favorite movie star a few days from now instead of right now (Loewenstein, 1987). They enjoy looking forward to an emotion-ally exciting event. Conversely, most would prefer to receive a painful shock today than 10 years from now. They want to get it over with. Most people don't object to waiting a couple of weeks for good news, but they want to know bad news as quickly as possible (Lovallo & Kahneman, 2000). Dreading the bad news only makes it worse.

....

4. If you want to invite someone to be a guest speaker for your favorite organization, when should you make the invitation? Why?
5. Why do many people prefer to bet on a lottery than a roulette wheel, which produces immediate results?

Answers

4. Make the invitation far in advance. Far in advance, the advantages of an action outweigh the disadvantages. When the time is close, the details of the task become more salient, and people find an excuse for not participating.
5. Someone who bets on a lottery enjoys the long period of anticipating how exciting the win might be.

....

module   11.1

In Closing

Many Types of Motivation

People do some strange things. Sometimes, they are motivated by curiosity, the desire to have something unusual to talk about with friends, perhaps even a desire for fame. As you will see in later modules of this chapter, even clearly adaptive behaviors such as hunger and sex are based on multiple and complex motives.

SUMMARY

* *Characteristics of motivated behaviors.* Motivation is the process that determines variations in the reinforcement value of an outcome. (page 375)
* *Motivation as drive reduction.* Some aspects of motivation can be described as drive reduction, but people strive for new experiences that do not reduce any apparent drive. (page 375)

* *Motivation as a way of maintaining homeostasis.* Many motivated behaviors tend to maintain body conditions and stimulation at a near-constant, or homeostatic, level. In addition, behaviors anticipate future needs. (page 375)
* *Motivation as incentive.* Motivations are partly under the control of incentives—external stimuli that pull us toward certain actions. Both drives and incentives control most motivated behaviors. (page 375)

- *Motivation conflict.* In general, biological needs take priority over other motivations but not always. Researchers can use conflicts as a way to measure motivation. (page 377)

- *Delayed gratification.* People vary in whether they choose a larger reward later over a smaller one now. It is often easier to choose the delayed reward if you make the choice far in advance. (page 378)

KEY TERMS

allostasis (page 375)

drive (page 375)

extrinsic motivation (page 376)

hierarchy of needs (page 377)

homeostasis (page 375)

incentive (page 375)

intrinsic motivation (page 376)

motivation (page 375)

overjustification effect (page 376)

self-actualization (page 377)

Hunger Motivation

> • How do we decide how much to eat and when?

Small birds eat only what they need at the moment, storing almost no fat at all. The advantage is that they remain light and fast enough to escape predators. The disadvantage is that they starve if they can't find food later. Bears follow a different strategy. Their food is abundant when nuts and berries are in season, but at other times, they find almost nothing to eat. Their evolved strategy is to eat as much as they can whenever they can and then live off their stored fat.

Few humans eat as gluttonously as bears, but we too have apparently evolved a strategy of eating more than we need at the moment in case food is scarce tomorrow, as it frequently has been during human history. Today, however, prosperous countries have abundant food, and many people overeat (Pinel, Assanand, & Lehman, 2000).

Our eating also depends on social motives. Imagine you visit your boyfriend's or girlfriend's family, and you want to make a good impression. "Dinner's ready!" someone calls. You go to the dining room and find a huge meal, which your hosts clearly expect you to enjoy. Do you explain that you are not hungry because you already made a pig of yourself at lunch? Probably not.

THE PHYSIOLOGY OF HUNGER AND SATIETY

Hunger is a partly homeostatic drive that keeps fuel available for the body. When supplies drop, specialized brain mechanisms trigger behaviors that lead to eating. How does your brain know how much fuel you need?

The problem is more complex than keeping fuel in your car's gas tank. When the fuel gauge shows that the tank is running low, you fill it with gas. By contrast, your stomach and intestines are not the only places where you store fuel. Fuel is present throughout your body, especially in the fat cells and liver cells, and more circulates in your blood. Furthermore, each meal has a different density of nutrients from any other. Fortunately, you don't have to know exactly how much to eat. You have mechanisms that control short-term changes in hunger and long-term mechanisms that correct for short-term fluctuations in your intake.

Short-Term Regulation of Hunger

Ordinarily, the main factor for ending a meal is distension of the stomach and intestines. We feel full when the digestive system is full (Seeley, Kaplan, & Grill, 1995). The stomach signals its distension by nerves to the brain, and the intestines signal distension by releasing a hormone (Deutsch & Ahn, 1986; Gibbs, Young, & Smith, 1973). With familiar foods, we also calibrate approximately how much nutrition we are getting per amount swallowed (Deutsch & Gonzalez, 1980).

When the stomach is empty, it stimulates hunger by releasing a hormone, *ghrelin* (GRELL-in). The other main factor in the onset of hunger is a drop in how much glucose enters the cells (Figure 11.4). Glucose, *the most abundant sugar in your blood, is an important source of energy for the body and almost the only source for the brain.* One could say, with only mild oversimplification, that hunger is a mechanism that motivates you to supply enough glucose. The body makes glucose from almost any food. If you eat too much, your body converts excess blood glucose into fats and other stored fuels. If you eat too little, you convert stored fuels back into blood glucose. The flow of glucose from the blood into cells depends on insulin, a hormone released by the pancreas.

The hormone insulin *increases the flow of glucose and several other nutrients into body cells.* At the beginning of a meal, before the nutrients begin to enter the blood, the brain sends messages to the pancreas to increase its secretion of insulin. Insulin promotes the movement of glucose and other nutrients out of the blood and into the cells that need fuel and into cells that store nutrients for future use.

As the meal continues, the digested food enters the blood, and almost as fast as it enters, insulin moves excess nutrients out of the blood and into the liver or fat cells. This process holds down

Mealtime is more than an opportunity to satisfy hunger: It is an occasion to share a pleasant experience with family or friends, to discuss the events of the day, and even to pass on cultural traditions from one generation to the next.

© Annie Griffiths Belt/CORBIS

FIGURE 11.4 Varying secretions of insulin regulate the flow of nutrients from the blood into the cells or from storage back into the blood.

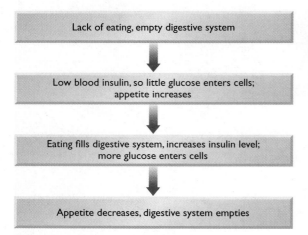

```
                                    ┌──────────────┐
                                    │ Other        │
                                    │ influences,  │
                                    │ e.g., stomach│──────┐
                                    │ distension   │      ▼
                                    └──────────────┘  ┌─────────┐
                                                      │ Satiety │
┌──────────┐      ┌──────────────┐                    └─────────┘
│ Just     │      │ Increasing   │
│ finished │─────▶│ levels of    │──┤
│ meal     │      │ glucose and  │  │
└──────────┘      │ other        │  ▼
                  │ nutrients in │  ┌──────────┐      ┌────────────────────┐
                  │ blood        │  │ Pancreas │      │ Excess glucose ...  │
                  └──────────────┘  │ secretes │─────▶│                     │
                                    │ more     │      │                     │
                                    │ insulin  │      │                     │
                                    └──────────┘      └────────────────────┘
```

Other influences, e.g., stomach distension → Satiety

Just finished meal → Increasing levels of glucose and other nutrients in blood → Satiety; → Pancreas secretes more insulin → Excess glucose and other nutrients in blood are converted to fats and other substances and stored in body cells. Surge in blood nutrients is dampened. Energy stores are developed for future needs.

the surge of nutrients in the blood (Woods, 1991). Hours after a meal, when blood glucose levels start to drop, the pancreas secretes another hormone, *glucagon,* that stimulates the liver to release stored glucose back into the blood.

As insulin levels rise and fall, hunger decreases and increases, as shown in Figure 11.5. Insulin affects hunger partly by controlling the flow of glucose and also by a more direct effect. Insulin stimulates neurons of the hypothalamus that signal satiety (Brüning et al., 2000). The importance of insulin has a consequence for dieting. Since about 1970, companies that produce soft drinks and packaged foods have been adding high-fructose corn syrup as a sweetener. Fructose tastes sweeter than other sugars, so you need fewer calories of fructose to achieve the same taste. However, fructose does not stimulate as much insulin release as other sugars do (Teff et al., 2004). Therefore, fructose does not trigger a feeling of satiety. People who average at least one soft drink per day

are more likely than average to gain weight (Dhingra et al., 2007; Liebman et al., 2006).

6. Insulin levels fluctuate over the course of a day. Would they be higher in the middle of the day, when people tend to be hungry, or late at night, when most are less hungry?

Answer

6. Insulin levels are higher in the middle of the day (LeMagnen, 1981). As a result, much of your meal is stored as fats, and you become hungry again. At night, when insulin levels are lower, you draw from your fat supplies to make more glucose.

Long-Term Regulation of Hunger

Stomach distension and the other mechanisms for ending a meal are far from perfect. For your next meal, you may eat a bit more or less than you need. If you misjudged in the same direction meal after meal, you would develop a problem.

You have long-term mechanisms to correct short-term errors. After overeating, you feel less hungry until you get back to your normal weight. If you eat too little, you feel hungrier than usual until you get back to normal. Most people's weight fluctuates from day to day but remains stable from month to month.

Your mean weight is called a **set point**—*a level that the body works to maintain* (Figure 11.6). The mechanism depends on *the hormone* **leptin,** *which the body's fat cells release in amounts proportional to their mass.* When the

```
┌───────────────────────────────────────────┐
│  Lack of eating, empty digestive system    │
└───────────────────────────────────────────┘
                      │
                      ▼
┌───────────────────────────────────────────┐
│ Low blood insulin, so little glucose        │
│ enters cells; appetite increases            │
└───────────────────────────────────────────┘
                      │
                      ▼
┌───────────────────────────────────────────┐
│ Eating fills digestive system, increases    │
│ insulin level; more glucose enters cells     │
└───────────────────────────────────────────┘
                      │
                      ▼
┌───────────────────────────────────────────┐
│ Appetite decreases, digestive system empties │
└───────────────────────────────────────────┘
```

Lack of eating, empty digestive system → Low blood insulin, so little glucose enters cells; appetite increases → Eating fills digestive system, increases insulin level; more glucose enters cells → Appetite decreases, digestive system empties

FIGURE 11.5 A feedback system between eating and insulin levels maintains homeostatic control of nutrition.

← Weight gain
← Set point
← Weight loss

FIGURE 11.6 For most people, weight fluctuates around a set point, just as a diving board bounces up and down from a central position.

body gains fat, the extra leptin alters activity in neurons of the hypothalamus, causing meals to satisfy hunger faster. Leptin is your fat cells' way of saying, "The body has enough fat already, so eat less." Leptin also triggers the start of puberty: When the body reaches a certain weight, the increased leptin levels combine with other forces to induce the hormonal changes of puberty (Chehab, Mounzih, Lu, & Lim, 1997).

Those few people who lack the genes to produce leptin become obese (Farooqi et al., 2001). Their brains get no signals from their fat supplies, so they act as if they have no fat and are starving. They also fail to enter puberty (Clément et al., 1998). Leptin injections greatly reduce obesity for these few people (Williamson et al., 2005). However, most obese people produce large amounts of leptin but apparently fail to respond to it. Injections of even larger amounts decrease their appetite somewhat, but at the risk of inducing Type II (adult-onset) diabetes (B. Cohen, Novick, & Rubinstein, 1996).

Concept Check

7. What hormones influence appetite, and which body parts release them?
8. Over the past few decades, the average age of starting puberty has become younger. What is one explanation, based on this chapter?

Answers

7. Insulin, released by the pancreas; ghrelin, released by the stomach; and leptin, released by fat cells.
8. People have been gaining weight and therefore producing more leptin. Leptin facilitates the onset of puberty.

Brain Mechanisms

Your appetite at any moment depends on the taste and appearance of the food, the contents of your stomach and intestines, the availability of glucose to the cells, and your body's fat supplies. It also depends on your health, body temperature, time of day, and social influences. The key areas for integrating all this information and thereby determining your hunger level include several parts of the hypothalamus (Figure 11.7).

Within the hypothalamus, an area called the arcuate nucleus has one set of neurons that receive hunger signals (e.g., "the food looks good"

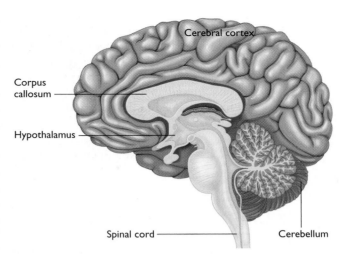

FIGURE 11.7 The hypothalamus, a small area on the underside of the brain, helps regulate eating, drinking, sexual behavior, and other motivated activities.

and "my stomach is empty") and other neurons that receive satiety signals (e.g., "my insulin level is high" and "my fat cells are supplying leptin"). The combined output from the arcuate nucleus directs other parts of the hypothalamus to enhance or weaken the taste of food, salivation responses, swallowing, and digestion (Mendieta-Zéron, López, & Diéguez, 2008). Damage in the hypothalamus can lead to severe undereating or overeating. Figure 11.8 shows an example of a rat with damage to one part of the hypothalamus, the ventromedial nucleus.

Reeves & Plum, "Hyperphagia, rage, and dementia accompanying a ventromedial hypothalamic neoplasm." *Archives of Neurology* 1969, Vol. 20, 616–624

FIGURE 11.8 A rat with a damaged ventromedial hypothalamus (left) has a constantly high insulin level that causes it to store most of its meal as fat. Because the nutrients do not circulate in the blood, the rat quickly becomes hungry again. This rat's excess fat prevents it from grooming its fur.

9. After damage to the ventrome-dial hypothalamus, an animal's weight eventually reaches a higher than usual level and then fluctuates around that amount. What has happened to the set point?

Concept Check

Answer

9. The set point has increased.

SOCIAL AND CULTURAL INFLUENCES ON EATING

Physiological mechanisms account for only part of our eating habits. Social factors are important also. When you eat with friends, you linger over the meal. You eat a few more bites after you thought you were done, and then a few more. Someone wants dessert, so you have one, too. On the average, you sit at the table two or three times as long with friends as you would alone (Bell & Pliner, 2003), and you eat almost twice as much food (de Castro, 2000). Exceptions occur, of course. If you think someone is watching and likely to scold you for overeating, you show restraint (Herman, Roth, & Polivy, 2003).

Overeating has spread in other cultures as they became, as some people put it, "Coca-Colonized" by Western cultures (J. M. Friedman, 2000). Consider the Native American Pima of Arizona (Figure 11.9). Most Pima adults are seriously obese, probably because of several genes (Norman et al., 1998), and most also have high blood pressure and Type II diabetes. However, their ancestors—with the same genes—were not obese. They ate the fruits and vegetables that grow in the Sonoran Desert, which are available only briefly during the year. To survive, they had to eat as much as they could whenever they could and conserve their energy as much as possible. Beginning in the 1940s, they switched to the same diet as other Americans, rich in calories and available year round. The Pima still eat massive quantities and conserve their energy by being relatively inactive, and the result is weight gain. We see here a superb example of the combined influence of genetics and environment. The Pima weight problem depends on both their genes and the change in diet.

EATING TOO MUCH OR TOO LITTLE

Obesity has become widespread but not universal. Why do some people become obese, whereas others do not? At the other extreme, why do some people eat too little? Abnormal eating reflects a combination of social and physiological influences.

Obesity

Obesity is *the excessive accumulation of body fat.* Physicians calculate a *body mass index,* defined as weight in kilograms divided by height in meters squared (kg ÷ m²). A ratio over 25 is considered overweight, over 30 is obese, and over 40 is extremely obese (National Institutes of Health, 2000). About 30% of U.S. adults are obese, and another 35% are overweight (Marx, 2003). Obesity increases the risk of diabetes, coronary heart disease, cancer, sleep apnea, and other diseases (Kopelman,

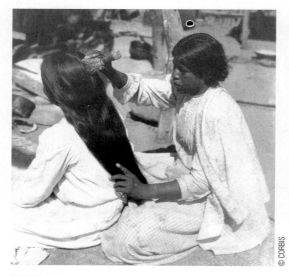

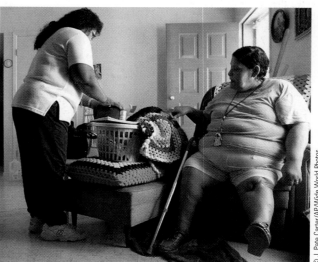

FIGURE 11.9 Until the 1940s, the Native American Pima ate their traditional diet of desert plants and remained thin. Today, they eat the typical U.S. diet while remaining relatively inactive, and the result is high prevalence of obesity.

Many people with obesity feel distressed and suffer from low self-esteem because of how other people treat them.

though each by itself has only a modest effect (Thorleifsson et al., 2009). But how do those genes alter behavior?

Many overweight people eat more than they admit, maybe even more than they admit to themselves. In one admirably simple study, researchers collected supermarket receipts and found that overweight families bought more food per person than average and especially more high-fat food (Ransley et al., 2003). However, in addition to consuming more energy, they also have low energy output, including a low metabolic rate.

One group of investigators compared the infants of twelve overweight mothers and six normal-weight mothers over their first year of life. The babies weighed about the same at birth, but six babies of the overweight mothers were inactive compared to the other babies and became overweight within their first year. During their first 3 months, they expended about 20% less energy per day than the average for other babies (S. B. Roberts, Savage, Coward, Chew, & Lucas, 1988).

Low energy expenditure is a good predictor of weight gain in adults as well. Researchers found that mildly obese people are less active than other people and spend more time sitting, even after they lose weight (J. A. Levine et al., 2005). Evidently, inactivity is a long-term habit, not a reaction to being heavy.

2000). For information about obesity, visit the Obesity Society's website; find a current link to it at **www.cengage.com/psychology/kalat**. People become overweight because they take in more calories than they use. But *why* do they do that?

The Limited Role of Emotional Disturbances

Emotional distress produces temporary fluctuations in eating and body weight for almost anyone. An eating binge distracts people from their worries and cheers them up (Heatherton & Baumeister, 1991). Eating binges are particularly common among people who have been dieting to lose weight (Greeno & Wing, 1994). Evidently, dieters actively inhibit their desire to eat until a stressful experience breaks their inhibitions and releases a pent-up desire to eat.

If distress provokes eating binges, could psychological distress cause obesity? The evidence indicates only a small influence. In one study, 19% of the people with a history of serious depression became obese compared to 15% of other people (R. S. McIntyre, Konarski, Wilkins, Soczynska, & Kennedy, 2006). However, many people report psychological distress *after* becoming obese because other people treat them unkindly (M. A. Friedman & Brownell, 1996).

Genetics and Energy Output

A few medical conditions produce obesity along with other problems, such as mental retardation (Cummings et al., 2002; Whitwell et al., 2007). Among otherwise healthy people, at least 20 to 30 genes influence the probability of obesity, al-

Portion Size

If a restaurant brings you more food than you wanted, do you feel obligated to eat it, so it won't go to waste? If you dine at an all-you-can-eat buffet (sometimes called an "all-night buffet"), do you try to get your money's worth? One contributor to obesity is the availability of so much tasty food.

A puzzling observation is that the French have less cardiovascular disease than Americans do despite eating a diet richer in fats. One explanation is meal size. On the average, French restaurants serve smaller meals than American restaurants, even when they are part of the same international chain, such as McDonald's or Pizza Hut (Rozin, Kabnick, Pete, Fischler, & Shields, 2003). French supermarkets also sell items in smaller sizes. People seem to have a predisposition—you might call it a default setting—to eat one portion of a food, whatever the size of that portion might be. To explore the role of portion size, researchers tried offering free snacks in the lobby of a building, varying the size of the snacks from one day to another. When they offered soft pretzels, most people ate one pretzel. When researchers offered pretzels already cut in half, most people ate half a pretzel. Similarly, in the lobby of another building, the researchers sometimes offered 3-g Tootsie Rolls and sometimes 12-g Tootsie Rolls. On the average, people ate more, by weight, on the days with big Tootsie Rolls (Geier, Rozin, & Doros, 2006).

It's not just the restaurants that offer large portions. The popular cookbook, *Joy of Cooking*, has been revised periodically. Of the recipes that have appeared in each edition, most have been revised to recommend larger portion sizes and to include ingredients with more calories. Recipes that called for an average of 268 calories per serving in 1936 provided 384 calories in the 2006 edition (Wansink & Payne, 2009).

10. Without denying the importance of genetics, what evidence indicates important nongenetic influences on eating and weight gain?

Answer

10. People eat more in social groups than when eating alone. People eat more when portion sizes are larger. Also, a change in diet led to much weight gain by the Pima.

Losing Weight

People trying to lose weight have a conflict between the motive to enjoy eating now and the motive to feel good about losing weight later. For people who struggle to lose weight, diets and most other interventions produce only small or temporary benefits (Stice, Shaw, & Marti, 2006). Nevertheless, advertisements for various diet programs report that many people lost a significant amount of weight. Let's assume they are telling the truth. If you hear that X number of people lost weight on some diet, how useful is that information? It's almost useless unless you also know how long they kept it off and how many other people tried the diet without losing weight. A review of the literature found that about as many people gain weight on a diet as lose (Mann et al., 2007).

More successful treatments require a change of lifestyle, including increased exercise as well as decreased eating. That combination does help, although still only 20–40% of participants keep the weight off for 2 years or more (Powell, Calvin, & Calvin, 2007). Appetite-suppressant drugs help some people, although many people quit taking the pills or overeat in spite of them. For any treatment, a weekly or biweekly follow-up by a therapist, dietician, or other concerned person increases the probability of continued efforts (Digenio, Mancuso, Gerber, & Dvorak, 2009).

Although most of the statistics about weight loss sound discouraging, you probably know people who did manage to lose weight and then kept it off. We hear about more dieting failures than successes for a simple reason: People who lose weight and keep it off don't keep seeking help (Schachter, 1982). The people who fail to lose weight show up at one weight-loss clinic after another. Therefore, the patients who have difficulties seem disproportionately common.

Social Pressures About Weight and Body Dimensions

Are you satisfied with your weight? Weight dissatisfaction is common, especially among women, including both White and Black women (Grabe & Hyde, 2006). The pressure to be thin and attractive begins with such things as Barbie dolls. Barbie has an impossible height to waist ratio. A woman that thin at the waist would die, and a woman nearly that thin would have no breast development. Researchers have found that repeated exposure to the doll causes 5- to 7-year-old girls to express dissatisfaction in their own bodies (Dittmar, Halliwell, & Ive, 2006).

Dissatisfaction in one's body often translates into worries about eating. Before we proceed, try these questions. In each case, circle one of the choices.

try it yourself

- *Ice cream* belongs best with: delicious   fattening
- *Chocolate cake* belongs best with: guilt   celebration
- *Heavy cream* belongs best with: whipped   unhealthy
- *Fried eggs* belong best with: breakfast   cholesterol

On questions like these, U.S. people, especially women, are more likely to circle *fattening, guilt, unhealthy,* and *cholesterol*—indicating food worries—whereas people in Japan, Belgium, and France usually circle *delicious, celebration, whipped,* and *breakfast.* U.S. people try to eat highly healthful foods but nevertheless worry about their diet (Rozin, Fischler, Imada, Sarubin, & Wrzesniewski, 1999).

April Fallon and Paul Rozin (1985) asked women to indicate on a diagram which body figure they thought men considered most attractive. The investigators also asked men which female figure *they* considered most attractive. As Figure 11.10 shows, women thought that men preferred thinner women than most men actually do. The same study also found that men

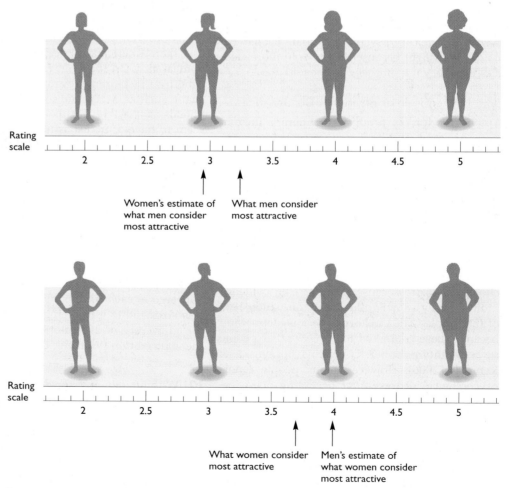

FIGURE 11.10 In a study by Fallon and Rozin (1985), women and men were asked which figure they considered most attractive and which figure they believed the opposite sex considered most attractive. Each sex incorrectly estimated the other's preferences.

thought women preferred heavier men than most women actually do.

Anorexia Nervosa

The Duchess of Windsor once said, "You can't be too rich or too thin." She may have been right about too rich, but she was wrong about too thin. Some people are so strongly motivated to be thin that they threaten their health.

Anorexia nervosa is *a condition in which someone refuses to eat enough to maintain a stable weight, intensely fears gaining weight, and misperceives his or her body as fatter than it actually is. Anorexia* means "loss of appetite," although the problem here is more a refusal to eat than a loss of appetite. The term *nervosa,* meaning "for reasons of the nerves," distinguishes this condition from digestive disorders. In the United States, anorexia nervosa occurs in a little less than 1% of women at some point in life and in about 0.3% of men (Hudson, Hiripi, Pope, & Kessler, 2007). It usually begins in the teenage years. As with other psychological conditions, anorexia nervosa comes in all degrees, but in its most severe form, it damages the heart muscle. Unlike other starving people, those with anorexia run long distances, compete at sports, work diligently on their school assignments, and sleep little. Most are perfectionists who take pride in the extreme self-control they demonstrate by refusing to eat (Halmi et al., 2000).

Most people with anorexia enjoy the taste of food and even enjoy preparing it. The problem is more a fear of eating than a lack of hunger. People with anorexia usually deny or understate their problem. Even when they become dangerously thin, they often describe themselves as "looking fat" and "needing to lose weight."

The causes of anorexia are unknown. Several genes are associated with an increased probability of anorexia, although none of them produces a large effect by itself (K. M. O. Brown et al., 2007). Many biochemical abnormalities have been demonstrated in the brains of people with anorexia, but the abnormalities are probably more the result than the cause of severe weight loss (Ferguson & Pigott, 2000). After weight returns to normal, most of the biochemical measures do, too.

Cultural influences are strong but not the whole story. Anorexia is more common in cultures that emphasize thinness, such as the United States, Canada, and northern Europe. Immigrants from southern Europe, Africa, or the Arab countries have increased risk of anorexia after living in a culture with higher incidence (Lindberg & Hjern, 2003). However, society's pressure cannot be the complete explanation, as most women who go on severe diets do not develop anorexia. Occasional

A fun house mirror temporarily distorts anyone's appearance. People with anorexia nervosa report a similar distortion of body image at all times, describing themselves as much fatter than they really are.

cases of anorexia nervosa have been documented in non-Westernized cultures of Africa and Southeast Asia, as well as in Europe hundreds of years ago, long before the emphasis on being thin (Keel & Klump, 2003). In some of those cases, society exerted other pressures, such as fasting for religious reasons. So the cultural influences that contribute to anorexia vary, but we need to explain why some people react so much more strongly than others.

Family influences are also important. Anorexia is reported more often in upper-middle-class families, possibly because people from poorer families are less likely to seek help and less likely to show up in the statistics (Becker, Franko, Speck, & Herzog, 2003). Anorexia is also more common in families that set high demands and encourage perfectionism and in families with much negative emotion and discord (Pike et al., 2007). Many of these families include a parent with anxiety or depression (Lindberg & Hjern, 2003). Most people with anorexia have no psychiatric history before the onset of anorexia, but many develop depression and anxiety disorders later (Berkman, Lohr, & Bulik, 2007).

This teenage girl, posing with her mother, was elected "best body in the senior class" during the worst period of her anorexia. Society encourages women to be extremely, even dangerously, thin.

Psychologists have tried various kinds of therapy, preferably including the whole family. Individuals who are identified and treated during the early teenage years generally progress better than those treated later, and those with the severest weight loss are the hardest to treat successfully (Steinhausen, Grigoroiu-Serbanescu, Boyadjieva, Neumärker, & Metzke, 2009).

....

11. In what way is a patient with anorexia strikingly different from typical starving people?

Answer

11. Unlike typical starving people, those with anorexia have high levels of activity. Also, they refuse to eat.

....

Bulimia Nervosa

Another eating disorder is **bulimia nervosa** (literally, "ox hunger"), in which people—again, mostly women—alternate *between self-deprivation and periods of excessive eating when they feel they have lost their ability to control themselves.* To compensate for overeating, they may force themselves to vomit or use laxatives or enemas, or they

may go through long periods of dieting and exercising. That is, they "binge and purge." In extreme eating binges, people have been known to consume up to 20,000 calories at a time (Schlesier-Stropp, 1984). A meal of a cheeseburger, fries, and a milkshake constitutes about 1,000 calories, so imagine eating that meal 20 times at one sitting. Most binges feature sweets and fats (Latner, 2003), so a better illustration of 20,000 calories would be 7 liters of chocolate fudge topping.

In the United States, about 1% of adult women and about 0.1% of adult men have bulimia nervosa (Hoek & van Hoeken, 2003). The incidence increased steadily for several decades, although it has leveled out since about 1990 (Crowther, Armey, Luce, Dalton, & Leahey, 2008). Most people recover fully or partly from bulimia, but many have lingering problems of depression (Berkman et al., 2007).

Culture is a major contributor. Bulimia was rare until the mid-1900s, and it has not been recorded in any cultures without a strong Western influence (Keel & Klump, 2003). Of course, eating binges are impossible without huge amounts of tasty food.

The most spectacular example of cultural influence comes from the Fiji Islands, where women have traditionally been heavy but content with their bodies. The idea of dieting to lose weight was unknown until the introduction of television, with many American programs, in 1995. Since then, many have begun dieting, self-induced vomiting, and binge eating. These people said they were trying to lose weight to be more like the women they saw on television (Becker, Burwell, Gilman, Herzog, & Hamburg, 2002; Becker, Burwell, Navara, & Gilman, 2003).

One hypothesis is that people with bulimia starve themselves for a while, fight their persistent feelings of hunger, and then go on an eating binge (Polivy & Herman, 1985). That idea may be on the right track, but it is incomplete. Of the people who starve themselves for days or weeks, some do develop eating binges, but others do not (Stice, 2002). The results may depend on what someone eats after a period of deprivation. Whereas most people end a fast by eating meat, fish, or eggs, people with bulimia start with desserts or snack foods (Latner, 2003). In some ways, bulimia resembles drug addiction (Hoebel, Rada, Mark, & Pothos, 1999). Overeating provides a "high" similar to that from drugs, and some drug users withdrawing from a drug turn to overeating as a substitute. Moreover, when an addict abstains from a drug for a while and then returns to it, the first new use of the drug can be highly reinforcing. By this reasoning, the cycles of abstention and overeating become addictive because the first big meal after a period of abstention is extremely reinforcing.

To test this idea, researchers put laboratory rats on a regimen of no food for 12 hours, including the first 4 hours of their waking day, followed by a meal of sweet syrup. With each repetition of this schedule, the rats ate more and more of that rich meal. Furthermore, if they were then deprived of this accustomed meal, they shook their heads and chattered their teeth in a pattern like that of rats going through morphine withdrawal (Colantuoni et al., 2001, 2002). Obviously, the rats in this study do not fully model the complexities of human bulimia, but they suggest that a pattern of deprivation followed by overeating provides strong reinforcement that overwhelms other motivations.

12. Under what circumstances would an eating binge produce an experience similar to taking an addictive drug?

Answer

12. Eating a meal high in sweets and fats right after a deprivation period produces an experience comparable to those produced by addictive drugs.

module 11.2

In Closing

The Complexities of Hunger

The research in this module underscores the idea that our motivations reflect a complex mixture of physiological, social, and cognitive forces. People become overweight for a variety of reasons relating to both genetics and culture, and they then try to lose weight mostly for social reasons, such as trying to look attractive. Sometimes, the physiological factors and the social factors collide, as when normal-weight people try to make themselves thinner and thinner.

The overall point is this: All our motivations interact and combine. How much we eat and what and when we eat depend not only on our need for food but also on social needs and the need for self-esteem.

SUMMARY

- *Short-term regulation of hunger.* Meals end by several mechanisms, principally distension of the stomach and intestines. Hunger resumes when the cells begin to receive less glucose and other nutrients. The hormone insulin regulates the flow of nutrients from the blood to storage. (page 381)
- *Long-term regulation of hunger.* An individual meal can be larger or smaller than necessary to provide the energy that the body needs. The body's fat cells secrete the hormone leptin in proportion to their mass; an increase of leptin decreases hunger. (page 382)
- *Causes of being overweight.* Some people are predisposed to obesity for genetic reasons. Whether they become obese or how obese they become depends on the kinds and

amounts of food available. Obese people tend to be inactive and remain so even after losing weight. (page 384)
- *Weight-loss techniques.* Most people fail to lose weight for the long term by dieting. A combination of diet and exercise works better, although the success rate is still disappointing. (page 386)
- *Anorexia nervosa and bulimia nervosa.* People suffering from anorexia nervosa deprive themselves of food, sometimes to a dangerous point. People suffering from bulimia nervosa alternate between periods of strict dieting and brief but spectacular eating binges. Cultural pressure to become thin contributes to both conditions. (page 387)

KEY TERMS

anorexia nervosa (page 387)

bulimia nervosa (page 388)

glucose (page 381)

insulin (page 381)

leptin (page 382)

obesity (page 384)

set point (page 382)

Sexual Motivation

- What do people do sexually?
- Why do people's sexual orientations differ?

Sexual motivation, like hunger, depends on both a physiological drive and incentives. Also like hunger, the sex drive increases during times of deprivation, at least up to a point, and it can be inhibited for many reasons. However, the sex drive differs from hunger in important ways. We do not need to be around food to feel hungry, but many people need a partner to feel sexual arousal. We eat in public, but we have sexual activities in private.

Ultimately, hunger and sex serve important biological functions that we ordinarily don't even think about during the acts themselves. We evolved mechanisms that make us enjoy eating because eating keeps us alive. Similarly, we evolved mechanisms that make sex feel good because it leads to reproduction.

Alfred C. Kinsey was an outstanding interviewer who put people at ease so they could speak freely but was also alert to probable lies. However, he did not obtain a random or representative sample of the population.

WHAT DO PEOPLE DO AND HOW OFTEN?

Researchers have many reasons for studying the frequency of various sexual behaviors. For example, if we want to predict the spread of AIDS, we need to know how many people are having unsafe sex and with how many partners. In addition to the scientific and medical reasons for studying sex, let's admit it: We're curious, aren't we?

The Kinsey Survey

The first important survey of human sexual behavior was conducted by Alfred C. Kinsey, an insect biologist who agreed to teach the biological portion of Indiana University's course on marriage. When he found that the library included little information about human sexuality, he conducted a survey. What started as a small-scale project for teaching purposes grew into a survey of 18,000 people.

Although Kinsey's sample was large, he obtained most of his interviews from members of cooperative organizations, ranging from fraternities to nunneries, mostly in the U.S. Midwest. Later researchers, using more care to get representative samples of the population, obtained significantly different results.

Nevertheless, Kinsey did document the variability of human sexual behavior (Kinsey, Pomeroy, & Martin, 1948; Kinsey, Pomeroy, Martin, & Gebhard, 1953). He found some people who had rarely or never experienced orgasm. He also found a middle-aged man who reported an average of four or five orgasms per day (with a wide variety of male, female, and nonhuman partners) and several women who sometimes had 50 or more orgasms within 20 minutes.

Kinsey found that most people were unaware of how much sexual behavior varies. When he asked people whether they believed that "excessive masturbation" causes physical and mental illness, most said "yes." (In fact, it does not.) He then asked what constitutes "excessive." For each person, excessive meant a little more than what he or she did. One young man who masturbated once a month said he

thought three times a month would cause mental illness. A man who masturbated three times daily said he thought five times a day would be excessive. (In reaction, Kinsey defined *nymphomaniac* as "someone who wants sex more than you do.")

Sexual customs vary sharply from one society to another. At a Hmong festival, unmarried women toss tennis balls to potential suitors.

Later Surveys

Kinsey did not try to interview a random sample of the population because he assumed that most people would refuse to cooperate. He may have been right in the 1940s, but in later years, researchers identified random samples and got most people to cooperate (Fay, Turner, Klassen, & Gagnon, 1989; Laumann, Gagnon, Michael, & Michaels, 1994).

(Some advice if anyone ever asks you to participate in a sex survey: Legitimate researchers present their credentials to show their affiliation with a research institute. They also take precautions to guarantee the confidentiality of responses. Do not trust "researchers" who fail to show their credentials. Be especially wary of sex surveys by telephone. It is hard to distinguish a legitimate survey from an obscene phone call in disguise.)

A survey of a random sample of almost 3,500 U.S. adults (Laumann et al., 1994) explored what people enjoy. Figure 11.11 shows the percentage of men and women who describe various sexual activities as "very appealing." The most popular sexual activity is vaginal intercourse, followed by watching one's partner undress and then by oral sex. Note an ambiguity: When 13% of men say they find group sex "very appealing," do they mean they have frequently enjoyed it or that they have fantasies about it?

Note that more men than women report enjoying every activity listed. A broader survey of 27,500 people found that in each of 29 countries, a higher percentage of men than women reported pleasure and satisfaction with their sex life (Laumann et al., 2006).

Figure 11.12 presents the results from a large-scale international survey of sexual behavior. As the figure shows, sexual activity declines with age, but even beyond age 70, about half of men and nearly a quarter of women remain sexually active (Brock et al., 2003). The main reasons for loss of sexual activity are health problems and the death of one's partner (Kontula & Haavio-Mannila, 2009).

Variations by Culture and Cohort

For most of human history, premarital sex was uncommon and considered scandalous in most of the world. Since the early to mid-1900s, many factors have challenged thinking about premarital sex. It had been that people reached puberty at about age 15 or 16 and got married before age 20.

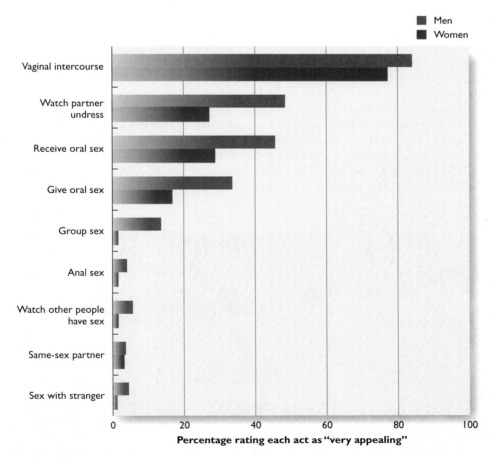

FIGURE 11.11 The percentage of U.S. adults who rate various sexual activities as "very appealing" as opposed to "somewhat appealing," "not appealing," or "not at all appealing." (Based on data of Laumann, Gagnon, Michael, & Michaels, 1994)

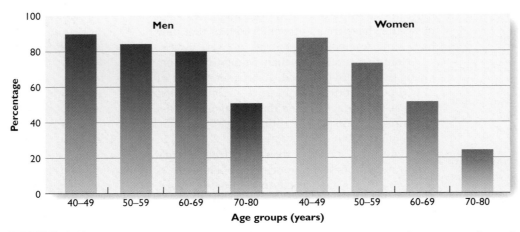

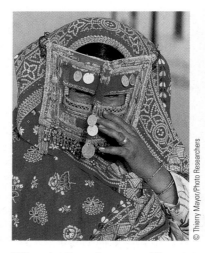

FIGURE 11.12 In a survey of four countries, the percentage of people reporting at least occasional sexual intercourse declines with advancing age. (From Brock et al., 2003)

In the United States today, because of improved health and nutrition, the mean age of puberty is about 10 to 12, and for economic reasons, most people postpone marriage until 25 to 30. Because of the introduction of reliable contraception, intercourse does not have to lead to an unwanted pregnancy. Finally, movies and television bombard us with implications that other people are having casual sex with multiple partners. Under the circumstances, abstinence until marriage has become the exception, not the rule.

Still, the results vary enormously among cultures and subcultures. A survey of four U.S. colleges found that the percentage of undergraduates who have had sexual intercourse ranged from 54% at one college to 90% at another (Davidson, Moore, Earle, & Davis, 2008). At universities in Turkey, the percentage ranged from 32% of the men and 9% of the women at one college to 84% of the men and 33% of the women at another college (Askum & Ataca, 2007). Figure 11.13 shows the relationship between mean age

of marriage and age of first sexual intercourse for men and women in various countries (Parish, Laumann, & Mojola, 2007). For women in many countries in Asia and Africa, the age of marriage equals the age of first sex. That is, nearly all women are virgins until marriage. In a few Asian and African countries, women's mean age of sex is just slightly less than the age of marriage, reflecting the fact that many women have sex with their fiancées during the months prior to marriage. In all of these countries, more men than women have sex before marriage, some with prostitutes, reflecting the ancient double standard that sex before marriage is acceptable for men but not women. In Figure 11.13, note the results for the United States and five European countries, in which both men and women have sex, on the average, 10 or more years before marriage.

Customs also vary by historical era. A survey in the United States in the 1990s found the results shown in Figure 11.14 (Laumann et al., 1994). On the average, people in their 40s reported more sex partners in their lifetime than did people in their 50s. Obviously, if you have had a certain number of partners by age 40, your total can't decrease as you get older. The 40-year-olds were different people from the 50-year-olds, and they had been young during an era of greater sexual freedom. This is a cohort effect, like the ones described in chapter 5. Surveys in Finland, Brazil, and India have also found trends toward greater sexual freedom in more recent generations (Kontula & Haavio-Mannila, 2009; Paiva, Aranha, & Bastos, 2008; Sandhya, 2009).

Different cultures have very different standards regarding public display of the human body and premarital sex.

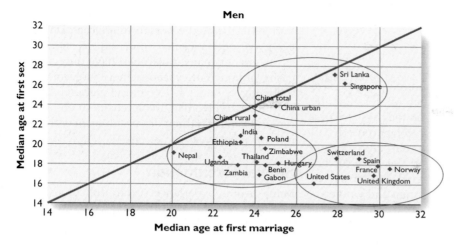

Men

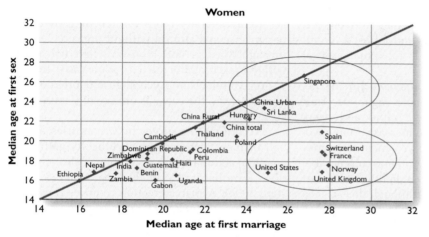

Women

FIGURE 11.13 Mean age of first sexual intercourse and mean age of marriage for people in various countries. (From Parish, W. L., Laumann, E. O., & Mojola, S. A., 2007. Sexual behavior in China: Trends and comparisons. *Population and Development Review, 33,* 745.)

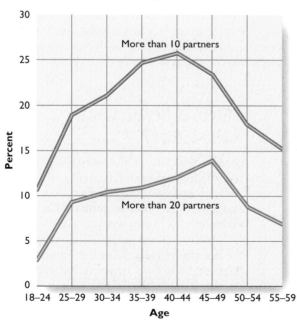

FIGURE 11.14 The percentage of U.S. men and women reporting more than 10 or 20 sex partners in their lives. (Based on data of Laumann et al., 1994)

Among men, levels of the hormone testosterone relate only weakly to levels of frequency of sexual activity, but one interesting pattern has been reported: Single men have higher testosterone levels than men in a committed relationship, such as marriage, except for men who are in a committed relationship but still seeking additional sex partners (M. McIntyre, Gangestad, et al., 2006). How shall we interpret these results? One possibility is that when a man becomes completely faithful to a partner, his testosterone level drops. However, a longitudinal study supported a different interpretation: Men whose testosterone levels start lower are more likely to enter into a committed, monogamous relationship (van Anders & Watson, 2006).

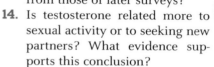

13. Why did Kinsey's results differ from those of later surveys?

14. Is testosterone related more to sexual activity or to seeking new partners? What evidence supports this conclusion?

Answers

13. Kinsey interviewed a nonrandom, nonrepresentative sample of people.

14. Testosterone relates more to seeking partners. Men with higher testosterone levels are less likely to commit themselves to a monogamous relationship.

Sexual Behavior in the Era of AIDS

During the 1980s, a new factor entered into people's sexual motivations: the fear of **acquired immune deficiency syndrome (AIDS),** *a sexually transmitted disease that attacks the body's immune system.* For HIV (human immunodeficiency virus)—the virus that causes AIDS—to spread from one person to another, it must enter the other person's blood. (The virus does not survive long outside body fluids.) The three common routes of transmission are transfusions of contaminated blood, sharing needles used for intravenous injections of illegal drugs, and sexual contact. Of types of sexual contact, anal intercourse is the riskiest, but vaginal intercourse is risky also. Touching and kissing do not spread the virus unless both people have open wounds that exchange blood.

For generations, people have known how to avoid contracting syphilis, gonorrhea, and other sexually transmitted diseases: Avoid sex with someone who might be infected or use a condom. If people had consistently followed this advice, we could have eliminated those diseases long ago. The same advice is now offered to combat AIDS, and the amount of compliance varies. Information campaigns have produced clear benefits but not enough to eradicate the disease.

In the United States, AIDS spread first among male homosexuals and later among heterosexuals. In parts of Africa, it affects one fifth or more of the adult population. One difficulty is that people remain symptom-free for years, so they can spread the virus long before they know they

have it and before their partners have reason to suspect it.

Sexual Arousal

Sexual motivation depends on both physiological and cognitive influences—that is, not just the "plumbing" of the body but also the presence of a suitable partner, a willingness to be aroused, and a lack of anxiety. William Masters and Virginia Johnson (1966), who pioneered the study of human sexual response, discovered similarities in physiological arousal between men and women.

They observed hundreds of people masturbating or having sexual intercourse in a laboratory and monitored their physiological responses, including heart rate, breathing, muscle tension, blood engorgement of the genitals and breasts, and nipple erection. Masters and Johnson identified four physiological stages in sexual arousal (Figure 11.15).

During the first stage, *excitement,* a man's penis becomes erect and a woman's vagina becomes lubricated. Breathing becomes rapid and deep. Heart rate and blood pressure increase. Many people experience a flush of the skin, which sometimes resembles a measles rash. Women's nipples become erect, and the breasts swell slightly for women who have not nursed a baby. Although this stage is referred to as excitement, nervousness interferes with it, as do stimulant drugs, including coffee.

During the second stage, called the *plateau,* excitement remains high. This stage lasts for varying lengths of time depending on a person's age and the intensity of the stimulation. Excitement becomes intense in the third stage, until a sudden release of tension known as *climax* or *orgasm,* which is felt throughout the entire body. During the fourth and final stage, *resolution,* the person relaxes.

As Figure 11.15 shows, the pattern of excitation varies from one person to another. During a given episode, a woman may experience no orgasm, one, or many. Most men have only one orgasm, although they can achieve orgasm again following a rest (or refractory) period. Among both men and women, the intensity of an orgasm ranges from something like a sigh to an extremely intense experience.

Sexual Dysfunction

Many people experience sexual difficulties, such as decreased interest in sex (Laumann et al., 2003). Those with decreased interest miss an opportunity for pleasure and risk jeopardizing their relationship with a partner.

Many people—more women than men—experience sexual arousal without orgasm. They go through Masters and Johnson's first two stages without reaching the third. In some cases, the lack of orgasm relates to psychological depression, but in most cases, the cause is unknown (Laumann et al., 2003).

According to a survey in 27 countries, almost half of men have occasional difficulty getting an erection, and many more say they wish their erections were harder (Mulhall, King, Glina, & Hvidsten, 2008). A man's erection requires relaxation of the smooth muscles controlling blood flow to the penis. The drug sildenafil (trade name Viagra) relaxes those muscles and facilitates an erection (Rowland & Burnett, 2000). Other men, especially young men, have premature ejaculations, advancing from excitement to orgasm sooner than they or their partners wish. Many women, especially older women, have trouble providing sufficient vaginal lubrication. Unfortunately, most people hesitate to discuss sexual problems with their physicians, and physicians seldom ask.

SEXUAL ANATOMY AND IDENTITY

Gender identity is *the sex that a person regards him- or herself as being.* Most people with male genitals have a male identity, and most with female genitals have a female identity, but exceptions do occur.

In the earliest stages of development, the human fetus has a "unisex" appearance (Figure 11.16). One structure subsequently develops into either a penis or a clitoris. Another structure develops into either a scrotum or labia. The direction of development depends on hormonal influences during prenatal development (McFadden, 2008). Beginning in the 7th or 8th week

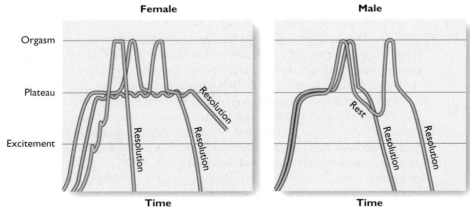

FIGURE 11.15 Sexual arousal usually proceeds through four stages—excitement, plateau, orgasm, and resolution. Each color represents the response of a different individual. Note the variation. (After Masters & Johnson, 1966)

Undifferentiated before sixth week

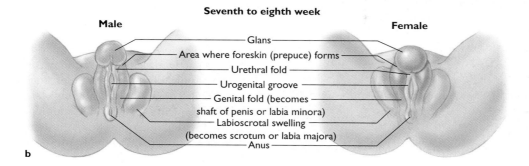

- Genital tubercle
- Urethral fold
- Urethral groove
- Genital fold
- Anal pit

a

Seventh to eighth week

Male   Female

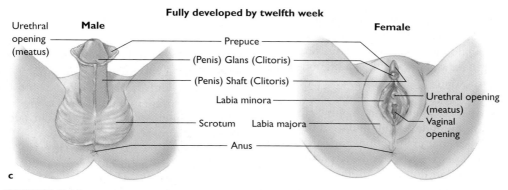

- Glans
- Area where foreskin (prepuce) forms
- Urethral fold
- Urogenital groove
- Genital fold (becomes shaft of penis or labia minora)
- Labioscrotal swelling (becomes scrotum or labia majora)
- Anus

b

Fully developed by twelfth week

Male   Female

- Urethral opening (meatus)
- Prepuce
- (Penis) Glans (Clitoris)
- (Penis) Shaft (Clitoris)
- Labia minora
- Scrotum   Labia majora
- Urethral opening (meatus)
- Vaginal opening
- Anus

c

FIGURE 11.16 Male and female genitals look the same for the first 6 or 7 weeks after conception (a). Differences emerge over the next couple of months (b) and are clear at birth (c).

after conception, *genetic male fetuses secrete higher levels of the hormone* **testosterone** than do females (although both sexes produce some), and over the next couple of months, the testosterone causes the tiny fetal structures to grow into a penis and a scrotum. In genetic female fetuses, with lower levels of testosterone, the structures develop into clitoris and labia instead. Levels of the *hormone* **estrogen** *increase more in females* than in males at this time. Estrogen is important for internal female development but has little effect on development of the external anatomy—penis versus clitoris and scrotum versus labia.

Remember: In humans and other mammals, high testosterone levels produce a male external anatomy, and low testosterone levels produce a female anatomy. Within normal limits, the amount of circulating estrogen does not determine whether one develops a male or female external appearance. Estrogen is important, however, for normal development of the internal female organs.

About 1 child in 2,000 is born with genitals that are hard to classify as male or female, and 1 or 2 in 100 have a slightly ambiguous external anatomy (Blackless et al., 2000). The most common cause is overactive adrenal glands in a genetic female. Adrenal glands secrete testosterone as well as other hormones, and if a genetic female is exposed to elevated amounts of testosterone during prenatal development, she develops a sexual anatomy that looks intermediate between male and female (Money & Ehrhardt, 1972). Less frequently, a genetic male develops an intermediate appearance because of an alteration in the gene that controls testosterone receptors (Misrahi et al., 1997). *People with an anatomy that appears intermediate between male and female* are known as **intersexes** (Figure 11.17). The Intersex Society of North America is devoted to increasing understanding and acceptance of people with ambiguous genitals. (A current link to their website can be found at **www.cengage.com/psychology/kalat.**)

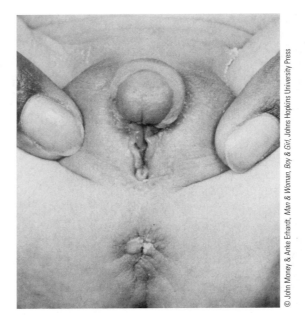

FIGURE 11.17 External genitals of a 3-month-old genetic female who was masculinized before birth by excess androgens from the adrenal gland.

© John Money & Anke Ehrhardt, *Man & Woman, Boy & Girl*, Johns Hopkins University Press

How should parents and others treat intersexed people? For decades, the standard medical recommendation was, when in doubt, call the child female and perform surgery to make her anatomy look female. This surgery includes creating or lengthening a vagina and reducing the ambiguous penis/clitoris to the size of an average clitoris. Many cases require repeated surgery to obtain a satisfactory appearance.

This recommendation was based on the assumption that any child who looks like a girl and is treated like a girl will develop a female gender identity. No one ever had much evidence for that assumption, and later experience has contradicted it. Follow-up studies on girls who were partly masculinized at birth, but reared as females, found that they are more likely than other girls to prefer boy-typical toys (cars, guns, and tools) to girl-typical toys

A group of intersexed adults gathered to provide mutual support and protest against involuntary surgical intervention for intersexes. To emphasize that they do not consider intersexuality shameful, they requested that their names be used. Left to right: Martha Coventry, Max Beck, David Vandertie, Kristi Bruse, and Angela Moreno.

Courtesy of Intersex Society of North America/Accord Alliance

(dolls, cosmetics, dishes) despite their parents' attempts to encourage interest in the girl-typical toys (Berenbaum, Duck, & Bryk, 2000; Nordenström, Servin, Bohlin, Larsson, & Wedell, 2002; Pasterski et al., 2005). This trend is not limited to girls with a medical abnormality: Researchers measured testosterone levels in the amniotic fluid of pregnant women and found that it predicted how much their daughters played with boy-typical toys when they were 6 to 10 years old (Auyeung et al., 2009).

The effects of prenatal hormones continue to influence development beyond childhood. Girls who were partly masculinized at birth continue to have male-typical interests at adolescence (Berenbaum, 1999). Those who had the highest levels of testosterone during prenatal development tend to have the lowest romantic interest in men during both adolescence and adulthood (Meyer-Bahlburg, Dolezal, Baker, & New, 2008). Some have a homosexual or bisexual orientation, and some have low interest in sex with any partner, male or female (Zucker et al., 1996).

There is, of course, nothing wrong with a girl being interested in boys' activities or being uninterested in sex with men. The point is that we can't count on rearing patterns to control psychological development. Prenatal hormones evidently influence interests and activities in addition to external anatomy.

Furthermore, the genital surgery—reducing or removing the penis/clitoris to make an intersex look more female—decreases sexual pleasure and the capacity for orgasm (Minto, Liao, Woodhouse, Ransley, & Creighton, 2003). An artificial vagina may be satisfactory to a male partner, but it provides no sensation or pleasure to the woman, and it requires frequent attention to prevent scar tissue. Finally, intersexed individuals object that, in many cases, physicians lied to them about the surgery and the reasons for it. Today, more and more physicians recommend that parents raise the child as the gender the genitals most resemble and perform no surgery until and unless the individual requests it. Many intersexed individuals prefer to remain as they are, without surgery (Dreger, 1998).

....

15. If a human fetus were exposed to very low levels of both testosterone and estrogen throughout prenatal development, how would the sexual anatomy appear?

Concept Check

16. If a human fetus were exposed to high levels of both testosterone and estrogen throughout prenatal development, how would the sexual anatomy appear?

Answers

15. A fetus exposed to very low levels of both testosterone and estrogen throughout prenatal development would develop a female appearance.

16. A fetus exposed to high levels of both testosterone and estrogen would develop a male appearance. High levels of testosterone lead to male anatomy; low levels lead to female anatomy. The level of estrogen is not decisive for external anatomy.

SEXUAL ORIENTATION

Sexual orientation is *someone's tendency to respond sexually to male or female partners or both or neither.* People vary in their sexual orientations, just as they do in their food preferences and other motivations. Those who prefer partners of their own sex have a homosexual (gay or lesbian) orientation.

Homosexual or bisexual behavior has also been observed in hundreds of animal species, although not all. Biologists had assumed that animal homosexuality occurred only in captivity, only if an individual could not find a partner of the other sex, or only in hormonally abnormal animals, but the evidence has refuted each of these hypotheses (Bagemihl, 1999). So, if "natural" means that something occurs in nature, then homosexuality is natural.

How many people have a homosexual orientation? You may have heard people confidently assert "10%." That number is derived from Kinsey's report that about 13% of the men and 7% of the women he interviewed in the 1940s and 1950s stated a predominantly homosexual orientation. The often-quoted figure of 10% is the mean of Kinsey's results for men and women. However, Kinsey did not have a random sample.

In a random sample of 3,500 U.S. adults, 2.8% of men and 1.4% of women described themselves as having a homosexual (gay or lesbian) orientation (Laumann et al., 1994). As Figure 11.18 demonstrates, the results depend on the phrasing of the question. Many people who do not consider themselves gay or lesbian have had at least one adult homosexual experience, and still more (especially males) had one in early adolescence (Laumann et al., 1994). Even higher percentages say they have felt some sexual attraction to a member of their own sex (Dickson, Paul, & Herbison, 2003).

Attitudes toward homosexual relationships have varied among cultures and among historical eras.

If you have frequently heard the prevalence of homosexual orientations estimated at 10%, you may be skeptical of the report that only 1 to 3% of people identify themselves as gay or lesbian. However, three other large surveys reported that 1 to 2%, 3%, or 6% of U.S. men were either gay or bisexual (Billy, Tanfer, Grady, & Klepinger, 1993; Cameron, Proctor, Coburn, & Forde, 1985; Fay et al., 1989). Surveys in other countries have reported similar or slightly lower percentages, as shown in Figure 11.19 (Izazola-Licea, Gortmaker, Tolbert, De Gruttola, & Mann, 2000; Sandfort, de

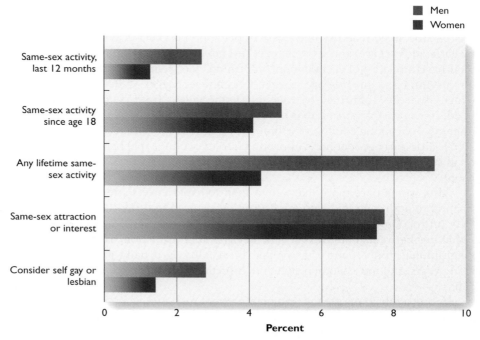

FIGURE 11.18 The percentages of U.S. adults who report sexual activity or interest in sexual activity with people of their own sex. (Based on data of Laumann et al., 1994)

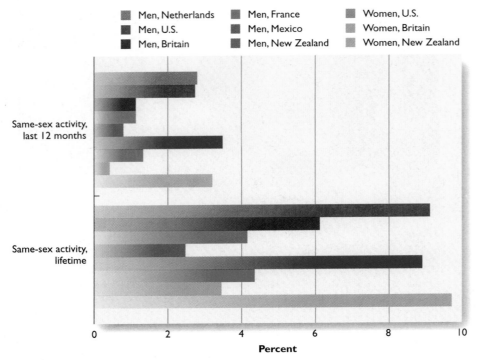

Legend:
- Men, Netherlands
- Men, U.S.
- Men, Britain
- Men, France
- Men, Mexico
- Men, New Zealand
- Women, U.S.
- Women, Britain
- Women, New Zealand

Same-sex activity, last 12 months

Same-sex activity, lifetime

Percent (x-axis: 0, 2, 4, 6, 8, 10)

FIGURE 11.19 Comparisons of the results of surveys conducted in six countries, in which people were asked about homosexual experiences. (Based on data of Dickson, Paul, & Herbison, 2003; Izazola-Licea, Gortmaker, Tolbert, De Gruttola, & Mann, 2000; Laumann, Gagnon, Michael, & Michaels, 1994; Sandfort, de Graaf, Bijl, & Schnabel, 2001; Spira et al., 1993; Wellings, Field, Johnson, & Wadsworth, 1994)

Graaf, Bijl, & Schnabel, 2001; Spira & Bajos, 1993; Wellings, Field, Johnson, & Wadsworth, 1994).

Differences Between Men and Women

Sexual orientation differs on the average between men and women in several regards. Most men become aware of being homosexual or heterosexual by early adolescence, and later changes are rare. Most (not all) homosexual men have a history of "gender-nonconforming" (i.e., feminine-type) behaviors beginning at an early age (Rieger, Linsenmeier, Gygax, & Bailey, 2008), which observers confirmed by watching home videos from people's childhood. In contrast, a fair number of women develop a homosexual (lesbian) orientation in young adulthood without any previous indications (Diamond, 2007). Girls' early gender-nonconforming (i.e., masculine-type) behaviors are relatively poor predictors of sexual orientation in women (Udry & Chantala, 2006).

Also, women are more likely than men to experience some sexual attraction to both men and women. Psychologists used to think that bisexuality (*attraction to both sexes*) was just a temporary transition by someone switching between homosexual and heterosexual attraction. However, a longitudinal study found that female bisexuality is usually stable over many years, and more women switch *to* bisexuality than *from* it (Diamond, 2008).

In one study, homosexual and heterosexual men and women watched a series of short pornographic films while the experimenters measured penis erection in the men and vaginal secretions by the women. (They tested people one at a time, so don't picture a mixed group watching these films with devices attached to their genitals.) Each film showed two men, two women, or a man and a woman. Among male observers, the results

were clear: Heterosexual men showed the greatest arousal while watching two women, less to watching a woman and a man, and little or no arousal while watching two men. Homosexual men showed the reverse—greatest arousal while watching two men. Women's responses were less clear. Most women, both lesbians and heterosexuals, showed responses to each kind of film (Chivers, Rieger, Latty, & Bailey, 2004).

Another study focused on men who regarded themselves as bisexual. All had a history of sexual experiences with both male and female partners. They watched films of sex acts between two men and other films of two women, while the researchers measured penis erections. Although each of them said he was sexually interested in both men and women, every one of them showed strong arousal—penis erection—to just one or the other. Most found the films of men arousing, although a few responded to the film of women. The researchers concluded that although bisexual behavior is moderately common among men, very few men have strong sexual fantasies and excitement about both male and female partners (Rieger, Chivers, & Bailey, 2005).

17. The vast majority of men, both homosexual and heterosexual, say they could not imagine switching sexual orientations. How does that fit with the research just described?

Concept Check

Answer

17. Studies of physiological arousal indicate that nearly all men respond either just to men or just to women. Although some men engage in sexual activities with both men and women, the orientation seems to be strongly one way or the other.

Possible Influences on Sexual Orientation

The available research suggests that genetic factors contribute to sexual orientation for both men and women. Figure 11.20 shows the results of studies concerning homosexuality in twins and other relatives of adult gays and lesbians (Bailey & Pillard, 1991; Bailey, Pillard, Neale, & Agyei, 1993). Note that homosexuality is more prevalent in their monozygotic (identical) twins than in their dizygotic (fraternal) twins. Another study with a

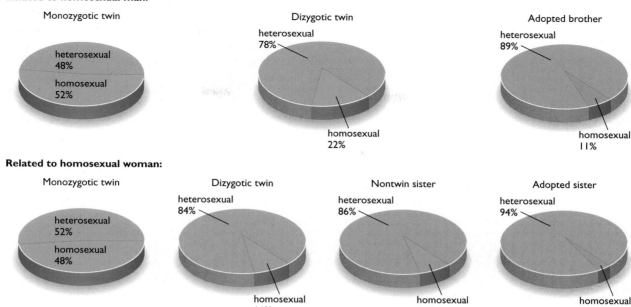

Related to homosexual man:

Monozygotic twin

heterosexual
48%

homosexual
52%

Dizygotic twin

heterosexual
78%

homosexual
22%

Adopted brother

heterosexual
89%

homosexual
11%

Related to homosexual woman:

Monozygotic twin

heterosexual
52%

homosexual
48%

Dizygotic twin

heterosexual
84%

homosexual
16%

Nontwin sister

heterosexual
86%

homosexual
14%

Adopted sister

heterosexual
94%

homosexual
6%

FIGURE 11.20 The probability of a homosexual orientation is higher among monozygotic twins of adult homosexuals than among their fraternal twins. The probability is higher among dizygotic twins than among adopted brothers or sisters who grew up together. These data suggest a genetic role in sexual orientation. (Based on results of Bailey & Pillard, 1991; Bailey, Pillard, Neale, & Agyei, 1993)

smaller sample showed the same trends (Kendler, Thornton, Gilman, & Kessler, 2000).

That trend suggests a genetic influence (not genetic "control") on homosexuality, and researchers have found a few genes that are more common in heterosexual than homosexual men (Mustanski et al., 2005). However, a genetic explanation raises an evolutionary question: How could a gene that increases homosexuality be widespread? Any gene that decreases the probability of reproducing becomes rare. One possible explanation relates to the finding that female relatives of gay men tend to have larger than average families (Camperio-Ciani, Corna, & Capiluppi, 2004). Male relatives of gay men also tend to be highly appealing to women (Zietsch et al., 2008). Even if gay men themselves have few children, increased reproduction by their brothers and sisters could spread genes that sometimes lead to homosexuality. However, a common estimate is that the average homosexual man has one fifth as many children as the average heterosexual man, and it would be surprising if the brothers and sisters have enough extra children to offset this decrease. Another possibility is that sexual orientation depends on the activation or inactivation of a gene rather than a genetic mutation. Environmental events can attach a methyl group (CH_3) to a gene and inactivate it, and a parent can pass an inactivated gene to the next generation (Bocklandt,

Horvath, Vilain, & Hamer, 2006). Such events could happen repeatedly regardless of evolutionary selection against individuals with the inactivated genes.

Another factor in sexual orientation is biological but not genetic: The probability of a homosexual orientation is slightly elevated among men who have an older brother. Having an older sister doesn't make a difference, nor does having an older adopted brother. It also doesn't make any difference whether the older brother lived in the same house with the younger brother or somewhere else. What matters is whether the mother had previously given birth to another son (Bogaert, 2006). One hypothesis to explain this tendency is that the first son sometimes causes the mother's immune system to build up antibodies that impair development of later sons (Bogaert, 2003).

Regardless of whether the original basis is genetics, prenatal environment, or something else, the question arises of how the body differs. Adult hormone levels are *not* different. On the average, adult homosexual people are similar to heterosexual people in their levels of testosterone and estrogen. Altering someone's hormone levels alters the strength of the sex drive but not sexual orientation (Tuiten et al., 2000). By analogy, changing your insulin or glucose levels affects your hunger but has little effect on what you consider good food.

However, it is possible that prenatal sex hormones influence later sexual orientation (McFadden, 2008). Presumably, if they do, they have some effect on the brain. One widely quoted and often misunderstood study reported a small but measurable difference between the brains of homosexual and heterosexual men. Let's examine the evidence.

What's the Evidence?
Sexual Orientation and Brain Anatomy

Animal studies have demonstrated that one section of the anterior hypothalamus is generally larger in males than in females. This brain area is necessary for the display of male-typical sexual activity in many mammalian species, and its size depends on prenatal hormones. Might part of the anterior hypothalamus differ between homosexual and heterosexual men?

Hypothesis INAH3, a particular cluster of neurons in the anterior hypothalamus, will be larger on average in the brains of heterosexual men than in the brains of homosexual men or heterosexual women.

Method Simon LeVay (1991) examined the brains of 41 adults who died at ages 26–59. AIDS was the cause of death for all 19 of the homosexual men in the study, 6 of the 16 heterosexual men, and 1 of the 6 heterosexual women. No brains of homosexual women were available for study. LeVay measured the sizes of four clusters of neurons in the anterior hypothalamus, including two clusters for which sex differences are common and two that are the same between the sexes.

Results Three of the four neuron clusters did not consistently vary in size among the groups LeVay studied. However, area INAH3 was on the average about twice as large in heterosexual men as it was in homosexual men and

about the same size in homosexual men as in heterosexual women. Figure 11.21 shows results for two representative individuals. The size of this area was about the same in heterosexual men who died of AIDS as in heterosexual men who died of other causes, so AIDS probably did not control the size of this area.

Interpretation These results suggest that the size of the INAH3 area may be related to heterosexual versus homosexual orientation, at least for some individuals. However, individuals within each group showed much variation. The anatomy does not correlate perfectly with behavior.

Like most studies, this one has its limitations: We do not know whether the people that LeVay studied were typical of others. One later study found that the INAH3 of homosexual men was intermediate in size between that of heterosexual men and heterosexual women (Byne et al., 2001). That study extended our knowledge by finding that the INAH3 varied among people because of differences in the size of neurons there, not the number of neurons.

Another limitation is that LeVay's study does not tell us whether brain anatomy influenced people's sexual orientation or whether their sexual activities altered brain anatomy. As mentioned in chapter 3, extensive experience modifies brain anatomy, even in adults.

So where does the research leave us? The evidence points to both genetics and prenatal environment, which probably alter certain aspects of brain anatomy in small ways. However, we need to know far more about how these biological factors interact with experience. At this point, we don't even know what kinds of experience are most relevant.

Uncertainty and tentative conclusions are not unusual in psychology. If you decide to become a psychologist, you will need to get used to the words "maybe" and "probably." As mentioned in chapter 2, most psychologists avoid the word "prove." Results merely increase or decrease their confidence in a conclusion.

18. Most studies find that gay men have approximately the same levels of testosterone in their blood as heterosexual men of the same age. Do such results conflict with the suggestion that prenatal hormonal conditions can predispose certain men to homosexuality?

Answer

18. Not necessarily. The suggestion is that prenatal hormones can alter early brain development. In adulthood, hormone levels are about average, but certain aspects of brain development have already been determined.

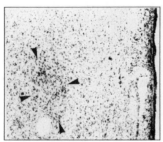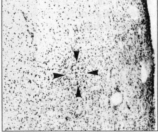

FIGURE 11.21 One section of the anterior hypothalamus (marked by arrows) is larger on the average in the brains of heterosexual men (a) than in the brains of homosexual men (b) or heterosexual women. Review Figure 11.7 for the location of the hypothalamus. (© S. LeVay, 1991, "A difference in hypothalamic structure between heterosexual and homosexual men," *Science 253*, 2034–2037)

In Closing

The Biology and Sociology of Sex

Studies of sexual motivation remind us that important motives have multiple determinants, both biological and social. We engage in sexual activity because it feels good, and we have evolved mechanisms that make it feel good because sex leads to reproduction. On the other hand, it often makes good biological sense to postpone reproduction until a safer time, so it is no wonder that nervousness decreases sexual arousal. We also engage in sexual activity because it cements a relationship with another person. Sex is one of the most powerful ways of drawing people together or tearing their relationship apart.

Society regulates sexual behavior strictly. The rules vary from one culture to another, but every culture has definite expectations about what people will do, when, and with whom. In short, we cannot make much sense of complex human behaviors without considering a range of biological and social influences.

SUMMARY

* *Variability in human sexual behavior.* Alfred Kinsey, who conducted the first extensive survey of human sexual behavior, found that sexual activity varies more widely than most people realize. (page 390)
* *More recent surveys.* Both men and women cite vaginal intercourse as their most preferred sexual activity. Most people remain sexually active even into their 70s if they remain healthy and have a healthy, willing partner. (page 391)
* *Sexual arousal.* Sexual arousal proceeds through four stages: excitement, plateau, orgasm, and resolution. (page 394)
* *Development of genitals.* In the early stages of development, the human fetus possesses anatomical structures that may develop into either male genitals (if testosterone levels are high enough) or female genitals (if testosterone levels are lower). (page 394)

* *Prevalence of homosexuality.* According to surveys in several countries, about 2 to 4% of adult men and somewhat fewer women regard themselves as primarily or exclusively homosexual. Sexual orientation varies in degree from exclusively homosexual to exclusively heterosexual with many intermediate gradations. (page 397)
* *Differences between men and women.* Nearly all men show a strong sexual response to either males or females but not both. Bisexuality is more common in women than men. (page 398)
* *Origins of sexual orientation.* Genetic influences and prenatal environment affect sexual orientation. On the average, heterosexual and homosexual men differ in the size of one structure in the hypothalamus that contributes to certain aspects of sexual behavior. Less is known about the role of experience in the development of sexual orientation. (page 398)

KEY TERMS

acquired immune deficiency syndrome (AIDS) (page 393)

bisexuality (page 398)

estrogen (page 395)

gender identity (page 394)

intersexes (page 395)

sexual orientation (page 397)

testosterone (page 395)

Work Motivation

• Why do some people try harder than others?

Sports competition is not a new idea. Archeologists in Mexico excavated an ancient human civilization from about 1400 B.C. and discovered, to their surprise, a ball court complete with nets (Hill, Blake, & Clark, 1998).

People compete against each other and against their own previous performance: Can I run farther, bicycle faster, or achieve a higher score than the last time? Striving for excellence on the job is similar. One of the key interests of employers and industrial/organizational psychologists is to understand what motivates workers to exert their full efforts. We shall consider "work" and "jobs" broadly, including schoolwork as well as employment.

GOALS AND DEADLINES

If you had no deadlines to meet, how hard would you work? When you have a deadline, do you sometimes wait until shortly before the deadline to start working in earnest? For example, are you reading this chapter now because you have to take a test on it tomorrow? (If so, don't feel too embarrassed. I wouldn't be sitting here revising this chapter right now except for the deadline my publisher gave me!)

Procrastination (putting off work until tomorrow) is a problem for many students and workers. Here is an experiment that beautifully illustrates the phenomenon.

What's the Evidence?
The Value of Deadlines

A professor set firm deadlines for one class and let another class choose their own deadlines to see whether those with evenly spaced deadlines would outperform those who had the opportunity to procrastinate (Ariely & Wertenbroch, 2002).

Critical Thinking

Hypothesis Students who are required, or who require themselves, to spread out their work will do better than those with an opportunity to wait until the end of the semester.

Method A professor taught two sections of the same course. Students were not randomly assigned to sections, but the students in the two sections had about equal academic records. The professor told one class that they had to write three papers, the first due after one third of the semester, the second after two thirds, and the third at the end of the semester. The other class was told that they could choose their own deadlines. They might make their three papers due after each third of the semester, all three at the end of the semester, or whatever else they chose. However, they had to decide by the second day of class, and whatever deadlines they chose would be enforced. That is, a paper that missed a deadline would be penalized, even though the student could have chosen a later deadline. At the end of the course, the professor graded all the papers blind to when they had been submitted.

Results If you were in the class that could choose the deadlines, what would you do? Twelve of the fifty-one students set all three deadlines on the final day of the semester. Presumably, they reasoned that they would try to finish their papers earlier, but they would

have the opportunity for extra time if they needed it. Other students, however, saw that if they set their deadlines at the end, they would expose themselves to a temptation that would be hard to resist, so they imposed earlier deadlines. Some spaced the deadlines evenly at one third, two thirds, and the end of the semester, and others compromised, setting deadlines for the first two papers later than one third and two thirds but not at the end of the semester.

On average, the students in the section with assigned deadlines got better grades than those who were allowed to choose their own deadlines. Of those permitted to choose their own deadlines, those who set their deadlines at approximately one third, two thirds, and the end of the semester did about the same as those with assigned deadlines and much better than those who set all their deadlines at the end.

Interpretation If the professor had studied only one class and let them choose their own deadlines, we could draw no conclusion from the finding that those who spread out their deadlines did the best. It could mean that early deadlines help, but it could also mean that better students set earlier deadlines. However, the early-deadline students merely matched the assigned-deadline students, whereas the late-deadline students did significantly worse. Therefore, the conclusion follows that setting deadlines does help. If you are required to do part of your work at a time, you manage your time to accomplish it. If your deadlines are all at the end, you face a powerful temptation to delay your work.

19. What conclusion would have followed if the early-deadline students did better than the late-deadline students did but that the class on the average did as well as the assigned-deadline students?

Concept Check

Answer

19. If students in the two sections had equal performance overall, we could not conclude that deadlines help. Instead, the conclusion would be that brighter students tend to set earlier deadlines.

Overcoming Procrastination

Given the importance of working steadily toward a goal, how can we overcome the temptation to procrastinate? Part of the answer is confidence. People who worry about failing have trouble getting started. A little encouragement or praise often helps (Fritzsche, Young, & Hickson, 2003).

You increase your likelihood of an action if you state a definite plan of when, where, and how you will do it. Generally, if you think about what you will do 10 years from now, you imagine only vague generalities. If you think about what you will do tomorrow morning, you imagine it with specific details. Conversely, if you imagine some task only as a vague abstraction, you are likely to postpone it. If you imagine the task in detail, you are likely to begin it sooner (McCrea, Liberman, Trope, & Sherman, 2008). For example, suppose you set a goal to exercise more and eat a healthier diet. Fine, but if you mean it, be more specific. Decide what kind of exercise you will do, when, and where. If you want to eat a healthier diet, decide to eat a salad instead of a hamburger for lunch tomorrow, or vow to buy fruits and vegetables the next time you go to the store. If you set specific plans, then the relevant situation will evoke the behavior (Milne, Orbell, & Sheeran, 2002; Verplanken & Faes, 1999).

If you find yourself procrastinating something, a good strategy is to make a decision about something else first, even something unimportant. For example, which do you like better, elephants or hippopotamuses? Where would you prefer to go on vacation, Hawaii or the Caribbean? Just after people have made quick, no-cost decisions like these, they become more likely than usual to take action of almost any kind, such as buying a new computer (Xu & Wyer, 2008). They get into the mind-set of deciding and acting instead of delaying and doing nothing.

Also try this: First, identify some activity that you do less often than you think you should—such as flossing your teeth, cleaning your room, or calling your grandparents. *Please choose an activity.* Now, estimate how likely you are to complete that activity at least once in the next week. *Please make that estimate.* If you have followed instructions, you have just increased your actual probability of engaging in that behavior! *Simply estimating your probability of doing some desirable activity increases your probability of that action* (Levav & Fitzsimons, 2006). Psychologists call this phenomenon the mere measurement effect.

20. How could you increase your probability of getting a good start on writing a term paper?

21. How could someone use the mere measurement effect to persuade you to do something?

Answers

20. First, find some way to boost your confidence. Then make specific plans, such as, "I will spend Monday night at the library looking for materials."

21. If someone asks you how likely you are to vote for a candidate, give money to a charity, or buy a new car, answering the question increases your probability of doing so.

High and Low Goals

Which of these goals would be best?

- I will work for an A in every course (a difficult goal).
- I will work for at least a C average (an easy goal).
- I will do my best (a vague goal).

The research says that "do your best" is the same as no goal at all. Although it sounds nice, you are never behind schedule on achieving it, so it doesn't motivate extra work. The most effective goals are difficult but realistic (Locke & Latham, 2002). For example, you might set the goal of getting the best grades you have ever received in a semester or of improving on your best previous score in some kind of athletic competition. People who set high but realistic goals are said to have a high need for achievement. *They feel good when they accomplish something that they weren't sure they could achieve.* Something accomplished too easily doesn't give that same feeling (Labroo & Kim, 2009). People with a low need for achievement either set no goals, or goals so low they can achieve them easily, or goals so unrealistically high that they have an excuse for not reaching them. One way psychologists measure need for achievement is by showing people pictures, asking people to tell stories about the pictures, and counting the number of references to accomplishments and success.

Many companies set goals for their workers, and again, the goals are most effective if they are high but realistic. Suppose a company announces that it will provide a generous bonus for all employees if profits increase by 10% this year. The employees will work to reach that level if they see a realistic chance of achieving it. If they think that an extraordinary effort could achieve only a 7 or 8% increase and that nothing less than 10% will qualify for the bonus, they will give up.

For any goal to be effective, certain conditions are necessary (Locke & Latham, 2002). One is to take the goal seriously, preferably by committing to it publicly. If you want to get better grades next

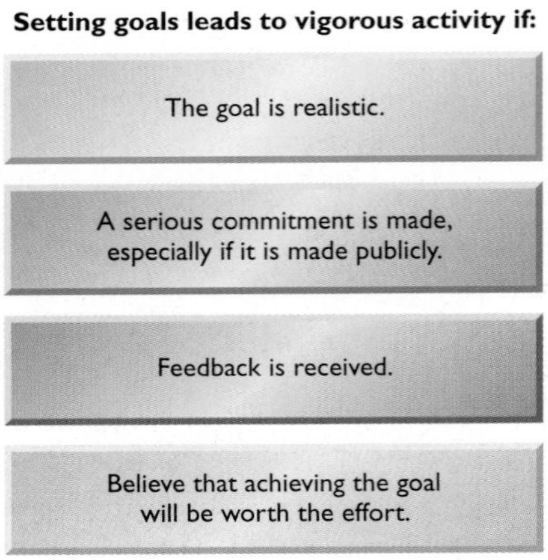

Setting goals leads to vigorous activity if:

The goal is realistic.

A serious commitment is made, especially if it is made publicly.

Feedback is received.

Believe that achieving the goal will be worth the effort.

FIGURE 11.22 The conditions under which goals are most effective in motivating vigorous efforts.

semester, tell your friends about it. Also you should receive frequent feedback about your progress. If you are aiming for all As and you get a B on a test in one course, you know you have to study harder in that course. If your goal is to increase profits by 10% and you learn that they are currently up 9%, you know you need to work a little harder. Finally, you have to believe that the reward will be worth your effort. Do you care enough about your grades to make sacrifices in your social life? Do you trust your boss to pay the bonuses as promised? Some employees do, but others consider their bosses lying, cheating scoundrels (Craig & Gustafson, 1998) (see Figure 11.22).

22. Under what conditions would people be most likely to keep their New Year's resolutions?

Answer

22. A New Year's resolution is like any other goal: People are more likely to keep it if it is realistic, if they state the resolution publicly, and if they receive feedback on how well they are doing.

Realistic Goals

Given that the best goals are high but realistic, what goal is realistic? Most Americans regard themselves as healthier than average, smarter, more creative, and better than average at almost everything. As part of their optimism, they underestimate the time needed for holiday shopping, writing a term paper, remodeling their kitchen, or completing almost any other task. Companies underestimate how long they will need to bring a product to market, reorganize their sales staff, or finish a building (Dunning, Heath, & Suls, 2005). Governments underestimate the time and cost of major projects. Americans are not alone. The Sydney Opera House in Australia was expected to be complete by 1963 at a cost of $7 million. It was finally completed in 1973 at a cost of $102 million.

One group of senior college students were asked to estimate "realistically" how soon they would complete their senior honors thesis—a major research paper. They were also asked what would be the latest time they might finish if ev-

erything went wrong. On the average, they actually finished their papers 1 week *later* than what they said was the worst-case scenario (Buehler, Griffin, & Ross, 1994).

The message is not to become discouraged but to allow yourself more time than you think you need—and get started sooner than you think is necessary. Major tasks usually take more work than expected.

23. If you are supervising employees who say they can finish a challenging job in 6 weeks, should you promise them a bonus for finishing in 6 weeks?

Answer

23. Your employees probably underestimate how long the task will take, and a goal of finishing in 6 weeks may be unrealistic. You might offer a bonus for finishing in 6 weeks, but you should also offer a decent incentive for finishing in 7 or 8.

Persistence Toward Goals

Why do some people become fabulously successful while others lag behind? Many people with the ability to succeed give up after a few discouragements, but others keep on trying. John Irving, one of America's most successful novelists, is dyslexic. By his own assessment, he succeeded only because of hard work and a willingness to undertake many revisions (Amabile, 2001).

You will hear people say, "Never give up." That is a good motto, usually. People who persist longer toward their goals tend to be more successful, happier, and more resilient in the face of stress. However, what happens when success becomes impossible? Despite your best efforts, you did not make the team. You did not get accepted by your favorite college. The person you wanted to date has married someone else. At some point, you have to let it go. People who have difficulty giving up after their goals become impossible tend to have problems in both physical and mental health (G. E. Miller & Wrosch, 2007). You should never give up . . . until success is impossible. Then you should give up.

JOB DESIGN AND JOB SATISFACTION

People work harder, more effectively, and with more satisfaction at some jobs than at others. Why?

Two Approaches to Job Design

Imagine that you are starting or reorganizing a company, and you must decide how to divide the workload. Should you make the jobs challenging and interesting at the risk of being difficult? Or should you make them simple and foolproof at the risk of being boring?

The answer depends on what you assume about the workers and their motivations. *According to the* scientific-management approach to job design, also known as *Theory X, most employees are lazy, indifferent, and uncreative.* Therefore, employers should make the work as foolproof as possible and supervise the workers to make sure they are doing each task the right way to save time and avoid injury (Figure 11.23). The employer leaves nothing to chance or to the worker's own initiative (McGregor, 1960).

According to an alternative view, the human-relations approach to job design, also known as *Theory Y, employees like variety in their job, a sense of accomplishment, and a sense of responsibility* (McGregor, 1960). Therefore, employers should enrich the jobs, giving each employee responsibility for meaningful tasks. For example, a financial services corporation that followed the scientific-management approach would have each employee keep just one kind of records for many clients, developing expertise at a narrow task. The same company, reorganized according to the human-relations approach, might put each employee in charge of fewer clients, keeping track of all the information about those clients. Employees with enriched jobs generally report greater satisfaction (Campion & McClelland, 1991). From the employer's standpoint, the enriched jobs have many advantages but two disadvantages: It takes longer to train the workers than it would with simpler jobs, and the workers performing enriched jobs expect to be paid more!

Which approach is better? It depends. Consider an analogy to education: Professor X tells students exactly what to read and when and precisely what to do to get a good grade. (This course is analogous to the scientific-management approach.) Professor Y outlines the general issues, provides a list of suggested readings, lets the students control class discussion, and invites students to create their own ideas for projects. (This course is analogous to the human-relations approach, though perhaps more extreme.) Which class would you like better?

If you are highly interested in the topic and have ideas of your own, you would love Professor Y's course and would consider Professor X's course tedious and insulting. But if you are taking the course just to satisfy a requirement, you might appreciate the precise structure of Professor X's class. The same is true of jobs. Some workers, especially the younger and brighter ones, thrive on the challenge of an enriched job, but others prefer a simple, stable set of tasks (Arnold & House, 1980; Campion & Thayer, 1985; Hackman & Lawler, 1971).

24. "I want my employees to enjoy their work and to feel pride in their achievements." Does that statement reflect a belief in the human-relations approach or the scientific-management approach?

Answer

24. It reflects the human-relations approach.

Job Satisfaction

Your choice of career profoundly affects the quality of your life. Between the ages of 20 and 70, you will spend about half of your waking hours on the job. You want to spend that time on a job you like. How much you like your job correlates moderately well with how well you perform it (Judge, Thoresen, Bono, & Patton, 2001). The causation probably goes in several directions: High job satisfaction improves performance, good performance improves job satisfaction, and highly conscientious people tend to be satisfied with life and successful on their job (Judge et al., 2001; Tett & Burnett, 2003).

However, the correlation is not high. You can probably imagine several explanations. For example, some people with excellent job performance are not highly satisfied because they want a better job.

Obviously, job satisfaction depends largely on the job itself, including the interest level, the pay, coworkers, and management. It also depends on the worker's personality. Some people are just easier to please than others. Comparisons of identical and fraternal twins indicate that job satisfaction is highly heritable (Arvey, McCall, Bouchard, Taubman, & Cavanaugh, 1994). If your close relatives say they are happy with their jobs, you probably are also, even though you have a different job. You don't inherit your job, but you inherit your disposition. Some people find much to like about their jobs, and others find much to complain about (Ilies & Judge, 2003; Judge & Larsen, 2001; Thoresen, Kaplan, Barsky, Warren, & de Chermont, 2003).

On the average, older workers express higher job satisfaction than younger workers do (Pond & Geyer, 1991) (see Figure 11.24). One possible explanation is that older workers have better, higher paying jobs. Another is that today's young people are harder to satisfy than their elders ever were (Beck & Wilson, 2000). Another possibility is that many

FIGURE 11.23 Psychologists have conducted research to determine the best, safest, most efficient ways to perform even simple tasks. For example, the drawing on the left shows the right way to lift a brick, and the drawing on the right shows the wrong way, according to Gilbreth (1911).

Possible reasons why older workers report greater job satisfaction than younger workers

Better pay
Greater responsibility
Greater challenges
Comfort of status quo
Less perceived likelihood of getting a better job
Previous experience in less suitable jobs

FIGURE 11.24 Psychologists propose several reasons why most older workers report higher job satisfaction than younger workers do.

young workers start in the wrong job and find a more suitable one later. Yet another is that many young people are still considering the possibility of changing jobs. By middle age, most people reconcile themselves to whatever jobs they have.

Pay and Job Satisfaction

An employer who wants to keep workers satisfied gives careful attention to the pay scale. Obviously, workers want to be paid well, but they also need to perceive the pay scale as fair. In one classic experiment, some workers were led to believe that they had been hired in spite of less than average qualifications for the job. They worked harder than average, apparently to convince the employer that they deserved the job, but perhaps also to convince themselves that they earned their pay (J. S. Adams, 1963).

Employees who perceive their bosses as operating unfairly often start looking for another job. They also stop doing the "good citizen" behaviors that help the company, such as keeping the building tidy, helping other workers, and attending extra meetings after working hours (Simons & Roberson, 2003). At the opposite extreme, some workers develop an emotional commitment to their company or organization, which leads them to work loyally and energetically, well beyond what they are paid to do (Meyer, Becker, & Vandenberghe, 2004; Seo, Barrett, & Bartunek, 2004).

Money is certainly part of anyone's work motivation. Presumably, you would quit your job if your employer stopped paying you. However, pay is not the complete motivation. Many people take a lower paying job because it offers a sense of accomplishment or highly pleasant working conditions. Even after people retire, many find that they miss the work. For many people, work is an enjoyable, important part of who they are.

25. What are some factors that contribute to high job satisfaction?

Concept Check

Answer

25. Factors associated with high job satisfaction include high ability to perform the job, a happy personality, a perception that the pay scale is fair, and old age.

LEADERSHIP

How hard you are motivated to work also depends on how you perceive your organization's leadership. Some employers inspire deep loyalties and intense efforts, whereas others barely get their workers to do the minimum. (The same is true of college professors, athletic coaches, and political leaders.)

What does good leadership require? Early psychological research found no consistent personality difference between effective and ineffective leaders. Effective leaders were not consistently more gregarious, outspoken, or anything else. You know there has to be something wrong here. If good and poor leaders really do not differ, we could choose company executives, college presidents, or state governors at random. Later researchers concluded that no single personality factor is decisive because what matters is a combination of many qualities. A good leader has the right combination of personality, intelligence, expertise, motives, values, and people-handling skills (Zaccaro, 2007).

Furthermore, what constitutes good leadership depends on the situation. Just as no one is creative in all situations—a creative poet probably can't propose creative solutions to an automobile repair problem—no one is a good leader in all situations (Vroom & Jago, 2007). A good leader of a committee meeting gives everyone a chance to express an opinion before putting an issue to a vote. Someone leading a field trip for a class of 6-year-olds makes the decisions and tells the children what to do. A dictatorial approach would almost always fail in a committee meeting, and asking the 6-year-olds to debate and vote is not ordinarily the best way to plan a day.

Industrial-organizational psychologists distinguish between transformational and transactional leadership styles. A **transformational leader** *articulates a vision of the future, intellectually stimulates subordinates, and motivates them to use their imagination to advance the organization.* A **transactional leader** *tries to make the organization more efficient at doing what it is al-*

ready doing by providing rewards (mainly pay) for effective work. A leader can be either of these, both, or neither. People who are described as transformational leaders are perceived as effective in almost any organization (Lowe, Kroeck, & Sivasubramaniam, 1996). This result should not be surprising. You would hardly describe your leader as "a visionary who intellectually stimulates me and motivates me to reach my potential" and then say your leader is doing a bad job overall. Transactional leaders are often effective in organizations where activities stay the same from year to year (Lowe et al., 1996).

26. Do transformational leaders emphasize intrinsic or extrinsic motivation? Which do transactional leaders emphasize?

Answer

26. A transformational leader emphasizes intrinsic motivation, the desire to achieve excellence. A transactional leader applies rewards to get workers to do their current jobs efficiently and so emphasizes extrinsic motivation.

module

11.4

In Closing

Work as Another Kind of Motivation

Work motivation has important points in common with hunger, sex, and other motivations. For example, they are all marked by persistent and varied behaviors to reach a goal. However, work also has some special features. One is the aspect of striving for excellence. Work is often competitive in a way that eating and sex are not. (Oh, I suppose you could compete at eating or sex, but most people don't.) Striving for excellence is never fully satisfied. Those who achieve their goals in business or other competitive endeavors usually respond by setting new, higher goals. In short, any kind of motivation requires a kind of striving, but each kind of striving has its own special features.

SUMMARY

- *Deadlines.* In general, people who are forced to meet deadlines manage their time to do so. If it is possible to postpone all work until later, many find it hard to resist that temptation. Setting deadlines for parts of one's own work can help. (page 402)
- *Overcoming procrastination.* People get started toward their goals if they set specific plans about what they will do, when, and where. Making any kind of decision helps end procrastination. (page 402)
- *Goal setting.* Setting a goal motivates strong effort if the goal is high but realistic. Other important factors include making a serious commitment to the goal, receiving feedback on progress, and believing that the goal will bring a fair reward. (page 403)
- *Making goals realistic.* People tend to underestimate how much time and effort they will need to achieve their goals. It is best to plan for more time and resources than seem necessary and to start as quickly as possible. (page 404)

- *Job design.* According to the scientific-management approach, jobs should be made simple and foolproof. According to the human-management approach, jobs should be made interesting enough to give workers a sense of achievement. (page 404)
- *Job satisfaction.* Job satisfaction is moderately correlated with good performance on the job for several reasons. People with a happy disposition are more likely than others to be satisfied with their jobs, as are older workers in general. Job satisfaction also requires a perception that the pay scale is fair. (page 405)
- *Leadership.* The demands of leadership depend on the situation. Leaders who inspire their associates are perceived as effective in almost any organization. Those perceived as using rewards to get employees to do their work efficiently are effective in situations when the business is stable. (page 406)

exploration and study

Why Does This Matter to Me?

SOCIAL RESPONSIBILITY AND PSYCHOLOGY

Many environmental and societal problems are caused by human behavior. Psychologists can help steer the course of our future toward more socially responsible and sustainable outcomes. Students of today need to be ever mindful of the link between human behavior and its impact on the environment and our communities.

"Motivated Behaviors" and Environmental Responsibility: A Step Further

People are becoming more concerned about conserving natural resources by recycling, minimizing use of fossil fuels, and so forth. Implementing good intentions is difficult, however, because people see little or no immediate consequence to their actions. Based on material in this chapter, can you suggest ways to motivate yourself or others?

Your Work Environment

Do you work, and if so, is your workplace trying to be socially and environmentally responsible? What would motivate your employers to embrace more sustainable practices? Visit www.cengage.com/psychology/kalat for some workplace sustainability tips.

Join the iChapters Plant a Tree Drive!

To show its support of the environmental movement, iChapters is planting a tree on behalf of each fan of the iChapters Facebook Page and for every 10 questions answered correctly in our quiz.
http://www.ichapters.com/plantatree/

Exploration and Study

SUGGESTIONS FOR FURTHER EXPLORATION

In addition to the study materials provided at the end of each module, you may supplement your review of this chapter with the following book and website suggestions or by using one or more of the book's electronic resources, which include its companion website, interactive Cengage Learning eBook, and CengageNOW. Brief descriptions of these resources follow. For more information, visit **www.cengage.com/psychology/kalat**.

ADDITIONAL RESOURCES

The book's companion website, accessible from **www.cengage.com/psychology/kalat**, provides a wide range of study resources such as an interactive glossary, flashcards, tutorial quizzes, updated web links, and Try It Yourself activities.

    CengageNOW with Critical Thinking Videos is an easy-to-use resource that helps you study in less time to get the grade you want. An online study system, CengageNOW gives you the option of taking a diagnostic pretest for each chapter. The system uses the results of each pretest to create personalized chapter study plans for you. The Personalized Study Plans

- Help you save study time by identifying areas on which you should concentrate and give you one-click access to corresponding pages of the interactive Cengage Learning eBook;

- Provide interactive exercises and study tools to help you fully understand chapter concepts; and
- Include a posttest for you to take to confirm that you are ready to move on to the next chapter.

Find critical thinking videos like this one in your CengageNOW product, which offer an opportunity for you to learn more about psychological research on different topics.

Weight Control

Books

Diamond, J. (1997). *Why is sex fun?* New York: Basic Books. Exploration of the "why" of sex. Why did we evolve to reproduce sexually? Why is human sex in several ways different from that of other animals?

Websites

Links to the websites described below are kept current and can be found at **www.cengage.com/psychology/kalat.**

Obesity

Check all kinds of information about this serious problem.

Sexual Behavior

See the latest research reports by the research institute that Kinsey founded.

Intersexes

Information from a support group for people with ambiguous genitalia.

© Sonya Farrell/Riser/Getty Images

12 chapter

Emotions, Stress, and Health

Consider This:

Suppose your romantic partner asks, "How much do you love me?" You reply, "Oh, compared to other loving couples, probably about average." "What?" your partner screams. "Average? Average!" You are in deep trouble, even though your answer was probably true. (That's what "average" means!)

If that was the wrong answer, what could you answer? "Forty-two cubic meters per second"? No, we don't measure love in physical units. So instead, you say, "I love you more than you can possibly imagine. More than any other person has ever loved." That

Would you make more intelligent decisions if you could thoroughly suppress your emotions, like the fictional character Spock? After brain damage that impairs emotion, people make worse than average decisions.

was a good answer, and now your partner is happy, even though the answer is almost certainly false.

When we are talking about emotions—love, hate, happiness, sadness, fear, anger, whatever—measurement is a serious problem. Psychologists make reasonably good measurements of sensation, perception, learning, memory, and cognition. As we now move to the areas of emotion, social behavior, and personality, the measurement problems become more severe, and consequently, the progress has been slower. In this chapter, we consider what psychologists have learned so far about emotions despite the difficulties.

The Nature of Emotion

- How does arousal relate to emotion?
- How many kinds of emotions do people have?
- How do emotions influence our thinking?

Imagine trying to list all the emotions you feel during a day. You might feel frightened, angry, sad, joyful, disgusted, worried, bored, ashamed, frustrated, contemptuous, embarrassed, surprised, and confused. But which of those states are really emotions? And how many are *different* emotions instead of overlapping or synonymous conditions?

Although most people think they know what they mean by the term *emotion,* defining it is difficult. Psychologists usually define it in terms of a combination of cognitions, physiology, feelings, and actions (Keltner & Shiota, 2003; Plutchik, 1982). For example, you might have the *cognition* "he was unfair to me," *physiological* changes that include increased heart rate, a *feeling* you call anger, and *behaviors* such as a clenched fist. However, that definition implies that the four kinds of components always occur together. Do they? Many psychologists maintain instead that you could feel fear, anger, or other emotions without knowing why; that is, you could have the physiological, feeling, and behavioral aspects of emotion without the cognition (Berkowitz, 1990; Parkinson, 2007; Ruys & Stapel, 2008).

For the way most people use the term *emotion,* the key component is the feeling. If you say you feel frightened but don't know why, most people would agree that you are experiencing an emotion. If you say, "I recognize that this is a dangerous situation," but you feel nothing, your experience is unemotional.

MEASURING EMOTIONS

As stated in chapter 1, research progress depends on good measurement. Psychologists measure emotions by self-reports, behavioral observations, and physiological measures. Each method has its strengths and weaknesses.

Self-Reports

Psychologists most often measure emotions by asking people how happy they are, how nervous, and so forth. Self-reports are quick and easy, but their accuracy is limited. If you rated your happiness 4 yesterday and 7 today, it seems clear that you have become happier. But if your friend rates her happiness 6, are you happier today than she is? Maybe, maybe not.

Behavioral Observations

We infer emotion from people's behavior and its context. If we see someone shriek and run away, we infer fear. When you were an infant, your parents must have inferred your emotions before you could report them verbally. They had to in order to teach you the words for emotions! At some point, you screamed and someone said you were "afraid." At another time, you smiled and someone said you were "happy."

We especially watch facial expressions. People sometimes control their expressions voluntarily. However, *very brief, sudden emotional expressions*, called **microexpressions**, are harder to control. For example, someone who is pretending to be calm or happy may show occasional brief signs of anger, fear, or sadness (Ekman, 2001). With practice (or a videotape that can be played slowly), psychologists identify emotions that people would like to hide. However, microexpressions are infrequent, and we cannot rely on them for much information (Porter & ten Brinke, 2008).

Physiological Measures

Originally, the term *emotion* referred to turbulent motion. Centuries ago, people described thunder as an "emotion of the atmosphere." Eventually, people limited the term to body motions and their associated feelings, but the idea still includes turbulent arousal.

Any stimulus that arouses emotion alters the activity of the **autonomic nervous system**, *the section of the nervous system that controls the organs* such as the heart and intestines. The word *autonomic* means "independent" (autonomous). Biologists once believed that the autonomic nervous system was independent of the brain and spinal cord. We now know that the brain and spinal cord regulate the autonomic nervous system, but the term *autonomic* remains.

Ordinarily, an emotional state elicits a tendency toward vigorous action, even if we suppress that tendency. Here, a soldier disarms a mine.

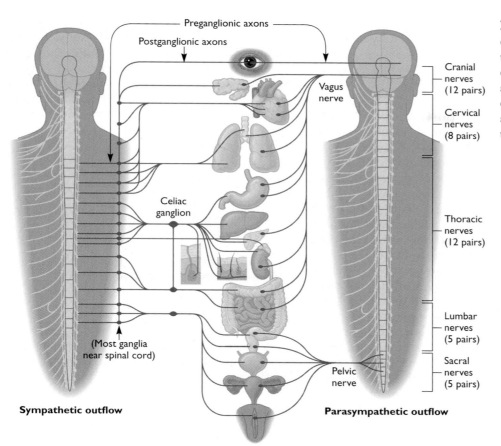

Preganglionic axons

Postganglionic axons

Vagus nerve

Celiac ganglion

(Most ganglia near spinal cord)

Pelvic nerve

Sympathetic outflow

Parasympathetic outflow

Cranial nerves (12 pairs)

Cervical nerves (8 pairs)

Thoracic nerves (12 pairs)

Lumbar nerves (5 pairs)

Sacral nerves (5 pairs)

FIGURE 12.1 The autonomic nervous system consists of the sympathetic and parasympathetic nervous systems, which sometimes act in opposing ways and sometimes cooperate. The sympathetic nervous system readies the body for emergency action. The parasympathetic nervous system supports digestive and other nonemergency functions.

The autonomic nervous system has two branches, the sympathetic and the parasympathetic nervous systems (Figure 12.1). *Two chains of neuron clusters just to the left and right of the spinal cord* comprise the sympathetic nervous system, *which arouses the body for vigorous action.* It is often called the "fight-or-flight" system because it increases your heart rate, breathing rate, sweating, and flow of epinephrine (EP-i-NEF-rin; also known as adrenaline), thereby preparing you for vigorous activity. Different situations activate different parts of the sympathetic nervous system to facilitate different kinds of activity.

The parasympathetic nervous system consists of *neurons whose axons extend from the medulla* (see Figure 12.1) *and the lower part of the spinal cord to neuron clusters near the organs. The parasympathetic nervous system decreases the*

The sympathetic nervous system prepares the body for a vigorous burst of activity.

heart rate and promotes digestion and other non-emergency functions. Both the sympathetic and parasympathetic systems send axons to the heart, the digestive system, and most other organs. A few organs, such as the adrenal gland, receive only sympathetic input.

Both systems are constantly active, although one system can temporarily dominate. If you spot some danger at a distance (in either time or space), you pay increased attention to it with mainly parasympathetic activity. If the danger is close enough to require action, you shift to vigorous sympathetic activity (Löw, Lang, Smith, & Bradley, 2008). Many situations activate parts of both systems (Berntson, Cacioppo, & Quigley, 1993). Some emergency situations increase your heart rate and sweating (sympathetic responses) and also promote bowel and bladder evacuation (parasympathetic responses). Have you ever been so frightened that you thought you might lose your bladder control?

Researchers measure sympathetic nervous system arousal as an indicator of strong emotion. For example, moment-by-moment changes in the electrical conductivity across the skin indicate instantaneous changes in the amount of sweating, a sympathetic nervous system response. Strong emotions also make people breathe faster (Gomez, Zimmermann, Guttormsen-Schär, & Danuser, 2005). However, remember that the sympathetic nervous system is the fight-*or*-flight system, so its responses could indicate anger, fear, or any other intense emotion. Physiological measurements do not tell us *which* emotion someone is feeling.

Brain measurements are also not very specific. Figure 12.2 summarizes the results of many studies using PET and fMRI brain scans (see chapter 3) to measure which brain areas became active when different emotions were aroused in various ways (Phan, Wager, Taylor, & Liberzon, 2002). As you can see, the areas aroused by a given emotion largely overlap those aroused by other emotions.

....

1. Why should we not insist on verbal reports to infer or measure emotions?
2. Why are physiological measurements more helpful for determining the intensity of an emotion than for identifying which emotion is present?

Answers

1. It would be impossible to teach a child (or anyone else) the words for emotions unless we had already inferred the emotions from the individual's behavior.
2. The sympathetic nervous system is aroused by either anger or fear (fight or flight), and therefore, its arousal indicates the strength of one or the other but does not identify which one. Also, different emotions activate overlapping brain areas.

....

EMOTION, AROUSAL, AND ACTION

How do emotional cognitions, feelings, behavior, and arousal relate to one another? William James, the founder of American psychology, proposed one of psychology's first theories.

The James-Lange Theory of Emotions

According to common sense, you feel sad and therefore you cry. You become afraid and therefore you tremble. You feel angry and therefore your face turns red. In 1884 William James and Carl Lange independently proposed the opposite. According to the James-Lange theory, *your interpretation of a stimulus evokes autonomic changes and sometimes muscle actions. Your perception of those changes is the feeling aspect of your emotion.* In James's original article, he said simply that the situation (e.g., the sight of a bear) gives rise to an action (e.g., running away), and your perception of the action is the emotion. That is, you don't run away because you are afraid; you feel afraid because you perceive yourself running away. In response to his critics, he

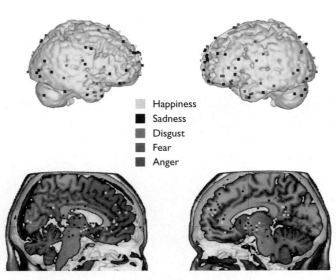

Happiness
Sadness
Disgust
Fear
Anger

FIGURE 12.2 Researchers aroused emotions in various ways and then used PET or fMRI scans to identify which brain areas became aroused. No brain area appears specific to one type of emotion. (© Phan, K. L., Wager, T., Taylor, S. F., & Liberzon, I (2002). "Functional neuroanatomy of emotion: A meta-analysis of emotion activation studies in PET and fMRI." *NeuroImage, 16,* 331–348. Photo reprinted with the permission of the author and publisher.)

clarified his view (James, 1894): Obviously, the sight of a bear doesn't automatically cause you to run away. You first appraise the situation. If it is a caged bear or a trained circus bear, you do not run. If it appears dangerous, you do run. So your appraisal of the situation is the cognitive aspect of the emotion. Your perception of yourself running away, with heart rate and breathing rate soaring, is what you *feel* as the emotion. That is,

Situation →   Appraisal →   Actions →   Perception of the actions
           = cognitive   = physiological   = feeling aspect of the
             aspect of the   and behavioral   emotion
             emotion   aspects

Given this interpretation, the James-Lange theory seems reasonable. Indeed, it is hard to imagine where the feeling aspect would come from if the body didn't react in some way. Furthermore, much evidence supports the theory. The main types of evidence are that people with little physical reaction feel little emotion, and people who feel a stronger reaction feel an enhanced emotion.

Effects of Decreased Reaction

According to the James-Lange theory, people with weak physiological responses still identify emotional situations cognitively, but they should have little emotional feeling. People with paralyzed muscles because of spinal cord injuries report normal or nearly normal emotions (Cobos, Sánchez, García, Vera, & Vila, 2002). However, people with weakened autonomic responses report weaker emotional feelings. In pure autonomic failure, *an uncommon condition with unknown cause, the autonomic nervous system stops regulating the organs.* That is, nothing in the nervous system influences heart rate, breathing rate, and so forth. One effect is that a patient who stands up quickly faints because none of the usual reflexes kick in to prevent gravity from drawing blood from the head. With regard to emotions, affected people still recognize that some situation calls for anger, fear, or sadness, but they report that their emotions feel less intense than before (Critchley, Mathias, & Dolan, 2001). The cognitive aspect of emotion remains, but the feeling is weak, exactly as the James-Lange theory predicts.

Effects of Increased Perceived Arousal

Suppose researchers mold your posture and breathing pattern into the pattern typical of some emotion. Will you then feel that emotion? Have someone read these instructions to you, or read them to someone else and check what happens:

> Lower your eyebrows toward your cheeks. Sigh. Close your mouth and push your lower lip slightly upward. Sigh again. Sit back in your chair and draw your feet under the chair. Be sure you feel no tension in your legs or feet. Sigh again. Fold your hands in your lap, cupping one in the other. Drop your head, letting your rib cage fall, letting most of your body go limp, except for a little tension in the back of your neck and across your shoulder blades. Sigh again.

Most people who follow these directions report starting to feel sad (Flack, Laird, & Cavallaro, 1999; Philippot, Chapelle, & Blairy, 2002). Instructions to hold the posture and breathing pattern characteristic of happiness, anger, or fear induce those emotions, too, although the instructions for fear sometimes induce anger and those for anger sometimes induce fear. Fear and anger are physiologically similar.

With studies like this, one worry is that the participants guess what the experimenter is trying to demonstrate. (Recall the idea of "demand characteristics" from chapter 2.) One group of researchers found a clever way to conceal the purpose of the study. They told participants they were studying how people with paralyzed arms learn to write. The participants were told to hold a pen either with their teeth or with their protruded lips, as in Figure 12.3, and then to make check marks to rate the funniness of cartoons.

When they held the pen with their teeth, their faces were forced into a near smile, and they rated the cartoons as very funny. When they held the pen with their lips, they could not smile, and they rated the cartoons as less funny (Strack, Martin, & Stepper, 1988). Try holding a pen one way and then the other while reading newspaper cartoons. Do you notice a difference? However, although a smile slightly facilitates happiness or amusement, it is not necessary for them. Children who are born with a facial paralysis that prevents them from smiling still feel joy and show a sense of humor (G. Miller, 2007b).

FIGURE 12.3 Facial expression can influence mood. When people hold a pen with their teeth (a), they rate cartoons as funnier than when they hold it with their lips (b).

In a similar study, researchers said they were studying people's ability to do two tasks at once. The motor task was to hold together the tips of two golf tees, which they attached to the participants' eyebrows. The only way to hold them together is to frown; so without saying "frown," they got people to frown. The cognitive task was to rate the pleasantness of photos. While people were frowning, they rated most photos less pleasant than people usually do (Larsen, Kasimatis, & Frey, 1992).

....

3. According to the James-Lange theory, do you run away from something because you are afraid of it?

4. What happens to emotions in people with conditions that weaken their autonomic responses? What happens when people adopt postures and breathing patterns characteristic of a particular emotion? How do these results relate to the James-Lange theory?

Answers

3. No. According to the James-Lange theory, you feel fear because you are running away.

4. People with pure autonomic failure have no systematic autonomic changes, and their emotions feel weak. People who adopt postures and breathing patterns characteristic of a certain emotion become slightly more likely to feel that emotion. These results confirm the predictions of the James-Lange theory.

Schachter and Singer's Theory of Emotions

All right, once you get your body into a hunched-over posture with tension only in your neck and you are constantly sighing, you feel sad. But how did you get into that posture in the first place? Ordinarily, your appraisal of the situation entered into the process.

Furthermore, how do you know whether you are angry or frightened? Anger and fear produce very similar physiological responses. Your autonomic changes don't tell you which emotion you are experiencing (Lang, 1994).

Because of such considerations, Stanley Schachter and Jerome Singer (1962) proposed a theory of how we identify one emotion from another. According to Schachter and Singer's theory of emotions (Figure 12.4), *the intensity of the physiological state—that is, the degree of sympathetic nervous system arousal—determines the intensity of the emotion, but a cognitive appraisal of the situation identifies the type of emotion.* A given type of arousal might produce an

experience of fear, anger, joy, or none of these depending on the situation. Schachter and Singer saw their theory as an alternative to the James-Lange theory, but it really addresses a different question.

The ideal test of Schachter and Singer's theory would be to wire you to someone else so that whenever the other person's heart rate, breathing rate, and so forth changed, yours would, too, at the same time and to the same degree. Then, when the other person felt an emotion, researchers would ask whether you feel it, too. That procedure is impossible with current technology, so Schachter and Singer (1962) tried a simpler procedure.

What's the Evidence?
The Cognitive Aspect of Emotion

Hypothesis A drug that increases arousal will enhance whatever emotion a situation arouses, but the type of emotion will depend on the situation.

Method The experimenters put college students into different situations but gave some of them injections of epinephrine (adrenalin) to induce (they hoped) the same physiological condition regardless of the situation. (Epinephrine mimics the effects of the sympathetic nervous system.) They tried to influence some participants to attribute their increased arousal to the situation and others to attribute it to the injection.

Specifically, the experimenters told some participants that the injections would produce no important side effects. These participants would presumably notice their arousal and attribute it to the situation, feeling intense emotions. Oth-

Cognitive appraisal of the situation: This calls for fear.

Perception of autonomic responses: My heart is beating fast and I'm breathing hard. My fear must be intense.

FIGURE 12.4 According to Schachter and Singer's theory, physiological arousal determines the intensity of an emotion, but a cognitive appraisal determines which emotion one feels.

ers were told to expect side effects such as increased heart rate and butterflies in the stomach. When they felt the changes, they would presumably attribute them to the injections and not consider them emotional experiences. Additional participants were given one set of instructions or the other but injected with a placebo instead of epinephrine.

Participants were then placed in different situations to elicit euphoria or anger. Each student in the euphoria situation waited in a room with a playful young man who flipped paper wads into a trash can, sailed paper airplanes, built a tower with manila folders, shot paper wads at the tower with a rubber band, played with a Hula-Hoop, and tried to get the other student to join his play. Each participant in the anger situation was asked to answer a questionnaire full of such insulting items as these:

Which member of your immediate family does not bathe or wash regularly?

With how many men (other than your father) has your mother had extramarital relationships?

4 or fewer   5–9   10 or more

Results Many students in the euphoria situation joined the playful partner (Figure 12.5). One jumped up and down on the desk, and another opened a window and threw paper wads at passersby. The anger situation was less effective than expected, although a few students muttered angry comments or refused to complete the questionnaire.

Recall that some of the participants had been informed beforehand that the injections would produce certain autonomic effects, including tremors and increased heart rate. No matter which situation they were in, they showed only slight emotional responses. When they felt themselves sweating and their hands trembling, they said to themselves, "Aha! I'm getting the side effects, just as they said I would."

Interpretation Unfortunately, this experiment has problems that limit the conclusions. Recall that some participants were injected with a placebo instead of epinephrine. These participants showed about as much euphoria in the euphoria situation and as much anger in the anger situation as did the participants injected with epinephrine. Therefore, the epinephrine injections apparently had nothing to do with the results. If so, we are left with this unexciting summary of the results: People in a situation designed to induce euphoria act happy, and those in an anger situation act angry (Plutchik & Ax, 1967). However, if they attribute their arousal to an injection, their response is more restrained.

Despite the problems in Schachter and Singer's experiment, the idea behind it is reasonable, and other research since then has supported it in many, though not all, cases. That idea, to reiterate, is that the arousal you perceive in yourself determines the intensity of the emotion, although not the identity of the emotion. To illustrate with one example, young heterosexual men were asked to rate the attractiveness of each woman in the *Sports Illustrated* swimsuit issue. (They participated in the name of science, of course.) While they were viewing each photo, they heard sounds. Some were told (correctly) that they were listening to random sounds, and others were told (incorrectly) that they were hearing their own heartbeats. The rate of the sounds fluctuated haphazardly. Men who thought they were hearing their own heartbeats gave high ratings to the women they saw when they thought their heartbeat was accelerating (Crucian et al., 2000). That is, a man who thought his heart was beating faster assumed he was excited about a particular woman. Experiments like this suggest that the emotion we perceive depends on a cognitive attribution we make based on the situation. However, results of such experiments vary depending on details of the procedure (Reisenzein, 1983).

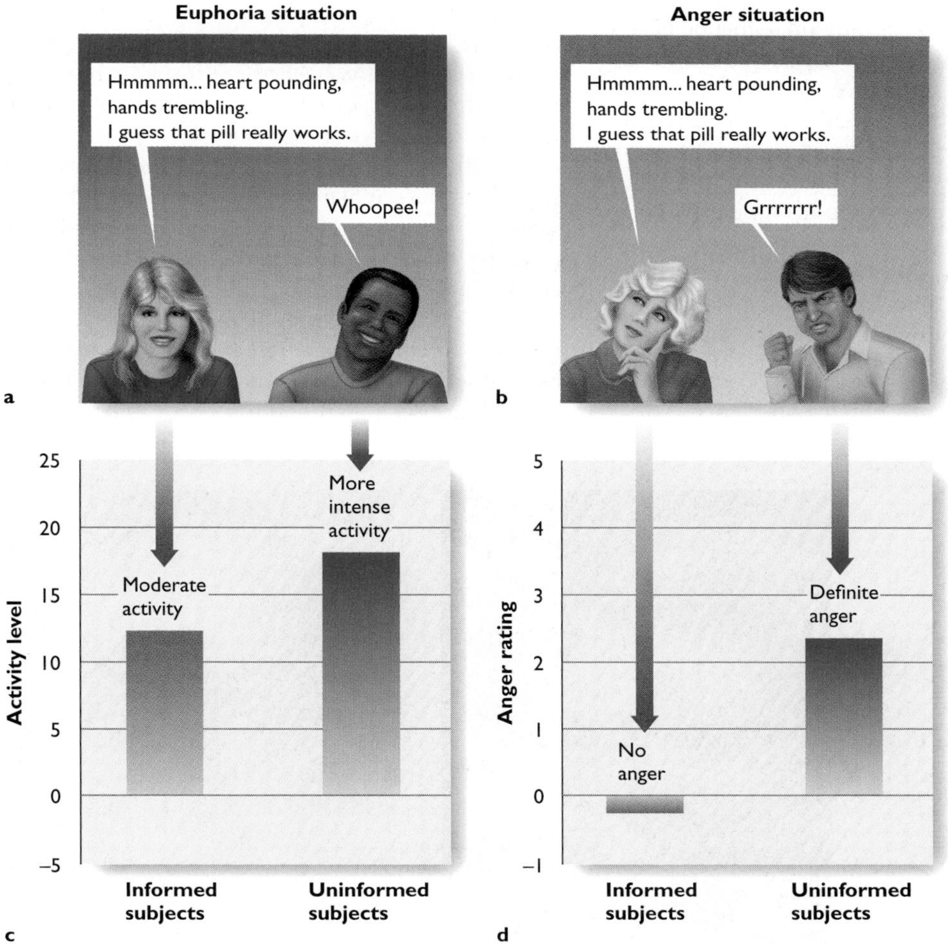

Euphoria situation

Anger situation

FIGURE 12.5 (a and b) In Schachter and Singer's experiment, people who were uninformed about the effects of epinephrine reported strong emotions appropriate to the situation. (c and d) According to Schachter and Singer, autonomic arousal controls the strength of an emotion, but cognitive factors tell us which emotion we are experiencing.

5. You are going on a first date with someone you hope will find you exciting. According to Schachter and Singer's theory, should you plan a date walking through an art gallery or riding on roller coasters?

Concept Check

Answer

5. According to Schachter and Singer's theory, you should plan a date riding on roller coasters. If your date gets emotionally excited, he or she may attribute the arousal to you. (However, if you are dating someone who gets nauseated on roller coasters, you should change your strategy!)

DO WE HAVE A FEW "BASIC" EMOTIONS?

How many emotions do humans experience? Do we have a few "basic" emotions that combine to form other experiences, like the elements of chemistry? Some psychologists have proposed a short list, such as happiness, sadness, anger, fear, disgust, and surprise. Others add more candidates, such as contempt, shame, guilt, interest, hope, pride, relief, frustration, love, awe, boredom, jealousy, regret, and embarrassment (Keltner & Buswell, 1997). Japanese people include *amae,* translated as "the pleasant feeling of depending on someone else" or "the feeling of comfort in another person's acceptance." The Japanese believe that people in other cultures have this emotional experience, too, but fail to notice or emphasize it (Doi, 1981; Niiya, Ellsworth, & Yamaguchi, 2006). Hindus include heroism, amusement, peace, and wonder (Hejmadi, Davidson, & Rozin, 2000).

How can we decide what is a basic emotion (if there is such a thing)? Psychologists generally consider the following criteria:

- Basic emotions should emerge early in life without requiring much experience. For example, nostalgia and pride emerge slowly and seem less basic than fear, anger, or joy (M. Lewis, 1995). The problem with this criterion is that all emotional expressions emerge gradually. Infants' expressions at first do not distinguish among distress, anger, and fear (Messinger, 2002).

- Basic emotions should be similar across cultures. Because most emotions look similar throughout human cultures, this criterion does not eliminate much.

- Each basic emotion should have its own facial expression and characteristic physiology. Most of the research has focused on this last criterion.

Producing Facial Expressions

Does each emotion have its own special expression? And why do we have facial expressions of emotions anyway?

Emotional expressions are not altogether arbitrary, as shown in Figure 12.6. When you are frightened, you open your eyes wide, increasing your ability to see dangers, and you inhale deeply, preparing for possible action. If you see something disgusting, you partly close your eyes and turn your nose away from the offending object, thus decreasing your exposure to it (Susskind et al., 2008). Furthermore, the wide-open eyes of a frightened face make you look more childlike and worthy of sympathy, whereas the narrowed eyes of anger make you look more adultlike and menacing (Sacco & Hugenberg, 2009).

In addition, emotional expressions are specialized for communication in monkeys and apes as well as in humans (Redican, 1982) (see Figure 12.7). Emotional expressions occur mostly in a

Figure 12.6 (a) A disgust expression decreases your exposure to something foul. (b) A fear expression increases your readiness to see dangers and take necessary actions.

a

b

Rainer Elstermann/Stone/Getty Images

Digital Vision/Alamy

FIGURE 12.7 Chimpanzees and humans have special facial expressions.

:-{}   :'(:-#   8-)
:-)   :-(:-/   :-0
:)   :(:*)   :O
!-)   :-x   ;-)
:'-(:-D   ;)   @}->--

In speech, we add gestures, facial expressions, or tone of voice to indicate emotion. At a keyboard, we sometimes add "emoticon" symbols.

social context. For example, Olympic medal winners generally smile if they are waiting for the awards ceremony with others but not if they are waiting alone (Fernández-Dols & Ruiz-Belda, 1997). Even 10-month-old infants smile more when their mothers are watching than when they are not (S. S. Jones, Collins, & Hong, 1991). Robert Provine (2000) spent many hours in shopping malls and elsewhere recording and observing laughter. He found that people laughed almost entirely when they were with friends and that the speakers laughed more than the listeners. People laughed mostly while saying something that wasn't even funny, such as, "Can I join you?" or "It was nice meeting you too." The laughter was a way to express friendliness.

Intentional emotional expressions seldom exactly match the spontaneous expressions. For example, the smile of a truly happy person includes movements of the mouth muscles and the muscles surrounding the eyes (Figure 12.8a). Volun-

tary smiles (Figure 12.8b) generally do not include the muscles around the eyes (Ekman & Davidson, 1993). *The full expression including the muscles around the eyes* is called the Duchenne smile, named after Duchenne de Boulogne, the first person to describe it.

Because the Duchenne smile is hard to produce voluntarily, it is a good indicator of someone's true feelings. Researchers have found that women with a Duchenne smile in their college yearbooks are more likely than other women to have happy, long-lasting marriages and to report feeling happy and competent long after their college years (Harker & Keltner, 2001).

Do we learn how to make appropriate facial expressions, or are they part of our biological heritage? Charles Darwin (1872/1965) asked missionaries and other people in remote places to describe the facial expressions of the people they saw. He reported that people everywhere had similar facial expressions, including expressions of grief, determination, anger, surprise, terror, and disgust. A century later, Irenäus Eibl-Eibesfeldt (1973, 1974) photo-

a   b

FIGURE 12.8 (a) A spontaneous, happy smile uses both the mouth muscles and the muscles surrounding the eyes. This expression is sometimes called the *Duchenne smile*. (b) A voluntary smile ordinarily includes only the mouth muscles. Most people cannot voluntarily activate the eye muscles associated with the Duchenne smile.

FIGURE 12.9 This laughing girl was born deaf and blind. (From Eibl-Eibesfeldt, 1973)

FIGURE 12.10 A boy who has been blind since birth covers his face in embarrassment. He prevents others from seeing his face, even though he has never experienced sight himself. (From Eibl-Eibesfeldt, 1973)

graphed people in various cultures, documenting smiling, frowning, laughing, and crying throughout the world, even in children who were born deaf and blind (Figures 12.9 and 12.10). The facial muscles responsible for emotional expressions show little variation from one person to another (Waller, Cray, & Burrows, 2008).

Eibl-Eibesfeldt also found that people everywhere express a friendly greeting by briefly raising their eyebrows (Figure 12.11). The mean duration of that expression is the same in all cultures: one third of a second from start to finish.

Understanding Facial Expressions

The similarity of facial expressions across cultures implies that they are unlearned, but researchers needed to test this assumption by asking whether people throughout the world interpret certain facial expressions the same way. Researchers interested in the hypothesis of a few basic emotions used photos of people showing six facial expressions, as shown in Figure 12.12. Look at each face and try to name its expression. (Please try now.)

After researchers translated the labels into other languages, people in other cultures also identified them, though somewhat less accurately (Ekman, 1992). Evidently, these facial expressions have nearly the same meaning throughout the world. Variations in the expressions have been compared to regional "accents." For example, the Chinese tend to restrain their expressions of pride and disgust, whereas Americans express them more fully (Camras, Chen, Bakeman, Norris, & Cain, 2006; Stipek, 1998). Just as you understand the speech from your own region better than that from elsewhere, you recognize facial expressions a bit more accurately among people from your own culture (Elfenbein, Beaupré, Lévesque, & Hess, 2007). Still, most people identify expressions fairly accurately even when viewing faces from an unfamiliar culture (Ekman & Friesen, 1984; Russell, 1994). Try the online activity Universal Emotions.

FIGURE 12.11 Like this man from New Guinea, people throughout the world raise their eyebrows as a greeting. (From Eibl-Eibesfeldt, 1973)

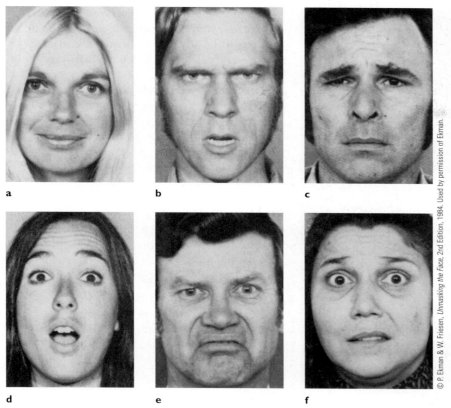

a   b   c

d   e   f

FIGURE 12.12 Paul Ekman has used these faces in experiments testing people's ability to recognize emotional expressions. Can you identify them? Check answer A on page 428. (From Ekman & Friesen, 1984)

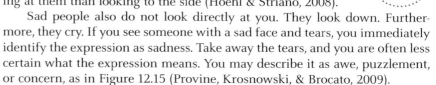

a

b

FIGURE 12.13 The same facial expression can look like sadness or fear depending on the person's posture. (Source: From Angry, disgusted, or afraid? by Aviezer, H., Hassin, R. R., Ryan, J., Grady, C., Susskind, J., Anderson, A., et al. (2008). *Psychological Science, 19,* 724–732. Reproduced with permission of Blackwell Publishing Ltd.)

The research almost certainly underestimates our ability to recognize emotional expressions. It is artificial to ask people to recognize emotion from a facial photograph. We do better with films (Ambadar, Schooler, & Cohn, 2005; Bould, Morris, & Wink, 2008), and we ordinarily supplement facial information by noticing gestures, posture, context, tone of voice, and sometimes even smell (K. Edwards, 1998; Leppänen & Hietanen, 2003; Zhou & Chen, 2009). People can recognize emotions moderately well from body posture alone (Van den Stock, Righart, & de Gelder, 2007), and the combination of face and posture works better than either one alone. Consider Figure 12.13. Although the facial expression is one of sadness for both parts, most people interpret the expression as sadness for the photo on the left and fear for the photo on the right (Aviezer et al., 2008).

Another issue: The faces in Figure 12.12 are all posed looking at the viewer. From the standpoint of experimental design, putting all the faces in the same position seems right. However, frightened people look at what frightens them. They look directly at you only if they are afraid of *you*. Examine the photos in Figure 12.14. Which expression is easier to identify? Most observers identify sad or frightened expressions faster when they see someone looking away (Adams & Kleck, 2003). In contrast, happy and angry expressions are easier to identify if the person is looking directly forward (Adams & Kleck, 2005). Even 7-month-old infants respond more strongly to an angry face looking at them than looking to the side (Hoehl & Striano, 2008).

Sad people also do not look directly at you. They look down. Furthermore, they cry. If you see someone with a sad face and tears, you immediately identify the expression as sadness. Take away the tears, and you are often less certain what the expression means. You may describe it as awe, puzzlement, or concern, as in Figure 12.15 (Provine, Krosnowski, & Brocato, 2009).

try it yourself

6. Researchers often show a set of photographs and ask observers to identify the emotions. In what way might this procedure underestimate the accuracy of recognizing emotions?

Concept Check

Fear

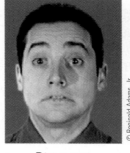 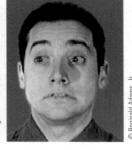

a   Direct gaze   b   Averted gaze

FIGURE 12.14 What emotions are these faces expressing? Most people identify fearful expressions more easily when the person is looking away.

People can, with a little less accuracy, also identify an expression of contempt, which is a little different from disgust. People also readily identify expressions of pride from facial expression and posture (Tracy & Robins, 2004; Tracy, Robins, & Lagattuta, 2005). From videotapes, though not from still photographs, most people can identify expressions of peace and heroism, which Hindu people generally list as emotions (Hejmadi et al., 2000). So if the ability to identify an expression is evidence for a basic emotion, our list should grow.

Also, we readily identify the facial expressions of sleepiness and confusion, although we probably would not classify either of them as an emotion (Keltner & Shiota, 2003; Rozin & Cohen, 2003). So the fact that we recognize facial expressions of surprise and disgust is not strong enough evidence to regard surprise or disgust as emotions.

....

7. Why is the ability to recognize the expressions of six emotions not good evidence that these are basic emotions?

Answer

7. Most everyday expressions do not neatly into those six categories. Also, we can identify facial expressions of other states, which may or may not be emotions.

....

An Alternative to Basic Emotions

Many psychologists doubt that it makes sense to talk about basic emotions at all (Barrett, 2006). If fear, anger, or anything else is a basic emotion, we should expect that when people show the facial expression of that emotion, they should ordinarily also show the gestures, postures, vocal intonation, and everything else that goes along with that emotion. However, people frequently show part of one emotional expression, part of another, and a posture or gesture that doesn't fit either one (Scherer & Ellgring, 2007).

Instead of considering an emotional expression as a unit, we might think of it as a compound of parts that can occur separately. As shown in Figure 12.16, you widen your eyes for a novel, surprising event. You turn down the corners of your mouth to indicate displeasure and furrow your eyebrows to indicate a desire to change something. You compress your lips when you feel in control of a situation. The expression we call anger is the sum of these components, but any of the components can occur on its own (Ortony & Turner, 1990; Scherer, 1992).

Instead of basic emotions, we might regard emotion as a series of dimensions. According to

Comstock Images/Jupiter Images

FIGURE 12.15 Tears make a face look much sadder than it would be without them.

Answer

6. We ordinarily have many other cues, such as change over time, gestures, posture, tone of voice, and context. Also, it is easier to recognize expressions of sadness and fear if the person looks down or to the side.

....

Do Facial Expressions Indicate Basic Emotions?

The question is whether we have basic emotions and, if so, what they are. The research shows that people throughout the world recognize facial expressions of joy, sadness, fear, anger, disgust, and surprise. However, the photos in Figure 12.12 were carefully posed to be the best possible examples of six expressions. With photos like these, people identify the expressions quickly and accurately (Tracy & Robins, 2008). In everyday life, most expressions show a mixture of emotions. If we take photographs of spontaneous everyday expressions, observers show poor agreement when they try to label one emotion per face (Naab & Russell, 2007).

Furthermore, the ability of people to recognize expressions of six emotions could not tell us whether people have precisely six basic emotions.

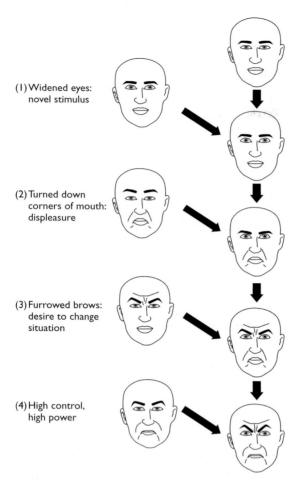

(1) Widened eyes: novel stimulus

(2) Turned down corners of mouth: displeasure

(3) Furrowed brows: desire to change situation

(4) High control, high power

FIGURE 12.16 What we usually regard as a single expression—in this case, anger—may be analyzed as a compound of independent parts. (Figure 5.3 from Scherer, K. R., 1992. "What does facial expression express?" In K. T. Strongman, Ed., *International Review of Studies on Emotion*, Vol. 2, pp. 139–165. Chichester, England: John Wiley & Sons, Ltd.)

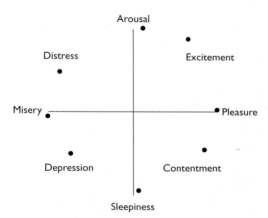

FIGURE 12.17 According to the circumplex model of emotion, emotional feelings occur along a continuum of arousal and another continuum of pleasure. (Figure 1 from Russell, J. A., 1980. "A circumplex model of affect," *Journal of Personality and Social Psychology, 39,* 1161–1178. Reproduced by permission of the American Psychological Association.)

the "circumplex" model, emotions range on a continuum from pleasure to misery and along another continuum from arousal to sleepiness (Russell, 1980). Figure 12.17 shows this idea. Note that this model deals with the feeling aspect of emotion, not the cognitive aspects. For example, both anger and fear would fit near "distress" on this graph, even though we associate anger and fear with different cognitions. Other psychologists have proposed different descriptions but maintain the idea that emotions range along continuous dimensions (D. Watson, Wiese, Vaidya, & Tellegen, 1999).

8. In what way does research on facial expressions support the idea of basic emotions?
9. How could we explain facial expressions without the idea of basic emotions?

Concept Check

Answers

8. Because people throughout the world can recognize the meaning of a few facial expressions, they appear to be universal among humans.
9. A facial expression, such as that for anger, can be described as a combination of independent components.

USEFULNESS OF EMOTIONS

Are emotions *useful* for anything? Presumably, they must be, or we would not have evolved the capacity to feel them. One function is that emotions focus our attention on important information. If you see an array of stimuli, your eyes and your attention turn at once toward the strongly pleasant or unpleasant images, even if you are trying to pay attention to something else (Schupp et al., 2007). You also remember emotionally arousing information better than neutral information (L. J. Levine & Pizarro, 2004). When you are distracted, you forget much of what you see and hear, but if you see or hear something frightening, you usually remember it despite the distraction (Kern, Libkuman, Otani, & Holmes, 2005).

Emotions or moods also adjust our priorities. If you see something frightening, you concentrate on the danger, as if you hardly saw anything else (Adolphs, Denburg, & Tranel, 2001; Mathews & Mackintosh, 2004). If you are running away from a mad attacker with a chainsaw, you don't stop to smell the roses. When you are in a happy mood, you expand your focus. According to Barbara Fredrickson's (2001) **broaden-and-build hypothesis** of positive emotions, *a happy mood increases your readiness to explore new ideas and opportunities.* You think creatively, notice the details in the background that you ordinarily overlook, and increase your pursuit of new experiences that will help maintain your happy mood (Fredrickson & Losada, 2005). An exception to this rule is that if you are happy because you are about to receive a particular treat, such as a chocolate pie, you might focus your attention more narrowly. It is when you are happy without any particular goal in mind, such as after watching a comedy film, that you are most likely to broaden your attention (Gable & Harmon-Jones, 2008).

Although major depression impairs reasoning, a mildly sad mood is helpful under some conditions. As discussed in chapter 11, most people overestimate their own abilities and underestimate how long a task will take. People in a happy mood are especially prone to that error. Sad people cautiously examine the evidence before making a decision. In one study, students listened to a weaker and a stronger argument concerning possible increases in student fees at their university. Students in a sad mood were more persuaded by the stronger argument, whereas students in a happy mood found both arguments about equally persuasive (Bless, Bohner, Schwarz, & Strack, 1990). In another study, slightly sad people were less likely than average to form "false memories," as described in chapter 7 (Storbeck & Clore, 2005).

10. What is one apparent "advantage" of feeling sad?

Answer

10. In some regards, sad people are more realistic and more likely to consider evidence slowly and carefully before making a decision.

Emotions and Moral Reasoning

People often advise us not to let our emotions get in the way of our decisions. Emotions sometimes impair decisions, but they also sometimes help (Beer, Knight, & D'Esposito, 2006). In particular, they often provide a guide when we have to make a quick decision about right and wrong.

Let's begin with two moral dilemmas. These are difficult decisions on which well-meaning people disagree.

The Trolley Dilemma. A trolley car with defective brakes is coasting downhill toward five people standing on the tracks. You could throw a switch to divert the trolley onto a different track, where one person is standing. If you flip the switch, the trolley will kill one instead of five. Should you do it?

The Footbridge Dilemma. Another trolley with defective brakes is coasting downhill and about to kill five people. This time you are standing on a footbridge over the track. You see a way to save those five people: A fat person is beside you, leaning over. If you push him off the bridge, he will land on the track and block the trolley. (You are, let's assume, too thin to block it yourself.) Again your action would kill one to save five. Should you do it? (Figure 12.18)

Most people say "yes" to flipping the switch in the first dilemma, but either say "no" or hesitate for a long time in the second dilemma (Greene, Sommerville, Nystrom, Darley, & Cohen, 2001). Logically, the answers should be the same because you kill one person to save five. Of course, the situations are not quite comparable. What if you pushed someone to his death and the trolley killed the others anyway? Or what if they jumped out of the way, so that killing him was unnecessary? However, even if you were fully confident that pushing one man off a bridge would save five others, it would still be emotionally repulsive.

After people make moral decisions in cases like these, they often have trouble stating a reason for their decisions (Cushman, Young, & Hauser, 2006). They seem to make their decisions quickly and emotionally and then look for an explanation afterward. The emotional guidance usually works. In an occasional bizarre case, maybe it makes sense to push a stranger off a bridge to save five others, but ordinarily, pushing someone off a bridge is a horrendously bad idea. Your emotional reaction is a quick guide to making a decision that is almost always right.

Decisions by People with Impaired Emotions

Antonio Damasio (1994) described patients who suffered impoverished or inappropriate emotions following brain damage. One was the famous patient Phineas Gage, who in 1848 survived an accident in which an iron bar shot through his head. Nearly one-and-a-half centuries later, researchers examined his skull (which is still on display in a Boston museum) and reconstructed the route that the bar must have taken through his brain (H. Damasio, Grabowski, Frank, Galaburda, & Damasio, 1994). As you can see in Figure 12.19, the accident damaged part of his prefrontal cortex. During the months after this accident, Gage often showed little emotion, and he made poor, impulsive decisions. However, the reports at the time provided little detail. Over the years, people retold this story and elaborated on it. If you have read about this case before, you may have read some exaggerations (Kotowicz, 2007).

A patient known to us as "Elliot" provides a more recent example (A. R. Damasio, 1994). Elliot suffered damage to his prefrontal cortex as a result of

FIGURE 12.18 (a) Should you flip a switch so the trolley goes down a track with one person instead of five? (b) Should you push a fat person off a bridge to save five people?

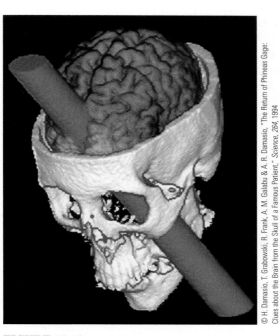

© H. Damasio, T. Grabowski, R. Frank, A. M. Galabu & A. R. Damasio, "The Return of Phineas Gage: Clues about the Brain from the Skull of a Famous Patient," *Science, 264,* 1994

FIGURE 12.19 In the 1990s, researchers used modern technology to reconstruct the path that an iron bar must have made through the brain of Phineas Gage, who survived this injury in 1848. The damage impaired Gage's judgment and decision-making ability.

surgery to remove a brain tumor. After the operation, he showed almost no emotional expression, no impatience, no frustration, no joy from music or art, and almost no anger. He described his brain surgery and the resulting deterioration of his life with calm detachment, as if describing events that happened to a stranger. Besides his impaired emotions, he had trouble making or following reasonable plans. He could discuss the probable outcome of each possible choice but still had trouble deciding. As a result, he could not keep a job, invest his money intelligently, or maintain normal friendships.

Other people with damage to the frontal and temporal cortex also make poor, impulsive decisions and process emotional information slowly (Levenson & Miller, 2007). Many fail to make the moral judgments that most other people make. For example, they decide with little hesitation that it is okay to push a stranger off the bridge to save five others on the tracks. They also fail to show guilt after being unfair to someone or embarrassment after doing something silly. It is as if they don't care about other people's opinions or outcomes (Krajbich, Adolphs, Tranel, Denburg, & Camerer, 2009; Sturn, Ascher, Miller, & Levenson, 2008).

According to Damasio (1994), impaired decision making stems from weak emotions. Ordinarily, when you or I consider possible decisions, we contemplate the possible outcomes and imagine

how each outcome might feel. If you consider a job offer from a company that fired your best friend, you imagine the unpleasant scene when you face your friend. People with temporal or frontal lobe damage don't easily imagine the emotional outcomes. As Damasio (1999, p. 55) said, "Emotions are inseparable from the idea of good and evil." If you cannot imagine feeling good or bad, proud or guilty, you make bad decisions.

11. In what way does prefrontal cortex damage interfere with decision making?

Answer

11. People with damage to the prefrontal cortex cannot imagine feeling good or bad after various outcomes; therefore, they see little reason to prefer one outcome to another.

EMOTIONAL INTELLIGENCE

Is reasoning about emotional issues different from reasoning about anything else? The observations on patient Elliot imply a difference, as he answers questions normally as long as they have nothing to do with emotional consequences. Casual observations in everyday life also suggest that reasoning about emotional topics might be special. Some people know the right thing to say to make someone else feel better. They notice subtle signals in people's facial expressions that indicate who needs reassurance or a pat on the back. They know when a smile is sincere or fake. They foresee whether their romantic attachments are going well or about to break up.

Psychologists therefore speak of **emotional intelligence,** *the ability to perceive, imagine, and understand emotions and to use that information in making decisions* (Mayer & Salovey, 1995, 1997). Part of emotional intelligence is detecting other people's emotions and knowing the right thing to say to manage emotional situations. Another aspect is being aware of one's own emotions and expressing or restraining them depending on the situation (Mayer, 2001; Swinkels & Giuliano, 1995).

The idea of emotional intelligence quickly became popular, but the evidence behind the idea is still not strong. If the concept is going to be useful, emotional intelligence must have enough in common with other kinds of intelligence to deserve being called intelligence. However, it should not overlap too heavily with academic intelligence, or we would have no reason to talk about it separately. First, we need a way to measure emotional intelligence. Several psychologists have devised pencil-and-paper tests. Here are two example questions, reworded slightly (Mayer, Caruso, & Salovey, 2000):

1. A man has been so busy at work that he spends little time with his wife and daughter. He feels guilty for spending so little time with them, and they feel hurt. Recently, a relative who lost her job moved in with them. A few weeks later, they told her she had to leave because they needed their privacy.
On a scale from 1 to 5, where 5 is highest, rate how much this man feels:
Depressed _____
Frustrated _____
Guilty _____
Energetic _____
Liking _____
Joyous _____
Happy _____

2. A driver hit a dog that ran into the street. The driver and the dog's owner hurried to check on the dog.
On a scale from 1 to 5, where 5 means "extremely likely" and 1 means "extremely unlikely," how would the driver and the dog's owner probably feel?
The owner would feel angry at the driver _____
The owner would feel embarrassed at not training the dog better _____
The driver would feel guilty for not driving more carefully _____
The driver would feel relieved that it was a dog and not a child _____

To each of these questions, you might answer, "It depends!" You need more information about the people and the situation. Indeed, one of the key aspects of emotional intelligence is knowing what additional information to request. Still, you could do your best to answer the questions as stated. The problem then is, gulp, what are the correct answers? In fact, are there any correct answers, or do they vary depending on culture and circumstances? Unlike mathematics, which has clear right and wrong answers, these questions do not.

The usual way to determine the right answers is "consensus": Researchers ask many people each question. Suppose on item 2, on the part about the driver feeling guilty, 70% say "5" (it is extremely likely that the driver will feel guilty). That becomes the best answer. However, an answer of

"4" isn't utterly wrong and is certainly better than an answer of "1." Suppose 20% of people answer "4," 5% answer "3," 4% answer "2," and 1% answer "1." Instead of counting anything absolutely right or wrong, the test adds .70 point for everyone who answered 5, .20 for everyone who answered 4, and so on. In other words, you always get part credit on any question, and you get more credit depending on how many other people agreed with you.

The main objection is that this scoring system doesn't give much credit on difficult items. Suppose on a given item, only 23% of people choose the best answer, and 21%, 20%, 19%, and 17% choose the other answers. For this item, the best answer is worth only .06 more than the worst answer. In fact, we could imagine an item on which almost everyone is wrong, and only the true emotional geniuses choose some answer that is really correct. Because it is an uncommon answer, it will be considered wrong.

In short, an emotional intelligence question as currently constituted does not do a good job of identifying an emotional "genius." However, it does identify people who fail to answer easy questions. That by itself is worth something. People with certain kinds of brain damage or psychiatric disorders do poorly even on easy questions about emotional situations (Adolphs, Baron-Cohen, & Tranel, 2002; Blair et al., 2004; J. Edwards, Jackson, & Pattison, 2002; Townshend & Duka, 2003). So the test identifies "emotional stupidity," even if it doesn't identify exceptional emotional intelligence.

The key criteria for any test are reliability and validity, as discussed in chapter 9. The authors of the current tests of emotional intelligence claim that the tests have high reliability (Mayer, Salovey, Caruso, & Sitarenios, 2001), but other researchers find problems with many of the test items and report much lower reliability (Føllesdal & Hagtvet, 2009). With regard to validity, high emotional intelligence scores are associated with many valued outcomes, including high quality of friendships (Lopes et al., 2004), ability to detect the emotional content of someone's voice (Trimmer & Cuddy, 2008), and avoidance of alcohol and illegal drug use (Brackett, Mayer, & Warner, 2004).

However, emotional intelligence is a useful concept only if it predicts such outcomes better than we already could with other tests. People who do well on Verbal IQ tests generally also do well on emotional intelligence tests (Zeidner, Shani-Zinovich, Matthews, & Roberts, 2005), and so do people who score high on personality tests measuring agreeableness and conscientiousness (Brackett et al., 2004; Gannon & Ranzijn, 2005). What do emotional intelligence scores predict that we couldn't already predict from a combination of Verbal IQ and a personality test? A couple of studies concluded "not much" (Amelang & Steinmayr, 2006; Gannon & Ranzijn, 2005). So either emotional intelligence is not a useful concept, or we need to improve our measurements of it.

....

12. What is the main objection to "consensus" scoring?

Answer

items.
12. A test based on consensus scoring can't easily identify the truly outstanding individuals because it doesn't give much credit on difficult

....

In Closing

Research on Emotions

Research on emotions is fascinating but difficult. Of the various components of emotion, the cognitive and feeling aspects are the hardest to measure. Behavioral and physiological measures are more objective, but they have their own problems. The best solution is to approach each problem in multiple ways. Any kind of study has flaws and limitations, but if several different kinds of research point to the same conclusion, we gain confidence in the overall idea. That principle is, indeed, important throughout psychology: Seldom is any study fully decisive, so we strive for independent lines of research that converge on the same conclusion.

SUMMARY

- *Measuring emotions.* Emotions are inferred, not observed directly. Researchers rely on self-reports, observations of behavior, and measurements of physiological changes. (page 412)

- *Emotions and autonomic arousal.* Many emotional states are associated with increased arousal of the sympathetic nervous system, which readies the body for emergency action. (page 412)

- *James-Lange theory.* According to the James-Lange theory of emotions, the feeling aspect of an emotion is the perception of a change in the body's physiological state. (page 414)

- *Evidence supporting the James-Lange theory.* People who lose control of their autonomic responses generally report weakened emotional feelings. Molding someone's posture and breathing pattern into the pattern typical for some emotion facilitates that emotion. (page 415)

- *Schachter and Singer's theory.* According to Schachter and Singer's theory, autonomic arousal determines the intensity of an emotion but does not determine which emotion occurs. We identify an emotion on the basis of how we perceive the situation. (page 416)

- *Do we have basic emotions?* Certain psychologists propose that we have a few basic emotions. The main evidence is that people throughout the world can recognize the same emotional expressions. However, most everyday expressions do not fit neatly into a few categories. Also, it is not obvious whether we should consider disgust and surprise as emotions. The fact that we recognize expressions of disgust and surprise is not decisive because we also recognize expressions of sleepiness and confusion, which most people do not regard as emotions. (page 418)

- *Facial expressions.* People produce facial expressions of emotion as a means of communicating their probable social behaviors. Many human facial expressions have similar meanings in cultures throughout the world. For several reasons, most of the research probably underestimates people's ability to recognize emotions. (page 418)

- *Alternative views.* Instead of speaking of a list of basic emotions, an alternative is to consider emotions as varying along continuous dimensions. (page 422)

- *Usefulness of emotions.* Emotions call our attention to important information and adjust our priorities to our situation in life. (page 423)

- *Emotions and moral decisions.* When we face a moral decision, we often react emotionally for or against one of the choices. Those quick emotional feelings may be an evolved mechanism to steer our behavior toward what is usually the right choice. (page 424)

- *Effects of brain damage.* We make many decisions by imagining the emotional consequences of the possible outcomes. People with brain damage that impairs their emotions have trouble making good decisions. (page 424)

- *Emotional intelligence.* People need skills to judge other people's emotions and the probable emotional outcomes of their own actions. The ability to handle such issues may constitute an "emotional intelligence." However, it is not clear that current measurements of emotional intelligence predict much that we could not already predict based on academic intelligence and certain aspects of personality. (page 425)

KEY TERMS

autonomic nervous system (page 412)

broaden-and-build hypothesis (page 423)

Duchenne smile (page 419)

emotional intelligence (page 425)

James-Lange theory (page 414)

microexpressions (page 412)

parasympathetic nervous system (page 413)

pure autonomic failure (page 415)

Schachter and Singer's theory of emotions (page 416)

sympathetic nervous system (page 413)

ANSWERS TO OTHER QUESTION IN THE MODULE (page 421)

A. The faces express (a) happiness, (b) anger, (c) sadness, (d) surprise, (e) disgust, and (f) fear.

A Survey of Emotions

- What makes people frightened, angry, happy, or sad?
- How do our emotions affect our actions?

The first module posed difficult theoretical questions, but we do not have to wait until we answer them. We can proceed to issues of practical importance to almost everyone, especially clinical psychologists: How can we control our fear and anger and increase our happiness?

FEAR AND ANXIETY

Fear and anxiety feel about the same. *Fear* generally refers to the response to an immediate danger, whereas *anxiety* is a vague, long-lasting sense that "something bad might happen." Is there a "right" level of anxiety? It depends on the situation. Presumably, evolution enabled us to readjust our anxiety based on our dangerous experiences.

Measuring Anxiety

Most emotion research relies on self-reports, but anxiety researchers also use an operational definition based on behavior: **Anxiety** is *an increase in the startle reflex.* The startle reflex is the quick, automatic response that almost any animal makes after a sudden loud noise. Within a fifth of a second after the noise, you tense your muscles, especially your neck muscles, close your eyes, and mobilize your sympathetic nervous system to prepare for escape if necessary. The startle reflex itself is automatic, but experiences and context modify it.

Imagine yourself sitting with friends in a familiar place on a nice, sunny day when you hear a sudden loud noise. You startle, but not strongly. Now imagine yourself walking alone at night through a graveyard when you think you see someone walking toward you . . . and then you hear the same loud noise. Your startle response will be greater. The increase in the startle reflex is a reliable, objective measurement of anxiety. As you would expect, the startle reflex is enhanced for people with anxiety disorders, especially post-traumatic stress disorder (Grillon, Morgan, Davis, & Southwick, 1998; Pole, Neylan, Best, Orr, & Marmar, 2003).

Learned associations also alter the startle reflex in laboratory animals. Suppose a rat frequently sees a "danger" stimulus—say, a light—before receiving a shock. Now, that danger stimulus enhances the startle reflex to a loud noise. The increase in the startle reflex is taken as a measure of anxiety, and research based on this measure has identified the amygdala (uh-MIG-duh-luh), as shown in Figure 12.20, as the key brain area for learning fears and anxiety (Antoniadis, Winslow, Davis, & Amaral, 2007; Wilensky, Schafe, Kristensen, & LeDoux, 2006). The figure shows a human brain, although much of the research has been conducted with laboratory animals.

People with amygdala damage report that they still feel fear and other emotions (A. K. Anderson & Phelps, 2002). However, they no longer respond quickly the way other people do to subtle or complex emotional information (Baxter & Murray, 2002; Whalen, 1998). For example, they are impaired at recognizing emotional expressions (A. Anderson & Phelps, 2000) and have trouble inferring emotions from people's tone of voice (Scott et al., 1997). They rate all faces about equally trust-

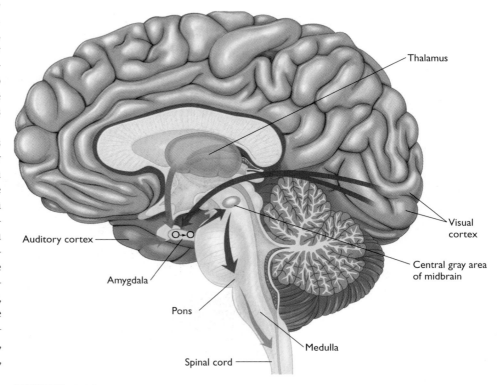

FIGURE 12.20 Structures in the pons and medulla control the startle response. The amygdala sends information that modifies activity in the pons and medulla. This drawing shows a human brain, although most research has been with rats.

worthy (Adolphs, Tranel, & Damasio, 1998) and almost all drawings about equally attractive (Adolphs & Tranel, 1999). Most people remember emotionally disturbing pictures better than emotionally neutral ones, but people with amygdala damage remember both kinds of photos about equally (LaBar & Phelps, 1998).

13. What method could one use to compare anxiety levels of non-human animals, preverbal children, or others who cannot answer in words?

Answer

13. One could measure the strength of the startle reflex.

Anxiety, Arousal, and Lie Detection

Let's consider an attempt to use physiological measurement of anxiety for a practical purpose: The **polygraph**, or "lie-detector test," *records indications of sympathetic nervous system arousal, such as blood pressure, heart rate, breathing rate, and electrical conduction of the skin* (Figure 12.21). (Slight sweating increases electrical conduction of the skin.) The assumption is that when people lie, they feel nervous and therefore increase their sympathetic nervous system arousal.

(A bit of trivia: William Marston, the inventor of the polygraph, was also the originator of the *Wonder Woman* cartoons. Wonder Woman used a "lasso of truth" to force people to stop lying.)

The polygraph sometimes accomplishes its goal simply because an accused person hooked up to a polygraph confesses, "Oh, what's the use. You're going to figure it out now anyway, so I may as well tell you. . . ." But if people do not confess, how effectively does a polygraph detect lying?

In one study, investigators selected 50 criminal cases where two suspects took a polygraph test and one suspect later confessed to the crime (Kleinmuntz & Szucko, 1984). Thus, they had data from 100 people who were considered plausible suspects at the time, of whom 50 were later shown to be guilty and 50 shown to be innocent. Six professional polygraph administrators examined the polygraph results and judged which suspects appeared to be lying. Figure 12.22 shows the results. The polygraph administrators identified 76% of the guilty suspects as liars but also classified 37% of the innocent suspects as liars.

Other research on the polygraph has produced varying results. In an ideal study, some suspects are innocent and others are guilty, all are seriously worried about being convicted, and the investigators eventually determine for certain who was guilty. Few such studies have been done, and those few have produced unimpressive results. Although many police officers still believe in polygraph testing, most researchers regard the accuracy as too uncertain for important decisions (Fiedler, Schmid, & Stahl, 2002). Polygraph results are almost never admissible as evidence in U.S. or European courts. The U.S. Congress passed a law in 1988 prohibiting private employers from giving polygraph tests to employees or job applicants, except under special circumstances, and a commission of the U.S. National Academy of Sciences in 2002 concluded that polygraphs should not be used for national security clearances.

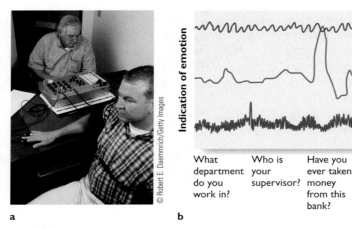

FIGURE 12.21 A polygraph operator (a) asks a series of nonthreatening questions to establish baseline readings of the subject's autonomic responses (b) and then asks questions relevant to an investigation.

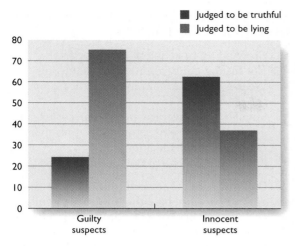

Legend:
- Judged to be truthful
- Judged to be lying

FIGURE 12.22 Polygraph examiners correctly identified 76% of guilty suspects as lying. However, they also identified 37% of innocent suspects as lying. (Based on data of Kleinmuntz & Szucko, 1984)

Alternative Methods of Detecting Lies

The guilty-knowledge test, *a modified version of the polygraph test,* produces more accurate results by *asking questions that should be threatening only to someone who knows the facts of a crime that have not been publicized* (Lykken, 1979). Instead of asking, "Did you rob the gas station?" the interrogator asks, "Was the gas station robbed at 8 P.M.? At 10:30? At midnight? At 1:30 in the morning? Did the robber carry a gun? A knife? A club? Was the getaway car green? Red? Blue?" Someone who shows heightened arousal only in response to the correct details of the crime is presumed to have "guilty knowledge" that only the guilty person or someone who had talked to the guilty person would possess. The guilty-knowledge test, when properly administered, identifies most guilty people and rarely classifies an innocent person as guilty (Iacono & Patrick, 1999).

Another approach is to avoid technology and simply observe people more carefully. Paul Ekman (2001) conducted extensive research to see how people react when they lie. For example, he asked people to watch either a pleasant movie or a disturbing documentary about burns and amputations and then, regardless of the content of the movie, to say they found the movie pleasant. So they all said the same words, but some were lying. Based on this and similar designs, Ekman found that people who are lying try to maintain a calm, happy expression but show microexpressions (brief involuntary emotional expressions), such as slight expressions of fear or a brief partial shrug of the shoulders. These microexpressions identify liars more accurately than the polygraph does.

Researchers also report that when people lie, they tend to provide fewer details than when the same people are telling the truth, perhaps to avoid saying something that could be shown to be wrong (DePaolo et al., 2003).

One final comment: All methods of detecting lying, from the polygraph to microexpressions, assume that people are nervous about lying. They fail with experienced, confident liars or people who have come to believe their own lies.

....

14. What does a polygraph measure?
15. What is the main objection to polygraph tests?

Concept Check

Answers

14. The polygraph measures several aspects of sympathetic nervous system activity, such as heart rate, breathing rate, and electrical conduction of the skin (an indicator of sweating).
15. A polygraph too often identifies an innocent person as lying.

ANGER AND AGGRESSIVE BEHAVIOR

During World War II, nearly all the industrialized nations were at war, the Nazis were exterminating the Jews, and the United States was preparing a nuclear bomb that it later dropped on Japan. Meanwhile, Mohandas K. Gandhi was in jail for leading a nonviolent protest march against British rule in India. The charge against Gandhi was, ironically, "disturbing the peace." Someone asked Gandhi what he thought of Western civilization. He replied that he thought it might be a good idea.

Human beings are capable of ghastly acts of cruelty but also of nobility, heroism, and courageous opposition to violence. The struggle to understand violence is among the most important goals facing humanity in general and psychology in particular.

Relationship of Anger to Aggression

Anger is associated with a desire to harm people or drive them away. Aggressive behavior is observable in nonhuman animals—or little boys on a playground—but most adults restrain their physical aggression. Surveys across a variety of cultures find that people experience anger frequently but seldom even consider striking anyone (Ramirez, Santisteban, Fujihara, & Van Goozen, 2002).

Participants in one study kept an "anger diary" for a week (Averill, 1983). A typical entry was, "My roommate locked me out of the room when I went to the shower." They also described how they reacted, such as, "I talked to my roommate about it," or "I did nothing about it." Very few admitted threatening to attack, much less actually attacking.

Causes of Anger

According to the frustration-aggression hypothesis, *the main cause of anger (and therefore aggression) is frustration—an obstacle that stands in the way of doing something or obtaining some expected reinforcer* (Dollard, Miller, Doob, Mowrer, & Sears, 1939). Many instances of anger easily fit this description. However, frustration makes you angry only when you believe the other person acted intentionally. You might feel angry at someone who ran down the hall and bumped into you but probably not at someone who slipped on a wet spot and bumped into you.

Leonard Berkowitz (1983, 1989) proposed a more comprehensive theory: Any unpleasant event—frustration, pain, heat, foul odors, bad news, whatever—excites both the impulse to fight and the impulse to flee. That is, it excites the sympathetic nervous system and its fight-or-flight response. Your choice between fight and flight depends on the circumstances. If you have won many fights, have seldom been punished, and think the person who just spilled coffee on you looks easy to beat, you express your anger. If you think you have little chance of winning a fight, you suppress your anger. And if the one who bumped into you is your boss or the loan and scholarship officer at your college, you smile and apologize for getting in the way.

Individual Differences in Anger and Aggression

Why are some people angry or aggressive more often than others? One hypothesis has been that low self-esteem leads to violence. According to this idea, people who think little of themselves try to build themselves up by tearing someone else down. The data on this point are mixed. Some studies find a small but significant relationship between aggressive behaviors and low self-esteem (Donnellan, Trzesniewski, Robins, Moffitt, & Caspi, 2005). Other studies find little effect or find a relationship between aggressiveness and narcissism—excessive self-centeredness (Baumeister, Campbell, Krueger, & Vohs, 2003; Baumeister, Smart, & Boden, 1996).

Another hypothesis not consistently supported is a link between violence and mental illness. Drug and alcohol abuse are highly associated with violence, and many mental patients abuse alcohol or other drugs. However, those without drug or alcohol abuse are no more likely than average to be violent (Hodgins, Mednick, Brennan, Schulsinger, & Engberg, 1996).

If low self-esteem and mental illness do not predict violence, what does? Genetic factors interact with environmental influences. People with low levels of the brain protein monoamine oxidase (MAO) react more aggressively than average when they feel they have been cheated (McDermott, Tingley, Cowden, Frazzetto, & Johnson, 2009). The tendency toward aggression is particularly strong among people who have both the gene for low MAO production and a history of being abused in childhood. Figure 12.23 shows the results of one study (Caspi et al., 2002). Of boys who had both childhood maltreatment and a low level of MAO, more than 80% developed conduct disorder, a condition marked by aggressive and antisocial behaviors. By comparison, fewer than 5% of boys in the overall population develop conduct disorder (Shaffer et al., 1996). Childhood maltreatment by itself had little effect, and the gene by itself had little effect, but the combination led to problems.

Several other factors are associated with a tendency toward violent behavior (Davidson, Putnam, & Larson, 2000; D. O. Lewis et al.,

1985; Lynam, 1996; Osofsky, 1995; Raine, Lencz, Bihrle, LaCasse, & Colletti, 2000):

- Growing up in a violent neighborhood
- Not feeling guilty after hurting someone
- Weaker than normal physiological responses to arousal
- Smaller than average prefrontal cortex and decreased release of serotonin to this area
- A history of suicide attempts
- Frequently watching violence on television

Culture is also a powerful influence. A fascinating study documented the influence of culture on aggressive behavior even in nonhuman primates. Researchers observed one troop of baboons for 25 years. At one point, all the most aggressive males in the troop tried to take food from a neighboring troop. The food happened to be contaminated, and all the aggressive males died. The troop then consisted of females, juveniles, and the least aggressive males. They got along well, stress levels decreased, and health improved. Over the years, new males occasionally entered the troop and adopted this troop's customs. Years later, none of the original males remained there, but the troop continued its nonaggressive tradition (Sapolsky & Share, 2004).

16. Is genetic predisposition a powerful contributor to aggressive behavior?

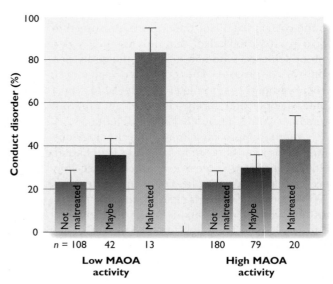

Figure 12.23 Children with low MAO type A levels who are maltreated have a high probability of showing aggressive and antisocial behaviors. (Figure 2A, page 852, from Caspi, A., McClay, J., Moffitt, T. E., Mill, J. Martin, J., Craig, I. W., et al., 2002. "Role of genotype in the cycle of violence in maltreated children," *Science, 297,* 851–854.)

Answer

16. It depends. One study found that a particular gene predisposed boys to conduct disorder only if they also suffered childhood maltreatment.

Sexual Aggression and Violence in Relationships

Most acts of violence occur between people who know each other well, including romantic couples. A review of the extensive research within heterosexual couples reported that women commit *more* acts of violence against men than men do against women (Archer, 2000). Almost everyone finds that result surprising. After all, we hear of battered women's clinics but not battered men's clinics. The explanation is that most researchers defined violence to include slaps, pushes, and other minor acts. Men inflict most of the serious injuries.

Rape is *sexual activity without the consent of the partner.* In one survey, about 10% of adult women reported that they had been forcibly raped, and another 10% said they had involuntary sex while incapacitated by alcohol or other drugs (Testa, Livingston, Vanzile-Tamsen, & Frone, 2003). However, the statistics vary considerably from one study to another. Recall from chapter 2 that slight changes in the wording of a survey question can enormously influence people's answers. Surveys that ask about "unwanted" sex report very high numbers because many people interpret "unwanted" to include times when they weren't in the mood but agreed to sex to please a partner (Hamby & Koss, 2003). Not only most women but also most men say they have sometimes had sex when they did not want to (Struckman-Johnson, Struckman-Johnson, & Anderson, 2003).

Even with a narrowly worded definition, surveys find rape to be far more widespread than the crime statistics indicate. Of all sexual assaults that legally qualify as rape, only about half the victims call the experience rape, and far fewer report the event to the police (Fisher, Daigle, Cullen, & Turner, 2003). Most women who have involuntary sex with a boyfriend or other acquaintance do not call the event rape, especially if alcohol was involved (Kahn, Jackson, Kully, Badger, & Halvorsen, 2003). In some cases, the man does not realize that the woman considered his behavior abusive.

What kind of man commits rape? Most rapists have a history of other acts of violence and criminality (Hanson, 2000). Sexually aggressive men tend to be high users of pornography (Vega & Malamuth, 2007), and rapists are much more

likely than other men to enjoy violent pornography (Donnerstein & Malamuth, 1997). Another element in rape is extreme self-centeredness, or lack of concern for others (Dean & Malamuth, 1997).

HAPPINESS, JOY, AND POSITIVE PSYCHOLOGY

Positive psychology is *the study of the features that enrich life, such as happiness, hope, creativity, courage, spirituality, and responsibility* (Seligman & Csikszentmihalyi, 2000). Happiness is hard to measure. Unlike fear and anger, happiness produces only small and inconsistent physiological responses. The best behavioral indicator of happiness is a smile, but people are often happy without smiling, and people often smile to be polite without feeling happy. Because the behavioral and physiological measures are so meager, researchers rely almost entirely on people's self-reports to measure happiness or **subjective well-being,** *which is a self-evaluation of one's life as pleasant, interesting, and satisfying* (Diener, 2000).

What factors influence happiness or subjective well-being? Ask some people question 1 and other people question 2.

1. What would make you happier than you are now?
2. What makes you happy?

To the question of what would make you happier, most U.S. students mention money, a good job, more time to relax, or a boyfriend or girlfriend (or a "better" boyfriend or girlfriend). To the question of what makes you happy, common answers include relationships with friends and family, exercise, music, a sense of accomplishing something well, religious faith, and enjoyment of nature.

Influence of Wealth

Although many people say more money would make them happier, few say their money does make them happy. How important is money for happiness?

Here is one way to ask: Researchers equipped people with devices that buzzed at unpredictable times to ask them to indicate their mood at the moment. On the average, low-income people reported feeling happy almost as frequently as high-income people. A likely reason is that wealthy people spend more hours at work-related activities and fewer hours on leisure (Kahneman, Krueger, Schkade, Schwarz, & Stone, 2006).

Another way to ask the question is to interview people who recently became wealthy. As you might guess, people who have just won a lottery call themselves very happy. As you might not guess, people who won a lottery a few months ago no longer rate themselves especially happy (Diener, Suh, Lucas, & Smith, 1999; Myers, 2000). One explanation is that lottery winners get used to their new level of happiness, so a given rating doesn't mean what it used to. Also, people are greedy. According to one newspaper survey, people earning $25,000 a year thought $50,000 a year would make them happy, but those earning $50,000 a year said they would need $100,000 a year, and those earning $100,000 a year wanted $200,000 (Csikszentmihalyi, 1999).

Another way to examine the effect of wealth is to survey people about their wealth and how happy they are overall. Most surveys have found a low correlation, around .20, and for years, psychologists concluded that money doesn't buy happiness. However, a reanalysis came to a different conclusion: Most people in these surveys are near the middle for both wealth and happiness, and therefore, the overall correlation doesn't show much relationship between wealth and happiness. However, if we compare people at a wider range of wealth, we find that, on the average, wealthy people are happier than poor people, with the middle class in between (Lucas & Schimmack, 2009). Impoverished people are particularly unhappy if they know their friends and relatives are doing better (Fliessbach et al., 2007) or if they are in poor health (D. M. Smith, Langa, Kabeto, & Ubel, 2005). Many poor people are happy, and so are many sick people, but it is hard to be happy if you are both poor and sick.

Cross-cultural research indicates that, in general, people in richer countries rate themselves happier than those in poorer countries, as shown in Figure 12.24, and countries that became wealthier over time also experience an increase in rated happiness (Inglehart, Foa, Peterson, & Welzel, 2008). An exception to this rule is that people in Latin American countries report themselves happier than their wealth would predict. Another exception is the countries of Eastern Europe, which at the time of the survey were shifting from communist to noncommunist governments and therefore undergoing turmoil in their political, economic, and belief systems.

In addition to wealth, the mean level of happiness of various countries correlates positively with religiousness and with tolerance for minority groups (Inglehart et al., 2008). It is possible that a tolerant attitude leads to happiness, but the evidence definitely shows that feeling happy makes one more tolerant. When things are going badly, people start defending their most traditional beliefs (Ashton-James, Maddux, Galinsky, & Chartrand, 2009). Happiness also tends to be greatest in countries where women have opportunities and status similar to men (Basabe et al., 2002). According to a saying popular in the southeastern United States, "If momma ain't happy, there ain't nobody happy."

17. Under what circumstances are poor people most likely to be unhappy?

Answer

17. Poor people are unhappiest if they have friends and relatives who are wealthier and also if they are sick as well as poor.

Other Influences on Happiness

One of the strongest influences on happiness is people's temperament or personality. In one study, most pairs of identical twins reported almost the same level of happiness, even if they differed in their wealth, education, and job prestige (Lykken & Tellegen, 1996). Most people fluctuate around a particular level of happiness for most of their lives (Diener, Lucas, & Scollon, 2006). (Abraham Lincoln said, "Most people are about as happy as they make up their minds to be.") High subjective well-being correlates strongly with personality factors that are themselves largely influenced by genetics, such as extraversion (enjoying the company of other people), emotional stability (not easily feeling depressed or nervous), and conscientiousness (Weiss, Bates, & Luciano, 2008).

Several factors influence happiness less than we might expect. Wouldn't you guess that especially good-looking people would be happier than average? If you are good looking, more people

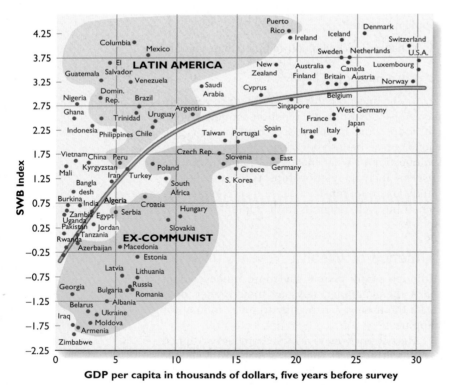

FIGURE 12.24 For each country, the mean level of individual wealth is represented on the x-axis and an index of subjective well-being is on the y-axis. Surveys were conducted in different countries in different years. (Source: Figure 2, pg. 269, from Inglehart, R., Foa, R., Peterson, C., Welzel, C. (2008). Development, freedom, and rising happiness, *Perspectives on Psychological Science, 3,* 264-285.)

smile at you, want to be your friend, and so forth. However, researchers have found only a small positive correlation between attractiveness and happiness among college students—except that highly attractive people are generally happier with their romantic life (Diener, Wolsic, & Fujita, 1995).

We might also guess that weather would make a difference. People rate themselves slightly happier on sunny days than cloudy days (Denissen, Butalid, Penke, & van Aken, 2008), but on the average, people in a cold state like Michigan rate themselves about as happy as those in sunny southern California (Schkade & Kahneman, 1998). Either people in a cold climate get used to it, or they mean something different when they rate themselves "happy."

Certain major life events do produce long-term changes in life satisfaction. People who get divorced show a gradual decrease in happiness in the years leading up to the divorce. They recover slowly and incompletely over the next few years (Diener & Seligman, 2004; Lucas, 2005). People who lose a spouse through death also show decreased happiness leading up to the event because of the spouse's failing health and slow, incomplete recovery afterward. Figure 12.25 shows the mean results. Naturally, the results vary from one person to another. Losing a job is a similar blow to life satisfaction, and many people do not fully recover (Lucas, Clark, Georgellis, & Diener, 2004). Suffering a long-term disability, such as paralysis, produces a sharp drop in life satisfaction from which many people fail to recover at all (Lucas, 2007).

Many aspects of life correlate with happiness or subjective well-being. In the following list, remember that correlations do not demonstrate causation, so alternative explanations are possible.

- Married people tend to be happier than unmarried people (DeNeve, 1999; Myers, 2000), and college students with close friendships and romantic attachments are usually happier than those without such attachments (Diener & Seligman, 2002). One explanation is that close social contacts are helpful in many ways (Cacioppo, Hawkley, & Berntson, 2003). Another is that happy people are more likely than sad people to get married or develop friendships (Lyubomirsky, King, & Diener, 2005). (Would you want to marry or become close friends with someone who was mostly sad?)
- Happy people are more likely than average to have goals in life other than the goal of making money (Csikszentmihalyi, 1999; Diener et al., 1999). One reason the money goal does not lead to happiness is that most people who

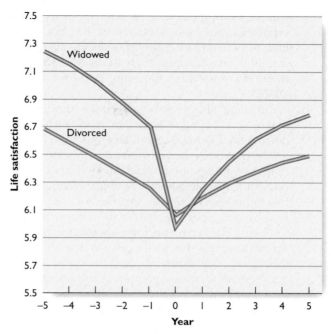

FIGURE 12.25 For each person, 0 marks the year of loss of a spouse through divorce or death. On the average, life satisfaction declines until the loss and gradually but incompletely recovers afterward. (From "Beyond money: Toward an economy of well-being," by E. Diener and M. E. P. Seligman from *Psychological Science in the Public Interest, 5,* 1–31. Copyright © 2004 Blackwell Publishing. Reprinted by permission.)

strive to be rich do not succeed! (Nickerson, Schwarz, Diener, & Kahneman, 2003).
- Generally, health and happiness go together (DeNeve, 1999; Myers, 2000). Health improves happiness, and a happy disposition probably leads to good health.
- Religious people tend to be happier than nonreligious people (Myers, 2000). Faith supports hopeful attitudes. In addition, unhappy people tend to be more critical of religious teachings and less likely to accept them.
- People who have happy friends tend also to be happy. In this case, one massive longitudinal study suggests a cause-and-effect relationship: If your friends or other people with whom you have frequent contact become happier, then within a few months, you will probably become happier also, and a few months later, your other friends will start becoming happier (Fowler & Christakis, 2008). Evidently, happiness is contagious!

If you want to improve your happiness, your best strategy is to change your activities. In one study, researchers identified students who reported a recent improvement in their living circumstances (e.g., more money or a better roommate) and other students who reported a recent improvement in their activities (e.g., joining a club or starting better study habits). Both groups reported about equal happiness at first, but by the end of the semester, those who had changed their activities were happier than those who changed their circumstances (Sheldon & Lyubomirsky, 2006).

Among the possible activities that might make you happier, here are two with well-documented benefits. First, take out time once a week—not more, or you won't take it seriously—to list five things about which you feel grateful. In one study, people who wrote about feeling grateful improved their life satisfaction, optimism, health, and exercise habits (Emmons & Mc-Cullough, 2003). Second, once a week, perform an act of kindness for someone you hardly know (Sheldon & Lyubomirsky, 2004). In one study, experimenters asked people to rate their happiness in the morning and then gave them money, instructing them to spend it by evening. Some (chosen randomly) were told to spend it on themselves. Others were told to buy a gift for someone else. When they were questioned again that evening, those who gave presents were happier, on the average, than those who spent the money on themselves (Dunn, Aknin, & Norton, 2008). In the words of a Chinese proverb, if you want happiness for an hour, take a nap. If you want happiness for a day, go fishing. If you want happiness for a year, inherit a fortune. If you want happiness for a lifetime, help somebody.

Age

Other things being equal, would you expect older people to become happier than when they were younger, less happy, or about the same? You may be surprised to learn that, compared to younger people, most people over age 65 report more happiness and less fear, anger, and sadness. They continue showing that trend as long as they remain healthy (Mroczek, 2004; Mroczek & Spiro, 2005). Older people are also likelier than younger people to enjoy the choices they make, including the products they buy (Kim, Healey, Goldstein, Hasher, & Wiprzycka, 2008).

Brain studies confirm these self-reports. In one study, young and old adults viewed photos while investigators recorded their brain activity. The amygdala of young adults responded more strongly to sad or frightening photos, whereas that of older adults responded more strongly to pleasant photos (Mather et al., 2004). In another study, while people were playing a game, a signal of the possibility to gain money produced equal effects on the brains of young and old, but a signal of the threat of losing money produced bigger responses in the brains of younger people (Larkin et al., 2007). Researchers have found that older peo-

ple tend to have increased connections to the amygdala from the frontal cortex, providing a possible means to actively suppress their responses to unpleasant information (St. Jacques, Dolcos, & Cabeza, 2009).

What explains these trends? The most popular hypothesis is that older people deliberately regulate their mood. They attend to happy events and turn away from unpleasant ones, especially if they are already in an unhappy mood (Isaacowitz, Toner, Goren, & Wilson, 2008). Support for this view comes from evidence that although older people usually direct their gaze away from emotionally negative photos, distraction (which weakens voluntary control) causes them to reverse that trend and stare at the negative photos (Knight et al., 2007).

....

18. List some factors that correlate with happiness.

Answer

18. Happiness correlates positively (though not in all cases strongly) with wealth, health, living in a country that tolerates minority groups and gives high status to women, having close personal relationships, having goals in life, being religious, having happy friends, expressing gratitude, and helping others. It also increases in old age.

....

SADNESS

If you ask people what makes them happy, you get many answers, but if you ask what makes them sad, most answers fit a pattern: People feel sad from a sense of loss. It could be death of a loved one, breakup of a romantic relationship, failure of health, or financial setbacks, but whatever someone has lost, they see little prospect of recovering it.

Crying

Severely sad people often react by crying. Just as cultures differ in their attitudes toward loud public laughter, they also differ in attitudes about adult crying. Adults in the United States cry—or at least admit to crying—far more often than those in China. Women reported crying more than men in each of 30 cultures in one survey (Becht & Vingerhoets, 2002).

Many people say that crying relieves tension and makes them feel better, but the evidence says otherwise. While people are crying, sympathetic nervous system arousal and other signs of tension visibly increase. Relaxation occurs when people *stop* crying (Gross, Fredrickson, & Levenson, 1994). Even then, they may be no more relaxed than if they had not cried at all. In one experiment, one group was encouraged to cry and another was instructed to hold back their tears while watching a sad film. Contrary to the idea that crying relieves tension, the two groups had equal tension at the end, and those who cried reported more depression (Kraemer & Hastrup, 1988). The function of crying may be to elicit sympathy and social support (Provine et al., 2009). It produces no demonstrable health benefits (Rottenberg, Bylsma, & Vingerhoets, 2008).

---

19. What evidence conflicts with the idea that crying relieves tension?

Answer

19. People who cried during a sad movie had no less tension than people who restrained their crying, and they reported feeling more depressed.

OTHER EMOTIONS

As mentioned in the previous module, psychologists have no consensus on how many types of emotion people have or even whether emotions fall into distinct categories. We can list all the elements of chemistry, but not everything comes in distinct elements. Here, briefly, let us consider a few other emotional experiences.

Many psychologists consider surprise an emotion. It occurs when events do not match expectations. When people are surprised, they become more sensitive to dangers and turn their attention toward anything that suggests a threat (Schützwohl & Borgstedt, 2005). They also tend to remember previous events that were surprising (Parzuchowski & Szymkow-Sudziarska, 2008).

Anger, disgust, and contempt are reactions to different kinds of offenses. Anger occurs when someone interferes with your rights or expectations. Disgust is literally *dis* (bad) + *gust* (taste). In the English language, we use the term loosely to refer to almost anything displeasing (Royzman & Sabini, 2001), but narrowly speaking, **disgust** refers to *a reaction to something that would make you feel contaminated if it got into your mouth* (Rozin, Lowery, et al., 1999). Most people find the idea of eating feces or insects highly disgusting. We also react with disgust, including a facial expression of disgust, to moral offenses, such as when one person cheats another (Chapman, Kim, Susskind, & Anderson, 2009; Danovitch & Bloom, 2009). In general, disgust is a feeling that something or someone is unclean (S. Schnall, Benton, & Harvey, 2008). **Contempt** is *a reaction to a violation of community standards,* such as when someone fails to do a fair share of the work or claims credit for something another person did (Rozin, Lowery, et al., 1999).

Embarrassment, shame, guilt, and pride are the "self-conscious" emotions. They occur when you think about how other people regard you or might regard you if they knew what you had done. People who feel guilty want to pay back the person they wronged, and if they can't rectify the situation, they feel as if they deserve punishment (Nelissen & Zeelenberg, 2009). The distinctions among embarrassment, shame, and guilt are not sharp, and different cultures draw the distinctions in different ways. For example, the Japanese use a word we translate as *shame* far more often than the word we translate as *embarrassment* (Imahori & Cupach, 1994). For English speakers, most causes of **embarrassment** fall into three categories (Sabini, Siepmann, Stein, & Meyerowitz, 2000):

- *mistakes,* such as thinking someone was flirting with you when in fact they were flirting with the person behind you
- *being the center of attention,* such as having people sing "Happy Birthday" to you
- *sticky situations,* such as having to ask someone for a major favor

Sometimes, people also feel embarrassed out of sympathy for someone else who is in an embarrassing situation (Shearn, Spellman, Straley, Meirick, & Stryker, 1999). Imagining how the other person feels causes you embarrassment, too.

module 12.2

In Closing

Emotions and the Richness of Life

We try to feel happy as much as possible and try to avoid feeling sad, angry, or frightened, right? Well, usually but not always. People voluntarily go to movies that they know will make them sad or frightened. They ride roller coasters that advertise how scary they are. Some people seem to enjoy being angry. Alcoholics and drug abusers experience wild swings of emotion, and many who quit say that although life is better since they quit, they miss the emotional swings. All of our emotions, within limits, provide richness to our experiences.

SUMMARY

- *Fear and anxiety.* Anxiety can be measured objectively by variations in the startle reflex after a loud noise. Processing emotional information, including anxiety, depends on a brain area called the amygdala. (page 429)

- *Polygraph.* The polygraph measures the activity of the sympathetic nervous system through such variables as heart rate, breathing rate, blood pressure, and electrical conductance of the skin. The polygraph is sometimes used as a "lie detector." However, because the responses of honest people overlap those of liars, the polygraph makes many mistakes. (page 430)

- *Anger.* People experience anger more often than violence. Anger arises when we perceive that someone has done something intentionally that blocks our intended actions. (page 431)

- *Individual differences in aggression.* One identified gene increases the probability of aggressive behavior but mainly among those who had abusive experiences in childhood. (page 432)

- *Positive psychology.* Positive psychology is the study of features that enrich life. (page 433)

- *Happiness and joy.* Happiness level is usually fairly stable over time. However, it decreases for years, sometimes permanently, after the death of a close loved one, divorce, loss of a job, or a disability. (page 433)

- *Increasing happiness.* Happiness increases from changes in activities, such as listing things to feel grateful about and helping other people. (page 435)

- *Sadness.* Sadness is a reaction to a loss. Crying is a way of communicating sadness or distress to others. (page 436)

- *Other emotions.* Anger, disgust, and contempt are reactions to different types of offenses. Embarrassment, shame, guilt, and pride depend on how we believe others will react to our actions. (page 437)

KEY TERMS

anxiety (page 429)

contempt (page 437)

disgust (page 437)

embarrassment (page 437)

frustration-aggression hypothesis (page 432)

guilty-knowledge test (page 431)

polygraph (page 430)

positive psychology (page 433)

rape (page 433)

subjective well-being (page 433)

Stress, Health, and Coping

• What is stress and how does it affect health?

• How can we deal more effectively with stress?

Imagine you meet a man suffering from multiple sclerosis. Would you say, "It's his own fault. He's being punished for his sins"? I presume not. However, many people in previous times believed just that. We congratulate ourselves today on having learned not to blame the victim.

Or have we? We think that cigarette smokers are at least partly at fault if they develop lung cancer. We note that AIDS is most common among people with a history of intravenous drug use or unsafe sex. If women drink alcohol during pregnancy, we hold them partly to blame if their infants have deformities or mental retardation. As we learn more and more about the causes of various illnesses, we expect people to accept more responsibility for their own health, although it is also easy to overstate the effect of behavior on health. Even if you are careful about your diet, exercise regularly, and avoid known risks, you could become ill anyway.

Health psychology *addresses how people's behavior influences health,* including such issues as why people smoke, why they sometimes ignore their physician's advice, and how they can reduce pain. In this module, we focus on stress, the effects of stress on health, and means of coping with stress.

Our emotions affect physiological processes and thereby influence health.

STRESS

Have you ever gone without sleep several nights in a row trying to meet a deadline? Or waited in a dangerous area for someone who was supposed to pick you up? Or had a close friend suddenly not want to see you anymore? Or tried to explain why you no longer want to date someone? These experiences and countless others cause stress.

Selye's Concept of Stress

Hans Selye, an Austrian-born physician who worked at McGill University in Montreal, noticed that a wide variety of illnesses produce the same symptoms—fever, inactivity, sleepiness, and loss of appetite. He noted that stressful experiences sometimes produce those symptoms, too. He inferred that these symptoms were the body's response to an illness or challenge, its way of fighting the difficulty. According to Selye (1979), stress is *the nonspecific response of the body to any demand made upon it.* All demands on the body evoke responses that prepare for fighting some kind of problem.

When people say, "I've been under a lot of stress lately," they usually refer to unpleasant experiences. Selye's concept of stress is broader, including any experience that changes a person's life. Getting married and being promoted are presumably pleasant experiences, but they also require changes in your life, so in Selye's sense, they produce stress. However, Selye's definition does not include the effects of poverty, racism, a lifelong disability, or anything else that is unchanging. An alternative definition of stress is *"an event or events that are interpreted as threatening to an individual and which elicit physiological and behavioral responses"* (McEwen, 2000, p. 173). Because this definition highlights what an individual interprets as threatening, it recognizes that some event might be stressful to you and not someone else or to you at one time and not at another. For example, seeing a snake in your backyard could terrify you but not bother someone who recognizes it as harmless. A critical word from your boss ordinarily disturbs you but not as much if you know why your boss is in a bad mood.

Measuring Stress

To do research on stress, we need to measure it. One approach is to give people a checklist of stressful experiences. For example, the Social Readjustment Rating Scale lists 43 life-change events (Holmes & Rahe, 1967). The authors of this test asked a group of people to rate how stressful each event would be, and on that basis, they assigned each event a certain number of points, such as 100 for death of a spouse and 11 for a traffic ticket. On this questionnaire, you check each event you experienced recently, and then a psychologist totals your points to measure your stress.

Checklists of this sort have serious problems. One is the assumption that many small stressors add to the same as one large stressor. For example, graduating from college, getting unexpected money, moving to a new address, and starting a new job are all considered stressors. According to the checklist, this combination rates almost twice as many points as you would get from a divorce. That assumption is implausible. Another problem is the ambiguity of many items. You get 44 points for "change in health of a family member." You would certainly check that item if you discover that your 5-year-old son or daughter has diabetes. Should you also check it if your aunt, whom you seldom see, recovers nicely from a bout of influenza? Apparently, you get to decide what counts and what doesn't.

Moreover, a given event has different meanings depending on how people interpret the event and what they can do about it (Lazarus, 1977). Becoming pregnant is not equally stressful to a 27-year-old married woman and an unmarried 16-year-old. Losing a job is shattering for a 50-year-old, disappointing to a 17-year-old, and trivial for an actor who works in many plays each year and never expects any of them to last long. How would you feel about winning a silver medal in the Olympics? Most of us would feel great, but many silver medal winners look sad, disappointed that they didn't win the gold (Medver, Madey, & Gilovich, 1995). What matters is not the event itself but what it means to someone.

The effects of stress depend not only on the unpleasant events ("hassles") that we have to deal with but also the pleasant events ("uplifts") that brighten our day and help to cancel out the unpleasant events (Kanner, Coyne, Schaefer, & Lazarus, 1981). Table 12.1 presents one example of this approach. Given that the stressfulness of an event depends on our interpretation of the event, the best way to measure someone's stress is through a careful, well-structured interview that evaluates all the pluses and minuses in someone's life (G. W. Brown, 1989).

TABLE 12.1 Ten Common Hassles and Uplifts

Hassles	Uplifts
1. Concerns about weight	1. Relating well with your spouse or lover
2. Health of a family member	2. Relating well with friends
3. Rising prices of common goods	3. Completing task
4. Home maintenance	4. Feeling healthy
5. Too many things to do	5. Getting enough sleep
6. Misplacing or losing things	6. Eating out
7. Yard work or outside home maintenance	7. Meeting your responsibilities
8. Property, investment, or taxes	8. Visiting, phoning, or writing someone
9. Crime	9. Spending time with family
10. Physical appearance	10. Home (inside) pleasing to you

Adapted from "Comparison of Two Modes of Stress Measurement: Daily Hassles and Uplifts Versus Major Life Events," by A. D. Kanner, J. C. Coyne, C. Schaefer, and R. S. Lazarus, *Journal of Behavioral Medicine*, 1981, 4, p. 14. Copyright (c) 1981 Plenum Publishing Corporation. Reprinted by permission of Springer-Verlag via RightsLink.

....

20. According to Selye's definition of stress, is getting married stressful? Would constant quarreling with your family be stressful?

21. Why are checklists an unsatisfactory way to measure stress?

The stressfulness of an event depends on how we interpret it. Most people would be delighted to finish second in an Olympic event, but someone who was hoping to finish first may consider it a defeat.

HOW STRESS AFFECTS HEALTH

People who have recently endured severe stress, such as the death of a husband or wife, have an increased risk of medical problems, ranging from life-threatening illnesses to tooth decay (Hugoson, Ljungquist, & Breivik, 2002; Lillberg et al., 2003; Manor & Eisenbach, 2003). How does stress lead to health problems?

Indirect Effects

Health problems by people under stress do not necessarily imply that the stress itself caused the illness. Many people who are under severe stress also suffer from poor diet, substance abuse, and other conditions that impair health (Gallo & Matthews, 2003; Repetti, Taylor, & Seeman, 2002).

Stress can influence health by altering people's behavior. For example, people who have just lost a husband or wife lose their appetite (Shahar, Schultz, Shahar, & Wing, 2001). They don't sleep well, they forget to take their medications, and some—especially men—increase their alcohol intake (Byrne, Raphael, & Arnold, 1999). One study examined adults who had endured serious stress during childhood, such as physical or sexual abuse. The childhood experiences correlated strongly with risk-taking behaviors in adulthood, such as smoking, drinking excessively, using illegal drugs, overeating, and having unsafe sex (Felitti et al., 1998). The childhood stress led to risky adult behaviors, and the behaviors led to health problems.

Stress also impairs health in roundabout ways. Back in the 1940s, a midwife who delivered three female babies on a Friday the 13th announced that all three were hexed and would die before their 23rd birthday. The first two did die young. As the third woman approached her 23rd birthday, she checked into a hospital and informed the staff of her fears. The staff noted that she dealt with her anxiety by extreme hyperventilation (deep breathing). Shortly before her birthday, she hyperventilated to death.

How did this happen? Ordinarily, when people do not breathe voluntarily, the carbon dioxide in their blood triggers reflexive breathing. By extreme hyperventilation, this woman exhaled so much carbon dioxide that she did not have enough left to trigger reflexive breathing. When she stopped breathing voluntarily, she stopped breathing altogether (Clinicopathologic Conference, 1967). This is a clear example of an indirect effect of emotions on health: The fact that she believed the hex caused its fulfillment.

Direct Effects

Stress also affects health more directly. Your sympathetic nervous system readies your body for brief vigorous activity, but your body reacts differently to a prolonged stressor. Perhaps you have a miserable job, or you live in a war zone, or you worry that a nearby nuclear power plant might have an accident. If you have a constant problem, your fight-or-flight system gives up, and you instead activate your adrenal glands to release the *hormone* cortisol, *which enhances metabolism and increases the supply of sugar and other fuels to the cells.* The increased fuel enables cells to sustain a high, steady level of activity to combat stress. A moderate, brief increase in cortisol also enhances attention and memory (Abercrombie, Kalin, Thurow, Rosenkranz, & Davidson, 2003; Beckner, Tucker, Delville, & Mohr, 2006). Cortisol also activates parts of your immune system, preparing it to fight anything from infections to tumors (Benschop et al., 1995; Connor & Leonard, 1998). Presumably, the reason is that throughout our evolutionary history, stressful situations often led to injury, so the immune system must be ready to fight infections. Your immune system fights infections by producing a fever because most bacteria do not reproduce well at elevated temperatures (Kluger, 1991). As you divert more energy to your immune system, you have less for other functions, and you become sleepy and listless. Note the result: Prolonged stress *by itself*, acting through the immune system, leads to fever, fatigue, and sleepiness (Maier & Watkins, 1998). You may think you are ill, even if you are not.

Still more prolonged stress creates problems. You feel withdrawn, your performance declines, and you complain about low quality of life (Evans, Bullinger, & Hygge, 1998). Prolonged high release of cortisol damages the hippocampus, a key brain area for memory (deQuervain, Roozendaal, Nitsch, McGaugh, & Hock, 2000; Kleen, Sitomer, Killeen, & Conrad, 2006; Kuhlmann, Piel, & Wolf, 2005). Eventually, stress exhausts the immune system, and you become more vulnerable to illness (S. Cohen et al., 1998).

22. How do the short-term effects of cortisol differ from the effects of prolonged cortisol?

Answer

22. Short-term, moderate increases in cortisol enhance memory and increase immune responses. (For example, many college students have increased immune system activity during the stressful time of taking final exams.) Prolonged cortisol damages the hippocampus, impairs memory, and exhausts the immune system.

Heart Disease

An upholsterer repairing the chairs in a physician's waiting room once noticed that the fronts of the seats wore out before the backs. To figure out why, the physician began watching patients in the waiting room. He noticed that his heart patients habitually sat on the front edges of their seats, waiting impatiently to be called in for their appointments. This observation led the physician to hypothesize a link between heart disease and an impatient, success-driven personality, now known as the Type A personality (M. Friedman & Rosenman, 1974).

People with **Type A personality** are *highly competitive, insisting on winning always. They are impatient, always in a hurry, and often hostile.* By contrast, people with a **Type B personality** are *more easygoing, less hurried, and less hostile.* Are you a Type A or a Type B? Test yourself by answering the questions in Figure 12.26.

Heart disease correlates with Type A behavior, especially with hostility, but it is a weak link (Eaker, Sullivan, Kelly-Hayes, D'Agostino, & Benjamin, 2004). The best way to conduct the research is to measure hostility now and heart problems later. (We want to know how hostility affects heart problems, not how heart problems affect hostility.) A study of that kind found a correlation of only .08 (Rutledge & Hogan, 2002). Even that weak effect may not indicate an emotional influence. Many people with high hostility also smoke, drink excessively, and eat a high-fat diet. Each of those behaviors increases the risk of heart problems (Krantz, Sheps, Carney, & Natelson, 2000).

The strongest known psychological influence on heart disease is social support. People with strong friendships and family ties usually take better care of themselves and keep their heart rate and blood pressure under control (Uchino, Cacioppo, & Kiecolt-Glaser, 1996). People who learn techniques for managing stress lower their blood pressure and decrease their risk of heart disease (Linden, Lenz, & Con, 2001).

Variations in the prevalence of heart disease across cultures may depend on behavior (R. V. Levine, 1990). In some cultures, people walk fast, talk fast, wear watches, and tend to everything in a hurry. In other, more relaxed cultures, people are

Measuring the Type A Personality

_____ 1. Do you find it difficult to restrain yourself from hurrying others' speech (finishing their sentences for them)?

_____ 2. Do you often try to do more than one thing at a time (such as eat and read simultaneously)?

_____ 3. Do you often feel guilty if you use extra time to relax?

_____ 4. Do you tend to get involved in a great number of projects at once?

_____ 5. Do you find yourself racing through yellow lights when you drive?

_____ 6. Do you need to win in order to derive enjoyment from games and sports?

_____ 7. Do you generally move, walk, and eat rapidly?

_____ 8. Do you agree to take on too many responsibilities?

_____ 9. Do you detest waiting in lines?

_____ 10. Do you have an intense desire to better your position in life and impress others?

FIGURE 12.26 If you answer "yes" to most of these items, Friedman and Rosenman (1974) would say that you probably have a Type A personality. But they would also take into account how you explain your answers, so this questionnaire gives only a rough estimate of your personality. (From *Type A Behavior and Your Heart*, by Meyer Friedman and Ray H. Rosenman, copyright © 1974 by Meyer Friedman. Used by permission of Alfred A. Knopf, a division of Random House, Inc. and Penguin Group UK.)

People in some cultures (a) live at a frantic pace. In other cultures (b), no one cares what time it is. Heart disease is more common in cultures with a hectic pace.

seldom in a rush. Almost nothing happens on schedule, but no one seems to care. As you might guess, heart disease is more common in countries with a hurried pace.

....

23. People with a Type A personality have an increased risk of stress-related heart disease. Yet, when they fill out the Social Readjustment Rating Scale, their scores are often low. Why might that scale understate the stress levels of Type A people?

Concept Check

Answer

23. The Social Readjustment Rating Scale measures life changes but not constant sources of stress such as the pressures of work.

....

Cancer

Behavior also influences cancer, at least indirectly. Women who examine their breasts regularly detect breast cancer at an early stage, when treatment is more helpful. Latina women in the United States have a higher rate of cervical cancer than other women, partly because they are less likely than other women to see doctors regularly for Pap smear tests (Meyerowitz, Richardson, Hudson, & Leedham, 1998). Preventing or treating cancer requires behavioral as well as medical interventions.

Does stress contribute directly to cancer? One study of 673 breast-cancer patients found no relationship between stressful events prior to the disease and the patients' survival times (Maunsell, Brisson, Mondor, Verreault, & Deschênes, 2001). However, another study found that highly stressful events decrease the probable survival time of people who already have cancer (Palesh et al., 2007).

Posttraumatic Stress Disorder

A profound result of severe stress is posttraumatic stress disorder (PTSD), *marked by prolonged anxiety and depression.* This condition has been recognized in postwar periods throughout history under such terms as "battle fatigue" and "shell shock." It also occurs in rape or assault victims, torture victims, survivors of life-threatening accidents, and witnesses to a murder. People with PTSD suffer from frequent nightmares, outbursts of anger, unhappiness, and guilt. A brief reminder of the tragic experience triggers a flashback that borders on panic. Mild problems seem unduly stressful, even years after the event (Solomon, Mikulincer, & Flum, 1988).

However, most people who endure traumatic events do not develop PTSD. Most suffer badly for a few weeks and then gradually recover (McFarlane, 1997). Many psychologists have assumed that the more intense the initial reaction to a stressful event, the more likely the person is to develop PTSD. If so, an immediate intervention, such as talking to a therapist, should reduce the likelihood of PTSD. Although this idea sounds reasonable, the evidence does not support it. The intensity of someone's response in the first week or so after a trauma is a poor predictor of PTSD (Harvey & Bryant, 2002), and most studies find that talking to a therapist right after a traumatic event has little effect on the development of PTSD (McNally, Bryant, & Ehlers, 2003). Some studies find that it makes people feel worse (Bootzin & Bailey, 2005; Lilienfeld, 2007).

Perhaps some people are simply more vulnerable than others. Most PTSD victims have a smaller than average hippocampus, and their brains differ from the average in several other ways (Stein, Hanna, Koverola, Torchia, & McClarty, 1997; Yehuda, 1997). Given that stress releases cortisol and that high levels of cortisol damage the hippocampus, it would seem likely that high stress caused the smaller hippocampus. However, one study compared identical twins in which one twin developed PTSD after wartime experiences and the other was not in battle and did not develop PTSD. The results: The severer the PTSD symptoms, the smaller the hippocampus of *both* the twin with PTSD and the twin without it (Gilbertson et al., 2002). These results imply that the hippocampus was already small before the trauma, perhaps for genetic reasons.

....

24. What conclusion would follow if researchers had found that the twin without PTSD had a normal size hippocampus?

Concept Check

Answer

24. If the twin without PTSD had a normal hippocampus, the conclusion would be that severe stress had damaged the hippocampus of the twin with PTSD.

....

COPING WITH STRESS

How you react to an event depends not only on the event itself but also on how you interpret it (Frijda, 1988; Lazarus, Averill, & Opton, 1970). Was it better or worse than you had expected? Was it a one-time event or the start of a trend? Your reaction also depends on your personality.

People who devote a short time each day to relaxation report diminished stress. Exercise works off excess energy, allowing greater relaxation.

Some people keep their spirits high in the face of tragedy, whereas others are devastated by minor setbacks. Coping with stress is the process of developing ways to get through difficult times.

People cope with stress in many ways, grouped into three categories. One is **problem-focused coping**, *in which people do something to control the situation.* The problem-focused methods are usually the most effective (Gross, 2001). Another category is **reappraisal**, *or reinterpreting a situation to make it seem less threatening.* The third category is **emotion-focused coping**, *in which people try to control their emotional reaction.* Suppose you are nervous about an upcoming test. Studying harder would be a problem-focused method of coping. Deciding that your grade on this test is not important would be an example of reappraisal. Deep breathing exercises would be an emotion-focused method.

The distinction is not a firm one, however (E. A. Skinner, Edge, Altman, & Sherwood, 2003). For example, one way of coping is to seek help and support from friends. Their support helps calm emotions (emotion-focused) but also may help deal with the problem itself (problem-focused).

Problem-Focused Coping

Gaining a sense of control over a situation makes it less stressful. Suppose a snowstorm has trapped you in a small cabin. You have food and fuel, but you have no idea how long you will be stuck. The snow melts 5 days later, enabling you to leave. Contrast that with a case where you decide to isolate yourself in a cabin for 5 days so you can finish a painting. In both cases, the physical circumstances are the same—5 days in a cabin. But when you do something voluntarily, you know what to expect, you know that you can quit, and you feel less stress.

When hospital patients or nursing-home residents are told what to expect and are given the chance to make some decisions for themselves, they feel better, their alertness and memory improve, and on the average, they live longer (Rodin, 1986; D. H. Shapiro, Schwartz, & Astin, 1996). Hospital patients who are told exactly what to expect show less anxiety and recover more quickly than average (Van Der Zee, Huet, Cazemier, & Evers, 2002). Many people find that religious faith helps by giving a sense of control over matters that are otherwise uncontrollable. A longitudinal study of 92,000 women found a slight tendency for religious people to live longer, presumably because of reduced stress (Schnall et al., 2008).

How does a sense of prediction or control reduce stress? First, we fear an unpredictable event may grow so intense that it might become unbearable. Second, when an event is predictable, we prepare for it at the appropriate time and relax at other times.

Thinking that you have control is calming, even if you really don't. In several studies, people had to sit through painfully loud noises while doing a difficult task. Those who were told they could press an "escape button" to turn off the noise did significantly better than those without an escape button, even though most people did not press the button—and therefore did not know whether the button worked (Glass, Singer, & Pennebaker, 1977; Sherrod, Hage, Halpern, & Moore, 1977).

In another study, two groups of people received painfully hot stimuli to their arms while playing a video game. Participants in one group knew they had no control over the pain. Those in the other group were told (incorrectly) that they could decrease the painful stimuli if they made the correct joystick response quickly enough. In fact, the painful stimuli varied randomly, but whenever it decreased, these people assumed they were responding "quickly enough." Those who *thought* they were in control reported feeling less pain, and brain scans confirmed that the pain-sensitive areas of the brain responded less strongly (Salomons, Johnstone, Backonja, & Davidson, 2004).

People also gain a sense of control by rehearsing a problem in their imagination. The better you predict the situation, the more easily you can rehearse your responses. In one study, pregnant women described what would happen as they went through labor and delivery. Those with the most accurate and detailed descriptions showed the least anxiety (G. P. Brown, MacLeod, Tata, & Goddard, 2002).

Many self-help books advise you to "visualize yourself succeeding" at something. The research says that visualizing yourself getting good grades, winning prizes, or receiving honors accomplishes nothing. What helps is to visualize yourself doing the work that will achieve success. As a student, you might visualize yourself studying in the library or writing a long research paper. By imagining the work, you begin it sooner, organize your time better, and finish sooner (S. E. Taylor, Pham, Rivkin, & Armor, 1998). You also gain a feeling of control, which makes the task less stressful.

Sometimes, a good way to reduce stress is to get a small-scale preview of an upcoming experience. You **inoculate** yourself against stressful events by *exposing yourself to small amounts of the events* (Janis, 1983; Meichenbaum, 1985; Meichenbaum & Cameron, 1983). Armies have soldiers practice combat skills under realistic conditions. A police trainee might pretend to intervene while two people enact a violent quarrel. If you are nervous about going to your landlord with a complaint, you might practice what you plan to say while your friend plays the part of the landlord. Inoculation has helped young people suffering from "dating anxiety." Some people are so nervous about saying or doing the wrong thing that they avoid dating opportunities. By role-playing, they practice dating behaviors with assigned partners and reduce their apprehension (Jaremko, 1983).

25. Which would disrupt your studying more, your own radio or your roommate's radio? Why?

26. Suppose you are nervous about giving a speech before a group of 200 strangers. How could you inoculate yourself to reduce the stress?

Concept Check

Practicing self-defense serves as an inoculation against fear. The thought of being attacked is less frightening if you know how to handle a situation.

© Cindy Charles

Answers

25. Your roommate's radio would be more disruptive. You can turn your own radio on or off, switch stations, or reduce the volume. You have no such control over your roommate's radio.

26. Practice giving your speech to a small group of friends, preferably in the room where you will deliver it.

Coping by Reappraisal

Suppose you are in a situation that offers no control. You applied for admission to graduate schools, and now you are waiting for the replies. You underwent medical tests, and you are nervously waiting for the results. While you are waiting, unable to control the outcome, what can you do?

An effective approach is to reappraise the situation: "Here is an opportunity for me to rise to the occasion, to show how strong I can be. Even if the news is bad, I can still make the best of this situation." People who recover well from tragedies and defeats say that they try to see the positive side of any event (Tugade & Fredrickson, 2004). Most people say they would rather maintain a moderately optimistic outlook on a situation than a completely accurate one (Armor, Massey, & Sackett, 2008).

Here is an example of reappraisal: Students were asked to restrain their emotions by whatever means they chose while examining a series of pictures that included some disturbing images, such as injured people and crying children. Those who restrained their emotions most successfully relied on reinterpreting the pictures. For example, they might regard a picture of an injured person as "someone about to receive good medical care" (Jackson, Malmstadt, Larson, & Davidson, 2000).

Emotion-Focused Coping

Emotion-focused strategies do not attempt to solve some underlying problem, but they help you manage your reaction to it. If you feel some unpleasant emotion—fear, anger, sadness, or disgust—would it help to simply suppress your emotion and act as if you are doing okay? Any kind of self-regulation takes effort, and the more effort you put into suppressing your emotional expressions, the less energy you'll have available for something else (Segerstrom & Nes, 2007). Most Europeans and North Americans find it difficult and unpleasant to suppress their emotions. However, people in Asian cultures routinely practice emotional suppression and find it much less burdensome (Butler, Lee, & Gross, 2007). In addition to actively suppressing emotions, other ways of handling them include social support, relaxation, exercise, and distraction.

Social support. When you feel bad, do you turn to others for support? This tendency varies across cultures more than you might expect. An American might discuss personal problems with a friend without necessarily expecting the friend to help. In Asian cultures, anyone who knows about your problem feels obligated to help. Many Asians avoid telling people about their difficulties for fear of burdening them with an obligation (Kim, Sherman, & Taylor, 2008).

If you were expecting something painful, would you feel better if someone held your hand? Researchers recorded women's reactions while they were watching signals that indicated the likelihood of receiving an electric shock. (When they saw a certain signal, it meant they had a 20% chance of receiving a shock.) At various times, each woman held her husband's hand, an unfamiliar man's hand, or no hand. As shown in Figure 12.27, on the average, a woman reported less unpleasantness and lower arousal while holding her husband's hand. Holding the hand of an unfamiliar person helped a little but not as much. Women who reported a highly satisfactory marriage received more benefit from holding their husband's hand than did women reporting a less satisfactory marriage (Coan, Schaefer, & Davidson, 2006).

Writing about stressful experiences can be helpful if you concentrate on finding solutions instead of just reliving the emotions. In one experiment, college students in one group spent half an hour per day for 3 to 5 days writing about a deeply upsetting experience, while participants in the control group wrote about unemotional topics. All the writings were confidential, so no one received any feedback or advice. The students were communicating only with themselves. Follow-up studies found that during the succeeding months, those who had written about their upsetting experiences showed better health, better grades, and less alcohol use than those in the control group (Pennebaker, 1997). Further research found that the benefits of writing about one's problems result mainly from people's attempts to understand how to handle similar situations better the next time (Pennebaker & Graybeal, 2001). Writing about pleasant emotional experiences also improves mood and health over the next few months (Burton & King, 2004).

Relaxation. Relaxation is an excellent way to reduce unnecessary anxiety. Here are some suggestions (Benson, 1985):

- Find a quiet place, or at least a spot where the noise is not too disturbing.
- Adopt a comfortable position, relaxing your muscles. If you are not sure how to do so, start with the opposite: *Tense* all your muscles so you notice how they feel. Then relax them one by one, starting from your toes and working toward your head.
- Reduce sources of stimulation, including your own thoughts. Focus your eyes on a simple, unexciting object. Or repeat something—a sentence, a phrase, a prayer, perhaps the Hindu syllable *om*—whatever feels comfortable to you.
- Don't worry about anything, not even about relaxing. If worrisome thoughts pop into your head, dismiss them with "oh, well."

People who practice this technique, a form of meditation, report that they feel less stress. Many improve their overall health (Benson, 1977, 1985). One study found that people who went through a 12-week meditation program had a long-lasting decrease in anxiety and depression compared with a control group who spent the same amount of time listening to lectures on how to reduce stress (Sheppard, Staggers, & John, 1997).

Exercise. Exercise also reduces stress. It may seem contradictory to say that both relaxation and exercise reduce stress, but exercise helps people relax. If you are tense about something that you have to do tomorrow, your best approach may be to put your energy to use: Exercise and relax afterward.

People in good physical condition react less strongly than other people do to stressful events (Crews & Landers, 1987). An event that would elevate heart rate enormously in other people elevates it only moderately in someone who has been exercising regularly. The exercise should be consistent, almost daily, but it does not need to be vigorous. In fact, strenuous activity often worsens someone's mood (Salmon, 2001).

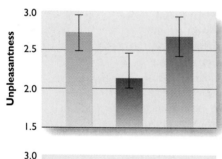

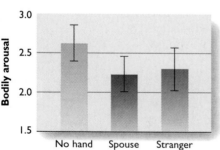

FIGURE 12.27 On the average, a woman exposed to the threat of an upcoming shock reported less distress while holding her husband's hand. (Figure 2, pg. 1036, from Coan, J. A., Schaefer, H. S., Davidson, R. J. (2006). Lending a hand: Social regulation of the neural response to a threat. *Psychological Science, 17,* 1032–1039.)

Part of the effect of exercise depends on people's expectations. Researchers studied the female room attendants at seven hotels. They randomly identified some of the hotels to inform these women (correctly) that their daily activities constitute good exercise that meets recommendations for a healthy, active lifestyle. When the researchers followed up 4 weeks later, they found that the women who were told that they were getting good exercise had in fact lost weight, and their blood pressure had decreased, even though they reported no actual change in their activities either at the hotel or outside it (Crum & Langer, 2007). Activity is more helpful if you think of it as healthy exercise than if you think of it as dull work.

Distraction. Distraction is another emotion-focused strategy, although usually not a powerful one. Many people find that they can reduce dental or postsurgical pain by playing video games or by watching comedies on television. The Lamaze method teaches pregnant women to suppress the pain of childbirth by concentrating on breathing exercises. Hospitalized patients handle their pain better if they distract themselves with a view or pleasant music (Fauerbach, Lawrence, Haythornthwaite, & Richter, 2002). Many people distract themselves from stressful or sad events by going shopping and buying themselves presents (Cryder, Lerner, Gross, & Dahl, 2008; Hama, 2001).

The effectiveness of distraction depends partly on people's expectations. In one experiment, college students were asked to hold their fingers in ice water until the sensation became too painful to endure (Melzack, Weisz, & Sprague, 1963). Some of them listened to music of their own choice and were told that listening to music would reduce the pain. Others also listened to music but were given no suggestion that it would ease the pain. Still others heard nothing but were told that a special "ultrasonic sound" was being transmitted that would lessen the pain. The group that heard music and expected it to reduce the pain tolerated the pain better than either of the other two groups did. Evidently, neither the music nor the suggestion of reduced pain is as effective as both are together.

27. Some people control anxiety with tranquilizers. In which of the three categories of coping strategy do these drugs belong?

Answer

27. Using tranquilizers is an example of emotion-focused coping.

Individual Differences

All of us can learn to handle stress better by using some of the techniques just described. In addition, some people seem to handle it better naturally (Haas, Omura, Constable, & Canli, 2007). They also remain happy and productive most of the time. Psychologists paid little attention to this phenomenon until the late 1990s, but now it has emerged as an important research topic.

Happy, optimistic people have many advantages. One is that they bounce back from painful experiences. One research difficulty is that if an investigator measures optimism and health at the same time, we have no way of knowing which one influenced the other. (Being healthy could make people optimistic just as easily as being optimistic could improve health.) A better design is to measure optimism first and health years later. In one study, investigators measured optimism for more than 5,000 city employees. Three years later, they asked them about recent major stressful events, such as death of a spouse or child. The researchers also examined work records to see how many sick-leave days each person took shortly after these traumatic events. They found that the more optimistic people took fewer sick days and returned more quickly to their normal activities (Kivimäki et al., 2005). That is, they were less devastated.

module 12.3

In Closing

Health Is Mental as Well as Medical

In this module, we have considered the ways people try to deal with stressful situations. But how well do these strategies work? The answer is that they work well for many people but at a cost. The cost is that coping with serious stressors requires energy. Many people who have had to cope with long-lasting stressors break their diets, resume smoking and drinking habits that they had abandoned long ago, and find it difficult to concentrate on challenging cognitive tasks (Muraven & Baumeister, 2000).

Still, in spite of the costs, an amazing number of people say that the experience of battling a chronic illness, tending to a loved one with a severe illness, or dealing with other painful experiences has brought them personal strength and an enhanced feeling of meaning in life (Folkman & Moskowitz, 2000). They found positive moments even in the midst of fear and loss. Not everyone rises to the occasion, but many do.

SUMMARY

- *Selye's concept of stress.* According to Hans Selye, stress is "the nonspecific response of the body to any demand made upon it." Any event, pleasant or unpleasant, that brings about change in a person's life produces some measure of stress. One problem with this definition is that it omits lifelong problems, such as coping with racism. (page 439)
- *Difficulties of measuring stress.* Stress checklists are problematic because many items are ambiguous. Also, the stressfulness of an event depends on the person's interpretation of the event and ability to cope with it. (page 440)
- *Indirect effects on health.* Stress affects health indirectly because people exposed to stressful events often change their eating, sleeping, and drinking habits. (page 441)
- *Direct effects on health.* Stress causes increased secretion of the hormone cortisol. Brief, moderate elevations of cortisol enhance memory and immune system responses. However, prolonged cortisol damages health by impairing the hippocampus and by exhausting the immune system. (page 441)
- *Heart disease and cancer.* Research has found only a small link between emotional responses and the onset of heart disease. A link to the onset of cancer remains uncertain, but reducing stress improves survival time and improves quality of life. (page 442)
- *Posttraumatic stress disorder.* After severe traumatic experiences, some people have long-lasting changes in experience. Some people are more vulnerable than others to this outcome. (page 443)
- *Coping styles.* Most strategies for dealing with stress fall into three major categories: trying to fix the problem, reappraisal, and trying to control emotions. (page 444)
- *Prediction and control.* Events are generally less stressful when people think they can predict or control them. (page 444)
- *Reappraisal.* Interpreting a situation in a new, less threatening way reduces tension. (page 445)
- *Emotion-focused coping.* Relaxation, exercise, and distraction reduce excess anxiety. (page 445)
- *Individual differences.* Optimistic people tend to handle stress more effectively than others. (page 447)

KEY TERMS

cortisol (page 441)

emotion-focused coping (page 444)

health psychology (page 439)

inoculation (page 445)

posttraumatic stress disorder (PTSD) (page 443)

problem-focused coping (page 444)

reappraisal (page 444)

stress (page 439)

Type A personality (page 442)

Type B personality (page 442)

Why Does This Matter to Me?

SOCIAL RESPONSIBILITY AND PSYCHOLOGY

Many environmental and societal problems are caused by human behavior. Psychologists can help steer the course of our future toward more socially responsible and sustainable outcomes. Students of today need to be ever mindful of the link between human behavior and its impact on the environment and our communities.

"Emotions, Stress, and Health" and Social Responsibility: A Step Further

Do you think there is a link between environmental hazards (pollution, noise, overcrowding) and mental health? How would you test, for instance, whether living in an urban environment predicts depression? Would your test show only a correlation or lack of correlation, or could you devise a causational experiment?

Help Reduce Stress in Your Community

Do you have a dog? Pet therapy programs may help reduce stress in heart patients among others. Visit www.cengage.com/psychology/kalat for a link to information and resources to certifiy you and your dog for animal-assisted therapy.
http://www.charityguide.org/volunteer/fewhours/pet-therapy.htm

Join the iChapters Plant a Tree Drive!

To show its support of the environmental movement, iChapters is planting a tree on behalf of each fan of the iChapters Facebook Page and for every 10 questions answered correctly in our quiz.
http://www.ichapters.com/plantatree/

Exploration and Study

SUGGESTIONS FOR FURTHER EXPLORATION

In addition to the study materials provided at the end of each module, you may supplement your review of this chapter with the following book and website suggestions or by using one or more of the book's electronic resources, which include its companion website, interactive Cengage Learning eBook, and CengageNOW. Brief descriptions of these resources follow. For more information, visit **www.cengage.com/psychology/kalat**.

ADDITIONAL RESOURCES

The book's companion website, accessible from **www.cengage.com/psychology/kalat**, provides a wide range of study resources such as an interactive glossary, flashcards, tutorial quizzes, updated web links, and Try It Yourself activities. For example, the exercise on universal emotions ties to what you've learned in this chapter.

CengageNOW with Critical Thinking Videos is an easy-to-use resource that helps you study in less time to get the grade you want. An online study system, CengageNOW gives you the option of taking a diagnostic pretest for each chapter. The system uses the results of each pretest to create personalized chapter study plans for you. The Personalized Study Plans

- Help you save study time by identifying areas on which you should concentrate and give you one-click access to corresponding pages of the interactive Cengage Learning eBook;
- Provide interactive exercises and study tools to help you fully understand chapter concepts; and
- Include a posttest for you to take to confirm that you are ready to move on to the next chapter.

Critical Thinking

Find critical thinking videos like this one in your CengageNOW product, which offer an opportunity for you to learn more about psychological research on different topics.

Fear Conditioning

Books

Damasio, A. (1999). *The feeling of what happens.* New York: Harcourt Brace. Ambitious treatment of the role of emotions in thinking and consciousness.

Haidt, J. (2006). *The happiness hypothesis.* New York: Basic Books. Excellent discussion of research on happiness and other emotions, especially on how they relate to moral behavior.

Provine, R. (2000). *Laughter.* New York: Viking Press. Pioneering observations of who laughs, when, and why. Highly recommended.

Websites

Links to the websites described below are kept current and can be found at **www.cengage.com/ psychology/kalat**.

Violence

The Minnesota Center Against Violence and Abuse (MINCAVA) maintains hundreds of links to sites that provide information about all forms of violence.

Emotions and Artificial Intelligence

Would it be possible to build a robot with emotions? Here is a site for people who like to think about that question.

© Alain Le Bot/Photononstop/Photolibrary

Social Psychology

Consider This:

In the *Communist Manifesto*, Karl Marx and Friedrich Engels wrote, "Mankind are more disposed to suffer, while evils are sufferable, than to right themselves by abolishing the forms to which they are accustomed. But when a long train of abuses and usurpations, pursuing invariably the same object, evinces a design to reduce them under absolute despotism, it is their right, it is their duty, to throw off such government." Fidel Castro wrote, "A little rebellion, now and then, is a good thing." Do you agree with those statements? Why or why not? Can you think of anything that would change your mind?

Oh, pardon me. . . . That first statement is not from the *Communist Manifesto*. It is from the United States' Declaration of Independence. Sorry. And that second quotation is from Thomas Jefferson, not Castro. Do you agree more with these statements now that you know they came from democratic revolutionaries instead of communist revolutionaries?

What influences your opinions? This question is one example of the issues that interest **social psychologists**—*the psychologists who study social behavior and how people influence one another.* Social psychology includes the study of attitudes, persuasion, self-understanding, and almost all everyday behaviors of relatively normal people in their relationships with others.

Influence depends not only on what someone says but also on what the listeners think of the speaker.

© AP Photo/Rich Pedroncelli

452

Cooperation and Competition

• What determines whether we cooperate or compete with others?

The custom of living in groups dates back to before the origin of the human species, as almost all primates (monkeys and apes) live in groups. Group life has many advantages, including defense against predators and protection of food and supplies. Human societies provide another feature not seen in other mammals: an extraordinary division of labor. If you had to make your own shelter and clothing, find your own food and water, and tend to your own medical problems, how long would you survive? Most of us wouldn't last long. Together, we accomplish vastly more than any of us could alone.

Furthermore, people go beyond mere cooperation. Most of us at least occasionally give to charity, volunteer our time for worthy projects, offer directions to a stranger who appears lost, and in other ways help people who will never pay us back. Why do people behave in cooperative, moral ways?

DEVELOPING MORALITY AND COOPERATION

Psychologists once regarded morality as a set of arbitrary, learned rules, such as learning to stop at a red light and go at a green light. Lawrence Kohlberg (1969; Kohlberg & Hersh, 1977) proposed instead that moral reasoning is a process that naturally matures through a series of stages, similar to Piaget's stages of cognitive development. For example, children younger than about 6 years old say that accidentally breaking something valuable is worse than intentionally breaking a less valuable object. Older children and adults attend more to people's intentions. The change is a natural unfolding, according to Kohlberg, not a matter of memorizing rules.

In George Bernard Shaw's (1911) play *The Doctor's Dilemma,* two men are dying. The only doctor in town has enough medicine to save one of them but not both. One man is an artistic genius but dishonest, rude, and disagreeable. The other is just ordinary but honest and decent. The doctor, forced to choose between them, saves the honest but untalented man. Did he make the right choice? According to Kohlberg, this is the wrong question. The right question is *why* he made that choice. In the play, the doctor chose this man because he hoped to marry the wife of the artistic genius after letting that man die. (You can evaluate the quality of the doctor's moral reasoning for yourself.)

To measure the maturity of someone's moral judgments, Kohlberg devised a series of moral dilemmas—*problems that pit one moral value against another.* Each dilemma is accompanied by a question such as, "Did this person do the right thing, and why or why not?" Kohlberg was not concerned about the choices people make because well-meaning people disagree on the answer. More revealing are their explanations, which are categorized into six stages, grouped into three levels (Table 13.1). Because few people respond consistently at stage 6, many authorities combine stages 5 and 6. To emphasize: Kohlberg's stages do not represent moral versus immoral decisions but moral versus less moral *reasons* for a decision.

People begin at Kohlberg's first stage and progress through the others in order, although few reach the highest stages. (The order of progression is an important point: If people were just as likely to progress in the order 3-5-4 as in the order 3-4-5, then we would have no justification for calling one stage higher than another.) Although people fluctuate from one time to another, we can classify them in terms of their average level.

1. For the moral dilemma described at the top of Table 13.1, suppose someone says that Heinz was wrong to steal the drug to save his wife's life. Which level of moral reasoning is characteristic of this judgment?

Concept Check

Answer

1. It depends. In Kohlberg's system, any judgment can represent either a high or a low level of moral reasoning. We evaluate a person's moral reasoning by the explanation, not by the decision itself.

Limitations of Kohlberg's Views

Kohlberg's theory has limitations. Let us consider two issues: (a) different orientations to morality and (b) the relationship between moral reasoning and behavior.

Moral Reasoning Not Centered on Justice

Kohlberg assumed that judgments of right and wrong depend on "justice." In many non-Western cultures, such as India, people seldom talk about justice. They speak instead of a natural sense of duty toward others (Shweder, Mahapatra, & Miller, 1987). They also focus on spiritual purity as a major aspect of morality (Haidt, 2007).

Even people in Western cultures don't always reason in terms of justice. Carol Gilligan (1977, 1979) has emphasized a "caring" orientation—that is, what would help or hurt other people. At one point during the Vietnam War, a group of soldiers were ordered to kill unarmed civilians. One soldier refused to shoot. In terms of justice, he acted at a high moral level. However, his actions made no difference, as other soldiers killed all the civilians. In terms of caring, he would have been more moral if he had found a way to hide a few potential victims (Linn & Gilligan, 1990).

TABLE 13.1 Responses to One of Kohlberg's Moral Dilemmas by People at Six Levels of Moral Reasoning

The dilemma: Heinz's wife was near death from cancer. A druggist had recently discovered a drug that might be able to save her. The druggist was charging $2000 for the drug, which cost him $200 to make. Heinz could not afford to pay for it, and he could borrow only $1000 from friends. He offered to pay the rest later. The druggist refused to sell the drug for less than the full price paid in advance: "I discovered the drug, and I'm going to make money from it." Late that night, Heinz broke into the store to steal the drug for his wife. Did Heinz do the right thing?

Level/Stage	Typical Answer	Description of Stage
The Level of Preconventional Morality		
1. Punishment and obedience orientation	"No. If he steals the drug, he might go to jail." "Yes. If he can't afford the drug, he can't afford a funeral, either."	Decisions are based on their immediate consequences. Whatever is rewarded is "good" and whatever is punished is "bad." If you break something and are punished, then what you did was bad.
2. Instrumental relativist orientation	"He can steal the drug and save his wife, and he'll be with her when he gets out of jail."	It is good to help other people, but only because they may one day return the favor: "You scratch my back and I'll scratch yours."
The Level of Conventional Morality		
3. Interpersonal concordance, or "good boy/nice girl" orientation	"People will understand if you steal the drug to save your wife, but they'll think you're cruel and a coward if you don't."	The "right" thing to do is whatever pleases others, especially those in authority. Be a good person so others will think you are good. Conformity to the dictates of public opinion is important.
4. "Law and order" orientation	"No, because stealing is illegal." "Yes. It is the husband's duty to save his wife even if he feels guilty afterward for stealing the drug."	You should respect the law—simply because it is the law—and work to strengthen the social order that enforces it.
The Level of Postconventional or Principled Morality		
5. Social-contract legalistic orientation	"The husband has a right to the drug even if he can't pay now. If the druggist won't charge it, the government should look after it."	The "right" thing to do is whatever people have agreed is the best thing for society. As in stage 4, you respect the law, but in addition recognize that a majority of the people can agree to change the rules. Anyone who makes a promise is obligated to keep the promise.
6. Universal ethical principle orientation	"Although it is legally wrong to steal, the husband would be morally wrong not to steal to save his wife. A life is more precious than financial gain."	In special cases it may be right to violate a law that conflicts with higher ethical principles, such as justice and respect for human life. Among those who have obeyed a "higher law" are Jesus, Mahatma Gandhi, and Martin Luther King, Jr.

Source: Kohlberg, 1981

Moral Reasoning and Moral Behavior

The movie *Schindler's List* portrays a German man who risked his life to save Jewish people from the Nazi Holocaust. If you or I had been Germans at the time, would we have done the same? I don't know. Knowing the right thing is not the same as doing it.

Kohlberg's approach concentrated on moral reasoning, not behavior. People are moderately consistent in their answers to hypothetical questions about moral dilemmas. They are less consistent in actual behavior. Researchers find that people seldom carefully reason out their moral decisions. Usually, they decide immediately and then try to think of a moral justification. Consider the following: Mark and his sister Julie are college students. During one summer, they traveled together, and one night, they stayed at a cabin in the woods. They decided it would be fun to have sex together, so they did. Julie was taking birth-control pills, but Mark used a condom anyway just to be sure. Both enjoyed the experience, and neither felt hurt in any way. They decided not to do it again but to keep it as their little secret. They feel

Sometimes, the two "voices" of moral reasoning—justice and caring—conflict with each other. From a caring standpoint, you want to help someone in distress. From a justice standpoint, you may think it wrong to encourage begging.

closer than ever as brother and sister. Was their action okay?

Almost everyone reacts vigorously and immediately that the decision was wrong. Why? Mark and Julie used two reliable methods of birth control, and both said they enjoyed the experience and did not feel hurt. So if their act was wrong,

Polish social worker Irena Sendler saved about 2,500 Jewish children by smuggling them out of danger during World War II. Few people take such heroic actions, even though we know what is right.

why was it wrong? When you said (I assume) that they were wrong, did you carefully reason it out, or did you decide impulsively and then look for a justification? Many, maybe most, of our moral decisions are based on emotions, not just logic (Haidt, 2001, 2007). Consequently, moral reasoning, as evaluated by Kohlberg's methods, correlates poorly with actual behavior (Krebs & Denton, 2005).

Although many people give answers that qualify as stages 4, 5, and 6, moral *behavior* at those levels is uncommon, and we can understand why (Krebs, 2000). Most behavior follows reasoning at stages 1, 2, and 3: Seek rewards, avoid punishments, cooperate with others who cooperate with you, and punish those who don't cooperate. Behavior at stages 4, 5, and 6 benefits other people whom you will never meet. You gain indirectly by building a reputation, but you don't gain immediately.

Still, most people recognize a moral imperative, even if they know their behavior falls short of it. You *want* to behave morally. Imagine the following: You and another student show up for a research study. The researchers explain that two studies are available. One study sounds appealing. The other is difficult and painful. You are invited to flip a coin, examine it by yourself in private, and then announce who gets to be in the pleasant study. In this situation, nearly 90% of students claim they won the toss and get to be in the pleasant experiment. Obviously, many are lying. However, suppose you were asked whether you want to flip the coin and announce the results or let the experimenter do it. Now most people say, "Let the experimenter do it" (Batson & Thompson, 2001). They avoid putting themselves in a situation in which they know they will be tempted to cheat.

ALTRUISTIC BEHAVIOR

Why do we sometimes engage in altruistic behavior—*helping others despite some cost or risk to ourselves?* It seems so natural that we take it for granted, but altruism is uncommon in other animal species. Let's qualify that: In almost every species, animals devote great energies and risk their lives to help their babies or other relatives. But they seldom do much to help unrelated individuals.

In one study, each chimpanzee could pull either of two ropes. Sometimes, it could pull one rope to get food or pull another to get nothing. It almost always chose the rope with food. At other times, one rope brought food, and the other rope brought food to *both* itself and a chimp it saw in another cage. The chimp in control seemed indifferent to the other chimp, even when the other chimp made begging gestures. Usually, the chimp pulled whichever rope was on the right regardless of whether it fed the other chimp or not (Silk et al., 2005).

Given that altruism is uncommon in the rest of the animal kingdom, why do people do so much to help one another? You may reply that we help others because it feels good. Yes, but why does it feel good? Did we evolve genes that make altruistic behavior feel good? If so, why? No one has found such a gene, and if someone did, a theoretical mystery would remain about how natural selection could favor such a gene. You may reply that an altruistic gene helps the species. Yes, but if a gene helps those who *don't* have the gene as much as or more than those who do, the gene won't spread in the population. If we consider the issue in nongenetic terms, the same problem arises: If you learn a habit of helping others, including people who are not altruistic themselves, they profit and you do not. Why would you learn to act that way? We shall consider two answers based on research with games.

The Prisoner's Dilemma and Similar Situations

Do you cooperate with others and help them generously? For most of us, the honest answer is "it depends" (Fehr & Fischbacher, 2003). To investigate how situations evoke cooperation or competition, many researchers in psychology and economics have used the **prisoner's dilemma**, *a situation where people choose between a cooperative act and a competitive act that benefits themselves but hurts others.* Here is the original version of this dilemma: You and a partner are arrested and charged with armed robbery. The police take you into separate rooms and urge each of you to confess. If neither of you confesses, the police do not have enough evidence to convict you of armed robbery, but they can convict you of a lesser offense with a sentence of 1 year in prison. If either confesses and testifies against the other, the confessor goes free and the other gets 20 years in prison. If you both confess, you each get 5 years in prison. Each of you knows that the other person has the same options. Figure 13.1 illustrates the choices.

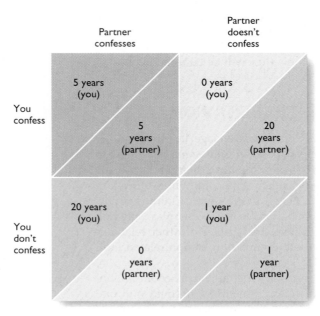

FIGURE 13.1 In the prisoner's dilemma, each person has an incentive to confess. But if both people confess, they suffer worse than if both had refused to confess.

If your partner does not confess, you can confess and go free. (Your partner gets 20 years in prison, but let's assume you care only about yourself.) If your partner confesses, you still gain by confessing because you will get only 5 years in prison instead of 20. So you confess. Your partner, reasoning the same way, also confesses, and you both get 5 years in prison. If you had both kept quiet, you would have served only 1 year in prison. The situation led both people to uncooperative behavior.

If you and your partner could discuss your strategy, you would agree not to confess. Then, when the police took you to separate rooms, you would each hope that the other keeps the bargain. But can you be sure? Maybe your partner will double-cross you and confess. If so, you should confess, too. And if your partner does keep the bargain, what should you do? Again, it's to your advantage to confess! We're back where we started.

The two of you are most likely to cooperate if you stay in constant communication (Nemeth, 1972). If you overhear each other, you know that, if one confesses, the other will retaliate. This kind of situation occurs in real life among nations as well as individuals. During the arms race between the United States and the Soviet Union, both sides wanted an agreement to stop building nuclear weapons. However, if one country kept the agreement while the other cheated by making additional weapons, the cheater could build a military advantage. The only way to keep an agreement was to allow each side to inspect the other. Each side needed to observe the other and also needed to be observed (even spied upon, to some extent) to reassure the other side. If either side doubted that the other was keeping its word, the agreement would fail.

The prisoner's dilemma can also be stated in terms of gains. Suppose you and another person have a choice between two moves, which we call *cooperate* and *compete*. Depending on your choices, here are the payoffs:

Here are the payoffs:

	Other person cooperates	Other person competes
You cooperate	Both win $1	Other person gains $2; you lose $2
You compete	You gain $2; other person loses $2	Both lose $1

Suppose you play this game only once with someone you will never meet. Both of you will reveal your answers by telephone to a third person. Which move do you choose? If the other person cooperates, your winning choice is *com-*

pete because you will get $2 instead of $1. If the other person competes, again you gain by competing because you will lose just $1 instead of $2. Logically, you should choose to compete, and so should the other person. Therefore, you both lose $1. (Advice: Try to avoid situations like this!)

Effective Strategies

If you and another person play repeatedly, the strategy changes drastically. The most dependable strategy is reciprocity, also called "tit for tat": Start with the *cooperate* move. If the other person cooperates, too, then continue cooperating. If the other person makes a *compete* move, retaliate with a *compete* move on your next turn. (Your retaliation should teach the other person not to take advantage of you.) You can try this strategy and others on Bryn Mawr's website, where you can compete against a computer opponent. Find a current link to the website at **www.cengage.com/ psychology/kalat**.

If you use the tit-for-tat strategy, you will never beat the other person, but both of you will do reasonably well. Business deals work like this in real life. You offer to sell me something, so I send you the money. If we keep our promises, we are willing to do business again.

Most individuals cooperate in prisoner's dilemma-type situations, especially when real rewards are at stake. Culture makes a difference, however. For example, Chinese people cooperate more than Americans on the average (Wong & Hong, 2005). Curiously, groups are more likely than individuals to compete instead of cooperating (Wildschut, Pinter, Vevea, Insko, & Schopler, 2003). Think of conflicts between nations or the ways in which competing political parties sometimes treat each other.

Let's consider another situation of cooperation versus competition known as the Trust game. The researchers give you (player A) $10 (or euros, pesos, or whatever) and the same amount to player B. Now you can, if you choose, transfer any or all of that money to player B. If so, it will be doubled, so that B gains $20. B then has an opportunity to transfer $0–10 back to you, which will be doubled. If you each transfer the full amount, you both gain $20. However, do you trust B? If you transfer $10 and B transfers nothing, B goes home with $30 and you get nothing.

A further complication: You don't know who B is, and B doesn't know who you are. Also, you will play repeatedly with a variety of partners, sometimes in the role of player A and sometimes as player B. How would you behave? Most people start off by cooperating. Player A transfers most of the $10 to B, and B returns the same or almost as much to A. However, some people are untrustworthy from the start (King-Casas et al., 2008). After the first round, your behavior depends on how people have treated you in the past. When people cooperate with you or treat you kindly, in this situation or any other, you become more likely to trust and help others (Bartlett & DeSteno, 2006). However, if someone cheats you—for example, you transfer $10 to B, who returns nothing to you—you become less trusting and less cooperative. You stop transferring money when you are player A, and you return less when you are player B. Cheating spreads within the population, and soon, no one transfers any money (Fehr & Fischbacher, 2003). In other settings, too, including a classroom, if people see someone get away with cheating, cheating spreads (Gino, Ayal, & Ariely, 2009).

Why don't business deals break down like that in real life? In real life, people are not anonymous. You develop a reputation, and so do others. You cooperate with people who cooperate, and you refuse to do business with those who don't (Nowak & Sigmund, 2005; D. S. Wilson, Near, & Miller, 1996). Thus, here is our first explanation for why people act altruistically: *They want a reputation for being fair and helpful.* As a result, other people will be pleased to deal with them and offer them help when they need it. In fact, people often choose to do business only with the most cooperative partners they can find. The result is a competition to develop the highest reputation for cooperation (McNamara, Barta, Fromhage, & Houston, 2008).

Why is altruistic behavior uncommon among nonhumans? For reputations to develop, individuals must recognize one another over long delays (Burtsev & Turchin, 2006). Recall from chapter 4 that people have an amazing ability to recognize other people's faces, even after delays of many years. Why have we evolved that ability? It is to keep track of whom to trust and whom to avoid. Most other species have poorer ability to recognize other individuals. In those that do recognize one another, a certain amount of sharing and cooperation does occur (Schutt, 2008).

Religious people tend to be more cooperative than average and more likely to help others. Researchers have related this tendency to maintaining reputation. Religious people tend to be highly cooperative toward others of their own religion and less toward outsiders. They also tend to become more cooperative when reminded of the concept of God, suggesting that they are interested in maintaining their "reputation" in the eyes of God (Norenzayan & Shariff, 2008).

If you lost interest in your reputation, would you become less cooperative? Researchers manipulated people's expectations of future social relationships. They told some people (randomly assigned) that their answers to a questionnaire revealed that they were the type of people who end up alone in life. Their friends will drift away, and their marriage, if any, won't last. (In fact, no questionnaire reveals any such thing. Even if it did, an ethical psychologist wouldn't tell people this prediction without offering counseling. However, the participants in this study seemed to believe what they were told.) The result was that the people who expected to be alone in life became less likely to contribute to a worthy cause, less likely to help someone with a simple chore, and more likely to give uncooperative responses in the prisoner's dilemma game (Twenge, Baumeister, DeWall, Ciarocco, & Bartels, 2007). After the experiment, the researchers of course told people that they weren't really doomed to a life of isolation!

Cultural Transmission

If you have been thinking about why people help one another, you might point out that other people teach us to cooperate. Again, researchers have demonstrated this tendency with games. One version is the Public Goods game. Imagine that you and three others play this game anonymously. The researcher gives each of you $20 (or 20 euros or whatever) to start. Each of you can contribute as much as you choose to the common pool. After all have made their contributions, the researchers increase the amount in the common pool by 60% and then divide it equally among all four players regardless of how much each contributed. That is, if each of you contributes the full $20, the total of $80 becomes $128 (80 x 1.6), and each person's share is $32, a nice profit over your original $20. However, a free rider could keep the $20 and take one fourth of the wealth earned by other people's contributions. You play this game repeatedly, and each time you are in a different group, so you never interact with the same person twice. How much would you contribute? Most people contribute less and less as the game continues.

However, the results change if we alter the rules: At the end of each round, each of you learns how much each other player contributed, and you have the option to punish. For a charge of $1 to yourself, you can subtract $3 from the player you want to punish. If you contributed most of your money to the common pool, and so did two others, you might be willing to pay for the opportunity to punish the uncooperative person who contributed little or nothing. It is considered "altruistic punishment" because you gain nothing, except a feeling of justice. The punished person might learn a lesson, but if so, the benefit is to the next group of people that he or she plays with. Many people do administer punishments, and the result is a high

level of cooperation across almost all individuals. No one wants to be the lowest contributor to the common pool for fear of being punished (Fehr & Gächter, 2002). So we have identified a second reason for human altruistic behavior: *We learn to cooperate because others who cooperate will punish us if we don't.* It is interesting what goes together here: Our ability to cooperate, which we consider a noble trait, is possible only because of our eagerness to wreak revenge (a rather base motive) when someone behaves selfishly.

However, the results just described don't always work. Sometimes, a punished noncooperator seeks revenge by punishing cooperators. In that case, those who avoid using punishment come out ahead (Dreber, Rand, Fudenberg, & Nowak, 2008). In countries where people don't have a strong tradition of cooperating, punishment and counterpunishment often get out of hand until no one cooperates, everyone punishes, and no one prospers (Herrmann, Thöni, & Gächter, 2008).

....

2. Theoretically, how can we explain why people sometimes act altruistically toward people they have never met? Why do they tend to be even more cooperative with people they have known for a long time?

Concept Check

3. You have read two explanations for humans' altruistic behavior. Why do both of them require individual recognition?

Answers

2. Even with a stranger, you behave altruistically to develop a reputation for cooperating. With a familiar person, you know the person will return your favors and probably retaliate if you fail to cooperate.

3. One explanation is that cooperating builds a reputation, and a reputation requires individuals to recognize one another. The other explanation is that people who cooperate will punish those who do not. Again, to retaliate, they need to recognize who has failed to cooperate.

....

ACCEPTING OR DENYING RESPONSIBILITY TOWARD OTHERS

Other people can encourage us to do something we would not have done on our own. They can also inhibit us from doing something that we would have done on our own. We look around to see what others are doing—or *not* doing—and we say, "Okay, I'll do that, too." Why do people sometimes work together and sometimes ignore the needs of others?

Bystander Helpfulness and Apathy

Suppose while you are waiting at a bus stop, you see me trip and fall down, not far away. I am not screaming in agony, but I don't get up either, so you are not sure whether I need help. Would you come over and offer to help? Or would you stay there and ignore me? Before you answer, try imagining the situation in two ways: First, you and I are the only people in sight. Second, many other people are nearby, none of them rushing to my aid. Does the presence of those other people make any difference to you? (It doesn't to me. I am in the same pain regardless of how many people ignore me.)

Late one night in March 1964, Kitty Genovese was stabbed to death near her apartment in Queens, New York. A newspaper article at the time reported that 38 of her neighbors heard her screaming for more than half an hour, but none of them called the police, each of them either declining to get involved or assuming that someone else had already called the police. Later investigations of the crime indicated that this report was greatly exaggerated (Manning, Levine, & Collins, 2007). Genovese was attacked twice in half an hour. About six people saw the first attack, and at least one or two did call the police, who did nothing. She went into the building on her own, and her attacker returned half an hour later, out of sight of witnesses, while she was too weak to scream loudly.

Although the original newspaper article was full of errors, it prompted widespread interest in why people often fail to help a person in distress. Are we less likely to act when we know that someone else could act? Bibb Latané and John Darley (1969) proposed that being in a crowd decreases our probability of action because of **diffusion of responsibility**: *We feel less responsibility to act when other people are equally able to act.*

In an experiment designed to test this hypothesis, a young woman ushered one or two students into a room and asked them to wait for the start of a market research study (Latané & Darley, 1968, 1969). She went into the next room, closing the door behind her. Then she played a tape recording that sounded as though she climbed onto a chair, fell off, and then moaned, "Oh . . . my foot . . . I can't move it. Oh . . . my ankle . . ." Of the participants who were waiting alone, 70% went next door and offered to help. Of the participants who were waiting with someone else, only 13% offered to help.

In another study, investigators entered 400 Internet chat groups of different sizes and in each

People watch other people's responses to decide how they should respond. When a group of sidewalk Santas—who had gathered in Manhattan to promote a back-rub business—came to the aid of an injured cyclist, a few Santas made the first move and the others followed.

one asked, "Can anyone tell me how to look at someone's profile?" (That is, how can I check the autobiographical sketch that each chat room user posts?) The researchers found that the more people in a chat room at the time, the longer the wait before anyone answered the question. In large groups, the researchers sometimes had to post the same question repeatedly (Markey, 2000).

Diffusion of responsibility is one explanation. Each person thinks, "It's not my responsibility to help any more than someone else's." A second possible explanation is that the presence of other people who are doing nothing provides information (or misinformation). The situation is ambiguous: "Do I need to act or not?" Other people's inaction implies that the situation requires no action. In fact, the others are just as uncertain as you are, and they draw conclusions from *your* inaction. Social psychologists use the term **pluralistic ignorance** to describe *a situation in which people say nothing, and each person falsely assumes that others have a better informed opinion.* The presence of other people exerts both normative and informational influences: Their inactivity implies that doing nothing is acceptable (a norm) and that the situation is not an emergency (information).

Social Loafing

When you take a test, you work alone, and your success depends on your own effort. In other cases, however, you are part of a team. If you work for a company that gives workers a share of the profits, your rewards depend on other workers' productivity as well as your own. Do you work as hard as you can when the rewards depend on the group's productivity?

In many cases, you do not. In one experiment, students were told to scream, clap, and make as much noise as possible, like cheerleaders at a sports event. Sometimes, each student screamed and clapped alone; sometimes, students acted in groups; and sometimes, they acted alone but *thought* other people were screaming and clapping, too. (They wore headphones so

During a catastrophe, people abandon their usual tendencies toward bystander apathy and social loafing.

they could not hear anyone else.) Most of the students who screamed and clapped alone made more noise than those who were or thought they were part of a group (Latané, Williams, & Harkins, 1979). Social psychologists call this phenomenon social loafing—*the tendency to "loaf" (or work less hard) when sharing work with other people.*

Social loafing has been demonstrated in many situations. Suppose you are asked to "name all the uses you can think of for a brick" (e.g., crack nuts, anchor a boat, use as a doorstop) and write each one on a card. You probably fill out many cards by yourself but fewer if you are tossing cards into a pile along with other people's suggestions (Harkins & Jackson, 1985). You don't bother submitting ideas that you assume other people have already suggested.

At this point, you may be thinking, "Wait a minute. When I'm playing basketball or soccer, I try as hard as I can. I don't think I loaf." You are right; social loafing is rare in team sports because observers, including teammates, watch your performance. People work hard in groups if they expect other people to notice their effort or if they think they can contribute something that other group members cannot (Shepperd, 1993; K. D. Williams & Karau, 1991).

4. Given what we have learned about social loafing, why are most people unlikely to work hard to clean the environment?

5. In a typical family, one or two members have jobs, but their wages benefit all. Why do those wage earners *not* engage in social loafing?

Concept Check

Answers

4. Social loafing is likely because many one-person contributions, such as picking up litter, would not earn individual credit or recognition. Also, each person thinks, "What good could one person do with such a gigantic problem?"

5. The main reason is that the wage earners see they can make a special contribution that the others (children, injured, or retired) cannot. Also, others can easily observe their contributions.

13.1

module

In Closing

Is Cooperative Behavior Logical?

Either we have evolved a tendency to help others, or we learn to. The research on the prisoner's dilemma and similar games attempts to demonstrate that cooperation and mutual aid are logical under certain conditions. You cooperate to develop a good reputation so that others will cooperate with you and not penalize you.

Do you find this explanation completely satisfactory? Sometimes, you make an anonymous contribution to a worthy cause with no expectation of personal gain, not even an improvement of your reputation. You simply wanted to help that cause. You occasionally help someone you'll never see again while no one else is watching. Perhaps these acts require no special explanation. You have developed habits of helping for all the reasons that investigators have identified. Once you developed those habits, you generalize them to other circumstances, even when they do you no good. Yes, perhaps. Or maybe researchers are still overlooking something. Conclusions in psychology are almost never final. You are invited to think about these issues yourself and develop your own hypotheses.

SUMMARY

- *Kohlberg's view of moral reasoning.* From infancy through adulthood, people gradually develop tendencies toward altruistic and cooperative behavior. Lawrence Kohlberg argued that we should evaluate moral reasoning on the basis of the reasons people give for a decision rather than the decision itself. (page 453)
- *Challenges to Kohlberg's views.* Kohlberg concentrated on justice and ignored other views of morality. People's answers to Kohlberg's dilemmas correlate only weakly with their actual behavior. We make many, perhaps most, moral decisions by quick emotional responses, not by careful deliberation. (page 453)
- *The prisoner's dilemma.* In the prisoner's dilemma, two people can choose to cooperate or compete. The *compete* move seems best from the individual's point of view, but it is harmful to the group. (page 456)

- *Effective strategies.* If someone plays the prisoner's dilemma repeatedly with the same partner, an effective strategy is tit for tat: Cooperate unless the other person competes, and then retaliate. (page 457)
- *Reasons for cooperation.* Studies of the prisoner's dilemma and other situations demonstrate two rational reasons for cooperation: A cooperative person enhances his or her reputation and therefore gains cooperation from others. Also, people who cooperate punish those who do not. (page 457)
- *Bystander apathy.* People are less likely to help someone if other people are in an equally good position to help. (page 459)
- *Social loafing.* Most people work less hard when they are part of a group than when they work alone, except when they think they can make a unique contribution or if they think others are evaluating their contribution. (page 459)

KEY TERMS

altruistic behavior (page 455)

diffusion of responsibility (page 459)

moral dilemma (page 453)

pluralistic ignorance (page 459)

prisoner's dilemma (page 456)

social loafing (page 460)

social psychologists (page 452)

Social Perception and Cognition

- What factors influence our judgments of others?
- How can we measure stereotypes that people do not want to admit?
- How can we overcome prejudices?
- How do we explain the causes of our own behavior and that of others?

What's your first impression of this man: rich or poor; businessman, professional athlete, or manual laborer? Many first impressions are accurate.

People generally measure their success by comparing themselves to others. You cheer yourself up by noting that you are doing better than some of your friends. You motivate yourself to try harder by comparing yourself to someone more successful (Suls, Martin, & Wheeler, 2002).

To make these comparisons, we need accurate information about other people. We also need that information to form expectations about how others will act and whom we can trust. Social perception and cognition are *the processes we use to learn about others and make inferences from that information.* Social perception and cognition influence our observations, memory, and thinking.

FIRST IMPRESSIONS

Other things being equal, *the first information we learn about someone influences us more than later information does* (E. E. Jones & Goethals, 1972). This tendency is known as the primacy effect. (We also encountered this term in chapter 7 on memory, where it refers to the tendency to remember well the first items on a list.) For example, if you hear both favorable and unfavorable reports about a restaurant, the first reports you hear influence you the most (Russo, Carlson, & Meloy, 2006).

We form first impressions with amazing speed and more accuracy than you might guess. In one study, college students viewed three 2-second videos of various professors lecturing, without sound, and rated how good they thought these professors were. Their mean rating correlated .6 with the end-of-semester ratings by the students in those classes (Ambady & Rosenthal, 1993). (These results suggest that students' evaluations of professors depend more on nonverbal communication than on the content of the lectures!) In another study, people watching 10-second videos of couples could in most cases guess how much romantic interest they felt (Place, Todd, Penke, & Asendorpf, 2009). People watching 1-minute videos of strangers guessed their wealth, with a correlation of .25 (Kraus & Keltner, 2009). People examining photos of company executives could guess how profitable the company was (Rule & Ambady, 2008). First impressions can be even faster: Researchers flashed photographs on a screen for a tenth of a second each and asked observers to judge each person's attractiveness, likability, and competence. Judgments made in this split second correlated better than .5 with judgments made at leisure (Willis & Todorov, 2006). You may have heard the expression, "You only have one chance to make a first impression." The research suggests that you have only a split second to make that impression!

First impressions can become self-fulfilling prophecies, *expectations that change behavior in a way that increases the probability of the predicted event.* Suppose a psychologist hands you a cell phone and asks you to talk with someone, while showing you a photo supposedly of that person. Unknown to the person you are talking to, the psychologist might hand you a photo of a very attractive member of the opposite sex or a much less attractive photo. Not surprisingly, you act friendlier to someone you regard as attractive. Furthermore, if you think you are talking to someone attractive, that person reacts by becoming more cheerful and talkative. In short, your first impression changes how you act and influences the other person to live up to (or down to) your expectations (M. Snyder, Tanke, & Berscheid, 1977).

6. Why do some professors avoid looking at students' names when they grade essay exams?

Concept Check

6. They want to avoid being biased by their first impressions of the students.

STEREOTYPES AND PREJUDICES

A stereotype is *a belief or expectation about a group of people.* A prejudice is *an unfavorable attitude toward a group of people.* It is usually associated with discrimination, which is *unequal treatment of different groups,* such as minority groups, the physically disabled, people who are obese, or gays and lesbians.

Stereotypes affect us in subtle, unconscious ways. Imagine yourself in this experiment: You are given sets of five words to arrange into sentences. Here are three examples:

CAR REPAIRS OLD THIS NEEDS

CLOUDY GRAY SKY THE WAS

OFFER GAMES SMALL BINGO PRIZES

Easy, right? You think the experiment is over, and now you are walking out. The real point of the experiment is to watch you walk out! People in one experimental condition—the one you were in—unscrambled sentences that included words associated with the stereotype of old people, such as *old, gray,* and *bingo.* On the average, people who have just been thinking about old people tend to walk more slowly than usual, like their stereotype of old people (Bargh, Chen, & Burrows, 1996). In a similar study, students who had been thinking about old people before filling out an attitude questionnaire expressed attitudes more consistent with their stereotypes of old people, such as defending more government support for health care (Kawakami, Dovidio, & Dijksterhuis, 2003).

It is possible to develop false stereotypes because of our tendency to remember the unusual, such as an unusual person doing something unusual. If you remember one left-handed redhead who cheated you, you might form a false stereotype about left-handed redheads—an illusory correlation, as discussed in chapter 2. However, some stereotypes are correct. For example, who do you think gets into more fistfights on the average—men or women? If you answered "men," you are supporting a stereotype, but you are correct. Similarly, who do you think is more likely to be sensitive to the subtle social connotations in everyday conversation—a liberal arts major or an engineering major? Again, if you said "liberal arts major," you are endorsing a stereotype, but the research supports you (Ottati & Lee, 1995).

The stereotype of old people as inactive has many exceptions.

Indeed, whenever we say that culture influences behavior, we imply that members of those cultures behave differently on the average and therefore that a stereotype about them is partly correct. In some cases, members of both cultures agree on the stereotypes but express them in different words. For example, many Americans describe the Chinese as "inhibited," whereas Chinese call themselves "self-controlled." U.S. businesspeople complain that Mexicans "don't show up on time," whereas Mexicans complain that people from the United States "are always in a rush" (Y. T. Lee & Duenas, 1995).

However, agreeing that a stereotype is correct on the average does not mean it fits all individuals (Banaji & Bhaskar, 2000). For example, some 80- and 90-year-olds are far more alert and active than the stereotype of old age suggests. If we form stereotypes, we need to recognize exceptions to the rule.

Implicit Measures of Stereotypes and Prejudice

Decades ago, Americans admitted their prejudices openly. Today, almost all people believe in fair treatment for everyone, or so they say. But are people as unprejudiced as they claim to be? Researchers have sought methods of measuring subtle prejudices that people do not want to admit, even to themselves.

One method is the Implicit Association Test (IAT), which *measures reactions to combinations of categories, such as flowers and pleasant.* If you respond quickly, you probably see the two categories as related. Imagine this example: You rest your left and right forefingers on a computer keyboard. When you hear a word, you should press with your left finger if it is an unpleasant word, such as *death, fail,* or *shame,* and press with your right finger if it is a pleasant word, such as *joy, love,* or *success.* After a while, the instructions change. Now you should press the left key if you hear the name of an insect and the right key if you hear the name of a flower. Next you combine two categories: Press the left key for unpleasant words or insects and the right key for pleasant words or flowers. Then the pairings switch: Press the left key for unpleasant words or flowers and the right key for pleasant words or insects. The procedure continues, alternating between the two instructions.

Most people respond faster to the combination "pleasant or flowers" than to "pleasant or insects." The conclusion is that most people like flowers more than insects. The procedure may seem more trouble than it is worth, as people readily tell us that they like flowers and not insects. However, this research established the validity of the method, which researchers then used to measure other preferences (Greenwald, Nosek, & Banaji, 2003).

Imagine yourself in this experiment: You view a computer screen that sometimes shows a photo and sometimes a word. If it is a photo of a Black person or a pleasant word, press the left key. If it is a photo of a White person or an unpleasant word, press the right key. After you respond that way for a while, the rule switches to the opposite pairing.

Figure 13.2 illustrates the procedures and Figure 13.3 summarizes the results for a group of White college students. Most responded faster to the combinations *Black/unpleasant* and *White/pleasant,* even though they claimed to have no racial prejudice (Phelps et al., 2000). This implicit preference of White people toward other Whites is stable over time (Baron & Banaji, 2006), and it correlates positively, though not strongly, with people's behavior in real-world situations (W. A. Cunningham, Preacher, & Banaji, 2001; Greenwald, Nosek, & Sriram, 2006; Nosek, 2007). On the average, older Whites show a stronger bias than younger Whites do (Stewart, von Hippel, & Radvansky, 2009). However, the Implicit Association Test probably over-

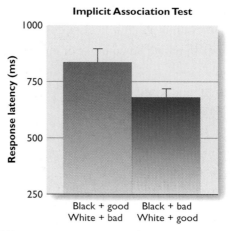

Implicit Association Test

FIGURE 13.3 On the average, White students who claimed to have no racial prejudice responded slower if they had to make one response for "Black face or pleasant word" and a different response for "White face or unpleasant word" than if the pairings were reversed—Black and unpleasant, White and pleasant. (From "Performance on Indirect Measures of Race Evaluation Predicts Amygdala Activation" by E. A. Phelps, K. J. O'Connor, W. A. Cunningham, E. S. Funayama, J. C. Gatenby, J. C. Gore & M. R. Banaji, *Journal of Cognitive Neuroscience,* 2000, *12,* 729–738. Copyright © 2000 MIT Press. Reprinted by permission.)

states people's prejudices, simply because it requires people to pay attention to race (M. A. Olson & Fazio, 2003).

Researchers made available a simplified version of the Implicit Association Test on a website, which you can try yourself: find a current link to the site at **www .cengage.com/psychology/kalat.**

What results would you predict for Black participants? Although most Black people state a more favorable explicit attitude to Blacks than to Whites, the Implicit Association Test indicates nearly equal responses to Blacks and Whites—that is, on the average, little or no prejudice (Stewart et al., 2009).

The IAT also gauges implicit attitudes toward men and women. Most women show a strong implicit preference for women over men. Men, however, show an almost equal preference for women and men (Nosek & Banaji, 2001; Rudman & Goodwin, 2004). Evidently, women like other women more than men like other men.

The results of the Implicit Association Test are important for showing that even well-meaning people have prejudices that they do not recognize (Greenwald & Banaji, 1995). That result is important to remember when people insist that we should evaluate college applicants or job applicants "entirely on the basis of their

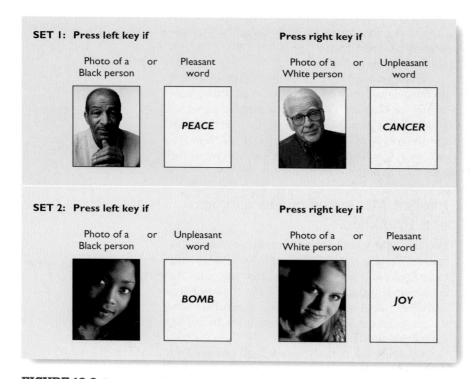

FIGURE 13.2 Procedures for an Implicit Association Test to measure prejudices.

qualifications." It is difficult to evaluate qualifications and ignore prejudices, especially when the qualifications are unclear (Crosby, Iyer, Clayton, & Downing, 2003). Consider this example (Dovidio & Gaertner, 2000): Each White college student was asked to evaluate the folder for someone applying for a job as a peer counselor. One third of the applications described strong experience and qualifications for the job, one third were marginal, and one third had weak qualifications. Of each kind of application (strong, marginal, or weak), half mentioned membership in a nearly all-White fraternity, and the other half mentioned membership in the Black Student Union. So each student read what appeared to be a strong White, strong Black, marginal White, marginal Black, weak White, or weak Black application. The following graph shows the mean results. The students were slightly more generous with well-qualified or poorly qualified Black applicants than with equally qualified Whites. The big difference, however, was for the marginal applications. The students evaluated the ambiguous qualifications more positively if they thought they applied to White applicants than Black applicants. Other studies have found similar results (Vanman, Saltz, Nathan, & Warren, 2004).

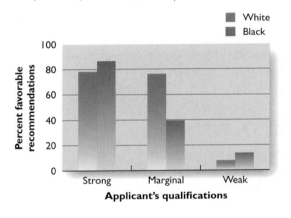

7. What is the advantage of the Implicit Association Test over asking people about their racial prejudices?

Answer

7. The Implicit Association Test reveals prejudices that people don't want to admit, even to themselves.

Prejudice as an Emotional Response

Although most people today *consciously endorse the idea of treating all groups equally, many people nevertheless harbor negative feelings and unintentionally discriminate.* When these conflicting feelings pertain to race, psychologists use the term aversive racism, also known as subtle prejudice, modern racism, symbolic racism, and racial ambivalence (Sears & Henry, 2003). This kind of racism is called "aversive" because it is unpleasant to the person who acts this way. Similarly, many people have ambivalent sexism, *an overt belief in equal treatment of the sexes joined with a lingering idea that women should be treated differently* (Glick & Fiske, 2001).

Fighting against showing prejudice causes tension, and as a result, many Whites feel anxiety about dealing with Blacks. They want to appear unprejudiced but fear that they will fail. Whites who have had little previous contact with Blacks are especially likely to show physiological arousal, such as increased heart rate, when talking with Blacks (Blascovich, Mendes, Hunter, Lickel, & Kowai-Bell, 2001). Researchers asked White college students a series of questions about their contacts with Blacks and possible anxiety about such encounters. Then they asked the students to return 1 week later for a session of interacting with a Black student. The White students with the greatest anxiety were the least likely to return for that session (Plant & Devine, 2003).

In another experiment, White college students were asked to spend some time working with a Black person. Various individuals, randomly assigned, received instructions to try to have a positive experience or to try to avoid the appearance of prejudice. Those who were told to try for a positive experience performed better and felt better. Trying to "avoid seeming prejudiced" is evidently a tiring experience, and those who were given this instruction showed an impaired performance on cognitive tasks *after* the interracial session (Trawalter & Richeson, 2006).

Many Whites advocate being "color blind"—ignoring group differences and treating everyone the same. That attitude is effortful, requiring people to ignore group differences or pretend not to notice. An alternative strategy is multiculturalism— *accepting, recognizing, and enjoying the differences among groups.* Research shows advantages of the multiculturalism approach for Whites and Blacks alike. Whites who are encouraged to adopt a multiculturalist attitude show less prejudice both in their overt behavior and on the Implicit Association Test (Richeson & Nussbaum, 2004). When a company or other organization endorses a multiculturalist position, minorities feel more comfortable within that organization (Plaut, Thomas, & Goren, 2009).

Overcoming Prejudice

After people form a prejudice, what can overcome it? Increasing contact between groups usually helps. Brief, superficial contact doesn't do much good, but prolonged, close contact does. A study of White and Black college students who were assigned to be roommates found that they spent little time together at first, but over the course of a semester, they formed more favorable attitudes and felt less anxiety about interracial interactions (Shook & Fazio, 2008).

A particularly effective technique is to get groups to work toward a common goal (Dovidio & Gaertner, 1999). Many years ago, psychologists demonstrated the power of this technique using two arbitrarily chosen groups (Sherif, 1966). At a summer camp at Robbers' Cave, Oklahoma, 11- and 12-year-old boys were divided into two groups in separate cabins. The groups competed for prizes in sports, treasure hunts, and other activities. With each competition, the antagonism between the two groups grew more intense. The boys made threatening posters, shouted insults, and engaged in food fights.

Up to a point, the "counselors" (experimenters) tolerated the hostility. Then they tried to reverse it by stopping the competitions and setting common goals. First, they asked the two groups to work together to find and repair a leak in the water pipe that supplied the camp. Then they had the two groups pool their treasuries to rent a movie that both groups wanted to see. Later, they had the boys pull together to get a truck out of a rut. Gradually, hostility turned into friendship—except for a few holdouts who nursed their hatred to the bitter end! The point is that competition breeds hostility, and cooperation leads to friendship.

The media also play a role in strengthening or weakening prejudices. In 1994 Rwanda (in south-central Africa) had a vicious civil war in which the majority Hutus, urged on by their government and Rwanda's primary radio station, killed three fourths of the Tutsi minority. (Televisions and newspapers are rare in Rwanda, and radio is the primary means of communication and entertainment.) Today, the Hutus and surviving Tutsis live in an uneasy truce. A radio soap opera, made available on an experimental basis to some villages and not others, described a fictional place in which one group attacked another group, but leaders spoke out against violence, and people from the two groups formed friendships. The people in villages that heard this soap opera showed increased sympathy, trust, and cooperation, breaking down the barriers between Hutus and Tutsis (Paluck, 2009).

8. What would be an improvement on the advice "try to avoid seeming prejudiced"?

Answer

8. It is better to try to have a positive experience and to enjoy cultural differences. Increased contact helps overcome intergroup tensions, especially if people work together for a common goal.

ATTRIBUTION

Yesterday, you won the state lottery, and today, classmates who previously ignored you want to be your friends. You draw inferences about their reasons. **Attribution** is *the set of thought processes we use to assign causes to our own behavior and that of others.*

Internal Versus External Causes

Fritz Heider, the founder of attribution theory, emphasized the distinction between internal and external causes of behavior (Heider, 1958). **Internal attributions** are *explanations based on someone's individual characteristics, such as attitudes, personality traits, or abilities.* **External attributions** are *explanations based on the situation, including events that presumably would influence almost anyone.* An example of an internal attribution is that your brother walked to work this morning "because he likes the exercise." An external attribution would be that he walked "because his car wouldn't start." Internal attributions are also known as *dispositional* (i.e., something about the person's disposition led to the behav-

People who work together for a common goal can overcome prejudices that initially divide them.

ior). External attributions are also known as *situational* (i.e., something about the situation led to the behavior).

You make internal attributions when someone does something you consider surprising. For example, if I say I would like to visit Hawaii, you draw no conclusions about me. However, if I say I would like to visit northern Norway in winter, you wonder what is special about my interests. When a man gets angry in public, most people assume he had a reason. When a woman gets equally angry in public, her behavior is more surprising, and people attribute it to her personality (Brescoll & Uhlmann, 2008).

This tendency sometimes leads to misunderstandings between members of different cultures. Each person views the other's behavior as "something I would not have done" and therefore as grounds for making an attribution about personality. For example, some cultures expect people to cry loudly at funerals, whereas others expect more restraint. People who are unfamiliar with other cultures may attribute a behavior to someone's personality, when in fact it is a dictate of culture.

We sometimes attribute a behavior to personality, when in fact it is customary in someone's culture. In the United States, a funeral usually calls for reserved behavior. Many other places expect loud wailing.

Harold Kelley (1967) proposed that we rely on three types of information when making an internal or an external attribution for someone's behavior:

- **Consensus information** *(how the person's behavior compares with other people's behavior)*. If someone behaves the same way you believe other people would in the same situation, you make an external attribution, recognizing that the situation led to the behavior. When a behavior seems unusual, you look for an internal attribution pertaining to the person. (You can be wrong if you misunderstand the situation.)
- **Consistency information** *(how the person's behavior varies from one time to the next)*. If someone almost always seems friendly, you make an internal attribution ("a friendly person"). If someone's friendliness varies, you make an external attribution, such as an event that elicited a good or bad mood.
- **Distinctiveness** *(how the person's behavior varies from one situation to another)*. If your friend is pleasant to all but one individual, you assume that person has done something to irritate your friend (an external attribution).

9. Classify the following as either internal or external attributions:
   a. She contributed money to charity because she is generous.
   b. She contributed money to charity because she wanted to impress her boss, who was watching.
   c. She contributed money to charity because she owed a favor to the man who was asking for contributions.
10. Juanita returns from watching *The Return of the Son of Sequel Strikes Back Again Part 2* and says it was excellent. Most other people disliked the movie. Will you make an internal or external attribution for Juanita's opinion? Why? (distinctiveness, consensus, or consistency?)

Answers

9. **a.** internal;   **b.** external;   **c.** external. An internal attribution relates to a stable aspect of personality or attitudes; an external attribution relates to the current situation.
10. You probably will make an internal attribution because of *consensus*. When one person's behavior differs from others, we make an internal attribution.

The Fundamental Attribution Error

A common error is *to make internal attributions for people's behavior even when we see evidence for an external influence on behavior*. This tendency is known as the **fundamental attribution error** (Ross, 1977). It is also known as the *correspondence bias,* meaning a tendency to assume a strong similarity between someone's current actions and his or her dispositions.

Imagine yourself in a classic study demonstrating this phenomenon. You are told that U.S. college students were randomly assigned to write essays praising or condemning Fidel Castro, then the communist leader of Cuba. You read an essay that defends Castro, criticizes the United States for its long embargo against Cuba, and compares Cuba favorably to other Latin American countries. What's your guess about the actual attitude of the student who wrote this essay?

very anti-Castro   neutral   very pro-Castro

Most U.S. students in one study guessed that the author of a pro-Castro essay was at least mildly pro-Castro, even though they were informed, as you were, that the author had been required to praise Castro (E. E. Jones & Harris, 1967). In a later study, experimenters explained that one student in a creative writing class had been assigned to write a pro-Castro essay and an anti-Castro essay at different times in the course. Then the participants read the two essays and estimated the writer's true beliefs. Most thought that the writer had changed attitudes between the two essays (Allison, Mackie, Muller, & Worth, 1993). That is, even when people are told of a powerful external reason for someone's behavior, they seem to believe the person probably had internal reasons as well (McClure, 1998). Similarly, when they see a famous actor or athlete endorse some product, they believe the celebrity really does favor that product, even though they know the manufacturer paid the celebrity for the endorsement (Cronley, Kardes, Goddard, & Houghton, 1999).

....

11. How would the fundamental attribution error affect people's attitudes toward actors and actresses who portrayed likable and contemptible characters? **Concept Check**

Answer

characters.

11. Because of the fundamental attribution error, people would tend to think that performers who portray likable characters are themselves likable, and those who play contemptible people probably resemble those

....

Cultural Differences in Attribution and Related Matters

The fundamental attribution error relates to culture. In general, people of Western cultures rely more on internal (personality) attributions in situations, whereas people in China and other Asian countries tend to make more external (situational) attributions. For example, how would you explain the behavior of the fish designated with an arrow in this drawing? Most Americans say this fish is leading the others, whereas many Chinese say the other fish are chasing it (Hong, Morris, Chiu, & Benet-Martinez, 2000). That is, the cultures differ in whether they think the fish controls its own behavior or obeys the influence of the others. **try it yourself**

Richard Nisbett and his colleagues noted other cases in which Asian people tend to focus more on the situation and less on individual personality than do most people in Western cultures (Nisbett, Peng, Choi, & Norenzayan, 2001). As a result, they expect more change and less consistency in people's

behavior from one situation to another. Asians are also more likely to accept contradictions and look for compromises instead of viewing one position as correct and another as incorrect. Here are a few examples:

- When given a description of a conflict, such as one between mother and daughter, Chinese students are more likely than Americans to see merit in both arguments instead of siding with one or the other (Peng & Nisbett, 1999).
- Far more Chinese than English-language proverbs include apparent self-contradictions, such as "beware of your friends, not your enemies" and "too humble is half proud" (Peng & Nisbett, 1999).
- Chinese people are more likely than Americans to expect events to change and to predict that current trends—whatever they might be—will reverse themselves. For example, if life seems to have been getting better lately, most Americans predict that things will continue getting better, whereas Chinese predict that things will get worse (Ji, Nisbett, & Su, 2001).
- In one study, people were told about an event and then told the final outcome. Americans often expressed surprise when Koreans said the outcome was to be expected. That is, in this study, the Koreans showed a stronger hindsight bias (chapter 7)—the tendency to say, "I knew it all along" (Choi & Nisbett, 2000).

The reported differences are interesting. Still, an important question remains: To the extent that Asian people respond differently from Western-culture people, is that difference due to ancient traditions or current conditions? Perhaps Asians notice the influence of their environment more just because their environment looks different from that of Western countries. Most Asian cities are more cluttered than American and European cities (Figure 13.4). Researchers found that Japanese students tended to notice the background of photographs more than Americans, who focused heavily on objects in the foreground. However, after Americans viewed a series of pictures of Japanese cities, they too began paying more attention to the backgrounds (Miyamoto, Nisbett, & Masuda, 2006). The question remains whether Asians pay more attention to backgrounds because of the way they build their cities or whether they build their cities that way because of a cultural tendency in their perception and thinking.

The Actor-Observer Effect

Here is another common bias related to the fundamental attribution error: *People are more likely to make internal attributions for other people's be-*

FIGURE 13.4 On the average, Asian cities are more crowded and cluttered than U.S. and European cities.

havior and more likely to make external attributions for their own (E. E. Jones & Nisbett, 1972). This tendency is called the **actor-observer effect.** You are an "actor" when you try to explain the causes of your own behavior and an "observer" when you try to explain someone else's behavior.

In one study, investigators asked college students to rate themselves, their fathers, their best friends, and Walter Cronkite (a television news announcer at the time) on several personality traits. For each trait (e.g., "leniency"), the participants were given three choices: (a) the person possesses the trait, (b) the person possesses the opposite trait, and (c) the person's behavior "depends on the situation." Participants checked "depends on the situation"—an external attribution—most frequently for themselves, less frequently for their fathers and friends, and least often for Walter Cronkite (Nisbett, Caputo, Legant, & Marecek, 1973). Figure 13.5 shows the results.

Why do you or I explain our own behavior differently from that of others? I am aware of many of the influences on my behavior. If I have an emergency and I am rushing to get somewhere, I might honk at other drivers and pass everyone I can. Because they don't know my situation, they probably assume I am always rude. Similarly, when someone honks and speeds past me, all I know is what I see (Pronin, 2008). I don't know that person's circumstances, so I assume he or she is habitually aggressive.

Another explanation is perceptual. We see other people as objects in our visual field, and we tend to think that whatever we are watching is the cause of the action. Researchers have found that if you watch a videotape of your own behavior, you tend to explain the behavior in terms of personality more than situational factors, just as you do when you watch other people (Storms, 1973).

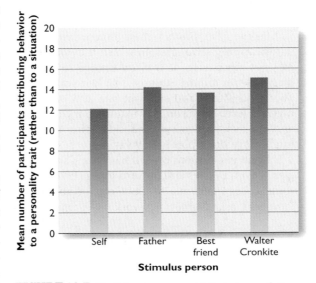

FIGURE 13.5 Participants were most likely to say that their own behavior depended on the situation and least likely to say "it depends" for the person they knew the least. (Based on data of Nisbett, Caputo, Legant, & Marecek, 1973)

A further application of this idea: Suppose you watch a videotape of a conversation between two people. The actual conversation is planned so that both people participate equally. However, you are randomly given one of two versions of the videotape, with the camera focused on one person or the other. You tend to perceive that the person you are watching dominates the conversation. Similarly, if you watch a videotape of an interrogation between a detective and a suspect, you judge the suspect's confession to be more voluntary if the camera focuses on the suspect and more coerced if the camera focuses on the detective (Lassiter, Geers, Munhall, Ploutz-Snyder, & Breitenbecher, 2002).

Using Attributions to Manage Perceptions of Ourselves

Even if you generally attribute your own behavior largely to external causes, you vary your attributions to try to present yourself in a favorable light. For example, you might credit your good grades to your intelligence and hard work (an internal attribution) but blame your bad grades on unfair tests (an external attribution). *Attributions that we adopt to maximize credit for success and minimize blame for failure* are called self-serving biases (D. T. Miller & Ross, 1975; van der Pligt & Eiser, 1983). Self-serving biases are robust. Even students who have learned about them usually think the biases apply to other people more than themselves (Pronin, Gilovich, & Ross, 2004). Self-serving biases are, however, less prominent among Chinese, Japanese, and other East Asian people, presumably because their culture defines self-worth in terms of fitting into the group rather than outcompeting one's peers (Balcetis, Dunning, & Miller, 2008; Heine & Hamamura, 2007).

People also protect their images with self-handicapping strategies, in which they *intentionally put themselves at a disadvantage to provide an excuse for failure.* Suppose you fear you will do poorly on a test. You stay out late at a party the night before. Now you can blame your low score on your lack of sleep without admitting that you might have done poorly anyway.

In an experiment on self-handicapping strategies, Steven Berglas and Edward Jones (1978) asked some college students to work on solvable problems and asked others to work on a mixture of solvable and unsolvable problems. (The students did not know that some of the problems were impossible.) The experimenters told all the students that they had done well. The students who had been given solvable problems (and had solved them) felt good about their success. Those who had worked on unsolvable problems were unsure in what way they had "done well." They had no confidence that they could continue to do well.

Next the experimenters told the participants that the purpose of the experiment was to investigate the effects of drugs on problem solving and that they were now going to hand out another set of problems. The participants could choose between taking a drug that supposedly impaired problem-solving abilities and another drug that supposedly improved them. The participants who had worked on unsolvable problems the first time were more likely than the others to choose the drug that supposedly impaired performance. Because they did not expect to do well on the second set of problems anyway, they provided themselves with an excuse.

- - - - - - - - - -

12. Who is more likely to make the fundamental attribution error, Americans or Chinese?

13. If instead of watching someone, you close your eyes and imagine yourself in that person's position, will you be more likely to explain the behavior with internal or external attributions? Why?

14. Why would people sometimes intentionally do something likely to harm their own performance?

Answers

14. People sometimes do something to harm their own performance, especially if they expect to do poorly anyway.

13. You will be more likely to give an external attribution because you will become more like an actor and less like an observer.

12. Americans and others from Western cultures are more likely to make the fundamental attribution error because the Chinese tend to attribute behavior more to situational factors than do Westerners.

- - - - - - - - - -

In Closing

How Social Perceptions Affect Behavior

We are seldom fully aware of the reasons for our own behavior, much less someone else's, but we make our best guesses. If someone you know passes by without saying "hello," you might attribute that person's behavior to absentmindedness, indifference, or hostility. You might attribute someone's friendly response to your own personal charm, the other person's extraverted personality, or that person's devious and manipulative personality. The attributions you make are sure to influence your own social behaviors.

SUMMARY

- *First impressions.* Other things being equal, we pay more attention to the first information we learn about someone than to later information. First impressions form rapidly, and in some cases, they are surprisingly accurate. (page 462)
- *Stereotypes.* Stereotypes are generalized beliefs about groups of people. Stereotypes influence our behavior in subtle ways, often without our awareness. (page 463)
- *Prejudice.* A prejudice is an unfavorable stereotype. Many people do not admit their prejudices, even to themselves. Indirect measures demonstrate subtle prejudices even in people who deny having them. (page 463)
- *Overcoming prejudice.* Trying to have a good experience with someone works better than trying to avoid showing prejudice. Accepting and enjoying group differences usually work better than trying to see everyone as the same. Spending time together and working together for a common goal weaken prejudices between groups. (page 465)
- *Attribution.* Attribution is the set of thought processes by which we assign internal or ex-
ternal causes to behavior. According to Harold Kelley, we are likely to attribute behavior to an internal cause if it is consistent over time, different from most other people's behavior, and directed toward a variety of other people or objects. (page 466)
- *Fundamental attribution error.* People frequently attribute people's behavior to internal causes, even when they see evidence of external influences. (page 467)
- *Cultural differences.* People in Asian cultures are less likely than those in Western cultures to attribute behavior to consistent personality traits and more likely to attribute it to the situation. (page 468)
- *Actor-observer effect.* We are more likely to attribute internal causes to other people's behavior than to our own. (page 468)
- *Self-serving bias and self-handicapping.* People sometimes try to protect their self-esteem by attributing their successes to skill and their failures to outside influences. They sometimes place themselves at a disadvantage to provide an excuse for failure. (page 470)

KEY TERMS

actor-observer effect (page 469)

ambivalent sexism (page 465)

attribution (page 466)

aversive racism (page 465)

consensus information (page 467)

consistency information (page 467)

discrimination (page 463)

distinctiveness (page 467)

external attribution (page 466)

fundamental attribution error (page 467)

Implicit Association Test (page 463)

internal attribution (page 466)

multiculturalism (page 465)

prejudice (page 463)

primacy effect (page 462)

self-fulfilling prophecy (page 462)

self-handicapping strategies (page 470)

self-serving biases (page 470)

social perception and cognition (page 462)

stereotypes (page 463)

Attitudes and Persuasion

> • What are some effective ways to influence attitudes?

"If you want to change people's behavior, you have to change their attitudes first." Do you agree? Suppose you do. Now answer two more questions: (a) What is your attitude about paying higher taxes? (b) If the government raises taxes, will you pay them?

I assume you said that you have an unfavorable attitude about higher taxes, but if the taxes are raised, you will pay them. Thus, by changing the law, the government could change your behavior without changing your attitude. Frequently, behaviors change more easily than attitudes.

So, what effects do attitudes have on behavior? And what leads people to change their attitudes?

ATTITUDES AND BEHAVIOR

An **attitude** is *a like or dislike that influences our behavior* (Allport, 1935; Petty & Cacioppo, 1981). Your attitudes include an evaluative or emotional component (how you feel about something), a cognitive component (what you know or believe), and a behavioral component (what you are likely to do). *Persuasion* is an attempt to alter your attitudes or behavior.

Attitude Measurement

Psychologists commonly measure attitudes through attitude scales. On a Likert scale (named after psychologist Rensis Likert), you would check a point along a line from 1, meaning "strongly disagree," to 7, meaning "strongly agree," for each statement, as illustrated in Figure 13.6.

Indicate your level of agreement with the items below, using the following scale:

	Strongly disagree		Neutral			Strongly agree
1. Labor unions are necessary to protect the rights of workers.	1	2	3	4	5	6	7
2. Labor union leaders have too much power.	1	2	3	4	5	6	7
3. If I worked for a company with a union, I would join the union.	1	2	3	4	5	6	7
4. I would never cross a picket line of striking workers.	1	2	3	4	5	6	7
5. Striking workers hurt their company and unfairly raise prices for the consumer.	1	2	3	4	5	6	7
6. Labor unions should not be permitted to engage in political activity.	1	2	3	4	5	6	7
7. America is a better place for today's workers because of the efforts by labor unions in the past.	1	2	3	4	5	6	7

Note: Items 2, 5, and 6 are scored the opposite of 1, 3, 4, and 7.

FIGURE 13.6 This Likert scale assesses attitudes toward labor unions.

The attitudes that people report do not always match their behaviors. For example, many people say one thing and do another with regard to cigarettes, alcohol, safe sex, wearing seat belts in a car, and studying hard for tests. One reason is that people sometimes answer attitude questionnaires impulsively, especially on questions they regard as unimportant (van der Pligt, de Vries, Manstead, & van Harreveld, 2000). A second reason is that people's answers to an attitude question fluctuate (Lord & Lepper, 1999). For example, what is your attitude toward politicians? While you are thinking about the public servants you admire most, you rate politicians favorably. Later, when you are thinking about corrupt or incompetent politicians, you answer differently.

Your attitudes are most likely to match your behavior if you have had much personal experience with the topic of the attitude (Glasman & Albarracín, 2006). For example, if you have had extensive experience dealing with mental patients, then you know how you react to them, and you state your attitude accordingly. Someone with less experience is stating a hypothetical attitude, which is less reliable.

15. What test or method mentioned earlier in this chapter demonstrates mixed or contradictory attitudes?

Answer

15. Some people express one attitude openly but demonstrate another attitude on the Implicit Association Test.

Cognitive Dissonance and Attitude Change

Much research asks whether people's attitudes change their behavior. The theory of cognitive dissonance reverses the direction: It holds that a change in people's behavior alters their attitudes (Festinger, 1957). **Cognitive dissonance** is *a state of unpleasant tension that people experience* *when they hold contradictory attitudes or when their behavior contradicts their stated attitudes, especially if the inconsistency distresses them.*

Suppose you pride yourself on honesty but find yourself saying something you do not believe. You feel tension, which you can reduce in three ways: You can change what you are saying to match your attitudes, change your attitude to match what you are saying, or find an explanation that justifies your behavior under the circumstances (Wicklund & Brehm, 1976). Although all of these options are possible, most research focuses on how cognitive dissonance changes people's attitudes.

Imagine yourself as a participant in this classic experiment on cognitive dissonance (Festinger & Carlsmith, 1959). The experimenters say they are studying motor behavior. They show you a board full of pegs. Your task is to take each peg out of the board, rotate it one fourth of a turn, and return it to the board. When you finish all the pegs, you start over, rotating all the pegs again as quickly and accurately as possible for an hour. As you proceed, an experimenter silently takes notes. You find your task immensely tedious. In fact, the researchers intentionally chose this task because it was so boring.

At the end of the hour, the experimenter thanks you for participating and "explains" (falsely) that the study's purpose is to determine whether people's performance depends on their attitudes toward the task. You were in the neutral-attitude group, but those in the positive-attitude group are told before they start that they will enjoy the experience.

In fact, the experimenter continues, right now the research assistant is supposed to give that instruction to the next participant, a young woman waiting in the next room. The experimenter excuses himself to find the research assistant and returns distraught. The assistant is nowhere to be found, he says. He turns to you and asks, "Would you be willing to tell the next participant that you thought this was an interesting, enjoyable experiment? If so, I will pay you." Assume that you consent, as most students in the study did. After you tell that woman in the next room that you enjoyed the study, what would you actually think of the study, assuming the experimenter paid you $1? What if he paid you $20? (This study occurred in the 1950s. In today's money, that $20 would be worth more than $150.)

After you have told the woman how much fun the experiment was, you leave, believing the study is over. As you walk down the hall, a representative of the psychology department greets you and explains that the department wants to find out what kinds of experiments are being con-

ducted and whether they are educationally worthwhile. (The answers to these questions are the real point of the experiment.) Two questions are how much you enjoyed the experiment and whether you would be willing to participate in a similar experiment later.

The students who received $20 said they thought the experiment was boring and that they wanted nothing to do with another such experiment. However, contrary to what you might guess, those who received $1 said they enjoyed the experiment and would be willing to participate again (Figure 13.7).

Why? According to the theory of cognitive dissonance, if you accept $20 to tell a lie, you experience little conflict. You are lying, but you are doing it for the $20. However, if you tell a lie for only $1, do you really want to think you can be bribed so cheaply? You feel a conflict between your true attitude and what you had said about the experiment. You experience cognitive dissonance—an unpleasant tension. You reduce your tension by changing your attitude, deciding that the experiment really was interesting after all. ("I learned a lot of interesting things about myself, like . . . uh . . . how good I am at rotating pegs.")

The idea of cognitive dissonance attracted much attention and inspired a great deal of research (Aronson, 1997). Here are two examples:

- An experimenter left a child in a room with toys but forbade the child to play with one particular toy. If the experimenter threatened the child with severe punishment for playing with the toy, the child avoided it but still regarded it as desirable. However, if the experimenter merely said that he or she would be disappointed if the child played with that toy, the child avoided the toy and said (even weeks later) that it was not a good toy (Aronson & Carlsmith, 1963).
- An experimenter asked college students to write an essay defending a position that the experimenter knew, from previous informa-

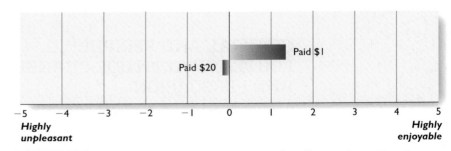

FIGURE 13.7 Participants were paid either $1 or $20 for telling another subject that they enjoyed an experiment (which was actually boring). Later, they were asked for their real opinions. Participants who were paid the smaller amount said that they enjoyed the study. (Based on data from Festinger & Carlsmith, 1959)

tion, contradicted the students' beliefs. For example, college students who favored freer access to alcohol might be asked to write essays on why the college should increase restrictions on alcohol. Those who were told they must write the essays did not change their views significantly, but those who were asked to "please" voluntarily write the essay generally came to agree with what they wrote (Croyle & Cooper, 1983).

The general principle is that, if you entice people to do something by means of a minimum reward or a tiny threat so that they are acting almost voluntarily, they change their attitudes to support what they are doing and reduce cognitive dissonance. This procedure is a powerful method of attitude change because people are actively participating, not just listening.

So if you want to change people's behavior, do you have to change their attitudes first? The results of cognitive dissonance experiments say quite the opposite: If you change people's behavior, their attitudes will change, too.

....

16. Suppose your parents pay you to get a good grade in a boring course. According to cognitive dissonance theory, are you more likely to develop a positive attitude toward your studies if your parents pay you $10 or $100?

Concept Check

Answer

16. You will come to like your studies more if you are paid $10. If you are paid only $10, you won't be able to tell yourself that you are studying harder only for the money. Instead, you will tell yourself that you must be really interested. The theory of intrinsic and extrinsic motivation (chapter 11) leads to the same prediction: If you study hard without any strong external reason, you perceive that you have internal reasons for studying.

....

CENTRAL AND PERIPHERAL ROUTES OF ATTITUDE CHANGE AND PERSUASION

Some of our attitudes come from careful examination of the evidence, and some have only a superficial basis. Richard Petty and John Cacioppo (1981, 1986) proposed the following distinction: *When people take a decision seriously, they invest the necessary time and effort to evaluate the evidence and logic behind each message.* Petty and Cacioppo call this logical approach the **central route to persuasion**. This method is generally most successful with people who are intelligent enough and motivated enough to evaluate complicated evidence. In contrast, *when people listen to a message on a topic they consider unimportant, they attend to more superficial factors* such as the speaker's appearance and reputation or the sheer length of someone's speech. This approach is the **peripheral route to persuasion**. The peripheral route also influences people when they are too tired or distracted to pay careful attention to the argument (Petty & Briñol, 2008).

Suppose someone is trying to convince you that it would be a good idea to institute a special comprehensive examination for all graduating seniors at some other college. The speaker repeats the same weak argument several times and persuades you. However, if you thought it was a proposed requirement at *your* college, you would listen carefully and evaluate the logic more accurately (Moons, Mackie, & Garcia-Marques, 2009).

....

17. You listen to a discussion about the best kinds of seafood for people to eat. Later, you hear a discussion about the best kind of cat food. You don't have a cat. In which case will you follow the central route to persuasion?

Concept Check

Answer

17. You will pay more attention to the evidence and logic, following the central route to persuasion, for the discussion about what seafood is best for people to eat.

....

Special Techniques of Persuasion

A great many people will try to persuade you to buy something, contribute to some cause, or do something else that may or may not be in your best interests. Robert Cialdini (1993) has described many techniques, all of which fall under the category of peripheral routes to persuasion. Let's consider a few of them. The goal here is not so much to teach you how to persuade others as to teach you how to recognize and resist certain kinds of manipulation.

Liking and Similarity

People are more successful persuading you if you like them or see them as similar to yourself. Suppose someone you don't know calls you and immediately asks, "How are you today?" You reply, "Okay." The reply: "Oh, I'm so glad to hear that!"

Grigory Rasputin's unsavory influence on the czar of Russia led to the Communist revolution. However, people who are told Rasputin resembled them, even in trivial ways, soften their criticisms.

Many hotels try to influence guests to agree to use towels more than once instead of having the hotel replace them daily. A typical message in the room points out that reusing towels saves energy, reduces the use of detergents that pollute the water supply, and in general, contributes to protecting the environment. Researchers found that more guests agree to reuse their towels if the message adds that most other guests have agreed to reuse their towels. It works even better to say that most other guests using *this room* have agreed (N. J. Goldstein, Cialdini, & Griskevicius, 2008). People are generally unaware of the power of this kind of influence, and most people deny that they paid any attention to what other people were doing (Nolan, Schultz, Cialdini, Goldstein, & Griskevisius, 2008).

18. A salesperson calls at your door and says that several of your neighbors (whom the salesperson names) have bought the product and recommended you as another possible customer. What techniques of persuasion is this salesperson using?

Answer

18. The salesperson is relying on endorsement by a group that you presumably like and trust. Also, you are likely to be persuaded by people similar to yourself.

Is this caller, who doesn't even know you, really delighted that you are "okay"? Or is this an attempt to seem friendly so that you will be more likely to buy something?

Salespeople, politicians, and others also try to emphasize the ways in which they are similar to you. For example, "I grew up in a small town, much like this one." To illustrate the influence of similarity, students were asked to read a very unflattering description of Grigory Rasputin, the "mad monk of Russia," and then rate Rasputin on several scales. All students read the same description except for Rasputin's birth date: In some cases, Rasputin's birth date had been changed to match the student's own birth date. Students who thought Rasputin had the same birth date as their own were more likely than others to rate him as "strong" and "effective" (Finch & Cialdini, 1989).

Social Norms

We'll consider conformity in more detail later in this chapter, but you already know the idea: People tend to do what others are doing. A powerful influence technique is to show that many other people are doing what you want them to do. A bartender or singer with a tip jar ordinarily puts a few dollars in at the start to imply that other people have already left tips.

Reciprocation

Civilization is based on the concept of reciprocation: If you do me a favor, then I owe you one. However, it is possible to misuse this principle. Suppose someone gives you a gift and then tells you what you should do in return. You may feel obligated, even if you didn't want the present. Many companies hand out free samples, confident that many of those who accept the samples will feel obligated to buy something in return.

Here's another version of reciprocation as a form of persuasion: An alumni organization once called me asking for contributions. Their representative told me that many other alumni were pledging $1,000, and he hoped he could count on me for the same. No, I explained, $1,000 is a lot of money, and I wasn't prepared to make that kind of contribution. Oh, he responded, with a tone that implied "too bad you don't have a *good* job like our other alumni." He then said that if I couldn't afford $1,000, how about $500? The suggestion was that we should compromise! He was giving in $500 from his original proposal, so I should give in $500 from my end.

Foot in the Door

Sometimes, someone *starts with a modest request, which you accept, and follows it with a larger request*. This procedure is called the **foot-in-the-door technique.** When Jonathan Freedman and Scott Fraser (1966) asked suburban residents in Palo Alto, California, to put a small "Drive Safely" sign in their windows, most agreed to do so. A couple of weeks later, other researchers asked the same residents to let them set up a large "Drive Safely" billboard in their front yards for 10 days. They also made the request to residents who had not been approached by the first researchers. Of those who had already agreed to display the small sign, 76% agreed to the billboard. Only 17% of the others agreed. Those who agreed to the first request felt they were already committed to the cause, and to be consistent, they agreed to further participation. Another study found that people who agreed to fill out a 20-minute survey became more willing a month later to take a 40-minute survey on the same topic. However, although this tendency was strong for Americans, it was weak for Chinese students. An interpretation was that

Chinese culture puts less emphasis on the individual, including less emphasis on individual consistency from one time to another (Petrova, Cialdini, & Sills, 2006).

Bait and Switch

Someone using the bait-and-switch technique *first offers an extremely favorable deal, gets the other person to commit to the deal, and then makes additional demands.* Alternatively, the person might offer a product at a very low price to get customers to the store but then claim to be out of the product and try to sell them something else. For example, a car dealer offers you an exceptionally good price on a new car and a generous price for the trade-in of your old car. The deal seems too good to resist. After you have committed yourself to buying this car, the dealer checks with the boss, who rejects the deal. Your salesperson comes back saying, "I'm so sorry. I forgot that this car has some special features that raise the value. If we sold it for the price I originally quoted, we'd lose money." So you agree to a higher price. Then the company's used car specialist looks at your old car and "corrects" the trade-in value to a lower amount. Still, you have committed yourself, so you don't back out. You leave with a deal that you would not have accepted at the start.

That's Not All!

In the that's-not-all technique, *someone makes an offer and then improves the offer before you have a chance to reply.* The television announcer says, "Here's your chance to buy this amazing combination paper shredder and coffeemaker for only $39.95. But wait, there's more! We'll throw in a can of dog deodorant! Also this handy windshield wiper cleaner and a solar-powered flashlight and a subscription to *Modern Lobotomist!* If you call now, you get this amazing offer, which usually costs $39.95, for only $19.95! Call now!" People who hear the first offer and then the "improved" offer are more likely to comply than are people who hear the "improved" offer from the start (Burger, 1986).

You may notice a similarity among the last three techniques. In the foot-in-the-door, bait-and-switch, and that's-not-all techniques, the persuader starts with one proposal and then switches to another. The first one changes the listener's state of mind for the second one.

19. Identify each of the following as an example of the foot-in-the-door technique, the bait-and-switch technique, or the that's-not-all technique.

   a. A credit card company offers you a card with a low introductory rate. After a few months, the interest rate on your balance doubles.

   b. A store marks its prices "25% off" and then scratches that out and marks them "50% off!"

   c. A friend asks you to help carry some supplies over to the elementary school for an afternoon tutoring program. When you get there, the principal says that one of the tutors is late and asks whether you could take her place until she arrives. You agree and spend the rest of the afternoon tutoring. The principal then talks you into coming back every week as a tutor.

Answer

19. a. bait-and-switch technique; b. that's-not-all technique; c. foot-in-the-door technique.

The Role of Fear

Some attempts at persuasion use threats, such as, "If you don't send money to support our cause, our political opponents will gain power and do terrible things." One organization sent out appeals with a message on the envelope, "Every day an estimated 800 dolphins, porpoises, and whales will die . . . unless you act now!" Strong fear often enhances persuasion (Dillard & Anderson, 2004), but people disregard statements that seem exaggerated or unrealistic (Leventhal, 1970).

A fear message is effective only if people believe their actions will be effective. For example, a message about the dangers of influenza motivates people to get immunized. Messages about the dangers of AIDS are less effective in motivating people to practice safe sex (Albarracín et al., 2005), perhaps because using condoms consistently is more difficult than getting a flu shot once a year. Messages about global warming are frightening, but people doubt that one person's behavior has a big effect.

Fear messages sometimes backfire. For example, an antidrug campaign might say that drug use is spreading wildly, or a conservation organization might say that pollution and destruction of the environment are out of control. The intended message is, "Take this problem seriously and act now." The unintended message that people sometimes hear is, "The problem is hopeless" (Cialdini, 2003).

Delayed Influence

Some messages have little influence at first but more later. We consider two examples.

The Sleeper Effect

Suppose you hear an idea from someone with poor qualifications. Because of what you think of the speaker, you reject the idea. Weeks later, you forget where you heard the idea (*source amnesia*) and remember only the idea itself. At that point, its persuasive impact may increase (Kumkale & Abarracín, 2004). If you completely forget the source, you might even claim it as your own idea! Psychologists use the term **sleeper effect** to describe *delayed persuasion by an initially rejected message.*

Minority Influence

Delayed influence also occurs when a minority group proposes a worthwhile idea. It could be an ethnic, religious, political, or any other kind of minority. The majority rejects the idea at first but reconsiders it later. If the minority continually repeats a single simple message and its members seem united, it has a good chance of eventually influencing the majority. The minority's influence often increases gradually, even if the majority hesitates to admit that the minority has swayed them (Wood, Lundgren, Ouellette, Busceme, & Blackstone, 1994). By expressing its views, the minority also prompts the majority to generate new ideas of its own (Nemeth, 1986). That is, by demonstrating the possibility of disagreement, the minority opens the way for other people to offer additional views. Suppose you disagree with what everyone else is saying, but you hesitate to speak out. Then someone else voices an objection different from what you meant to say, and now you feel more comfortable expressing your own idea.

One powerful example of minority influence is that of the Socialist Party of the United States, which ran candidates for elective offices from 1900 through the 1950s. The party never received more than 6% of the vote in any presidential election. No Socialist candidate was elected senator or governor, and only a few were elected to the House of Representatives (Shannon, 1955). Beginning in the 1930s, the party's support dwindled, until eventually it stopped nominating candidates. Was that because they had failed? No! Most of their major proposals had been enacted into law (Table 13.2). Of course, the Democrats and Republicans who voted for these changes claimed credit for the ideas.

20. At a meeting of your student government, you suggest a new method of testing and grading students. The other members immediately reject your plan. Should you give up?

Answer

20. The fact that your idea was rejected does not mean that you should give up. If you and a few allies continue to present this plan, showing apparent agreement among yourselves, the majority may eventually adopt a similar plan—probably without giving you credit for it.

Differences in Resistance to Persuasion

You may be more easily influenced at some times than at others. *Simply informing people that they are about to hear a persuasive speech activates their resistance and weakens the persuasion* (Petty & Cacioppo, 1977). This tendency is called the **forewarning effect.** Actually, the results are somewhat complex. Suppose you have a strongly unfa-

TABLE 13.2 Political Proposals of the U.S. Socialist Party, Around 1900

Proposal	Eventual Fate of Proposal
Women's right to vote	Established by 19th Amendment to U.S. Constitution; ratified in 1920
Old-age pensions	Included in the Social Security Act of 1935
Unemployment insurance	Included in the Social Security Act of 1935; also guaranteed by the other state and federal legislation
Health and accident insurance	Included in part in the Social Security Act of 1935 and in the Medicare Act of 1965
Increased wages, including minimum wage	First minimum-wage law passed in 1938; periodically updated since then
Reduction of working hours	Maximum 40-hour workweek (with exceptions) established by the Fair Labor Standards Act of 1938
Public ownership of electric, gas, and other utilities and of the means of transportation and communication	Utilities not owned by government but heavily regulated by federal and state government since the 1930s
Initiative, referendum, and recall (mechanisms for private citizens to push for changes in legislation and for removal of elected officials)	Adopted by most state governments

Sources: Foster, 1968; and Leuchtenburg, 1963

vorable attitude toward something—increased tuition at your college, for example. Now someone tells you that a well-informed person is going to try to persuade you in favor of higher tuition. At once, before the speech even begins, your attitudes shift slightly in the direction of favoring higher tuition! Exactly why is unclear; perhaps you are telling yourself, "I guess there must be some good reason for that opinion." Then when you hear the speech itself, it does have some influence, and your attitudes will shift still further toward favoring it (or at least toward neutrality), but your attitudes do not shift as much as those of someone who had not been forewarned. The warning alerts you to resist the persuasion, to criticize weak arguments, and to reject weak evidence (Wood & Quinn, 2003).

In the closely related inoculation effect, *people first hear a weak argument and then a stronger argument supporting the same conclusion.* After they have rejected the first argument, they usually reject the second one also. In one experiment, people listened to speeches *against* brushing their teeth after every meal. Some of them heard just a strong argument (e.g., "Brushing your teeth too frequently wears away tooth enamel, leading to serious disease"). Others first heard a weak argument and then the strong argument 2 days later. Still others first heard an argument *for* brushing teeth and then the strong argument against it. Only those who heard the weak argument against brushing resisted the influence of the strong argument. The other two groups found it highly persuasive (McGuire & Papageorgis, 1961). So if you want to convince people, start with your strong evidence.

21. If you want your children to preserve the beliefs and attitudes you try to teach them, should you give them only arguments that support those beliefs or should you also expose them to attacks on those beliefs? Why?

Answer

21. You should expose them to weak attacks on their beliefs so that they will learn how to resist such attacks.

Coercive Persuasion

Finally, let's consider the most unfriendly kinds of persuasion. Suppose the police suspect you of a crime, and they want you to confess. You waive your rights to an attorney and talk with them. After all, what do you have to lose? You're innocent, so you have nothing to hide. First the police claim your crime is horrendous and you face a stiff sentence. Then they offer sympathy and excuses, implying that if you confess, you can get a much lighter sentence. They claim to have solid evidence of your guilt anyway, so you may as well confess because they can convict you even if you don't. They tell you that you failed a polygraph test. You stay in isolation, without food or sleep for many hours, with no promise of when, if ever, this ordeal will end. Apparently, confession is the only way you can get them to stop badgering you. Might you confess, even though you are innocent? You think, "Oh, well, eventually they will realize their mistake. They can't really convict me, because they won't have any other evidence."

Many innocent people do confess under these conditions. Unfortunately, juries consider a confession extremely strong evidence, even if they know it was coerced (Kassin & Gudjonsson, 2004). To test the effects of coercive persuasion, researchers set up this experiment: They asked pairs of students to work independently on logic problems. For half of the pairs, one of them (a confederate of the experimenter) asked for help, which the first person usually gave. Later, they were told that offering help was considered cheating. For the other pairs, the confederate did not ask for help and therefore no cheating occurred. After both completed the problems, the experimenter entered the room and accused the participant of cheating. For some, the experimenter merely made the accusation and asked for a confession. Under those conditions, 46% of the guilty students and 6% of the innocent ones signed a confession. (Why any innocent students confessed here is a mystery.) Other students were exposed to coercive techniques. The experimenter threatened to report the student to the professor, who would deal with this event as harshly as any other case of academic cheating. However, the experimenter suggested they could settle the problem quickly if the student signed a confession. Under these circumstances, 87% of the guilty students and 43% of the innocent ones agreed to confess, as illustrated in Figure 13.8 (Russano, Meissner, Narchet, & Kassin, 2005). The message is that coercive techniques increase confessions by guilty people, and also by innocent people, and therefore make the confessions unreliable evidence.

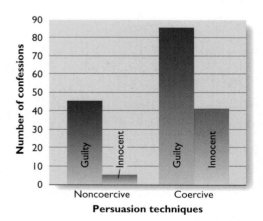

FIGURE 13.8 Coercive persuasion techniques increased the number of confessions by both guilty and innocent people. (Based on data of Russano, Meissner, Narchet, & Kassin, 2005)

In Closing

Persuasion and Manipulation

Broadly defined, attitudes influence almost everything we do. When you form an attitude about something of little consequence, it is understandable that you follow the peripheral route, paying little attention to the complexities of the evidence. When you are dealing with important matters, however, you usually follow the central route, examining the facts as carefully as you can. It is important to be alert to some of the influences that might throw you off course, such as the foot-in-the-door technique, bait and switch, and cognitive dissonance. Advertisers, politicians, and others try to polish their techniques of persuasion, and not everyone has your best interest at heart.

SUMMARY

- *Attitudes.* An attitude is a like or dislike of something or somebody that influences our behavior. (page 472)
- *Cognitive dissonance.* Cognitive dissonance is a state of unpleasant tension that arises from contradictory attitudes or from a behavior that conflicts with an attitude. When people's behavior does not match their attitudes, they try to eliminate the inconsistency by changing their behavior or their attitudes. (page 472)
- *Two routes to persuasion.* When people consider a topic of little importance to them, they are easily persuaded by the speaker's appearance and other superficial factors. When people care about the topic, they pay more attention to logic and to the quality of the evidence. (page 474)
- *Methods of influence.* Someone you like or consider similar to yourself is more persuasive than other people. Being told that most people favor some idea or action makes it appealing. Occasionally, a person gives something as an inducement for others to reciprocate by doing what the first person wants. In the foot-in-the-door, bait-and-switch, and that's-not-all techniques, a first request makes people more likely to accept a second request. (page 474)
- *Influence of fear.* Messages that appeal to fear are effective if people perceive the danger as real and think they can do something about it. (page 476)
- *Sleeper effect.* When people reject a message because of their low regard for the person who proposed it, they sometimes forget where they heard the idea and later come to accept it. (page 477)
- *Minority influence.* Although a minority may have little influence at first, it can, through persistent repetition of its message, eventually persuade the majority to adopt its position or consider other ideas. (page 477)
- *Forewarning and inoculation effects.* If people have been warned that someone will try to persuade them of something or if they have previously heard a weak version of the persuasive argument, they tend to resist the argument. (page 477)
- *Coercive persuasion.* Techniques designed to pressure a suspect into confessing decrease the reliability of the confession because, under these circumstances, many innocent people confess also. (page 478)

KEY TERMS

attitude (page 472)

bait-and-switch technique (page 476)

central route to persuasion (page 474)

cognitive dissonance (page 472)

foot-in-the-door technique (page 475)

forewarning effect (page 477)

inoculation effect (page 478)

peripheral route to persuasion (page 474)

sleeper effect (page 477)

that's-not-all technique (page 476)

Interpersonal Attraction

- How do we choose our partners?
- Do men and women choose for the same reasons?
- Why do some marriages succeed and others fail?

William Proxmire, a former U.S. senator, used to give Golden Fleece Awards to those who, in his opinion, most flagrantly wasted the taxpayers' money. He once bestowed an award on psychologists who had received a federal grant to study how people fall in love. According to Proxmire, the research was pointless because people do not want to understand love. They prefer, he said, to let such matters remain a mystery.

This module presents the information Senator Proxmire thought you didn't want to know.

ESTABLISHING RELATIONSHIPS

Of all the people you meet, how do you choose those who become your friends or romantic attachments? How do they choose you?

Proximity and Familiarity

Proximity means *closeness*. (It comes from the same root as *approximate*.) Not surprisingly, *we are most likely to become friends with people who live or work in proximity to us*. One professor assigned students to seats randomly and followed up on them a year later. Students most often became friends with those who sat in adjacent seats (Back, Schmulkle, & Egloff, 2008). One reason proximity is important is that people who live nearby discover what they have in common. Another reason is the mere exposure effect, the principle that *the more often we come in contact with someone or something, the more we tend to like that person or object* (Saegert, Swap, & Zajonc, 1973; Zajonc, 1968).

However, familiarity does not always lead to liking. Researchers contacted people who were about to go on a first date arranged by an online dating service. They asked how much each person expected to like the person they were about to date and how much the two of them seemed to have in common. Prior to the date, most people gave moderately high ratings on both questions. The researchers asked the same questions after the date. A few people's ratings went up, but more went down, and some went all the way to the bottom (Norton, Frost, & Ariely, 2007). Becoming familiar with someone gives you a chance to find out what you have in common, but it also gives you a chance to see the other person's flaws.

Physical Attractiveness

What characteristics do you look for in a potential romantic partner? Most people have many of the same priorities regardless of whether they are male or female, homosexual or heterosexual (Holmberg & Blair, 2009). Those priorities include intelligence, honesty, a sense of humor, and of course, physical attractiveness.

In a study long ago, psychologists arranged blind dates for 332 freshman couples for a dance before the start of classes. They asked participants to fill out questionnaires, but the experimenters ignored the questionnaires and paired students at random. Midway through the dance, the experimenters separated the men and women and asked them to rate how much they liked their dates. The only factor that influenced the ratings was physical attractiveness (Walster, Aronson, Abrahams, & Rottman, 1966). Similarities of attitudes, personality, and intelligence counted for almost nothing. Surprising? Hardly. During the brief time they had spent together at the dance, the couples had little opportunity to learn much about each other. Intelligence, honesty, and other character values are critical for a lasting relationship but not for the first hour of the first date (Keller, Thiessen, & Young, 1996).

Later studies examined a speed-dating situation, in which people briefly meet 10 to 25 other people in one evening and then report which potential partners they might like to meet for a more extended date. For both men and women, physical attractiveness was by far the main influence on their choices (Finkel & Eastwick, 2008).

Possible Biological Value of Attractiveness: Birds

Why do we care about physical appearance? We take its importance so much for granted that we don't even understand the question, so for a moment let's consider other species.

In many bird species, early in the mating season, females shop around and choose a brilliantly colored male that sings vigorously from the treetops. In several species, females also prefer males with especially long tails (Figure 13.9). From an evolutionary standpoint, aren't these foolish choices? The popular males are those that risk their lives by singing loudly from the treetops, where they call the attention of hawks and eagles. They waste energy by growing bright feathers. (It takes more energy to produce bright than dull colors.) A long tail may look pretty, but it interferes with flying. Why does the female prefer a mate who wastes energy and endangers his life?

Biologists eventually decided that wasting energy and risking life were precisely the point (Zahavi & Zahavi, 1997). Only a healthy, vigorous

© CMCD/PhotoDisc

FIGURE 13.9 In some bird species, males with long tails attract more mates. Only a healthy male can afford this trait that impairs his flying ability.

male has enough energy to make bright, colorful feathers (Blount, Metcalfe, Birkhead, & Surai, 2003; Faivre, Grégoire, Préault, Cézilly, & Sorci, 2003). Only a strong male can fly despite a long tail, and only a strong male would risk predation by singing from an exposed perch. A colorful, singing male is showing off: "Look at me! I am so healthy and vigorous that I can afford to take crazy risks and waste energy!" The female, we presume, does not understand why she is attracted to colorful loudmouths. She just is because, throughout her evolutionary history, most females who chose such partners reproduced more successfully than those who chose dull-colored, quiet, inactive males.

So it would seem, theoretically. The problem is that although a male's bright colors and vigorous singing do indicate health, his health depends more on his luck in finding a good feeding place than on his genes. The same is true for fish as well as birds (Brooks, 2000; E. J. A. Cunningham & Russell, 2000).

Possible Biological Value of Attractiveness: Humans

Although individual preferences vary somewhat, most people agree rather closely on which faces are attractive and which are not (Hönekopp, 2006). Are attractive people more likely than others to be healthy and fertile? Theoretically, they should be. Certainly, many illnesses decrease people's attractiveness. Also, *good-looking* generally means *normal,* and normal appearance probably indicates *good genes.* Suppose a computer takes photographs of many people and averages their faces. The resulting composite face has about an average nose, average distance between the eyes, and so forth, and most people rate this face "highly attractive" (Langlois & Roggman, 1990; Langlois, Roggman, & Musselman, 1994; Rhodes, Sumich, & Byatt, 1999) (see Figure 13.10). The average person may not be highly attractive, but a highly attractive person has average features. An attractive face has few irregularities—no crooked teeth, skin blemishes, or asymmetries, and no facial hair on women (Fink & Penton-Voak, 2002).

Why is normal attractive? First, normal implies healthy. Presumably, the genes for an average face spread in the population because of their link to success. Any face far different from the

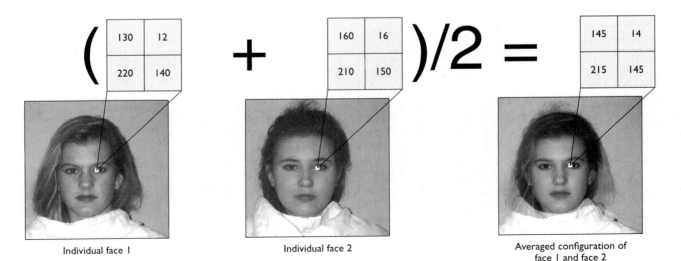

Individual face 1   Individual face 2   Averaged configuration of face 1 and face 2

FIGURE 13.10 A computer measured the gray value of each point on each picture. It then produced a new picture with the average of the grays at each point. This set of photos illustrates the procedure for two original faces. The numbers are for illustrative purposes only. Most people rate the resulting face as highly attractive. (© Langlois, Roggman, & Musselman, "Average faces," *Psychological Science*, Vol. 5, No.4.)

average might indicate an undesirable mutation. Second, we like anything that is familiar. If you have recently seen many faces that are thinner than usual, fatter than usual, or in some other way distorted, your judgment of "attractive" is shifted slightly in the direction of the faces you have just seen (Rhodes, Jeffery, Watson, Clifford, & Nakayama, 2003).

Do attractive people tend to be healthier or more fertile than others? Researchers obtained photos of hundreds of teenagers from long ago. They asked other people to rate the faces for attractiveness, and they obtained medical records for the people in the photos. The ratings of attractiveness had little relationship to health. People who were rated attractive were more likely to marry, especially to marry early, but unattractive people who did marry were just as likely to have children (Kalick, Zebrowitz, Langlois, & Johnson, 1998). Evidently, at least for this sample, attractiveness did not predict health or fertility. Other studies have found a low but statistically reliable correlation between facial attractiveness and health for women but not for men (Weeden & Sabini, 2005).

If facial attractiveness is a weak cue to health, what about the rest of the body? People with much abdominal fat are considered less attractive, and they tend to be less healthy (Weeden & Sabini, 2005), although lower body fat may be beneficial for a pregnant woman (Lassek & Gaulin, 2008). Theorists have proposed a more precise hypothesis that men should prefer women with a narrow waist and wide hips—a waist-to-hip ratio of about 0.7—because medical researchers believe women with that ratio are most likely to be healthy and fertile. Examine the drawings of women's figures in Figure 13.11. Which one do you consider most attractive? Most people in the United States rate thinner women as the most attractive (Tassinary & Hansen, 1998). In non-Westernized cultures of Tanzania and southeastern Peru, most men regarded heavier women as the most attractive (Marlowe & Wetsman, 2001; Yu & Shepard, 1998). In short, preferences for female shape vary somewhat across cultures and do not necessarily match what researchers consider healthy or fertile.

Where do all these studies leave us? Theoretically, it would make sense for good looks to indicate healthful genes. However, so far, researchers have not found a strong link. Still, even a weak relationship means something. For your first evaluation of a partner, you can rely on appearance, which is a weak indicator of health and good genes, or on no information at all. We see how a preference for good appearance might have evolved.

22. According to evolutionary theory, attractiveness is a sign of good health. Why would it be difficult for an unhealthy individual to produce "counterfeit" attractiveness?

23. According to evolutionary theory, a face with average features is attractive. Why?

Answers

23. Average features must have been successful for our ancestors for the genes to spread in the population. Therefore, average features are a sign of probable health.

22. Attractive features such as bright feathers in a bird or large muscles in a man require much energy. It would be difficult for an unhealthy individual to devote enough energy to produce such features.

Similarity

Although physical appearance is important, it is clearly not enough. You will find yourself physically attracted to many people who would be unsuitable as your long-term partner. As you get to

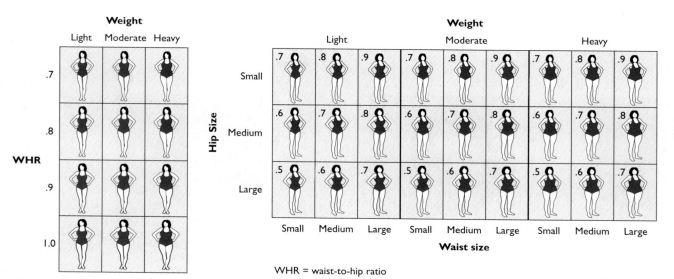

FIGURE 13.11 Which of these female figures do you find most attractive? Average ratings vary across cultures. (From "A Critical Test of the Waist-to-Hip-Ratio Hypothesis of Female Physical Attractiveness" by L. G. Tassinary & K. A. Hansen, *Psychological Science*, 1998, 9, 150–155. Copyright © 1998 Blackwell Publishers. Reprinted by permission.)

Even when friends differ in some ways, they generally have much in common, such as interests, attitudes, and level of education.

know someone, your reaction to his or her personality alters your appraisal of physical attractiveness. Someone whom you come to respect and admire seems more attractive than before. Someone whom you find deceitful and cruel begins to look unattractive (Kniffin & Wilson, 2004).

Most romantic partners and close friends resemble each other in age, physical attractiveness, political and religious beliefs, intelligence, education, and attitudes (Eastwick, Finkel, Mochon, & Ariely, 2007; Laumann, 1969; L. Lee et al., 2008; Montoya, 2008; Rushton & Bons, 2005). The only known point on which similarity doesn't help is smell: Many women (unconsciously) prefer a romantic partner who does not smell too much like herself, her brothers, and other members of her family. That tendency is presumably a way to decrease the chance of mating with a close relative. Curiously, women taking birth-control pills fail to show this tendency. Perhaps it occurs

only when women have a chance of becoming pregnant (Roberts, Gosling, Carter, & Petrie, 2008).

As a relationship matures, people's interests become more and more alike (Anderson, Keltner, & John, 2003). Couples who have much in common enjoy the relationship more because they share many activities and agree more often than disagree.

Members of minority groups face special difficulties. If your ethnic or religious group is greatly outnumbered where you live, your choice of potential friends or romantic partners may be limited to members of your group who do not share your interests or members of other groups who do (Hamm, 2000).

Attraction and Modern Technology

The Internet has added a new dimension to dating. Through Internet dating services, people meet individuals they never would have met otherwise. A potential couple can learn each other's background and evaluate what they have in common before deciding whether to meet on a real date. The system is not perfect. Many people still pay more attention to appearance than to substance, and many people are less than honest in describing themselves online. Still, these dating services help many people find good matches (Mahfouz, Philaretou, & Theocharous, 2008).

Some people also have Internet contacts without an intention of meeting face to face. They establish an online character (who may or may not look like the real person) who interacts with someone else's online character, sometimes even having on-screen sex. Most people who have this

In virtual worlds such as Second Life, people create virtual representations of themselves. Some people claim to have fallen in love in such online communities. This man's first wife divorced him because she considered his online relationship to be infidelity. He then married (in real life) the woman he had previously known only online.

kind of relationship rate their real-life relationships as not very close (Scott, Mottarella & Lavooy, 2006). Perhaps people who have trouble in their face-to-face relationships turn to online relationships as a substitute. Another possibility is that the online relationships cause their real-life relationships to suffer.

The Equity Principle

According to exchange or equity theories, *social relationships are transactions in which partners exchange goods and services.* In some cases, the businesslike nature of a romantic relationship is unmistakable. In the Singles' Ads of many newspapers, people seeking a relationship describe what they have to offer and what they expect in return. Most people who describe themselves as attractive or wealthy describe high expectations for a mate. People with less to offer make fewer demands (Waynforth & Dunbar, 1995).

As in business, a relationship is most stable if both partners believe the deal is fair. It is easiest to establish a fair deal if the partners are about equally attractive and intelligent, contribute about equally to the finances and the chores, and so forth. For most couples, one partner contributes more in one way, and the other contributes more in another way.

The equity principle applies readily in the early stages of friendships or romances but less so later. For example, you might nurse your spouse or lifelong friend through a long illness without worrying about whether you are still getting a fair deal.

....

24. Someone your own age from another country moves next door. Neither of you speaks the other's language. What factors will tend to strengthen the likelihood of your becoming friends? What factors will tend to weaken it?

Concept Check

Answer

24. Proximity and familiarity will strengthen the likelihood of your becoming friends. The similarity principle will weaken it. Because of the difference in languages, you will have little chance to discover similarities in interests or attitudes. In fact, proximity will probably not be as potent a force as usual because it serves largely as a means of enabling people to discover what they have in common.

....

SPECIAL CONCERNS IN SELECTING A MATE

Choosing a partner for marriage or long-term partnership has special features because of the extra dimension of raising children. Yes, I know, not everyone wants to get married, not all married couples want children, and many unmarried people rear children. The following discussion does not apply to everyone—almost nothing in psychology does!—but it applies to those who hope to marry and have children.

Imagine that two people have expressed a desire to date you, and you have reason to believe the date could lead to a long-term relationship and eventual marriage. You have to choose between the two, and you cannot date both. Here are the choices for women: Man A is extraordinarily good-looking. He works as a waiter at a small restaurant and has no ambition to do anything more. Man B is about average looking. He patented an invention and sold it for a fortune. He was recently accepted to a prestigious medical school, and he is said to have an outstanding career ahead as a medical researcher.

The choices for men: Woman A is extraordinarily good-looking. She works as a waitress at a small restaurant and has no ambition to do anything more. Woman B is about average looking. She patented an invention and sold it for a fortune. She was recently accepted to a prestigious medical school, and she is said to have an outstanding career ahead as a medical researcher.

I have offered these choices to my own classes, and you probably can guess the results: Nearly all of the women chose man B. The men were divided, but most chose woman A. The same trends occur in all cultures for which we have data (Buss, 2000). Both men and women prefer a physically attractive partner, but women have the additional concern of preferring a partner who can be a good provider. Most men are less concerned about a woman's potential job success.

Another worldwide trend is that many men will accept almost any partner for a short-term sexual relationship, whereas most women either refuse a short-term sexual relationship or accept only a very appealing partner (Buss, 2000). Also, more men seek sexual variety. As shown in Figure 13.12, in all of the 52 nations that were surveyed, more men than women hoped for more than one sexual partner (Schmitt et al., 2003). Another trend pertains to jealousy: In many cultures, men are more insistent on women's sexual fidelity than women insist on men's. In China, men and women are equally insistent on the other's sexual fidelity, and in Sweden, both seem equally toler-

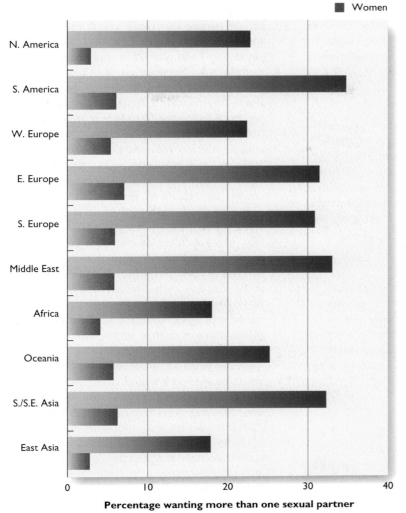

Percentage wanting more than one sexual partner

FIGURE 13.12 In all 52 countries, a higher percentage of men than women wanted more than one sexual partner within the next month. (Source: Based on data of Schmitt et al., 2003)

causing her to have sex with many partners would provide no advantage.

A man's other way of spreading his genes is to devote his energies to supporting one woman and helping her rear their children. However, this strategy succeeds only if the woman he marries is fertile. Because a young woman will be fertile for longer than an older woman, men increase their probable contribution to the gene pool if they marry young women. In contrast, a woman can be less concerned about the age of her partner because men remain fertile into old age. However, she should prefer a man who can provide food and other resources.

A man's strategy of helping one woman rear her children also depends on her sexual fidelity. If she is not, he may be spreading another man's genes and not his own. A woman does not need to be equally jealous if her husband has a brief sexual affair as long as he continues supporting her and her children.

However, even if we accept these descriptions of male and female behavior, they might not be products of genetics and natural selection. An alternative view is that people learn these preferences (Eagly & Wood, 1999). Yes, of course, the brain is subject to natural selection just as much as any other organ, but we need not assume that evolution has micromanaged our behavior with specific mechanisms for each decision.

Furthermore, many psychologists question the descriptions of male and female behavior just discussed. For example, the strength of women's preference for financially secure men varies from culture to culture depending on women's own financial status (Kasser & Sharma, 1999). Much of the evidence that men have stronger sexual jealousy than women rests on surveys of college students discussing hypothetical situations. Most surveys of older, more experienced people report that men and women are about equally angry over a partner's sexual infidelity and about equally hurt if a partner forms an emotional attachment to someone else (M. C. Green & Sabini, 2006).

ant of infidelity, but researchers have found no culture where women demand more fidelity from men than men demand from women (Buss, Larsen, Westen, & Semmelroth, 1992; Buunk, Angleitner, Oubaid, & Buss, 1996).

Those trends are clear, but the explanation is not. One hypothesis is that we have evolved to act this way (Bjorklund & Shackelford, 1999; Buss, 2000; Gangestad, 2000; Geary, 2000). The argument goes as follows. First, consider short-term sexual relationships: A man who has a quick sexual relationship has some chance of spreading his genes if the woman becomes pregnant and manages to rear the child successfully. Therefore, hypothetical genes that cause men to act this way would spread in the population. For a woman, having sex with many partners cannot give her more babies than sex with one partner. So a gene

Finally, is it really true that women gain nothing from having sex with multiple partners? Sarah Hrdy (2000) has pointed out a number of potential benefits:

- Her husband might be infertile.
- Another man might have better genes than her husband and give her better children.
- The other man may provide her with additional resources and protection.
- If she has sex with many men, all of them may provide a modest amount of care and protection for her children.
- She might be able to "trade up," leaving her husband and joining the new partner.

A general point is that we cannot reconstruct the social life of our ancestors with confidence. Mating customs vary from one human culture to another and even from one chimpanzee troop to another (Parish & deWaal, 2000). So reconstructing the evolution of human social behavior is uncertain. The case for evolutionary influence on mate choices would be stronger if someone found genes that alter preferences. (For example, imagine a gene that causes men to prefer old women or women to prefer impoverished men.) Without evidence of genetic variation in mate choice, discussions of the evolution of social behavior remain speculative.

25. Suppose astronauts discover beings on another planet, similar to us except that all men have exactly the same wealth and women remain fertile all their lives instead of losing fertility at menopause. What would an evolutionary theorist predict about the mate preferences of men and women on this planet?

Concept Check

Answer

25. If all men are equally wealthy, women would select men on another basis, such as appearance. If women's fertility lasts as late in life as men's does, then the men on this planet should not have a strong preference for younger women.

MARRIAGE

Answer each of these true–false questions about marriage:

try it yourself

(T F) 1. Men gain more advantages from marriage than women do.

(T F) 2. Divorce lowers the economic standard of living for both husband and wife.

(T F) 3. Single people have more sex than married people and enjoy it more.

(T F) 4. Living together before marriage decreases the probability of divorce.

(T F) 5. Having children usually increases marital satisfaction.

(T F) 6. Marriages are happier if the wife stays at home than if she has a job.

(T F) 7. Whenever you are angry at your partner, you should vent your anger openly.

The answer is that all of them are false (Caldwell & Woolley, 2008; Fincham, 2003). If you missed some, don't feel bad. Most marriage counselors also answered wrong on about half of these and similar items (Caldwell & Woolley, 2008). Let's go through these items quickly:

1. Men gain advantages from marriage (including improved health), but most women gain, too (especially financially).

2. In most cases, divorce lowers the wife's standard of living but not the man's.

3. Single people may brag about their sex life more, but most married people find sex more satisfying, both physically and emotionally.

4. Couples who live together first have a higher probability of divorce. One possible explanation is that certain religions strongly discourage both living together before marriage and divorce. Another explanation is that some couples decide too casually to live together and then drift into a decision to marry.

5. Marital happiness usually declines when a couple has children because they need to spend so much of their time on child care instead of each other. Marital satisfaction usually increases after the children grow up and leave home (Gorchoff, John, & Helson, 2008).

6. Marriages tend to be more stable financially if the wife has a job. The wife may or may not feel better as a result of the job depending on the type of work. On the average, marital happiness doesn't change much, one way or the other, as a result of the wife's job.

7. Venting your anger at your spouse makes your spouse feel bad and makes you feel bad, too. Your spouse will retaliate by screaming at you. Nothing good will come of it (Fincham, 2003). If you have a complaint against your partner—an annoying habit, for example—state it politely, not angrily.

Is it possible to predict which marriages will succeed and which will not? To some extent, yes. Psychologists studied recently married couples and compared the results to how the marriages developed later. In most cases, a couple that divorced within 7 years made frequent negative comments about each other, even early in their marriage. Any sign of contempt—such as rolling the eyes or sarcasm—is a particularly bad sign. Apparently, they married in the hope of working out their problems, but matters just grew worse. Most couples who divorced after more than 7 years did not express hostility early in their marriage but also did not show as much love and affection as other couples whose marriages were going to last (Gottman, Coan, Carrere, & Swanson, 1998; Gottman & Levenson, 2000; Huston, Niehuis, & Smith, 2001).

Apparently, other subtle cues, hard to quantify, also distinguish successful from less successful marriages. In one fascinating study, people watched 3-minute videotaped conversations between married couples and estimated how satisfied each couple was. Their estimates were then compared to reports by the couples themselves. People who reported that their own marriages were either highly satisfying or highly unsatisfy-

riages remain strong for a lifetime. A romantic relationship changes over the years, just as individual lives do. Dating couples and newlyweds have the intense excitement of learning about each other and doing new things together. The mere sight of the other person brings a rush of excitement (Bartels & Zeki, 2000; Kim & Hatfield, 2004). *Sexual desire, romance, and friendship increase in parallel.* This stage of a relationship is called passionate love (Diamond, 2004; Hatfield & Rapson, 1993). As time passes, the relationship develops into companionate love, *marked by sharing, care, and protection* (Gonzaga, Turner, Keltner, Campos, & Altemus, 2006; Hatfield & Rapson, 1993). The couple feels more confident and secure in their relationship. The passion may remain, but it is no longer the main bond holding the couple together. Generally, people with strong companionate love have high satisfaction with life (Kim & Hatfield, 2004).

In a mature, lasting relationship, a couple can count on each other for care and affection through both good and bad times.

ing were the best at judging the quality of other couples' marriages. Marriage counselors and marriage researchers lagged behind, as did unmarried people (Ebling & Levenson, 2003).

When you hear about how many marriages end in divorce, it is easy to despair, but many mar-

26. If you have a troubled relationship with a boyfriend or girlfriend, will you have a good chance of working out your problems after you get married?

Answer

26. No. Couples who have a mixture of positive and negative feelings toward each other before marriage have a much increased probability of divorce.

module   13.4

In Closing

Choosing Your Partners Carefully

Life is like a roller-coaster ride in the dark: It has lots of ups and downs, and you never know what is going to happen next. You want to ride with someone you like and trust. However, many people choose their friends and spouses poorly. In some regards, forming impressions of romantic partners is especially difficult. A person you date is trying to make a good impression, and you *hope* to like the person. As the relationship progresses, another factor kicks in: Remember from the section on persuasion that anyone you like tends to be highly persuasive. In short, it is easy to form an attachment and later regret it.

SUMMARY

- *Forming relationships.* People generally choose friends and romantic partners who live near them. In the early stage of romantic attraction, physical appearance is the key factor, but similarity of interests and goals becomes more serious later. Relationships are most likely to thrive if each person believes that he or she is getting about as good a deal as the other person is. (page 480)

- *Physical attractiveness.* Theoretically, physical attractiveness should be a cue to someone's health and therefore desirability as a mate. Someone with approximately average features is attractive, presumably because average features have been associated with successful breeding in the past. However, attractiveness is a only a weak predictor of human health. (page 480)

- *Men's and women's preferences in marriage partners.* In every human culture, men prefer young, attractive women, and women prefer men who are good providers. Evolutionary theorists believe humans evolved to have these preferences to improve chances of reproducing. However, it is also plausible that people learn these preferences. (page 484)

- *Marriage.* Marriage and similar relationships often break up because of problems that were present from the start. (page 486)
- *Romantic love.* The early stages of a romantic relationship are marked by passionate love. Later, the relationship develops into companionate love. (page 487)

KEY TERMS

companionate love (page 487)

exchange (or equity) theories (page 484)

mere exposure effect (page 480)

passionate love (page 487)

proximity (page 480)

Interpersonal Influence

> • How are we influenced by other people's actions or inactions?

People influence us constantly. First, they provide us with *information* (or misinformation). For example, if you approach a building and find crowds quickly fleeing from it, they probably know something you don't. Second, people set *norms* that define the expectations of a situation. For example, if you find yourself in a clean, well-kept neighborhood, you do your part to keep things clean. In a neighborhood where graffiti cover the walls, you feel less restraint against littering (Keizer, Lindenberg, & Steg, 2008). Third, people influence us just by suggesting a possible action. Seeing people yawn makes you feel like yawning, too. Why? They haven't given you any new information, and you don't necessarily wish to resemble them. You copy just because seeing a yawn suggested the possibility.

CONFORMITY

Conformity means *altering one's behavior to match other people's behavior or expectations.* The pressure to conform often exerts an overwhelming normative influence. For example, Koversada, Croatia, used to be an officially nudist town. If a first-time visitor walked around the city wearing clothes, other people stopped and stared, shaking their heads with disapproval. The visitor felt as awkward and self-conscious as a naked person would be in a city of clothed people. Most visitors quickly undressed (Newman, 1988).

If you exclaim, "I wouldn't conform," compare your own clothing right now to what others around you are wearing. Professors have sometimes noted the irony of watching a class full of students in blue jeans insisting that they do not conform to other people's style of dress (C. R. Snyder, 2003). Do you think you conform about as much as most other people do or more or less? *Most* U.S. students insist that they conform *less* than average. One group were asked, "Here is what most students at your college think about this issue . . . Now, what do you think?" Regardless of what they were told the others thought, most students said they agreed with that position . . . while insisting that it was really their own opinion, and they weren't just going along with the crowd (Pronin, Berger, & Molouki, 2007). Clearly, conformity is a powerful influence whether we want to admit it or not.

Conformity to an Obviously Wrong Majority

Early research suggested that we conform our opinions mostly in ambiguous situations when we are unsure of our own judgment (Sherif, 1935). Would we also conform if we saw that everyone else was wrong? To answer that question, Solomon Asch (1951, 1956) conducted a now-famous series of experiments. He asked groups of students to look at a vertical bar, as shown in Figure 13.13, which was defined as the model. He showed them three other vertical bars (right half of Figure 13.13) and asked them which bar was the same length as the model. As you can see, the task is simple. Asch asked the students to give their answers aloud. He repeated the procedure with 18 sets of bars.

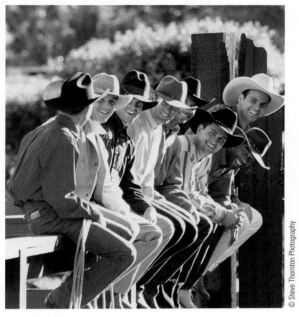

People conform to one another in their clothing and other customs.

Only one student in each group was a real participant. The others were confederates who had been instructed to give incorrect answers on 12 of the 18 trials. Asch arranged for the real participant to be the next-to-last person in the group to announce his answer so that he would hear most of the confederates' incorrect responses before giving his own (Figure 13.14). Would he go along with the crowd?

To Asch's surprise, 37 of the 50 participants conformed to the majority at least once, and 14 conformed on most of the trials. When faced with a unanimous wrong answer by the other group

FIGURE 13.13 In Asch's conformity studies, a participant was asked which of three lines matched another line. Before answering, the participant heard other people answer incorrectly.

FIGURE 13.14 Three of the participants in one of Asch's experiments on conformity. The one in the middle looking uncomfortable is the real participant. The others are the experimenter's confederates. (From Asch, 1951)

nonconformists were interesting, too. Some were nervous but felt duty bound to say how the bars looked to them. A few seemed socially withdrawn. Still others were supremely self-confident, as if to say, "I'm right and everyone else is wrong. It happens all the time." Asch (1951, 1955) found that the amount of conforming influence depended on the size of the opposing majority. In a series of studies, he varied the number of confederates who gave incorrect answers from 1 to 15. He found that people conformed to a group of 3 or 4 just as readily as to a larger group (Figure 13.15). However, a participant conformed much less if he or she had an ally. Being a minority of one is painful, but being in a minority of two is not as bad (Figure 13.16).

members, the mean participant conformed on 4 of the 12 trials. Asch (1955) was disturbed by these results: "That we have found the tendency to conformity in our society so strong . . . is a matter of concern. It raises questions about our ways of education and about the values that guide our conduct" (p. 34).

Why did people conform so readily? When they were interviewed after the experiment, some said they thought the rest of the group was correct or they guessed that an optical illusion was influencing the appearance of the bars. Others said they knew their conforming answers were wrong but went along with the group for fear of ridicule. They were subject to a normative influence. The

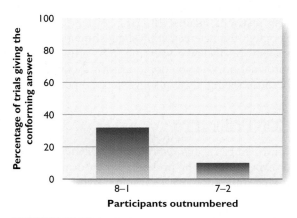

FIGURE 13.16 In Asch's experiments, participants who were faced with a unanimous incorrect majority conformed on 32% of trials. Participants who had one ally giving the correct answer were less likely to conform.

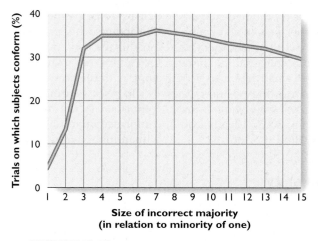

FIGURE 13.15 Asch found that conformity became more frequent as group size increased to about three, and then it leveled off. (Adapted from "Opinion and Social Pressure" by Solomon Asch, *Scientific American*, November 1955. Copyright © 1955 by Scientific American, Inc. All rights reserved.)

27. Are you more likely to conform to a group when you are outnumbered 5 to 1, 10 to 1, or 10 to 2?

Concept Check

Answer

27. You would be about equally likely to conform when outnumbered 5 to 1 or 10 to 1. Any group of 3 or more produces about the same urge to conform. However, having even one ally decreases the pressure, so you would be less likely to conform when outnumbered 10 to 2.

Variation in Conformity

Over the years since Asch's experiments, many similar studies have been conducted. In the United States, most studies show a decrease in the amount of conformity since the 1950s. In most Asian countries, the percentage of conforming answers tends to be relatively high, partly because people are trying to be polite and not embarrass the others by pointing out their error (R. Bond & Smith, 1996). That is, when researchers use the same procedure in different cultures, they may not be testing the same psychological processes.

Are people in certain cultures more prone to conformity as a general rule? The cultures of southern Asia, including China and Japan, are often described as more "collectivist" in contrast to the "individualist" cultures of the United States, Canada, Australia, and most of Europe. According to this view, Western culture encourages originality, competition, and individual freedom, whereas Eastern culture favors subordination of the individual to the welfare of the family or society. Originally, this contrast was based on observations of the Japanese during and shortly after World War II. However, Japan is a far different place today from what it was then. Acting collectively is a common response of any country when under attack or recovering from attack (Takano & Osaka, 1999). Shortly after terrorists crashed four passenger planes on September 11, 2001, U.S. citizens showed a strong collectivist "we're all in this together" attitude.

Many studies have contrasted Japanese and U.S. attitudes, mostly using college students and relying on questions like those in Table 13.3. A few investigators have directly observed conformist, cooperative, and competitive behaviors in various countries. Most studies have found no significant difference between Japanese and American attitudes, and some have even found Japanese students slightly *more* individualistic than Americans (M. H. Bond, 2002; Oyserman, Coon, & Kemmelmeier, 2002; Takano & Osaka, 1999).

Some researchers therefore suggest that the "collectivist" notion is wrong, at least for modern-day Japan (Takano & Osaka, 1999). Others point out that each country has multiple subcultures (A. P. Fiske, 2002). People in rural Japan are certainly different from those in Tokyo. Also, we need to measure collectivism or individualism more carefully (M. H. Bond, 2002). For example, you might find fault with some of the items in Table 13.3. In any case, we should beware of the generalization that all Asian cultures are collectivist or conformist.

---

28. What is one possible explanation for why collectivism may have been a more prominent aspect of Japanese thinking in the past than it is today?

Answer

28. During and shortly after World War II, the people of Japan were under attack or recovering from attack. In that situation, people of any country are motivated to work collectively.

TABLE 13.3 Examples of Questions to Measure Collectivist Versus Individualist Attitudes

T	F	I take pride in accomplishing what no one else can accomplish.
T	F	It is important to me that I perform better than others on a task.
T	F	I am unique—different from others in many respects.
T	F	I like my privacy.
T	F	To understand who I am, you must see me with members of my group.
T	F	I would help, within my means, if a relative were in financial difficulty.
T	F	Before making a decision, I always consult with others.
T	F	I have respect for the authority figures with whom I interact.

Note: The first four items measure individualism; the second four measure collectivist attitudes.
Source: From Oyserman, Coon, & Kemmelmeier, 2002.

OBEDIENCE TO AUTHORITY

Ordinarily, if someone ordered you to hurt another person, you would refuse. However, certain situations exert powerful pressure.

Decades ago, psychologist Philip Zimbardo and his colleagues paid college students to play the roles of guards and prisoners for 2 weeks during a vacation period. The researchers set up the basement of a university building as a prison but gave the students only minimal instructions on how to conduct themselves. Within 6 days, the researchers had to cancel the study because many of the "guards" were physically and emotionally bullying the "prisoners" (Haney, Banks, & Zimbardo, 1973). Why? None of the students were habitually cruel in everyday life. However, in this situation, they could get away with cruelty without any penalties or retaliation. Also, they presumably inferred that cruelty was expected. After all, what would be the point of "playing prison" for 2 weeks while behaving politely?

Although we should beware of drawing too broad a conclusion from this single study, as the results would differ with changes in instructions or procedure, we can see parallels in real life. In 2003 American soldiers admitted brutally degrading Iraqi prisoners at the Abu Ghraib prison. Early speculation attributed their actions to "a few bad apples" among the soldiers. Later, it became apparent that none of them were habitually cruel. They were ill trained as prison guards, lightly supervised, under constant stress and discomfort, and in almost constant danger. Further, they had the usual military custom of obedience to authority and conformity to their peers. No one can excuse their terrible actions, but the actions probably stemmed more from the evil situation than from inherently evil people (S. T. Fiske, Harris, & Cuddy, 2004).

What's the Evidence?
The Milgram Experiment

A more extensive series of studies examined how people would react if an experimenter asked them to deliver shocks to another person, starting with weak shocks and progressing to stronger ones. At what point, if any, would they refuse? This research by Stanley Milgram (1974) was inspired by reports of atrocities in the Nazi concentration camps during World War II. People who had committed the atrocities defended themselves by saying they were only obeying orders. International courts rejected that defense, and outraged people throughout the world told themselves, "If I had been there, I would have refused to follow such orders" and "It couldn't happen here."

What do you think? Could it happen here?

Hypothesis When an authority figure gives normal people instructions to do something that might hurt another person, some of them will obey.

Method Two adult male participants arrived at the experimental room—the real participant and a confederate of the experimenter pretending to be a participant. They were not college students. The experimenters wanted results that would generalize to a broad population. They also wanted to minimize the risk that the participants would suspect the true purpose of the experiment. The experimenter told the participants that in this study on learning, one participant would be the "teacher" and the other was the "learner." The teacher would read lists of words through a microphone to the learner, who would sit in a nearby room. The teacher would then test the learner's memory for the words. Whenever the learner made a mistake, the teacher was to deliver an electric shock as punishment.

The experiment was rigged so that the real participant was always the teacher and the confederate was always the learner. The teacher watched as the learner was strapped into the escape-proof shock device (Figure 13.17). The learner never received shocks, but the teacher was led to believe that he did. In fact, before the start of the study, the experimenter had the teacher feel a sample shock from the machine.

At the start of the experiment, the teacher read the words and the learner made many mistakes. The teacher operated a shock generator with levers to deliver shocks ranging from 15 volts to 450 volts in 15-volt increments (Figure 13.18). The experimenter instructed the teacher to begin by punishing the learner with the 15-volt switch for his first mistake and increase by 15 volts for each successive mistake.

FIGURE 13.18 The "teacher" in Milgram's experiment flipped switches on this box, apparently delivering stronger and stronger shocks for each successive error that the "learner" made. Although the device looked realistic, it did not actually shock the learner.

As the voltage went up, the learner in the next room cried out in pain and kicked the wall. In one version of the experiment, the learner complained that he had a heart condition. If a teacher asked who would take responsibility for any harm done to the learner, the experimenter replied that he, the experimenter, would take responsibility but insisted, "while the shocks may be painful, they are not dangerous." When the shocks reached 150 volts, the learner called out in pain and begged to be let out of the experiment, complaining that his heart was bothering him. Beginning at 270 volts, he screamed in agony. At 300 volts, he shouted that he would no longer answer any questions. After 330 volts, he made no response at all. Still, the experimenter ordered the teacher to continue asking questions and delivering shocks. Remember, the learner was not really being shocked. The screams of pain came from a tape recording.

Results Of 40 participants, 25 delivered shocks all the way to 450 volts. Most of those who quit did so fairly early. Most of those who went beyond 150 volts and everyone who continued beyond 330 persisted all the way to 450. Those who delivered the maximum shock were not sadists but normal adults recruited from the community through newspaper ads. They were paid a few dollars for their services, and if they asked, they were told that they could keep the money even if they quit. (Not many asked.) People from all walks of life obeyed the experimenter's orders, including blue-collar workers, white-collar workers, and professionals. Most of them grew upset and agitated while they were supposedly delivering shocks to the screaming learner.

Interpretation The level of obedience depended on certain factors of the situation. One was that the experimenter agreed to take responsibility. (Remember the diffusion of responsibility principle.) Also, the experimenter started with a small request, a 15-volt shock, and gradually progressed to stronger shocks.

FIGURE 13.17 In Milgram's experiment, a rigged selection chose a confederate of the experimenter to be the "learner." Here the learner is strapped to a device that supposedly delivers shocks.

FIGURE 13.19 In one variation of the procedure, the experimenter asked the teacher to hold the learner's hand on the shock plate. This close contact with the learner decreased obedience to less than half its usual level. (From Milgram's 1965 film, *Obedience*)

It is easy to agree to the small request, and after you have agreed to that one, it is easy to agree to the next one.

Figures 13.19 and 13.20 illustrate the results of some variations in procedure. Participants were more obedient to an experimenter who remained in the same room than to one who left. They were less obedient if they needed to force the learner's hand back onto the shock plate. If additional "teachers" divided the task—the other "teachers" being confederates of the experimenter—a participant was likely to obey if the others obeyed but unlikely if the others did not.

Still, the remarkable conclusion remains that, under a variety of conditions, many normal people followed orders from an experimenter they had just met, even though they thought they might hurt or even kill someone. Imagine how much stronger the pressure to obey orders from a government or military leader would be.

Ethical Issues Milgram's experiment told us something about ourselves that we did not want to hear. No longer could we say, "What happened in Nazi Germany could never happen here." We found that most of us do follow orders, even offensive ones. We are indebted to Milgram's study for this important, if unpleasant, information.

However, although I am glad to know about Milgram's results, I doubt that I would have enjoyed participating in his experiment. Most people were emotionally drained, and some were visibly upset to discover how readily they had obeyed orders to deliver dangerous shocks to another person.

A few years after Milgram's studies, the U.S. government established regulations to protect people participating in research. Actually, Milgram's studies had little influence on these regulations; they were enacted in response to abusive experiments in medicine (Benjamin & Simpson, 2009). Nevertheless, the rules were extended to psychological research. In addition, psychologists became more sensitive to the ethics of research, and the American Psychological Association established clear rules about what an experimenter can ask someone to do. Today, before the start of any psychological experiment—even the simplest and most innocuous—the experimenter must submit a plan to an institutional committee that can approve or reject the ethics of the experiment. One of the main rules is *informed consent*. Before you participate in a research study, you must be informed of what is about to happen, and you must agree to it.

Could anyone replicate Milgram's research today? Psychologists long assumed it would be impossible because of the ethical restraints. However, a psychologist found a way to rep-

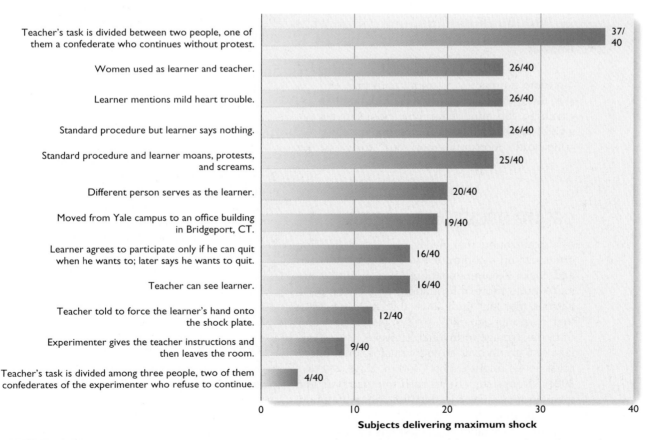

FIGURE 13.20 Milgram varied his procedure in many ways. Division of responsibility increased obedience. An implication of personal responsibility decreased obedience.

licate the essential aspect of the research. Milgram reported that most of the people who went beyond 150 volts continued all the way to 450. The teacher's tension and stress accumulated as the learner screamed and protested at the higher voltages. So Burger (2009) repeated the procedure but stopped it at 150 volts. Replicating that much of the experiment provides valuable information without the severe ethical objections. The result was that most people continued as far as 150 volts, just as they had in Milgram's research more than 40 years earlier. Women and men showed about equal compliance (Burger, 2009). The level of obedience was a bit lower than in Milgram's era, probably because of societal trends toward greater individualism, assertiveness, and self-esteem (Twenge, 2009). Still, the finding remains that most normal people were willing to follow orders that might hurt someone.

(It is interesting to speculate about what would have happened under other conditions that Milgram didn't try. Would people quit earlier if they thought they were shocking a child? What if they were told that they would eventually trade places so that the previous learner would start delivering shocks to the teacher? How do you think the teachers would behave then? What other changes in procedure can you imagine that might influence the degree of obedience?)

29. In what way did the obedience in Milgram's experiment resemble the foot-in-the-door procedure? How did it resemble Skinner's shaping procedure?

Answer

29. As with the foot-in-the-door procedure, Milgram started with a small request (give a small shock) and then built up. Skinner's shaping procedure also starts with an easy task and then builds to something more difficult.

GROUP DECISION MAKING

An organization that needs to reach a decision often sets up a committee to consider the issues and make recommendations. A committee has more time, more information, and fewer peculiarities than any individual has. Research finds that a group generally makes better decisions than the average individual. However, the advantage of a group over an individual is often not as great as we might expect (Sorkin, Hays, & West, 2001). Groups sometimes rush to a decision, and many groups show social loafing. Some individuals conform to the majority opinion and discard their own, possibly better, opinions.

Group Polarization

If nearly all the people who compose a group lean in the same direction on a particular issue, then a group discussion will move the group as a whole even further in that direction. This phenomenon is known as group polarization. Note that it requires a fairly homogeneous group. If the group has several disagreeing factions, the trends are less predictable (Rodrigo & Ato, 2002).

The term *polarization* does not mean that the group breaks up into fragments favoring different positions. Rather, it means that the members of a group move *together* toward one pole (extreme position) or the other. For example, a group of people who are opposed to abortion or in favor of animal rights or opposed to gun regulations will, after discussing the issue among themselves, generally become more extreme in their views than they had been at the start (Lamm & Myers, 1978).

Group polarization demonstrates both informational and normative influences (Isenberg, 1986). During the discussion, if most of the members were already leaning in the same direction, they hear new arguments favoring that side of the issue and few or none for the opposition (Kuhn & Lao, 1996). Also, as the members of the group become aware of the consensus during the discussion, the pressure to conform is especially powerful for those who do not feel fully accepted by the group (Noel, Wann, & Branscombe, 1995).

30. Is a jury more likely to reach a biased or extreme decision than a single individual would be?

Answer

30. It depends. Group polarization would probably move a nearly unanimous jury toward a unanimous verdict. However, a jury that starts out divided would not experience group polarization. Most research has found that juries and similar groups are no more extreme than the average individual (Kerr, MacCoun, & Kramer, 1996).

Groupthink

An extreme form of group polarization, known as groupthink, occurs when *the members of a group suppress their doubts about a group's decision for fear of making a bad impression or disrupting group harmony* (Janis, 1972, 1985). The main elements leading to groupthink are overconfidence by the leadership, underestimation of the problems, and pressure to conform. Sometimes, dissenters conform on their own, and sometimes, the leadership actively urges them to conform.

A dramatic example of groupthink led to the Bay of Pigs fiasco of 1962. President John F. Kennedy and his advisers were considering a plan to support a small-scale invasion of Cuba at the Bay of Pigs. They assumed that a small group of Cuban exiles could overwhelm the Cuban army and trigger a spontaneous rebellion of the Cuban people against their government. Most of the advisers who doubted this assumption kept quiet. The one who did express doubts was told that he should loyally support the president. Within a few hours after the invasion began, all the invaders were killed or captured. The decision makers then wondered how they could have made such a stupid decision.

Groupthink often occurs in business decisions, especially in highly prosperous and successful companies. The leaders become overconfident, and their critics become hesitant to speak up. For example, after British Airways discovered that 60% of its passengers were non-British, its leaders decided to remove the British flag from the tailfins of the planes. This decision not only angered the British public but also outraged the employees who resented what seemed a pointless expense of £60 million to change the company's logo while the company was firing workers to save costs (Eaton, 2001).

Groupthink is not easy to avoid. We generally admire government or business leaders who are

Many organizations try to resist the tendency toward groupthink, which stifles dissenting views. During the Renaissance, European kings sometimes called on a "fool" (or court jester) to describe some proposal in a fresh and possibly amusing light. In a court composed largely of yes-men, the fool was the only one who could point out the folly of a proposed action without fear of reprisals.

decisive and confident. Groupthink occurs when they become *too* decisive and confident, failing to consider all the risks. One strategy is for a leader to consult with advisers individually so they are not influenced by what they hear other advisers saying. A message for all of us is to be concerned when anyone in power seems too sure of success.

In Closing

Fix the Situation, Not Human Nature

If we want to prevent people from panicking when a fire breaks out in a crowded theater, the best solution is to build more exits. Similarly, it is difficult to teach people to behave ethically or intelligently when they are under strong pressure to conform. For example, the more shocks a person has already given someone in Milgram's obedience study, the harder it is to quit. In a group where everyone else seems united behind the leader's decision, it is difficult to speak up in opposition. To avoid the temptation to make bad decisions, we need to choose our situations carefully.

SUMMARY

- *Social influence.* People influence our behavior by offering information and by setting norms of expected conduct. We also follow others' examples just because they suggested a possible action. (page 489)
- *Conformity.* Many people conform to the majority view even when they are confident that the majority is wrong. An individual is as likely to conform to a group of three as to a larger group, but an individual with an ally is less likely to conform. (page 489)
- *Cultural differences.* Although some cultures tend to be more collectivist or conforming than others, it is an overgeneralization to regard all Asian cultures as collectivist or to assume that all members of a society are equally collectivist. (page 490)
- *Obedience.* In Milgram's obedience study, many people followed directions in which they thought they were delivering painful shocks to another person. (page 491)
- *Group polarization.* Groups of people who lean mostly in the same direction on a given issue often make more extreme decisions than most people would have made on their own. (page 494)
- *Groupthink.* Groupthink occurs when members of a cohesive group fail to express their opposition to a decision for fear of making a bad impression or harming the cohesive spirit of the group. (page 494)

KEY TERMS

conformity (page 489)

group polarization (page 494)

groupthink (page 494)

exploration and study

Why Does This Matter to Me?

SOCIAL RESPONSIBILITY AND PSYCHOLOGY

Many environmental and societal problems are caused by human behavior. Psychologists can help steer the course of our future toward more socially responsible and sustainable outcomes. Students of today need to be ever mindful of the link between human behavior and its impact on the environment and our communities.

"Social Psychology" and Social Responsibility: A Step Further

It is difficult to persuade people to do something with uncertain and delayed benefits, such as conserving resources to benefit the environment in the long run. What techniques can you suggest to improve the attempts in this regard?

Community-Based Social Marketing

- Visit Aceti Associates' website for a set of barrier/motivation inventories that shed light on the difficulties of motivating people toward sustainable behavior. It also lists proven strategies for catalyzing such behavior change.
- More information and resources for those working to foster sustainable behaviors can be found at the Fostering Sustainable Behavior website. Registration is required.

Find current links to the above websites at www.cengage.com/psychology/kalat.

Join the iChapters Plant a Tree Drive!

To show its support of the environmental movement, iChapters is planting a tree on behalf of each fan of the iChapters Facebook Page and for every 10 questions answered correctly in our quiz.
http://www.ichapters.com/plantatree/

Exploration and Study

SUGGESTIONS FOR FURTHER EXPLORATION

In addition to the study materials provided at the end of each module, you may supplement your review of this chapter with the following book and website suggestions or by using one or more of the book's electronic resources, which include its companion website, interactive Cengage Learning eBook, and CengageNOW. Brief descriptions of these resources follow. For more information, visit **www.cengage.com/psychology/kalat**.

ADDITIONAL RESOURCES

The book's companion website, accessible from www.cengage.com/psychology/kalat, provides a wide range of study resources such as an interactive glossary, flashcards, tutorial quizzes, updated web links, and Try It Yourself activities.

CengageNOW with Critical Thinking **Videos** is an easy-to-use resource that helps you study in less time to get the grade you want. An online study system, CengageNOW gives you the option of taking a diagnostic pretest for each chapter. The system uses the results of each pretest to create personalized chapter study plans for you. The Personalized Study Plans

- Help you save study time by identifying areas on which you should concentrate and give you one-click access to corresponding pages of the interactive Cengage Learning eBook;
- Provide interactive exercises and study tools to help you fully understand chapter concepts; and
- Include a posttest for you to take to confirm that you are ready to move on to the next chapter.

Find critical thinking videos like this one in your CengageNOW product, which offer an opportunity for you to learn more about psychological research on different topics.

Implicit Association

Books

Goldstein, N. J., Martin, S. J., & Cialdini, R. B. (2008). *Yes! 50 scientifically proven ways to be persuasive.* This book describes research-backed techniques of persuasion, which could be useful to you both in attempting to persuade others and in resisting unwelcome attempts to persuade you.

Milgram, S. (1975). *Obedience to authority.* New York: Harper & Row. This describes Milgram's classic experiments on obedience.

Zimbardo, P. (2007). *The Lucifer Effect: Understanding how good people turn evil.* New York: Random House. In the Stanford prison experiment, normal college students treated others brutally. At Abu Ghraib, U.S. soldiers cruelly tortured their prisoners. Why? This book explores the issue.

Websites

Links to the websites described below are kept current and can be found at **www.cengage.com/psychology/kalat**.

Social Psychology Network

This huge database includes more than 13,000 links to resources about social behavior.

Prisoner's Dilemma

Play the prisoner's dilemma game with a computer opponent. Try different strategies to see which works best.

Implicit Association Test

Test your own prejudices and attitudes with the Implicit Association Test.

Koji Aoki/Getty Images

14 chapter Personality

Consider This: Several thousand people have the task of assembling the world's largest jigsaw puzzle, which contains more than a trillion pieces. Connie Conclusionjumper scrutinizes 20 pieces, stares off into space, and announces, "When the puzzle is fully assembled, it will be a picture of the Sydney Opera House!" Prudence Plodder says, "Well, I don't know what the whole puzzle will look like, but I think I've found two little pieces that fit together."

Which of the two has made the greater contribution to completing the puzzle? We could argue either way. Clearly, the task requires an enormous number of little, unglamorous accomplishments like Prudence's. But if Connie is right, her flash of insight will be extremely valuable for assembling all the pieces. Of course, if the puzzle turns out to be a picture of a sailboat at sunset, then Connie will have misled us and wasted our time.

Some psychologists have offered grand theories about the nature of personality. Others have tried to classify personality types and understand why people act differently in specific situations. In this chapter, we explore several methods of approaching personality ranging from large-scale theories to small-scale descriptions. In the first module, we consider some famous personality theorists, including Sigmund Freud. The second module concerns descriptions of personality. Any description is, of course, a theory, but it differs from the kinds of theories in the first module. The final module describes personality measurements.

© AP/Wide World Photos

This three-dimensional jigsaw puzzle of the ocean liner *Titanic* consists of 26,000 pieces. Understanding personality is an even more complex puzzle.

Personality Theories

> • How can we best describe the overall structure of personality?

Every individual is virtually an enemy of civilization. . . . Thus civilization has to be defended against the individual. . . . For the masses are lazy and unintelligent . . . and the individuals composing them support one another in giving free rein to their indiscipline.

—Sigmund Freud (1927/1961, pp. 6–8)

It has been my experience that persons have a basically positive direction. In my deepest contacts with individuals in therapy, even those whose troubles are most disturbing, whose behavior has been most anti-social, whose feelings seem most abnormal, I find this to be true.

—Carl Rogers (1961, p. 26)

What is human nature? The 17th-century philosopher Thomas Hobbes argued that humans are by nature selfish. Life in a state of nature, he said, is "nasty, brutish, and short." We need the government to protect ourselves from one another. The 18th-century political philosopher Jean-Jacques Rousseau disagreed, maintaining that people are naturally good and that governments are the problem, not the solution. Rational people acting freely, he maintained, would advance the welfare of all.

The debate between those two viewpoints survives in theories of personality (Figure 14.1). Sigmund Freud held that people are born with sexual and destructive impulses that must be held in check if civilization is to survive. Carl Rogers believed that people seek good and noble goals after they have been freed from unnecessary restraints.

Hobbes	Rousseau
Humans are selfish	Humans are good
Government is required for protection	Government is a corrupting influence

Freud	Rogers
Natural impulses are detrimental to society	Natural impulses are noble and good

FIGURE 14.1 Sigmund Freud, like the philosopher Thomas Hobbes, stressed the more destructive aspects of human nature. Carl Rogers, like Jean-Jacques Rousseau, emphasized the more favorable aspects.

Which point of view is correct? Way down deep, are we good, bad, both, or neither? What is the basic nature of human personality?

The term *personality* comes from the Latin word *persona*, meaning "mask." In the plays of ancient Greece and Rome, actors wore masks to indicate their characters. Unlike a mask, however, the term *personality* implies something stable. **Personality** consists of *all the consistent ways in which the behavior of one person differs from that of others, especially in social situations.* (Differences in learning, memory, sensation, or muscle control are generally not considered personality.)

SIGMUND FREUD AND THE PSYCHODYNAMIC APPROACH

Sigmund Freud (1856–1939), an Austrian physician, developed the first psychodynamic theory. *A psychodynamic theory relates personality to the interplay of conflicting forces within the individual, including unconscious ones.* That is, internal forces that we do not understand push us and pull us.

Freud's influence extends into sociology, literature, art, religion, and politics. And yet, here we are, about three fourths of the way through this text on psychology, and until now, I have barely mentioned Freud. Why?

The reason is that Freud's influence within psychology has declined substantially. According to one psychologist, Frederick Crews (1996, p. 63), "independent studies have begun to converge toward a verdict that was once considered a sign of extremism or even of neurosis: that there is literally nothing to be said, scientifically or therapeutically, to the advantage of the entire Freudian system or any of its constituent dogmas." Think about that: *nothing* to be said in favor of *any* of Freud's theories. Needless to say,

Sigmund Freud interpreted dreams, slips of the tongue, and so forth to infer unconscious thoughts and motivations.

The fame of Sigmund Freud far exceeds that of any other psychologist. His picture has appeared on the Austrian 50-schilling bill and bimetal millennial coin.

of explaining and dealing with personality, based on the interplay of conscious and unconscious forces, as psychoanalysis. To this day, psychoanalysts remain loyal to some version of Freud's methods and theories, although their views have of course developed over the decades.

Psychoanalysis started as a simple theory: Each of us has an unconscious mind and a conscious mind. The unconscious is the repository of memories, emotions, and thoughts, many of them illogical, that affect our behavior even though we cannot talk about them. According to this theory, traumatic experiences and unresolved childhood conflicts force thoughts and emotions into the unconscious. The goal of psychoanalysts is to bring those memories back to consciousness, producing catharsis and enabling the person to overcome irrational impulses.

As Freud listened to his patients, however, he became convinced that the traumatic events they recalled could not account for their abnormal behavior. Some patients reacted strongly to events that others took in stride. Why? At first, in the early 1890s, Freud attributed their overreactions to sexual difficulties (Macmillan, 1997). For a while, he recommended increased sexual activity as a cure for certain kinds of anxiety disorders. In contrast, people suffering from nervous exhaustion, he said, were suffering from the results of masturbation. His evidence for this idea was that all his patients who were suffering from nervous exhaustion had masturbated (!). You can see the problem with this evidence.

Freud soon abandoned these hypotheses and suggested instead that the ultimate cause of psychological disorders was traumatic childhood sexual experiences, either seduction by other children or sexual abuse by adults. Freud's patients did not report any such memories, but Freud put together parts of the patients' dream reports, slips of the tongue, and so forth and claimed that they pointed to early sexual abuse.

A few years later, he abandoned the idea that psychological disorders resulted from childhood sexual abuse. According to Freud's own description of these events, he decided that his patients had "misled" him into believing they were sexually abused in early childhood (Freud, 1925). Why did Freud abandon his early theory? According to one view (Masson, 1984), Freud simply lost the courage to defend his theory. According to other scholars, however, Freud never had any evidence for it (Esterson, 2001; Powell & Boer, 1994;

not everyone agrees with that statement. Still, the decline of Freud's influence is striking. Even psychologists who remain loyal to Freud's ideas admit that they feel isolated from the mainstream of psychological research (Bornstein, 2005).

Freud's Search for the Unconscious

Freud would have preferred to be a professor of cultural history or anthropology. In Austria at the time, however, universities offered few positions to Jews. The only professions readily open to him were law, business, and medicine. Freud chose medicine, but his interests within medicine were more theoretical than practical.

Early in his career, Freud worked with the psychiatrist Josef Breuer, who was treating a young woman with a fluctuating variety of physical complaints. As she talked with Breuer about her past, she remembered various emotionally traumatic experiences. Breuer, and later Freud, said that remembering these experiences produced catharsis, a release of pent-up emotional tension, thereby relieving her illness. However, later scholars who reexamined the medical records found that this woman who was so central to the history of psychoanalysis showed little or no benefit from the treatment (Ellenberger, 1972).

Regardless of whether the "talking cure" had been successful in this case, Freud began applying it to other patients. He referred to his method

Schatzman, 1992). Freud had inferred his patients' sexual abuse from their symptoms and dreams despite their own denials of abuse. It was hardly fair, therefore, to complain that the patients had misled him into believing they had been abused.

When he abandoned his ideas about early sexual abuse, he replaced them with theories focusing on children's sexual fantasies. Although he did not fully develop his views of girls' early sexual development, he was explicit about boys: During early childhood, every boy goes through an Oedipus complex, *when he develops a sexual interest in his mother and competitive aggression toward his father.* (Oedipus—EHD-ah-puhs—in the ancient Greek play by Sophocles unknowingly murdered his father and married his mother.) Most boys negotiate through this stage and emerge with a healthy personality, but some have sexual fantasies that they fail to resolve, leading to long-term personality difficulties.

What evidence did he have for this view? Again, he had none. He reconsidered the same statements his patients made to him earlier and reinterpreted them. Just as his patients denied having been sexually abused in childhood, they also denied what he inferred about their childhood sexual fantasies. Freud considered his patients' protests to be signs of emotional resistance and therefore confirmation that his interpretations were correct. Freud's main evidence for his interpretations was simply that he could construct a coherent story linking a patient's symptoms, dreams, and so forth to the sexual fantasies that Freud inferred (Esterson, 1993).

Theories about childhood sexual fantasies are difficult to test, to say the least. Developmental psychologists report that they virtually never see evidence of an Oedipus complex in children. Although some psychoanalysts still see merit in the idea (Luborsky & Barrett, 2006), most put little emphasis on it.

....

1. What was Freud's original view of the cause of childhood conflicts, and what view did he substitute? What evidence did he have for either view?

Answer

1. Initially, Freud pointed to childhood sexual abuse. Later, he said the problem was childhood sexual fantasies, such as the Oedipus complex. His only evidence was that he thought he could infer these childhood events from his patients' dreams and symptoms.

....

Stages of Psychosexual Development in Freud's Theory of Personality

Right or wrong, Freud's theory is so well known that you should understand it. One of his central points was that psychosexual interest and pleasure begin in infancy. He used the term psychosexual pleasure broadly to include *all strong, pleasant excitement arising from body stimulation.* He maintained that how we deal with our psychosexual development influences nearly all aspects of our personality.

According to Freud (1905/1925), people have a *psychosexual energy,* which he called libido (lih-BEE-doh), from a Latin word meaning "desire." During infancy, libido is focused in the mouth. As the child grows older, libido flows to other body parts. Children go through five stages of psychosexual development, and each leaves its mark on the adult personality. If normal sexual development is blocked or frustrated at any stage, Freud said, part of the libido becomes fixated at that stage, and the person *continues to be preoccupied with the pleasure area associated with that stage.* Table 14.1 summarizes these stages.

TABLE 14.1 Freud's Stages of Psychosexual Development

Stage (approximate ages)	Sexual Interests	Effects of Fixation at This Stage
Oral stage (birth to 1½ years)	Sucking, swallowing, biting	Lasting concerns with dependence and independence; pleasure from eating, drinking, and other oral activities
Anal stage (1½ to 3 years)	Expelling feces, retaining feces	Orderliness or sloppiness, stinginess or wastefulness, stubbornness
Phallic stage (3 to 5 or 6 years)	Touching penis or clitoris; Oedipus complex	Difficulty feeling closeness. Males: fear of castration Females: penis envy
Latent period (5 or 6 to puberty)	Sexual interests suppressed	—
Genital stage (puberty onward)	Sexual contact with other people	—

The Oral Stage

In the oral stage, from birth to about age 1½ *the infant derives intense psychosexual pleasure from stimulation of the mouth, particularly while sucking at the mother's breast.* According to Freud, someone fixated at this stage continues to receive great pleasure from eating, drinking, and smoking and may also have lasting concerns with dependence and independence.

The Anal Stage

At about age 1½, children enter the anal stage, when *they get psychosexual pleasure from the sensations of bowel movements.* If toilet training is too strict—or too lenient—the child becomes fixated at this stage. Someone fixated at the anal stage goes through life "holding things back"—being orderly, stingy, and stubborn—or less commonly, goes to the opposite extreme, becoming messy and wasteful.

According to Freud, if normal sexual development is blocked at the oral stage, the child seeks pleasure from drinking and eating and later from kissing and smoking. Perhaps this smoker's mother weaned him too quickly—or let him nurse too long. Like many of Freud's ideas, this one is difficult to test.

Masterfile

© Jeff Greenberg/PhotoEdit

The Phallic Stage

Beginning at about age 3, in the phallic stage, children begin to *play with their genitals* and according to Freud become sexually attracted to the opposite-sex parent. Freud claimed that boys are afraid of being castrated, whereas girls develop "penis envy." These ideas have always been controversial, and no clear evidence supports them.

The Latent Period

From about age 5 or 6 until adolescence, Freud said, most children enter a latent period in which they *suppress their psychosexual interest.* At this time, they play mostly with peers of their own sex. The latent period is evidently a product of European culture and does not appear in all societies.

The Genital Stage

Beginning at puberty, young people *take a strong sexual interest in other people.* This is known as the genital stage. According to Freud, anyone who has fixated a great deal of libido in an earlier stage has little libido left for the genital stage. But people who have successfully negotiated the earlier stages now derive primary satisfaction from sexual intercourse.

Evaluation of Freud's Stages

It is undeniable that infants get pleasure from sucking, that toddlers go through toilet training, that older children begin to notice their genitals, and that adolescents become interested in sexual contact with other people. However, the idea of fixation at various stages, central to much of Freud's thinking, is difficult to test (Grünbaum, 1986; Popper, 1986). When it has been tested, the results have been inconclusive. For example, the characteristics of being orderly, stingy, and stubborn, which Freud attributed to anal fixation, correlate with one another, suggesting that they relate to a single personality trait. However, we have no evidence connecting them to toilet training (Fisher & Greenberg, 1977).

....

2. If someone has persistent problems with independence and dependence, Freud would suggest a fixation at which psychosexual stage?

Concept Check

Answer

2. Freud would interpret this behavior as a fixation at the oral stage.

....

Structure of Personality

Personality, Freud claimed, consists of three aspects: id, ego, and superego. (Actually, he used German words that mean *it, I,* and *over-I.* A translator used Latin equivalents instead of English words.) The id consists of *sexual and other bio-*

logical drives that demand immediate gratification. The ego is *the rational, decision-making aspect of the personality.* The superego contains *the memory of rules and prohibitions we learned from our parents and others,* such as, "Nice little boys and girls don't do that." If the id produces sexual desires that the superego considers repugnant, the result is guilty feelings. Most psychologists today find it difficult to imagine the mind in terms of three warring factions and therefore regard Freud's description as only a metaphor.

. . . .

3. What kind of behavior would Freud expect of someone with a strong id and a weak superego? What behavior would Freud expect of someone with an unusually strong superego?

Concept Check

Answer

3. Someone with a strong id and a weak superego could be expected to give in to a variety of sexual and other impulses that other people would inhibit. Someone with an unusually strong superego would be unusually inhibited and dominated by feelings of guilt.

. . . .

Defense Mechanisms Against Anxiety

According to Freud, *the ego defends itself against anxieties by relegating unpleasant thoughts and impulses to the unconscious mind.* Among the defense mechanisms that the ego employs are repression, denial, rationalization, displacement, regression, projection, reaction formation, and sublimation. He saw these as normal processes that sometimes went to extremes. His daughter, Anna, developed and elaborated descriptions of these mechanisms.

Repression

The defense mechanism of repression is *motivated forgetting*—rejecting unacceptable thoughts, desires, and memories and banishing them to the unconscious. For example, someone sees a murder and forgets it, or someone has an unacceptable sexual impulse and becomes unaware of it.

Is repression a real phenomenon? Psychoanalysts defend the concept, but the evidence is shaky. As discussed in chapter 7, most people who endure miserable experiences remember them well, unless they were very young at the time. In fact, emotionally traumatic events are highly memorable. Laboratory investigations attempting to demonstrate repression have produced, at best, weak and ambiguous evidence (Holmes, 1990). People can and often do intentionally suppress unwanted thoughts and memories (Erdelyi, 2006). However, intentional suppression is different from Freud's concept of repression, which was an unconscious mechanism producing lost memories, distorted perceptions, and pathological behaviors. According to most research, people who intentionally suppress unpleasant memories *improve* their psychological adjustment. They do not face the problems Freud saw as linked to repression (Rofé, 2008). The evidence suggests much reason to be skeptical of repression.

Denial

The refusal to believe information that provokes anxiety ("This can't be happening") is denial. Whereas repression is the motivated forgetting of information, denial is an assertion that the information is incorrect. For example, someone with an alcohol problem may insist, "I'm not an alcoholic. I can take it or leave it." A patient who is told that he or she has a fatal illness may refuse to accept the diagnosis.

Rationalization

When people *attempt to prove that their actions are rational and justifiable and thus worthy of approval,* they are using rationalization. For example, a student who wants to go to the movies says, "More studying won't do me any good anyway." Someone who misses a deadline to apply for a job says, "I didn't really want that job."

Displacement

By diverting a behavior or thought away from its natural target toward a less threatening target, displacement lets people engage in the behavior with less anxiety. For example, if you are angry with your employer, you might yell at someone else.

Regression

A *return to a more immature level of functioning,* regression is an effort to avoid the anxiety of facing one's current role in life. By adopting a childish role, a person escapes responsibility and returns to an earlier, more secure, way of life. For example, after a new sibling is born, an older child may cry or pout. An adult who has just gone through a divorce or lost a job may move in with his or her parents.

Projection

Attributing one's own undesirable characteristics to other people is known as projection. If someone tells you to stop being angry, you might reply, "I'm not angry! You're the one who's angry!" Suggesting that other people have your faults might make the faults seem less threatening. For example, someone who secretly enjoys pornography might accuse other people of enjoying it. However, the research finds that people using projection do not ordinarily decrease their anxiety or their awareness of their own faults (Holmes, 1978; Sherwood, 1981).

Reaction Formation

To keep undesirable characteristics repressed, people may use reaction formation to *present themselves as the opposite of what they really are to hide the unpleasant truth either from themselves or others.* In other words, they go to the opposite extreme. A man troubled by doubts about his religious faith might try to convert others to the faith. Someone with unacceptable aggressive tendencies might join a group dedicated to preventing violence.

Sublimation

The transformation of sexual or aggressive energies into culturally acceptable, even admirable, behaviors is sublimation. According to Freud, sublimation lets someone express an impulse without admitting its existence. For example, painting and sculpture may represent a sublimation of sexual impulses. Someone may sublimate aggressive impulses by becoming a surgeon. However, if the true motives of a painter are sexual and the true motives of a surgeon are violent, they are well hidden indeed. Sublimation is the one proposed defense mechanism that is associated with socially constructive behavior.

---

4. Match these Freudian defense mechanisms with the situations that follow: repression, regression, denial, projection, rationalization, reaction formation, displacement, sublimation.

    a. A man who is angry with his neighbor goes deer hunting.
    b. A smoker insists there is no convincing evidence that smoking impairs health.
    c. Someone who secretly enjoys pornography works to outlaw it.
    d. A man who beats his wife writes a book arguing that people have an instinctive need for aggressive behavior.
    e. A woman forgets a doctor's appointment for a test for cancer.
    f. Someone who has difficulty dealing with others resorts to pouting and crying.

Concept Check

g. A boss takes credit for an employee's idea because "If I get the credit, our department will look good and all employees will benefit."
h. Someone with an impulse to shout obscenities writes novels.

Answers

4. a. displacement; b. denial; c. reaction formation; d. projection; e. repression; f. regression; g. rationalization; h. sublimation.

Evaluating Freud

Freud was an extremely persuasive speaker and writer. Although his influence within psychology has declined, his ideas continue to inspire vigorous supporters, including many in other disciplines, who apply Freudian interpretations to literature, politics, and so forth (Merlino, Jacobs, Kaplan, & Moritz, 2008). Many people regard the following as enduring contributions of Freud's ideas (Luborsky & Barrett, 2006; Westen, 1998):

- Much of mental life is unconscious. We don't always know why we're doing something.
- Conflicting motives influence much of our behavior. Some of those conflicts trace back to unresolved problems in early childhood.
- Our relationships with other people can resemble the relationships we had with other people in the past, such as our parents. (This concept is known as *transference*.)
- People develop through stages of psychosexual interest and relationships with the social world.

How much credit should Freud receive for these ideas? It's debatable. Consider the idea of unconscious processes. The kinds of unconscious processes that current research supports are very different from Freud's concepts. For example, implicit memory (chapter 7) and priming (chapters 7 and 8) are unconscious in the sense that people are unaware of certain influences on their behavior. However, these processes are unconscious because of weak stimuli, not because of repression. Freud's ideas about the unconscious did not lead to any of the research on implicit memory or priming. If anything, psychological researchers may have avoided considering unconscious processes because of their association with Freud's speculations.

The idea behind the psychoanalytic couch is for the client to relax and say everything that comes to mind. Freud's couch is pictured here.

Undeniably, much of our behavior reflects conflicting motives. That idea, however, is hardly original to Freud. Furthermore, most conflicts relate to the here and now. (I'd like to take a trip, but I'd also like to save money. I'd like to have a chocolate fudge sundae, but I'd also like to lose weight.) To agree that people have conflicting motives does not mean agreeing that our conflicts reflect an Oedipus conflict or any other problem dating back to early childhood.

The idea of transference should count as an insight by Freud. You might react emotionally to a therapist (or anyone else) who reminds you of a parent. Let's give Freud credit for that one.

What about the stages of psychosexual development? Yes, babies enjoy sucking and toddlers go through toilet training. But that observation doesn't amount to much unless we also believe Freud's concept of fixation at different psychosexual stages. That idea remains a speculation with no strong evidence to support it.

Finally, even if some of Freud's concepts vaguely resemble certain modern ideas, pointing out that similarity is a case of "damning with faint praise." Freud's goal was not to make generalizations such as "people often have conflicting motives." He thought he had found a way to uncover people's unconscious thoughts and motives. In that regard, most psychological researchers are unconvinced.

Neo-Freudians

Psychologists known as **neo-Freudians** *remained faithful to parts of Freud's theory while modifying other parts.* One of the most influential was the German physician Karen Horney (HOR-nigh; 1885–1952), who believed that Freud exaggerated the role of the sex drive in human behavior and misunderstood women's motivations. She believed, for example, that children had conflict with their parents because of parental intimidation, not because of sexual desires. Horney emphasized the social and cultural influences on personality that spur anxiety. Still, she emphasized many Freudian concepts such as repression. Her views were more a revision than a rejection of Freud's theories.

Karen Horney, a neo-Freudian, revised some of Freud's theories and paid greater attention to cultural influences. She pioneered the study of feminine psychology.

Other theorists, including Carl Jung and Alfred Adler, disagreed more sharply with Freud. Although Jung and Adler were at one time associates of Freud, each broke with Freud's theory in substantial ways and should not be classified as neo-Freudians.

CARL JUNG AND THE COLLECTIVE UNCONSCIOUS

Carl G. Jung (YOONG; 1875–1961), a Swiss physician, was an early member of Freud's inner circle. Freud regarded Jung like a son, the "heir apparent" or "crown prince" of the psychoanalytic movement, until their father–son relationship deteriorated (Alexander, 1982).

Carl G. Jung rejected Freud's concept that dreams hide their meaning from the conscious mind: "To me dreams are a part of nature, which harbors no intention to deceive, but expresses something as best it can" (Jung, 1965, p. 161).

Jung's theory of personality emphasized people's search for a spiritual meaning in life and the continuity of human experience, past and present. In contrast to Freud, who traced much of adult personality to childhood events, Jung stressed the possibility of personality changes in adulthood under the influence of the goals people set.

Jung was impressed that many of his patients described dreams with no clear relation to anything in their own lives. Rather, they were similar to images that are common in the myths, religions, and artworks of cultures throughout the world. He suggested that these images arise from inborn aspects of human nature. If you dream about a beetle, Jung might relate your dream to the important role beetles have played in human mythology dating back to the ancient Egyptians. If you dream about a baby, he might relate the symbolism to the possibility of psychological rebirth (Lawson, 2008).

According to Jung, people have not only a conscious mind and a "personal unconscious" (equivalent to Freud's unconscious) but also a collective unconscious mind. The **collective unconscious**, present at birth, pertains to *the cumulative experience of preceding generations.* Whereas the conscious mind and the personal unconscious vary from one person to another, the collective unconscious does not. It contains **archetypes**, which are *vague images*—or at least the predisposition to form images—*that have always been part of the human experience.* As evidence for this view, Jung pointed out similarities in the art of cultures throughout the world (Figure 14.2) as well as similarities in their myths and folklore.

Exactly how did the collective experiences of our ancestors become part of our unconscious minds? Jung offered little by way of explanation, and our current understanding of biology offers no route by which an experience could get directly into the genes. A more realistic hypothesis is that ancient people who thought in certain

FIGURE 14.2 Carl Jung was fascinated that similar images appear in the artworks of different cultures. One recurring image is the circular mandala, a symbol of unity and wholeness. These mandalas are: (a) a Hindu painting from Bhutan; (b) a mosaic from Beth Alpha Synagogue, Israel; (c) a tie-dye tapestry created in California; and (d) a Navajo sand painting from the southwestern United States.

ways had advantages and therefore survived long enough to become our ancestors. As a result, we evolved a tendency to think in those same ways.

Another of Jung's contributions was the idea of psychological types. He believed that people's personalities fell into a few distinct categories, such as extraverted or introverted. Although the results of personality testing do not support this idea, the authors of the Myers-Briggs personality test have revived it, as we shall see in the third module of this chapter.

5. How does Jung's idea of the collective unconscious differ from Freud's idea of the unconscious?

Answer

5. Jung's collective unconscious is the same for all people and is present at birth. Freud believed the unconscious developed from repressed experiences.

ALFRED ADLER AND INDIVIDUAL PSYCHOLOGY

Alfred Adler emphasized the ways in which personality depended on people's goals, especially their way of striving for a sense of superiority.

Alfred Adler (1870–1937), an Austrian physician who, like Jung, was an early associate of Freud, broke away because he believed Freud overemphasized the sex drive and neglected other influences. They parted company in 1911, with Freud insisting that women experience "penis envy" and Adler replying that women were more likely to envy men's status and power.

Adler founded a rival school of thought, which he called **individual psychology**. Adler did not mean "psychology of the individual." Rather, he meant *"indivisible psychology," a psychology of the person as a whole rather than parts* such as id, ego, and superego. Adler emphasized the importance of conscious, goal-directed behavior.

Adler's Description of Personality

Several of Adler's early patients were acrobats who had suffered childhood injuries to an arm or leg. After they worked to overcome their disabilities, they continued until they developed unusual strength and coordination. Perhaps, Adler surmised, people in general try to overcome weaknesses and transform them into strengths (Adler, 1932/1964).

As infants, Adler noted, we are small, dependent, and surrounded by others who seem so superior. We try to overcome that feeling of inferiority. Occasional experiences with failure goad us to try harder. However, persistent failures and excessive criticism produce an **inferiority complex**, *an exaggerated feeling of weakness, inadequacy, and helplessness.*

According to Adler, everyone has a natural **striving for superiority**, *a desire to seek personal excellence and fulfillment.* Each person creates a master plan for achieving a sense of superiority. A typical strategy is to seek success in business, sports, or other competitive activities. People also strive for success in other ways. Someone who withdraws from life gains a sense of accomplishment or superiority from being uncommonly self-sacrificing. Someone who constantly complains about illnesses or disabilities wins a measure of control over friends and family. Another person may commit crimes to savor the attention the crimes bring. People also get a feeling of superiority by making excuses. If you marry someone who is likely to thwart your ambitions, perhaps your underlying motivation is to maintain an illusion: "I could have been a great success if my spouse hadn't prevented me." Failure to study can have a similar motivation: "I could have done well on this test, but my friends talked me into partying the night before." According to Adler, people often engage in self-defeating behavior because they are not fully aware of their goals and strategies.

Adler tried to determine people's real motives. For example, he would ask someone who complained of a backache, "How would your life be different if you could get rid of your backache?" Those who eagerly said they would become more active were presumably trying to overcome their ailment. Those who said they could not imagine how their life would change, or said only that they would get less sympathy from others, were presumably exaggerating their discomfort if not imagining it.

---

6. How could we explain self-handicapping (from chapter 13) in Adler's theory?

Answer

6. In Adler's theory, people sometimes put themselves at a disadvantage to provide an excuse for failure so that in their imagination they can maintain a sense of superiority.

Adler's View of Psychological Disorders

According to Adler, seeking success for yourself alone is unhealthy (Adler, 1928/1964). The healthiest goal is to seek success for a larger group, such as your family, your community, your nation, or better yet, all of humanity. Adler was ahead of his time, and many psychologists since then have rediscovered this idea (Crocker & Park, 2004).

According to Adler, people's needs for one another require a **social interest**, *a sense of solidarity and identification with other people.* Note that social interest does not mean a desire to socialize. It means an interest in the welfare of society. People with social interest want to cooperate, not compete. In equating mental health with social interest, Adler saw mental health as a positive state, not just a lack of impairments. In Adler's view, people with excessive anxieties are not suffering from an illness. Rather, they have set immature goals, are following a faulty style of life, and show little social interest. Their response to new opportunity is, "Yes, but . . ." (Adler, 1932/1964).

For example, one of Adler's patients was a man who lived in conflict with his wife because he was constantly trying to impress and dominate her (Adler, 1927). When discussing his problems, the man revealed that he had been slow to mature and did not reach puberty until age 17. Other teenagers had ignored him or treated him like a child. Though he was now physically normal, he was overcompensating for those years of feeling inferior by trying to seem bigger and more important than he really was.

Adler's Legacy

Adler's influence exceeds his fame, and he probably would be glad for that. His concept of the inferiority complex has become part of the common culture. He was the first to talk about mental health as a positive state of activity and accomplishment rather than merely the absence of impairments. Many later psychologists have endorsed this idea (Keyes, 2007). Various later forms of therapy drew upon Adler's emphasis on understanding the assumptions that people make and how those assumptions influence behavior. Many psychologists also followed Adler by urging people to take responsibility for their own behavior. According to Adler, the key to a healthy personality was not just freedom from disorders but a desire for the welfare of other people.

THE LEARNING APPROACH

How did you develop your personality? As discussed in chapter 13, many social situations influence and constrain your behavior. You learn much of what we call personality in terms of what to do in one situation after another (Mischel, 1973,

1981). Because situations vary, so does your behavior. You might be honest about returning a lost wallet to its owner but lie to your professor about why your paper is late. The learning approach to personality emphasizes the ways in which we learn our social behaviors, one situation at a time. As described in the Social Learning section of chapter 6, we learn social behaviors by vicarious reinforcement and punishment. That is, we copy behaviors that were successful for other people and avoid behaviors that failed for others. Also, we imitate the people whom we respect and want to resemble.

Let's consider how this idea applies to masculine and feminine tendencies. Beginning in early childhood, most boys prefer to spend their time with other boys, and most girls prefer to spend their time with other girls. The result is to magnify the differences between boys and girls. Researchers see a slight tendency for girls to prefer dolls and boys to prefer toy cars and trucks beginning even before age 1 year (Alexander, Wilcox, & Woods, 2009), but that tendency grows from year to year, influenced by playmates of the same sex (Golombok et al., 2008). Children also tend to identify more with adults of their own gender. In one experiment, children watched adults choose between an apple and a banana. If all the men chose one fruit and all the women chose the other, the boys wanted what the men had and the girls wanted what the women had (Perry & Bussey, 1979).

As we learn people's expectations for us, we develop a **gender role**, *the pattern of behavior that a person is expected to follow because of being male or female.* A gender role is the psychological

Children learn gender roles partly by imitating adults, but they probably learn more from other children.

FIGURE 14.3 Gender roles vary greatly among cultures and even from one time period to another for a single culture. Here, a Palestinian man (a) and a Vietnamese woman (b) plow the fields. Men in Bangladesh (c) and women in Thailand (d) do the wash.

aspect of being male or female, as opposed to sex, which is the biological aspect. We know that gender role is at least partly learned because of the variation among cultures (Figure 14.3). For example, some cultures define cooking as women's work, and others define it as men's work. Men wear their hair short in some cultures and long in others. We also see changes in gender differences over time. For example, in the United States, the prevalence of heart disease has increased among women, and the prevalence of depression has increased for men. Those changes imply changes in gender roles as culture has changed (Dedovic, Wadiwalla, Engert, & Pruessner, 2009). Gender role impacts personality in detailed ways. For example, women tend to be more sensitive to other people's feelings than men are (Bekker & van Assen, 2008). Men, however, tend to be more tolerant of other men's quirky habits—more willing, for example, to stay with an assigned college roommate than to insist on switching (Benenson et al., 2009).

7. Suppose someone observes your behavior over a period of time and reports that your personality seems "inconsistent." How does the learning approach to personality explain that inconsistency?

Answer

7. You learn your behaviors one situation at a time. You may have learned to be friendly in one situation and not another or honest in one situation and not another.

HUMANISTIC PSYCHOLOGY

Another perspective on personality, humanistic psychology, *deals with consciousness, values, and abstract beliefs, including spiritual experiences and the beliefs that people live and die for.* According to humanistic psychologists, personality depends on people's beliefs and perceptions of the world. If you *believe* that a particular experience was highly meaningful, then it *was* highly meaningful. A psychologist can understand you only by asking you to interpret and evaluate the events of your life. (In theology, a *humanist* glorifies human potentials, generally denying or de-emphasizing a supreme being. The term *humanistic psychologist* implies nothing about someone's religious beliefs.)

Humanistic psychology emerged in the 1950s and 1960s as a protest against behaviorism and psychoanalysis, the dominant psychological viewpoints at the time (Berlyne, 1981). Behaviorists and psychoanalysts often emphasize the less noble aspects of people's thoughts and actions, whereas humanistic psychologists see people as essentially good and striving to achieve their potential. Also, behaviorism and psychoanalysis, despite their differences, both assume *determinism* (the belief that every behavior has a cause) and *reductionism* (the attempt to explain behavior in terms of its component elements).

Humanistic psychologists do not try to explain behavior in terms of its parts or hidden causes. They claim that people make deliberate, conscious decisions. For example, people might devote themselves to a great cause, sacrifice their own well-being, or risk their lives. To the humanistic psychologist, ascribing such behavior to past reinforcements or unconscious thought processes misses the point.

Humanistic psychologists generally study the special qualities of a given individual as opposed to studying groups. Their research consists mostly of recording narratives, more like a biographer than like a scientist. Their data are qualitative, not quantitative, and often difficult to evaluate.

Carl Rogers and the Goal of Self-Actualization

Carl Rogers, an American psychologist, studied theology before turning to psychology, and the influence of those early studies is apparent in his view of human nature. Rogers became the most influential humanistic psychologist.

Rogers (1980) regarded human nature as basically good. He said people have a natural drive toward self-actualization, *the achievement of one's full potential.* According to Rogers, it is as natural for people to strive for excellence as it is for a plant to grow. The drive for self-actualization is the basic drive behind the development of personality. Rogers's concept of self-actualization is similar to Adler's concept of striving for superiority.

Children evaluate themselves and their actions beginning at an early age. They learn that their actions can be good or bad. They develop a self-concept, *an image of what they really are,* and an ideal self, *an image of what they would like to be.* Rogers measured self-concept and ideal self by handing someone a stack of cards containing statements such as "I am honest" and "I am suspicious of others." The person would then sort the statements into piles representing *true of me* and *not true of me* or arrange them in a continuum from *most true of me* to *least true of me.* (This method is known as a *Q-sort.*) Then Rogers would provide an identical stack of cards and ask the person to sort them into two piles: *true of my ideal self* and *not true of my ideal self.* In this manner, he could compare someone's self-concept

Carl Rogers maintained that people naturally strive toward positive goals without special urging. He recommended that people relate to one another with unconditional positive regard.

to his or her ideal self. People who perceive much discrepancy between the two generally feel distress. Humanistic psychologists try to help people overcome their distress by improving their self-concept or by revising their ideal self.

To promote human welfare, Rogers maintained that people should relate to one another with unconditional positive regard, a relationship that Thomas Harris (1967) described as "I'm OK—You're OK." Unconditional positive regard is *the complete, unqualified acceptance of another person as he or she is,* much like the love of a parent for a child. If you feel unconditional positive regard, you might disapprove of someone's actions or intentions, but you would still accept and love the person. (This view resembles the Christian advice to "hate the sin but love the sinner.") The alternative is *conditional positive regard,* the attitude that "I shall like you only if . . . ." People who are treated with conditional positive regard feel restrained about opening themselves to new ideas or activities for fear of losing someone else's support.

Abraham Maslow and the Self-Actualized Personality

Abraham Maslow, another humanistic psychologist, complained that most psychologists concentrate on disordered personalities, assuming that personality is either normal or worse than normal. Maslow insisted, as Alfred Adler had, that personality can differ from normal in positive, desirable ways. He proposed that people's highest need is *self-actualization,* the fulfillment of an individual's potential.

As a first step toward describing the self-actualized personality, Maslow (1962, 1971) made a list of people who in his opinion were approaching their full potential. His list included people he knew personally as well as some from history. He sought to discover what, if anything, they had in common.

Abraham Maslow, one of the founders of humanistic psychology, introduced the concept of a "self-actualized personality," a personality associated with high productivity and enjoyment of life.

Harriet Tubman, identified by Maslow as having a self-actualized personality, was a leader of the Underground Railroad, a system for helping slaves escape from the southern states before the Civil War. Maslow defined the self-actualized personality by first identifying admirable people, such as Tubman, and then determining what they had in common.

According to Maslow (1962, 1971), people with a self-actualized (or self-actualizing) personality show the following characteristics:

- An accurate perception of reality: They perceive the world as it is, not as they would like it to be. They accept uncertainty and ambiguity.

- Independence, creativity, and spontaneity: They make their own decisions, even if others disagree.
- Acceptance of themselves and others: They treat people with unconditional positive regard.
- A problem-centered outlook rather than a self-centered outlook: They think about how to solve problems, not how to make themselves look good. They concentrate on significant philosophical or political issues, not just on getting through the day.
- Enjoyment of life: They are open to positive experiences, including "peak experiences" when they feel truly fulfilled and content.
- A good sense of humor.

Critics have noted that, because Maslow's description is based on his own choice of examples, it may simply reflect the characteristics that he himself admired. That is, his reasoning was circular: He defined certain people as self-actualized and then inquired what they had in common to figure out what "self-actualized" means (Neher, 1991). In any case, Maslow paved the way for other attempts to define a healthy personality as something more than a personality without disorder.

....

8. What does humanistic psychology have in common with the ideas of Alfred Adler?

Concept Check

Answer

8. Adler emphasized the importance of people's beliefs and the possibility of a better than normal personality. Humanistic psychology is based on Adler's approach.

....

14.1   module

In Closing

In Search of Human Nature

The three most comprehensive personality theorists—Freud, Jung, and Adler—lived and worked in Austria in the early 1900s. Here we are, a century later, and most specialists in personality research neither accept those theories nor try to replace them with anything better. Recall from chapter 1 that a good research question is interesting and answerable. Fundamental questions about human nature are extraordinarily interesting but not easily answerable. Most researchers today try to answer smaller questions about specific, measurable aspects of behavior, as the next two modules will describe. After researchers answer many of the smaller questions, perhaps they may return to the big questions of "what makes people tick?"

SUMMARY

- *Personality theories as views of human nature.* Personality consists of the stable, consistent ways in which each person's behavior differs from that of others. Theories of personality relate to conceptions of whether people are naturally good or bad. (page 500)

- *Psychodynamic theories.* Several historically influential theories have described personality as the outcome of unconscious internal forces. (page 500)

- *Freud.* Sigmund Freud, the founder of psychoanalysis, proposed that much of what we do and say has hidden meanings. However, most psychologists today are skeptical of his attempts to understand those hidden meanings. (page 500)

- *Freud's psychosexual stages.* Freud believed that many unconscious thoughts and motives are sexual in nature. He proposed that people progress through stages or periods of psychosexual development—oral, anal, phallic, latent, and genital—and that frustration at any stage fixates the libido at that stage. (page 502)

- *Defense mechanisms.* Freud and his followers argued that people defend themselves against anxiety by such mechanisms as denial, repression, projection, and reaction formation. (page 504)

- *Jung.* Carl Jung believed that all people share a collective unconscious that represents the entire experience of humanity. (page 506)

- *Adler.* Alfred Adler proposed that people's primary motivation is a striving for superiority. Each person adopts his or her own method of striving, and to understand people, we need to understand their goals and beliefs. (page 508)

- *Adler's view of a healthy personality.* According to Adler, the healthiest style of life is one that emphasizes social interest—that is, concern for the welfare of others. (page 508)

- *The learning approach.* Much of what we call personality is learned through individual experience, imitation, or vicarious reinforcement and punishment. (page 509)

- *Humanistic psychology.* Humanistic psychologists emphasize conscious, deliberate decision making. (page 510)

KEY TERMS

anal stage (page 502)

archetypes (page 506)

catharsis (page 501)

collective unconscious (page 506)

defense mechanism (page 504)

denial (page 504)

displacement (page 504)

ego (page 504)

fixation (page 502)

gender role (page 509)

genital stage (page 503)

humanistic psychology (page 510)

id (page 503)

ideal self (page 511)

individual psychology (page 508)

inferiority complex (page 508)

latent period (page 503)

libido (page 502)

neo-Freudians (page 506)

Oedipus complex (page 502)

oral stage (page 502)

personality (page 500)

phallic stage (page 503)

projection (page 504)

psychoanalysis (page 501)

psychodynamic theory (page 500)

psychosexual pleasure (page 502)

rationalization (page 504)

reaction formation (page 505)

regression (page 504)

repression (page 504)

self-actualization (page 511)

self-concept (page 511)

social interest (page 508)

striving for superiority (page 508)

sublimation (page 505)

superego (page 504)

unconditional positive regard (page 511)

unconscious (page 501)

- What traits provide the best description of personality?
- Why do people differ in their personalities?

Like this man playing the role of a woman in Japanese kabuki theater, actors can present personalities that are very different from their private ones. All of us occasionally display temporary personalities that are different from our usual selves.

Did you ever wonder *why* people differ in personality? Why don't we all have the "best" personality—whatever that is? If there were such a thing as a best personality, presumably natural selection would have established it for all of us, so the likely conclusion is that there is no best personality for all people in all situations (Nettle, 2006). Highly aggressive behavior is sometimes successful, but it also entails a risk of injury. Is fearfulness helpful or harmful? It depends; some situations really are dangerous. Is it a good thing to trust other people? Up to a point, yes, but dishonest people take advantage of anyone who is too trusting. A society works best if people have a variety of personalities.

Psychologists study personalities in two ways, called the nomothetic and the idiographic approaches. The word *nomothetic* (NAHM-uh-THEHT-ick) comes from the Greek *nomothetes,* meaning "legislator," and the **nomothetic approach** *seeks general laws about various aspects of personality* based on studies of groups of people. For example, we might make the nomothetic statement that people vary in a trait called *extraversion,* and the more extraverted someone is, the more likely that person will introduce himself or herself to a stranger.

In contrast, the word *idiographic* is based on the root *idio-,* meaning "individual." The **idiographic approach** concentrates on *intensive studies of individuals* (Allport, 1961). For example, a psychologist might study one person's goals, moods, and reactions. The conclusions would apply to this person and perhaps no one else.

PERSONALITY TRAITS AND STATES

Meteorologists distinguish between climate (the usual conditions) and weather (the current conditions). For example, the climate in Scotland is moister and cooler than the climate in Texas, but on a given day, the weather could be warm in Scotland and cool in Texas. Similarly, psychologists distinguish between long-lasting personality conditions and temporary fluctuations.

A consistent, long-lasting tendency in behavior, such as shyness, hostility, or talkativeness, is known as a **trait**. In contrast, a **state** is *a temporary activation of a particular behavior.* For example, being afraid right now is a state; being nervous most of the time is a trait. Being quiet in a library is a state; being quiet habitually is a trait. A trait, like a climatic condition, manifests itself as an average over time. Both traits and states are descriptions of behavior, not explanations. To say that someone is nervous and quiet does not explain anything. It merely describes what we are trying to explain.

9. Suppose someone becomes nervous as soon as he sits down in a dentist's chair. Is this experience "trait anxiety" or "state anxiety"?

Answer

9. It is state anxiety because it is evoked by a particular situation. Trait anxiety is a tendency to become nervous in many situations.

THE SEARCH FOR BROAD PERSONALITY TRAITS

According to the **trait approach to personality,** *people have consistent characteristics in their behavior.* Psychologists have described, studied, and measured many personality traits. Let's consider one example: belief in a just world. People who have a strong **belief in a just world** *maintain that life is fair and people usually get what they deserve* (Lerner, 1980). Here are examples of questions to measure this belief reworded from a standard questionnaire (Lipkus, 1991). Indicate your degree of agreement from 1 (complete disagreement) to 6 (complete agreement). The higher your score (scores range from 6 to 36), the greater your belief in a just world:

People usually get the rewards and punishments they deserve.

Most people who meet with misfortune did something to bring it on themselves.

Most of the lucky breaks I get are earned.

Promotions go to the people who work hardest.

People who have no job or no money have only themselves to blame.

Only rarely does an innocent person go to prison.

It is comforting to believe that life is fundamentally fair, that good deeds are rewarded and bad deeds punished. People with a strong belief in a just world usually handle stressful situations well, confident that things will turn out favorably after all (Bègue & Muller, 2006; Otto, Boos, Dalbert, Schöps, & Hoyer, 2006). They are more likely than average to offer help to a person in distress or to seek revenge against whoever caused the harm, presumably to restore a sense of justice (Furnham, 2003; Kaiser, Vick, & Major, 2004). However, if someone has been harmed and cannot be helped, people with a strong belief in a just world feel threatened, and to defend their belief, they often blame the victim (Hafer & Bègue, 2005). ("She shouldn't have been walking in that neighborhood." "He shouldn't have been out so late at night.") The point is that a personality trait—in this case, belief in a just world—manifests itself in many ways.

. . . .

10. Accident victims often respond, "It could have been worse." How might this reaction relate to a belief in a just world?

Answer

10. It seems unjust for an innocent person to sustain an injury. Minimizing the damage makes the injustice seem less.

. . . .

Issues in Personality Measurement

In personality as in other areas of psychology, research progress depends on good measurement. The problem in measuring personality is that behavior fluctuates depending on the situation. If we measure risk taking, we find that many people take risks in one situation but not in others. For example, someone might smoke cigarettes but avoid other kinds of risk (Hanoch, Johnson, & Wilke, 2006). To measure personality by observations, we would have to watch people in a huge variety of situations. Instead, researchers use questionnaires to ask people how they usually behave.

Devising a useful questionnaire is more difficult than you might think. When people rate their own personality, can we trust them to be accurate? Most Americans rate themselves above average in self-esteem and most other desirable aspects of personality, as well as intelligence, acceptance of minority groups, creativity, sense of humor, and almost anything else you can imagine. The British tend to be more modest, and Asians are still more modest (Furnham, Hosoe, & Tang, 2002). Because psychologists compare the scores of one person with another, Americans who try to answer honestly, rating themselves as about average, are considered to have a *low* opinion of themselves (Baumeister, Campbell, Krueger, & Vohs, 2003).

One way to check the validity of a personality questionnaire is to compare questionnaire results to behaviors recorded in diary form. In one study, 170 college students filled out questionnaires about several personality dimensions, including aggressiveness and spontaneity. Then they kept daily records of such behaviors as yelling at someone (aggression) and buying something on the spur of the moment (spontaneity). Both kinds of data rely on self-reports, but the daily behavior records are more detailed, closer in time to the actual events, and presumably more accurate. The questionnaire results correlated about .4 with daily reports of aggressive behavior but less well with reports of spontaneous acts (Wu & Clark, 2003). That is, the questionnaire results were moderately accurate but not great.

An Example of Measurement Problems: Self-Esteem

Let's consider the personality dimension of **self-esteem,** *one's evaluation of one's own abilities, performance, and worth.* People in general, and Americans in particular, like to have high self-esteem. They do what they can to maintain it, including trying to improve their skills, if they think they can, or reminding themselves that they are more successful than many other people (Nussbaum & Dweck, 2008). Psychologists generally expect that high self-esteem should lead to increased productivity and other good outcomes. However, programs to raise people's self-esteem have often had disappointing results. On the plus side, people who increase their self-esteem are better able to cope with stress (Creswell et al., 2005; Marsh & Craven,

2006). However, raising people's self-esteem generally has little effect on aggressive behavior and sometimes *decreases* school and job performance (Baumeister et al., 2003). Psychologists also expect that all successful people should have high self-esteem, but many studies reported that young women, including many who seem bright and accomplished, report somewhat lower self-esteem than comparable men.

Much of the discrepancy between expectations and data depends on how we measure self-esteem (Blascovich & Tomaka, 1991). Here is one set of items from a self-esteem questionnaire:

- I feel that I have a number of good qualities.
- I can do things as well as most other people.
- At times I think I'm no good at all.
- I'm a failure.

An answer of "true" to the first two or "false" to the second two would count toward a high self-esteem score. Contrast those items to another self-esteem questionnaire, on which you are to answer from 1 (rarely or never) to 5 (usually or always):

- I feel that I am a beautiful person.
- I think that I make a good impression on others.
- I think that I have a good sense of humor.
- I feel that people really like me very much.

Do those items measure self-esteem or bragging? Here are some true–false items from a third test of self-esteem:

- There are lots of things about myself I'd change if I could.
- I'm often sorry for the things I do.
- I'm not doing as well in school as I'd like.
- I wish I could change my physical appearance.

Do "true" answers on these items indicate low self-esteem or do they indicate high goals? Someone who says "true" is presumably striving for self-improvement. Someone who says "false" thinks himself or herself to be just about perfect already. In short, some of the self-esteem questions measure **narcissism**—that is, *self-centeredness.* Narcissism correlates with being indifferent to the welfare of others and sometimes aggressive toward others. If we measure self-esteem without the narcissistic tendencies, it correlates with kinder and less aggressive behaviors toward others (Locke, 2009).

How concerned should we be that many young women report low self-esteem? Again, it depends on how someone measured self-esteem. According to a careful analysis of answers to individual items, women's self esteem is equal to men's or higher with regard to academics, emotion, social acceptance, moral behavior, and many other regards. They tend to have lower self-esteem

only with regard to athletic ability (where, in fact, more men concentrate their efforts) and physical appearance, presumably because women strive for a higher standard than men do (Gentile, Grabe, Dolan-Pascoe, Twenge, & Wells, 2009).

The message, in short, is this: Personality is difficult to measure, and we should look carefully at how it was measured before we draw any broad conclusions.

....

11. If someone's questionnaire results indicate "low self-esteem," what else might the results actually mean other than low self-esteem?

Answer

11. Depending on the questionnaire items, what appears to be low self-esteem might indicate high goals and therefore lack of satisfaction with one's current performance.

....

THE BIG FIVE MODEL OF PERSONALITY

Psychologists have devised questionnaires to measure belief in a just world, self-esteem, and hundreds of other traits. Are some of these more important than others? Remember the principle of parsimony from chapter 2: If we can adequately describe personality with a few traits, we should not measure more.

One way to begin is to examine our language. The English language probably has a word for every important personality trait. Although this assumption is not a logical necessity, it seems reasonable considering how much attention people pay to other people's personalities. Gordon Allport and H. S. Odbert (1936) plodded through an English dictionary and found almost 18,000 words that might be used to describe personality. They deleted from this list words that were merely evaluations, such as *nasty*, and terms referring to temporary states, such as *confused.* (At least, we hope that being confused is temporary.) In the remaining list, they looked for clusters of synonyms, such as *affectionate, warm,* and *loving,* and kept only one of these terms. When they found opposites, such as *honest* and *dishonest,* they also kept just one term. (*Honesty* and *dishonesty* are different extremes of one dimension, not separate traits.) After eliminating synonyms and antonyms, Raymond Cattell (1965) narrowed the original list to 35 traits.

Derivation of the Big Five Personality Traits

Although some of the 35 personality traits that Cattell identified are not exactly synonyms or antonyms of one another, many of them overlap. Psychologists looked for clusters of traits that correlate strongly with one another (but don't correlate with the other clusters). Using this approach, researchers found what they call the **big five personality traits:** *neuroticism, extraversion, agreeableness, conscientiousness, and openness to new experience* (McCrae & Costa, 1987). The case for these five traits is that (a) each correlates with many personality dimensions for which our language has a word and (b) none of these traits correlates highly with any of the other four, so they are not measuring the same thing. The big five dimensions are described in the following list (Costa, McCrae, & Dye, 1991):

Neuroticism is *a tendency to experience unpleasant emotions frequently.* Some personality researchers prefer the term *emotional stability,* which is the mirror image of neuroticism. That is, anyone who is high in one is low in the other. Neuroticism correlates positively with anxiety, hostility, depression, self-consciousness, and frequent conflicts with other people. People high in neuroticism tend to have troubles in their health, jobs, and marriages (Roberts, Kuncel, Shiner, Caspi, & Goldberg, 2007).

Extraversion is *a tendency to seek stimulation and to enjoy the company of other people.* Extraverted people are more likely than average to move to big cities where they will have contact with many other people (Jokela, Elovainio, Kivimäki, & Keltikangas-Järvinen, 2008). The opposite of extraversion is introversion. Extraversion is associated with warmth, gregariousness, assertiveness, impulsiveness, and a need for excitement. The unpleasant side of extraversion is an increased chance of alcohol abuse and other risky behaviors (Martsh & Miller, 1997). The pleasant side is that extraverts tend to be happy (Francis, Brown, Lester, & Philipchalk, 1998). The relationship goes in both directions: Feeling happy makes people more outgoing, and outgoing behavior makes people feel happy (Lucas, Le, & Dyrenforth, 2008). In one study, people who pretended to be extraverted reported feeling happier afterward (Fleeson, Malanos, & Achille, 2002).

Active, outgoing behavior ⟷ Happy feelings

Agreeableness is *a tendency to be compassionate toward others.* It implies a concern for the welfare of other people and is closely related to Adler's concept of social interest. People high in agreeableness trust other people and expect other people to trust them. They are more likely than average to have stable marriages and stable employment (Roberts et al., 2007).

Conscientiousness is *a tendency to show self-discipline, to be dutiful, and to strive for achievement and competence.* People high in conscientiousness work hard and complete their tasks on time (Judge & Ilies, 2002). They tend to exercise and eat a healthy diet. They avoid tobacco, excessive alcohol, and risky sex (Bogg & Roberts, 2004). They tend to have successful jobs, successful marriages, and greater than average life expectancy (Roberts et al., 2007).

Openness to experience is *a tendency to enjoy new intellectual experiences and new ideas.* People high in this trait enjoy modern art,

unusual music, and thought-provoking films and books. They enjoy meeting different kinds of people and exploring new ideas (McCrae, 1996). In one study, young adults listed their favorite songs. Then another person listened to those songs and tried to guess the personality of the person who chose them. From music alone, they guessed people's openness to experience with a correlation above .6 (Rentfrow & Gosling, 2006).

Table 14.2 summarizes the big five model.

Table 14.2 The Big Five Model of Personality

Trait	Description	Typical True–False Question to Measure It
Neuroticism	Prone to unpleasant emotions	I have many worries.
Extraversion	Seeking excitement and social contact	I make friends easily.
Agreeableness	Compassionate and trusting	I believe others have good intentions.
Conscientiousness	Self-disciplined and dutiful	I complete most tasks on time or early.
Openness	Stimulated by new ideas	I believe art is important for its own sake.

Courtesy of Morimura Yasumasa

The Japanese artist Morimura Yasumasa re-creates famous paintings, substituting his own face for the original. People high in "openness to experience" delight in new, unusual artforms such as this.

12. Some psychologists suggest that we should divide extraversion into two traits—which they call *ambition* and *sociability*—changing the big five into the big six. How should psychologists determine whether to do so?

13. If you wanted to predict someone's happiness, which personality trait would you measure? What if you wanted to predict how long someone would live?

Answers

12. They should determine whether measures of ambition correlate strongly with measures of sociability. If so, then ambition and sociability can be considered two aspects of a single trait, extraversion. If not, then they are indeed separate personality traits.

13. Extraversion correlates significantly with happiness. To predict longevity, you could measure someone's conscientiousness. Conscientious people tend to follow recommendations about good diet, exercise, and avoiding risky behaviors.

Cross-cultural studies offer partial support to the big five approach. Several studies have found results consistent with the big five model for people in other cultures using other languages (McCrae & Costa, 1997; Yamagata et al., 2006). However, some studies do find cross-cultural differences (Panayiotou, Kokkinos, & Spanoudis, 2004). A study in China identified traits corresponding to extraversion, neuroticism, conscientiousness, and loyalty to Chinese traditions (Cheung et al., 1996).

Criticisms

Most research on the five-factor model has concentrated on descriptions of behavior, with little observation of actual behavior. The research methods could overlook certain personality traits because of quirks of the English language. For example, we identify extraversion–introversion as a big factor because it relates to so many words in the English language—sociability, warmth, friendliness, gregariousness, happiness, and so forth. Sense of humor does not emerge as a major personality trait because the language has few synonyms for it. Critics of the big five approach point to personality dimensions that the model seems to overlook (Paunonen & Jackson, 2000): sense of humor, religiousness, manipulativeness, honesty, sexiness, thriftiness, conservativeness, masculinity–femininity, and snobbishness.

On the other end, some critics believe that five is more traits than we need. Openness to ex-

perience has a modest positive correlation with extraversion, and conscientiousness correlates negatively with neuroticism, so perhaps we could get by with just neuroticism, extraversion, and agreeableness (Eysenck, 1992).

Overall, how should we evaluate the five-factor description? The answer depends on our purposes. The five-factor description accounts for enough of the variability in human behavior to be useful, and it is now the basis for most research in personality. However, for some purposes, three factors may be enough, and for other purposes, more may be necessary. It depends on how much precision we want in describing and predicting people's behavior.

THE ORIGINS OF PERSONALITY

A description of personality differences is not an explanation. What makes some people more extraverted, neurotic, agreeable, conscientious, or open to experience than other people are?

Heredity and Environment

If you want evidence that heredity can influence personality, you need look no further than the nearest pet dog. For centuries, people have selectively bred dogs for their personalities, ranging from the friendliest lap dogs to those capable of furious attacks.

To measure the influences of heredity and environment on human personality, researchers rely mostly on studies of twins and adopted children (Bouchard & McGue, 2003). As Figure 14.4 shows, five studies conducted in separate locations indicated greater similarities in extraversion between monozygotic pairs

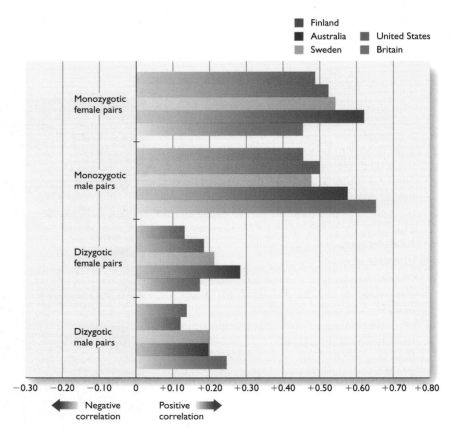

FIGURE 14.4 The length of each bar indicates the strength of a correlation between pairs of twins in their degree of extraversion. Correlations (similarities) were greater between monozygotic twins (who share all their genes) than between dizygotic twins (who share half their genes). (Based on data summarized by Loehlin, 1992)

than dizygotic pairs (Loehlin, 1992). Studies in Australia and the United States found a similar pattern for neuroticism, with monozygotic (identical) twins resembling each other much more than dizygotic (fraternal) twins, who resembled each other no more than brothers or sisters born at different times (Lake, Eaves, Maes, Heath, & Martin, 2000).

Modern methods make it possible to search for specific genes linked to particular personality traits. Several studies have identified genes apparently linked to neuroticism or to the specific aspect of neuroticism known as *harm avoidance* or anxiety-proneness (Fullerton et al., 2003). However, each of the genes identified so far makes only a small contribution.

Also, researchers compare the personalities of parents, their biological children, and their adopted children. As Figure 14.5 shows, parents' extraversion levels correlate moderately with those of their biological children but hardly at all with their adopted children. Similarly, biologically related brothers or sisters growing up together resemble each other moderately in personality, and unrelated children adopted into the same family do not (Loehlin, 1992). The results shown in Figures 14.4 and 14.5 pertain to extraversion; other studies provide a largely similar pattern for other personality traits (Heath, Neale, Kessler, Eaves, & Kendler, 1992; Loehlin, 1992; Viken, Rose, Kaprio, & Koskenvuo, 1994).

The low correlations between adopted children and adoptive parents imply that children learn rather little of their personalities by imitating their parents. (Recall from chapter 5 that Judith Harris made this same point.) Many researchers believe that much of the variation among people's personalities relates to the **unshared environment**, *the aspects of environment that differ from one individual to another, even within a family.* Unshared environment includes the effects of a particular playmate, a particular teacher, an injury or illness, or any other isolated experience. Because of its idiosyncratic nature, unshared environment is difficult to investigate.

....

14. What evidence would indicate an important role of the *shared environment*—the influences that are the same for all children within a family?

Answer

14. If the personalities of adopted children within a family correlated highly with one another, we would conclude that the similarity reflected the shared environment. The weakness of such correlations is the main evidence for the importance of the unshared environment.

....

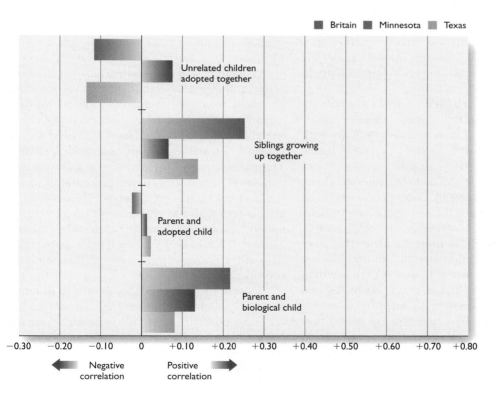

Britain **Minnesota** **Texas**

Unrelated children adopted together

Siblings growing up together

Parent and adopted child

Parent and biological child

−0.30 −0.20 −0.10 0 +0.10 +0.20 +0.30 +0.40 +0.50 +0.60 +0.70 +0.80

◄ Negative correlation   Positive correlation ►

FIGURE 14.5 The length and direction of each bar indicate the correlations between pairs of people in their degree of extraversion. Biological relatives (siblings or parent and child) showed low positive correlations. People related by adoption had close to zero correlations. (Based on data summarized by Loehlin, 1992)

Influences of Age, Culture, and Cohort

Do you think your personality now resembles what it was in childhood? In some aspects, it probably does. In one study, investigators followed people's behavior from age 3 to 26. Children who were fearful and easily upset at age 3 were more nervous and inhibited than others at age 26. Those who were impulsive and restless at age 3 tended to have trouble with others from then on and felt alienated from society. Those who were confident, friendly, and eager to explore their environment at 3 tended to be confident adults, eager to take charge of events (Caspi et al., 2003).

Will your personality change much in the future? According to the research, the older people get, the more slowly they change. In childhood, answers on a personality questionnaire correlate a modest .34 with a second test given 6 or 7 years later. By college age, the correlation is .54. It increases to .64 at age 30 and .74 at age 60 (Roberts & DelVecchio, 2000). Why personality becomes more fixed as we grow older is not known, but you can probably imagine a few hypotheses.

Although the differences that occur over age are not large, the trends are fairly consistent. One trend, found in cultures throughout the world, is that middle-aged people are more likely than teenagers to be highly conscientious (Donnellan & Lucas, 2008; McCrae et al., 2000). A simple hypothesis is that adults are forced, whether they like it or not, to hold a job, pay the bills, repair the house, care for children, and take responsibility in other ways.

Most people reach their peak of social vitality and sensation seeking during adolescence or early adulthood and then decline gradually with further age (Roberts, Walton, & Viechtbauer, 2006). Again, this trend occurs across cultures (Donnellan & Lucas, 2008; Labouvie-Vief, Diehl, Tarnowski, & Shen, 2000). Older people also tend to be less neurotic—that is, more emotionally stable—and more agreeable (Cramer, 2003; McCrae et al., 2000). In most countries that have been examined, young adults on the average score higher on openness to new experience than older people (Donnellan & Lucas, 2008; Roberts et al., 2006). This trend is no surprise, as we see that young people enjoy new types of music, new kinds of food, new styles of clothing, and so forth (Sapolsky, 1998), whereas older people stay with old habits. Figure 14.6 shows mean changes in six aspects of personality over age (Roberts et al., 2006). Note that this research distinguished between two aspects of extraversion—social vitality and social dominance.

Does personality vary among cultures or countries? That is, might the typical or average personality in one country differ from that in another? An extensive study of 49 cultures asked people to rate the personality of the average member of their culture. These reports defined the stereotype of the average American, German, Indonesian, and so forth, and many of the results were what you might expect. For example, Australian and Puerto Rican people describe typical members of their society as extraverted, and Japanese people describe the typical Japanese person as introverted. People in each culture also answered questionnaires about their own personality. The average self-description correlated almost zero with ratings of the typical member of society (Terrcciano et al., 2005). That is, most Australian and Puerto Rican people described themselves as only average in extraversion despite regarding the average person of their society as highly extraverted. From these data, the researchers concluded that national stereotypes are almost totally inaccurate.

However, this research method has a problem. If you rate the extraversion or conscientiousness of the typical member of your society, you do so relative to people from other societies. But if you answer how extraverted or conscientious *you* are, you do so relative to the average member of your own society. For example, if you are a fairly extraverted person relative to all the people in the world, but you live in Puerto Rico, you might rate yourself as only average relative to other Puerto Ricans.

A better way of comparing personalities across cultures is to examine actual behavior. Researchers measured conscientiousness from observations of such items as the accuracy of clocks in public places and postal workers' speed and accuracy when selling stamps and making change. These objective measures of conscientiousness correlated significantly with perceptions of national character (i.e., stereotypes). They correlated almost zero with the average self-rating of conscientiousness by people within each society (Heine, Buchtel, & Norenzayan, 2008). That is, personality does differ among cultures after all if we measure it properly.

Within the United States, people in different areas vary slightly, on the average, in personality. "Creative productivity" tends to be highest in the Northeast, Midwest, and West Coast. People in the Southeast are more likely to defend their reputation violently. People in cities tend to be more extraverted than those in rural areas. These are just a few of the differences. One reason for the differences is that the reputation of a place tends to attract like-minded people. If you read

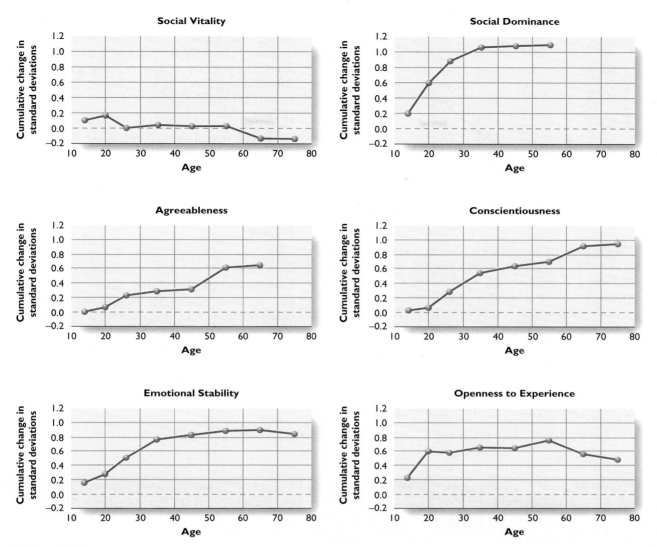

FIGURE 14.6 Six aspects of personality show different patterns of change over age based on the means of longitudinal research studies. The numbers along the vertical axis represent changes from the earliest age tested, measured in terms of standard deviations. (From Roberts, Walton, & Viechtbauer, 2006)

about people in Portland, Oregon, and think, "those sound like my kind of people," you might want to move there, too. Another factor is that extraverts tend to seek exciting places with many opportunities to socialize, such as a large city, whereas people high in neuroticism tend to seek less threatening places (Rentfrow, Gosling, & Potter, 2008).

Finally, does personality change from one generation to the next? Remember the Flynn effect from chapter 9: Over the years, people's performance on IQ tests has gradually increased so that each generation does better on the tests than the previous generation. Researchers have also found generational differences in personality. For example, over the years, beginning in the 1950s, measurements of anxiety have steadily increased (Twenge, 2000). On the Child Manifest

Anxiety Scale, the mean score in the 1950s was 15.1, and the mean for children in mental hospitals was 20.1. By the 1980s, the mean for *all* children was 23.3! Do we really have that much more anxiety than in past generations? Perhaps people's answers do not mean what they used to. The more disturbing possibility is that we really do live in an age of anxiety. Compared to past generations, more children today have to live through their parents' divorce, and fewer live in a neighborhood with many friends and relatives. Might those social changes have raised the average anxiety level to what used to characterize the top 10%? The answer is uncertain, but today's researchers worry about why people worry so much.

Generations also differ in other aspects of personality. As shown in Figure 14.7, from the

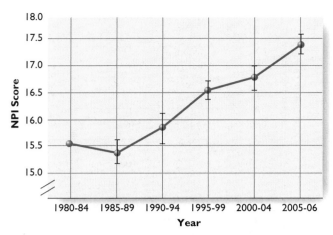

FIGURE 14.7 The mean level of narcissism has increased steadily since the 1980s. (Figure 2, page 883, from Twenge, J. M., Konrath, S., Foster, J. D., Campbell, W. K., & Bushman, B. J. (2008). Egos inflating over time: A cross-temporal meta-analysis of the narcissistic personality inventory. *Journal of Personality, 76,* 875–901)

1980s to 2006, American college students showed a steady increase in measures of narcissism (Twenge, Konrath, Foster, Campbell, & Bushman, 2008). Narcissism relates to self-confidence, which is generally a good thing, but it also relates to risk taking, selfishness, and troubled romantic relationships. The general point here is that the era in which you live exerts a major influence on personality development.

15. What evidence suggests that national stereotypes are *more* accurate indicators of personality trends than are the mean of self-reports by people within each nation?

Answer

15. Ratings of the national character, especially conscientiousness, correlate with observed behaviors, such as the speed of postal clerks. The average of self-reports does not correlate significantly with observed behaviors. When people rate themselves, they compare themselves to others within the country, and therefore, their ratings are not necessarily a good gauge of what the country as a whole does.

14.2 module

In Closing

The Challenges of Classifying Personality

Personality descriptions refer to averages over time. We don't expect anyone to be equally extraverted at all times, equally neurotic, or anything else. What you do at any moment depends largely on the situation. In a sufficiently novel situation, you may be surprised by the actions of people you know well and even by your own behavior. The variation across situations makes the measurement of general tendencies difficult. Research progress always depends on good measurement, and you can see why progress in understanding personality is slow.

SUMMARY

- *Nomothetic and idiographic research.* Nomothetic studies examine large numbers of people briefly, whereas idiographic studies examine one or a few individuals intensively. (page 514)
- *Traits and states.* Traits are personality characteristics that persist over time; states are temporary tendencies in response to particular situations. (page 514)

- *Measurement problems.* Personality researchers rely mostly on self-reports, which are not entirely accurate. (page 515)
- *Five major traits.* Much of personality can be explained by these five traits: neuroticism, extraversion, agreeableness, conscientiousness, and openness to new experience. (page 516)

- *Determinants of personality.* Studies of twins and adopted children indicate that heredity contributes to the observed differences in personality. Family environment evidently contributes rather little. Much of personality relates to unshared environment, the special experiences that vary from one person to another even within a family. (page 518)
- *Changes over age.* Compared to younger people, older people tend to be higher in conscientiousness and agreeableness. They are somewhat lower in extraversion and neuroticism. Openness to experience decreases with age in most countries. (page 520)
- *Changes over generations.* Measurements of anxiety have gradually increased over the decades so that normal people now report anxiety levels that used to characterize people in mental hospitals. (page 521)

KEY TERMS

agreeableness (page 517)

belief in a just world (page 514)

big five personality traits (page 516)

conscientiousness (page 517)

extraversion (page 517)

idiographic approach (page 514)

narcissism (page 516)

neuroticism (page 516)

nomothetic approach (page 514)

openness to experience (page 517)

self-esteem (page 515)

state (page 514)

trait (page 514)

trait approach to personality (page 514)

unshared environment (page 519)

Personality Assessment

• What inferences can we draw from the results of a personality test?

A new P. T. Barnum Psychology Clinic has just opened at your local shopping mall and is offering a grand opening special on personality tests. You would like to know more about yourself, so you sign up. Here is Barnum's true–false test:

Questionnaire for Universal Assessment of Zealous Youth (QUAZY)

1. I have never met a cannibal I didn't like.	T	F
2. Robbery is the only felony I have ever committed.	T	F
3. I eat "funny mushrooms" less frequently than I used to.	T	F
4. I don't care what people say about my nose-picking habit.	T	F
5. Sex with vegetables no longer disgusts me.	T	F
6. This time I am quitting glue-sniffing for good.	T	F
7. I generally lie on questions like this one.	T	F
8. I spent much of my childhood sucking on computer cables.	T	F
9. I find it impossible to sleep if I think my bed might be clean.	T	F
10. Naked bus drivers make me nervous.	T	F
11. I spend my spare time playing strip solitaire.	T	F

You turn in your answers. A few minutes later, a computer prints out your personality profile:

> You have a need for other people to like and admire you, and yet you tend to be critical of yourself. While you have some personality weaknesses, you are generally able to compensate for them. You have considerable unused capacity that you have not turned to your advantage. Disciplined and self-controlled on the outside, you tend to be worrisome and insecure on the inside. At times, you have serious doubts as to whether you have made the right decision or done the right thing. You prefer a certain amount of change and variety and become dissatisfied when hemmed in by restrictions and limitations. You also pride yourself as an independent thinker and do not accept others' statements without satisfactory proof. But you have found it unwise to be too frank in revealing yourself to others. At times you are extraverted, affable, and sociable, while at other times you are introverted, wary, and reserved. Some of your aspirations tend to be rather unrealistic. (Forer, 1949, p. 120)

Do you agree with this assessment? Did it capture your personality? Several experiments have been conducted along these lines with psychology classes (Forer, 1949; Marks & Kammann, 1980; Ulrich, Stachnik, & Stainton, 1963). Students filled out a questionnaire that looked reasonable, not like the ridiculous questions above (which were included just to amuse you). Several days later, each student received a sealed envelope with his or her name on it. Inside was a personality profile supposedly based on the student's answers to the questionnaire. The students were asked, "How accurately does this profile describe you?" About 90% rated it as good or excellent, and some expressed amazement at its accuracy. They didn't know that everyone had received exactly the same personality profile—the same one you just read.

The students accepted this personality profile partly because it vaguely describes almost everyone and partly because people accept almost *any*

People tend to accept almost any personality assessment, especially if it is stated in vague terms that people can interpret to fit themselves.

statement that a psychologist makes about them (Marks & Kammann, 1980). This *tendency to accept vague descriptions of our personality is known as the* Barnum effect, named after P. T. Barnum, the circus owner who specialized in fooling people out of their money.

The conclusion: Psychological testing must be done carefully. If we want to know whether a test measures someone's personality, we cannot simply ask that person's opinion. Psychologists need to design a test carefully and then determine its reliability and validity.

STANDARDIZED PERSONALITY TESTS

A standardized test is *one that is administered according to rules that specify how to interpret the results.* An important step for standardizing a test is to determine the distribution of scores. We need to know the mean score and the range of scores for a representative sample of the population and how they differ for special populations, such as people with severe depression. Given such information, we can determine whether a particular score on a personality test is within the normal range or whether it is more typical of people with some disorder.

Most of the tests published in popular magazines have not been standardized. A magazine may herald an article: "Test Yourself: How Good Is Your Marriage?" or "Test Yourself: How Well Do You Control the Stress in Your Life?" After you compare your answers to the scoring key, the article may tell you that "if your score is greater than 80, you are doing very well . . . if it is below 20, you need to work on improving yourself!"—or some such nonsense. Unless the magazine states otherwise, you can assume that the author pulled the scoring norms out of thin air with no supporting research.

Over the years, psychologists have developed an enormous variety of tests to measure normal and abnormal personality. We shall examine a few prominent examples.

AN OBJECTIVE PERSONALITY TEST: THE MINNESOTA MULTIPHASIC PERSONALITY INVENTORY

The most widely used personality test, the Minnesota Multiphasic Personality Inventory (mercifully abbreviated MMPI), consists of *true–false questions intended to measure certain personality dimensions and clinical conditions.* The original MMPI, developed in the 1940s and still in use, has 550 items. *The second edition,* MMPI–2, published in 1990, has 567. Example items are "my mother never loved me" and "I think I would like the work of a pharmacist." (The items stated in this text are rewordings of actual items.)

The MMPI was devised *empirically*—that is, based on evidence rather than theory (Hathaway & McKinley, 1940). The authors wrote hundreds of questions that they thought might relate to personality. They put these questions to people with various psychological disorders and to a group of hospital visitors, who were assumed to be psychologically normal. The researchers selected the items that most people in any clinical group answered differently from most normal people. They assumed, for example, that if your answers resemble those of people with depression, you probably are depressed also. The MMPI includes scales for depression, paranoia, schizophrenia, and others.

Some of the items on the MMPI make sense theoretically, but others do not. For example, some items on the Depression scale ask about feelings of helplessness or worthlessness, which are an important part of depression. But two other items are "I attend religious services frequently" and "occasionally I tease animals." If you answer *false* to either of those items, you get a point on the Depression scale! These items were included simply because more depressed people than others answered *false.* The reason is not obvious, except that depression makes people inactive, unlikely to do anything they don't have to do.

Revision of the Test

The MMPI was standardized in the 1940s. As time passed, the meaning of certain items or their answers changed. For example, how would you respond to the following item?

I believe I am important.　　　T　　F

In the 1940s, fewer than 10% of all people marked *true.* At the time, the word *important* meant about the same thing as *famous,* and people who called themselves important were thought to have an inflated view of themselves. Today, we stress that every person is important.

What about this item?

I like to play drop the handkerchief.　　T　　F

Drop the handkerchief, a game similar to tag, fell out of popularity in the 1950s. Most people today have never heard of the game, much less played it.

To bring the MMPI up to date, psychologists eliminated obsolete items and added new ones to deal with drug abuse, suicidal thoughts, and other issues (Butcher, Graham, Williams, & Ben-Porath, 1990). Then they tried out the new MMPI–2 on a large representative sample of the U.S. population. That is, they restandardized the test. The MMPI–2 has 10 clinical scales, as shown in Table 14.3. The items of any type are scattered throughout the test so that people won't see that "oh, this seems to be

TABLE 14.3 The 10 MMPI–2 Clinical Scales

Scale	Typical Item
Hypochondria (Hs)	I have chest pains several times a week. (T)
Depression (D)	I am glad that I am alive. (F)
Hysteria (Hy)	My heart frequently pounds so hard I can hear it. (T)
Psychopathic Deviation (Pd)	I get a fair deal from most people. (F)
Masculinity–Femininity (Mf)	I like to arrange flowers. (T = female)
Paranoia (Pa)	There are evil people trying to influence my mind. (T)
Psychasthenia (Obsessive–Compulsive) (Pt)	I save nearly everything I buy, even after I have no use for it. (T)
Schizophrenia (Sc)	I see, hear, and smell things that no one else knows about. (T)
Hypomania (Ma)	When things are dull I try to get some excitement started. (T)
Social Introversion (Si)	I have the time of my life at parties. (F)

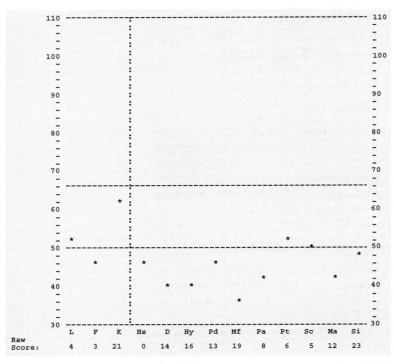

FIGURE 14.8 This is the MMPI–2 profile of a middle-aged man with no psychological problems. Someone with a disorder would have a score above 65 on one or more scales. (Source: Minnesota Multiphasic Personality Inventory–2, © by the Regents of the University of Minnesota. Data courtesy of R. J. Huber.)

a set of items about depression." Most people get at least a few points on each scale. A score above a certain level indicates probable difficulty. Figure 14.8 shows how MMPI–2 scores are plotted.

Culture and the MMPI

Can a single test measure personality for all kinds of people? In particular, is the MMPI a fair measure of personality for people of different ethnic and cultural backgrounds?

In general, the means and ranges on each scale are about the same for many ethnic groups, even after translation into different languages (Negy, Leal-Puente, Trainor, & Carlson, 1997). However, differences do occur. For example, Mexicans are more likely than U.S. people to say *true* to "Life is a constant strain for me." Presumably, the reason is that life really is more difficult for many people in Mexico. On several scales of the MMPI–2, the Mexican means differ from the U.S. means (Lucio, Ampudia, Durán, León, & Butcher, 2001). Consequently, the scoring standards for a personality test should differ from one country to another.

Detecting Deception

If you take the MMPI, could you lie to make yourself look mentally healthier than you really are? Yes. Could someone catch your lies? Probably.

The designers of the MMPI and MMPI–2 included items designed to identify lying (Woychyshyn, McElheran, & Romney, 1992). For example, consider the items "I like every person I have ever met" and "occasionally I get angry at someone." If you answer *true* to the first question and *false* to the second, you are either a saint or a liar. The test authors, convinced that liars outnumber saints, count such answers on a "lie" scale. If you get too many points on that scale, a psychologist distrusts your answers to the other items. Strangely enough, some people lie to try to look bad. For example, a criminal defendant might want to be classified as mentally ill. The MMPI includes items to detect that kind of faking also (Bagby, Nicholson, Bacchiochi, Ryder, & Bury, 2002).

Several other questionnaires also try to detect deception. Suppose an employer's questionnaire asks you how much experience you have had at various skills, including "determining myopic weights for periodic tables." You're not sure what that means, but you want the job. Do you claim to have extensive experience? If so, your claimed expertise will count *against* you because "determining myopic weights for periodic tables" is nonsense. The employer asked about it just to see whether you were exaggerating your qualifications on other items.

....

16. Suppose a person thinks "Black is my favorite color" would be a good true–false item for the Depression scale of the MMPI. How would a researcher decide whether to include it?

17. Why does the MMPI include some items that ask about common flaws, such as, "Sometimes I think more about my own welfare than that of others"?

Answers

17. Such items are intended to detect lying. If you answered *false*, you would get a point on a lying scale.

16. Researchers would determine whether people with depression are more likely than other people to answer *true*. If so, the item could be included.

....

THE NEO PI-R

A more recent personality test is based on the five-factor personality model described in the second module. An early version of this test measured neuroticism, extraversion, and openness to experience, abbreviated NEO. A revised test added scales for conscientiousness and agreeableness, but kept the name NEO, which is now considered just the name of the test and not an abbreviation. (It's like the company AT&T, which no longer stands for American Telephone and Telegraph. After all, how many people use telegraphs anymore?) The **NEO PI-R (NEO personality inventory-revised)** *includes 240 items to measure neuroticism, extraversion, openness, agreeableness, and conscientiousness*. A typical conscientiousness item resembles this:

	Very inaccurate	Moderately inaccurate	Neither	Moderately accurate	Very accurate
I keep my promises.					

Scores on this test have reliability of about .9. They correlate with observable behaviors, too. For example, students who score high on conscientiousness tend to spend much time studying (Chamorro-Premuzic, & Furnham, 2008). People who score high on extraversion make efforts to meet new people, and people high in openness are more likely than others to attend an art gallery (Church et al., 2008). The test has been translated into several other languages and seems to work reasonably well in other cultures (Wu, Lindsted, Tsai, & Lee, 2007). It is intended mainly to measure normal personality, as contrasted to the MMPI, which is often used to identify possible clinical problems.

....

18. For what purposes might the NEO PI-R be more suitable, and for what purposes might the MMPI be more suitable?

Answer

18. The NEO PI-R is designed to measure normal personality. The MMPI is set up to detect possible abnormalities.

....

THE MYERS-BRIGGS TYPE INDICATOR

The **Myers-Briggs Type Indicator (MBTI)** is *a test of normal personality, loosely based on Carl Jung's theories.* Jung emphasized the distinction between extraversion, which he defined as attending to the outside world, and introversion, concentrating on one's inner world. He thought each person was throughout life either extraverted or introverted. Unlike the MMPI, which gives people scores ranging continuously from zero upward on each scale, the MBTI classifies people as types. In addition to being either extraverted or introverted, each person is classed as sensing or intuitive, thinking or feeling, and judging or perceiving. For example, you might be classified as introverted-intuitive-thinking-judging. The test identifies a total of 16 personality types (McCaulley, 2000). The MBTI is more popular with businesses, which use it to describe the personalities of their employees, than with most psychologists, who are skeptical of dividing people into distinct categories. Some counselors also use the MBTI to help students choose a possible career, although other tests are more suitable for that purpose (Pulver & Kelly, 2008). You can take a simplified version of the MBTI on the Human Metrics' website and see how it classifies you. But remember the Barnum

effect: The description may be reasonably accurate, but most people are inclined to accept almost any personality report they receive. Find a link to the Human Metrics' website at **www.cengage.com/psychology/kalat.**

I've heard it said that there are two kinds of people—the kind who believe there are two kinds of people and the kind who don't believe it. It is tempting to divide people into personality types, but is it true that people fall into discrete groups? It would make sense to divide people into extraverted and introverted types if most people's scores were far to one end of the scale or the other. In fact, most people get scores close to the middle. If you change your answer to one or two questions, you might switch from one personality type to the other according to this test (Pittenger, 2005). Although the MBTI is a reasonable test in many regards, its insistence on putting people into distinct categories seems hard to defend.

PROJECTIVE TECHNIQUES

Many people are reluctant to confide embarrassing information, either on a personality test or in an interview. To avoid embarrassment, sometimes people seeking help say, "Let me tell you about my friend's problem and ask what my friend should do." They then describe their own problem. They are "projecting" their problem onto someone else in Freud's sense of the word—that is, attributing it to someone else.

Rather than discouraging projection, psychologists often make use of it with **projective techniques,** which are *designed to encourage people to project their personality characteristics onto ambiguous stimuli.* Let's consider two well-known projective techniques: the Rorschach Inkblots and the Thematic Apperception Test.

....

19. Which of the following is a projective technique?

a. A psychologist gives a child a set of puppets with instructions to act out a story about a family.
b. A psychologist hands you a stack of cards, each containing one word, and asks you to sort the cards into a stack that applies to you and a stack that does not.

Answer

19. The puppet activity could be a projective technique if the child projects his or her own concerns onto the puppets. Sorting cards is an objective measure, not a projective test.

....

The Rorschach Inkblots

The Rorschach Inkblots, *a projective technique based on people's interpretations of 10 ambiguous inkblots,* is the most famous and most widely used projective personality technique. It was created by Hermann Rorschach (ROAR-shock), a Swiss psychiatrist, who showed people inkblots and asked them to say whatever came to mind (Pichot, 1984). Other psychiatrists and psychologists gradually developed the Rorschach into the projective technique we know today.

Administering the Rorschach

The Rorschach Inkblot Technique consists of ten cards similar to the one in Figure 14.9, five of them in color. A psychologist hands you a card and asks, "What might this be?" The instructions are intentionally vague on the assumption that you reveal more about your personality in an ill-defined situation.

Sometimes, people's answers are revealing either immediately or in response to a psychologist's probes. Here is an example (Aronow, Reznikoff, & Moreland, 1995):

Client: Some kind of insect; it's not pretty enough to be a butterfly.

Psychologist: Any association to that?

Client: It's an ugly black butterfly, no colors.

Psychologist: What does that make you think of in your own life?

Client: You probably want me to say "myself." Well, that's probably how I thought of myself when I was younger—I never thought of myself as attractive—my sister was the attractive one. I was the ugly duckling—I did get more attractive as I got older.

Evaluation of the Rorschach

When you describe what you see in a picture, your answer undoubtedly relates to your experiences, concerns, and personality. But how accurately can psychologists perceive that relationship? And when they perceive a relationship, did they really get the information from the Rorschach or from something they already knew about you?

One man described a particular inkblot as "like a bat that has been squashed on the pavement under the heel of a giant's boot" (Dawes, 1994, p. 149). Psychologist Robyn Dawes initially was impressed with how the Rorschach had revealed this client's sense of being overwhelmed and crushed by powers beyond his control. But then he realized that he had already known the man was depressed. If a client with a history of

violence had made the same response, he would have focused on the aggressive nature of the giant's foot stomp. For other clients, he would have made still other interpretations. Psychologists often believe the Rorschach gave them an insight, when in fact it just confirmed an opinion they already had (Wood, Nezworski, Lilienfeld, & Garb, 2003).

James Exner (1986) developed methods to standardize the interpretations of Rorschach responses, such as counting the number of times a client mentions aggressive themes. Experienced clinicians using this system achieve a reasonably high level of agreement in their interpretations (Viglione & Taylor, 2003), and most individuals' scores are consistent over time (Grønnerød, 2003). However, serious problems remain (Garb, Wood, Lilienfeld, & Nezworski, 2005; Lilienfeld, Wood, & Garb, 2000; Wood et al., 2003):

- The test identifies *most* people as psychologically disturbed.
- An evaluation depends on your *total number* of pathological answers, not what percentage of your answers are abnormal. Highly intelligent or talkative people say more than other people do and thus are more likely to say something that seems "disturbed."
- Several scales of the test have low or unknown validity.
- Most important, the Rorschach rarely gives information that could not be obtained more easily in other ways. In most cases, psychologists who are given biographical and MMPI information plus Rorschach results make no better personality judgments than psychologists who are given the biographical and MMPI information alone.

Critics of the Rorschach stop short of calling it completely invalid. Their point is that it is not valid enough to make important decisions about an individual, such as which parent should get custody of a child or which prisoners should get parole (Wood et al., 2003). Other psychologists continue to defend the Rorschach, insisting that when it is used properly, its reliability and validity are comparable to those of other psychological tests (Society for Personality Assessment, 2005). The problem is that many other tests also have validity too low for making important decisions about people. Personality measurement is, frankly, difficult. The controversy will surely continue.

20. Why are highly talkative people more likely than others to have their Rorschach answers considered disturbed?

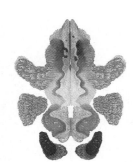

FIGURE 14.9 In the Rorschach Inkblot Technique, people examine an abstract pattern and say what it looks like.

Answer

The Thematic Apperception Test

The Thematic Apperception Test (TAT) consists of pictures like the one shown in Figure 14.10. *The person is asked to make up a story for each picture, describing what events led up to this scene, what is happening now, and what will happen in the future.* Christiana Morgan and Henry Murray devised this test to measure people's needs. It was revised and published by Murray (1943) and later revised by others. It includes 31 pictures, including some showing women, some showing men, some with both or neither, and one that is totally blank. A psychologist selects a few cards to use with a given client (Lilienfeld et al., 2000).

The assumption is that when you tell a story about a person in the drawing, you probably identify with the person, and so the story is really about yourself. You might describe events and concerns in your own life, including some that you might be reluctant to discuss openly. For example, one young man told the following story about a picture of a man clinging to a rope:

> This man is escaping. Several months ago he was beat up and shanghaied and taken aboard ship. Since then, he has been mistreated and unhappy and has been looking for a way to escape. Now the ship is anchored near a tropical island and he is climbing down a rope to the water. He will get away successfully and swim to shore. When he gets there, he will be met by a group of beautiful native women with whom he will live the rest of his life in luxury and never tell anyone what happened. Sometimes he will feel that he should go back to his old life; but he will never do it. (Kimble & Garmezy, 1968, pp. 582–583)

This young man had entered divinity school to please his parents but was unhappy there. He was wrestling with a secret desire to escape to a new life with greater worldly pleasures. In his story, he described someone doing what he wanted to do.

Psychologists use the TAT in various inconsistent ways. Many therapists interpret the results according to their clinical judgment, without any clear rules. If you took the TAT with two psychologists, they might reach different conclusions about you (Cramer, 1996). As with the Rorschach, one criticism is that the test seldom provides information that goes beyond what we could get in other ways (Lilienfeld et al., 2000).

The TAT is also used to measure people's need for achievement by counting all the times they mention achievement. The test is similarly used to measure power and affiliation needs. These results are useful for research purposes, although not necessarily for making decisions about an individual (Lilienfeld et al., 2000).

FIGURE 14.10 In the Thematic Apperception Test, people tell a story about what is going on in a picture, including what led up to this event, what is happening now, and what will happen in the future. (From the *Thematic Apperception Test* by Henry A. Murray, 1943. © 1971 by the President and Fellows of Harvard College.)

Handwriting as a Projective Technique

Based on the theory that your personality affects everything you do, some psychologists (and others) have tried analyzing people's handwriting. For example, perhaps people who dot their i's with a dash—*i̇*—are especially energetic, or perhaps people who draw large loops above the line—as in *allow*—are highly idealistic. Carefully collected data, however, show only random relationships between handwriting and personality (Tett & Palmer, 1997).

IMPLICIT PERSONALITY TESTS

The research provides only weak support for the projective tests, but the motivation behind them remains: Psychologists would like to measure personality aspects that people cannot or will not discuss openly. So the search for another kind of personality test continues.

Recall from chapter 7 the distinction between explicit and implicit memory. If you listen to a list of words and then try to repeat them, what you recall is explicit memory. If you unknowingly use words from the list in your later conversation, your use of those words constitutes implicit memory. Implicit memory occurs even when you are not aware of remembering something.

Many researchers are trying to develop an implicit personality test—one that measures some aspect of your personality without your awareness. One example is the Implicit Association Test. In the last chapter, we considered how this test could be used to measure prejudices that people do not want to admit. It can also be used to detect other emotional reactions. For example, someone who is nervous around other people might pair social words (*party, friend, companion*) more readily with unpleasant words than with pleasant words. Someone with an intense fear of spiders might pair spiders with unpleasant words more strongly than most others do (Ellwart, Rinck, & Becker, 2006).

Another example of an implicit personality test is the Emotional Stroop Test. Recall the Stroop effect from chapter 8: People are asked to look at a display like this and read the color of the ink instead of reading the words:

purple brown green blue yellow purple yellow red brown

With the Emotional Stroop Test, *someone examines a list of words, some of which relate to a possible source of worry or concern, and tries to say the color of the ink of each word.* For example, say the color of the ink of each of these words as fast as you can:

cancer venom defeat hospital rattler failure fangs blood
loser slither nurses bite jobless cobra inadequate disease

If you have a snake phobia, you might pause longer than other people when you try to read the color of snake-related words—*venom, rattler, fangs, slither, bite, cobra.* You can collect results for yourself at the Online Try It Yourself activity Emotional Stroop Test.

The Emotional Stroop Test has shown that violent offenders have long delays on words like *anger* and *hate* (P. Smith & Waterman, 2003), pain sufferers respond slowly for words related to pain (Crombez, Hermans, & Adriaensen, 2000), suicide attempters respond slowly to death-related words, and drug addicts have delays on words related to addiction (Cox, Fadardi, & Pothos, 2006). However, the differences are not large, and the Emotional Stroop Test is not reliable enough to make decisions about an individual.

21. On the preceding sample items of an Emotional Stroop Test, if you had the greatest delay in naming the ink color for *cancer, hospital, blood, nurses,* and *disease,* what would these results imply about your emotions?

Answer

21. The results would suggest that you are worried about health-related matters.

USES AND MISUSES OF PERSONALITY TESTS

Personality tests serve several functions. Researchers use them to investigate how personality develops. Clinicians use them to help identify disorders and to measure improvement during therapy. Many businesses use the MBTI to promote mutual understanding, and some use tests to help select which job applicants to hire. Using personality tests for job selection has positive but low validity. For example, the NEO-PI-R measures conscientiousness (among other factors), and conscientiousness correlates about .15 with job performance and cooperativeness (Hough & Oswald, 2008; Morgeson et al., 2007). Low neuroticism also correlates with good job performance, although less consistently than conscientiousness does (Barrick, Mount, & Judge, 2001).

Should businesses make important decisions based on tests with such unimpressive validity? It is certainly a reasonable question, although one could argue that even low validity is better than sheer guesswork. A further problem is that people can fake good scores. If you are taking a test and you want to make a good impression on a prospective employer, you might pretend to be more conscientious, more agreeable, and less neurotic than you really are. (On a cognitive test, you can't pretend to be smarter than you really are.) In many cases, faking lowers the validity of personality tests. However, in some situations, it might not be so bad (Morgeson et al., 2007). If the employer wants to hire salespeople to push a flawed or useless product, the ability to lie might be a plus!

How useful are personality tests for diagnosing psychological disorders? They are useful up to a point but sometimes misleading. Suppose someone's MMPI personality profile resembles the profile typical for schizophrenia. Identifying schizophrenia or any other unusual condition is a signal-detection problem, as in chapter 4: We want to report a stimulus when it is present but not when it is absent. People without schizophrenia outnumber people with schizophrenia by about 100 to 1. Suppose a particular personality profile on some test is characteristic of 95% of people with schizophrenia and 5% of everyone else. As Figure 14.11 shows, 5% of the total population is a larger group than 95% of the people with schizophrenia. Thus, if we label as "schizophrenic" everyone with a high score, we are wrong more often than right. (Recall the representativeness heuristic and the issue of base-rate information discussed in chapter 8: Someone who seems representative of people in a rare category does not necessarily belong to that category.) Therefore, although the personality test provides a helpful clue, a psychologist looks for evidence beyond the test score before drawing a conclusion.

22. Is a personality test more likely to be accurate in identifying common disorders or rare disorders?

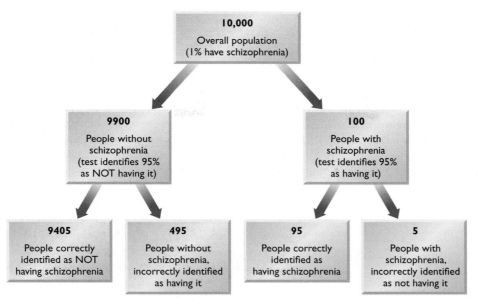

FIGURE 14.11 Assume that a certain profile occurs in 95% of people with schizophrenia and 5% of other people. If we relied entirely on this test, we would correctly identify 95 schizophrenic people and misidentify 495 normal people.

Answer

22. It is more likely to be accurate with common disorders, such as depression. If a condition is rare, let's say 1% or 0.1%, the chance of a false positive (saying that a normal person has the disorder) could easily exceed the probability of correctly identifying someone with the disorder.

PERSONALITY TESTS IN ACTION: CRIMINAL PROFILING

Personality traits are moderately (but only moderately) accurate predictors of people's behavior in certain situations. Can we go in the other direction? Can we observe behavior and infer someone's personality traits? In particular, consider crime. Although you might not have thought of it this way, psychological profiling of criminals is an application of personality testing. It assumes that people who commit similar crimes have similar personalities or backgrounds, and therefore, an investigator can observe a crime and infer something useful about the criminal. In 1956 the New York city police asked psychiatrist James Brussel to help them find the "mad bomber" who had planted more than 30 bombs over 16 years. Brussel examined the evidence and told police the mad bomber hated the power company, Con Ed. The bomber was probably unmarried, foreign-born—probably Slavic—50–60 years old, and living in Bridgeport, Connecticut. Brussel said to look for a man who dresses neatly and wears a buttoned double-breasted suit. That evidence led police directly to a suspect, George Metesky, who was wearing a buttoned double-breasted suit! Metesky confessed, and criminal profiling established itself as a powerful tool.

Well, that's the way James Brussel told the story, anyway. Remember from chapter 7 about memory distortions and hindsight bias? Brussel apparently distorted his memory of what he told the police. According to police records, Brussel didn't say the bomber was Slavic; he said German. Metesky in fact was Lithuanian. Brussel didn't say the bomber lived in Bridgeport, Connecticut; he said White Plains, New York, and the police spent much time searching for suspects in White Plains. Metesky in fact lived in Waterbury, Connecticut. Brussel said the bomber was 40–50 years old and revised his memory when Metesky turned out to be a bit older. Brussel also said the bomber had a facial scar, had a night job, and was an expert on civil or military ordnance (none of which was true). And Metesky was not wearing a buttoned double-breasted suit when the police arrested him. He was wearing pajamas. Nothing that Brussel said led the police to Metesky. They found him because a clerk from Con Ed patiently went through years of letters the company had received until she found a threatening letter that resembled messages the mad bomber had planted (Foster, 2000).

Brussel's *reported* success in helping the police (which wasn't really a success at all) inspired a growing interest in criminal profiling, and today, FBI profilers consult with police on a thousand or so cases per year. How accurate are their profiles?

Researchers examined 21 criminal profiles that various police departments obtained. Most statements in those profiles were vague, ambiguous, or useless to investigators, such as, "The offender felt no remorse" (Alison, Smith, Eastman, & Rainbow, 2003). Most of the "evidence" to support profiling consists of anecdotes about statements profilers made that turned out to be correct. It is tempting to remember the successes and forget the failures, as in the confirmation bias discussed in chapter 9 (Snook, Cullen, Bennell, Taylor, & Gendreau, 2008). The *number* of correct statements is useless information unless we know the *percentage* correct. We also need to know whether professional profilers' surmises are more accurate than other people's guesses. Only a few studies have investigated these questions. Let's examine one of the best such studies.

What's the Evidence?

Criminal Profiling

Richard Kocsis and his associates first did a study of profiling in a murder case. They provided extensive details about the murder to five professional profilers and larger numbers of police officers, psychologists, college students, and self-declared psychics. Then each of these people tried to guess the sex, height, age, religion, and so forth of the murderer in 30 multiple-choice questions (with varying numbers of choices per item). Researchers compared the answers to facts about the actual murderer, who had in fact been caught, although the profilers and other participants did not know about him. Random guessing would produce 8.1 correct answers for the 30 items. Of the tested groups, professional profilers did the best, at 13.8 correct, and psychics did the worst, at 11.3, but none of the groups did well (Kocsis, Irwin, Hayes, & Nunn, 2000).

However, one could object that it is hard to profile a criminal from a single crime. Kocsis (2004) therefore did a similar study concerning someone who had committed a series of 13 cases of arson (setting fires).

Hypothesis Professional profilers will guess correctly more facts about the arsonist than other people will.

Method As in Kocsis's first study, most profilers refused to participate, but he did find three who were willing. Other groups were police officers with much experience investigating arson, professional fire investigators, and sophomore chemistry majors. Each person examined all the evidence that police had assembled before they identified the culprit. The evidence included photos and descriptions of the crime scenes, statements by witnesses, fingerprints, shoe prints, information from investigators about how the fires were set, and so forth. Then each participant answered 33 questions about the probable arsonist. All were questions to which the researcher knew the answer, and all were items that would be potentially helpful in a police investigation. Examples (reworded slightly for brevity):

- The offender is: (1) male, (2) female.
- The offender is: (1) thin, (2) average, (3) solid/muscular, (4) fat.
- The offender was: (1) highly familiar with some of the crime locations, (2) somewhat familiar, (3) unfamiliar.
- The offender is: (1) single, (2) married, (3) living with someone, (4) divorced.
- The offender is: (1) a student, (2) unemployed, (3) employed part time, (4) a blue-collar worker, (5) a semiskilled worker, (6) a skilled or white-collar worker.
- The offender's alcohol use is: (1) none, (2) low, (3) medium, (4) in binges, (5) high.
- The offender: (1) has a previous criminal record, (2) has no previous criminal record.

The study also included a group of community college students who received *no* information about the crimes (except that they were arson), but they were asked to guess about the arsonist anyway. For example, without knowing anything, one might guess that the offender is probably male.

Results Questions had between two and nine choices each, and random guessing would produce a bit more than 10 correct answers. Figure 14.12 shows the results. The three professional profilers did the best, but only 3-4 items better than the chemistry majors. (Chemistry majors were selected for this study to represent people who are inexperienced with criminal investigations but smart. Take a bow, chemistry majors.) Police and firefighters, despite their experience, did not do significantly better than the control group, who had no information about the crimes.

Interpretation This study has clear limitations, especially that it included only three professional profilers, just one criminal, and a set of questions that may not have been ideal. Still, the profilers did better than the other groups, so it appears that the field is not entirely bogus. It is noteworthy that police officers experienced in investigating arson cases were no more accurate than people who had no information about the crimes. Evidently, police experience by itself doesn't help in this situation. A few similar studies have been done with similar results: Professional profilers do a bit better than other people, but not by much, and police investigators do no better than inexperienced people. In no case did anyone answer a very high percentage of questions correctly (Snook, Eastwood, Gendreau, Goggin, & Cullen, 2007).

A critical question remains: Did the profilers do well *enough*? On the average, they answered 23 questions correctly, which is closer to the scores of people who knew nothing (16+) than it is to a perfect score (33). If profilers provide the police with a mixture of correct and incorrect information, is the net result to advance the investigation or lead the police astray?

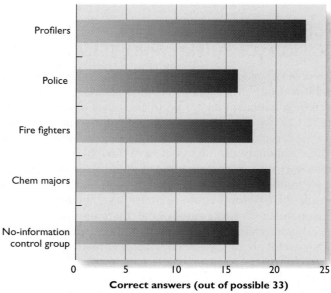

FIGURE 14.12 Of 33 multiple-choice questions, many of them with only two or three choices, profilers answered a mean of 23 items correctly. Random guessing would produce 10 correct. People with no information about the crime guessed more than 16 correct. (Source: Based on data from Kocsis, 2004)

23. Note the use of a control group who knew nothing about the crime. Why was this group necessary? We already knew how many answers someone would get right by random guessing.

Concept
Check

Answer

23. No one would guess randomly. Even someone who knew nothing about the specific crimes would guess that the criminal was male, just because men commit more violent crimes than women. One would probably also guess the person has a previous criminal record of some sort, and alcohol consumption probably isn't "none." In many other questions, some guesses are more likely than others regardless of the details of the crime.

We should not conclude that criminal profiling is impossible. However, the results of the research so far are unimpressive. Why, then, do many police investigators insist they find criminal profiles useful? Many criminal profiles include vague statements that apply to many people: The criminal is about the same age as the victim, average in appearance, does not look out of context in the area, possibly unemployed, has a pornography collection, and is probably a very confused person (Alison, Smith, & Morgan, 2003). In one study, researchers gave police officers a criminal profile that an FBI profiler had prepared for the investigation of a particular murder, plus a description of the actual murderer (who had been caught), and asked the officers how well the profile fit the actual criminal. Most rated it between 5 and 6 on a scale of 1 to 7. The researchers then gave a different group of police officers the same profile, plus a completely different, fictional description of the murderer, changing his age, relationship to the victim, childhood history, and everything else. Most of this group also rated it between 5 and 6 (Alison et al., 2003). In short, the actual facts about the criminal made little difference to how highly the police rated the profile.

module 14.3

In Closing

Possibilities and Limits of Personality Tests

One of most people's main topics of conversation could be described uncharitably as "gossip" or more kindly as "understanding other people." Knowing about other people is important. You need to know whom to trust and whom to distrust.

Given this focus on personality, most of us tend to believe that personality is highly stable and governs a great deal of behavior. If so, someone should be able to look at a crime scene and infer the personality of the perpetrator. Psychologists should be able to listen to people's answers to the Rorschach Inkblots and discern their innermost secrets. So it might seem, but the research suggests we should be cautious. Personality is somewhat consistent over time and situations, but it is like climate—a trend over a long period of time and not always a good guide to what is happening at the moment. Our actions depend on our situations at least as much as they depend on our personalities.

SUMMARY

- *People's tendency to accept personality test results.* Because most people accept almost any interpretation of their personality based on a personality test, tests must be carefully scrutinized to ensure that they are measuring what they claim to measure. (page 524)

- *Standardized personality tests.* A standardized test is administered according to explicit rules, and its results are interpreted in a prescribed fashion based on the norms for the population. (page 524)

- *The MMPI.* The MMPI, a widely used personality test, consists of a series of true–false questions selected in an effort to distinguish among various personality types. The MMPI–2 is a modern version. (page 525)
- *Detection of lying.* The MMPI and other tests guard against lying by including items about common faults and rare virtues. Anyone who denies common faults or claims rare virtues is probably lying. (page 526)
- *Projective techniques.* A projective technique, such as the Rorschach Inkblots or the Thematic Apperception Test, lets people describe their concerns indirectly while talking about ambiguous stimuli. The results from projective techniques have unimpressive validity for making decisions about any individual. (page 527)

- *Implicit personality tests.* The Emotional Stroop Test measures people's delays in naming the color of ink on the assumption that they will pause longer if the word has emotional meaning to them. So far, such tests are useful for research but not for decisions about an individual. (page 529)
- *Uses and misuses of personality tests.* Personality tests can help assess personality, but their results should be interpreted in conjunction with other evidence. (page 530)
- *Criminal profiling.* Some psychologists try to aid police investigations by constructing personality profiles of the kind of person who would commit a certain crime. Research has been limited, and so far, it suggests low accuracy of personality profiles. (page 531)

KEY TERMS

Barnum effect (page 524)

Emotional Stroop Test (page 530)

Minnesota Multiphasic Personality Inventory (MMPI) (page 525)

MMPI–2 (page 525)

Myers-Briggs Type Indicator (MBTI) (page 527)

NEO PI-R (NEO personality inventory-revised) (page 526)

projective techniques (page 527)

Rorschach Inkblots (page 528)

standardized test (page 524)

Thematic Apperception Test (TAT) (page 529)

exploration and study

Why Does This Matter to Me?

SOCIAL RESPONSIBILITY AND PSYCHOLOGY

Many environmental and societal problems are caused by human behavior Psychologists can help steer the course of our future toward more socially responsible and sustainable outcomes. Students of today need to be ever mindful of the link between human behavior and its impact on the environment and our communities.

"Personality" and Social Responsibility: A Step Further

If we want to organize people to accomplish worthy goals, such as conserving natural resources, what would be helpful to know about their personality? Would personality tests provide that information? How much, if anything, could the insights of psychoanalysis contribute?

Media for Sustainability

On Facebook, there are many causes that you can join that support service projects or sustainable outcomes. However, perhaps you feel you have unique attributes (e.g., organizational skills or a friendly personality that has amassed you more than 200 friends on the Facebook). If so, consider starting your own local cause using the tools provided on the Facebook Causes page; find a current link to this website at www.cengage.com/psychology/kalat.

Join the iChapters Plant a Tree Drive!

To show its support of the environmental movement, iChapters is planting a tree on behalf of each fan of the iChapters Facebook Page and for every 10 questions answered correctly in our quiz.
http://www.ichapters.com/plantatree/

SUGGESTIONS FOR FURTHER EXPLORATION

In addition to the study materials provided at the end of each module, you may supplement your review of this chapter with the following book and website suggestions or by using one or more of the book's electronic resources, which include its companion website, interactive Cengage Learning eBook, and CengageNOW. Brief descriptions of these resources follow. For more information, visit **www.cengage.com/psychology/kalat**.

ADDITIONAL RESOURCES

The book's companion website, accessible from **www.cengage.com/psychology/kalat**, provides a wide range of study resources such as an interactive glossary, flashcards, tutorial quizzes, updated web links, and Try It Yourself activities. For example, the exercise on the Emotional Stroop Test ties to what you've learned in this chapter.

CengageNOW with Critical Thinking Videos is an easy-to-use resource that helps you study in less time to get the grade you want. An online study system, CengageNOW gives you the option of taking a diagnostic pretest for each chapter. The system uses the results of each pretest to create personalized chapter study plans for you. The Personalized Study Plans

- Help you save study time by identifying areas on which you should concentrate and give you one-click access to corresponding pages of the interactive Cengage Learning eBook;
- Provide interactive exercises and study tools to help you fully understand chapter concepts; and
- Include a posttest for you to take to confirm that you are ready to move on to the next chapter.

Find critical thinking videos like this one in your CengageNOW product, which offer an opportunity for you to learn more about psychological research on different topics.

Books

Crews, F. C. (1998). *Unauthorized Freud.* New York: Viking Press. Devastating criticisms of Sigmund Freud's use and misuse of evidence.

Freud, S. (1924). *Introductory lectures on psychoanalysis.* New York: Boni and Liveright. Read Freud's own words and form your own opinion.

Hicks, S. J., & Sales, B. D. (2006). *Criminal profiling.* Washington, DC: American Psychological Association. A review of research on this interesting, controversial topic.

Websites

Links to the websites described below are kept current and can be found at **www.cengage.com/psychology/kalat**.

Personality Measures and the Big Five

This site offers a wealth of information about personality traits and research, including links to many research sites.

The Myers-Briggs Type Indicator

This website lets you take a shorter, simplified version of the Myers-Briggs test and see how it classifies your personality.

Personality Traits

Manchan/Photographer's Choice/Getty Images

15 chapter

Abnormality, Therapy, and Social Issues

Consider This:

Over the past 4 months, George has injured dozens of people whom he hardly knew. Two of them had to be sent to the hospital. George expresses no guilt, no regrets. He says he would hit every one of them again if he got the chance. What should society do with George?

1. Send him to jail.

2. Commit him to a mental hospital.

3. Give him an award for being the best defensive player in the league.

You cannot answer the question unless you know the context of George's behavior. Behavior that seems normal at a party is bizarre at a business meeting. Behavior that earns millions for a rock singer might earn a trip to the mental hospital for someone else.

Even knowing the context of someone's behavior may not tell us whether it is normal. Suppose your rich Aunt Tillie starts passing out money to strangers on a

© Jay Mallin

A protestor who spends years of his life picketing the White House in search of peace is statistically abnormal and puts himself at risk of harm. Still, most of us would not call him psychologically abnormal.

street corner and plans to continue until she has exhausted her fortune. Should the court commit her to a mental hospital and make you the trustee of her estate? (If so, for whose sake—hers or yours?)

A man claiming to have a message from God asks permission to address the United Nations. A psychiatrist is sure that antipsychotic drugs can relieve this man of his disordered thinking, but the man insists that he is perfectly sane. Should we force him to take the drugs, ignore him, or place his speech on the agenda of the United Nations?

Abnormal Behavior: An Overview

• What do we mean by "abnormal" behavior?

Many students in medical school contract what is called "medical students' disease." Imagine reading a medical textbook that describes, say, Cryptic Ruminating Umbilicus Disorder (CRUD): "The symptoms are hardly noticeable until the condition becomes hopeless. The first symptom is a pale tongue." (You go to the mirror. You can't remember what your tongue is supposed to look like, but it *does* look a little pale.) "Later, a hard spot forms in the neck." (You feel your neck. "Wait! I never felt *this* before! I think it's something hard!") "Just before the arms and legs fall off, the person has shortness of breath, increased heart rate, and sweating." (Already distressed, you *do* have shortness of breath, your heart *is* racing, and you *are* sweating profusely.)

Sooner or later, most medical students misunderstand the description of some disease and confuse it with their own normal condition. When my brother was in medical school, he diagnosed himself as having a rare, fatal illness, checked himself into a hospital, and wrote out his will. (He finished medical school and is still doing fine today, decades later.)

Students of psychological disorders are particularly vulnerable to medical students' disease. As you read this chapter and the next one, you may decide that you are suffering from one of the disorders you read about. Perhaps you are, but recognizing a little of yourself in the description of a psychological disorder does not mean that you have the disorder. Most people feel nervous occasionally, and most have mood swings, strange habits, or beliefs that strike other people as odd. A diagnosis of a psychological disorder should be reserved for people whose problems seriously interfere with their lives.

DEFINING ABNORMAL BEHAVIOR

How should we define abnormal behavior? To try to be completely objective, we might define it as any behavior significantly different from the average. However, by that definition, unusually happy or successful people are abnormal, and severe depression would be normal if it became common enough.

Another way to define abnormal would be to let people decide for themselves whether they are troubled. That is, anyone who complains of feeling miserable has a problem. Fair enough, but what about certain people who insist that they do *not* have a problem? Imagine someone who babbles incoherently while claiming to be obeying messages from another planet. Most of us would call the behavior abnormal, even if this person does not.

The American Psychiatric Association (1994) defined abnormal behavior as any behavior that leads to distress (including distress to others), disability, or an increased risk of death, pain, or loss of freedom. This definition includes too much. When Dr. Martin Luther King Jr. fought for the rights of African Americans, he risked death, pain, and loss of freedom, but we regard his acts as heroic, not abnormal. Presumably, we want to limit

a

b

What we consider abnormal depends on the context. (a) People dressed as witches ski down a mountain as part of an annual festival in Belalp, Switzerland, in which dressing as witches is supposed to chase away evil spirits. (b) A woman walks through a public park carrying a snake. Unusual behavior is not necessarily a sign of psychological disorder.

Edvard Munch (1864–1944), *Self Portrait, The Night Wanderer*, 1923–1924, Munch Museum, Oslo, Norway. The uncurtained windows and the bare room emphasize the feeling of loneliness and isolation.

In ancient Greece, behavior changes were explained in terms of an imbalance among four fluids: An excess of blood caused a sanguine (courageous and loving) personality. An excess of phlegm caused a phlegmatic (calm) personality. Too much yellow bile made one choleric (easily angered). Too much black bile made one melancholic (sad). Although the theory is obsolete, the terms *sanguine, phlegmatic, choleric,* and *melancholic* persist. This theory was an early attempt at a biological explanation of personality and abnormality.

Traditional Chinese philosophy held that personality progresses through five states of change, analogous to the seasons: Winter rain helps the trees (wood) grow in spring. The trees burn (fire) in summer, and the ashes return to earth in late summer. The earth can be mined for metal in autumn, and melted metal becomes a liquid, like water, completing the cycle. According to this view, personality also cycles with the season, and an excessive response could cause too much fear, anger, and so forth. Figure 15.1 illustrates the idea.

our concept of "abnormal behavior" to conditions that are undesirable.

Could we define abnormal behavior as behavior that is undesirable? If so, who gets to decide what is undesirable? Totalitarian governments have been known to put political dissidents in mental hospitals because the dissidents' behavior was undesirable—from the government's point of view. Several decades ago, the American Psychiatric Association considered homosexuality a mental illness, until researchers showed how many homosexual people were well adjusted.

In short, every definition has problems. It is sometimes easy to agree that a certain person has a psychological disorder. In other cases, we find room for disagreement.

Views of Abnormality

Over the years, people have had many views of what abnormal behavior is and what causes it. One recurrent idea is demon possession, a popular idea in medieval Europe and still a widespread idea in much of the world today (Cohen & Barrett, 2008). Although the idea conflicts with the scientific worldview, we understand its appeal: When someone's behavior changes drastically, we feel like saying, "That's not the person I knew."

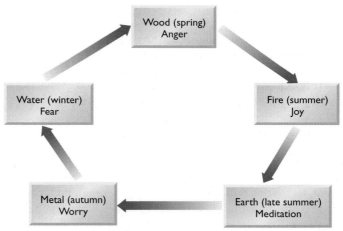

FIGURE 15.1 In traditional Chinese philosophy, personality cycles through five stages or elements, just as the seasons do. An excessive response could lead to abnormalities.

The Biopsychosocial Model

In Western cultures today, the predominant view is the biopsychosocial model, which emphasizes that *abnormal behavior has three major aspects: biological, psychological, and sociological.* Many researchers and therapists focus mainly on one aspect or another of this model, but few deny that all three aspects are important.

The *biological* roots of abnormal behavior include genetic factors, abnormal brain development, and excesses or deficiencies in the activity of various neurotransmitters or hormones. Additional influences include brain damage, infectious diseases, brain tumors, poor nutrition, inadequate sleep, and the overuse of drugs, including nonprescription medications.

The *psychological* component of abnormality includes reactions to stressful events and other experiences. For example, people who are known to have been physically or sexually abused in childhood are more likely than others to develop psychological problems in adulthood (J. G. Johnson, Cohen, Brown, Smailes, & Bernstein, 1999). The psychological aspect also includes favorable experiences that help people remain resilient. Anxiety and depression are less common for people who have a strong network of social support.

Finally, behavior must be understood in a *social* and cultural context. Certain kinds of psychological disorder are more common in some social settings than in others. For example, as mentioned in chapter 11, cultures that pressure women to be extremely thin increase the risk of anorexia nervosa. Alcohol abuse is common in Las Vegas but uncommon among Mormons. Behavior that is considered acceptable in one society might be labeled abnormal in another.

The key point about the biopsychosocial model is that the three aspects interact with one another. Genetic and other biological factors alter the way people react to experiences, and the outcomes are modified by culture.

....

1. Of the three aspects of the biopsychosocial model, which one did the ancient Greek theory emphasize? Which does traditional Chinese philosophy emphasize?

Answer

1. The Greek theory emphasized the biological aspect, and Chinese philosophy emphasizes the psychological aspect, with some credit to biological influences. Neither paid much attention to sociological or cultural influences, presumably because neither group was much aware of differences between one culture and another.

....

Cultural Influences on Abnormality

In some cultures, we see certain types of abnormal behavior that seldom if ever occur elsewhere. In part of Sudan some years ago, women had low status and very limited rights. If a woman's husband mistreated her, she had no defense. However, people in this society believed that a woman could be possessed by a demon that caused her to lose control and scream "crazy" things that she "could not possibly believe," including insults against her own husband (!). Her husband could not scold or punish her because, after all, it was not she who was speaking, but a demon. The standard way to remove the demon was to provide the woman with luxurious food, new clothing, an opportunity to spend much time with other women, and almost anything else she demanded until the demon departed. You can imagine how common demon possession became (Constantinides, 1977).

More examples: *Koro*, said to be common in China, is a fear that a man's penis will retract into the body, causing death. Some men have been known to hold onto their penis constantly to prevent it from disappearing into the body (Bracha, 2006). You have probably heard the expression "to run amok." *Running amok* occurs in parts of Southeast Asia, where someone (usually a young man) runs around engaging in indiscriminate violent behavior (Berry, Poortinga, Segal, & Dasen, 1992). Such behavior is considered an understandable reaction to psychological stress. Does running amok remind you of anything common in North America or Europe? How about the celebrations that occur after a sports team wins a major championship? Like running amok, people often regard such wild displays as temporary responses to overwhelming emotion.

For another example, one Australian psychiatrist found that three mental patients in a hospital had cut off one of their ears. Assuming that this behavior must be a common symptom of mental illness, he contacted other psychiatrists to ask how often they had seen the same thing. He found that ear removal occurred only at his own hospital. Apparently, after one patient cut off his ear, the other two copied (Alroe & Gunda, 1995). The point is that just as we learn from other people how to behave normally, we also learn possible ways to behave abnormally.

Suggestion may also be a major influence in **dissociative identity disorder (DID)**, previously known as *multiple personality disorder,* in which *someone alternates among distinct personalities.* (Alternating among different personalities is *not* schizophrenia, although the media often mislabel it as such.) Dissociative identity disorder was extremely rare before the 1950s, when a few cases received much publicity. Chris Sizemore was featured in the book and movie *The Three Faces of Eve,* written by her psychiatrists (Thigpen & Cleckley, 1957). Sizemore ("Eve") eventually told her own story, which was very different from her psychiatrists' version (Sizemore & Huber, 1988; Sizemore & Pittillo, 1977). A few other cases of dissociative identity disorder also received extensive publicity, such as the case of *Sybil,* although one of the psychiatrists associated with that case later said he thought the author of the book distorted the facts about Sybil to improve book sales (Borch-Jacobsen, 1997). In the 1970s through the 1990s, therapists reported more and more cases. One hypothesis is that the publicity

Fans sometimes celebrate a major sports victory with a destructive rampage. In some ways, this behavior is like running amok. It is an abnormal behavior copied from other people's example.

Chris Sizemore, whose story was told in *The Three Faces of Eve*, exhibited a total of 22 personalities, including her final, permanent identity.

CLASSIFYING PSYCHOLOGICAL DISORDERS

How many kinds of psychological disorders exist? Centuries ago, physicians drew few distinctions between one disease and another, and they prescribed many of the same treatments (e.g., leeches) for almost any ailment. Medical progress depended on separating one disorder from another so that researchers could find the causes and best treatment for each. Presumably, the same should be true for psychological disorders. If we are going to find the causes of depression, for example, psychologists need to agree on what they mean by *depression* and how it differs from other disorders.

To standardize their definitions, psychiatrists and psychologists developed *a reference book called* the *Diagnostic and Statistical Manual of Mental Disorders (DSM)*—now in its fourth edition and therefore known as *DSM–IV*—which *sets specific criteria for each psychological diagnosis*, including depression, alcohol intoxication, exhibitionism, pathological gambling, anorexia nervosa, sleepwalking disorder, stuttering, and hundreds of others. The latest edition of this book is called a Text Revision of *DSM–IV* and therefore is labeled *DSM–IV–TR* (American Psychiatric Association, 2000).

DSM-IV *Classifications*

The clinicians and researchers who use *DSM–IV* classify each client along five separate *axes* (lists). A person may have one disorder, several, or none. The axis that gets the most attention is *Axis I, clinical disorders*. Table 15.1 lists the major categories of disorder listed on Axis I. Each disorder on Axis I represents in some way a deterioration of functioning. Previous chapters discussed attention-deficit disorder, eating disorders, and sleep disorders, which are listed on Axis I. In chapter 16, we concentrate on three common Axis I disorders—anxiety disorders, substance-abuse disorders, and mood disorders—as well as schizophrenia and autism, which are less common but often incapacitating when they occur.

Axis II includes personality disorders and mental retardation. A **personality disorder** is *a maladaptive, inflexible way of dealing with the environment and other people,* such as being unusually self-centered. The concept of personality disorder is in flux. The authors of *DSM-IV* believed that personality disorders fell into a few discrete categories. Table 15.2 lists some examples. Psychologists had little evidence for separate types of per-

about Eve and Sybil led to the increased prevalence. Some therapists suggested to patients that perhaps they had other personalities. In some cases, they used hypnosis to explore that possibility, inadvertently implanting a suggestion while people were in a state of increased suggestibility (Lilienfeld et al., 1999). The suggestions may have exaggerated small tendencies until they became full-blown disorders. If so, this is another example of a cultural influence on abnormal behavior.

Culture also influences the expression of more widespread disorders. Depressed people in different cultures have much in common with one another, except that those in Europe and North America complain more about how they feel, whereas those in China and similar cultures complain more about their physical symptoms such as fatigue, pain, and sleeplessness (Ryder et al., 2008). Conduct disorder and other conditions marked by antisocial behavior occur throughout the world, but their prevalence depends on cultural influences. Conduct disorder is much more prevalent among Puerto Rican youth in New York, where they feel less comfortable with local culture, than among Puerto Rican youth living in Puerto Rico (Bird et al., 2001; Canino & Alegria, 2008). Several other disorders are more common in some cultures and less common in others, as we shall see in the next chapter.

2. In what way might dissociative identity disorder resemble koro and running amok?

Answer

2. In each case, people are reacting to real problems, but the way they react depends on suggestions or expectations from other people.

TABLE 15.1 Some Major Categories of Psychological Disorders According to Axis I of DSM–IV

Category	Examples and Descriptions
Disorder usually first evident in childhood	*Attention deficit hyperactivity disorder:* impulsivity, impaired attention *Tourette's disorder:* repetitive movements such as blinking, twitching, chanting sounds or words *Elimination disorders:* bedwetting, urinating or defecating in one's clothes *Stuttering:* frequent repetition or prolongation of sounds while trying to speak
Substance-related disorders	Abuse of alcohol, cocaine, opiates, or other drugs
Schizophrenia	Deterioration of daily functioning along with a combination of hallucinations, delusions, or other symptoms
Delusional (paranoid) disorder	Unjustifiable beliefs, such as "everyone is talking about me behind my back"
Mood disorders	*Major depressive disorder:* Repeated episodes of depressed mood and lack of energy *Bipolar disorder:* Alternation between periods of depression and mania
Anxiety disorders	*Panic disorder:* Repeated attacks of intense terror *Phobia:* Severe anxiety and avoidance of a particular object or situation
Somatoform disorders	*Conversion disorder:* Physical ailments caused partly by psychological factors but not faked *Hypochondriasis:* Exaggerated complaints of illness *Somatization disorder:* Complaints of pain or other ailments without any physical disorder
Dissociative disorders	Loss of personal identity or memory without brain damage
Sexual disorders	*Pedophilia:* Sexual attraction to children *Voyeurism:* Sexual arousal primarily from watching others undress or have sexual relations *Exhibitionism:* Sexual arousal from exposing one's genitals in public
Eating disorders	*Anorexia nervosa:* Refusal to eat, fear of fatness *Bulimia nervosa:* Binge eating alternating with severe dieting
Sleep disorders	*Sleep terror disorder:* Repeated sudden awakenings in a state of panic *Insomnia:* Frequently not getting enough sleep to feel well rested the next day
Impulse control disorders	Frequently acting on impulses that others would inhibit, such as stealing, gambling foolishly, or hitting people

sonality disorders, but they hoped later research would support the idea. In fact, not much research has ensued, and so far, it indicates that all of the personality disorders overlap. Many people with personality disorders have a combination of several on the list, not just one (Lenzenweger, Johnson, & Willett, 2004). It is also common for someone to be diagnosed with one personality disorder at one time and a different one later. The next edition, *DSM-V*, may not list separate personality disorders. Instead, it might ask a therapist to evaluate each person on several dimensions, such as antisocial tendencies, narcissism, and avoidance (D. Watson & Clark, 2006; Widiger & Trull, 2007).

One distinction between Axis I and Axis II disorders is that Axis II disorders tend to be lifelong, whereas Axis I disorders represent a deterio-

ration of functioning. However, the personality disorders listed in Axis II change from time to time more than psychologists had assumed (Clark, 2009). A stronger reason for distinguishing Axis II from Axis I is that Axis II disorders are seldom the main reason for consulting a therapist. (Most people do not seek treatment for narcissism or other personality disorders, except when other people insist on it.) By listing Axis II disorders separately, *DSM–IV* encourages the therapist to notice them. A therapist fills out a diagnosis on Axis I and then comes to the question of what, if anything, to list on Axis II. It is possible to list "no diagnosis," but at least the therapist pauses to consider the possibilities.

Axis III, general medical conditions, lists physical disorders, such as diabetes, head trauma, or

TABLE 15.2 Some Major Categories of Psychological Disorders According to Axis II of DSM–IV

Category and Examples	Descriptions
Mental Retardation	Intellectual functioning significantly below average; inability to function effectively and independently
Personality Disorders	
Antisocial personality disorder	Lack of affection for others; high probability of harming others without feeling guilty; apparent weakness of most emotions
Borderline personality disorder	Lack of stable self-image; trouble establishing lasting relationships or maintaining lasting decisions; repeated self-endangering behaviors
Histrionic personality disorder	Excessive emotionality and attention seeking
Narcissistic personality disorder	Exaggerated opinion of one's own importance and disregard for others. (Narcissus was a figure in Greek mythology who fell in love with his own image.)
Avoidant personality disorder	Avoidance of social contact; lack of friends
Dependent personality disorder	Preference for letting other people make decisions; lack of initiative and self-confidence

alcoholic cirrhosis of the liver. A psychotherapist needs to know about these disorders because they influence behavior and sometimes interfere with treatment. *Axis IV, psychosocial and environmental problems,* indicates how much stress the person has had to endure. Stress intensifies a psychological disorder and thus affects the course of treatment. *Axis V, global assessment of functioning,* evaluates a person's overall level of functioning on a scale from 1 (serious attempt at suicide or complete inability to take care of oneself) to 100 (happy, productive, with many interests). Some people with a psychological disorder are able to proceed with their normal work and social activities, but other people are not.

3. In what way does *DSM-IV* help psychologists do research on Axis I disorders?
4. Why does this advantage probably not apply to personality disorders?

Concept Check

Answers

3. Carefully classifying disorders helps ensure that psychologists who say they are studying the same disorder, such as depression, really are.
4. The research suggests no real distinction among different personality disorders. Most people who have one of the personality disorders also, at least to some degree.

Pros and Cons of DSM-IV

DSM–IV has helped standardize psychiatric diagnoses so that psychologists in different places mean approximately the same thing when they say *depression, schizophrenia,* and so forth. Researchers collect information about what kind of person is most likely to develop each disorder, whether the disorder is more common in certain times and places than others, what treatments are effective, and so forth. Although *DSM-IV* is certainly imperfect, psychologists need some sort of manual to standardize diagnosis.

One criticism is that *DSM–IV* includes many minor disorders that pose little threat of developing into anything serious (Kutchins & Kirk, 1997). For example, if you don't enjoy sex as much as most other people seem to, you might seek help. To receive help, you will be diagnosed with *hypoactive sexual desire disorder.* If you are a woman who would like help in dealing with premenstrual distress, a therapist might diagnose you with *premenstrual dysphoric disorder* (Daw, 2002). The result is that almost anyone who wants a little help can be labeled mentally ill. Partly because of the large number of diagnoses, surveys have found that about a quarter of all people in the United States qualify for a psychiatric diagnosis in any given year, and almost half qualify at some time in life (Kessler, Berglund, Demler, Jin, & Walters, 2005; Kessler, Chiu, Demler, & Walters, 2005). The most common disorders are anxiety disorders, mood disorders (e.g., depression), impulse control problems (including attention-deficit disorder and conduct disorder), and substance abuse, as shown in Figure 15.2.

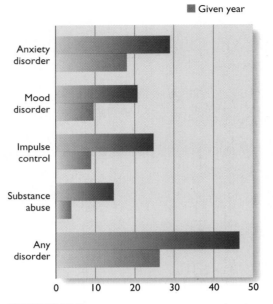

Lifetime
Given year

Anxiety disorder

Mood disorder

Impulse control

Substance abuse

Any disorder

0   10   20   30   40   50

FIGURE 15.2 In this survey, just over one fourth of U.S. adults suffer a psychological disorder in any given year, and nearly half do at some time in life. This figure combines results for men and women of all adult ages. (Based on data of Kessler, Berglund, et al., 2005; Kessler, Chiu, et al., 2005)

A more fundamental question concerns *DSM–IV's* assumption that disorders occur in categories. As already mentioned, the personality disorders apparently do not fit into distinct categories. Even for Axis I disorders, not every client fits neatly into a single category (Ahn, Flanagan, Marsh, & Sanislow, 2006). So far, no laboratory test separates one psychiatric disorder from another. Behavioral symptoms are often ambiguous, too. It is not unusual for a client to fit several diagnoses partly and none perfectly (Kupfer, First, & Regier, 2002). Of all people with any psychiatric diagnosis, nearly half qualify for at least one additional diagnosis, and people with a serious disorder are especially likely to have additional disorders (Kessler, Chiu, et al., 2005).

5. What are some criticisms of *DSM–IV*?

Concept
Check

Answer

5. One criticism is that *DSM-IV* lists many minor problems and risks giving too many people the stigma of a mental illness. Also, many of the disorders overlap.

15.1   module

In Closing

Is Anyone Normal?

According to the studies described in this module, nearly half of all people in the United States will have a *DSM–IV* disorder at some point in life. If those statistics are even close to accurate, one implication is obvious: Most of the people who qualify for a psychological diagnosis are not a rare group who would stand out immediately from everyone else. At some point in your life, you may have a bout of some kind of psychological distress. If so, remember that you have plenty of company.

Almost everyone has an unpleasant mood or behaves strangely at times. The difference between normal and abnormal is one of degree. Many people who qualify for a *DSM-IV* diagnosis are not much different from a great many other people who do not.

© Bob Daemmrich/The Image Works

SUMMARY

- *Normal and abnormal behavior.* The American Psychiatric Association defines behavior as abnormal if it leads to distress, disability, or increased risk of harm. However, any definition of abnormal behavior has difficulties. (page 538)
- *Views of abnormality.* In the past, people have described abnormal behavior in many ways, including spirit possession. The standard view today is that abnormal behavior results from a combination of biological, psychological, and social influences. (page 539)
- *Cultural influences.* Every culture provides examples not only of how to behave normally but also of how to behave abnormally. Symptoms of a disorder vary among cultures, and cultures influence the prevalence of various disorders. (page 540)
- *The Diagnostic and Statistical Manual.* Psychological disorders are classified in the *Diagnostic and Statistical Manual of Mental Disorders, Fourth Edition (DSM–IV)*. This manual classifies disorders along five axes. Axes I and II contain psychological disorders; Axis III lists physical ailments that can affect behavior; Axes IV and V provide the means of evaluating a person's stress level and overall functioning. (page 541)
- *Axis I disorders.* Axis I of *DSM–IV* lists a wide variety of disorders, including anxiety disorders, substance abuse, and depression. (page 541)
- *Axis II disorders.* Axis II of *DSM–IV* lists mental retardation and various personality disorders. (page 541)
- *Personality disorders.* Personality disorders are stable characteristics that impair a person's effectiveness or ability to get along with others. Examples of personality disorders are excessive dependence on others and excessive self-centeredness. Different personality disorders overlap substantially. (page 541)
- *Pros and cons of DSM–IV. DSM–V* is important for helping therapists and researchers standardize their diagnoses. However, it has been criticized for giving psychiatric labels to people with minor difficulties or understandable reactions to stressful situations. (page 543)

KEY TERMS

biopsychosocial model (page 539)

Diagnostic and Statistical Manual of Mental Disorders, Fourth Edition (DSM-IV) (page 541)

dissociative identity disorder (page 540)

personality disorder (page 541)

- What methods do therapists use to combat psychological disorders?
- How effective are these methods?

Observation

If I don't drive around the park, I'm pretty sure to make my mark.

If I'm in bed each night by ten, I may get back my looks again.

If I abstain from fun and such, I'll probably amount to much.

But I shall stay the way I am, Because I do not give a damn.

—Dorothy Parker (1944)[1]

Psychotherapy is *a treatment of psychological disorders by methods that include a personal relationship between a trained therapist and a client.* But psychotherapy does little good unless the client gives the proverbial damn.

Psychotherapy is used for people with the disorders listed in *DSM–IV* and also for people who just need to talk about some concern or worry. Some psychotherapy clients are virtually incapacitated by their problems, but others are reasonably happy, successful people who would like to function even more successfully.

The discussion here focuses on psychotherapy as it is practiced in the United States and Europe. Most Chinese consider it shameful to discuss personal or family matters with a stranger (Bond, 1991). Psychologists in India adapt their practice to local customs. For example, to maintain a close relationship with a client, they have to respect beliefs in astrology and other concepts that most Western psychologists dismiss (Clay, 2002).

HISTORICAL TRENDS IN PSYCHOTHERAPY

Psychotherapy has changed greatly since the mid-1900s for both scientific and economic reasons (Sanchez & Turner, 2003). Before World War II, almost all psychotherapists were psychiatrists. In the 1940s and 1950s, most therapists used Freudian methods and expected to see each patient frequently, perhaps daily, for months or years. No one had done much research to determine whether the treatment was effective, mainly because therapists had little incentive to undertake such research. People who wanted therapy paid for it themselves, as most people had no health insurance, and health insurance seldom if ever included psychiatric care. Because of the lack of research on the effectiveness of psychotherapy, clients had little choice but to trust whatever their therapists claimed. Some clients received a diagnosis such as depressed or schizophrenic, but many were given either no diagnosis at all or a vague diagnosis like "neurotic" or "psychotic."

Today, all of that has changed. Not only psychiatrists but also clinical psychologists, social workers, and others provide services for distressed people. Although some continue to rely on Freud's methods, most use other procedures. Many changes can be traced to the influence of health maintenance organizations (HMOs) and other insurance programs that now pay for mental health care. HMOs try to restrain costs and make sure that money is spent effectively. If the man down the street wants to see his therapist every day for the rest of his life, receiving what looks like a quack treatment, no one will object if he is paying the bills himself. However, if he is under the same health insurance program that you are, then you are helping to pay his fees. Suddenly, you and your insurance company want to know whether his treatment is effective enough to justify the cost. Generally, insurance companies will pay for more treatment if someone has a diagnosed mental disorder. They limit the treatment to a moderate number of sessions and support only therapies that appear effective according to the best available evidence. The consequences have been, as you might guess:

- Therapists have listed more and more diagnoses of mental disorder so that more clients can qualify for insurance help. The previous module mentioned the huge number of diagnoses listed in *DSM–IV,* and now you understand why.
- Therapists try to streamline the process to achieve good results in a few sessions if possible.
- Psychologists have conducted extensive research on the effectiveness of psychotherapy. In particular, they have worked to determine **empirically supported treatments,** *which are therapies demonstrated to be helpful* (APA Presidential Task Force on Evidence-Based Practice, 2006). Many therapists follow published manuals that specify exactly how to treat various disorders.
- In many cases, HMOs have also produced unwelcome changes to psychological care because they sometimes fail to authorize adequate care (Hamm, Reiss, Paul, & Bursztajn, 2007). That is, sometimes HMOs stand in the way of good care instead of facilitating it.

Table 15.3 summarizes these changes.

Psychotherapists today employ a great variety of methods. Different therapists treating the same problem approach it in strikingly different ways.

---

[1] Quote from "Observations" by Dorothy Parker, copyright 1928, renewed © 1956 by Dorothy Parker from *The Portable Dorothy Parker,* by Dorothy Parker, introduction by Brendan Gill. Used by permission of Viking Penguin, a division of Penguin Books USA Inc.

TABLE 15.3 Changes in Psychotherapy Between the 1950s and the 21st Century

Aspect of Therapy	1950s	Early 21st Century
Payment	By the patient or family	By health insurance
Types of therapist	Psychiatrists	Psychiatrists, clinical psychologists, others
Types of treatment	Mostly Freudian	Many types; emphasis on evidence-based treatments
Duration of treatment	Usually long, often years	A few sessions if effective; more if necessary
Diagnoses	Usually vague, such as "neurosis" or "psychosis." Often, no diagnosis.	Many diagnoses. Each clearly described in *DSM–IV*.
Treatment decisions	By the therapist and patient	Sometimes by the HMO

We shall review some of the most common types of therapy, exploring what they have in common as well as how they differ. In addition to the "talk" therapies discussed here, many clients receive antidepressants or other medications. Chapter 16 discusses those treatments in the context of specific disorders, such as depression.

....

6. How has treatment of psychological disorders changed since the 1950s?

7. What is one major reason psychotherapists have added so many diagnoses to *DSM–IV*?

Answers

7. It is possible to get health insurance to pay for treatment if someone has a disorder diagnosed in *DSM–IV*.

6. In the 1950s, psychiatrists conducted almost all psychotherapy. Today, clinical psychologists and other specialists also provide treatment. Today's therapists use a variety of empirically supported treatments, with less reliance on Freudian methods. Therapists try to achieve good results in just a few sessions, when possible, instead of proceeding for months or years. Today's therapists provide diagnoses for more disorders and define their diagnoses more carefully.

....

PSYCHOANALYSIS

Psychodynamic therapies *attempt to relate personality to the interplay of conflicting impulses within the individual, including some that the individual does not consciously recognize.* For exam-

ple, both Sigmund Freud's procedure (looking for sexual motives) and Alfred Adler's procedure (looking for power and superiority motives) are considered psychodynamic despite the differences between them. Here we focus on the procedure developed by Freud, although its practitioners have modified and developed it further since Freud's time.

Psychoanalysis, the first of the "talk" therapies, is *a method based on identifying unconscious thoughts and emotions and bringing them to consciousness to help people understand their thoughts and actions.* Psychoanalysis is therefore an "insight-oriented therapy" in contrast to therapies that focus on changing thoughts and behaviors (Figure 15.3). Psychoanalysis was the dominant form of psychotherapy in the United States in the mid-1900s. Over the years, it has declined in popu-

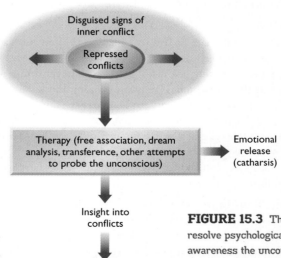

FIGURE 15.3 The goal of psychoanalysis is to resolve psychological problems by bringing to awareness the unconscious thought processes that created the difficulty. *Analysis* literally means "to loosen or break up, to look at the parts."

A psychotherapist, like this military psychologist in a Haitian refugee camp, tries to help people overcome problems.

larity and influence in the United States, although it remains more widespread in parts of Europe.

Freud believed that psychological problems result from unconscious thought processes and that the way to control self-defeating behavior is to make those processes conscious. Bringing them to consciousness, he thought, would produce catharsis, *a release of pent-up emotions associated with unconscious thoughts and memories.* (Whether catharsis is actually helpful is, however, uncertain. Expressing strong fear and anger does not make people feel good.) To bring unconscious material to consciousness, Freud used dream analysis, as discussed in chapter 10, free association, and transference.

Free Association

In free association, the client starts thinking about a particular symptom or problem and then reports everything that comes to mind—a word, a phrase, a visual image. The client is instructed not to omit or censor anything or even to speak in complete sentences. The psychoanalyst listens for links and themes that might tie the patient's fragmentary remarks together. The assumption is that nothing happens without a cause, and every jump from one thought to another reveals a relationship between them.

Here is a paraphrased excerpt from a free-association session:

> A man begins by describing a conference he had with his boss the previous day. He did not like the boss's policy, but he was in no position to contradict the boss. He dreamed something about an ironing board, but that was all he remembered of the dream. He comments that his wife has been complaining about the way their maid irons. He thinks his wife is being unfair; he hopes she does not fire the maid. He complains that his boss did not give him credit for some work he did recently. He recalls a childhood episode: He jumped off a cupboard and bounced off his mother's behind while she was leaning over to do some ironing. She told his father, who gave him a spanking. His father never let him explain; he was always too strict. (Munroe, 1955, p. 39)

To a psychoanalyst, the links in this story suggest that the man is associating his wife with his mother. His wife was unfair to the maid about the ironing, just as his mother had been unfair to him. Moreover, his boss is like his father, never giving him a chance to explain his errors and never giving him credit for what he did well.

Transference

Some clients express love or hatred for their therapist because he or she unconsciously reminds them of someone else. In this transference reaction, clients *transfer onto the therapist the behaviors and feelings they originally established toward their father, mother, or another important person in their lives.* Transference often provides clues to the client's feelings about that person.

Psychoanalysts offer interpretations of what the client says—that is, they *explain the underlying meaning*—and sometimes argue with a client about interpretations. They may regard the client's disagreement as resistance. For example, a client who has begun to touch on an extremely anxiety-provoking topic may turn the conversation to something trivial or may simply "forget" to come to the next session.

Psychoanalysts today modify Freud's approach in many ways. The goal is still to bring about a major reorganization of the personality, changing a person from the inside out, by helping people understand the hidden reasons behind their actions.

8. What methods do psychoanalysts use to try to gain access to the unconscious?

Concept Check

Answer

8. Psychoanalysts use free association and transference to infer the contents of the unconscious. They also use dream analysis, as discussed in chapter 10.

BEHAVIOR THERAPY

Behavior therapists assume that human behavior is learned and that someone who has learned an abnormal behavior can extinguish it or learn a competing response. They identify the behavior that needs to be changed, such as a fear or bad habit, and then set about changing it through reinforcement and other principles of learning. They may try to understand the causes of a behavior as a first step toward changing it, but unlike psychoanalysts, they are more interested in changing behaviors than in understanding their hidden meanings.

Behavior therapy *begins with clear, well-defined behavioral goals, such as eliminating test anxiety, and then attempts to achieve those goals through learning.* Setting clear goals enables the therapist to judge whether the therapy is succeeding. If the client shows no improvement after a few sessions, the therapist tries a different procedure.

One example of behavior therapy is for children who continue wetting the bed after the usual age of toilet training. Occasionally, this problem lingers to age 5, 10, or beyond. Many bed-wetters have small bladders and thus have difficulty getting through the night without urinating. Also, many are unusually deep sleepers who do not wake up when they need to urinate (Stegat, 1975).

The most effective procedure uses classical conditioning to train the child to wake up at night when the bladder is full. A small battery-powered device is attached to the child's underwear at night (Figure 15.4). When the child urinates, the device detects the moisture and produces a pulsing vibration that awakens the child. (Alternative devices work on the same principle but produce loud noises.) According to one interpretation, the vibration acts as an unconditioned stimulus (UCS) that evokes the unconditioned response (UCR) of waking up. In this instance, the body itself generates the conditioned stimulus (CS): the sensation produced by a full bladder (Figure 15.5). Whenever that sensation is present, it serves as a signal that the vibration is imminent. After a few pairings (or more), the sensation of a full bladder is enough to wake the child.

FIGURE 15.4 A small device called a Potty Pager fits into a child's underwear and vibrates when it becomes moist. This awakens the child, who then learns to awaken when the bladder is full.

Courtesy of Ideas for Living, Inc.

Actually, the situation is a little more complicated. When children learn to awaken to go to the toilet, the child gains rewards and avoids discomfort. Thus, the learning includes operant conditioning as well as classical conditioning (Ikeda, Koga, & Minami, 2006). In addition, many children begin sleeping through the night without needing to urinate. Through a series of hormonal mechanisms, the body stops producing so much urine at night (Butler et al., 2007). In any case, the alarm method is an application of behavior therapy, successful for at least two thirds of bed-wetting children, sometimes after as few as one or two nights.

9. Contrast the goals and methods of behavior therapy with those of psychoanalysis.
10. If we interpret the alarm method for bed-wetting as classical conditioning, what is the conditioned stimulus? What is the unconditioned stimulus? What is the conditioned response?

Concept Check

Answers

9. Psychoanalysts try to infer unconscious thoughts and motives and try to trace current behavior to experiences of long ago. Behavior therapists pay little attention to thoughts of any kind, conscious or unconscious. They set specific goals and try to change current behavior regardless of how the behavior originated.
10. The conditioned stimulus is the sensation of a full bladder. The unconditioned stimulus is the alarm. The conditioned response (and unconditioned response) is waking up.

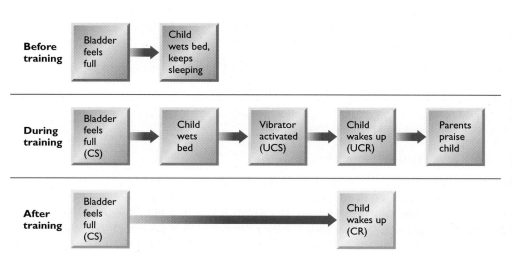

Before training

Bladder feels full → Child wets bed, keeps sleeping

During training

Bladder feels full (CS) → Child wets bed → Vibrator activated (UCS) → Child wakes up (UCR) → Parents praise child

After training

Bladder feels full (CS) → Child wakes up (CR)

FIGURE 15.5 A child can be trained not to wet the bed by using classical conditioning techniques. At first, the sensation of a full bladder (the CS) produces no response, and the child wets the bed. This causes a vibration or other alarm (the UCS), and the child wakes up (the UCR). By associating the sensation of a full bladder with the vibration, the child soon begins waking up (CR) in response to the sensation of a full bladder.

THERAPIES THAT FOCUS ON THOUGHTS AND BELIEFS

Suppose someone asks for your opinion on something and then asks someone else also. How do you react? You might think, "It's perfectly reasonable to get several opinions." Or you might feel hurt by the implication that your opinion wasn't good enough. Suppose someone invites several of your friends to a party but not you. Do you shrug your shoulders or do you take it as an insult? Your emotions depend not only on the events of life but also on how you interpret them. Some therapists focus on the thoughts and beliefs that underlie emotional reactions. Unlike psychoanalysts, these therapists are more concerned about their clients' conscious thoughts than their unconscious thoughts and more concerned about their clients' thoughts today than during early childhood.

Cognitive Therapies

Cognitive therapy *seeks to improve people's psychological well-being by changing their thoughts and beliefs—their cognitions* (Beck, 1976; Hollon & Beck, 1979). A cognitive therapist identifies distressing thoughts and encourages the client to explore the evidence behind them. Usually, the client discovers that the beliefs are unjustified. Cognitive therapy also encourages people to monitor their daily activities and determine which ones provide opportunities for pleasure or a sense of accomplishment. The therapist helps the client overcome specific problems, develop better social skills, and take a more active role in life.

A related approach, **rational-emotive behavior therapy,** *assumes that thoughts (rationality) lead to emotions. The problem therefore is not the unpleasant emotions themselves but the irrational thoughts that lead to them.* Rational-emotive therapists believe that abnormal behavior often results from irrational "internal sentences" such as these (Ellis, 1987):

- I must perform certain tasks successfully.
- I must perform well at all times.
- I must have the approval of certain people at all times.
- Others must treat me fairly and with consideration.
- I must live under easy, gratifying conditions.

The word *must* makes these beliefs irrational. Rational-emotive therapists try to identify irrational beliefs (which people may never have verbalized) and then contradict them. They urge clients to substitute other more realistic internal sentences. Here is an excerpt from a rational-emotive therapy session with a 25-year-old physicist:

Client: The whole trouble is that I am really a phony. I am living under false pretenses. And the longer it goes on, the more people praise me and make a fuss over my accomplishments, the worse I feel.

Therapist: What do you mean you are a phony? I thought that you told me, during our last session, that your work has been examined at another laboratory and that some of the people there think your ideas are of revolutionary importance.

Client: But I have wasted so much time. I could be doing very much better. . . . Remember that book I told you I was writing . . . it's been three weeks now since I've spent any time on it. And this is simple stuff that I should be able to do with my left hand while I am writing a technical paper with my right. I have heard Bob Oppenheimer reel off stuff extemporaneously to a bunch of newspaper reporters that is twice as good as what I am mightily laboring on in this damned book!

Therapist: Perhaps so. And perhaps you're not quite as good—yet—as Oppenheimer or a few other outstanding people in your field. But the real point, it seems to me, is that . . . here you are, at just twenty-five, with a Ph.D. in a most difficult field, with an excellent job, much good work in process, and what well may be a fine professional paper and a good popular book also in progress. And just because you're not another Oppenheimer or Einstein quite yet, you're savagely berating yourself.

Client: Well, shouldn't I be doing much better than I am?

Therapist: No, why the devil should you? As far as I can see, you are not doing badly at all. But your major difficulty—the main cause of your present unhappiness—is your utterly perfectionistic criteria for judging your performance. (Ellis & Harper, 1961, pp. 99–100)

....

11. Of the therapies discussed so far, which ones are most concerned with people's emotions, and which one is least concerned?

Answer

11. Psychoanalysis and rational-emotive therapy are both concerned with people's emotions, though in different ways. Behavior therapy is more concerned with what people do than with how they feel about it.

....

Cognitive-Behavior Therapy

Many therapists combine important features of both behavior therapy and cognitive therapy to form cognitive-behavior therapy. Cognitive-behavior therapists *set explicit goals for changing people's behavior, but they place more emphasis than most behavior therapists do on changing people's interpretation of their situation.* For example, most of us become very upset if we see a video news report showing a fatal automobile accident. We would be much less upset if someone told us that the film was a special-effects simulation (Meichenbaum, 1995). Similarly, cognitive-behavior therapists try to help clients distinguish between serious problems and imagined or exaggerated problems. They help clients change their interpretations of past events, current concerns, and future possibilities. They then try to change clients' behavior in dealing with the concerns worth taking seriously. Cognitive-behavior therapy has become one of the most widespread forms of therapy in the United States.

A plane crash is very upsetting if we regard it as real, but not if we regard it as fictional, as in this scene from the television series *Lost*. The impact of any event depends not just on the event itself but also on its context and how we interpret it.

TOUCHSTONE/ABC/THE KOBAL COLLECTION

HUMANISTIC THERAPY

As we saw in chapter 14, humanistic psychologists believe that people can decide deliberately what kind of person to be. They also believe that we naturally strive to achieve our full potential. However, people sometimes come to dislike themselves because they feel criticism and rejection. They become distressed by the incongruence

(mismatch) between their perceptions of their real self and their ideal self. That incongruence becomes a problem, causing people to lose confidence in their ability to cope. According to humanistic therapists, once people are freed from the inhibiting influences of a rejecting society, they can solve their own problems.

The best-known version of humanistic therapy, pioneered by Carl Rogers, is person-centered therapy, also known as *nondirective* or *client-centered* therapy. *The therapist listens to the client with total acceptance and unconditional positive regard.* Most of the time, the therapist paraphrases and clarifies what the client has said, conveying the message, "I'm trying to understand your experience from your point of view." The therapist strives to be genuine, empathic, and caring, rarely offering any interpretation or advice. Here is an example (shortened from Rogers, 1951, pp. 46–47):

Client: I've never said this before to anyone. This is a terrible thing to say, but if I could just find some glorious cause that I could give my life for I would be happy. I guess maybe I haven't the guts—or the strength—to kill myself—and I just don't want to live.

Counselor: At the present time things look so black to you that you can't see much point in living.

Client: Yes. I wish people hated me, because then I could turn away from them and could blame them. But no, it is all in my hands. I either fight whatever it is that holds me in this terrible conflict, or retreat clear back to the security of my dream world where I could do things, have clever friends, be a pretty wonderful sort of person.

Counselor: It's really a tough struggle, digging into this like you are, and at times the shelter of your dream world looks more attractive and comfortable.

Client: My dream world or suicide.

Counselor: Your dream world or something more permanent than dreams.

Client: Yes. (A long pause. Complete change of voice.) So I don't see why I should waste your time. I'm not worth it. What do you think?

Counselor: It's up to you, Gil. It isn't wasting my time. I'd be glad to see you, whenever you come, but it's how you feel about it. If you want to come twice a week, once a week, it's up to you.

Client: You're not going to suggest that I come in oftener? You're not alarmed and think I ought to come in every day until I get out of this?

Counselor: I believe you are able to make your own decision. I'll see you whenever you want to come.

Client: I don't believe you are alarmed about . . . I see. I may be afraid of myself, but you aren't afraid for me.

The therapist provides an atmosphere in which the client freely explores feelings of guilt, anxiety, and hostility. By accepting the client's feelings, the therapist conveys the message, "You can make your own decisions. Now that you are more aware of certain problems, you can deal with them constructively yourself." Few therapists today rely purely on person-centered therapy, but most users of other therapy methods have adopted its emphasis on the close, caring, honest relationship between therapist and client (Hill & Nakayama, 2000).

12. Answer the following questions with reference to psychoanalysis, cognitive therapy, humanistic therapy, and behavior therapy.

    a. With which type of therapy is the therapist least likely to offer advice and interpretations of behavior?

    b. Which type focuses more on changing what people do than on exploring what they think?

    c. Which two types of therapy try to change what people think?

Answers

12. a. humanistic therapy; b. behavior therapy; c. psychoanalysis and cognitive therapy.

FAMILY SYSTEMS THERAPY

In family systems therapy, *the guiding assumptions are that most people's problems develop in a family setting and that the best way to deal with them is to improve family relationships and communication.* Family systems therapy is not an alternative to other forms of therapy. A family therapist uses behavior therapy, cognitive therapy, or other techniques. What distinguishes family therapists is that they prefer to talk with two or more members of a family together. Even when they talk with someone alone, they focus on how the individual fits into the family and how other family members react. Solving most problems requires changing the family dynamics as well as any individual's behavior (Clarkin & Carpenter, 1995; Rohrbaugh, Shoham, Spungen, & Steinglass, 1995).

For example, a young woman with anorexia nervosa may have excessively demanding parents or other family difficulties. Treating only this woman herself would be pointless. A therapist needs to enlist her parents' help to monitor her eating without blame, criticism, or dominance (Eisler et al., 2000).

For another example, a young widow came to a therapist because her daughter, then 5 years old, had cried every day since her father died 3 years ago. The therapist soon discovered that the girl's problem related to the family dynamics. She almost never cried at school and not always at home. She cried about many things and not just about the death of her father, whom she barely remembered anymore. The crying was a way to get the mother's attention. Her older brother was expected to be the strong "man of the house" although he was only 7 years old. Meanwhile, the mother was sad herself and overburdened with taking care of two children. She often cried alone, hiding it from her children. A family systems therapist helped each family member understand their role within the family and the needs of the others (Drell et al., 2009). In short, this kind of problem is a problem of the family, not of one individual within the family.

© Ed Quinn/CORBIS

A patient with anorexia nervosa (fourth from the right) responds best to treatment if her whole family participates.

TRENDS IN PSYCHOTHERAPY

Hundreds of types of therapy are available, including some that are quite different from the five discussed thus far (Table 15.4). About half of U.S. psychotherapists profess no strong allegiance to any single form of therapy. Instead, they practice eclectic therapy, meaning that they *use a combination of methods and approaches* (Wachtel, 2000). An eclectic therapist might use behavior therapy with one client and rational-emotive therapy with another or might start with one therapy and then shift to another if the first is ineffective. The therapist would use insights from several approaches, including person-centered therapy's emphasis on a caring relationship between therapist and client.

Because health insurance companies insist on limiting costs, psychotherapists have sought methods for quick and inexpensive help, such as brief therapy and group therapy. Self-help groups provide a no-cost alternative.

TABLE 15.4 Comparison of Five Types of Psychotherapy

Type of Psychotherapy	Theory of What Causes Psychological Disorders	Goal of Treatment	Therapeutic Methods	Role of Therapist
Psychoanalysis	Unconscious thoughts and motivations	To bring unconscious thoughts to consciousness to achieve insight	Free association, dream analysis, and other methods of probing the unconscious mind	To interpret associations
Cognitive therapies	Irrational beliefs and unrealistic goals	To establish realistic goals, expectations, and interpretations of a situation	Dialogue with the therapist	To help the client reexamine assumptions
Humanistic (person-centered) therapy	Reactions to a rejecting society; incongruence between self-concept and ideal self	To enable client to make personal decisions; to promote self-acceptance	Client-centered interviews	To focus the client's attention; to provide unconditional positive regard
Behavior therapy	Learned inappropriate maladaptive behaviors	To change behaviors	Positive reinforcement and other learning techniques	To develop, direct, and evaluate the behavior therapy program
Family system therapy	Distorted communication and confused roles within a family	To improve the life of each individual by improving functioning of the family	Counseling sessions with the whole family or with the individual talking about life in the family	To promote better family communication and understanding

Brief Therapy

Some types of psychotherapy require a major commitment of time and money. The cost of a session varies, but it is not cheap. A physician who sees many patients per hour—a dermatologist, for example—might charge a moderate amount per visit, but a therapist who sees just one person per hour charges more. A therapy that continues "as long as necessary" might drag on for years at mounting cost.

However, some clients improve much faster than others (Baldwin, Berkeljon, Atkins, Olsen, & Nielsen, 2009). About half of all people who enter psychotherapy show significant improvement within eight sessions (K. I. Howard, Kopta, Krause, & Orlinsky, 1986). As a result, many therapists place limits on the duration of therapy. At the start of brief therapy, or time-limited therapy, the therapist and client reach an agreement about what they can expect from each other and how long the treatment will last—such as once per week for 2 months. As the deadline approaches, both therapist and client are strongly motivated to reach a successful conclusion. (The same issue arose in the motivation chapter. Without deadlines, few people apply themselves diligently.)

Moreover, clients who know the deadline in advance do not feel deserted or rejected when the therapy ends. They may return for an occasional extra session months later, but for a time, they must get along without help. Most clients with mild to moderate problems respond well to brief therapy.

Unfortunately, many HMOs insist on extremely brief therapy, in some cases as few as three sessions. A very short deadline changes the treatment strategy. Instead of exploring all the client's problems, the therapist concentrates on encouraging strengths, so the client can deal with the problems as well as possible. Even very brief therapy is often successful but not always. Many people need more help than their insurance provides.

Group Therapy

The pioneers of psychotherapy saw their clients individually. Individual treatment has advantages, such as privacy. However, therapists today frequently treat clients in groups. Group therapy *is administered to several people at once.* It first became popular as a method of providing help to people who could not afford individual sessions. (Spreading the costs among five to ten people reduces the cost for each.) Soon therapists discovered other advantages to group therapy. Just meeting other people with similar problems is reassuring. People learn, "I am not so odd after all." Also, many clients seek help because of troubled or failed relationships. A group therapy session lets them examine how they relate to others, practice social skills, and receive feedback (Ballinger & Yalom, 1995).

Self-Help Groups

A self-help group, such as Alcoholics Anonymous, *operates much like group therapy, except without a therapist.* Each participant both gives and receives help. People who have experienced a problem can offer special insights to others with the same problem. They are especially well prepared when someone says, "You just don't understand." They reply, "Oh, yes, we do!" Self-

(a) Individual therapy offers complete privacy and the opportunity to pursue individual problems in depth. (b) In group therapy, participants can explore how they relate to other people.

tions consistently show improved mental and physical health over the next few months, especially those with much variation and flexibility in what they write (Campbell & Pennebaker, 2003; Pennebaker & Seagal, 1999). Apparently, writing about a difficult experience helps people make sense of it and eventually put it behind them. In many cases, writing about emotions prompts people to make decisions and change their way of life. Also, after people state their problems in writing, they tend to spend less time brooding about them (Sloan, Marx, Epstein, & Dobbs, 2008).

13. Brief therapy is a goal or policy for many therapists. Why would it be less important in self-help groups such as Alcoholics Anonymous?

Concept Check

Answer

13. One advantage of brief therapy is that it limits the expense. Expense is not an issue for self-help groups because they charge nothing other than a voluntary contribution toward rental of the facilities.

help groups have another advantage: The members can phone one another for help at almost any time. The service is supported by voluntary contributions, so each person pays only what he or she can afford.

Some self-help groups consist of current or former mental patients. The members enjoy talking to others who have gone through a similar experience, either in addition to or instead of seeing a therapist. The Mental Patients' Association in Canada consists of former patients who were frustrated with their treatment (or lack of treatment) in mental hospitals (Chamberlin, 1978). Members share experiences, provide support, and work together to defend the rights and welfare of mental patients. In some places, mental patients or former mental patients have organized self-help centers as an alternative to mental hospitals. These are small, homelike environments that may or may not include professional therapists. Instead of treating people as patients who need medical help, they expect people to take responsibility for their own actions. In many cases, these facilities produce results equal to or better than those of mental hospitals, and the clients certainly like them better (Greenfield, Stoneking, Humphreys, Sundby, & Bond, 2008).

The ultimate in self-help is to deal with your own problems without any therapist or group. In a series of studies, James Pennebaker and his colleagues have found that people with mild problems can do themselves an amazing amount of good just by organizing their thoughts about their emotional difficulties. Research participants are randomly assigned to two groups. One group writes about their intense and difficult emotional experiences for 15 minutes on 3 or more days. The other group spends the same time writing about unemotional events. The people writing about their emo-

What's the Evidence?

How Effective Is Psychotherapy?

Critical Thinking

The rise of HMOs and other insurance programs heightened interest in measuring the effectiveness of psychotherapy. Hans Eysenck (1952) pointed out that most psychological crises are temporary, and most people recover within a year or two with or without therapy. *Improvement without therapy* is called **spontaneous remission.** Psychotherapy is effective only if it does better than what we could expect by spontaneous remission.

In other chapters, most What's the Evidence? sections highlighted one or two studies. Here, the section highlights a general research approach. Hundreds of research studies similar to this have been conducted, although they vary in their details (Kazdin, 1995).

Hypothesis Psychologically troubled people who receive psychotherapy will show greater improvements in their condition than similar people who do not receive therapy.

Method For the results to be meaningful, participants must be randomly assigned to the therapy and nontherapy groups. Comparing people who sought therapy to those who did not seek it would be improper because the two groups might differ in the severity of their problems or their motivation for overcoming them. In the best studies, people who contact a clinic about receiving therapy are all given a preliminary examination and then randomly assigned to receive therapy at once or wait for therapy later. In some studies, people are randomly assigned to several different kinds of therapy

a

b

Because everyone's moods and behavior fluctuate over time, an apparent improvement between (a) the start of therapy and (b) the end is hard to interpret. How much of the improvement is due to the therapy and how much would have occurred without it?

groups as well as a waiting-list group. A few months later, the investigators compare the amount of improvement shown by people in each group. Because of ethical considerations, such research is usually limited to people with mild to moderate problems. It would be difficult to ask someone with a severe problem to wait several months for treatment.

How should the investigators measure the amount of improvement? They cannot rely on the therapists' judgments any more than someone could ask professors to evaluate the effectiveness of their own courses. For similar reasons, researchers cannot ask the clients, who might overstate their improvement. Therefore, researchers ask a "blind" observer to evaluate clients without knowing which ones received therapy. Or they ask each client to take a standardized personality test, such as the MMPI. None of these measures are perfect, of course, and they probably underestimate certain aspects of improvement.

Results Here, we do not focus on the results of any one study. Most experiments have included only a modest number of people, such as 10 or 20 receiving therapy and a similar number on the waiting list. To draw a conclusion, we pool the results from many similar experiments. Psychologists use a method called **meta-analysis**, *taking the results of many experiments, weighting each one in proportion to the number of participants, and determining the overall average effect.* According to one meta-analysis that pooled the results of 475 experiments, the average person in therapy shows greater improvement than 80% of similarly troubled people who do not receive therapy (M. L. Smith, Glass, & Miller, 1980). Figure 15.6 illustrates this effect.

Interpretation The results say that psychotherapy usually produces benefits but not always. However, even a collection of 475 studies has limitations, and critics have noted many ways in which individual studies either overstate or understate the effectiveness of psychotherapy (Staines & Cleland, 2007). One unavoidable limitation is that most re-search has dealt with mild disorders. Most research has also used brief treatments because it is hard to keep anyone on a waiting list for long. In addition, most of the research has examined behavior therapy or cognitive therapy because these methods use consistent methods and set specific goals. It is more difficult to evaluate psychoanalysis or person-centered therapy.

One could easily complain that investigators invested a great deal of effort for not much payoff. After 475 experiments, we can confidently say that therapy is usually better than no therapy for mild psychological disorders. This conclusion is like saying that medicine is usually better than no medicine, or education is usually better than no education. However, even if the conclusion seems unimpressive, it was necessary to satisfy HMOs and other organizations that wanted evidence for therapy's effectiveness. The research

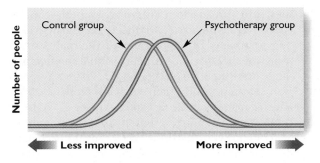

FIGURE 15.6 According to one review of 475 studies, the average person receiving psychotherapy shows more improvement than do 80% of similar, randomly assigned people who are not in therapy. This comparison lumps together all kinds of therapy and all kinds of disorders. (Smith, Mary Lee, Glass, Gene V., and Miller, Thomas I.: *The Benefits of Psychotherapy*, p. 88, Figure 1. © 1980 The Johns Hopkins University Press. Reprinted by permission of The Johns Hopkins University Press.)

also paved the way for more detailed studies about how therapy produces its benefits and under what circumstances it is most effective.

14. Although well-designed experiments on psychotherapy use a blind observer to rate clients' mental health, double-blind studies are difficult or impossible. Why?

Answer

14. A double-blind design requires that neither the subjects nor the observers know which subjects received the experimental treatment and which ones were in the control group. It is not possible to prevent subjects from knowing whether they have received psychotherapy. (It is, however, possible to use a treatment believed to be ineffective and call it psychotherapy.)

COMPARING THERAPIES AND THERAPISTS

Next, we would like to know which kinds of therapy are most effective and whether different therapies are best for different disorders. The practical problem for researchers is that therapists use hundreds of types of treatment for hundreds of psychological disorders. To test the effect of each treatment on each disorder would require tens of thousands of experiments, not counting replications. Furthermore, many clients have several problems, not just one, and many therapists use an eclectic trial-and-error approach instead of a single well-defined therapy (Goldfried & Wolfe, 1996).

Research has proceeded despite these difficulties, and it leads to a stunningly simple conclusion: For a wide variety of disorders, mostly relating to anxiety or depression, all the mainstream types of therapy appear nearly equal in effectiveness (Benish, Imel, & Wampold, 2008; Cuijpers, van Straten, Andersson, & van Oppen, 2008; Leichsenring & Leibing, 2003; Lipsey & Wilson, 1993; Stiles, Shapiro, & Elliott, 1986; Wampold et al., 1997). Even the differences that do occur are hard to interpret. For example, in some studies, one kind of treatment produced better immediate benefits and another produced greater long-term benefits, so the apparent advantage depended on the time of measurement (Sandell et al., 1999).

However, a few kinds of treatment produce more harm than good. For example, prolonged discussions of a stressful experience shortly after the event are more likely to cause than prevent posttraumatic stress disorder. "Scared straight" interventions tend to increase, not decrease, criminal behavior. Rebirthing (reenacting the moment of birth) has led to death or serious injury in several cases. Recovered memory therapies have led to false accusations that damaged family relationships. Group therapy for aggressive teenagers often backfires by helping them meet others with similar dispositions. The list goes on. The point is that we need to rely on good research to separate good treatments from neutral or harmful ones (Lilienfeld, 2007; Nicholson, Foote, & Gigerick, 2009). Clinical psychologists emphasize empirically supported therapies to distinguish them from fads, untested methods, and treatments likely to be ineffective or worse.

Similarities Among Psychotherapeutic Methods

What should we conclude from the observation that several forms of psychotherapy seem to be similar in their effectiveness? Evidently, different therapeutic methods have much in common despite the differences in their assumptions, methods, and goals. One feature is that all rely on a "therapeutic alliance"—a relationship between therapist and client characterized by acceptance, caring, respect, and attention. The relationship provides social support that helps clients deal with their problems and acquire social skills that they can apply to other relationships.

Second, in nearly all forms of therapy, at least in North America and Europe, clients talk openly and honestly about their beliefs and emotions, relationships with family members, and other issues that people ordinarily keep secret. They examine aspects of themselves that they usually take for granted. Third, the mere fact of entering therapy improves clients' morale. The therapist conveys the message "you are going to get better." Clients gain confidence. The expectation of improvement can lead to improvement.

Finally, every form of therapy requires clients to commit themselves to changes in their lifestyle. Simply by coming to the therapy session, they reaffirm their commitment to feel less depressed, overcome their fears, or conquer some bad habit. They make an effort so that they can report progress when they come for the next session. Improvement probably depends more on what clients do between sessions than on procedures in the sessions themselves. Table 15.5 highlights some similarities and differences among four major types of therapy.

15. Name four ways in which nearly all forms of psychotherapy are similar.

Table 15.5 Similarities and Differences Among Four Types of Psychotherapy

Procedure	Psychoanalysis	Behavior Therapy	Cognitive Therapy	Person-Centered Therapy
Therapeutic alliance	√	√	√	√
Discuss problems openly	√	√	√	√
Expect improvement	√	√	√	√
Commit to make changes	√	√	√	√
Probe unconscious	√			
Specific goals		√	√	
Emphasize new learning		√		
Reinterpret situation			√	
Unconditional positive regard				√
Change thinking	√		√	

Answer

15. Nearly all forms of psychotherapy include a "therapeutic alliance" (a close relationship between client and therapist), an effort to understand oneself and discuss personal difficulties openly, an expectation of improvement, and a commitment to make changes in one's life.

Comparisons Among Therapists

Researchers also have compared the effectiveness of therapists with different kinds of training. The U.S. magazine *Consumer Reports* (1995) surveyed its readers about their mental health and their contact with psychotherapy. Of the thousands who said they had sought help for a mental health problem within the previous 3 years, most said they were satisfied with the treatment and thought it had helped them. For measuring the effectiveness of psychotherapy, this study has some obvious problems: the lack of a random sample, the lack of a control group, and reliance on clients to evaluate their own improvement (Jacobson & Christensen, 1996). Nevertheless, the results indicated that people reported about equal satisfaction and benefits from talking with a psychiatrist, a psychologist, or a social worker (Seligman, 1995). They reported somewhat less satisfaction from consulting a marriage counselor or a general practice physician (Figure 15.7). A later survey of psychotherapy clients in Germany yielded similar results (Hartmann & Zepf, 2003).

The same general pattern emerged in a variety of other studies with different research methods: The type of therapist is

not critical to the amount of improvement. More experienced therapists tend to be slightly more accurate in diagnosing disorders (Spengler et al., 2009) but not necessarily more effective in their treatments (Christensen & Jacobson, 1994; Dawes, 1994).

These results do not mean that all therapists are equally good. Within any group of therapists—highly experience behavior therapists, inexperienced psychiatrists, or whatever—some individuals are much more effective than others. The differences *within* each group are large relative to the differences between groups (Staines,

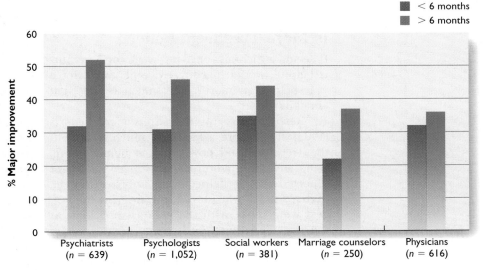

FIGURE 15.7 The percentage of *Consumer Reports* respondents who said they experienced great improvement in the problem that led them to treatment. (From "The Effectiveness of Psychotherapy: The Consumer Reports Study" by M. E. P. Seligman, *American Psychologist*, 1995, *50*, 965–974. Copyright © 1995 by the American Psychological Association. Reprinted by permission.)

Just talking to a sympathetic listener, even someone without training, is helpful for many people with mild to moderate problems.

2008). Furthermore, how much some client is likely to improve depends at least as much on the client as it does on the type of therapy or experience of the therapist (Bohart, 2000). For example, younger clients usually respond better than older ones (Payne & Marcus, 2008).

Is the conclusion, then, that if you are psychologically troubled, you may as well talk to your next-door neighbor as to a psychotherapist? No, for several reasons:

- The research comparing nonprofessionals to experienced therapists has examined clients with mild problems. We cannot assume that the same results would hold for more disabling conditions.
- Few of us know someone with enough patience to listen to hours of personal ramblings.
- Conversation with a professional psychotherapist is confidential (except under special circumstances, such as if you tell your therapist you are planning to kill someone). You can't count on a friend to keep your secrets.
- A well-trained psychotherapist can recognize symptoms of a brain tumor or other medical disorder and refer you to an appropriate medical specialist.

Is More Treatment Better?

If seeing a therapist once per week for 3 months is helpful, would meeting twice per week for a year help even more? How much is the right amount?

Respondents in the *Consumer Reports* (1995) study were asked how much treatment they received and how much it helped them. Generally, those who received longer treatment reported that it helped them more. However, perhaps those who stayed in treatment the longest were those with the greatest problems at the start and therefore had the greatest room for improvement.

A better research design examines a single group of clients repeatedly as all of them progress through a given number of therapy sessions. Figure 15.8 shows the results of one such study. According to both the researchers and the clients

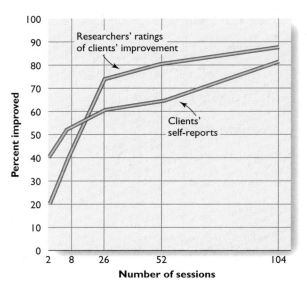

FIGURE 15.8 The relationship of the number of psychotherapy sessions to the percentage of clients who improved. (From "The Dose-Effect Relationship in Psychotherapy" by K. I. Howard et al., *American Psychologist*, 1986, *41*, 159–164. Copyright © 1986 by the American Psychological Association. Reprinted by permission of the author.)

themselves, progress was fast at first and then progressively slower (K. I. Howard et al., 1986). Later research has confirmed this pattern for most clients (Stulz, Lutz, Leach, Lucock, & Barkham, 2007). Evidently, brief treatment accomplishes much, but prolonged treatment accomplishes more.

A 5-year study conducted at Fort Bragg, North Carolina, examined the effects of extensive treatment. A government-supported program provided free clinical services for every teenager or child who needed psychological help and who had a parent in the military. Each client had a case manager who determined what treatment plan was best, made sure the client received every necessary type of help, and coordinated all the service providers to make sure that each one knew what the others were doing. The goal was to demonstrate that a well-planned, integrated program would be highly effective and perhaps save money by avoiding a wasteful overlap of services. Results were compared to those in a similar community that offered the usual less coordinated services. The result? The integrated program at Fort Bragg was no more beneficial, just more expensive (Bickman, 1996). We should not draw too strong a conclusion from this study or from any other single study. Still, most people had expected the integrated program to show clear advantages, and the results seem to imply that more therapy is not always better.

Advice for Potential Clients

At some point, you or someone close to you may be interested in seeing a psychotherapist. If so, here are some points to remember:

- Consulting a therapist does not mean that something is wrong with you. Many people simply need to talk with someone during a crisis.
- If you live in the United States, you can look up the telephone number for the Mental Health Association. Call and ask for a recommendation. You can specify how much you can pay, what kind of problem you have, and even what kind of therapist you prefer.

- Effective therapy depends on a good relationship between client and therapist. If you feel more comfortable talking with someone from your own culture, ethnic group, or religious background, look for such a therapist (La Roche & Christopher, 2008; Worthington, Kurusu, McCullough, & Sandage, 1996).
- Be skeptical of any therapist who seems overconfident. Clinical experience does not give anyone quick access to your private thoughts.
- Expect at least some improvement within 6 to 8 weeks. If you do not seem to be making progress, ask your therapist why. If you do not receive a convincing answer, consider seeing someone else.

module  15.2

In Closing

Trying to Understand Therapy

As you have seen, therapists differ enormously in their assumptions and methods. A psychoanalyst hopes to uncover your unconscious thoughts, memories, and motives on the assumption that knowing about them will help solve your problems. A cognitive or behavior therapist is more interested in changing your current thoughts and actions than in dwelling on the past. A person-centered therapist provides a warm, supportive setting, in which you can set your own goals and decide for yourself how to achieve them. Despite these major differences, all the common forms of therapy are almost equally effective. It is as if researchers found that when you are sick, one kind of medicine is as good as another.

Psychotherapy began with psychiatry, a branch of medicine, and we still treat it as analogous to medicine. That is, a client comes with a disorder, the therapist provides a treatment, and health insurance pays the bills. In some ways, this analogy fails, and therapy is more like education. A client is like a student, and the therapist is like an instructor who tries to provide direction, but the amount of progress depends on the client's own efforts. This is not to say that the therapist is irrelevant. However, the variation between one client and another is greater than the typical difference between one treatment and another.

SUMMARY

- *Psychoanalysis.* Psychoanalysts try to uncover the unconscious reasons behind self-defeating behaviors. To bring the unconscious to consciousness, they rely on free association, dream analysis, and transference. (page 547)
- *Behavior therapy.* Behavior therapists set specific goals for changing a client's behavior and use learning techniques to help a client achieve those goals. (page 548)
- *Cognitive therapies.* Cognitive therapists try to get clients to give up their irrational beliefs and unrealistic goals and to replace defeatist thinking with more favorable views of them-

selves and the world. Many therapists combine features of behavior therapy and cognitive therapy, attempting to change people's behaviors by altering how they interpret the situation. (page 550)
- *Humanistic therapy.* Humanistic therapists, including person-centered therapists, assume that people who accept themselves as they are can solve their own problems. Person-centered therapists listen with unconditional positive regard and seldom offer interpretations or advice. (page 551)

- *Family systems therapy.* In many cases, an individual's problem is part of an overall disorder of family communications and expectations. Family systems therapists try to work with a whole family. (page 552)
- *Brief therapy.* Many therapists set a time limit for treatment. Brief therapy is appropriate in many cases but not all. (page 553)
- *Group therapies and self-help groups.* Psychotherapy is sometimes provided to people in groups, often composed of individuals with similar problems. Self-help groups provide sessions similar to group therapy but without a therapist. (page 553)

- *Effectiveness of psychotherapy.* The average troubled person in therapy improves more than at least 80% of the troubled people not in therapy. In general, all mainstream therapies appear about equally effective, although a few "fad" therapies are useless or harmful. Therapists today emphasize empirically supported therapies. (page 554)
- *Similarities among therapies.* A wide variety of therapies share certain features: All rely on a caring relationship between therapist and client. All promote self-understanding. All improve clients' morale. And all require a commitment by clients to try to make changes in their lives. (page 556)

KEY TERMS

behavior therapy (page 548)

brief therapy (page 553)

catharsis (page 548)

cognitive therapy (page 550)

cognitive-behavior therapy (page 551)

eclectic therapy (page 552)

empirically supported treatments (page 546)

family systems therapy (page 552)

free association (page 548)

group therapy (page 553)

incongruence (page 551)

interpretation (page 548)

meta-analysis (page 555)

person-centered therapy (page 551)

psychoanalysis (page 547)

psychodynamic therapies (page 547)

psychotherapy (page 546)

rational-emotive behavior therapy (page 550)

self-help group (page 553)

spontaneous remission (page 554)

transference (page 548)

• How should society deal with psychological disorders?

Some nearsighted people lost in the woods were trying to find their way home. One of the few who wore glasses said, "I think I know the way. Follow me." The others burst into laughter. "That's ridiculous," said one. "How could anybody who needs glasses be our leader?"

In 1972 the Democratic Party nominated Senator Thomas Eagleton for vice president of the United States. Shortly after his nomination, he revealed that he had once received psychiatric treatment for depression. He was ridiculed mercilessly: "How could anybody who needed a psychiatrist be our leader?"

Although many people today receive psychiatric care, it still carries a stigma, and most people who have troubles decline to seek help from a psychologist or psychiatrist (Wang et al., 2005). All of us need to consider our reactions toward the idea of therapeutic help. We also need to deal with other issues. Who, if anyone, should receive psychiatric treatment involuntarily? Should mental patients have the right to refuse treatment? Under what circumstances, if any, should a criminal defendant be acquitted because of "insanity"? Can society as a whole take steps to prevent psychological disorders?

DEINSTITUTIONALIZATION

In the 1800s and early 1900s, growing numbers of people with severe psychological disturbances were confined in large mental hospitals supported by the government (Torrey & Miller, 2001). Most of these hospitals were understaffed and overcrowded. Residents included not only mental patients but also elderly people with Alzheimer's disease and others who could not care for themselves (Leff, 2002). Hospital attendants cooked all the food, washed the laundry, and did other chores without teaching residents the skills they would need if they were ever to leave. (Many never did.) Some hospitals were better than others, but most were grim places.

Since the 1950s, more and more hospitals moved toward deinstitutionalization, *the removal of patients from mental hospitals,* to give them the least restrictive care possible—an idea that many people had been advocating for 100 years or more (Tuntiya, 2007). The hope was that patients would live at home, free to live as normal a life as possible, while receiving outpatient care at community mental health centers, which are usually cheaper and more effective than large mental hospitals (Fenton, Hoch, Herrell, Mosher, & Dixon, 2002; Fenton, Mosher,

Herrell, & Blyler, 1998). Mental hospitals remain today, but they have fewer residents, who generally stay for shorter times than in the past. As a result of deinstitutionalization policies, as well as the advent of antidepressant and antipsychotic medications, the number of long-term mental patients declined substantially. For example, England and Wales had 130 psychiatric hospitals in 1975 but only 12 in 2000 (Leff, 2002). The United States had almost 200,000 people in mental hospitals in 1967 and fewer than 40,000 in 2007 (Scott, Lakin, & Larson, 2008).

But what happened to people after release from the mental hospitals? Some did get treatment at community mental health centers, as intended, but many did not. Some ended in nursing homes or prisons. Many became homeless, especially those who had lost contact with their relatives and those with substance-abuse problems (Odell & Commander, 2000). Some became almost completely isolated from society—so isolated that when they died, their bodies were not found until a few days later (Nilsson & Lögdberg, 2008). Deinstitutionalization was and is a good idea in principle but only if implemented well, including good opportunities for community health care.

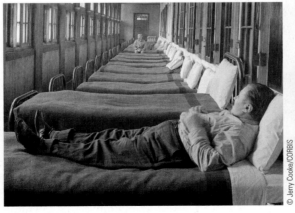

Most mental hospitals of the mid-1900s were unpleasant warehouses that provided minimal care.

Deinstitutionalization moved people out of mental hospitals, but many received little or no treatment after their release.

16. Why did deinstitutionalization seem like a good idea? For what reason has it often not worked well?

Answer

16. Deinstitutionalization appears to be a good idea because treatment in a community mental health center is more effective and less costly than treatment in a mental hospital. However, many people receive inadequate treatment after their release from the mental hospitals.

INVOLUNTARY COMMITMENT AND TREATMENT OF POTENTIALLY DANGEROUS PATIENTS

Suppose a family moves into the house next to yours, and their adult son, who lives at home, is a current or former mental patient. Are you in danger? If so, how much? The most extensive study of this question was conducted in Sweden, where researchers had access to the whole country's medical and criminal records. They found that 6.6% of people with severe mental illnesses committed violent crimes compared to 1.8% of everyone else. Another way of putting it is that people with severe mental illnesses, who constituted about 1.4% of the population, committed about 5% of the violent crimes (Fazel & Grann, 2006). However, not all mental patients are the same. As illustrated in Figure 15.9, people with mental illness who also abuse alcohol or other substances have a significantly increased probability of violent crimes (Elbogen & Johnson, 2009). Furthermore, mental patients who have already committed other crimes have a greatly increased probability of additional crimes (Baillargeon, Binswanger, Penn, Williams, & Murray, 2009). Mental patients who do not have a history of substance abuse or previous criminal activity are no more dangerous than anyone else, and those who are socially withdrawn have an especially low probability of being dangerous (Swanson et al., 2006).

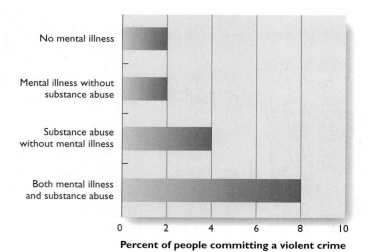

FIGURE 15.9 People with mental illness have an 8% chance of committing a violent crime within 2 to 3 years if they are also substance abusers. Those who are not substance abusers have about a 2% probability, similar to the rest of the population. (Based on data from Elbogen, E. B., & Johnson, S. C., 2009. The intricate link between violence and mental disorder. *Archives of General Psychiatry, 66,* 152–161.)

Suppose someone with a history of mental illness does appear to be dangerous and refuses to be treated. Should it be possible to require someone to accept treatment and perhaps confine that person to a mental hospital? In the United States, the law varies from state to state, but typically, a judge can order a mental patient who is dangerous to be involuntarily confined to a mental hospital. However, that decision is difficult. How extensive a history of offenses should be necessary, and under what circumstances could the person be released from the hospital? The decision to confine an unwilling person in a mental hospital is not generally made for that person's benefit but for what is believed to be the benefit of society (Dallaire, McCubbin, Morin, & Cohen, 2000).

Most states also permit involuntary commitment to a mental hospital for nondangerous patients who have become incompetent to make their own decisions or take care of their daily needs. That judgment is also difficult. Imagine someone who mutters incoherently, cannot keep a job, does not take care of personal hygiene, and harasses the neighbors. Is that person sufficiently incompetent to justify an involuntary commitment? If not, what would constitute incompetence? The problem is that, on the one hand, some seriously disordered people fail to recognize that they have a problem. On the other hand, some families have been known to commit annoying relatives to mental hospitals just to get them out of the way, and some psychiatrists have given strong medications to people with minor problems, doing more harm than good.

THE DUTY TO PROTECT

Suppose someone tells his psychotherapist that he plans to kill a woman who has refused his attentions. Months later, the client really does kill her. Should her family be able to sue the therapist and collect damages?

In the 1976 *Tarasoff* case, a California court ruled that *a therapist who has reason to believe that a client is dangerous to someone must warn the endangered person or take other steps to prevent harm.* Since then, the rule has become widely accepted in the United States and Canada, although its application remains unclear in many cases (Quattrocchi & Schopp, 2005). Therapists objected to this ruling for two reasons: First, it conflicts with the principle that everything said during a psychotherapy session is confidential. Second, it is difficult to know which clients are really dangerous. Many people (and not only those in therapy) have at some point said, "I'm so angry I could kill," without any actual intention to carry out that threat.

After decades of experience with the *Tarasoff* ruling, it is clear that the loss of confidentiality has not been disastrous to therapy. Therapists routinely explain to a new client that communications in therapy are confidential, except for statements that indicate danger to others. However, to decrease the risk of being sued, therapists now frequently decline to take potentially violent people as clients and frequently recommend involuntary commitment, even when someone's potential for danger is not clear (Buckner & Firestone, 2000).

THE INSANITY DEFENSE

Suppose someone slips a potent drug into your drink, and it causes you to hallucinate wildly. You see what looks like a hideous giant cockroach, and you kill it. Later, you discover it was not a cockroach but a person. Should you be convicted of murder? Of course not. You had no idea what you were doing. Now suppose your own brain chemistry did the same thing to you, causing you the same hallucination. You kill what you think is a giant cockroach, but it is actually a human being. Should you be convicted of murder?

The tradition since Roman times has been that you would be "not guilty by reason of insanity." You had no intention to do harm, and you did not know what you were doing. You should go to a mental hospital, not a prison. Most people agree with that principle in extreme cases. The problem is where to draw the line. Under what conditions is someone legally insane? *Insanity* is a legal term, not a psychological or medical term, and its definition depends on politics more than science.

One point of agreement is that the crime itself, no matter how atrocious, does not demonstrate insanity. Jeffrey Dahmer, arrested in 1991 for murdering and cannibalizing several men, was ruled sane and sentenced to prison. Theodore Kaczynski, arrested for mailing bombs for more than two decades, refused to plead insanity and probably would not have been ruled insane anyway. Bizarre crimes do not, in themselves, demonstrate insanity. Each of these murderers knew what he was doing and tried to avoid capture. Trying to avoid capture is generally taken as evidence that the person *did* understand what he or she was doing.

Lawyers, physicians, and psychologists have long struggled to establish a clear definition of insanity. The most famous definition, the M'Naghten rule, written in Great Britain in 1843, states:

> To establish a defense on the ground of insanity, it must be clearly proved that, at the time of the committing of the act, the party accused was laboring under such a defect of reason, from disease of the mind, as not to know the

nature and quality of the act he was doing; or if he did know it, that he did not know he was doing what was wrong. (Shapiro, 1985)

In other words, *to be regarded as insane under the M'Naghten rule, people must be so disordered that they do not understand what they are doing.* The rule in U.S. federal courts is similar: Insanity applies if "the defendant, as a result of severe mental disease or defect, was unable to appreciate the nature and quality or wrongfulness of his acts" (Knoll & Resnick, 2008). Regardless of exactly how the law is worded, an insanity verdict requires a difficult judgment about the defendant's state of mind at the time of the act. To help make that judgment, psychologists and psychiatrists are called as expert witnesses. If all the experts agree the defendant is insane, the prosecution ordinarily accepts the insanity plea. If the experts agree the defendant is not insane, the defense abandons the plea. The insanity cases that come to a jury trial are the difficult ones in which the experts disagree. In the United States, fewer than 1% of accused felons plead insanity, and of those, fewer than 25% are found not guilty (Knoll & Resnick, 2008). However, those cases generally receive much media attention, and because people hear about them, they assume such cases are common. (Remember the availability heuristic from chapter 8.) The insanity defense is equally rare in other countries.

Another common misconception is that defendants found not guilty by reason of insanity simply go free, where they are apt to commit further attacks. People found not guilty by reason of insanity are almost always committed to a mental hospital, and they usually stay at least as long in the hospital as they would have in prison (Silver, 1995). When they are released, it is usually a "conditional release" that requires them to follow certain rules, such as continuing to take their medicine (Vitacco et al., 2008).

a   b

Theodore Kaczynski (a), who once had a promising career as a mathematician, became (b) a recluse who mailed bombs that killed 3 and injured 23 others. However, committing bizarre acts of violence does not qualify someone as legally insane.

For more information about cases using the insanity defense, as well as other legal cases relevant to psychology, visit J. F. Hooper's Psychiatry & The Law website. Find a current link to this site at **www.cengage.com/psychology/kalat.**

17. Someone who has been involuntarily committed to a mental hospital escapes and commits a murder. Will this person be judged not guilty by reason of insanity?

Answer

17. Not necessarily. The court must also find that the psychological disorder meets the legal definition of insanity, which usually includes the idea that the disorder prevented the person from understanding what he or she was doing.

PREVENTING MENTAL ILLNESS

Which would you prefer, a treatment that relieves you of a disorder or a procedure that prevents you from developing one at all? Traditionally, psychologists and psychiatrists have focused on treatment, but prevention would be even better. **Prevention** is *avoiding a disorder from the start.* For example, in one study of "pessimistic" college students and another study with children of depressed parents, half of the participants received cognitive therapy and half did not. In both studies, fewer people in the therapy group became depressed over the next 2 or 3 years (Clarke et al., 2001; Seligman, Schulman, DeRubeis, & Hollon, 1999).

Let's distinguish prevention from intervention and maintenance. **Intervention** is *identifying a disorder in its early stages and relieving it,* and **maintenance** is *taking steps to keep it from becoming more serious.* For an example of maintenance, therapists identify people showing early signs of schizophrenia and try to block further deterioration (McGorry et al., 2002).

Just as our society puts fluoride into drinking water to prevent tooth decay and immunizes people against contagious diseases, it can take action to prevent certain types of psychological disorders (Albee, 1986; Wandersman & Florin, 2003). Here are some examples:

- **Early screening.** Most people do not seek a therapist's help until they have struggled with a problem on their own for years. Early detection increases the probability of a good outcome.
- **Ban toxins.** The sale of lead-based paint has been banned because children who eat flakes of it sustain brain damage. Many other toxins in the air and water have yet to be controlled.

- **Educate pregnant women about prenatal care.** The use of alcohol or other drugs during pregnancy damages the brain of a fetus, and bacterial and viral infections during pregnancy can impair fetal brain development.
- **Outlaw smoking in public places and educate people about the risks of smoking.** Improvements in physical health improve psychological well-being, too.
- **Help people get jobs.** People who lose their jobs lose self-esteem and increase their risk of depression and substance abuse.
- **Provide child care.** Improved, affordable day-care services relieve stress for both parents and children.
- **Improve educational opportunities.** Programs that get young people interested in their schoolwork help to decrease juvenile delinquency.

These techniques are aimed at prevention for the entire community. **Community psychologists,** who *focus on the needs of large groups rather than those of individuals,* have been among the leaders in seeking prevention. Unfortunately, prevention is often more difficult than it might seem. Many attempts to prevent PTSD by counseling tragedy victims and urging them to discuss their feelings have increased the rate of PTSD (Bootzin & Bailey, 2005). Of programs intended to prevent women from developing anorexia or bulimia nervosa, some have been effective, others ineffective, and some counterproductive (Mann et al., 1997; Stice & Shaw, 2004; C. B. Taylor et al., 2006). Attempts have been made to combat suicide by using television programs about the pain that suicide causes to friends and relatives. These programs have never decreased the suicide rate; in fact, the research controversy is about how much the programs *increased* the suicide rate (Joiner, 1999). One study compared suicidal patients receiving brief crisis intervention to others receiving more prolonged therapy. Those receiving more help had a *higher* rate of suicide (Moller, 1992). The general point is that we cannot take for granted that a procedure intended to prevent some disorder will succeed. Sometimes, talking about a behavior problem makes it more likely.

18. Why is it important to do careful research before initiating a new program to prevent a psychological disorder?

Answer

18. Some programs intended for prevention have been ineffective or counterproductive. It is important to test the effectiveness of a program before setting it up on a large scale.

In Closing

The Science and Politics of Mental Illness

Suppose you are a storekeeper. Someone dressed as Batman stands outside your store every day shouting gibberish at anyone who comes by. Your once-thriving business draws fewer and fewer customers each day. The disturbing man outside does not seem to be breaking any laws. He is not obviously dangerous, just annoying, and he wants nothing to do with psychologists or psychiatrists. Should he nevertheless be forced to accept treatment for his odd behavior? If not, what happens to your rights as a storekeeper?

Similarly, the insanity defense and all the other issues in this module are complicated questions that require political decisions by society as a whole, not just the opinions of psychologists or psychiatrists. Regardless of what career you enter, you will be a voter and potential juror, and you will have a voice in deciding these issues. The decisions deserve serious, informed consideration.

SUMMARY

* *Deinstitutionalization.* Today, few patients stay long in mental hospitals. However, many patients released from mental hospitals do not receive adequate alternative care. (page 561)
* *Involuntary commitment.* Laws on involuntary commitment to mental hospitals vary, but typically, people can be committed if they are judged to be dangerous or incompetent. It is difficult to frame laws that ensure treatment for those who need it while also protecting the rights of those who have good reasons for refusing it. (page 562)
* *Duty to warn.* The courts have ruled that a therapist who is convinced that a client is dangerous should warn the endangered person. (page 562)
* *The insanity defense.* Some defendants accused of a crime are acquitted for reasons of insanity, which is a legal rather than a medical or psychological concept. (page 563)
* *Prevention of psychological disorders.* Psychologists and psychiatrists are increasingly concerned about preventing psychological disorders. Many preventive measures require the cooperation of society as a whole. Methods of prevention based on good intentions do not always succeed. (page 564)

KEY TERMS

community psychologist (page 564)

deinstitutionalization (page 561)

intervention (page 564)

maintenance (page 564)

M'Naghten rule (page 563)

prevention (page 564)

Tarasoff (page 562)

Why Does This Matter to Me?

SOCIAL RESPONSIBILITY AND PSYCHOLOGY

Many environmental and societal problems are caused by human behavior. Psychologists can help steer the course of our future toward more socially responsible and sustainable outcomes. Students of today need to be ever mindful of the link between human behavior and its impact on the environment and our communities.

"Abnormality, Therapy, and Social Issues" and Social Responsibility: A Step Further

Many people are less productive than they might be because of mild anxieties and discouragement. How could we improve the mental health of people who do not have diagnosable disorders? Might greater contact with the natural environment help?

Nature and Health

Some therapists do believe that contact with the natural environment can help clients overcome small as well as large difficulties. For more information on wilderness therapy, visit www.cengage.com/psychology/kalat where you can find a list of websites that offer outdoor behavioral health care programs to research.

Join the iChapters Plant a Tree Drive!

To show its support of the environmental movement, iChapters is planting a tree on behalf of each fan of the iChapters Facebook Page and for every 10 questions answered correctly in our quiz.
http://www.ichapters.com/plantatree/

Exploration and Study

SUGGESTIONS FOR FURTHER EXPLORATION

In addition to the study materials provided at the end of each module, you may supplement your review of this chapter with the following book and website suggestions or by using one or more of the book's electronic resources, which include its companion website, interactive Cengage Learning eBook, and CengageNOW. Brief descriptions of these resources follow. For more information, visit **www.cengage.com/psychology/kalat**.

ADDITIONAL RESOURCES

The book's companion website, accessible from **www.cengage.com/psychology/kalat**, provides a wide range of study resources such as an interactive glossary, flashcards, tutorial quizzes, updated web links, and Try It Yourself activities.

    CengageNOW with Critical Thinking Videos is an easy-to-use resource that helps you study in less time to get the grade you want. An online study system, CengageNOW gives you the option of taking a diagnostic pretest for each chapter. The system uses the results of each pretest to create personalized

chapter study plans for you. The Personalized Study Plans

- Help you save study time by identifying areas on which you should concentrate and give you one-click access to corresponding pages of the interactive Cengage Learning eBook;
- Provide interactive exercises and study tools to help you fully understand chapter concepts; and
- Include a posttest for you to take to confirm that you are ready to move on to the next chapter.

Find critical thinking videos like this one in your CengageNOW product, which offer an opportunity for you to learn more about psychological research on different topics.

Anti-social Personality Disroder: George

Books

Lilienfeld, S. O., Lynn, S. J., & Lohr, J. M. (Eds.). (2003). *Science and pseudoscience in clinical psychology.* New York: Guilford Press. Most clinical psychologists today use empirically supported treatments. This book surveys some of the faddish quack treatments that are not based on evidence.

Porter, R., & Wright, D. (Eds.). (2003). *The confinement of the insane.* Cambridge, England: Cambridge University Press. A review of mental hospitals and the treatment of people with disorders from 1800 through the middle of the 20th century.

Seligman, M. E. P. (1993). *What you can change . . . and what you can't.* New York: Fawcett Columbine. Description of both the possibilities and the limitations of psychotherapy.

Websites

Links to the websites described below are kept current and can be found at **www.cengage.com/psychology/kalat**.

Landmark Cases in Forensic Psychiatry

In his excellent Forensic Psychiatry Resource page, James Hooper offers brief summaries of criminal and civil cases in which mental disorders became an issue.

© Barbara Stitzer / PhotoEdit

16 chapter

Specific Disorders and Treatments

Consider This: Do you ever wonder what it would feel like to be someone else? Just for the experience, would you be willing to "get inside the head" of someone with a mental illness, to feel what it would be like to have severe anxieties, depression, alcohol abuse, schizophrenia, or other disorders? Perhaps you have such a condition already, at least to a mild degree. But would you be willing to experience—temporarily—what it is like to have other or more severe disorders? It would not be pleasant. People with severe depression say you can't even imagine how bad it feels if you haven't been through it yourself.

In the first three modules of this chapter, we explore three of the most commonly diagnosed psychological disorders: anxiety disorders, substance abuse, and mood disorders. The final module is about schizophrenia and autism, which are less common but often disabling.

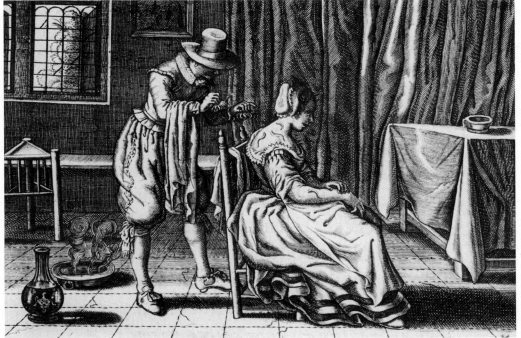

© Hulton Deutch Collection/Getty Images

In the early days of medicine, physicians provided the same treatments for all diseases (e.g., applying leeches to draw blood, as shown). Progress depended on differentiating particular disorders and developing individual treatments for each. Can we also find specific treatments for specific psychological disorders?

module

Anxiety Disorders

- Why do some people develop exaggerated fears?
- Why do some people develop strange habits of thought and action?

Many situations evoke anxiety or tension in almost anyone. Anxiety becomes a problem only if it is frequently more intense than the situation justifies.

You go to the beach, looking forward to an afternoon of swimming and surfing. Will you stay out of the water if someone tells you that a shark attacked a swimmer yesterday? What if the shark attack was a month ago? What if someone saw a small shark that did not attack anyone?

How much fear and caution are normal? Staying out of the water because you see a large shark is reasonable. Staying out because a small shark was present a few days ago is less sensible. If you refuse even to look at ocean photographs that might *remind* you of sharks, you have a serious problem. Excessive fear and caution are linked to some common psychological disorders.

DISORDERS WITH EXCESSIVE ANXIETY

Many psychological disorders are marked by anxiety and attempts to avoid anxiety. Anxiety is similar to fear, except that fear is tied to a specific situation. You might be afraid of a growling dog, but your fear subsides when you get away. Anxiety is a long-lasting apprehensive feeling you cannot easily escape.

How much anxiety is normal? It depends. If you are aware of a remote danger, you should pay attention to it but remain calm. If you are in immediate danger, different areas of your brain become active, your anxiety increases, and you mobilize your body for emergency action (Mobbs et al., 2007). If you live in a dangerous place or if you have been through some terrifying experiences, you might interpret remote dangers as immediate ones and show increased anxiety more quickly than other people do (Ganzel, Casey, Glover, Voss, & Temple, 2007). You have an anxiety disorder only if your anxiety is consistently more extreme than your circumstances warrant and great enough to interfere with your life. Figure 16.1 shows the preva-

lence of anxiety disorders in six countries (Bijl et al., 2003; Murali, 2001). We already considered posttraumatic stress disorder in chapter 12. Here we consider additional anxiety disorders.

Generalized Anxiety Disorder (GAD)

People with generalized anxiety disorder (GAD) are *almost constantly plagued by exaggerated worries*. They worry that "I might get sick," "My daughter might get sick," "I might lose my job," or "I might not be able to pay my bills." Although they have no more reason for worry than anyone else, they grow so tense, irritable, and fatigued that they have trouble working, maintaining social relationships, or enjoying life (Henning, Turk, Mennin, Fresco, & Heimberg, 2007). Because anxiety is a common symptom of so many other disorders, most people with the symptoms of GAD have (or used to have or will have) other disorders, too, such as depression, panic disorder, or phobia (Bruce, Machan, Dyck, & Keller, 2001). GAD responds fairly well to both antidepressant

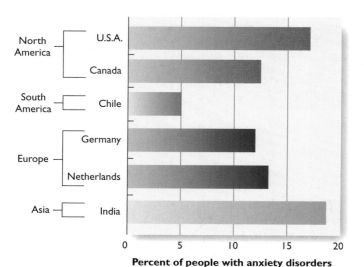

Percent of people with anxiety disorders

FIGURE 16.1 Percentage of people in six countries who have an anxiety disorder within a given year. (Based on data of Bijl, R. V., de Graaf, R., Hiripi, E., Kessler, R. C., Kohn, R., Offord, D. R., et al., 2003. The prevalence of treated and untreated mental disorders in five countries. *Health Affairs, 22*, 122–133; and Murali, M. S., 2001. Epidemiological study of prevalence of mental disorders in India. *Indian Journal of Community Medicine, 26,* 198.)

drugs (Rivas-Vazquez, 2001) and cognitive-behavioral therapy (Mitte, 2005).

Panic Disorder (PD)

Suddenly, you feel warm all over. You are breathing faster and faster but still can't seem to catch your breath. For no apparent reason, your heart is pounding harder than ever before. You are dizzy and nauseated, sweating profusely, and your hands are shaking. What is happening? You worry that you are having a heart attack. But within a few minutes, the episode is over and you feel normal again. You couldn't recover from a heart attack that fast. If it wasn't a heart attack, then what? Are you losing your mind?

This description fits a typical panic attack. People with *panic disorder (PD)* *have frequent periods of anxiety and occasional attacks of panic—rapid breathing, increased heart rate, chest pains, sweating, faintness, and trembling.*

Panic disorder occurs in 1 to 3% of adults at some time during their lives throughout the world. For reasons unknown, it is more common in Whites than in Blacks, including both African Americans and Blacks of Caribbean descent (Himle, Baser, Taylor, Campbell, & Jackson, 2009). One speculation is that strong religious faith helps many Blacks deal with anxiety situations. Panic disorder is more common in women than men, again for reasons unknown (Weissman, Warner, Wickramaratne, Moreau, & Olfson, 1997), and it is more common in adolescents and young adults than older adults. Adolescents have an especially strong anxiety reaction to stress because of increased production of certain hormone receptors (Shen et al., 2007). One study found that 8 of 24 people with panic disorder recovered completely within 11 years, while all of the others had less frequent panic attacks than before (Swoboda, Amering, Windhaber, & Katschnig, 2003).

Several studies have indicated a genetic contribution, although no single gene has a strong influence (Hettema, Neale, & Kendler, 2001; Kim, Lee, Yang, Hwang, & Yoon, 2009). A few studies have found a high overlap between panic disorder and *joint laxity* (the ability to bend fingers farther than usual, popularly called "double-jointedness"), which is believed to have a genetic basis (Bulbena et al., 2004; Gratacòs et al., 2001).

Psychologists have proposed several theories of panic disorder, none of which is fully established (Roth, Wilhelm, & Pettit, 2005). One is that people start having strong autonomic responses, such as rapid heartbeat, and interpret the arousal as a heart attack or other emergency. Their anxiety about the attack increases the arousal, thus further increasing the anxiety (Austin & Richards, 2001). Another theory is that a panic attack begins with hyperventilation, *rapid deep breathing.* Almost anything that causes hyperventilation makes the body react as if it were suffocating, thereby triggering other sympathetic nervous system responses such as sweating and increased heart rate (Coplan et al., 1998; Klein, 1993). If you became aroused after exercise, you would not react emotionally because you would attribute your arousal to the exercise (Esquivel, Schruers, Kuipers, & Griez, 2002). However, if you suddenly increase your breathing rate and don't know why, you may worry about the next attack and worry that it may embarrass you in public. Your worry increases the risk of further attacks (McNally, 2002). People who have repeated panic attacks start to associate them with places, events, activities, and internal states. Any situation that resembles those of previous panic attacks may trigger a new panic attack as a conditioned response (Bouton, Mineka, & Barlow, 2001).

Many people with panic disorder also develop agoraphobia (from *agora,* the Greek word for "marketplace"), *an excessive fear of open or public places,* or social phobia, *a severe avoidance of other people and a fear of doing anything in public.* People with panic disorder develop agoraphobia or social phobia because they are afraid of being incapacitated or embarrassed by a panic attack in a public place. In a sense, they are afraid of their own anxiety (McNally, 1990). To avoid the prospect of a public panic attack, they stay home as much as possible.

In most cases, panic disorder responds well to cognitive or cognitive-behavior therapy (Marchand et al., 2008). The procedures of cognitive-behavior therapy include teaching the patient to control breathing, countering the start of a panic with pleasant imagery, and learning to relax. For many, just knowing that panic attack does not mean heart attack helps greatly. Therapists also try to identify the thoughts and situations that trigger panic attacks and help a patient deal with those triggers. In addition, they help the person experience sweating and increased heart rate in a controlled setting, so the person learns that these physiological changes need not lead to a full-scale panic attack. Although this therapy may require several months, researchers find that at least three fourths of patients can stop their panic attacks altogether (Butler, Chapman, Forman, & Beck, 2006).

1. Some psychologists advise people with panic attacks to adopt the attitude, "If it happens, it happens." Why would they make this recommendation?

2. Which kinds of people are most likely to develop panic disorder?

Concept Check

Answers

2. Panic disorder is more common in women than men, Whites than Blacks, and young people than old people.

1. Worrying about anything—even panic attacks themselves—increases the risk of another panic attack.

DISORDERS WITH EXAGGERATED AVOIDANCE

People learn to avoid punishment. In some cases, their efforts become so extreme and persistent that they interfere with daily activities. Let's begin by discussing avoidance learning, which is relevant to phobias and compulsions. If you learn to do something for positive reinforcement, your responses extinguish when reinforcements cease, as discussed in chapter 6. Avoidance behaviors are different. Suppose you learn to press a lever to avoid electric shocks. Soon you are responding consistently and receiving no shocks. Now the experimenter disconnects the shock generator without telling you. The extinction procedure has begun, and you no longer need to press the lever. What will you do? You continue pressing, of course. As far as you can tell, nothing has changed, and the response still works. *Avoidance behaviors are highly resistant to extinction.* Once someone learns a response to avoid mishap, the response continues long after it ceases to be necessary.

You can see how this tendency would support superstitions. If you believe that Friday the 13th is dangerous, you are very cautious on that day. If nothing goes wrong, you are convinced that your caution was successful. If a misfortune happens anyway, it confirms your belief that Friday the 13th is dangerous. As long as you continue an avoidance behavior, you never learn whether it is useful or not!

3. Suppose you are an experimenter, and you have trained someone to press a lever to avoid shocks. Now you disconnect the shock generator. Other than telling the person what you have done, how could you facilitate extinction of the lever pressing?

Answer

3. Temporarily prevent the person from pressing the lever. Only by ceasing to press it does the person discover that pressing is not necessary.

A **phobia** is *an extreme, persistent fear that interferes with normal living.* It is not necessarily an irrational fear. Many people have phobias of snakes, spiders, lightning, heights, and other items that really are dangerous. What is irrational is the excessive degree of the fear, leading to panic in the presence of the feared object. In most cases, people with phobias are not so much afraid of the object itself but of their own reactions (Beck & Emery, 1985). They fear that they will have a heart attack or that they will embarrass themselves by trembling or fainting. Consequently, they do whatever they can to avoid the object or anything that reminds them of it.

Prevalence

According to an extensive study of U.S. adults, about 11% of people suffer a phobia at some time in life, and 5 to 6% have a phobia at any given time (Magee, Eaton, Wittchen, McGonagle, & Kessler, 1996). However, phobias vary from mild to extreme, so their apparent prevalence depends on how many marginal cases we include. As with other anxiety disorders, phobias are more common in women than men (Burke, Burke, Regier, & Rae, 1990).

Here are some common objects of phobias (Cox, McWilliams, Clara, & Stein, 2003):

- Open, public places (*agoraphobia*)
- Public speaking
- Heights (including elevators, being on a high floor of a building)
- Not being on solid ground (being in the air or on the water)
- Being with or being observed by strangers (*social phobia*)
- Being alone
- Dangers or reminders of dangers (snakes, spiders, other animals, blood, injections, storms, etc.)

Phobias

Terror is the only thing that comes close to how I feel when I think of moths. Their willowy, see-through wings always seem filthy. I remember being stuck in a car with a huge moth and my date, not knowing how terrified I was of moths, thought I was kidding when I told him I was afraid. It was terrible! I can feel it right now . . . feeling trapped and the moth with its ugly body flitting around so quickly, I couldn't anticipate where it would go next. Finally that creature hit me in the arm and I screamed—it felt dirty and sleazy and then it hit me in the face and I began to scream uncontrollably. I had the terrible feeling it was going to fly into my mouth while I was screaming, but I couldn't stop. (phobia patient quoted by Duke & Nowicki, 1979, p. 244)

Many people who watched the famous shower scene in the movie *Psycho* became afraid to take showers. Actress Janet Leigh, who portrayed the woman killed in that scene, subsequently avoided showers herself.

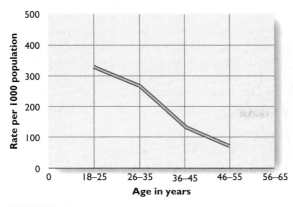

FIGURE 16.2 Most young people with phobias lose them by middle age. (Based on the data of Burke, Burke, Regier, & Rae, 1990)

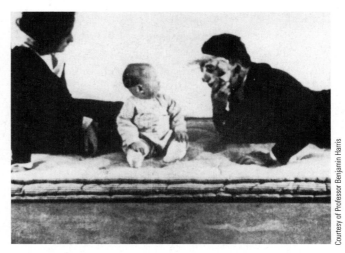

Courtesy of Professor Benjamin Harris

FIGURE 16.3 John B. Watson first demonstrated that Albert B. showed little fear of small animals. Then Watson paired a white rat with a loud, frightening noise. Albert became afraid of the white rat, as well as other small animals and odd-looking masks.

Figure 16.2 shows the prevalence of phobias by age. As with panic disorder, phobias are most common in young adults and less common with age.

Acquiring Phobias

Infants are born with a fear of sudden loud noises, and most of them quickly show a fear of abandonment. In contrast, no one is born with a phobia. Some phobias can be traced to a specific event. For example, one child got locked in a trunk and developed a phobia of closed spaces. Another person developed a phobia of water after diving into a lake and finding a corpse (Kendler et al., 1995). However, many people with phobias do not remember any personal event that started the phobia, and many people who have had traumatic experiences do not develop phobias (Field, 2006). It is likely that some people are more genetically predisposed than others to develop phobias (Kendler, Myers, & Prescott, 2002).

John B. Watson, one of the founders of behaviorism, was the first to demonstrate the possibility of learning fears (Watson & Rayner, 1920). Most people would consider it unethical to try to teach a child an intense fear, but Watson felt less restraint. (And this was before the day of institutional review boards that oversee the ethics of research.) Watson and Rosalie Rayner studied an 11-month-old child, "Albert B.," who had previously shown no fear of white rats or other animals (Figure 16.3). They set a white rat in front of him and then struck a large steel bar behind him with a hammer. The sound made Albert whimper and cover his face. After a few repetitions, the mere sight of the rat made Albert cry and crawl away. Watson and Rayner declared that they had created a strong fear similar to a phobia. Unfortunately, they made no attempt to extinguish Albert's fear.

Watson and Rayner's explanation of phobias ignored some important questions: Why do many people develop phobias toward objects that have never injured them? Why are some phobias much more common than others? And why are phobias so persistent? Although Watson and Rayner's study was unsatisfactory in many ways (B. Harris, 1979; Samelson, 1980), it led the way for later research.

4. In classical conditioning terms, what was the CS in Watson and Rayner's experiment? The UCS? The CR? The UCR?

Concept Check

Answer

4. The CS was the white rat. The UCS was the loud noise. The CR and the UCR were a combination of crying and other fear reactions.

What's the Evidence?

Learning Fear by Observation

Given that people aren't born with phobias, but many people develop phobias without a personal traumatic experience, maybe they learn their phobias from watching others. As noted in the discussion of social learning in chapter 6, we learn much by watching or listening to others. Susan Mineka and her colleagues demonstrated that monkeys learn fears by observing other monkeys (Mineka, 1987; Mineka, Davidson, Cook, & Keir, 1984). Her research shows how animal studies shed light on important human issues.

Critical Thinking

First Study

Hypothesis Monkeys that have seen other monkeys avoid a snake will develop a similar fear themselves.

Method Nearly all monkeys born in the wild show a fear of snakes, but laboratory monkeys do not. Mineka put a laboratory-reared monkey with a wild-born monkey and let them both see a snake (Figure 16.4a). The lab monkey watched the wild monkey show signs of fear. Later, Mineka tested the lab monkey by itself to see its response to a snake.

Results When the lab monkey saw its partner shriek and run away from the snake, it became frightened, too (Figure 16.4b). It continued to fear the snake when tested by itself, even months later.

Interpretation The lab monkey may have learned a fear of snakes because it saw that its partner was afraid of snakes. But Mineka considered another interpretation: Perhaps see-ing the other monkey's fear simply heightened the lab monkey's fear in general, including its fear of snakes (which happened to be the only fear that was tested). What was the critical experience—seeing the other monkey show fear *of snakes* or seeing the other monkey show fear *of anything?* To find out, Mineka conducted a second experiment.

Second Study

Hypothesis A monkey learns a fear from another monkey only if it sees *what* the other monkey fears.

Method A monkey reared in a lab watched a monkey reared in the wild through a window. The wild monkey looked through another window, where it saw a snake. The lab monkey saw the wild monkey's fear but did not see the snake. Later, the lab monkey was placed with a snake to see whether it would show fear.

Results The lab monkey showed no fear of the snake.

Interpretation To develop a fear of snakes, the observer monkey needed to see that the other monkey was frightened of snakes, not just that it was frightened (Figure 16.4c).

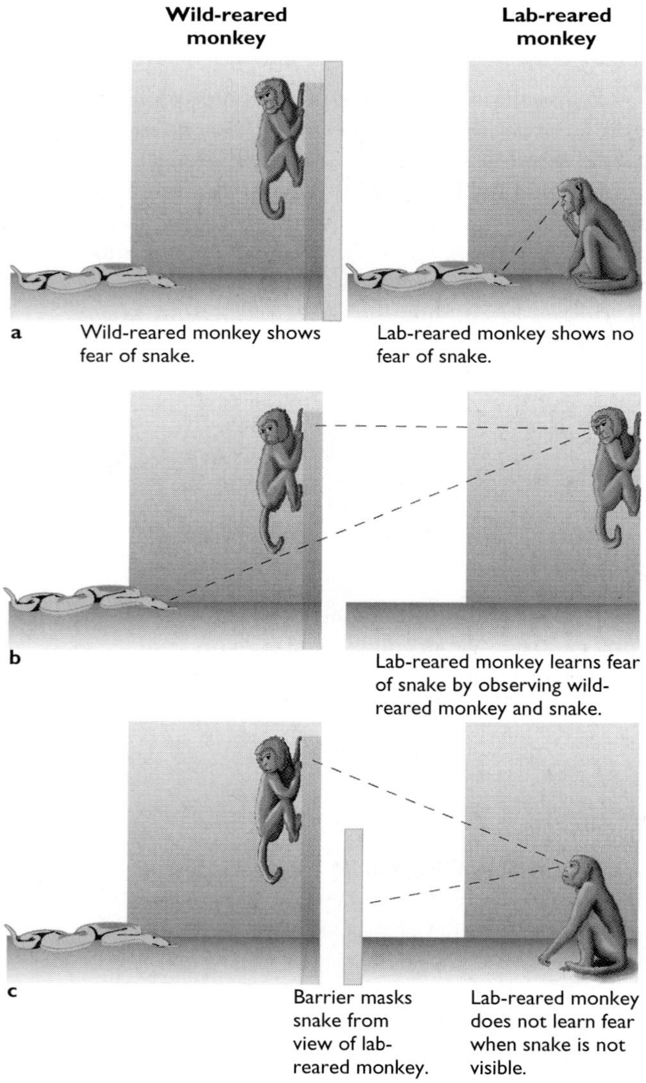

Note that the observer monkey had to see *what* the other monkey feared but not *why* it was afraid of the snake. Humans not only observe one another's fears but also explain why.

Some Phobias Are More Common Than Others

Imagine that you survey your friends. You can actually survey them, if you wish, but it's easy enough to imagine the results. You ask them:

- Are you afraid of snakes?
- Are you afraid of cars?
- Have you ever been bitten by a snake or seen someone else bitten?
- Have you ever been injured in a car accident or seen someone else injured?

I think you know what to expect. Far more people have been injured or seen someone injured by cars than by snakes, but far more are afraid of snakes than cars. Common phobias include open spaces, closed spaces, heights, lightning and thunder, certain animals, and illness. In contrast, few people have phobias of cars, guns, tools, or electricity—even though they produce many injuries. When my son Sam was a toddler, at least three times he stuck his finger into an electric outlet. He even had a name for it: "Smoky got me again." (I worried about him!) But he never developed a fear of electricity or gadgets.

Why do people develop fears of some objects more readily than other objects? One explanation is that although we are not born with many fears, we may be evolutionarily prepared to learn certain fears more easily than other fears (Öhman & Mineka, 2003; Seligman, 1971). Nearly every infant develops a fear of heights and of strangers,

Wild-reared monkey / **Lab-reared monkey**

a Wild-reared monkey shows fear of snake. / Lab-reared monkey shows no fear of snake.

b Lab-reared monkey learns fear of snake by observing wild-reared monkey and snake.

c Barrier masks snake from view of lab-reared monkey. / Lab-reared monkey does not learn fear when snake is not visible.

FIGURE 16.4 A lab-reared monkey learns to fear snakes from the reactions of a wild-reared monkey. But if the snake is not visible, the lab-reared monkey learns no fear.

especially unfamiliar men. Heights and unfamiliar adult males have been dangerous throughout mammalian evolution. Less universal but still widespread are the fears of snakes, darkness, and confined spaces, which have been dangerous throughout primate (monkey and ape) evolution. Cars, guns, and electricity became dangerous only within the last few generations of humans, a tiny amount of time in evolutionary terms. Our predisposition to develop fears and phobias corresponds to how long various items have been dangerous in our evolutionary history (Bracha, 2006).

Evidence supporting this view comes from both monkey and human studies. Monkeys who watch a videotape of another monkey running away from a snake learn to fear snakes; monkeys who watch another monkey running away from a flower learn no fear of flowers (Mineka, 1987). People who receive electric shocks paired with pictures of snakes quickly develop a strong and persistent response to snake pictures; people who receive shocks paired with pictures of houses show a much weaker response (Öhman, Eriksson, & Olofsson, 1975).

However, although people learn fears of snakes more easily than fears of houses, it is unfair to assume that this tendency must be built in evolutionarily. The participants were adults, after all. They had massive opportunities to learn that snakes are dangerous and houses are not. Another study asked 3-year-olds to find a particular object in a photograph. They consistently found a snake faster than they found a flower, a frog, or a caterpillar (LoBue & DeLoache, 2008). That result suggests a natural tendency to pay attention to snakes. However, another study found that people notice guns in a photo just as easily and quickly as snakes (Fox, Griggs, & Mouchlianitis, 2007). We certainly haven't evolved a tendency to pay attention to guns, so maybe our attention goes to anything we have learned is dangerous regardless of evolutionary predisposition.

In addition to possible evolutionary factors, we can consider other explanations for why snake and spider phobias are more common than car or tool phobias (Mineka & Zinbarg, 2006). For example, consider safe experiences. Okay, you have hurt yourself with tools and you have been in a car accident or seen others injured in a car accident. But how many times have you had safe experiences with tools and cars? It's presumably a huge number. In contrast, how often have you had safe experiences with snakes, spiders, or falling from high places? What counts in learning is not just the number of bad experiences but the ratio of bad experiences to safe experiences.

Another possible explanation relates to controllability. People most often develop phobias of objects that they cannot predict or control. If you

Many people are afraid of extreme heights, partly because the danger is hard to control.

are afraid of spiders, you must be constantly on the alert. You can never be sure they aren't around. Lightning is also unpredictable and uncontrollable. In contrast, you don't have to worry that hammers, saws, or electric outlets will take you by surprise. You must be on the alert for cars when you are near a road but not at other times.

5. Give three explanations for why more people develop phobias of snakes and spiders than cars and guns.

Answer

5. People may be born with a predisposition to learn fears of objects that have been dangerous throughout our evolutionary history. We more readily fear objects with which we have few safe experiences. We more readily fear objects that we cannot predict or control.

Behavior Therapy for Phobias

Well-established phobias last many years. Remembering the discussion about avoidance learning, you see why phobias are difficult to extinguish: If you have learned to press a lever to avoid shock, you may not stop pressing long enough to find out that the response is no longer necessary. Similarly, if you always avoid snakes or heights or closed places, you don't learn that your fear is exaggerated, and you will not extinguish your fear.

Recall behavior therapy from chapter 15: A therapist sets a specific goal and uses learning techniques to help the client achieve that goal. One common and usually successful type of behavior therapy for phobia is *systematic desensitization, a method of reducing fear by gradually exposing people to the object of their fear* (Wolpe, 1961). Someone with a phobia of snakes, for example, is exposed to pictures of a snake in the reassuring environment of the therapist's office. The therapist might start with a cartoon drawing and gradually work up to a black-and-white photograph, a color photograph, and then a real snake (Figure 16.5). Or the therapist might start with the snake itself (obviously, with the client's consent). The client is terrified at first, but the autonomic nervous system is not capable of sustaining a per-

FIGURE 16.5 In systematic desensitization for phobia, a therapist gradually exposes a client to the object of the phobia. The therapist demonstrates fearlessness in the presence of the object and encourages the client to do the same.

manent panic. Gradually, the person becomes calmer and in doing so learns, "It's not that bad after all. Here I am, not far from that horrid snake, and I'm not having a heart attack."

The process resembles Skinner's shaping procedure (see chapter 6). The person is given time to master one step before going on to the next. If the distress becomes too great, the client says "stop," and the therapist then goes back several steps. Some people complete the whole procedure in a single 1-hour session; others need more time. Systematic desensitization is often combined with social learning: The person with a phobia watches the therapist or other people display a fearless response to the object.

However, most therapists do not keep handy a supply of snakes, spiders, and so forth. Increasingly, they use virtual reality, which is highly effective (Coelho, Waters, Hine, & Wallis, 2009): The client is equipped with a helmet that displays a virtual-reality scene, as shown in Figure 16.6. Then,

without leaving the office, the therapist exposes the client to the feared object or situation. For example, a client with a phobia of heights can go up a glass elevator in a hotel or cross a narrow bridge over a chasm. This technology gives the therapist control of the situation, including the option of quickly increasing or decreasing the intensity of the display. Virtual reality also has the advantage of privacy. If a client is afraid of heights, virtual reality saves the client the embarrassment of going up the stairs or elevator of a public building.

6. How does systematic desensitization resemble extinction of a learned shock-avoidance response?

7. How does systematic desensitization relate to the James-Lange theory of emotions presented in chapter 12?

Answers

6. To extinguish a learned shock-avoidance response, prevent the response so that the individual learns that a failure to respond is not dangerous. Similarly, in systematic desensitization, the patient is prevented from fleeing the feared stimulus. He or she learns that the danger is not as great as imagined.

7. The procedure is compatible with the James-Lange theory of emotions, which holds that emotions follow from perceptions of body arousal. In systematic desensitization, as arousal of the autonomic nervous system decreases, the person perceives, "I am calming down. I must be less frightened than I thought I was."

FIGURE 16.6 Virtual reality lets a patient with a phobia of heights experience heights without leaving the therapist's office.

Obsessive-Compulsive Disorder

People with **obsessive-compulsive disorder** have two kinds of problems. An **obsession** is a *repetitive, unwelcome stream of thought*. For example, some people find themselves constantly imagining gruesome scenes, worrying that they are about to kill someone, dwelling on doubts about their religion, or thinking, "I hate my sister. I hate my sister." They find these thoughts alien and disturbing, but knowing "I don't really want to kill someone" or "I don't really hate my sister" doesn't stop the repetitive thoughts. A **compulsion** is a *repetitive, almost irresistible action*. Obsessions generally lead to compulsions, as an itching sensation leads to scratching. For example, someone obsessed about dirt and disease develops compulsions of continual cleaning and washing. Someone with obsessive worries about doing something shameful develops compulsive rituals that maintain excessive self-control. That is, the compulsion is an attempt to reduce the distress that the obsession caused.

An estimated 2 to 3% of all people in the United States suffer from obsessive-compulsive disorder at some time in life, mostly to a mild degree (Karno, Golding, Sorenson, & Burnam, 1988). More than half have obsessions without compulsions. Most have additional disorders, such as depression or generalized anxiety disorder (Torres et al., 2006). The disorder occurs most frequently among hardworking, perfectionist people of average or above-average intelligence. It usually develops between the ages of 10 and 25. The causes are not known. It tends to run in families, but no gene has been identified as being responsible. Several brain areas of people with obsessive-compulsive disorder tend to be larger than average, whereas other areas are smaller (Lázaro et al., 2008; Rotge et al., 2009). Several brain areas tend to be more active than normal, and several other brain areas tend to be less active (Chamberlain et al., 2008).

DSM-IV lists obsessive-compulsive disorder with the anxiety disorders, but it is associated with guilt at least as much as with anxiety. People with obsessive-compulsive disorder say they feel guilt and anxiety over persistent impulses—perhaps an impulse to engage in a sexual act that they consider shameful, an impulse to hurt someone, or an impulse to commit suicide. They decide, "Oh, what a terrible thought. I don't want to think that ever again." And so they resolve to avoid that thought or impulse.

However, trying to block out a thought only makes it more intrusive. As a child, the Russian novelist Leo Tolstoy once organized a club with an unusual qualification for membership: A prospective member had to stand alone in a corner *without thinking about a white bear* (Simmons, 1949). If you think that sounds easy, try it. Ordinarily, you go months between thoughts about polar bears, but when you try *not* to think about them, you can think of little else.

In one experiment, college students were asked to tape-record everything that came to mind during 5 minutes but to try *not* to think about white bears. If they did, they were to mention it and ring a bell. Participants reported thinking about bears a mean of more than six times during the 5 minutes (Wegner, Schneider, Carter, & White, 1987). Afterward, they reported that almost everything in the room reminded them of white bears. Evidently, attempts to suppress a thought are likely to backfire even with an emotionally trivial thought. You can imagine how hard it is with severely upsetting thoughts.

People with obsessive-compulsive disorder have any of several kinds of compulsions. One man collected newspapers under his bed until they raised the bed so high it almost touched the ceiling. Others have odd habits, such as touching everything they see, trying to arrange objects in a completely symmetrical manner, or walking back and forth through a doorway nine times before leaving a building. One person with obsessive-compulsive disorder could not go to sleep at night until he had counted the corners of every object in the room to make sure that the total number of corners was evenly divisible by 16. If it was not, he would add or remove objects until the room had an acceptable total of corners. (The Obsessive-Compulsive Foundation produces a button that reads "Every Member Counts"!) The most common compulsions are cleaning and checking.

Most people seldom think about polar bears. But if you try to avoid thinking about them, you can think of little else.

Cleaning Compulsion

Many religions recommend ritual washing to clean one's soul after any foul action or thought, and many people use compulsive cleaning as a way to improve their sense of purity. Consider the following study: You are asked to fill in missing letters to form English words in items like these:

S _ _ P
W _ _ H

Each of the items could be completed in more than one way to make a common word. At the end of the task, you get to choose either a pencil or an antiseptic wipe as your token reward for participation. The manipulation is this: Before the fill-in-the-letters task, some people are asked to recall a good deed from their past, and others are asked to recall something shameful they did. If you were in the "shameful" group, you would be more likely to fill in letters to form "cleaning" words, such as SOAP and WASH, and more likely to choose the antiseptic wipe instead of the pencil (Zhong & Liljenquist, 2006).

Here is an example of a severe cleaning compulsion (Nagera, 1976): "R.," a 12-year-old boy, had a longstanding habit of prolonged bathing and hand washing, dating from a film about germs he had seen in the second grade. At about age 12, he started to complain about "being dirty" and having "bad thoughts" that he would not describe. His hand washing and bathing became longer and more frequent. When he bathed, he carefully washed himself with soap and washcloth all over, including the inside of his mouth and the inside of each nostril. He even opened his eyes in the soapy water and carefully washed his eyeballs.

The only part he did not wash was his penis, which he covered with a washcloth as soon as he entered the tub.

In addition to his peculiar bathing habits, he developed some original superstitions. Whenever he did anything with one hand, he immediately did the same thing with the other hand. Whenever anyone mentioned a member of his family, he would mention the corresponding member of the other person's family. He always walked to school by the same route but was careful never to step on any spot where he had ever stepped before. You can imagine the strain on his memory. At school, he would wipe the palm of his hand on his pants after any "good" thought; at home, he would wipe his hand on his pants after any "bad" thought.

Checking Compulsion

An obsessive-compulsive checker double-checks everything. Before going to bed at night, he or she makes sure all the doors and windows are locked and all the water faucets and gas outlets are turned off. But then the question arises, "Did I *really* check them all, or did I only imagine it?" So everything has to be checked again and again. "After all, maybe I accidentally unlocked one of the doors while I was checking it." Obsessive-compulsive checkers may go on for hours and even then may not be satisfied.

Some have been known to check every door they pass to see whether anyone has been locked in. Others check trash containers and bushes to see whether anyone has abandoned a baby. One man worried he might drive his car over a pedestrian and then forget about it. He drove back and forth along a street to see whether he ran over any pedestrians the last time through (Pollak, 1979; Rachman & Hodgson, 1980).

Why do people with this problem continue checking? Part of the explanation is that they feel a strong responsibility to prevent harm to others. They continue checking to make sure nothing has gone wrong (Rachman, 2002; Szechtman & Woody, 2004). Another reason is that they do not trust their own memory. In one study, obsessive-compulsive patients took a memory test and estimated how many questions they answered correctly. Their actual percentage correct was as good as average, but their estimates of their own performance were well below average (Dar, Rish, Hermish, Taub, & Fux, 2000). So perhaps obsessive-compulsive patients continue checking what they have already checked because they do not trust their memory.

Why do they distrust their own memory? One study found that repeated checking makes the memories less distinct! Normal college students were asked to turn on and off the gas rings of a "virtual gas stove" on a computer. One group did it just once; the other group turned the rings on and off repeatedly. At the end, both groups were asked which rings they had turned off on the most recent trial. Those who had manipulated the controls repeatedly answered as correctly as the others but expressed less confidence in their answers. That is, the authors of this study suggest a vicious cycle: Not trusting your memory causes you to check repeatedly, and repeated checking makes the memory less distinct (van den Hout & Kindt, 2003).

Table 16.1 summarizes key differences between obsessive-compulsive cleaners and checkers. Table 16.2 lists some items from a questionnaire on obsessive-compulsive tendencies (Rachman & Hodgson, 1980). Try answering these questions yourself, or try guessing how a person with obsessive-compulsive disorder would answer them. (The few items listed here are not sufficient to diagnose someone as obsessive-compulsive. So don't obsess about it if you agree with all the obsessive-compulsive answers.)

TABLE 16.1 Obsessive-Compulsive Cleaners and Checkers

	Cleaners	Checkers
Sex distribution	Mostly female	About equally male and female
Dominant emotion	Anxiety, similar to phobia	Guilt, shame
Speed of onset	Usually rapid	More often gradual
Life disruption	Dominates life	Usually does not disrupt job and family life
Ritual length	Less than 1 hour at a time	Some go on indefinitely
Feel better after rituals?	Yes	Usually not

Source: From *Obsessions and Compulsions*, by Stanley J. Rachman and Ray J. Hodgson. Copyright © 1980 by Prentice-Hall, Inc. Reprinted by permission.

TABLE 16.2 Obsessive-Compulsive Tendencies

1. I avoid public telephones because of possible contamination.	T	F
2. I frequently get nasty thoughts and have difficulty getting rid of them.	T	F
3. I usually have serious thoughts about the simple everyday things I do.	T	F
4. Neither of my parents was very strict during my childhood.	T	F
5. I do not take a long time to dress in the morning.	T	F
6. One of my major problems is that I pay too much attention to detail.	T	F
7. I do not stick to a very strict routine when doing ordinary things.	T	F
8. I do not usually count when doing a routine task	T	F
9. Even when I do something very carefully, I often feel that it is not quite right.	T	F

Check typical answers on page 580.
Source: From *Obsessions and Compulsions*, by Stanley J. Rachman and Ray J. Hodgson. Copyright © 1980 by Prentice-Hall, Inc. Reprinted by permission.

Therapies

Nearly all people with obsessive-compulsive disorder realize that their thoughts and rituals are inappropriate. However, that understanding does not bring relief. Most people with obsessive-compulsive disorder improve over time with or without treatment (Skoog & Skoog, 1999). Still, no one wants to wait years for spontaneous recovery. The therapy best supported by the evidence is *exposure therapy with response prevention*: The person is exposed to a situation in which he or she ordinarily performs certain rituals but is prevented from performing them (Rosa-Alcázar, Sánchea-Meca, Gómez-Conesa, & Marín-Martínez, 2008). Someone might be prevented from cleaning the house or checking the doors and windows more than once before going to sleep. The point is to demonstrate that nothing catastrophic occurs if one leaves a little mess in the house or runs a slight risk of leaving a door unlocked. Antidepressant drugs are also helpful in many cases (Greist, Jefferson, Kobak, Katzelnick, & Serlin, 1995).

8. In what way do people with obsessive-compulsive disorder have an abnormal memory?
9. Suppose someone reports that a long-term therapy, lasting 10 years, cures many people of obsessive-compulsive disorder. Should we be impressed? Why or why not?

Concept Check

Answers

8. People with obsessive-compulsive disorder do not trust their memory, although its accuracy is normal.
9. We should not be impressed. Over a long enough time, most people recover from obsessive-compulsive disorder, even without treatment.

module 16.1

In Closing

Emotions and Avoidance

Phobias and obsessive-compulsive disorder illustrate some of the possible links between emotions and cognitions. At the risk of seriously oversimplifying, we could say that people with phobias experience emotional attacks because of their cognitions about a particular object, whereas people with obsessive-compulsive disorder experience repetitive cognitions for emotional reasons. In both conditions, most people know that their reactions are exaggerated, but mere awareness of the problem does not correct it. Dealing with such conditions requires attention to emotions, cognitions, and the links between them.

SUMMARY

- *Generalized anxiety disorder and panic disorder.* People with generalized anxiety disorder experience excessive anxiety much of the day, even when actual dangers are low. Panic disorder is characterized by episodes of disabling anxiety, high heart rate, and rapid breathing. (page 570)
- *Persistence of avoidance behaviors.* A learned shock-avoidance response can persist long after the possibility of shock has been removed. As with shock-avoidance responses, phobias and obsessive-compulsive disorder persist because people do not discover that their avoidance behaviors are unnecessary. (page 572)
- *Phobia.* A phobia is a fear so extreme that it interferes with normal living. Phobias are learned through observation as well as through experience. (page 572)
- *Common phobias.* People are more likely to develop phobias of certain objects (e.g.,

snakes) than of others (e.g., cars). The most common objects of phobias have menaced humans throughout evolutionary history. They pose dangers that are difficult to predict or control, and we generally have few safe experiences with them. (page 572)
- *Systematic desensitization of phobias.* A common therapy for phobia is systematic desensitization. The patient is taught to relax and is then gradually exposed to the object of the phobia. (page 575)
- *Obsessive-compulsive disorder.* People with obsessive-compulsive disorder try to avoid thoughts or impulses that cause distress. They also perform repetitive behaviors. (page 576)
- *Types of obsessive-compulsive disorder.* Two common compulsions are cleaning and checking. Cleaners try to avoid any type of contamination. Checkers constantly double-check themselves and invent elaborate rituals. (page 577)

KEY TERMS

agoraphobia (page 571)

compulsion (page 576)

generalized anxiety disorder (GAD) (page 570)

hyperventilation (page 571)

obsession (page 576)

obsessive-compulsive disorder (page 576)

panic disorder (PD) (page 571)

phobia (page 572)

social phobia (page 571)

systematic desensitization (page 575)

ANSWERS TO OTHER QUESTIONS IN THE MODULE

Typical answers for people with obsessive-compulsive disorder (page 579): 1. T; 2. T; 3. T; 4. F; 5. F; 6. T; 7. F; 8. F; 9. T

Substance-Related Disorders

- Why do people abuse alcohol and other drugs?
- What can be done to help people with substance-related disorders?

How would you like to volunteer for an experiment? I want to implant into your brain a little device that will automatically lift your mood. There are still a few kinks in it, but most people who have tried say that it makes them feel good at least some of the time, and some people say they like it a great deal.

I should tell you about the possible risks. My device will endanger your health and reduce your life expectancy. Some people believe it causes brain damage, but they haven't proved that charge, so I don't think you should worry about it. Your behavior will change a good bit, though. You may have difficulty concentrating, for example. The device affects some people more than others. If you happen to be strongly affected, you will have difficulty completing your education, getting or keeping a job, and carrying on a satisfactory personal life. But if you are lucky, you can avoid all that. Anyway, you can quit the experiment anytime you decide. You should know, though, that the longer the device remains in your brain, the harder it is to remove.

I cannot pay you for taking part in this experiment. In fact, *you* will have to pay *me*. But I'll give you a bargain rate: only $5 for the first week and then a little more each week as time passes. One other thing: Technically speaking, this experiment is illegal. We probably won't get caught, but if we do, we could both go to jail.

What do you say? Is it a deal? I presume you will say "no." I get very few volunteers. And yet, if I change the term *brain device* to *drug* and change *experiment* to *drug deal,* it is amazing how many volunteers come forward.

In chapter 3, we examined the effects of drugs on the brain and behavior. In this module, we focus on the process of addiction.

SUBSTANCE DEPENDENCE (ADDICTION)

Use and abuse of alcohol and other drugs come in all degrees, from the occasional social drinker to the person whose problems become ruinous. People who *find it difficult or impossible to quit a self-destructive habit* are said to have a dependence on it or an addiction to it. Two major questions are what causes occasional drug use to develop into an overwhelming craving, and why some people are more vulnerable than others.

Addictions vary in many ways, and many people convince themselves that they are not addicted because they still (usually) fulfill their daily activities or because they sometimes abstain. In fact, many people with alcoholism or other addictions keep their jobs and do them well at times. Many go days or weeks without using the substance. To decide whether you are addicted, ask, "Does the substance cause troubles in my life, and do I often take more than I had decided I would?"

Nearly all the drugs that commonly produce addictions stimulate dopamine receptors in a small brain area called the *nucleus accumbens,* which is apparently critical for attention and habit formation (Berridge & Robinson, 1998; Koob & LeMoal, 1997). Figure 16.7 shows its location. Some people have assumed this area is the brain's pleasure center. However, the synapses respond to almost any surprising event but hardly at all to pleasant but expected events (Waelti, Dickinson, & Schultz, 2001; Young, Joseph, & Gray, 1993). They also become active when a person or animal starts seeking a drug, long before receiving the effects of it (Phillips, Stuber, Heien, Wightman, & Carelli, 2003). So the role of the nucleus accum-

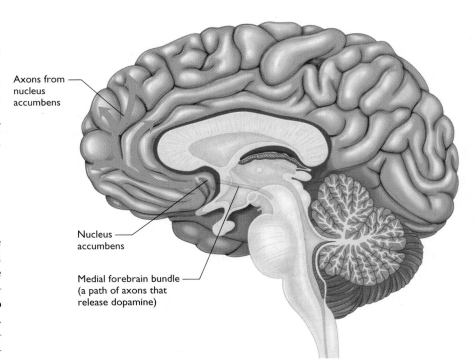

Axons from nucleus accumbens

Nucleus accumbens

Medial forebrain bundle (a path of axons that release dopamine)

FIGURE 16.7 The nucleus accumbens is a small brain area that is critical for the motivating effects of many experiences, including drugs, food, and sex. Most abused drugs increase the activity of the neurotransmitter dopamine in this area.

bens may relate more to attention than to pleasure. Indeed, it is reasonable to describe addiction as something that monopolizes people's attention (Robinson & Berridge, 2000).

Moreover, it is probably not helpful to say that something becomes addictive *because* it stimulates the nucleus accumbens. One could just as well say that it stimulates the nucleus accumbens because it has become addictive. For example, gambling and video game playing do not automatically stimulate the nucleus accumbens—they can't, because they aren't "substances"—but after people develop a strong gambling or video game habit, the activities come to stimulate the nucleus accumbens (Koepp et al., 1998).

Many substances can be addictive under certain circumstances—or at least, can satisfy an addiction that has already formed. In a hospital ward where alcoholics were being treated, one patient moved his bed into the men's room (Cummings, 1979). At first, the hospital staff ignored this curious behavior. Then, one by one, other patients moved their beds into the men's room. Eventually, the staff discovered what was happening. These men, deprived of alcohol, had discovered that by drinking about 30 liters of water per day and urinating the same amount (which was why they moved into the men's room), they could alter the acid-to-base balance of their blood enough to produce a sensation similar to drunkenness. (Do *not* try this yourself. Some people have died from an overdose of water!)

10. Why is it probably pointless to distinguish between substances that are and are not addictive?

Answer

10. Some people show addictions to gambling or video games, which are not substances at all. Some have managed to abuse water.

What Motivates Addictive Behavior?

After someone has become addicted, what motivation sustains the repetitive and insistent drug seeking? Most people who have become addicted to a drug say it seldom provides great pleasure. Why do they continue despite the costs and risks?

One possibility is that they really are still seeking pleasure. Even if the experience usually is not good, sometimes it is, and as discussed in chapter 6, behavior on a partial reinforcement schedule is highly persistent. In particular, the first use of a drug after a period of abstention produces intense effects, so the user learns to return to the substance after any attempt to quit (Hoebel, Rada, Mark, & Pothos, 1999; Hutcheson, Everitt, Robbins, & Dickinson, 2001).

A second hypothesis, not contradictory to the first, is that the motivation is to escape unpleasant feelings. Even for someone in the early stages of addiction, a brief period of abstention produces withdrawal symptoms, marked by discomfort and depression. Withdrawal symptoms from prolonged alcoholism include sweating, nausea, sleeplessness, and in severe cases, hallucinations and seizures. With opiate drugs, withdrawal symptoms include anxiety, restlessness, vomiting, diarrhea, and sweating. A user learns to take the drug to escape these feelings. Someone who *uses a drug to reduce unpleasant withdrawal symptoms* is said to have a **physical dependence**. A **psychological dependence** is a *strong repetitive desire for something without physical symptoms of withdrawal.* For example, habitual gamblers have a psychological dependence on placing bets, even though abstaining from gambling produces no withdrawal symptoms. A psychological dependence can be extremely insistent, and the distinction between physical and psychological dependence is not always helpful.

Many people report strong drug cravings long after the end of withdrawal symptoms, so we need to look further to explain addiction. Another hypothesis is that a drug user learns to associate the drug with relief from internal distress. That is, at first someone takes a drug to relieve withdrawal symptoms but later learns to use it to relieve other kinds of displeasure. Support for this idea comes from the observation that people who have quit drugs are most likely to relapse during periods of financial or social difficulties (Baker, Piper, McCarthy, Majeskie, & Fiore, 2004).

The relief-from-distress explanation is plausible, as far as it goes, but leaves the question of why addiction produces such obsessive use. After all, many people deal with stress by exercising, but few continue until they collapse and lose consciousness. Many cope with stress by shopping but not to the point of bankruptcy.

To account for the persistence of drug use far beyond what seems necessary to escape distress, Terry Robinson and Kent Berridge (2000, 2001) distinguish between "liking" and "wanting." Addicted drug users rarely get intense pleasure ("liking") from a drug, but they continue to want it anyway. By analogy, someone who plays video games by the hour *wants* to play but probably does not feel great pleasure. Addiction hijacks the brain areas that are important for motivation, attention, and learning (Kalivas, Volkow, & Seamans, 2005; Liu, Pu, & Poo, 2005; Volkow et al., 2006). Drug users show strong responses to drug-related stimuli but less than normal responses to other kinds of pleasure (Lubman et al., 2009). The same is true for laboratory animals: Rats that become heroin addicted work hard to get heroin but work less than average for other rewards (Kenny, Chen, Kitamura, Markou, & Koob, 2006). Furthermore, cocaine addiction impairs learning, including the ability to learn new behaviors that might compete with the drug addiction (Moussawi et al., 2009). In short, when the addictive drug doesn't provide much pleasure, nothing else does either.

....

11. According to one of the hypotheses just described, how do people learn to use drugs when they are feeling bad?

Concept Check

Answer

11. At first, they learn to use the drug to escape withdrawal symptoms caused by abstention from the drug itself. Later, they learn to use the drug to escape from other kinds of distress.

....

Is Substance Dependence a Disease?

You have no doubt heard people call alcoholism or drug abuse a disease. It is hard to confirm or deny that statement, however, without a clear definition of *disease*. Medical doctors assign no precise meaning to disease.

When people call alcoholism or drug dependence a disease, they apparently mean that people who abuse alcohol or other drugs should feel no guiltier about their condition than they would about having pneumonia. Although the disease label is reassuring, the concept has questionable implications. It implies an all-or-none distinction between people with the disease and those without it. The evidence suggests a continuum from no problem to severe problems (W. R. Miller & Brown, 1997; Polcin, 1997).

Also, because many untreated diseases grow worse and worse over time, the disease concept suggests that alcoholism or drug dependence becomes worse over time. In fact, the outcome varies. Various individuals deteriorate, remain steady, improve, or fluctuate (Sartor, Jacob, & Bucholz, 2003).

Furthermore, to regard substance dependence as a disease suggests a need for medical intervention. Alcoholism and drug dependence often respond well to family therapy and other nonmedical treatments (Liddle, Dakof, Turner, Henderson, & Greenbaum, 2008; Stanton & Shadish, 1997). By improving the person's family life, possibly improving the job situation, and helping the person develop new interests, family therapy decreases the compulsion for alcohol or drug use.

Nicotine Dependence

You have no doubt heard that the cigarette smoking habit depends on nicotine addiction. One type of evidence for this conclusion is that people find it easier to quit cigarettes if they have a replacement source of nicotine, such as a nicotine patch, nicotine chewing gum, or nicotine nasal spray (Rose, 1996).

"If so," you may wonder, "why have so many smokers switched to low-tar, low-nicotine cigarette brands? Wouldn't those brands fail to satisfy a nicotine craving?" Yes, they would *if* they delivered low nicotine! Most low-tar, low-nicotine cigarettes have the same kind of tobacco as other cigarettes but have a filter with a row of little air holes, as shown in Figure 16.8. The idea is that air entering these holes will dilute the tobacco smoke coming through the barrel of the cigarette. However, many smokers cover the air holes with their lips or fingers. In addition, because they think low-tar, low-nicotine cigarettes are safer, many smokers smoke more often and inhale more deeply (Lee, Chen, & Hsieh, 2008). Consequently, they inhale about as much tar and nicotine per day as people smoking regular cigarettes and incur the same health risks (Benowitz et al., 2005; Kozlowski, Frecker, Khouw, & Pope, 1980).

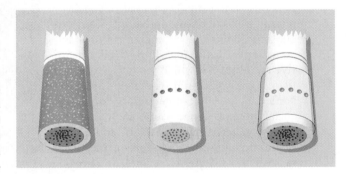

FIGURE 16.8 Cigarette butts of a regular cigarette, a low-nicotine cigarette smoked with the holes uncovered, and a low-nicotine cigarette smoked with the holes covered. The stain at the tip shows how much tar has come through.

ALCOHOLISM

Although most people drink alcohol in moderation, some let alcohol ruin their lives. **Alcoholism** is *the habitual overuse of alcohol.* Treating alcoholism is difficult, and the success rate is not impressive. If we could identify the problem earlier or identify young people who are at high risk for alcoholism, perhaps we could initiate effective prevention. At least, psychologists would like to try.

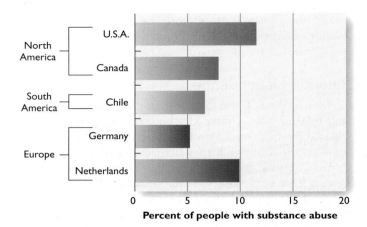

FIGURE 16.9 Percentage of people in five countries who have substance abuse disorder within a given year. (Based on data of Bijl, R. V., de Graaf, R., Hiripi, E., Kessler, R. C., Kohn, R., Offord, D. R., et al., 2003. The prevalence of treated and untreated mental disorders in five countries. *Health Affairs, 22,* 122–133.)

Genetics and Family Background

Twin studies have long indicated a strong genetic basis for alcoholism (True et al., 1999). Most alcoholics are also heavy cigarette smokers, and many abuse other drugs, too, so the genes that predispose to alcoholism probably predispose to addictive behavior in general. Researchers have identified at least six genes with a significant link to increased probability of addiction (Li & Burmeister, 2009). The outcome, of course, depends on the environment also. The prevalence of alcoholism and other kinds of substance abuse varies among cultures and subcultures. Figure 16.9 shows the data from five countries for which we have extensive data (Bijl et al., 2003). The genes linked to addiction increase susceptibility to various social influences that lead to addiction.

A genetic predisposition contributes mainly to early-onset alcoholism. Late-onset or Type I (or Type A) alcoholism *develops gradually over the years, affects about as many women as men, is generally less severe, and depends more on life experiences than genetics.* That is, Type I alcoholism often occurs in people with no family history. Early-onset or Type II (or Type B) alcoholism *develops rapidly, usually by age 25, is much more common in men than women, is usually more severe, and shows a stronger genetic basis* (Devor, Abell, Hoffman, Tabakoff, & Cloninger, 1994; McGue, 1999). Table 16.3 summarizes this distinction. Naturally, not everyone with alcoholism fits neatly into one category or the other.

The incidence of alcoholism is greater than average among people who grew up in families marked by conflict, hostility, and inadequate parental supervision of the children (Schulsinger, Knop, Goodwin, Teasdale, & Mikkelsen, 1986; Zucker & Gomberg, 1986). Women who were sexually abused in childhood are at increased risk for alcoholism (Kendler, Bulik, et al., 2000). Culture also plays an important role. For example, alcoholism is more prevalent in Irish culture, which tolerates it, than among Jews or Italians, who emphasize drinking in moderation (Cahalan, 1978; Vaillant & Milofsky, 1982).

Still, individuals differ. Not all children of alcoholic parents become alcoholics themselves, and not all children who grow up in a culture that tolerates heavy drinking become alcoholics. Can we identify people who are highly vulnerable to alcoholism?

Italian and Jewish cultures, which stress moderation, have a fair amount of alcohol use but not much abuse.

TABLE 16.3 Type I and Type II Alcoholism

	Severity	Gender Distribution	Genetics Basis	Onset
Type I (or Type A)	Generally less severe; better long-term outcome	Both males and females	Weaker genetic contribution	Gradual onset later in life
Type II (or Type B)	More severe, more likely to be associated with aggressive behavior and antisocial personality	Almost exclusively males	Strong evidence for genetic contribution	Rapid onset in teens or early 20s

What's the Evidence?

Ways of Predicting Alcoholism

Perhaps people's behavior might indicate who is more likely to develop alcoholism. One way to find such clues is to record the behaviors of young people and then, many years later, examine their alcohol use. However, this procedure requires decades of research and a huge sample of participants.

A more feasible approach is to compare people who have an alcoholic parent to people who have no alcoholic relatives. From previous studies, we know that more children of alcoholics will become alcoholics. Therefore, behaviors that are significantly more prevalent among the children of alcoholics may predict vulnerability to alcoholism. In the first study, experimenters tested whether alcohol provides more than the usual amount of reward to the sons of alcoholics (Levenson, Oyama, & Meek, 1987).

First Study

Hypothesis Drinking alcohol will provide relief for almost anyone in a stressful situation. It will provide more relief to the adult sons of alcoholic fathers than to other men of the same age.

The researchers did not study sons of alcoholic mothers because they were interested in genetics, not prenatal environment. If a mother drinks heavily during pregnancy, especially early pregnancy, she increases the risk of alcohol abuse in her children (Alati et al., 2006; Baer, Sampson, Barr, Connor, & Streissguth, 2003).

Method Half of the participants were sons of alcoholic fathers, and the others were from families with no known alcoholics. The young men were told that, at a certain time, they would receive an electric shock, and later, they would have to give a 3-minute speech entitled "What I Like and Dislike about My Body." (You can imagine the embarrassment and stress of that assignment.) They watched a clock tick off the waiting time. Alcohol was offered to half of each group at the start of the waiting period, and all of them drank it.

Results All of the men showed considerable stress as measured by heart rate, restlessness, and self-reports. Those who drank alcohol showed a lower heart rate and reported less anxiety. The easing of stress was more pronounced in those with an alcoholic father (Figure 16.10).

Interpretation Men who are genetically vulnerable to alcoholism experience greater stress-reducing effects from alcohol than other men of the same age. We do not know why that is true, but we might use the stress-reducing effects to predict vulnerability to alcoholism.

Second Study

Several other studies found that young men who are vulnerable to alcoholism have difficulty estimating their own degree of intoxication. This study tested whether young drinkers who underestimate their degree of intoxication are more likely than others to become alcoholics later in life (Schuckit & Smith, 1997).

Hypothesis Men who underestimate their intoxication after moderate drinking will be more likely than others to develop alcoholism later.

Method This study was limited to 18- to 25-year-old men with a close relative who was alcoholic. After each of them drank a fixed amount of alcohol, they were asked to walk and describe how intoxicated they felt. Experimenters measured the stagger or sway when the men walked. Ten years later, the experimenters located as many of these men as possible, interviewed them, and determined which ones had become alcoholics.

Results Of those who either did not sway much when walking or stated that they did not feel intoxicated, 51 of 81 (63%) became alcoholics within 10 years. Of those who clearly swayed and reported feeling intoxicated, 9 of 52 (17%) became alcoholics.

Interpretation Men who neither act nor feel intoxicated after a moderate amount of drinking are likely to continue drinking and to become alcoholics. By watching and interviewing young drinkers, psychologists can identify a high-risk population.

One limitation of these studies is clear: They examined only men. A study of a small sample of women found that daughters of alcoholics, like sons of alcoholics, tend to feel less intoxicated and show less body sway after drinking alcohol (Schuckit et al., 2000). We do not yet know how well that tendency predicts later alcoholism.

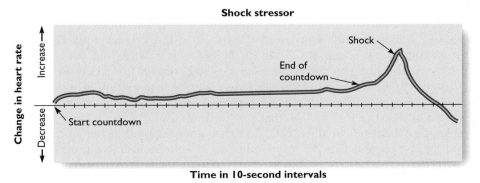

FIGURE 16.10 Changes in stress over time for a typical subject: The line goes up to indicate an increase in heart rate. Alcohol suppressed the signs of stress, especially for the sons of alcoholics. (From "Greater Reinforcement from Alcohol for Those at Risk: Parental Risk, Personality Risk, and Sex," by Levenson et al., *Journal of Abnormal Psychology*, 1987, *96*, 242–253. Copyright © 1987 by the American Psychological Association. Reprinted by permission of the author.)

12. What are two ways the sons of alcoholics differ from the sons of nonalcoholics?

Answer

12. Alcohol gives them more than the average amount of relief from stress, and they do not appear or feel as drunk as other people do after a moderate amount of drinking.

Treatments

> My mind is a dark place, and I should not be left alone there at night.
>
> —Participant at Alcoholics Anonymous Meeting

Of all the people who try to quit alcohol or other drugs on their own, an estimated 10 to 20% manage to succeed (S. Cohen et al., 1989), though not necessarily on the first try. Some people quit and relapse many times before eventual success. In many cases, however, people with a substance-abuse problem find that they cannot quit on their own. Eventually, they "hit bottom," discovering that they have damaged their health, their ability to hold a job, and their relationships with friends and family. At that point, they turn to either a mental health professional or a self-help group such as Alcoholics Anonymous. Combating alcoholism is difficult but not hopeless. Let's consider several approaches and controversies.

Alcoholics Anonymous

The most popular treatment for alcoholism in North America is Alcoholics Anonymous (AA), *a self-help group of people who are trying to abstain from alcohol use and help others do the same.* AA meetings are held regularly in community halls, church basements, and other available spaces. The meeting format varies but often includes study of the book *Alcoholics Anonymous* (Anonymous, 1955) and discussions of participants' individual problems. Some meetings feature an invited speaker. The group has a strong spiritual focus, including a reliance on "a Power greater than ourselves," but no affiliation with any particular religion. Although AA imposes no requirements on its members other than making an effort to quit alcohol, new members are strongly encouraged to attend 90 meetings during the first 90 days. The idea is to make a strong commitment. From then on, members attend as often as they like.

Millions of people have participated in the AA program. One reason for its appeal is that all its members have gone through similar experiences. If someone tries to make an excuse for drinking and says, "You just don't understand how I feel," others can retort, "Oh, yes we do!" A member who feels the urge to take a drink can phone a fellow member day or night for support. The only charge is a voluntary contribution toward the cost of renting the meeting place. AA has inspired Narcotics Anonymous (NA) and other "anonymous" self-help groups to help compulsive gamblers, compulsive eaters, and others.

Researchers find that people who regularly attend AA or NA meetings, and who have a strong commitment to the program, are more likely than other addicts to abstain from alcohol and drugs (Gossop, Stewart, & Marsden, 2008; Laffaye, McKellar, Ilgen, & Moos, 2008). However, we cannot draw a cause-and-effect conclusion, tempting as it might be. People are not randomly assigned to attendance or nonattendance at the meetings. Presumably, those who attend regularly differ in many ways from those who decline to participate or who try a few times and then quit.

Antabuse

In addition to or instead of attendance at AA meetings, some individuals with alcoholism seek medical treatment. Many years ago, investigators noticed that the workers in a certain rubber manufacturing plant drank very little alcohol. The investigators eventually linked this behavior to *disulfiram,* a chemical that was used in the manufacturing process. Ordinarily, the liver converts alcohol into a toxic substance, *acetaldehyde* (ASS-eh-TAL-de-HIDE) and then converts acetaldehyde into a harmless substance, *acetic acid.* Disulfiram, however, blocks the conversion of acetaldehyde to acetic acid. Whenever the workers exposed to disulfiram drank alcohol, they accumulated acetaldehyde and became ill. Over time, they learned to avoid alcohol.

Disulfiram, available under the trade name Antabuse, is now sometimes used in the treatment of alcoholism, but it is regarded as only moderately effective (Hughes & Cook, 1997). *Alcoholics who take a daily Antabuse pill become sick whenever they have a drink.* They develop headache, nausea, blurred vision, anxiety, and a sensation of heat in the face. The threat of sickness is more effective than the sickness itself (Fuller & Roth, 1979). By taking a daily Antabuse pill, a recovering alcoholic renews the decision not to drink. Those who do take a drink in spite of the threat become quite ill, at which point they decide either not to drink again or not to take the pill again! Several other medications are also moderately effective in helping people quit alcohol. In each case, the medication is most effective for people who are strongly motivated to quit (Krishnan-Sarin, Krystal, Shi, Pittman, & O'Malley, 2007; Mason, Goodman, Chabac, & Lehert, 2006).

13. About 50% of Southeast Asians have a gene that makes them unable to convert acetaldehyde to acetic acid. Would such people be more likely or less likely than others to become alcoholics?

Answer

13. They are less likely than others to become alcoholics. This gene is considered the probable reason that relatively few Asians become alcoholics (Harada, Agarwal, Goedde, Tagaki, & Ishikawa, 1982; Reed, 1985).

Harm Reduction

Most physicians agree with Alcoholics Anonymous that the only hope for an alcoholic is abstinence. Drinking in moderation, they insist, is out of the question. A few psychologists doubt that abstention is a realistic goal for everyone (Peele, 1998). The harm reduction approach *concentrates on decreasing the frequency of drug use and minimizing the harmful consequences to health and well-being,* even if the person does not abstain (MacCoun, 1998). Critics charge that the idea of reduced drinking discourages people from making a serious effort at abstinence. Defenders reply that when people find that they cannot quit, we should not give up on helping them.

Contingency Management

Another approach is a form of behavior therapy known as *contingency management.* Practitioners monitor alcohol use by a Breathalyzer or other drugs by urine samples. Whenever the test shows no alcohol or drugs, a therapist provides an immediate reinforcement. For example, teenagers might receive a movie pass or a voucher for a pizza (Kaminer, 2000).

A major strength of this approach is that many people who are not motivated to try other approaches do agree to receive rewards for being free of alcohol and drugs. The effectiveness of contingency management is surprising, as the rewards are small. That is, people could have abstained from alcohol and drugs and then used the money they saved to give themselves the same or greater rewards. Evidently, there is something powerful about testing negative for drugs and then receiving an immediate reinforcement.

OPIATE DEPENDENCE

Prior to 1900, opiate drugs such as morphine and heroin were considered less dangerous than alcohol (Siegel, 1987). In fact, many doctors urged patients with alcoholism to switch from alcohol to morphine. Then, around 1900, opiates became illegal in the United States, except by prescription to control pain. Since then, research on opiate use has been limited by the fact that only lawbreakers use opiates.

Opiate dependence often has a rapid onset in contrast to alcohol and tobacco dependence, which develop more slowly. Like alcoholism, opiate abuse shows a hereditary tendency. That is, the closer your genetic relationship to an opiate abuser, the higher your probability

of developing the same problem (Kendler, Karkowski, Neale, & Prescott, 2000).

Treatments

Some users of heroin and other opiates try to break their habit by going "cold turkey"—quitting completely, sometimes under medical supervision. Many people, however, experience a recurring urge to take the drug long after the withdrawal symptoms have subsided. To combat that urge, they can turn to self-help groups, contingency management, and other treatments. Cognitive-behavioral therapists emphasize the importance of identifying the locations and situations in which a person has the greatest cravings and the greatest temptation to relapse into drug use. Therapists then teach the person how to minimize exposure to those situations and how to handle the situations when avoiding them is impossible (Witkiewitz & Marlatt, 2004).

For those who cannot quit, researchers have sought to find a nonaddictive substitute that would satisfy the craving for opiates without harmful side effects. (Heroin was originally introduced as a substitute for morphine before physicians discovered that it is even more troublesome!)

The drug methadone (METH-uh-don) *is sometimes offered as a less dangerous substitute for opiates.* Methadone, which is chemically similar to morphine and heroin, can itself be addictive. (Table 16.4 compares methadone and morphine.) When methadone is taken as a pill, however, it enters the bloodstream gradually and departs gradually (Dole, 1980). (If morphine or heroin is taken as a pill, much of it is digested and

Heroin withdrawal resembles a week-long bout of severe flu, with aching limbs, intense chills, vomiting, and diarrhea. Unfortunately, even after people have endured withdrawal, they still sometimes crave the drug.

TABLE 16.4 Comparison of Methadone with Morphine

	Morphine	Methadone by Injection	Methadone Taken Orally
Addictive?	Yes	Yes	Weakly
Onset	Rapid	Rapid	Slow
"Rush"?	Yes	Yes	No
Relieves craving?	Yes	Yes	Yes
Rapid withdrawal symptoms?	Yes	Yes	No

never reaches the brain.) Thus, methadone does not produce the "rush" associated with injected opiates. It satisfies the craving without producing a strong "high" and blocks heroin or morphine

from reaching the same receptors. Although methadone satisfies the craving for opiates, it does not eliminate the addiction. If the dosage is reduced, the craving returns.

The drugs *buprenorphine* and *levo-α-acetyl-methadol acetate* (LAAM) have effects similar to methadone. Most buprenorphine users decrease their use of heroin and other drugs, decrease their criminal activities, and improve their health (Teesson et al., 2006).

14. Many methadone clinics carefully watch patients while they are taking their pills. Why?

Answer

14. Someone who didn't swallow the pill could dissolve it in water and inject it to get a "high" similar to that of heroin or morphine.

16.2 | module

In Closing

Substances, the Individual, and Society

Anxiety disorders and depression are serious problems for the people suffering with them and for their families and friends. Substance abuse is a big problem for everyone because it is closely linked to crime, unemployment, drunk driving, and other threats to society (Odgers et al., 2008).

SUMMARY

- *Substance dependence.* People who find it difficult or impossible to stop using a substance are said to be dependent on it or addicted to it. (page 581)
- *Addictive substances.* Nearly all addictive substances stimulate dopamine synapses in a brain area that is apparently associated with attention. (page 581)
- *Motivations behind addiction.* Some people continue using drugs frequently despite little apparent pleasure. One hypothesis is that they use the drugs to escape displeasure. Another is that frequent use of a drug modifies brain circuits to make the drug dominate attention. (page 582)

- *The disease concept.* Whether or not substance abuse is considered a disease depends on what we mean by disease. (page 583)
- *Predisposition to alcoholism.* People at risk for alcoholism find that alcohol relieves their stress more than it does for other people. People who underestimate their level of intoxication are more likely than others to become alcoholics later. (page 585)
- *Alcoholics Anonymous.* The self-help group Alcoholics Anonymous provides the most common treatment for alcoholism in North America. (page 586)

- *Antabuse.* Some alcoholics are treated with Antabuse, a prescription drug that makes them ill if they drink alcohol. (page 586)
- *The controlled drinking controversy.* Whether certain alcoholics can be trained to drink in moderation is controversial. (page 587)

- *Opiate abuse.* Some opiate users quit using opiates, suffer through the withdrawal symptoms, and manage to abstain from further use. Others substitute methadone or buprenorphine under medical supervision. (page 587)

KEY TERMS

Alcoholics Anonymous (AA) (page 586)

alcoholism (page 583)

Antabuse (page 586)

dependence (or addiction) (page 581)

harm reduction (page 587)

methadone (page 587)

physical dependence (page 582)

psychological dependence (page 582)

Type I (or Type A) alcoholism (page 584)

Type II (or Type B) alcoholism (page 584)

- What causes severe mood swings?
- What can be done to relieve them?

Ordinarily, most people feel happy when life is going well and sad when it is not. Some people, however, feel extremely bad or (less often) extremely good for weeks or months regardless of the events in their lives. Why?

DEPRESSION

People who say "I'm depressed," often mean "I'm discouraged. Life isn't going well for me right now." A **major depression** is a more *extreme condition, persisting most of each day for at least 2 weeks, usually more, while the person experiences little interest, pleasure, motivation, activity, or ability to concentrate.* Sadness is characteristic of depression, but lack of happiness is even more characteristic. People with depression no longer enjoy food or sex. Many say they cannot even imagine anything that would make them happy. In one study, people had a beeper that alerted them at unpredictable times to make a note in their journal of what they were doing and how they felt about it. People with depression reported about an average number of sad experiences but far fewer than average happy experiences (Peters, Nicolson, Berkhof, Delespaul, & deVries, 2003). In another study, people viewed pictures while researchers recorded their expressions. Depressed people responded about the same as others to sad pictures but showed almost no response to pleasant pictures (Sloan, Strauss, & Wisner, 2001).

Nearly all depressed people experience sleep abnormalities (Carroll, 1980; Healy & Williams, 1988) (see Figure 16.11). They enter REM sleep within 45 minutes after falling asleep—an unusually short time for most people—and have more frequent eye movements during their REM periods.

Normal sleep

← 90 minutes →

Depressed sleep

← 90 minutes →

FIGURE 16.11 Most people sleeping at their usual time progress slowly to stage 4 and then back through stages 3, 2, and REM. Depressed people enter REM sooner than average and awaken frequently during the night.

They wake up early and cannot get back to sleep. When morning comes, they feel poorly rested. Sleep difficulty is often an early sign of depression (Modell, Ising, Holsboer, & Lauer, 2005). A longitudinal study found that adolescents who had trouble sleeping were more likely than other adolescents to become depressed later (Roane & Taylor, 2008).

Depression is common from adolescence through old age. About 10% of U.S. adults are depressed within any given year (Kessler, Chiu, Demler, & Walters, 2005), and about 20% are depressed at some time in life (Kessler, Berglund, Demler, Jin, & Walters, 2005). Figure 16.12 shows the prevalence of major depression across various countries (Bijl et al., 2003; King et al., 2008; Murali, 2001; Tiwari & Wang, 2006). It is difficult, of course, to distinguish between differences in prevalence and differences in standards of diagnosis. Also, some of the samples were small.

The good news is that few people remain permanently depressed. Typically, people have an episode of depression that lasts a few months (less commonly, years) and then recover. The bad news is that depression is likely to return. Later episodes tend to be briefer but more frequent (Solomon et al., 1997). A common pattern is that an intensely stressful event triggers the first episode of depression, but later episodes seem to occur on their own with little evidence of stress. Later episodes also become more difficult to treat. It is as if the brain learns how to become depressed. It gets better and better at becoming depressed (Monroe & Harkness, 2005; Post, 1992). The same is true for epilepsy and migraine headaches: The more episodes one has had, the easier it is to have another one. An implication is that early treatment is important for depression.

In a variant form of depression known as **seasonal affective disorder (SAD)**, or **depression with a seasonal pattern** (Figure 16.13), *people repeatedly become depressed during a particular season of the year.* It is common in Scandinavia, which has huge differences between summer and winter (Haggarty et al., 2002), and almost universal among explorers who spend long times in Antarctica (Palinkas, 2003). Although annual winter depressions receive the most

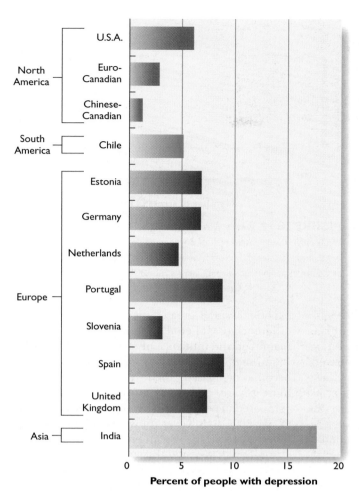

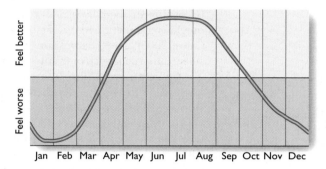

FIGURE 16.12 Percentage of people in various countries who have major depression within a given year. (Based on data from these sources: Bijl, R. V., de Graaf, R., Hiripi, E., Kessler, R. C., Kohn, R., Offord, D. R., et al., 2003. The prevalence of treated and untreated mental disorders in five countries. *Health Affairs, 22,* 122–133; King, M., Nazareth, I., Levy, G., Walker, C., Morris, R., Weich, S., et al., 2008. Prevalence of common mental disorders in general practice attendees across Europe. *British Journal of Psychiatry, 192,* 362–367; Murali, M. S., 2001. Epidemiological study of prevalence of mental disorders in India. *Indian Journal of Community Medicine, 26,* 198; Tiwari, S. K., & Wang, J. L., 2006. The epidemiology of mental and substance use-related disorders among White, Chinese, and other Asian populations in Canada. *Canadian Journal of Psychiatry, 51,* 904–912.)

FIGURE 16.13 Most people feel better during the summer than during the winter, when there are fewer hours of sunlight. The differences are greater for people with seasonal affective disorder (SAD).

publicity, annual summer depressions also occur (Faedda et al., 1993). Unlike other depressed patients, most people with seasonal affective disorder sleep and eat excessively during their depressed periods (Jacobsen, Sack, Wehr, Rogers, & Rosenthal, 1987). In contrast to other depressed patients who generally get sleepy early and wake up early, people with SAD tend to fall asleep late and awaken late (Teicher et al., 1997). The disorder is linked to a gene that affects circadian rhythms (Johansson et al., 2003).

The most effective treatment for seasonal affective disorder is sitting in front of a bright light for a few hours each day. Although the effects of light therapy are poorly understood, they are powerful, reliable, and inexpensive, with no side effects (Wirz-Justice, 1998). Preliminary results suggest that light therapy also helps some people with non-seasonal depression (Kripke, 1998; Putilov, Pinchasov, & Poljakova, 2005). To find more information about seasonal affective disorder and light therapy, visit SADA's website. Find a current link to this website at **www.cengage.com/psychology/kalat**.

Bipolar disorder, previously known as *manic-depressive disorder,* is a related condition in which someone *alternates between periods of depression and periods of mania, which are opposite extremes.* We consider bipolar disorder in more detail later.

15. How does major depression differ from ordinary sadness or discouragement?

16. What might you observe about people to determine which ones were most likely to become depressed later?

Concept Check

Answers

15. Major depression is more severe than sadness and lasts months. A person with major depression finds almost no pleasure in anything.

16. You could examine sleep patterns. Depressed people show certain sleep abnormalities, such as REM periods soon after going to sleep, and some of these sleep abnormalities occur long before depression itself.

Environmental and Genetic Influences on Depression

As a rule, people become depressed when bad things happen to them, especially events that leave them feeling helpless, humiliated, or guilty (Kendler, Hettema, Butera, Gardner, & Prescott, 2003). However, when various people have roughly the same experience, some become depressed and others do not. For example, of the people who lived in New York City during the terrorist attack on the World Trade Center in 2001, about 9% became seriously depressed within the next 6 months. Most of those were people with many other stressful events in their lives and a history of previous traumatic events (Person, Tracy, & Galea, 2006). Thus, depression usually results from a sequence of events, not a single event.

Genetic factors also influence people's likelihood of depression. If you become depressed before age 30, the probability is high that some of your close relatives are or will be depressed also (Kendler, Gardner, & Prescott, 1999; Lyons et al., 1998). If you become depressed later in life, the probability is high that some of your close relatives have problems with their blood circulation (Kendler, Fiske, Gardner, & Gatz, 2009). These results imply two sets of genes and two ways of becoming depressed—one of them related to brain functioning and the other related to blood flow. However, no gene is specific to depression. Many people with depression have relatives with substance abuse, antisocial personality disorder, attention-deficit disorder, bulimia nervosa, migraine headaches, and other disorders (Fu et al., 2002; Hudson et al., 2003; Kendler et al., 1995). Evidently, certain genes magnify the risk of a variety of physical and mental disorders.

While seeking to identify genes related to depression, researchers found inconsistent results. Then they considered the possibility that certain genes influence how people respond to stress instead of directly provoking depression. Figure 16.14 shows the results of a study examining different alleles (forms) of a gene controlling production of the neurotransmitter serotonin. One allele is called *s* (short), and the other is *l* (long). A person can have two *s* alleles (*s/s*), two *l* alleles (*l/l*), or one of each (*s/l*). Researchers compared people with different numbers of stressful experiences such as divorce and job loss. For young adults reporting no major stressors, the risk of depression was only moderate regardless of the genes. For those with stressful experiences, people with the *s/s* combination had the greatest probability of depression, and those with the *l/l* combination had the least. The greater the number of stressful

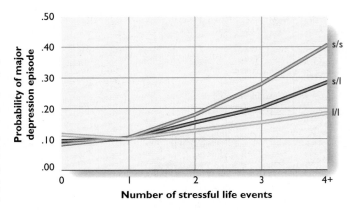

FIGURE 16.14 People with the *s/s* genes controlling serotonin levels have the greatest risk of depression, and those with the *l/l* genes have the least, but only for people who have had seriously stressful experiences. (From Caspi et al., 2003)

experiences, the greater the effect of the genetic difference (Caspi et al., 2003). That is, the *s* allele magnified the influence of stress. A further study found that when people with the *s/s* combination become depressed, their depression is usually more severe, and their episodes more frequent, compared to people with the other genes (Zalsman et al., 2006). However, most other studies have failed to replicate this interaction among genes, stress, and depression (Risch et al., 2009). The different results may stem from different ways of measuring stress (Monroe & Reid, 2008), or it may be that this gene really doesn't have much influence on depression.

17. Why might a particular gene appear to be linked to depression in one sample of people but not in another?

Answer

17. Perhaps certain genes increase the risk of depression among people who have experienced severe stress. Such genes would show no clear link to depression in people who had less stress. However, most studies have failed to replicate this promising hypothesis.

Gender Differences

Depression is uncommon before adolescence, but from adolescence on, it occurs about twice as often in women as in men, and the ratio is even higher for severe depression. Women experience depression more than men in all cultures for which we have data (Culbertson, 1997; Cyranowski, Frank, Young, & Shear, 2000; Silberg et al., 1999).

Why is depression more common in women than men? On the average, depressed women have about the same hormonal levels as other women (Roca, Schmidt, & Rubinow, 1999), so hormones are apparently not the answer. One hypothesis is that females encounter more negative events than males do (Hankin & Abramson, 2001). For example, severe sexual abuse in childhood increases the risk of later depression, and more girls than boys are sexually abused. The strongest evidence for the effects of sexual abuse comes from a study that compared pairs of twins in which one reported childhood sexual abuse and the other did not. On the average, the twin reporting sexual abuse had more depression than the other twin (E. C. Nelson et al., 2002). Of course, this conclusion presumes that both twins accurately reported childhood events.

Susan Nolen-Hoeksema (1990, 1991) has suggested that the excess of depression among women relates to how people react to emotional distress: When men start to feel sad, they generally try to distract themselves. They play basketball, watch a movie, or do something else instead of thinking about how they feel. Women are more likely to **ruminate**—*to think about their depressing experiences, talk about their feelings, and perhaps cry*. Ruminating interferes with problem solving, takes time away from pleasant social activities, and biases a person toward a pessimistic appraisal of the situation (Nolen-Hoeksema, Wisco, & Lyubomirsky, 2008). In one study, people watched a sad movie and then researchers randomly assigned them to ruminate about the film or distract themselves. Those who ruminated about the film felt worse afterward (Ciesla & Roberts, 2007).

An explanation in terms of rumination has the advantage of suggesting ways to help people avoid or minimize depression. It does not, however, explain *why* women ruminate more and distract themselves less than men do. Another difficult question: Do the ruminative thoughts *lead to* depression? Or are they an early symptom of depression?

Although ruminating about your unpleasant feelings tends to make them worse, thinking about the problem that led to the feelings can be helpful. The difference is this: If you think about some unfortunate event as if it were happening again, you feel worse. If you think about it as if you were an outside observer, you become calmer and you make plans to solve the problem (Ayduk & Kross, 2008).

Cognitive Aspects of Depression

Suppose you fail a test. Choose your probable explanation:

- The test was difficult. Probably other students did poorly, too.
- I had a weak background in this topic from my previous education compared to others.
- I didn't get a good chance to study.
- I'm just stupid. I always do badly no matter how hard I try.

The first three explanations attribute your failure to something temporary, specific, or correctable. However, the fourth attribution applies always and everywhere. If you make that attribution—and if you care about your grades—you are likely to feel depressed (Abramson, Seligman, & Teasdale, 1978; C. Peterson, Bettes, & Seligman, 1985).

In a given situation, you might have a good reason for one attribution or another. Still, everyone has an **explanatory style**, *a tendency to accept one kind of explanation for success or failure more often than others*. Most people are fairly consistent in how they explain their failures (Burns & Seligman, 1989). Recall from chapter 13 that an *internal attribution* cites a cause within the person. ("I studied poorly.") An *external attribution* identifies causes outside the person. ("The test was hard.")

Blaming yourself isn't always wrong, of course. However, taking the blame too consistently constitutes a *pessimistic* explanatory style, especially if your attributions for failure are global (applying to all situations) and stable (applying to all times). People with a pessimistic style are more likely than others to have been depressed in the past and more likely to become depressed in the future (Alloy et al., 1999; Haeffel et al., 2005). According to Aaron Beck (1973, 1987), people with depression put unfavorable interpretations on almost all their experiences. If someone walks by without comment, their likely response is, "See, people ignore me. They don't like me." After any kind of defeat, "I'm hopeless." Athletes with a pessimistic style tend to give up and try less after a defeat. Athletes with a more optimistic style try harder after a defeat because they believe they can overcome their defeats with hard work (Seligman, Nolen-Hoeksema, Thornton, & Thornton, 1990). (How do you react after a disappointment? Do you try harder or do you give up?)

Depression is most common among people who have little social support.

18. Would depressed people be more or less likely than others to buy a lottery ticket?

Answer

18. Depressed people are less likely than others to buy a lottery ticket because they regard their chances of success as remote on any task.

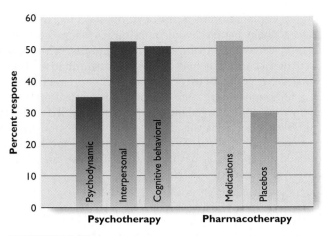

FIGURE 16.15 About one third of depressed patients recover without treatment, many others recover with treatment, and more than one third respond poorly to treatment. (From Hollon, S. D., Thase, M. E., and Markowitz, J. C., 2002. Treatment and prevention of depression, *Psychological Science in the Public Interest, 3,* 39–77. Reprinted by permission of Wiley-Blackwell Publishers.)

Treatments

The usual treatment for depression is psychotherapy or antidepressant drugs. Of people with depression who have no treatment or only a placebo, about one third will improve significantly over the next few months. *Improvement without treatment* is called spontaneous recovery. Of those who get interpersonal or cognitive-behavioral psychotherapy, more than half will improve. Psychodynamic therapy, including psychoanalysis, has been tested less often but appears less effective. Of those who take antidepressant drugs, more than half improve (Hollon, Thase, & Markowitz, 2002). Figure 16.15 shows the results. Psychotherapy and antidepressant drugs appear to help about the same percentage of people. Note that many of the people who recover with either psychotherapy or medication would have recovered spontaneously without treatment. A combination of psychotherapy and antidepressant drugs boosts the mean benefit but still leaves many people not responding.

Psychotherapy

Most of the research on psychotherapy for depression focuses on interpersonal therapy and cognitive therapy, as shown in Figure 16.15. Interpersonal therapy *focuses on improving people's social relationships and helping them cope with current or recent problems such as death of a loved one, divorce, or unemployment* (Hollon et al., 2002). Cognitive therapy, as discussed in chapter 15, focuses on changing people's thoughts and encouraging a more active life. According to Aaron Beck, a pioneer in cognitive therapy, depressed people

are guided by certain thoughts or assumptions of which they are only dimly aware. He refers to the "negative cognitive triad of depression":

- I am deprived or defeated.
- The world is full of obstacles.
- The future is devoid of hope.

Based on these "automatic thoughts," people who are depressed interpret ambiguous situations to their own disadvantage. When something goes wrong, they habitually blame themselves (Beck, 1991). The therapist focuses on a belief, such as "no one likes me," points out that it is a hypothesis, and invites the client to collect evidence to test it.

Psychologists today put less emphasis than Beck did on faulty reasoning and more on excessive emotions as the cause of depression (Johnson-Laird, Mancini, & Gangemi, 2006). Nevertheless, cognitive and cognitive-behavioral therapies are reasonably effective for depression. In addition to the focus on changing thoughts and beliefs, cognitive therapy also encourages people to become more active—to take part in more activities that might bring pleasure or a sense of accomplishment. Research has found that giving depressed people just this guidance toward greater activity produces good antidepressant effects (Jacobson et al., 1996). Think about a parallel finding in chapter 14: Introverts who pretend to be extraverted (i.e., more outgoing for the time being) report feeling happier. The same applies here: Just getting people to become more active helps relieve depression.

Antidepressant Medications

The common antidepressants include tricyclics, serotonin reuptake inhibitors, and monoamine oxidase inhibitors. Tricyclic drugs (e.g., imipramine, trade name Tofranil) *block the reabsorption of the neurotransmitters dopamine, norepinephrine, and serotonin after they are released by an axon's terminal* (Figure 16.16). Thus, tricyclics prolong the effect of these neurotransmitters on the receptors of the postsynaptic cell. Although they are effective for many people, they produce unpleasant side effects, including dry mouth, difficulty urinating, heart irregularities, and drowsiness (Horst & Preskorn, 1998). Many people quit the drugs or reduce the dosage because of the side effects.

Selective serotonin reuptake inhibitors (SSRIs) (e.g., fluoxetine, trade name Prozac) are similar to tricyclic drugs but more specific in their effects. They *block the reuptake of the neurotransmitter serotonin.* Their side effects are usually limited to mild nausea or headache (Feighner et al., 1991). Other common drugs in this category are sertraline (Zoloft), fluvoxamine (Luvox), citalopram (Celexa), and paroxetine (Paxil or Seroxat).

Monoamine (MAHN-oh-ah-MEEN) oxidase inhibitors (MAOIs) (e.g., phenelzine, trade name Nardil) *block the metabolic breakdown of released dopamine, norepinephrine, and serotonin* by the enzyme monoamine oxidase (MAO) (Figure 16.16c). Like the tricyclics and SSRIs, MAOIs prolong the ability of released neurotransmitters to stimulate the postsynaptic cell.

Other antidepressant drugs have little in common with each other except that they do not fit into the first three groups. These atypical antidepressants *are about as effective, on the average, as other antidepressants and produce milder side effects.* They act primarily on dopamine or norepinephrine synapses rather than serotonin, although their mechanism of effect is not entirely certain. The most common of these is buproprion, also known by the trade name Wellbutrin (Thase et al., 2005). Two studies found that 25 to 30% of patients who did not respond to one of the SSRI drugs improved after switching to one of the atypical antidepressants or a combination of an SSRI and an atypical antidepressant for an additional 12 to 14 weeks (Rush et al., 2006; Trivedi et al., 2006). However, neither study had a control group to consider the possibility that these patients might have improved spontaneously during that period of time.

You have probably heard about St. John's wort, *an herb with antidepressant effects.* It contains several chemicals that block the reuptake of dopamine and serotonin, as other antidepressant drugs do. Because St. John's wort is a naturally occurring substance, it is inexpensive and available without a doctor's prescription. Reports vary on its effectiveness, but it has drawbacks. Its strength varies from one batch to another because the Food and Drug Administration does not regulate the sale of herbs. Also, it has this unusual side effect: It activates a liver enzyme that breaks down toxic plant chemicals—a good thing to break down—but it also breaks down most medications (Moore et al., 2000). It is therefore risky for anyone in treatment for any medical condition.

19. Which type of antidepressant drug has effects similar to methylphenidate (Ritalin), discussed in chapter 3?
20. If you take prescription antidepressant drugs, would it help to take St. John's wort also?

Answers

19. The effects of methylphenidate (Ritalin) resemble those of buproprion (Wellbutrin). Both block the reuptake of dopamine. Buproprion, like methylphenidate, is sometimes prescribed for attention-deficit disorder. The effects of methylphenidate also overlap those of tricyclics.
20. It would be risky. St. John's wort activates an enzyme that breaks down nearly all medicines, including antidepressant drugs.

The effects of antidepressant drugs develop gradually. Nearly any benefit within the first 2 weeks is a *placebo effect,* which depends on the person's expectation of feeling better (Stewart et al., 1998). The effects of the drug itself begin after 2 to 3 weeks and increase over the next few weeks (Blaine, Prien, & Levine, 1983). Even then, part of the apparent drug effect is also a placebo effect or an effect of the passage of time. Figure 16.17 summarizes the results of many studies with many antidepressant drugs. People with mild to moderate depression respond about as well to placebos as they do to the drugs. The drugs provide a significant benefit for people with severe depression, mainly because those people are unlikely to respond well to placebos (Kirsch et al., 2008).

The fact that antidepressant drugs alter synaptic activity within an hour or so but need weeks to improve someone's mood tells us that the

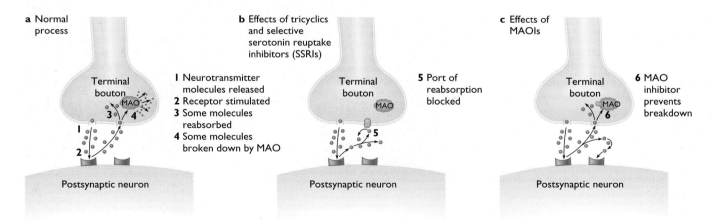

FIGURE 16.16 (a) Ordinarily, after the release of a neurotransmitter, some of the molecules are reabsorbed by the terminal bouton, and some are broken down by the enzyme monoamine oxidase (MAO). (b) Selective serotonin reuptake inhibitors (SSRIs) prevent reabsorption of serotonin. Tricyclic drugs prevent reabsorption of dopamine, norepinephrine, and serotonin. (c) MAO inhibitors (MAOIs) block the enzyme monoamine oxidase and thereby increase the availability of the neurotransmitter.

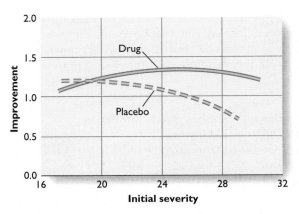

FIGURE 16.17 The mean amount of improvement varies depending on how severe the depression was before treatment. For people with mild to moderate depression, recovery is about equal with placebos or antidepressant drugs. The drugs show a significant benefit for severely depressed people because they do not respond well to placebos. (From Kirsch, I., Deacon, B. J., Heudo-Medina, T. B., Scoboria, A., Moore, T. J., & Johnson, B. T., 2008. Initial severity and antidepressant benefits: A meta-analysis of data submitted to the Food and Drug Administration. *PLoS Medicine, 5*(2), e45.)

explanation in terms of synapses must be incomplete. Some change within the brain must develop more slowly (Krishnan & Nestler, 2008). One promising hypothesis concerns cell growth. In several brain areas, neurons' cell bodies shrink visibly—well, visibly under a microscope—when people become depressed (Cotter, Mackay, Landau, Kerwin, & Everall, 2001). Most people with depression have low levels of *neurotrophins* (chemicals that stimulate growth and activity of neurons) in certain brain areas, and antidepressant treatments increase these levels (Sen, Duman, & Sanacora, 2008). Another promising hypothesis is that antidepressants promote the gradual growth of new circuits that increase communication in the hippocampus (Airan et al., 2007).

Choosing Between Psychotherapy and Antidepressant Drugs

Psychotherapy helps about the same percentage of patients as antidepressant drugs do. Nevertheless, each has its advantages and disadvantages (Hollon et al., 2005). Antidepressant drugs usually show benefits a little faster. They are also less expensive than psychotherapy and more convenient. (It's easier to take a pill than to drive somewhere and spend an hour with a therapist.) However, the drugs produce unpleasant side effects, such as dry mouth, difficulty urinating, or increased blood pressure. In addition, many peo-

ple find that after they stop taking the drugs, their depression returns a few months later. Psychotherapy shows slower benefits, but the benefits have a better chance of lasting long after the person ends therapy. Psychotherapy is particularly recommended for patients who report traumatic childhood experiences—such as death of their parents or prolonged neglect (Nemeroff et al., 2003).

Combining psychotherapy and antidepressant drugs helps, but not as much as you might guess. A combination has the advantages of acting fast and giving a good chance of long-term relief. However, combined treatment doesn't help a much higher percentage of patients than either treatment alone does (Hollon et al., 2005). In short, about 30% of people recover from depression fairly quickly by placebos or the passage of time. Another 20 to 30% recover with either psychotherapy or antidepressant drugs. And then some others are hard to treat. For that reason, therapists continue looking for new treatments.

Electroconvulsive Shock Therapy

Another treatment for depression is electroconvulsive therapy (ECT) (Figure 16.18): *A brief electrical shock is administered across the patient's head to induce a convulsion similar to epilepsy.* ECT, first used in the 1930s, was widely used in the 1940s and 1950s as a treatment for many psychiatric disorders. It fell out of favor because of its history of abuse. Some patients were subjected to ECT hundreds of times without informed consent, and sometimes, ECT was used more as a punishment than a therapy.

Beginning in the 1970s, ECT made a comeback in modified form, mostly for severely depressed people who fail to respond to antidepressant drugs or patients with strong suicidal tendencies (Scovern & Kilmann, 1980). For suicidal patients, ECT has the advantage of rapid effect, generally within 1 week. When a life is at stake, rapid relief is important. However, about half of those who show a good response will relapse into depression within 6 months unless they receive some other therapy to prevent it (Riddle & Scott, 1995).

ECT is now used only with patients who have given their informed consent. The shock is less intense than it had been, and the patient is given muscle relaxants to prevent injury and anesthetics to reduce discomfort. As

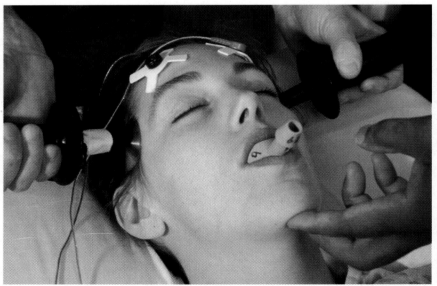

FIGURE 16.18 Electroconvulsive therapy is administered today only with the patient's informed consent. ECT is given in conjunction with muscle relaxants and anesthetics to minimize discomfort.

a rule, the procedure is applied every other day for about 2 weeks. Then the psychiatrist evaluates the progress and either stops the treatment or repeats it a few more times. Its most common side effect is temporary memory impairment.

How ECT works is uncertain, but it is not by causing people to forget depressing memories. ECT that is administered to just the frontal part of the brain or just the right hemisphere is as effective as the usual whole-brain ECT but without significant memory loss (Lisanby, Maddox, Prudic, Devanand, & Sackeim, 2000; Sackeim et al., 2000).

Other Treatments

Several free or inexpensive treatments have shown significant benefits in limited research. One method, already mentioned, is the use of bright lights. A second is to get consistent aerobic exercise, such as jogging or brisk walking, to increase blood flow to the brain (Leppämäki, Partonen, & Lönnqvist, 2002). However, although the evidence clearly shows that exercise correlates with less chance of depression, we cannot draw a cause-and-effect conclusion. Perhaps it is just that the people who are prone to depression are unlikely to exercise (De Moor, Boomsma, Stubbe, Willemsen, & de Geus, 2008).

A third possibility is to increase intake of seafood, which contains oils that are important for brain functioning. People who eat at least a pound (0.45 kg) of seafood per week have a decreased probability of mood disorders (Noaghiul & Hibbeln, 2003).

Also, to almost everyone's surprise, a full night of sleep deprivation provides quick relief for about 60% of people with depression. The benefits usually last only until the next night's sleep, but they sometimes last a few days (Wirz-Justice & Van den Hoofdakker, 1999). Sleep deprivation, bright light, or exercise can be combined with psychotherapy or antidepressant drugs to increase the benefits (Martiny, Lunde, Undén, Dam, & Bech, 2005; Putilov et al., 2005).

- -

21. What would be one major advantage of combining one night's sleep deprivation with either psychotherapy or antidepressant drugs? Concept Check

Answer

21. Sleep deprivation produces rapid relief, but its effects do not last long. Psychotherapy and antidepressant drugs take effect more slowly, but their benefits last longer.

- -

BIPOLAR DISORDER

People with bipolar disorder alternate between the extremes of mania and depression. In many respects, mania is the *opposite of depression.* In depression, people are inactive and inhibited. In mania, they are *constantly active and uninhibited.* People with a mild degree of mania ("hypomania") are energetic, life-of-the-party types, but people with more severe mania are dangerous to themselves and others. Some mental hospitals have to disable the fire alarms in certain wards because manic patients impulsively pull the alarm every time they pass it. People in a depressed phase feel helpless, guilt ridden, and sad. When they are manic, they are either excited or irritable. The symptoms of high activity and high distractibility overlap between mania and attention-deficit disorder with hyperactivity (ADHD). Many people qualify for a diagnosis of both ADHD and bipolar disorder (Tamam, Karakus, & Ozpoyraz, 2008).

Typically, longer episodes of depression alternate with briefer episodes of mania. Psychologists distinguish two types of bipolar disorder. People with bipolar I disorder *have had at least one episode of mania.* People with bipolar II disorder *have had episodes of major depression and hypomania, which is a milder degree of mania.* In the past, about 1% of all adults in the United States were diagnosed with bipolar disorder (Robins et al., 1984), but the disorder is defined a bit more loosely today and the diagnosis is applied to more people (Bih et al., 2008).

Twin studies indicate a strong hereditary component for bipolar disorder. In pairs of monozygotic twins in which one has bipolar disorder and the other does not, brain research suggests that the twin without bipolar disorder strongly activates parts of the frontal cortex to control mood and fight off distress. That is, both twins are vulnerable, but one has found a way to be resilient (Krüger et al., 2006).

A Self-Report

Many artists, writers, and composers have suffered from bipolar disorder. One such person was theatrical director Joshua Logan, who described his experiences as follows.

Depressive Phase

> I had no faith in the work I was doing or the people I was working with. . . . It was a great burden to get up in the morning and I couldn't wait to go to bed at night, even though I started not sleeping well. . . . I thought I was well but feeling low because of a hidden personal discouragement of some sort—something I couldn't quite put my

finger on. . . . I just forced myself to live through a dreary, hopeless existence that lasted for months on end. . . .

My depressions actually began around the age of thirty-two. I remember I was working on a play, and I was forcing myself to work. . . . I can remember that I sat in some sort of aggravated agony as it was read aloud for the first time by the cast. It sounded so awful that I didn't want to direct it. I didn't even want to see it. I remember feeling so depressed that I wished that I were dead without having to go through the shame and defeat of suicide. I couldn't sleep well at all, and sleep meant, for me, oblivion, and that's what I longed for and couldn't get. I didn't know what to do and I felt very, very lost. (Fieve, 1975, pp. 42–43)

Manic Phase

Here, Logan describes his manic experiences:

Finally, as time passed, the depression gradually wore off and turned into something else, which I didn't understand either. But it was a much pleasanter thing to go through, at least at first. Instead of hating everything, I started liking things—liking them too much, perhaps. . . . I put out a thousand ideas a minute: things to do, plays to write, plots to write stories about. . . .

I decided to get married on the spur of the moment. . . . I practically forced her to say yes. Suddenly we had a loveless marriage and that had to be broken up overnight. . . .

I can only remember that I worked constantly, day and night, never even seeming to need more than a few hours of sleep. I always had a new idea or another conference. . . . It was an exhilarating time for me.

It finally went too far. In the end I went over the bounds of reality, or law and order, so to say. I don't mean that I committed any crimes, but I could easily have done so if anyone had crossed me. I flew into rages if contradicted. I began to be irritable with everyone. Should a man, friend or foe, object to anything I did or said, it was quite possible that I could poke him in the jaw. I was eventually persuaded by the doctors that I was desperately ill and should go into the hospital. But it was not, even then, convincing to me that I was ill.

There I was, on the sixth floor of a New York building that had special iron bars around it and an iron gate that had slid into place and locked me away from the rest of the world. . . . I looked about and saw that there was an open window. I leaped up on the sill and climbed out of the window on the ledge on the sixth floor and said, "Unless you open the door, I'm going to climb down the outside of this building." At the time, I remember feeling so powerful that I might actually be able to scale the building. . . . They immediately opened the steel door, and I

climbed back in. That's where manic elation can take you. (Excerpts from Joshua Logan in *Moodswing,* by Ronald R. Fieve. Copyright © 1975 by Ronald R. Fieve. Published by William R. Morrow & Co.)

22. What are the similarities and differences between seasonal affective disorder and bipolar disorder? Concept Check

Answer

22. Both conditions have repetitive cycles. However, people with bipolar disorder swing back and forth between depression and mania, whereas people with seasonal affective disorder alternate between depression and normal mood.

Drug Therapies

Psychotherapy helps bipolar patients cope with life's difficulties (Hollon et al., 2002), but by itself, it seldom alleviates the main symptoms. Medications are an important aspect of the treatment.

Decades ago, Australian researcher J. F. Cade proposed that uric acid might help treat mania. To dissolve uric acid in water, he mixed it with lithium salts. The resulting mixture proved effective, but researchers discovered that the benefits depended on the lithium salts, not the uric acid. Lithium salts were slow to be adopted in the United States. The drug manufacturers had no interest in marketing lithium, which is a natural substance not available for patents. Also, the lith-

If treated, those who suffer from disorders such as bipolar disorder can lead highly functional and successful lives. Dr. Alice W. Flaherty is a neurologist who says having the disorder has made her more empathetic to her patients.

ium dosage must be carefully monitored. A low dose is useless, and a high dose causes nausea, blurred vision, and tremors.

Properly regulated dosages of lithium are now a common and effective treatment for bipolar disorder (Baldessarini & Tondo, 2000). People take the recommended doses of lithium for years without unfavorable consequences (Schou, 1997). Anticonvulsant drugs, such as valproate (Depakene, Depacote), are about equal to lithium in effectiveness (Hilty, Brady, & Hales, 1999). Researchers do not yet know how lithium or the anticonvulsant drugs alleviate bipolar disorder.

People usually recover from bipolar disorder faster in Taiwan (China) than in the United States (Strakowski et al., 2007). One reason is that U.S. patients with bipolar disorder are far more likely than the Taiwanese to abuse alcohol or other drugs. Another is that people in Taiwan are more likely to seek help quickly instead of waiting for the symptoms to become severe.

MOOD DISORDERS AND SUICIDE

Most severely depressed people and people with bipolar disorder consider suicide, and many attempt it. Suicides also occur for other reasons, though. Some people commit suicide because they feel guilt or disgrace. Some have committed suicide because of obedience to a cult leader (Maris, 1997). Others have a painful terminal illness and wish to hasten the end.

Across cultures, more men die by suicide, although women make more attempts (Canetto & Sakinofsky, 1998; Cross & Hirschfeld, 1986). Men are more likely to use violent means, whereas women are more likely to try something like a drug overdose, which is less certain to be fatal. Many people who attempt suicide are probably crying out for help without intending to die. Unfortunately, some do die and others become disabled.

Suicide has no dependable pattern. Some people give warning signals well in advance, but many do not, and some firmly deny they are considering suicide (Fawcett, 2001). One study found that most of the people who attempted suicide made the decision impulsively within 24 hours of the attempt (L. G. Peterson, Peterson, O'Shanick, & Swann, 1985). However, anyone who admits to having a plan of how to commit suicide is at seri-

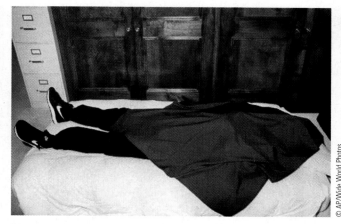

Members of the Heaven's Gate cult in San Diego committed mass suicide in 1997 when their leader assured them that death was the route to being rescued by an alien spacecraft.

ous risk. Table 16.5 lists additional risk factors. Similar patterns have been found in the United States and China, so they are apparently not culture specific (Cheng, 1995).

If you suspect that someone you know is thinking about suicide, what should you do? Treat the person like a normal human being who needs social support and friendship. Don't assume that he or she is so fragile that one wrong word will be disastrous. See *Websites* at the end of the chapter for more resources regarding suicide.

Table 16.5 People Most Likely to Attempt Suicide

- People who have recently endured the death of a spouse or a child, and men who recently have been divorced or separated (Blumenthal & Kupfer, 1986; Qin & Mortensen, 2003)

- People who have had major recent setbacks in their job, finances, or social life (Hendin, Maltsberger, Lipschitz, Haas, & Kyle, 2001)

- People with depression or bipolar disorder, especially those not in treatment and those who feel hopeless (Baldessarini, Tondo, & Hennen, 2001; Beck, Steer, Beck, & Newman, 1993)

- People who have made previous suicide attempts (Beck, Steer, & Brown, 1993)

- Drug or alcohol abusers (Beck & Steer, 1989)

- People who, during their childhood or adolescence, lost a parent by death or divorce (Adam, 1986)

- People with guns in their home (Brent, 2001)

- People with relatives who have committed suicide (Blumenthal & Kupfer, 1986)

16.3 module

In Closing

Mood and Mood Disorders

The capacity to feel sad is normal and appropriate. If you never felt sad, you might make bad decisions. Depression can be seen as the result of normal mechanisms that have gone to an extreme (Allen & Badcock, 2003). Depression seriously distorts thinking and mood. We need research to find further weapons to fight this monster.

SUMMARY

- *Symptoms of depression.* People with depression find little interest or pleasure in life, have trouble sleeping, lose interest in sex and food, and have difficulty concentrating. (page 590)
- *Episodes.* Depression occurs in episodes. Although the first episode is usually triggered by a stressful event, later episodes occur faster and more easily. (page 590)
- *Seasonal affective disorder.* People with seasonal affective disorder become depressed during one season of the year. Bright light usually relieves this condition. (page 590)
- *Predispositions.* Certain genes possibly magnify the depressive effects of stressful experiences. People with these genes are more likely than other people to become depressed after a stressful experience. (page 592)
- *Sex differences.* It is uncertain why more women than men become depressed. One hypothesis is that women are more likely to ruminate about their depression, whereas men distract themselves. (page 592)
- *Cognitive factors.* People who consistently blame themselves for their failures are likely to become depressed. (page 593)
- *Treatments.* At least 30% of depressed patients recover spontaneously within a few months. Another 20% or more recover with psychotherapy or antidepressant drugs. Many patients, however, do not respond quickly to either treatment. (page 594)

- *Psychotherapy.* Interpersonal therapy helps depressed people improve social relationships and deal with current life problems. Cognitive therapy attempts to change people's self-defeating thoughts and encourages active participation in life. (page 594)
- *Antidepressant drugs.* Several kinds of drugs prolong the activity of dopamine or serotonin at synaptic receptors. Although the drugs affect the synapses within an hour or so, their behavioral effects begin after 2 or 3 weeks of treatment. (page 594)
- *Advantages and disadvantages.* Psychotherapy's effects are more likely to produce long-lasting benefits, but antidepressant drugs are easier and less expensive. (page 596)
- *Other treatments.* Electroconvulsive therapy (ECT) helps many depressed people who fail to respond to antidepressant drugs. Additional treatments include exercise, bright light, and altered sleep schedules. (page 596)
- *Bipolar disorder.* People with bipolar disorder alternate between periods of depression and mania, when they engage in constant, uninhibited activity. Lithium salts are an effective treatment, as are certain anticonvulsant drugs. (page 597)
- *Suicide.* Although it is difficult to know who will attempt suicide, several warning signs are associated with an increased risk. (page 599)

KEY TERMS

atypical antidepressants (page 595)

bipolar disorder (page 591)

bipolar I disorder (page 597)

bipolar II disorder (page 597)

electroconvulsive therapy (ECT) (page 596)

explanatory style (page 593)

interpersonal therapy (page 594)

major depression (page 590)

mania (page 597)

monoamine oxidase inhibitors (MAOIs) (page 595)

ruminate (page 593)

seasonal affective disorder (SAD) (or depression with a seasonal pattern) (page 590)

selective serotonin reuptake inhibitors (SSRIs) (page 594)

spontaneous recovery (page 594)

St. John's wort (page 595)

tricyclic drugs (page 594)

Schizophrenia and Autism

- What is schizophrenia and what can be done about it?
- What is autism and what can be done about it?

Would you like to live in a world all your own? You become the supreme ruler who tells other people—and even inanimate objects—what to do. Your fantasies become realities.

Perhaps that world sounds like heaven to you, but it might not feel that way for long. Most of us enjoy the give and take of interactions with other people. We enjoy struggling to achieve our fantasies more than we would enjoy their immediate fulfillment.

Some people with schizophrenia live in a world of their own, confusing fantasy with reality. Others retreat into a private existence and pay little attention to others. In this module, we also consider autism, which is characterized by a lack of social contact.

SYMPTOMS OF SCHIZOPHRENIA

Many people mistakenly use the term *schizophrenia* when they mean *dissociative identity disorder,* or *multiple personality,* a condition in which people alternate among personalities. The term *schizophrenia* does come from Greek roots meaning "split mind," but the "split" in the term schizophrenia refers to a split between the intellectual and emotional aspects of one personality, as if the intellect were no longer in contact with the emotions (Figure 16.19). Someone suffering from schizophrenia may express strong inappropriate emotion or fail to show appropriate emotion. This separation of intellect and emotions is no longer considered a defining feature of schizophrenia, but it does occur.

Intellect

Emotions

FIGURE 16.19 The term *schizophrenia,* derived from Greek roots meaning "split mind," refers to a split between the intellectual and emotional aspects of a single personality.

To be diagnosed with schizophrenia, according to *DSM-IV, someone must exhibit a deterioration of daily activities, including work, social relations, and self-care. He or she must also exhibit at least two of the following: hallucinations, delusions, disorganized speech, grossly disorganized behavior, or a loss of normal emotional responses and social behaviors* (American Psychiatric Association, 1994). If someone's hallucinations or delusions are severe, then no other symptoms are necessary. Because the definition of schizophrenia calls for two or more symptoms from a list of five, it is possible for two people diagnosed with schizophrenia to have no symptoms in common. As we shall see, schizophrenia also results from several causes.

Before assigning a diagnosis of schizophrenia, a therapist must rule out other conditions that produce similar symptoms, including drug abuse, brain damage, neurological diseases, niacin deficiency, and food allergies. About half of all people with schizophrenia have substance abuse as well, and nearly half are depressed.

Positive and Negative Symptoms

Psychologists distinguish between positive and negative symptoms of schizophrenia. In this case, *positive* means *present* and *negative* means *absent;* they do not mean *good* and *bad.* Positive symptoms are *behaviors that are notable by their presence,* such as hallucinations and delusions. Negative symptoms are *behaviors notable for their absence,* including a lack of speech and emotional expression, a lack of ability to feel pleasure, and a general inability to take care of oneself.

Negative symptoms tend to be more consistent over time and more difficult to treat (Arndt, Andreasen, Flaum, Miller, & Nopoulos, 1995). People with many negative symptoms have an earlier onset of the disorder and worse performance in school and on the job (Andreasen, Flaum, Swayze, Tyrrell, & Arndt, 1990).

Hallucinations

Hallucinations are *perceptions that do not correspond to anything in the objective world.* The most common hallucination is to hear voices or other sounds that no one else hears. The voices may speak nonsense, or they may direct the person to do something. Hallucinating people sometimes think the voices are real, sometimes know the voices are unreal, and sometimes are not sure (Junginger & Frame, 1985). Auditory hallucinations occur at the same time as spontaneous activity in the auditory cortex and related brain areas (Shergill, Brammer, Williams, Murray, & McGuire, 2000).

Have you ever heard a voice when you knew you were alone? I once asked my class this question. At first, just a few people hesitantly raised their hands, and then more and more, until about one fourth of the class—and I, too—admitted to hearing a voice at least once. Often, the experience occurred while the person was lying in bed, not asleep but not fully awake either. Having an occasional auditory hallucination does not mean you are losing your mind.

Delusions

Delusions are *unfounded beliefs that are strongly held despite a lack of evidence for them.* Three common types are delusions of persecution, grandeur, and reference. A **delusion of persecution** is *a belief that dangerous enemies are persecuting you.* A **delusion of grandeur** is *a belief that you are unusually important,* perhaps a special messenger from God or a person of central importance to the future of the world. A **delusion of reference** is *a tendency to interpret all sorts of messages as if they were meant for yourself.* For example, someone may interpret a newspaper headline as a coded message or take a television announcer's comments as personal insults. Delusions are most common among people with impaired attention and a tendency to jump to conclusions (Bentall et al., 2009).

However, it is hazardous to diagnose someone with schizophrenia if the only symptoms are delusions. Suppose someone constantly sees evidence of government conspiracies in everyday events. Is that belief a delusion of persecution or merely an unusual opinion? Might it even be correct? Most people who believe they have been abducted by outer-space aliens seem normal in most other regards. Even if we confidently label their beliefs as false, we should not consider them mentally ill (Clancy, 2005). Members of religious minorities also have beliefs that other people regard as strange. Don't most of us have a belief or two that someone might consider unjustifiable?

Disordered Thinking

On the average, people with schizophrenia score significantly below average on cognitive tests, although 20 to 25% are unimpaired (Wexler et al., 2009). For example, the Wisconsin Card Sorting Task asks people to sort a stack of cards by one rule (e.g., in piles by color) and then shift to a different rule (e.g., in piles by number or shape). Most people with schizophrenia have trouble shifting, as do children and people with frontal cortex damage. People with schizophrenia also have trouble perceiving patterns in ambiguous displays, such as the faces shown in Figure 16.20 (Uhlhaas et al., 2006).

Another characteristic of schizophrenic thought is difficulty using abstract concepts. For instance, many people with schizophrenia give strictly literal responses when asked to interpret the meaning of proverbs. Here are some examples (Krueger, 1978, pp. 196–197):

> *Proverb:* People who live in glass houses shouldn't throw stones.
> *Interpretation:* "It would break the glass."
> *Proverb:* All that glitters is not gold.
> *Interpretation:* "It might be brass."
> *Proverb:* A stitch in time saves nine.
> *Interpretation:* "If you make one stitch for a small tear now, it will save nine later."

- -

23. If someone alternates between one personality and another, is that a case of schizophrenia?

24. What are typical "positive" and "negative" symptoms of schizophrenia?

Concept Check

Answers

23. No, that would be dissociative identity disorder (multiple personality).
24. Positive symptoms include hallucinations, delusions, and thought disorder. Negative symptoms include lack of speech and emotional expression, a lack of ability to feel pleasure, and a general inability to take care of oneself.

- -

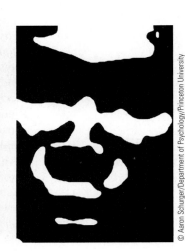

FIGURE 16.20 Patterns like these are known as Mooney faces. Most people with schizophrenia are slow to see the faces.

© Aaron Schurger/Department of Psychology/Princeton University

TYPES AND PREVALENCE

Depending on which symptoms are most prominent, psychiatrists and psychologists distinguish five major types of schizophrenia. These distinctions are useful for descriptive purposes, although they do not identify the underlying causes.

Types of Schizophrenia

Catatonic schizophrenia is characterized by a *prominent movement disorder, including either rigid inactivity or excessive activity.* Periods of extremely rapid, repetitive activity alternate with periods of total inactivity. During the inactive periods, the person may hold a rigid posture and resist attempts to alter it (Figure 16.21). Despite the inactivity, the brain is alert and the person may complain later about comments someone said at the time. Catatonic schizophrenia is less common today than decades ago (Stompe, Ortwein-Swoboda, Ritter, Schanda, & Friedmann, 2002), although periods of catatonia sometimes occur in patients with other disorders (Moskowitz, 2004).

FIGURE 16.21 Someone with catatonic schizophrenia alternates between periods of rigidity and periods of frantic activity.

Disorganized schizophrenia is characterized by *incoherent speech, absence of social relationships, and "silly" or odd behavior.* Here is a conversation with someone suffering from disorganized schizophrenia (Duke & Nowicki, 1979, p. 162):

Interviewer: How does it feel to have your problems?

Patient: Who can tell me the name of my song? I don't know, but it won't be long. It won't be short, tall, none at all. My head hurts, my knees hurt—my nephew, his uncle, my aunt. My God, I'm happy . . . not a care in the world. My hair's been curled, the flag's unfurled. This is my country, land that I love, this is the country, land that I love.

Interviewer: How do you feel?

Patient: Happy! Don't you hear me? Why do you talk to me? (barks like a dog).

According to one explanation, a major reason for incoherent speech is impaired working memory. If you tried to speak while your attention was distracted by a difficult task, your thoughts would seem incoherent, too (Kerns, 2007).

Paranoid schizophrenia is characterized by *elaborate hallucinations and delusions, especially delusions of persecution and delusions of grandeur.* As a rule, people with paranoid schizophrenia are more cognitively intact than those with other forms. They can generally take care of themselves well enough to get through the activities of the day. Some manage to complete college work and take good jobs.

Undifferentiated schizophrenia is characterized by the *basic symptoms—deterioration of daily functioning plus some combination of hallucinations, delusions, inappropriate emotions, thought disorders, and so forth.* However, the person does not have any of the special features that would qualify for the catatonic, disorganized, or paranoid types.

Residual schizophrenia is a diagnosis for people *who have had an episode of schizophrenia and who are partly recovered.* That is, the person has mild lingering symptoms.

Many people fall on the margin between two or more types of schizophrenia, perhaps switching back and forth between them. Switching is especially common between undifferentiated schizophrenia and the other types (Kendler, Gruenberg, & Tsuang, 1985).

25. Why are people more likely to switch between undifferentiated schizophrenia and one of the other types than, say, between disorganized schizophrenia and another type?

Answer

25. Whenever any of the special symptoms of catatonic, disorganized, or paranoid schizophrenia become less severe, the person is left with undifferentiated or residual schizophrenia. To shift between two of the other types, someone would have to lose the symptoms of one type and gain the symptoms of another.

Prevalence

About 1% of Americans have schizophrenia at some point in life (Narrow, Rae, Robins, & Regier, 2002). Some sources cite higher or lower figures depending on how many marginal cases they include. As well as researchers can reconstruct from historical records, the incidence of schizophrenia and severe mental illness in general began to increase in the late 1700s, especially in England and Ireland, and later in the United States. For generation after generation, people tried to convince themselves that mental illness wasn't really becoming more common but that it just appeared to increase because previous generations had not kept good records (Torrey & Miller, 2001). Nevertheless, they kept building new mental hospitals, which quickly became crowded to overflowing despite their uninviting accommodations. Since about 1950, the incidence of schizophrenia has stopped increasing. It appears to be decreasing in some parts of the world (Suvisaari, Haukka, Tanskanen, & Lönnqvist, 1999) and increasing in others (Healy et al., 2001). Part of the fluctuation is probably due to changes in patterns of diagnosis (Ösby et al., 2001). However, it is also likely that the incidence really does vary from one time and place to another, and if we can understand why, we may get major clues to the causes of schizophrenia (Torrey & Miller, 2001). Note that either an increase or decrease in incidence from one era to another implies nongenetic influences. (Evolution doesn't happen that fast.)

Schizophrenia occurs in all ethnic groups, but it is less common and usually less severe in Third World countries (El-Islam, 1982; Leff et al., 1987; Torrey, 1986; Wig et al., 1987). When people move from a less technologically advanced country to, say, Britain, their probability of developing schizophrenia increases (Coid et al., 2008). Perhaps some aspect of life in technologically advanced countries (diet?) increases the risk of schizophrenia. Another possibility is that people in Third World countries receive more social support from nearby relatives and friends.

Schizophrenia is most frequently diagnosed in young adults in their teens or 20s. It is more common in men than women by a ratio of about 7:5. Men are also more likely to be diagnosed younger and to have severer symptoms (Aleman, Kahn, & Selten, 2003). Once it begins, schizophrenia is usually a permanent condition, but not always. Some people have episodes of schizophrenia, like the episodes of depression, followed by a period of reasonably normal behavior (Harrow & Jobe, 2007).

CAUSES

Schizophrenia probably develops from a variety of influences. The prime candidates are genetics and prenatal environment, aggravated by difficulties later in life.

Genetics

The evidence for a genetic basis rests primarily on studies of twins and adopted children. Monozygotic ("identical") twins have much higher overlap than dizygotic twins or other relatives, indicating high heritability of schizophrenia (Cardno et al., 1999; Gottesman, 1991; Sullivan, Kendler, & Neale, 2003) (see Figure 16.22). Adopted children who develop schizophrenia have more biological relatives than adoptive relatives with schizophrenia (Kety et al., 1994). However, the data on adopted children are subject to another interpretation. A child's biological mother influences her baby's brain development not only through genes but also through prenatal environment. Many women with schizophrenia are impoverished. Many smoke and drink during pregnancy and fail to eat a good diet. Therefore, if some of their children develop schizophrenia, we cannot assume a genetic explanation.

The strongest evidence would be a demonstration linking schizophrenia to a specific gene. Researchers have found links to at least 14 genes with small effects (Callicott et al., 2005; Fanous et al., 2005; Gurling et al., 2006; Millar et al., 2005). For example, investigators found that one gene occurs in 70% of people with schizophrenia and 60% of everyone else (Saleem et al., 2001). The gene receiving the most attention is **DISC1**, *meaning disrupted in schizophrenia-1*, which controls the rate of production of new neurons in the hippocampus (Duan et al., 2007). Behaviorally, this gene relates to a lack of pleasure from social relationships (Tomppo et al., 2009). However, the results vary from one population to another. A study of thousands of people in various locations found no gene that was consistently different between people who do and do not have schizophrenia (Sanders et al., 2008).

A further problem with a genetic explanation is the question of why natural selection has not eliminated a gene responsible for schizophrenia. People with schizophrenia usually die younger than other people (Saha, Chant, & McGrath, 2007), they are less likely than others to have children, and their unaffected brothers and sisters do not compensate by reproducing more than average (Haukka, Suvisaari, & Lönnqvist, 2003).

Among the possible ways to explain these confusing and conflicting results, an appealing idea is that schizophrenia can arise from a mutation in any of a large number of genes (Keller, 2008). Ordinarily, mutation is too rare an event to account for much, but if we consider the large number of genes important for brain development, it's possible that mutations happen often enough to keep pace with the selection against them. If a large number of genes are relevant, we see why no one gene shows up as a consistent risk factor across populations.

Researchers have found deletions and duplications of tiny parts of a chromosome in about 15% of people with schizophrenia (International Schizophrenia Consortium, 2008; Stefansson et al., 2008). These are spontaneous errors of gene copying, which can even occur for one monozygotic twin and not the other (Bruder et al., 2008).

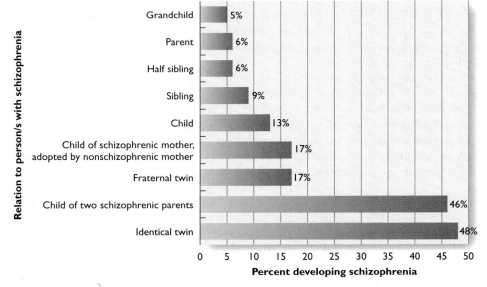

FIGURE 16.22 The relatives of a person with schizophrenia have an increased probability of developing schizophrenia themselves. (Based on data from Gottesman, 1991)

26. How do researchers explain how schizophrenia can have a strong genetic basis, even though no one can find any gene strongly linked with schizophrenia?

Answer

Prenatal Environment and the Neurodevelopmental Hypothesis

If schizophrenia can result from disruption of any of a large number of genes, maybe some cases don't result from genetic factors at all. In particular, difficulties in the prenatal environment can strongly influence brain development and therefore behavior. According to the neurodevelopmental hypothesis, *schizophrenia originates with nervous system impairments that develop before or around the time of birth because of either genetics or early environment* (McGrath, Féron, Burne, Mackay-Sim, & Eyles, 2003; Weinberger, 1996). Schizophrenia is known to be more common in any of these cases (Fatemi & Folsom, 2009):

- The patient's mother had a difficult pregnancy, labor, or delivery.
- The mother was poorly nourished during pregnancy.
- The mother had a bacterial or viral infection during pregnancy.
- The mother had an Rh-negative blood type and her baby was Rh-positive. The risk of schizophrenia is more than 2% for her second and later Rh-positive children, especially boys (Hollister, Laing, & Mednick, 1996).
- The patient was infected during childhood with the parasite *Toxoplasma gondii*, which attacks parts of the brain (Niebuhr et al., 2008). The usual route of infection with this parasite is handling cat feces (Leweke et al., 2004; Torrey & Yolken, 2005).

Furthermore, *a person born in the winter or early spring is slightly more likely to develop schizophrenia than a person born at other times* (Bradbury & Miller, 1985; Davies, Welham, Chant, Torrey, & McGrath, 2003). Investigators have demonstrated this season-of-birth effect only in the northern climates, not near the equator. Evidently, something about the weather contributes to some people's vulnerability to schizophrenia. No other psychological disorder has this characteristic. One possible explanation relates to the fact that influenza and other epidemics are most common in the fall. If a woman catches influenza or

another infection during the first or second trimester of pregnancy, her illness impairs the brain development in her fetus. A virus does not cross the placenta into the fetus, but the mother's fever can impair the fetus's brain development, and so can elevated activity of her immune system.

27. According to the neurodevelopmental hypothesis, what is one reason researchers cannot find a single gene responsible for schizophrenia?

Concept Check

Answer

Brain Abnormalities

Regardless of the relationship between genetic and environmental influences, the net outcome is a person with schizophrenia and, in many cases, mild brain abnormalities. Indications of brain abnormalities have been reported in patients in cultures as different as the United States and Nigeria (Ohaeri, Adeyinka, & Osuntokun, 1995) and in patients who have not yet taken any medications (Torrey, 2002). Brain scans indicate that the hippocampus and several areas of the cerebral cortex are a few percent smaller than normal in people with schizophrenia, especially those with the greatest behavioral deficits (Lui et al., 2009). The cerebral ventricles, which are fluid-filled cavities in the brain, are larger than normal in people with schizophrenia (Wolkin et al., 1998; Wright et al., 2000). Figure 16.23 shows an example of enlarged cerebral ventricles.

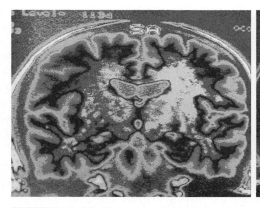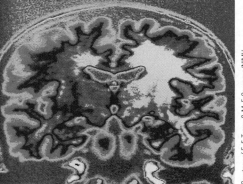

Courtesy of E. F. Torrey & M. F. Casanova/NIMH

FIGURE 16.23 The twin on the left has schizophrenia; the twin on the right does not. Note that the ventricles (near the center of each brain) are larger in the twin with schizophrenia. The ventricles are fluid-filled cavities. An enlargement of the ventricles implies a loss of brain tissue.

Most people with schizophrenia also have smaller than average neurons (Pierri, Volk, Auh, Sampson, & Lewis, 2001; Weinberger, 1999) and fewer than the average number of synapses, especially in the prefrontal cortex (Glantz & Lewis, 1997, 2000). They also have less than the average amount of myelin, a material that surrounds and insulates many axons (K. L. Davis et al., 2003). One area of the cortex with consistent impairments, the dorsolateral prefrontal cortex, is important for those aspects of working memory that are consistently impaired in schizophrenia, and it is one of the slowest areas of the brain to mature. Therefore, its malformation supports the view that schizophrenia is related to impaired brain maturation (Gur et al., 2000; Pearlson, Petty, Ross, & Tien, 1996; Sowell, Thompson, Holmes, Jernigan, & Toga, 1999).

However, these results must be interpreted cautiously. Many people with schizophrenia abuse alcohol or other drugs, and people with both schizophrenia and alcohol abuse have greater indications of brain damage than those with schizophrenia alone (Deshmukh, Rosenbloom, Pfefferbaum, & Sullivan, 2002; Mathalon, Pfefferbaum, Lim, Rosenbloom, & Sullivan, 2003; Sullivan et al., 2000). Unfortunately, most studies have not attempted to separate the effects of schizophrenia from those of alcohol abuse.

....

28. Suppose someone argues that the brain abnormalities in schizophrenia indicate that brain damage causes schizophrenia. What is an alternative explanation?

Answer

28. Perhaps schizophrenia leads to alcohol abuse, which in turn leads to brain abnormalities.

....

Later Events Triggering the Onset of Schizophrenia

Certain genes and abnormal prenatal environment predispose people to schizophrenia, but not everyone with a predisposition develops the disorder. We know this by comparing people who have schizophrenia to their brothers and sisters who do not. Those without schizophrenia show some of the same memory problems and other behavioral abnormalities that characterize schizophrenia (Chamchong, Dyckman, Austin, Clementz, & McDowell, 2008; Rasetti et al., 2009). Evidently, they too had whatever genes or other factors predispose people to schizophrenia. A longitudinal

study of young adults found that those who developed schizophrenia showed shrinkage of several brain areas that developed as the disorder progressed (Takahashi et al., 2009). That is, the disruption of neural development early in life doesn't do all the damage. It somehow leaves people vulnerable so that something later in life triggers further changes. These later events certainly need further investigation.

THERAPIES

Before the discovery of effective drugs to combat schizophrenia, the outlook was bleak. Many people spent years or decades in mental hospitals, growing more disoriented. Matters are better now, although far from ideal. Psychotherapy helps, presumably by controlling the stress that often aggravates schizophrenia (Sensky et al., 2000). However, nearly all patients with schizophrenia receive drugs as part of their treatment.

Medications

During the 1950s, researchers discovered the first effective **antipsychotic drug**—*that is, a drug that can relieve schizophrenia.* That drug was chlorpromazine (klor-PRAHM-uh-ZEEN, trade name Thorazine). Chlorpromazine and other antipsychotic drugs, including haloperidol (HAHL-o-PAIR-ih-dol, trade name Haldol), have enabled many people with schizophrenia to live active and productive lives. Although the drugs do not cure the disorder, a daily pill helps control it, much as insulin injections control diabetes.

Antipsychotic drugs take effect gradually and produce variable degrees of recovery. As a rule, the greater someone's deterioration before drug treatment begins, the less the recovery will be. Most of the improvement emerges in about a month (Szymanski, Simon, & Gutterman, 1983). When affected people stop taking the drugs, the symptoms return (Figure 16.24).

Typical antipsychotic drugs block dopamine synapses in the brain. Their therapeutic effectiveness is nearly proportional to their ability to block those synapses (Seeman & Lee, 1975). Furthermore, large doses of amphetamines, cocaine, or other drugs that stimulate dopamine activity produce the positive symptoms of schizophrenia. These observations led to the **dopamine hypothesis of schizophrenia**—that *the underlying cause of schizophrenia is excessive stimulation of certain types of dopamine synapses.* People with schizophrenia do not overproduce dopamine, but they could have increased release or increased numbers of dopamine receptors in certain brain areas (Hirvonen et al., 2006; Howes et al., 2009).

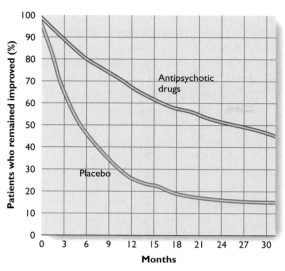

FIGURE 16.24 After recovery from schizophrenia, the percentage of schizophrenic patients who remained improved for the next 2½ years was higher in the group that received continuing drug treatment than in the placebo group. (Based on Baldessarini, 1984)

Nevertheless, dopamine may not be the entire explanation of schizophrenia. The brain's release of dopamine is regulated largely by the neurotransmitter glutamate, and several lines of evidence suggest that people with schizophrenia have deficient glutamate activity in the prefrontal cortex (D. A. Lewis & Gonzalez-Burgos, 2006). Prolonged use of *phencyclidine* ("angel dust"), which inhibits glutamate receptors, produces both the positive and negative symptoms of schizophrenia (Olney & Farger, 1995). Drugs that stimulate certain glutamate synapses facilitate relief from the negative symptoms of schizophrenia, such as social withdrawal (Heresco-Levy & Javitt, 2004).

Side Effects and Alternative Drugs

Antipsychotic drugs produce unwelcome side effects, including tardive dyskinesia (TAHRD-eev DIS-ki-NEE-zhuh), *a condition characterized by tremors and involuntary movements* (Kiriakakis, Bhatia, Quinn, & Marsden, 1998). Presumably, tardive dyskinesia relates to the fact that antipsychotic drugs alter activity at dopamine synapses, some of which control movement. Researchers have sought new drugs to combat schizophrenia without causing tardive dyskinesia.

Atypical antipsychotic drugs, such as risperidone and clozapine, *relieve schizophrenia without causing tardive dyskinesia*. These drugs produce effects on both dopamine and serotonin synapses. Atypical antipsychotic drugs relieve the negative symptoms of schizophrenia that most antipsychotic drugs fail to address (J. M. Davis,

Chen, & Glick, 2003). Clozapine is regarded by most psychiatrists as the most effective drug for relieving the symptoms of schizophrenia (McEvoy et al., 2006). However, the atypical antipsychotic drugs have side effects of their own, and it is not clear that they improve overall quality of life any better than the older drugs (P. B. Jones et al., 2006).

....

29. What is the advantage of the atypical antipsychotic drugs?

Answer

29. Atypical antipsychotic drugs relieve the negative symptoms of schizophrenia better than the older drugs do.

....

Family Matters

The intensity of any patient's symptoms varies from time to time. One hypothesis to explain the fluctuation is that patients react to variations in emotional stress, especially from their own family. Many young patients with schizophrenia live with their parents, and many parents grow understandably frustrated with an adult son or daughter who cannot hold a job, does not take care of even routine self-grooming, and seems unmotivated to change. Occasionally, a parent has an outburst of *hostile or critical comments,* known as expressed emotion. Many studies have found patients exposed to frequent criticism are likely to have frequent relapses of schizophrenic symptoms (Butzlaff & Hooley, 1998).

Most psychologists have assumed that the expressed emotion leads to the relapses. However, the evidence is correlational. Here is one more opportunity to remind you to beware of using correlational evidence to infer cause and effect: Perhaps the parents' high degree of criticism leads the patient to frequent relapses, or perhaps the patient's frequent relapses stimulate the parents to more criticism. One study examined both the parents' expressed emotion and the patient's behavior repeatedly over a year and a half. The amount of expressed emotion correlated better with the patient's *previous* levels of negative symptoms (social withdrawal etc.) than with the patient's *subsequent* levels of those symptoms (King, 2000). These results suggest that a parent's expressed emotion is more a reaction to the patient's behavior than a cause of it.

In any case, the families of people with schizophrenia need help, too. They need help for their own sake, as well as for making them more patient and more helpful to their son or daughter with schizophrenia. Research has confirmed that including the parents in the therapy program magnifies the benefits to the patients (Pitschel-Walz, Leucht, Bäuml, Kissling, & Engel, 2001).

AUTISM

Autism is another condition characterized by impaired social contact. Frankly, the similarities between autism and schizophrenia are superficial. In fact, in some ways, autism is the opposite of paranoid schizophrenia (Crespi & Badcock, 2008). For example, someone with paranoid schizophrenia sees other people's influence in everything. A rock on the street is a message; a newspaper left on a table is someone's attempt to communicate; a change in the weather is evidence of a giant conspiracy. Autistic people perceive social influence in almost nothing. They pay little attention to other people. We consider autism in this module because there is no other convenient place to put it. The main symptoms of autism are (Ritvo, 2006):

- *Impaired social relationships* (little eye contact; no seeking to share pleasures with others)
- *Impaired communication* (repetitive speech; no sustained conversations)
- *Stereotyped behaviors* (repetitive movements such as flapping fingers)

In addition to these primary symptoms, most individuals show a variety of other miscellaneous symptoms, including fluctuations of temperature regulation, insensitivity to pain, and decreased tendency to become dizzy after spinning with the lights on (Ritvo, 2006). (They show a normal tendency to dizziness with the lights off!) Another characteristic is a tendency to focus attention narrowly on one item to the exclusion of everything else (Bryson, 2005).

People with moderate difficulties in relating to others are diagnosed with *Asperger's syndrome*. About 1 person in 150 has either autism or Asperger's syndrome. Symptoms are highly variable, partly because some children with autism have other disorders as well, such as a specific phobia, obsessive-compulsive disorder, or attention-deficit disorder. One disorder they do *not* have is social phobia (Leyfer et al., 2006). (Social phobia implies enhanced fear of making a bad impression on others. People with autism pay little attention to others' reactions.)

Autism is usually noticed before age 2 and sometimes within the first weeks of life, as parents notice that their infant seems not to cuddle like other infants. Twin studies point to a strong genetic basis. One study found 92% concordance for autism or related problems in monozygotic ("identical") twins. That is, if one twin had autism or related problems, the probability was 92% that the other did also. For dizygotic twins, the concordance was only 10% (A. Bailey et al., 1995). To explain this huge discrepancy between monozygotic and dizygotic twins, one possibility is that autism depends on a combination of two or more genes. If autism requires two or three genes, the probability of getting the combination would be low for dizygotic twins. Another hypothesis arises from the observation that autism, like schizophrenia, is more common among children of older fathers (Reichenberg et al., 2006). As men age, some of their genes add a methyl (CH_3) group that alters gene expression without being a mutation in the usual sense. The process is known as *gene imprinting*. An imprinted gene would affect both monozygotic twins, but the chance is low that two dizygotic twins would receive the same imprinted gene.

Researchers have found many abnormalities of brain anatomy and chemistry that are common in autism but none that occur consistently. One of the most surprising is that about one fifth of autistic people have unusually large heads and brains—larger than 97% of everyone else (White, O'Reilly, & Frith, 2009). Evidently, they have more neurons but abnormal connections among them (Ke et al., 2009). Other abnormalities include decreased number of neurons in the cerebellum, small neuron size in the amygdala, and elevated levels of serotonin in the blood (Bauman & Kemper, 2005; Lam, Aman, & Arnold, 2006).

Given enough patience and special education, some individuals with autism develop well enough to live reasonably normal lives. Many drug therapies have been tried, but so far, the results have not been impressive. Autism remains a fascinating mystery.

- -

30. Of the most common symptoms of autism, which would be considered *negative symptoms* analogous to the negative symptoms of schizophrenia?

Answer

30. Impaired social relationships and impaired communication.

- -

In Closing

The Elusiveness of Schizophrenia and Autism

Whereas anxiety disorders, substance abuse, and depression overlap somewhat, and many people experience them at least occasionally, schizophrenia and autism stand apart. Most of us can imagine circumstances that would drive us to excess anxiety, depression, or addictive behaviors, but it is harder to imagine developing a break from reality or losing interest in social contact.

As you have read about schizophrenia and autism, you could easily become discouraged with how little we seem to know and how many major questions remain unanswered. An antidote to complete discouragement would be to read what the textbooks of 50 years ago had to say. At that time, schizophrenia and autism were blamed on bad parents, who gave their children confusing "come here, go away" messages or didn't show enough love. Those days, mercifully, have passed. We don't yet have all the answers that we seek, but at least we know what the answers are *not*. That progress is worth celebrating.

SUMMARY

- *Symptoms of schizophrenia.* A diagnosis of schizophrenia applies if someone has deteriorated in everyday functioning and shows at least two of the following symptoms: hallucinations (mostly auditory), delusions, disorganized speech, disorganized behavior, and loss of normal emotional responses and social behaviors. (page 601)

- *Positive and negative symptoms.* Positive symptoms are behaviors that attract attention by their presence, such as hallucinations and delusions. Negative symptoms are behaviors that are noteworthy for their absence, such as impaired emotional expression. (page 601)

- *Thought disorder of schizophrenia.* The thought disorder of schizophrenia is characterized by impaired use of abstract concepts. (page 602)

- *Types of schizophrenia.* Psychologists distinguish five types of schizophrenia: catatonic, disorganized, paranoid, undifferentiated, and residual. (page 603)

- *Genetic influences.* Much evidence indicates that it is possible to inherit a predisposition toward schizophrenia. A current hypothesis is that schizophrenia can result from changes in any of a large number of genes. (page 604)

- *Prenatal environment and the neurodevelopmental hypothesis.* Many researchers believe that schizophrenia originates with abnormal brain development before or around the time of birth because of either genetics or prenatal environment. Early abnormal development leaves a person vulnerable to further deterioration in adulthood. (page 605)

- *Brain abnormalities.* Many people with schizophrenia show indications of mild brain abnormalities, especially in the prefrontal cortex. However, some of the damage may be due to alcohol abuse. (page 605)

- *Antipsychotic drugs.* Drugs that alleviate schizophrenia block dopamine synapses. Results are best if treatment begins before someone has suffered serious deterioration. (page 606)

- *Neurotransmitters.* The effectiveness of dopamine blockers in alleviating schizophrenia suggests that the underlying problem relates to excessive dopamine activity. An alternative hypothesis is that part of the problem relates to a deficiency of glutamate. (page 606)

- *Autism.* Autism, a condition that begins in early childhood, is characterized by impaired social contact, impaired language, and stereotyped movements. (page 608)

KEY TERMS

antipsychotic drugs (page 606)

atypical antipsychotic drugs (page 607)

autism (page 608)

catatonic schizophrenia (page 603)

delusion (page 602)

delusion of grandeur (page 602)

delusion of persecution (page 602)

delusion of reference (page 602)

DISC1 (page 604)

disorganized schizophrenia (page 603)

dopamine hypothesis of schizophrenia (page 606)

expressed emotion (page 607)

hallucinations (page 601)

negative symptoms (page 601)

neurodevelopmental hypothesis (page 605)

paranoid schizophrenia (page 603)

positive symptoms (page 601)

residual schizophrenia (page 603)

schizophrenia (page 601)

season-of-birth effect (page 605)

tardive dyskinesia (page 607)

undifferentiated schizophrenia (page 603)

exploration and study

Why Does This Matter to Me?

SOCIAL RESPONSIBILITY AND PSYCHOLOGY

Many environmental and societal problems are caused by human behavior. Psychologists can help steer the course of our future toward more socially responsible and sustainable outcomes. Students of today need to be ever mindful of the link between human behavior and its impact on the environment and our communities.

"Specific Disorders and Treatments" and Social Responsibility: A Step Further

Stressful experiences aggravate mental illnesses. Eliminating stress from life is a hopeless task, but can we find ways to reduce it or help people cope with it?

A Lasting Impact

Does your school have a psychology club or organization such as Psi Chi or Psi Beta that you could join? If so, does it have a volunteering component? Is there a mental hospital or some other organization that aids those with mental illness in your community? Perhaps you could establish a relationship between your university's organization and your community's organization. Such a relationship could outlast your own educational career. Not only would it look good on your résumé, but it could make a lasting impact toward helping the mentally ill in your community.

Join the iChapters Plant a Tree Drive!

To show its support of the environmental movement, iChapters is planting a tree on behalf of each fan of the iChapters Facebook Page and for every 10 questions answered correctly in our quiz.
http://www.ichapters.com/plantatree/

Exploration and Study

SUGGESTIONS FOR FURTHER EXPLORATION

In addition to the study materials provided at the end of each module, you may supplement your review of this chapter with the following book and website suggestions or by using one or more of the book's electronic resources, which include its companion website, interactive Cengage Learning eBook, and CengageNOW. Brief descriptions of these resources follow. For more information, visit **www.cengage.com/psychology/kalat**.

ADDITIONAL RESOURCES

The book's companion website, accessible from **www.cengage.com/psychology/kalat**, provides a wide range of study resources such as an interactive glossary, flashcards, tutorial quizzes, updated web links, and Try It Yourself activities.

CengageNOW with Critical Thinking Videos is an easy-to-use resource that helps you study in less time to get the grade you want. An online study system, CengageNOW gives you the option of taking a diagnostic pretest for each chapter. The system uses the results of each pretest to create personalized chapter study plans for you. The Personalized Study Plans

- Help you save study time by identifying areas on which you should concentrate and give you one-click access to corresponding pages of the interactive Cengage Learning eBook;
- Provide interactive exercises and study tools to help you fully understand chapter concepts; and
- Include a posttest for you to take to confirm that you are ready to move on to the next chapter.

Find critical thinking videos like this one in your CengageNOW product, which offer an opportunity for you to learn more about psychological research on different topics.

Social Isolation

Books

Jamison, K. R. (1997). *An unquiet mind.* New York: Random House. A psychiatrist describes her own lifelong battle with bipolar disorder.

Websites

Links to the websites described below are kept current and can be found at **www.cengage.com/psychology/kalat**.

Psychological Disorders and More

The American Psychiatric Association offers facts about various disorders, drug therapies, how to choose a therapist, and much more.

National Clearinghouse for Alcohol and Drug Information

Here is comprehensive information for those who want to overcome a drug problem.

Harbor of Refuge

Postings by people with bipolar disorder for others with the same problem.

The Experience of Schizophrenia

This is the personal site of Ian Chovil, who began struggling with schizophrenia in late adolescence and suffered greatly until he began taking medication in 1990. He tells his own story in unsparing detail.

Walkers in Darkness

This long-established and award-winning site is dedicated to helping people with schizophrenia, bipolar illness, and related mood disorders. Included are descriptions of each disorder, information on medication and therapy, links to a variety of resources, forums, chat rooms, and mailing lists.

SAVE

The SAVE mission is to prevent suicide through public awareness and education, reduce stigma, and serve as a resource for those touched by suicide.

National Suicide Prevention Lifeline

The National Suicide Prevention Lifeline is a 24-hour, toll-free suicide prevention service available to anyone in suicidal crisis. The number (in the United States) is 1-800-273-TALK (8255).

Here we are at the end of the book. As I have been writing and revising, I have imagined you sitting there reading. I have imagined a student much like I was in college, reading about psychology for the first time and often growing excited about it. I remember periodically telling a friend or relative, "Guess what I just learned about psychology! Isn't this interesting?" (I still do the same today.) I also remember occasionally thinking, "Hmm. The book says such-and-so, but I'm not convinced. I wonder whether psychologists ever considered a different explanation. . . ." I started thinking about research I might do if I became a psychologist.

I hope you have had similar experiences yourself. I hope you have occasionally become so excited about something you read in this book that you thought about it and told other people about it. In fact, I hope you told your roommate so much about psychology that you started to become mildly annoying. I also hope you have sometimes doubted a conclusion, imagining a research project that might test it or improve on it. Psychology is still a work in progress.

Now, as I picture you reaching the end of the course, I'm not sure how you will react. You might be thinking, "Wow, I sure have learned a lot!" Or you might be thinking, "Is that *all*?" Maybe you are reacting both ways: "Yes, I learned a lot. But it seems like there should be more. I still don't understand what conscious experience is all about, and I don't understand why I react the way I do sometimes. And this book—*wonderful as it is!*—hardly mentioned certain topics. Why do we laugh? How do we sense the passage of time? Why do people like to watch sports? Why are some people religious and others not?"

I have two good reasons for not answering all your questions. One is that this is an introductory text, and it can't go on forever. If you want to learn more, you should take other psychology courses or do additional reading. The other reason is that psychologists do not know all the answers.

Perhaps someday, you will become a researcher yourself and add to our knowledge. If not, you can try to keep up to date on current developments in psychology by reading good books and magazine articles. The magazine *Scientific American Mind* is an excellent source. One of my main goals has been to prepare you to continue learning about psychology.

Try to read critically: Is a conclusion based on good evidence? If you read about a survey, were the questions worded clearly? How reliable and valid were the measurements? Did the investigators obtain a representative or random sample? If someone draws a cause-and-effect conclusion, was the evidence based on experiments or only correlations? Even if the evidence looks solid, is the author's explanation the best one?

Above all, remember that any conclusion is tentative. Psychological researchers seldom use the word *prove;* their conclusions are almost always tentative. I once suggested to my editor, half seriously, that we should include in the index to this book the entry "*maybe*—see pages 1–611." We did not include such an entry, partly because some people might not have noticed the humor, and partly because our understanding of psychology is not really that bad. Still, be leery of anyone who seems a little too certain about a great new insight in psychology. It is a long route from *maybe* to *definitely.*

Numbers in parentheses indicate the chapter in which a source is cited.

Abercrombie, H. C., Kalin, N. H., Thurow, M. E., Rosenkranz, M. A., & Davidson, R. J. (2003). Cortisol variation in humans affects memory for emotionally laden and neutral information. *Behavioral Neuroscience, 117,* 505–516. (12)

Abramson, L. Y., Seligman, M. E. P., & Teasdale, J. D. (1978). Learned helplessness in humans: Critique and reformulation. *Journal of Abnormal Psychology, 87,* 49–74. (16)

Ackil, J. K., Van Abbema, D. L., & Bauer, P. J. (2003). After the storm: Enduring differences in mother-child recollections of traumatic and nontraumatic events. *Journal of Experimental Child Psychology, 84,* 286–309. (7)

Adam, K. S. (1986). Early family influences on suicidal behavior. *Annals of the New York Academy of Sciences, 487,* 63–76. (16)

Adams, D. L., & Horton, J. C. (2002). Shadows cast by retinal blood vessels mapped in primary visual cortex. *Science, 298,* 572–576. (4)

Adams, J. S. (1963). Wage inequities, productivity, and work quality. *Industrial Relations, 3,* 9–16. (11)

Adams, R. B., & Kleck, R. E. (2003). Perceived gaze direction and the processing of facial displays of emotion. *Psychological Science, 14,* 644–647. (12)

Adams, R. B., & Kleck, R. E. (2005). Effects of direct and averted gaze on the perception of facially communicated emotion. *Emotion, 5,* 3–11. (12)

Adler, A. (1927). *Understanding human nature.* New York: Greenberg. (14)

Adler, A. (1964). Brief comments on reason, intelligence, and feeble-mindedness. In H. L. Ansbacher & R. R. Ansbacher (Eds.), *Superiority and social interest* (pp. 41–49). New York: Viking Press. (Original work published 1928) (14)

Adler, A. (1964). The structure of neurosis. In H. L. Ansbacher & R. R. Ansbacher (Eds.), *Superiority and social interest* (pp. 83–95). New York: Viking Press. (Original work published 1932) (14)

Adler, E., Hoon, M. A., Mueller, K. L., Chandrashekar, J., Ryba, N. J. P., & Zuker, C. S. (2000). A novel family of mammalian taste receptors. *Cell, 100,* 693–702. (4)

Adolph, K. E. (2000). Specificity of learning: Why infants fall over a veritable cliff. *Psychological Science, 11,* 290–295. (5)

Adolphs, R., Baron-Cohen, S., & Tranel, D. (2002). Impaired recognition of social emotions following amygdala damage. *Journal of Cognitive Neuroscience, 14,* 1264–1274. (12)

Adolphs, R., Denburg, N. L., & Tranel, D. (2001). The amygdala's role in long-term declarative memory for gist and detail. *Behavioral Neuroscience, 115,* 983–992. (12)

Adolphs, R., & Tranel, D. (1999). Preferences for visual stimuli following amygdala damage. *Journal of Cognitive Neuroscience, 11,* 610–616. (12)

Adolphs, R, Tranel, D., & Damasio, A. R. (1998). The human amygdala in social judgment. *Nature, 393,* 470–474. (12)

Agar, W. E., Drummond, F. H., Tiegs, O. W., & Gunson, M. M. (1954). Fourth (final) report on a test of McDougall's Lamarckian experiment on the training of rats. *Journal of Experimental Biology, 31,* 307–321. (2)

Aglioti, S. M., Cesari, P., Romani, M., & Urgesi, C. (2008). Action anticipation and motor resonance in elite basketball players. *Nature Neuroscience, 11,* 1109–1116. (8)

Ahn, W., Flanagan, E. H., Marsh, J. K., & Sanislow, C. A. (2006). Beliefs about essences and the reality of mental disorders. *Psychological Science, 17,* 759–766. (15)

Ainsworth, M. D. S. (1979). Attachment as related to mother-infant interaction. In J. S. Rosenblatt, R. A. Hinde, C. Beer, & M. Busnel (Eds.), *Advances in the study of behavior* (Vol. 9, pp. 1–51). New York: Academic Press. (5)

Ainsworth, M. D. S., Blehar, M., Waters, E., & Wall, S. (1978). *Patterns of attachment.* Hillsdale, NJ: Erlbaum. (5)

Airan, R. D., Meltzer, L. A., Roy, M., Gong, Y., Chen, H., & Deisseroth, K. (2007). High-speed imaging reveals neurophysiological links to behavior in an animal model of depression. *Science, 317,* 819–823. (16)

Åkerstedt, T. (2007). Altered sleep/wake patterns and mental performance. *Physiology and Behavior, 90,* 209–218. (10)

Alati, R., Al Mamum, A., Williams, G. M., O'Callaghan, M., Najman, J. M., & Bor, W. (2006). In utero alcohol exposure and prediction of alcohol disorders in early childhood. *Archives of General Psychiatry, 63,* 1009–1016. (16)

Albarracín, D., Gillette, J. C., Earl, A. N., Glasman, L. R., Durantini, M. R., & Ho, M. H. (2005). A test of major assumptions about behavior change: A comprehensive look at the effects of passive and active HIV-prevention interventions since the beginning of the epidemic. *Psychological Bulletin, 131,* 856–897. (13)

Albee, G. W. (1986). Toward a just society: Lessons from observations on the primary prevention of psychopathology. *American Psychologist, 41,* 891–898. (15)

Aleman, A., Kahn, R. S., & Selten, J. P. (2003). Sex differences in the risk of schizophrenia. *Archives of General Psychiatry, 60,* 565–571. (16)

Alexander, G. M., & Hines, M. (2002). Sex differences in response to children's toys in nonhuman primates (*Cercopithecus aethiops sabaeus*). *Evolution and Human Behavior, 23,* 467–479. (5)

Alexander, G. M., Wilcox, T., & Woods, R. (2009). Sex differences in infants' visual interest in toys. *Archives of Sexual Behavior, 38,* 427–433. (14)

Alexander, I. E. (1982). The Freud-Jung relationship—the other side of Oedipus and countertransference. *American Psychologist, 37,* 1009–1018. (14)

Alexander, K. W., Quas, J. A., Goodman, G. S., Ghetti, S., Edelstein, R. S., Redlich, A. D., et al. (2005). Traumatic impact predicts long-term memory for documented child sexual abuse. *Psychological Science, 16,* 33–40. (7)

Alison, L. J., Smith, M. D., Eastman, O., & Rainbow, L. (2003). Toulmin's philosophy of argument and its relevance to offender profiling. *Psychology, Crime and Law, 9,* 173–183. (14)

Alison, L., Smith, M. D., & Morgan, K. (2003). Interpreting the accuracy of offender profiles. *Psychology, Crime and Law, 9,* 185–195. (14)

Alkire, M. T., Hudetz, A. G., & Tononi, G. (2008). Consciousness and anesthesia. *Science, 322,* 876–880. (10)

Allen, N. B., & Badcock, P. B. T. (2003). The social risk hypothesis of depressed mood: Evolutionary, psychosocial, and neurobiological perspectives. *Psychological Bulletin, 129,* 887–913. (16)

Allison, S. T., Mackie, D. M., Muller, M. M., & Worth, L. T. (1993). Sequential correspondence biases and perceptions of change: The Castro studies revisited. *Personality and Social Psychology Bulletin, 19,* 151–157. (13)

Alloy, L. B., Abramson, L. Y., Whitehouse, W. G., Hogan, M. E., Tashman, N. A., Steinberg, D. L., et al. (1999). Depressogenic cognitive styles: Predictive validity, information processing and personality characteristics, and developmental origins. *Behaviour Research and Therapy, 37,* 503–531. (16)

Allport, G. W. (1935). Attitudes. In C. Murchison (Ed.), *A handbook of social psychology* (pp. 798–844). Worcester, MA: Clark University Press. (13)

Allport, G. W. (1961). *Pattern and growth in personality.* New York: Holt, Rinehart & Winston. (14)

Allport, G. W., & Odbert, H. S. (1936). Traitnames: A psycholexical study. *Psychological Monographs, 47*(Whole No. 211). (14)

Alpers, G. W., & Gerdes, A. B. M. (2007). Here is looking at you: Emotional faces predominate in binocular rivalry. *Emotion, 7,* 495–506. (10)

Alpert, J. L., Brown, L. S., & Courtois, C. A. (1998). Symptomatic clients and memories of childhood abuse. *Psychology, Public Policy, and Law, 4,* 941–995. (7)

Alroe, C. J., & Gunda, V. (1995). Self-amputation of the ear. *Australian and New Zealand Journal of Psychiatry, 29,* 508–512. (15)

Altmann, E. M., & Gray, W. D., (2002). Forgetting to remember: The functional relationship of decay and interference. *Psychological Science, 13,* 27–33. (7)

Alves, E., Summavielle, T., Alves, C. J., Comes-da-Silva, J., Barata, J. C., Fernandes, E., et al. (2007). Monoamine oxidase-B mediates ecstasy-induced neurotoxic effects to adolescent rat brain mitochondria. *Journal of Neuroscience, 27,* 10203–10210. (3)

Amabile, T. M. (2001). Beyond talent. *American Psychologist, 56,* 333–336. (11)

Amanzio, M., Pollo, A., Maggi, G., & Benedetti, F. (2001). Response variability to analgesics: A role for non-specific activation of endogenous opioids. *Pain, 90,* 205–215. (4)

Amato, P. R., & Keith, B. (1991). Parental divorce and the well-being of children: A meta-analysis. *Psychological Bulletin, 110,* 26–46. (5)

Ambadar, Z., Schooler, J. W., & Cohn, J. F. (2005). Deciphering the enigmatic face. *Psychological Science, 16,* 403–410. (12)

Ambady, N., & Rosenthal, R. (1993). Half a minute: Predicting teacher evaluations from thin slices of nonverbal behavior and physical attractiveness. *Journal of Personality and Social Psychology, 64,* 431–441. (13)

Ambady, N., Shih, M., Kim, A., & Pittinsky, T. L. (2001). Stereotype susceptibility in children: Effects of identity activation on quantitative performance. *Psychological Science, 12,* 385–390. (9)

Amedi, A., Floel, A., Knecht, S., Zohary, E., & Cohen, L. G. (2004). Transcranial magnetic stimulation of the occipital pole interferes with verbal processing in blind subjects. *Nature Neuroscience, 7,* 1266–1270. (3)

Amelang, M., & Steinmayr, R. (2006). Is there a validity increment for tests of emotional intelligence in explaining the variance of performance criteria? *Intelligence, 34,* 459–468. (12)

American Medical Association. (1986). Council report: Scientific status of refreshing recollection by the use of hypnosis. *International Journal of Clinical and Experimental Hypnosis, 34,* 1–12. (10)

American Psychiatric Association. (1994). *Diagnostic and statistical manual of mental disorders* (4th ed.). Washington, DC: Author. (15, 16)

American Psychiatric Association. (2000). *Diagnostic and statistical manual of mental disorders* (4th ed., Text revision.). Washington, DC: Author. (15)

Amzica, F., & Steriade, M. (1996). Progressive cortical synchronization of pontogeniculo-occipital potentials during rapid eye movement sleep. *Neuroscience, 72,* 309–314. (10)

Anderson, A., & Phelps, E. A. (2000). Expression without recognition: Contributions of the human amygdala to emotional communication. *Psychological Science, 11,* 106–111. (12)

Anderson, A. K., & Phelps, E. A. (2002). Is the human amygdala critical for the subjective experience of emotion? Evidence of intact dispositional affect in patients with amygdala lesions. *Journal of Cognitive Neuroscience, 14,* 709–720. (12)

Anderson, C., Keltner, D., & John, O. P. (2003). Emotional convergence between people over time. *Journal of Personality and Social Psychology, 84,* 1054–1068. (13)

Anderson, C. A., & Bushman, B. J. (2001). Effects of violent video games on aggressive behavior, aggressive cognition, aggressive affect, physiological arousal, and prosocial behavior: A meta-analytic review of the scientific literature. *Psychological Science, 12,* 353–359. (2)

Anderson, S. W., Bechara, A., Damasio, H., Tranel, D., & Damasio, A. R. (1999). Impairment of social and moral behavior related to early damage in human prefrontal cortex. *Nature Neuroscience, 2,* 1032–1037. (3)

Andreano, J. M., & Cahill, L. (2006). Glucocorticoid release and memory consolidation in men and women. *Psychological Science, 17,* 466–470. (7)

Andreasen, N. C., Flaum, M., Swayze, V. W., II, Tyrrell, G., & Arndt, S. (1990). Positive and negative symptoms in schizophrenia. *Archives of General Psychiatry, 47,* 615–621. (16)

Andrew, D., & Craig, A. D. (2001). Spinothalamic lamina I neurons selectively sensitive to histamine: A central neural pathway for itch. *Nature Neuroscience, 4,* 72–77. (4)

Andrews, T. J., Halpern, S. D., & Purves, D. (1997). Correlated size variations in human visual cortex, lateral geniculate nucleus, and optic tract. *Journal of Neuroscience, 17,* 2859–2868. (4)

Anglin, D., Spears, K. L., & Hutson, H. R. (1997). Flunitrazepam and its involvement in date or acquaintance rape. *Academy of Emergency Medicine, 4,* 323–326. (3)

Anonymous. (1955). *Alcoholics anonymous* (2nd ed.). New York: Alcoholics Anonymous World Services. (16)

Anseel, F., & Duyck, W. (2008). Unconscious applicants. *Psychological Science, 19,* 1059–1061. (1)

Antoniadis, E. A., Winslow, J. T., Davis, M., & Amaral, D. G. (2007). Role of the primate amygdala in fear-potentiated startle. *Journal of Neuroscience, 27,* 7386–7396. (12)

APA Presidential Task Force on Evidence-Based Practice. (2006). Evidence-based practice in psychology. *American Psychologist, 61,* 271–285. (15)

Araneda, R. C., Kini, A. D., & Firestein, S. (2000). The molecular receptive range of an odorant receptor. *Nature Neuroscience, 3,* 1248–1255. (4)

Archer, J. (2000). Sex differences in aggression between heterosexual partners: A meta-analytic review. *Psychological Bulletin, 126,* 651–680. (12)

Arden, R., & Plomin, R. (2006). Sex differences in variance of intelligence across childhood. *Personality and Individual Differences, 41,* 39–48. (9)

Ariely, D., & Wertenbroch, K. (2002). Procrastination, deadlines, and performance: Self-control by precommitment. *Psychological Science, 13,* 219–224. (11)

Arkes, H. R., & Ayton, P. (1999). The sunk cost and Concorde effects: Are humans less rational than lower animals? *Psychological Bulletin, 125,* 591–600. (8)

Armor, D. A., Massey, C., & Sackett, A. M. (2008). Prescribed optimism: Is it right to be wrong about the future? *Psychological Science, 19,* 329–331. (12)

Arndt, S., Andreasen, N. C., Flaum, M., Miller, D., & Nopoulos, P. (1995). A longitudinal study of symptom dimensions in schizophrenia. *Archives of General Psychiatry, 52,* 352–360. (16)

Arnell, K. M., Killman, K. V., & Fijavz, D. (2007). Blinded by emotion: Target misses follow attention capture by arousing distractors in RSVP. *Emotion, 7,* 465–477. (7)

Arnett, J. J. (2000). Emerging adulthood: A theory of development from the late teens through the twenties. *American Psychologist, 55,* 469–480. (5)

Arnold, H. J., & House, R. J. (1980). Methodological and substantive extensions to the job characteristics model of motivation. *Organizational Behavior and Human Performance, 25,* 161–183. (11)

Aronow, E., Reznikoff, M., & Moreland, K. L. (1995). The Rorschach: Projective technique or psychometric test? *Journal of Personality Assessment, 64,* 213–228. (14)

Aronson, E. (1997). The theory of cognitive dissonance: The evolution and vicissitudes of an idea. In C. McGarty & S. A. Haslam (Eds.), *The message of social psychology* (pp. 20–35). Cambridge, MA: Blackwell. (13)

Aronson, E., & Carlsmith, J. M. (1963). Effect of the severity of threat on the devaluation of forbidden behavior. *Journal of Abnormal and Social Psychology, 66,* 584–588. (13)

Arvey, R. D., McCall, B. P., Bouchard, T. J., Jr., Taubman, P., & Cavanaugh, M. A. (1994). Genetic influences on job satisfaction and work values. *Personality and Individual Differences, 17,* 21–33. (11)

Asch, S. E. (1951). Effects of group pressure upon the modification and distortion of judgments. In H. Guetzkow (Ed.), *Groups, leadership, and men* (pp. 177–190). Pittsburgh, PA: Carnegie Press. (13)

Asch, S. E. (1955, November). Opinions and social pressure. *Scientific American, 193*(5), 31–35. (13)

Asch, S. E. (1956). Studies of independence and conformity: I. A minority of one against a unanimous majority. *Psychological Monographs, 70*(9, Whole No. 416). (13)

Ash, R. (1986, August). An anecdote submitted by Ron Ash. *The Industrial-Organizational Psychologist, 23*(4), 8. (6)

Ashton-James, C. E., Maddux, W. W., Galinsky, A. D., & Chartrand, T. L. (2009). Who I am depends on how I feel. *Psychological Science, 20,* 340–346. (12)

Askum, D., & Ataca, B. (2007). Sexuality related attitudes and behaviors of Turkish university students. *Archives of Sexual Behavior, 36,* 741–752. (11)

Athos, E. A., Levinson, B., Kistler, A., Zemansky, J., Bostrom, A., Freimer, N., et al. (2007). Dichotomy and perceptual distortions in absolute pitch ability. *Proceedings of the National Academy of Sciences, USA, 104,* 14795–14800. (4)

Atkinson, R. C., & Shiffrin, R. M. (1968). Human memory: A proposed system and its control. In K. W. Spence & J. T. Spence (Eds.), *The psychology of learning and motivation* (Vol. 2, pp. 89–105). New York: Academic Press. (7)

Au, T. K., Knightly, L. M., Jun, S.-A., & Oh, J. W. (2002). Overhearing a language during childhood. *Psychological Science, 13,* 238–243. (8)

Austin, D. W., & Richards, J. C. (2001). The catastrophic misinterpretation model of panic disorder. *Behaviour Research and Therapy, 39,* 1277–1291. (16)

Auyeung, B., Baron-Cohen, S., Ashwin, E., Knickmeyer, R., Taylor, K., Hackett, G., et al. (2009). Fetal testosterone predicts sexually differentiated childhood behavior in girls and boys. *Psychological Science, 20,* 144–148. (11)

Averill, J. R. (1983). Studies on anger and aggression: Implications for theories of emotion. *American Psychologist, 38,* 1145–1160. (12)

Aviezer, H., Hassin, R. R., Ryan, J., Grady, C., Susskind, J., Anderson, A., et al. (2008). Angry, disgusted, or afraid? *Psychological Science, 19,* 724–732. (12)

Ayduck, Ö., & Kross, E. (2008). Enhancing the pace of recovery. *Psychological Science, 19,* 229–231. (16)

Babkoff, H., Caspy, T., Mikulincer, M., & Sing, H. C. (1991). Monotonic and rhythmic influences: A challenge for sleep deprivation research. *Psychological Bulletin, 109,* 411–428. (10)

Baccus, J. R., Baldwin, M. W., & Packer, D. J. (2004). Increasing implicit self-esteem through classical conditioning. *Psychological Science, 15,* 498–502. (6)

Back, M. D., Schmukle, S. C., & Egloff, B. (2008). Becoming friends by chance. *Psychological Science, 19,* 439–440. (13)

Baddeley, A. D. (2001). Is working memory still working? *American Psychologist, 56,* 851–864. (7)

Baddeley, A. D., & Hitch, G. (1974). Working memory. In G. H. Bower (Ed.), *Psychology of learning and motivation* (Vol. 8, pp. 47–89). New York: Academic Press. (7)

Baddeley, A., & Hitch, G. J. (1994). Developments in the concept of working memory. *Neuropsychology, 8,* 485–493. (7)

Baer, J. S., Sampson, P. D., Barr, H. M., Connor, P. D., & Streissguth, A. P. (2003). A 21-year longitudinal analysis of the effects of prenatal alcohol exposure on young adult drinking. *Archives of General Psychiatry, 60,* 377–385. (16)

Bagby, R. M., Nicholson, R. A., Bacchiochi, J. R., Ryder, A. G., & Bury, A. S. (2002). The predictive capacity of the MMPI-2 and PAI validity scales and indexes to detect coached and uncoached feigning. *Journal of Personality Assessment, 78,* 69–86. (14)

Bagemihl, B. (1999). *Biological exuberance.* New York: St. Martin's Press. (11)

Bahrick, H. (1984). Semantic memory content in permastore: 50 years of memory for Spanish learned in school. *Journal of Experimental Psychology: General, 113,* 1–29. (7)

Bailey, A., Le Couteur, A., Gottesman, I., Bolton, P., Simonoff, E., Yuzda, E., et al. (1995). Autism as a strongly genetic disorder: Evidence from a British twin study. *Psychological Medicine, 25,* 63–78. (16)

Bailey, J. M., & Pillard, R. C. (1991). A genetic study of male sexual orientation. *Archives of General Psychiatry, 48,* 1089–1096. (11)

Bailey, J. M., Pillard, R. C., Neale, M. C., & Agyei, Y. (1993) Heritable factors influence sexual orientation in women. *Archives of General Psychiatry, 50,* 217–223. (11)

Baillargeon, J., Binswanger, I. A., Penn, J. V., Williams, B. A., & Murray, O. J. (2009). Psychiatric disorders and repeat incarcerations: The revolving prison door. *American Journal of Psychiatry, 166,* 103–109. (15)

Baillargeon, R. (1986). Representing the existence and the location of hidden objects: Object permanence in 6- and 8-month-old infants. *Cognition, 23,* 21–41. (5)

Baillargeon, R. (1987). Object permanence in 3 1/2- and 4 1/2-month-old infants. *Developmental Psychology, 23,* 655–664. (5)

Baillargeon, R., Li, J., Ng, W., & Yuan, S. (2009). An account of infants' physical reasoning. In A. Woodward & A. Needham (Eds.), *Learning and the infant* (pp. 66–116). New York: Oxford University Press. (5)

Baird, J. C. (1982). The moon illusion: A reference theory. *Journal of Experimental Psychology: General, 111,* 304–315. (4)

Baker, T. B., Piper, M. E., McCarthy, D. E., Majeskie, M. R., & Fiore, M. C. (2004). Addiction motivation reformulated: An affective processing model of negative reinforcement. *Psychological Review, 111,* 33–51. (16)

Baker, T. B., & Tiffany, S. T. (1985). Morphine tolerance as habituation. *Psychological Bulletin, 92,* 78–108. (6)

Baker-Ward, L., Gordon, B. N., Ornstein, P. A., Larus, D. M., & Clubb, P. A. (1993). Young children's long-term retention of a pediatric examination. *Child Development, 64,* 1519–1533. (7)

Bakermans-Kranenburg, M. J., van IJzendoorn, M. H., & Juffer, F. (2003). Less is more: Meta-analyses of sensitivity and attachment interventions in early childhood. *Psychological Bulletin, 129,* 195–215. (5)

Balcetis, E., Dunning, D., & Miller, R. L. (2008). Do collectivists know themselves better than individualists? Cross-cultural studies of the holier than thou phenomenon. *Journal of Personality and Social Psychology, 95,* 1252–1267. (13)

Baldessarini, R. J. (1984). Antipsychotic drugs. In T. B. Karasu (Ed.), *The psychiatric therapies: I. The somatic therapies* (pp. 119–170). Washington, DC: American Psychiatric Press. (16)

Baldessarini, R. J., & Tondo, L. (2000). Does lithium treatment still work? *Archives of General Psychiatry, 57,* 187–190. (16)

Baldessarini, R. J., Tondo, L., & Hennen, J. (2001). Treating the suicidal patient with bipolar disorder. *Annals of the New York Academy of Sciences, 932,* 24–38. (16)

Baldwin, S. A., Berkeljon, A., Atkins, D. C., Olsen, J. A., & Nielsen, S. L. (2009). Rates of change in naturalistic psychotherapy: Contrasting dose-effect and good-enough level models of change. *Journal of Consulting and Clinical Psychology, 77,* 203–211. (15)

Ballinger, B., & Yalom, I. (1995). Group therapy in practice. In B. Bongar & L. E. Beutler (Eds.), *Comprehensive textbook of psychotherapy: Theory and practice* (pp. 189–204). Oxford, England: Oxford University Press. (15)

Banaji, M. R., & Bhaskar, R. (2000). Implicit stereotypes and memory: The bounded rationality of social beliefs. In D. L. Schacter & E. Scarry (Eds.), *Memory, brain, and belief* (pp. 139–175). Cambridge, MA: Harvard University Press. (13)

Bandura, A. (1977). *Social learning theory.* Upper Saddle River, NJ: Prentice Hall. (6)

Bandura, A. (1986). *Social foundations of thought and action.* Upper Saddle River, NJ: Prentice Hall. (6)

Bandura, A., Barbaranelli, C., Caprara, G. V., & Pastorelli, C. (2001). Self-efficacy beliefs as shapers of children's aspirations and career trajectories. *Child Development, 72,* 187–206. (6)

Bandura, A., Ross, D., & Ross, S. A. (1963). Imitation of film-mediated aggressive models. *Journal of Abnormal and Social Psychology, 66,* 3–11. (6)

Banks, W. P., & Isham, E. A. (2009). We infer rather than perceive the moment we decided to act. *Psychological Science, 20,* 17–21. (10)

Baptista, L. F., & Petrinovich, L. (1984). Social interaction, sensitive phases and the song template hypothesis in the white-crowned sparrow. *Animal Behaviour, 32,* 172–181. (6)

Bargh, J. A., Chen, M., & Burrows, L. (1996). The automaticity of social behavior: Direct effects of trait concept and stereotype activation on action. *Journal of Personality and Social Psychology, 71,* 230–244. (13)

Barnett, R. C., & Hyde, J. S. (2001). Women, men, work, and family. *American Psychologist, 56,* 781–796. (5)

Barnier, A. J., & McConkey, K. M. (1998). Posthypnotic responding away from the hypnotic setting. *Psychological Science, 9,* 256–262. (10)

Baron, A., & Galizio, M. (2005). Positive and negative reinforcement: Should the distinction be preserved? *Behavior Analyst, 28,* 85–98. (6)

Baron, A. S., & Banaji, M. R. (2006). The development of implicit attitudes. *Psychological Science, 17,* 53–58. (13)

Baron, J., & Norman, M. F. (1992). SATs, achievement tests, and high-school class rank as predictors of college performance. *Educational and Psychological Measurement, 52,* 1047–1055. (9)

Barrett, L. F. (2006). Are emotions natural kinds? *Perspectives on Psychological Science, 1,* 28–58. (12)

Barrett, L. F., Tugade, M. M., & Engle, R. W. (2004). Individual differences in working memory capacity and dual-process theories of the mind. *Psychological Bulletin, 130,* 553–573. (7)

Barrick, M. R., Mount, M. K., & Judge, T. A. (2001). Personality and performance at the beginning of the new millennium: What do we know and where do we go next? *International Journal of Selection and Assessment, 9,* 9–29. (14)

Bartels, A., & Zeki, S. (2000). The neural basis of romantic love. *NeuroReport, 11,* 3829–3834. (13)

Bartlett, F. C. (1932). *Remembering.* Cambridge, England: Cambridge University Press. (7)

Bartlett, M. Y., & DeSteno, D. (2006). Gratitude and prosocial behavior. *Psychological Science, 17,* 319–325. (12)

Bartoshuk, L. M. (1991). Taste, smell, and pleasure. In R. C. Bolles (Ed.), *The hedonics of taste* (pp. 5–28). Hillsdale, NJ: Erlbaum. (4)

Bartoshuk, L. M., Duffy, V. B., Lucchina, L. B., Prutkin, J., & Fast, K. (1998). PROP (6-n-propyl-thiouracil) supertasters and the saltiness of NaCl. *Annals of the New York Academy of Sciences, 855,* 793–796. (1)

Basabe, N., Paez, D., Valencia, J., Gonzalez, J. L., Rimé, B., & Diener, E. (2002). Cultural dimensions, socioeconomic development, climate, and emotional hedonic level. *Cognition and Emotion, 16,* 103–125. (12)

Batson, C. D., & Thompson, E. R. (2001). Why don't people act morally? Motivational considerations. *Current Directions in Psychological Science, 10,* 54–57. (13)

Bauer, P. J. (2005). Developments in declarative memory. *Psychological Science, 16,* 41–47. (7)

Bauer, P. J. (2007). Recall in infancy: A neurodevelopmental approach. *Current Directions in Psychological Science, 16,* 142–146. (5)

Bauer, P. J., Wenner, J. A., & Kroupina, M. G. (2002). Making the past present: Later verbal accessibility of early memories. *Journal of Cognition and Development, 3,* 21–47. (7)

Bauman, M. L., & Kemper, T. L. (2005). Structural brain anatomy in autism: What is the evidence? In M. L. Bauman & T. L. Kemper (Eds.), *The neurobiology of autism* (pp. 121–135). Baltimore: Johns Hopkins University Press. (16)

Baumeister, R. F. (2008). Free will in scientific psychology. *Perspectives on Psychological Science, 3,* 14–19. (1)

Baumeister, R. F., Campbell, J. D., Krueger, J. I., & Vohs, K. D. (2003). Does high self-esteem cause better performance, interpersonal success, happiness, or healthier lifestyles? *Psychological Science in the Public Interest, 4,* 1–44. (12, 14)

Baumeister, R. F., Smart, L., & Boden, J. M. (1996). Relation of threatened egotism to violence and aggression: The dark side of high self-esteem. *Psychological Review, 103,* 5–33. (12)

Baumeister, R. F., Vohs, K. D., & Funder, D. C. (2007). Psychology as the science of self-reports and finger movements. *Perspectives on Psychological Science, 2,* 396–403. (6)

Baumrind, D. (1971). Current patterns of parental authority. *Developmental Psychology Monographs, 4*(1, Pt. 2). (5)

Baumrind, D., Larzelere, R. E., & Cowan, P. A. (2002). Ordinary physical punishment: Is it harmful? Comment on Gershoff (2002). *Psychological Bulletin, 128,* 580–589. (6)

Baxter, M. G., & Murray, E. A. (2002). The amygdala and reward. *Nature Reviews Neuroscience, 3,* 563–573. (3, 12)

Bayley, T. M., Dye, L., & Hill, A. J. (2009). Taste aversions in pregnancy. In S. Reilly & T. R. Schachtman (Eds.), *Conditioned taste aversion* (pp. 497–512). New York: Oxford University Press. (6)

Beauchamp, G. K., Cowart, B. J., Mennella, J. A., & Marsh, R. R. (1994). Infant salt taste: Developmental, methodological, and contextual factors. *Developmental Psychobiology, 27,* 353–365. (1)

Becht, M. C., & Vingerhoets, A. J. J. M. (2002). Crying and mood change: A cross-cultural study. *Cognition and Emotion, 16,* 87–101. (12)

Beck, A. T. (1973). *The diagnosis and management of depression.* Philadelphia: University of Pennsylvania Press. (16)

Beck, A. T. (1976). *Cognitive therapy and the emotional disorders.* New York: New American Library. (15)

Beck, A. T. (1987). Cognitive models of depression. *Journal of Cognitive Psychotherapy: An International Quarterly, 1,* 5–37. (16)

Beck, A. T. (1991). Cognitive therapy: A 30-year retrospective. *American Psychologist, 46,* 368–375. (16)

Beck, A. T., & Emery, G. (1985). *Anxiety disorders and phobias.* New York: Basic Books. (16)

Beck, A. T., & Steer, R. A. (1989). Clinical predictors of eventual suicide: A 5- to 10-year prospective study of suicide attempters. *Journal of Affective Disorders, 17,* 203–209. (16)

Beck, A. T., Steer, R. A., Beck, J. S., & Newman, C. F. (1993). Hopelessness, depression, suicidal ideation, and clinical diagnosis of depression. *Suicide and Life-Threatening Behavior, 23,* 139–145. (16)

Beck, A. T., Steer, R. A., & Brown, G. (1993). Dysfunctional attitudes and suicidal ideation in psychiatric outpatients. *Suicide and Life-Threatening Behavior, 23,* 11–20. (16)

Beck, K., & Wilson, C. (2000). Development of affective organizational commitment: A cross-sequential examination of change with tenure. *Journal of Vocational Behavior, 56,* 114–136. (11)

Becker, A. E., Burwell, R. A., Gilman, S. E., Herzog, D. B., & Hamburg, P. (2002). Eating behaviours and attitudes following prolonged exposure to television among ethnic Fijian adolescent girls. *British Journal of Psychiatry, 180,* 509–514. (11)

Becker, A. E., Burwell, R. A., Navara, K., & Gilman, S. E. (2003). Binge eating and binge eating disorder in a small-scale, indigenous society: The view from Fiji. *International Journal of Eating Disorders, 34,* 423–431. (11)

Becker, A. E., Franko, D. L., Speck, A., & Herzog, D. B. (2003). Ethnicity and differential access to care for eating disorder symptoms. *International Journal of Eating Disorders, 33,* 205–212. (11)

Beckett, C., Maughan, B., Rutter, M., Castle, J., Colvert, E., Groothues, C., et al. (2006). Do the effects of early severe deprivation on cognition persist into early adolescence? Findings from the English and Romanian adoptees study. *Child Development, 77,* 696–711. (9)

Beckner, V. E., Tucker, D. M., Delville, Y., & Mohr, D. C. (2006). Stress facilitates consolidation of verbal memory for a film but does not affect retrieval. *Behavioral Neuroscience, 120,* 518–527. (12)

Beeman, M. J., & Chiarello, C. (1998). Complementary right- and left-hemisphere language comprehension. *Current Directions in Psychological Science, 7,* 2–8. (3)

Beer, J. S., Knight, R. T., & D'Esposito, M. (2006). Controlling the integration of emotion and cognition. *Psychological Science, 17,* 448–453. (12)

Bègue, L., & Muller, D. (2006). Belief in a just world as moderator of hostile attributional bias. *British Journal of Social Psychology, 45,* 117–126. (14)

Behrens, K. Y., Hesse, E., & Main, M. (2007). Mothers' attachment status as determined by the adult attachment interview predicts their 6-year-olds' reunion responses: A study conducted in Japan. *Developmental Psychology, 43,* 1553–1567. (5)

Behrens, M., Foerster, S., Staehler, F., Raguse, J.-D., & Meyerhof, W. (2007). Gustatory expression pattern of the human TAS2R bitter receptor gene family reveals a heterogenous population of bitter responsive taste receptor cells. *Journal of Neuroscience, 27,* 12630–12640. (4)

Behrens, T. E. J., Hunt, L. T., Woolrich, M. W., & Rushworth, M. F. S. (2008). Associative learning of social value. *Nature, 456,* 245–249. (6)

Bekker, M. H. J., & van Assen, M. A. L. M. (2008). Autonomy-connectedness and gender. *Sex Roles, 59,* 532–544. (14)

Bell, R., & Pliner, P. L. (2003). Time to eat: The relationship between the number of people eating and meal duration in three lunch settings. *Appetite, 41,* 215–218. (11)

Bellugi, U., Lichtenberger, L., Jones, W., Lai, Z., & St. George, M. (2000). I. The neurocognitive profile of Williams syndrome: A complex pattern of strengths and weaknesses. *Journal of Cognitive Neuroscience, 12*(Suppl.), 7–29. (8)

Bellugi, U., & St. George, M. (2000). Preface. *Journal of Cognitive Neuroscience, 12*(Suppl.), 1–6. (8)

Belsky, J. (1996). Parent, infant, and social-contextual antecedents of father-son attachment security. *Developmental Psychology, 32,* 905–913. (5)

Bem, D. J., & Honorton, C. (1994). Does psi exist? Replicable evidence for an anomalous process of information transfer. *Psychological Bulletin, 115,* 4–18. (2)

Bem, S. L. (1974). The measurement of psychological androgyny. *Journal of Consulting and Clinical Psychology, 42,* 155–162. (5)

Benenson, J. F., Markovits, H., Fitzgerald, C., Geoffroy, D., Flemming, J., Kahlenberg, S. M., et al. (2009). Males' greater tolerance of same-sex peers. *Psychological Science, 20,* 184–190. (14)

Benish, S. G., Imel, Z. E., & Wampold, B. E. (2008). The relative efficacy of bona fide psychotherapies for treating post-traumatic stress disorder: A meta-analysis of direct comparisons. *Clinical Psychology Review, 28,* 746–758. (15)

Benjamin, L. T., Jr., & Simpson, J. A. (2009). The power of the situation. *American Psychologist, 64,* 12–19. (13)

Benowitz, N. L., Jacob, P., III, Bernert, J. T., Wilson, W., Wang, L., Allen, F., et al. (2005). Carcinogen exposure during short-term switching from regular to "light" cigarettes. *Cancer Epidemiology, Biomarkers, and Prevention, 14,* 1376–1383. (16)

Benschop, R. J., Godaert, G. L. R., Geenen, R., Brosschot, J. F., DeSmet, M. B. M., Olff, M., et al. (1995). Relationships between cardiovascular and immunologic changes in an experimental stress model. *Psychological Medicine, 25,* 323–327. (12)

Benson, H. (1977). Systemic hypertension and the relaxation response. *New England Journal of Medicine, 296,* 1152–1156. (12)

Benson, H. (1985). Stress, health, and the relaxation response. In W. D. Gentry, H. Benson, & C. J. de Wolff (Eds.), *Behavioral medicine: Work, stress and health* (pp. 15–32). Dordrecht, The Netherlands: Martinus Nijhoff. (12)

Bentall, R. P., Rowse, G., Shryane, N., Kinderman, P., Howard, R., Blackwood, N., et al. (2009). The cognitive and affective structure of paranoid delusions. *Archives of General Psychiatry, 66,* 236–247. (16)

Berenbaum, S. A. (1999). Effects of early androgens on sex-typed activities and interests in adolescents with congenital adrenal hyperplasia. *Hormones and Behavior, 35,* 102–110. (11)

Berenbaum, S. A., Duck, S. C., & Bryk, K. (2000). Behavioral effects of prenatal versus postnatal androgen excess in children with 21-hydroxylase-deficient congenital adrenal hyperplasia. *Journal of Clinical Endocrinology and Metabolism, 85,* 727–733. (5, 11)

Berger, R. J., & Phillips, N. H. (1995). Energy conservation and sleep. *Behavioural Brain Research, 69,* 65–73. (10)

Berglas, S., & Jones, E. E. (1978). Drug choice as a self-handicapping strategy in response to noncontingent success. *Journal of Personality and Social Psychology, 36,* 405–417. (13)

Berkman, N. D., Lohr, K. N., & Bulik, C. M. (2007). Outcomes of eating disorders: A systematic review of the literature. *International Journal of Eating Disorders, 40,* 293–309. (11)

Berkowitz, L. (1983). Aversively stimulated aggression: Some parallels and differences in research with animals and humans. *American Psychologist, 38,* 1135–1144. (12)

Berkowitz, L. (1989). Frustration-aggression hypothesis: Examination and reformulation. *Psychological Bulletin, 106,* 59–73. (12)

Berkowitz, L. (1990). On the formulation and regulation of anger and aggression: A cognitive neoassociationistic analysis. *American Psychologist, 45,* 494–503. (12)

Berlyne, D. E. (1981). Humanistic psychology as a protest movement. In J. R. Royce & L. P. Mos (Eds.), *Humanistic psychology: Concepts and criticisms* (pp. 261–293). New York: Plenum Press. (14)

Berman, M. G., Jonides, J., & Kaplan, S. (2008). The cognitive benefits of interacting with nature. *Psychological Science, 19,* 1207–1212. (8)

Bernstein, D. M., Atance, C., Loftus, G. R., & Meltzoff, A. (2004). We saw it all along. *Psychological Science, 15,* 264–267. (7)

Bernstein, I. L. (1991). Aversion conditioning in response to cancer and cancer treatment. *Clinical Psychology Review, 11,* 185–191. (6)

Berntsen, D., & Rubin, D. C. (2002). Emotionally charged autobiographical memories across the lifespan: The recall of happy, sad, traumatic and involuntary memories. *Psychology and Aging, 17,* 636–652. (7)

Berntson, G. G., Cacioppo, J. T., & Quigley, K. S. (1993). Cardiac psychophysiology and autonomic space in humans: Empirical perspectives and conceptual implications. *Psychological Bulletin, 114,* 296–322. (12)

Berridge, K. C., & Robinson, T. E. (1995). The mind of an addicted brain: Neural sensitization of wanting versus liking. *Current Directions in Psychological Science, 4,* 71–76. (6)

Berridge, K. C., & Robinson, T. E. (1998). What is the role of dopamine in reward: Hedonic impact, reward learning, or incentive salience? *Brain Research Reviews, 28,* 309–369. (16)

Berry, J. W., Poortinga, Y. H., Segal, H., & Dasen, P. R. (1992). *Cross-cultural psychology.* Cambridge, England: Cambridge University Press. (15)

Bertenthal, B. I., Longo, M. R., & Kosobud, A. (2006). Imitative response tendencies following observation of intransitive actions. *Journal of Experimental Psychology: Human Perception and Performance, 32,* 210–225. (6)

Bertolino, A., Blasi, G., Latorre, V., Rubino, V., Rampino, A., Sinibaldi, L., et al. (2006). Additive effects of genetic variation in dopamine regulating genes on working memory cortical activity in human brain. *Journal of Neuroscience, 26,* 3918–3922. (9)

Bialystok, E., Craik, F., & Luk, G. (2008). Cognitive control and lexical access in younger and older bilinguals. *Journal of Experimental Psychology: Learning, Memory, and Cognition, 34,* 859–873. (8)

Bialystok, E., Craik, F. I., & Ryan, J. (2006). Executive control in a modified antisaccade task: Effects of aging and bilingualism. *Journal of Experimental Psychology: Learning, Memory, and Cognition, 32,* 1341–1354. (8)

Bickman, L. (1996). A continuum of care: More is not always better. *American Psychologist, 51,* 689–701. (15)

Bih, S.-H., Chien, I-C., Chou, Y.-J., Lin, C.-H., Lee, C.-H., & Chou, P. (2008). The treated prevalence and incidence of bipolar disorder among national health insurance enrollees in Taiwan, 1996–2003. *Social Psychiatry and Psychiatric Epidemiology, 43,* 860–865. (16)

Bijl, R. V., de Graaf, R., Hiripi, E., Kessler, R. C., Kohn, R., Offord, D. R., et al. (2003). The prevalence of treated and untreated mental disorders in five countries. *Health Affairs, 22,* 122–133. (16)

Billy, J. O. G., Tanfer, K., Grady, W. R., & Klepinger, D. H. (1993, March/April). The sexual behavior of men in the United States. *Family Planning Perspectives, 25,* 52–60. (11)

Binet, A., & Simon, T. (1905). Méthodes nouvelles pour le diagnostic du niveau intellectuel des anormaux [New methods for the measurement of the intellectual level of the abnormal]. *L'Année Psychologique, 11,* 191–244. (9)

Bird, H. R., Canino, G. J., Davies, M., Zhang, H., Ramirez, R., & Lahey, B. B. (2001). Prevalence and correlates of antisocial behaviors among three ethnic groups. *Journal of Abnormal Child Psychology, 29,* 465–478. (15)

Bishop, E. G., Cherny, S. S., Corley, R., Plomin, R., DeFries, J. C., & Hewitt, J. K. (2003). Development genetic analysis of general cognitive ability from 1 to 12 years in a sample of adoptees, biological siblings, and twins. *Intelligence, 31,* 31–49. (9)

Bjerkedal, T., Kristensen, P., Skjeret, G. A., & Brevik, J. I. (2007). Intelligence test scores and birth order among young Norwegian men (conscripts) analyzed within and between families. *Intelligence, 35,* 503–514. (5)

Bjorklund, D. F., & Pellegrini, A. D. (2000). Child development and evolutionary psychology. *Child Development, 71,* 1687–1708. (5)

Bjorklund, D. F., & Shackelford, T. K. (1999). Differences in parental investment contribute to important differences between men and women. *Current Directions in Psychological Science, 8,* 86–92. (13)

Blackless, M., Charuvastra, A., Derryck, A., Fausto-Sterling, A., Lauzanne, K., & Lee, E. (2000). How sexually dimorphic are we? Review and synthesis. *American Journal of Human Biology, 12,* 151–166. (11)

Blackwell, A., & Bates, E. (1995). Inducing agrammatic profiles in normals: Evidence for the selective vulnerability of morphology under cognitive resource limitation. *Journal of Cognitive Neuroscience, 7,* 228–257. (8)

Blaine, J. D., Prien, R. F., & Levine, J. (1983). The role of antidepressants in the treatment of affective disorders. *American Journal of Psychotherapy, 37,* 502–520. (16)

Blair, R. J. R., Mitchell, D. G. V., Peschardt, K. S., Colledge, E., Leonard, R. A., Shine, J. H., et al. (2004). Reduced sensitivity to others' fearful expressions in psychopathic individuals. *Personality and Individual Differences, 37,* 1111–1122. (12)

Blake, R., & Logothetis, N. K. (2002). Visual competition. *Nature Reviews Neuroscience, 3,* 13–23. (10)

Blakemore, C., & Sutton, P. (1969). Size adaptation: A new aftereffect. *Science, 166,* 245–247. (4)

Blascovich, J., Mendes, W. B., Hunter, S. B., Lickel, B., & Kowai-Bell, N. (2001). Perceiver threat in social interactions with stigmatized others. *Journal of Personality and Social Psychology, 80,* 253–267. (13)

Blascovich, J., & Tomaka, J. (1991). Measures of self-esteem. In J. P. Robinson, R. R. Shaver, & L. S. Wrightsman (Eds.), *Measures of personality and social psychological attitudes* (Vol. 1, pp. 115–160). San Diego, CA: Academic Press. (14)

Blasi, G., Mattay, V. S., Bertolino, A., Elvevåg, B., Callicott, J. H., Das, S., et al. (2005). Effect of catechol-O-methyltransferase val[158]met genotype on attentional control. *Journal of Neuroscience, 25,* 5038–5045. (8)

Bless, H., Bohner, G., Schwarz, N., & Strack, F. (1990). Mood and persuasion: A cognitive response analysis. *Personality and Social Psychology Bulletin, 16,* 331–345. (12)

Blount, J. D., Metcalfe, N. B., Birkhead, T. R., & Surai, P. F. (2003). Carotenoid modulation of immune function and sexual attractiveness in zebra finches. *Science, 300,* 125–127. (13)

Blum, D. (1994). *The monkey wars.* New York: Oxford University Press. (2)

Blum, G. S., & Barbour, J. S. (1979). Selective inattention to anxiety-linked stimuli. *Journal of Experimental Psychology: General, 108,* 182–224. (4)

Blumenthal, S. J., & Kupfer, D. J. (1986). Generalizable treatment strategies for suicidal behavior. *Annals of the New York Academy of Sciences, 487,* 327–340. (16)

Boakes, R. A., & Nakajima, S. (2009). Conditioned taste aversions based on running or swimming. In S. Reilly & T. R. Schachtman (Eds.), *Conditioned taste aversion* (pp. 159–178). New York: Oxford University Press. (6)

Bocklandt, S., Horvath, S., Vilain, E., & Hamer, D. H. (2006). Extreme skewing of X chromosome inactivation in mothers of homosexual men. *Human Genetics, 118,* 691–694. (11)

Bogaert, A. F. (2003). The interaction of fraternal birth order and body size in male sexual orientation. *Behavioral Neuroscience, 117,* 381–384. (11)

Bogaert, A. F. (2006). Biological versus nonbiological older brothers and men's sexual orientation. *Proceedings of the National Academy of Sciences, USA, 103,* 10771–10774. (11)

Bogg, T., & Roberts, B. W. (2004). Conscientiousness and health-related behaviors: A meta-analysis of the leading behavioral contributors to mortality. *Psychological Bulletin, 130,* 887–919. (14)

Bohart, A. C. (2000). The client is the most important common factor: Clients' self-healing capacities and psychotherapy. *Journal of Psychotherapy Integration, 10,* 127–149. (15)

Bonanno, G. A., & Mancini, A. D. (2008). The human capacity to thrive in the face of potential trauma. *Pediatrics, 121,* 369–375. (5)

Bond, M. H. (1991). *Beyond the Chinese face.* New York: Oxford University Press. (15)

Bond, M. H. (2002). Reclaiming the individual from Hofstede's ecological analysis—A 20-year odyssey: Comment on Oyserman et al. (2002). *Psychological Bulletin, 128,* 73–77. (13)

Bond, R., & Smith, P. B. (1996). Culture and conformity: A meta-analysis of studies using Asch's (1952, 1956) line judgment task. *Psychological Bulletin, 119,* 111–137. (13)

Bonnie, R. J. (1997). Research with cognitively impaired subjects: Unfinished business in the regulation of human research. *Archives of General Psychiatry, 54,* 105–111. (2)

Boot, W. R., Kramer, A. F., Simons, D. J., Fabiani, M., & Gratton, G. (2008). The effects of video game playing on attention, memory, and executive control. *Acta Psychologica, 129,* 387–398. (8)

Bootzin, R. R., & Bailey, E. T. (2005). Understanding placebo, nocebo, and iatrogenic treatment effects. *Journal of Clinical Psychology, 61,* 871–880. (12, 15)

Borch-Jacobsen, M. (1997, April 24). Sybil—The making of a disease: An interview with Dr. Herbert Spiegel. *New York Review of Books,* no. 7, 60–64. (15)

Borden, V. M. H., & Rajecki, D. W. (2000). First-year employment outcomes of psychology baccalaureates: Relatedness, preparedness, and prospects. *Teaching of Psychology, 27,* 164–168. (1)

Boring, E. G. (1930). A new ambiguous figure. *American Journal of Psychology, 42,* 444–445. (4)

Bornstein, R. F. (2005). Reconnecting psychoanalysis to mainstream psychology: Challenges and opportunities. *Psychoanalytic Psychology, 22,* 323–340. (14)

Bouchard, T. J., Lykken, D. T., McGue, M., Segal, N. L., & Tellegen, A. (1990). Sources of psychological differences: The Minnesota study of twins reared apart. *Science, 250,* 223–228. (5)

Bouchard, T. J., Jr., & McGue, M. (1981). Familial studies of intelligence: A review. *Science, 212,* 1055–1059. (9)

Bouchard, T. J., Jr., & McGue, M. (2003). Genetic and environmental influences on human psychological differences. *Journal of Neurobiology, 54,* 4–45. (5, 14)

Bould, E., Morris, N., & Wink, B. (2008). Recognizing subtle emotional expressions: The role of facial movements. *Cognition and Emotion, 22,* 1569–1587. (12)

Bouton, M. E. (1994). Context, ambiguity, and classical conditioning. *Current Directions in Psychological Science, 3,* 49–53. (6)

Bouton, M. E., Mineka, S., & Barlow, D. H. (2001). A modern learning theory perspective on the etiology of panic disorder. *Psychological Review, 108,* 4–32. (16)

Bowlby, J. (1973). *Attachment and loss: Vol. II. Separation.* New York: Basic Books. (5)

Bowmaker, J. K. (1998). Visual pigments and molecular genetics of color blindness. *News in Physiological Sciences, 13,* 63–69. (4)

Bowmaker, J. K., & Dartnall, H. J. A. (1980). Visual pigments of rods and cones in a human retina. *Journal of Physiology* (London), *298,* 501–511. (4)

Boyke, J., Driemeyer, J., Gaser, C., Büchel, C., & May, A. (2008). Training-induced brain structure changes in the elderly. *Journal of Neuroscience, 28,* 7031–7035. (3)

Bracha, H. S. (2006). Human brain evolution and the "neuroevolutionary time-depth principle": Implications for the reclassification of fear-circuitry-related traits in *DSM–V* and for studying resilience to warzone-related posttraumatic stress disorder. *Progress in Neuro-Psychopharmacology and Biological Psychiatry, 30,* 827–853. (15, 16)

Brackett, M. A., Mayer, J. D., & Warner, R. M. (2004). Emotional intelligence and its relation to everyday behaviour. *Personality and Individual Differences, 36,* 1387–1402. (12)

Bradbury, T. N., & Miller, G. A. (1985). Season of birth in schizophrenia: A review of evidence, methodology, and etiology. *Psychological Bulletin, 98,* 569–594. (16)

Braden, J. P., & Niebling, B. C. (2005). Using the joint test standards to evaluate the validity evidence for intelligence tests. In D. P. Flanagan & P. L. Harrison (Eds.), *Contemporary intellectual assessment* (pp. 615–630). New York: Guilford Press. (9)

Bradley, D. C., Troyk, P. R., Berg, J. A., Bak, M., Cogan, S., Erickson, R., et al. (2005). Visuotopic mapping through a multichannel stimulating implant in primate V1. *Journal of Neurophysiology, 93,* 1659–1670. (4)

Brainard, M. S., & Doupe, A. J. (2000). Auditory feedback in learning and maintenance of vocal behaviour. *Nature Reviews Neuroscience, 1,* 31–40. (6)

Brang, D., Edwards, L., Ramachandran, V. S., & Coulson, S. (2008). Is the sky 2? Contextual priming in grapheme-color synesthesia. *Psychological Science, 19,* 421–428. (4)

Brédart, S., Delchambre, M., & Laureys, S. (2006). One's own face is hard to ignore. *Quarterly Journal of Experimental Psychology, 59,* 46–52. (8)

Bregman, A. S. (1981). Asking the "what for" question in auditory perception. In M. Kubovy & J. R. Pomerantz (Eds.), *Perceptual organization* (pp. 99–118). Hillsdale, NJ: Erlbaum. (4)

Brennan, P. A., & Zufall, F. (2006). Pheromonal communication in vertebrates. *Nature, 444,* 308–315. (4)

Brent, D. A. (2001). Firearms and suicide. *Annals of the New York Academy of Sciences, 932,* 225–239. (16)

Brescoll, V. L., & Uhlmann, E. L. (2008). Can an angry woman get ahead? *Psychological Science, 19,* 268–275. (13)

Breslau, N., Dickens, W. T., Flynn, J. R., Peterson, E. L., & Lucia, V. C. (2006). Low birthweight and social disadvantage: Tracking their relationship with children's IQ during the period of school attendance. *Intelligence, 34,* 351–362. (9)

Brewer, M. B., & Chen, Y.-R. (2007). Where (who) are collectives in collectivism? Toward conceptual clarification of individualism and collectivism. *Psychological Review, 114,* 131–151. (5)

Brock, G., Laumann, E., Glasser, D. B., Nicolosi, A., Gingell, C., & King, R. for the GSSAB Investigator's Group. (2003). *Prevalence of sexual dysfunction among mature men and women in USA, Canada, Australia and New Zealand.* Poster session presented at the meeting of the American Urological Association, Chicago, April 26–May 1, 2003. Retrieved from http://www.pfizerglobalstudy.com/Posters/GSSAB%20AUA%202003_poster_FINAL.pdf. (11)

Brody, N. (2003). Construct validation of the Sternberg Triarchic Abilities Test: Comment and reanalysis. *Intelligence, 31,* 319–329. (9)

Brooks, R. (2000). Negative genetic correlation between male sexual attractiveness and survival. *Nature, 406,* 67–70. (13)

Brower, K. J., & Anglin, M. D. (1987). Adolescent cocaine use: Epidemiology, risk factors, and prevention. *Journal of Drug Education, 17,* 163–180. (3)

Brown, A. S. (2003). A review of the déjà vu experience. *Psychological Bulletin, 129,* 394–413. (10)

Brown, G. P., MacLeod, A. K., Tata, P., & Goddard, L. (2002). Worry and the simulation of future outcomes. *Anxiety, Stress and Coping, 15,* 1–17. (12)

Brown, G. W. (1989). Life events and measurement. In G. W. Brown & T. O. Harris (Eds.), *Life events and illness* (pp. 3–45). New York: Guilford Press. (12)

Brown, J. (1977). *Mind, brain, and consciousness.* New York: Academic Press. (8)

Brown, K. M. O., Bujac, S. R., Mann, E. T., Campbell, D. A., Stubbins, M. J., & Blundell, J. E. (2007). Further evidence of association of OPRD1 & HTR1D polymorphisms with susceptibility to anorexia nervosa. *Biological Psychiatry, 61,* 367–373. (11)

Brown, R., & McNeill, D. (1966). The "tip of the tongue." *Journal of Verbal Learning and Verbal Behavior, 5,* 325–337. (7)

Bruce, S. E., Machan, J. T., Dyck, I., & Keller, M. B. (2001). Infrequency of "pure" GAD: Impact of psychiatric comorbidity on clinical course. *Depression and Anxiety, 14,* 219–225. (16)

Bruck, M., Cavanagh, P., & Ceci, S. J. (1991). Fortysomething: Recognizing faces at one's 25th reunion. *Memory and Cognition, 19,* 221–228. (4)

Bruder, C. E. G., Piotrowski, A., Gijsbers, A. A. C. J., Andersson, R., Erickson, S., Diaz de Stahl, T., et al. (2008). Phenotypically concordant and discordant monozygotic twins display different DNA copy-number-variation profiles. *American Journal of Human Genetics, 82,* 763–771. (16)

Bruner, J. S., & Potter, M. C. (1964). Interference in visual recognition. *Science, 144,* 424–425. (8)

Brüning, J. C., Gautham, D., Burks, D. J., Gillette, J., Schubert, M., Orban, P. C., et al. (2000). Role of brain insulin receptor in control of body weight and reproduction. *Science, 289,* 2122–2125. (11)

Bryant, F. B., & Guilbault, R. L. (2002). "I knew it all along" eventually: The development of

hindsight bias in the Clinton impeachment verdict. *Basic and Applied Social Psychology, 24,* 27–41. (7)

Brysbaert, M., Vitu, F., & Schroyens, W. (1996). The right visual field advantage and the optimal viewing position effect: On the relation between foveal and parafoveal word recognition. *Neuropsychology, 10,* 385–395. (8)

Bryson, S. E. (2005). The autistic mind. In M. L. Bauman & T. L. Kemper (Eds.), *The neurobiology of autism* (pp. 34–44). Baltimore: Johns Hopkins University Press. (16)

Buck, L., & Axel, R. (1991). A novel multigene family may encode odorant receptors: A molecular basis for odor recognition. *Cell, 65,* 175–187. (4)

Buckner, F., & Firestone, M. (2000). "Where the public peril begins": 25 years after *Tarasoff. Journal of Legal Medicine, 21,* 187–222. (15)

Buehler, R., Griffin, D., & Ross, M. (1994). Exploring the "planning fallacy": Why people underestimate their task completion times. *Journal of Personality and Social Psychology, 67,* 366–381. (11)

Bulbena, A., Gago, J., Martin-Santos, R., Porta, M., Dasquens, J., & Berrios, G. E. (2004). Anxiety disorder and joint laxity: A definitive link. *Neurology, Psychiatry and Brain Research, 11,* 137–140. (16)

Burger, J. M. (1986). Increasing compliance by improving the deal: The that's-not-all technique. *Journal of Personality and Social Psychology, 51,* 277–283. (13)

Burger, J. M. (2009). Replicating Milgram: Would people still obey today? *American Psychologist, 64,* 1–11. (13)

Burke, D. M., Locantore, J. K., Austin, A. A., & Chae, B. (2004). Cherry pit primes Brad Pitt. *Psychological Science, 15,* 164–170. (8)

Burke, K. A., Franz, T. M., Miller, D. N., & Schoenbaum, G. (2008). The role of the orbitofrontal cortex in the pursuit of happiness and more specific rewards. *Nature, 454,* 340–344. (6)

Burke, K. C., Burke, J. D., Jr., Regier, D. A., & Rae, D. S. (1990). Age at onset of selected mental disorders in five community populations. *Archives of General Psychiatry, 47,* 511–518. (16)

Burns, B. D. (2004). The effects of speed on skilled chess performance. *Psychological Science, 15,* 442–447. (8)

Burns, M. O., & Seligman, M. E. P. (1989). Explanatory style across the life span: Evidence for stability over 52 years. *Journal of Personality and Social Psychology, 56,* 471–477. (16)

Burr, D. C., Morrone, M. C., & Ross, J. (1994). Selective suppression of the magnocellular visual pathway during saccadic eye movements. *Nature, 371,* 511–513. (8)

Burton, C. M., & King, L. A. (2004). The health benefits of writing about intensely positive experiences. *Journal of Research in Personality, 38,* 150–163. (12)

Burton, H., Snyder, A. Z., Conturo, T. E., Akbudak, E., Ollinger, J. M., & Raichle, M. E. (2002). Adaptive changes in early and late blind: A fMRI study of Braille reading. *Journal of Neurophysiology, 87,* 589–607. (3)

Burtsev, M., & Turchin, P. (2006). Evolution of cooperative strategies from first principles. *Nature, 440,* 1041–1044. (13)

Bushman, B. J., & Anderson, C. A. (2001). Media violence and the American public: Scientific facts versus media misinformation. *American Psychologist, 56,* 477–489. (2)

Buss, D. M. (2000). Desires in human mating. *Annals of the New York Academy of Sciences, 907,* 39–49. (13)

Buss, D. M., Larsen, R. J., Westen, D., & Semmelroth, J. (1992). Sex differences in jealousy: Evolution, physiology, and psychology. *Psychological Science, 3,* 251–255. (13)

Butcher, J. N., Graham, J. R., Williams, C. L., & Ben-Porath, Y. S. (1990). *Development and use of the MMPI-2 content scales.* Minneapolis: University of Minnesota Press. (14)

Butcher, L. M., Davis, O. S. P., Craig, I. W., & Plomin, R. (2007). Genome-wide quantitative trait locus association scan of general cognitive ability using pooled DNA and 500K single nucleotide polymorphism microarrays. *Genes, Brain and Behavior, 7,* 435–446. (9)

Butler, A. C., Chapman, J. E., Forman, E. M., & Beck, A. T. (2006). The empirical status of cognitive-behavioral therapy: A review of meta-analyses. *Clinical Psychology Review, 26,* 17–31. (16)

Butler, E. A., Lee, T. L., & Gross, J. J. (2007). Emotion regulation and culture: Are the social consequences of emotion suppression culture-specific? *Emotion, 7,* 30–48. (13)

Butler, R. J., Holland, P., Gasson, S., Norfolk, S., Houghton, L., & Penney, M. (2007). Exploring potential mechanisms in alarm treatment for primary nocturnal enuresis. *Scandinavian Journal of Urology and Nephrology, 41,* 407–413. (15)

Butzlaff, R. L., & Hooley, J. M. (1998). Expressed emotion and psychiatric relapse. *Archives of General Psychiatry, 55,* 547–552. (16)

Buunk, B. P., Angleitner, A., Oubaid, V., & Buss, D. M. (1996). Sex differences in jealousy in evolutionary and cultural perspective: Tests from The Netherlands, Germany, and the United States. *Psychological Science, 7,* 359–363. (13)

Buxbaum, L. J. (2006). On the right (and left) track: Twenty years of progress in studying hemispatial neglect. *Cognitive Neuropsychology, 23,* 184–201. (10)

Byne, W., Tobet, S., Mattiace, L. A., Lasco, M. S., Kemether, E., Edgar, M. A., et al. (2001). The interstitial nuclei of the human anterior hypothalamus: An investigation of variation with sex, sexual orientation, and HIV status. *Hormones and Behavior, 40,* 86–92. (11)

Byrne, G. J. A., Raphael, B., & Arnold, E. (1999). Alcohol consumption and psychological distress in recently widowed older men. *Australian and New Zealand Journal of Psychiatry, 33,* 740–747. (12)

Cacioppo, J. T., Hawkley, L. C., & Berntson, G. G. (2003). The anatomy of loneliness. *Current Directions in Psychological Science, 12,* 71–74. (12)

Cahalan, D. (1978). Subcultural differences in drinking behavior in U.S. national surveys and selected European studies. In P. E. Nathan, G. A. Marlatt, & T. Løberg (Eds.), *Alcoholism: New directions in behavioral research and treatment* (pp. 235–253). New York: Plenum Press. (16)

Cahill, L. (2006). Why sex matters for neuroscience. *Nature Reviews Neuroscience, 7,* 477–484. (3, 5)

Caldwell, B. E., & Woolley, S. R. (2008). Marriage and family therapists' endorsement of myths about marriage. *American Journal of Family Therapy, 36,* 367–387. (13)

Caldwell, J. A., Mu, Q., Smith, J. K., Mishory, A., Caldwell, J. L., Peters, G., et al. (2005). Are individual differences in fatigue vulnerability related to baseline differences in cortical activation? *Behavioral Neuroscience, 119,* 694–707. (10)

Callaghan, T., Rochat, P., Lillard, A., Claux, M. L., Odden, H., Itakura, S., et al. (2005). Synchrony in the onset of mental-state reasoning. *Psychological Science, 16,* 378–384. (5)

Callicott, J. H., Straub, R. E., Pezawas, L., Egan, M. F., Mattay, V. S., Hariri, A. R., et al. (2005). Variation in DISC1 affects hippocampal structure and function and increases risk for schizophrenia. *Proceedings of the National Academy of Sciences, USA, 102*, 8627–8632. (16)

Cameron, P., Proctor, K., Coburn, W., & Forde, N. (1985). Sexual orientation and sexually transmitted disease. *Nebraska Medical Journal, 70*, 292–299. (11)

Campbell, R. S., & Pennebaker, J. W. (2003). The secret life of pronouns: Flexibility in writing style and physical health. *Psychological Science, 14*, 60–65. (15)

Campbell, S. S., & Tobler, I. (1984). Animal sleep: A review of sleep duration across phylogeny. *Neuroscience and Biobehavioral Reviews, 8*, 269–300. (10)

Camperio-Ciani, A., Corna, F., & Capiluppi, C. (2004). Evidence for maternally inherited factors favouring male homosexuality and promoting female fecundity. *Proceedings of the Royal Society of London*, B, *271*, 2217–2221. (11)

Campion, M. A., & McClelland, C. L. (1991). Interdisciplinary examination of the costs and benefits of enlarged jobs: A job design quasi-experiment. *Journal of Applied Psychology, 76*, 186–198. (11)

Campion, M. A., & Thayer, P. W. (1985). Development and field evaluation of an interdisciplinary measure of job design. *Journal of Applied Psychology, 70*, 29–43. (11)

Campion, M. A., & Thayer, P. W. (1989). How do you design a job? *Personnel Journal, 68*, 43–46. (1)

Campos, J. J., Bertenthal, B. I., & Kermoian, R. (1992). Early experience and emotional development. *Psychological Science, 3*, 61–64. (5)

Camras, L. A., Chen, Y., Bakeman, R., Norris, K., & Cain, T. R. (2006). Culture, ethnicity and children's facial expressions: A study of European American, mainland Chinese, Chinese American, and adopted Chinese girls. *Emotion, 6*, 103–114. (12)

Canetto, S. S., & Sakinofsky, I. (1998). The gender paradox in suicide. *Suicide and Life-Threatening Behavior, 28*, 1–23. (16)

Canino, G., & Alegria, M. (2008). Psychiatric diagnosis—Is it universal or relative to culture? *Journal of Child Psychology and Psychiatry, 49*, 237–250. (15)

Cannon, W. B. (1929). Organization for physiological homeostasis. *Physiological Reviews, 9*, 399–431. (11)

Cao, Q., Zang, Y., Zhu, C., Cao, X., Sun, L., Zhou, X., et al. (2008). Alerting deficits in children with attention deficit/hyperactivity disorder: Event-related fMRI evidence. *Brain Research, 1219*, 159–168. (8)

Cardno, A. G., Marshall, E. J., Coid, B., Macdonald, A. M., Ribchester, T. R., Davies, N. J., et al. (1999). Heritability estimates for psychotic disorders. *Archives of General Psychiatry, 56*, 162–168. (16)

Carey, S. (1978). The child as word learner. In M. Halle, J. Bresnan, & G. A. Miller (Eds.), *Linguistic theory and psychological reality* (pp. 264–293). Cambridge, MA: MIT Press. (8)

Carlson, S. M., & Meltzoff, A. N. (2008). Bilingual experience and executive functioning in young children. *Developmental Science, 11*, 282–298. (8)

Carlsson, K., Petrovic, P., Skare, S., Petersson, K. M., & Ingvar, M. (2000). Tickling expectations: Neural processing in anticipation of a sensory stimulus. *Journal of Cognitive Neuroscience, 12*, 691–703. (4)

Carney, R. N., & Levin, J. R. (1998). Coming to terms with the keyword method in introductory psychology: A "neuromnemonic" example. *Teaching of Psychology, 25*, 132–134. (7)

Carr, J. (2008). The everyday life of adults with Down syndrome. *Journal of Applied Research in Intellectual Disabilities, 21*, 389–397. (9)

Carroll, B. J. (1980). Implications of biological research for the diagnosis of depression. In J. Mendlewicz (Ed.), *New advances in the diagnosis and treatment of depressive illness* (pp. 85–107). Amsterdam: Excerpta Medica. (16)

Carroll, J. B. (1993). *Human cognitive abilities.* Cambridge, England: Cambridge University Press. (9)

Carroll, J. B. (2003). The higher-stratum structure of cognitive abilities: Current evidence supports *g* and about ten broad factors. In H. Nyborg (Ed.), *The scientific study of general intelligence: Tribute to Arthur R. Jensen* (pp. 5–21). Oxford, England: Elsevier. (9)

Carstensen, L. L., Mikels, J. A., & Mather, M. (2006). Aging and the intersection of cognition, motivation, and emotion. In J. E. Birren & K. W. Schaie (Eds.), *Handbook of the psychology of aging* (6th ed., pp. 343–362). Burlington, MA: Elsevier. (5)

Caspi, A., McClay, J., Moffitt, T. E., Mill, J., Martin, J., Craig, I. W., et al. (2002). Role of genotype in the cycle of violence in maltreated children. *Science, 297*, 851–854. (5, 12)

Caspi, A., Sugden, K., Moffit, T. E., Taylor, A., Craig, I. W., Harrington, H. L., et al. (2003). Influence of life stress on depression: Moderation by a polymorphism in the 5-HTT gene. *Science, 301*, 386–389. (14, 16)

Cassia, V. M., Turati, C., & Simion, F. (2004). Can a nonspecific bias toward top-heavy patterns explain newborns' face preference? *Psychological Science, 15*, 379–383. (5)

Caterina, M. J., Rosen, T. A., Tominaga, M., Brake, A. J., & Julius, D. (1999). A capsaicin-receptor homologue with a high threshold for noxious heat. *Nature, 398*, 436–441. (4)

Catmur, C., Walsh, V., & Heyes, C. (2007). Sensorimotor learning configures the human mirror system. *Current Biology, 17*, 1527–1531. (3)

Cattell, R. B. (1965). *The scientific analysis of personality.* Chicago: Aldine. (14)

Cattell, R. B. (1987). *Intelligence: Its structure, growth and action.* Amsterdam: North-Holland. (14)

Center for Psychology Workforce Analysis and Research. (2007). Doctorate Employment Survey. Washington, DC: American Psychological Association. (1)

Cepeda, N. J., Pashler, H., Vul, E., Wixted, J. T., & Rohrer, D. (2006). Distributed practice in verbal recall tasks: A review and quantitative synthesis. *Psychological Bulletin, 132*, 354–380. (7)

Cepeda, N. J., Vul, E., Rohrer, D., Wixted, J. T., & Pashler, H. (2008). Spacing effects in learning. *Psychological Science, 19*, 1095–1102. (7)

Cesarini, D., Dawes, C. T., Fowler, J. H., Johanesson, M., Lichtenstein, P., & Wallace, B. (2008). Heritability of cooperative behavior in the trust game. *Proceedings of the National Academy of Sciences, USA, 105*, 3721–3726. (5)

Chabris, C. F., & Glickman, M. E. (2006). Sex differences in intellectual performance: Analysis of a large cohort of competitive chess players. *Psychological Science, 17*, 1040–1046. (5)

Chamberlain, S. R., Menzies, L., Hampshire, A., Suckling, J., Fineberg, N. A., del Campo, N., et al. (2008). Orbitofrontal dysfunction in patients with obsessive-compulsive disorder and their unaffected relatives. *Science, 321*, 421–422. (16)

Chamberlin, J. (1978). *On our own.* New York: Hawthorn. (15)

Chamchong, J., Dyckman, K. A., Austin, B. P., Clementz, B. A., & McDowell, J. E. (2008). Common neural circuitry supporting volitional saccades and its disruption in schizophrenia. *Biological Psychiatry, 64*, 1042–1050. (16)

Chamorro-Premuzic, T., & Furnham, A. (2008). Personality, intelligence and approaches to

learning as predictors of academic performance. *Personality and Individual Differences, 44*, 1596–1603. (14)

Chao, M. M., Chen, J., Roisman, G. I., & Hong, Y.-y. (2007). Essentializing race. *Psychological Science, 18*, 341–348. (5)

Chapman, H. A., Kim, D. A., Susskind, J. M., & Anderson, A. K. (2009). In bad taste: Evidence for the oral origins of moral disgust. *Science, 323*, 1222–1226. (12)

Chase-Lansdale, P., Moffitt, R. A., Lohrman, B. J., Cherlin, A. J., Coley, R. L., Pittman, L. D., et al. (2003). Mothers' transitions from welfare to work and the well-being of preschoolers and adolescents. *Science, 299*, 1548–1552. (5)

Chaudhari, N., Landin, A. M., & Roper, S. D. (2000). A metabotropic glutamate receptor variant functions as a taste receptor. *Nature Neuroscience, 3*, 113–119. (4)

Chee, M. W. L., Tan, J. C., Zheng, H., Parimal, S., Weissman, D. H., Zagorodnov, V., et al. (2008). Lapsing during sleep deprivation is associated with distributed changes in brain activation. *Journal of Neuroscience, 28*, 5519–5528. (10)

Cheetham, E. (1973). *The prophecies of Nostradamus.* New York: Putnam's. (2)

Chehab, F. F., Mounzih, K., Lu, R., & Lim, M. E. (1997). Early onset of reproductive function in normal female mice treated with leptin. *Science, 275*, 88–90. (11)

Chemelli, R. M., Willie, J. T., Sinton, C. M., Elmquist, J. K., Scammell, T., Lee, C., et al. (1999). Narcolepsy in orexin knockout mice: Molecular genetics of sleep regulation. *Cell, 98*, 437–451. (10)

Chen, D., & Haviland-Jones, J. (2000). Human olfactory communication of emotion. *Perceptual and Motor Skills, 91*, 771–781. (5)

Chen, Z., Williams, K. D., Fitness, J., & Newton, N. C. (2008). When hurt will not heal. *Psychological Science, 19*, 789–795. (4)

Cheng, A. T. A. (1995). Mental illness and suicide. *Archives of General Psychiatry, 52*, 594–603. (16)

Cheng, C. (2005). Processes underlying gender-role flexibility: Do androgynous individuals know more or know how to cope? *Journal of Personality, 73*, 645–673. (5)

Cheryan, S., & Bodenhausen, G. V. (2000). When positive stereotypes threaten intellectual performance: The psychological hazards of "model minority" status. *Psychological Science, 11*, 399–402. (9)

Cheung, F. M., Leung, K., Fang, R. M., Song, W. Z., Zhang, J. X., & Zhang, J. P. (1996). Development of the Chinese Personality Assessment Inventory (CPAI). *Journal of Cross-Cultural Psychology, 27*, 181–199. (14)

Chivers, M. L., Rieger, G., Latty, E., & Bailey, J. M. (2004). A sex difference in the specificity of sexual arousal. *Psychological Science, 15*, 736–744. (11)

Choi, I., & Nisbett, R. E. (2000). Cultural psychology of surprise: Holistic theories and recognition of contradiction. *Journal of Personality and Social Psychology, 79*, 890–905. (13)

Choi, Y. Y., Shamosh, N. A., Cho, S. H., DeYoung, C. G., Lee, M. J., Lee, J.-M., et al. (2008). Multiple bases of human intelligence revealed by cortical thickness and neural activation. *Journal of Neuroscience, 28*, 10323–10329. (9)

Chomsky, N. (1980). *Rules and representations.* New York: Columbia University Press. (8)

Christensen, A., & Jacobson, N. S. (1994). Who (or what) can do psychotherapy: The status and challenge of nonprofessional therapies. *Psychological Science, 5*, 8–14. (15)

Church, A. T., Katigbak, M. S., Reyes, J. A. S., Salanga, M. G. C., Miramontes, L. A., & Adams, N. B. (2008). Prediction and cross-situational consistency of daily behavior across cultures: Testing trait and cultural psychology perspectives. *Journal of Research in Personality, 42*, 1199–1215. (14)

Churchland, P. S. (1986). *Neurophilosophy.* Cambridge, MA: MIT Press. (10)

Cialdini, R. B. (1993). *Influence: The psychology of persuasion* (Rev. ed.). New York: Morrow. (6, 13)

Cialdini, R. B. (2003). Crafting normative messages to protect the environment. *Current Directions in Psychological Science, 12*, 105–109. (13)

Ciesla, J. A., & Roberts, J. E. (2007). Rumination, negative cognition, and their interactive effects on depressed mood. *Emotion, 7*, 555–565. (16)

Cimino, K. (2007, June 20). After it blooms, it will smell as bad as a blooming corpse. *News and Observer* (Raleigh, NC), p. 4B. (11)

Cislo, A. M. (2008). Ethnic identity and self-esteem: Contrasting Cuban and Nicaraguan young adults. *Hispanic Journal of Behavioral Sciences, 30*, 230–250. (5)

Clancy, S. A. (2005). *Abducted: How people come to believe they were kidnapped by aliens.* Cambridge, MA: Harvard University Press. (16)

Clark, C. A. C., Woodward, L. J., Horwood, L. J., & Moor, S. (2008). Development of emotional and behavioral regulation in children born extremely preterm and very preterm: Biological and social influences. *Child Development, 79*, 1444–1462. (5)

Clark, L. A. (2009). Stability and change in personality disorder. *Current Directions in Psychological Science, 18*, 27–31. (15)

Clarke, G. N., Hornbrook, M., Lynch, F., Polen, M., Gale, J., Beardslee, W., et al. (2001). A randomized trial of a group cognitive intervention for preventing depression in adolescent offspring of depressed patients. *Archives of General Psychiatry, 58*, 1127–1134. (15)

Clarkin, J. F., & Carpenter, D. (1995). Family therapy in historical perspective. In B. Bongar & L. E. Beutler (Eds.), *Comprehensive textbook of psychotherapy: Theory and practice* (pp. 205–227). Oxford, England: Oxford University Press. (15)

Clay, R. A. (2002, May). An indigenized psychology. *Monitor on Psychology, 33*(5), 58–59. (15)

Clearfield, M. W., & Nelson, N. M. (2006). Sex differences in mothers' speech and play behavior with 6-, 9-, and 14-month-old infants. *Sex Roles, 54*, 127–137. (5)

Clément, K., Vaisse, C., Lahlou, N., Cabrol, S., Pelloux, V., Cassuto, D., et al. (1998). A mutation in the human leptin receptor gene causes obesity and pituitary dysfunction. *Nature, 392*, 398–401. (11)

Clements, W. A., & Perner, J. (1994). Implicit understanding of belief. *Cognitive Development, 9*, 377–395. (5)

Clinicopathologic conference. (1967). *Johns Hopkins Medical Journal, 120*, 186–199. (12)

Coan, J. A., Schaefer, H. S., & Davidson, R. J. (2006). Lending a hand: Social regulation of the neural response to threat. *Psychological Science, 17*, 1032–1039. (12)

Coatsworth, J. D., Maldonado-Molina, M., Pantin, H., & Szapocznik, J. (2005). A person-centered and ecological investigation of acculturation strategies in Hispanic immigrant youth. *Journal of Community Psychology, 33*, 157–174. (5)

Cobos, P., Sánchez, M., García, C., Vera, M. N., & Vila, J. (2002). Revisiting the James versus Cannon debate on emotion: Startle and autonomic modulation in patients with spinal cord injuries. *Biological Psychology, 61*, 251–269. (12)

Cocodia, E. A., Kim, J. S., Shin, H.-S., Kim, J. W., Ee, J., Wee, M. S. W., et al. (2003). Evidence that rising population intelligence is impacting in

formal education. *Personality and Individual Differences, 35*, 797–810. (9)

Coelho, C. M., Waters, A. M., Hine, T. J., & Wallis, G. (2009). The use of virtual reality in acrophobia research and treatment. *Journal of Anxiety Disorders, 23*, 563–574. (16)

Cohen, B., Novick, D., & Rubinstein, M. (1996). Modulation of insulin activities by leptin. *Science, 274*, 1185–1188. (11)

Cohen, D. (2001). Cultural variation: Considerations and implications. *Psychological Bulletin, 127*, 451–471. (5)

Cohen, E., & Barrett, J. L. (2008). Conceptualizing spirit possession: Ethnographic and experimental evidence. *Ethos, 36*, 246–267. (15)

Cohen, J. D., Noll, D. C., & Schneider, W. (1993). Functional magnetic resonance imaging: Overview and methods for psychological research. *Behavior Research Methods, Instruments, and Computers, 25*, 101–113. (3)

Cohen, N. J., & Squire, L. R. (1980). Preserved learning and retention of pattern-analyzing skill in amnesia: Dissociation of knowing how and knowing that. *Science, 210*, 207–211. (7)

Cohen, S., Frank, E., Doyle, W. J., Skoner, D. P., Rabin, B. S., & Swaltney, J. M., Jr. (1998). Types of stressors that increase susceptibility to the common cold in healthy adults. *Health Psychology, 17*, 214–223. (12)

Cohen, S., Lichtenstein, E., Prochaska, J. O., Rossi, J. S., Gritz, E. R., Carr, C. R., et al. (1989). Debunking myths about self-quitting: Evidence from 10 prospective studies of persons who attempt to quit smoking by themselves. *American Psychologist, 44*, 1355–1365. (16)

Cohen Kadosh, R., Henik, A., Catena, A., Walsh, V., & Fuentes, L. J. (2009). Induced cross-modal synaesthetic experience without abnormal neuronal connections. *Psychological Science, 20*, 258–265. (10)

Coid, J. W., Kirkbride, J. B., Barker, D., Cowden, F., Stamps, R., Yang, M., et al. (2008). Raised incidence rates of all psychoses among migrant groups. *Archives of General Psychiatry, 65*, 1250–1258. (16)

Colantuoni, C., Rada, P., McCarthy, J., Patten, C., Avena, N. M., Chadeayne, A., et al. (2002). Evidence that intermittent, excessive sugar intake causes endogenous opioid dependence. *Obesity Research, 10*, 478–488. (11)

Colantuoni, C., Schwenker, J., McCarthy, J., Rada, P., Ladenheim, B., Cadet, J. L., et al. (2001). Excessive sugar intake alters binding to dopamine and mu-opioid receptors in the brain. *NeuroReport, 12*, 3549–3552. (11)

Colcombe, S., & Kramer, A. F. (2003). Fitness effects on the cognitive function of older adults: A meta-analytic study. *Psychological Science, 14*, 125–130. (5)

Collins, A. M., & Loftus, E. F. (1975). A spreading-activation theory of semantic processing. *Psychological Review, 82*, 407–428. (8)

Collins, A. M., & Quillian, M. R. (1969). Retrieval time from semantic memory. *Journal of Verbal Learning and Verbal Behavior, 8*, 240–247. (8)

Collins, A. M., & Quillian, M. R. (1970). Does category size affect categorization time? *Journal of Verbal Learning and Verbal Behavior, 9*, 432–438. (8)

Collins, W. A., Maccoby, E. E., Steinberg, L., Hetherington, E. M., & Bornstein, M. H. (2000). Contemporary research on parenting: The case for nature and nurture. *American Psychologist, 55*, 218–232. (5)

Colom, R., & García-López, O. (2003). Secular gains in fluid intelligence: Evidence from the Culture-Fair Intelligence Test. *Journal of Biosocial Science, 35*, 33–39. (9)

Colom, R., Juan-Espinosa, M., Abad, F., & Garciá, L. F. (2000). Negligible sex differences in general intelligence. *Intelligence, 28*, 57–68. (9)

Conners, C. K., & Schulte, A. C. (2002). Learning disorders. In K. L. Davis, D. Charney, J. T. Coyle, & C. Nemeroff (Eds.), *Neuropsychopharmacology* (pp. 597–612). Philadelphia: Lippincott, Williams, & Wilkins. (9)

Connine, C. M., Blasko, D. G., & Hall, M. (1991). Effects of subsequent sentence context in auditory word recognition: Temporal and linguistic constraints. *Journal of Memory and Language, 30*, 234–250. (8)

Connor, T. J., & Leonard, B. E. (1998). Depression, stress and immunological activation: The role of cytokines in depressive disorders. *Life Sciences, 62*, 583–606. (12)

Constantinides, P. (1977). Ill at ease and sick at heart: Symbolic behavior in a Sudanese healing cult. In I. Wilson (Ed.), *Symbols and sentiments* (pp. 61–84). New York: Academic Press. (15)

Consumer Reports. (1995, November). Mental health: Does therapy help? *Consumer Reports,* pp. 734–739. (15)

Cooper, J., & Cooper, G. (2002). Subliminal motivation: A story revisited. *Journal of Applied Social Psychology, 32*, 2213–2227. (4)

Coplan, J. D., Goetz, R., Klein, D. F., Papp, L. A., Fyer, A. J., Leibowitz, M. R., et al. (1998). Plasma cortisol concentrations preceding lactate-induced panic. *Archives of General Psychiatry, 55*, 130–136. (16)

Corallo, G., Sackur, J., Dehaene, S., & Sigman, M. (2008). Limits on introspection. *Psychological Science, 19*, 1110–1117. (8)

Corkin, S. (1984). Lasting consequences of bilateral medial temporal lobectomy: Clinical course and experimental findings in H. M. *Seminars in Neurology, 4*, 249–259. (7)

Corkin, S. (2002). What's new with the amnesic patient H. M.? *Nature Reviews Neuroscience, 3*, 153–159. (7)

Cosmelli, D., David, O., Lachaux, J.-P., Martinerie, J., Garnero, L., Renault, B., et al. (2004). Waves of consciousness: Ongoing cortical patterns during binocular rivalry. *NeuroImage, 23*, 128–140. (10)

Costa, P. T., Jr., McCrae, R. R., & Dye, D. A. (1991). Facet scales for agreeableness and conscientiousness: A revision of the NEO personality inventory. *Personality and Individual Differences, 12*, 887–898. (14)

Cotter, D., Mackay, D., Landau, S., Kerwin, R., & Everall, I. (2001). Reduced glial cell density and neuronal size in the anterior cingulate cortex in major depressive disorder. *Archives of General Psychiatry, 58*, 545–553. (16)

Courage, M. L., & Howe, M. L. (2002). From infant to child: The dynamics of cognitive change in the second year of life. *Psychological Bulletin, 128*, 250–277. (5)

Cowan, R. L. (2007). Neuroimaging research in human MDMA users: A review. *Psychopharmacology, 189*, 539–556. (3)

Cox, B. J., McWilliams, L. A., Clara, I. P., & Stein, M. B. (2003). The structure of feared situations in a nationally representative sample. *Journal of Anxiety Disorders, 17*, 89–101. (16)

Cox, J. J., Reimann, F., Nicholas, A. K., Thornton, G., Roberts, E., Springell, K., et al. (2006). An *SCN9A* channelopathy causes congenital inability to experience pain. *Nature, 444*, 894–898. (4)

Cox, W. M., Fadardi, J. S., & Pothos, E. M. (2006). The addiction-Stroop test: Theoretical considerations and procedural recommendations. *Psychological Bulletin, 132*, 443–476. (14)

Craig, A. D., Bushnell, M. C., Zhang, E. T., & Blomqvist, A. (1994). A thalamic nucleus specific for pain and temperature sensation. *Nature, 372,* 770–773. (4)

Craig, S. B., & Gustafson, S. B. (1998). Perceived leader integrity scale: An instrument for assessing employee perceptions of leader integrity. *Leadership Quarterly, 9,* 127–145. (11)

Craik, F. I. M., & Lockhart, R. S. (1972). Levels of processing: A framework for memory research. *Journal of Verbal Learning and Verbal Behavior, 11,* 671–684. (7)

Cramer, P. (1996). *Storytelling, narrative, and the Thematic Apperception Test.* New York: Guilford Press. (14)

Cramer, P. (2003). Personality change in later adulthood is predicted by defense mechanism use in early adulthood. *Journal of Research in Personality, 37,* 76–104. (14)

Credé, M., & Kuncel, N. R. (2008). Study habits, skills, and attitudes. *Perspectives on Psychological Science, 3,* 425–453. (9)

Crespi, B., & Badcock, C. (2008). Psychosis and autism as diametrical disorders of the social brain. *Behavioral and Brain Sciences, 31,* 241–261. (16)

Creswell, J. D., Welch, W. T., Taylor, S. E., Sherman, D. K., Gruenwald, T. L., & Mann, T. (2005). Affirmation of personal values buffers neuroendocrine and psychological stress responses. *Psychological Science, 16,* 846–851. (14)

Crews, D. J., & Landers, D. M. (1987). A meta-analytic review of aerobic fitness and reactivity to psychosocial stressors. *Medicine and Science in Sports and Exercise, 19,* S114–S120. (12)

Crews, F. (1996). The verdict on Freud. *Psychological Science, 7,* 63–68. (14)

Crinion, J., Turner, R., Grogan, A., Hanakawa, T., Noppeney, U., Devlin, J. T., et al. (2006). Language control in the bilingual brain. *Science, 312,* 1537–1540. (8)

Critchley, H. D., Mathias, C. J., & Dolan, R. J. (2001). Neuroanatomical basis for first- and second-order representations of bodily states. *Nature Neuroscience, 4,* 207–212. (12)

Crocetti, E., Rubini, M., Luyckx, K., & Meeus, W. (2008). Identity formation in early and middle adolescents from various ethnic groups: From three dimensions to five statuses. *Journal of Youth and Adolescence, 37,* 983–996. (5)

Crocker, J., & Park, L. E. (2004). The costly pursuit of self-esteem. *Psychological Bulletin, 130,* 392–414. (14)

Crombez, G., Hermans, D., & Adriaensen, H. (2000). The emotional Stroop task and chronic pain: What is threatening for chronic pain sufferers? *European Journal of Pain* (London), *4,* 37–44. (14)

Cronley, M. L., Kardes, F. R., Goddard, P., & Houghton, D. C. (1999). Endorsing products for the money: The role of correspondence bias in celebrity advertising. *Advances in Consumer Research, 26,* 627–631. (13)

Crosby, F. J., Iyer, A., Clayton, S., & Downing, R. A. (2003). Affirmative action: Psychological data and the policy debates. *American Psychologist, 58,* 93–115. (13)

Cross, C. K., & Hirschfeld, R. M. A. (1986). Psychosocial factors and suicidal behavior. *Annals of the New York Academy of Sciences, 487,* 77–89. (16)

Crowley, K., Callanen, M. A., Tenenbaum, H. R., & Allen, E. (2001). Parents explain more often to boys than to girls during shared scientific thinking. *Psychological Science, 12,* 258–261. (5)

Crowther, J. H., Armey, M., Luce, K. H., Dalton, G. R., & Leahey, T. (2008). The point prevalence of bulimic disorders from 1990 to 2004. *International Journal of Eating Disorders, 41,* 491–497. (11)

Croyle, R. T., & Cooper, J. (1983). Dissonance arousal: Physiological evidence. *Journal of Personality and Social Psychology, 45,* 782–791. (13)

Crucian, G. P., Hughes, J. D., Barrett, A. M., Williamson, D. J. G., Bauer, R. M., Bowers, D., et al. (2000). Emotional and physiological responses to false feedback. *Cortex, 36,* 623–647. (12).

Crum, A. J., & Langer, E. J. (2007). Mind-set matters. *Psychological Science, 18,* 165–171. (12)

Cryder, C. E., Lerner, J. S., Gross, J. J., & Dahl, R. E. (2008). Misery is not miserly: Sad and self-focused individuals spend more. *Psychological Science, 19,* 525–530. (12)

Csikszentmihalyi, M. (1999). If we are so rich, why aren't we happy? *American Psychologist, 54,* 821–827. (12)

Cuijpers, P., van Straten, A., Andersson, G., & van Oppen, P. (2008). Psychotherapy for depression in adults: A meta-analysis of comparative outcome studies. *Journal of Consulting and Clinical Psychology, 76,* 909–922. (15)

Culbertson, F. M. (1997). Depression and gender. *American Psychologist, 52,* 25–31. (16)

Cumming, G. (2008). Replication and *p* intervals. *Perspectives on Psychological Science, 3,* 286–300. (2)

Cummings, D. E., Clement, K., Purnell, J. Q., Vaisse, C., Foster, K. E., Frayo, R. S., et al. (2002). Elevated plasma ghrelin levels in Prader-Willi syndrome. *Nature Medicine, 8,* 643–644. (11)

Cummings, N. A. (1979). Turning bread into stones: Our modern antimiracle. *American Psychologist, 34,* 1119–1129. (16)

Cunningham, E. J. A., & Russell, A. F. (2000). Egg investment is influenced by male attractiveness in the mallard. *Nature, 404,* 74–77. (13)

Cunningham, W. A., Preacher, K. J., & Banaji, M. R. (2001). Implicit attitude measures: Consistency, stability, and convergent validity. *Psychological Science, 12,* 163–170. (13)

Cushman, F., Young, L., & Hauser, M. (2006). The role of conscious reasoning and intuition in moral judgment. *Psychological Science, 17,* 1082–1089. (12)

Cynkar, A. (2007, June). The changing gender composition of psychology. *Monitor on Psychology, 38*(6), 46. (1)

Cyranowski, J. M., Frank, E., Young, E., & Shear, K. (2000). Adolescent onset of the gender difference in lifetime rates of major depression. *Archives of General Psychiatry, 57,* 21–27. (16)

Czeisler, C. A., Johnson, M. P., Duffy, J. F., Brown, E. N., Ronda, J. M., & Kronauer, R. E. (1990). Exposure to bright light and darkness to treat physiologic maladaptation to night work. *New England Journal of Medicine, 322,* 1353–1359. (10)

Czeisler, C. A., Moore-Ede, M. C., & Coleman, R. M. (1982). Rotating shift work schedules that disrupt sleep are improved by applying circadian principles. *Science, 217,* 460–463. (10)

Dadds, M. R., Bovbjerg, D. H., Redd, W. H., & Cutmore, T. R. H. (1997). Imagery in human classical conditioning. *Psychological Bulletin, 122,* 89–103. (6)

Daley, T. C., Whaley, S. E., Sigman, M. D., Espinosa, M. P., & Neumann, C. (2003). IQ on the rise: The Flynn effect in rural Kenyan children. *Psychological Science, 14,* 215–219. (9)

Dallaire, B., McCubbin, M., Morin, P., & Cohen, D. (2000). Civil commitment due to mental illness and dangerousness: The union of law and psychiatry within a treatment-control system. *Sociology of Health and Illness, 22,* 679–699. (15)

Dallenbach, K. M. (1951). A puzzle picture with a new principle of concealment. *American Journal of Psychology, 64,* 431–433. (4)

Damaser, E. C., Shor, R. E., & Orne, M. E. (1963). Physiological effects during hypnotically requested emotions. *Psychosomatic Medicine, 25,* 334–343. (10)

Damasio, A. (1999). *The feeling of what happens.* New York: Harcourt Brace. (12)

Damasio, A. R. (1994). *Descartes' error: Emotion, reason, and the human brain.* New York: G. P. Putnam's Sons. (3, 12)

Damasio, H., Grabowski, T., Frank, R., Galaburda, A. M., & Damasio, A. R. (1994). The return of Phineas Gage: The skull of a famous patient yields clues about the brain. *Science, 264,* 1102–1105. (12)

Damron-Rodriguez, J. (1991). Commentary: Multicultural aspects of aging in the U.S.: Implications for health and human services. *Journal of Cross-Cultural Gerontology, 6,* 135–143. (5)

Daniel, M. H. (1997). Intelligence testing: Status and trends. *American Psychologist, 52,* 1038–1045. (9)

Danovitch, J., & Bloom, P. (2009). Children's extension of disgust to physical and moral events. *Emotion, 9,* 107–112. (12)

Dapretto, M., Davies, M. S., Pfeifer, J. H., Scott, A. A., Sigman, M., Bookheimer, S. Y., et al. (2006). Understanding emotions in others: Mirror neuron dysfunction in children with autism spectrum disorders. *Nature Neuroscience, 9,* 28–30. (3)

Dar, R., Rish, S., Hermish, H., Taub, M., & Fux, M. (2000). Realism of confidence in obsessive-compulsive checkers. *Journal of Abnormal Psychology, 109,* 673–678. (16)

Dar-Nimrod, I., & Heine, S. J. (2006). Exposure to scientific theories affects women's math performance. *Science, 314,* 435. (9)

Darst, C. R., & Cummings, M. E. (2006). Predator learning favours mimicry of a less-toxic model in poison frogs. *Nature, 440,* 208–211. (6)

Darwin, C. (1859). *On the origin of species by means of natural selection.* New York: D. Appleton. (1)

Darwin, C. (1871). *The descent of man.* New York: D. Appleton. (1)

Darwin, C. (1965). *The expression of emotions in man and animals.* Chicago: University of Chicago Press. (Original work published 1872) (12)

Das, J. P. (2002). A better look at intelligence. *Current Directions in Psychological Science, 11,* 28–33. (9)

Davenport, J. L., & Potter, M. C. (2004). Scene consistency in object and background perception. *Psychological Science, 15,* 559–564. (8)

Davidson, J. K., Sr., Moore, N. B., Earle, J. R., & Davis, R. (2008). Sexual attitudes and behavior at four universities: Do region, race, and/or religion matter? *Adolescence, 43,* 189–220. (11)

Davidson, R. J., Putnam, K. M., & Larson, C. L. (2000). Dysfunction in the neural circuitry of emotion regulation—A possible prelude to violence. *Science, 289,* 591–594. (12)

Davies, G., Welham, J., Chant, D., Torrey, E. F., & McGrath, J. (2003). A systematic review and meta-analysis of Northern Hemisphere season of birth studies in schizophrenia. *Schizophrenia Bulletin, 29,* 587–593. (16)

Davis, J. M., Chen, N., & Glick, I. D. (2003). A meta-analysis of the efficacy of second-generation antipsychotics. *Archives of General Psychiatry, 60,* 553–564. (16)

Davis, K. L., Stewart, D. G., Friedman, J. I., Buchsbaum, M., Harvey, P. D., Hof, P. R., et al. (2003). White matter changes in schizophrenia. *Archives of General Psychiatry, 60,* 443–456. (16)

Davis, O. S. P., Arden, R., & Plomin, R. (2008). *g* in middle childhood: Moderate genetic and shared environmental influence using diverse measures of general cognitive ability at 7, 9, and 10 years in a large population sample of twins. *Intelligence, 36,* 68–80. (9)

Daw, J. (2002, October). Is PMDD real? *Monitor on Psychology, 33*(9), 58–60. (15)

Dawes, R. M. (1994). *House of cards: Psychology and psychotherapy.* New York: Free Press. (14, 15)

Day, R. H. (1972). Visual spatial illusions: A general explanation. *Science, 175,* 1335–1340. (4)

Day, S. (2005). Some demographic and socio-cultural aspects of synesthesia. In L. C. Robertson & N. Sagiv (Eds.), *Synesthesia* (pp. 11–33). Oxford, England: Oxford University Press. (4)

Day, W. F., Jr., & Moore, J. (1995). On certain relations between contemporary philosophy and radical behaviorism. In J. T. Todd & E. K. Morris (Eds.), *Modern perspectives on B. F. Skinner and contemporary behaviorism* (pp. 75–84). Westport, CT: Greenwood Press. (6)

de Castro, J. M. (2000). Eating behavior: Lessons from the real world of humans. *Nutrition, 16,* 800–813. (1, 11)

de Groot, A. D. (1966). Perception and memory versus thought: Some old ideas and recent findings. In B. Kleinmuntz (Ed.), *Problem solving* (pp. 19–50). New York: Wiley. (8).

De Moor, M. H. M., Boomsma, D. I., Stubbe, J. H., Willemsen, G., & de Geus, E. J. C. (2008). Testing causality in the association between regular exercise and symptoms of anxiety and depression. *Archives of General Psychiatry, 65,* 897–905. (16)

de Quervain, D. J.-F., & Papassotiropoulos, A. (2006). Identification of a genetic cluster influencing memory performance and hippocampal activity in humans. *Proceedings of the National Academy of Sciences, USA, 103,* 4270–4274. (9)

de Waal, F. B. M. (2002). Evolutionary psychology: The wheat and the chaff. *Current Directions in Psychological Science, 11,* 187–191. (1, 5)

de Wit, H., Crean, J., & Richards, J. B. (2000). Effects of *d*-amphetamine and ethanol on a measure of behavioral inhibition in humans. *Behavioral Neuroscience, 114,* 830–837. (8)

Deacon, S., & Arendt, J. (1996). Adapting to phase shifts: II. Effects of melatonin and conflicting light treatment. *Physiology and Behavior, 59,* 675–682. (10)

Deacon, T. W. (1997). *The symbolic species.* New York: W. W. Norton. (8)

Dean, K. E., & Malamuth, N. M. (1997). Characteristics of men who aggress sexually and of men who imagine aggressing: Risk and moderating variables. *Journal of Personality and Social Psychology, 72,* 449–455. (12)

Deary, I. J. (2002). *g* and cognitive elements of information processing: An agnostic view. In R. J. Sternberg & E. L. Grigorenko (Eds.), *The general intelligence factor: How general is it?* (pp. 151–181). Mahwah, NJ: Erlbaum. (9)

Deary, I. J., Batty, G. D., Pattie, A., & Gale, C. R. (2008). More intelligent, more dependable children live longer. *Psychological Science, 19,* 874–880. (9)

Deary, I. J., Strand, S., Smith, P., & Fernandes, C. (2007). Intelligence and educational achievement. *Intelligence, 35,* 13–21. (9)

Deary, I. J., Whiteman, M. C., Starr, J. M., Whalley, L. J., & Fox, H. C. (2004). The impact of childhood intelligence on later life: Following up the Scottish mental surveys of 1932 and 1947. *Journal of Personality and Social Psychology, 86,* 130–147. (9)

DeCasper, A. J., & Fifer, W. P. (1980). Of human bonding: Newborns prefer their mothers' voices. *Science, 208,* 1174–1177. (5)

Deci, E. L. (1971). Effects of externally mediated rewards on intrinsic motivation. *Journal of Personality and Social Psychology, 18,* 105–115. (11)

Dedovic, K., Wadiwalla, M., Engert, V., & Pruessner, J. C. (2009). The role of sex and gender socialization in stress reactivity. *Developmental Psychology, 45,* 49–55. (14)

Deese, J. (1959). On the prediction of occurrence of particular verbal intrusions in immediate recall. *Journal of Experimental Psychology, 58,* 17–22. (7)

DeFelipe, C., Herrero, J. F., O'Brien, J. A., Palmer, J. A., Doyle, C. A., Smith, A. J. H., et al. (1998). Altered nociception, analgesia and aggression in mice lacking the receptor for substance P. *Nature, 392,* 394–397. (4)

Dehaene, S., Naccache, L., Cohen, L., LeBihan, D., Mangin, J.-F., Poline, J. B., et al. (2001). Cerebral mechanisms of word masking and unconscious repetition priming. *Nature Neuroscience, 4,* 752–758. (10)

DeLoache, J. S. (1989). The development of representation in young children. *Advances in Child Development and Behavior, 22,* 1–39. (5)

DeLoache, J. S., Miller, K. F., & Rosengren, K. S. (1997). The credible shrinking room: Very young children's performance with symbolic and nonsymbolic relations. *Psychological Science, 8,* 308–313. (5)

Dement, W. C. (1972). *Some must watch while some must sleep.* Stanford, CA: Stanford Alumni Association. (10)

Dement, W., & Kleitman, N. (1957a). Cyclic variations in EEG during sleep and their relation to eye movements, body motility, and dreaming. *Electroencephalography and Clinical Neurophysiology, 9,* 673–690. (10)

Dement, W., & Kleitman, N. (1957b). The relation of eye movements during sleep to dream activity: An objective method for the study of dreaming. *Journal of Experimental Psychology, 53,* 339–346. (10)

DeNeve, K. M. (1999). Happy as an extraverted clam? The role of personality for subjective well-being. *Current Directions in Psychological Science, 8,* 141–144. (12)

Denissen, J. J. A., Butalid, L., Penke, L., & van Aken, M. A. G. (2008). The effects of weather on daily mood. A multilevel approach. *Emotion, 8,* 662–667. (12)

Dennett, D. C. (2003). *Freedom evolves.* New York: Viking Press. (1)

DePaolo, B. M., Lindsay, J. J., Malone, B. E., Muhlenbruck, L., Charlton, K., & Cooper, H. (2003). Cues to deception. *Psychological Bulletin, 129,* 74–118. (12)

deQuervain, D. J.-F., Roozendaal, B., Nitsch, R. M., McGaugh, J. L., & Hock, C. (2000). Acute cortisone administration impairs retrieval of long-term declarative memory in humans. *Nature Neuroscience, 3,* 313–314. (12)

Deshmukh, A., Rosenbloom, M. J., Pfefferbaum, A., & Sullivan, E. V. (2002). Clinical signs of cerebellar dysfunction in schizophrenia, alcoholism, and their comorbidity. *Schizophrenia Research, 57,* 281–291. (16)

Detterman, D. K. (1979). Detterman's laws of individual differences research. In R. J. Sternberg & D. K. Detterman (Eds.), *Human intelligence* (pp. 165–175). Norwood, NJ: Ablex. (9)

Deutsch, D., Henthorn, T., Marvin, E., & Xu, H. S. (2006). Absolute pitch among American and Chinese conservatory students: Prevalence differences, and evidence for a speech-related critical period. *Journal of the Acoustical Society of America, 119,* 719–722. (4)

Deutsch, J. A., & Ahn, S. J. (1986). The splanchnic nerve and food intake regulation. *Behavioral and Neural Biology, 45,* 43–47. (11)

Deutsch, J. A., & Gonzalez, M. F. (1980). Gastric nutrient content signals satiety. *Behavioral and Neural Biology, 30,* 113–116. (11)

Devane, W. A., Hanuš, L., Breuer, A., Pertwee, R. G., Stevenson, L. A., Griffin, G., et al. (1992). Isolation and structure of a brain constituent that binds to the cannabinoid receptor. *Science, 258,* 1946–1949. (3)

Devor, E. J., Abell, C. W., Hoffman, P. L., Tabakoff, B., & Cloninger, C. R. (1994). Platelet MAO activity in Type I and Type II alcoholism. *Annals of the New York Academy of Sciences, 708,* 119–128. (16)

Dewhurst, S. A., & Robinson, C. A. (2004). False memories in children. *Psychological Science, 15,* 782–786. (7)

Dewsbury, D. A. (1998). Celebrating E. L. Thorndike a century after *Animal Intelligence. American Psychologist, 53,* 1121–1124. (6)

Dewsbury, D. A. (2000a). Introduction: Snapshots of psychology circa 1900. *American Psychologist, 55,* 255–259. (1)

Dewsbury, D. A. (2000b). Issues in comparative psychology at the dawn of the 20th century. *American Psychologist, 55,* 750–753. (6)

Dhingra, R., Sullivan, L., Jacques, P. F., Wang, T. J., Fox, C. S., Meigs, J. B., et al. (2007). Soft drink consumption and risk of developing cardiometabolic risk factors and the metabolic syndrome in middle-aged adults in the community. *Circulation, 116,* 480–488. (11)

Diamond, A., & Kirkham, N. (2005). Not quite as grown up as we like to think. *Psychological Science, 16,* 291–297. (5)

Diamond, L. M. (2004). Emerging perspectives on distinctions between romantic love and sexual desire. *Current Directions in Psychological Science, 13,* 116–119. (13)

Diamond, L. M. (2007). A dynamical systems approach to the development and expression of female same-sex sexuality. *Perspectives in Psychological Science, 2,* 142–161. (11)

Diamond, L. M. (2008). Female bisexuality from adolescence to adulthood: Results from a 10-year longitudinal study. *Developmental Psychology, 44,* 5–14. (11)

Dick, F., Bates, E., Wulfeck, B., Utman, J. A., Dronkers, N., & Gernsbacher, M. A. (2001). Language deficits, localization, and grammar: Evidence for a distributive model of language breakdown in aphasic patients and neurologically intact individuals. *Psychological Review, 108,* 759–788. (3)

Dickens, W. T., & Flynn, J. R. (2001). Heritability estimates versus large environmental effects: The IQ paradox resolved. *Psychological Review, 108,* 346–369. (5)

Dickens, W. T., & Flynn, J. R. (2006). Black Americans reduce the racial IQ gap. *Psychological Science, 17,* 913–920. (9)

Dickson, N., Paul, C., & Herbison, P. (2003). Same-sex attraction in a birth cohort: Prevalence and persistence in early adulthood. *Social Science and Medicine, 56,* 1607–1615. (11)

Diener, E. (2000). Subjective well-being. *American Psychologist, 55,* 34–43. (12)

Diener, E., Lucas, R. E., & Scollon, C. N. (2006). Beyond the hedonic treadmill. *American Psychologist, 61,* 305–314. (12)

Diener, E., & Seligman, M. E. P. (2002). Very happy people. *Psychological Science, 13,* 81–84. (12)

Diener, E., & Seligman, M. E. P. (2004). Beyond money: Toward an economy of well-being. *Psychological Science in the Public Interest, 5,* 1–31. (12)

Diener, E., Suh, E. M., Lucas, R. E., & Smith, H. L. (1999). Subjective well-being: Three decades of progress. *Psychological Bulletin, 125,* 276–302. (12)

Diener, E., Wolsic, B., & Fujita, F. (1995). Physical attractiveness and subjective well-being. *Journal of Personality and Social Psychology, 69,* 120–129. (12)

Digenio, A. G., Mancuso, J. P., Gerber, R. A., & Dvorak, R. V. (2009). Comparison of methods for delivering a lifestyle modification program for obese patients. *Annals of Internal Medicine, 150*, 255–262. (11)

Dijksterhuis, A., & Bargh, J. A. (2001). The perception-behavior expressway: Automatic effects of social perception on social behavior. *Advances in Experimental Social Psychology, 33*, 1–40. (6)

Dijksterhuis, A., & Nordgren, L. F. (2006). A theory of unconscious thought. *Perspectives on Psychological Science, 1*, 95–109. (8)

DiLalla, D. L., Carey, G., Gottesman, I. I., & Bouchard, T. J., Jr. (1996). Heritability of MMPI personality indicators of psychopathology in twins reared apart. *Journal of Abnormal Psychology, 105*, 491–499. (5)

Dillard, J. P., & Anderson, J. W. (2004). The role of fear in persuasion. *Psychology and Marketing, 21*, 909–926. (13)

DiMarzo, V., Goparaju, S. K., Wang, L., Liu, J., Bátkai, S., Járai, Z., et al. (2001). Leptin-regulated endocannabinoids are involved in maintaining food intake. *Nature, 410*, 822–825. (3)

Dimberg, U., Thunberg, M., & Elmehed, K. (2000). Unconscious facial reactions to emotional facial expressions. *Psychological Science, 11*, 86–89. (4)

Dinstein, I., Hasson, U., Rubin, N., & Heeger, D. J. (2007). Brain areas selective for both observed and executed movements. *Journal of Neurophysiology, 98*, 1415–1427. (3)

Dittmar, H., Halliwell, E., & Ive, S. (2006). Does Barbie make girls want to be thin? The effect of experimental exposure to images of dolls on the body image of 5- to 8-year-old girls. *Developmental Psychology, 42*, 283–292. (11)

Dobelle, W. H. (2000). Artificial vision for the blind by connecting a television camera to the visual cortex. *ASAIO Journal, 46*, 3–9. (4)

Dobrzecka, C., Szwejkowska, G., & Konorski, J. (1966). Qualitative versus directional cues in two forms of differentiation. *Science, 153*, 87–89. (6)

Doi, T. (1981). *The anatomy of dependence.* Tokyo: Kodansha International. (12)

Dole, V. P. (1980). Addictive behavior. *Scientific American, 243*(6), 138–154. (16)

Dollard, J., Miller, N. E., Doob, L. W., Mowrer, O. H., & Sears, R. R. (1939). *Frustration and aggression.* New Haven, CT: Yale University Press. (12)

Domhoff, G. W. (1996). *Finding meaning in dreams: A quantitative approach.* New York: Plenum Press. (10)

Domhoff, G. W. (1999). Drawing theoretical implications from descriptive empirical findings on dream content. *Dreaming, 9*, 201–210. (10)

Domhoff, G. W. (2001). A new neurocognitive theory of dreams. *Dreaming, 11*, 13–33. (10)

Domhoff, G. W. (2003). *The scientific study of dreams.* Washington, DC: American Psychological Association. (2, 10)

Domhoff, G. W., & Schneider, A. (2008). Similarities and differences in dream content at the cross-cultural, gender, and individual levels. *Consciousness and Cognition, 17*, 1257–1265. (10)

Donnellan, M. B., & Lucas, R. E. (2008). Age differences in the big five across the life span: Evidence from two national samples. *Psychology and Aging, 23*, 558–566. (14)

Donnellan, M. B., Trzesniewski, K. H., Robins, R. W., Moffitt, T. E., & Caspi, A. (2005). Low self-esteem is related to aggression, antisocial behavior, and delinquency. *Psychological Science, 16*, 328–335. (12)

Donnerstein, E., & Malamuth, N. (1997). Pornography: Its consequences on the observer. In L. B. Schlesinger & E. Revitch (Eds.), *Sexual*

dynamics of antisocial behavior (2nd ed., pp. 30–49). Springfield, IL: Charles C Thomas. (12)

Dovidio, J. F., & Gaertner, S. L. (1999). Reducing prejudice: Combating intergroup biases. *Current Directions in Psychological Science, 8*, 101–105. (13)

Dovidio, J. F., & Gaertner, S. L. (2000). Aversive racism and selection decisions: 1989 and 1999. *Psychological Science, 11*, 315–319. (13)

Doyle, J. M., & Kao, G. (2007). Are racial identities of multiracials stable? *Social Psychology Quarterly, 70*, 405–423. (5)

Dreber, A., Rand, D. G., Fudenberg, D., & Nowak, M. A. (2008). Winners don't punish. *Nature, 452*, 348–351. (13)

Dreger, A. D. (1998). *Hermaphrodites and the medical invention of sex.* Cambridge, MA: Harvard University Press. (11)

Drell, M., Fuchs, C., Fishel-Ingram, P., Greenberg, G. S., Griffies, S., & Morse, P. (2009). The clinical exchange: The girl who cried every day for 3 years. *Journal of Psychotherapy Integration, 19*, 1–33. (15)

Drewnowski, A., Henderson, S. A., Shore, A. B., & Barratt-Fornell, A. (1998). Sensory responses to 6-n-propylthiouracil (PROP) or sucrose solutions and food preferences in young women. *Annals of the New York Academy of Sciences, 855*, 797–801. (1)

Drews, F. A., Pasupathi, M., & Strayer, D. L. (2008). Passenger and cell phone conversations in simulated driving. *Journal of Experimental Psychology: Applied, 14*, 392–400. (8)

Driver, J., & Mattingley, J. B. (1998). Parietal neglect and visual awareness. *Nature Neuroscience, 1*, 17–22. (10)

Duan, X., Chang, J. H., Ge, S., Faulkner, R. L., Kim, J. Y., Kitabatake, Y., et al. (2007). Disrupted-in-schizophrenia 1 regulated integration of newly generated neurons in the adult brain. *Cell, 130*, 1146–1158. (16)

Dubois, F. (2007). Mate choice copying in monogamous species: Should females use public information to choose extrapair males? *Animal Behaviour, 74*, 1785–1793. (6)

Duckworth, A. L., & Seligman, M. E. P. (2005). Self-discipline outdoes IQ in predicting academic performance of adolescents. *Psychological Science, 16*, 939–944. (9)

Ducommun, C. Y., Michel, C. M., Clarke, S., Adriani, M., Seeck, M., Landis, T., et al. (2004). Cortical motion deafness. *Neuron, 43*, 765–777. (3)

Duke, M., & Nowicki, S., Jr. (1979). *Abnormal psychology: Perspectives on being different.* Monterey, CA: Brooks/Cole. (16)

Dunn, E. W., Aknin, L. B., & Norton, M. I. (2008). Spending money on others promotes happiness. *Science, 319*, 1687–1688. (12)

Dunning, D., Heath, C., & Suls, J. M. (2005). Flawed self-assessment: Implications for health, education, and the workplace. *Psychological Science in the Public Interest, 5*, 69–106. (11)

Durbin, C. E., Hayden, E. P., Klein, D. N., & Olino, T. M. (2007). Stability of laboratory-assessed temperamental emotionality traits from ages 3 to 7. *Emotion, 7*, 388–399. (5)

Durgin, F. H. (2000). The reverse Stroop effect. *Psychonomic Bulletin and Review, 7*, 121–125. (8)

Dywan, J., & Bowers, K. (1983). The use of hypnosis to enhance recall. *Science, 22*, 184–185. (10)

Eagly, A. H., & Crowley, M. (1986). Gender and helping behavior: A meta-analytic review of the social psychological literature. *Psychological Bulletin, 100*, 283–308. (5)

Eagly, A. H., Johannesen-Schmidt, M. C., & van Engen, M. L. (2003). Transformational, transactional, and laissez-faire leadership styles:

A meta-analysis comparing women and men. *Psychological Bulletin, 129*, 569–591. (5)

Eagly, A. H., & Wood, W. (1999). The origins of sex differences in human behavior. *American Psychologist, 54*, 408–423. (13)

Eaker, E. D., Sullivan, L. M., Kelly-Hayes, M., D'Agostino, R. B., Sr., & Benjamin, E. J. (2004). Anger and hostility predict the development of atrial fibrillation in men in the Framingham Offspring Study. *Circulation, 109*, 1267–1271. (12)

Earnest, D. J., Liang, F.-Q., Ratcliff, M., & Cassone, V. M. (1999). Immortal time: Circadian clock properties of rat suprachiasmatic cell lines. *Science, 283*, 693–695. (10)

Eastwick, P. W., Finkel, E. J., Mochon, D., & Ariely, D. (2007). Selective versus unselective romantic desire. *Psychological Science, 18*, 317–319. (13)

Eaton, J. (2001). Management communication: The threat of groupthink. *Corporate Communications, 6*, 183–192. (13)

Eaves, L. J., Martin, N. G., & Heath, A. C. (1990). Religious affiliation in twins and their parents: Testing a model of cultural inheritance. *Behavior Genetics, 20*, 1–22. (5)

Ebbinghaus, H. (1913). *Memory.* New York: Teachers College Press. (Original work published 1885) (7)

Ebling, R., & Levenson, R. W. (2003). Who are the marital experts? *Journal of Marriage and the Family, 65*, 130–142. (13)

Educational Testing Service. (1994). *GRE 1994–95 guide.* Princeton, NJ: Author. (9)

Edwards, J., Jackson, H. J., & Pattison, P. E. (2002). Emotion recognition via facial expression and affective prosody in schizophrenia: A methodological review. *Clinical Psychology Review, 22*, 789–832. (12)

Edwards, K. (1998). The face of time: Temporal cues in facial expressions of emotion. *Psychological Science, 9*, 270–276. (12)

Eibl-Eibesfeldt, I. (1973). *Der vorprogrammierte Mensch* [The preprogrammed human]. Vienna: Verlag Fritz Molden. (12)

Eibl-Eibesfeldt, I. (1974). *Love and hate.* New York: Schocken Books. (12)

Eich, E. (1995). Searching for mood dependent memory. *Psychological Science, 6*, 67–75. (7).

Eich, E., & Macaulay, D. (2000). Are real moods required to reveal mood-congruent and mood-dependent memory? *Psychological Science, 11*, 244–248. (7)

Eichenbaum, H. (2002). *The cognitive neuroscience of memory.* New York: Oxford University Press. (7)

Eigsti, I.-M., Zayas, V., Mischel, W., Shoda, Y., Ayduk, O., Dadlani, M. B., et al. (2006). Predicting cognitive control from preschool to late adolescence and young adulthood. *Psychological Science, 17*, 478–484. (8).

Eimas, P. D., Siqueland, E. R., Jusczyk, P., & Vigorito, J. (1971). Speech perception in infants. *Science, 171*, 303–306. (5)

Eisenberger, N. I., Lieberman, M. D., & Williams, K. D. (2003). Does rejection hurt? An fMRI study of social exclusion. *Science, 302*, 290–292. (4)

Eisenberger, R., & Cameron, J. (1996). Detrimental effects of reward: Reality or myth? *American Psychologist, 51*, 1153–1166. (11)

Eisler, I., Dare, C., Hodes, M., Russell, G., Dodge, E., & LeGrange, D. (2000). Family therapy for adolescent anorexia nervosa: The results of a controlled comparison of two family interventions. *Journal of Child Psychology and Psychiatry and Allied Disciplines, 41*, 727–736. (15)

Ekman, P. (1992). Facial expressions of emotion: New findings, new questions. *Psychological Science, 3*, 34–38. (12)

Ekman, P. (2001). *Telling lies* (3rd ed.). New York: W. W. Norton. (12)

Ekman, P., & Davidson, R. J. (1993). Voluntary smiling changes regional brain activity. *Psychological Science, 4*, 342–345. (12)

Ekman, P., & Friesen, W. V. (1984). *Unmasking the face* (2nd ed.). Palo Alto, CA: Consulting Psychologists Press. (12)

El-Islam, M. F. (1982). Rehabilitation of schizophrenics by the extended family. *Acta Psychiatrica Scandinavica, 65*, 112–119. (16.)

El-Sheikh, M., Buckhalt, J. A., Mize, J., & Acebo, C. (2006). Marital conflict and disruption of children's sleep. *Child Development, 77*, 31–43. (5)

Elbogen, E. B. & Johnson, S. C. (2009). The intricate link between violence and mental disorder. *Archives of General Psychiatry, 66*, 152–161. (15)

Eldridge, L. L., Engel, S. A., Zeineh, M. M., Bookheimer, S. Y., & Knowlton, B. J. (2005). A dissociation of encoding and retrieval processes in the human hippocampus. *Journal of Neuroscience, 25*, 3280–3286. (7)

Elfenbein, H. A., Beaupré, M., Lévesque, M., & Hess, U. (2007). Toward a dialect theory: Cultural differences in the expression and recognition of posed facial expressions. *Emotion, 7*, 131–146. (12)

Elia, J., Ambrosini, P. J., & Rapoport, J. L. (1999). Treatment of attention-deficit hyperactivity disorder. *New England Journal of Medicine, 340*, 780–788. (8)

Elicker, J., Englund, M., & Sroufe, L. A. (1992). Predicting peer competence and peer relationships in childhood from early parent-child relationships. In R. D. Parke & G. W. Ladd (Eds.), *Family-peer relationships* (pp. 77–106). Hillsdale, NJ: Erlbaum. (5)

Elkind, D. (1984). *All grown up and no place to go.* Reading, MA: Addison-Wesley. (5)

Elkins, G., Marcus, J., Bates, J., Rajab, M. H., & Cook, T. (2006). Intensive hypnotherapy for smoking cessation: A prospective study. *International Journal of Clinical and Experimental Hypnosis, 54*, 303–315. (10)

Ellenberger, H. F. (1972). The story of "Anna O": A critical review with new data. *Journal of the History of the Behavioral Sciences, 8*, 267–279. (14)

Elliot, A. J., Maier, M. A., Moller, A. C., Friedman, R., & Meinhardt, J. (2007). Color and psychological functioning: The effect of red on performance attainment. *Journal of Experimental Psychology: General, 136*, 154–168. (1)

Elliott, C. (1997). Caring about risks: Are severely depressed patients competent to consent to research? *Archives of General Psychiatry, 54*, 113–116. (2)

Elliott, R., Sahakian, B. J., Matthews, K., Bannerjea, A., Rimmer, J., & Robbins, T. W. (1997). Effects of methylphenidate on spatial working memory and planning in healthy young adults. *Psychopharmacology, 131*, 196–206. (8)

Ellis, A. (1987). The impossibility of achieving consistently good mental health. *American Psychologist, 42*, 364–375. (15)

Ellis, A., & Harper, R. A. (1961). *A guide to rational living.* Upper Saddle River, NJ: Prentice Hall. (15)

Ellwart, T., Rinck, M., & Becker, E. S. (2006). From fear to love: Individual differences in implicit spider associations. *Emotion, 6*, 18–27. (14)

Else-Quest, N. M., Hyde, J. S., Goldsmith, H. H., & Van Hulle, C. A. (2006). Gender differences in temperament: A meta-analysis. *Psychological Bulletin, 132*, 33–72. (5)

Emery, C. E., Jr. (1997, November/December). UFO survey yields conflicting conclusions. *Skeptical Inquirer, 21*, 9. (2)

Emmons, R. A., & McCullough, M. E. (2003). Counting blessings versus burdens: An experimental investigation of gratitude and subjective well-being in daily life. *Journal of Personality and Social Psychology, 84*, 377–389. (12)

Engle, R. W., Tuholski, S. W., Laughlin, J. E., & Conway, A. R. A. (1999). Working memory, short-term memory, and general fluid intelligence: A latent-variable approach. *Journal of Experimental Psychology: General, 128*, 309–331. (7)

Enns, J. T., & Rensink, R. A. (1990). Sensitivity to three-dimensional orientation in visual search. *Psychological Science, 1*, 323–326. (8)

Erdelyi, M. H. (2006). The unified theory of repression. *Behavioral and Brain Sciences, 29*, 499–551. (14)

Erel, O., & Burman, B. (1995). Interrelatedness of marital relations and parent-child relations: A meta-analytic review. *Psychological Bulletin, 118*, 108–132. (5)

Erev, I., Wallsten, T. S., & Budescu, D. V. (1994). Simultaneous over- and underconfidence: The role of error in judgment processes. *Psychological Review, 101*, 519–527. (8)

Ericsson, K. A., & Charness, N. (1994). Expert performance: Its structure and acquisition. *American Psychologist, 49*, 725–747. (8)

Ericsson, K. A., Chase, W. G., & Faloon, S. (1980). Acquisition of a memory skill. *Science, 208*, 1181–1182. (7)

Ericsson, K. A., Krampe, R. T., & Tesch-Römer, C. (1993). The role of deliberate practice in the acquisition of expert performance. *Psychological Review, 100*, 363–406. (8)

Erikson, E. H. (1963). *Childhood and society* (2nd ed.). New York: W. W. Norton. (5)

Ernhart, C. B., Sokol, R. J., Martier, S., Moron, P., Nadler, D., Ager, J. W., et al. (1987). Alcohol teratogenicity in the human: A detailed assessment of specificity, critical period, and threshold. *American Journal of Obstetrics and Gynecology, 156*, 33–39. (5)

Ernst, C., & Angst, J. (1983). *Birth order: Its influence on personality.* New York: Springer-Verlag. (5)

Eschenko, O., Mölle, M., Born, J., & Sara, S. J. (2006). Elevated sleep spindle density after learning or after retrieval in rats. *Journal of Neurophysiology, 26*, 12914–12920. (10)

Esquivel, G., Schruers, K., Kuipers, H., & Griez, E. (2002). The effects of acute exercise and high lactate levels on 35% CO$_2$ challenge in healthy volunteers. *Acta Psychiatrica Scandinavica, 106*, 394–397. (16)

Esterson, A. (1993). *Seductive mirage.* Chicago: Open Court. (10, 14)

Esterson, A. (2001). The mythologizing of psychoanalytic history: Deception and self-deception in Freud's accounts of the seduction theory episode. *History of Psychology, 12*, 329–352. (14)

Etcoff, N. L., Ekman, P., Magee, J. J., & Frank, M. G. (2000). Lie detection and language comprehension. *Nature, 405*, 139. (3)

Euston, D. R., Tatsuno, M., & McNaughton, B. L. (2007). Fast-forward playback of recent memory sequences in prefrontal cortex during sleep. *Science, 318*, 1147–1150. (10)

Evans, G. W., Bullinger, M., & Hygge, S. (1998). Chronic noise exposure and physiological response: A prospective study of children living under environmental stress. *Psychological Science, 9*, 75–77. (12)

Evans, G. W., & Schamberg, M. A. (2009). Childhood poverty, chronic stress, and adult working memory. *Proceedings of the National Academy of Sciences, USA, 106*, 6545–6549. (9)

Exner, J. E., Jr. (1986). *The Rorschach: A comprehensive system* (2nd ed.). New York: Wiley. (14)

Eysenck, H. J. (1952). The effects of psychotherapy: An evaluation. *Journal of Consulting Psychology, 16*, 319–324. (15)

Eysenck, H. J. (1992). Four ways five factors are not basic. *Personality and Individual Differences, 13*, 667–673. (14)

Fabiano, G. A., Pelham, W. E., Jr., Gnag, E. M., Burrows-MacLean, L., Coles, E. K., Chaco, A., et al. (2007). The single and combined effects of multiple intensities of behavior modification and methylphenidate for children with attention deficit hyperactivity disorder in a classroom setting. *School Psychology Review, 36*, 195–216. (6)

Faedda, G. L., Tondo, L., Teicher, M. H., Baldessarini, R. J., Gelbard, H. A., & Floris, G. F. (1993). Seasonal mood disorders: Patterns of seasonal recurrence in mania and depression. *Archives of General Psychiatry, 50*, 17–23. (16)

Fagan, J. F., & Holland, C. R. (2007). Racial equality in intelligence: Predictions from a theory of intelligence as processing. *Intelligence, 35*, 319–334. (9)

Fagan, J. F., & Holland, C. R. (2009). Culture-fair prediction of academic achievement. *Intelligence, 37*, 62–67. (9)

Fagen, Z. M., Mitchum, R., Vezina, P., & McGehee, D. S. (2007). Enhanced nicotinic receptor function and drug abuse vulnerability. *Journal of Neuroscience, 27*, 8771–8778. (3)

Faivre, R., Grégoire, A., Préault, M., Cézilly, F., & Sorci, G. (2003). Immune activation rapidly mirrored in a secondary sexual trait. *Science, 300*, 103. (13)

Falleti, M. G., Maruff, P., Collie, A., Darby, D. G., & McStephen, M. (2003). Qualitative similarities in cognitive impairment associated with 24 h of sustained wakefulness and a blood alcohol concentration of 0.05%. *Journal of Sleep Research, 12*, 265–274. (10)

Fallon, A. E., & Rozin, P. (1985). Sex differences in perceptions of desirable body shape. *Journal of Abnormal Psychology, 94*, 102–105. (11)

Fan, P. (1995). Cannabinoid agonists inhibit the activation of 5-HT3 receptors in rat nodose ganglion neurons. *Journal of Neurophysiology, 73*, 907–910. (3)

Fanous, A. H., van den Oord, E. J., Riley, S. H., Aggen, S. H., Neale, M. C., O'Neill, F. A., et al. (2005). Relationship between a high-risk haplotype in the *DTNBP1* (dysbindin) gene and clinical features of schizophrenia. *American Journal of Psychiatry, 162*, 1824–1832. (16)

Fantz, R. L. (1963). Pattern vision in newborn infants. *Science, 140*, 296–297. (5)

Farah, M. J. (1992). Is an object an object an object? Cognitive and neuropsychological investigations of domain specificity in visual object recognition. *Current Directions in Psychological Science, 1*, 164–169. (4)

Farber, S. L. (1981). *Identical twins reared apart: A reanalysis.* New York: Basic Books. (9)

Farmer-Dougan, V. (1998). A disequilibrium analysis of incidental teaching. *Behavior Modification, 22*, 78–95. (6)

Farnè, A., Buxbaum. L. J., Ferraro, M., Frassinetti, F., Whyte, J., Veramonti, T., et al. (2006). Patterns of spontaneous recovery of neglect and associated disorders in acute right brain-damaged patients. *Journal of Neurology, Neurosurgery, and Psychiatry, 75*, 1401–1410. (10)

Farooqi, I. S., Keogh, J. M., Kamath, S., Jones, S., Gibson, W. T., Trussell, R., et al. (2001). Partial leptin deficiency and human adiposity. *Nature, 414*, 34–35. (11)

Farris, C., Treat, T. A., Viken, R. J., & McFall, R. M. (2008). Perceptual mechanisms that characterize gender differences in decoding women's sexual intent. *Psychological Science, 19*, 348–354. (5)

Fatemi, S. H., & Folsom, T. D. (2009). The neurodevelopmental hypothesis of schizophrenia revisited. *Schizophrenia Bulletin, 35*, 528–548. (16)

Fauerbach, J. A., Lawrence, J. W., Haythornthwaite, J. A., & Richter, L. (2002). Coping with the stress of a painful medical procedure. *Behaviour Research and Therapy, 40*, 1003–1015. (12)

Faust, M., Kravetz, S., & Babkoff, H. (1993). Hemispheric specialization or reading habits: Evidence from lexical decision research with Hebrew words and sentences. *Brain and Language, 44*, 254–263. (8)

Fawcett, J. (2001). Treating impulsivity and anxiety in the suicidal patient. *Annals of the New York Academy of Sciences, 932*, 94–102. (16)

Fay, R. E., Turner, C. F., Klassen, A. D., & Gagnon, J. H. (1989). Prevalence and patterns of same-gender sexual contact among men. *Science, 243*, 338–348. (11)

Fazel, S., & Grann, M. (2006). The population impact of severe mental illness on violent crime. *American Journal of Psychiatry, 163*, 1397–1403. (15)

Feeney, D. M. (1987). Human rights and animal welfare. *American Psychologist, 42*, 593–599. (2)

Fehr, E., & Fischbacher, U. (2003). The nature of human altruism. *Nature, 425*, 785–791. (13)

Fehr, E., & Gächter, S. (2002). Altruistic punishment in humans. *Nature, 415*, 137–140. (13)

Feighner, J. P., Gardner, E. A., Johnston, J. A., Batey, S. R., Khayrallah, M. A., Ascher, J. A., et al. (1991). Double-blind comparison of buproprion and fluoxetine in depressed outpatients. *Journal of Clinical Psychiatry, 52*, 329–335. (16)

Felitti, V. J., Anda, R. F., Nordenberg, D., Williamson, D. F., Spitz, A. M., Edwards, V., et al. (1998). Relationship of childhood abuse and household dysfunction to many of the leading causes of death in adults. *American Journal of Preventive Medicine, 14*, 245–258. (12)

Feng, J., Spence, I., & Pratt, J. (2007). Playing an action video game reduces gender differences in spatial cognition. *Psychological Science, 18*, 850–855. (5)

Fenton, W. S., Hoch, J. S., Herrell, J. M., Mosher, L., & Dixon, L. (2002). Cost and cost-effectiveness of hospital vs. residential crisis care for patients who have serious mental illness. *Archives of General Psychiatry, 59*, 357–364. (15)

Fenton, W. S., Mosher, L. R., Herrell, J. M., & Blyler, C. R. (1998). Randomized trial of general hospital and residential alternative care for patients with severe and persistent mental illness. *American Journal of Psychiatry, 155*, 516–522. (15)

Ferguson, C. P., & Pigott, T. A. (2000). Anorexia and bulimia nervosa: Neurobiology and pharmacotherapy. *Behavior Therapy, 31*, 237–263. (11)

Fernald, D. (1984). *The Hans legacy: A story of science*. Hillsdale, NJ: Erlbaum. (2)

Fernandez, E., & Turk, D. C. (1992). Sensory and affective components of pain: Separation and synthesis. *Psychological Bulletin, 112*, 205–217. (4)

Fernández-Dols, J. M., & Ruiz-Belda, M. A. (1997). Spontaneous facial behavior during intense emotional episodes: Artistic truth and optical truth. In J. A. Russell & J. M. Fernández-Dols (Eds.), *The psychology of facial expression* (pp. 255–274). Cambridge, England: Cambridge University Press. (12)

Ferreira, F., Bailey, K. G. D., & Ferraro, V. (2002). Good-enough representations in language comprehension. *Current Directions in Psychological Science, 11*, 11–15. (8)

Festinger, L. (1957). *A theory of cognitive dissonance*. Stanford, CA: Stanford University Press. (13)

Festinger, L., & Carlsmith, J. M. (1959). Cognitive consequences of forced compliance. *Journal of Abnormal and Social Psychology, 58*, 203–210. (13)

Fiedler, K., Schmid, J., & Stahl, T. (2002). What is the current truth about polygraph lie detection? *Basic and Applied Social Psychology, 24*, 313–324. (12)

Field, A. P. (2006). Is conditioning a useful framework for understanding the development and treatment of phobias? *Clinical Psychology Review, 26*, 857–875. (16)

Fieve, R. R. (1975). *Moodswing*. New York: Morrow. (16)

Finch, J. F., & Cialdini, R. B. (1989). Another indirect tactic of (self-) image imagement: Boosting. *Personality and Social Psychology Bulletin, 15*, 222–232. (13)

Fincham, F. D. (2003). Marital conflict: Correlates, structure, and context. *Current Directions in Psychological Science, 12*, 23–27. (13)

Fink, B., & Penton-Voak, I. (2002). Evolutionary psychology of facial attractiveness. *Current Directions in Psychological Science, 11*, 154–158. (13)

Finkel, E. J., & Eastwick, P. W. (2008). Speed-dating. *Current Directions in Psychological Science, 17*, 193–197. (13)

Fisher, B. S., Daigle, L. E., Cullen, F. T., & Turner, M. G. (2003). Acknowledging sexual victimization as rape: Results from a national-level survey. *Justice Quarterly, 20*, 535–574. (12)

Fisher, S., & Greenberg, R. P. (1977). *The scientific credibility of Freud's theories and therapy*. New York: Basic Books. (14)

Fisher, S. E., Vargha-Khadem, F., Watkins, K. E., Monaco, A. P., & Pembrey, M. E. (1998). Localisation of a gene implicated in a severe speech and language disorder. *Nature Genetics, 18*, 168–170. (8)

Fiske, A. P. (2002). Using individualism and collectivism to compare cultures—A critique of the validity and measurement of the constructs: Comment on Oyserman et al. (2002). *Psychological Bulletin, 128*, 78–88. (13)

Fiske, S. T., Harris, L. T., & Cuddy, A. J. C. (2004). Why ordinary people torture enemy prisoners. *Science, 306*, 1482–1483. (13)

Flack, W. F., Jr., Laird, J. D., & Cavallaro, L. A. (1999). Separate and combined effects of facial expressions and bodily postures on emotional feelings. *European Journal of Social Psychology, 29*, 203–217. (12)

Flatz, G. (1987). Genetics of lactose digestion in humans. *Advances in Human Genetics, 16*, 1–77. (5)

Flavell, J. (1986). The development of children's knowledge about the appearance–reality distinction. *American Psychologist, 41*, 418–425. (5)

Fleeson, W., Malanos, A. B., & Achille, N. M. (2002). An intraindividual process approach to the relationship between extraversion and positive affect: Is acting extraverted as "good" as being extraverted? *Journal of Personality and Social Psychology, 83*, 1409–1422. (14)

Fletcher, R., & Voke, J. (1985). *Defective colour vision*. Bristol, England: Hilger. (4)

Fliessbach, K., Weber, B., Trautner, P., Dohmen, T., Sunde, U., Elger, C. E., et al. (2007). Social comparison affects reward-related brain activity in the human ventral striatum. *Science, 318*, 1305–1308. (12)

Fligstein, D., Barabasz, A., Barabasz, M., Trevisan, M. S., & Warner, D. (1998). Hypnosis enhances recall memory: A test of forced and non-forced conditions. *American Journal of Clinical Hypnosis, 40*, 297–305. (10)

Flor, H., Elbert, T., Knecht, S., Wienbruch, C., Pantev, C., Birbaumer, N., et al. (1995). Phantom-limb pain as a perceptual correlate of cortical reorganization following arm amputation. *Nature, 375*, 482–484. (4)

Flynn, J. R. (1984). The mean IQ of Americans: Massive gains 1932 to 1978. *Psychological Bulletin, 95*, 29–51. (9)

Flynn, J. R. (1998). IQ gains over time: Toward finding the causes. In U. Neisser (Ed.), *The rising curve* (pp. 25–66). Washington, DC: American Psychological Association. (9)

Flynn, J. R. (1999). Searching for justice: The discovery of IQ gains over time. *American Psychologist, 54*, 5–20. (9)

Fodor, J. (1998). When is a dog a DOG? *Nature, 396*, 325–327. (8)

Fogel, S. M., Nader, R., Cote, K. A., & Smith, C. T. (2007). Sleep spindles and learning potential. *Behavioral Neuroscience, 121*, 1–10. (10)

Folkman, S., & Moskowitz, J. T. (2000). Positive affect and the other side of coping. *American Psychologist, 55*, 647–654. (12)

Føllesdal, H., & Hagtvet, K. A. (2009). Emotional intelligence: The MSCEIT from the perspective of generalizability theory. *Intelligence, 37*, 94–105. (12)

Forer, B. R. (1949). The fallacy of personal validation: A classroom demonstration of gullibility. *Journal of Abnormal and Social Psychology, 44*, 118–123. (14)

Foster, D. (2000). *Author unknown*. New York: Henry Holt. (14)

Foster, W. Z. (1968). *History of the Communist Party of the United States*. New York: Greenwood Press. (13)

Fotopoulou, A., Solms, S., & Turnbull, O. (2004). Wishful reality distortions in confabulation: A case report. *Neuropsychologia, 47*, 727–744. (7)

Foulkes, D. (1999). *Children's dreaming and the development of consciousness*. Cambridge, MA: Harvard University Press. (10)

Fowler, J. H., Baker, L. A., & Dawes, C. T. (2008). Genetic variation in political participation. *American Political Science Review, 102*, 233–248. (5)

Fowler, J. H., & Christakis, N. A. (2008). Dynamic spread of happiness in a large social network: Longitudinal analysis over 20 years in the Framingham Heart Study. *British Medical Journal, 337*, a2338. (12)

Fox, E., Griggs, L., & Mouchlianitis, E. (2007). The detection of fear-relevant stimuli: Are guns noticed as quickly as snakes? *Emotion, 7*, 691–696. (16)

Fox, N., A., Nichols, K. E., Henderson, H. A., Rubin, K., Schmidt, L., Hamer, D., et al. (2005). Evidence for a gene–environment interaction in predicting behavioral inhibition in middle childhood. *Psychological Science, 16*, 921–926. (5)

Francis, L. J., Brown, L. B., Lester, D., & Philipchalk, R. (1998). Happiness as stable extraversion: A cross-cultural examination of the reliability and validity of the Oxford Happiness Inventory among students in the U.K., U.S.A., Australia, and Canada. *Personality and Individual Differences, 24*, 167–171. (14)

Frank, M. J., & Claus, E. D. (2006). Anatomy of a decision: Striato-orbitofrontal interactions in reinforcement learning, decision making, and reversal. *Psychological Review, 113*, 300–326. (3)

Fredrickson, B. L. (2001). The role of positive emotion in psychology: The broaden-and-build theory of positive emotions. *American Psychologist, 56*, 218–226. (12)

Fredrickson, B. L., & Losada, M. F. (2005). Positive affect and the complex dynamics of human flourishing. *American Psychologist, 60*, 678–686. (12)

Freedman, J. L., & Fraser, S. C. (1966). Compliance without pressure: The foot in the door technique. *Journal of Personality and Social Psychology, 4*, 195–202. (13)

French, A. R. (1988). The patterns of mammalian hibernation. *American Scientist, 76*, 568–575. (10)

French, S. E., Seidman, E., Allen, L., & Aber, J. L. (2006). The development of ethnic identity during adolescence. *Developmental Psychology, 42*, 1–10. (5)

Frensch, P. A., & Rünger, D. (2003). Implicit learning. *Current Directions in Psychological Science, 12*, 13–18. (7)

Freud, S. (1925). An autobiographical study. In J. Strachey, A. Freud, A. Strachey, & A. Tyson (Eds.), *The standard edition of the complete psychological works of Sigmund Freud* (Vol. 20, pp. 7–70). London: Hogarth Press and the Institute of Psycho-Analysis. (14)

Freud, S. (1925). *Three contributions to the theory of sex* (A. A. Brill, Trans.). New York: Nervous and Mental Disease Publishing. (Original work published 1905) (14)

Freud, S. (1935). *A general introduction to psychoanalysis* (Rev. ed.). New York: Liveright. (10)

Freud, S. (1955). *The interpretation of dreams* (J. Strachey, Trans.). New York: Basic Books. (Original work published 1900) (10)

Freud, S. (1961). *The future of an illusion* (J. Strachey, Trans.). New York: W. W. Norton. (Original work published 1927) (14)

Frey, S. H., Bogdanov, S. Smith, J. C., Watrous, S., & Breidenbach, W. C. (2008). Chronically deafferented sensory cortex recovers a grossly typical organization after allogenic hand transplantation. *Current Biology, 18*, 1530–1534. (3)

Fried, I., Katz, A., McCarthy, G., Sass, K. J., Williamson, P., Spencer, S. S., et al. (1991). Functional organization of human supplementary motor cortex studied by electrical stimulation. *Journal of Neuroscience, 11*, 3656–3666. (10)

Friedman, J. M. (2000). Obesity in the new millennium. *Nature, 404*, 632–634. (11)

Friedman, M., & Rosenman, R. H. (1974). *Type-A behavior and your heart.* New York: Knopf. (12)

Friedman, M. A., & Brownell, K. D. (1996). A comprehensive treatment manual for the management of obesity. In V. B. Van Hasselt & M. Hersen (Eds.), *Sourcebook of psychological treatment manuals for adult disorders* (pp. 375–422). New York: Plenum Press. (11)

Frijda, N. H. (1988). The laws of emotion. *American Psychologist, 45*, 349–358. (12)

Fritz, C. O., Morris, P. E., Bjork, R. A., Gelman, R., & Wickens, T. D. (2000). When further learning fails: Stability and change following repeated presentation of text. *British Journal of Psychology, 91*, 493–511. (7)

Fritzsche, B. A., Young, B. R., & Hickson, K. C. (2003). Individual differences in academic procrastination tendency and writing success. *Personality and Individual Differences, 35*, 1549–1557. (11)

Fu, Q., Heath, A. C., Bucholz, K. K., Nelson, E., Goldberg, J., Lyons, M. J., et al. (2002). Shared genetic risk of major depression, alcohol dependence, and marijuana dependence. *Archives of General Psychiatry, 59*, 1125–1132. (16)

Fuchs, T., Haney, A., Jechura, T. J., Moore, F. R., & Bingman, V. P. (2006). Daytime naps in night-migrating birds: Behavioural adaptation to seasonal sleep deprivation in the Swainson's thrush, *Catharus ustulatus. Animal Behaviour, 72*, 951–958. (10)

Fuligni, A. J. (1998). The adjustment of children from immigrant families. *Current Directions in Psychological Science, 7*, 99–103. (5)

Fuller, R. K., & Roth, H. P. (1979). Disulfiram for the treatment of alcoholism: An evaluation in 128 men. *Annals of Internal Medicine, 90*, 901–904. (16)

Fullerton, J., Cubin, M., Tiwari, H., Wang, C., Bomhra, A., Davidson, S., et al. (2003). Linkage analysis of extremely discordant and concordant sibling pairs identifies quantitative-trait loci that influence variation in the human personality trait neuroticism. *American Journal of Human Genetics, 72*, 879–890. (14)

Furman, L. M. (2008). Attention-deficit hyperactivity disorder (ADHD): Does new research support old concepts? *Journal of Child Neurology, 23*, 775–784. (8)

Furnham, A. (2003). Belief in a just world: Research progress over the last decade. *Personality and Individual Differences, 34*, 795–817. (14)

Furnham, A., Hosoe, T., & Tang, T. L.-P. (2002). Male hubris and female humility? A crosscultural study of ratings of self, parental, and sibling multiple intelligence in America, Britain, and Japan. *Intelligence, 30*, 101–115. (14)

Furukawa, T. (1997). Cultural distance and its relationship to psychological adjustment of international exchange students. *Psychiatry and Clinical Neurosciences, 51*, 87–91. (1)

Gable, P. A., & Harmon-Jones, E. (2008). Approach-motivated positive affect reduces breadth of attention. *Psychological Science, 19*, 476–482. (12)

Gabrieli, J. D. E., Cohen, N. J., & Corkin, S. (1988). The impaired learning of semantic knowledge following bilateral medial temporal-lobe resection. *Brain and Cognition, 7*, 157–177. (7)

Gage, F. H. (2000). Mammalian neural stem cells. *Science, 287*, 1433–1438. (3)

Gailliot, M. T., Stillman, T. F., Schmeichel, B. J., Maner, J. K., & Plant, E. A. (2008). Mortality salience increases adherence to salient norms and values. *Personality and Social Psychology Bulletin, 34*, 993–1003. (5)

Galdi, S., Arcuri, L., & Gawronski, B. (2008). Automatic mental associations predict future choices of undecided decision-makers. *Science, 321*, 1100–1102. (8)

Galef, B. G., Jr. (1998). Edward Thorndike: Revolutionary psychologist, ambiguous biologist. *American Psychologist, 53*, 1128–1134. (6)

Gallistel, C. R., & Gibbon, J. (2000). Time, rate, and conditioning. *Psychological Review, 107*, 289–344. (6)

Gallo, L. C., & Matthews, K. A. (2003). Understanding the association between socioeconomic status and physical health: Do negative emotions play a role? *Psychological Bulletin, 129*, 10–51. (12)

Galton, F. (1978). *Hereditary genius.* New York: St. Martin's Press. (Original work published 1869) (1, 9)

Gangestad, S. W. (2000). Human sexual selection, good genes, and special design. *Annals of the New York Academy of Sciences, 907*, 50–61. (13)

Gannon, N., & Ranzijn, R. (2005). Does emotional intelligence predict unique variance in life satisfaction beyond IQ and personality? *Personality and Individual Differences, 38*, 1353–1364. (12)

Ganzel, B., Casey, B. J., Glover, G., Voss, H. V., & Temple, E. (2007). The aftermath of 9/11: Effects of intensity and recency of trauma on outcome. *Emotion, 7*, 227–238. (16)

Garb, H. N., Wood, J. N., Lilienfeld, S. O., & Nezworski, M. T. (2005). Roots of the Rorschach controversy. *Clinical Psychology Review, 25*, 97–118. (14)

Garcia, J. (1990). Learning without memory. *Journal of Cognitive Neuroscience, 2*, 287–305. (6)

Garcia, J., Ervin, F. R., & Koelling, R. A. (1966). Learning with prolonged delay of reinforcement. *Psychonomic Science, 5*, 121–122. (6)

Garcia, J., & Koelling, R. A. (1966). Relation of cue to consequence in avoidance learning. *Psychonomic Science, 4*, 123–124. (6)

Garcia Coll, C. T. (1990). Developmental outcome of minority infants: A process-oriented look into our beginnings. *Child Development, 61*, 270–289. (5)

Gardner, H. (1985). *Frames of mind.* New York: Basic Books. (9)

Gardner, H. (1999). *Intelligence reframed.* New York: Basic Books. (9)

Gardner, M. (1978). Mathematical games. *Scientific American, 239*(5), 22–32. (8)

Gardner, M. (1994). Notes of a fringe watcher: The tragedies of false memories. *Skeptical Inquirer, 18*, 464–470. (7)

Gardner, M., & Steinberg, L. (2005). Peer influence on risk taking, risk preference, and risky decision making in adolescence and adulthood: An experimental study. *Developmental Psychology, 41*, 625–635. (5)

Gardner, R. A., & Gardner, B. T. (1969). Teaching sign language to a chimpanzee. *Science, 165*, 664–672. (8)

Gaser, C., & Schlaug, G. (2003). Brain structures differ between musicians and non-musicians. *Journal of Neuroscience, 23*, 9240–9245. (8)

Geary, D. C. (2000). Evolution and proximate expression of human paternal investment. *Psychological Bulletin, 126*, 55–77. (13)

Geier, A. B., Rozin, P., & Doros, G. (2006). Unit bias. *Psychological Science, 17*, 521–525. (11)

Gelman, R. (1982). Accessing one-to-one correspondence: Still another paper about conservation. *British Journal of Psychology, 73*, 209–220. (5)

Genoux, D., Haditsch, U., Knobloch, M., Michalon, A., Storm, D., & Mansuy, I. M. (2002). Protein phosphatase 1 is a molecular constraint on learning and memory. *Nature, 418*, 970–975. (7)

Gentile, B., Grabe, S., Dolan-Pascoe, B., Twenge, J. M., & Wells, B. E. (2009). Gender differences in domain-specific self-esteem: A meta-analysis. *Review of General Psychology, 13*, 34–45. (14)

Geraerts, E., Bernstein, D. M., Merckelbach, H., Linders, C., Raymaekers, L., & Loftus, E. F. (2008). Lasting false beliefs and their behavioral consequences. *Psychological Science, 19*, 749–753. (7)

Geraerts, E., Schooler, J. W., Merckelbach, H., Jelicic, M., Hauer, B. J. A., & Ambadar, Z. (2007). The reality of recovered memories. *Psychological Science, 18*, 564–568. (7)

German, T. P., & Barrett, H. C. (2005). Functional fixedness in a technologically sparse culture. *Psychological Science, 16*, 1–5. (8)

Gershoff, E. T. (2002). Corporal punishment by parents and associated child behaviors and experiences: A meta-analytic and theoretical review. *Psychological Bulletin, 128*, 539–579. (6)

Geschwind, N. (1979). Specializations of the human brain. In *Scientific American* (Ed.), *The brain: A Scientific American book.* San Francisco: W. H. Freeman. (8)

Gibbs, J., Young, R. C., & Smith, G. P. (1973). Cholecystokinin decreases food intake in rats. *Journal of Comparative and Physiological Psychology, 84*, 488–495. (11)

Gibson, J. J. (1968). What gives rise to the perception of movement? *Psychological Review, 75*, 335–346. (4)

Giebel, H. D. (1958). Visuelles Lernvermögen bei Einhufern [Visual learning capacity in hoofed animals]. *Zoologische Jahrbücher Abteilung für Allgemeine Zoologie, 67*, 487–520. (1)

Gigerenzer, G. (2004). Dread risk, September 11, and fatal traffic accidents. *Psychological Science, 15*, 286–287. (8)

Gigerenzer, G. (2008). Why heuristics work. *Perspectives on Psychological Science, 3*, 20–29. (8)

Gigi, A., Babai, R., Katzav, E., Atkins, S., & Hendler, T. (2007). Prefrontal and parietal regions are involved in naming of objects seen from unusual viewpoints. *Behavioral Neuroscience, 121,* 836–844. (3)

Gil-da-Costa, R., Martin, A., Lopes, M. A., Muñoz, M., Fritz, J. B., & Braun, A. R. (2006). Species-specific calls activate homologs of Broca's and Wernicke's areas in the macaque. *Nature Neuroscience, 9,* 1064–1070. (8)

Gilbertson, M. W., Shenton, M. E., Ciszewski, A., Kasai, K., Lasko, N. B., Orr, S. P., et al. (2002). Smaller hippocampal volume predicts pathological vulnerability to psychological trauma. *Nature Neuroscience, 5,* 1242–1247. (12)

Gilbreth, F. B. (1911). *Motion study.* London: Constable. (11)

Gillath, O., Shaver, P. R., Baek, J. M., & Chun, D. S. (2008). Genetic correlates of adult attachment style. *Personality and Social Psychology Bulletin, 34,* 1396–1405. (5)

Gilligan, C. (1977). In a different voice: Women's conceptions of self and morality. *Harvard Educational Review, 47,* 481–517. (13)

Gilligan, C. (1979). Woman's place in man's life cycle. *Harvard Educational Review, 49,* 431–446. (13)

Gino, F., Ayal, S., & Ariely, D. (2009). Contagion and differentiation in unethical behavior. *Psychological Science, 20,* 393–398. (13)

Giros, B., Jaber, M., Jones, S. R., Wightman, R. M., & Caron, M. G. (1996). Hyperlocomotion and indifference to cocaine and amphetamine in mice lacking the dopamine transporter. *Nature, 379,* 606–612. (3)

Glantz, L. A., & Lewis, D. A. (1997). Reduction of synaptophysin immunoreactivity in the prefrontal cortex of subjects with schizophrenia. *Archives of General Psychiatry, 54,* 660–669. (16)

Glantz, L. A., & Lewis, D. A. (2000). Decreased dendritic spine density on prefrontal cortical pyramidal neurons in schizophrenia. *Archives of General Psychiatry, 57,* 65–73. (16)

Glasman, L. R., & Albarracín, D. (2006). Forming attitudes that predict future behavior: A meta-analysis of the attitude–behavior relation. *Psychological Bulletin, 132,* 778–822. (13)

Glass, D. C., Singer, J. E., & Pennebaker, J. W. (1977). Behavioral and physiological effects of uncontrollable environmental events. In D. Stokols (Ed.), *Perspectives on environment and behavior* (pp. 131–151). New York: Plenum Press. (12)

Glass, M. (2001). The role of cannabinoids in neurodegenerative diseases. *Progress in Neuro-Psychopharmacology and Biological Psychiatry, 25,* 743–765. (3)

Glick, P., & Fiske, S. T. (2001). Ambivalent sexism. *Advances in Experimental Social Psychology, 33,* 115–188. (13)

Goldberg, W. A., Prause, J., Lucas-Thompson, R., & Himsel, A. (2008). Maternal employment and children's achievement in context: A meta-analysis of four decades of research. *Psychological Bulletin, 134,* 77–108. (5)

Goldfried, M. R., & Wolfe, B. E. (1996). Psychotherapy practice and research: Repairing a strained alliance. *American Psychologist, 51,* 1007–1016. (15)

Goldin-Meadow, S., McNeill, D., & Singleton, J. (1996). Silence is liberating: Removing the handcuffs on grammatical expression in the manual modality. *Psychological Review, 103,* 34–55. (8)

Goldin-Meadow, S., & Mylander, C. (1998). Spontaneous sign systems created by deaf children in two cultures. *Nature, 391,* 279–281. (8)

Goldstein, A. (1980). Thrills in response to music and other stimuli. *Physiological Psychology, 8,* 126–129. (3, 4)

Goldstein, D. G., & Gigerenzer, G. (2002). Models of ecological rationality: The recognition heuristic. *Psychological Review, 109,* 75–90. (8)

Goldstein, E. B. (1989). *Sensation and perception* (3rd ed.). Belmont, CA: Wadsworth. (4)

Goldstein, E. B. (2007). *Sensation and perception* (7th ed.). Belmont, CA: Wadsworth. (4)

Goldstein, M. H., & Schwade, J. A. (2008). Social feedback to infants' babbling facilitates rapid phonological learning. *Psychological Science, 19,* 515–523. (8)

Goldstein, N. J., Cialdini, R. B., & Griskevicius, V. (2008). A room with a viewpoint: Using social norms to motivate environmental conservation in hotels. *Journal of Consumer Research, 35,* 472–482. (13)

Golombok, S., Perry, B., Burston, A., Murray, C., Mooney-Somers, J., Stevens, M., et al. (2003). Children with lesbian parents: A community study. *Developmental Psychology, 39,* 20–33. (5)

Golombok, S., Rust, J., Zervoulis, K., Croudace, T., Golding, J., & Hines, M. (2008). Developmental trajectories of sex-typed behavior in boys and girls: A longitudinal general population study of children aged 2.5–8 years. *Child Development, 79,* 1583–1593. (14)

Gomez, P., Zimmermann, P., Guttormsen-Schär, S., & Danuser, B. (2005). Respiratory responses associated with affective processing of film stimuli. *Biological Psychology, 68,* 223–235. (12)

Gómez-Pinilla, F. (2008). Brain foods: The effects of nutrients on brain function. *Nature Reviews Neuroscience, 9,* 568–578. (2)

Gong, L. (2007). Ethnic identity and identification with the majority group: Relations with national identity and self-esteem. *International Journal of Intercultural Relations, 31,* 503–523. (5)

Gonzaga, G. C., Turner, R. A., Keltner, D., Campos, B., & Altemus, M. (2006). Romantic love and sexual desire in close relationships. *Emotion, 6,* 163–179. (13)

Goodall, J. (1971). *In the shadow of man.* Boston: Houghton Mifflin. (2)

Goodman, G. S., Ghetti, S., Quas, J. A., Edelstein, R. S., Alexander, K. W., Redlich, A. D., et al. (2003). A prospective study of memory for child sexual abuse: New findings relevant to the repressed-memory controversy. *Psychological Science, 14,* 113–118. (7)

Gorchoff, S. M., John, O. P., & Helson, R. (2008). Contextualizing change in marital satisfaction during middle age. *Psychological Science, 19,* 1194–1200. (13)

Gordon, P. C., Hendrick, R., & Levine, W. H. (2002). Memory-load interference in syntactic processing. *Psychological Science, 13,* 425–430. (8)

Gossop, M., Stewart, D., & Marsden, J. (2008). Attendance at Narcotics Anonymous and Alcoholics Anonymous meetings, frequency of attendance and substance use outcomes after residential treatment for drug dependence: A 5-year follow-up study. *Addiction, 103,* 119–125. (16)

Gothe, J., Brandt, S. A., Irlbacher, K., Röricht, S., Sabel, B. A., & Meyer, B.-U. (2002). Changes in visual cortex excitability in blind subjects as demonstrated by transcranial magnetic stimulation. *Brain, 125,* 479–490. (3)

Gottesman, I. I. (1991). *Schizophrenia genesis.* New York: W. H. Freeman. (16)

Gottfredson, L. S. (2002a). *g: Highly general and highly practical.* In R. J. Sternberg & E. L. Grigorenko (Eds.), *The general intelligence factor: How general is it?* (pp. 331–380). Mahwah, NJ: Erlbaum. (9)

Gottfredson, L. S. (2002b). Where and why g matters: Not a mystery. *Human Performance, 15,* 25–46. (9)

Gottfredson, L. S. (2003). Dissecting practical intelligence theory: Its claims and evidence. *Intelligence, 31,* 343–397. (9)

Gottfredson, L. S. (2004). Intelligence: Is it the epidemiologists' elusive "fundamental cause" of social class inequalities in health? *Journal of Personality and Social Psychology, 86,* 174–199. (9)

Gottman, J. M., Coan, J., Carrere, S., & Swanson, C. (1998). Predicting marital happiness and stability from newlywed interactions. *Journal of Marriage and the Family, 60,* 5–22. (13)

Gottman, J. M., & Levenson, R. W. (2000). The timing of divorce: Predicting when a couple will divorce over a 14-year period. *Journal of Marriage and the Family, 62,* 737–745. (13)

Grabe, S., & Hyde, J. S. (2006). Ethnicity and body dissatisfaction among women in the United States: A meta-analysis. *Psychological Bulletin, 132,* 622–640. (11)

Graf, P., & Mandler, G. (1984). Activation makes words more accessible, but not necessarily more retrievable. *Journal of Verbal Learning and Verbal Behavior, 23,* 553–568. (7)

Gratacòs, M., Nadalm, M., Martín-Santos, R., Pujana, M. A., Gago, J., Peral, B., et al. (2001). A polymorphic genomic duplication on human chromosome 15 is a susceptibility factor for panic and phobic disorders. *Cell, 106,* 367–379. (16)

Graziadei, P. P. C., & deHan, R. S. (1973). Neuronal regeneration in the frog olfactory system. *Journal of Cell Biology, 59,* 525–530. (3)

Green, D. M., & Swets, J. A. (1966). *Signal detection theory and psychophysics.* New York: Wiley. (4)

Green, J. P., & Lynn, S. J. (2005). Hypnosis versus relaxation: Accuracy and confidence in dating international news events. *Applied Cognitive Psychology, 19,* 679–691. (10)

Green, J. P., Lynn, S. J., & Montgomery, G. H. (2008). Gender-related differences in hypnosis-based treatments for smoking: A follow-up meta-analysis. *American Journal of Clinical Hypnosis, 50,* 259–271. (10)

Green, M. C., & Sabini, J. (2006). Gender, socioeconomic status, age, and jealousy: Emotional responses to infidelity in a national sample. *Emotion, 6,* 330–334. (13)

Greenberg, J., Martens, A., Jonas, E., Eisenstadt, D., Pyszczynski, T., & Solomon, S. (2003). Psychological defense in anticipation of anxiety. *Psychological Science, 14,* 516–519. (5)

Greene, J. D., Sommerville, R. B., Nystrom, L. E., Darley, J. M., & Cohen, J. D. (2001). An fMRI investigation of emotional engagement in moral judgment. *Science, 293,* 2105–2108. (12)

Greenfield, T. K., Stoneking, B. C., Humphreys, K., Sundby, E., & Bond, J. (2008). A randomized trial of a mental health consumer-managed alternative to civil commitment for acute psychiatric crisis. *American Journal of Community Psychology, 42,* 135–144. (15)

Greenhoot, A. F., Ornstein, P. A., Gordon, B. N., & Baker-Ward, L. (1999). Acting out the details of a pediatric check-up: The impact of interview condition and behavioral style on children's memory reports. *Child Development, 70,* 363–380. (7)

Greeno, C. G., & Wing, R. R. (1994). Stress-induced eating. *Psychological Bulletin, 115,* 444–464. (11)

Greenwald, A. G., & Banaji, M. R. (1995). Implicit social cognition: Attitudes, self-esteem, and stereotypes. *Psychological Review, 102,* 4–27. (13)

Greenwald, A. G., & Draine, S. C. (1997). Do subliminal stimuli enter the brain unnoticed? Tests with a new method. In J. D. Cohen & J. W. Schooler (Eds.), *Scientific approaches to consciousness* (pp. 83–108). Mahwah, NJ: Erlbaum. (4)

Greenwald, A. G., Nosek, B. A., & Banaji, M. R. (2003). Understanding and using the Implicit Association Test: I. An improved scoring algorithm. *Journal of Personality and Social Psychology, 85*, 197–216. (13)

Greenwald, A. G., Nosek, B. A., & Sriram, N. (2006). Consequential validity of the Implicit Association Test. *American Psychologist, 61*, 56–61. (13)

Greenwald, A. G., Spangenberg, E. R., Pratkanis, A. R., & Eskanazi, J. (1991). Double-blind tests of subliminal self-help audiotapes. *Psychological Science, 2*, 119–122. (4)

Greist, J. H., Jefferson, J. W., Kobak, K. A., Katzelnick, D. J., & Serlin, R. C. (1995). Efficacy and tolerability of serotonin transport inhibitors in obsessive-compulsive disorder. *Archives of General Psychiatry, 52*, 53–60. (16)

Griffith, R. M., Miyagi, O., & Tago, A. (1958). The universality of typical dreams: Japanese vs. Americans. *American Anthropologist, 60*, 1173–1179. (10)

Grillon, C., Morgan, C. A., III, Davis, M., & Southwick, S. M. (1998). Effects of darkness on acoustic startle in Vietnam veterans with PTSD. *American Journal of Psychiatry, 155*, 812–817. (12)

Grissmer, D. W., Williamson, S., Kirby, S. N., & Berends, M. (1998). Exploring the rapid rise in the Black achievement scores in the United States (1970–1990). In U. Neisser (Ed.), *The rising curve* (pp. 251–285). Washington, DC: American Psychological Association. (9)

Grønnerød, C. (2003). Temporal stability in the Rorschach method: A meta-analytic review. *Journal of Personality Assessment, 80*, 272–293. (14)

Gross, J. J. (2001). Emotion regulation in adulthood: Timing is everything. *Current Directions in Psychological Science, 10*, 214–219. (12)

Gross, J. J., Fredrickson, B. L., & Levenson, R. W. (1994). The psychophysiology of crying. *Psychophysiology, 31*, 460–468. (12)

Grossman, E. D., & Blake, R. (2001). Brain activity evoked by inverted and imagined biological motion. *Vision Research, 41*, 1475–1482. (4)

Grünbaum, A. (1986). Précis of *The foundations of psychoanalysis:* A philosophical critique. *Behavioral and Brain Sciences, 9*, 217–284. (14)

Guilleminault, C., Heinzer, R., Mignot, E., & Black, J. (1998). Investigations into the neurologic basis of narcolepsy. *Neurology, 50*(Suppl. 1), S8–S15. (10)

Guiso, L., Monte, F., Sapienza, P., & Zingales, L. (2008). Culture, gender, and math. *Science, 320*, 1164–1165. (5)

Gur, R. E., Cowell, P. E., Latshaw, A., Turetsky, B. I., Grossman, R. I., Arnold, S. E., et al. (2000). Reduced dorsal and orbital prefrontal gray matter volumes in schizophrenia. *Archives of General Psychiatry, 57*, 761–768. (16)

Gurling, H. M. D., Critchley, H., Datta, S. R., McQuillin, A., Blaveri, E., Thirumalai, S., et al. (2006). Genetic association and brain morphology studies and the chromosome 8p22 pericentriolar material 1 (*PCM1*) gene in susceptibility to schizophrenia. *Archives of General Psychiatry, 63*, 844–854. (16)

Gustavson, C. R., Kelly, D. J., Sweeney, M., & Garcia, J. (1976). Prey-lithium aversions: I. Coyotes and wolves. *Behavioral Biology, 17*, 61–72. (6)

Gvilia, I., Xu, F., McGinty, D., & Szymusiak, R. (2006). Homeostatic regulation of sleep: A role for preoptic area neurons. *Journal of Neuroscience, 26*, 9426–9433. (10)

Haarmeier, T., Thier, P., Repnow, M., & Petersen, D. (1997). False perception of motion in a patient who cannot compensate for eye movements. *Nature, 389*, 849–852. (4)

Haas, B. W., Omura, K., Constable, R. T., & Canli, T. (2007). Is automatic emotion regulation associated with agreeableness? *Psychological Science, 18*, 130–132. (12)

Habermas, T., & Bluck, S. (2000). Getting a life: The emergence of the life story in adolescence. *Psychological Bulletin, 126*, 748–769. (5)

Hackman, J. R., & Lawler, E. E., III (1971). Employee reactions to job characteristics. *Journal of Applied Psychology, 55*, 259–286. (11)

Haeffel, G. J., Abramson, L. Y., Voelz, Z. R., Metalsky, G. I., Halberstadt, L., Dykman, B. M., et al. (2005). Negative cognitive styles, dysfunctional attitudes, and the remitted depression paradigm: A search for the elusive cognitive vulnerability to depression factor among remitted depressives. *Emotion, 5*, 343–348. (16)

Hafer, C. L., & Bègue, L. (2005). Experimental research on just-world theory: Problems, developments, and future challenges. *Psychological Bulletin, 131*, 128–167. (14)

Haggard, P., Clark, S., & Kalogeras, J. (2002). Voluntary action and conscious awareness. *Nature Neuroscience, 5*, 382–385. (10)

Haggard, P., & Eimer, M. (1999). On the relation between brain potentials and the awareness of voluntary movements. *Experimental Brain Research, 126*, 128–133. (10)

Haggard, P., & Libet, B. (2001). Conscious intention and brain activity. *Journal of Consciousness Studies, 8*, 47–63. (10)

Haggarty, J. M., Cernovsky, Z., Husni, M., Minor, K., Kermean, P., & Merskey, H. (2002). Seasonal affective disorder in an arctic community. *Acta Psychiatrica Scandinavica, 105*, 378–384. (16)

Haidt, J. (2001). The emotional dog and its rational tail: A social intuitionist approach to moral judgment. *Psychological Review, 108*, 814–834. (13)

Haidt, J. (2007). The new synthesis in moral psychology. *Science, 316*, 998–1002. (13)

Haist, F., Gore, J. B., & Mao, H. (2001). Consolidation of human memory over decades revealed by functional magnetic resonance imaging. *Nature Neuroscience, 4*, 1139–1145. (7)

Hakuta, K., Bialystok, E., & Wiley, E. (2003). Critical evidence: A test of the critical-period hypothesis for second-language acquisition. *Psychological Science, 14*, 31–38. (8)

Hall, C. S., & Van de Castle, R. L. (1966). *The content analysis of dreams*. New York: Appleton-Century-Crofts. (10)

Hall, J. A., & Matsumoto, D. (2004). Gender differences in judgments of multiple emotions from facial expressions. *Emotion, 4*, 201–206. (12)

Hall, L. J., & McGregor, J. A. (2000). A follow-up study of the peer relationships of children with disabilities in an inclusive school. *Journal of Special Education, 34*, 114–126. (9)

Halmi, K. A., Sunday, S. R., Strober, M., Kaplan, A., Woodside, D. B., Fichter, M., et al. (2000). Perfectionism in anorexia nervosa: Variation by clinical subtype, obsessionality, and pathological eating behavior. *American Journal of Psychiatry, 157*, 1799–1805. (11)

Halpern, D. F., Benbow, C. P., Geary, D. C., Gur, R. C., Hyde, J. S., & Gernsbacher, M. A. (2007). The science of sex differences in science and mathematics. *Psychological Science in the Public Interest, 8*, 1–51. (5)

Halpern, S. D., Andrews, T. J., & Purves, D. (1999). Interindividual variation in human visual performance. *Journal of Cognitive Neuroscience, 11*, 521–534. (4)

Hama, Y. (2001). Shopping as a coping behavior for stress. *Japanese Psychological Research, 43*, 218–224. (12)

Hamann, S. B., & Squire, L. R. (1997). Intact perceptual memory in the absence of conscious memory. *Behavioral Neuroscience, 111*, 850–854. (7)

Hambrick, D. Z., & Engle, R. W. (2002). Effects of domain knowledge, working memory capacity, and age on cognitive performance: An investigation of the knowledge-is-power hypothesis. *Cognitive Psychology, 44*, 339–387. (7)

Hamby, S. L., & Koss, M. P. (2003). Shades of gray: A qualitative study of terms used in the measurement of sexual victimization. *Psychology of Women Quarterly, 27*, 243–255. (12)

Hamilton, S. P., Fyer, A. J., Durner, M., Heiman, G. A., Baisre de Leon, A., Hodge, S. E., et al. (2003). Further genetic evidence for a panic disorder syndrome mapping to chromosome 13q. *Proceedings of the National Academy of Sciences, USA, 100*, 2550–2555. (16)

Hamm, J. V. (2000). Do birds of a feather flock together? The variable bases for African American, Asian American, and European American adolescents' selection of similar friends. *Developmental Psychology, 36*, 209–219. (13)

Hamm, R. M., Reiss, D. M., Paul, R. K., & Bursztajn, H. J. (2007). Knocking at the wrong door: Insured workers' inadequate psychiatric care and workers' compensation claims. *Journal of Law and Psychiatry, 30*, 416–426. (15)

Hammock, E. A. D., & Young, L. J. (2005). Microsatellite instability generates diversity in brain and sociobehavioral traits. *Science, 308*, 1630–1634. (5)

Han, C. J., & Robinson, J. K. (2001). Cannabinoid modulation of time estimation in the rat. *Behavioral Neuroscience, 115*, 243–246. (3)

Haney, C., Banks, C., & Zimbardo, P. (1973). Interpersonal dynamics in a simulated prison. *International Journal of Criminology and Penology, 1*, 69–97. (13)

Hankin, B. L., & Abramson, L. Y. (2001). Development of gender differences in depression: An elaborated cognitive vulnerability-transactional stress theory. *Psychological Bulletin, 127*, 773–796. (16)

Hanoch, Y., Johnson, J. G., & Wilke, A. (2006). Domain specificity in experimental measures and participant recruitment. *Psychological Science, 17*, 300–304. (14)

Hanson, R. K. (2000). Will they do it again? Predicting sex-offense recidivism. *Current Directions in Psychological Science, 9*, 106–109. (12)

Harada, S., Agarwal, D. P. Goedde, H. W., Tagaki, S., & Ishikawa, B. (1982). Possible protective role against alcoholism for aldehyde dehydrogenase isozyme deficiency in Japan. *Lancet, ii*, 827. (16)

Harinck, F., Van Dijk, E., Van Beest, I., & Mersmann, P. (2007). When gains loom larger than losses. *Psychological Science, 18*, 1099–1105. (8)

Hariri, A. R., Mattay, V. S., Tessitore, A., Kolachana, B., Fera, F., Goldman, D., et al. (2002). Serotonin transporter genetic variation and the response of the human amygdala. *Science, 297*, 400–403. (3)

Harker, L. A., & Keltner, D. (2001). Expressions of positive emotion in women's college yearbook pictures and their relationship to personality and life outcomes across adulthood. *Journal of Personality and Social Psychology, 80*, 112–124. (12)

Harkins, S. G., & Jackson, J. M. (1985). The role of evaluation in eliminating social loafing. *Journal of Personality and Social Psychology, 11*, 457–465. (13)

Harley, B., & Wang, W. (1997). The critical period hypothesis: Where are we now? In A. M. B. deGroot & J. F. Knoll (Eds.), *Tutorials in bilingualism* (pp. 19–51). Mahwah, NJ: Erlbaum. (8)

Harlow, H. F., Harlow, M. K., & Meyer, D. R. (1950). Learning motivated by a manipulative drive. *Journal of Experimental Psychology, 40*, 228–234. (11)

Harper, L. V. (2005). Epigenetic inheritance and the intergenerational transfer of experience. *Psychological Bulletin, 131*, 340–360. (5)

Harris, B. (1979). What ever happened to Little Albert? *American Psychologist, 34,* 151–160. (16)

Harris, J. R. (1995). Where is the child's environment? A group socialization theory of development. *Psychological Review, 102,* 458–489. (5)

Harris, J. R. (1998). *The nurture assumption.* New York: Free Press. (5)

Harris, J. R. (2000). Context-specific learning, personality, and birth order. *Current Directions in Psychological Science, 9,* 174–177. (5)

Harris, R. J., Schoen, L. M., & Hensley, D. L. (1992). A cross-cultural study of story memory. *Journal of Cross-Cultural Psychology, 23,* 133–147. (7)

Harris, T. (1967). *I'm OK—You're OK.* New York: Avon. (14)

Harrow, M., & Jobe, T. H. (2007). Factors involved in outcome and recovery in schizophrenia patients not on antipsychotic medications: A 15-year multifollow-up study. *Journal of Nervous and Mental Disease, 195,* 406–414. (16)

Hartmann, S., & Zepf, S. (2003). Effectiveness of psychotherapy in Germany: A replication of the *Consumer Reports* study. *Psychotherapy Research, 13,* 235–242. (15)

Harvey, A. G., & Bryant, R. A. (2002). Acute stress disorder: A synthesis and critique. *Psychological Bulletin, 128,* 886–902. (12)

Hassabis, D., Kumaran, D., Vann, S. D., & Maguire, E. A. (2007). Patients with hippocampal amnesia cannot imagine new experiences. *Proceedings of the National Academy of Sciences, 104,* 1726–1731. (7)

Hastie, R., Schkade, D. A., & Payne, J. W. (1999). Juror judgments in civil cases: Hindsight effects on judgments of liability for punitive damages. *Law and Human Behavior, 23,* 597–614. (7)

Hatfield, E., & Rapson, R. L. (1993). *Love, sex, and intimacy.* New York: HarperCollins. (13)

Hathaway, S. R., & McKinley, J. C. (1940). A multiphasic personality schedule (Minnesota): I. Construction of the schedule. *Journal of Psychology, 10,* 249–254. (14)

Haueisen, J., & Knösche, T. R. (2001). Involuntary motor activity in pianists evoked by music perception. *Journal of Cognitive Neuroscience, 13,* 786–792. (6)

Hauk, O., Johnsrude, I., & Pulvermüller, F. (2004). Somatotopic representation of action words in human motor and premotor cortex. *Neuron, 41,* 301–307. (8)

Haukka, J., Suvisaari, J., & Lönnqvist, J. (2003). Fertility of patients with schizophrenia, their siblings, and the general population: A cohort study from 1950 to 1959 in Finland. *American Journal of Psychiatry, 160,* 460–463. (16)

Hauri, P. (1982). *The sleep disorders.* Kalamazoo, MI: Upjohn. (10)

Hayes, J., Schimel, J., & Williams, T. J. (2008). Fighting death with death. *Psychological Science, 19,* 501–507. (5)

Healy, D., Savage, M., Michael, P., Marris, M., Hirst, D., Carter, M., et al. (2001). Psychiatric bed utilization: 1896 and 1996 compared. *Psychological Medicine, 31,* 779–790. (16)

Healy, D., & Williams, J. M. G. (1988). Dysrhythmia, dysphoria, and depression: The interaction of learned helplessness and circadian dysrhythmia in the pathogenesis of depression. *Psychological Bulletin, 103,* 163–178. (16)

Heath, A. C., Neale, M. C., Kessler, R. C., Eaves, L. J., & Kendler, K. S. (1992). Evidence for genetic influences on personality from self-reports and informant ratings. *Journal of Personality and Social Psychology, 63,* 85–96. (5, 14)

Heatherton, T. G., & Baumeister, R. F. (1991). Binge eating as escape from self-awareness. *Psychological Bulletin, 110,* 86–108. (11)

Heck, A., Collins, J., & Peterson, L. (2001). Decreasing children's risk taking on the playground. *Journal of Applied Behavior Analysis, 34,* 349–352. (6)

Hedges, L. V., & Nowell, A. (1995). Sex differences in mental test scores, variability, and numbers of high-scoring individuals. *Science, 269,* 41–45. (9)

Heider, F. (1958). *The psychology of interpersonal relations.* New York: Wiley. (13)

Heine, S. J., Buchtel, E. E., & Norenzayan, A. (2008). What do cross-national comparisons of personality traits tell us? *Psychological Science, 19,* 309–313. (14)

Heine, S. J., & Hamamura, T. (2007). In search of East Asian self-enhancement. *Personality and Social Psychology Review, 11,* 4–27. (13)

Heit, E. (1993). Modeling the effects of expectations on recognition memory. *Psychological Science, 4,* 244–251. (7)

Heitz, R. P., & Engle, R. W. (2007). Focusing the spotlight: Individual differences in visual attention control. *Journal of Experimental Psychology: General, 136,* 217–240. (7)

Hejmadi, A., Davidson, R. J., & Rozin, P. (2000). Exploring Hindu Indian emotion expressions. *Psychological Science, 11,* 183–187. (12)

Henderlong, J., & Lepper, M. R. (2002). The effects of praise on children's intrinsic motivation: A review and synthesis. *Psychological Bulletin, 128,* 774–795. (11)

Henderson, J. M. (2007). Regarding scenes. *Current Directions in Psychological Science, 16,* 219–222. (8)

Henderson, J. M., & Hollingworth, A. (2003). Global transsaccadic change blindness during scene perception. *Psychological Science, 14,* 493–497. (8)

Hendin, H., Maltsberger, J. T., Lipschitz, A., Haas, A. P., & Kyle, J. (2001). Recognizing and responding to a suicide crisis. *Annals of the New York Academy of Sciences, 932,* 169–186. (16)

Hendrie, H. C. (2001). Exploration of environmental and genetic risk factors for Alzheimer's disease: The value of cross-cultural studies. *Current Directions in Psychological Science, 10,* 98–101. (7)

Henning, E. R., Turk, C. L., Mennin, D. S., Fresco, D. M., & Heimberg, R. G. (2007). Impairment and quality of life in individuals with generalized anxiety disorder. *Depression and Anxiety, 24,* 342–349. (16)

Heresco-Levy, U., & Javitt, D. C. (2004). Comparative effects of glycine and D-cycloserine on persistent negative symptoms in schizophrenia: A retrospective analysis. *Schizophrenia Research, 66,* 89–96. (16)

Hergenhahn, B. R. (1992). *An introduction to the history of psychology* (2nd ed.). Belmont, CA: Wadsworth. (1)

Herkenham, M., Lynn, A. B., deCosta, B. R., & Richfield, E. K. (1991). Neuronal localization of cannabinoid receptors in the basal ganglia of the rat. *Brain Research, 547,* 267–274. (3)

Herkenham, M., Lynn, A. B., Little, M. D., Johnson, M. R., Melvin, L. S., deCosta, B. R., et al. (1990). Cannabinoid receptor localization in brain. *Proceedings of the National Academy of Sciences, USA, 87,* 1932–1936. (3)

Herman, C. P., Roth, D. A., & Polivy, J. (2003). Effects of the presence of others on food intake: A normative interpretation. *Psychological Bulletin, 129,* 873–886. (11)

Herman, J., Roffwarg, H., & Tauber, E. S. (1968). Color and other perceptual qualities of REM and NREM sleep. *Psychophysiology, 5,* 223. (10)

Herrmann, B., Thöni, C., & Gächter, S. (2008). Antisocial punishment across societies. *Science, 319,* 1362–1367. (13)

Hershkowitz, I., & Terner, A. (2007). The effects of repeated interviewing on children's forensic statements of sexual abuse. *Applied Cognitive Psychology, 21,* 1131–1143. (7)

Hertenstein, M. J. (2002). Touch: Its communicative functions in infancy. *Human Development, 45,* 70–94. (5)

Herz, R. (2007). *The scent of desire.* New York: HarperCollins. (4)

Herz, R. S., & von Clef, J. (2001). The influence of verbal labeling on the perception of odors: Evidence for olfactory illusions? *Perception, 30,* 381–391. (4)

Hespos, S. J., & Baillargeon, R. (2007). Young infants' actions reveal their developing knowledge of support variables. *Cognition, 107,* 304–316. (5)

Hess, T. M. (2005). Memory and aging in context. *Psychological Bulletin, 131,* 383–406. (5)

Hetherington, E. M. (1989). Coping with family transitions. Winners, losers, and survivors. *Child Development, 60,* 1–14. (5)

Hetherington, E. M., Bridges, M., & Insabella, G. M. (1998). What matters? What does not? *American Psychologist, 53,* 167–184. (5)

Hetherington, E. M., Stanley-Hagan, M., & Anderson, E. R. (1989). Marital transitions: A child's perspective. *American Psychologist, 44,* 303–312. (10)

Hettema, J. M., Neale, M. C., & Kendler, K. S. (2001). A review and meta-analysis of the genetic epidemiology of anxiety disorders. *American Journal of Psychiatry, 158,* 1568–1578. (16)

Hildreth, K., Sweeney, B., & Rovee-Collier, C. (2003). Differential memory-preserving effects of reminders at 6 months. *Journal of Experimental Child Psychology, 84,* 41–62. (5)

Hilgard, E. R. (1973). A neodissociation interpretation of pain reduction in hypnosis. *Psychological Review, 80,* 396–411. (10)

Hill, C. E., & Nakayama, E. Y. (2000). Client-centered therapy: Where has it been and where is it going? A comment on Hathaway (1948). *Journal of Clinical Psychology, 56,* 861–875. (15)

Hill, J. L., Waldfogel, J., Brooks-Gunn, J., & Han, W.-J. (2005). Maternal employment and child development: A fresh look using newer methods. *Developmental Psychology, 41,* 833–850. (5)

Hill, W. D., Blake, M., & Clark, J. E. (1998). Ball court design dates back 3,400 years. *Nature, 392,* 878–879. (11)

Hillis, A. E., Kleinman, J. T., Newhart, M., Heidler-Gary, J., Gottesman, R., Barker, P. B., et al. (2006). Restoring cerebral blood flow reveals neural regions critical for naming. *Journal of Neuroscience, 26,* 8069–8073. (8)

Hilty, D. M., Brady, K. T., & Hales, R. E. (1999). A review of bipolar disorder among adults. *Psychiatric Services, 50,* 201–213. (16)

Himle, J. A., Baser, R. E., Taylor, R. J., Campbell, R. D., & Jackson, J. S. (2009). Anxiety disorders among Africans, Blacks of Caribbean descent, and non-Hispanic Whites in the United States. *Journal of Anxiety Disorders, 23,* 578–590. (16)

Hirvonen, J., van Erp, T. G. M., Huttunen, J., Aalto, S., Någren, K., Huttunen, M., et al. (2006). Brain dopamine D_1 receptors in twins discordant for schizophrenia. *American Journal of Psychiatry, 163,* 1747–1753. (16)

Hobson, J. A. (2005). Sleep is of the brain, by the brain and for the brain. *Nature, 437,* 1254–1256. (10)

Hobson, J. A., & McCarley, R. W. (1977). The brain as a dream state generator: An activation-synthesis hypothesis of the dream process. *American Journal of Psychiatry, 134,* 1335–1348. (10)

Hodgins, S., Mednick, S. A., Brennan, P. A., Schulsinger, F., & Engberg, M. (1996). Mental disorder and crime. *Archives of General Psychiatry, 53,* 489–496. (12)

Hoebel, B. G., Rada, P. V., Mark, G. P., & Pothos, E. (1999). Neural systems for reinforcement and inhibition of behavior: Relevance to eating, addiction, and depression. In D. Kahneman, E. Diener, & N. Schwartz (Eds.), *Well-being: Foundations of hedonic psychology* (pp. 560–574). New York: Russell Sage Foundation. (11, 16)

Hoehl, S., & Striano, T. (2008). Neural processing of eye gaze and threat-related emotional facial expressions in infancy. *Child Development, 79,* 1752–1760. (12)

Hoek, H. W., & van Hoeken, D. (2003). Review of the prevalence and incidence of eating disorders. *International Journal of Eating Disorders, 34,* 383–396. (11)

Hoffrage, U., Hertwig, R., & Gigerenzer, G. (2000). Hindsight bias: A by-product of knowledge updating? *Journal of Experimental Psychology: Learning, Memory, and Cognition, 26,* 566–581. (7)

Holcombe, A. O., & Cavanagh, P. (2001). Early binding of feature pairs for visual perception. *Nature Neuroscience, 4,* 127–128. (3)

Holden, G. W., & Miller, P. C. (1999). Enduring and different: A meta-analysis of the similarity in parents' child rearing. *Psychological Bulletin, 125,* 223–254. (5)

Holland, R. W., Hendriks, M., & Aarts, H. (2005). Smells like clean spirit. *Psychological Science, 16,* 689–693. (8)

Hollingsworth, D. E., McAuliffe, S. P., & Knowlton, B. J. (2001). Temporal allocation of visual attention in adult attention deficit hyperactivity disorder. *Journal of Cognitive Neuroscience, 13,* 298–305. (8)

Hollister, J. M., Laing, P., & Mednick, S. A. (1996). Rhesus incompatibility as a risk factor for schizophrenia in male adults. *Archives of General Psychiatry, 53,* 19–24. (16)

Hollon, S. D., & Beck, A. T. (1979). Cognitive therapy of depression. In P. C. Kendall & S. D. Hollon (Eds.), *Cognitive-behavioral interventions* (pp. 153–203). New York: Academic Press. (15)

Hollon, S. D., Jarrett, R. B., Nierenberg, A. A., Thase, M. E., Trivedi, M., & Rush, A. J. (2005). Psychotherapy and medication in the treatment of adult and geriatric depression: Which monotherapy or combined treatment? *Journal of Clinical Psychiatry, 66,* 455–468. (16)

Hollon, S. D., Thase, M. E., & Markowitz, J. C. (2002). Treatment and prevention of depression. *Psychological Science in the Public Interest, 3,* 39–77. (16)

Holmberg, D., & Blair, K. L. (2009). Sexual desire, communication, satisfaction, and preferences of men and women in same-sex versus mixed-sex relationships. *Journal of Sex Research, 46,* 57–66. (13)

Holmes, D. S. (1978). Projection as a defense mechanism. *Psychological Bulletin, 85,* 677–688. (14)

Holmes, D. S. (1987). The influence of meditation versus rest on physiological arousal: A second examination. In M. A. West (Ed.), *The psychology of meditation* (pp. 81–103). Oxford, England: Clarendon Press. (10)

Holmes, D. S. (1990). The evidence for repression: An examination of sixty years of research. In J. L. Singer (Ed.), *Repression and dissociation* (pp. 85–102). New York: Wiley. (7, 14)

Holmes, T., & Rahe, R. (1967). The social readjustment rating scale. *Journal of Psychosomatic Research, 11,* 213–218. (12)

Homa, D. (1983). An assessment of two extraordinary speed-readers. *Bulletin of the Psychonomic Society, 21,* 123–126. (8)

Hönekopp, J. (2006). Once more: Is beauty in the eye of the beholder? Relative contributions of private and shared taste to judgments of facial attractiveness. *Journal of Experimental Psychology: Human Perception and Performance, 32,* 199–209. (13)

Hong, Y., Morris, M. W., Chiu, C., & Benet-Martinez, V. (2000). Multicultural minds: A dynamic constructivist approach to culture and cognition. *American Psychologist, 55,* 709–720. (13)

Hoover, D. W., & Milich, R. (1994). Effects of sugar ingestion expectancies on mother-child interactions. *Journal of Abnormal Child Psychology, 22,* 501–515. (2)

Horn, J. L. (1968). Organization of abilities and the development of intelligence. *Psychological Review, 75,* 242–259. (9)

Horn, J. L., & Donaldson, G. (1976). On the myth of intellectual decline in adulthood. *American Psychologist, 31,* 701–719. (9)

Horne, J. A. (1988). *Why we sleep.* Oxford, England: Oxford University Press. (10)

Horne, J. A., Brass, C. G., & Pettitt, A. N. (1980). Circadian performance differences between morning and evening "types." *Ergonomics, 23,* 29–36. (10)

Horst, W. D., & Preskorn, S. H. (1998). Mechanisms of action and clinical characteristics of three atypical antidepressants: Venlafaxine, nefazodone, bupropion. *Journal of Affective Disorders, 51,* 237–254. (16)

Hough, L. M., & Oswald, F. L. (2008). Personality testing and industrial-organizational psychology: Reflections, progress, and prospects. *Industrial and Organizational Psychology, 1,* 272–290. (14)

Howard, K. I., Kopta, S. M., Krause, M. S., & Orlinsky, D. E. (1986). The dose-effect relationship in psychotherapy. *American Psychologist, 41,* 159–164. (15)

Howard, R. W. (1999). Preliminary real-world evidence that average human intelligence really is rising. *Intelligence, 27,* 235–250. (9)

Howe, C. Q., & Purves, D. (2005). *Perceiving geometry.* New York: Springer. (4)

Howe, C. Q., Yang, Z., & Purves, D. (2005). The Poggendorff illusion explained by natural scene geometry. *Proceedings of the National Academy of Sciences, USA, 102,* 7707–7712. (4)

Howe, M. L., & Courage, M. L. (1993). On resolving the enigma of infantile amnesia. *Psychological Bulletin, 113,* 305–326. (7)

Howe, M. L., & Courage, M. L. (1997). The emergence and early development of autobiographical memory. *Psychological Review, 104,* 499–523. (7)

Howes, O. D., Montgomery, A. J., Asselin, M.-C., Murray, R. M., Valli, I., Tabraham, P., et al. (2009). Elevated striatal dopamine function linked to prodromal signs of schizophrenia. *Archives of General Psychiatry, 66,* 13–20. (16)

Hrdy, S. B. (2000). The optimal number of fathers. *Annals of the New York Academy of Sciences, 907,* 75–96. (13)

Hróbjartsson, A., & Gøtzsche, P. C. (2001). Is the placebo powerless? *New England Journal of Medicine, 344,* 1594–1602. (4)

Hsee, C. K., & Tang, J. N. (2007). Sun and water: On a modulus-based measurement of happiness. *Emotion, 7,* 213–218. (2)

Hu, P., Stylos-Allan, M., & Walker, M. P. (2006). Sleep facilitates consolidation of emotional declarative memory. *Psychological Science, 17,* 891–898. (10)

Hubbs-Tait, L., Nation, J. R., Krebs, N. F., & Bellinger, D. C. (2005). Neurotoxicants, micronutrients, and social environments: Individual and combined effects on children's development. *Psychological Science in the Public Interest, 6,* 57–121. (5)

Hubel, D. H., & Wiesel, T. N. (1968). Receptive fields and functional architecture of monkey striate cortex. *Journal of Physiology* (London), *195,* 215–243. (4)

Huber, R., Ghilardi, M. F., Massimini, M., & Tononi, G. (2004). Local sleep and learning. *Nature, 430,* 78–81. (10)

Hudson, J. I., Hiripi, E., Pope, H. G., Jr., & Kessler, R. C. (2007). The prevalence and correlates of eating disorders in the National Comorbidity Survey Replication. *Biological Psychiatry, 61,* 348–358. (11)

Hudson, J. I., Mangweth, B., Pope, H. G., Jr., De Col, C., Hausmann, A., Gutweniger, S., et al. (2003). Family study of affective spectrum disorder. *Archives of General Psychiatry, 60,* 170–177. (16)

Hudson, W. (1960). Pictorial depth perception in sub-cultural groups in Africa. *Journal of Social Psychology, 52,* 183–208. (4)

Huff, D. (1954). *How to lie with statistics.* New York: W. W. Norton. (2)

Hughes, J. C., & Cook, C. C. H. (1997). The efficacy of disulfiram: A review of outcome studies. *Addiction, 92,* 381–395. (16)

Hughes, J., Smith, T. W., Kosterlitz, H. W., Fothergill, L. A., Morgan, B. A., & Morris, H. R. (1975). Identification of two related pentapeptides from the brain with potent opiate antagonist activity. *Nature, 258,* 577–579. (3)

Hugoson, A., Ljungquist, B., & Breivik, T. (2002). The relationship of some negative events and psychological factors to periodontal disease in an adult Swedish population 50 to 80 years of age. *Journal of Clinical Periodontology, 29,* 247–253. (12)

Hull, C. L. (1932). The goal gradient hypothesis and maze learning. *Psychological Review, 39,* 25–43. (1)

Hull, C. L. (1943). *Principles of behavior: An introduction to behavior theory.* New York: D. Appleton. (11)

Hunter, J. E. (1997). Needed: A ban on the significance test. *Psychological Science, 8,* 3–7. (2)

Hur, Y.-M., Bouchard, T. J., Jr., & Eckert, E. (1998). Genetic and environmental influences on self-reported diet: A reared-apart twin study. *Physiology and Behavior, 64,* 629–636. (5)

Hur, Y.-M., Bouchard, T. J., Jr., & Lykken, D. T. (1998). Genetic and environmental influence on morningness–eveningness. *Personality and Individual Differences, 25,* 917–925. (5)

Hurovitz, C. S., Dunn, S., Domhoff, G. W., & Fiss, H. (1999). The dreams of blind men and women: A replication and extension of previous findings. *Dreaming, 9,* 183–193. (10)

Huston, T. L., Niehuis, S., & Smith, S. E. (2001). The early marital roots of conjugal distress and divorce. *Current Directions in Psychological Science, 10,* 116–119. (13)

Hutcheson, D. M., Everitt, B. J., Robbins, T. W., & Dickinson, A. (2001). The role of withdrawal in heroin addiction: Enhances reward or promotes avoidance? *Nature Neuroscience, 4,* 943–947. (16)

Hyde, J. (2005). The gender similarities hypothesis. *American Psychologist, 60,* 581–592. (5)

Hyde, J. S., Lindberg, S. M., Linn, M. C., Ellis, A. B., & Williams, C. C. (2008). Gender similarities characterize math performance. *Science, 321,* 494–495. (5)

Hyde, K. L., & Peretz, I. (2004). Brains that are out of tune but in time. *Psychological Science, 15,* 356–360. (4)

Iacono, W. G., & Patrick, C. J. (1999). Polygraph ("lie detector") testing: The state of the art. In A. K. Hess & I. B. Weiner (Eds.), *The handbook of forensic psychology* (pp. 440–473). New York: Wiley. (12)

Iggo, A., & Andres, K. H. (1982). Morphology of cutaneous receptors. *Annual Review of Neuroscience, 5*, 1–31. (4)

Ikeda, K., Koga, A., & Minami, S. (2006). Evaluation of a cure process during alarm treatment for nocturnal enuresis. *Journal of Clinical Psychology, 62*, 1245–1257. (15)

Ikonomidou, C., Bittigau, P., Ishimaru, M. J., Wozniak, D. F., Koch, C., Genz, K., et al. (2000). Ethanol-induced apoptotic neurodegeneration and fetal alcohol syndrome. *Science, 287*, 1056–1060. (5)

Ilies, R., & Judge, T. A. (2003). On the heritability of job satisfaction: The mediating role of personality. *Journal of Applied Psychology, 88*, 750–759. (11)

Imahori, T. T., & Cupach, W. R. (1994). A cross-cultural comparison of the interpretation and management of face: U.S. American and Japanese responses to embarrassing predicaments. *International Journal of Intercultural Relations, 18*, 193–219. (12)

Imhoff, M. C., & Baker-Ward, L. (1999). Preschoolers' suggestibility: Effects of developmentally appropriate language and interviewer supportiveness. *Journal of Applied Developmental Psychology, 20*, 407–429. (7)

Inglehart, R., Foa, R., Peterson, C., & Welzel, C. (2008). Development, freedom, and rising happiness. *Perspectives on Psychological Science, 3*, 264–285. (12)

Inouye, S. T., & Kawamura, H. (1979). Persistence of circadian rhythmicity in a mammalian hypothalamic "island" containing the suprachiasmatic nucleus. *Proceedings of the National Academy of Sciences, USA, 76*, 5962–5966. (10)

International Schizophrenia Consortium. (2008). Rare chromosomal deletions and duplications increase risk of schizophrenia. *Nature, 455*, 237–241. (16)

Irvine, R. J., Keane, M., Felgate, P., McCann, U. D., Callaghan, P. D., & White, J. M. (2006). Plasma drug concentrations and physiological measures in "dance party" participants. *Neuropsychopharmacology, 31*, 424–430. (3)

Irwin, D. E., & Brockmole, J. R. (2004). Suppressing *where* but not *what*: The effect of saccades on dorsal- and ventral-stream visual processing. *Psychological Science, 15*, 467–473. (8)

Isaacowitz, D. M., Toner, K., Goren, D., & Wilson, H. R. (2008). Looking while unhappy. *Psychological Science, 19*, 848–853. (12)

Isenberg, D. J. (1986). Group polarization: A critical review and meta-analysis. *Journal of Personality and Social Psychology, 50*, 1141–1151. (13)

Iverson, J. M., & Goldin-Meadow, S. (2005). Gesture paves the way for language development. *Psychological Science, 16*, 367–371. (8)

Ivry, R. B., & Diener, H. C. (1991). Impaired velocity perception in patients with lesions of the cerebellum. *Journal of Cognitive Neuroscience, 3*, 355–366. (3)

Iyengar, S. S., & Lepper, M. R. (2000). When choice is demotivating. *Journal of Personality and Social Psychology, 79*, 995–1006. (8)

Iyengar, S. S., Wells, R. E., & Schwartz, B. (2006). Doing better but feeling worse. *Psychological Science, 17*, 143–150. (8)

Izazola-Licea, J. A., Gortmaker, S. L., Tolbert, K., De Gruttola, V., & Mann, J. (2000). Prevalence of same-gender sexual behavior and HIV in a probability household survey of Mexican men. *Journal of Sex Research, 37*, 37–43. (11)

Jackson, D. C., Malmstadt, J. R., Larson, C. L., & Davidson, R. J. (2000). Suppression and enhancement of emotional responses to unpleasant pictures. *Psychophysiology, 37*, 515–522. (12)

Jacobs, B., Schall, M., & Scheibel, A. B. (1993). A quantitative dendritic analysis of Wernicke's area in humans: II. Gender, hemispheric, and environmental factors. *Journal of Comparative Neurology, 327*, 97–111. (8)

Jacobs, B. L. (1987). How hallucinogenic drugs work. *American Scientist, 75*, 386–392. (3)

Jacobs, K. M., Mark, G. P., & Scott, T. R. (1988). Taste responses in the nucleus tractus solitarius of sodium-deprived rats. *Journal of Physiology, 406*, 393–410. (1)

Jacobsen, F. M., Sack, D. A., Wehr, T. A., Rogers, S., & Rosenthal, N. E. (1987). Neuroendocrine 5-hydroxytryptophan in seasonal affective disorder. *Archives of General Psychiatry, 44*, 1086–1091. (16)

Jacobson, N. S., & Christensen, A. (1996). Studying the effectiveness of psychotherapy: How well can clinical trials do the job? *American Psychologist, 51*, 1031–1039. (15)

Jacobson, N. S., Dobson, K. S., Truax, P. A., Addis, M. E., Koerner, K., Gollan, J. K., et al. (1996). A component analysis of cognitive-behavior therapy for depression. *Journal of Consulting and Clinical Psychology, 64*, 295–304. (16)

James, W. (1890). *The principles of psychology.* New York: Henry Holt. (1)

James, W. (1894). The physical basis of emotion. *Psychological Review, 1*, 516–529. (12)

James, W. (1961). *Psychology: The briefer course.* New York: Harper. (Original work published 1892) (10)

Jancke, D., Chavane, F., Naaman, S., & Grinvald, A. (2004). Imaging cortical correlates of illusion in early visual cortex. *Nature, 428*, 423–426. (10)

Janis, I. L. (1972). *Victims of groupthink.* Boston: Houghton Mifflin. (13)

Janis, I. L. (1983). Stress inoculation in health care. In D. Meichenbaum & M. E. Jaremko (Eds.), *Stress reduction and prevention* (pp. 67–99). New York: Plenum Press. (12)

Janis, I. L. (1985). Sources of error in strategic decision making. In J. M. Pennings & associates (Eds.), *Organizational strategy and change* (pp. 157–197). San Francisco: Jossey-Bass. (13)

Jaremko, M. E. (1983). Stress inoculation training for social anxiety, with emphasis on dating anxiety. In D. Meichenbaum & M. E. Jaremko (Eds.), *Stress reduction and prevention* (pp. 419–450). New York: Plenum Press. (12)

Jerome, L., & Segal, A. (2001). Benefit of long-term stimulants on driving in adults with ADHD. *Journal of Nervous and Mental Disease, 189*, 63–64. (8)

Ji, L-J., Nisbett, R. E., & Su, Y. (2001). Culture, change, and prediction. *Psychological Science, 12*, 450–456. (13)

Jiang, Y., Costello, P., & He, S. (2007). Processing of invisible stimuli. *Psychological Science, 18*, 349–355. (10)

Johanek, L. M., Meyer, R. A., Hartke, T., Hobelmann, J. G., Maine, D. N., LaMotte, R. H., et al. (2007). Psychophysical and physiological evidence for parallel afferent pathways mediating the sensation of itch. *Journal of Neuroscience, 27*, 7490–7497. (4)

Johansson, C., Willeit, M., Smedh, C., Ekholm, J., Paunio, T., Kieseppä, T., et al. (2003). Circadian clock-related polymorphisms in seasonal affective disorder and their relevance to diurnal preference. *Neuropsychopharmacology, 28*, 734–739. (16)

Johansson, P., Hall, L., Sikström, S., & Olsson, A. (2005). Failure to detect mismatches between intention and outcome in a simple decision task. *Science, 310*, 116–119. (8)

Johns, M., Schmader, T., & Martens, A. (2005). Knowing is half the battle. *Psychological Science, 16*, 175–179. (9)

Johnson, J. G., Cohen, P., Brown, J., Smailes, E. M., & Bernstein, D. P. (1999). Childhood maltreatment increases risk for personality disorders during early adulthood. *Archives of General Psychiatry, 56*, 600–606. (15)

Johnson, M. K., Hashtroudi, S., & Lindsay, D. S. (1993). Source monitoring. *Psychological Bulletin, 114*, 3–28. (7)

Johnson, W., & Bouchard, T. J., Jr. (2005). The structure of human intelligence: It is verbal, perceptual, and image rotation (VPR), not fluid and crystallized. *Intelligence, 33*, 393–416. (9)

Johnson, W., & Bouchard, T. J., Jr. (2007). Sex differences in mental abilities: *g* masks the dimensions on which they lie. *Intelligence, 35*, 23–39. (9)

Johnson, W., Bouchard, T. J., Jr., Krueger, R. F., McGue, M., & Gottesman, I. I. (2004). Just one *g*: Consistent results from three test batteries. *Intelligence, 32*, 95–107. (9)

Johnson, W., Carothers, A., & Deary, I. J. (2008). Sex differences in variability in general intelligence. *Perspectives on Psychological Science, 3*, 518–531. (9)

Johnson, W., te Nijenhuis, J., & Bouchard, T. J., Jr. (2008). Still just 1 *g*: Consistent results from five test batteries. *Intelligence, 36*, 81–95. (9)

Johnson-Laird, P. N., Mancini, F., & Gangemi, A. (2006). A hyper-emotion theory of psychological illnesses. *Psychological Review, 113*, 822–841. (16)

Johnston, J. C., & McClelland, J. L. (1974). Perception of letters in words: Seek not and ye shall find. *Science, 184*, 1192–1194. (8)

Johnston, J. J. (1975). Sticking with first responses on multiple-choice exams: For better or for worse? *Teaching of Psychology, 2*, 178–179. (8)

Johnstone, H. (1994, August 8). Prince of memory says victory was on the cards. *The Times* (London), p. 2. (7)

Joiner, T. E., Jr. (1999). The clustering and contagion of suicide. *Current Directions in Psychological Science, 8*, 89–92. (15)

Joint Committee on Standards for Educational and Psychological Testing of the American Educational Research Association, the American Psychological Association, and the National Council on Measurement in Education. (1999). *Standards for educational and psychological testing.* Washington, DC: American Educational Research Association. (9)

Jokela, M., Elovainio, M., Kivimäki, M., & Keltikangas-Järvinen, L. (2008). Temperament and migration patterns in Finland. *Psychological Science, 19*, 831–837. (14)

Jones, C. M., Braithwaite, V. A., & Healy, S. D. (2003). The evolution of sex differences in spatial ability. *Behavioral Neuroscience, 117*, 403–411. (5)

Jones, E. E., & Goethals, G. R. (1972). Order effects in impression formation: Attribution context and the nature of the entity. In E. Jones, D. Kanouse, H. Kelley, R. Nisbett, S. Valins, & B. Wiener (Eds.), *Attribution: Perceiving the causes of behavior* (pp. 27–46). Morristown, NJ: General Learning Press. (13)

Jones, E. E., & Harris, V. A. (1967). The attribution of attitudes. *Journal of Experimental Social Psychology, 13*, 1–24. (13)

Jones, E. E., & Nisbett, R. E. (1972). The actor and the observer: Divergent perception of the causes of behavior. In E. Jones, D. Kanouse, H. Kelley, R. Nisbett, S. Valins, & B. Wiener (Eds.), *Attribution: Perceiving the causes of behavior* (pp. 79–94). Morristown, NJ: General Learning Press. (13)

Jones, J. T., Pelham, B. W., Carvallo, M., & Mirenberg, M. C. (2004). How do I love thee? Let me count the Js: Implicit egotism and interpersonal attraction. *Journal of Personality and Social Psychology, 87,* 665–683. (1)

Jones, P. B., Barnes, T. R. E., Davies, L., Dunn, G., Lloyd, H., Hayhurst, K. P., et al. (2006). Randomized controlled trial of the effect on quality of life of second- vs. first-generation antipsychotic drugs in schizophrenia. *Archives of General Psychiatry, 63,* 1079–1087. (16)

Jones, S. S., Collins, K., & Hong, H. W. (1991). An audience effect on smile production in 10-month-old infants. *Psychological Science, 2,* 45–49. (12)

Joseph, R. (1988). Dual mental functioning in a split-brain patient. *Journal of Clinical Psychology, 44,* 770–779. (3)

Joseph, R. (2000). Fetal brain behavior and cognitive development. *Developmental Review, 20,* 81–98. (5)

Jouvet, M., Michel, F., & Courjon, J. (1959). Sur un stade d'activité électrique cérébrale rapide au cours du sommeil physiologique [On a state of rapid electrical cerebral activity during physiological sleep]. *Comptes Rendus des Séances de la Société de Biologie, 153,* 1024–1028. (10)

Judge, T. A., & Ilies, R. (2002). Relationship of personality to performance motivation: A meta-analytic review. *Journal of Applied Psychology, 87,* 797–807. (14)

Judge, T. A., & Larsen, R. J. (2001). Dispositional affect and job satisfaction: A review and theoretical extension. *Organizational Behavior and Human Decision Processes, 86,* 67–98. (11)

Judge, T. A., Thoresen, C. J., Bono, J. E., & Patton, G. K. (2001). The job satisfaction–job performance relationship: A qualitative and quantitative review. *Psychological Bulletin, 127,* 376–407. (11)

Juhasz, B. J. (2005). Age-of-acquisition effects in word and picture identification. *Psychological Bulletin, 131,* 684–712. (5)

Jung, C. G. (1965). *Memories, dreams, reflections* (A. Jaffe, Ed.). New York: Random House. (14)

Junginger, J., & Frame, C. L. (1985). Self-report of the frequency and phenomenology of verbal hallucinations. *Journal of Nervous and Mental Disease, 173,* 149–155. (16)

Jusczyk, P. W. (2002). How infants adapt speech-processing capacities to native-language structure. *Current Directions in Psychological Science, 11,* 15–18. (5)

Juslin, P., Winman, A., & Olsson, H. (2000). Naive empiricism and dogmatism in confidence research: A critical examination of the hard–easy effect. *Psychological Review, 107,* 384–396. (8)

Just, M. A., & Carpenter, P. A. (1987). *The psychology of reading and language comprehension.* Boston: Allyn & Bacon. (8)

Kagan, J., Reznick, J. S., & Snidman, N. (1988). Biological bases of childhood shyness. *Science, 240,* 167–171. (5)

Kagan, J., & Snidman, N. (1991). Infant predictors of inhibited and uninhibited profiles. *Psychological Science, 2,* 40–44. (5)

Kahn, A. S., Jackson, J., Kully, C., Badger, K., & Halvorsen, J. (2003). Calling it rape: Differences in experiences of women who do or do not label their sexual assault as rape. *Psychology of Women Quarterly, 27,* 233–242. (12)

Kahneman, D., Krueger, A. B., Schkade, D., Schwarz, N., & Stone, A. A. (2006). Would you be happier if you were richer? A focusing illusion. *Science, 312,* 1908–1910. (12)

Kahneman, D., & Tversky, A. (1973). On the psychology of prediction. *Psychological Review, 80,* 237–251. (8)

Kaiser, C. R., Vick, S. B., & Major, B. (2004). A prospective investigation of the relationship between just-world beliefs and the desire for revenge after September 11, 2001. *Psychological Science, 15,* 503–506. (14)

Kalick, S. M., Zebrowitz, L. A., Langlois, J. H., & Johnson, R. M. (1998). Does human facial attractiveness honestly advertise health? *Psychological Science, 9,* 8–13. (13)

Kalivas, P. W., Volkow, N., & Seamans, J. (2005). Unmanageable motivation in addiction: A pathology in prefrontal-accumbens glutamate transmission. *Neuron, 45,* 647–650. (16)

Kamin, L. J. (1969). Predictability, surprise, attention, and conditioning. In B. A. Campbell & R. M. Church (Eds.), *Punishment and aversive behavior* (pp. 279–296). New York: Appleton-Century-Crofts. (6)

Kaminer, Y. (2000). Contingency management reinforcement procedures for adolescent substance abuse. *Journal of the American Academy of Child and Adolescent Psychiatry, 39,* 1324–1326. (16)

Kanaya, T., Scullin, M. H., & Ceci, S. J. (2003). The Flynn effect and U.S. policies. *American Psychologist, 58,* 778–790. (9)

Kanazawa, S. (2004). General intelligence as a domain-specific adaptation. *Psychological Review, 111,* 512–523. (9)

Kane, M. J., Brown, L. H., McVay, J. C., Silvia, P. J., Myin-Germeys, I., & Kwapil, T. R. (2007). For whom the mind wanders, and when. *Psychological Science, 18,* 614–621. (7)

Kane, M. J., & Engle, R. W. (2000). Working-memory capacity, proactive interference, and divided attention: Limits on long-term memory retrieval. *Journal of Experimental Psychology: Learning, Memory, and Cognition, 26,* 336–358. (7)

Kanizsa, G. (1979). *Organization in vision.* New York: Praeger. (4)

Kanner, A. D., Coyne, J. C., Schaefer, C., & Lazarus, R. S. (1981). Comparison of two modes of stress measurement: Daily hassles and uplifts versus major life events. *Journal of Behavioral Medicine, 4,* 1–39. (12)

Kanwisher, N. (2000). Domain specificity in face perception. *Nature Neuroscience, 3,* 759–763. (4)

Karno, M., Golding, J. M., Sorenson, S. B., & Burnam, A. (1988). The epidemiology of obsessive-compulsive disorder in five U.S. communities. *Archives of General Psychiatry, 45,* 1094–1099. (16)

Kasser, T., & Sharma, Y. S. (1999). Reproductive freedom, educational equality, and females' preference for resource-acquisition characteristics in mates. *Psychological Science, 10,* 374–377. (13)

Kasser, T., & Sheldon, K. M. (2000). Of wealth and death. Materialism, mortality salience, and consumption behavior. *Psychological Science, 11,* 348–351. (5)

Kassin, S. M., & Gudjonsson, G. H. (2004). The psychology of confessions: A review of the literature and issues. *Psychological Science in the Public Interest, 5,* 33–67. (13)

Katz, S., Lautenschlager, G. J., Blackburn, A. B., & Harris, F. H. (1990). Answering reading comprehension items without passages on the SAT. *Psychological Science, 1,* 122–127. (9)

Kauffman, S. A. (2008). *Reinventing the sacred.* New York: Basic Books. (1)

Kaufman, A. S. (2001). WAIS–III IQs, Horn's theory, and generational changes from young adulthood to old age. *Intelligence, 29,* 131–167. (9)

Kaufman, L., & Rock, I. (1989). The moon illusion thirty years later. In M. Hershenson (Ed.), *The moon illusion* (pp. 193–234). Hillsdale, NJ: Erlbaum. (4)

Kawakami, K., Dovidio, J. F., & Dijksterhuis, A. (2003). Effect of social category priming on personal attitudes. *Psychological Science, 14,* 315–319. (13)

Kazdin, A. E. (1995). Methods of psychotherapy research. In B. Bongar & L. E. Beutler (Eds.), *Comprehensive textbook of psychotherapy: Theory and practice* (pp. 405–433). Oxford, England: Oxford University Press. (15)

Ke, X., Tang, T., Hong, S., Hang, Y., Zou, B., Zi, H., et al. (2009). White matter impairments in autism: Evidence from voxel-based morphometry and diffusion tensor imaging. *Brain Research, 1265,* 171–177. (16)

Kee, N., Teixeira, C. M., Wang, A. H., & Frankland, P. W. (2007). Preferential incorporation of adult-generated granule cells into spatial memory networks in the dentate gyrus. *Nature Neuroscience, 10,* 355–362. (3, 7)

Keel, P. K., & Klump, K. L. (2003). Are eating disorders culture-bound syndromes? Implications for conceptualizing their etiology. *Psychological Bulletin, 129,* 747–769. (11)

Keele, S. W., & Ivry, R. B. (1990). Does the cerebellum provide a common computation for diverse tasks? *Annals of the New York Academy of Sciences, 608,* 179–207. (3)

Keizer, K., Lindenberg, S., & Steg, L. (2008). The spreading of disorder. *Science, 322,* 1681–1685. (13)

Keller, M. C. (2008). The evolutionary persistence of genes that increase mental disorders risk. *Current Directions in Psychological Science, 17,* 395–399. (16)

Keller, M. C., Fredrickson, B. L., Ybarra, O., Cote, S., Johnson, K., Mikels, J., et al. (2005). A warm heart and a clear head. *Psychological Science, 16,* 724–731. (2)

Keller, M. C., Thiessen, D., & Young, R. K. (1996). Mate assortment in dating and married couples. *Personality and Individual Differences, 21,* 217–221. (13)

Kelley, H. H. (1967). Attribution theory in social psychology. In D. Levine (Ed.), *Nebraska Symposium on Motivation* (Vol. 15, pp. 192–238). Lincoln: University of Nebraska Press. (13)

Keltner, D., & Buswell, B. N. (1997). Embarrassment: Its distinct form and appeasement functions. *Psychological Bulletin, 122,* 250–270. (12)

Keltner, D., & Shiota, M. N. (2003). New displays and new emotions: A commentary on Rozin and Cohen (2003). *Emotion, 3,* 86–91. (12)

Kendler, K. S., Bulik, C. M., Silberg, J., Hettema, J. M., Myers, J., & Prescott, C. A. (2000). Childhood sexual abuse and adult psychiatric and substance abuse disorders in women. *Archives of General Psychiatry, 57,* 953–959. (16)

Kendler, K. S., Fiske, A., Gardner, C. O., & Gatz, M. (2009). Delineation of two genetic pathways to major depression. *Biological Psychiatry, 65,* 808–811. (16)

Kendler, K. S., Gardner, C. O., & Prescott, C. A. (1999). Clinical characteristics of major depression that predict risk of depression in relatives. *Archives of General Psychiatry, 56,* 322–327. (16)

Kendler, K. S., Gruenberg, A. M., & Tsuang, M. T. (1985). Subtype stability in schizophrenia. *American Journal of Psychiatry, 142,* 827–832. (16)

Kendler, K. S., Hettema, J. M., Butera, F., Gardner, C. O., & Prescott, C. A. (2003). Life event dimensions of loss, humiliation, entrapment, and danger in the prediction of onsets of major depression and generalized anxiety. *Archives of General Psychiatry, 60,* 789–796. (16)

Kendler, K. S., Karkowski, L. M., Neale, M. C., & Prescott, C. A. (2000). Illicit psychoactive substance use, heavy use, abuse, and dependence in a US population-based sample of male twins. *Archives of General Psychiatry, 57,* 261–269. (16)

Kendler, K. S., Myers, J., & Prescott, C. A. (2002). The etiology of phobias. *Archives of General Psychiatry, 59,* 242–248. (16)

Kendler, K. S., Thornton, L. M., Gilman, S. E., & Kessler, R. C. (2000). Sexual orientation in a U.S. sample of twin and nontwin sibling pairs. *American Journal of Psychiatry, 157,* 1843–1846. (11)

Kendler, K. S., Walters, E. E., Neale, M. C., Kessler, R. C., Heath, A. C., & Eaves, L. J. (1995). The structure of the genetic and environmental risk factors for six major psychiatric disorders in women. *Archives of General Psychiatry, 52,* 374–383. (16)

Kenny, P. J., Chen, S. A., Kitamura, O., Markou, A., & Koob, G. F. (2006). Conditioned withdrawal drives heroin consumption and decreases reward sensitivity. *Journal of Neuroscience, 26,* 5894–5900. (16)

Keppel, G., & Underwood, B. J. (1962). Proactive inhibition in short-term retention of single items. *Journal of Verbal Learning and Verbal Behavior, 1,* 153–161. (7)

Kerchner, G. A., & Nicoll, R. A. (2008). Silent synapses and the emergence of a postsynaptic mechanism for LTP. *Nature Reviews Neuroscience, 9,* 813–825. (7)

Kern, R. P., Libkuman, T. M., Otani, H., & Holmes, K. (2005). Emotional stimuli, divided attention, and memory. *Emotion, 5,* 408–417. (12)

Kerns, J. G. (2007). Experimental manipulation of cognitive control processes causes an increase in communication disturbances in healthy volunteers. *Psychological Medicine, 37,* 995–1004. (16)

Kerr, N. L., MacCoun, R. J., & Kramer, G. P. (1996). Bias in judgment: Comparing individuals and groups. *Psychological Review, 103,* 687–719. (13)

Kerr, R., & Booth, B. (1978). Specific and varied practice of motor skill. *Perceptual and Motor Skills, 46,* 395–401. (7)

Kessler, R. C., Berglund, P., Demler, O., Jin, R., & Walters, E. E. (2005). Lifetime prevalence and age-of-onset distributions of *DSM–IV* disorders in the National Comorbidity Survey Replication. *Archives of General Psychiatry, 62,* 593–602. (15, 16)

Kessler, R. C., Chiu, W. T., Demler, O., & Walters, E. E. (2005). Prevalence, severity, and comorbidity of 12-month *DSM–IV* disorders in the National Comorbidity Survey Replication. *Archives of General Psychiatry, 62,* 617–627. (15, 16)

Kety, S. S., Wendler, P. H., Jacobsen, B., Ingraham, L. J., Jansson, L., Faber, B., et al. (1994). Mental illness in the biological and adoptive relatives of schizophrenic adoptees. *Archives of General Psychiatry, 51,* 442–455. (16)

Keyes, C. L. M. (2007). Promoting and protecting mental health as flourishing. *American Psychologist, 62,* 95–108. (14)

Keysar, B., Barr, D. J., & Horton, W. S. (1998). The egocentric basis of language use: Insights from a processing approach. *Current Directions in Psychological Science, 7,* 46–50. (5)

Keysar, B., & Henly, A. S. (2002). Speakers' overestimation of their effectiveness. *Psychological Science, 13,* 207–212. (5)

Khan, U., & Dhar, R. (2007). Where there is a way, is there a will? The effect of future choices on self-control. *Journal of Experimental Psychology: General, 136,* 277–288. (11)

Kiefer, A. K., & Sekaquaptewa, D. (2007). Implicit stereotypes, gender identification, and math-related outcomes. *Psychological Science, 18,* 13–18. (9)

Kim, H., Baydar, N., & Greek, A. (2003). Testing conditions influence the race gap in cognition

and achievement estimated by household survey data. *Journal of Applied Developmental Psychology, 23,* 567–582. (9)

Kim, H. S., Sherman, D. K., & Taylor, S. E. (2008). Culture and social support. *American Psychologist, 63,* 518–526. (12)

Kim, J., & Hatfield, E. (2004). Love types and subjective well-being: A cross-cultural study. *Social Behavior and Personality, 32,* 173–182. (13)

Kim, J. E., & Moen, P. (2001). Is retirement good or bad for subjective well-being? *Current Directions in Psychological Science, 10,* 83–86. (5)

Kim, S. (1989). *Inversions.* San Francisco: W. H. Freeman. (4)

Kim, S., Healey, M. K., Goldstein, D., Hasher, L., & Wiprzycka, U. J. (2008). Age differences in choice satisfaction. *Psychology and Aging, 23,* 33–38. (12)

Kim, Y.-K., Lee, H.-J., Yang, J.-C., Hwang, J.-A., & Yoon, H.-K. (2009). A tryptophan hydroxylase 2 gene polymorphism is associated with panic disorder. *Behavior Genetics, 39,* 170–175. (16)

Kimble, G. A. (1961). *Hilgard and Marquis' conditioning and learning* (2nd ed.). New York: Appleton-Century-Crofts. (6)

Kimble, G. A. (1967). Attitudinal factors in classical conditioning. In G. A. Kimble (Ed.), *Foundations of conditioning and learning* (pp. 642–659). New York: Appleton-Century-Crofts. (1)

Kimble, G. A. (1993). A modest proposal for a minor revolution in the language of psychology. *Psychological Science, 4,* 253–255. (6)

Kimble, G. A., & Garmezy, N. (1968). *Principles of general psychology* (3rd ed.). New York: Ronald Press. (14)

King, M. L., Jr. (1964, November 13). Speech at Duke University, Durham, NC. (5)

King, M., Nazareth, I., Levy, G., Walker, C., Morris, R., Weich, S., et al. (2008). Prevalence of common mental disorders in general practice attendees across Europe. *British Journal of Psychiatry, 192,* 362–367. (16)

King, S. (2000). Is expressed emotion cause or effect in the mothers of schizophrenic young adults? *Schizophrenia Research, 45,* 65–78. (16)

King-Casas, B., Sharp, C., Lomax-Bream, L., Lorenz, T., Fonagy, P., & Montague, P. R. (2008). The rupture and repair of cooperation in borderline personality disorder. *Science, 321,* 806–810. (13)

Kinsey, A. C., Pomeroy, W. B., & Martin, C. E. (1948). *Sexual behavior in the human male.* Philadelphia: Saunders. (11)

Kinsey, A. C., Pomeroy, W. B., Martin, C. E., & Gebhard, P. H. (1953). *Sexual behavior in the human female.* Philadelphia: Saunders. (11)

Kiriakakis, V., Bhatia, K. P., Quinn, N. P., & Marsden, C. D. (1998). The natural history of tardive dyskinesia: A long-term follow-up of 107 cases. *Brain, 121,* 2053–2066. (16)

Kirsch, I., Deacon, B. J., Huedo-Medina, T. B., Scoboria, A., Moore, T. J., & Johnson, B. T. (2008). Initial severity and antidepressant benefits: A meta-analysis of data submitted to the Food and Drug Administration. *PLoS Medicine, 5*(2), e45. (16)

Kirsch, I., & Lynn, S. J. (1998). Dissociation theories of hypnosis. *Psychological Bulletin, 123,* 100–115. (10)

Kirsch, I., & Braffman, W. (2001). Imaginative suggestibility and hypnotizability. *Current Directions in Psychological Science, 10,* 57–61. (10)

Kivimäki, M., Vahtera, J., Elovainio, M., Helenius, H., Singh-Manoux, A., & Pentti, J. (2005). Optimism and pessimism as predictors of change in health after death or onset of severe illness in family. *Health Psychology, 24,* 413–421. (12)

Kleen, J. K., Sitomer, M. T., Killeen, P. R., & Conrad, C. D. (2006). Chronic stress impairs spatial memory and motivation for reward without

disrupting motor ability and motivation to explore. *Behavioral Neuroscience, 120,* 842–851. (12)

Klein, D. F. (1993). False suffocation alarms, spontaneous panics, and related conditions. *Archives of General Psychiatry, 50,* 306–317. (16)

Kleinmuntz, B., & Szucko, J. J. (1984). A field study of the fallibility of polygraphic lie detection. *Nature, 308,* 449–450. (12)

Kleiser, R., Seitz, R. J., & Krekelberg, B. (2004). Neural correlates of saccadic suppression in humans. *Current Biology, 14,* 386–390. (8)

Kleitman, N. (1963). *Sleep and wakefulness* (Rev. and enlarged ed.). Chicago: University of Chicago Press. (10)

Kluger, A. N., & Tikochinsky, J. (2001). The error of accepting the "theoretical" null hypothesis: The rise, fall, and resurrection of commonsense hypotheses in psychology. *Psychological Bulletin, 127,* 408–423. (2)

Kluger, M. J. (1991). Fever: Role of pyrogens and cryogens. *Physiological Reviews, 71,* 93–127. (12)

Kniffin, K. M., & Wilson, D. S. (2004). The effect of nonphysical traits on the perception of physical attractiveness. *Evolution and Human Behavior, 25,* 88–101. (13)

Knight, M., Seymour, T. L., Gaunt, J. T., Baker, C., Nesmith, K., & Mather, M. (2007). Aging and goal-directed emotional attention: Distraction reverses emotional biases. *Emotion, 7,* 705–714. (12)

Knoll, J. L., IV, & Resnick, P. J. (2008). Insanity defense evaluations: Toward a model for evidence-based practice. *Brief Treatment and Crisis Intervention, 8,* 92–110. (15)

Knuttinen, M.-G., Power, J. M., Preston, A. R., & Disterhoft, J. F. (2001). Awareness in classical differential eyeblink conditioning in young and aging humans. *Behavioral Neuroscience, 115,* 747–757. (6)

Kochanska, G., Aksan, N., & Joy, M. E. (2007). Children's fearfulness as a moderator of parenting in early socialization: Two longitudinal studies. *Developmental Psychology, 43,* 222–237. (5)

Kocsis, R. N. (2004). Psychological profiling of serial arson offenses: An assessment of skills and accuracy. *Criminal Justice and Behavior, 31,* 341–361. (14)

Kocsis, R. N., Irwin, H. J., Hayes, A. F., & Nunn, R. (2000). Expertise in psychological profiling: A comparative assessment. *Journal of Interpersonal Violence, 15,* 311–331. (14)

Koepp, M. J., Gunn, R. N., Lawrence, A. D., Cunningham, V. J., Dagher, A., Jones, T., et al. (1998). Evidence for striatal dopamine release during a video game. *Nature, 393,* 266–268. (3, 16)

Kohlberg, L. (1969). Stage and sequence: The cognitive-developmental approach to socialization. In D. A. Goslin (Ed.), *Handbook of socialization theory and research* (pp. 347–480). Chicago: Rand McNally. (13)

Kohlberg, L. (1981). *The meaning and measurement of moral development.* Worcester, MA: Clark University. (13)

Kohlberg, L., & Hersh, R. H. (1977). Moral development: A review of the theory. *Theory into Practice, 16,* 53–59. (13)

Koke, L. C., & Vernon, P. A. (2003). The Sternberg Triarchic Abilities Test (STAT) as a measure of academic achievement and general intelligence. *Personality and Individual Differences, 35,* 1803–1807. (9)

Kontula, O., & Haavio-Mannila, E. (2009). The impact of aging on human sexual activity and sexual desire. *Journal of Sex Research, 46,* 46–56. (11)

Koob, G. F., & LeMoal, M. (1997). Drug abuse: Hedonic homeostatic dysregulation. *Science, 278,* 52–58. (16)

Kopelman, P. G. (2000). Obesity as a medical problem. *Nature, 404,* 635–643. (11)

Koppenaal, R. J. (1963). Time changes in the strengths of A-B, A-C lists: Spontaneous recovery? *Journal of Verbal Learning and Verbal Behavior, 2,* 310–319. (7)

Koriat, A., Bjork, R. A., Sheffer, L., & Bar, S. K. (2004). Predicting one's own forgetting: The role of experience-based and theory-based processes. *Journal of Experimental Psychology: General, 133,* 643–656. (7)

Korman, M., Doyon, J., Doljansky, J., Carrier, J., Dagan, Y., & Karni, A. (2007). Daytime sleep condenses the time course of motor memory consolidation. *Nature Neuroscience, 10,* 1206–1213. (10)

Kornell, N., & Bjork, R. A. (2008). Learning concepts and categories. *Psychological Science, 19,* 585–592. (7)

Kotowicz, Z. (2007). The strange case of Phineas Gage. *History of the Human Sciences, 20,* 115–131. (12)

Koyano, W. (1991). Japanese attitudes toward the elderly: A review of research findings. *Journal of Cross-Cultural Gerontology, 4,* 335–345. (5)

Kozel, N. J., & Adams, E. H. (1986). Epidemiology of drug abuse: An overview. *Science, 234,* 970–974. (3)

Kozlowski, L. T., Frecker, R. C., Khouw, V., & Pope, M. A. (1980). The misuse of "less hazardous" cigarettes and its detection: Hole blocking of ventilated filters. *American Journal of Public Health, 70,* 1202–1203. (16)

Kraemer, D. L., & Hastrup, J. L. (1988). Crying in adults: Self-control and autonomic correlates. *Journal of Social and Clinical Psychology, 6,* 53–68. (12)

Krähenbühl, S., & Blades, M. (2006). The effect of question repetition within interviews on young children's eyewitness recall. *Journal of Experimental Child Psychology, 94,* 57–67. (7)

Krajbich, I., Adolphs, R., Tranel, D., Denburg, N. L., & Camerer, C. F. (2009). Economic games quantify diminished sense of guilt in patients with damage to the prefrontal cortex. *Journal of Neuroscience, 29,* 2188–2192. (12)

Krantz, D. S., Sheps, D. S., Carney, R. M., & Natelson, B. H. (2000). Effects of mental stress in patients with coronary artery disease. *Journal of the American Medical Association, 283,* 1800–1802. (12)

Kraus, M. W., & Keltner, D. (2009). Signs of socioeconomic status. *Psychological Science, 20,* 99–106. (13)

Krebs, D. L. (2000). The evolution of moral dispositions in the human species. *Annals of the New York Academy of Sciences, 907,* 132–148. (13)

Krebs, D. L., & Denton, K. (2005). Toward a more pragmatic approach to morality: A critical evaluation of Kohlberg's model. *Psychological Review, 112,* 629–649. (13)

Kreiner, D. S., Altis, N. A., & Voss, C. W. (2003). A test of the effect of reverse speech on priming. *Journal of Psychology, 137,* 224–232. (4)

Kreitzer, A. C., & Regehr, W. G. (2001). Retrograde inhibition of presynaptic calcium influx by endogenous cannabinoids at excitatory synapses onto Purkinje cells. *Neuron, 29,* 717–727. (3)

Krendl, A. C., Richeson, J. A., Kelley, W. M., & Heatherton, T. F. (2008). The negative consequences of threat. *Psychological Science, 19,* 168–175. (9)

Kreskin. (1991). *Secrets of The Amazing Kreskin.* Buffalo, NY: Prometheus. (2)

Kripke, D. F. (1998). Light treatment for nonseasonal depression: Speed, efficacy, and combined treatment. *Journal of Affective Disorders, 49,* 109–117. (16)

Kripke, D. F., Garfinkel, L., Wingard, D. L., Klauber, M. R., & Marler, M. R. (2002). Mortality associated with sleep duration and insomnia. *Archives of General Psychiatry, 59,* 131–136. (2)

Krishnan, V., & Nestler, E. J. (2008). The molecular neurobiology of depression. *Nature, 455,* 894–902. (16)

Krishnan-Sarin, S., Krystal, J. H., Shi, J., Pittman, B., & O'Malley, S. S. (2007). Family history of alcoholism influences naloxone-induced reduction in alcohol drinking. *Biological Psychiatry, 62,* 694–697. (16)

Krueger, D. W. (1978). The differential diagnosis of proverb interpretation. In W. E. Fann, I. Karacan, A. D. Pokorny, & R. L. Williams (Eds.), *Phenomenology and treatment of schizophrenia* (pp. 193–201). New York: Spectrum. (16)

Krueger, J. M., Rector, D. M., Roy, S., Van Dongen, H. P. A., Belenky, G., & Panksepp, J. (2008). Sleep as a fundamental property of neuronal assemblies. *Nature Reviews Neuroscience, 9,* 910–919. (10)

Krueger, R. F., Markon, K. E., & Bouchard, T. J., Jr. (2003). The extended genotype: The heritability of personality accounts for the heritability of recalled family environments in twins reared apart. *Journal of Personality, 71,* 809–833. (5)

Kruger, J., Wirtz, D., & Miller, D. T. (2005). Counterfactual thinking and the first instinct fallacy. *Journal of Personality and Social Psychology, 88,* 725–735. (8)

Krüger, S., Alda, M., Young, L. T., Goldapple, K., Parikh, S., & Mayberg, H. S. (2006). Risk and resilience markers in bipolar disorder: Brain responses to emotional challenge in bipolar patients and their healthy siblings. *American Journal of Psychiatry, 163,* 257–264. (16)

Krupa, D. J., Thompson, J. K., & Thompson, R. F. (1993). Localization of a memory trace in the mammalian brain. *Science, 260,* 989–991. (3)

Kübler-Ross, E. (1975). *Death: The final stage of growth.* Englewood Cliffs, NJ: Prentice Hall. (5)

Kuhl, P. K., Andruski, J. E., Chistovich, I. A., Chistovich, L. A., Kozhevnikova, E. V., Ryskina, V. L., et al. (1997). Cross-language analysis of phonetic units in language addressed to infants. *Science, 277,* 684–686. (8)

Kuhlmann, S., Piel, M., & Wolf, O. T. (2005). Impaired memory retrieval after psychosocial stress in healthy young men. *Journal of Neuroscience, 25,* 2977–2982. (12)

Kuhn, D., & Lao, J. (1996). Effects of evidence on attitudes: Is polarization the norm? *Psychological Science, 7,* 115–120. (13)

Kumaran, D., & Maguire, E. A. (2005). The human hippocampus: Cognitive maps or relational memory? *Journal of Neuroscience, 25,* 7254–7259. (10)

Kumkale, G. T., & Albarracín, D. (2004). The sleeper effect in persuasion: A meta-analytic review. *Psychological Bulletin, 130,* 143–172. (13)

Kunar, M. A., Carter, R., Cohen, M., & Horowitz, T. S. (2008). Telephone conversation impairs sustained visual attention via a central bottleneck. *Psychonomic Bulletin and Review, 15,* 1135–1140. (8)

Kupfer, D. J., First, M. B., & Regier, D. A. (2002). *A research agenda for DSM–V.* Washington, DC: American Psychiatric Association. (15)

Kurihara, K., & Kashiwayanagi, M. (1998). Introductory remarks on umami taste. *Annals of the New York Academy of Sciences, 855,* 393–397. (4)

Kuroshima, H., Kuwahata, H., & Fujita, K. (2008). Learning from others' mistakes in capuchin monkeys (*Cebus apella*). *Animal Cognition, 11,* 611–623. (6)

Kutchins, H., & Kirk, S. A. (1997). *Making us crazy.* New York: Free Press. (15)

La Grand, R., Mondloch, C. J., Maurer, D., & Brent, H. P. (2004). Impairment in holistic face processing following early visual displacement. *Psychological Science, 15,* 762–768. (4)

La Roche, M., & Christopher, M. S. (2008). Culture and empirically supported treatments: On the road to a collision? *Culture and Psychology, 14,* 333–356. (15)

LaBar, K. S., & Phelps, E. A. (1998). Arousal-mediated memory consolidation: Role of the medial temporal lobe in humans. *Psychological Science, 9,* 490–493. (12)

Labouvie-Vief, G., Diehl, M., Tarnowski, A., & Shen, J. (2000). Age differences in adult personality: Findings from the United States and China. *Journal of Gerontology: Psychological Sciences, 55B,* P4–P17. (14)

Labroo, A. A., & Kim, S. (2009). The "instrumentality" heuristic. *Psychological Science, 20,* 127–134. (11)

Lackner, J. R. (1993). Orientation and movement in unusual force environments. *Psychological Science, 4,* 134–142. (4)

Laeng, B., Svartdal, F., & Oelmann, H. (2004). Does color synesthesia pose a paradox for early-selection theories of attention? *Psychological Science, 15,* 277–281. (4)

Laffaye, C., McKellar, J. D., Ilgen, M. A., & Moos, R. H. (2008). Predictors of 4-year outcome of community residential treatment for patients with substance use disorders. *Addiction, 103,* 671–680. (16)

Lahti, T. A., Leppämäki, S., Ojanen, S.-M., Haukka, J., Tuulio-Henriksson, A., Lönnqvist, J., et al. (2006). Transition into daylight saving time influences the fragmentation of the rest–activity cycle. *Journal of Circadian Rhythms, 4,* 1. (10)

Lai, C. S. L., Fisher, S. E., Hurst, J. A., Vargha-Khadem, F., & Monaco, A. P. (2001). A forkhead-domain gene is mutated in a severe speech and language disorder. *Nature, 413,* 519–523. (8)

Lake, R. I. E., Eaves, L. J., Maes, H. H. M., Heath, A. C., & Martin, N. G. (2000). Further evidence against the environmental transmission of individual differences in neuroticism from a collaborative study of 45,850 twins and relatives on two continents. *Behavior Genetics, 30,* 223–233. (5, 14)

Lam, K. S. L., Aman, M. G., & Arnold, L. E. (2006). Neurochemical correlates of autistic disorder: A review of the literature. *Research in Developmental Disabilities, 27,* 254–289. (16)

Lamb, M. E., Orbach, Y., Hershkowitz, I., Horowitz, D., & Abbott, C. B. (2007). Does the type of prompt affect the accuracy of information provided by alleged victims of abuse in forensic interviews? *Applied Cognitive Psychology, 21,* 1117–1130. (7)

Lambie, J. A., & Marcel, A. J. (2002). Consciousness and the varieties of emotion experience: A theoretical framework. *Psychological Review, 109,* 219–259. (12)

Lamm, H., & Myers, D. G. (1978). Group-induced polarization of attitudes and behavior. *Advances in Experimental Social Psychology, 11,* 145–195. (13)

Land, E. H., Hubel, D. H., Livingstone, M. S., Perry, S. H., & Burns, M. M. (1983). Colour-generating interactions across the corpus callosum. *Nature, 303,* 616–618. (4)

Land, E. H., & McCann, J. J. (1971). Lightness and retinex theory. *Journal of the Optical Society of America, 61,* 1–11. (4)

Lang, A. J., Craske, M. G., Brown, M., & Ghaneian, A. (2001). Fear-related state dependent memory. *Cognition, 15,* 695–703. (7)

Lang, P. J. (1994). The varieties of emotional experience: A meditation on James-Lange theory. *Psychological Review, 101,* 211–221. (12)

Langer, E. J. (1975). The illusion of control. *Journal of Personality and Social Psychology, 32,* 311–328. (5)

Langlois, J. H., & Roggman, L. A. (1990). Attractive faces are only average. *Psychological Science, 1,* 115–121. (13)

Langlois, J. H., Roggman, L. A., & Musselman, L. (1994). What is average and what is not average about average faces? *Psychological Science, 5,* 214–220. (13)

Langworthy, R. A., & Jennings, J. W. (1972). Oddball, abstract olfactory learning in laboratory rats. *Psychological Record, 22,* 487–490. (1)

Lansford, J. E., Malone, P. S., Castellino, D. R., Dodge, K. A., Pettit, G. S., & Bates, J. E. (2006). Trajectories of internalizing, externalizing, and grades for children who have and have not experienced their parents' divorce or separation. *Journal of Family Psychology, 20,* 292–301. (5)

Lappe, C., Herholz, S. C., Trainor, L. J., & Pantev, C. (2008). Cortical plasticity induced by short-term unimodal and multimodal musical training. *Journal of Neuroscience, 28,* 9632–9639. (3)

Larkin, G. R. S., Gibbs, S. E. B., Khanna, K., Nielsen, L., Carstensen, L. L., & Knutson, B. (2007). Anticipation of monetary gain but not loss in healthy older adults. *Nature Neuroscience, 10,* 787–791. (12)

Larkina, M., Güler, O. E., Kleinknecht, E., & Bauer, P. J. (2008). Maternal provision of structure in a deliberate memory task in relation to their preschool children's recall. *Journal of Experimental Child Psychology, 100,* 235–251. (5)

Larsen, L., Hartmann, P., & Nyborg, H. (2008). The stability of general intelligence from early adulthood to middle age. *Intelligence, 36,* 29–34. (9)

Larsen, R. J., Kasimatis, M., & Frey, K. (1992). Facilitating the furrowed brow—An unobtrusive test of the facial feedback hypothesis applied to unpleasant affect. *Cognition and Emotion, 6,* 321–338. (12)

Larson, R. W. (2001). How U.S. children and adolescents spend time: What it does (and doesn't) tell us about their development. *Current Directions in Psychological Science, 10,* 160–164. (5)

Larzelere, R. E., & Kuhn, B. R. (2005). Comparing child outcomes of physical punishment and alternative disciplinary tactics: A meta-analysis. *Clinical Child and Family Psychology Review, 8,* 1–37. (6)

Larzelere, R. E., Kuhn, B. R., & Johnson, B. (2004). The intervention selection bias: An underrecognized confound in intervention research. *Psychological Bulletin, 120,* 289–303. (2)

Lashley, K. (1923). The behavioristic interpretation of consciousness. *Psychological Bulletin, 30,* 237–272, 329–353. (10)

Lashley, K. S. (1951). The problem of serial order in behavior. In L. A. Jeffress (Ed.), *Cerebral mechanisms in behavior* (pp. 112–146). New York: Wiley. (8)

Lassek, W. D., & Gaulin, S. J. C. (2008). Waist-hip ratio and cognitive ability: Is gluteofemoral fat a privileged store of neurodevelopmental processes? *Evolution and Human Behavior, 29,* 26–34. (13)

Lassiter, G. D., Geers, A. L., Munhall, P. J., Ploutz-Snyder, R. J., & Breitenbecher, D. L. (2002). Illusory causation: Why it occurs. *Psychological Science, 13,* 299–305. (13)

Latané, B., & Darley, J. M. (1968). Group inhibition of bystander intervention in emergencies. *Journal of Personality and Social Psychology, 10,* 215–221. (13)

Latané, B., & Darley, J. M. (1969). Bystander "apathy." *American Scientist, 57,* 244–268. (13)

Latané, B., Williams, K., & Harkins, S. (1979). Many hands make light the work: The causes and consequences of social loafing. *Journal of Personality and Social Psychology, 37,* 823–832. (13)

Latner, J. D. (2003). Macronutrient effects on satiety and binge eating in bulimia nervosa and binge eating disorder. *Appetite, 40,* 309–311. (11)

Lau, H. C., Rogers, R. D., Haggard, P., & Passingham, R. E. (2004). Attention to intention. *Science, 303,* 1208–1210. (10)

Lau, H. C., Rogers, R. D., & Passingham, R. E. (2006). On measuring the perceived onsets of spontaneous actions. *Journal of Neuroscience, 26,* 7265–7271. (10)

Laugerette, F., Gaillard, D., Passilly-Degrace, P., Niot, I., & Besnard, P. (2007). Do we taste fat? *Biochimie, 89,* 265–269. (4)

Laumann, E. O. (1969). Friends of urban men: An assessment of accuracy in reporting their socio-economic attributes, mutual choice, and attitude development. *Sociometry, 32,* 54–69. (13)

Laumann, E. O., Gagnon, J. H., Michael, R. T., & Michaels, S. (1994). *The social organization of sexuality: Sexual practices in the United States.* Chicago: University of Chicago Press. (11)

Laumann, E. O., Nicolosi, A., Glasser, D. B., Paik, A., Buvat, J., Gingell, C., et al. for the GSSAB Investigators' Group. (2003). *Prevalence of sexual problems among men and women aged 40 to 80 years: Results of an international survey.* Paper presented at the second international consultation on erectile and sexual dysfunctions, Paris.

Laumann, E. O., Paik, A., Glasser, D. B., Kang, J.-H., Wang, T., Levinson, B., et al. (2006). A cross-national study of subjective sexual well-being among older women and men: Findings from the global study of sexual attitudes and behaviors. *Archives of Sexual Behavior, 35,* 145–161. (11)

Laursen, B., Coy, K. C., & Collins, W. A. (1998). Reconsidering changes in parent-child conflict across adolescence: A meta-analysis. *Child Development, 69,* 817–832. (5)

Laws, G., Byrne, A., & Buckley, S. (2000). Language and memory development in children with Down syndrome at mainstream schools and special schools: A comparison. *Educational Psychology, 20,* 447–457. (9)

Lawson, T. T. (2008). *Carl Jung, Darwin of the mind.* London: Karnac. (14)

Lázaro, L., Caldú, X., Junqué, C., Bargalló, N., Andrés, S., Morer, A., et al. (2008). Cerebral activation in children and adolescents with obsessive-compulsive disorder before and after treatment: A functional MRI study. *Journal of Psychiatric Research, 42,* 1051–1059. (16)

Lazarus, R. S. (1977). Cognitive and coping processes in emotion. In A. Monat & R. S. Lazarus (Eds.), *Stress and coping* (pp. 145–158). New York: Columbia University Press. (12)

Lazarus, R. S., Averill, J. R., & Opton, E. M., Jr. (1970). Towards a cognitive theory of emotion. In M. B. Arnold (Ed.), *Feelings and emotions* (pp. 207–232). New York: Academic Press. (12)

Lea, A. J., Barrera, J. P., Tom, L. M., & Blumstein, D. T. (2008). Heterospecific eavesdropping in a nonsocial species. *Behavioral Ecology, 19,* 1041–1046. (6)

Lee, J.-M., Chen, S.-H., & Hsieh, C.-J. (2008). Does perceived safety of light cigarettes encourage smokers to smoke more or to inhale more deeply? *International Journal of Public Health, 53,* 236–244. (11)

Lee, L., Loewenstein, G., Ariely, D., Hong, J., & Young, J. (2008). If I'm not hot, are you hot or not? *Psychological Science, 19,* 669–677. (13)

Lee, M. G., Hassani, O. K., & Jones, B. E. (2005). Discharge of identified orexin/hypocretin neurons across the sleep–waking cycle. *Journal of Neuroscience, 25,* 6716–6720. (10)

Lee, R. A., Su, J., & Yoshida, E. (2005). Coping with intergenerational family conflict among Asian American college students. *Journal of Counseling Psychology, 52,* 389–399. (5)

Lee, S.-H., Blake, R., & Heeger, D. J. (2005). Traveling waves of activity in primary visual cortex during binocular rivalry. *Nature Neuroscience, 8,* 22–23. (10)

Lee, Y. T., & Duenas, G. (1995). Stereotype accuracy in multicultural business. In Y. T. Lee, L. J. Jussim, & C. R. McCauley (Eds.), *Stereotype accuracy* (pp. 157–186). Washington, DC: American Psychological Association. (13)

Leff, J. (2002). The psychiatric revolution: Care in the community. *Nature Reviews Neuroscience, 3,* 821–824. (15)

Leff, J., Wig, N. N., Ghosh, A., Bedi, H., Menon, D. K., Kuipers, L., et al. (1987). Expressed emotion and schizophrenia in North India: III. Influence of relatives' expressed emotion on the course of schizophrenia in Changigarh. *British Journal of Psychiatry, 151,* 166–173. (16)

Legge, G. E., Ahn, S. J., Klitz, T. S., & Luebker, A. (1997). Psychophysics of reading: XVI. The visual span in normal and low vision. *Vision Research, 37,* 1999–2010. (8)

Leichsenring, F., & Leibing, E. (2003). The effectiveness of psychodynamic therapy and cognitive behavior therapy in the treatment of personality disorders: A meta-analysis. *American Journal of Psychiatry, 160,* 1223–1232. (15)

Leinders-Zufall, T., Lane, A. P., Puche, A. C., Ma, W., Novotny, M. V., Shipley, M. T., et al. (2000). Ultrasensitive pheromone detection by mammalian vomeronasal neurons. *Nature, 405,* 792–796. (4)

Lekeu, F., Wojtasik, V., Van der Linden, M., & Salmon, E. (2002). Training early Alzheimer patients to use a mobile phone. *Acta Neurologica Belgica, 102,* 114–121. (7)

LeMagnen, J. (1981). The metabolic basis of dual periodicity of feeding in rats. *Behavioral and Brain Sciences, 4,* 561–607. (11)

Lenneberg, E. H. (1967). *Biological foundations of language.* New York: Wiley. (8)

Lenneberg, E. H. (1969). On explaining language. *Science, 164,* 635–643. (8)

Lenton, A. P., Fasolo, B., & Todd, P. M. (2008). "Shopping" for a mate: Expected versus experienced preferences in online mate choice. *IEEE Transactions on Professional Communication, 51,* 169–182. (8)

Lenzenweger, M. F., Johnson, M. D., & Willett, J. B. (2004). Individual growth curve analysis illuminates stability and change in personality disorder features. *Archives of General Psychiatry, 61,* 1015–1024. (15)

Leonard, L. B. (2007). Processing limitations and the grammatical profile of children with specific language impairment. In R. V. Kail (Ed.), *Advances in child development and behavior* (Vol. 35, pp. 139–171). Oxford, England: Elsevier. (8)

Leppämäki, S., Partonen, T., & Lönnqvist, J. (2002). Bright-light exposure combined with physical exercise elevates mood. *Journal of Affective Disorders, 72,* 139–144. (16)

Leppänen, J. M., & Hietanen, J. K. (2003). Affect and face perception: Odors modulate the recognition advantage of happy faces. *Emotion, 3,* 315–326. (12)

Lerner, M. J. (1980). *The belief in a just world: A fundamental delusion.* New York: Plenum Press. (14)

Lesko, A. C., & Corpus, J. H. (2006). Discounting the difficult: How high math-identified women respond to stereotype threat. *Sex Roles, 54,* 113–125. (9)

Lett, B. T., Grant, V. L., Koh, M. T., & Smith, J. F. (2001). Wheel running simultaneously produces conditioned taste aversion and conditioned place preference in rats. *Learning and Motivation, 32,* 129–136. (6)

Leuchtenberg, W. E. (1963). *Franklin D. Roosevelt and the New Deal 1932–1940.* New York: Harper & Row. (13)

Levav, J., & Fitzsimons, G. J. (2006). When questions change behavior. *Psychological Science, 17,* 207–213. (11)

LeVay, S. (1991). A difference in hypothalamic structure between heterosexual and homosexual men. *Science, 253,* 1034–1037. (11)

Levenson, R. W., & Miller, B. L. (2007). Loss of cells—Loss of self. *Current Directions in Psychological Science, 16,* 289–294. (12)

Levenson, R. W., Oyama, O. N., & Meek, P. S. (1987). Greater reinforcement from alcohol for those at risk: Parental risk, personality risk, and sex. *Journal of Abnormal Psychology, 96,* 242–253. (16)

Leventhal, H. (1970). Findings and theory in the study of fear communication. In L. Berkowitz (Ed.), *Advances in experimental social psychology* (Vol. 5, pp. 119–186). New York: Academic Press. (13)

Levine, J. A., Lanningham-Foster, L. M., McCrady, S. K., Krizan, A. C., Olson, L. R., Kane, P. H., et al. (2005). Interindividual variation in posture allocation: Possible role in human obesity. *Science, 307,* 584–586. (11)

Levine, L. J., & Pizarro, D. A. (2004). Emotion and memory research: A grumpy overview. *Social Cognition, 5,* 530–554. (12)

Levine, R. V. (1990). The pace of life. *American Scientist, 78,* 450–459. (12)

Levine, S. C., Vasilyeva, M., Lourenco, S. F., Newcombe, N. S., & Huttenlocher, J. (2005). Socioeconomic status modifies the sex difference in spatial skill. *Psychological Science, 16,* 841–845. (5)

Levinson, D. J. (1986). A conception of adult development. *American Psychologist, 41,* 3–13. (5)

Levy, B. J., McVeigh, N. D., Marful, A., & Anderson, M. C. (2007). Inhibiting your native language. *Psychological Science, 18,* 29–34. (8)

Levy, J., Pashler, H., & Boer, E. (2006). Central interference in driving. *Psychological Science, 17,* 228–235. (8)

Leweke, F. M., Gerth, C. W., Koethe, D., Klosterkötter, J., Ruslanova, I., Krivogorsky, B., et al. (2004). Antibodies to infectious agents in individuals with recent onset schizophrenia. *European Archives of Psychiatry and Clinical Neuroscience, 254,* 4–8. (16)

Lewis, D. A., & Gonzalez-Burgos, G. (2006). Pathophysiologically based treatment interventions in schizophrenia. *Nature Medicine, 12,* 1016–1022. (16)

Lewis, D. O., Moy, E., Jackson, L. D., Aaronson, R., Restifo, N., Serra, S., et al. (1985). Biopsychosocial characteristics of children who later murder: A prospective study. *American Journal of Psychiatry, 142,* 1161–1167. (12)

Lewis, M. (1995). Self-conscious emotions. *American Scientist, 83,* 68–78. (12)

Lewis, M., Sullivan, M. W., Stanger, C., & Weiss, M. (1991). Self development and self-conscious emotions. In S. Chess & M. E. Hertzig (Eds.), *Annual progress in child psychiatry and child development 1990* (pp. 34–51). New York: Brunner/Mazel. (5)

Leyfer, O. T., Folstein, S. E., Bacalman, S., Davis, N. O., Dinh, E., Morgan, J., et al. (2006). Comorbid psychiatric disorders in children with autism: Interview development and rates of disorders. *Journal of Autism and Developmental Disorders, 36,* 849–861. (16)

Li, M. D., & Burmeister, M. (2009). New insights into the genetics of addiction. *Nature Reviews Neuroscience, 10,* 225–231. (16)

Li, W., Howard, J. D., Parrish, T. B., & Gottfried, J. A. (2008). Aversive learning enhances perceptual and cortical discrimination of indiscriminable odor cues. *Science, 319,* 1842–1845. (6)

Libet, B., Gleason, C. A., Wright, E. W., & Pearl, D. K. (1983). Time of conscious intention to act in relation to onset of cerebral activities (readiness potential): The unconscious initiation of a freely voluntary act. *Brain, 106,* 623–642. (10)

Lickliter, R., & Bahrick, L. E. (2000). The development of infant intersensory perception: Advantages of a comparative convergent-operations approach. *Psychological Bulletin, 126,* 260–280. (3)

Liddle, H. A., Dakof, G. A., Turner, R. M., Henderson, C. E., & Greenbaum, P. E. (2008). Treating adolescent drug abuse: A randomized trial comparing multidimensional family therapy and cognitive behavior therapy. *Addiction, 103,* 1660–1670. (16)

Liebman, M., Pelican, S., Moore, S. A., Holmes, B., Wardlaw, M. K., Melcher, L. M., et al. (2006). Dietary intake-, eating behavior-, and physical activity-related determinants of high body mass index in the 2003 Wellness IN the Rockies cross-sectional study. *Nutrition Research, 26,* 111–117. (11)

Lien, M.-C., Ruthruff, E., & Johnston, J. C. (2006). Attentional limitations in doing two tasks at once. *Current Directions in Psychological Science, 15,* 89–93. (8)

Lilie, J. K., & Rosenberg, R. P. (1990). Behavioral treatment of insomnia. *Progress in Behavior Modification, 25,* 152–177. (10)

Lilienfeld, S. O. (2007). Psychological treatments that cause harm. *Perspectives on Psychological Science, 2,* 53–70. (12, 15)

Lilienfeld, S. O., Lynn, S. J., Kirsch, I., Chaves, J. F., Sarbin, T. R., Ganaway, G. K., et al. (1999). Dissociative identity disorder and the sociocognitive model: Recalling the lessons of the past. *Psychological Bulletin, 125,* 507–523. (15)

Lilienfeld, S. O., Wood, J. M., & Garb, H. N. (2000). The scientific status of projective tests. *Psychological Science in the Public Interest, 1,* 27–66. (14)

Lillberg, K., Verkasalo, P. K., Kaprio, J., Teppo, L., Helenius, H., & Koskenvuo, M. (2003). Stressful life events and risk of breast cancer in 10,808 women: A cohort study. *American Journal of Epidemiology, 157,* 415–423. (12)

Lim, M. M., Wang, Z., Olazábal, D. E., Ren, X., Terwilliger, E. F., & Young, L. J. (2004). Enhanced partner preference in a promiscuous species by manipulating the expression of a single gene. *Nature, 429,* 754–757. (5)

Lin, L., Faraco, J., Li, R., Kadotani, H., Rogers, W., Lin, X., et al. (1999). The sleep disorder canine narcolepsy is caused by a mutation in the hypocretin (orexin) receptor 2 gene. *Cell, 98,* 365–376. (10)

Lincoln, G. A., Clarke, I. J., Hut, R. A., & Hazlerigg, D. G. (2006). Characterizing a mammalian circadian pacemaker. *Science, 314,* 1941–1944. (10)

Lindberg, L., & Hjern, A. (2003). Risk factors for anorexia nervosa: A national cohort study. *International Journal of Eating Disorders, 34,* 397–408. (11)

Linden, W., Lenz, J. W., & Con, A. H. (2001). Individualized stress management for primary hypertension: A randomized trial. *Archives of Internal Medicine, 161,* 1071–1080. (12)

Lindsay, D. S., Hagen, L., Read, J. D., Wade, K. A., & Garry, M. (2004). True photographs and false memories. *Psychological Science, 15,* 149–154. (7)

Lindsay, D. S., & Read, J. D. (1994). Psychotherapy and memories of childhood sexual abuse: A cognitive perspective. *Applied Cognitive Psychology, 8,* 281–338. (7)

Linn, R., & Gilligan, C. (1990). One action, two moral orientations—The tension between justice and care voices in Israeli selective conscientious objectors. *New Ideas in Psychology, 8,* 189–203. (13)

Lipkus, I. (1991). The construction and preliminary validation of a global Belief in a Just World scale and the exploratory analysis of the multidimensional Belief in a Just World scale. *Personality and Individual Differences, 12,* 1171–1178. (14)

Lipsey, M. W., & Wilson, D. B. (1993). The efficacy of psychological, educational, and behavioral treatment. *American Psychologist, 48,* 1181–1209. (15)

Lipton, P. (2005). Testing hypotheses: Prediction and prejudice. *Science, 307,* 219–221. (2)

Lisanby, S. H., Maddox, J. H., Prudic, J., Devanand, D. P., & Sackeim, H. A. (2000). The effects of electroconvulsive therapy on memory of autobiographical and public events. *Archives of General Psychiatry, 57,* 581–590. (16)

Liu, Q., Pu, L., & Poo, M. (2005). Repeated cocaine exposure *in vivo* facilitates LTP induction in midbrain dopamine neurons. *Nature, 437,* 1027–1031. (16)

LoBue, V., & DeLoache, J. S. (2008). Detecting the snake in the grass. *Psychological Science, 19,* 284–289. (16)

Locke, E. A., & Latham, G. P. (2002). Building a practically useful theory of goal setting and task motivation. *American Psychologist, 57,* 705–717. (11)

Locke, J. L. (1994). Phases in the child's development of language. *American Scientist, 82,* 436–445. (8)

Locke, K. D. (2009). Aggression, narcissism, self-esteem, and the attribution of desirable and humanizing traits to self versus others. *Journal of Research in Personality, 43,* 99–102. (14)

Loeb, J. (1973). *Forced movements, tropisms, and animal conduct.* New York: Dover. (Original work published 1918) (6)

Loeber, S., Croissant, B., Heinz, A., Mann, K., & Flor, H. (2006). Cue exposure in the treatment of alcohol dependence: Effects on drinking outcome, craving and self-efficacy. *British Journal of Clinical Psychology, 45,* 515–529. (6)

Loehlin, J. C. (1992). *Genes and environment in personality development.* Newbury Park, CA: Sage. (5, 14)

Loehlin, J. C., Horn, J. M., & Willerman, L. (1989). Modeling IQ change: Evidence from the Texas adoption project. *Child Development, 60,* 993–1004. (9)

Loewenstein, G. (1987). Anticipation and the valuation of delayed consumption. *The Economic Journal, 97,* 666–684. (11)

Loewi, O. (1960). An autobiographic sketch. *Perspectives in Biology, 4,* 3–25. (3)

Loftus, E. (2003). Our changeable memories: Legal and practical implications. *Nature Reviews Neuroscience, 4,* 231–234. (7)

Loftus, E. F. (1975). Leading questions and the eyewitness report. *Cognitive Psychology, 7,* 560–572. (7)

Loftus, E. F. (1993). The reality of repressed memories. *American Psychologist, 48,* 518–537. (7)

Loftus, E. F., Feldman, J., & Dashiell, R. (1995). The reality of illusory memories. In D. L. Schacter (Ed.), *Memory distortion* (pp. 47–68). Cambridge, MA: Harvard University Press. (7)

636

Loftus, G. R. (1996). Psychology will be a much better science when we change the way we analyze data. *Current Directions in Psychological Science, 5,* 161–171. (2)

Logothetis, N. K. (2008). What we can do and what we cannot do with fMRI. *Nature, 453,* 869–878. (3)

Long, G. M., & Toppine, T. C. (2004). Enduring interest in perceptual ambiguity: Alternating views of reversible figures. *Psychological Bulletin, 130,* 748–768. (4)

Longstreth, L. E. (1981). Revisiting Skeels' final study: A critique. *Developmental Psychology, 17,* 620–625. (9)

Lopes, P. N., Brackett, M. A., Nezlak, J. B., Schütz, A., Sellin, I., & Salovey, P. (2004). Emotional intelligence and social interaction. *Personality and Social Psychology Bulletin, 30,* 1018–1034. (12)

Lord, C. G., & Lepper, M. R. (1999). Attitude representation theory. *Advances in Experimental Social Psychology, 31,* 265–343. (13)

Lotto, R. B., & Purves, D. (2002). The empirical basis of color perception. *Consciousness and Cognition, 11,* 609–629. (4)

Lotze, M., Grodd, W., Birbaumer, N., Erb, M., Huse, E., & Flor, H. (1999). Does use of a myoelectric prosthesis prevent cortical reorganization and phantom limb pain? *Nature Neuroscience, 2,* 501–502. (4)

Lovallo, D., & Kahneman, D. (2000). Living with uncertainty: Attractiveness and resolution timing. *Journal of Behavioral Decision Making, 13,* 179–190. (11)

Löw, A., Lang, P. J., Smith, J. C., & Bradley, M. M. (2008). Both predator and prey. *Psychological Science, 19,* 865–873. (12)

Low, K. S. D., Yoon, M. J., Roberts, B. W., & Rounds, J. (2005). The stability of vocational interests from early adolescence to middle adulthood: A quantitative review of longitudinal studies. *Psychological Bulletin, 131,* 713–737. (5)

Lowe, K. B., Kroeck, K. G., & Sivasubramaniam, N. (1996). Effectiveness correlates of transformational and transactional leadership: A meta-analytic review of the MLQ literature. *Leadership Quarterly, 7,* 385–425. (11)

Lubman, D. I., Yücell, M., Kettle, J. W. L., Scaffidi, A., Mackenzie, T., Simmons, J. G., et al. (2009). Responsiveness to drug cues and natural rewards in opiate addiction. *Archives of General Psychiatry, 66,* 205–213. (16)

Luborsky, L., & Barrett, M. S. (2006). The history and empirical status of key psychoanalytic concepts. *Annual Review of Clinical Psychology, 2,* 1–19. (14)

Lucas, R. E. (2005). Time does not heal all wounds. *Psychological Science, 16,* 945–950. (12)

Lucas, R. E. (2007). Long-term disability is associated with lasting changes in subjective well-being: Evidence from two nationally representative longitudinal studies. *Journal of Personality and Social Psychology, 92,* 717–730. (12)

Lucas, R. E., Clark, A. E., Georgellis, Y., & Diener, E. (2004). Unemployment alters the set point for life satisfaction. *Psychological Science, 15,* 8–13. (12)

Lucas, R. E., Le, K., & Dyrenforth, P. S. (2008). Explaining the extraversion/positive affect relation: Sociability cannot account for extraverts' greater happiness. *Journal of Personality, 76,* 385–414. (14)

Lucas, R. E., & Schimmack, U. (2009). Income and well-being: How big is the gap between the rich and the poor? *Journal of Research in Personality, 43,* 75–78. (12)

Luciano, M., Wright, M. J., Smith, G. A., Geffen, G. M., Geffen, L. B., & Martin, N. G. (2001). Genetic covariance among measures of information processing speed, working memory, and IQ. *Behavior Genetics, 31,* 581–592. (9)

Lucio, E., Ampudia, A., Durán, C., León, I., & Butcher, J. N. (2001). Comparison of the Mexican and American norms of the MMPI–2. *Journal of Clinical Psychology, 57,* 1459–1468. (14)

Luck, S. J., & Vogel, E. K. (1997). The capacity of visual working memory for features and conjunctions. *Nature, 390,* 279–281. (7)

Lui, S., Deng, W., Huang, X., Jiang, L., Ma, X., Chen, H., et al. (2009). Association of cerebral deficits with clinical symptoms in antipsychotic-naïve first-episode schizophrenia: An optimized voxel-based morphometry and resting state functional connectivity study. *American Journal of Psychiatry, 166,* 196–205. (16)

Luthar, S. S., Cicchetti, D., & Becker, B. (2000). The construct of resilience: A critical evaluation and guidelines for future work. *Child Development, 71,* 543–562. (5)

Lyamin, O. I., Kosenko, P. O., Lapierre, J. L., Mukhametov, L. M., & Siegel, J. M. (2008). Fur seals display a strong drive for bilateral slow-wave sleep while on land. *Journal of Neuroscience, 28,* 12614–12621. (10)

Lyamin, O. I., Mukhametov, L. M., Siegel, J. M., Nazarenko, E. A., Polyakova, I. G., & Shpak, O. V. (2002). Unihemispheric slow wave sleep and the state of the eyes in a white whale. *Behavioural Brain Research, 129,* 125–129. (10)

Lyamin, O., Pryaslova, J., Lance, V., & Siegel, J. (2005). Continuous activity in cetaceans after birth. *Nature, 435,* 1177. (10)

Lykken, D. T. (1979). The detection of deception. *Psychological Bulletin, 86,* 47–53. (12)

Lykken, D. T., Bouchard, T. J., Jr., McGue, M., & Tellegen, A. (1993). Heritability of interests: A twin study. *Journal of Applied Psychology, 78,* 649–661. (5)

Lykken, D. T., McGue, M., Tellegen, A., & Bouchard, T. J. (1992). Emergenesis: Genetic traits that may not run in families. *American Psychologist, 47,* 1565–1577. (5)

Lykken, D., & Tellegen, A. (1996). Happiness is a stochastic phenomenon. *Psychological Science, 7,* 186–189. (11)

Lynam, D. R. (1996). Early identification of chronic offenders: Who is the fledgling psychopath? *Psychological Bulletin, 120,* 209–234. (12)

Lynn, R. (2009). What has caused the Flynn effect? Secular increases in the developmental quotients of infants. *Intelligence, 37,* 16–24. (9)

Lynn, R., & Harvey, J. (2008). The decline of the world's IQ. *Intelligence, 36,* 112–120. (9)

Lyons, M. J., Eisen, S. A., Goldberg, J., True, W., Lin, N., Meyer, J. M., et al. (1998). A registry-based twin study of depression in men. *Archives of General Psychiatry, 55,* 468–472. (16)

Lyubomirsky, S., King, L., & Diener, E. (2005). The benefits of frequent positive affect: Does happiness lead to success? *Psychological Bulletin, 131,* 803–855. (12)

MacCallum, F., & Golombok, S. (2004). Children raised in fatherless families from infancy: A follow-up of children of lesbian and single heterosexual mothers at early adolescence. *Journal of Child Psychology and Psychiatry, 45,* 1407–1419. (5)

MacCoun, R. J. (1998). Toward a psychology of harm reduction. *American Psychologist, 53,* 1199–1208. (16)

Macey, P. M., Henderson, L. A., Macey, K. E., Alger, J. R., Frysinger, R. C., Woo, M. A., et al. (2002). Brain morphology associated with obstructive sleep apnea. *American Journal of Respiratory and Critical Care Medicine, 166,* 1382–1387. (10)

Machin, S., & Pekkarinen, T. (2008). Global sex differences in test score variability. *Science, 322,* 1331–1332. (9)

Macknik, S. L., King, M., Randi, J., Robbins, A., Teller, Thompson, J., & Martinez-Conde, S. (2008). Attention and awareness in stage magic: Turning tricks into research. *Nature Reviews Neuroscience, 9,* 871–879. (8)

Macmillan, M. (1997). *Freud evaluated.* Cambridge, MA: MIT Press. (14)

MacQuitty, J. (1996, August 1). Lily the stink loses its 33-year reputation by a nose. *The Times* (London), pp. 1–2. (11)

Madson, L. (2005). Demonstrating the importance of question wording on surveys. *Teaching of Psychology, 32,* 40–43. (2)

Magee, W. J., Eaton, W. W., Wittchen, H. -U., McGonagle, K. A., & Kessler, R. C. (1996). Agoraphobia, simple phobia, and social phobia in the National Comorbidity Survey. *Archives of General Psychiatry, 53,* 159–168. (16)

Magen, E., Dweck, C. S., & Gross, J. J. (2008). The hidden-zero effect. *Psychological Science, 19,* 648–649. (8)

Magnuson, K. A., & Duncan, G. J. (2006). The role of socioeconomic resources in the Black–White test score gap among young children. *Developmental Review, 26,* 365–399. (9)

Maguire, E. A., & Frith, C. D. (2003). Lateral asymmetry in the hippocampal response to the remoteness of autobiographical memories. *Journal of Neuroscience, 23,* 5302–5307. (7)

Maguire, E. A., Gadian, D. G., Johnsrude, I. S., Good, C. D., Ashburner, J., Frackowiak, R. S. J., et al. (2000). Navigation-related structural change in the hippocampi of taxi drivers. *Proceedings of the National Academy of Sciences, USA, 97,* 4398–4403. (3)

Mahfouz, A. Y., Philaretou, A. G., & Theocharous, A. (2008). Virtual social interactions: Evolutionary, social psychological and technological perspectives. *Computers in Human Behavior, 24,* 3014–3026. (14)

Mahowald, M. W., & Schenck, C. H. (2005). Insights from studying human sleep disorders. *Nature, 437,* 1279–1285. (10)

Maier, S. F., & Watkins, L. R. (1998). Cytokines for psychologists: Implications of bidirectional immune-to-brain communication for understanding behavior, mood, and cognition. *Psychological Review, 105,* 83–107. (12)

Maki, R. H. (1990). Memory for script actions: Effects of relevance and detail expectancy. *Memory and Cognition, 18,* 5–14. (7)

Malamed, F., & Zaidel, E. (1993). Language and task effects on lateralized word recognition. *Brain and Language, 45,* 70–85. (8)

Maldonado, R., Saiardi, A., Valverde, O., Samad, T. A., Roques, B. P., & Borrelli, E. (1997). Absence of opiate rewarding effects in mice lacking dopamine D2 receptors. *Nature, 388,* 586–589. (3)

Malmberg, A. B., Chen, C., Tonegawa, S., & Basbaum, A. I. (1997). Preserved acute pain and reduced neuropathic pain in mice lacking PKC. *Science, 278,* 179–283. (4)

Malmquist, C. P. (1986). Children who witness parental murder: Posttraumatic aspects. *Journal of the American Academy of Child Psychiatry, 25,* 320–325. (7)

Malpass, R. S. (2006). A policy evaluation of simultaneous and sequential lineups. *Psychology, Public Policy, and Law, 12,* 394–418. (7)

Mangan, M. A. (2004). A phenomenology of problematic sexual behavior. *Archives of Sexual Behavior, 33,* 287–293. (10)

Mann, T., Nolen-Hoeksema, S., Huang, K., Burgard, D., Wright, A., & Hanson, K. (1997). Are two interventions worse than none? Joint primary and secondary prevention of eating disorders in college females. *Health Psychology, 16,* 215–225. (15)

Mann, T., Tomiyama, A. J., Westling, E., Lew, A.-M., Samuels, B., & Chatman, J. (2007). Medicare's search for effective obesity treatments. *American Psychologist, 62*, 220–233. (11)

Manning, R., Levine, M., & Collins, A. (2007). The Kitty Genovese murder and the social psychology of helping. *American Psychologist, 62*, 555–562. (13)

Manor, O., & Eisenbach, Z. (2003). Mortality after spousal loss: Are there socio-demographic differences? *Social Science and Medicine, 56*, 405–413. (12)

Maquet, P., Laureys, S., Peigneux, P., Fuchs, S., Petiau, C., Phillips, C., et al. (2000). Experience-dependent changes in cerebral activation during human REM sleep. *Nature Neuroscience, 3*, 831–836. (10)

Marchand, A., Coutu, M.-F., Dupuis, G., Fleet, R., Borgeat, F., Todorov, C., et al. (2008). Treatment of panic disorder with agoraphobia: Randomized placebo-controlled trial of four psychosocial treatments combined with imipramine or placebo. *Cognitive Behaviour Therapy, 37*, 146–159. (16)

Marcia, J. E. (1980). Identity in adolescence. In J. Adelson (Ed.), *Handbook of adolescent psychology* (pp. 159–187). New York: Wiley. (5)

Marcus, G. F., Vijayan, S., Rao, S. B., & Vishton, P. M. (1999). Rule learning by seven-month-old infants. *Science, 283*, 77–80. (8)

Marian, V., & Neisser, U. (2000). Language-dependent recall of autobiographical memories. *Journal of Experimental Psychology: General, 129*, 361–368. (7)

Marin, R. H., Perez, M. F., Duero, D. G., & Ramirez, O. A. (1999). Preexposure to drug administration context blocks the development of tolerance to sedative effects of diazepam. *Pharmacology Biochemistry and Behavior, 64*, 473–477. (6)

Maris, R. W. (1997). Social suicide. *Suicide and Life-Threatening Behavior, 27*, 41–49. (16)

Markey, P. M. (2000). Bystander intervention in computer-mediated intervention. *Computers in Human Behavior, 16*, 183–188. (13)

Marks, D., & Kammann, R. (1980). *The psychology of the psychic.* Buffalo, NY: Prometheus. (2, 14)

Marler, P. (1997). Three models of song learning: Evidence from behavior. *Journal of Neurobiology, 33*, 501–516. (6)

Marler, P., & Peters, S. (1981). Sparrows learn adult song and more from memory. *Science, 213*, 780–782. (6)

Marler, P., & Peters, S. (1982). Long-term storage of learned birdsongs prior to production. *Animal Behaviour, 30*, 479–482. (6)

Marler, P., & Peters, S. (1987). A sensitive period for song acquisition in the song sparrow, *Melospiza melodia*: A case of age-limited learning. *Ethology, 76*, 89–100. (6)

Marler, P., & Peters, S. (1988). Sensitive periods for song acquisition from tape recordings and live tutors in the swamp sparrow, *Melospiza georgiana. Ethology, 77*, 76–84. (6)

Marlowe, F., & Wetsman, A. (2001). Preferred waist-to-hip ratio and ecology. *Personality and Individual Differences, 30*, 481–489. (13)

Marriott, F. H. C. (1976). Abnormal colour vision. In H. Davson (Ed.), *The eye* (2nd ed., pp. 533–547). New York: Academic Press. (4)

Marsh, E. J., Meade, M. L., & Roediger, H. L., III. (2003). Learning facts from fiction. *Journal of Memory and Language, 49*, 519–536. (7)

Marsh, H. W., & Byrne, B. M. (1991). Differentiated additive androgyny model: Relations between masculinity, femininity, and multiple dimensions of self-concept. *Journal of Personality and Social Psychology, 61*, 811–828. (5)

Marsh, H. W., & Craven, R. G. (2006). Reciprocal effects of self-concept and performance from a multidimensional perspective. *Perspectives on Psychological Science, 1*, 133–163. (14)

Marshall, J. C., & Halligan, P. W. (1995). Seeing the forest but only half the trees? *Nature, 373*, 521–523. (10)

Marshall, L., Helgadóttir, H., Mölle, M., & Born, J. (2006). Boosting slow oscillations during sleep potentiates memory. *Nature, 444*, 610–613. (10)

Martens, A., Johns, M., Greenberg, J., & Schimel, J. (2006). Combating stereotype threat: The effect of self-affirmation on women's intellectual performance. *Journal of Experimental Social Psychology, 42*, 236–243. (9)

Martin, D. J., & Lynn, S. J. (1996). The hypnotic simulation index: Successful discrimination of real versus simulating participants. *International Journal of Clinical and Experimental Hypnosis, 44*, 338–353. (10)

Martindale, C. (2001). Oscillations and analogies: Thomas Young, MD, FRS, genius. *American Psychologist, 56*, 342–345. (4)

Martínez, K., & Colom, R. (2009). Working memory capacity and processing efficiency predict fluid but not crystallized and spatial intelligence: Evidence supporting the neural noise hypothesis. *Personality and Individual Differences, 46*, 281–286. (9)

Martiny, K., Lunde, M., Undén, M., Dam, H., & Bech, P. (2005). Adjunctive bright light in non-seasonal major depression: Results from clinician-rated depression scales. *Acta Psychiatria Scaninavica, 112*, 117–125. (16)

Martsh, C. T., & Miller, W. R. (1997). Extraversion predicts heavy drinking in college students. *Personality and Individual Differences, 23*, 153–155. (14)

Marx, J. (2003). Cellular warriors at the battle of the bulge. *Science, 299*, 846–849. (11)

Masicampo, E. J., & Baumeister, R. F. (2008). Toward a physiology of dual-process reasoning *Psychological Science, 19*, 255–260. (1)

Maslow, A. H. (1962). *Toward a psychology of being.* Princeton, NJ: Van Nostrand. (14)

Maslow, A. H. (1970). *Motivation and personality* (2nd ed.). New York: Harper & Row. (11)

Maslow, A. H. (1971). *The farther reaches of human nature.* New York: Viking Press. (14)

Mason, B. J., Goodman, A. M., Chabac, S., & Lehert, P. (2006). Effect of oral acamprosate on abstinence in patients with alcohol dependence in a double-blind, placebo-controlled trial: The role of patient motivation. *Journal of Psychiatric Research, 40*, 383–393. (16)

Mason, D. A., & Frick, P. J. (1994). The heritability of antisocial behavior: A meta-analysis of twin and adoption studies. *Journal of Psychopathology and Behavioral Assessment, 16*, 301–323. (5)

Mason, M. F., Norton, M. I., Van Horn, J. D., Wegner, D. M., Grafton, S. T., & Macrae, C. N. (2007). Wandering minds: The default network and stimulus-independent thought. *Science, 315*, 393–395. (3)

Massimini, M., Ferrarelli, F., Huber, R., Esser, S. K., Singh, H., & Tononi, G. (2005). Breakdown of cortical effective connectivity during sleep. *Science, 309*, 2228–2232. (10)

Masson, J. M. (1984). *The assault on truth.* New York: Farrar, Straus and Giroux. (14)

Masters, W. H., & Johnson, V. E. (1966). *Human sexual response.* Boston: Little, Brown. (11)

Mathalon, D. H., Pfefferbaum, A., Lim, K. O., Rosenbloom, M. J., & Sullivan, E. V. (2003). Compounded brain volume deficits in schizophrenia-alcoholism comorbidity. *Archives of General Psychiatry, 60*, 245–252. (16)

Matheny, A. P., Jr. (1989). Children's behavioral inhibition over age and across situations: Genetic similarity for a trait to change. *Journal of Personality, 57*, 215–235. (5)

Mather, M., Canli, T., English, T., Whitfield, S., Wais, P., Ochsner, K., et al. (2004). Amygdala responses to emotionally valenced stimuli in older and younger adults. *Psychological Science, 15*, 259–263. (12)

Mathews, A., & Mackintosh, B. (2004). Take a closer look: Emotion modifies the boundary extension effect. *Emotion, 4*, 36–45. (12)

Matsumoto, D. (1994). *People: Psychology from a cultural perspective.* Pacific Grove, CA: Brooks/Cole. (2)

Matsunami, H., Montmayeur, J.-P., & Buck, L. B. (2000). A family of candidate taste receptors in human and mouse. *Nature, 404*, 601–604. (4)

Mattson, M. P., & Magnus, T. (2006). Ageing and neuronal variability. *Nature Reviews Neuroscience, 7*, 278–294. (5)

Maunsell, E., Brisson, J., Mondor, M., Verreault, R., & Deschênes, L. (2001). Stressful life events and survival after breast cancer. *Psychosomatic Medicine, 63*, 306–315. (12)

May, C. P., Hasher, L., & Stoltzfus, E. R. (1993). Optimal time of day and the magnitude of age differences in memory. *Psychological Science, 4*, 326–330. (10)

Mayberry, R. I., Lock, E., & Kazmi, H. (2002). Linguistic ability and early language exposure. *Nature, 415*, 1026–1029. (8)

Mayer, J. D. (2001). Emotion, intelligence, and emotional intelligence. In J. P. Forgas (Ed.), *Handbook of affect and social cognition* (pp. 410–431). Mahwah, NJ: Erlbaum. (12)

Mayer, J. D., Caruso, D. R., & Salovey, P. (2000). Emotional intelligence meets traditional standards for an intelligence. *Intelligence, 27*, 267–298. (12)

Mayer, J. D., & Salovey, P. (1995). Emotional intelligence and the construction and regulation of feelings. *Applied and Preventive Psychology, 4*, 197–208. (12)

Mayer, J. D., & Salovey, P. (1997). What is emotional intelligence? In P. Salovey & D. J. Sluyter (Eds.). *Emotional development and emotional intelligence* (pp. 3–34). New York: Basic Books. (12)

Mayer, J. D., Salovey, P., Caruso, D. R., & Sitarenios, G. (2001). Emotional intelligence as a standard intelligence. *Emotion, 1*, 232–242. (12)

Mazzoni, G., & Memon, A. (2003). Imagination can create false autobiographical memories. *Psychological Science, 14*, 186–188. (7)

McCall, V. W., Yates, B., Hendricks, S., Turner, K., & McNabb, B. (1989). Comparison between the Stanford-Binet: L-M and the Stanford-Binet: Fourth edition with a group of gifted children. *Contemporary Educational Psychology, 114*, 93–96. (9)

McCall, W. A. (1939). *Measurement.* New York: Macmillan. (9)

McCaulley, M. H. (2000). Myers-Briggs Type Indicator: A bridge between counseling and consulting. *Consulting Psychology Journal: Practice and Research, 52*, 117–132. (14)

McClelland, J. L. (1988). Connectionist models and psychological evidence. *Journal of Memory and Language, 27*, 107–123. (8)

McClelland, J. L., & Rumelhart, D. E. (1981). An interactive activation model of context effects in letter perception: Part 1. An account of basic findings. *Psychological Review, 88*, 375–407. (8)

McClintock, M. K. (1971). Menstrual synchrony and suppression. *Nature, 229*, 244–245. (4)

McClure, J. (1998). Discounting causes of behavior: Are two reasons better than one? *Journal of Personality and Social Psychology, 74*, 7–20. (13)

McCormick, M. C. (1985). The contribution of low birth weight to infant mortality and childhood morbidity. *New England Journal of Medicine, 312*, 82–90. (6)

McCornack, R. L. (1983). Bias in the validity of predicted college grades in four ethnic minority groups. *Educational and Psychological Measurement, 43*, 517–522. (9)

McCourt, K., Bouchard, T. J., Jr., Lykken, D. T., Tellegen, A., & Keyes, M. (1999). Authoritarianism revisited: Genetic and environmental influences examined in twins reared apart and together. *Personality and Individual Differences, 27*, 985–1014. (5)

McCrae, R. R. (1996). Social consequences of experiential openness. *Psychological Bulletin, 120*, 323–337. (14)

McCrae, R. R., & Costa, P. T., Jr. (1987). Validation of the five-factor model of personality across instruments and observers. *Journal of Personality and Social Psychology, 52*, 81–90. (14)

McCrae, R. R., & Costa, P. T., Jr. (1997). Personality trait structure as a human universal. *American Psychologist, 52*, 509–516. (14)

McCrae, R. R., Costa, P. T., Jr., Ostendorf, F., Angleitner, A., Hrebíčková, M., Avia, M. D., et al. (2000). Nature over nurture: Temperament, personality, and life span development. *Journal of Personality and Social Psychology, 78*, 173–186. (14)

McCrea, S. M., Liberman, N., Trope, Y., & Sherman, S. J. (2008). Construal level and procrastination. *Psychological Science, 19*, 1308–1314. (11)

McCrink, K., & Wynn, K. (2004). Large-number addition and subtraction by 9-month-old infants. *Psychological Science, 15*, 776–781. (5)

McDermott, R., Tingley, D., Cowden, J., Frazzetto, G., & Johnson, D. D. P. (2009). Monoamine oxidase A gene (MAOA) predicts behavioral aggression following provocation. *Proceedings of the National Academy of Sciences, USA, 106*, 2118–2123. (12)

McDougall, W. (1938). Fourth report on a Lamarckian experiment. *British Journal of Psychology, 28*, 321–345, 365–395. (2)

McElheny, V. (2004). Three Nobelists ask: Are we ready for the next frontier? *Cerebrum, 5*, 69–81. (1)

McEvoy, J. P., Lieberman, J. A., Stroup, T. S., Davis, S. M., Meltzer, H. Y., & Rosenheck, R. A. (2006). Effectiveness of clozapine versus olanzapine, quetiapine, and risperidone in patients with chronic schizophrenia who did not respond to prior atypical antipsychotic treatment. *American Journal of Psychiatry, 163*, 600–610. (16)

McEwen, B. S. (2000). The neurobiology of stress: From serendipity to clinical relevance. *Brain Research, 886*, 172–189. (12)

McFadden, D. (2008). What do sex, twins, spotted hyenas, ADHD, and sexual orientation have in common? *Perspectives on Psychological Science, 3*, 309–323. (11)

McFarlane, A. C. (1997). The prevalence and longitudinal course of PTSD. *Annals of the New York Academy of Sciences, 821*, 10–23. (12)

McGorry, P. D., Yung, A. R., Phillips, L. J., Yuen, H. P., Francey, S., Cosgrave, E. M., et al. (2002). Randomized controlled trial of interventions designed to reduce the risk of progression to first-episode psychosis in a clinical sample with subthreshold symptoms. *Archives of General Psychiatry, 59*, 921–928. (15)

McGovern, P. E., Glusker, D. L., Exner, L. J., & Voigt, M. M. (1996). Neolithic resinated wine. *Nature, 381*, 480–481. (3)

McGrath, J. J., Féron, F. P., Burne, T. H. J., Mackay-Sim, A., & Eyles, D. W. (2003). The neurodevelopmental hypothesis of schizophrenia: A review of recent developments. *Annals of Medicine, 35*, 86–93. (16)

McGregor, D. M. (1960). *The human side of enterprise.* New York: McGraw-Hill. (11)

McGue, M. (1999). The behavioral genetics of alcoholism. *Current Directions in Psychological Science, 8*, 109–115. (16)

McGue, M., & Bouchard, T. J., Jr. (1998). Genetic and environmental influences on human behavioral differences. *Annual Review of Neuroscience, 21*, 1–24. (9)

McGue, M., Elkins, I., Walden, B., & Iacono, W. G. (2005). Perceptions of the parent–adolescent relationship: A longitudinal investigation. *Developmental Psychology, 41*, 971–984. (5)

McGuire, S., & Clifford, J. (2000). Genetic and environmental contributions to loneliness in children. *Psychological Science, 11*, 487–491. (5)

McGuire, S., Clifford, J., Fink, J., Basho, S., & McDonnell, A. (2003). Children's reactions to the unfamiliar in middle childhood and adolescence: An observational twin/sibling study. *Personality and Individual Differences, 35*, 339–354. (5)

McGuire, W. J., & Papageorgis, D. (1961). The relative efficacy of various types of prior belief-defense in producing immunity against persuasion. *Journal of Abnormal and Social Psychology, 62*, 327–337. (13)

McGurk, H., Caplan, M., Hennessy, E., & Moss, P. (1993). Controversy, theory, and social context in contemporary day care research. *Journal of Child Psychology, 34*, 3–23. (6)

McGurk, H., & MacDonald, J. (1976). Hearing lips and seeing voices. *Nature, 264*, 746–748. (8)

McIntyre, M., Gangestad, S. W., Gray, P. B., Chapman, J. F., Burnham, T. C., O'Rourke, M. T., et al. (2006). Romantic involvement often reduces men's testosterone levels—But not always: The moderating effect of extrapair sexual interest. *Journal of Personality and Social Psychology, 91*, 642–651. (11)

McIntyre, R. S., Konarski, J. Z., Wilkins, K., Soczynska, J. K., & Kennedy, S. H. (2006). Obesity in bipolar disorder and major depressive disorder: Results from a national community health survey on mental health and well-being. *Canadian Journal of Psychiatry, 51*, 274–280. (11)

McKelvey, M. W., & McKenry, P. C. (2000). The psychosocial well-being of Black and White mothers following marital dissolution. *Psychology of Women Quarterly, 24*, 4–14. (5)

McKinnon, J. D., & Bennett, C. E. (2005). *We the people: Blacks in the United States.* Washington, DC: U.S. Census Bureau. (9)

McMurtry, P. L., & Mershon, D. H. (1985). Auditory distance judgments in noise, with and without hearing protection. *Proceedings of the Human Factors Society* (Baltimore), pp. 811–813. (4)

McNally, R. J. (1990). Psychological approaches to panic disorder: A review. *Psychological Bulletin, 108*, 403–419. (16)

McNally, R. J. (2002). Anxiety sensitivity and panic disorder. *Biological Psychiatry, 52*, 938–946. (16)

McNally, R. J., Bryant, R. A., & Ehlers, A. (2003). Does early psychological intervention promote recovery from posttraumatic stress? *Psychological Science in the Public Interest, 4*, 45–77. (12)

McNamara, J. M., Barta, Z., Fromhage, L., & Houston, A. I. (2008). The coevolution of choosiness and cooperation. *Nature, 451*, 189–192. (13)

McNamara, P., McLaren, D., Smith, D., Brown, A., & Stickgold, R. (2005). A "Jekyll and Hyde" within: Aggressive versus friendly interactions in REM and non-REM dreams. *Psychological Science, 16*, 130–136. (10)

Mechelli, A., Crinion, J. T., Noppeney, U., O'Doherty, J., Ashburner, J., Frackowiak, R. S., et al. (2004). Structural plasticity in the bilingual brain. *Nature, 431*, 757. (8)

"The medals and the damage done." (2004). *Nature, 430*, 604. (3)

Meddis, R., Pearson, A. J. D., & Langford, G. (1973). An extreme case of healthy insomnia. *EEG and Clinical Neurophysiology, 35*, 213–214. (10)

Medver, V. H., Madey, S. F., & Gilovich, T. (1995). When less is more: Counterfactual thinking and satisfaction among Olympic athletes. *Journal of Personality and Social Psychology, 69*, 603–610. (12)

Meeter, M., & Murre, J. M. J. (2004). Consolidation of long-term memory: Evidence and alternatives. *Psychological Bulletin, 130*, 843–857. (7)

Mehl, M. R., Vazire, S., Ramirez-Esparza, M., Slatcher, R. B., & Pennebaker, J. W. (2007). Are women really more talkative than men? *Science, 317*, 82. (5)

Meichenbaum, D. (1985). *Stress inoculation training.* New York: Pergamon Press. (12)

Meichenbaum, D., & Cameron, R. (1983). Stress inoculation training. In D. Meichenbaum & M. E. Jaremko (Eds.), *Stress reduction and prevention* (pp. 115–154). New York: Plenum Press. (12)

Meichenbaum, D. H. (1995). Cognitive-behavioral therapy in historical perspective. In B. Bongar & L. E. Beutler (Eds.), *Comprehensive textbook of psychotherapy: Theory and practice* (pp. 140–158). Oxford, England: Oxford University Press. (15)

Melchers, K. G., Ungor, M., & Lachnit, H. (2005). The experimental task influences cue competition in human causal learning. *Journal of Experimental Psychology: Animal Behavior Processes, 31*, 477–483. (6)

Meltzoff, A. N., & Moore, M. K. (1977). Imitation of facial and manual gestures by human neonates. *Science, 198*, 75–78. (3)

Melzack, R., & Wall, P. D. (1965). Pain mechanisms: A new theory. *Science, 150*, 971–979. (4)

Melzack, R., Weisz, A. Z., & Sprague, L. T. (1963). Stratagems for controlling pain: Contributions of auditory stimulation and suggestion. *Experimental Neurology, 8*, 239–247. (12)

Mendelsohn, A., Chalamish, Y., Solomonovich, A., & Dudai, Y. (2008). Mesmerizing memories: Brain substrates of episodic memory suppression in posthypnotic amnesia. *Neuron, 57*, 159–170. (10)

Mendieta-Zéron, H., López, M., & Diéguez, C. (2008). Gastrointestinal peptides controlling body weight homeostasis. *General and Comparative Endocrinology, 155*, 481–495. (11)

Merckelbach, H, Dekkers, T., Wessel, I., & Roefs, A. (2003). Dissociative symptoms and amnesia in Dutch concentration camp survivors. *Comprehensive Psychiatry, 44*, 65–69. (7)

Merlino, J. P., Jacobs, M. S., Kaplan, J. A., & Moritz, K. L. (Eds.). (2008). *Freud at 150: 21st-century essays on a man of genius.* Lanham, MD: Rowman & Littlefield. (14)

Mershon, D. H., & King, L. E. (1975). Intensity and reverberation as factors in the auditory perception of egocentric distance. *Perception and Psychophysics, 18*, 409–415. (4)

Meshi, D., Drew, M. R., Saxe, M., Ansorge, M. S., David, D., Santarelli, L., et al. (2006). Hippocampal neurogenesis is not required for behavioral effects of environmental enrichment. *Nature Neuroscience, 9*, 729–731. (3)

Mesmer, F. A. (1980). *Mesmerism: A translation of the original medical and scientific writings of F. A. Mesmer.* Los Altos, CA: Kaufmann. (5)

Messinger, D. S. (2002). Positive and negative: Infant facial expressions and emotions. *Current Directions in Psychological Science, 11,* 1–6. (12)

Meyer, J. P., Becker, T. E., & Vandenberghe, C. (2004). Employee commitment and motivation: A conceptual analysis and integrative model. *Journal of Applied Psychology, 89,* 991–1007. (11)

Meyer-Bahlburg, H. F. L., Dolezal, C., Baker, S. W., & New, M. I. (2008). Sexual orientation in women with classical or non-classical congenital adrenal hyperplasia as a function of degree of prenatal androgen excess. *Archives of Sexual Behavior, 37,* 85–99. (11)

Meyer-Lindenberg, A., Mervis, C. B., & Berman, K. F. (2006). Neural mechanisms in Williams syndrome: A unique window to genetic influences on cognition and behaviour. *Nature Reviews Neuroscience, 7,* 380–393. (8)

Meyerowitz, B. E., Richardson, J., Hudson, S., & Leedham, B. (1998). Ethnicity and cancer outcomes: Behavioral and psychosocial considerations. *Psychological Bulletin, 123,* 47–70. (12)

Mezzanotte, W. S., Tangel, D. J., & White, D. P. (1992). Waking genioglossal electromyogram in sleep apnea patients versus normal controls (a neuromuscular compensatory mechanism). *Journal of Clinical Investigation, 89,* 1571–1579. (10)

Mikulincer, M., Shaver, P. R., & Pereg, D. (2003). Attachment theory and affect regulation: The dynamics, development, and cognitive consequences of attachment-related strategies. *Motivation and Emotion, 27,* 77–102. (5)

Milar, K. S. (2000). The first generation of women psychologists and the psychology of women. *American Psychologist, 55,* 616–619. (1)

Milgram, S. (1974). *Obedience to authority.* New York: Harper & Row. (13)

Milich, R., Wolraich, M., & Lindgren, S. (1986). Sugar and hyperactivity: A critical review of empirical findings. *Clinical Psychology Review, 6,* 493–513. (2)

Milkman, K. L., Rogers, T., & Bazerman, M. H. (2008). Harnessing our inner angels and demons. *Perspectives on Psychological Science, 3,* 324–338. (11)

Millar, J. K., Pickard, B. S., Mackie, S., James, R., Christie, S., Buchanan, S. R., et al. (2005). DISC1 and PDE4B are interacting genetic factors in schizophrenia that regulate cAMP signaling. *Science, 310,* 1187–1191. (16)

Miller, C. T., Dibble, E., & Hauser, M. D. (2001). Amodal completion of acoustic signals by a nonhuman primate. *Nature Neuroscience, 4,* 783–784. (4)

Miller, D. T., & Ross, M. (1975). Self-serving biases in the attribution of causality: Fact or fiction? *Psychological Bulletin, 82,* 213–225. (13)

Miller, G. (2007a). Animal extremists get personal. *Science, 318,* 1856–1858. (2)

Miller, G. (2007b). The mystery of the missing smile. *Nature, 316,* 826–827. (12)

Miller, G. A. (1956). The magical number seven, plus or minus two: Some limits on our capacity for processing information. *Psychological Review, 63,* 81–97. (7)

Miller, G. E., & Wrosch, C. (2007). You've gotta know when to fold 'em. *Psychological Science, 18,* 773–777. (11)

Miller, L. C., & Fishkin, S. A. (1997). On the dynamics of human bonding and reproductive success: Seeking windows on the adapted-for human–environmental interface. In J. A. Simpson & D. T. Kenrick (Eds.), *Evolutionary social psychology* (pp. 197–235). Mahwah, NJ: Erlbaum. (2)

Miller, R. J., Hennessy, R. T., & Leibowitz, H. W. (1973). The effect of hypnotic ablation of the background on the magnitude of the Ponzo perspective illusion. *International Journal of Clinical and Experimental Hypnosis, 21,* 180–191. (10)

Miller, W. R., & Brown, S. A. (1997). Why psychologists should treat alcohol and drug problems. *American Psychologist, 52,* 1269–1279. (16)

Milne, S. E., Orbell, S., & Sheeran, P. (2002). Combining motivational and volitional interventions to promote exercise participation: Protection motivation theory and implementation intentions. *British Journal of Health Psychology, 7,* 163–184. (11)

Milner, B. (1959). The memory defect in bilateral hippocampal lesions. *Psychiatric Research Reports, 11,* 43–52. (7)

Milton, J., & Wiseman, R. (1999). Does psi exist? Lack of replication of an anomalous process of information. *Psychological Bulletin, 125,* 387–391. (2)

Minde, K., Minde, R., & Vogel, W. (2006). Culturally sensitive assessment of attachment in children aged 18–40 months in a South African township. *Infant Mental Health Journal, 27,* 544–558. (5)

Mineka, S. (1987). A primate model of phobic fears. In H. Eysenck & I. Martin (Eds.), *Theoretical foundations of behavior therapy* (pp. 81–111). New York: Plenum Press. (16)

Mineka, S., Davidson, M., Cook, M., & Keir, R. (1984). Observational conditioning of snake fear in rhesus monkeys. *Journal of Abnormal Psychology, 93,* 355–372. (16)

Mineka, S., & Zinbarg, R. (2006). A contemporary learning theory perspective on the etiology of anxiety disorders. *American Psychologist, 61,* 10–26. (16)

Mingroni, M. A. (2004). The secular rise in IA: Giving heterosis a closer look. *Intelligence, 32,* 65–83. (9)

Minto, C. L., Liao, L.-M., Woodhouse, C. R. J., Ransley, P. G., & Creighton, S. M. (2003). The effect of clitoral surgery on sexual outcome in individuals who have intersex conditions with ambiguous genitalia: A cross-sectional study. *Lancet, 361,* 1252–1257. (11)

Mischel, W. (1973). Toward a cognitive social learning reconceptualization of personality. *Psychological Review, 80,* 252–283. (14)

Mischel, W. (1981). Current issues and challenges in personality. In L. T. Benjamin, Jr. (Ed.), *The G. Stanley Hall Lecture Series* (Vol. 1, pp. 81–99). Washington, DC: American Psychological Association. (14)

Misrahi, M., Meduri, G., Pissard, S., Bouvattier, C., Beau, I., Loosfelt, H., et al. (1997). Comparison of immunocytochemical and molecular features with the phenotype in a case of incomplete male pseudohermaphroditism associated with a mutation of the luteinizing hormone receptor. *Journal of Clinical Endocrinology and Metabolism, 82,* 2159–2165. (11)

Mitchell, D. B. (2006). Nonconscious priming after 17 years: Invulnerable implicit memory? *Psychological Science, 17,* 925–929. (8)

Mitte, K. (2005). Meta-analysis of cognitive-behavioral treatments for generalized anxiety disorder: A comparison with psychotherapy. *Psychological Bulletin, 131,* 785–795. (16)

Mitte, K. (2008). Memory bias for threatening information in anxiety and anxiety disorders. *Psychological Bulletin, 134,* 886–911. (7)

Miyamoto, Y., Nisbett, R. E., & Masuda, T. (2006). Culture and the physical environment. *Psychological Science, 17,* 113–119. (13)

Mobbs, D., Petrovic, P., Marchant, J. L., Hassabis, D., Weiskopf, N., Seymour, B., et al. (2007). When fear is near: Threat imminence elicits prefrontal-periaqueductal gray shifts in humans. *Science, 317,* 1079–1083. (16)

Mochizuki, T., Crocker, A., McCormack, S., Yanagisawa, M., Sakurai, T., & Scammell, T. E. (2004). Behavioral state instability in orexin knock-out mice. *Journal of Neuroscience, 24,* 6291–6300. (10)

Modell, S., Ising, M., Holsboer, F., & Lauer, C. J. (2005). The Munich vulnerability study on affective disorders: Premorbid polysomnographic profile of affected high-risk probands. *Biological Psychiatry, 58,* 694–699. (16)

Moffitt, T. E., Caspi, A., & Rutter, M. (2006). Measured gene–environment interactions in psychopathology. *Perspectives on Psychological Science, 1,* 5–27. (1, 5)

Mogle, J. A., Lovett, B. J., Stawski, R. S., & Sliwinski, M. J. (2008). What's so special about working memory? *Psychological Science, 19,* 1071–1077. (7)

Mojtabai, R., & Olfson, M. (2008). National trends in psychotherapy by office-based psychiatrists. *Archives of General Psychiatry, 65,* 962–970. (1)

Moller, H. J. (1992). Attempted suicide: Efficacy of different aftercare strategies. *International Clinical Psychopharmacology, 6*(Suppl. 6), 58–59. (15)

Mondloch, C. J., Leis, A., & Maurer, D. (2006). Recognizing the face of Johnny, Suzy, and me: Insensitivity to the spacing among features at 4 years of age. *Child Development, 77,* 234–243. (5)

Money, J., & Ehrhardt, A. A. (1972). *Man & woman, boy & girl.* Baltimore: Johns Hopkins University Press. (11)

Monk, T. H., & Aplin, L. C. (1980). Spring and autumn daylight time changes: Studies of adjustment in sleep timings, mood, and efficiency. *Ergonomics, 23,* 167–178. (10)

Monroe, S. M., & Harkness, K. L. (2005). Life stress, the "kindling" hypothesis, and the recurrence of depression: Considerations from a life stress perspective. *Psychological Review, 112,* 417–445. (16)

Monroe, S. M., & Reid, M. W. (2008). Gene–environment interactions in depression research. *Psychological Science, 19,* 947–956. (16)

Montgomery, G., & Kirsch, I. (1996). Mechanisms of placebo pain reduction: An empirical investigation. *Psychological Science, 7,* 174–176. (4)

Monti-Bloch, L., Jennings-White, C., Dolberg, D. S., & Berliner, D. L. (1994). The human vomeronasal system. *Psychoneuroendocrinology, 19,* 673–686. (4)

Montoya, A. G., Sorrentino, R., Lucas, S. E., & Price, B. H. (2002). Long-term neuropsychiatric consequences of "ecstasy" (MDMA): A review. *Harvard Review of Psychiatry, 10,* 212–220. (3)

Montoya, R. M. (2008). I'm hot, so I'd say you're not: The influence of objective physical attractiveness on mate selection. *Personality and Social Psychology Bulletin, 34,* 1315–1331. (13)

Moons, W. G., Mackie, D. M., & Garcia-Marques, T. (2009). The impact of repetition-induced familiarity on agreement with weak and strong arguments. *Journal of Personality and Social Psychology, 96,* 32–44. (13)

Moorcroft, W. (1993). *Sleep, dreaming, and sleep disorders: An introduction* (2nd ed.). Lanham, MD: University Press of America. (10)

Moorcroft, W. H. (2003). *Understanding sleep and dreaming.* New York: Kluwer. (10)

Moore, B. C. J. (1989). *An introduction to the psychology of hearing* (3rd ed.). London: Academic Press. (4)

Moore, D. S., & Johnson, S. P. (2008). Mental rotation in human infants. *Psychological Science, 19,* 1063–1066. (5)

Moore, E. G. J. (1986). Family socialization and the IQ test performance of traditionally and transracially adopted Black children. *Developmental Psychology, 22,* 317–326. (9)

Moore, J. (1995). Some historical and conceptual relations among logical positivism, behaviorism, and cognitive psychology. In J. T. Todd & E. K. Morris (Eds.), *Modern perspectives on B. F. Skinner and contemporary behaviorism* (pp. 51–74). Westport, CT: Greenwood Press. (6)

Moore, L. B., Goodwin, B., Jones, S. A., Wisely, G. B., Serabjit-Singh, C. J., Willson, T. M., et al. (2000). St. John's wort induces hepatic drug metabolism through activation of the pregnane X receptor. *Proceedings of the National Academy of Sciences, USA, 97*, 7500–7502. (16)

Morewedge, C. K., Gilbert, D. T., & Wilson, T. D. (2005). The least likely of times. *Psychological Science, 16*, 626–630. (8)

Morewedge, C. K., & Norton, M. I. (2009). When dreaming is believing: The (motivated) interpretation of dreams. *Journal of Personality and Social Psychology, 96*, 249–264. (10)

Morgeson, F. P., Campion, M. A., Dipboye, R. L., Hollenbeck, J. R., Murphy, K., & Schmitt, N. (2007). Are we getting fooled again? Coming to terms with limitations in the use of personality tests for personnel selection. *Personnel Psychology, 60*, 1029–1049. (14)

Morris, G., & Baker-Ward, L. (2007). Fragile but real: Children's capacity to use newly acquired words to convey preverbal memories. *Child Development, 78*, 448–458. (7)

Moscovitch, M. (1985). Memory from infancy to old age: Implications for theories of normal and pathological memory. *Annals of the New York Academy of Sciences, 444*, 78–96. (7)

Moscovitch, M. (1989). Confabulation and the frontal systems: Strategic versus associative retrieval in neuropsychological theories of memory. In H. L. Roediger, III, & F. I. M. Craik (Eds.), *Varieties of memory and consciousness: Essays in honour of Endel Tulving* (pp. 133–160). Hillsdale, NJ: Erlbaum. (7)

Moscovitch, M. (1992). Memory and working-with-memory: A component process model based on modules and central systems. *Journal of Cognitive Neuroscience, 4*, 257–267. (7)

Moskowitz, A. K. (2004). "Scared stiff": Catatonia as an evolutionary-based fear response. *Psychological Review, 111*, 984–1002. (16)

Moskowitz, B. A. (1978). The acquisition of language. *Scientific American, 239*(5), 92–108. (8)

Moss, E., Cyr, C., Bureau, J.-F., Tarabulsy, G. M., & Dubois-Comtois, K. (2005). Stability of attachment during the preschool period. *Developmental Psychology, 41*, 773–783. (5)

Moulin, C. J. A., Conway, M. A., Thompson, R. G., James, N., & Jones, R. W. (2005). Disordered memory awareness: Recollective confabulation in two cases of persistent déjà vecu. *Neuropsychologia, 43*, 1362–1378. (10)

Moussawi, K., Pacchioni, A., Moran, M., Olive, M. F., Gass, J. T., Lavin, A., et al. (2009). *N*-acetylcysteine reverses cocaine-induced metaplasticity. *Nature Neuroscience, 12*, 182–189. (16)

Mroczek, D. K. (2004). Positive and negative affect at midlife. In O. G. Brim, C. D. Ryff, & R. C. Kessler (Eds.), *How healthy are we?* (pp. 205–226). Chicago: University of Chicago Press. (12)

Mroczek, D. K., & Spiro, A. (2005). Change in life satisfaction during adulthood: Findings from the veterans affairs normative aging study. *Journal of Personality and Social Psychology, 88*, 189–202. (12)

Mulhall, J., King, R., Glina, S., & Hvidsten, K. (2008). Importance of and satisfaction with sex among men and women worldwide: Results of the Global Better Sex Survey. *Journal of Sexual Medicine, 5*, 788–795. (11)

Müller, M. M., Malinowski, P., Gruber, T., & Hillyard, S. A. (2003). Sustained division of the attentional spotlight. *Nature, 424*, 309–312. (8)

Munroe, R. (1955). *Schools of psychoanalytic thought*. New York: Dryden Press. (15)

Murali, M. S. (2001). Epidemiological study of prevalence of mental disorders in India. *Indian Journal of Community Medicine, 26*, 198. (16)

Muraven, M., & Baumeister, R. F. (2000). Self-regulation and depletion of limited resources: Does self-control resemble a muscle? *Psychological Bulletin, 126*, 247–259. (12)

Murphy, G. L., & Medin, D. L. (1985). The role of theories in conceptual coherence. *Psychological Review, 92*, 289–316. (8)

Murray, H. A. (1943). *Thematic Apperception Test manual*. Cambridge, MA: Harvard University Press. (14)

Must, O., te Nijenhuis, J., Must, A., & van Vianen, A. E. M. (2009). Comparability of IQ scores over time. *Intelligence, 37*, 25–33. (9)

Mustanski, B. S., DuPree, M. G., Nievergelt, C. M., Bocklandt, S., Schork, N. J., & Hamer, D. H. (2005). A genomewide scan of male sexual orientation. *Human Genetics, 116*, 272–278. (11)

Myers, D. G. (2000). The funds, friends, and faith of happy people. *American Psychologist, 55*, 56–67. (12)

Naab, P. J., & Russell, J. A. (2007). Judgments of emotion from spontaneous facial expressions of New Guineans. *Emotion, 7*, 736–744. (12)

Nadig, A. S., & Sedivy, J. C. (2002). Evidence of perspective-taking constraints in children's on-line reference resolution. *Psychological Science, 13*, 329–336. (5)

Nagera, H. (1976). *Obsessional neuroses*. New York: Aronson. (16)

Nairne, J. S., Pandeirada, J. N. S., & Thompson, S. R. (2008). Adaptive memory: The comparative value of survival processing. *Psychological Science, 19*, 176–180. (7)

Nairne, J. S., Thompson, S. R., & Pandeirada, J. N. S. (2007). Adaptive memory: Survival processing enhances retention. *Journal of Experimental Psychology: Learning, Memory, and Cognition, 33*, 263–273. (7)

Narrow, W. E., Rae, D. S., Robins, L. N., & Regier, D. A. (2002). Revised prevalence estimates of mental disorders in the United States. *Archives of General Psychiatry, 59*, 115–123. (16)

Nash, M. (1987). What, if anything, is regressed about hypnotic age regression? A review of the empirical literature. *Psychological Bulletin, 102*, 42–52. (10)

Nash, M. R., Johnson, L. S., & Tipton, R. D. (1979). Hypnotic age regression and the occurrence of transitional object relationships. *Journal of Abnormal Psychology, 88*, 547–555. (10)

National Institutes of Health. (2000). *The practical guide: Identification, evaluation, and treatment of overweight and obesity in adults* (NIH Publication No. 00-4084). Washington, DC: Author. (11)

Nebes, R. D. (1974). Hemispheric specialization in commissurotomized man. *Psychological Bulletin, 81*, 1–14. (3)

Nedjam, Z., Dalla Barba, G., & Pillon, B. (2000). Confabulation in a patient with fronto-temporal dementia and a patient with Alzheimer's disease. *Cortex, 36*, 561–577. (7)

Negy, C., Leal-Puente, L., Trainor, D. J., & Carlson, R. (1997). Mexican American adolescents' performance on the MMPIA. *Journal of Personality Assessment, 69*, 205–214. (14)

Neher, A. (1991). Maslow's theory of motivation: A critique. *Journal of Humanistic Psychology, 31*, 89–112. (14)

Neisser, U. (1997). Rising scores on intelligence tests. *American Scientist, 85*, 440–447. (9)

Nelissen, R. M. A., & Zeelenberg, M. (2009). When guilt evokes self-punishment: Evidence for the existence of a *Dobby effect*. *Emotion, 9*, 118–122. (12)

Nelson, E. C., Heath, A. C., Madden, P. A. F., Cooper, L., Dinwiddie, S. H., Bucholz, K. K., et al. (2002). Association between self-reported childhood sexual abuse and adverse psychosocial outcomes: Results from a twin study. *Archives of General Psychiatry, 59*, 139–145. (16)

Nelson, K., & Fivush, R. (2004). The emergence of autobiographical memory: A social cultural developmental theory. *Psychological Review, 111*, 486–511. (7)

Nemeroff, C. B., Heim, C. M., Thase, M. E., Klein, D. N., Rush, A. J., Schatzberg, A. F., et al. (2003). Differential responses to psychotherapy versus pharmacotherapy in patients with chronic forms of major depression and childhood trauma. *Proceedings of the National Academy of Sciences, USA, 100*, 14293–14296. (16)

Nemeth, C. (1972). A critical analysis of research utilizing the prisoner's dilemma paradigm for the study of bargaining. In L. Berkowitz (Ed.), *Advances in experimental social psychology* (Vol. 6, pp. 203–234). New York: Academic Press. (13)

Nemeth, C. J. (1986). Differential contributions of majority and minority influence. *Psychological Review, 93*, 23–32. (13)

Nettelbeck, T., & Wilson, C. (2004). The Flynn effect: Smarter not faster. *Intelligence, 32*, 85–93. (9)

Nettle, D. (2006). The evolution of personality variation in humans and other animals. *American Psychologist, 61*, 622–631. (14)

Newcombe, N. S., Lloyd, M. E., & Ratliff, K. R. (2007). Development of episodic and autobiographical memory: A cognitive neuroscience perspective. In R. V. Kail (Ed.), *Advances in child development and behavior* (Vol. 35, pp. 37–85). Oxford, England: Elsevier. (7)

Newcombe, N. S., Sluzenski, J., & Huttenlocher, J. (2005). Preexisting knowledge versus on-line learning. *Psychological Science, 16*, 222–227. (5)

Newman, B. (1988, September 9). Dressing for dinner remains an issue in the naked city. *The Wall Street Journal*, p. 1. (13)

Nguyen, H.-H. D., & Ryan, A. M. (2008). Does stereotype threat affect test performance of minorities and women? A meta-analysis of experimental evidence. *Journal of Applied Psychology, 93*, 1314–1334. (9)

NICHD Early Child Care Research Network. (2006). Child-care effect sizes for the NICHD study of early child care and youth development. *American Psychologist, 61*, 99–116. (5)

Nicholson, H., Foote, C., & Gigerick, S. (2009). Deleterious effects of psychotherapy and counseling in the schools. *Psychology in the Schools, 46*, 232–237. (15)

Nickerson, C., Schwarz, N., Diener, E., & Kahneman, D. (2003). Zeroing in on the dark side of the American Dream: A closer look at the negative consequences of the goal for financial success. *Psychological Science, 14*, 531–536. (12)

Nickerson, R. S., & Adams, M. J. (1979). Long-term memory for a common object. *Cognitive Psychology, 11*, 287–307. (7)

Niebuhr, D. W., Millikan, A. M., Cowan, D. N., Yolken, R., Li, Y., & Weber, N. S. (2008). Selected infectious agents and risk of schizophrenia among U.S. military personnel. *American Journal of Psychiatry, 165*, 99–106. (16)

Nielsen, T. A., Zadra, A. L., Simard, V., Saucier, S., Stenstrom, P., Smith, C., et al. (2003). The typical dreams of Canadian university students. *Dreaming, 13*, 211–235. (10)

Nietzel, M.T., & Bernstein, D.A. (1987) *Introduction to clinical psychology.* Upper Saddle River, NJ: Prentice Hall. (9)

Nieuwenstein, M. R., & Potter, M. C. (2006). Temporal limits of selection and memory encoding. *Psychological Science, 17,* 471–475. (8)

Niiya, Y., Ellsworth, P. C., & Yamaguchi, S. (2006). Amae in Japan and the United States: An exploration of a "culturally unique" emotion. *Emotion, 6,* 279–295. (12)

Niki, K., & Luo, J. (2002). An fMRI study on the time-limited role of the medial temporal lobe in long-term topographical autobiographic memory. *Journal of Cognitive Neuroscience, 14,* 500–507. (7)

Nikles, C. D., II, Brecht, D. L., Klinger, E., & Bursell, A. L. (1998). The effects of current-concern and nonconcern-related waking suggestions on nocturnal dream content. *Journal of Personality and Social Psychology, 75,* 242–255. (10)

Nilsson, L.-L., & Lögdberg, B. (2008). Dead and forgotten—Postmortem time before discovery as indicator of social isolation and inadequate mental healthcare in schizophrenia. *Schizophrenia Bulletin, 102,* 337–339. (15)

Nisbett, R. E., Caputo, C., Legant, P., & Marecek, J. (1973). Behavior as seen by the actor and as seen by the observer. *Journal of Personality and Social Psychology, 27,* 154–164. (13)

Nisbett, R. E., Peng, K., Choi, I., & Norenzayan, A. (2001). Culture and systems of thought: Holistic versus analytic cognition. *Psychological Review, 108,* 291–310. (13)

Noaghiul, S., & Hibbeln, J. R. (2003). Cross-national comparisons of seafood consumption and rates of bipolar disorders. *American Journal of Psychiatry, 160,* 2222–2227. (16)

Noel, J. G., Wann, D. L., & Branscombe, N. R. (1995). Peripheral ingroup membership status and public negativity toward outgroups. *Journal of Personality and Social Psychology, 68,* 127–137. (13)

Nolan, J. M., Schultz, P. W., Cialdini, R. B., Goldstein, N. J., & Griskevicius, V. (2008). Normative social influence is underdetected. *Personality and Social Psychology Bulletin, 34,* 913–923. (13)

Nolen-Hoeksema, S. (1990). *Sex differences in depression.* Stanford, CA: Stanford University Press. (16)

Nolen-Hoeksema, S. (1991). Responses to depression and their effects on the duration of depressive episodes. *Journal of Abnormal Psychology, 100,* 569–582. (16)

Nolen-Hoeksema, S., Wisco, B. E., & Lybomirsky, S. (2008). Rethinking rumination. *Perspectives on Psychological Science, 3,* 400–424. (16)

Norcross, J. C., Kohout, J. L., & Wicherski, M. (2005). Graduate study in psychology: 1971 to 2004. *American Psychologist, 60,* 959–975. (1)

Nordenström, A., Servin, A., Bohlin, G., Larsson, A., & Wedell, A. (2002). Sex-typed toy play behavior correlates with the degree of prenatal androgen exposure assessed by CYP21 genotype in girls with congenital adrenal hyperplasia. *Journal of Clinical Endocrinology and Metabolism, 87,* 5119–5124. (5, 11)

Norenzayan, A., & Shariff, A. F. (2008). The origin and evolution of religious prosociality. *Science, 322,* 58–62. (13)

Norman, R. A., Tataranni, P. A., Pratley, R., Thompson, D. B., Hanson, R. L., Prochazka, M., et al. (1998). Autosomal genomic scan for loci linked to obesity and energy metabolism in Pima Indians. *American Journal of Human Genetics, 62,* 659–668. (11)

Norton, A., Winner, E., Cronin, K., Overy, K., Lee, D. J., & Schlaug, G. (2005). Are there pre-existing neural, cognitive, or motoric markers for musical ability? *Brain and Cognition, 59,* 124–134. (3)

Norton, M. I., Frost, J. H., & Ariely, D. (2007). Less is more: The lure of ambiguity, or why familiarity breeds contempt. *Journal of Personality and Social Psychology, 92,* 97–105. (13)

Nosek, B. A. (2007). Implicit–explicit relations. *Current Directions in Psychological Science, 16,* 65–69. (13)

Nosek, B. A., & Banaji, M. R. (2001). The go/no-go association task. *Social Cognition, 19,* 625–664. (13)

Nowak, M. A., & Sigmund, K. (2005). Evolution of indirect reciprocity. *Nature, 437,* 1291–1298. (13)

Nussbaum, A. D., & Dweck, C. S. (2008). Defensiveness versus remediation: Self-theories and modes of self-esteem maintenance. *Personality and Social Psychology Bulletin, 34,* 599–612. (14)

Oakes, L. M., Ross-Sheehy, S., & Luck, S. J. (2007). The development of visual short-term memory in infancy. In L. M. Oakes & P. J. Bauer (Eds.), *Short- and long-term memory in infancy and early childhood* (pp. 75–102). New York: Oxford University Press. (5)

Oberauer, K., Süss, H.-M., Wilhelm, O., & Wittman, W. W. (2003). The multiple faces of working memory. *Intelligence, 31,* 167–193. (7)

O'Connor, A. R., & Moulin, C. J. A. (2008). The persistence of erroneous familiarity in an epileptic male: Challenging perceptual theories of déjà vu activation. *Brain and Cognition, 68,* 144–147. (7)

O'Kane, G., Kensinger, E. A., & Corkin, S. (2004). Evidence for semantic learning in profound amnesia: An investigation with patient H. M. *Hippocampus, 14,* 417–425. (7)

Odell, S. M., & Commander, M. J. (2000). Risk factors for homelessness among people with psychotic disorders. *Social Psychiatry and Psychiatric Epidemiology, 35,* 396–401. (15)

Odgers, C. L., Caspi, A., Nagin, D. S., Piquero, A. R., Slutske, W. S., Milne, B. J., et al. (2008). Is it important to prevent early exposure to drugs and alcohol among adolescents? *Psychological Science, 19,* 1037–1044. (16)

Ohaeri, J. U., Adeyinka, A. O., & Osuntokun, B. O. (1995). Computed tomographic density changes in schizophrenic and manic Nigerian subjects. *Behavioural Neurology, 8,* 31–37. (16)

Ohayon, M. M. (1997). Prevalence of *DSM–IV* diagnostic criteria of insomnia: Distinguishing insomnia related to mental disorders from sleep disorders. *Journal of Psychiatric Research, 31,* 333–346. (10)

Öhman, A., Eriksson, A., & Olofsson, C. (1975). One-trial learning and superior resistance to extinction of autonomic responses conditioned to potentially phobic objects. *Journal of Comparative and Physiological Psychology, 88,* 619–627. (16)

Öhman, A., & Mineka, S. (2003). The malicious serpent: Snakes as a prototypical stimulus for an evolved module of fear. *Current Directions in Psychological Science, 12,* 5–9. (16)

Okasha, M., McCarron, P., McEwen, J., & Smith, G. D. (2001). Age at menarche: Secular trends and association with adult anthropometric measures. *Annals of Human Biology, 28,* 68–78. (5)

Olausson, H., Lamarre, Y., Backlund, H., Morin, C., Wallin, B. G., Starck, G., et al. (2002). Unmyelinated tactile afferents signal touch and project to insular cortex. *Nature Neuroscience, 5,* 900–904. (3)

Oliet, S. H. R., Baimoukhametova, D. V., Piet, R., & Bains, J. S. (2007). Retrograde regulation of GABA transmission by the tonic release of oxytocin and endocannabinoids governs postsynaptic firing. *Journal of Neuroscience, 27,* 1325–1333. (3)

Olney, J. W., & Farger, N. B. (1995). Glutamate receptor dysfunction and schizophrenia. *Archives of General Psychiatry, 52,* 998–1007. (16)

Olson, M. A., & Fazio, R. H. (2001). Implicit attitude formation through classical conditioning. *Psychological Science, 12,* 413–417. (6)

Olson, M. A., & Fazio, R. H. (2003). Relations between implicit measures of prejudice: What are we measuring? *Psychological Science, 14,* 636–639. (13)

Orne, M. T. (1951). The mechanisms of hypnotic age regression: An experimental study. *Journal of Abnormal and Social Psychology, 46,* 213–225. (10)

Orne, M. T. (1959). The nature of hypnosis: Artifact and essence. *Journal of Abnormal and Social Psychology, 58,* 277–299. (10)

Orne, M. T. (1969). Demand characteristics and the concept of quasi-controls. In R. Rosenthal & R. L. Rosnow (Eds.), *Artifact in behavioral research* (pp. 143–179). New York: Academic Press. (2)

Orne, M. T. (1979). On the simulating subject as a quasi-control group in hypnosis research: What, why, and how. In E. Fromm & R. E. Shor (Eds.), *Hypnosis: Developments in research and new perspectives* (2nd ed., pp. 519–565). New York: Aldine. (10)

Orne, M. T., & Evans, F. J. (1965). Social control in the psychological experiment: Antisocial behavior and hypnosis. *Journal of Personality and Social Psychology, 1,* 189–200. (10)

Orne, M. T., & Scheibe, K. E. (1964). The contribution of nondeprivation factors in the production of sensory deprivation effects: The psychology of the "panic button." *Journal of Abnormal and Social Psychology, 68,* 3–12. (2)

Ornstein, P. A., Baker-Ward, L., Gordon, B. N., Pelphrey, K. A., Tyler, C. S., & Gramzow, E. (2006). The influence of prior knowledge and repeated questioning on children's long-term retention of the details of a pediatic examination. *Developmental Psychology, 42,* 332–344. (7)

Ortony, A., & Turner, T. J. (1990). What's basic about basic emotions? *Psychological Review, 97,* 315–331. (12)

Ösby, U., Hammar, N., Brandt, L., Wicks, S., Thinsz, Z., Ekbom, A., et al. (2001). Time trends in first admissions for schizophrenia and paranoid psychosis in Stockholm County, Sweden. *Schizophrenia Research, 47,* 247–254. (16)

Osofsky, J. D. (1995). The effects of exposure to violence on young children. *American Psychologist, 50,* 782–788. (12)

O'Toole, B. I. (1990). Intelligence and behaviour and motor vehicle accident mortality. *Accident Analysis and Prevention, 22,* 211–221. (9)

Ottati, V., & Lee, Y. T. (1995). Accuracy: A neglected component of stereotype research. In Y. T. Lee, L. J. Jussim, & C. R. McCauley (Eds.), *Stereotype accuracy* (pp. 29–59). Washington, DC: American Psychological Association. (13)

Otto, K., Boos, A., Dalbert, C., Schöps, D., & Hoyer, J. (2006). Posttraumatic symptoms, depression, and anxiety of flood victims: The impact of the belief in a just world. *Personality and Individual Differences, 40,* 1075–1084. (14)

Otto, R. K., & Heilbrun, K. (2002). The practice of forensic psychology. *American Psychologist, 57,* 5–18. (1)

Owen, A. M., Coleman, M. R., Boly, M., Davis, M. H., Laureys, S., & Pickard, J. D. (2006). Detecting awareness in the vegetative state. *Science, 313,* 1402. (10)

Oxley, D. R., Smith, K. B., Alford, J. R., Hibbing, M. V., Miller, J. L., Scalora, M., et al. (2008). Political attitudes vary with physiological traits. *Science, 321,* 1667–1670. (3)

Oyserman, D., Coon, H. M., & Kemmelmeier, M. (2002). Rethinking individualism and collectivism: Evaluation of theoretical assumptions and meta-analyses. *Psychological Bulletin, 128,* 3–72. (13)

Padgham, C. A. (1975). Colours experienced in dreams. *British Journal of Psychology, 66,* 25–28. (10)

Paiva, V., Aranha, F., & Bastos, F. I. (2008). Opinions and attitudes regarding sexuality: Brazilian national research, 2005. *Revista de Saúde Pública, 42*(Suppl. 1). (11)

Paivandy, S., Bullock, E. E., Reardon, R. C., & Kelly, F. D. (2008). The effects of decision-making style and cognitive thought patterns on negative career thoughts. *Journal of Career Assessment, 16,* 474–488. (8)

Paladini, C. A., Fiorillo, C. D., Morikawa, H., & Williams, J. T. (2001). Amphetamine selectively blocks inhibitory glutamate transmission in dopamine neurons. *Nature Neuroscience, 4,* 275–281. (3)

Palesh, O., Butler, L. D., Koopman, C., Giese-Davis, J., Carlson, R., & Spiegel, D. (2007). Stress history and breast cancer recurrence. *Journal of Psychosomatic Research, 63,* 233–239. (12)

Palinkas, L. A. (2003). The psychology of isolated and confined environments. *American Psychologist, 58,* 353–363. (10, 16)

Paluck, E. L. (2009). Reducing intergroup prejudice and conflict using the media: A field experiment in Rwanda. *Journal of Personality and Social Psychology, 96,* 574–587. (13)

Panayiotou, G., Kokkinos, C. M., & Spanoudis, G. (2004). Searching for the "big five" in a Greek context: The NEO-FFI under the microscope. *Personality and Individual Differences, 36,* 1841–1854. (14)

Panikashvili, D., Simeonidou, C., Ben-Shabat, S., Hanuš, L. Breuer, A., Mechoulam, R., et al. (2001). An endogenous cannabinoid (2-AG) is neuroprotective after brain injury. *Nature, 413,* 527–531. (3)

Papini, M. R. (2002). Pattern and process in the evolution of learning. *Psychological Review, 109,* 186–201. (1)

Parasuraman, R., Greenwood, P. M., Kumar, R., & Fossella, J. (2005). Beyond heritability: Neurotransmitter genes differentially modulate visuospatial attention and working memory. *Psychological Science, 16,* 200–207. (7)

Parish, A. R., & deWaal, F. B. M. (2000). The other "closest living relative." *Annals of the New York Academy of Sciences, 907,* 97–113. (13)

Parish, W. L., Laumann, E. O., & Mojola, S. A. (2007). Sexual behavior in China: Trends and comparisons. *Population and Development Review, 33,* 729–756. (11)

Park, G., Lubinski, D., & Benbow, C. P. (2008). Ability differences among people who have commensurate degrees matter for scientific creativity. *Psychological Science, 19,* 957–961. (9)

Parke, R. D., Berkowitz, L., Leyens, J. P., West, S. G., & Sebastian, R. J. (1977). Some effects of violent and nonviolent movies on the behavior of juvenile delinquents. In L. Berkowitz (Ed.), *Advances in experimental social psychology* (Vol. 10, pp. 135–172). New York: Academic Press. (2)

Parker, D. (1944). *The portable Dorothy Parker.* New York: Viking Press. (15)

Parker, E. S., Cahill, L., & McGaugh, J. L. (2006). A case of unusual autobiographical remembering. *Neurocase, 12,* 35–49. (7)

Parkinson, B. (2007). Getting from situations to emotions: Appraisal and other routes. *Emotion, 7,* 21–25. (12)

Parmeggiani, P. L. (1982). Regulation of physiological functions during sleep in mammals. *Experientia, 38,* 1405–1408. (10)

Parrott, A. C. (1999). Does cigarette smoking cause stress? *American Psychologist, 54,* 817–820. (3)

Parzuchowski, M., & Szymkow-Sudziarska, A. (2008). Well, slap my thigh: Expression surprise facilitates memory of surprising material. *Emotion, 8,* 430–434. (12)

Pascual-Leone, A., Wasserman, E. M., Sadato, N., & Hallett, M. (1995). The role of reading activity on the modulation of motor control outputs to the reading hand in Braille readers. *Annals of Neurology, 38,* 910–915. (8)

Pashler, H., & Harris, C. R. (2001). Spontaneous allocation of visual attention: Dominant role of uniqueness. *Psychonomic Bulletin and Review, 8,* 747–752. (8)

Pasterski, V. L., Geffner, M. E., Brain, C., Hindmarsh, P., Brook, C., & Hines, M. (2005). Prenatal hormones and postnatal socialization by parents as determinants of male-typical toy play in girls with congenital adrenal hyperplasia. *Child Development, 76,* 264–278. (5, 11)

Pate, J. L., & Rumbaugh, D. M. (1983). The language-like behavior of Lana chimpanzee: Is it merely discrimination and paired-associate learning? *Animal Learning and Behavior, 11,* 134–138. (8)

Patterson, C. J. (1994). Lesbian and gay families. *Current Directions in Psychological Science, 3,* 62–64. (5)

Patterson, D. R. (2004). Treating pain with hypnosis. *Current Directions in Psychological Science, 13,* 252–255. (10)

Paulhus, D. L., Trapnell, P. D., & Chen, D. (1999). Birth order effects on personality and achievement within families. *Psychological Science, 10,* 482–488. (5)

Paunonen, S. V., & Jackson, D. N. (2000). What is beyond the big five? Plenty! *Journal of Personality, 68,* 821–835. (14)

Paus, T., Marrett, S., Worsley, K. J., & Evans, A. C. (1995). Extraretinal modulation of cerebral blood flow in the human visual cortex: Implications for saccadic suppression. *Journal of Neurophysiology, 74,* 2179–2183. (8)

Pavlov, I. P. (1960). *Conditioned reflexes.* New York: Dover. (Original work published 1927) (6)

Payne, J. W., Samper, A., Bettman, J. R., & Luce, M. F. (2008). Boundary conditions on unconscious thought in complex decision making. *Psychological Science, 19,*1118–1123. (8)

Payne, K. T., & Marcus, D. K. (2008). The efficacy of group therapy for older adult clients: A meta-analysis. *Group Dynamics: Theory, Research, and Practice, 12,* 268–278. (15)

Pearce, J. M. (1994). Similarity and discrimination: A selective review and a connectionist model. *Psychological Review, 101,* 587–607. (6)

Pearl, P. L., Weiss, R. E., & Stein, M. A. (2001). Medical mimics. *Annals of the New York Academy of Sciences, 931,* 97–112. (8)

Pearlson, G. D., Petty, R. G., Ross, C. A., & Tien, A. Y. (1996). Schizophrenia—a disease of heteromodal association cortex. *Neuropsychopharmacology, 14,* 1–17. (16)

Peele, S. (1998, March/April). All wet. *The Sciences, 38*(2), 17–21. (16)

Peigneux, P., Laureys, S., Fuchs, S., Collette, F., Perrin, F., Reggers, J., et al. (2004). Are spatial memories strengthened in the human hippocampus during slow wave sleep? *Neuron, 44,* 535–545. (10)

Penfield, W., & Rasmussen, T. (1950). *The cerebral cortex of man.* New York: Macmillan. (3)

Peng, K., & Nisbett, R. E. (1999). Culture dialectics, and reasoning about contradiction. *American Psychologist, 54,* 741–754. (13)

Pelham, B. W., Mirenberg, M. C., & Jones, J. K. (2002). Why Susie sells seashells by the seashore: Implicit egotism and major life decisions. *Journal of Personality and Social Psychology, 82,* 469–487. (1)

Pelham, W. E., Jr., & Fabiano, G. A. (2008). Evidence-based psychosocial treatments for attention-deficit/hyperactivity disorder. *Journal of Clinical Child and Adolescent Psychology, 37,* 184–214. (8)

Pennebaker, J. W. (1997). Writing about emotional experiences as a therapeutic process. *Psychological Science, 8,* 162–166. (12)

Pennebaker, J. W., & Graybeal, A. (2001). Patterns of natural language use: Disclosure, personality, and social integration. *Current Directions in Psychological Science, 10,* 90–93. (12)

Pennebaker, J. W., & Seagal, J. D. (1999). Forming a story: The health benefits of narrative. *Journal of Clinical Psychology, 55,* 1243–1254. (15)

Perani, D., & Abutalebi, J. (2005). The neural basis of first and second language processing. *Current Opinion in Neurobiology, 15,* 202–206. (4)

Peretz, I., Cummings, S., & Dube, M. P. (2007). The genetics of congenital amusia (tone deafness): A family-aggregation study. *American Journal of Human Genetics, 81,* 582–588. (4)

Perez, E. A. (1995). Review of the preclinical pharmacology and comparative efficacy of 5-hydroxytryptamine-3 receptor antagonists for chemotherapy-induced emesis. *Journal of Clinical Oncology, 13,* 1036–1043. (3)

Pérez, M. F., Maglio, L. E., Marchesini, G. R., Molina, J. C., & Ramirez, O. A. (2002). Environmental changes modify the expression of diazepam withdrawal. *Behavioural Brain Research, 136,* 75–81. (6)

Perry, D. G., & Bussey, K. (1979). The social learning theory of sex differences: Imitation is alive and well. *Journal of Personality and Social Psychology, 37,* 1699–1712. (14)

Person, C., Tracy, M., & Galea, S. (2006). Risk factors for depression after a disaster. *Journal of Nervous and Mental Disease, 194,* 659–666. (16)

Pert, C. B., & Snyder, S. H. (1973). The opiate receptor: Demonstration in nervous tissue. *Science, 179,* 1011–1014. (3, 4)

Pessiglione, M., Schmidt, L., Draganski, B., Kalisch, R., Lau, H., Dolan, R. J., et al. (2007). How the brain translates money into force: A neuroimaging study of subliminal motivation. *Science, 316,* 904–906. (4)

Pesta, B. J., & Poznanski, P. J. (2008). Black–White differences on IQ and grades: The mediating role of elementary cognitive tasks. *Intelligence, 36,* 323–329. (9)

Peters, F., Nicolson, N. A., Berkhof, J., Delespaul, P., & deVries, M. (2003). Effects of daily events on mood states in major depressive disorder. *Journal of Abnormal Psychology, 112,* 203–211. (16)

Peterson, C., Bettes, B. A., & Seligman, M. E. P. (1985). Depressive symptoms and unprompted causal attributions: Content analysis. *Behaviour Research and Therapy, 23,* 379–382. (16)

Peterson, L. G., Peterson, M., O'Shanick, G. J., & Swann, A. (1985). Self-inflicted gunshot wounds: Lethality of method versus intent. *American Journal of Psychiatry, 142,* 228–231. (16)

Peterson, L. R., & Peterson, M. J. (1959). Short-term retention of individual verbal items. *Journal of Experimental Psychology, 58,* 193–198. (7)

Petkov, C. I., Kayser, C., Steudel, T., Whittingstall, K., Augath, M., & Logothetis, N. K. (2008). A voice region in the monkey brain. *Nature Neuroscience, 11,* 367–374. (8)

Petrill, S. A., Luo, D., Thompson, L. A., & Detterman, D. K. (1996). The independent prediction of general intelligence by elementary cognitive tasks: Genetic and environmental influences. *Behavior Genetics, 26,* 135–147. (9)

Petrill, S. A., Plomin, R., Berg, S., Johansson, B., Pedersen, N. L., Ahern, F., et al. (1998). The genetic and environmental relationship between general and specific cognitive abilities in twins age 80 and older. *Psychological Science, 9,* 183–189. (9)

Petrova, P. K., Cialdini, R. B., & Sills, S. J. (2006). Consistency-based compliance across cultures. *Journal of Experimental Psychology, 43,* 104–111. (13)

Petty, R. E., & Briñol, P. (2008). Persuasion: From single to multiple to metacognitive processes. *Perspectives on Psychological Science, 3,* 137–147. (13)

Petty, R. E., & Cacioppo, J. T. (1977). Effects of forewarning of persuasive intent and involvement on cognitive responses and persuasion. *Personality and Social Psychology Bulletin, 5,* 173–176. (13)

Petty, R. E., & Cacioppo, J. T. (1981). *Attitudes and persuasion: Classic and contemporary approaches.* Dubuque, IA: William C. Brown. (13)

Petty, R. E., & Cacioppo, J. T. (1986). *Communication and persuasion: Central and peripheral routes to attitude change.* New York: Springer-Verlag. (13)

Pexman, P. M., Hargreaves, I. S., Edwards, J. D., Henry, L. C., & Goodyear, B. G. (2007). The neural consequences of semantic richness. *Psychological Science, 18,* 401–406. (3)

Pezze, M. A., Bast, T., & Feldon, J. (2003). Significance of dopamine transmission in the rat medial prefrontal cortex for conditioned fear. *Cerebral Cortex, 13,* 371–380. (6)

Pfungst, O. (1911). *Clever Hans.* New York: Holt. (2)

Phan, K. L., Wager, T., Taylor, S. F., & Liberzon, I. (2002). Functional neuroanatomy of emotion: A meta-analysis of emotion activation studies in PET and fMRI. *NeuroImage, 16,* 331–348. (12)

Phelps, E. A., O'Connor, K. J., Cunningham, W. A., Funayama, E. S., Gatenby, J. C., Gore, J. C., et al. (2000). Performance on indirect measures of race evaluation predicts amygdala activation. *Journal of Cognitive Neuroscience, 12,* 729–738. (13)

Phelps, M. E., & Mazziotta, J. C. (1985). Positron emission tomography: Human brain function and biochemistry. *Science, 228,* 799–809. (1, 3)

Philippot, P., Chapelle, G., & Blairy, S. (2002). Respiratory feedback in the generation of emotions. *Cognition and Emotion, 16,* 605–627. (12)

Phillips, P. E. M., Stuber, G. D., Heien, M. L. A. V., Wightman, R. M., & Carelli, R. M. (2003). Subsecond dopamine release promotes cocaine seeking. *Nature, 422,* 614–618. (16)

Phillips, T. M., & Pittman, J. F. (2007). Adolescent psychological well-being by identity style. *Journal of Adolescence, 30,* 1021–1034. (5)

Phinney, J. S. (1990). Ethnic identity in adolescents and adults: Review of research. *Psychological Bulletin, 108,* 499–514. (5)

Piaget, J. (1954). *The construction of reality in the child* (M. Cook, Trans.). New York: Basic Books. (Original work published 1937) (5)

Pichot, P. (1984). Centenary of the birth of Hermann Rorschach. *Journal of Personality Assessment, 48,* 591–596. (14)

Pierri, J. N., Volk, C. L. E., Auh, S., Sampson, A., & Lewis, D. A. (2001). Decreased somal size of deep layer 3 pyramidal neurons in the prefrontal cortex of subjects with schizophrenia. *Archives of General Psychiatry, 58,* 466–473. (16)

Pike, J. J., & Jennings, N. A. (2005). The effects of commercials on children's perceptions of gender appropriate toy use. *Sex Roles, 52,* 83–91. (5)

Pike, K. M., Hilbert, A., Wilfley, D. E., Fairburn, C. G., Dohm, F.-A., Walsh, B. T., et al. (2007). Toward an understanding of risk factors for anorexia nervosa: A case-control study. *Psychological Medicine, 38,* 1443–1453. (11)

Pind, J., Gunnarsdóttir, E. K., & Jóhannesson, H. S. (2003). Raven's standard progressive matrices: New school age norms and a study of the test's validity. *Personality and Individual Differences, 34,* 375–386. (9)

Pinel, J. P. J., Assanand, S., & Lehman, D. R. (2000). Hunger, eating, and ill health. *American Psychologist, 55,* 1105–1116. (11)

Pinker, S. (1994). *The language instinct.* New York: Morrow. (8)

Piolino, P., Desgranges, B., Benali, K., & Eustache, F. (2002). Episodic and semantic remote autobiographical memory in ageing. *Memory, 10,* 239–257. (7)

Pitschel-Walz, G., Leucht, S., Bäuml, J., Kissling, W., & Engel, R. R. (2001). The effect of family interventions on relapse and rehospitalization in schizophrenia—A meta-analysis. *Schizophrenia Bulletin, 27,* 73–92. (16)

Pittenger, D. J. (2005). Cautionary comments regarding the Myers-Briggs Type Indicator. *Consulting Psychology Journal: Practice and Research, 57,* 210–221. (14)

Place, S. S., Todd, P. M., Penke, L., & Asendorpf, J. B. (2009). The ability to judge the romantic interest of others. *Psychological Science, 20,* 22–26. (13)

Plant, E. A., & Devine, P. G. (2003). The antecedents and implications of interracial anxiety. *Personality and Social Psychology Bulletin, 29,* 790–801. (13)

Plaut, D. C., & Booth, J. R. (2000). Individual and developmental differences in semantic priming: Empirical and computational support for a single-mechanism account of lexical priming. *Psychological Review, 107,* 786–823. (8)

Plaut, V. C., Thomas, K. M., & Goren, M. J. (2009). Is multiculturalism or color blindness better for minorities? *Psychological Science, 20,* 444–446. (13)

Plomin, R., Corley, R., DeFries, J. C., & Fulker, D. W. (1990). Individual differences in television viewing in early childhood: Nature as well as nurture. *Psychological Science, 1,* 371–377. (5)

Plomin, R., DeFries, J. C., McClearn, G. E., & McGuffin, P. (Eds.). (2001). *Behavioral genetics* (4th ed.) New York: Worth. (9)

Plomin, R., Fulker, D. W., Corley, R., & DeFries, J. C. (1997). Nature, nurture, and cognitive development from 1 to 16 years: A parent-offspring adoption study. *Psychological Science, 8,* 442–447. (9)

Plomin, R., & Kovas, Y. (2005). Generalist genes and learning disabilities. *Psychological Bulletin, 131,* 592–617. (9)

Plomin, R., & Spinath, F. M. (2004). Intelligence: Genetics, genes, and genomics. *Journal of Personality and Social Psychology, 86,* 112–129. (9)

Plous, S. (1993). *The psychology of judgment and decision making.* Philadelphia: Temple University Press. (8)

Plous, S. (1996). Attitudes toward the use of animals in psychological research and education. *American Psychologist, 51,* 1167–1180. (2)

Plutchik, R. (1982). A psychoevolutionary theory of emotions. *Social Science Information, 21,* 529–553. (12)

Plutchik, R., & Ax, A. F. (1967). A critique of "determinants of emotional state" by Schachter and Singer (1962). *Psychophysiology, 4,* 79–82. (12)

Pockett, S., & Miller, A. (2007). The rotating spot method of timing subjective events. *Consciousness and Cognition, 16,* 241–254. (10)

Polcin, D. L. (1997). The etiology and diagnosis of alcohol dependence: Differences in the professional literature. *Psychotherapy, 34,* 297–306. (16)

Pole, N., Neylan, T. C., Best, S. R., Orr, S. P., & Marmar, C. R. (2003). Fear-potentiated startle and posttraumatic stress symptoms in urban police officers. *Journal of Traumatic Stress, 16,* 471–479. (12)

Polivy, J., & Herman, C. P. (1985). Dieting and binging: A causal analysis. *American Psychologist, 40,* 193–201. (11)

Polk, T. A., Drake, R. M., Jonides, J. J., Smith, M. R., & Smith, E. E. (2008). Attention enhances the neural processing of relevant features and suppresses the processing of irrelevant features in humans: A functional magnetic resonance imaging study of the Stroop task. *Journal of Neuroscience, 28,* 13786–13792. (8)

Pollak, J. M. (1979). Obsessive-compulsive personality: A review. *Psychological Bulletin, 86,* 225–241. (16)

Pond, S. B., III, & Geyer, P. D. (1991). Differences in the relation between job satisfaction and perceived work alternatives among older and younger blue-collar workers. *Journal of Vocational Behavior, 39,* 251–262. (11)

Poole, D. A., & White, L. T. (1993). Two years later: Effect of question repetition and retention interval on the eyewitness testimony of children and adults. *Developmental Psychology, 29,* 844–853. (7)

Pope, H. G., Jr., Gruber, A. J., Hudson, J. I., Huestis, M. A., & Yurgelun-Todd, D. (2001). Neuropsychological performance in long-term cannabis users. *Archives of General Psychiatry, 58,* 909–915. (3)

Pope, K. S. (1996). Memory, abuse, and science: Questioning claims about the false memory syndrome epidemic. *American Psychologist, 51,* 957–974. (7)

Popper, K. (1986). Predicting overt behavior versus predicting hidden states. *Behavioral and Brain Sciences, 9,* 254–255. (14)

Porter, J., Craven, B., Khan, R. M., Chang, S.-J., Kang, I., Judkewicz, B., et al. (2007). Mechanisms of scent-tracking in humans. *Nature Neuroscience, 10,* 27–29. (4)

Porter, S., Birt, A. R., Yuille, J. C., & Lehman, D. R. (2000). Negotiating false memories: Interviewer and rememberer characteristics relate to memory distortion. *Psychological Science, 11,* 507–510. (7)

Porter, S., & ten Brinke, L. (2008). Reading between the lies. *Psychological Science, 19,* 508–514. (12)

Post, R. M. (1992). Transduction of psychosocial stress into the neurobiology of recurrent affective disorder. *American Journal of Psychiatry, 149,* 999–1010. (16)

Posthuma, D., De Geus, E. J. C., Baaré, W. F. C., Pol, H. E. H., Kahn, R. S., & Boomsma, D. I. (2002). The association between brain volume and intelligence is of genetic origin. *Nature Neuroscience, 5,* 83–84. (9)

Povinelli, D. J., & deBlois, S. (1992). Young children's (*Homo sapiens*) understanding of knowledge formation in themselves and others. *Journal of Comparative Psychology, 106,* 228–238. (5)

Powell, L. H., Calvin, J. E., III, & Calvin, J. E., Jr. (2007). Effective obesity treatments. *American Psychologist, 62,* 234–246. (11)

Powell, R. A., & Boer, D. P. (1994). Did Freud mislead patients to confabulate memories of abuse? *Psychological Reports, 74,* 1283–1298. (14)

Pratkanis, A. R. (1992, Spring). The cargo-cult science of subliminal perception. *Skeptical Inquirer, 16,* 260–272. (4)

Principe, G. F., Kanaya, T., Ceci, S. J., & Singh, M. (2006). Believing is seeing. *Psychological Science, 17,* 243–248. (7)

Pronin, E. (2008). How we see ourselves and how we see others. *Science, 320,* 1177–1180. (13)

Pronin, E., Berger, J., & Molouki, S. (2007). Alone in a crowd of sheep: Asymmetric perceptions of conformity and their roots in an introspection error. *Journal of Personality and Social Psychology, 92*, 585–595. (13)

Pronin, E., Gilovich, T., & Ross, L. (2004). Objectivity in the eye of the beholder: Divergent perceptions of bias in self versus others. *Psychological Review, 111*, 781–799. (13)

Provine, R. (2000). *Laughter.* New York: Viking Press. (2, 12)

Provine, R. R., Krosnowski, K. A., & Brocato, N. W. (2009). Tearing: Breakthrough in human emotional signaling. *Evolutionary Psychology, 7*, 52–56. (12)

Public Agenda. (2001). *Medical research: Red flags.* Retrieved February 8, 2007, from http://www.publicagenda.org/charts/support-stem-cell-research-can-vary-dramatically-depending-question-wording-o. (2)

Pulver, C. A., & Kelly, K. R. (2008). Incremental validity of the Myers-Briggs Type Indicator in predicting academic major selection of undecided university students. *Journal of Career Assessment, 16*, 441–455. (14)

Purves, D., & Lotto, R. B. (2003). *Why we see what we do: An empirical theory of vision.* Sunderland, MA: Sinauer Associates. (4)

Purves, D., Williams, S. M., Nundy, S., & Lotto, R. B. (2004). Perceiving the intensity of light. *Psychological Review, 111*, 142–158. (4)

Putilov, A. A., Pinchasov, B. B., & Poljakova, E. Y. (2005). Antidepressant effects of mono- and combined non-drug treatments for seasonal and non-seasonal depression. *Biological Rhythm Research, 36*, 405–421. (16)

Pyers, J. E., & Emmorey, K. (2008). The face of bimodal bilingualism. *Psychological Science, 19*, 531–536. (8)

Pyszczynski, T., Greenberg, J., & Solomon, S. (2000). Proximal and distal defense: A new perspective on unconscious motivation. *Current Directions in Psychological Science, 9*, 156–160. (5)

Qin, P., & Mortensen, P. B. (2003). The impact of parental status on the risk of completed suicide. *Archives of General Psychiatry, 60*, 797–802. (16)

Quadrel, M. J., Fischhoff, B., & Davis, W. (1993). Adolescent (in)vulnerability. *American Psychologist, 48*, 102–116. (5)

Quas, J. A., Malloy, L. C., Melinder, A., Goodman, G. S., D'Mello, M., & Schaaf, J. (2007). Developmental differences in the effects of repeated interviews and interview bias on young children's event memory and false reports. *Developmental Psychology, 43*, 823–837. (7)

Quattrocchi, M. R., & Schopp, R. F. (2005). Tarasaurus rex: A standard of care that could not adapt. *Psychology, Public Policy, and Law, 11*, 109–137. (15)

Quinn, P. C., & Liben, L. S. (2008). A sex difference in mental rotation in young infants. *Psychological Science, 19*, 1067–1070. (5)

Quiroga, R. Q., Mukamel, R., Isham, E. A., & Fried, I. (2008). Human single-neuron responses at the threshold of conscious recognition. *Proceedings of the National Academy of Sciences, USA, 105*, 3599–3604. (10)

Rachman, S. (2002). A cognitive theory of compulsive checking behavior. *Behaviour Research and Therapy, 40*, 625–639. (16)

Rachman, S. J., & Hodgson, R. J. (1980). *Obsessions and compulsions.* Upper Saddle River, NJ: Prentice Hall. (16)

Rahman, Q., Andersson, D., & Govier, E. (2005). A specific sexual orientation-related difference in navigation strategy. *Behavioral Neuroscience, 119*, 311–316. (5)

Raine, A., Lencz, T., Bihrle, S., LaCasse, L., & Colletti, P. (2000). Reduced prefrontal gray matter volume and reduced autonomic activity in antisocial personality disorder. *Archives of General Psychiatry, 57*, 119–127. (12)

Rainville, P., Duncan, G. H., Price, D. D., Carrier, B., & Bushnell, M. C. (1997). Pain affect encoded in human anterior cingulate but not somatosensory cortex. *Science, 277*, 968–971. (5)

Rainville, P., Hofbauer, R. K., Bushnell, M. C., Duncan, G. H., & Price, D. D. (2002). Hypnosis modulates activity in brain structures involved in the regulation of consciousness. *Journal of Cognitive Neuroscience, 14*, 887–901. (10)

Raison, C. L., Klein, H. M., & Steckler, M. (1999). The moon and madness reconsidered. *Journal of Affective Disorders, 53*, 99–106. (2)

Ramachandran, V. S. (2003, May). Hearing colors, tasting shapes. *Scientific American, 288*(5), 52–59. (4)

Ramachandran, V. S., & Blakeslee, S. (1998). *Phantoms in the brain.* New York: Morrow. (4)

Ramachandran, V. S., & Hirstein, W. (1998). The perception of phantom limbs: The D. O. Hebb lecture. *Brain, 121*, 1603–1630. (4)

Ramey, C. T., & Ramey, S. L. (1998). Early intervention and early experience. *American Psychologist, 33*, 109–120. (9)

Ramirez, J. M., Santisteban, C., Fujihara, T., & Van Goozen, S. (2002). Differences between experience of anger and readiness to angry action: A study of Japanese and Spanish students. *Aggressive Behavior, 28*, 429–438. (12)

Ramirez-Amaya, V., Marrone, D. F., Gage, F. H., Worley, P. F., & Barnes, C. A. (2006). Integration of new neurons into functional neural networks. *Journal of Neuroscience, 26*, 12237–12241. (3)

Ramsey-Rennels, J. L., & Langlois, J. H. (2006). Infants' differential processing of female and male faces. *Current Directions in Psychological Science, 15*, 59–62. (5)

Ransley, J. K., Donnelly, J. K., Botham, H., Khara, T. N., Greenwood, D. C., & Cade, J. E. (2003). Use of supermarket receipts to estimate energy and fat content of food purchased by lean and overweight families. *Appetite, 41*, 141–148. (11)

Rasch, B., & Born, J. (2008). Reactivation and consolidation of memory during sleep. *Current Directions in Psychological Science, 17*, 188–192. (10)

Rasetti, R., Mattay, V. S., Wiedholz, L. M., Kolachana, B. S., Hariri, A. R., Callicott, J. H., et al. (2009). Evidence that altered amygdala activity in schizophrenia is related to clinical state and not genetic risk. *American Journal of Psychiatry, 166*, 216–225. (16)

Rattenborg, N. C., Amlaner, C. J., & Lima, S. L. (2000). Behavioral, neurophysiological and evolutionary perspectives on unihemispheric sleep. *Neuroscience and Biobehavioral Reviews, 24*, 817–842. (10)

Rattenborg, N. C., Mandt, B. H., Obermeyer, W. H., Winsauer, P. J., Huber, R., Wikelski, M., et al. (2004). Migratory sleeplessness in the white-crowned sparrow (*Zonotrichia leucophrys gambelii*). *PLoS Biology, 2*, 924–936. (3)

Rauscher, F. H., Shaw, G. L., & Ky, K. N. (1993). Music and spatial task performance. *Nature, 365*, 611. (2)

Raven, J. (2000). The Raven's Progressive Matrices: Change and stability over culture and time. *Cognitive Psychology, 41*, 1–48. (9)

Raymond, J. E. (2003). New objects, not new features, trigger the attentional blink. *Psychological Science, 14*, 54–59. (8)

Rayner, K. (1998). Eye movements in reading and information processing: 20 years of research. *Psychological Bulletin, 124*, 372–422. (8)

Rayner, K., Foorman, B. R., Perfetti, C. A., Pesetsky, D., & Seidenberg, M. S. (2001). How psychological science informs the teaching of reading. *Psychological Science in the Public Interest, 2*, 31–74. (8)

Rayner, K., White, S. J., Johnson, R. L., & Liversedge, S. P. (2006). Raeding wrods with jubmled lettres. *Psychological Science, 17*, 192–193. (8)

Raz, A., Kirsch, I., Pollard, J., & Nitkin-Kaner, Y. (2006). Suggestion reduces the Stroop effect. *Psychological Science, 17*, 91–95. (8)

Rechtschaffen, A., & Bergmann, B. M. (1995). Sleep deprivation in the rat by the disk-over-water method. *Behavioural Brain Research, 69*, 55–63. (5)

Redding, R. E. (2001). Sociopolitical diversity in psychology. *American Psychologist, 56*, 205–215. (5)

Redican, W. K. (1982). An evolutionary perspective on human facial displays. In P. Ekman (Ed.), *Emotion in the human face* (pp. 212–280). Cambridge, England: Cambridge University Press. (12)

Reed, A. E., Mikels, J. A., & Simon, K. I. (2008). Older adults prefer less choice than younger adults. *Psychology and Aging, 23*, 671–675. (8)

Reed, J. M., & Squire, L. R. (1999). Impaired transverse patterning in human amnesia is a special case of impaired memory for two-choice discrimination tasks. *Behavioral Neuroscience, 113*, 3–9. (7)

Reed, T. E. (1985). Ethnic differences in alcohol use, abuse, and sensitivity: A review with genetic interpretation. *Social Biology, 32*, 195–209. (16)

Reichenberg, A., Gross, R., Weiser, M., Bresnahan, M., Silverman, J., Harlap, S., et al. (2006). Advancing paternal age and autism. *Archives of General Psychiatry, 63*, 1026–1032. (16)

Reicher, G. M. (1969). Perceptual recognition as a function of meaningfulness of stimulus material. *Journal of Experimental Psychology, 81*, 275–280. (8)

Reinius, B., Saetre, P., Leonard, J. A., Blekhman, R., Merino-Martinez, R., Gilad, Y., et al. (2008). An evolutionarily conserved sexual signature in the primate brain. *PLoS Genetics, 4*, e1000100. (5)

Reisenzein, R. (1983). The Schachter theory of emotions: Two decades later. *Psychological Bulletin, 94*, 239–264. (12)

Reneman, L., de Win, M. M. L., van den Brink, W., Booij, J., & den Heeten, G. J. (2006). Neuroimaging findings with MDMA/ecstasy: Technical aspects, conceptual issues and future prospects. *Journal of Psychopharmacology, 20*, 164–175. (3)

Reneman, L., Lavalaye, J., Schmand, B., de Wolff, F. A., van den Brink, W., den Heeten, G. J., et al. (2001). Cortical serotonin transporter density and verbal memory in individuals who stopped using 3,4-methylenedioxymethamphetamine (MDMA or "ecstasy"). *Archives of General Psychiatry, 58*, 901–906. (3)

Rensink, R. A., O'Regan, J. K., & Clark, J. J. (1997). To see or not to see: The need for attention to perceive changes in scenes. *Psychological Science, 8*, 368–373. (8)

Rentfrow, P. J., & Gosling, S. D. (2006). Message in a ballad. *Psychological Science, 17*, 236–242. (14)

Rentfrow, P. J., Gosling, S. D., & Potter, J. (2008). A theory of the emergence, persistence, and expression of geographic variation in psychological characteristics. *Perspectives on Psychological Science, 3*, 339–369. (14)

Repetti, R. L., Taylor, S. E., & Seeman, T. E. (2002). Risky families: Family social environments and the mental and physical health of offspring. *Psychological Bulletin, 128*, 330–366. (12)

Repovš, G., & Baddeley, A. (2006). The multi-component model of working memory: Explorations in experimental cognitive psychology. *Neuroscience, 139,* 5–21. (7)

Rescorla, R. A. (1968). Probability of shock in the presence and absence of CS in fear conditioning. *Journal of Comparative and Physiological Psychology, 66,* 1–5. (6)

Rescorla, R. A. (1988). Pavlovian conditioning: It's not what you think it is. *American Psychologist, 43,* 151–160. (6)

Restle, F. (1970). Moon illusion explained on the basis of relative size. *Science, 167,* 1092–1096. (4)

Revusky, S. (2009). Chemical aversion treatment of alcoholism. In S. Reilly & T. R. Schachtman (Eds.), *Conditioned taste aversion* (pp. 445–472). New York: Oxford University Press. (6)

Reyna, V. F., & Farley, F. (2006). Risk and rationality in adolescent decision making: Implications for theory, practice, and public policy. *Psychological Science in the Public Interest, 7,* 1–44. (5)

Rhodes, G., Jeffery, L., Watson, T. L, Clifford, C. W. G., & Nakayama, K. (2003). Fitting the mind to the world: Face adaptation and attractiveness aftereffects. *Psychological Science, 14,* 558–566. (13)

Rhodes, G., Sumich, A., & Byatt, G. (1999). Are average facial configurations attractive only because of their symmetry? *Psychological Science, 10,* 52–58. (13)

Rhodes, R. A., Murthy, N. V., Dresner, M. A., Selvaraj, S., Stavrakakis, N., Babar, S., et al. (2007). Human 5-HT transporter availability predicts amygdala reactivity *in vivo. Journal of Neuroscience, 27,* 9233–9237. (3)

Riccio, D. C. (1994). Memory: When less is more. *American Psychologist, 49,* 917–926. (7)

Riccio, D. C., Millin, P. M., & Gisquet- Verrier, P. (2003). Retrograde amnesia: Forgetting back. *Current Directions in Psychological Science, 12,* 41–44. (7)

Rice, M. E., & Cragg, S. J. (2004). Nicotine amplifies reward-related dopamine signals in striatum. *Nature Neuroscience, 7,* 583–584. (3)

Richard, C., Honoré, J., Bernati, T., & Rousseaux, M. (2004). Straight-ahead pointing correlates with long-line bisection in neglect patients. *Cortex, 40,* 75–83. (10)

Richeson, J. A., & Nussbaum, R. J. (2004). The impact of multiculturalism versus color-blindness on racial bias. *Journal of Experimental Social Psychology, 40,* 417–423. (13)

Riddle, W. J. R., & Scott, A. I. F. (1995). Relapse after successful electroconvulsive therapy: The use and impact of continuation antidepressant drug treatment. *Human Psychopharmacology, 10,* 201–205. (16)

Rieger, G., Chivers, M. L., & Bailey, J. M. (2005). Sexual arousal patterns of bisexual men. *Psychological Science, 16,* 579–584. (11)

Rieger, G., Linsenmeier, J. A. W., Gygax, L., & Bailey, J. M. (2008). Sexual orientation and childhood gender nonconformity: Evidence from home videos. *Developmental Psychology, 44,* 46–58. (11)

Rilling, J. K., Glasser, M. F., Preuss, T. M., Ma, X., Zhao, T., Hu, X., et al. (2008). The evolution of the arcuate fasciculus revealed with comparative DTI. *Nature Neuroscience, 11,* 426–428. (8)

Risch, N., Herrell, R., Lehner, T., Liang, K.-Y., Eaves, L., Hoh, J., et al. (2009). Interaction between the serotonin transporter gene (*5-HTTLPR*), stressful life events, and risk of depression. *Journal of the American Medical Association, 301,* 2462–2471. (16)

Ritvo, E. R. (2006). *Understanding the nature of autism and Asperger's syndrome.* London: Jessica Kingsley. (16)

Rivas-Vazquez, R. A. (2001). Antidepressants as first-line agents in the current pharmacotherapy of anxiety disorders. *Professional Psychology: Research and Practice, 32,* 101–104. (16)

Roane, B. M., & Taylor, D. J. (2008). Adolescent insomnia as a risk factor for early adult depression and substance abuse. *Sleep, 31,* 1351–1356. (16)

Roberts, B. W., & DelVecchio, W. F. (2000). The rank-order consistency of personality traits from childhood to old age: A quantitative review of longitudinal studies. *Psychological Bulletin, 126,* 3–25. (14)

Roberts, B. W., Kuncel, N. R., Shiner, R., Caspi, A., & Goldberg, L. R. (2007). The power of personality. *Perspectives on Psychological Science, 2,* 313–345. (14)

Roberts, B. W., Walton, K. E., & Viechtbauer, W. (2006). Patterns of mean-level change in personality traits across the life course: A meta-analysis of longitudinal studies. *Psychological Bulletin, 132,* 1–25. (14)

Roberts, S. B., Savage, J., Coward, W. A., Chew, B., & Lucas, A. (1988). Energy expenditure and intake in infants born to lean and overweight mothers. *New England Journal of Medicine, 318,* 461–466. (11)

Roberts, S. C., Gosling, L. M., Carter, V., & Petrie, M. (2008). MHC-correlated odour preferences in humans and the use of oral contraceptives. *Proceedings of the Royal Society,* B, 275, 2715–2722. (13)

Robertson, I. H. (2005, Winter). The deceptive world of subjective awareness. *Cerebrum, 7*(1), 74–83. (3)

Robertson, L. C. (2003). Binding, spatial attention and perceptual awareness. *Nature Reviews Neuroscience, 4,* 93–102. (3)

Robins, L. N., Helzer, J. E., Weissman, M. M., Orvaschel, H., Gruenberg, E., Burke, J. D., Jr., et al. (1984). Lifetime prevalence of specific psychiatric disorders in three sites. *Archives of General Psychiatry, 41,* 949–958. (16)

Robinson, T. E., & Berridge, K. C. (2000). The psychology and neurobiology of addiction: An incentive-sensitization view. *Addiction, 95*(Suppl. 2), S91–S117. (16)

Robinson, T. E., & Berridge, K. C. (2001). Incentive-sensitization and addiction. *Addiction, 96,* 103–114. (16)

Roca, C. A., Schmidt, P. J., & Rubinow, D. R. (1999). Gonadal steroids and affective illness. *Neuroscientist, 5,* 227–237. (16)

Rock, I., & Kaufman, L. (1962). The moon illusion, II. *Science, 136,* 1023–1031. (4)

Rodd, J., Gaskell, G., & Marslen-Wilson, W. (2002). Making sense of semantic ambiguity: Semantic competition in lexical access. *Journal of Memory and Language, 46,* 245–266. (8)

Rodgers, J. L. (2001). What causes birth order-intelligence patterns? *American Psychologist, 56,* 505–510. (5)

Rodgers, J. L., Cleveland, H. H., van den Oord, E., & Rowe, D. C. (2000). Resolving the debate over birth order, family size, and intelligence. *American Psychologist, 55,* 599–612. (5)

Rodgers, J. L., & Wänström, L. (2007). Identification of a Flynn effect in the NLSY: Moving from the center to the boundaries. *Intelligence, 35,* 187–196. (9)

Rodin, J. (1986). Aging and health: Effects of the sense of control. *Science, 233,* 1271–1276. (5, 12)

Rodrigo, M. F., & Ato, M. (2002). Testing the group polarization hypothesis by using logit models. *European Journal of Social Psychology, 32,* 3–18. (13)

Roediger, H. L., III, & Karpicke, J. D. (2006). Test-enhanced learning. *Psychological Science, 17,* 249–255. (7)

Roediger, H. L., III, & McDermott, K. B. (1995). Creating false memories: Remembering words not presented in lists. *Journal of Experimental Psychology: Learning, Memory, and Cognition, 21,* 803–814. (7)

Roediger, H. L., III, & McDermott, K. B. (2000). Tricks of memory. *Current Directions in Psychological Science, 9,* 123–127. (7)

Roenneberg, T., Kuehnle, T., Pramstaller, P. P., Ricken, J., Havel, M., Guth, A., et al. (2004). A marker for the end of adolescence. *Current Biology, 14,* R1038–R1039. (10)

Roenneberg, T., Kumar, C. J., & Merrow, M. (2007). The human circadian clock entrains to sun time. *Current Biology, 17,* R44–R45. (10)

Rofé, Y. (2008). Does repression exist? Memory, pathogenic, unconscious and clinical evidence. *Review of General Psychology, 12,* 63–85. (14)

Rogers, C. R. (1951). *Client-centered therapy.* Boston: Houghton Mifflin. (15)

Rogers, C. R. (1961). *On becoming a person.* Boston: Houghton Mifflin. (14)

Rogers, C. R. (1980). *A way of being.* Boston: Houghton Mifflin. (14)

Rogers, T. B. (1995). *The psychological testing enterprise: An introduction.* Pacific Grove, CA: Brooks/Cole. (9)

Rogler, L. H. (2002). Historical generations and psychology. *American Psychologist, 57,* 1013–1023. (5)

Rohrbaugh, M., Shoham, V., Spungen, C., & Steinglass, P. (1995). Family systems therapy in practice: A systemic couples therapy for problem drinking. In B. Bongar & L. E. Beutler (Eds.), *Comprehensive textbook of psychotherapy: Theory and practice* (pp. 228–253). Oxford, England: Oxford University Press. (15)

Rohrer, D., & Pashler, H. (2007). Increasing retention without increasing study time. *Current Directions in Psychological Science, 16,* 183–186. (7)

Roisman, G. I., Collins, W. A., Sroufe, L. A., & Egeland, B. (2005). Predictors of young adults' representations of and behavior in their current romantic relationship: Prospective tests of the prototype hypothesis. *Attachment and Human Development, 7,* 105–121. (5)

Romero, A. J., & Roberts, R. E. (2003). Stress within a bicultural context for adolescents of Mexican descent. *Cultural Diversity and Ethnic Minority Psychology, 9,* 171–184. (5)

Ronen, T., & Rosenbaum, M. (2001). Helping children to help themselves: A case study of enuresis and nail biting. *Research on Social Work Practice, 11,* 338–356. (6)

Rönkä, A., Oravala, S., & Pulkkinen, L. (2003). Turning points in adults' lives: The effects of gender and the amount of choice. *Journal of Adult Development, 10,* 203–215. (5)

Rönnlund, M., & Nilsson, L.-G. (2008). The magnitude, generality, and determinants of Flynn effects on forms of declarative memory and visuospatial ability: Time-sequential analyses of data from a Swedish cohort study. *Intelligence, 36,* 192–209. (9)

Rosa-Alcázar, A. I., Sánchez-Meca, J., Gómez-Conesa, A., & Marín-Martínez, F. (2008). Psychological treatment of obsessive-compulsive disorder: A meta-analysis. *Clinical Psychology Review, 28,* 1310–1325. (16)

Rosch, E. (1978). Principles of categorization. In E. Rosch & B. B. Lloyd (Eds.), *Cognition and categorization* (pp. 27–48). Hillsdale, NJ: Erlbaum. (8)

Rosch, E., & Mervis, C. B. (1975). Family resemblances: Studies in the internal structure of categories. *Cognitive Psychology, 7,* 573–605. (8)

Rose, J. E. (1996). Nicotine addiction and treatment. *Annual Review of Medicine, 47,* 493–507. (16)

Rose, J. E., Brugge, J. F., Anderson, D. J., & Hind, J. E. (1967). Phase-locked response to low-frequency tones in single auditory nerve fibers of the squirrel monkey. *Journal of Neurophysiology, 30,* 769–793. (4)

Rosen, V. M., & Engle, R. W. (1997). The role of working memory capacity in retrieval. *Journal of Experimental Psychology: General, 126,* 211–227. (7)

Rosenbaum, R. S., Köhler, S., Schacter, D. L., Moscovitch, M., Westmacott, R., Black, S. E., et al. (2005). The case of K. C.: Contributions of a memory-impaired person to memory theory. *Neuropsychologia, 43,* 989–1021. (7)

Ross, L. (1977). The intuitive psychologist and his shortcomings: Distortions in the attribution process. In L. Berkowitz (Ed.), *Advances in experimental social psychology* (Vol. 10, pp. 173–220). New York: Academic Press. (13)

Rosselli, M., & Ardila, A. (2003). The impact of culture and education on non-verbal neuropsychological measurements: A critical review. *Brain and Cognition, 52,* 326–333. (9)

Rotge, J.-Y., Guehl, D., Dilharreguy, B., Tignol, J., Bioulac, B., Allard, M., et al. (2009). Meta-analysis of brain volume changes in obsessive-compulsive disorder. *Biological Psychiatry, 65,* 75–83. (16)

Roth, B. L., Lopez, E., & Kroeze, W. K. (2000). The multiplicity of serotonin receptors: Uselessly diverse molecules or an embarrassment of riches? *The Neuroscientist, 6,* 252–262. (3)

Roth, W. T., Wilhelm, F. H., & Pettit, D. (2005). Are current theories of panic falsifiable? *Psychological Bulletin, 131,* 171–192. (16)

Rothbaum, F., Weisz, J., Pott, M., Miyake, K., & Morelli, G. (2000). Attachment and culture: Security in the United States and Japan. *American Psychologist, 55,* 1093–1104. (5)

Rottenberg, J., Bylsma, L. M., & Vingerhoets, A. J. J. M. (2008). Is crying beneficial? *Current Directions in Psychological Science, 17,* 400–404. (12)

Rotton, J., & Kelly, I. W. (1985). Much ado about the full moon: A meta-analysis of lunar-lunacy research. *Psychological Bulletin, 97,* 286–306. (2)

Routh, D. K. (2000). Clinical psychology training: A history of ideas and practices prior to 1946. *American Psychologist, 55,* 236–241. (1)

Rovee-Collier, C. (1997). Dissociations in infant memory: Rethinking the development of explicit and implicit memory. *Psychological Review, 104,* 467–498. (5)

Rovee-Collier, C. (1999). The development of infant memory. *Current Directions in Psychological Science, 8,* 80–85. (5)

Rowe, J. W., & Kahn, R. L. (1987). Human aging: Usual and successful. *Science, 237,* 143–149. (5)

Rowland, D. L., & Burnett, A. L. (2000). Pharmacotherapy in the treatment of male sexual dysfunction. *Journal of Sex Research, 37,* 226–243. (11)

Royzman, E. B., & Sabini, J. (2001). Something it takes to be an emotion: The interesting case of disgust. *Journal for the Theory of Social Behavior, 31,* 29–59. (12)

Rozin, P. (1996). Sociocultural influences on human food selection. In E. D. Capaldi (Ed.), *Why we eat what we eat* (pp. 233–263). Washington, DC: American Psychological Association. (1)

Rozin, P., & Cohen, A. B. (2003). High frequency of facial expressions corresponding to confusion, concentration, and worry in an analysis of naturally occurring facial expressions of Americans. *Emotion, 3,* 68–75. (12)

Rozin, P., & Fallon, A. E. (1987). A perspective on disgust. *Psychological Review, 94,* 23–41. (1)

Rozin, P., Fallon, A., & Augustoni-Ziskind, M. L. (1986). The child's conception of food: The development of categories of acceptable and rejected substances. *Journal of Nutrition Education, 18,* 75–81. (1)

Rozin, P., Fischler, C., Imada, S., Sarubin, A., & Wrzesniewski, A. (1999). Attitudes to food and the role of food in life in the U.S.A., Japan, Flemish Belgium and France: Possible implications for the diet-health debate. *Appetite, 33,* 163–180. (11)

Rozin, P., Kabnick, K., Pete, E., Fischler, C., & Shields, C. (2003). The ecology of eating: Smaller portion sizes in France than in the United States help explain the French paradox. *Psychological Science, 14,* 450–454. (11)

Rozin, P., & Kalat, J. W. (1971). Specific hungers and poison avoidance as adaptive specializations of learning. *Psychological Review, 78,* 459–486. (1, 6)

Rozin, P., Lowery, L., Imada, S., & Haidt, J. (1999). The CAD triad hypothesis: A mapping between three moral emotions (contempt, anger, disgust) and three moral codes (community, autonomy, divinity). *Journal of Personality and Social Psychology, 76,* 574–586. (12)

Rozin, P., Markwith, M., & Ross, B. (1990). The sympathetic magical law of similarity, nominal realism and neglect of negatives in response to negative labels. *Psychological Science, 1,* 383–384. (8)

Rozin, P., Markwith, M., & Stoess, C. (1997). Moralization and becoming a vegetarian: The transformation of preferences into values and the recruitment of disgust. *Psychological Science, 8,* 67–73. (1)

Rozin, P., Millman, L., & Nemeroff, C. (1986). Operation of the laws of sympathetic magic in disgust and other domains. *Journal of Personality and Social Psychology, 50,* 703–712. (1)

Rozin, P., & Pelchat, M. L. (1988). Memories of mammaries: Adaptations to weaning from milk. *Progress in Psychobiology and Physiological Psychology, 13,* 1–29. (5)

Rubenstein, R., & Newman, R. (1954). The living out of "future" experiences under hypnosis. *Science, 119,* 472–473. (10)

Rubia, K., Oosterlaan, J., Sergeant, J. A., Brandeis, D., & v. Leeuwen, T. (1998). Inhibitory dysfunction in hyperactive boys. *Behavioural Brain Research, 94,* 25–32. (8)

Ruch, J. (1984). *Psychology: The personal science.* Belmont, CA: Wadsworth. (5)

Rudman, L. A., & Goodwin, S. A. (2004). Gender differences in automatic in-group bias: Why do women like women more than men like men? *Journal of Personality and Social Psychology, 87,* 494–509. (13)

Rule, N. O., & Ambady, N. (2008). The face of success: Inferences from chief executive officers' appearance predict company profits. *Psychological Science, 19,* 109–111. (13)

Rumbaugh, D. M., & Washburn, D. A. (2003). *Intelligence of apes and other rational beings.* New Haven, CT: Yale University Press. (6)

Rumelhart, D. E., & McClelland, J. L. (1982). An interactive activation model of context effects in letter perception: Part 2. The contextual enhancement effect and some tests and extensions of the model. *Psychological Review, 89,* 60–94. (8)

Rumelhart, D. E., McClelland, J. L., & the PDP Research Group. (1986). *Parallel distributed processing.* Cambridge, MA: MIT Press. (8)

Rusak, B. (1977). The role of the suprachiasmatic nuclei in the generation of circadian rhythms in the golden hamster, *Mesocricetus auratus. Journal of Comparative Physiology A, 118,* 145–164. (10)

Rush, A. J., Trivedi, M. H., Wisniewski, S. R., Stewart, J. W., Nierenberg, A. A., Thase, M. E., et al. (2006). Bupropion-SR, sertraline, or venlafaxine-XR after failure of SSRIs for depression. *New England Journal of Medicine, 354,* 1231–1242. (16)

Rushton, J. P., & Bons, T. A. (2005). Mate choice and friendship in twins. *Psychological Science, 16,* 555–559. (13)

Russano, M. B., Meissner, C. A., Narchet, F. M., & Kassin, S. M. (2005). Investigating true and false confessions within a novel experimental paradigm. *Psychological Science, 16,* 481–486. (13)

Russell, J. A. (1980). A circumplex model of affect. *Journal of Personality and Social Psychology, 39,* 1161–1178. (12)

Russell, J. A. (1994). Is there universal recognition of emotion from facial expression? A review of the cross-cultural studies. *Psychological Bulletin, 115,* 102–141. (12)

Russo, J. E., Carlson, K. A., & Meloy, M. G. (2006). Choosing an inferior alternative. *Psychological Science, 17,* 899–904. (13)

Rutledge, T., & Hogan, B. E. (2002). A quantitative review of prospective evidence linking psychological factors with hypertension development. *Psychosomatic Medicine, 64,* 758–766. (12)

Ruys, K. I., & Stapel, D. A. (2008). The secret life of emotions. *Psychological Science, 19,* 385–391. (4, 12)

Ryan, J. D., Althoff, R. R., Whitlow, S., & Cohen, N. J. (2000). Amnesia is a deficit in relational memory. *Psychological Science, 11,* 454–461. (7)

Ryan, R. M., & Deci, E. L. (2000). Self-determination theory and the facilitation of intrinsic motivation, social development, and well-being. *American Psychologist, 55,* 68–78. (11)

Ryder, A. G., Yang, J., Zhu, X., Yao, S., Yi, J., Heine, S. J., et al. (2008). The cultural shaping of depression: Somatic symptoms in China, psychological symptoms in North America? *Journal of Abnormal Psychology, 117,* 300–313. (15)

Sabini, J., Siepmann, M., Stein, J., & Meyerowitz, M. (2000). Who is embarrassed by what? *Cognition and Emotion, 14,* 213–240. (12)

Sacco, D. F., & Hugenberg, K. (2009). The look of fear and anger: Facial maturity modulation recognition of fearful and angry expressions. *Emotion, 9,* 39–49. (12)

Sackeim, H. A., Prudic, J., Devanand, D. P., Nobler, M. S., Lisanby, S. H., Peyser, S., et al. (2000). A prospective, randomized, double-blind comparison of bilateral and right unilateral electroconvulsive therapy at different stimulus intensities. *Archives of General Psychiatry, 57,* 425–434. (16)

Sackett, P. R., Borneman, M. J., & Connelly, B. S. (2008). High-stakes testing in higher education and employment. *American Psychologist, 63,* 215–227. (9)

Sadato, N., Pascual-Leone, A., Grafman, J., Deiber, M.-P., Ibañez, V., & Hallett, M. (1998). Neural networks for Braille reading by the blind. *Brain, 121,* 1213–1229. (3)

Sadato, N., Pascual-Leone, A., Grafman, J., Ibañez, V., Deiber, M.-P., Dold, G., et al. (1996). Activation of the primary visual cortex by Braille reading in blind subjects. *Nature, 380,* 526–528. (3)

Saegert, S., Swap, W., & Zajonc, R. B. (1973). Exposure, context, and interpersonal attraction. *Journal of Personality and Social Psychology, 25,* 234–242. (13)

Saffran, J. R. (2003). Statistical language learning: Mechanisms and constraints. *Current Directions in Psychological Science, 12,* 110–114. (8)

Saffran, J. R., Aslin, R. N., & Newport, E. L. (1996). Statistical learning by 8-month-old infants. *Science, 274,* 1926–1928. (8)

Saha, S., Chant, D., & McGrath, J. (2007). A systematic review of mortality in schizophrenia. *Archives of General Psychiatry, 64,* 1123–1131. (16)

Saleem, Q., Dash, D., Gandhi, C., Kishore, A., Benegal, V., Sherrin, T., et al. (2001). Association of CAG repeat loci on chromosome 22 with schizophrenia and bipolar disorder. *Molecular Psychiatry, 6,* 694–700. (16)

Sales, B. D., & Folkman, S. (2000). *Ethics in research with human participants.* Washington, DC: American Psychological Association. (1)

Salmon, P. (2001). Effects of physical exercise on anxiety, depression, and sensitivity to stress: A unifying theory. *Clinical Psychology Review, 21,* 33–61. (12)

Salomons, T. V., Johnstone, T., Backonja, M.-M., & Davidson, R. J. (2004). Perceived controllability modulates the neural response to pain. *Journal of Neuroscience, 24,* 7199–7203. (12)

Salthouse, T. A. (2006). Mental exercise and mental aging. *Perspectives on Psychological Science, 1,* 68–87. (8)

Samelson, F. (1980). J. B. Watson's Little Albert, Cyril Burt's twins, and the need for a critical science. *American Scientist, 35,* 619–625. (16)

Samuel, A. G. (2001). Knowing a word affects the fundamental perception of the sounds within it. *Psychological Science, 12,* 348–351. (8)

Sanchez, L. M., & Turner, S. M. (2003). Practicing psychology in the era of managed care. *American Psychologist, 58,* 116–129. (15)

Sandell, R., Blomberg, J., Lazar, A., Schubert, J., Carlsson, J., & Broberg, J. (1999). Wie die Zeit vergeht: Langzeitergebnisse von Psychoanalysen und analytischen Psychotherapien. [As time goes by: Long-term outcomes of psychoanalysis and long-term psychotherapy.] *Forum der Psychoanalyse, 15,* 327–347. (15)

Sanders, A. R., Duan, J., Levinson, D. F., Shi, J., He, D., Hou, C., et al. (2008). No significant association of 14 candidate genes with schizophrenia in a large European ancestry sample: Implications for psychiatric genetics. *American Journal of Psychiatry, 165,* 497–506. (16)

Sanders, R. E., Gonzalez, D. J., Murphy, M. D., Pesta, B. J., & Bucur, B. (2002). Training content variability and the effectiveness of learning: An adult age assessment. *Aging, Neuropsychology, and Cognition, 9,* 157–174. (7)

Sandfort, T. G. M., de Graaf, R., Bijl, R. V., & Schnabel, P. (2001). Same-sex sexual behavior and psychiatric disorders. *Archives of General Psychiatry, 58,* 85–91. (11)

Sandhya, S. (2009). The social context of marital happiness in urban Indian couples: Interplay of intimacy and conflict. *Journal of Marital and Family Conflict, 35,* 74–96. (11)

Sapolsky, R. M. (1998, March 30). Open season. *The New Yorker, 74*(6), 57–58, 71–72. (14)

Sapolsky, R. M., & Share, L. J. (2004). A pacific culture among wild baboons: Its emergence and transmission. *PLoS Biology, 2,* 534–541. (12)

Sapp, F., Lee, K., & Muir, D. (2000). Three-year-olds' difficulty with the appearance–reality distinction: Is it real or is it apparent? *Developmental Psychology, 36,* 547–560. (5)

Sartor, C. E., Jacob, T., & Bucholz, K. K. (2003). Drinking course in alcohol-dependent men from adolescence to midlife. *Journal of Studies on Alcohol, 64,* 712–719. (16)

Saucier, D. M., Green, S. M., Leason, J., MacFadden, A., Bell, S., & Elias, L. J. (2002). Are sex differences in navigation caused by sexually dimorphic strategies or by differences in the ability to use the strategies? *Behavioral Neuroscience, 116,* 403–410. (5)

Saults, J. S., & Cowan, N. (2007). A central capacity limit to the simultaneous storage of visual and auditory arrays in working memory. *Journal of Experimental Psychology: General, 136,* 663–684. (7)

Savage-Rumbaugh, E. S. (1990). Language acquisition in a nonhuman species: Implications for the innateness debate. *Developmental Psychology, 23,* 599–620. (8)

Savage-Rumbaugh, E. S., Murphy, J., Sevcik, R. A., Brakke, K. E., Williams, S. L., & Rumbaugh, D. M. (1993). Language comprehension in ape and child. *Monographs of the Society for Research in Child Development, 58*(Serial no. 233). (8)

Savage-Rumbaugh, E. S., Sevcik, R. A., Brakke, K. E., & Rumbaugh, D. M. (1992). Symbols: Their communicative use, communication, and combination by bonobos *(Pan paniscus).* In L. P. Lipsitt & C. Rovee-Collier (Eds.), *Advances in infancy research* (Vol. 7, pp. 221–278). Norwood, NJ: Ablex. (8)

Savani, K., Markus, H. R., & Conner, A. L. (2008). Let your preference be your guide? Preferences and choices are more tightly linked for North Americans than for Indians. *Journal of Personality and Social Psychology, 95,* 861–876. (8)

Scalera, G., & Bavieri, M. (2009). Role of conditioned taste aversion on the side effects of chemotherapy in cancer patients. In S. Reilly & T. R. Schachtman (Eds.), *Conditioned taste aversion* (pp. 513–541). New York: Oxford University Press. (6)

Scarborough, E., & Furomoto, L. (1987). *Untold lives: The first generation of American women psychologists.* New York: Columbia University Press. (1)

Scarr, S. (1997). Rules of evidence: A larger context for the statistical debate. *Psychological Science, 8,* 16–17. (2)

Scarr, S. (1998). American child care today. *American Psychologist, 53,* 95–108. (5)

Schachter, D. L. (1987). Implicit memory: History and current status. *Journal of Experimental Psychology: Learning, Memory, and Cognition, 13,* 501–518. (7)

Schacter, D. L., Verfaellie, M., Anes, M. D., & Racine, C. (1998). When true recognition suppresses false recognition: Evidence from amnesic patients. *Journal of Cognitive Neuroscience, 10,* 668–679. (7)

Schachter, S. (1982). Recidivism and self-cure of smoking and obesity. *American Psychologist, 37,* 436–444. (11)

Schachter, S., & Singer, J. (1962). Cognitive, social, and physiological determinants of emotional state. *Psychological Review, 69,* 379–399. (12)

Schatzman, M. (1992, March 21). Freud: Who seduced whom? *New Scientist,* pp. 34–37. (14)

Schellenberg, E. G. (2004). Music lessons enhance IQ. *Psychological Science, 15,* 511–514. (9)

Schellenberg, E. G. (2006). Long-term positive associations between music lessons and IQ. *Journal of Educational Psychology, 98,* 457–468. (9)

Schellenberg, E. G., & Trehub, S. E. (2003). Good pitch memory is widespread. *Psychological Science, 14,* 262–266. (4)

Schenck, C. H., & Mahowald, M. W. (1996). Long-term, nightly benzodiazepine treatment of injurious parasomnias and other disorders of disrupted nocturnal sleep in 170 adults. *American Journal of Medicine, 100,* 333–337. (10)

Scherer, K. R. (1992). What does facial expression express? In K. T. Strongman (Ed.), *International review of studies on emotion* (Vol. 2, pp. 139–165). Chichester, England: Wiley. (12)

Scherer, K. R., & Ellgring, H. (2007). Multimodal expression of emotion: Affect programs or componential appraisal patterns? *Emotion, 7,* 158–171. (12)

Schiffman, S. S., & Erickson, R. P. (1971). A psychophysical model for gustatory quality. *Physiology and Behavior, 7,* 617–633. (4)

Schkade, D. A., & Kahneman, D. (1998). Does living in California make people happy? *Psychological Science, 9,* 340–346. (12)

Schlesier-Stropp, B. (1984). Bulimia: A review of the literature. *Psychological Review, 95,* 247–257. (11)

Schmidt, F. L., & Hunter, J. E. (1981). Employment testing: Old theories and new research findings. *American Psychologist, 36,* 1128–1137. (9)

Schmidt, F. L., & Hunter, J. E. (1998). The validity and utility of selection methods in personnel psychology: Practical and theoretical implications of 85 years of research findings. *Psychological Bulletin, 124,* 262–274. (9)

Schmidt, R. A., & Bjork, R. A. (1992). New conceptualizations of practice: Common principles in three paradigms suggest new concepts for training. *Psychological Science, 3,* 207–217. (7)

Schmitt, A. P., & Dorans, N. J. (1990). Differential item functioning for minority examinees on the SAT. *Journal of Educational Measurement, 27,* 67–81. (9)

Schmitt, D. P., & 118 members of the International Sexuality Description Project. (2003). Universal sex differences in the desire for sexual variety: Tests from 52 nations, 6 continents, and 13 islands. *Journal of Personality and Social Psychology, 85,* 85–104. (13)

Schmolck, H., Buffalo, E. A., & Squire, L. R. (2000). Memory distortions develop over time. *Psychological Science, 11,* 39–45. (7)

Schnall, E., Wassertheil-Smoller, S., Swencionis, C., Zemon, V., Tinker, L., O'Sullivan, J., et al. (in press). The relationship between religion and cardiovascular outcomes and all-cause mortality in the women's health initiative observational study. *Psychology and Health.* (12)

Schnall, S., Benton, J., & Harvey, S. (2008). With a clean conscience. *Psychological Science, 19,* 1219–1222. (12)

Schneider, P., Scherg, M., Dosch, G., Specht, H. J., Gutschalk, A., & Rupp, A. (2002). Morphology of Heschl's gyrus reflects enhanced activation in the auditory cortex of musicians. *Nature Neuroscience, 5,* 688–694. (3, 8)

Schnider, A. (2003). Spontaneous confabulation and the adaptation of thought to ongoing reality. *Nature Reviews Neuroscience, 4,* 662–671. (7)

Schooler, C. (1972). Birth order effects: Not here, not now! *Psychological Bulletin, 78,* 161–175. (5)

Schooler, C. (1998). Environmental complexity and the Flynn effect. In U. Neisser (Ed.), *The rising curve* (pp. 67–79). Washington, DC: American Psychological Association. (9)

Schou, M. (1997). Forty years of lithium treatment. *Archives of General Psychiatry, 54,* 9–13. (16)

Schredl, M. (2000). Continuity between waking life and dreaming: Are all waking activities reflected equally often in dreams? *Perceptual and Motor Skills, 90,* 844–846. (10)

Schuckit, M. A., & Smith, T. L. (1997). Assessing the risk for alcoholism among sons of alcoholics. *Journal of Studies on Alcohol, 58,* 141–145. (16)

Schuckit, M. A., Smith, T. L., Kalmijn, J., Tsuang, J., Hesselbrock, V., Bucholz, K., et al. (2000). Response to alcohol in daughters of alcoholics: A pilot study and a comparison with sons of alcoholics. *Alcohol and Alcoholism, 35,* 242–248. (16)

Schulsinger, F., Knop, J., Goodwin, D. W., Teasdale, T. W., & Mikkelsen, U. (1986). A prospective study of young men at high risk for alcoholism. *Archives of General Psychiatry, 43,* 755–760. (16)

Schumm, W. R. (2008). Re-evaluation of the "no differences" hypothesis concerning gay and lesbian parenting as assessed in eight early (1979–1986) and four later (1997–1998) dissertations. *Psychological Reports, 103,* 275–304. (5)

Schupp, H. T., Stockburger, J., Codispoti, M., Junghöfer, M., Weike, A. I., & Hamm, A. O. (2007). Selective visual attention to emotion. *Journal of Neuroscience, 27,* 1082–1089. (12)

Schutt, B. (2008, November). The curious bloody lives of vampire bats. *Natural History, 117*(9), 22–27. (13)

Schützwohl, A., & Borgstedt, K. (2005). The processing of affectively valenced stimuli: The role of surprise. *Cognition and Emotion, 19,* 583–600. (12)

Schwartz, B. (2004). *The paradox of choice.* New York: HarperCollins. (8)

Schwartz, B., Ward, A., Monterosso, J., Lyubomirsky, S., White, K., & Lehman, D. R. (2002). Maximizing versus satisficing: Happiness is a matter of choice. *Journal of Personality and Social Psychology, 83,* 1178–1197. (8)

Schwartz, C. E., Wright, C. I., Shin, L. M., Kagan, J., & Rauch, S. L. (2003). Inhibited and uninhibited infants "grown up": Adult amygdalar response to novelty. *Science, 300,* 1952–1953. (5)

Scott, N., Lakin, K. C., & Larson, S. A. (2008). The 40th anniversary of deinstitutionalization in the United States: Decreasing state institutional populations, 1967–2007. *Intellectual and Developmental Disabilities, 46,* 402–405. (15)

Scott, S. K., Young, A. W., Calder, A. J., Hellawell, D. J., Aggleton, J. P., & Johnson, M. (1997). Impaired auditory recognition of fear and anger following bilateral amygdala lesions. *Nature, 385,* 254–257. (12)

Scott, T. R., & Verhagen, J. V. (2000). Taste as a factor in the management of nutrition. *Nutrition, 16,* 874–885. (1)

Scott, V. M., Mottarella, K. E., & Lavooy, M. J. (2006). Does virtual intimacy exist? A brief exploration into reported levels of intimacy in online relationships. *CyberPsychology and Behavior, 9,* 759–761. (13)

Scovern, A. W., & Kilmann, P. R. (1980). Status of electroconvulsive therapy: Review of the outcome literature. *Psychological Bulletin, 87,* 260–303. (16)

Scripture, E. W. (1907). *Thinking, feeling, doing* (2nd ed.). New York: G. P. Putnam's Sons. (1)

Seamon, J. G., Lee, I. A., Toner, S. K., Wheeler, R. H., Goodkind, M. S., & Birch, A. D. (2002). Thinking of critical words during study is unnecessary for false memory in the Deese, Roediger, and McDermott procedure. *Psychological Science, 13,* 526–531. (7)

Sears, D. O., & Henry, P. J. (2003). The origins of symbolic racism. *Journal of Personality and Social Psychology, 85,* 259–275. (13)

Seeley, R. J., Kaplan, J. M., & Grill, H. J. (1995). Effect of occluding the pylorus on intraoral intake: A test of the gastric hypothesis of meal termination. *Physiology and Behavior, 58,* 245–249. (11)

Seeman, P., & Lee, T. (1975). Antipsychotic drugs: Direct correlation between clinical potency and presynaptic action on dopamine neurons. *Science, 188,* 1217–1219. (16)

Segerstrom, S. C., & Nes, L. S. (2007). Heart rate variability reflects self-regulatory strength, effort, and fatigue. *Psychological Science, 18,* 275–281. (12)

Seidman, L. J., Valera, E. M., & Makris, N. (2005). Structural brain imaging of attention-deficit/hyperactivity disorder. *Biological Psychiatry, 57,* 1263–1272. (8)

Sekuler, A. B., & Bennett, P. J. (2001). Generalized common fate: Grouping by common luminance changes. *Psychological Science, 12,* 437–444. (4)

Seligman, M. E. P. (1970). On the generality of the laws of learning. *Psychological Review, 77,* 406–418. (6)

Seligman, M. E. P. (1971). Phobias and preparedness. *Behavior Therapy, 2,* 307–320. (16)

Seligman, M. E. P. (1995). The effectiveness of psychotherapy: The *Consumer Reports* study. *American Psychologist, 50,* 965–974. (15)

Seligman, M. E. P., & Csikszentmihalyi, M. (2000). Positive psychology. *American Psychologist, 55,* 5–14. (12)

Seligman, M. E. P., Nolen-Hoeksema, S., Thornton, N., & Thornton, K. M. (1990). Explanatory style as a mechanism of disappointing athletic performance. *Psychological Science, 1,* 143–146. (16)

Seligman, M. E. P., Schulman, P., DeRubeis, R. J., & Hollon, S. D. (1999). The prevention of depression and anxiety. *Prevention and Treatment, 2,* article 8. (15)

Selye, H. (1979). Stress, cancer, and the mind. In J. Taché, H. Selye, & S. B. Day (Eds.), *Cancer, stress, and death* (pp. 11–27). New York: Plenum Press. (12)

Semmler, C., Brewer, N., & Wells, G. L. (2004). Effects of postidentification feedback on eyewitness identification and nonidentification confidence. *Journal of Applied Psychology, 89,* 334–346. (7)

Sen, S., Duman, R., & Sanacora, G. (2008). Serum brain-derived neurotrophic factor, depression, and antidepressant medications: Meta-analyses and implications. *Biological Psychiatry, 64,* 527–532. (16)

Senghas, A., & Coppola, M. (2001). Children creating language: How Nicaraguan sign language acquired a spatial grammar. *Psychological Science, 12,* 323–328. (8)

Senghas, A., Kita, S., & Özyürek, A. (2004). Children creating core properties of language: Evidence from an emerging sign language in Nicaragua. *Science, 305,* 1779–1782. (8)

Sensky, T., Turkington, D., Kingdon, D., Scott, J. L., Scott, J., Siddle, R., et al. (2000). A randomized controlled trial of cognitive-behavioral therapy for persistent symptoms in schizophrenia resistant to medication. *Archives of General Psychiatry, 57,* 165–172. (16)

Seo, M.-G., Barrett, L. F., & Bartunek, J. M. (2004). The role of affective experience in work motivation. *Academy of Management Review, 29,* 423–439. (11)

Sergent, C., & Dehaene, S. (2004). Is consciousness a gradual phenomenon? *Psychological Science, 15,* 720–728. (10)

Shaffer, D., Fisher, P., Dulcan, M. K., Davies, M., Piacentini, J., Schwab-Stone, M. E., et al. (1996). The NIMH Diagnostic Interview Schedule of Children version 2.3 (DISC-2.3): Description, acceptability, prevalence rates, and performance in the MECA study. *Journal of the American Academy of Child and Adolescent Psychiatry, 35,* 865–877. (12)

Shafir, E. B., Smith, E. E., & Osherson, D. N. (1990). Typicality and reasoning fallacies. *Memory and Cognition, 18,* 229–239. (8)

Shafto, M., & MacKay, D. G. (2000). The Moses, mega-Moses, and Armstrong illusions: Integrating language comprehension and semantic memory. *Psychological Science, 11,* 372–378. (8)

Shah, A. M., & Wolford, G. (2007). Buying behavior as a function of parametric variation of number of choices. *Psychological Science, 18,* 369–370. (8)

Shahar, D. R., Schultz, R., Shahar, A., & Wing, R. R. (2001). The effect of widowhood on weight change, dietary intake, and eating behavior in the elderly population. *Journal of Aging and Health, 13,* 186–199. (12)

Shamosh, N. A., DeYoung, C. G., Green, A. E., Reis, D. L., Johnson, M. R., Conway, A. R. A., et al. (2008). Individual differences in delay discounting. *Psychological Science, 19,* 904–911. (9)

Shannon, D. A. (1955). *The Socialist Party of America.* New York: Macmillan. (13)

Shapiro, D. H., Jr., Schwartz, C. E., & Astin, J. A. (1996). Controlling ourselves, controlling our world. *American Psychologist, 51,* 1213–1230. (12)

Shapiro, D. L. (1985). Insanity and the assessment of criminal responsibility. In C. P. Ewing (Ed.), *Psychology, psychiatry, and the law: A clinical and forensic handbook* (pp. 67–94). Sarasota, FL: Professional Resource Exchange. (15)

Shapiro, K. L., Caldwell, J., & Sorensen, R. E. (1997). Personal names and the attentional blink: A visual "cocktail party" effect. *Journal of Experimental Psychology: Human Perception and Performance, 23,* 504–514. (8)

Sharot, T., Delgado, M. R., & Phelps, E. A. (2004). How emotion enhances the feeling of remembering. *Nature Neuroscience, 7,* 1376–1380. (7)

Shaw, G. B. (1911). *The doctor's dilemma.* New York: Brentano's. (13)

Shaw, P., Eckstrand, K., Sharp, W., Blumenthal, J., Lerch, J. P., Greenstein, D., et al. (2007). Attention-deficit/hyperactivity disorder is characterized by a delay in cortical maturation. *Proceedings of the National Academy of Sciences, USA, 104,* 19649–19654. (8)

Shayer, M., Ginsburg, D., & Coe, R. (2007). Thirty years on—A large anti-Flynn effect? The Piagetian test Volume and Heaviness norms 1975–2003. *British Journal of Educational Psychology, 77,* 25–41. (9)

Shearn, D., Spellman, L., Straley, B., Meirick, J., & Stryker, K. (1999). Empathic blushing in friends and strangers. *Motivation and Emotion, 23,* 307–316. (12)

Sheldon, K., & Lyubomirsky, S. (2004). Achieving sustainable new happiness: Prospects, practices, and prescriptions. In P. A. Linley & S. Joseph (Eds.), *Positive psychology in practice* (pp. 127–145). Hoboken, NJ: Wiley. (12)

Sheldon, K. M., & Lyubomirsky, S. (2006). Achieving sustainable gains in happiness: Change your actions, not your circumstances. *Journal of Happiness Studies, 7,* 55–86. (12)

Shen, H., Gong, Q. H., Aoki, C., Yuan, M., Ruderman, Y., Dattilo, M., et al. (2007). Reversal of neurosteroid effects at $\alpha 4 \beta 2 \delta$ GABA$_A$ receptors triggers anxiety at puberty. *Nature Neuroscience, 10,* 469–477. (16)

Shenkin, S. D., Starr, J. M., & Deary, I. J. (2004). Birth weight and cognitive ability in childhood: A systematic review. *Psychological Bulletin, 130,* 989–1013. (5)

Shepard, R. N. (1990). *Mind sights.* New York: W. H. Freeman. (4)

Shepard, R. N., & Metzler, J. N. (1971). Mental rotation of three-dimensional objects. *Science, 171,* 701–703. (8)

Sheppard, W. D., II, Staggers, F. J., Jr., & John, L. (1997). The effects of a stress management program in a high security government agency. *Anxiety, Stress, and Coping, 10,* 341–350. (12)

Shepperd, J. A. (1993). Productivity loss in performance groups: A motivation analysis. *Psychological Bulletin, 113,* 67–81. (13)

Shergill, S. S., Brammer, M. J., Williams, S. C. R., Murray, R. M., & McGuire, P. K. (2000). Mapping auditory hallucinations in schizophrenia using functional magnetic resonance imaging. *Archives of General Psychiatry, 57,* 1033–1038. (16)

Sherif, M. (1935). A study of some social factors in perception. *Archives of Psychology, 27,* 1–60. (13)

Sherif, M. (1966). *In common predicament.* Boston: Houghton Mifflin. (13)

Sherrod, D. R., Hage, J. N., Halpern, P. L., & Moore, B. S. (1977). Effects of personal causation and perceived control on responses to an aversive environment: The more control, the better. *Journal of Experimental Social Psychology, 13,* 14–27. (12)

Sherwood, G. G. (1981). Self-serving biases in person perception: A reexamination of projection as a mechanism of defense. *Psychological Bulletin, 90,* 445–459. (14)

Shih, M., Pittinsky, T. L., & Ambady, N. (1999). Stereotype susceptibility: Identity salience and shifts in quantitative performance. *Psychological Science, 10,* 80–83. (9)

Shih, M., & Sanchez, D. T. (2005). Perspectives and research on the positive and negative implications of having multiple racial identities. *Psychological Bulletin, 131,* 569–591. (5)

Shimaya, A. (1997). Perception of complex line drawings. *Journal of Experimental Psychology: Human Perception and Performance, 23,* 25–50. (4)

Shinskey, J. L., & Munakata, Y. (2005). Familiarity breeds searching. *Psychological Science, 16,* 595–600. (5)

Shogren, E. (1993, June 2). Survey finds 4 in 5 suffer sex harassment at school. *Los Angeles Times,* p. A10. (2)

Shook, N. J., & Fazio, R. H. (2008). Interracial roommate relationships. *Psychological Science, 19,* 717–723. (13)

Shrager, Y., Levy, D. A., Hopkins, R. O., & Squire, L. R. (2008). Working memory and the organization of brain systems. *Journal of Neuroscience, 28,* 4818–4822. (7)

Shweder, R., Mahapatra, M., & Miller, J. G. (1987). Culture and moral development. In J. Kagan & S. Lamb (Eds.), *The emergence of morality in young children* (pp. 1–83). Chicago: University of Chicago Press. (13)

Siegel, J. M. (2005). Clues to the functions of mammalian sleep. *Nature, 437,* 1264–1271. (10)

Siegel, S. (1977). Morphine tolerance as an associative process. *Journal of Experimental Psychology: Animal Behavior Processes, 3,* 1–13. (6)

Siegel, S. (1983). Classical conditioning, drug tolerance, and drug dependence. *Research Advances in Alcohol and Drug Problems, 7,* 207–246. (6)

Siegel, S. (1987). Alcohol and opiate dependence: Reevaluation of the Victorian perspective. *Research Advances in Alcohol and Drug Problems, 9,* 279–314. (16)

Siepka, S. M., Yoo, S. H., Park, J., Song, W. M., Kumar, V., Hu, Y. N., et al. (2007). Circadian mutant overtime reveals F-box protein FBXL3 regulation of cryptochrome and period gene expression. *Cell, 129,* 1011–1023. (10)

Sigman, M., & Whaley, S. E. (1998). The role of nutrition in the development of intelligence. In U. Neisser (Ed.), *The rising curve* (pp. 155–182). Washington, DC: American Psychological Association. (9)

Silberg, J., Pickles, A., Rutter, M., Hewitt, J., Simonoff, E., Maes, H., et al. (1999). The influence of genetic factors and life stress on depression among adolescent girls. *Archives of General Psychiatry, 56,* 225–232. (16)

Silk, J. B., Brosnan, S. F., Vonk, J., Henrich, J., Povinelli, D. J., Richardson, A. S., et al. (2005). Chimpanzees are indifferent to the welfare of unrelated group members. *Nature, 437,* 1357–1359. (13)

Silva, E. J., & Duffy, J. F. (2008). Sleep inertia varies with circadian phase and sleep stage in older adults. *Behavioral Neuroscience, 122,* 929–935. (10)

Silver, E. (1995). Punishment or treatment? Comparing the lengths of confinement of successful and unsuccessful insanity defendants. *Law and Human Behavior, 19,* 375–388. (15)

Silverstein, L. B., & Auerbach, C. F. (1999). Deconstructing the essential father. *American Psychologist, 54,* 397–407. (5)

Simcock, G., & Hayne, H. (2002). Breaking the barrier? Children fail to translate their preverbal memories into language. *Psychological Science, 13,* 225–231. (7)

Simmons, E. J. (1949). *Leo Tolstoy.* London: Lehmann. (16)

Simner, J., & Ward, J. (2006). The taste of words on the tip of the tongue. *Nature, 444,* 438. (4)

Simon, N. W., Mendez, I. A., & Setlow, B. (2007). Cocaine exposure causes long-term increases in impulsive choice. *Behavioral Neuroscience, 121,* 543–549. (3)

Simons, D. J., & Levin, D. T. (2003). What makes change blindness interesting? *The Psychology of Learning and Motivation, 42,* 295–322. (8)

Simons, T., & Roberson, Q. (2003). Why managers should care about fairness: The effects of aggregate justice perceptions on organizational outcomes. *Journal of Applied Psychology, 88,* 432–443. (11)

Simpson, C. A., & Vuchinich, R. E. (2000). Reliability of a measure of temporal discounting. *Psychological Record, 50,* 3–16. (11)

Singer, T., Seymour, B., O'Doherty, J., Kaube, H., Dolan, R. J., & Frith, C. D. (2004). Empathy for pain involves the affective but not sensory components of pain. *Science, 303,* 1157–1162. (4)

Singh, M., Hoffman, D. D., & Albert, M. K. (1999). Contour completion and relative depth: Petter's rule and support ratio. *Psychological Science, 10,* 423–428. (4)

Sirin, S. R., & Fine, M. (2007). Hyphenated selves: Muslim American youth negotiating identities on the fault lines of global conflict. *Applied Developmental Science, 11,* 151–163. (5)

Sizemore, C. C., & Huber, R. J. (1988). The twenty-two faces of Eve. *Individual Psychology, 44,* 53–62. (15)

Sizemore, C. C., & Pittillo, E. S. (1977). *I'm Eve.* Garden City, NY: Doubleday. (15)

Skeels, H. M. (1966). Adult status of children with contrasting early life experiences. *Monographs of the Society for Research in Child Development, 31,* 1–65. (9)

Skinner, B. F. (1938). *The behavior of organisms.* New York: D. Appleton-Century. (6)

Skinner, B. F. (1990). Can psychology be a science of mind? *American Psychologist, 45,* 1206–1210. (6)

Skinner, E. A., Edge, K., Altman, J., & Sherwood, H. (2003). Searching for the structure of coping: A review and critique of category systems for classifying ways of coping. *Psychological Bulletin, 129,* 216–269. (12)

Skoog, G., & Skoog, I. (1999). A 40-year follow-up of patients with obsessive-compulsive disorder. *Archives of General Psychiatry, 56,* 121–127. (16)

Sloan, D. M., Marx, B. P., Epstein, E. M., & Dobbs, J. L. (2008). Expressive writing buffers against maladaptive rumination. *Emotion, 8,* 302–306. (15)

Sloan, D. M., Strauss, M. E., & Wisner, K. L. (2001). Diminished response to pleasant stimuli by depressed women. *Journal of Abnormal Psychology, 110,* 488–493. (16)

Smith. D. M., Langa, K. M., Kabeto, M. U., & Ubel, P. A. (2005). Health, wealth, and happiness. *Psychological Science, 16,* 663–666. (12)

Smith, K. (2007). Looking for hidden signs of consciousness. *Nature, 446,* 355. (10)

Smith, L. T. (1975). The interanimal transfer phenomenon: A review. *Psychological Bulletin, 81,* 1078–1095. (2)

Smith, M. L. (1988). Recall of spatial location by the amnesic patient H. M. *Brain and Cognition, 7,* 178–183. (7)

Smith, M. L., Glass, G. V., & Miller, T. I. (1980). *The benefits of psychotherapy.* Baltimore: Johns Hopkins University Press. (15)

Smith, M. W. (1974). Alfred Binet's remarkable questions: A cross-national and cross-temporal analysis of the cultural biases built into the Stanford-Binet intelligence scale and other Binet tests. *Genetic Psychology Monographs, 89,* 307–334. (9)

Smith, P., & Waterman, M. (2003). Processing bias for aggression words in forensic and nonforensic samples. *Cognition and Emotion, 17,* 681–701. (14)

Smith, S. M., & Moynan, S. C. (2008). Forgetting and recovering the unforgettable. *Psychological Science, 19,* 462–468. (7)

Snook, B., Cullen, R. M., Bennell, C., Taylor, P. J., & Gendreau, P. (2008). The criminal profiling illusion: What's behind the smoke and mirrors? *Criminal Justice and Behavior, 35,* 1257–1276. (14)

Snook, B., Eastwood, J., Gendreau, P., Goggin, C., & Cullen, R. M. (2007). Taking stock of criminal profiling: A narrative review and meta-analysis. *Criminal Justice and Behavior, 34,* 437–453. (14)

Snyder, C. R. (2003). "Me conform? No way": Classroom demonstrations for sensitizing students to their conformity. *Teaching of Psychology, 30,* 59–61. (13)

Snyder, M., Tanke, E. D., & Berscheid, E. (1977). Social perception and interpersonal behavior: On the self-fulfilling nature of social stereotypes. *Journal of Personality and Social Psychology, 35,* 656–666. (13)

Society for Personality Assessment. (2005). The status of the Rorschach in clinical and forensic practice: An official statement by the Board of Trustees of the Society for Personality Assessment. *Journal of Personality Assessment, 85,* 219–237. (14)

Solanto, M. V., Abikoff, H., Sonuga-Barke, E., Schachar, R., Logan, G. D., Wigal, T., et al. (2001). The ecological validity of delay aversion and response inhibition as measures of impulsivity in AD/HD: A supplement to the NIMH multimodal treatment study of AD/HD. *Journal of Abnormal Child Psychology, 29,* 215–228. (8)

Solms, M. (1997). *The neuropsychology of dreams.* Mahwah, NJ: Erlbaum. (10)

Solms, M. (2000). Dreaming and REM sleep are controlled by different brain mechanisms. *Behavioral and Brain Sciences, 23,* 843–850. (10)

Solomon, D. A., Keller, M. B., Leon, A. C., Mueller, T. I., Shea, T., Warshaw, M., et al. (1997). Recovery from major depression. *Archives of General Psychiatry, 54,* 1001–1006. (16)

Solomon, Z., Mikulincer, M., & Flum, H. (1988). Negative life events, coping responses, and combat-related psychopathology: A prospective study. *Journal of Abnormal Psychology, 97,* 302–307. (12)

Song, H., & Schwarz, N. (2008). If it's hard to read, it's hard to do. *Psychological Science, 19,* 986–988. (8)

Song, H., & Schwarz, N. (2009). If it's difficult to pronounce, it must be risky. *Psychological Science, 20,* 135–138. (8)

Song, H., Stevens, C. F., & Gage, F. H. (2002). Neural stem cells from adult hippocampus develop essential properties of functional CNS neurons. *Nature Neuroscience, 5,* 438–445. (3)

Sonuga-Barke, E. J. S. (2004). Causal models of attention-deficit/hyperactivity disorder: From common simple deficits to multiple developmental pathways. *Biological Psychology, 57,* 1231–1238. (8)

Soon, C. S., Brass, M., Heinze, H.-J., & Haynes, J.-D. (2008). Unconscious determinants of free decisions in the human brain. *Nature Neuroscience, 11,* 543–545. (10)

Sorkin, R. D., Hays, C. J., & West, R. (2001). Signal-detection analysis of group decision making. *Psychological Review, 108,* 183–203. (13)

Sowell, E. R., Thompson, P. M., Holmes, C. J., Jernigan, T. L., & Toga, A. W. (1999). *In vivo* evidence for post-adolescent brain maturation in frontal and striatal regions. *Nature Neuroscience, 2,* 859–861. (16)

Spalding, K. L., Bhardwaj, R. D., Buchholz, B. A., Druid, H., & Frisén, J. (2005). Retrospective birth dating of cells in humans. *Cell, 122,* 133–143. (3)

Spanos, N. P. (1987–1988). Past-life hypnotic regression: A critical view. *Skeptical Inquirer, 12,* 174–180. (10)

Spear, L. P. (2000). Neurobehavioral changes in adolescence. *Current Directions in Psychological Science, 9,* 111–114. (5)

Spearman, C. (1904). "General intelligence," objectively determined and measured. *American Journal of Psychology, 15,* 201–293. (9)

Speer, J. R. (1989). Detection of plastic explosives. *Science, 243,* 1651. (8)

Spelke, E. S. (2005). Sex differences in intrinsic aptitude for mathematics and science? *American Psychologist, 60,* 950–958. (5)

Spellman, B. (2005, March). Could reality shows become reality experiments? *APS Observer, 18*(3), 34–35. (2)

Spence, J. T. (1984). Masculinity, femininity, and gender-related traits: A conceptual analysis and critique of current research. *Progress in Experimental Personality Research, 13,* 1–97. (5)

Spengler, P. M., White, M. J., Ægisdóttir, S., Maugherman, A. S., Anderson, L. A., Cook, R. S., et al. (2009). The meta-analysis of clinical judgment project: Effects of experience on judgment accuracy. *The Counseling Psychologist, 3,* 350–399. (15)

Sperry, R. W. (1967). Split-brain approach to learning problems. In G. C. Quarton, T. Melnechuk, & F. O. Schmitt (Eds.), *The neurosciences: A study program* (pp. 714–722). New York: Rockefeller University Press. (3)

Spira, A., & Bajos, N. (1993). *Les comportements sexuels en France* [Sexual behaviors in France]. Paris: La documentation Française. (11)

Squire, L. R., Haist, F., & Shimamura, A. P. (1989). The neurology of memory: Quantitative assessment of retrograde amnesia in two groups of amnesic patients. *Journal of Neuroscience, 9,* 828–839. (7)

St. Jacques, P. L., Dolcos, F., & Cabeza, R. (2009). Effects of aging on functional connectivity of the amygdala for subsequent memory of negative pictures. *Psychological Science, 20,* 74–84. (12)

Staddon, J. (1993). *Behaviorism.* London: Duckworth. (6)

Staddon, J. E. R. (1999). Theoretical behaviorism. In W. O'Donohue & R. Kitchener (Eds.), *Handbook of behaviorism* (pp. 217–241). San Diego, CA: Academic Press. (6)

Staines, G. L. (2008). The relative efficacy of psychotherapy: Reassessing the methods-based paradigm. *Review of General Psychiatry, 12,* 330–343. (15)

Staines, G. L., & Cleland, C. M. (2007). Bias in meta-analytic estimates of the absolute efficacy of psychotherapy. *Review of General Psychiatry, 11,* 329–347. (15)

Stalnaker, T. A., Roesch, M. R., Franz, T. M., Calu, D. J., Singh, T., & Schoenbaum, G. (2007). Cocaine-induced decision-making deficits are mediated by miscoding in basolateral amygdala. *Nature Neuroscience, 10,* 949–951. (3)

Stams, G.-J. J. M., Juffer, F., & van IJzendoorn, M. H. (2002). Maternal sensitivity, infant attachment, and temperament in early childhood predict adjustment in middle childhood: The case of adopted children and their biologically unrelated parents. *Developmental Psychology, 38,* 806–821. (5)

Stanton, M. D., & Shadish, W. R. (1997). Outcome, attrition, and family-couples treatment for drug abuse: A meta-analysis and review of the controlled, comparative studies. *Psychological Bulletin, 122,* 170–191. (16)

Starr, C., & Taggart, R. (1992). *Biology: The unity and diversity of life* (6th ed.). Belmont, CA: Wadsworth. (3)

Ste-Marie, D. M. (1999). Expert–novice differences in gymnastic judging: An information-processing perspective. *Applied Cognitive Psychology, 13,* 269–281. (8)

Steblay, N. M., & Bothwell, R. K. (1994). Evidence for hypnotically refreshed testimony. *Law and Human Behavior, 18,* 635–651. (10)

Steele, C. M., & Aronson, J. (1995). Stereotype threat and the intellectual test performance of African Americans. *Journal of Personality and Social Psychology, 69,* 797–811. (9)

Stefansson, H., Rujescu, D., Cichon, S., Pietiläinen, O. P. H., Ingason, A., Steinberg, S., et al. (2008). Large recurrent microdeletions associated with schizophrenia. *Nature, 455,* 232–236. (16)

Stegat, H. (1975). Die Verhaltenstherapie der Enuresis und Enkopresis [Behavior therapy for enuresis and encopresis]. *Zeitschrift für Kinder- und Jugend-psychiatrie, 3,* 149–173. (15)

Stein, M. B., Hanna, C., Koverola, C., Torchia, M., & McClarty, B. (1997). Structural brain changes in PTSD. *Annals of the New York Academy of Sciences, 821,* 76–82. (12)

Steinhausen, H.-C., Grigoroiu-Serbanescu, M., Boyadjieva, S., Neumärker, K.-J., & Metzke, C. W. (2009). The relevance of body weight in the medium-term to long-term course of adolescent anorexia nervosa. Findings from a multisite study. *International Journal of Eating Disorders, 42,* 19–25. (11)

Stella, N., Schweitzer, P., & Piomelli, D. (1997). A second endogenous cannabinoid that modulates long-term potentiation. *Nature, 382,* 677–678. (3)

Sternberg, K. J., Baradaran, L. P., Abbott, C. B., Lamb, M. E., & Guterman, E. (2006). Type of violence, age, and gender differences in the effects of family violence on children's behavior problems: A mega-analysis. *Developmental Review, 26,* 89–112. (5)

Sternberg, R. J. (1985). *Beyond IQ.* Cambridge, England: Cambridge University Press. (9)

Sternberg, R. J. (1997). The concept of intelligence and its role in lifelong learning and success. *American Psychologist, 52,* 1030–1037. (9)

Sternberg, R. J. (2002). Beyond *g:* The theory of successful intelligence. In R. J. Sternberg & E. L. Grigorenko (Eds.), *The general intelligence factor: How general is it?* (pp. 447–479). Mahwah, NJ: Erlbaum. (9)

Sternberg, R. J., Nokes, C., Geissler, P. W., Prince, R., Okatcha, F., Bundy, D. A., et al. (2001). The relationship between academic and practical intelligence: A case study in Kenya. *Intelligence, 29,* 401–418. (9)

Stevens, S. S. (1961). To honor Fechner and repeal his law. *Science, 133,* 80–86. (1)

Stevens, W. D., Hasher, L., Chiew, K. S., & Grady, C. L. (2008). A neural mechanism underlying memory failure in older adults. *Journal of Neuroscience, 28,* 12820–12824. (7)

Stewart, B. D., von Hippel, W., & Radvansky, G. A. (2009). Age, race, and implicit prejudice. *Psychological Science, 20,* 164–168. (13)

Stewart, I. (1987). Are mathematicians logical? *Nature, 325,* 386–387. (9)

Stewart, J. W., Quitkin, F. M., McGrath, P. J., Amsterdam, J., Fava, M., Fawcett, J., et al. (1998). Use of pattern analysis to predict differential relapse of remitted patients with major depression during 1 year of treatment with fluoxetine or placebo. *Archives of General Psychiatry, 55,* 334–343. (16)

Stice, E. (2002). Risk and maintenance factors for eating pathology: A meta-analytic review. *Psychological Bulletin, 128,* 825–848. (11)

Stice, E., & Shaw, H. (2004). Eating disorder prevention programs: A meta-analytic review. *Psychological Bulletin, 130,* 206–227. (15)

Stice, E., Shaw, H., & Marti, C. N. (2006). A meta-analytic review of obesity prevention programs for children and adolescents: The skinny on interventions that work. *Psychological Bulletin, 132,* 667–691. (11)

Stickgold, R. (2005). Sleep-dependent memory consolidation. *Nature, 437,* 1272–1278. (10)

Stickgold, R., Malia, A., Maguire, D., Roddenberry, D., & O'Connor, M. (2000). Replaying the game: Hypnagogic images in normals and amnesics. *Science, 290,* 350–353. (7)

Stiles, W. B., Shapiro, D. A., & Elliott, R. (1986). "Are all psychotherapies equivalent?" *American Psychologist, 41,* 165–180. (15)

Stipek, D. (1998). Differences between Americans and Chinese in the circumstances evoking pride, shame, and guilt. *Journal of Cross-Cultural Psychology, 29,* 616–629. (12)

Stompe, T., Ortwein-Swoboda, G., Ritter, K., Schanda, H., & Friedmann, A. (2002). Are we witnessing the disappearance of catatonic schizophrenia? *Comprehensive Psychiatry, 43,* 167–174. (16)

Stone, V. E., Nisenson, L., Eliassen, J. C., & Gazzaniga, M. S. (1996). Left hemisphere representations of emotional facial expressions. *Neuropsychologia, 34,* 23–29. (3)

Stoolmiller, M. (1999). Implications of the restricted range of family environments for estimates of heritability and nonshared environment in behavior–genetic adoption studies. *Psychological Bulletin, 125,* 392–409. (5)

Storbeck, J., & Clore, G. L. (2005). With sadness comes accuracy; with happiness, false memory. *Psychological Science, 16,* 785–791. (12)

Storms, M. D. (1973). Videotape and the attribution process: Reversing actors' and observers' points of view. *Journal of Personality and Social Psychology, 27,* 165–175. (13)

Strack, F., Martin, L. L., & Stepper, S. (1988). Inhibiting and facilitating conditions of the human smile: A nonobtrusive test of the facial feedback hypothesis. *Journal of Personality and Social Psychology, 54,* 768–777. (12)

Strakowski, S. M., Tsai, S.-Y., DelBello, M. P., Chen, C.-C., Fleck, D. E., Adler, C. M., et al. (2007). Outcome following a first manic episode: Cross-national US and Taiwan comparison. *Bipolar Disorders, 9,* 820–827. (16)

Strange, B. A., Kroes, M. C. W., Roiser, J. P., Yan, G. C. Y., & Dolan, R. J. (2008). Emotion-induced retrograde amnesia is determined by a 5-HTT genetic polymorphism. *Journal of Neuroscience, 28,* 7036–7039. (7)

Strange, D., Sutherland, R., & Garry, M. (2004). A photographic memory for false autobiographical events: The role of plausibility in children's false memories. *Australian Journal of Psychology, 56*(Suppl. S), 137. (7)

Strauch, I., & Lederbogen, S. (1999). The home dreams and waking fantasies of boys and girls between ages 9 and 15: A longitudinal study. *Dreaming, 9*, 153–161. (10)

Streissguth, A. P., Sampson, P. D., & Barr, H. M. (1989). Neurobehavioral dose-response effects of prenatal alcohol exposure in humans from infancy to adulthood. *Annals of the New York Academy of Sciences, 562*, 145–158. (5)

Strenze, T. (2007). Intelligence and socioeconomic success: A meta-analytic review of longitudinal research. *Intelligence, 35*, 401–426. (9)

Struckman-Johnson, C., Struckman-Johnson, D., & Anderson, P. B. (2003). Tactics of sexual coercion: When men and women won't take no for an answer. *Journal of Sex Research, 40*, 76–86. (12)

Stulz, N., Lutz, W., Leach, C., Lucock, M., & Barkham, M. (2007). Shapes of early change in psychotherapy under routine outpatient conditions. *Journal of Consulting and Clinical Psychology, 75*, 864–874. (15)

Sturm, V. E., Ascher, E. A., Miller, B. L., & Levenson, R. W. (2008). Diminished self-conscious emotional responding in frontotemporal lobar degeneration patients. *Emotion, 8*, 861–869. (12)

Stuss, D. T., Alexander, M. P., Palumbo, C. L., Buckle, L., Sayer, L., & Pogue, J. (1994). Organizational strategies of patients with unilateral or bilateral frontal lobe injury in word list learning tasks. *Neuropsychology, 8*, 355–373. (7)

Sudzak, P. D., Glowa, J. R., Crawley, J. N., Schwartz, R. D., Skolnick, P., & Paul, S. M. (1986). A selective imidazobenzodiazepine antagonist of ethanol in the rat. *Science, 234*, 1243–1247. (3)

Sullivan, E. V., Deshmukh, A., Desmond, J. E., Mathalon, D. H., Rosenbloom, M. J., Lim, K. O., et al. (2000). Contribution of alcohol abuse to cerebellar volume deficits in men with schizophrenia. *Archives of General Psychiatry, 57*, 894–902. (16)

Sullivan, P. F., Kendler, K. S., & Neale, M. C. (2003). Schizophrenia as a complex trait: Evidence from a meta-analysis of twin studies. *Archives of General Psychiatry, 60*, 1187–1192. (16)

Suls, J., Martin, R., & Wheeler, L. (2002). Social comparisons: Why, with whom, and with what effect? *Current Directions in Psychological Science, 11*, 159–163. (13)

Sundet, J. M., Barlaug, D. G., & Torjussen, T. M. (2004). The end of the Flynn effect? A study of secular trends in mean intelligence test scores of Norwegian conscripts during half a century. *Intelligence, 32*, 349–362. (9)

Sundet, J. M., Eriksen, W., & Tambs, K. (2008). Intelligence correlations between brothers decrease with increasing age difference. *Psychological Science, 19*, 843–847. (9)

Susskind, J. M., Lee, D. H., Cusi, A., Feiman, R., Grabski, W., & Anderson, A. K. (2008). Expressing fear enhances sensory acquisition. *Nature Neuroscience, 11*, 843–850. (12)

Suvisaari, J. M., Haukka, J. K., Tanskanen, A. J., & Lönnqvist, J. K. (1999). Decline in the incidence of schizophrenia in Finnish cohorts born from 1954 to 1965. *Archives of General Psychiatry, 56*, 733–740. (16)

Swanson, J. W., Swartz, M. S., Van Dorn, R. A., Elbogen, E. B., Wagner, H. R., Rosenheck, R. A. (2006). A national study of violent behavior in persons with schizophrenia. *Archives of General Psychiatry, 63*, 490–499. (15)

Sweet, S. S., & Pianka, E. R. (2003, November). The lizard kings. *Natural History, 112*(9), 40–45. (6)

Sweetland, J. D., Reina, J. M., & Taffi, A. F. (2006). WISC–III verbal/performance discrepancies among a sample of gifted children. *Gifted Child Quarterly, 50*, 7–10. (9)

Swinkels, A., & Giuliano, T. A. (1995). The measurement and conceptualization of mood awareness: Monitoring and labeling one's mood states. *Personality and Social Psychology Bulletin, 21*, 934–949. (12)

Swinton, S. S. (1987). *The predictive validity of the restructured GRE with particular attention to older students* (GRE Board Professional Rep. No. 83-25P. ETS Research Rep. 87-22). Princeton, NJ: Educational Testing Service. (9)

Swoboda, H., Amering, M., Windhaber, J., & Katschnig, H. (2003). The long-term course of panic disorder—an 11 year follow-up. *Journal of Anxiety Disorders, 17*, 223–232. (16)

Szechtman, H., & Woody, E. (2004). Obsessive-compulsive disorder as a disturbance of security motivation. *Psychological Review, 111*, 111–127. (16)

Szechtman, H., Woody, E., Bowers, K. S., & Nahmias, C. (1998). Where the imagined appears real: A positron emission tomography study of auditory hallucinations. *Proceedings of the National Academy of Sciences, USA, 95*, 1956–1960. (10)

Szrek, H., & Baron, J. (2007). The value of choice in insurance purchasing. *Journal of Economic Psychology, 28*, 529–544. (8)

Szymanski, H. V., Simon, J. C., & Gutterman, N. (1983). Recovery from schizophrenic psychosis. *American Journal of Psychiatry, 140*, 335–338. (16)

Takahashi, T., Wood, S. J., Yung, A. R., Soulsby, B., McGorry, P. D., Suzuki, M., et al. (2009). Progressive gray matter reduction of the superior temporal gyrus during transition to psychosis. *Archives of General Psychiatry, 66*, 366–376. (16)

Takano, Y., & Osaka, E. (1999). An unsupported common view: Comparing Japan and the U.S. on individualism/collectivism. *Asian Journal of Social Psychology, 2*, 311–341. (13)

Takehara-Nishiuchi, K., & McNaughton, B. L. (2008). Spontaneous changes of neocortical code for associative memory during consolidation. *Science, 322*, 960–963. (7)

Talarico, J. M., & Rubin, D. C. (2003). Confidence, not consistency, characterizes flashbulb memories. *Psychological Science, 14*, 455–461. (7)

Tamam, L., Karakus, G., & Ozpoyraz, N. (2008). Comorbidity of adult attention-deficit hyperactivity disorder and bipolar disorder: Prevalence and clinical correlates. *European Archives of Psychiatry and Clinical Neuroscience, 258*, 385–393. (16)

Tanaka, J. W., Curran, T., & Sheinberg, D. L. (2005). The training and transfer of real-world perceptual expertise. *Psychological Science, 16*, 145–151. (8)

Tarr, M. J., & Gauthier, I. (2000). FFA: A flexible fusiform area for subordinate-level visual processing automatized by experience. *Nature Neuroscience, 3*, 764–769. (3)

Tashiro, A., Makino, H., & Gage, F. H. (2007). Experience-specific functional modification of the dentate gyrus through adult neurogenesis: A critical period during an immature stage. *Journal of Neuroscience, 27*, 3252–3259. (7)

Tassinary, L. G., & Hansen, K. A. (1998). A critical test of the waist-to-hip-ratio hypothesis of female physical attractiveness. *Psychological Science, 9*, 150–155. (13)

Taylor, C. B., Bryson, S., Luce, K. H., Cunning, D., Doyle, A. C., Abascal, L. B., et al. (2006). Prevention of eating disorders in at-risk college-age women. *Archives of General Psychiatry, 63*, 881–888. (15)

Taylor, S. E., Pham, L. B., Rivkin, I. D., & Armor, D. A. (1998). Harnessing the imagination: Mental simulation, self-regulation, and coping. *American Psychologist, 53*, 429–439. (12)

Teasdale, T. W., & Owen, D. R. (2005). A long-term rise and recent decline in intelligence test performance: The Flynn effect in reverse. *Personality and Individual Differences, 39*, 837–843. (9)

Teasdale, T. W., & Owen, D. R. (2008). Secular declines in cognitive test scores: A reversal of the Flynn effect. *Intelligence, 36*, 121–126. (9)

Teesson, M., Ross, J., Darke, S., Lynskey, M., Ali, R., Ritter, A., et al. (2006). One year outcomes for heroin dependence: Findings from the Australian Treatment Outcome Study (ATOS). *Drug and Alcohol Dependence, 83*, 174–180. (16)

Teff, K. L., Elliott, S. S., Tschöp, M., Kieffer, T. J., Rader, D., Heiman, M., et al. (2004). Dietary fructose reduces circulating insulin and leptin, attenuates postprandial suppression of ghrelin, and increases triglycerides in women. *Journal of Clinical Endocrinology and Metabolism, 89*, 2963–2972. (11)

Teicher, M. H., Glod, C. A., Magnus, E., Harper, D., Benson, G., Krueger, K., et al. (1997). Circadian rest–activity disturbances in seasonal affective disorder. *Archives of General Psychiatry, 54*, 124–130. (16)

Terr, L. (1988). What happens to early memories of trauma? A study of twenty children under age five at the time of documented traumatic events. *Journal of the American Academy of Child and Adolescent Psychiatry, 27*, 96–104. (7)

Terracciano, A., Abdel-Khalek, A. M., Ádám, N., Admaoovová, L., Ahn, C.-k., Ahn, H.-n., et al. (2005). National character does not reflect mean personality levels in 49 cultures. *Science, 310*, 96–100. (14)

Terrace, H. S., Petitto, L. A., Sanders, R. J., & Bever, T. G. (1979). Can an ape create a sentence? *Science, 206*, 891–902. (8)

Testa, M., Livingston, J. A., Vanzile-Tamsen, C., & Frone, M. R. (2003). The role of women's substance use in vulnerability to forcible and incapacitated rape. *Journal of Studies on Alcohol, 64*, 756–764. (12)

Tetlock, P. E. (1994, July 2). *Good judgment in world politics: Who gets what right, when and why?* Address presented at the sixth annual convention of the American Psychological Society, Washington, DC. (8)

Tett, R. P., & Burnett, D. D. (2003). A personality trait-based interactionist model of job performance. *Journal of Applied Psychology, 88*, 500–517. (11)

Tett, R. P., & Palmer, C. A. (1997). The validity of handwriting elements in relation to self-report personality trait measures. *Personality and Individual Differences, 22*, 11–18. (14)

Thanickal, T. C., Moore, R. Y., Nienhuis, R., Ramanathan, L., Gulyani, S., Aldrich, M., et al. (2000). Reduced number of hypocretin neurons in human narcolepsy. *Neuron, 27*, 469–474. (10)

Thase, M. E., Haight, B. R., Richard, N., Rockett, C. B., Mitton, M., Modell, J. G., et al. (2005). Remission rates following antidepressant therapy with bupropion or selective serotonin reuptake inhibitors: A meta-analysis of original data from 7 randomized controlled trials. *Journal of Clinical Psychiatry, 66*, 974–981. (16)

Theeuwes, J. (2004). No blindness for things that do not change. *Psychological Science, 15*, 65–70. (8)

Thieman, T. J. (1984). A classroom demonstration of encoding specificity. *Teaching of Psychology, 11*, 101–102. (7)

Thierry, G., & Wu, Y. J. (2007). Brain potentials reveal unconscious translation during foreign-language comprehension. *Proceedings of the National Academy of Sciences, USA, 104*, 12530–12535. (8)

Thigpen, C., & Cleckley, H. (1957). *The three faces of Eve*. New York: McGraw-Hill. (15)

Thomas, A., & Chess, S. (1980). *The dynamics of psychological development.* New York: Brunner/Mazel. (5)

Thompson, C. R., & Church, R. M. (1980). An explanation of the language of a chimpanzee. *Science, 208,* 313–314. (8)

Thoresen, C. J., Kaplan, S. A., Barsky, A. P., Warren, C. R., & de Chermont, K. (2003). The affective underpinnings of job perceptions and attitudes: A meta-analytic review and integration. *Psychological Bulletin, 129,* 914–945. (11)

Thorleifsson, G., Walters, G. B., Gudbjartsson, D. F., Steinthorsdottir, V., Sulem, P., Helgadottir, A., et al. (2009). Genome-wide association yields new sequence variants at seven loci that associate with measures of obesity. *Nature Genetics, 41,* 18–24. (11)

Thorndike, E. L. (1918). The nature, purposes, and general methods of measurements of educational products. In E. J. Ashbaugh, W. A. Averill, L. P. Ayres, F. W. Ballou, E. Bryner, B. R. Buckingham, et al. (Eds.), *The seventeenth yearbook of the National Society for the Study of Education. Part II: The measurement of educational products* (pp. 16–24). Bloomington, IL: Public School Publishing Company. (9)

Thorndike, E. L. (1970). *Animal intelligence.* Darien, CT: Hafner. (Original work published 1911) (6)

Timberlake, W., & Farmer-Dougan, V. A. (1991). Reinforcement in applied settings: Figuring out ahead of time what will work. *Psychological Bulletin, 110,* 379–391. (6)

Tinbergen, N. (1951). *The study of instinct.* Oxford, England: Oxford University Press. (3)

Tishkoff, S. A., Reed, F. A., Ranciaro, A., Voight, B. F., Babbitt, C. C., Silverman, J. S., et al. (2006). Convergent adaptation of human lactase persistence in Africa and Europe. *Nature Genetics, 39,* 31–40. (5)

Titchener, E. B. (1910). *A textbook of psychology.* New York: Macmillan. (1)

Tiwari, S. K., & Wang, J. L. (2006). The epidemiology of mental and substance use-related disorders among White, Chinese, and other Asian populations in Canada. *Canadian Journal of Psychiatry, 51,* 904–912. (16)

Todd, J. J., Fougnie, D., & Marois, R. (2005). Visual short-term memory load suppresses temporo-parietal junction activity and induces inattentional blindness. *Psychological Science, 16,* 965–972. (8)

Todes, D. P. (1997). From the machine to the ghost within. *American Psychologist, 52,* 947–955. (6)

Toh, K. L., Jones, C. R., He, Y., Eide, E. J., Hinz, W. A., Virshup, D. M., et al. (2001). An h*Per2* phosphorylation site mutation in familial advanced sleep phase syndrome. *Science, 291,* 1040–1043. (10)

Tolman, E. C. (1938). The determinants of behavior at a choice point. *Psychological Review, 45,* 1–41. (1)

Tolstoy, L. (1978). *Tolstoy's letters: Vol. I. 1828–1879.* New York: Charles Scribner's Sons. (Original works written 1828–1879) (5)

Tombaugh, C. W. (1980). *Out of the darkness, the planet Pluto.* Harrisburg, PA: Stackpole. (4)

Tomppo, L., Hennah, W., Miettunen, J., Järvelin, M.-R., Veijola, J., Ripatti, S., et al. (2009). Association of variants in *DISC1* with psychosis-related traits in a large population cohort. *Archives of General Psychiatry, 66,* 134–141. (16)

Toomey, R., Lyons, M. J., Eisen, S. A., Xian, H., Chantarujikapong, S., Seidman, L. J., et al. (2003). A twin study of the neuropsychological consequences of stimulant abuse. *Archives of General Psychiatry, 60,* 303–310. (3)

Torres, A. R., Prince, M. J., Bebbington, P. E., Bhugra, D., Brugha, T. S., Farrell, M., et al. (2006). Obsessive-compulsive disorder: Prevalence, comorbidity, impact, and help-seeking in the British national psychiatric morbidity survey of 2000. *American Journal of Psychiatry, 163,* 1978–1985. (16)

Torrey, E. F. (1986). Geographic variations in schizophrenia. In C. Shagass, R. C. Josiassen, W. H. Bridger, K. J. Weiss, D. Stoff, & G. M. Simpson (Eds.), *Biological psychiatry 1985* (pp. 1080–1082). New York: Elsevier. (16)

Torrey, E. F. (2002). Studies of individuals with schizophrenia never treated with antipsychotic medications: A review. *Schizophrenia Research, 58,* 101–115. (16)

Torrey, E. F., & Miller, J. (2001). *The invisible plague: The rise of mental illness from 1750 to the present.* New Brunswick, NJ: Rutgers University Press. (15, 16)

Torrey, E. F., & Yolken, R. H. (2005). *Toxoplasma gondii* as a possible cause of schizophrenia. *Biological Psychiatry, 57,* 128S. (16)

Townshend, J. M., & Duka, T. (2003). Mixed emotions: Alcoholics' impairments in the recognition of specific emotional facial expressions. *Neuropsychologia, 41,* 773–782. (12)

Tracy, J. L., & Robins, R. W. (2004). Show your pride: Evidence for a discrete emotion expression. *Psychological Science, 15,* 194–197. (12)

Tracy, J. L., & Robins, R. W. (2008). The automaticity of emotion recognition. *Emotion, 8,* 81–95. (12)

Tracy, J. L., Robins, R. W., & Lagattuta, K. H. (2005). Can children recognize pride? *Emotion, 5,* 251–257. (12)

Trawalter, S., & Richeson, J. A. (2006). Regulatory focus and executive function after interracial interactions. *Journal of Experimental Social Psychology, 42,* 406–412. (13)

Treisman, A. (1999). Feature binding, attention and object perception. In G. W. Humphreys, J. Duncan, & A. Treisman (Eds.), *Attention, space and action* (pp. 91–111). Oxford, England: Oxford University Press. (3)

Treisman, A., & Souther, J. (1985). Search asymmetry: A diagnostic for preattentive processing of separable features. *Journal of Experimental Psychology: General, 114,* 285–310. (8)

Trevena, J. A., & Miller, J. (2002). Cortical movement preparation before and after a conscious decision to move. *Consciousness and Cognition, 11,* 162–190. (10)

Trimmer, C. G., & Cuddy, L. L. (2008). Emotional intelligence, not music training, predicts recognition of emotional speech prosody. *Emotion, 8,* 838–849. (12)

Trivedi, M. H., Fava, M., Wisniewski, S. R., Thase, M. E., Quitlein, F., Warden, D., et al. (2006). Medication augmentation after failure of SSRIs for depression. *New England Journal of Medicine, 354,* 1243–1252. (16)

Tronick, E. Z., Morelli, G. A., & Ivey, P. K. (1992). The Efe forager infant and toddler's pattern of social relationships: Multiple and simultaneous. *Developmental Psychology, 28,* 568–577. (5)

True, W. R., Xian, H., Scherer, J. F., Madden, P. A. F., Bucholz, K. K., Heath, A. C., et al. (1999). Common genetic vulnerability for nicotine and alcohol dependence in men. *Archives of General Psychiatry, 56,* 655–661. (16)

Tsao, D. Y., Freiwald, W. A., Tootell, R. B. H., & Livingstone, M. S. (2006). A cortical region consisting entirely of face-selective cells. *Science, 311,* 670–674. (3)

Tse, D., Langston, R. F., Kakeyama, M., Bethus, I., Spooner, P. A., Wood, E. R., et al. (2007). Schemas and memory consolidation. *Science, 316,* 76–82. (7)

Tuerk, P. W. (2005). Research in the high-stakes era. *Psychological Science, 16,* 419–425. (9)

Tugade, M. M., & Fredrickson, B. L. (2004). Resilient individuals use positive emotions to bounce back from negative emotional experiences. *Journal of Personality and Social Psychology, 86,* 320–333. (12)

Tuiten, A., Van Honk, J., Koppeschaar, H., Bernaards, C., Thijssen, J., & Verbaten, R. (2000). Time course of effects of testosterone administration on sexual arousal in women. *Archives of General Psychiatry, 57,* 149–153. (11)

Tulving, E. (1989). Remembering and knowing the past. *American Scientist, 77,* 361–367. (7)

Tulving, E., & Thomson, D. M. (1973). Encoding specificity and retrieval processes in episodic memory. *Psychological Review, 80,* 352–373. (7)

Tuntiya, N. (2007). Free-air treatment for mental patients: The deinstitutionalization debate of the nineteenth century. *Sociological Perspectives, 50,* 469–488. (15)

Turkheimer, E., Haley, A., Waldron, M., D'Onofrio, B., & Gottesman, I. I. (2003). Socioeconomic status modifies heritability of IQ in young children. *Psychological Science, 14,* 623–628. (9)

Tversky, A., & Kahneman, D. (1981). The framing of decisions and the psychology of choice. *Science, 211,* 453–458. (8)

Tversky, A., & Kahneman, D. (1983). Extensional versus intuitive reasoning: The conjunctional fallacy in probability judgment. *Psychological Review, 90,* 293–315. (8)

Twenge, J. M. (2000). The age of anxiety? Birth cohort change in anxiety and neuroticism, 1952–1993. *Journal of Personality and Social Psychology, 79,* 1007–1021. (14)

Twenge, J. M. (2006). *Generation me.* New York: Free Press. (5)

Twenge, J. M. (2009). Change over time in obedience: The jury's still out, but it might be decreasing. *American Psychologist, 64,* 28–31. (13)

Twenge, J. M., Baumeister, R. F., DeWall, C. N., Ciarocco, N. J., & Bartels, J. M. (2007). Social exclusion decreases prosocial behavior. *Journal of Personality and Social Psychology, 92,* 56–66. (13)

Twenge, J. M., Konrath, S., Foster, J. D., Campbell, W. K., & Bushman, B. J. (2008). Egos inflating over time: A cross-temporal meta-analysis of the narcissistic personality inventory. *Journal of Personality, 76,* 875–901. (14)

Uchino, B. N., Cacioppo, J. T., & Kiecolt-Glaser, J. K. (1996). The relationship between social support and physiological processes: A review with emphasis on underlying mechanisms and implications for health. *Psychological Bulletin, 119,* 488–531. (12)

Udolf, R. (1981). *Handbook of hypnosis for professionals.* New York: Van Nostrand Reinhold. (10)

Udry, J. R., & Chantala, K. (2006). Masculinity–femininity predicts sexual orientation in men but not in women. *Journal of Biosocial Science, 38,* 797–809. (11)

Uhlhaas, P. J., Linden, D. E. J., Singer, W., Haenschel, C., Lindner, M., Maurer, K., et al. (2006). Dysfunctional long-range coordination of neural activity during Gestalt perception in schizophrenia. *Journal of Neuroscience, 26,* 8168–8175. (16)

Ulrich, R. E., Stachnik, T. J., & Stainton, N. R. (1963). Student acceptance of generalized personality interpretations. *Psychological Reports, 13,* 831–834. (14)

Ulrich, R. S. (1984). View through a window may influence recovery from surgery. *Science, 224,* 420–421. (4)

Unsworth, N., Heitz, R. P., & Parks, N. A. (2008). The importance of temporal distinctiveness for forgetting over the short term. *Psychological Science, 19,* 1078–1081. (7)

U.S. Department of Labor. (2008). *Occupational outlook handbook* (2008–2009 ed.). Retrieved November 9, 2008, from www.bls.gov/oco/ocos056.htm. (1)

Vaillant, G. E., & Milofsky, E. S. (1982). The etiology of alcoholism: A prospective viewpoint. *American Psychologist, 37,* 494–503. (16)

Valli, K., Strandholm, T., Sillanmäki, L., & Revonsuo, A. (2008). Dreams are more negative than real life: Implications for the function of dreaming. *Cognition and Emotion, 22,* 833–861. (10)

Vallines, I., & Greenlee, M. W. (2006). Saccadic suppression of retinotopically localized blood oxygen level-dependent responses in human primary visual area V1. *Journal of Neuroscience, 26,* 5965–5969. (8)

van Anders, S. M., & Watson, N. V. (2006). Relationship status and testosterone in North American heterosexual and non-heterosexual men and women: Cross-sectional and longitudinal data. *Psychoneuroendocrinology, 31,* 715–723. (11)

Van Boven, L., & Ashworth, L. (2007). Looking forward, looking back: Anticipation is more evocative than retrospection. *Journal of Experimental Psychology: General, 136,* 289–300. (8)

Van Cantfort, T. E., Gardner, B. T., & Gardner, R. A. (1989). Developmental trends in replies to Wh-questions by children and chimpanzees. In R. A. Gardner, B. T. Gardner, & T. E. Van Cantfort (Eds.), *Teaching sign language to chimpanzees* (pp. 198–239). Albany: State University of New York Press. (8)

van den Hout, M., & Kindt, M. (2003). Repeated checking causes memory distrust. *Behaviour Research and Therapy, 41,* 301–316. (16)

Van den Stock, J., Righart, R., & de Gelder, B. (2007). Body expressions influence recognition of emotions in the face and voice. *Emotion, 7,* 487–494. (12)

van der Pligt, J., de Vries, N. K., Manstead, A. S. R., & van Harreveld, F. (2000). The importance of being selective: Weighing the role of attribute importance in attitudinal judgment. *Advances in Experimental Social Psychology, 32,* 135–200. (13)

van der Pligt, J., & Eiser, J. R. (1983). Actors' and observers' attributions, self-serving bias, and positivity. *European Journal of Social Psychology, 13,* 95–104. (13)

Van der Werf, Y. D., Altena, E., Schoonheim, M. M., Sanz-Arigita, E. J., Vis, J. C., De Rijke, W., et al. (2009). Sleep benefits subsequent hippocampal functioning. *Nature Neuroscience, 12,* 122–123. (10)

Van Der Zee, K. I., Huet, R. C. G., Cazemier, C., & Evers, K. (2002). The influence of the premedication consult and preparatory information about anesthesia on anxiety among patients undergoing cardiac surgery. *Anxiety, Stress, and Coping, 15,* 123–133. (12)

van IJzendoorn, M. H., Juffer, F., & Poelhuis, C. W. K. (2005). Adoption and cognitive development: A meta-analytic comparison of adopted and nonadopted children's IQ and school performance. *Psychological Bulletin, 131,* 301–316. (9)

Vandello, J. A., Bosson, J. K., Cohen, D., Burnaford, R. M., & Weaver, J. R. (2008). Precarious manhood. *Journal of Personality and Social Psychology, 95,* 1325–1339. (5)

Vanman, E. J., Saltz, J. L., Nathan, L. R., & Warren, J. A. (2004). Racial discrimination by low-prejudiced Whites. *Psychological Science, 15,* 711–714. (13)

Vasterling, J., Duke, L. M., Brailey, K., Constans, J. I., Allain, A. N., & Sutker, P. B. (2002). Attention, learning, and memory performances and intellectual resources in Vietnam veterans: PTSD and no disorder comparisons. *Neuropsychology, 16,* 5–14. (9)

Vega, V., & Malamuth, N. M. (2007). Predicting sexual aggression: The role of pornography in the context of general and specific risk factors. *Aggressive Behavior, 33,* 104–117. (12)

Velluti, R. A. (1997). Interactions between sleep and sensory physiology. *Journal of Sleep Research, 6,* 61–77. (10)

Verplanken, B., & Faes, S. (1999). Good intentions, bad habits, and effects of forming implementation intentions on healthy eating. *European Journal of Social Psychology, 29,* 591–604. (11)

Verrey, F., & Beron, J. (1996). Activation and supply of channels and pumps by aldosterone. *News in Physiological Sciences, 11,* 126–133. (1)

Viglione, D. J., & Taylor, N. (2003). Empirical support for interrater reliability of Rorschach Comprehensive System scoring. *Journal of Clinical Psychology, 59,* 111–121. (14)

Viken, R. J., Rose, R. J., Kaprio, J., & Koskenvuo, M. (1994). A developmental genetic analysis of adult personality: Extraversion and neuroticism from 18 to 59 years of age. *Journal of Personality and Social Psychology, 66,* 722–730. (5, 14)

Visser, B. A., Ashton, M. C., & Vernon, P. A. (2006). Beyond *g*: Putting multiple intelligences theory to the test. *Intelligence, 34,* 487–502. (9)

Vitacco, M. J., Van Rybroek, G. J., Erickson, S. K., Rogstad, J. E., Tripp, A., Harris, L., et al. (2008). Developing services for insanity acquittees conditionally released into the community: Maximizing success and minimizing recidivism. *Psychological Services, 5,* 118–125. (15)

Vogel, E. K., McCollough, A. W., & Machizawa, M. G. (2005). Neural measures reveal individual differences in controlling access to working memory. *Nature, 438,* 500–503. (5)

Vohs, K. D., & Schooler, J. W. (2008). The value of believing in free will: Encouraging a belief in determinism increases cheating. *Psychological Science, 19,* 49–54. (1)

Vokey, J. R., & Read, J. D. (1985). Subliminal messages: Between the devil and the media. *American Psychologist, 40,* 1231–1239. (4)

Volkow, N. D., Wang, G.-J., & Fowler, J. S. (1997). Imaging studies of cocaine in the human brain and studies of the cocaine addict. *Annals of the New York Academy of Sciences, 820,* 41–55. (3)

Volkow, N. D., Wang, G.-J., Fowler, J., Gatley, S. J., Logan, J., Ding, Y.-S., et al. (1998). Dopamine transporter occupancies in the human brain induced by therapeutic doses of oral methylphenidate. *American Journal of Psychiatry, 155,* 1325–1331. (3)

Volkow, N. D., Wang, G.-J., Telang, F., Fowler, J. S., Logan, J., Childress, A.-R., et al. (2006). Cocaine cues and dopamine in dorsal striatum: Mechanism of craving in cocaine addiction. *Journal of Neuroscience, 26,* 6583–6588. (16)

Vroom, V. H., & Jago, A. G. (2007). The role of the situation in leadership. *American Psychologist, 62,* 17–24. (11)

Vuilleumier, P. (2000). Faces call for attention: Evidence from patients with visual extinction. *Neuropsychologia, 38,* 693–700. (10)

Vyazovskiy, V. V., Cirelli, C., Pfister-Genskow, M., Faraguna, U., & Tononi, G. (2008). Molecular and electrophysiological evidence for net synaptic potentiation in wake and depression in sleep. *Nature Neuroscience, 11,* 200–208. (10)

Vygotsky, L. S. (1978). *Mind in society.* Cambridge, MA: Harvard University Press. (5)

Wachholtz, A. B., & Pargament, K. I. (2008). Migraines and meditation: Does spirituality matter? *Journal of Behavioral Medicine, 31,* 351–366. (10)

Wachtel, P. L. (2000). Psychotherapy in the twenty-first century. *American Journal of Psychotherapy, 54,* 441–450. (15)

Wade, K. A., Garry, M., Read, J. D., & Lindsay, D. S. (2002). A picture is worth a thousand lies: Using false photographs to create false childhood memories. *Psychonomic Bulletin and Review, 9,* 597–603. (7)

Waelti, P., Dickinson, A., & Schultz, W. (2001). Dopamine responses comply with basic assumptions of formal learning theory. *Nature, 412,* 43–48. (16)

Wagner, A. D., Desmond, J. E., Demb, J. B., Glover, G. H., & Gabrieli, J. D. E. (1997). Semantic repetition priming for verbal and pictorial knowledge: A functional MRI study of left inferior prefrontal cortex. *Journal of Cognitive Neuroscience, 9,* 714–726. (3)

Wagstaff, G. F., Brunas-Wagstaff, J., Cole, J., Knapton, L., Winterbottom, J., Crean, V., et al. (2004). Facilitating memory with hypnosis, focused meditation, and eye closure. *International Journal of Clinical and Experimental Hypnosis, 52,* 434–455. (10)

Wainright, J. L., Russell, S. T., & Patterson, C. J. (2004). Psychosocial adjustment, school outcomes, and romantic relationships of adolescents with same-sex parents. *Child Development, 75,* 1886–1898. (5)

Wald, G. (1968). Molecular basis of visual excitation. *Science, 162,* 230–239. (4)

Waller, B. M., Cray, J. J., Jr., & Burrows, A. M. (2008). Selection for universal facial emotion. *Emotion, 8,* 435–439. (12)

Waller, N. G., Kojetin, B. A., Bouchard, T. J., Jr., Lykken, D. T., & Tellegen, A. (1990). Genetic and environmental influences on religious interests, attitudes, and values: A study of twins reared apart and together. *Psychological Science, 1,* 138–142. (5)

Walsh, R., & Shapiro, S. L. (2006). The meeting of meditative disciplines and Western psychology. *American Psychologist, 61,* 227–239. (10)

Walster, E., Aronson, E., Abrahams, D., & Rottman, L. (1966). Importance of physical attractiveness in dating behavior. *Journal of Personality and Social Psychology, 4,* 508–516. (13)

Walum, H., Westberg, L., Henningsson, S., Neiderhiser, J. M., Reiss, D., Igl, W., et al. (2008). Genetic variation in the vasopressin receptor 1a gene (*AVPR1A*) associates with pair-bonding behavior in humans. *Proceedings of the National Academy of Sciences, USA, 105,* 14153–14156. (5)

Wampold, B. E., Mondin, G. W., Moody, M., Stich, F., Benson, K., & Ahn, H. (1997). A meta-analysis of outcome studies comparing bona fide psychotherapies: Empirically, "All must have prizes." *Psychological Bulletin, 122,* 203–215. (15)

Wandersman, A., & Florin, P. (2003). Community interventions and effective prevention. *American Psychologist, 58,* 441–448. (15)

Wang, P. S., Lane, M., Olfson, M., Pincus, H. A., Wells, K. B., & Kessler, R. C. (2005). Twelve-month use of mental health services in the United States. *Archives of General Psychiatry, 62,* 629–640. (15)

Wansink, B., & Payne, C. R. (2009). The joy of cooking too much: 70 years of calorie increases in classic recipes. *Annals of Internal Medicine, 150,* 291. (11)

Wansink, B., & van Ittersum, K. (2003). Bottoms up! The influence of elongation on pouring and consumption volume. *Journal of Consumer Research, 30,* 455–463. (5)

Warren, R. M. (1970). Perceptual restoration of missing speech sounds. *Science, 167,* 392–393. (4, 8)

Warren, R. M. (1999). *Auditory perception.* Cambridge, England: Cambridge University Press. (4)

Washington, E. (2006). *Female socialization: How daughters affect their legislator fathers' voting on women's issues* (Working Paper No. 11924). Cambridge, MA: National Bureau of Economic Research. (2)

Wason, P. C. (1960). On the failure to eliminate hypotheses in a conceptual task. *Quarterly Journal of Experimental Psychology, 12,* 129–140. (8)

Waters, E., Merrick, S., Treboux, D., Crowell, J., & Albersheim, L. (2000). Attachment security in infancy and early adulthood: A twenty-year longitudinal study. *Child Development, 71,* 684–689. (5)

Watson, D., & Clark, L. A. (2006). Clinical diagnosis at the crossroads. *Clinical Psychology, 13,* 210–215. (15)

Watson, D., Wiese, D., Vaidya, J., & Tellegen, A. (1999). The two general activation systems of affect: Structural findings, evolutionary considerations, and psychobiological evidence. *Journal of Personality and Social Psychology, 76,* 820–838. (12)

Watson, J. B. (1913). Psychology as the behaviorist views it. *Psychological Review, 20,* 158–177. (1)

Watson, J. B. (1919). *Psychology from the standpoint of a behaviorist.* Philadelphia: Lippincott. (1)

Watson, J. B. (1925). *Behaviorism.* New York: W. W. Norton. (1, 6)

Watson, J. B., & Rayner, R. (1920). Conditioned emotional reactions. *Journal of Experimental Psychology, 3,* 1–14. (16)

Watson, J. M., Balota, D. A., & Roediger, H. L., III (2003). Creating false memories with hybrid lists of semantic and phonological associates: Over-additive false memories produced by converging associative networks. *Journal of Memory and Language, 49,* 95–118. (7)

Waynforth, D., & Dunbar, R. I. M. (1995). Conditional mate choice strategies in humans: Evidence from "lonely hearts" advertisements. *Behaviour, 132,* 755–779. (13)

Weeden, J., & Sabini, J. (2005). Physical attractiveness and health in Western societies: A review. *Psychological Bulletin, 131,* 635–653. (13)

Wegner, D. M. (2002). *The illusion of conscious will.* Cambridge, MA: MIT Press. (1)

Wegner, D. M., Schneider, D. J., Carter, S. R., III, & White, T. L. (1987). Paradoxical effects of thought suppression. *Journal of Personality and Social Psychology, 53,* 5–13. (16)

Weinberger, D. R. (1996). On the plausibility of "the neurodevelopmental hypothesis" of schizophrenia. *Neuropsychopharmacology, 14,* 1S–11S. (16)

Weinberger, D. R. (1999). Cell biology of the hippocampal formation in schizophrenia. *Biological Psychiatry, 45,* 395–402. (16)

Weiss, A., Bates, T. C., & Luciano, M. (2008). Happiness is a personal(ity) thing. *Psychological Science, 19,* 205–210. (12)

Weissman, M. M., Leaf, P. J., & Bruce, M. L. (1987). Single parent women: A community study. *Social Psychiatry, 22,* 29–36. (5)

Weissman, M. M., Warner, V., Wickramaratne, P., Moreau, D., & Olfson, M. (1997). Offspring of depressed parents. *Archives of General Psychiatry, 54,* 932–940. (16)

Weller, A., & Weller, L. (1997). Menstrual synchrony under optimal conditions: Bedouin families. *Journal of Comparative Psychology, 111,* 143–151. (4)

Wellings, K., Field, J., Johnson, A., & Wadsworth, J. (1994). *Sexual behavior in Britain: The national survey of sexual attitudes and lifestyles.* New York: Penguin. (11)

Wells, G. L., Malpass, R. S., Lindsay, R. C. L., Fisher, R. P., Turtle, J. W., & Fulero, S. M. (2000). From the lab to the police station. *American Psychologist, 55,* 581–598. (7)

Wells, G. L., Memon, A., & Penrod, S. D. (2006). Eyewitness evidence: Improving its probative value. *Psychological Science in the Public Interest, 7,* 45–75. (7)

Wells, G. L., Olson, E. A., & Charman, S. D. (2003). Distorted retrospective eyewitness reports as functions of feedback and delay. *Journal of Experimental Psychology: General, 9,* 42–52. (7)

Wender, P. H., Wolf, L. E., & Wasserstein, J. (2001). Adults with ADHD. *Annals of the New York Academy of Sciences, 931,* 1–16. (8)

Werker, J. F., & Tees, R. C. (2005). Speech perception as a window for understanding plasticity and commitment in language systems of the brain. *Developmental Psychology, 46,* 233–251. (8)

Westen, D. (1998). The scientific legacy of Sigmund Freud: Toward a psychodynamically informed psychological science. *Psychological Bulletin, 124,* 333–371. (14)

Westerberg, C. E., & Marsolek, C. J. (2006). Do instructional warnings reduce false recognition? *Applied Cognitive Psychology, 20,* 97–114. (7)

Wethington, E., Kessler, R. C., & Pixley, J. E. (2004). Turning points in adulthood. In O. G. Brim, C. D. Ryff, & R. C. Kessler (Eds.), *How healthy are we?* (pp. 586–613). Chicago: University of Chicago Press. (5)

Wexler, B. E., Zhu, H., Bell, M. D., Nicholls, S. S., Fulbright, R. K., Gore, J. C., et al. (2009). Neuropsychological near normality and brain abnormality in schizophrenia. *American Journal of Psychiatry, 166,* 189–195. (16)

Whalen, P. J. (1998). Fear, vigilance, and ambiguity: Initial neuroimaging studies of the human amygdala. *Current Directions in Psychological Science, 7,* 177–188. (12)

Wheeler, D. D. (1970). Processes in word recognition. *Cognitive Psychology, 1,* 59–85. (8)

Wheeler, M. E., & Treisman, A. M. (2002). Binding in short-term visual memory. *Journal of Experimental Psychology: General, 131,* 48–64. (3)

White, S., O'Reilly, H., & Frith, U. (2009). Big heads, small details and autism. *Neuropsychologia, 47,* 1274–1281. (16)

White, S. J., Johnson, R. L., Liversedge, S. P., & Rayner, K. (2008). Eye movements when reading transposed text: The importance of word-beginning letters. *Journal of Experimental Psychology: Human Perception and Performance, 34,* 1261–1276. (8)

Whitwell, J. L., Sampson, E. L., Loy, C. T., Warren, J. E., Rossor, M. N., Fox, N. C., et al. (2007). VBM signatures of abnormal eating behaviours in frontotemporal lobar degeneration. *NeuroImage, 35,* 207–213. (11)

Wichman, A. L., Rodgers, J. L., & MacCallum, R. C. (2006). A multilevel approach to the relationship between birth order and intelligence. *Personality and Social Psychology Bulletin, 32,* 117–127. (5)

Wicklund, R. A., & Brehm, J. W. (1976). *Perspectives on cognitive dissonance.* Hillsdale, NJ: Erlbaum. (13)

Widiger, T. A., & Trull, T. J. (2007). Plate tectonics in the classification of personality disorders. *American Psychologist, 62,* 71–83. (15)

Wig, N. N., Menon, D. K., Bedi, H., Leff, J., Kuipers, L., Ghosh, A., et al. (1987). Expressed emotion and schizophrenia in North India: II. Distribution of expressed emotion components among relatives of schizophrenic patients in Aarhus and Chandigarh. *British Journal of Psychiatry, 151,* 160–165. (16)

Wildschut, T., Pinter, B., Vevea, J. L., Insko, C. A., & Schopler, J. (2003). Beyond the group mind: A quantitative review of the interindividual-intergroup discontinuity effect. *Psychological Bulletin, 129,* 698–722. (13)

Wilensky, A. E., Schafe, G. E., Kristensen, M. P., & LeDoux, J. E. (2006). Rethinking the fear circuit. *Journal of Neuroscience, 26,* 12387–12396. (12)

Wilkins, L., & Richter, C. P. (1940). A great craving for salt by a child with corticoadrenal insufficiency. *Journal of the American Medical Association, 114,* 866–868. (1)

Williams, C. L., Barnett, A. M., & Meck, W. H. (1990). Organizational effects of early gonadal secretions on sexual differentiation in spatial memory. *Behavioral Neuroscience, 104,* 84–97. (5)

Williams, K. D., & Karau, S. J. (1991). Social loafing and social compensation: The effects of expectations of co-worker performance. *Journal of Personality and Social Psychology, 61,* 570–581. (13)

Williams, L. M. (1994). Recall of childhood trauma: A prospective study of women's memories of child sexual abuse. *Journal of Consulting and Clinical Psychology, 61,* 1167–1176. (7)

Williams, M. A., Visser, T. A., Cunnington, R., & Mattingley, J. B. (2008). Attenuation of neural responses in primary visual cortex during the attentional blink. *Journal of Neuroscience, 28,* 9890–9894. (8)

Williams, R. W., & Herrup, K. (1988). The control of neuron number. *Annual Review of Neuroscience, 11,* 423–453. (3)

Williams, W. M. (1998). Are we raising smarter children today? School- and home-related influences on IQ. In U. Neisser (Ed.), *The rising curve* (pp. 125–154). Washington, DC: American Psychological Association. (9)

Williamson, D. A., Ravussin, E., Wong, M.-L., Wagner, A., DiPaoli, A., Caglayan, S., et al. (2005). Microanalysis of eating behavior of three leptin deficient adults treated with leptin therapy. *Appetite, 45,* 75–80. (11)

Willis, J., & Todorov, A. (2006). First impressions: Making up your mind after a 100-ms exposure to a face. *Psychological Science, 17,* 592–598. (13)

Wilson, D. S., Near, D., & Miller, R. R. (1996). Machiavellianism: A synthesis of the evolutionary and psychological literatures. *Psychological Bulletin, 119,* 285–299. (13)

Wilson, J. R., & the editors of *Life.* (1964). *The mind.* New York: Time. (4)

Wilson, R. I., & Nicoll, R. A. (2002). Endocannabinoid signaling in the brain. *Science, 296,* 678–682. (3)

Wilson, R. S. (1987). Risk and resilience in early mental development. In S. Chess & A. Thomas (Eds.), *Annual progress in child psychiatry and child development 1986* (pp. 69–85). New York: Brunner/Mazel. (5)

Winer, G. A., & Cottrell, J. E. (1996). Does anything leave the eye when we see? Extramission beliefs of children and adults. *Current Directions in Psychological Science, 5,* 137–142. (4)

Winer, G. A., Cottrell, J. E., Gregg, V., Fournier, J. S., & Bica, L. A. (2002). Fundamentally misunderstanding visual perception: Adults' belief in visual emissions. *American Psychologist, 57,* 417–424. (4)

Winner, E. (1986, August). Where pelicans kiss seals. *Psychology Today,* 24–35. (5)

Winner, E. (2000). Giftedness: Current theory and research. *Current Directions in Psychological Science, 9,* 153–156. (9)

Winocur, G., & Hasher, L. (1999). Aging and time-of-day effects on cognition in rats. *Behavioral Neuroscience, 113,* 991–997. (10)

Winocur, G., & Hasher, L. (2004). Age and time-of-day effects on learning and memory in a non-matching-to-sample test. *Neurobiology of Aging, 25,* 1107–1115. (10)

Winocur, G., Moscovitch, M., & Sekeres, M. (2007). Memory consolidation or transformation: Context manipulation and hippocampal representations of memory. *Nature Neuroscience, 10,* 555–557. (7)

Wirz-Justice, A. (1998). Beginning to see the light. *Archives of General Psychiatry, 55,* 861–862. (16)

Wirz-Justice, A., & Van den Hoofdakker, R. H. (1999). Sleep deprivation in depression: What do we know, where do we go? *Biological Psychiatry, 46,* 445–453. (16)

Witkiewitz, K., & Marlatt, G. A. (2004). Relapse prevention for alcohol and drug problems: That was Zen, this is Tao. *American Psychologist, 59,* 224–235. (16)

Wolfe, J. M., Horowitz, T. S., & Kenner, N. M. (2005). Rare items often missed in visual searches. *Nature, 435,* 439–440. (4)

Wolkin, A., Rusinek, H., Vaid, G., Arena, L., Lafargue, T., Sanfilipo, M., et al. (1998). Structural magnetic resonance image averaging in schizophrenia. *American Journal of Psychiatry, 155,* 1064–1073. (16)

Wolman, B. B. (1989). *Dictionary of behavioral science* (2nd ed.). San Diego, CA: Academic Press. (9)

Wolpe, J. (1961). The systematic desensitization treatment of neuroses. *Journal of Nervous and Mental Disease, 132,* 189–203. (16)

Wolraich, M. L., Lindgren, S. D., Stumbo, P. J., Steglink, L. D., Appelbaum, M. I., & Kiritsy, M. C. (1994). Effects of diets high in sucrose or aspartame on the behavior and cognitive performance of children. *New England Journal of Medicine, 330,* 301–307. (2)

Wong, R. Y., & Hong, Y. (2005). Dynamic influences of culture on cooperation in the prisoner's dilemma. *Psychological Science, 16,* 429–434. (13)

Wood, J. M., Nezworski, T., Lilienfeld, S. O., & Garb, H. N. (2003). *What's wrong with the Rorschach?* San Francisco: Jossey-Bass. (14)

Wood, W., & Eagly, A. H. (2002). A cross-cultural model of the behavior of women and men: Implications for the origins of sex differences. *Psychological Bulletin, 128,* 699–727. (5)

Wood, W., Lundgren, S., Ouellette, J. A., Busceme, S., & Blackstone, T. (1994). Minority influence: A meta-analytic review of social influence processes. *Psychological Bulletin, 115,* 323–345. (13)

Wood, W., & Quinn, J. M. (2003). Forewarned and forearmed? Two meta-analytic syntheses of forewarnings of influence appeals. *Psychological Bulletin, 129,* 119–138. (13)

Woodhill, B. M., & Samuels, C. A. (2003). Positive and negative androgyny and their relationship with psychological health and well-being. *Sex Roles, 48,* 555–565. (5)

Wooding, S., Kim, U., Bamshad, M. J., Larsen, J., Jorde, L. B., & Drayna, D. (2004). Natural selection and molecular evolution in *PTC*, a bitter-taste receptor gene. *American Journal of Human Genetics, 74,* 637–646. (1)

Woods, J. H., & Winger, G. (1997). Abuse liability of flunitrazepam. *Journal of Clinical Psychopharmacology, 17*(Suppl. 3), S1–S57. (3)

Woods, S. C. (1991). The eating paradox: How we tolerate food. *Psychological Review, 98,* 488–505. (11)

Woodworth, R. S. (1934). *Psychology* (3rd ed.). New York: Henry Holt. (1)

Worthington, E. L., Jr., Kurusu, T. A., McCullough, M. E., & Sandage, S. J. (1996). Empirical research on religion and psychotherapeutic processes and outcomes: A 10-year review and research prospectus. *Psychological Bulletin, 119,* 448–487. (15)

Woychyshyn, C. A., McElheran, W. G., & Romney, D. M. (1992). MMPI validity measures: A comparative study of original with alternative indices. *Journal of Personality Assessment, 58,* 138–148. (14)

Wright, D. B., & Skagerberg, E. M. (2007). Postidentification feedback affects real eyewitnesses. *Psychological Science, 18,* 172–178. (7)

Wright, I. C., Rabe-Hesketh, S., Woodruff, P. W. R., David, A. S., Murray, R. M., & Bullmore, E. T. (2000). Meta-analysis of regional brain volumes in schizophrenia. *American Journal of Psychiatry, 157,* 16–25. (16)

Wright, L. (1994). *Remembering Satan.* New York: Knopf. (7)

Wu, K. D., & Clark, L. A. (2003). Relations between personality traits and self-reports of daily behavior. *Journal of Research in Personality, 37,* 231–256. (14)

Wu, K., Lindsted, K. D., Tsai, S.-Y., & Lee, J. W. (2007). Chinee NEO-PI-R in Taiwanese adolescents. *Personality and Individual Differences, 44,* 656–667. (14)

Wundt, W. (1902). *Outlines of psychology* (C. H. Judd, Trans.). New York: Gustav Sechert. (Original work published 1896) (1)

Wundt, W. (1961). Contributions to the theory of sensory perception. In T. Shipley (Ed.), *Classics in psychology* (pp. 51–78). New York: Philosophical Library. (Original work published 1862) (1, 10)

Xu, A. J., & Wyer, R. S., Jr. (2008). The comparative mind set. *Psychological Science, 19,* 859–864. (11)

Yamagata, S., Suzuki, A., Ando, J., One, Y., Kijima, N., Yoshimura, K., et al. (2006). Is the genetic structure of human personality universal? A cross-cultural twin study from North America, Europe, and Asia. *Journal of Personality and Social Psychology, 90,* 987–998. (14)

Yamagishi, T., Hashimoto, H., & Schug, J. (2008). Preferences versus strategies as explanations for culture-specific behavior. *Psychological Science, 19,* 579–584. (5)

Yang, K.-S. (2003). Beyond Maslow's culture-bound linear theory: A preliminary statement of the double-Y model of basic human needs. *Nebraska Symposium on Motivation, 49,* 175–255. (11)

Yarsh, T. L., Farb, D. H., Leeman, S. E., & Jessell, T. M. (1979). Intrathecal capsaicin depletes substance P in the rat spinal cord and produces prolonged thermal analgesia. *Science, 206,* 481–483. (4)

Yehuda, R. (1997). Sensitization of the hypothalamic-pituitary-adrenal axis in posttraumatic stress disorder. *Annals of the New York Academy of Sciences, 821,* 57–75. (12)

Ying, Y.-W., Han, M., & Wong, S. L. (2008). Cultural orientation in Asian American adolescents: Variation by age and ethnic density. *Youth and Society, 39,* 507–523. (5)

Yoo, S.-S., Hu, P. T., Gujar, N., Jolesz, F. A., & Walker, M. P. (2007). A deficit in the ability to form new human memories without sleep. *Nature Neuroscience, 10,* 385–392. (10)

Young, A. M. J., Joseph, M. H., & Gray, J. A. (1993). Latent inhibition of conditioned dopamine release in rat nucleus accumbens. *Neuroscience, 54,* 5–9. (16)

Yu, D. W., & Shepard, G. H., Jr. (1998). Is beauty in the eye of the beholder? *Nature, 396,* 321–322. (13)

Yunesian, M., Aslani, A., Vash, J. H., & Yazdi, A. B. (2008). Effects of transcendental meditation on mental health: A before-after study. *Clinical Practice and Epidemiology in Mental Health, 4,* 25. (10)

Zaccaro, S. J. (2007). Trait-based perspectives of leadership. *American Psychologist, 62,* 6–16. (11)

Zadra, A. L., Nielsen, T. A., & Donderi, D. C. (1998). Prevalence of auditory, olfactory, and gustatory experiences in home dreams. *Perceptual and Motor Skills, 87,* 819–826. (10)

Zahavi, A., & Zahavi, A. (1997). *The handicap principle.* New York: Oxford University Press. (13)

Zahn, T. P. Rapoport, J. L., & Thompson, C. L. (1980). Autonomic and behavioral effects of dextroamphetamine and placebo in normal and hyperactive prepubertal boys. *Journal of Abnormal Child Psychology, 8,* 145–160. (8)

Zajonc, R. B. (1968). Attitudinal effects of mere exposure. *Journal of Personality and Social Psychology, 9*(Monograph Suppl. 2, Pt. 2). (13)

Zalsman, G., Huang, Y.-y., Oquendo, M. A., Burke, A. K., Hu, X.-z., Brent, D. A., et al. (2006). Association of a triallelic serotonin transporter gene promoter region (5-HTTLPR) polymorphism with stressful life events and severity of depression. *American Journal of Psychiatry, 163,* 1588–1593. (16)

Zaragoza, M. S., Payment, K. E., Ackil, J. K., Drivdahl, S. B., & Beck, M. (2001). Interviewing witnesses: Forced confabulation and confirmatory feedback increase false memories. *Psychological Science, 12,* 473–477. (7)

Zehr, D. (2000). Portrayals of Wundt and Titchener in introductory psychology texts: A content analysis. *Teaching of Psychology, 27,* 122–126. (1)

Zeidner, M., Shani-Zinovich, I., Matthews, G., & Roberts, R. D. (2005). Assessing emotional intelligence in gifted and non-gifted high school students: Outcomes depend on the measure. *Intelligence, 33,* 369–391. (12)

Zepelin, H., & Rechtschaffen, A. (1974). Mammalian sleep, longevity, and energy metabolism. *Brain, Behavior, and Evolution, 10,* 425–470. (10)

Zhang, W., & Luck, S. J. (2008). Discrete fixed-resolution representations in visual working memory. *Nature, 453,* 233–235. (8)

Zhang, X., & Firestein, S. (2002). The olfactory receptor gene superfamily of the mouse. *Nature Neuroscience, 5,* 124–133. (4)

Zhong, C.-B., & Liljenquist, K. (2006). Washing away your sins: Threatened morality and physical cleansing. *Science, 313,* 1451–1452. (16)

Zhou, W., & Chen, D. (2009). Fear-related chemosignals modulate recognition of fear in ambiguous facial expressions. *Psychological Science, 20,* 177–183. (12)

Zhu, Y., Fenik, P., Zhen, G., Mazza, E., Kelz, M., Aston-Jones, G., et al. (2007). Selective loss of catecholaminergic wake-active neurons in a murine sleep apnea model. *Journal of Neuroscience, 27,* 10060–10071. (10)

Zietsch, B. P., Morley, K. I., Shekar, S. N., Verwej, K. J. H., Keller, M. C., Macgregor, S., et al. (2008). Genetic factors predisposing to homosexuality may increase mating success in heterosexuals. *Evolution and Human Behavior, 29,* 424–433. (11)

Zihl, J., von Cramon, D., & Mai, N. (1983). Selective disturbance of movement vision after bilateral brain damage. *Brain, 106,* 313–340. (3)

Zimmer, H. D. (2008). Visual and spatial working memory. *Neuroscience and Biobehavioral Reviews, 8,* 1373–1395. (7)

Zimmer-Gembeck, M. J., Siebenbruner, J., & Collins, W. A. (2004). A prospective study of intraindividual and peer influences on adolescents' heterosexual romantic and sexual behavior. *Archives of Sexual Behavior, 33,* 381–394. (5)

Zucker, K. J., Bradley, S. J., Oliver, G., Blake, J., Fleming, S., & Hood, J. (1996). Psychosexual development of women with congenital adrenal hyperplasia. *Hormones and Behavior, 30,* 300–318. (11)

Zucker, R. A., & Gomberg, E. S. L. (1986). Etiology of alcoholism reconsidered. *American Psychologist, 41,* 783–793. (16)

Zuriff, G. E. (1995). Continuity over change within the experimental analysis of behavior. In J. T. Todd & E. K. Morris (Eds.), *Modern perspectives on B. F. Skinner and contemporary behaviorism* (pp. 171–178). Westport, CT: Greenwood Press. (6)

Attention tendency to respond to some stimuli more than others or to remember some more than others, 275–281

  attention-deficit disorder, 71–72, 280–281

  and bilingualism, 304

  and emotions, 423

  and intelligence, 316

  limits of, 277–279, *277, 278, 279*

  and memory, 245, 247–248

  preattentive vs. attentive processes, 275–277, *276*

Attentional blink brief period after perceiving a stimulus, during which it is difficult to attend to another stimulus, 279

Attention-deficit disorder (ADD) condition marked by easy distraction from important tasks, impulsiveness, moodiness, and failure to follow through on plans, 71–72, 280–281

Attention-deficit hyperactivity disorder (ADHD) condition marked by easy distraction from important tasks, impulsiveness, moodiness, and failure to follow through on plans, plus excessive activity and fidgetiness, 71–72, 280–281

Attentive process procedure that extracts information from one part of the visual field at a time, 276–277, *276*

Attitudes likes or dislikes that influence our behavior toward a person or thing, 472–474, *472, 473. See also* Persuasion

Attraction, 480–488

  equity theory, 484

  and mate selection, 484–486

  and physical attractiveness, 480–482

  and proximity, 480

  and similarity, 482–483

  and technology, 483–484

Attribution thought processes we use to assign causes to our own behavior and to the behavior of others, 466–470

Atypical antidepressants drugs that relieve depression for some patients who do not respond to other antidepressants, generally with only mild side effects, 595

Atypical antipsychotic drugs drugs such as clozapine and risperidone that relieve schizophrenia without causing tardive dyskinesia, 607

Audition. *See* Hearing

Authoritarian parents those who exert firm controls on their children, generally without explaining the reasons for the rules and without providing much warmth, 187

Authoritative parents those who are demanding and impose firm controls but who are also warm and responsive to the child's communications, 187

Authority, obedience to, 491–494, *492, 493*

Autism condition characterized by poor social relationships, impaired communication, and stereotyped behaviors, 80, 608

Autonomic nervous system section of the nervous system that controls the functioning of the internal organs, such as the heart, 77–78, 83–84, *84*, 412–414

Availability heuristic strategy of assuming that how easily one can remember examples of some kind of event indicates how common the event actually is, 289–290, *289*

Aversive racism consciously expressing the idea that all people are equal but nevertheless unintentionally discriminating against some groups, 465

Avoidance learning learning to make a response that avoids pain or some similar outcome, 572

Axon single, long, thin, straight fiber that transmits information from a neuron to other neurons or to muscle cells, 64, *64*

Bait-and-switch technique procedure of first offering an extremely favorable deal and then making additional demands after the other person has committed to the deal, 476

Barnum effect tendency to accept vague statements about one's personality, 524

Base-rate information data about the frequency or probability of a given item, 288

Basic emotions, 418–423

Basic research procedures that seek knowledge for its own sake, regardless of whether a practical application is obvious, 22

Beck, Max, *396*

Behavioral neuroscientist. *See* Biopsychologist

Behaviorism field of psychology that concentrates on observable, measurable behaviors and not on mental processes, 21, 196–199, *196*

  history of, 21, *21*, 197–198

  and humanistic psychology, 511

  and psychotherapy, 548–549, *549*

Behaviorist psychologist who insists that psychologists should study only observable, measurable behaviors, not mental processes, 196. *See also* Behaviorism

Behavior modification (or applied behavior analysis) procedure for determining the reinforcers that sustain an unwanted behavior and then reducing the reinforcements for the unwanted behavior and providing suitable reinforcers for more acceptable behaviors, 220–221

Behavior therapy treatment that begins with clear, well-defined behavioral goals, such as eliminating test anxiety, and then attempts to achieve those goals through learning, 548–549, *549*

Belief in a just world idea that life is fair and people usually get what they deserve, 514–515

Benzodiazepines, 72–73, 75

Bias tendency for test scores to exaggerate a difference between groups or to report a nonexistent difference, 330–334, *331, 332, 333*

Biculturalism ability to alternate between membership in one culture and membership in another, 185

Big five personality traits five traits that account for a great deal of human personality differences: neuroticism, extraversion, agreeableness, conscientiousness, and openness to new experience, 516–518, *517*

Bilingualism ability to use two languages about equally well, 304

Bimodal distribution, 54, *54*

Binding problem question of how separate brain areas combine forces to produce a unified perception of a single object, 87–88, *88*

Binocular cues visual cues that depend on the action of both eyes, 133

Binocular rivalry alteration between seeing the pattern in the left retina and the pattern in the right retina, 342–343, *343*

Biopsychologist (or behavioral neuroscientist) specialist who tries to explain behavior in terms of biological factors, such as electrical and chemical activities in the nervous system, the effects of drugs and hormones, genetics, and evolutionary pressures, 11–12

Biopsychosocial model concept that abnormal behavior has three major aspects: biological, psychological, and sociological, 539–540

Bipolar cells, 101, *101*, 103

Bipolar disorder condition in which a person alternates between periods of depression and periods of mania, 591, 597–599, *598*

Bipolar I disorder condition characterized by episodes of minor depression and at least one episode of mania, 597

Bipolar II disorder condition characterized by episodes of major depression and hypomania, which is a milder degree of mania, 597

Biracialism, 185–186, *186*

Birdsong learning, 226–227, *226*

Birth order, 186–187, *187*, 327

Bisexuality condition of being sexually aroused and attracted by both males and females, 398. *See also* Sexual orientation

Blind observer observer who can record data without knowing what the researcher has predicted, 40

Blind spot area where the optic nerve exits the retina, 103, *103*

Blocking effect tendency of a previously established association to one stimulus to block the formation of an association to an added stimulus, 208, *208*

Bobo doll experiment, 228, *228*

Body weight, 384–388, *384, 385, 386, 387, 388*

Bonobos, *299*, 300, *300*

Bottom-up-process sensory activity in which tiny elements combine to produce larger items, 128, 275–276

Brain, 77–89

  and anxiety, 429–430, *429*

  and attention, 275

  and autism, 608

  and autonomic nervous system, 83–84

  binding problem, 87–88

  cerebral cortex, 78–81

  and circadian rhythms, 353, *354*

  and cutaneous senses, 115–116, *116, 117*

  and depression, 594–596

  development of, 78, *78*

  and dreaming, 362

  and emotions, 414, *414*, 436

  and expertise, 293

  hemispheric connections, 85–87, *86, 87*

  and hunger, 383–384, *383*

  and hypnosis, 365, *366*

  and language, 301–302, *301*, 304

  measurement techniques, 82–83, *82, 83*

  and memory, 242, 248, 263–267, *264*

  mind-brain problem, 5–6

  and motor control, 81–82

  and nervous system, 77–78, *77*

  and olfaction, 119, *119*

  and pain, 114

  plasticity of, 84–85

  and reading, 308–309

  and schizophrenia, 605–606, *605*

  and sexual orientation, 400, *400*

  and sleep, 357

  and stress, 441, 443

  subcortical areas, 81

  and substance-related disorders, 581–582, *581*

  and vision, 99, 103–104, *103, 104*

Brain death condition in which the brain shows no activity and no response to any stimulus, 343

Brief therapy treatment that begins with an agreement about what the therapist and the client can expect from each other and how long the treatment will last; also known as time-limited therapy, 553

Brightness contrast increase or decrease in an object's apparent brightness because of the effects of objects around it, 126

Broaden-and-build hypothesis idea that a happy mood increases your readiness to explore new ideas and opportunities, 423

Broca's aphasia condition characterized by inarticulate speech and by difficulties with both using and understanding grammatical devices such as prepositions, conjunctions, word endings, complex sentence structures, and so forth, 301–302, *301*

Bruse, Kristi, *396*

Bulimia nervosa condition in which a person alternates between self-starvation and excessive eating, 388–389

Burden of proof obligation to present evidence to support one's claim, 29

Bystander responses, 459, *459*

Caffeine, 75

Calkins, Mary, 22, *22*

Cancer, 443

Capsaicin chemical that stimulates the release of substance P, 115

Caring orientation, 454–455

Drug tolerance progressively weaker effects of a drug after repeated use, 205–206

DSM-IV (Diagnostic and Statistical Manual of Mental Disorders, Fourth Edition) book that lists the acceptable labels for all psychological disorders, with a description of each and guidelines on how to distinguish it from similar disorders, 541–544, *542, 543, 544*

Dualism view that the mind is separate from the brain, 5–6

Duchenne smile spontaneous expression that includes movement of both the mouth muscles and certain muscles near the eyes, 419, *419*

Ear, 109–110, *110. See also* Hearing

Ebbinghaus, Hermann, 235–236, *259*

Eclectic therapy treatment that uses a combination of methods and approaches, 552

Ecstasy (MDMA), 74, 76

ECT (electroconvulsive therapy) treatment using a brief electrical shock that is administered across the patient's head to induce a convulsion similar to epilepsy, sometimes used as a treatment for certain types of depression, 596–597

EEG (electroencephalograph) device that measures and amplifies slight electrical changes on the scalp that reflect brain activity, 82, *82*, 357, *357*

Ego according to Freud, the rational, decision-making aspect of personality, 504

Egocentric thinking not taking the perspective of another person; tending to view the world as centered around oneself, 164, 170

Electroconvulsive therapy (ECT) treatment using a brief electrical shock that is administered across the patient's head to induce a convulsion similar to epilepsy, sometimes used as a treatment for certain types of depression, 596–597

Electroencephalograph (EEG) device that measures and amplifies slight electrical changes on the scalp that reflect brain activity, 82, *82*, 357, *357*

Electromagnetic spectrum continuum of all the frequencies of radiated energy, 98, *98*

Embarrassment emotional reaction to mistakes, being the center of attention, or "sticky situations," 437

Emotional intelligence ability to perceive, imagine, and understand emotions and to use that information in decision making, 425–426

Emotional Stroop Test procedure in which someone tries to say the color of ink for a number of words, some of which might pertain to a source of worry or concern, 530

Emotion-focused coping methods in which people try to weaken their emotional reaction, 444, 445–447

Emotions, 411–438
anger, 431–433, 437
anxiety, 429–431
basic, 418–423
emotional intelligence, 425–426
and facial expressions, 415–416, *415*, 418–422, *418, 419, 420, 421, 433*
gender differences, 181
happiness, 433–436, *434, 435*
and health, *439*
and hunger, 385
James-Lange theory, 414–416
measurement, 411, 412–414
and memory, 248, *248*
and moral reasoning, 424, *424*, 453, 455
and pain, 114
and prejudice, 465
sadness, 436–437
Schachter and Singer's theory, 416–418, *416, 417*
and stress coping strategies, 445–447
usefulness of, 423–425

Empirically supported treatments therapies demonstrated to be helpful, 546

Encoding, 247–254, 268

Encoding specificity principle tendency for the associations formed at the time of learning to be more effective retrieval cues than other associations, 251–252, *251, 252*, 268

Endocrine system set of glands that produce hormones and release them into the bloodstream, 83–84, *85*

Endorphins chemicals produced by the brain that have effects resembling those of opiates, such as inhibiting pain, 69, 73, 115

Environment. *See* Nature-nurture issue

Epilepsy condition characterized by abnormal rhythmic activity of brain neurons, 86, 347

Epinephrine (adrenaline), 248, 413

Episodic buffer, 244

Episodic memory memory for specific events in a person's life, 240, 247

Equilibration establishment of harmony or balance between assimilation and accommodation, 161

Equity theories (or exchange theories) theories maintaining that social relationships are transactions in which partners exchange goods and services, 484

Ergonomist. *See* Human factors specialist

Erikson, Erik, *173*

ESP (extrasensory perception) alleged ability of certain people to acquire information without using any sense organ and without receiving any form of physical energy, 33–35

Estrogen family of hormones present in higher quantities in females than in males, 395

Estrogens, 83–84

Ethics, 50–51

Ethnic background, 22–23, *23*, 185–186, *185, 186*, 331–332

Evidence, 4, 29–36
and falsifiability, 29
and parsimony, 31–35
and replicability, 31
and scientific method, 29–31, *30, 31*
See also Data analysis; Research; Research examples

Evolution gradual change in the frequency of various genes from one generation to the next, 12, 22
and attraction, 485–486
and genetics, 151–152
and preparedness, 223
and sexual orientation, 399

Evolutionary explanation account that relates behavior to the evolutionary history of the species, 63. *See also* Evolution

Evolutionary psychologist one who tries to explain behavior in terms of the evolutionary history of the species, including reasons evolution might have favored a tendency to act in particular ways, 12, 22. *See also* Evolution

Exchange theories (or equity theories) theories maintaining that social relationships are transactions in which partners exchange goods and services, 484

Excitation, 65. *See also* Action potential

Excitement stage of sexual arousal, 394

Exercise, *444*, 446–447, 597

Experimental group group that receives the treatment that an experiment is designed to test, 47, 48

Experimenter bias tendency of an experimenter to unintentionally distort procedures or results based on the experimenter's own expectations of the outcome of the study, 39–40

Experiments studies in which the investigator manipulates at least one variable while measuring at least one other variable, 35, 47–50, *48. See also* Research; Research examples

Expertise, 293–294, *294*, 317

Explanatory style tendency to accept one kind of explanation for success or failure more often than others, 593

Explicit memory (or direct memory) memory that a person can state, generally recognizing that it is the correct answer, 237, 265

Expressed emotion hostile or critical comments directed toward a person with a psychiatric disorder such as schizophrenia, 607

External attribution explanation for someone's behavior based on the current situation, including events that presumably would influence almost anyone, 466–467

Extinction (a) in classical conditioning, the dying out of the conditioned response after repeated presentations of the conditioned stimulus without the unconditioned stimulus; (b) in operant conditioning, the weakening of a response after a period without reinforcement, 202–203, *203*, 215, 219

Extrasensory perception (ESP) alleged ability of certain people to acquire information without using any sense organ and without receiving any form of physical energy, 33–35

Extraversion tendency to seek stimulation and to enjoy the company of other people, 517

Extrinsic motivation motivation based on the rewards and punishments that an act may bring, 376

Eye, 98–99, *99. See also* Vision

Eye movements, 308–309

Eyewitness memory, 238–240

Face recognition, 126, *126*, 156, *156, 157*

Facial expressions, 415–416, *415*, 418–422, *418, 419, 420, 421, 433*

False memory report that someone believes to be a memory but that does not actually correspond to real events, 262–263, *263*

Falsifiable with reference to a theory, making sufficiently precise predictions for which we can at least imagine evidence that would contradict the theory (if anyone had obtained such evidence), 29

Family, 186–191
and anorexia nervosa, 387
birth order, 186–187, *187*
divorce, 190
nontraditional, 189–190, *189*
parental employment, 188–189, *189*
parenting style, 187–188
and schizophrenia, 607–608

Family systems therapy treatment based on the assumptions that most people's problems develop in a family setting and that the best way to deal with them is to improve family relationships and communication, 552, *552*

Fear, 429, 476. *See also* Anxiety

Feature detector neuron in the visual system of the brain that responds to the presence of a certain simple feature, such as a horizontal line, 126–128, *127, 128*

Fetal alcohol syndrome condition marked by stunted growth of the head and body; malformations of the face, heart, and ears; and nervous system damage, including seizures, hyperactivity, learning disabilities, and mental retardation, 153, *153*

Fetus organism more developed than an embryo but not yet born (from about 8 weeks after conception until birth in humans), 152

Figure and ground object and its background, 128–129, *129*

First impressions, 462–463

Fixation (a) in vision, a period when the eyes are steady; (b) in Freud's theory, a persisting preoccupation with an immature psychosexual interest as a result of frustration at that stage of psychosexual development, 308–309, 502, 503

Fixed-interval schedule rule for delivering reinforcement for the first response that the subject makes after a specified period of time has passed, 218, *218*

Fixed-ratio schedule rule for delivering reinforcement only after the subject has made a specific number of correct responses, 218, *218*

Flashbulb memories, 248

Fluid intelligence basic power of reasoning and using information, including the ability to perceive relationships, solve unfamiliar problems, and gain new types of knowledge, 317, 319

Latent period according to Freud, a period in which psychosexual interest is suppressed or dormant, 503

Law of effect Thorndike's theory that a response followed by favorable consequences becomes more probable and a response followed by unfavorable consequences becomes less probable, 210–211

Leadership, 406–407

Learning, 195–231
  behaviorism, 21, 196–199
  birdsong, 226–227
  classical conditioning, 200–209
  conditioned taste aversions, 223–226
  operant conditioning, 210–221
  and sleep, 355
  social learning, 227–230, 509–510
  variations in, 223, 231

Learning and motivation study of how behavior depends on the outcomes of past behaviors and on current motivations, 11. *See also* Learning; Motivation

Learning approach to personality, 509–510

Learning curve graphical representation of the changes in behavior that occur over the course of learning, 210

Lens flexible structure that can vary its thickness to enable the eye to focus on objects at different distances, 98–99, *99*

Leptin hormone released by fat cells; among other effects, it signals the brain to decrease meal size, 382–383

Levels-of-processing principle concept that the number and types of associations established during learning determine the ease of later retrieval of a memory, 250

Libido in Freud's theory, psychosexual energy, 502

Light therapy, 591, 597

Likert scale, 472, *472*

Limbic system, 81

Linear perspective, 134, *134*, 136–137

Lithium, 598–599

Loeb, Jacques, 197

Loewi, Otto, 67–68, 69

Longitudinal study study of a single group of individuals over time, 159, *159*

Long-term memory relatively permanent store of information, 240, 241, 242–243

Loss, 436–437

Loudness perception that depends on the amplitude of a sound wave, 109

LSD (lysergic acid diethylamide), 74, 76

Magnetoencephalograph (MEG) device that records rapid magnetic changes during brain activity, 82

Mainstreaming, 325, *326*

Maintenance treating a disorder to keep it from becoming more serious, 564

Major depression condition lasting most of the day, day after day, with a loss of interest and pleasure and a lack of productive activity, 590

Mania condition in which people are constantly active, uninhibited, and either excited or irritable, 597

Manifest content according to Freud, content that appears on the surface of a dream, 361–362

MAOIs (monoamine oxidase inhibitors) drugs that block the metabolic breakdown of released dopamine, norepinephrine, and serotonin, thus prolonging the effects of these neurotransmitters on the receptors of the postsynaptic cell, 595

MAO (monoamine oxidase), 432, *432*

Marijuana, 73–74, *73*, 75

Marriage, 435, 486–488, *487*

Maslow, Abraham, 511–512, *511*

Maslow's hierarchy of needs proposal that motivations range from the most insistent needs to the ones that receive attention only when all others are under control, 377–378, *377*, *378*

Mate selection, 484–486

Maximizing thoroughly considering every possibility to find the best one, 287–288, *288*

MBTI (Myers-Briggs Type Indicator) test of normal personality, based loosely on the theories of Carl Jung, 527

MDMA (methylenedioxymethamphetamine, ecstasy), 74, 76

Mean sum of all the scores reported in a study divided by the total number of scores, 53–54, *54*

Measurement, 4
  attitudes, 472, *472*
  emotional intelligence, 425–426
  emotions, 411, 412–414
  stress, 440

Measures of central score, 53–54, *54*

Measures of variation, 55, *55*, *56*

Median middle score in a list of scores arranged from highest to lowest, 54, *54*

Meditation method of inducing a calm, relaxed state through the use of special techniques, 370, *370*

Medulla structure that is located in the hindbrain and is an elaboration of the spinal cord; controls many muscles in the head and several life-preserving functions, such as breathing, 81

MEG (magnetoencephalograph) device that records rapid magnetic changes during brain activity, 82

Melatonin, 353

Memory process of retaining information or the information retained, 234–269
  children as eyewitnesses, 239–240
  consolidation, 243, 254–255
  and drugs, 73
  Ebbinghaus's studies, 235–236, *235*, *236*
  encoding, 247–254
  forgetting, 259–268
  and hypnosis, 367, *367*
  implicit, 237–238
  importance of, 234
  infancy, 158, *158*
  information-processing model, 240–243
  and intelligence, 316
  old age, 178
  retrieval, 255–257
  and schizophrenia, 603
  and sleep, 355
  and suspect lineups, 238–239
  testing methods, 236–237, *238*
  working memory, 243–245

Mental age average age of other children whose intellectual performance matches that of a given child, 320

Mental illness. *See* Abnormal behavior

Mental imagery, 274–275, *275*

Mentally challenged people, 325

Mere exposure effect principle that the more often we come into contact with someone or something, the more we tend to like that person or object, 480

Mere measurement effect increased probability of actually doing something as a result of estimating the likelihood of doing it, 403

Mesmer, Franz Anton, 364, *364*

Meta-analysis method of taking the results of many experiments, weighting each one in proportion to the number of participants, and determining the overall average effect, 31, 555

Methadone, 73

Methadone drug commonly offered as a less dangerous substitute for opiates, 587–588, *588*

Methamphetamine, 71

Method of loci mnemonic device that calls for linking the items on a list with a memorized list of places, 253–254, *254*

Methodological behaviorist psychologist who studies only measurable, observable events but sometimes uses those observations to make inferences about internal events, 196, *196*

Methylphenidate (Ritalin), 71–72, 75

Microexpressions very brief, involuntary expressions of fear, anger, or other emotions, 412, 431

Midlife transition period when people reassess their personal goals, set new ones, and prepare for the rest of life, 178

Milgram experiments, 492–494, *492*, *493*

Mind-brain problem philosophical question of how the conscious mind is related to the physical nervous system, including the brain, 5–6

Minimally conscious state condition in which someone has brief periods of purposeful actions and speech comprehension, 343

Minnesota Multiphasic Personality Inventory (MMPI) standardized test consisting of true-false items intended to measure various personality dimensions and clinical conditions such as depression, 525–526, *525*, *526*

Minority influence, 477

Minority students, 22–23, *23*

Mirror neurons cells that are activated while you perform a movement and also while you watch someone else perform the same movement, 80–81, *81*

MMPI (Minnesota Multiphasic Personality Inventory) standardized test consisting of true-false items intended to measure various personality dimensions and clinical conditions such as depression, 525–526, *525*, *526*

M'Naghten rule rule that a defendant is not criminally responsible if, at the time of committing an unlawful act, the person was laboring under such a defect of reason, from disease of the mind, as not to know the nature and quality of the act he was doing; or if he did know it, that he did not know he was doing wrong, 563

Mnemonic device any memory aid that is based on encoding each item in a special way, 253–254, *254*

Modeling, 227–228

Mode score that occurs most frequently in a distribution of scores, 54, *54*

Monism view that consciousness is inseparable from the physical brain, 6

Monoamine oxidase inhibitors (MAOIs) drugs that block the metabolic breakdown of released dopamine, norepinephrine, and serotonin, thus prolonging the effects of these neurotransmitters on the receptors of the postsynaptic cell, 595

Monoamine oxidase (MAO), 432, *432*

Monocular cues visual cues to distance that are just as effective with one eye as with both, 133, *134*

Monozygotic twins (literally, "one-egg" twins) twins who develop from the same fertilized egg, 148–149, *148*, *149*

Mood disorders, 590–600
  bipolar disorder, 591, 597–599, *598*
  depression, 590–597
  and suicide, 599, *599*

Moon illusion apparent difference between the size of the moon at the horizon and its size when viewed higher in the sky, 138–139, *138*

Moral dilemma problem that pits one moral value against another, 424, *424*, 453, 454

Moral reasoning, 453–454, *454*
  and emotions, 424, *424*, 453

Moreno, Angela, 396

Morpheme linguistic unit of meaning, 307, *307*

Morphine, 73, 75

Motion parallax apparently swift motion of objects close to a moving observer and the apparently slow motion of objects farther away, 134, 135

Motivation process that determines the reinforcement value of an outcome, 374–380
  and brain, 81
  conflicting, 377–379, *377*, *378*
  and drugs, 71, 72
  views of, 375–377, *376*, *377*
  and work, 402–407, *404*, *405*, *406*
  See also Hunger; Work motivation

Movement perception, 132–133, *133*

Multiculturalism attitude of accepting, recognizing, and enjoying differences among groups, 465

Multiple intelligences Gardner's theory that intelligence is composed of numerous unrelated forms of intelligent behavior, 317–318, *318*

Multiple personality disorder. *See* Dissociative identity disorder

Multiplier effect when a small initial advantage in some behavior, possibly genetic in origin, alters the environment and magnifies that advantage, 147–148, 155

Myelin insulating sheath that speeds the transmission of impulses along an axon, 64, 606

Myers-Briggs Type Indicator (MBTI) test of normal personality, based loosely on the theories of Carl Jung, 527

Myopia, 100

Narcissism, excessive self-centeredness, 516
and aggression, 432, 433

Narcolepsy condition characterized by suddenly falling asleep, or at least feeling very sleepy, during the day, 359

Narcotics drugs that produce drowsiness, insensitivity to pain, and decreased responsiveness to events, 73

Naturalistic observation careful examination of what many people or nonhuman animals do under natural conditions, 41, *41*

Nature-nurture issue question of the relative roles played by heredity (nature) and environment (nurture) in determining differences in behavior, 6–7, 145, 147–148
behaviorism on, 198–199
and intelligence, 334–336
and interaction, 151
multiplier effects, 147–148
and personality, 518–519, *518*, *519*

Necker cube, 129, *129*

Need for achievement personality trait marked by feeling good after accomplishing something that one wasn't sure of completing, 403

Negative punishment decrease in the future probability of a response because it led to the absence of something such as food, 214

Negative reinforcement increase in the future probability of a response because it led to the absence of something such as pain, 214

Negative symptoms characteristics notable for their absence, 601

Neo-Freudians personality theorists who have remained faithful to parts of Freud's theory while modifying other parts, 506

NEO PI-R (NEO personality inventory-revised) personality test including 240 items to measure neuroticism, extraversion, openness, agreeableness, and conscientiousness, 526–527

Nerve deafness hearing loss that results from damage to the cochlea, the hair cells, or the auditory nerve, 110

Nervous system, 77–78, *77*. *See also* Brain

Neurocognitive theory approach that treats dreams as just another example of thinking, except that they occur under special conditions, 362

Neurodevelopmental hypothesis idea that schizophrenia originates with impaired development of the nervous system before or around the time of birth, possibly but not necessarily for genetic reasons, 605

Neurons cells of the nervous system that receive information and transmit it to other cells by conducting electrochemical impulses, 63–65
distribution of, *63*
parts of, 64–65, *64*
and plasticity, 84
types of, *64*

Neuroscience, 22, 63–70
action potential, 65–66
and drugs, 71–76
neurons, 63–65
neurotransmitters, 66–69

synapses, 66–68
See also Brain

Neuroticism tendency to experience unpleasant emotions relatively frequently, 516–517

Neurotransmitters chemicals that are stored in the terminal of an axon and that, when released, activate receptors of other neurons, 66–69, *67*, *68*
chart, *69*
and drugs, 71, 72, 73, 74, *75*
and pain, 115, *116*
research examples, 67–68, *69*

Neurotrophins, 596

Nicotine, 72, 75, 583, *583*

Night terror condition in which a person awakens screaming and sweating with a racing heart rate, sometimes flailing with the arms and pounding the walls, 359

95% confidence interval range within which the true population mean lies with 95% certainty, 56–57, *57*

Nitric oxide, 69

Nomothetic approach approach to the study of individual differences that seeks general laws about how an aspect of personality affects behavior, 514

Nontraditional families, 189–190, *189*

Norepinephrine, 69

Normal distribution (or normal curve) symmetrical frequency of scores clustered around the mean, 53

Norms description of the frequencies of occurrence of particular scores, 324
and persuasion, 475

Nostradamus, 33–34, *34*

Nucleus accumbens, 581–582, *581*

Obedience to authority, 491–494, *492*, *493*

Obesity excessive accumulation of body fat, 383, *384*, *385*

Object permanence concept that objects continue to exist even when one does not see, hear, or otherwise sense them, 162–163, *162*, *163*

O'Brien, Dominic, 235, *235*

Observational studies, 41–47
case histories, 41
correlational studies, 43–47
naturalistic observations, 41
surveys, 41–43
vs. experiments, *48*

Obsession repetitive, unwelcome stream of thought, 576

Obsessive-compulsive disorder condition with repetitive thoughts and actions, 576–579, *578*, *579*

Occam's razor, 31

Occipital lobe rear portion of each cerebral hemisphere, critical for vision, 78

Oedipus complex according to Freud, a young boy's sexual interest in his mother accompanied by competitive aggression toward his father, 502

Old age, 178–179, *179*, 352, *352*

Olfaction sense of smell; the detection of chemicals in contact with the membranes inside the nose, 118–120, *119*, *120*

Olfactory receptors, 118, *119*

Omission training learning to suppress a behavior that would lead to the omission of an event such as food, 214

Ontogenic explanation. *See* Developmental explanation

Open-mindedness, 32

Openness to experience tendency to enjoy new intellectual experiences, the arts, fantasies, and anything that exposes a person to new ideas, 517, *517*

Operant conditioning (or instrumental conditioning) process of changing behavior by following a response with reinforcement, 210–221
applications of, 219–221
phenomena of, 215–216
reinforcement/punishment, 212–215
shaping, 216–219
and social learning, 227
Thorndike's studies, 210–211, *210*, *211*
vs. classical conditioning, *215*

Operation according to Piaget, a mental process that can be reversed, 164

Operational definition definition that specifies the operations (or procedures) used to produce or measure something; a way to give it a numerical value, 37

Opiates either drugs derived from the opium poppy or synthetic drugs that produce effects similar to those of opium derivatives, 73, 75, 587–588, *587*, *588*

Opponent-process theory theory that we perceive color in terms of a system of paired opposites: red versus green, yellow versus blue, and white versus black, 105–106, *105*, *106*

Optical illusion misinterpretation of a visual stimulus as being larger or smaller, or straighter or more curved, than it really is, *3*

Optic chiasm, 103

Optic nerve set of axons that extend from the ganglion cells of the eye to the thalamus and several other areas of the brain, 103

Optimism, 404

Oral stage Freud's first stage of psychosexual development; here, psychosexual pleasure focuses on the mouth, 502, *503*

Orexin (hypocretin), 359

Orgasm (climax) stage of sexual arousal, 394

Otoliths, 113–114

Overconfidence, 290

Overgeneralization, 303

Overjustification effect tendency of people who are given more extrinsic motivation than necessary to perform a task to experience a decline in their intrinsic motivation, 376

p < .05 statement that the probability that randomly generated results would resemble the observed results is less than 5%, 56

Pain, 114–116, *115*, *116*, 365, *365*, 366

Panic disorder (PD) disorder characterized by frequent bouts of moderate anxiety and occasional attacks of sudden increased heart rate, chest pains, difficulty breathing, sweating, faintness, and trembling, 571–572

Paranoid schizophrenia type of schizophrenia characterized by the basic symptoms plus strong or elaborate hallucinations and delusions, 603

Parasympathetic nervous system neurons located in the medulla and the bottom of the spinal cord; these neurons send messages to the internal organs to prepare the body for digestion and related processes, 83, *84*, 413–414, *413*

Parental employment, 188–189, *189*

Parentese, 301

Parenting style, 187–188

Parietal lobe portion of each cerebral hemisphere; the main receiving area for the sense of touch and for the awareness of one's own body and perception of location of the body in space, 79, 87

Parkinson's disease condition that affects about 1% of people over the age of 50; the main symptoms are difficulty initiating voluntary movement, slowness of movement, tremors, rigidity, and depressed mood, 68–69

Parsimony (literally, stinginess) scientists' preference for the theory that explains the results using the simplest assumptions, 31–35, 216, 516

Passionate love relationship characterized by strong sexual desire, romance, and friendship, 487

Past life memories, 368

Pattern recognition, 125–131, 293–294, *294*

Pavlov, Ivan P., 200, *200*, 206, 207

Pavlovian conditioning. *See* Classical conditioning

PCP (phencyclidine, angel dust), 74, 76, 607

Peer pressure, 175–176

Perception interpretation of sensory information, 123–140
depth, 133–135, *133*, *134*, 135–137, *135*
minimal stimuli, 123–125, *123*, *124*

Psychological dependence strong repetitive desire for something without any physical symptoms of withdrawal, 582

Psychological disorders. *See* Abnormal behavior

Psychology systematic study of behavior and experience:
definitions, 3
essential points in, 3–4
philosophical issues in, 4–7
specialization in, 13–14, *13*
types of, 7–13, *7*, *9*

Psychometric approach measurement of individual differences in abilities and behaviors, 315–316, *315*, *316*

Psychophysical function mathematical description of the relationship between the physical properties of a stimulus and its perceived properties, 19, *19*

Psychosexual pleasure according to Freud, any strong, pleasant enjoyment arising from body stimulation, 502

Psychotherapy treatment of psychological disorders by methods that include a personal relationship between a trained therapist and a client, 546–560
behavior therapy, 548–549, *549*
cognitive-behavior therapy, 551, 571, 594
cognitive therapy, 550, 571, 594
comparisons, *553*, 556–559, *557*, *558*
and depression, 594, 596
effectiveness of, 554–556, *555*
family systems therapy, 552, *552*
historical trends, 546–547, *547*
humanistic therapy, 551–552
psychoanalysis, 501, 511, 547–548, *547*
trends in, 552–554

PTSD (posttraumatic stress disorder) condition in which people who have endured extreme stress feel prolonged anxiety and depression, 429, 443

Puberty, 175, 383

Punishment event that decreases the probability that a response will be repeated, 213–215, 229, 230

Pupil adjustable opening in the eye through which light enters, 98

Pure autonomic failure uncommon condition with unknown cause in which the autonomic nervous system stops regulating the organs, 415

Q-sort, 511

Racial differences. *See* Ethnic background

Radical behaviorist one who denies that internal, private events are causes of behavior, 196

Random assignment chance procedure for assigning subjects to groups so that every subject has the same probability as any other subject of being assigned to a particular group, 48

Random sample group of people picked in random fashion so that every individual in the population has an equal chance of being selected, 38

Range statement of the highest and lowest scores in a distribution of scores, 55

Rape sexual activity without the consent of the partner, 433

Rapid eye movement (REM) sleep stage of sleep characterized by rapid eye movements, a high level of brain activity, and deep relaxation of the postural muscles; also known as paradoxical sleep, 356

Rational-emotive behavior therapy treatment based on the assumption that thoughts (rationality) lead to emotions and that problems arise not from the unpleasant emotions themselves but from the irrational thoughts that lead to them, 550

Rationalization attempting to prove that one's actions are rational and justifiable and thus worthy of approval, 504

Reaction formation presenting oneself as the opposite of what one really is in an effort to reduce anxiety, 505

Readiness potential increased motor cortex activity prior to the start of a movement, 347

Reading, 307–309, *307*, *308*, *309*

Reappraisal reinterpreting a situation to make it seem less threatening, 444, 445

Reasoning. *See* Cognition

Recency effect tendency to remember the final or most recent items, 249

Receptor specialized cell that converts environmental energies into signals for the nervous system, 98

Recessive gene gene whose effects appear only if the dominant gene is absent, 146–147

Reciprocation, 475

Recognition method of testing memory by asking someone to choose the correct item from a set of alternatives, 236–237, 238–239

Reconstruction putting together an account of past events based partly on memories and partly on expectations of what must have happened, 255–256, 266

Recovered memory report of a long-lost memory, prompted by clinical techniques, 260–263, *263*

Reductionism, 511

Reflexes rapid, automatic responses to stimuli, 81

Regression return to a more juvenile level of functioning as a means of reducing anxiety or in response to emotionally trying circumstances, 504

Rehearsal, 444

Reinforcement event that increases the future probability of the most recent response, 210, 212–215, 229, 230

Reinforcer event that follows a response and increases the later probability or frequency of that response, 212

Relationships. *See* Attraction; Marriage; Social support

Relaxation, *444*, 446

Relearning method (or savings method) method of testing memory by measuring how much faster someone can relearn something than learn something for the first time, 237

Reliability repeatability of a test's scores, 327, *327*, 330

Religion, 435, 444, 457

REM behavior disorder, 356

REM (rapid eye movement) sleep stage of sleep characterized by rapid eye movements, a high level of brain activity, and deep relaxation of the postural muscles; also known as paradoxical sleep, 356

Replicable result result that can be repeated (at least approximately) by any competent investigator who follows the same procedures used in the original study, 31, 35

Representativeness heuristic tendency to assume that, if an item is similar to members of a particular category, it is probably a member of that category itself, 288–289, *289*

Representative sample selection of the population chosen to match the entire population with regard to specific variables, 38

Repression according to Freudian theory, motivated forgetting, the process of moving an unacceptable memory, motivation, or emotion from the conscious mind to the unconscious mind, 261, 504

Research, 37–52
case histories, 41
correlational studies, 43–47
development, 158–161, *159*
ethical considerations, 50–51
experiments, 47–50
general principles of, 37–41
measurement, 4
naturalistic observations, 41
surveys, 41–43
See also Data analysis; Research examples

Research examples:
acquired characteristics, 48–50, *49*
alcoholism, 585–586, *585*
classical conditioning, 204–205, *205*
conformity, 492–494, *492*, *493*
consciousness and action, 347–349, *347*, *348*

criminal profiling, 532–533
deadlines, 402
emotions, 416–417, *417*
feature detectors, 126–127, *127*
hypnosis, 367–369, *367*, *368*
mental imagery, 274–275, *275*
neurotransmitters, 67–68, *69*
object permanence, 162–163, *162*, *163*
phobias, 573–577, *574*
psychotherapy effectiveness, 554–556, *555*
recovered memory, 262–263
sexual orientation, 400, *400*
stereotype threat, 333–334, *333*
theory of mind, 164–165, *165*, *166*

Residual schizophrenia condition in which someone has had an episode of schizophrenia and is now partly, but not fully, recovered, 603

Resilience, 153

Resolution stage of sexual arousal, 394

Resting potential electrical polarization that ordinarily occurs across the membrane of an axon that is not undergoing an action potential, 65

Restless leg syndrome (periodic limb movement disorder) condition that occurs during sleep, marked by unpleasant sensations in the legs and many repetitive leg movements strong enough to interrupt sleep, 360

Retina layer of visual receptors covering the back surface of the eyeball, 98

Retinaldehydes, 102

Retinal disparity difference in the apparent position of an object as seen by the left and right retinas, 133

Retinex theory concept that color perception results from the cerebral cortex's comparison of various retinal patterns, 106

Retrieval cues information associated with remembered material, which can be useful for helping to recall that material, 250

Retroactive interference impairment that a newer memory produces on an older one, 260, *260*

Retrograde amnesia loss of memory for events that occurred before the brain damage, 264, *265*

Reuptake, 66

Reversible figure stimulus that you can perceive in more than one way, 129, *129*

Risk-taking behaviors, 72, 175–176, *177*, 368–369, *369*

Ritalin (methylphenidate), 71–72, 75

RNA, 145

Rods visual receptors that are adapted for vision in dim light, 100, *100*, 101, *101*, 102

Rogers, Carl, 511, *511*

Rohypnol (flunitrazepam), 72–73, 76

Role models, 230, *230*

Rorschach Inkblots projective personality technique; people are shown 10 inkblots and asked what each might be depicting, 528–529, *528*

Ruminate to think about one's depressing experiences, talk about one's feelings, and perhaps cry, 593

Saccade quick jump in the focus of the eyes from one point to another, 308–309

Sadness, 436–437

SAD (seasonal affective disorder) (or depression with a seasonal pattern) condition in which people become seriously depressed in one season of the year, such as winter, 590–591, *591*

Sampling, 37–39, *38*, *39*, 41–42

Satisficing searching only until you find something that is good enough (satisfactory), 287–288

Savings method (or relearning method) method of testing memory by measuring how much faster someone can relearn something than learn something for the first time, 237

Scaffolding, 170

Scatter plot graph in which each dot represents a given individual, with one measurement for that individual on the x-axis (horizontal) and another measurement on the y-axis (vertical), 44–45, *45*

Schachter and Singer's theory of emotions theory that the intensity of sympathetic arousal determines the intensity of an emotion but that cognitive factors determine the type of emotion, 416–418, *416, 417*

Schedule of reinforcement rule or procedure linking the pattern of responses to the reinforcements, 217–218, *218*

Schema (pl.: schemata) organized way of interacting with objects in the world, 161

Schizophrenia condition marked by deterioration of daily activities over a period of at least 6 months, plus hallucinations, delusions, flat or inappropriate emotions, certain movement disorders, or thought disorders, 501–508, *601, 603, 607*
  causes of, 604–606, *604, 605*
  prevalence of, 603–604
  symptoms of, 601–602, *602*
  treatment for, 606–608
  types of, 603

School psychologist specialist in the psychological condition of students, 10

Scientific-management approach view that most employees are lazy, indifferent, and uncreative, so jobs should be made simple and foolproof; also known as Theory X, 405

Scientific method, 29–31, *30, 31*

SD (standard deviation) measurement of the amount of variation among scores in a normal distribution, 55, *56*, 60

Seasonal affective disorder (SAD) (or depression with a seasonal pattern) condition in which people become seriously depressed in one season of the year, such as winter, 590–591, *591*

Season-of-birth effect tendency for people born in the winter months to be slightly more likely than other people to develop schizophrenia, 605

Secondary reinforcer event that becomes reinforcing because it has previously been associated with a primary reinforcer, 212–213, *213*

Second law of thermodynamics, 32

Selective attrition tendency of some kinds of people to be more likely than others to drop out of a study, 159

Selective serotonin reuptake inhibitors (SSRIs) drugs that block the reuptake of the neurotransmitter serotonin by the terminal bouton, 594–595, *595*

Self-actualization achievement of one's full potential, 377, 511–512, *512*

Self-concept image of what one really is, 511

Self-efficacy perception of one's own ability to perform a task successfully, 229–230

Self-esteem evaluation of one's own abilities, performance, and worth, 515–516
  and aggression, 432

Self-fulfilling prophecy expectation that alters one's behavior in such a way as to increase the probability of the predicted event, 462

Self-handicapping strategies techniques for intentionally putting oneself at a disadvantage to provide an excuse for an expected failure, 470

Self-help group assembly of people with similar problems, who operate much like group therapy but without a therapist, 553–554

Self-recognition, 163, *164*

Self-reinforcement, 230

Self-serving biases attributions that people adopt to maximize their credit for their successes and to minimize their blame for their failures, 470

Semantic memory memory of general principles, 240

Semicircular canals, 113

Sendler, Irena, *455*

Sensation conversion of energy from the environment into a pattern of response by the nervous system, 78–79, 97
  chemical senses, 117–121, *118, 119, 120*
  cutaneous senses, 114–117, *114, 115, 116, 117*
  hearing, 109–112, *109, 110, 111, 112*, 131, 156–157, *157*
  historical study of, 19
  synesthesia, 120–121

vestibular sense, 113–114, *113*, 132, 362
  See also Vision

Senses. *See* Sensation

Sensitive period time early in life during which some kind of learning occurs most readily, 226

Sensorimotor stage according to Piaget, the first stage of intellectual development; an infant's behavior is limited to making simple motor responses to sensory stimuli, 162–163, *162, 163, 164*

Sentences, 305–306

Sequential design procedure in which researchers start with groups of people of different ages, studied at the same time, and then study them again at one or more later times, 160

Serotonin, 69, 71, 74, 594–595, *595*

Set point level of some variable (e.g., weight) that the body works to maintain, 382–383, *382*

Sex chromosomes pair of chromosomes that determine whether an individual will develop as a female or as a male, 146–147

Sex-limited gene gene that affects one sex more strongly than the other, even though both sexes have the gene, 147

Sex-linked gene (or X-linked gene) gene located on the X chromosome, 147

Sex roles different activities expected of males and females. *See* Gender roles

Sexuality, 390–401
  and aggression, 433
  and anatomy, 394–396, *395, 396*
  and attraction, 484–486
  Freud on, 501
  sexual behavior, 390–394, *390, 391, 392, 393*
  sexual orientation, 397–400, *397, 398, 399, 400*

Sexual orientation person's tendency to react sexually toward either males or females, 397–400, *397, 398, 399, 400*

Shame, 437

Shaping technique for establishing a new response by reinforcing successive approximations, 216–219, *216, 217, 218*

Short-term memory temporary storage of a limited amount of information, 240, 241, 242

Signal-detection theory study of people's tendencies to make hits, correct rejections, misses, and false alarms, 123–124, *124*

Sign language, 304

Similarity in Gestalt psychology, the tendency to perceive objects that resemble each other as belonging to a group, 129, *130*

Similarity (social psychology), 474–475, 482–483, *483*

Single-blind study research in which either the observer or the subjects are unaware of which subjects received which treatment, 40, *40*

Skeletal responses movements of the muscles that move the limbs, trunk, and head, 210

Skepticism, 2, 28

Skin, 114, *114*. *See also* Cutaneous senses

Skinner, B. F., 216–217, *216*

Sleep, 351–363
  abnormalities of, 358–360, *359*
  circadian rhythms, 351–353, *352, 353, 354*
  and depression, 590, *590*
  dreaming, 356, 360–363, *360, 361*
  reasons for, 354–355, *355*
  stages of, 356–358, *356, 357, 358*

Sleep apnea condition causing a person to have trouble breathing while asleep, 358–359

Sleeper effect delayed persuasion by an initially rejected message, 240, 477

Sleep spindles waves of brain activity at about 12 to 14 per second, 357

Sleep talking, 359

Sleepwalking, 359

Smell, 118–120, *119, 120*

Social/emotional development, 173–180
  adolescence, 175–177, *176, 177*
  adulthood, 177–178

and death, 179
  Erikson's stage summary, 173–174, *173*
  infancy, 174–175
  old age, 178–179, *179*

Social interest sense of solidarity and identification with other people, 508–509

Social-learning approach view that people learn by observing and imitating the behavior of others and by imagining the consequences of their own behavior, 227–230, *227, 228, 229, 230*

Social loafing tendency to work less hard ("loaf") when sharing work with other people, 459–460

Social perception and cognition process of gathering and remembering information about others and making inferences based on that information, 462–471
  attribution, 466–470
  first impressions, 462–463
  prejudice, 463–466

Social phobia severe avoidance of other people and an especially strong fear of doing anything in public, 571

Social psychologist psychologist who studies social behavior and how individuals influence other people and are influenced by other people, 12, 452

Social support, 442, 446, *446*, 604

Somatic nervous system, 77

Somatosensory system, 114. *See also* Cutaneous senses

Sound localization, 112, *112*

Sound waves vibrations of the air or of another medium, 109, *109*

Source amnesia forgetting where or how you learned something, 240–241

Spanking, 213

SPAR method systematic way to monitor and improve understanding of a text by surveying, processing meaningfully, asking questions, and reviewing, 253

Spatial neglect tendency to ignore the left side of the body, the left side of the world, and the left side of objects, 346, *346*

Spinal cord part of the central nervous system that communicates with sensory neurons and motor neurons below the level of the head, 81, *81*

Split-brain surgery, 86–87, *87*

Spontaneous recovery temporary return of an extinguished response after a delay, 204, 594

Spontaneous remission improvement of a psychological condition without therapy, 554

Sports psychologists, 22

Spreading activation process by which the activation of one concept also activates or primes other concepts that are linked to it, 282–283, *282, 283*

SSRIs (selective serotonin reuptake inhibitors) drugs that block the reuptake of the neurotransmitter serotonin by the terminal bouton, 594–595, *595*

Stage of concrete operations according to Piaget, the ability to deal with the properties of concrete objects but not hypothetical or abstract questions, 168

Stage of formal operations according to Piaget, the stage when children develop the ability to deal with abstract, hypothetical situations, which demand logical, deductive reasoning and systematic planning, 168

Standard deviation (SD) measurement of the amount of variation among scores in a normal distribution, 55, *56*, 60

Standardization process of establishing rules for administering a test and for interpreting the scores, 324

Standardized test test that is administered according to specified rules, and its scores are interpreted in a prescribed fashion, 324, 524–525

Stanford-Binet IQ test first important IQ test in the English language, 320–321, *320*, 324

Startle reflex, 429

State temporary activation of a particular behavior, 514

State-dependent memory tendency to remember something better if your body is in the same condition during recall as it was during the original learning, 251